STRUCTURED
COBOL
PROGRAMMING

EIGHTH EDITION

NANCY STERN
Hofstra University

ROBERT A. STERN
Nassau Community College

JOHN WILEY & SONS, INC.
New York   Chichester   Brisbane   Toronto   Singapore   Weinheim

Acquisitions Editor   Beth Lang Golub
Marketing Manager   Leslie Hines
Senior Production Editor   Tony VenGraitis
Production Service and Designer   HRS Electronic Text Management
Assistant Manufacturing Manager   Mark Cirillo
Senior Illustration Coordinator   Anna Melhorn
Cover Photo   Bob Pizaro/Comstock, Inc.
Cover Design   HRS Electronic Text Management

This book was set in 10/12 Palatino by CRWaldman Graphic Communications and printed and bound by Donnelley/Willard. The cover was printed by Phoenix Color.

Recognizing the importance of preserving what has been written, it is a policy of John Wiley & Sons, Inc. to have books of enduring value published in the United States printed on acid-free paper, and we exert our best efforts to that end.

Library of Congress Cataloging in Publication Data
Stern, Nancy B.
    Structured COBOL programming / Nancy Stern, Robert A. Stern.—
8th ed.
        p.   cm.
    Includes bibliographical references.
    ISBN 0-471-13886-X (alk. paper)
    1. COBOL (Computer program language)   2. Structured programming.
I. Stern, Robert A.   II. Title.
QA76.73.C25S75 1997
005.13'3—dc20   96-9924
                                                                              CIP

Printed in the United States of America

10 9 8 7 6 5 4

To Lori Anne and Melanie

PREFACE

OVERALL MARKET

This book is intended for readers with no previous programming or computer experience as well as for those with some background in the computing field. It has been specifically designed for use in college courses on COBOL both in two-year and four-year schools.

OBJECTIVES OF THIS BOOK

1. To teach students how to design programs so that they are easy to read, debug, modify, and maintain.
2. To provide students with the ability to write well-designed elementary, intermediate, and advanced structured COBOL programs in their entirety. These include both batch and interactive programs.
3. To familiarize students with information processing and systems concepts that will help them interact with users and systems analysts when designing programs.
4. To focus on the key elements of the most recent COBOL standard, called COBOL 85, that facilitate and promote the writing of well-designed structured programs. We highlight where COBOL 85 features differ from COBOL 74, the previous standard. We also specify changes that will be incorporated in the next standard, which is currently referred to as COBOL 9x.
5. To familiarize students with programming tools such as pseudocode and hierarchy charts that make program logic more structured, modular, and top-down. We also provide information on the flowchart, which is an older tool, but one that is still used by some for planning purposes.
6. To teach students useful techniques for maintaining and modifying older "legacy" programs.

HOW THIS BOOK DIFFERS FROM *STRUCTURED COBOL PROGRAMMING*, SEVENTH EDITION

The eighth edition of *Structured COBOL Programming* builds on the strengths of the previous seven editions and includes some changes and additions we think have significantly improved the text. The dual emphasis on structured program design and syntax is retained, as is the focus on top-down modular programming and documentation. In this edition we highlight pseudocode as the primary program planning tool.

The following are some of the specific changes we have made:

1. *COBOL 85 program design elements are the focus of this text.* Some more structured types of processing are available beginning with COBOL 85. Since there are still some COBOL 74 users of this text, we focus on COBOL 85 design elements, but where these differ from COBOL 74, we include those differences in the margins.

   One main change that impacts most of the programs in the new edition relates to the method used for reading records. For COBOL 74 users, we explain the concept of a priming READ, which remains one way of structuring programs. But for COBOL 85 users, we emphasize the following method for designing programs:

```
PERFORM UNTIL ARE-THERE-MORE-RECORDS = 'NO '
    READ INPUT-FILE
        AT END
            MOVE 'NO ' TO ARE-THERE-MORE-RECORDS
        NOT AT END
            PERFORM 200-CALC-RTN
    END-READ
END-PERFORM
```

Our COBOL 85 programs use the above structure and, in the margin, show the COBOL 74 structure that includes a priming READ.

We also focus on scope terminators using COBOL 85 and illlustrate their use extensively.

The EVALUATE verb, in-line PERFORMs, and clauses such as NOT AT END and NOT INVALID KEY are emphasized throughout the text. Here, again, we do not abandon COBOL 74 but illustrate how it differs from COBOL 85.

COBOL 9x features that have already been approved for use in the new standard are explained in detail as well.

To facilitate the reader's understanding of these three standards, we use icons to highlight a feature that relates specifically to a particular standard:

2. *Interactive and batch processing.* We focus on batch processing through Chapter 4. Beginning in Chapter 5, we use the ACCEPT and DISPLAY verbs and explain the differences between batch and interactive processing. In Chapter 6, we introduce the SCREEN SECTION and illustrate how users can create fully interactive programs. From Chapter 6 on, every chapter includes interactive elements and at least one end-of-chapter Programming Assignment that requires interactive processing. Topics that specifically relate to interactive issues are highlighted with the use of an interactive icon:

3. *A streamlined text.* In many schools, COBOL courses are in transition. Some are one-semester courses and others have a two-semester sequence. This book begins, in Chapter 1, by explaining the fact that a very large number of programs have been written in COBOL and continue to be written in COBOL, so that, despite the claims of some pundits, COBOL is not a dying language, but a language in transition. We make the assumption that most programming courses in colleges and universities introduce students to the fundamentals of the language and then provide them with enough information to learn advanced concepts on their own. Thus, we have streamlined the text by omitting some topics that are only infrequently covered in many courses. For example, double- and triple-level arrays are introduced in a chapter on arrays, but are not emphasized here. Relative file processing is introduced along with indexed file processing in a single chapter.

Because we realize that some instructors may wish to have additional coverage of more advanced topics, we provide supplements that can be downloaded from our Web site on the Internet.

We believe that the result is a new text, which includes appropriate coverage of all topics without being overpowering in either depth or breadth.

4. *Pseudocode and flowcharting.* In this edition, we focus primarily on pseudocode. We introduce flowcharts and illustrate them in Chapter 5. After that, the planning

tool we use predominantly is pseudocode. We believe that pseudocode is a more current planning tool, but for those who still prefer flowcharting, there is enough in this edition to help students plan programs with flowcharts.

5. *The Internet.* Our Web site is www.wiley.com/cobol/. We use our Web site to provide late-breaking information to our readers on COBOL 9x and other aspects of COBOL. We also use the Web site to provide supplementary material that can be downloaded. This includes advanced topics, the *COBOL Syntax Reference Guide*, and other additions to the text. Finally, we use our Web site to link to other Web sites that include COBOL references. References in the text that point to Web sites include a Net icon:

6. *Object-oriented COBOL and other issues for the twenty-first century.* We include a full chapter on object-oriented COBOL, with examples, which is expected to be part of the COBOL 9x standard. We also discuss COBOL issues that relate to the future. For example, the two-digit year that is commonly used in many existing COBOL programs becomes problematic for the next century. Two-digit years have traditionally assumed a year in the 1900s. How will we distinguish between 2084 and 1984? This issue, and others like it, are addressed in the text.

7. *A focus on maintaining existing COBOL programs.* Many students begin their programming careers as maintenance programmers. To date, little or no attention has been given in textbooks to the techniques used to modify and update existing legacy code. We include a Programming Assignment in each chapter that focuses on maintenance issues.

8. *Record layouts.* Rather than use the traditional pictorial record layout for describing input and output disk files, we describe our records using a format that has become a standard for depicting database records. You will see these new record layouts throughout the text.

9. *Intrinsic functions.* Intrinsic functions are now a part of the COBOL 85 extended standard. Many texts add them as a final chapter. We believe intrinsic functions are important enough to be integrated into the text. We introduce them in Chapter 7, along with arithmetic verbs, and use them throughout the book.

10. *Debugging tips have been enhanced.* We continue to include an end-of-chapter series of Debugging Exercises that provide users with program code that needs correction. We also highlight Debugging Tips in the text that help users avoid program errors. The Debugging icon is used to point to these items:

11. *Illustrated programs, Practice Programs, and Programming Assignments have been redesigned to reflect changes to the COBOL standard and to more appropriately depict real-world problems.*

FEATURES OF THE TEXT

FORMAT

The format of this text is designed to be as helpful as possible. Each chapter begins with:

1. **A detailed chapter outline.**
   Before beginning a chapter, you can get an overview of its contents by looking at

this outline. In addition, after you have read the chapter, you can use the outline as a summary of the overall organization.

2. **A list of objectives.**
   This list helps you see what the chapter is intended to teach even before you read it.

The material is presented in a step-by-step manner with numerous examples and illustrations. Within each chapter there are self-tests, with solutions, that are designed to help you evaluate your own understanding of the material presented. We encourage you to take these tests as you go along. They will help pinpoint and resolve any misunderstandings you may have.

END-OF-CHAPTER MATERIAL

Each chapter ends with learning aids consisting of:

1. *Chapter Summary.*
2. *Key Terms List.* This is a list of all new terms defined in the chapter. Appendix E is a glossary that lists all key terms in the text along with their definitions.
3. *Chapter Self-Test*—with solutions so you can test yourself on your understanding of the chapter as a whole.
4. *Practice Program.* A full program is illustrated. We recommend you read the definition of the problem and try to code the program yourself. Then compare your solution to the one illustrated.
5. *Review Questions.* These are general questions that may be assigned by your instructor for homework.
6. *Debugging Exercises.* These are program excerpts with errors in them. You are asked to correct the coding. The errors highlighted are those commonly made by students and entry-level programmers.
7. *Programming Assignments.* The assignments appear in increasing order of difficulty. They include a full set of specifications similar to those that programmers are actually given in the "real world." You are asked to code and debug each program using test data. You will need to either create your own test data or receive a set from your instructor.

   Programming Assignments in each chapter include at least one interactive program (designated with an icon) and a maintenance program that students will need to modify or update. Appendix B includes sample test data that can be used for Programming Assignment 2 in each chapter.

A syntax reference guide and a disk containing all programs illustrated in the book also accompany this text. The disk also contains data sets for all Programming Assignments. Alternatively, both the syntax reference guide and the disk can be downloaded from the Internet.

INSTRUCTIONAL AIDS

Two instructor's resource manuals are available. One contains (1) solutions to all text questions and (2) course outlines. The second contains hard-copy solutions to all Programming Assignments from the text. This latter manual is packaged with a disk that contains (1) the solutions to Programming Assignments and (2) test data for the Programming Assignments. A student data disk containing Practice Programs illustrated in the book, along with data for all Programming Assignments, is also provided. Instructors are free to distribute these disks to their students. The data disk's contents can also be downloaded from the Internet.

A computerized test bank and set of transparency masters are also available. An electronic multimedia slide presentation package, designed using PowerPoint, is available as a lecture enhancer or as a student study tool.

Three PC compilers are available for purchase with the text:

- Micro Focus Personal COBOL for DOS packaged with a student manual prepared by John Crawford of California State Polytechnical University and Micro Focus Personal COBOL for Windows, also packaged with a student manual. The Micro Focus compilers are distributed by John Wiley & Sons only to colleges and universities in North America. To obtain these compilers *outside of North America*, please contact Micro Focus Publishing at mfpublg@microfocus.com or Micro Focus Publishing, 2465 East Bayshore Rd., Palo Alto, CA 94303 USA.
- An educational version of Ryan McFarland's RM/COBOL-85. This is packaged with a student manual prepared by James Janossy.

To obtain review copies of the compilers, please contact your local Wiley sales representative or call Wiley at 1-800-225-5945.

For online help, an email address (techhelp@wiley.com) is available for faculty only who may experience difficulty installing or using these compilers. If you are a student, please ask your instructor for help.

Wiley's Web site for this book is www.wiley.com/cobol/; it contains late-breaking information as well as supplements that can be downloaded, and linkages to other COBOL sites.

The reviewers who provided many helpful suggestions throughout the development of this project are acknowledged on page xi, along with all of those who helped bring this project to fruition.

We update our programming texts every few years and welcome your comments, criticisms, and suggestions. We can be reached c/o:

Nancy Stern
Robert A. Stern
BCIS Department
Hofstra University
Hempstead, NY 11550

You can also contact us using CompuServe's EasyPlex electronic mail service. Our user id is 76505,1222.

Our Internet address is acsnns@hofstra.edu.

Nancy Stern
Robert A. Stern

ACKNOWLEDGMENTS

Our special thanks to (1) the following individuals at John Wiley & Sons: Beth Lang Golub, Editor; Joe Heider, Publisher; Ann Berlin, Vice President of Production and Manufacturing; David Kear, Supplements Editor; and Kiersta Fricke, Media Editor; (2) Shelley Flannery, Copy Editor; (3) Jim Ley, University of Wisconsin at Stout, for preparation of the Instructor's Manual and for invaluable suggestions; (4) Jan Ewing, Steve Knapp, Samuel Bartos, and William J. Cataldi of Ewing Systems and Rosann Kelly, Hofstra University, for technical proofreading; (5) Ed Burke, Lorraine Burke, Erica Smythe, and Karen Mahakian of HRS for design specifications and project management; (6) Aaron Seligman, Nassau Community College, for numerous useful suggestions; (7) Donald E. Carr, Eastern Kentucky University, for the Test Bank; (8) Herbert Rebhun, University of Houston–Downtown, for the PowerPoint electronic slides; (9) Charles Hamilton of Beat Media Broadcasting, Internet consultant, (10) Carol L. Eisen for her invaluable assistance in the preparation of the manuscript; and (11) Mike McCandless for permission to use material from the Micro Focus Personal COBOL for Windows manual in our Chapter 18.

We thank the following reviewers for their many helpful suggestions: Fred Harold, Florida Atlantic University; Jerry Hattaway, Troy State University; Alfred L. McKinney, Louisiana State University at Shreveport; James P. Ley, University of Wisconsin at Stout; Susan Stohl, Glendale Community College.

A special word of thanks to Hofstra University for giving us the opportunity to experiment with some new ideas and techniques, and to our students, whose interesting and insightful questions helped us improve our pedagogic approach.

The following acknowledgment has been reproduced from COBOL Edition, U.S. Department of Defense, at the request of the Conference on Data Systems Languages.

"Any organization interested in reproducing the COBOL report and specifications in whole or in part, using ideas taken from this report as the basis for an instruction manual or for any other purpose is free to do so. However, all such organizations are requested to reproduce this section as part of the introduction to the document. Those using a short passage, as in a book review, are requested to mention 'COBOL' in acknowledgment of the source, but need not quote this entire section.

"COBOL is an industry language and is not the property of any company or group of companies, or of any organization or group of organizations.

"No warranty, expressed or implied, is made by any contributor or by the COBOL Committee as to the accuracy and functioning of the programming system and language. Moreover, no responsibility is assumed by any contributor or by the committee, in connection therewith.

"Procedures have been established for the maintenance of COBOL. Inquiries concerning the procedures for proposing changes should be directed to the Executive Committee of the Conference on Data Systems Languages.

CONTENTS

Accompanying this text are a COBOL Syntax Reference Guide, coding sheets, and Printer Spacing Charts.

This text is available with three packages entitled *Getting Started with RM/COBOL-85*, 2nd edition, and *Getting Started with Micro Focus Personal COBOL* (two versions)—either Personal COBOL for DOS or Personal COBOL for Windows. Each package contains a manual and an educational version of the compiler.

UNIT I
The Basics

CHAPTER 1

An Introduction to Structured Program Design in COBOL

▓ OBJECTIVES

To familiarize you with

1. Why COBOL is such a popular business-oriented language.
2. Programming practices and techniques.
3. A history of how COBOL evolved and the use of the current ANS standard versions of COBOL.
4. An overview of the four divisions of a COBOL program.

▓ CONTENTS

COMPUTER PROGRAMMING: AN OVERVIEW

TYPES OF COMPUTER PROGRAMS

A **program** is a set of instructions that enable a computer to process data. There are two types of computer programs: **operating system programs**, which control the overall operations of the computer, and **applications programs**, which actually perform tasks required by users. The term used to describe all types of programs is called **software**.

An applications program operates on **input** data and converts it to meaningful **output** information. The following is an illustration of how a computer processes data:

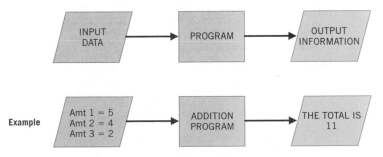

A computer can process data only as efficiently and effectively as it is programmed.

The set of instructions in an applications program is written by a computer professional called an **applications programmer** or **software developer**.

APPLICATIONS PROGRAMS

As noted, an applications program is written by an applications **programmer** or software developer to provide users with the information they need. Some applications programs are written to obtain a quick solution to a one-time problem; others are written to be run periodically on a regularly scheduled basis. An applications program to display the average grade for a set of exams entered as incoming data would be an example of a one-time job. An applications program to print student transcripts each semester would be an example of a program that is run periodically on a regular basis.

In general, applications programs read input, process it, and produce information or output that the user needs. Applications programs are generally used to computerize business procedures. A set of computerized business procedures in an application area is called an **information system**.

Interactive vs. Batch Processing

Some applications are processed interactively, as the data is transacted, while other data is collected and processed later, in batches. Interactive applications typically accept input data from a PC, workstation, or terminal. The input is processed immediately and the output is displayed on a screen and/or printed. This type of interactive processing is used when data must be current at all times and output is required immediately after processing. A Point-of-Sale system in which receipts are computer generated when sales are transacted is an example of an interactive application.

Other applications process large volumes of input at periodic intervals. Payroll procedures used to update the master collection of payroll information prior to printing pay checks are often performed in batch mode at periodic intervals. We will see that COBOL is ideally suited for both interactive and batch processing applications.

When an applications program is written for a specific user it is called a **customized program**. COBOL is ideally suited as a language for writing customized applications programs. Although we will focus on COBOL for applications programming in this text, we now provide a brief description of another type of applications software called an applications package.

If the tasks to be performed by a program are relatively standard, such as preparing a budget, an **applications package** might be purchased as an alternative to writing a customized program in a language such as COBOL. Such packages are sold by software vendors. Typically, documentation is provided by the manufacturer in the form of a user's manual, which explains how to use the package. For example, Lotus for Windows is a widely used package for applications such as budgeting, scheduling, and preparing trial balances.

If a package exists that can be used *as is* for an application, purchasing it will almost always be cheaper and easier than writing a customized program. But if an application has special requirements, then writing a customized program may be preferable to modifying an existing package.

MACHINE LANGUAGE PROGRAMS

All programs to be executed by the computer must be in **machine language**. It would be very tedious and cumbersome for the programmer or software developer to code instructions in this form. He or she would need to reference actual addresses or locations in memory and use complex instruction codes.

SYMBOLIC PROGRAMS

Since programming or software development in machine language is so difficult, programming languages have evolved that enable the programmer to write English-like or symbolic instructions. However, before symbolic instructions can be executed or run, they must be translated or **compiled** by the computer into machine language. The computer itself uses a translator program or **compiler** to perform this conversion into machine language.

There are numerous **symbolic programming languages** that can be translated into machine language. COBOL is one such language that is used extensively for commercial applications. Other symbolic programming languages include Visual Basic, Pascal, and C++.

THE APPLICATIONS PROGRAM DEVELOPMENT PROCESS

The process of developing programs is similar for all applications regardless of the symbolic programming language used. An overview of the steps involved in the program development process follows. Each of these steps will then be discussed in detail.

PROGRAM DEVELOPMENT PROCESS

1. Determine Program Specifications
   Programmers, along with systems analysts who are responsible for the overall computerized design of business procedures, work with users to develop program specifications. Program specifications include input and output layouts describing the precise format of data along with the step-by-step processing requirements for converting input to output.

2. Design the Program Using Program Planning Tools
   Programmers use design or program planning tools such as flowcharts, pseudocode, and hierarchy charts to help map out the structure and logic of a program before the program is actually coded.

3. Code and Enter the Program
   The programmer writes and then keys or enters the source program into the computer system using a keyboard.

4. Compile the Program
   The programmer makes certain that the program has no rule violations.

5. Test the Program
   The programmer develops sample data and uses the program to operate on it to ensure that processing is correct.

6. Document the Program
   The programmer writes procedure manuals for users and computer operators so they can run the program on a regularly scheduled basis.

Most novices believe that computer programming begins with coding or writing program instructions and ends with program testing. You will find, however, that programmers who begin with the coding phase often produce poorly designed or inadequate programs. The steps involved in programming should be developmental, where coding is undertaken only *after* the program requirements have been fully specified and the logic to be used has been carefully planned.

Moreover, there are steps required *after* a program has been coded and tested. Each program must be documented with a formal set of procedures and instructions that specify how it is to be used. This **documentation** is meant for (1) those who will be working with the output, (2) computer operators who will run the program on a regularly scheduled basis, and (3) maintenance programmers who may need to make modifications to the program at a later date.

DETERMINE PROGRAM SPECIFICATIONS

When a company decides to computerize a business application or information system such as payroll or accounts receivable, a systems analyst or a software developer is typically assigned the task of designing the entire computerized application. This systems analyst works closely with users to determine such factors as output needs, how many programs are required, and input requirements. A **user** is the businessperson who, when the application is computerized, will depend on or use the output.

When a systems analyst decides what customized programs are required, he or she prepares **program specifications** to be given to the programmers or software developers so that they can perform their tasks. Typically, the program specifications consist of:

1. **Record layout forms** to describe the formats of the input and output data on disk or other storage medium. Figure 1.1 illustrates two examples of record layouts. (We will use version (b) for most of our illustrations.) They indicate:
    a. The data items or field names within each record.
    b. The location of each data item within the record.
    c. The size of each data item.
    d. For numeric data items, the number of decimal positions. For example, 999.99 is a five-digit field with three integer and two decimal places. See Figure 1.1*a*.
    e. In some organizations, standard names of the fields to be used in a program are specified on the record layouts. In other organizations, names of fields are assigned by the programmer or software developer. In Figure 1.1 we use fields whose precise COBOL names have been defined by the programmer.

2. **Printer Spacing Charts** for printed output. Printed output requires a format not typically needed for other types of output:
    a. Headings are usually printed that contain report and page titles, dates, page numbers, and so on.
    b. Data must be spaced neatly across the page, allowing for margins.
    c. Sometimes additional lines for error messages or totals are required.

Figure 1.1 Sample record layouts.

(a)

CODE-IN	EMPLOYEE-NO-IN	REGULAR-HRS-IN	OVERTIME-HRS-IN	HOURLY-RATE-IN

1	2 3	7 8	11 12	15 16	19
99	99999	99.99	99.99	99.99

(b)

Employee Record Layout			
Field	**Size**	**Data Type**	**No. of Decimal Positions (if Numeric)**
CODE-IN	2	Numeric	0
EMPLOYEE-NO-IN	5	Numeric	0
REGULAR-HRS-IN	4	Numeric	2
OVERTIME-HRS-IN	4	Numeric	2
HOURLY-RATE-IN	4	Numeric	2

Figure 1.2   Sample Printer Spacing Chart.

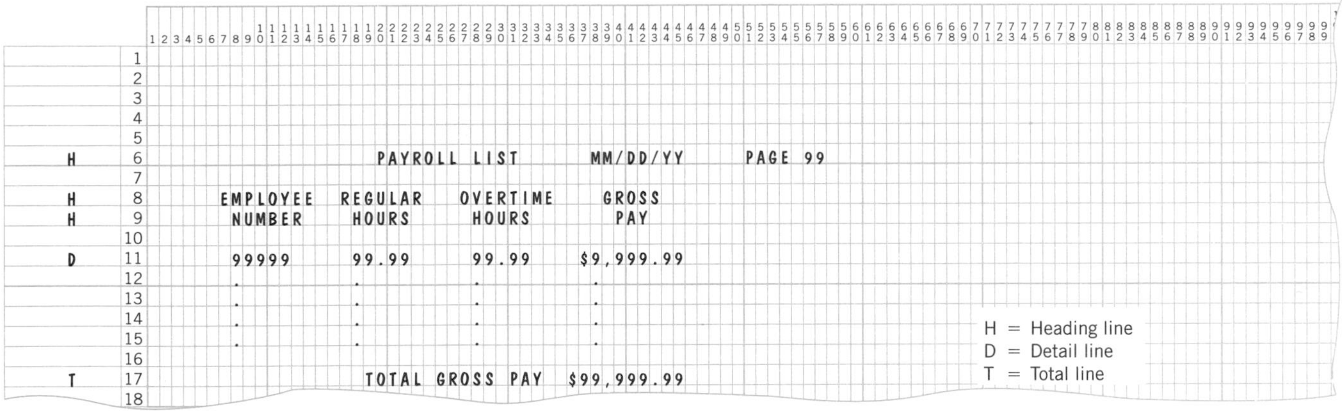

A Printer Spacing Chart, as illustrated in Figure 1.2, is a tool used for determining the proper spacing of printed output. It specifies the precise print positions to be used in the output. It also includes all data items to be printed and their formats.

The record layout forms for keyed input and disk output are prepared either by a systems analyst or a software developer. If output is to be printed, a Printer Spacing Chart is prepared to indicate the precise format of the output. Along with these layout forms, a set of notes is prepared indicating the specific requirements of the program.

Illustrative programs and assignments in this text will include samples of these program specifications so that you will become familiar with them as you read through the book. This will help you learn what you can expect to receive from a systems analyst or what you may need if you, as the programmer, will be preparing these specifications yourself.

DESIGN THE PROGRAM USING PROGRAM PLANNING TOOLS

Before a programmer begins to code, he or she should *plan the logic* to be used in the program. Just as an architect draws a blueprint before undertaking the construction of a building, a programmer should use a planning tool before a program is coded.

Originally, programmers used program flowcharts to plan the logic in a program. A program **flowchart** is a conventional block diagram providing a pictorial representation of the logic to be used in a program. **Pseudocode** is written with English-like expressions rather than diagrams and is specifically suited for depicting logic in a *structured program*. **Hierarchy** or **structure charts** are used to show the relationships among sections in a program. Today, more software developers use pseudocode and hierarchy charts in place of flowcharts to plan a program's logic.

In most of our illustrations, we will depict the logic flow to be used in a program with pseudocode and a hierarchy chart. We end this first chapter with a brief overview of all planning tools including flowcharts; in Chapter 5 we provide an in-depth discussion of these tools.

CODE AND ENTER THE PROGRAM

After the logic of a program has been planned, the programmer writes a set of instructions, called the **source program**, in a symbolic programming language. Symbolic programs *cannot* be executed or run by the computer until they have been compiled or translated into machine language. The source program is generally *keyed* into a computer using a keyboard and then *stored* on disk or other storage medium.

Figure 1.3 The compilation process.

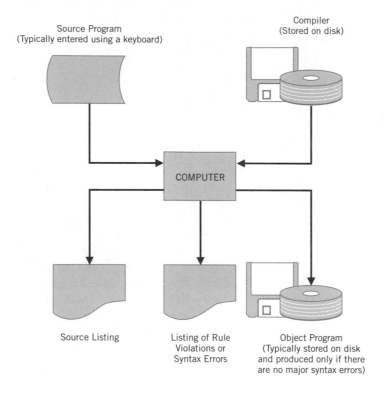

COMPILE THE SOURCE PROGRAM

After the source program has been entered on a keyboard or read from a disk, the computer must translate it into a machine language program called the **object program** before execution can occur. A program called a compiler translates source progams into object programs, which are executable. Figure 1.3 illustrates the compilation process.

TEST THE PROGRAM

Programs must be tested or **debugged** to ensure that they have no errors. There are several methods used to test or debug a program.

Debugging During the Compile and Test Phases

Compile-Time Errors

When the computer compiles a COBOL program, errors detected by the compiler will be listed. Any violation of a programming rule is called a **syntax error**. For example, if the COBOL instruction to add two numbers is spelled AD instead of ADD, the computer will print a message indicating that a syntax error has occurred. If such errors are very serious, then execution of the program cannot begin until the errors are corrected.

Execution Errors

Note that the syntax errors detected during a compilation are just one type of programming error. **Logic errors** can occur as well. These are detected during program execution, not during compilation, and result in incorrect output. One type of logic error is when the *sequence* of programming steps is not specified properly. Another type of logic error occurs when the wrong instruction is coded. If you include an ADD instruction instead of a MULTIPLY, for example, this would result in a logic error. Another type of execution error is called a **run-time error**, which occurs if the computer cannot execute an instruction. Examples of run-time errors are (1) an attempt to divide by zero and (2) reading from a file that cannot be found.

Execution errors are detected by the programmer when the program is tested during run-time. After all syntax errors have been corrected, the object program is loaded into storage and linked to the system. Then the program is run or tested with *sample or test data* to see if it will process the data correctly. The test run should read the sample data as input and produce the desired output. The programmer then checks the output to be sure it is correct. If it is not correct, a logic error has occurred. If the program cannot be executed in its entirety, this would be the result of a run-time error.

Sample data should be prepared carefully to ensure that during program testing or debugging all conditions provided for in a program are actually tested. If not, a program that has begun to be used on a regularly scheduled production basis may eventually produce logic or run-time errors.

If there are no errors in the source program when it is compiled, or if only minor violations of rules have been made, all instructions will be translated into machine language. The object program can then be executed, or tested during run-time. Figure 1.4 illustrates the steps involved in coding and testing a program.

Debugging Techniques

We have seen that after a program has been planned and coded, it must be compiled and after syntax errors are corrected it must be executed with test data. It is not unusual for errors to occur during either compilation or execution. As noted, eliminating these errors is called debugging. Several methods of debugging should be used by the programmer:

Desk Checking

Programmers should carefully review a program for typographical or spelling errors *before* it is keyed in and again after it has been keyed. **Desk checking** will minimize the overall time it takes to debug a program. Frequently, programmers fail to see the need for this phase, on the assumption that it is better to let the computer find errors. Omitting the desk checking phase can, however, result in undetected *logic* errors that could take hours or even days to debug later on. Experienced programmers carefully review their programs before and after keying them.

Correcting Syntax Errors

After a program has been translated or compiled, the computer will print a source listing along with diagnostic messages that point to any rule violations or syntax errors. The programmer must then correct the errors and recompile the program before it can be run with test data.

Program Walkthroughs

After a program has been successfully compiled, programmers test the logic by executing it with test data. It is best, however, to "walk through" the program first to see if it will produce the desired results. In a program **walkthrough**, the programmer manually steps through the logic of the program using the test data to see if the correct results will be obtained. This is done *prior to* machine execution. Such walkthroughs can help the programmer find logic and run-time errors more easily. Sometimes structured walkthroughs are performed directly from pseudocode, even *prior to* the actual coding of a program, in an effort to minimize the need for program changes later on.

Frequently, programming teams work together to test the logic in their programs using the walkthrough approach. This method of debugging can save considerable time.

Figure 1.4 Steps involved in coding and testing a program.

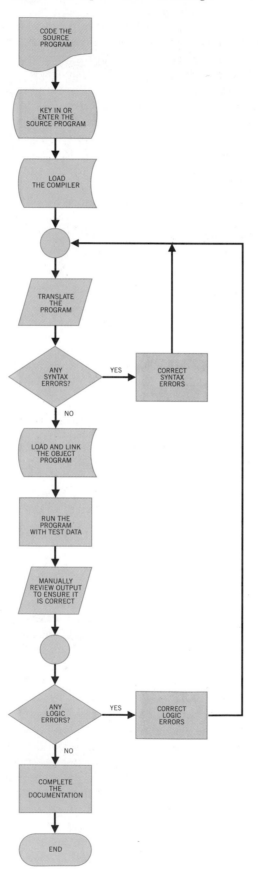

Detecting Logic and Run-time Errors by Executing the Program

Detecting logic and run-time errors by executing the program is usually the most difficult and time-consuming part of debugging. Chapters 5 and 11 focus on additional techniques used for finding and correcting logic and run-time errors in COBOL programs.

The preparation of test data is an extremely critical aspect of debugging. The programmer should prepare data that will test *every possible condition* the program is likely to encounter. It is not uncommon for a program that has been thought to be fully tested and that has been operational for some time to suddenly produce errors. Most often, these problems arise because a specific condition not previously encountered has occurred and the program did not test for that situation.

DOCUMENT THE PROGRAM

Before a program is ready to be released to the operating staff for regular production runs, it must be fully documented. That is, the users and operators must be supplied with a formal, written set of procedures called documentation, which explains, in detail, how the program is to be executed and how the output is to be used. Experienced programmers should begin preparing documentation early on, and then build on it throughout the development process.

THE NATURE OF COBOL

COBOL IS A BUSINESS-ORIENTED LANGUAGE

COBOL is one of the most widespread commercial applications languages in use today. The reasons for its success are discussed in this section.

The name COBOL is an abbreviation for *COmmon Business-Oriented Language*. As a business-oriented language COBOL is designed specifically for commercial applications, such as payroll and inventory, that typically operate on a large volume of data. Commercial languages such as COBOL that are best suited for processing large volumes of data are somewhat less suitable for handling scientific problems where complex calculations are required.

COBOL IS A STANDARD LANGUAGE

COBOL is a common programming language, meaning that COBOL compilers are available in a standard form for most computers. The same COBOL program may be compiled and run on a variety of machines, such as an IBM AS/400 and a VAX 8500, or even a personal computer (PC), with only minor variations.

COBOL is a standard language, which means that all compilers, regardless of the computers on which they run, have the same syntax rules.

Because the COBOL language is so widely used, computers of a future generation will undoubtedly support it. COBOL is very often used on microcomputers as well. Available with this text are PC-based packages entitled *Getting Started with RM/COBOL-85* and *Getting Started with Micro Focus Personal COBOL*—DOS and Windows versions. Each package includes an educational version of the compiler and a manual.

COBOL IS AN ENGLISH-LIKE LANGUAGE

In summary, the meaning of the name COBOL suggests two of its basic advantages. It is *common* or standard, and it is *business-oriented*. There are, however, additional reasons why it is such a popular language.

COBOL is an English-like language. All instructions can be coded using English words rather than complex codes. To add two numbers together, for example, we use the word ADD. Similarly, the rules for programming in COBOL conform to many of the rules for writing in English, making it easier to learn.

COBOL Is a User-Friendly Language

Because users are frequently able to understand the English-like instructions of COBOL, it is considered a user-friendly language. This means that it is not overly technical like some other languages. Users who rely on computer output but have no programming expertise may be able to understand the logic and instructions in a COBOL program.

A HISTORY OF COBOL AND THE ANS VERSIONS

When It Began

COBOL was developed in 1959 by a group called the CODASYL Committee. CODASYL is an abbreviation for *CO*nference on *DA*ta *SY*stems *L*anguages. This committee included representatives from academia, user groups, and computer manufacturers. The ultimate objective of this committee was to develop a *standard* business-oriented language for which all major manufacturers would provide compilers. The Department of Defense convened this conference since it, as well as other government agencies, was dissatisfied with the lack of standards in the computing field.

The American National Standards (ANS) Versions of COBOL

As a result of the CODASYL effort, the first COBOL compilers became available in 1960. But as years passed, users became dissatisfied with the wide variations among COBOL compilers produced by the different computer manufacturers.

The **American National Standards Institute (ANSI)** is an organization that develops standards in numerous technical fields. It is currently the overseeing organization for COBOL standards. Like CODASYL, ANSI's COBOL committee consists of representatives from academia, user groups, and computer manufacturers.

In 1968, the first American National Standards (ANS) version of COBOL was developed and approved. Beginning in 1968, all major computer manufacturers and software suppliers provided compilers that adhered to the COBOL language formats specified in this ANS version of COBOL. In 1974, a second version of ANS COBOL was developed to make the language even more efficient and standardized. The 1985 version of ANS COBOL is now most widely used; it goes beyond the previous versions in increasing the versatility and the structure of the language.[1]

All versions of ANS COBOL are very similar, although there are some variations. This text focuses on COBOL 85 but when there are differences between COBOL 85 and the previous standard, COBOL 74, we indicate them. You should determine what COBOL standard your computer uses so that you will be more attuned to the variations among the different versions cited in this text.

Note that an individual COBOL compiler (whether it is a 68, 74, or 85 version) may include **enhancements**, which provide the programmer with additional options not necessarily part of the standard. The reference manual for each compiler indicates these enhancements as shaded entries to distinguish them from the ANS standard.

---

[1] Copies of the ANS COBOL standard can be obtained from the American National Standards Institute, 1430 Broadway, New York, NY 10118.

The next version of COBOL will be produced during this decade and is currently referred to as COBOL 9x. At the end of each chapter we include changes that are likely to be included in that new standard.

WEB SITE
The Internet site www.ansi.org includes COBOL 9x updates.

THE FUTURE OF COBOL

The future of COBOL has been the subject of much discussion in recent years. It is, after all, a language that has been in existence for over 40 years while newer languages now have many more features that make them more suitable for PC-based applications.

But COBOL is likely to remain an important language in the years ahead. Consider the following facts:

1. According to the Datapro Information Services Group, an estimated 150 billion lines of COBOL source code are currently in use, with programmers adding about five billion lines each year.
2. According to the Datapro Information Services Group, 42.7 percent of all applications development programmers in medium to large U.S. companies use COBOL.
3. International Data Corporation reports that revenues for COBOL desktop development are expected to be $176.4 million by 1998; these revenues have increased from $86.3 million in 1993 at an average growth rate of 15.4 percent a year.

These facts suggest that COBOL will remain an important language in the years ahead for two reasons: (1) older, mainframe-based ''legacy'' systems will need to be maintained by maintenance programmers who know COBOL and (2) COBOL is still being used by many organizations for new application development.

SELF-TEST Self-test questions are provided throughout the text, with solutions that follow, to help you assess your understanding of the material presented.

1. A program must be in _____ language to be executed or run by a computer.
2. Programs are typically written in a _____ language rather than in machine language because _____ .
3. Programs written in a language other than machine language must be _____ before execution can occur.
4. The process of converting a source program into machine language is called _____ .
5. The program written in a programming language such as COBOL is called the _____ program.
6. The object program is the _____ .
7. A _____ converts a source program into a(n) _____ program.
8. The errors that are detected during compilation denote _____ ; they are usually referred to as _____ errors.
9. Before executing a program with test data, the logic of the program can be checked manually using a technique called a _____ .
10. COBOL is an abbreviation for _____ .
11. COBOL is a common language in the sense that _____ .
12. (T or F) COBOL is ideally suited for scientific as well as business problems.

Solutions

1. machine
2. symbolic; machine languages are very complex
3. translated or compiled
4. compilation or translation

5. source or applications
6. set of instructions that has been converted into machine language
7. compiler or translator program; object or machine language
8. any violation of programming rules in the use of the symbolic programming language; syntax
9. program walkthrough
10. Common Business-Oriented Language
11. it can be used on many computers
12. F—It is ideally suited for business applications.

TECHNIQUES FOR IMPROVING PROGRAM DESIGN

STRUCTURED PROGRAMMING USING MODULAR DESIGN FOR CODING PARAGRAPHS

When programming became a major profession in the 1960s and 1970s, the primary goal of programmers or software developers was getting programs to work. Although this is still a programmer's main objective, writing programs so that they are easy to read, debug, and modify is just as important. That is, as the computer field evolves, more and more attention is being given to programming style and technique, as well as to making programs as efficient as possible.

The most important technique for improving the design of a program in any language is called **structured programming**. This technique uses logical control constructs that make programs easier to read, debug, and modify if changes are required. Moreover, structured programs are easier to evaluate so that programming managers are better able to assess the program's logic.

For those of you who have had some previous programming experience, you may have encountered nonstructured techniques that include frequent use of GO TOs or branch points to skip to different sections of programs. These GO TOs often make it very difficult to follow the logic of a program; they can also complicate the debugging process.

One major purpose of structured programming is to simplify debugging by eliminating branch points in a program. For that reason, structured programming is sometimes referred to as GO-TO-less programming, where a GO TO statement is the COBOL code for a branch. Using the techniques of structured programming, the GO TO or branch statement is avoided entirely. In COBOL, this means writing programs where sequences are controlled by PERFORM statements. (In other languages, this would mean writing programs where sequences are controlled by DO or WHILE statements.)

Using this structured technique, each section of a program can be written and even debugged independently without too much concern for where it enters the logic flow. This concept may seem a little abstract at this point, but we will clarify it as we go along.

The typical structured program is subdivided into paragraphs or **modules**, where a main module calls in other modules as needed. That is, the programmer codes one main module, and when some other set of instructions is required, it is coded as a separate module that is called in and executed by a PERFORM statement. The terms "paragraph," "routine," and "module" are used interchangeably in this text.

In a modularized program, each module can be tested independently. Moreover, it is feasible for different programmers to code different modules or sections of a large and complex program. The main module simply calls for the execution of the other modules or sections as needed.

THE TOP-DOWN APPROACH FOR CODING MODULES

Another common technique for making programs easier to read and more efficient is called **top-down programming**. The term implies that proper program design is best achieved by developing major modules or procedures before minor ones. Thus, in a top-down program, the main routines are coded first and are followed by intermediate routines and then minor ones.

By coding modules in this top-down manner, the overall organization of the program is given primary attention. Details are deferred or saved for minor modules, which are coded last. Top-down programming is analogous to designing a term paper by developing an outline first, which gets more and more detailed only after the main organization or structure has been established. This standardized top-down technique complements the structured approach for achieving efficient program design.

In this text we will use structured techniques in all our programs and avoid the use of GO TOs. In addition, we will code in a top-down format so that you will learn to program in a style that is widely accepted as a standardized and effective one. Chapter 5 discusses in depth the design features used in structured and top-down programs.

A SAMPLE PROGRAM

AN OVERVIEW OF THE FOUR DIVISIONS

Every COBOL program consists of four separate *divisions*, each with a specific function:

THE FOUR DIVISIONS

Name	Purpose
IDENTIFICATION DIVISION	Identifies the program to the computer. It also can provide documentation about the program.
ENVIRONMENT DIVISION	Defines the file-names and describes the specific computer equipment that will be used by the program.
DATA DIVISION	Describes the input and output formats to be used by the program. It also defines any constants and work areas necessary for the processing of data.
PROCEDURE DIVISION	Contains the instructions necessary for reading input, processing it, and creating output.

The structure and organization of a COBOL program are best explained by an illustration. Note that this illustration is intended to familiarize you with a sample COBOL program; do not expect to be able to code an entire program yourself until you have read the next few chapters.

DEFINITION OF THE PROBLEM

A software developer in a large company is assigned the task of calculating and printing weekly wages or gross pay for all nonsalaried personnel. See Figure 1.5. The employee name, hourly rate, and number of hours worked are supplied as input for each employee, and the weekly wages figure is to be computed as follows:

WEEKLY-WAGES = HOURS -WORKED × HOURLY-RATE

Before processing can begin, the input must be in a form that is ''readable'' or under-

Figure 1.5 Systems specifications for sample program.

standable to the computer. The input may have been keyed using the keyboard of a PC or terminal and then stored as a **file** or collection of data. A file is most often stored on disk.

INPUT LAYOUT

Assume that employee data is entered as a file on disk. As we will see, the device used for entering the input does not really affect the program's logic. The data file entered as input has the format specified in the record layout form in Figure 1.6. A **record** is a unit within the file that contains data for an individual employee. The record layout depicted in Figure 1.6*b* will be our preferred representation.

The employee record consists of three data items called **fields**. We call the three fields EMPLOYEE-NAME-IN, HOURS-WORKED-IN, and HOURLY-RATE-IN. From the record layout in Figure 1.6, you can see that positions 1 through 20 of each record contain EMPLOYEE-NAME-IN. If any name contains less than 20 characters, the **low-order**, or rightmost, **positions** are left blank. Name fields are typically alphabetic or **alphanumeric**, which means they can contain any character (e.g., O'CONNOR, SMITH 3rd). We typically define all nonnumeric fields as alphanumeric.

Alphabetic and alphanumeric data are always entered from left to right. HOURS-WORKED-IN will be placed in positions 21–22 and HOURLY-RATE-IN in positions 23–25. If HOURS-WORKED-IN is a single digit (0–9), then 0 will be placed in the leftmost or **high-order position** of the field (00–09). Thus, if HOURS-WORKED-IN equals 7, the data would be entered as 07. Numeric data is always right-justified in this way. We typically define as numeric only those fields used in arithmetic operations.

Figure 1.6 Input disk record layout for sample program.

(a) Pictorial Representation of the Input Record Layout

EMPLOYEE-NAME-IN	HOURS-WORKED-IN	HOURLY-RATE-IN (DOLLARS) (CENTS)
1 20	21 22	23 24 25

(b) Text-Based Representation of the Input Record Layout

EMPLOYEE-DATA **Record Layout**			
Field Name	**Size**	**Data Type**	**No. of Decimal Positions (if Numeric)**
EMPLOYEE-NAME-IN	20	Alphanumeric	
HOURS-WORKED-IN	2	Numeric	0
HOURLY-RATE-IN	3	Numeric	2

Note: We typically define all nonnumeric fields as alphanumeric.

The HOURLY-RATE-IN figure, as a dollars and cents amount, is to be interpreted as a field with two decimal positions. That is, 925 in record positions 23–25 will be interpreted by the computer as 9.25. The decimal point is *not* entered on the record, since it would waste a storage position. Instead, COBOL uses **implied decimal points** to represent numbers with decimal components that are to be used in arithmetic operations.

We use the suffix -IN with each field name of EMPLOYEE-RECORD to reinforce the fact that these are input fields. This is a recommended naming convention, *not* a required one. Because all our employee records have exactly the same format, we say that this file has **fixed-length records**. Files are frequently represented in column-and-row format, where columns represent fields and rows represent records, as depicted in Figure 1.6b.

Output Layout

A file or collection of employee records with the above format will be read as input to the program. Then WEEKLY-WAGES-OUT will be calculated by the computer as HOURS-WORKED-IN multiplied by HOURLY-RATE-IN. Suppose we wanted to store this new WEEKLY-WAGES-OUT field as part of a file. A computed figure cannot be added directly to our input file. That is, we usually do not add output data directly to an input record. Instead, we create an output file that contains the input along with the computed WEEKLY-WAGES-OUT.

If we wanted this WEEKLY-WAGES-OUT field as part of a payroll file, we would create an output file that contained all input data *in addition to* the computed wage figure. The output PAYROLL-FILE could be stored on a second disk file. Or we could print the output as a file called PAYROLL-LISTING that would include the input fields along with the computed weekly wages. Our sample program will create printed output. The Printer Spacing Chart in Figure 1.7 illustrates the format for each printed or detail (D) line.

Figure 1.7 indicates the print positions we will use for the output. Print positions 1–20 are left blank, as a left margin, and the name is printed in positions 21–40. The X's indicate that an alphanumeric field is to be printed in 21–40. NAME-OUT is the field name we will assign to this output area.

Print positions 41–50 are left blank for readability to separate one field from another, and the hours worked are printed in 51–52. The 9's are used to specify the positions where numeric data is to be printed. Similarly, the hourly rate is printed in positions 61–64 and weekly wages in positions 71–76. The entries in parentheses are the names of the fields that will be printed.

As illustrated in Figure 1.5, the file or collection of records that serves as input to the system will be called EMPLOYEE-DATA. For each record read as input, the computer will calculate WEEKLY-WAGES-OUT from the two input fields HOURS-WORKED-IN and HOURLY-RATE-IN. The input data along with the computed figures for each record will be used to create the output print file called PAYROLL-LISTING. All fields within each print record, or line, of the PAYROLL-LISTING file have the suffix -OUT to make it clear that they are output fields.

Figure 1.7 Printer Spacing Chart for sample program.

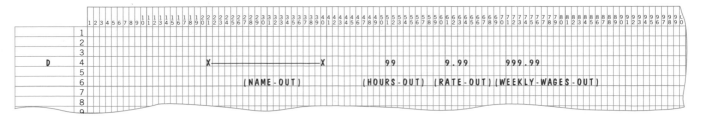

THE PROGRAM ILLUSTRATED

Reviewing the Specifications

The systems specifications in Figure 1.5 illustrate the relationship between input and output files. The program specifications in Figures 1.6 and 1.7 illustrate the input and output record layouts. Once these specifications have been prepared, the programmer should plan the program's design. This means mapping out the logic to be used in the program. Figure 1.8 illustrates a sample pseudocode that explains the logic to be used in the program. The techniques used to write a pseudocode are explained in detail in Chapter 5. We include this planning tool here because we believe you should become familiar with reading it even before you prepare your own.

After the program has been designed or planned using pseudocode, it is ready to be written or coded. You will recall that a program is a set of instructions that operate on input to produce output. Figure 1.9 is a simplified COBOL 85 program that will read employee disk records and create a printed payroll report containing the computed wages for each employee along with the input data. Sample input test data and its corresponding printout are illustrated in Figure 1.10.

Coding Rules

Note that the program is divided into four major divisions. The IDENTIFICATION, ENVIRONMENT, DATA, and PROCEDURE DIVISIONs are coded on lines (or serial numbers) 01, 03, 07, and 26, respectively. Every COBOL program *must* contain these four divisions in this order. For the sake of consistency, we use uppercase letters in all our coding and we distinguish the number zero from the letter O by slashing zeros.

The first 29 lines of this program are similar regardless of which COBOL compiler you use. Some instruction formats used in the rest of the program are not part of the COBOL 74 standard, although if you use a COBOL 74 compiler it is likely to have these formats as enhancements. In the next section we illustrate the last 19 lines of the same program using only the standard instruction format for COBOL 74. This program will run with any COBOL compiler, but we recommend that it be used only by COBOL 74 programmers.

Figure 1.8 Pseudocode for sample COBOL 85 program.

```
START
        Open the files
        PERFORM UNTIL no more records (Are-There-More-Records = 'NO ')
            READ input record
                AT END
                        Move 'NO ' to Are-There-More-Records
                NOT AT END
                        Clear the output area
                        Move input fields to output fields
                        Calculate Wages as Rate multiplied by Hours
                        Write the output record
            END-READ
        END-PERFORM
        Close the files
STOP
```

Figure 1.9 Sample COBOL 85 program on coding form.

COBOL Program Sheet

System						Punching Instructions							Sheet	of
Program	**FIRST SAMPLE PROGRAM**			Graphic						Card Form #			Identification	
Programmer	**N. STERN**		Date	Punch									73] [80	

```
Sequence                Cont.  A   B                           COBOL Statement
(Page)  (Serial)
1    3 4   6 7 8     12      16      20      24      28      32      36      40      44      48      52      56      60      64      68

001  0 1      IDENTIFICATION DIVISION.
001  0 2      PROGRAM-ID. SAMPLE.
001  0 3      ENVIRONMENT DIVISION.
001  0 4      INPUT-OUTPUT SECTION.
001  0 5      FILE-CONTROL.     SELECT EMPLOYEE-DATA     ASSIGN TO EMP-DAT.
001  0 6                        SELECT PAYROLL-LISTING   ASSIGN TO PRINTER.
001  0 7      DATA DIVISION.
001  0 8      FILE SECTION.
001  0 9      FD  EMPLOYEE-DATA      LABEL RECORDS ARE STANDARD.
001  1 0      01  EMPLOYEE-RECORD.
001  1 1          05   EMPLOYEE-NAME-IN     PICTURE X(20).
001  1 2          05   HOURS-WORKED-IN      PICTURE 9(2).
001  1 3          05   HOURLY-RATE-IN       PICTURE 9V99.
001  1 4      FD  PAYROLL-LISTING      LABEL RECORDS ARE OMITTED.
001  1 5      01  PRINT-REC.
001  1 6          05                    PICTURE X(20).
001  1 7          05   NAME-OUT          PICTURE X(20).
001  1 8          05                    PICTURE X(10).
001  1 9          05   HOURS-OUT         PICTURE 9(2).
001  2 0          05                    PICTURE X(8).
00121             05   RATE-OUT          PICTURE 9.99.
00122             05                    PICTURE X(6).
00123             05   WEEKLY-WAGES-OUT  PICTURE 999.99.
00124     WORKING-STORAGE SECTION.
00125     01  ARE-THERE-MORE-RECORDS     PICTURE XXX VALUE 'YES'.
00126     PROCEDURE DIVISION.
00127     100-MAIN-MODULE.
00128         OPEN INPUT EMPLOYEE-DATA
00129              OUTPUT PAYROLL-LISTING
00130         PERFORM UNTIL ARE-THERE-MORE-RECORDS = 'NO '
00131             READ EMPLOYEE-DATA
00132                 AT END
00133                     MOVE 'NO ' TO ARE-THERE-MORE-RECORDS
00134                 NOT AT END
00135                     PERFORM 200-WAGE-ROUTINE
00136             END-READ
00137         END-PERFORM
00138         CLOSE EMPLOYEE-DATA
00139               PAYROLL-LISTING
00140         STOP RUN.
00141     200-WAGE-ROUTINE.
00142         MOVE SPACES TO PRINT-REC
00143         MOVE EMPLOYEE-NAME-IN TO NAME-OUT
00144         MOVE HOURS-WORKED-IN TO HOURS-OUT
00145         MOVE HOURLY-RATE-IN TO RATE-OUT
00146         MULTIPLY HOURS-WORKED-IN BY HOURLY-RATE-IN
00147             GIVING WEEKLY-WAGES-OUT
00148         WRITE PRINT-REC.
```

Figure 1.10 Sample input test data and its corresponding printout.

Sample Input

```
ROBERT FROST          45500
WILLIAM SHAKESPEARE 50550
JOHN DUNNE            35425
JANE AUSTIN           55600
MARK TWAIN            30450
```

Sample Output

```
ROBERT FROST                  45        5.00        225.00
WILLIAM SHAKESPEARE           50        5.50        275.00
JOHN DUNNE                    35        4.25        148.75
JANE AUSTIN                   55        6.00        330.00
MARK TWAIN                    30        4.50        135.00
```

The IDENTIFICATION and ENVIRONMENT DIVISIONs

In this program, the IDENTIFICATION DIVISION has, as its only entry, the PROGRAM-ID. That is, the IDENTIFICATION DIVISION of this program serves to name the program. We will see that there are other entries used for documentation purposes that may be included in the IDENTIFICATION DIVISION, but PROGRAM-ID is the only *required* entry.

The ENVIRONMENT DIVISION assigns the input and output files to specific devices in the INPUT-OUTPUT SECTION. The input file, called EMPLOYEE-DATA, will be on a disk in a file called EMP-DAT. Similarly, PAYROLL-LISTING is the output file and is assigned to the printer, called PRINTER in our program (but it may be called by a different name at your computer center—SYSLST and SYS$OUTPUT are common names).

The DATA DIVISION

The FILE SECTION of the DATA DIVISION describes the format of the input and output files. The *File Description*, or FD, for EMPLOYEE-DATA describes the input disk file, which in this case has identifying disk labels (LABEL RECORDS ARE STANDARD).

The record format for the input file is called EMPLOYEE-RECORD. It has three input fields—EMPLOYEE-NAME-IN, HOURS-WORKED-IN, and HOURLY-RATE-IN. Each field has a corresponding PICTURE clause denoting the size and type of data that will appear in the field.

EMPLOYEE-NAME-IN is a data field containing 20 characters. PICTURE X(20) indicates that the size of the field is 20 characters. The X in the PICTURE clause means that the field can contain any alphanumeric character, including a space. Similarly, HOURS-WORKED-IN is a two-position numeric field. PICTURE 9(2) indicates the type and size of data: 9 denotes numeric data, and (2) denotes a two-position area. HOURLY-RATE-IN is a three-position numeric field with an implied decimal point. That is, PICTURE 9V99 indicates a *three-position* numeric field with an implied or assumed decimal point after the first position; the V means an implied decimal point. Thus 925 in this field will be interpreted by the computer as 9.25. The decimal point does *not* appear in the input disk record, but the V in the PICTURE clause ensures that the number will be treated by the computer as if a decimal point had been included.

The output print file called PAYROLL-LISTING does not have a record label because print files can be checked manually. It has a record format called PRINT-REC, which is subdivided into eight fields, each with an appropriate PICTURE clause.

The fields that have blank field names set aside space in the record but are not used in the PROCEDURE DIVISION. We will set them up so that they will actually contain blanks. They are used in the print record so that output fields to be printed will be separated from one another by spaces or blanks. With COBOL 74, you must use the word FILLER instead of a blank field name.

The first unused area with no field name is defined with a PICTURE of X(20), which means it has 20 characters.

The word FILLER is required with COBOL 74 and optional with COBOL 85, which permits you to leave the field name blank.

Thus, to obtain a 20-character blank area for a left margin we say 05 PICTURE X(20) or 05 FILLER PICTURE X(20). NAME-OUT will follow in print positions 21–40 as noted on the Printer Spacing Chart in Figure 1.7. The next entry 05 PICTURE X(10) means that the following field is a 10-position blank area that will separate the name from HOURS-OUT, which is two numeric positions. After the next eight-position blank area, a RATE-OUT field is denoted as PICTURE 9.99. This is a *four-position field* that actually contains a decimal point. Printed numeric fields with decimal values should always include the decimal point.

Note that HOURLY-RATE-IN and RATE-OUT have different PICTURE clauses. (HOURLY-RATE-IN has a PICTURE of 9V99.) Suppose we read a value of 123 into HOURLY-RATE-IN; it will be stored as 1$\wedge$23 with the *decimal point implied*. All numeric fields are decimally aligned in arithmetic and move operations. When we move HOURLY-RATE-IN to RATE-OUT, the result will be 1.23 in RATE-OUT *with the actual decimal point printing* because RATE-OUT has a PICTURE of 9.99. (With COBOL, decimal points are omitted but implied in input files, while they are actually included in output print files.) Then a six-position blank field will be followed by a six-position WEEKLY-WAGES-OUT field with the decimal point printing again.

The first three data fields of PRINT-REC (NAME-OUT, HOURS-OUT, and RATE-OUT) will contain data copied directly from each input record. The last field, WEEKLY-WAGES-OUT, must be computed.

The field or data item called ARE-THERE-MORE-RECORDS is defined in the WORKING-STORAGE SECTION of the DATA DIVISION. This field is initialized with a value of 'YES'. The quote marks are always used to designate a nonnumeric value. The field called ARE-THERE-MORE-RECORDS will be used in the PROCEDURE DIVISION as an end-of-file indicator, sometimes referred to as a "flag" or "switch." That is, it will always have a value of 'YES' until the last data record has been read and processed, at which time a 'NO ' will be moved into it. When this field contains 'YES', it means there are still more records to process; when it contains 'NO ', there are no more input records.

The data-name ARE-THERE-MORE-RECORDS was chosen because the field is used to indicate when the last data record has been read and processed. Any field name could have been used, but the name ARE-THERE-MORE-RECORDS is both descriptive and self-explanatory. This indicator field will be programmed to contain the value 'YES' when there are still records to process; we set it to 'NO ' only when there are *no* more input records.

The PROCEDURE DIVISION

The PROCEDURE DIVISION contains the set of instructions to be executed by the computer. Each instruction is executed in the order in which it appears on the coding sheets. The PROCEDURE DIVISION is divided into two paragraphs or modules, 100-MAIN-MODULE and 200-WAGE-ROUTINE. In our COBOL 85 programs, we include a period only at the end of the last instruction in a module. We will consider margin rules later.

The first PROCEDURE DIVISION entry is the following:

```
OPEN INPUT EMPLOYEE-DATA
     OUTPUT PAYROLL-LISTING
```

This instruction accesses the devices assigned to the files and indicates to the computer which file is input and which is output. It extends to two lines for readability but is treated as a single unit or statement. We use periods only for the last statement in the paragraph, although it is permissible to end each statement with a period.

The second instruction begins with a PERFORM verb on line 30 and ends on line 37 with an END-PERFORM scope terminator:

```
PERFORM UNTIL ARE-THERE-MORE-RECORDS = 'NO '
    .
    .
END-PERFORM
```

This instruction indicates that all statements from lines 31 to 36 are to be executed or performed repeatedly until the end-of-file indicator, ARE-THERE-MORE-RECORDS, is equal to a value of 'NO ', meaning there are no more records to process.

Within the PERFORM UNTIL ... END-PERFORM we first read a record. If a record is successfully read, it is processed at 200-WAGE-ROUTINE and the PERFORM UNTIL ... END-PERFORM is repeated. If there are no more records to process when the READ instruction is executed, the AT END clause is processed and 'NO ' is moved to ARE-THERE-MORE-RECORDS. Then the PERFORM UNTIL ... END-PERFORM is terminated.

The PERFORM UNTIL ... END-PERFORM is called a **loop** because the instructions within it are executed repeatedly until ARE-THERE-MORE-RECORDS is set equal to 'NO ' when an AT END condition is reached.

The statements within this loop are indented for ease of reading. Let us look at the READ statement within the PERFORM UNTIL ... END-PERFORM more closely:

```
READ EMPLOYEE-DATA
    AT END
            MOVE 'NO ' TO ARE-THERE-MORE-RECORDS
    NOT AT END
            PERFORM 200-WAGE-ROUTINE
END-READ
```

This is an instruction that causes the computer to read *one* data record into an area of storage referred to as the input area. Note that data must be in storage in order to be operated on. If there are no more records to be read when this READ statement is executed, the value 'NO ' will be moved to the field called ARE-THERE-MORE-RECORDS; otherwise the field remains unchanged at its initial value of 'YES'. Given that there are input records to process at the beginning of the run, the first attempt to read a record will cause data to be transmitted from disk to storage for processing. After a record has been successfully read, the AT END clause is executed. The PERFORM instruction following the NOT AT END clause is executed when the READ brings input into main memory. This will occur every time the PERFORM loop is executed except when there is no more input to process. The END-READ is a COBOL 85 scope terminator that specifies the end of the READ statement. Scope terminators are a COBOL 85 structured programming addition that are not part of the COBOL 74 standard.

Suppose the first input record is as follows:

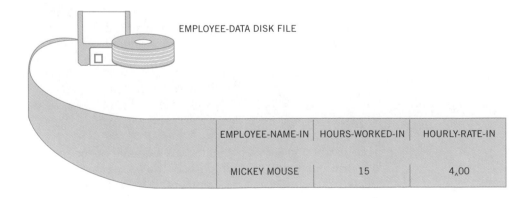

EMPLOYEE-DATA DISK FILE

EMPLOYEE-NAME-IN	HOURS-WORKED-IN	HOURLY-RATE-IN
MICKEY MOUSE	15	4.00

The READ instruction reads the preceding record into primary storage or main memory and makes it available to the Central Processing Unit or CPU for processing. This record is stored in a symbolic storage address called EMPLOYEE-RECORD, which is a data-name that is defined by the programmer in the DATA DIVISION. When this first record is read, primary storage or main memory will contain the following:

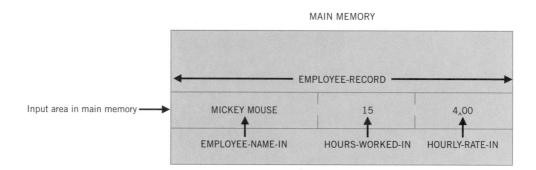

Thus, READ ... NOT AT END ... will cause all the statements within the paragraph named 200-WAGE-ROUTINE (from line 42 through line 48) to be executed.

Once ARE-THERE-MORE-RECORDS = 'NO ', the PERFORM UNTIL ... END-PERFORM is no longer executed. The statement to be operated on next is the one immediately following the PERFORM in 100-MAIN-MODULE. That is, the PERFORM UNTIL ... END-PERFORM causes repeated execution of 200-WAGE-ROUTINE until there are no more input records, at which time control returns to the statement following the PERFORM. The instructions on lines 38–40, CLOSE and STOP RUN, are executed only after all input records have been processed in 200-WAGE-ROUTINE.

In summary, the first instruction within 100-MAIN-MODULE in the PROCEDURE DIVISION is the OPEN statement and it activates the files. Then the PERFORM UNTIL ... END-PERFORM is executed. It reads a record and performs a process module if a record is successfully read. This PERFORM UNTIL ... END-PERFORM loop reads and processes records repeatedly until there are no more records, at which time 'NO ' is moved to the indicator called ARE-THERE-MORE-RECORDS. The process module, 200-WAGE-ROUTINE, is executed every time a record is successfully read; it moves data to the output area, calculates a weekly wage, and prints a line for every input record.

When there is no more input, the AT END clause of the READ is executed. 'NO ' is moved to ARE-THERE-MORE-RECORDS and the PERFORM UNTIL ... END-PERFORM loop is terminated. Then control returns to the statement after the PERFORM UNTIL ... END-PERFORM in 100-MAIN-MODULE. This is the CLOSE statement, which deactivates the files. The STOP RUN is executed as the last instruction, and the program is terminated. The first five steps—OPEN, PERFORM, the READ within the PERFORM, CLOSE, and STOP RUN—represent the main module of the PROCEDURE DIVISION. These statements appear within the module or paragraph labeled 100-MAIN-MODULE.

Let us look more closely at the instructions to be executed in the 200-WAGE-ROUTINE paragraph when a record has been successfully read. First, MOVE SPACES TO PRINT-REC clears out or initializes the output area called PRINT-REC with blanks or spaces. This ensures that all unnamed or FILLER areas will be blank. Then, EMPLOYEE-NAME-IN of the first disk record, which was read with the READ statement on line 31, is moved to NAME-OUT of the output area. The fields called HOURS-WORKED-IN and HOURLY-RATE-IN of this first record are also moved to the output area. WEEKLY-WAGES-OUT, an output field, is then calculated by multiplying HOURS-WORKED-IN by HOURLY-RATE-IN. The three MOVE and one MULTIPLY instructions executed in 200-WAGE-ROUTINE for the first record produce the following results in primary storage or main memory:

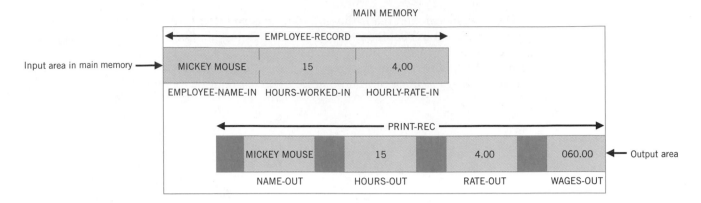

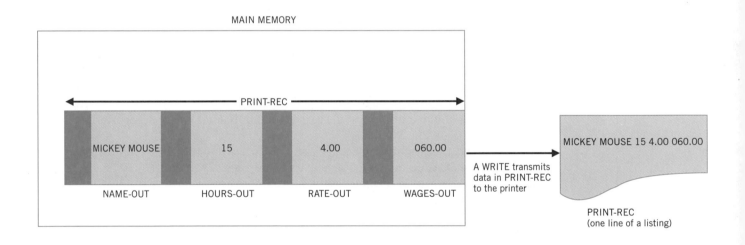

After the data has been moved to the area reserved in storage for output (called the output area), a WRITE instruction is executed. This WRITE statement takes the information in the output area and prints it:

Later on, we will see that we can add an ADVANCING clause to the WRITE statement to obtain double spacing of output lines: WRITE PRINT-REC AFTER ADVANCING 2 LINES.

The set of instructions delimited by the PERFORM UNTIL ... END-PERFORM will read and process the first disk record and print one output line. This PERFORM UNTIL ... END-PERFORM is a loop that gets executed repeatedly until ARE-THERE-MORE-RECORDS = 'NO '. When the PERFORM UNTIL ... END-PERFORM is repeated, the READ statement on line 31 is executed. If a successful READ is performed, which means that a record for processing is actually read, the instructions within the NOT AT END ... END-READ scope process the second record and print another output line.

The sequence of instructions within the PERFORM UNTIL ... END-PERFORM are repeated until the field called ARE-THERE-MORE-RECORDS is set equal to 'NO ', which will occur only after all input records have been read. That is, the PERFORM UNTIL ... END-PERFORM gets executed repeatedly until a READ instruction produces an AT END condition, which means there is no more input. Then 'NO ' is moved to ARE-THERE-MORE-RECORDS and the PERFORM UNTIL ... END-PERFORM loop is complete. The instructions following the END-PERFORM—the CLOSE and the STOP RUN on lines 38–40—are then executed and the program is terminated. The STOP RUN, as the last instruction in the module or paragraph, ends with a period.

The Use of Periods

All statements in the first three divisions end with a period. The PROCEDURE DIVISION entry and the module names end with a period, as does the last statement in each module. In our COBOL 85 programs, all other PROCEDURE DIVISION entries do not have periods. We will discuss punctuation in more detail later on.

Figure 1.9, then, represents an entire sample COBOL 85 program. It will run on any computer, although minor changes may be necessary in the SELECT statements because some compilers have specific requirements for the ASSIGN clause. You may want to key in and run this program on your system just to familiarize yourself with COBOL. Figure 1.11 is the computer-produced source listing of the same program. This program can

Figure 1.11 Computer listing of sample program.

```
01    IDENTIFICATION DIVISION.
02    PROGRAM-ID. SAMPLE.
03    ENVIRONMENT DIVISION.
04    INPUT-OUTPUT SECTION.
05    FILE-CONTROL. SELECT EMPLOYEE-DATA     ASSIGN TO EMP-DAT.
06                  SELECT PAYROLL-LISTING  ASSIGN TO PRINTER.
07    DATA DIVISION.
08    FILE SECTION.
09    FD  EMPLOYEE-DATA      LABEL RECORDS ARE STANDARD.
10    01  EMPLOYEE-RECORD.
11        05  EMPLOYEE-NAME-IN   PICTURE X(20).
12        05  HOURS-WORKED-IN    PICTURE 9(2).
13        05  HOURLY-RATE-IN     PICTURE 9V99.
14    FD  PAYROLL-LISTING   LABEL RECORDS ARE OMITTED.
15    01  PRINT-REC.
16        05                     PICTURE X(20).
17        05  NAME-OUT           PICTURE X(20).
18        05                     PICTURE X(10).
19        05  HOURS-OUT          PICTURE 9(2).
20        05                     PICTURE X(8).
21        05  RATE-OUT           PICTURE 9.99.
22        05                     PICTURE X(6).
23        05  WEEKLY-WAGES-OUT   PICTURE 999.99.
24    WORKING-STORAGE SECTION.
25    01  ARE-THERE-MORE-RECORDS  PICTURE XXX VALUE 'YES'.
26    PROCEDURE DIVISION.
27    100-MAIN-MODULE.
28        OPEN INPUT EMPLOYEE-DATA
29             OUTPUT PAYROLL-LISTING
30        PERFORM UNTIL ARE-THERE-MORE-RECORDS = 'NO '
31            READ EMPLOYEE-DATA
32                AT END
33                    MOVE 'NO ' TO ARE-THERE-MORE-RECORDS
34                NOT AT END
35                    PERFORM 200-WAGE-ROUTINE
36            END-READ
37        END-PERFORM
38        CLOSE EMPLOYEE-DATA
39              PAYROLL-LISTING
40        STOP RUN.
41    200-WAGE-ROUTINE.
42        MOVE SPACES TO PRINT-REC
43        MOVE EMPLOYEE-NAME-IN TO NAME-OUT
44        MOVE HOURS-WORKED-IN TO HOURS-OUT
45        MOVE HOURLY-RATE-IN TO RATE-OUT
46        MULTIPLY HOURS-WORKED-IN BY HOURLY-RATE-IN
47                GIVING WEEKLY-WAGES-OUT
48        WRITE PRINT-REC.
```

be run as is using a COBOL 85 compiler, which is the most commonly used compiler today. It will, however, require some modifications that we will discuss, if you are using a COBOL 74 compiler. Note that in COBOL, statements are English-like; also the structured organization of a program in COBOL makes it an easy language to read and learn.

COBOL 74 Variations—Only for Students with COBOL 74 Compilers

If you use a COBOL 85 compiler, skip this section.

Some programmers still use a COBOL 74 compiler. Unless a COBOL 74 compiler has enhancements, you cannot code (1) a PERFORM UNTIL ... END-PERFORM or (2) a READ ... NOT AT END ... END-READ instruction as in Figure 1.11. The COBOL 74 version of this sample program would have a PROCEDURE DIVISION as illustrated in Figure 1.12.

All COBOL programs begin by opening the input and output files. In COBOL 74 programs, we use an initial or **priming** READ to read the first record. Then a separate paragraph is executed until there are no more records. In this program, after the first record is read, 200-WAGE-ROUTINE is executed repeatedly until there is no more input. 200-WAGE-ROUTINE processes the first record read on line 30 and ends by reading a second record. When 200-WAGE-ROUTINE is executed a second time, the second record is processed and a third record read. This procedure is repeated until there is no more input and 'NO ' is moved to ARE-THERE-MORE-RECORDS on line 46.

The processing of 200-WAGE-ROUTINE is under the control of the PERFORM on line 32. When the READ in 200-WAGE-ROUTINE results in an AT END condition and ARE-THERE-MORE-RECORDS is set equal to 'NO ', the PERFORM on line 32 is no longer executed and the instructions following the PERFORM on lines 34 to 36 are then run. The two files are closed and the run terminated.

Note that COBOL 74 programs have more limitations than COBOL 85 programs:

COBOL 74	**COBOL 85**
1. Each instruction ends with a period.	1. Only the last instruction in a paragraph or module ends with a period.
2. The loop, PERFORM paragraph-name UNTIL ..., requires a separate module that is executed until the condition specified is met.	2. A loop can be coded within a module using an in-line PERFORM UNTIL ... END-PERFORM sequence.
3. READ statements cannot have a NOT AT END clause or an END-READ delimiter. This makes it necessary to code programs with a priming READ:	3. The sequence READ

                                AT END ...
                                    NOT AT END ...
                            END-READ

```
Priming READ ──→ READ ...
required              AT END ...
before PERFORM    PERFORM (paragraph) UNTIL
                           (no more records)
                      :
                      :
          (paragraph)
                      :
                      :
              READ ...
                  AT END ...  ←── Paragraph ends with a READ
```

makes it easier to include a single READ in a program within a sequence of steps executed by the PERFORM.

Figure 1.12   COBOL 74 program with a priming READ.

COBOL Program Sheet

System				Punching Instructions									Sheet	of	
Program	**FIRST SAMPLE PROGRAM**			Graphic							Card Form #			Identification	
Programmer	**N. STERN**		Date	Punch									73]		[80

Sequence (Page) (Serial)	Cont.	A	B	COBOL Statement

```
001 01  IDENTIFICATION DIVISION.
001 02  PROGRAM-ID. SAMPLE.
001 03  ENVIRONMENT DIVISION.
001 04  INPUT-OUTPUT SECTION.
001 05  FILE-CONTROL.    SELECT EMPLOYEE-DATA    ASSIGN TO EMP-DATA.
001 06                   SELECT PAYROLL-LISTING  ASSIGN TO PRINTER.
001 07  DATA DIVISION.
001 08  FILE SECTION.
001 09  FD  EMPLOYEE-DATA      LABEL RECORDS ARE STANDARD.
001 10  01  EMPLOYEE-RECORD.
001 11      05  EMPLOYEE-NAME-IN      PICTURE X(20).
001 12      05  HOURS-WORKED-IN       PICTURE 9(2).
001 13      05  HOURLY-RATE-IN        PICTURE 9V99.
001 14  FD  PAYROLL-LISTING   LABEL RECORDS ARE OMITTED.
001 15  01  PRINT-REC.
001 16      05  FILLER               PICTURE X(20).
001 17      05  NAME-OUT             PICTURE X(20).
001 18      05  FILLER               PICTURE X(10).
001 19      05  HOURS-OUT            PICTURE 9(2).
001 20      05  FILLER               PICTURE X(8).
00121       05  RATE-OUT             PICTURE 9.99.
00122       05  FILLER               PICTURE X(6).
00123       05  WEEKLY-WAGES-OUT     PICTURE 999.99.
00124  WORKING-STORAGE SECTION.
00125  01  ARE-THERE-MORE-RECORDS    PICTURE XXX VALUE 'YES'.
00126  PROCEDURE DIVISION.
00127  100-MAIN-MODULE.
00128      OPEN INPUT EMPLOYEE-DATA
00129           OUTPUT PAYROLL-LISTING.
00130      READ EMPLOYEE-DATA
00131          AT END MOVE 'NO ' TO ARE-THERE-MORE-RECORDS.
00132      PERFORM 200-WAGE-ROUTINE
00133          UNTIL ARE-THERE-MORE-RECORDS = 'NO '.
00134      CLOSE EMPLOYEE-DATA
00135            PAYROLL-LISTING.
00136      STOP RUN.
00137  200-WAGE-ROUTINE.
00138      MOVE SPACES TO PRINT-REC.
00139      MOVE EMPLOYEE-NAME-IN TO NAME-OUT.
00140      MOVE HOURS-WORKED-IN TO HOURS-OUT.
00141      MOVE HOURLY-RATE-IN TO RATE-OUT.
00142      MULTIPLY HOURS-WORKED-IN BY HOURLY-RATE-IN
00143          GIVING WEEKLY-WAGES-OUT.
00144      WRITE PRINT-REC.
00145      READ EMPLOYEE-DATA
00146          AT END MOVE 'NO ' TO ARE-THERE-MORE-RECORDS.
00147
```

Figure 1.13 Hierarchy or structure chart for sample program.

A BRIEF OVERVIEW OF PROGRAM PLANNING TOOLS

A program such as the one shown in Figure 1.9 would first be planned using either a flowchart or pseudocode to map out the logic and to ensure that the program to be written is well-designed. In Chapter 5 we discuss in detail the techniques used for planning a program. In Figure 1.8 in this chapter, we simply illustrated one of these planning tools (pseudocode).

The following are basic rules for reading the pseudocode in Figure 1.8.

RULES FOR INTERPRETING PSEUDOCODE

General Rules

1. A pseudocode begins with a START and ends with a STOP.

2. All instructions are read in sequence.

3. The instructions between the PERFORM ... END-PERFORM in the illustration are executed repeatedly UNTIL there are no more records to process.

Finally, Figure 1.13 illustrates a hierarchy or structure chart, which shows the relationships among modules in a program. This figure shows that there are two modules or paragraphs and that 200-WAGE-ROUTINE is the paragraph executed from 100-MAIN-MODULE. That is, within 100-MAIN-MODULE there is a PERFORM 200-WAGE-ROUTINE statement.

We will see in Chapter 5 that hierarchy charts are extremely useful for illustrating the logic flow in a program that has many PERFORM statements. As we write more complex programs, the hierarchy charts will become more detailed as well.

ENTERING AND RUNNING A COBOL PROGRAM ON YOUR COMPUTER

After your program is coded, you will key it into the computer using (1) a terminal linked to a mainframe or minicomputer or (2) a keyboard of a PC. If you are using a mainframe or minicomputer, you will need to obtain the log-on and authorization codes that will enable you to access the computer. You will also need to learn the system commands for accessing the COBOL compiler and executing COBOL programs. If you are using a PC that is part of a network, you will also need to learn log-on procedures.

In most instances, you will use a *text editor* for entering the program, which will enable you to easily correct any mistakes you make while typing. Most text editors have common features, such as commands for deleting lines, adding lines, and changing or replacing entries. You may use standard text editors or text editors designed specifically for entering COBOL programs.

Some COBOL text editors will automatically tab to position 8, which is the first position of a COBOL program. If you examine Figure 1.9, you will see that some instructions are coded beginning in position 8, which is marked A for Margin A, and some are coded beginning in position 12, which is marked B for Margin B. Alternatively, some COBOL compilers, like those used on the VAX, permit the programmer to use column 1 as Margin A and column 5 as Margin B. We discuss margin rules in detail in the next chapter.

 If you are using a microcomputer, you can use *any* text editor or word processing package for creating your COBOL program, but most PC-based COBOL compilers come with their own text editors. Then you will need to consult a user's manual for accessing your specific COBOL compiler. Our *Getting Started with RM/COBOL-85* and *Getting Started with Micro Focus Personal COBOL* manuals (Windows and DOS versions), available with this text, include methods used for keying and running RM/COBOL-85 and Micro Focus Personal COBOL programs, respectively.

Each computer has its own operating system commands for:

1. Logging on to the computer system.
2. Creating a COBOL program file-name.
3. Using a text editor to key in program and/or data files, make any corrections, save files, and exit the editor.
4. Calling in the COBOL compiler.
5. Translating the COBOL program.
6. Linking or loading the object program so it can be run.
7. Running the object program with test data.
8. Logging off.

CHAPTER SUMMARY
A. The Nature of COBOL
1. COBOL is one of the most widespread commercial programming languages in use today.
2. COBOL is an abbreviation for Common Business-Oriented Language.
3. It is an English-like language.
4. The American National Standards (ANS) versions of COBOL are 1968, 1974, and 1985. (This text focuses on COBOL 85 and indicates how it differs from COBOL 74. Changes expected to be included in the future 199x COBOL standard are indicated as well.)
B. Program Preparation and Debugging
1. Get program specifications from the systems analyst or prepare them yourself.
2. Use planning tools—flowcharts, pseudocode, hierarchy charts—for program design.
3. Code the program.
4. Compile the program and fix syntax errors.
5. Test the program using debugging techniques.
   a. Perform program walkthroughs.
   b. Check for logic and run-time errors during and after program execution.
6. Document the program.
C. Techniques for Improving Program Design
1. Structured programming.
   a. Referred to as GO-TO-less programming.
   b. Structured programs are subdivided into paragraphs or modules.
2. Top-Down Programming.
   a. Major modules or procedures are coded before minor ones.
   b. This is analogous to developing an outline before writing a report—the organization and structure are most important; details are filled in later.
D. The COBOL Divisions
1. IDENTIFICATION DIVISION.
   a. Identifies the program to the computer system.

    b. May provide some documentation as well.

    c. `PROGRAM-ID` is the only required entry within the division.

2. `ENVIRONMENT DIVISION`.

    Assigns a file-name to each file used in the program, and specifies the device that the file will use.

3. `DATA DIVISION`.

    a. Defines and describes the formats of all input, output, and work areas used for processing.

    b. `FILE SECTION`

        (1) Each file-name defined in the `ENVIRONMENT DIVISION` must be described in an `FD` in the `DATA DIVISION`.

        (2) Each record format within every file is defined as an `01` entry.

        (3) Fields within each record are described with a `PICTURE` clause that specifies the size and type of data.

    c. `WORKING-STORAGE SECTION`

        (1) Defines any work areas needed for processing.

        (2) An end-of-file indicator is coded in the `WORKING-STORAGE SECTION`; we will refer to this field as `ARE-THERE-MORE-RECORDS`. In our examples, the field called `ARE-THERE-MORE-RECORDS` will contain the value `'YES'` when there are input records to process, and a value of `'NO '` when there is no more data.

4. `PROCEDURE DIVISION`.

    a. Is subdivided into paragraphs or modules.

    b. Includes all instructions required to process input and produce output.

    c. All instructions are executed in sequence, but a `PERFORM UNTIL ... END-PERFORM` is a loop. The instructions within its range are executed repeatedly until the condition specified in the `UNTIL` clause is met. When the condition is met, the steps directly following the `END-PERFORM` are executed; after a paragraph is executed with a `PERFORM`, control returns to the next instruction, in sequence, following the `PERFORM`.

    d. Main module or paragraph.

    The following are typical entries in a main module.

        (1) Files are designated as `INPUT` or `OUTPUT` and activated in an `OPEN` statement.

        (2) A `PERFORM UNTIL ... END-PERFORM` is a loop that is executed repeatedly until `ARE-THERE-MORE-RECORDS = 'NO '`. The indicator, `ARE-THERE-MORE-RECORDS`, is set to `'NO '` only after the last input record has been read and processed and the `READ ... AT END` clause is executed.

        (3) Within the `PERFORM UNTIL ... END-PERFORM`, we code the following:

```
READ ...
    AT END ...
    NOT AT END ...
END-READ
```

        The `READ` attempts to read a record. If a record is successfully read, the `NOT AT END` clause is executed; this usually contains a `PERFORM` statement that executes a paragraph that processes the record. If there are no more records to process, the `AT END` clause is executed, which usually moves `'NO '` to `ARE-THERE-MORE-RECORDS` so that the `PERFORM UNTIL ... END-PERFORM` loop can be terminated.

        (4) A `CLOSE` statement deactivates all the files.

        (5) A `STOP RUN` terminates processing.

    e. Calculation or processing paragraphs.

        (1) Calculation or processing paragraphs are executed when a statement in the main module specifies `PERFORM` paragraph-name.

        (2) A calculation or processing paragraph is required to process each input record.

KEY TERMS

Alphanumeric field	Compile	Enhancements
American National Standards Institute (ANSI)	Compiler	Field
Applications package	Customized program	File
Applications program	Debug	Fixed-length record
Applications programmer	Desk checking	Flowchart
	Documentation	Hierarchy chart

High-order position
Implied decimal point
Information system
Input
Logic error
Loop
Low-order position
Machine language
Module
Object program
Operating system
  programs

Output
Priming READ
Printer Spacing Chart
Program
Program specifications
Programmer
Pseudocode
Record
Record layout form
Run-time error
Software
Software developer

Source program
Structure chart
Structured programming
Symbolic programming
  language
Syntax error
Top-down programming
User
Walkthrough

CHAPTER SELF-TEST

At the end of each chapter there is a self-test that covers the material in the entire chapter. The solutions follow the test.

1. All COBOL programs consist of ___(no.)___ divisions called _____ , _____ , _____ , and _____ .

2. The function of the IDENTIFICATION DIVISION is to _____ .

3. The function of the ENVIRONMENT DIVISION is to _____ .

4. The function of the DATA DIVISION is to _____ .

5. The function of the PROCEDURE DIVISION is to _____ .

6. Another term for incoming data is _____ and another term for outgoing information is _____ .

7. _____ and _____ are examples of computer input media.

8. Two techniques for simplifying the design of a COBOL program and facilitating debugging are called _____ and _____ .

9. A(n) _____ statement indicates which files are input and which are output.

10. (T or F) A PERFORM ... UNTIL instruction executes a series of steps repeatedly until some condition is met.

Solutions

1. four; IDENTIFICATION; ENVIRONMENT; DATA; PROCEDURE

2. identify the program

3. assign a file-name to each file and specify the device that each file will use

4. describe the input, output, and work areas used in the program

5. define the instructions and operations necessary to convert intput data into output

6. input; output

7. disk; data entered using a keyboard

8. structured programming; top-down programming

9. OPEN

10. T

REVIEW QUESTIONS

I. True-False Questions

_____ 1. A COBOL program that compiles without any syntax errors will always run properly.

_____ 2. Programs written in COBOL need not be compiled.

_____ 3. Although COBOL is a commercial programming language, it contains advanced mathematical functions that can be used for highly sophisticated scientific problems.

_____ 4. The sequence in which the four divisions in a COBOL program are written is IDENTIFICATION, DATA, ENVIRONMENT, PROCEDURE.

_____ 5. The division that specifies the computer devices to be used is the DATA DIVISION.

_____ 6. The division that seems to require the least programming effort is the IDENTIFICATION DIVISION.

_____ 7. Instructions are coded in the PROCEDURE DIVISION.

_____ 8. If 1370 is read into a field with a PICTURE clause of 99V99 it will be stored as 13ᴧ70.

_____ 9. If the preceding field were moved to an output area with a PICTURE of 99.99 it would be printed as 13.70.

_____ 10. Fields defined in WORKING-STORAGE can be given initial values.

II. General Questions

1. Define the following terms:
   - (a) Program.
   - (b) Compiler.
   - (c) Source program.
   - (d) Object program.

2. State the differences between a symbolic programming language and a machine language.

3. State the major reasons why COBOL is such a popular language.

4. What is the meaning of the term "structured programming"?

5. What is the meaning of the term "ANS COBOL"?

6. Indicate the difference between operating system software and applications software.

7. What is the meaning of the term "syntax error"?

8. What is the purpose of the PICTURE clause?

9. What is the purpose of the SELECT statement?

10. What is the purpose of the WORKING-STORAGE SECTION?

PROGRAMMING ASSIGNMENTS

Completing the following assignments will help you learn how to enter a program on your system. If you have access to a computer, enter one or more of these programs, compile, and debug them.

Before you begin, you will need to be provided with the following system-dependent information:

A. The method of accessing a computer at your center and using its text editor.

B. The operating system commands for entering a program, compiling it, and executing it.

C. The ASSIGN clause requirements for SELECT statements.

To run the program, you may use test data supplied by an instructor or you may create your own input.

1. Key in and run the program in Figure 1.9 using your own sample data file.

2. Figure 1.14 is an illustration of a sample COBOL program.
   - (a) Describe the input by providing a layout of the input record.
   - (b) Describe the output by providing a layout of the output record.
   - (c) Describe, in your own words, the processing that converts the input data into output.
   - (d) Key in and run the program using your own sample data file.

3. Figure 1.15 is an illustration of a sample COBOL program.
   - (a) Describe the input by providing a layout of the input record.
   - (b) Describe the output by providing a layout of the output record.
   - (c) Describe, in your own words, the processing that converts the input data into output.
   - (d) Key in and run the program using your own sample data file.

Figure 1.14 Program for Programming Assignment 2.

COBOL 85

```
IDENTIFICATION DIVISION.
PROGRAM-ID.  PROBLEM2.
ENVIRONMENT DIVISION.
INPUT-OUTPUT SECTION.
FILE-CONTROL.  SELECT SALES-FILE ASSIGN TO DISK1.
               SELECT PRINT-FILE ASSIGN TO PRINTER.
DATA DIVISION.
FILE SECTION.
FD  SALES-FILE LABEL RECORDS ARE STANDARD.
01  SALES-REC.
    05  NAME-IN               PICTURE X(15).
    05  AMOUNT-OF-SALES-IN     PICTURE 999V99.
FD  PRINT-FILE LABEL RECORDS ARE OMITTED.
01  PRINT-REC.
    05                         PICTURE X(20).
    05  NAME-OUT               PICTURE X(15).
    05                         PICTURE X(20).
    05  AMT-COMMISSION-OUT     PICTURE 99.99.
    05                         PICTURE X(72).
WORKING-STORAGE SECTION.
01  ARE-THERE-MORE-RECORDS     PICTURE XXX VALUE 'YES'.
PROCEDURE DIVISION.
100-MAIN-MODULE.
    OPEN INPUT SALES-FILE
         OUTPUT PRINT-FILE
    PERFORM    UNTIL ARE-THERE-MORE-RECORDS = 'NO '
               READ SALES-FILE
                   AT END
                           MOVE 'NO ' TO ARE-THERE-MORE-RECORDS
                   NOT AT END
                           PERFORM 200-COMMISSION-RTN
               END-READ
    END-PERFORM
    CLOSE  SALES-FILE
           PRINT-FILE
    STOP RUN.
200-COMMISSION-RTN.
    MOVE SPACES TO PRINT-REC
    MOVE NAME-IN TO NAME-OUT
    IF  AMOUNT-OF-SALES-IN IS GREATER THAN 100.00
        MULTIPLY .03 BY AMOUNT-OF-SALES-IN
            GIVING AMT-COMMISSION-OUT
    ELSE
        MULTIPLY .02 BY AMOUNT-OF-SALES-IN
            GIVING AMT-COMMISSION-OUT
    END-IF
    WRITE PRINT-REC.
```

COBOL 74 Substitutions

For COBOL 74, FILLER must be used instead of a blank field name

```
READ SALES-FILE
    AT END MOVE 'NO ' TO
        ARE-THERE-MORE-RECORDS.
PERFORM 200-COMMISSION-RTN
    UNTIL ARE-THERE-MORE-RECORDS
        = 'NO '.
CLOSE SALES-FILE
      PRINT-FILE.
STOP RUN.
```

Omit the END-IF scope terminator and end the preceding line with a period

```
READ SALES-FILE
    AT END MOVE 'NO ' TO
        ARE-THERE-MORE-RECORDS.
```

Figure 1.15 Program for Programming Assignment 3.

COBOL 85

```
IDENTIFICATION DIVISION.
PROGRAM-ID. PROBLEM3.
ENVIRONMENT DIVISION.
INPUT-OUTPUT SECTION.
FILE-CONTROL.    SELECT PAYROLL-IN  ASSIGN TO DISK1.
                 SELECT PAYROLL-OUT ASSIGN TO DISK2.
DATA DIVISION.
FILE SECTION.
FD  PAYROLL-IN LABEL RECORDS ARE STANDARD.
01  PAYROLL-REC.
    05 EMPLOYEE-NUMBER-IN    PICTURE 9(5).
    05 EMPLOYEE-NAME-IN      PICTURE X(20).
    05 LOCATION-CODE-IN      PICTURE 9999.
    05 ANNUAL-SALARY-IN      PICTURE 9(6).
FD  PAYROLL-OUT LABEL RECORDS ARE STANDARD.
01  RECORD-OUT.
    05 EMPLOYEE-NUMBER-OUT   PICTURE 9(5).
    05 EMPLOYEE-NAME-OUT     PICTURE X(20).
    05 ANNUAL-SALARY-OUT     PICTURE 9(6).
WORKING-STORAGE SECTION.
01  ARE-THERE-MORE-RECORDS   PICTURE X(3) VALUE 'YES'.
PROCEDURE DIVISION.
100-MAIN-MODULE.
    OPEN INPUT PAYROLL-IN
         OUTPUT PAYROLL-OUT
    PERFORM    UNTIL ARE-THERE-MORE-RECORDS = 'NO '
            READ PAYROLL-IN
                AT END
                            MOVE 'NO ' TO ARE-THERE-MORE-RECORDS
                NOT AT END
                            PERFORM 200-WAGE-ROUTINE
            END-READ
    END-PERFORM
    CLOSE   PAYROLL-IN
            PAYROLL-OUT
    STOP RUN.
200-WAGE-ROUTINE.
    MOVE EMPLOYEE-NUMBER-IN TO EMPLOYEE-NUMBER-OUT
    MOVE EMPLOYEE-NAME-IN TO EMPLOYEE-NAME-OUT
    ADD 1000, ANNUAL-SALARY-IN
        GIVING ANNUAL-SALARY-OUT
    WRITE RECORD-OUT.
```

COBOL 74 Substitutions

```
READ PAYROLL-IN
    AT END MOVE 'NO ' TO
        ARE-THERE-MORE-RECORDS.
PERFORM 200-WAGE-ROUTINE
    UNTIL ARE-THERE-MORE-RECORDS
        = 'NO '.
CLOSE PAYROLL-IN
    PAYROLL-OUT.
STOP RUN.
```

```
READ PAYROLL-IN
    AT END MOVE 'NO ' TO
        ARE-THERE-MORE-RECORDS.
```

CHAPTER 2

The IDENTIFICATION and ENVIRONMENT DIVISIONs

▰ OBJECTIVES

To familiarize you with

1. The basic structure of a COBOL program.
2. General coding and format rules.
3. IDENTIFICATION and ENVIRONMENT DIVISION entries.

▰ CONTENTS

BASIC STRUCTURE OF A COBOL PROGRAM

CODING A SOURCE PROGRAM

Recall that *all* COBOL programs consist of *four divisions*. In the next few chapters, we discuss each division in detail. After reading Chapters 2–4, you will be able to write elementary programs using all the divisions of a COBOL program. We begin with some basic rules for coding programs.

Each COBOL instruction is coded on a single line using 80 characters per line, where specific entries must appear in designated columns or positions. Originally, each COBOL line was keypunched into a single 80-column punched card. Today, each COBOL line is typed or keyed using a keyboard and displayed on a single line of a screen or monitor.

COBOL **coding** or **program sheets** are sometimes used to create an initial version of the program prior to keying it into the computer. Programmers use coding sheets in much the same way that some people create handwritten versions of their documents before typing. One main advantage of COBOL coding sheets is that they designate where the specific items of a program are to be placed. See Figure 2.1.

Most COBOL program sheets have 20 lines numbered 01–20 respectively in columns 4–6. They also have four or more additional unnumbered lines that can be used for insertions in case one or more entries have been accidentally omitted.

For every line written on the coding sheet, we will key in one line on a terminal or PC keyboard. The entire program is referred to as the *COBOL source program.*

Figure 2.1 Main body of a COBOL coding sheet.

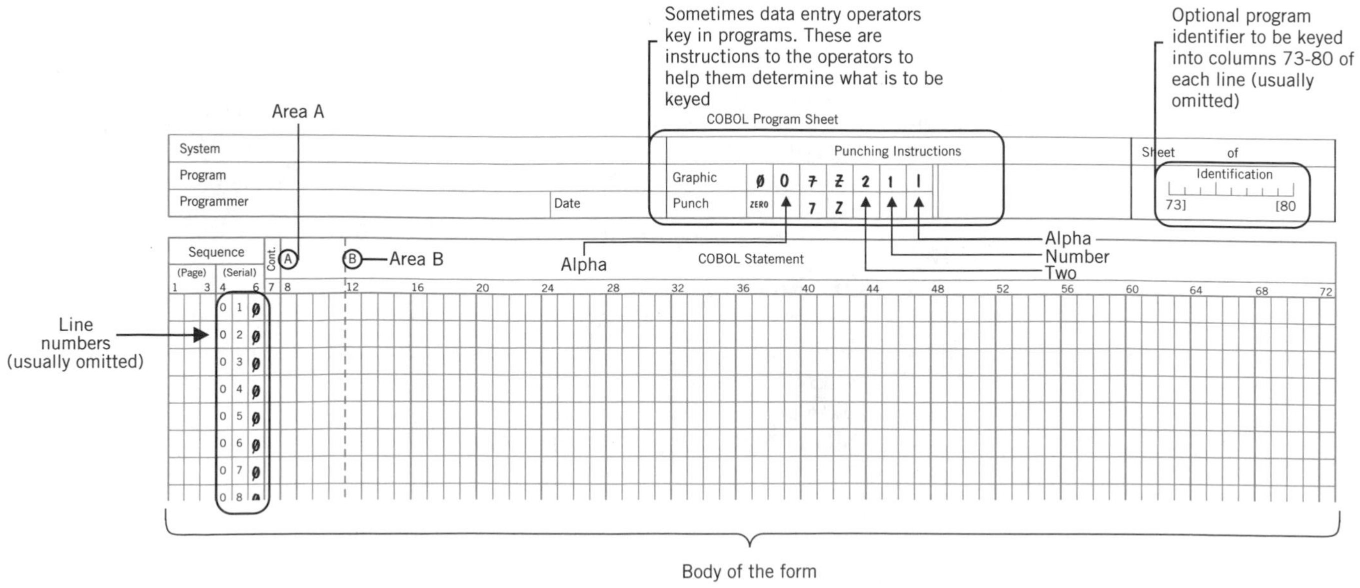

CODING RULES

The Main Body of a Program

Today, most software developers key their programs directly into the computer and do not use coding sheets. We will, however, consider the coding sheet here because the form itself illustrates some important rules about the language.

The main body of a program and the coding sheet itself are subdivided into 72 positions or columns because each COBOL instruction can be a maximum of 72 characters long. Each line of a coding sheet is equivalent to one line entered on a terminal or PC keyboard. Figure 2.2 illustrates how an excerpt of a COBOL program appears as two lines of code.

Optional Entries: Identification and Page and Serial Numbers

On the top right side of the coding sheet there is provision for a program identification, labeled positions 73–80. This identification entry may be entered into positions 73–80 of all program lines keyed from this form, but it is usually left blank. The rest of the data recorded on the top of the form is *not* keyed into the source program. It is for informational purposes only.

The page and serial (or line) numbers, positions 1–6, and the identification entry, positions 73–80, are *optional* in a COBOL program. In the past, when lines were keypunched onto cards, page and serial numbers would help ensure that the cards were properly sequenced. Similarly, identification numbers helped to ensure that the cards in the program deck were part of the correct program. Today, these entries are rarely used. Most compilers automatically provide line numbers for each keyed line. We will not include either of these entries in our programs.

Column 7: For Comments, Continuing Nonnumeric Literals, and Starting a New Page

Column 7 of a COBOL program is a **continuation position** labeled Cont. on a coding sheet. It has three primary purposes:

1. It can be used for designating an entire line as a comment by coding an * (asterisk) in column 7.
2. It can be used to force the printing of subsequent instructions on the next page of the source listing by coding a / (slash) in column 7.

Figure 2.2 Using a terminal or PC keyboard to enter a COBOL program.

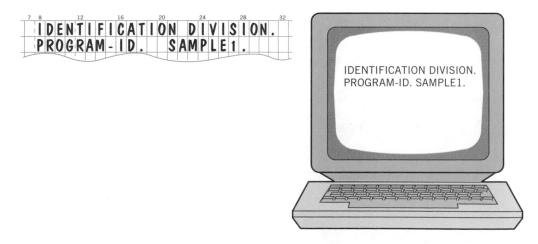

3. It can be used for the continuation of nonnumeric literals, as we will see in Chapter 3.

We will discuss the first two uses here.

Comments

Comment lines are useful for providing documentation on how a program will process data. Comments are also used to remind the programmer about specific aspects of the program and to provide useful information to any key users who might read the program. The following illustrates how comments can be used in a COBOL program:

```
 IDENTIFICATION DIVISION.
 PROGRAM-ID. SAMPLE.
 ********************************************************************************
 *      this program reads two input files, compares the part                  *
 *      numbers, and prints part numbers missing from either                   *
 *      file.                                                                   *
 ********************************************************************************
```

We also use comments throughout our programs to clarify the logic used. If column 7 of any line contains an *, that entire line is not compiled, but is printed on the listing for documentation purposes only. Finally, a comment line or a blank line with no entries at all can be used to separate entries in a program.

───── DEBUGGING TIP ─────

Use uppercase letters for instructions; use lowercase letters for comments to set them apart from instructions, making them easier to identify.

Page-Eject with a Slash (/) in Column 7

Column 7 can also be used to skip to the next page when the source listing is being printed. In long programs, for example, we might want each division printed on a separate page. To skip to a new page after each division, insert a line that is blank except for a slash (/) in column 7.

Areas A and B

Positions 8–72 of a standard COBOL program contain program statements. Column 8 is labeled *A* and column 12 is labeled *B*. These are referred to as *Areas*. Certain entries must begin in Area A and others must begin in Area B.

If an entry is to be coded in **Area A**, it may begin in position 8, 9, 10, or 11. Most often, Area A entries begin in position 8. If an entry is to be coded in **Area B**, it may begin anywhere after position 11. That is, it may begin in positions 12, 13, 14, and so on. Note that margin rules specify the *beginning* point of entries. A word that must *begin* in Area A may *extend* into Area B.

Example   AUTHOR, a paragraph-name in the IDENTIFICATION DIVISION, must begin in Area A. Any entry referring to AUTHOR may then follow in Area B as in the following:

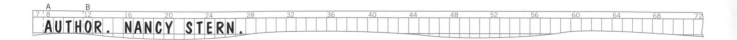

The A of AUTHOR is placed in column 8, or Area A. The word itself extends into Area B. The next entry must begin in Area B or in any position after column 11. In our example, the author's name begins in position 16.

TYPES OF COBOL ENTRIES

As we have seen, COBOL programs are divided into four **divisions** called the IDENTIFICATION, ENVIRONMENT, DATA, and PROCEDURE DIVISIONs. They must *always* appear in that order in a program. Some divisions are subdivided into **sections**. The DATA DIVISION, for example, which describes all storage areas for data processed in the program, is divided into two main sections: the FILE SECTION and the WORKING-STORAGE SECTION. The FILE SECTION of the DATA DIVISION describes the input and output areas, and the WORKING-STORAGE SECTION of the DATA DIVISION describes the intermediate work areas necessary for processing. Each section may be further subdivided into **paragraphs**.

All other entries in the program are considered COBOL **statements**. A statement or series of statements that ends with a period is referred to as a **sentence**. We will see that all statements in the first three divisions always end with a period. Statements in the PROCEDURE DIVISION may or may not end with periods.

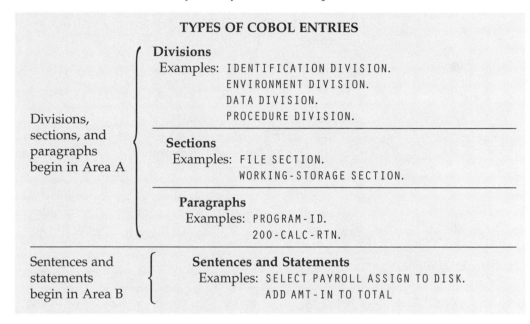

TYPES OF COBOL ENTRIES

Divisions, sections, and paragraphs begin in Area A

Divisions
Examples: IDENTIFICATION DIVISION.
ENVIRONMENT DIVISION.
DATA DIVISION.
PROCEDURE DIVISION.

Sections
Examples: FILE SECTION.
WORKING-STORAGE SECTION.

Paragraphs
Examples: PROGRAM-ID.
200-CALC-RTN.

Sentences and statements begin in Area B

Sentences and Statements
Examples: SELECT PAYROLL ASSIGN TO DISK.
ADD AMT-IN TO TOTAL

MARGIN RULES

1. Division, section, and paragraph-names begin in Area A.

2. All other statements, clauses, and sentences begin in Area B.

We will see that the great majority of COBOL entries, including all PROCEDURE DIVISION instructions, begin in Area B.

Figure 2.3 provides an example of these margin rules. The ENVIRONMENT DIVISION entry begins in Area A, as does the CONFIGURATION SECTION entry. SOURCE-COMPUTER and OBJECT-COMPUTER are paragraph-names, which must also begin in Area A. SOURCE-COMPUTER and OBJECT-COMPUTER must have COBOL sentences following them in Area B, either on the same line or the next line. Each sentence in this division ends with a period.

Note that ENVIRONMENT DIVISION, CONFIGURATION SECTION, and SOURCE-COMPUTER are each followed by a period, as are all division, section, and paragraph-names. A sentence, which consists of a statement or series of statements, must also end with a period.

Division and section names *must* always appear on a line with no other entry. Paragraph-names may appear on the same line as statements. Keep in mind that each period must be followed by at least one space.

Figure 2.3 Illustration of margin rules.

```
ENVIRONMENT DIVISION.
CONFIGURATION SECTION.
SOURCE-COMPUTER.
    IBM-ES9000.
OBJECT-COMPUTER.
    IBM-ES9000.
INPUT-OUTPUT SECTION.
FILE-CONTROL.
    SELECT SALE-FILE ASSIGN TO DISK1.
```

In the PROCEDURE DIVISION, several statements or sentences may appear on one line, but we will use the convention of coding one statement per line for ease of reading and debugging.

REVIEW OF COBOL CODING RULES

Columns	Use	Explanation
1–6	Sequence numbers or Page and Line numbers (optional)	Previously used for sequence-checking when programs were punched into cards. We will omit them.
7	Continuation, comment, or starting a new page	Used to denote a line as a comment (* in column 7), to cause the printer to skip to a new page when printing the source listing (a / in column 7), or to continue nonnumeric literals (see Chapter 3).
8–11	Area A	Some entries such as DIVISION, SECTION, and paragraph-names must begin in Area A.
12–72	Area B	Most COBOL entries, including PROCEDURE DIVISION statements and sentences, are coded in Area B.
73–80	Program identification (optional)	Used to identify the program. We will omit this entry.

REVIEW OF MARGIN RULES

1. Division and Section Names
   a. Begin in Area A.
   b. End with a period.
   c. Must appear on a line with no other entries.

2. Paragraph-names
   a. Begin in Area A.
   b. End with a period, which must always be followed by at least one space.
   c. May appear on lines by themselves or with other entries.

3. Sentences and Statements
   a. Begin in Area B.
   b. Sentences end with a period, which must always be followed by at least one space.
   c. May appear on lines by themselves or with other entries.
   d. A sentence consists of a statement or series of statements.
   e. For COBOL 85, we do not end `PROCEDURE DIVISION` statements with a period except for the last one in the paragraph. Periods are, however, permitted at the end of each full statement.

As noted, blank lines, as well as comments, are permitted anywhere in a COBOL program and should be used to improve readability.

─────── COBOL 9X CHANGES ───────

The rather rigid margin rules required in current programs will be eliminated in COBOL 9x.

CODING REQUIREMENTS OF THE IDENTIFICATION DIVISION

PARAGRAPHS IN THE IDENTIFICATION DIVISION

The `IDENTIFICATION DIVISION` is the smallest, simplest, and least significant division of a COBOL program. As the name indicates, it supplies identifying information about the program.

The `IDENTIFICATION DIVISION` has *no* effect on the execution of the program but is, nevertheless, *required* as a means of identifying the program to the computer.

The `IDENTIFICATION DIVISION` is divided into paragraphs, not sections. The following paragraphs may be coded:

Format

```
IDENTIFICATION DIVISION.
PROGRAM-ID.   program-name.
[AUTHOR.   [comment-entry] ...]
[INSTALLATION.   [comment-entry] ...]
[DATE-WRITTEN.   [comment-entry] ...]
[DATE-COMPILED.   [comment-entry] ...]
[SECURITY.   [comment-entry] ...]
```

The division name, `IDENTIFICATION DIVISION`, is coded in Area A. Paragraph-names are also coded in Area A, and each must be followed by a period. The above format is the same as the one that appears in COBOL reference manuals. The next section discusses the rules for interpreting instruction formats such as the preceding.

UNDERSTANDING INSTRUCTION FORMATS AS THEY APPEAR IN REFERENCE MANUALS

Programming texts, like this one, are written to help you learn the basic rules of a language. They do not, in general, attempt to be complete because that would require many more pages.

To learn *all* the rules of a language and all the options available, you would consult a *reference manual* that is available for each major compiler. Reference manuals are very concise and sometimes difficult to read. Nonetheless, most programmers find they often need to consult them.

We will use the same basic *instruction format* for presenting the syntax of a language as is used in reference manuals. This will not only familiarize you with COBOL's syntax but will help you to read and understand a COBOL reference manual. Instruction formats such as those used here are similar to those for other programming languages.

The following are instruction format rules that will assist you in interpreting the format for the IDENTIFICATION DIVISION entries just described:

RULES FOR INTERPRETING INSTRUCTION FORMATS

1. Uppercase words are COBOL reserved words that have special meaning to the compiler.

2. Underlined words are required in the paragraph.

3. Lowercase words represent user-defined entries.

4. Braces { } denote that one of the enclosed items is required.

5. Brackets [ ] mean the clause or paragraph is optional.

6. If punctuation is specified in the format, it is required.

7. The use of dots or ellipses (. . .) means that additional entries of the same type may be included if desired.

These rules appear on the inside of the front cover of this text for ease of reference.

We will use simplified formats here so as not to overwhelm you with too much detail. Thus, all our instruction formats will be correct but not necessarily complete. The full instruction formats for COBOL entries are included in a *COBOL Syntax Reference Guide* that accompanies this text.

--- WEB SITE ---

Our *COBOL Syntax Reference Guide* can also be downloaded from our Web page. Check Wiley's Internet site at http://www.wiley.com/cobol/ for more information.

EXAMPLES

The instruction format for the IDENTIFICATION DIVISION entries indicates that the only *required* paragraph is the **PROGRAM-ID**. That is, COBOL programs must be identified by a program name. All other paragraphs in the IDENTIFICATION DIVISION format are enclosed in brackets, meaning that they are optional. In fact, they could be entered as comments rather than paragraphs.

In summary, the first two entries of a program *must be* IDENTIFICATION DIVISION and PROGRAM-ID, with an appropriate program name as follows:

```
IDENTIFICATION DIVISION.
PROGRAM-ID. SAMPLE1.
```

PROGRAM-ID is followed by a period and then at least one space. The program name itself is coded in Area B. We use names of eight characters or less, letters and digits only, because such names are accepted on *all* systems. The two entries may also be coded as follows:

```
IDENTIFICATION DIVISION.
PROGRAM-ID.
    SAMPLE1.
```

Since PROGRAM-ID is a paragraph-name, the user-defined program name SAMPLE1 may appear *on the same line* as PROGRAM-ID, or *on the next line* in Area B. In either case, PROGRAM-ID and the program name must each be followed by a period.

As noted, the other paragraph-names listed in the instruction format are bracketed [ ] and are therefore optional. They can be used to help document the program. If you include any of these, however, as paragraphs rather than comments, they must be coded in the sequence specified in the instruction format. Each paragraph-name is followed by a period and at least one space. The actual entry following the paragraph-name is called a "comment entry" because it is treated as a comment; it can contain *any* character including a period.

If used, AUTHOR would include the name of the programmer; INSTALLATION would be the name of the company or the computer organization; DATE-WRITTEN is the date the program was coded. For most ANS COBOL users, the DATE-COMPILED paragraph can be coded with an actual date entered but is more often written simply as:

```
DATE-COMPILED.
```

On most computers, when DATE-COMPILED is coded *without* a comment-entry, the compiler itself will automatically *fill in the actual date of compilation*. Thus, if the program is compiled three different times on three separate dates, it is not necessary to keep revising this entry. The compiler itself will list the actual date of compilation if the entry DATE-COMPILED appears on a line by itself.

SECURITY would simply indicate whether the program is classified or confidential. This coding would not, however, actually control access to the program. That must be controlled by passwords or other operating system techniques.

In addition to PROGRAM-ID, any, or all, of the preceding paragraphs may be included in the IDENTIFICATION DIVISION. As paragraph-names, these entries are coded in Area A.

The IDENTIFICATION DIVISION, as well as the other divisions, frequently includes comments that describe the program. Recall that an * in column 7 may be used to designate any line as a comment line. Comments are extremely useful for documentation purposes.

The following is an example of IDENTIFICATION DIVISION coding:

```
IDENTIFICATION DIVISION.
PROGRAM-ID. EXHIBIT1.
AUTHOR. R. A. STERN.
INSTALLATION. COMPANY ABC
              ACCOUNTING DEPT.
DATE-WRITTEN. JAN. 1, 1998.
DATE-COMPILED.
SECURITY. CONFIDENTIAL.
*   this program will create a master payroll file, editing    *
*   the input data and producing an error list.                *
```

The comment entry for INSTALLATION, as well as the other entries, may extend to several lines. Each entry *within a paragraph* must, however, be coded in Area B.

--- COBOL 9X CHANGES ---

All paragraphs AUTHOR through SECURITY will be deleted from the 9x standard since they can easily be replaced with comments.

SELF-TEST

1. If an entry must begin in Area A, it may begin in position _____ ; if an entry must begin in Area B, it may begin in position _____ .

2. The four divisions of a COBOL program must appear in order as _____ , _____ , _____ , and _____ .

3. What entries must be coded beginning in Area A?

4. Most entries such as PROCEDURE DIVISION instructions are coded in Area _____ .

5. _____ and _____ must each appear on a separate line. All other entries may have several statements on the same line.

6. The first two entries of a COBOL program must always be _____ and _____ .

7. Each of the preceding entries must be followed by a _____ , which, in turn, must be followed by a _____ .

8. The first two entries of a program are both coded beginning in Area _____ .

9. Code the IDENTIFICATION DIVISION for a program called EXPENSES for a corporation, Dynamic Data Devices, Inc., written July 15, 1998. This program has a security classification and is available to authorized personnel only. It produces a weekly listing by department of all operating expenses.

10. The DATE-COMPILED paragraph usually does not include a comment entry because _____ .

Solutions

1. 8, 9, 10, or 11; 12, 13, 14, and so on
2. IDENTIFICATION; ENVIRONMENT; DATA; PROCEDURE
3. Division, section, and paragraph-names.
4. B
5. Division names; section names
6. IDENTIFICATION DIVISION.
   PROGRAM-ID. program-name.
7. period; space or blank
8. A
9. The following is a *suggested* solution:

```
IDENTIFICATION DIVISION.
PROGRAM-ID. EXPENSES.
AUTHOR. N. B. STERN.
INSTALLATION. DYNAMIC DATA DEVICES, INC.
DATE-WRITTEN. 7/15/98.
DATE-COMPILED.
SECURITY. AUTHORIZED PERSONNEL ONLY.
*    this program produces a weekly list by department    *
*    of all operating expenses.                           *
```

Note: Only the IDENTIFICATION DIVISION *and* PROGRAM-ID *are required. Note, too, that it is good form to use lowercase letters for comments.*

10. the computer itself can supply the date of the compilation (The current date is stored in main memory.)

THE SECTIONS OF THE ENVIRONMENT DIVISION

The **ENVIRONMENT DIVISION** is the only machine-dependent division of a COBOL program. It supplies information about the *computer equipment* to be used in the program. That is, the entries in this division will be dependent on (1) the computer system and (2) the specific devices or hardware used in the program.

The ENVIRONMENT DIVISION is composed of two sections:

SECTIONS OF THE ENVIRONMENT DIVISION

CONFIGURATION SECTION.
INPUT-OUTPUT SECTION.

The CONFIGURATION SECTION supplies information about the computer on which the COBOL program will be compiled and executed. The INPUT-OUTPUT SECTION supplies information about the specific devices used in the program. Printers and disk drives are devices that are typically referred to in the INPUT-OUTPUT SECTION of the ENVIRONMENT DIVISION.

The ENVIRONMENT DIVISION is the only division of a COBOL program that will change significantly if the program is to be run on a different computer. Since computers have various models and equipment, each will require different ENVIRONMENT DIVISION specifications. Throughout this discussion, we will use some *sample* statements, keeping in mind that such entries are dependent on the actual computer used and the devices that will be accessed by the program. You will need either (1) to ask your computer manager or instructor for the device specifications used at your computer center or (2) to check the COBOL manual for your PC compiler.

Interactive Processing.   We will see later on that interactive programs that (1) use keyed data as input and (2) display output on a screen do not need an ENVIRONMENT DIVISION at all.

CONFIGURATION SECTION

The **CONFIGURATION SECTION** of the ENVIRONMENT DIVISION indicates: (1) the **SOURCE-COMPUTER**—the computer that will be used for compiling the program—and (2) the **OBJECT-COMPUTER**—the computer that will be used for executing or running the program. SOURCE-COMPUTER and OBJECT-COMPUTER are paragraphs coded primarily for documentation purposes.

Recall that this text focuses on two existing versions of standard COBOL, the 1974 standard that we call COBOL 74 and the 1985 standard that we call COBOL 85. Officially, the CONFIGURATION SECTION is required for COBOL 74 users and is optional with COBOL 85. In actuality, however, most COBOL 74 compilers include an *enhancement* that permits the user to omit this section if desired. We will briefly consider the CONFIGURATION SECTION, but generally we omit it from our programs.

As noted, all section names, like division names, are coded in Area A. Thus, the CONFIGURATION SECTION, if coded, will follow the ENVIRONMENT DIVISION entry in Area A. SOURCE-COMPUTER and OBJECT-COMPUTER, as paragraph-names, would also be coded in Area A.

The SOURCE- and OBJECT-COMPUTER entries specify:

ENTRIES FOR SOURCE-COMPUTER AND OBJECT-COMPUTER PARAGRAPHS

1. The computer manufacturer.

2. The computer number.

3. The computer model number, if needed.

Consider the following sample entries:

```
ENVIRONMENT DIVISION.
CONFIGURATION SECTION.
SOURCE-COMPUTER. VAX-8800.
OBJECT-COMPUTER. VAX-8800.
```

Each paragraph-name is directly followed by a period and then a space. The designated computer, VAX-8800, is also followed by a period.

In the example, the source and object computers are the same. In general, this will be the case, since compilation and execution are usually performed on the same computer. If, however, the program will be compiled on one model computer and executed, at some future time, on another model computer, these entries will differ, as in the following example:

Example

```
ENVIRONMENT DIVISION.
CONFIGURATION SECTION.
SOURCE-COMPUTER. IBM-ES9000.
OBJECT-COMPUTER. VAX-8800.
```

In this illustration, the program will be compiled on an IBM computer and executed on a VAX.

INPUT-OUTPUT SECTION

The INPUT-OUTPUT SECTION of the ENVIRONMENT DIVISION follows the CONFIGURATION SECTION (if coded) and supplies information concerning the input and output devices used in the program. In the next section, we will discuss the FILE-CONTROL paragraph of the INPUT-OUTPUT SECTION. In the FILE-CONTROL paragraph, a file-name is designated and assigned to a device for each file used in the program.

ASSIGNING FILES TO DEVICES IN THE ENVIRONMENT DIVISION

OVERALL FORMAT

We have thus far discussed the following entries of the ENVIRONMENT DIVISION:

```
ENVIRONMENT DIVISION.
CONFIGURATION SECTION.
SOURCE-COMPUTER.
    computer and model number supplied by the manufacturer
OBJECT-COMPUTER.
    computer and model number supplied by the manufacturer
INPUT-OUTPUT SECTION.
FILE-CONTROL.
    entries that assign file-names to devices . . .
```

The FILE-CONTROL paragraph consists of SELECT statements, each of which is coded in Area B followed by a period. A SELECT statement defines a file-name and assigns a device name to that file. A **file** is the major collection of data for a given application.

For batch processing applications, we have an input file and an output file: one set of data serves as input and a second set of data serves as output. For interactive processing where input is entered using a keyboard, we would not establish an input file in the ENVIRONMENT DIVISION. If the output for an interactive program is printed or saved on disk, we would establish an output file only in the ENVIRONMENT DIVISION. If the output is displayed on a screen, then we would not establish *any* files in the ENVIRONMENT DIVISION—indeed we can omit the ENVIRONMENT DIVISION entirely.

The instruction format for a SELECT statement is as follows:

Format

SELECT   file-name-1
    ASSIGN TO   implementor-name-1

The **implementor-name** is a machine-dependent device specification that is typically provided by the computer center.

REVIEW OF INSTRUCTION FORMAT RULES

1. Uppercase words are reserved words; lowercase words are user-defined.

2. Underlined words are required in the statement.

Guidelines for SELECT Statement

We use two lines for a SELECT statement, with the second line indented for ease of reading.

File-Name Rules

The file-name assigned to each device must conform to the rules for forming user-defined words. A user-defined word is a word chosen by the programmer to represent some element in a program such as a file-name:

RULES FOR FORMING USER-DEFINED WORDS (Such as File-Names)

1. 1 to 30 characters.

2. Letters, digits, and hyphens (-) only.

3. No embedded blanks.

4. At least one alphabetic character.

5. May not begin or end with a hyphen.

6. No COBOL reserved words such as DATA, DIVISION, etc. (A full list of reserved words appears in Appendix A and in the *COBOL Syntax Reference Guide*.)

For each file used in the program, a SELECT statement must be specified. If a program requires a disk file as input and produces a printed report as an output file, two SELECT statements will be specified. One file-name will be assigned to the disk file and the other to the print file.

---- DEBUGGING TIP ----

File-names assigned by the programmer should be meaningful. SALES-IN, for example, would be a more appropriate file-name than S-IN. Also, avoid the use of device-specific file-names such as SALES-DISK. The medium used for storing a given file might change over time, so the use of a device-specific name could prove to be misleading.

If you look at the list of COBOL reserved words that may *not* be coded as user-defined names, you are apt to wonder about how to avoid inadvertently using such words. Note that very few reserved words include hyphens. If you develop the habit of including hyphenated names, which are apt to be clearer anyway, the risk of errors will be reduced.

Implementor-Names or Device Specifications

The implementor-names or device specifications vary widely among computers. We will consider both simplified versions and more detailed ones. You will need to obtain the exact device specifications for your system from your computer center, instructor, or PC manual.

Most systems enable the programmer to access frequently used devices by special device names. The following are common shorthand device specifications that you may be able to use with your system:

Printer	SYSLST or SYS$OUT or PRINTER
Disk	DISC or DISK followed by a disk file-name

For many systems the following entries would be valid for a program that reads input from a disk and prints a report as output:*

Example

```
FILE-CONTROL.
    SELECT TRANSACTION-FILE
        ASSIGN TO DISK 'DATA1'.
    SELECT REPORT-FILE
        ASSIGN TO PRINTER.
```

Sometimes the device specification or implementor-name can be any user-defined word that refers to a file-name on disk reserved for your data entries. Consider the following, which is valid on a DEC VAX system:

```
SELECT SALES-FILE
    ASSIGN TO SALES1.
```

During program execution, the user will be able to access data assigned to a disk file called SALES1. Some systems require the implementor-name to be enclosed in quotes (e.g., 'SALES1') when defining a disk name. In either case, the file will have a file-name of SALES1. That is, a directory of files on disk will include a SALES1 file. SALES1 is the name of the file (file-name) as it is known to the operating system, while SALES-FILE is the name of the file (file-name) as it is known in the COBOL program.

For VAX and PC users, you can skip the following section entirely.

MORE DETAILED DEVICE SPECIFICATIONS REQUIRED FOR SOME COMPUTERS

As noted, device specifications vary among computer manufacturers. The following expanded format of a SELECT statement is standard for some computers, specifically mainframes:

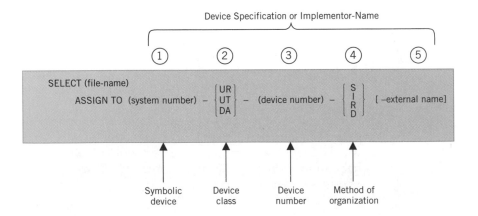

Examples

```
SELECT PAYROLL-IN
    ASSIGN TO SYS005-UR-1403-S.
SELECT SALES-OUT
    ASSIGN TO SYS006-UT-3400-S.
```

Shorter versions that may be acceptable include:

```
SELECT SALES-IN
    ASSIGN TO SYS007-DA-S.
```

The FILE-CONTROL paragraph may seem unnecessarily complex, but the entries are standard for each installation. The only user-defined word is the file-name.

---

*Consult your computer's specifications manual to see if you can use these device specifications.

Interpreting the Device Specification

In this section, we briefly explain the meaning of the five entries for the device specification just described. You may skip this section if you are not required to provide specific device assignments with your programs.

DEVICE SPECIFICATIONS

1. Symbolic Device
   Supplied by the computer center, which assigns a number to each device. SYSNNN is common, where NNN may be a number from 001 to 256.

2. Device Class {UR, UT, DA}
   The braces mean that any one of the following may be used:
   UR—unit-record (terminal or printer)
   UT—utility (sequential disk)
   DA—direct-access (disk)

3. Device Number
   Supplied by the computer manufacturer.

4. Method of Organization
   S for sequential (printer, terminal, or disk)
   I, R, or D may be used for disk files to be accessed randomly

5. External-Name (optional on many systems)

Let us consider the following illustration, using an arbitrary system number since this will depend on the installation.

Example A disk file, consisting of transaction data, may be assigned as follows for an IBM mainframe:

```
SELECT TRANS-FILE
       ASSIGN TO SYS004-DA-3330-S.
```

The file-name, TRANS-FILE, is supplied by the programmer. The remaining clause in the statement is necessary when using a disk drive. The disk is a DA or direct-access device with number 3330 that is assigned to SYS004 for this installation. This disk will be accessed sequentially, which means that records are read or written in the order they enter the system.

Remember that SELECT statements are coded in Area B.

SELECT STATEMENTS FOR PCs

1. Device Specification

For input or output files on disk, PC versions of COBOL use device names that specify:

(1) The drive on which the disk file appears followed by a colon (e.g., C:, D:, etc.). If your file is in a subdirectory, you must specify that as well (e.g., C:\COBOL8\SALES1).

(2) The file-name for that disk file, where the rules for forming file-names are dependent on the operating system. IBM-compatibles using Windows 3.x or DOS have file-names that are 1 to 8 characters with an optional 1- to 3-character file extension. Windows 95 file-names can be up to 256 characters if you are using a Windows 95 COBOL compiler.

The device name for these PC versions of COBOL is usually enclosed in quotes. Consider the following:

```
SELECT EMPLOYEE-FILE ASSIGN TO 'C:EMPFILE'.
SELECT INVENTORY-FILE ASSIGN TO 'C:\INVENTORY\INVFILE.DAT'.
```

2. ORGANIZATION IS LINE SEQUENTIAL

Disk files are most often created so that they resemble text files. That is, if each record in the file is 80 characters or less, the Enter key is pressed to designate the end of the record. This means that each record will appear *on a single line* of a screen or printout so that it is easier to read. If a disk record is more than 80 characters, say 120 characters, we still use the Enter key to designate the end of the record. In this case, each record will be displayed on two lines—the first line would have 80 characters and the second would have 40 characters.

In order to create disk files so that each record is on an independent line or lines, the SELECT statement must include the clause ORGANIZATION IS LINE SEQUENTIAL. In files designated with ORGANIZATION IS LINE SEQUENTIAL, the Enter key is used to end each record. Consider the following example:

```
SELECT SALES-FILE ASSIGN TO 'C:\SALES.DAT'
    ORGANIZATION IS LINE SEQUENTIAL.
```

When creating a disk file, use the ORGANIZATION IS LINE SEQUENTIAL clause to ensure that each record is on a separate line. Print files should also have this clause.

If this clause is omitted when using a PC version of COBOL, then records will *not* be on separate lines. If disk files were created so that each record is on a separate line or lines, and the ORGANIZATION IS LINE SEQUENTIAL clause is omitted, any effort to process the file will result in an error. In fact, omitting this clause is the most common input/output error encountered by students.

───────────────────── DEBUGGING TIP ─────────────────────

When processing data with a PC COBOL compiler, always use the ORGANIZATION IS LINE SEQUENTIAL clause with the SELECT statement for all files.

In summary, the entry in the SELECT statement that is most important to you is the file-name assigned. All other entries are standard for your computer. The file-name is again used in the DATA DIVISION to describe the file. It is also referenced in the PROCEDURE DIVISION to access the file.

The preceding discussion should serve as a general guide for users. Consult your specifications manual or instructor for the requirements of the SELECT statements for your computer.

CODING GUIDELINES FOR THE IDENTIFICATION AND ENVIRONMENT DIVISIONS

1. Use a blank comment line with an * in column 7, or a page eject symbol (/ in column 7) to separate divisions. You could use a blank line to separate sections as well.

2. Code a single statement per line for the sake of clarity and to make debugging easier.

3. In general, code paragraph-names on lines by themselves.

4. Be liberal in your use of comments—they can make programs easier to read and debug. Box lengthy comments using asterisks:

```
************************************************************
*                                                        *
*                  (Comments go here)                    *
*                                                        *
************************************************************
```

5. The sequence in which files are selected in SELECT statements is not critical,

but for documentation purposes, it is more logical to select and define the input file(s) first, followed by output file(s).

6. Code each SELECT on two lines. The best format is as follows:

```
SELECT  file-name
        ASSIGN TO   implementor-name.
```

7. Avoid the use of device-specific file-names such as SALES-DISK.

Figure 2.4 provides an overview of how sections and paragraphs are coded in a COBOL program:

Figure 2.4 Hierarchical structure of a COBOL program.

Division	**Sections**	**Paragraphs**	
IDENTIFICATION		PROGRAM-ID AUTHOR INSTALLATION DATE-WRITTEN DATE-COMPILED SECURITY	} Optional (With COBOL 9x, these can only be used as comments—we recommend you omit them.)
ENVIRONMENT	CONFIGURATION		
		SOURCE-COMPUTER OBJECT-COMPUTER SPECIAL-NAMES	} Optional
	INPUT-OUTPUT		
		FILE-CONTROL	
DATA	FILE WORKING-STORAGE		
PROCEDURE	sections and paragraphs have user-defined names		

— COBOL 9x CHANGES —

1. Although current versions of COBOL require strict adherence to margin rules, COBOL 9x will eliminate these restrictions. Coding rules for Margins A and B will become recommendations, not requirements.

2. The PROGRAM-ID paragraph will be the only one permitted in the IDENTIFICATION DIVISION; all other entries (e.g., AUTHOR through SECURITY) can be specified as comments.

3. The maximum length of user-defined names will increase from 30 to 60 characters.

CHAPTER SUMMARY   I. The IDENTIFICATION DIVISION

A. The IDENTIFICATION DIVISION and its paragraphs are used to define the program-name and to provide documentation; they do not affect the execution of the program.

B. The first two items to be coded in a program are:

```
IDENTIFICATION DIVISION.
PROGRAM-ID.   program-name.
```

C. A program name that is up to eight characters, letters and digits only, is acceptable on all computers.

D. All other paragraphs and identifying information in this division are optional. Paragraphs that may be included are as follows (be sure you code these in the sequence specified):

```
AUTHOR.
INSTALLATION.
DATE-WRITTEN.
DATE-COMPILED.
SECURITY.
```

For many systems, if no entry follows the DATE-COMPILED paragraph, the compiler will insert the date of compilation on the source listing. Comments can be substituted for all these paragraphs, if desired.

E. Comments can be included in the IDENTIFICATION DIVISION, as well as all other divisions, by coding an * in position 7. This makes the entire line a comment. We encourage you to use comments throughout your programs for documentation.

F. A slash (/) in column 7 will cause the subsequent lines to be printed on the next page of the source listing.

II. The ENVIRONMENT DIVISION

A. The format for the ENVIRONMENT DIVISION is as follows:

```
ENVIRONMENT DIVISION.
[CONFIGURATION SECTION.
[SOURCE-COMPUTER.  computer-name.]
[OBJECT-COMPUTER.  computer-name.]]
[INPUT-OUTPUT SECTION.
 FILE-CONTROL.
       SELECT file-name-1
            ASSIGN TO implementor-name-1.
            :
            :
                                             ]
```

Note: The entire ENVIRONMENT DIVISION is optional for COBOL 85.

Interactive Processing. Fully interactive programs that use keyed data as input and screen displays as output need not have an ENVIRONMENT DIVISION.

B. The CONFIGURATION SECTION is usually optional and we recommend you omit it. It supplies documentary information on the computer(s) being used.

C. The INPUT-OUTPUT SECTION is also optional but must be included if files are assigned to devices in a program. We will always include the INPUT-OUTPUT SECTION for printing and for batch processing.

D. The ENVIRONMENT DIVISION is the only division of a COBOL program that may vary depending on the computer used. Obtain the exact device specifications or disk file-name rules from your computer center, instructor, or PC COBOL manual.

If you look at the COBOL Syntax Reference Guide that accompanies this text you will find that the full format for the ENVIRONMENT DIVISION is far more extensive than specified in this chapter. We have extracted the most commonly used elements.

--- WEB SITE ---

If you do not have a *COBOL Syntax Reference Guide*, it can be downloaded from our Web page. Consult Wiley's Internet site at http://www.wiley.com/cobol/ for more information.

KEY TERMS

Area A	DATE-COMPILED	IDENTIFICATION
Area B	DATE-WRITTEN	DIVISION
AUTHOR	DIVISION	Implementor-name
Coding sheet	ENVIRONMENT DIVISION	INPUT-OUTPUT SECTION
CONFIGURATION SECTION	File	INSTALLATION
Continuation position	FILE-CONTROL	OBJECT-COMPUTER

Paragraph	Section	Sentence
PROGRAM-ID	SECURITY	SOURCE-COMPUTER
Program sheet	SELECT	Statement

CHAPTER SELF-TEST

1. The IDENTIFICATION DIVISION entry is always followed by the _____ paragraph.
2. The entries in the ENVIRONMENT DIVISION are dependent on _____ and _____ .
3. The two sections of the ENVIRONMENT DIVISION are the _____ SECTION and the _____ SECTION.
4. The device specifications in the ENVIRONMENT DIVISION (will, will not) change significantly if the program is run on a different computer.
5. Files are defined and assigned in the _____ paragraph of the INPUT-OUTPUT SECTION.
6. PC-based versions of COBOL should include the _____ clause with a SELECT statement.
7. For every device used in the program, a _____ -name must be specified.
8. The file-name used in the SELECT statement must conform to the rules for forming _____ .
9. SELECT statements are coded in Area _____ .
10. Code the IDENTIFICATION and ENVIRONMENT DIVISION entries for a program that reads an input transaction disk, creates an error listing for all erroneous records, and creates a master disk file that is organized sequentially.

Solutions

1. PROGRAM-ID
2. the computer; the specific devices used
3. CONFIGURATION; INPUT-OUTPUT
4. will—These are the only entries in a COBOL program that are apt to change significantly.
5. FILE-CONTROL
6. ORGANIZATION IS LINE SEQUENTIAL
7. file
8. user-defined words
9. B
10.
```
    IDENTIFICATION DIVISION.
    PROGRAM-ID. EDIT1.
    AUTHOR. N. B. STERN.
    ****************************************
    *     this program reads input         *
    *     records, creates a master disk   *
    *     and error listing.               *
    ****************************************
    ENVIRONMENT DIVISION.
    CONFIGURATION SECTION.
    SOURCE-COMPUTER. VAX-8800.
    OBJECT-COMPUTER. VAX-8800.
    INPUT-OUTPUT SECTION.
    FILE-CONTROL.
        SELECT TRANSACTION-FILE
            ASSIGN TO DISK 'DATA1'.
        SELECT ERROR-FILE
            ASSIGN TO DISK 'DATA2'.
        SELECT MASTER-FILE
            ASSIGN TO DISK 'DATA3'.
```

Note: ASSIGN clauses may vary depending on the computer system you are using.

PRACTICE PROGRAM

Code the IDENTIFICATION and ENVIRONMENT DIVISION entries for the following program:

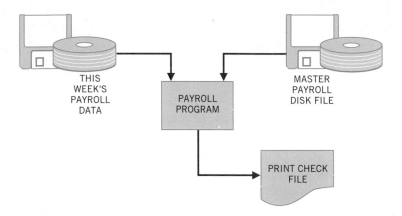

All SELECT statements are coded in Area B. The order in which the files are specified is not significant, but usually we SELECT input files before output files. The following is a suggested solution:

```
IDENTIFICATION DIVISION.
PROGRAM-ID. SAMPLE2.
AUTHOR. R. A. STERN.
***********************************************************
*** the program produces a printed report from      ***
*** a master disk file and the week's payroll data ***
***********************************************************
ENVIRONMENT DIVISION.
CONFIGURATION SECTION.
SOURCE-COMPUTER. VAX-8800.
OBJECT-COMPUTER. VAX-8800.
INPUT-OUTPUT SECTION.
FILE-CONTROL.   SELECT WEEKLY-WAGES
                    ASSIGN TO DISK 'DATA1'.
                SELECT PAYROLL
                    ASSIGN TO DISK 'DATA2'.
                SELECT PRINT-CHECKS
                    ASSIGN TO DISK 'DATA3'.
```

REVIEW QUESTIONS

I. True-False Questions

_____ 1. It is best to code only one statement on each coding line.

_____ 2. IDENTIFICATION DIVISION, PROGRAM-ID, and AUTHOR are the first three required entries of a COBOL program.

_____ 3. FILE 12 is a valid file-name.

_____ 4. A division name must appear as an independent item on a separate line.

_____ 5. Information supplied in the IDENTIFICATION DIVISION makes it easier for users to understand the nature of the program.

_____ 6. DATE-COMPILED is a paragraph-name that typically requires no additional entries.

_____ 7. Every period in a COBOL program must be followed by at least one space.

_____ 8. The INSTALLATION paragraph is restricted to one line.

_____ 9. The INPUT-OUTPUT SECTION of the ENVIRONMENT DIVISION assigns the file-names.

_____ 10. FILE-CONTROL is a required entry in the ENVIRONMENT DIVISION for programs that use files.

_____ 11. A file-name is an example of a user-defined word.

_____ 12. A maximum of three files may be defined in the INPUT-OUTPUT SECTION.

II. General Questions

Make necessary corrections to each of the following (1–4).

1. IDENTIFICATION DIVISION
   PROGRAM-ID SAMPLE1

2. ENVIRONMENT DIVISION.
       CONFIGURATION SECTION.

3. IDENTIFICATION DIVISION.
   AUTHOR.MARY DOE.
   PROGRAM-ID. SAMPLE4.

4. DATA DIVISION. FILE SECTION.

Make necessary corrections to each of the following and assume that the device specification, where noted, is correct (5–8).

5. ENVIRONMENT DIVISION
   CONFIGURATION SECTION.
   SOURCE-COMPUTER.   MODEL-120.

6. ENVIRONMENT DIVISION.
       :
       :
   INPUT OUTPUT SECTION

7. SELECT FILE A
       ASSIGN TO DISK1.

8. FILE CONTROL.
   SELECT FILEA
       ASSIGN TO PRINTER.

9. State which of the following entries are coded in Area A:
   (a) IDENTIFICATION DIVISION.
   (b) PROGRAM-ID.
   (c) (name of author)
   (d) FILE SECTION.
   (e) (COBOL statement) ADD TAX TO TOTAL.
   (f) ENVIRONMENT DIVISION.
   (g) CONFIGURATION SECTION.
   (h) SOURCE-COMPUTER.
   (i) FILE-CONTROL.
   (j) SELECT statement.

10. Why do you think AUTHOR through SECURITY paragraphs will no longer be part of the COBOL 9x standard? How could the information that pertains to these entries be added to a program?

PROGRAMMING ASSIGNMENTS

1. Code the IDENTIFICATION DIVISION for a program called UPDATE for the United Accounting Corp. The program must be written by 8/25/98 and completed by 10/25/98, and it has a top-secret security classification. The program will create a new master disk each month from the previous master disk and selected transaction disk records.

2. Consider the program excerpt in Figure 2.5. Code the IDENTIFICATION DIVISION. Include numerous paragraphs for documentation purposes. Also include comments that describe the program.

For the following problems, code the SELECT statements using the implementor-names relevant for your computer center.

3. Write the IDENTIFICATION and ENVIRONMENT DIVISION entries for the following program:

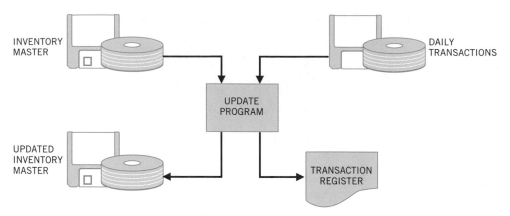

Program Specifications for Programming Assignment 3

Figure 2.5 Program for Programming Assignment 2.

COBOL 85

```
*** CODE IDENTIFICATION DIVISION HERE  ***
ENVIRONMENT DIVISION.
INPUT-OUTPUT SECTION.
FILE-CONTROL.
    SELECT TRANS-FILE    ASSIGN TO DISK.
    SELECT SALES-FILE    ASSIGN TO PRINTER.
DATA DIVISION.
FILE SECTION.
FD  TRANS-FILE  LABEL RECORDS ARE OMITTED.
01  TRANS-REC.
    05  NAME-IN          PIC X(20).
    05  UNIT-PRICE-IN    PIC 9(3)V99.
    05  QTY-SOLD-IN      PIC 999.
FD  SALES-FILE  LABEL RECORDS ARE STANDARD.
01  SALES-REC.
    05  NAME-OUT         PIC X(20).
    05  TOTAL-PRICE-OUT PIC 9(6)V99.
WORKING-STORAGE SECTION.
01  ARE-THERE-MORE-RECORDS  PIC X(3) VALUE 'YES'.
PROCEDURE DIVISION.
100-MAIN-MODULE.
    OPEN INPUT TRANS-FILE
         OUTPUT SALES-FILE
    PERFORM UNTIL ARE-THERE-MORE-RECORDS = 'NO '
        READ TRANS-FILE
            AT END
                 MOVE 'NO ' TO ARE-THERE-MORE-RECORDS
            NOT AT END
                 PERFORM 200-CALC-RTN
        END-READ
    END-PERFORM
    CLOSE TRANS-FILE
          SALES-FILE
    STOP RUN.
200-CALC-RTN.
    MOVE NAME-IN TO NAME-OUT
    MULTIPLY UNIT-PRICE-IN BY QTY-SOLD-IN GIVING TOTAL-PRICE-OUT
    WRITE SALES-REC.
```

COBOL 74 Substitutions

```
READ TRANS-FILE
    AT END MOVE 'NO ' TO
        ARE-THERE-MORE-RECORDS.
PERFORM 200-CALC-RTN
    UNTIL ARE-THERE-MORE-RECORDS
        = 'NO '.
```

```
READ TRANS-FILE
    AT END MOVE 'NO ' TO
        ARE-THERE-MORE-RECORDS.
```

4. Code the IDENTIFICATION DIVISION and the ENVIRONMENT DIVISION for a COBOL update program that uses an input transaction disk file and last week's master inventory disk file to create a current master inventory disk file.

5. Code the IDENTIFICATION DIVISION and the ENVIRONMENT DIVISION for a COBOL program that will use a sequential master billing disk to print gas bills and electric bills.

6. Consider the program excerpt in Figure 2.6. Code the IDENTIFICATION and ENVIRONMENT DIVISIONs for this program. Be as complete and as specific as possible. Include comments that describe the program.

Figure 2.6 Program for Programming Assignment 6.

COBOL 85

```
*      IDENTIFICATION AND ENVIRONMENT
*         DIVISION ENTRIES GO HERE
 DATA DIVISION.
 FILE SECTION.
 FD  STUDENT-FILE
     LABEL RECORDS ARE OMITTED.
 01  STUDENT-REC.
     05  NAME       PIC X(20).
     05  GRADE1     PIC 999.
     05  GRADE2     PIC 999.
     05  GRADE3     PIC 999.
 FD  TRANSCRIPT-FILE
     LABEL RECORDS ARE OMITTED.
 01  TRANSCRIPT-REC.
     05  NAME-OUT   PIC X(20).
     05  AVERAGE    PIC 999.
 WORKING-STORAGE SECTION.
 01  ARE-THERE-MORE-RECORDS  PIC X(3)  VALUE  'YES'.
*
 PROCEDURE DIVISION.
*
 100-MAIN-MODULE.
     OPEN INPUT STUDENT-FILE
          OUTPUT TRANSCRIPT-FILE
     PERFORM UNTIL ARE-THERE-MORE-RECORDS = 'NO '
         READ STUDENT-FILE
             AT END
                 MOVE 'NO ' TO ARE-THERE-MORE-RECORDS
             NOT AT END
                 PERFORM 200-CALC-RTN
         END-READ
     END-PERFORM
     CLOSE STUDENT-FILE
           TRANSCRIPT-FILE
     STOP RUN.
 200-CALC-RTN.
     MOVE NAME TO NAME-OUT
     ADD GRADE1, GRADE2, GRADE3
        GIVING AVERAGE
     DIVIDE 3 INTO AVERAGE
     WRITE TRANSCRIPT-REC.
```

COBOL 74 Substitutions

```
READ STUDENT-FILE
    AT END MOVE 'NO ' TO
        ARE-THERE-MORE-RECORDS.
PERFORM 200-CALC-RTN
    UNTIL ARE-THERE-MORE-RECORDS
        = 'NO '.
```

```
◄─── READ STUDENT-FILE
     AT END MOVE 'NO ' TO
         ARE-THERE-MORE-RECORDS.
```

CHAPTER 3

The DATA DIVISION

■■ **OBJECTIVES**

To familiarize you with

1. Systems design considerations that relate to programming.
2. The ways in which data is organized.
3. The rules for forming data-names and constants in COBOL.
4. How input and output files are defined and described in the DATA DIVISION.
5. How storage can be reserved for fields not part of input or output, such as constants and work areas.

■■ **CONTENTS**

SYSTEMS DESIGN CONSIDERATIONS

THE RELATIONSHIP BETWEEN A BUSINESS INFORMATION SYSTEM AND ITS PROGRAMS

Programs are not usually written as independent entities. Rather, they are part of an overall set of procedures called a computerized business information system. Each program, then, is really only *one part* of an information system.

A systems analyst is the computer professional responsible for the design of the overall computerized business information system. Thus, if the sales department of a major company is not running smoothly or is too costly to operate, the company's management may call on a systems analyst to design a more efficient business information system. Because such a design would typically include computerization of various aspects of the department's functions, the systems analyst should have considerable computer expertise.

The systems analyst first determines what the outputs from the entire system should be and then designs the inputs necessary to produce these outputs. The analyst also determines what programs are required to read input and to produce the required output. Each set of program specifications would include the input and output layouts for that specific aspect of the overall system. The analyst provides the programmer with these specifications so that he or she will know precisely what the input and output will look like. In smaller companies, programmers or software developers may serve as analysts themselves, designing systems and then writing the programs.

 ### INTERACTIVE AND BATCH PROCESSING

The two types of processing performed by computers are interactive processing and batch processing. With interactive processing, data is operated on and output is produced as soon as the input is entered. Point-of-Sale systems, for example, are used to key in a customer's account number and amount of sale when a transaction is made. This data automatically updates the master accounts receivable file so that a new balance due for the customer is calculated.

A master accounts receivable file is a major collection of data for the given application. Because changes to the accounts receivable file are made *when a transaction occurs*, we call this *interactive processing*. The transaction data is keyed into a PC or terminal; then the accounts receivable file is updated and a printed sales receipt is generated.

Batch processing operates on files, typically stored on disk, at periodic intervals. All or most of the data in the files is operated on during the batch procedure. For example, the process of producing customer bills from the master accounts receivable file would be an example of a batch operation. All customer records from the disk file are processed collectively at periodic intervals (i.e., once a month).

Interactive processing uses input/output instructions and record layouts that are different from those of batch processing. The way data is accepted from a terminal or PC keyboard is different from the way data is read from large disk files. In this text we will focus on both interactive and batch processing. This chapter emphasizes file concepts, and Chapter 5 emphasizes methods used to enter data interactively.

DESIGNING INPUT FOR APPLICATIONS USING BATCH PROCESSING

For most batch processing applications, each set of input and output typically consists of a *file*, which itself contains groups of **records**. A payroll file, for example, would be the major collection of payroll data for a company. It would consist of employee records, where each record contains data for a single employee:

A *record layout form* is used for describing each type of input or output in a program. If the output is a print file, a Printer Spacing Chart is prepared instead of a record layout form. This chart describes the precise format for each print line. Chapter 1 illustrates record layout forms and Printer Spacing Charts.

All our batch programs will be accompanied by record layouts and Printer Spacing Charts so that you will become very familiar with them. Interactive programs will include screen layouts to describe data entered or displayed on a screen.

FORMING DATA-NAMES

RULES

As we have seen from the program illustrations in the previous chapter, storage areas are reserved in memory for files, which consist of records. Each record is itself divided into fields of data such as Social Security Number, Name, and Salary.

Files, records, and fields are categories of data in a COBOL program. They are each assigned a user-defined name called a **data-name** or **identifier**. We will see later that there are other types of user-defined words as well. In COBOL, user-defined names must conform to the following rules:

RULES FOR FORMING USER-DEFINED DATA-NAMES

1. 1 to 30 characters.

2. Letters, digits, and hyphens (-) only. (We use uppercase letters in all our illustrations, but lowercase letters could be used.)

3. May not begin or end with a hyphen.

4. No embedded blanks are permitted (that is, no blanks within the data-name).

5. Must contain at least one alphabetic character.

6. May not be a COBOL **reserved word**. A reserved word, such as ADD, MOVE, or DATA, is one that has special meaning to the COBOL compiler.

COBOL 85 and COBOL 74 reserved words are listed in Appendix A and in your *COBOL Syntax Reference Guide*. If a compiler has features that go beyond the standard, it will have *additional* COBOL reserved words. All COBOL reserved words for your specific compiler will be listed in the COBOL compiler's reference manual.

The following are examples of valid user-defined data-names:

EXAMPLES OF VALID USER-DEFINED DATA-NAMES

```
DATE-IN            AMOUNT1-IN
NAME-OUT           AMOUNT-OF-TRANSACTION-OUT
LAST-NAME-IN
```

The suffixes -IN and -OUT are recommended naming conventions, but they are not required.

The following are examples of invalid user-defined data-names:

EXAMPLES OF INVALID USER-DEFINED DATA-NAMES

Data-Name	Reason It Is Invalid
EMPLOYEE NAME	There is an *embedded blank* between EMPLOYEE and NAME. EMPLOYEE-NAME is, however, okay.
DISCOUNT-%	%, as a special character, is invalid.
INPUT	INPUT is a COBOL reserved word.
123	A data-name must contain at least one alphabetic character.

Although reserved words cannot be used as data-names, they can be modified to be acceptable. INPUT-1, for example, would be a permissible data-name.

Consider the following record layout for an output disk file:

DATE OF TRANSACTION	AMOUNT	INVOICE NUMBER	CUSTOMER NAME

The fields may be named as follows: DATE-OF-TRANS-OUT, AMOUNT-OUT, INVOICE-NO-OUT, CUSTOMER-NAME-OUT. We use the suffix -OUT to designate these as output fields. Hyphens are used in place of embedded blanks for data-names that incorporate more than one word.

────── DEBUGGING TIP ──────

Each file, record, and field of data must be assigned a name in the COBOL program. Once a name is assigned, the *same* name must be used throughout when referring to the specific unit of data. CREDIT-AMT-IN, defined as a data-name in the DATA DIVISION, may *not* be referred to as CR-AMT-IN in the PROCEDURE DIVISION. To do so would result in a syntax error.

GUIDELINES

Use Meaningful Names

The data-names used should describe the type of data within the field. DATE-OF-TRANS-IN is a more meaningful data-name than D1, for example, although both names are valid. In any programming language, using data-names that describe the contents of the fields makes it easier to read, debug, and modify a program.

Use Prefixes or Suffixes Where Appropriate

Prefixes or suffixes are commonly used to indicate the type of data within a record. Thus NAME-OUT might be used as an output field to distinguish it from NAME-IN, which could be the same field on an input record. To make our program easier to read and more standardized, we will use prefixes or suffixes such as -IN and -OUT along with meaningful names. Later on, we will describe a heading line that includes fields with a prefix of HL-, a total line that includes fields with a prefix of TL-, and so on.

THE FILE SECTION OF THE DATA DIVISION

AN OVERVIEW

The **DATA DIVISION** is that part of a COBOL program that defines and describes fields, records, and files in storage. Any area of storage that is required for the processing of data must be established in the DATA DIVISION. We focus on the following two main sections of the DATA DIVISION in this text:

THE TWO MAIN SECTIONS OF THE DATA DIVISION[1]

1. **FILE SECTION**—defines all input and output files.

2. **WORKING-STORAGE SECTION**—reserves storage for fields not part of input or output but required for processing. These include constants, end-of-file indicators, and work areas.

The sections of the DATA DIVISION must be defined in the sequence shown.

Any program that (1) reads data from input files or (2) produces output files, requires a FILE SECTION to describe the input and output areas. Since batch programs typically read input files, operate on them, and produce output files, the FILE SECTION will be an essential part of all such programs.

Interactive Processing.   Interactive programs that just accept input from a keyboard and display output on a screen do not need SELECT statements or a FILE SECTION. We discuss interactive processing in Chapters 5 and 6.

──────────

[1]There are two other, lesser-used sections that are considered later on in this text. The LINKAGE SECTION, which can be part of the DATA DIVISION in programs that are linked to each other, is discussed in Chapter 16. The REPORT SECTION is discussed in Chapter 17.

Defining a File

As noted previously, a file is the overall collection of data pertaining to a specific application. The Megabuck Dept. Store, for example, may have an inventory file that contains all current information on items stocked by the company. The same company may also have an accounts receivable file of customer information, a payroll file of employee information, and so on. In summary, files appear as input or output in COBOL programs. Batch programs use at least one input and one output file.

A typical program may read an input file from disk and produce a printed output file of bills, checks, or summary totals. Other programs may be written to incorporate changes into a **master file**, which contains the *major collection* of data for a particular application. Thus, we may have an input file of master payroll records along with an input file of transaction records that contains changes to be made to the master. These changes may include new hires, salary increases for current employees, changes in the number of dependents, and so on. The two input files—the master payroll file and the transaction file—would be used to create a new master payroll file as output that incorporates all the changes. This process of using a file of transaction records along with an existing master file to produce a new master is called an **update procedure** and is a common programming application. The old master file and the transaction file of changes serve as input and a new master file with the changes incorporated would be the output file:

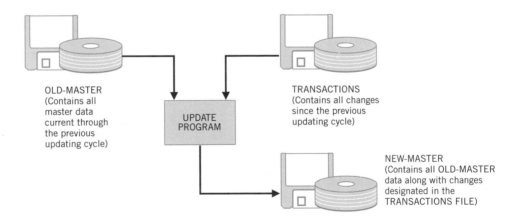

OLD-MASTER
(Contains all
master data
current through
the previous
updating cycle)

UPDATE
PROGRAM

TRANSACTIONS
(Contains all changes
since the previous
updating cycle)

NEW-MASTER
(Contains all OLD-MASTER
data along with changes
designated in the
TRANSACTIONS FILE)

Thus, for *each* form of input and output used in a batch application, we have *one* file. Three files would typically be used for the preceding update procedure: an input master file, an input transaction file, and a new output master file. We discuss this type of update procedure in detail in Chapter 13.

The FILE SECTION, as the name implies, describes all input and output files used in the program. Each file has already been defined in the ENVIRONMENT DIVISION in a SELECT statement, where the file-name is designated and an input or output device name is assigned to it. Thus, for every SELECT statement, we will have one file to describe in the FILE SECTION of the DATA DIVISION.

The FILE SECTION, then, describes the input and output areas used in the program. An *input area* is primary storage reserved for records from an incoming file. A READ instruction, in the PROCEDURE DIVISION, will transmit *one* record of the designated file to this input area. Similarly, an *output area* is primary storage reserved for a record to be produced in an output file. When a WRITE statement is executed, data stored in this output area is transmitted as *one* record to the specified output device. Most programs read one record, then process it, and produce output before reading the next record. Thus, a single input area, which will hold one record at a time, and a single output area for storing each output record—one at a time—are sufficient.

FILE DESCRIPTION ENTRIES

Each file is described in the FILE SECTION with an FD sentence that may consist of a series of clauses. After the clauses are specified, the FD sentence ends with a period. **FD** is an abbreviation for **File Description**. Each FD entry will describe a file defined in a SELECT statement in the ENVIRONMENT DIVISION. Thus, as an example, we may have:

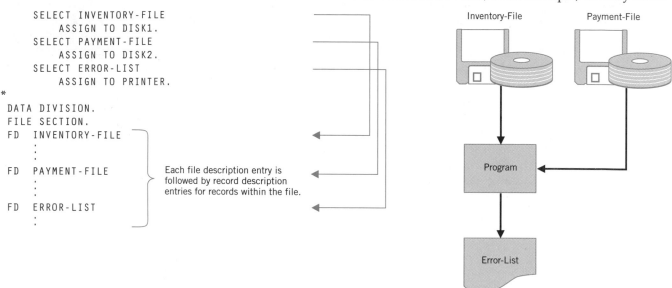

```
        SELECT INVENTORY-FILE
            ASSIGN TO DISK1.
        SELECT PAYMENT-FILE
            ASSIGN TO DISK2.
        SELECT ERROR-LIST
            ASSIGN TO PRINTER.
*
    DATA DIVISION.
    FILE SECTION.
    FD  INVENTORY-FILE
        :
        :
    FD  PAYMENT-FILE
        :
        :
    FD  ERROR-LIST
        :
```

Each file description entry is followed by record description entries for records within the file.

Inventory-File   Payment-File

Program

Error-List

Every FD entry will be followed by a file-name and certain clauses that describe the file and the format of its records. Since there are three SELECT statements in the preceding example, there will be three FD entries in the FILE SECTION, each with the same file-name as in the corresponding SELECT statement.

The two entries, DATA DIVISION and FILE SECTION, are coded in Area A. FD is also coded in Area A. The file-name, however, is typically coded in Area B. If FD clauses are used, no period follows the file-name. FD ACCTS-RECEIVABLE-FILE, for example, signals the compiler that the file called ACCTS-RECEIVABLE-FILE is about to be described.

Several clauses may be used to describe a file. These will follow the FD file-name, and no period will be written until the last clause is specified. Consider the following examples that include full FD entries:

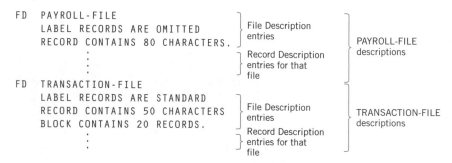

```
    FD  PAYROLL-FILE
        LABEL RECORDS ARE OMITTED
        RECORD CONTAINS 80 CHARACTERS.
        :
        :
    FD  TRANSACTION-FILE
        LABEL RECORDS ARE STANDARD
        RECORD CONTAINS 50 CHARACTERS
        BLOCK CONTAINS 20 RECORDS.
        :
```

File Description entries · Record Description entries for that file } PAYROLL-FILE descriptions

File Description entries · Record Description entries for that file } TRANSACTION-FILE descriptions

We will focus on File Description entries first and then consider Record Description entries for records within each file. Note that all these FD clauses are optional for COBOL 85.

LABEL RECORD(S) Clause—(Optional for COBOL 85, required for COBOL 74)

Format

```
LABEL {RECORD  IS } {OMITTED }
      {RECORDS ARE} {STANDARD}
```

Interpreting Instruction Formats

Each set of braces { } denotes that one of the enclosed items is required when the specific clause is used. We can, for example, code either `LABEL RECORD IS OMITTED` or `LABEL RECORDS ARE OMITTED`.

What Is a Label Record?

Data on magnetic media such as disk cannot be "read" as one reads a book, a line on a terminal, or a printed report. That is, data is stored on disk as magnetized bits or binary digits that cannot be seen by the naked eye. *Label records,* then, are usually created as the first and last records of a disk file to provide identifying information about the file.

Since the data on a disk is not visible, these label records can be used to check if the correct file is being accessed for a specific program. Labels are created on output files so that, when the same file is later read as input, the labels may be checked to ensure that the file being accessed is the correct one. That is, labels are *created* on output files and *checked* on input files. The COBOL compiler will call in the routine for writing labels on output files or for checking labels on input files if the following entry is included:

```
LABEL RECORDS ARE STANDARD
```

This **LABEL RECORDS** clause will result in the following:

1. For output files, the first record on a disk file will be created as a standard 80-position **header label** identifying the file to the system; similarly, the last record on the disk file will be created as a **trailer label**.
2. For input files, these labels will be computer-checked to ensure that the file being processed is the correct one.

The information that should appear on the labels will need to be supplied to the system. This is done with operating system commands, which are separate from the COBOL program.

With COBOL 85, the `LABEL RECORDS` clause is optional. The process of creating and checking labels could be handled entirely by the operating system. When the `LABEL RECORDS` clause is not included, the computer assumes that `LABEL RECORDS ARE STANDARD`. *The clause must, however, appear with all `FD`s when using COBOL 74.*

The clause `LABEL RECORDS ARE STANDARD` is permitted only for magnetic media such as disk. Printed files do *not* use label records, since identifying information is unnecessary where data is visible to the human eye. The following entry, then, is used for such files:

```
LABEL RECORDS ARE OMITTED
```

Sometimes a disk file may include the entry `LABEL RECORDS ARE OMITTED`. In that case, label records will be neither created on output files nor checked on input files.

If an output disk file is created with standard labels, then `LABEL RECORDS` should be `STANDARD` when reading that same file as input at some later date.

Example 1   A print file called `EMPLOYEE-FILE` would include the following:

```
FD  EMPLOYEE-FILE
    LABEL RECORDS ARE OMITTED
```

Example 2   A disk file called INVENTORY-FILE would include the following:

```
FD   INVENTORY-FILE
     LABEL RECORDS ARE STANDARD
```

RECORD CONTAINS Clause—(Optional)

Format

RECORD CONTAINS integer-1 CHARACTERS

The **RECORD CONTAINS** clause indicates the size of each record. A print file, for example, may have the following entry:

RECORD CONTAINS 80 CHARACTERS

Interpreting Instruction Formats

Note that in the instruction format, only the word RECORD is underlined. This means that the other words are optional. The clause RECORD 80 could be coded, then, instead of the preceding because CONTAINS and CHARACTERS are not required. Coding the full statement is, however, more user-friendly. Note that the only user-defined entry in this clause is the integer specified.

Record Size for Print Files

Printers vary in the number of characters they can print per line. PC printers usually print 80 or 100 characters per line; mainframe and minicomputer line printers usually print 132 or 100 characters per line.

Record Size for Disk Files

For disk files, the RECORD CONTAINS clause varies. One of the advantages of storing data on magnetic media (such as disk) is that records can be any size.

DEBUGGING TIP

The RECORD CONTAINS clause in the File Description entry is always *optional*, but we recommend that you use it because it provides a check on record size. For example, if the RECORD CONTAINS clause indicates 80 CHARACTERS in the record, but the PICTURE clauses mistakenly add up to 81 characters, a syntax error will occur during the compilation. If the RECORD CONTAINS clause were not included, the inclusion of an 81st position in the record would *not* be detected until the program is actually run. It is easier to detect and fix errors at compile-time rather than at run-time.

Example 3   An FD entry for a disk file called SALES-FILE with 150-character records may be:

```
FD   SALES-FILE
     LABEL RECORDS ARE STANDARD
     RECORD CONTAINS 150 CHARACTERS
```

BLOCK CONTAINS Clause—(Optional)

Format

BLOCK CONTAINS integer-1 RECORDS

What Is Blocking?

The **BLOCK CONTAINS** clause is included in the File Description entry only for files on magnetic media such as disk, which may have records that have been blocked. **Blocking** is a technique that increases the speed of input/output operations and makes more effective use of storage space on disk. A group of logical records is included within one block to maximize the efficient use of a disk area. That is, reading in a block of 10 disk records, for example, is more efficient than reading in each disk record separately. Even though a disk file may be blocked, the program processes records in the standard way, that is, one logical record at a time. If there are 10 disk records per block, we say that the physical record (or block) consists of 10 logical records.

By indicating BLOCK CONTAINS n RECORDS for an input disk, the computer is able to read the full block correctly. Similarly, by indicating the number of records in a block for an output disk, the computer is able to create the correct block of records. Thus, the BLOCK CONTAINS clause of a disk file is the *only* entry used to read or write a block of records. *No additional COBOL statements are necessary.* The operating system handles blocking of output records and deblocking of input records when reading them.

The BLOCK CONTAINS clause itself is *omitted* when records are not blocked, as with print files; it is also sometimes omitted with some disk files. Typically, the systems analyst or programmer determines the most efficient block size to use.

Suppose we have an input file with the following FD entries:

```
FD  TRANSACTION-FILE
    LABEL RECORDS ARE STANDARD
    RECORD CONTAINS 50 CHARACTERS
    BLOCK CONTAINS 20 RECORDS.
```

With a record size of 50 and a block of 20, 1000 characters (50 × 20) are read into the input area reserved for this file. For the initial read, the first 50 characters in main memory are processed. For the next read, the second 50 characters in memory are processed. This will continue until the entire block is accessed and processed; *then* the next block is read and the procedure is repeated.

The BLOCK CONTAINS entry is optional for COBOL 85 *even when records are blocked.* This is because operating system commands can be used to indicate the blocking factor. In general, we will omit this clause in our programs.

The three clauses discussed are the most commonly used entries in the FD, but they are not the only ones. For most applications in COBOL, they are quite adequate. Table 3.1 provides a summary of these clauses. After all clauses within the FD are coded, place a period at the end. Note that no other period will appear in the FD.

Table 3.1

Summary of FD Entries			
Clause	**Entries**	**Optional or Required**	**Use**
LABEL RECORD(S)	[IS / ARE] {OMITTED / STANDARD}	Optional for COBOL 85; required for COBOL 74	STANDARD is specified if header and trailer labels are used on disk; OMITTED is used for print files
RECORD CONTAINS	(integer) CHARACTERS	Optional	Indicates the number of characters in the record
BLOCK CONTAINS	(integer) RECORDS	Optional for COBOL 85; required for COBOL 74	Indicates the blocking factor for disk

> **RULES FOR CODING FILE DESCRIPTION ENTRIES**
>
> 1. FD is coded in Area A.
>
> 2. All other entries should be coded in Area B.
>
> 3. No period is coded until the last clause has been specified.
>
> 4. Commas are always optional in a program to separate clauses. If used, they must be followed by at least one blank. We recommend you omit them.
>
> 5. We recommend that each clause appear on a separate line for clarity and ease of debugging.

You will see from the instruction format that the words IS and ARE are *not underlined* in any clause, which means that they may be omitted. Thus, to say LABEL RECORDS STANDARD, for example, is acceptable. Finally, clauses may appear in any sequence in an FD.

Example 4   The following is a correctly coded File Description specification, even though the sequence of clauses is not the same as previously described:

```
FD   INVENTORY-IN
     RECORD CONTAINS 100 CHARACTERS
     LABEL RECORDS ARE OMITTED
     BLOCK CONTAINS 10 RECORDS.
```

SELF-TEST
1. What is the purpose of the DATA DIVISION?
2. What are the two primary sections of a DATA DIVISION?
3. What is the purpose of the FILE SECTION of the DATA DIVISION?
4. File-names must be from one to ___(no.)___ characters in length, contain at least one _____ , and have no _____ .
5. File-names (*must, need not*) be unique.
6. For every file defined in a SELECT statement, there will be one _____ entry in the FILE SECTION.
7. The three clauses that may be used with an FD entry are _____ , _____ , and _____ .
8. For print files, LABEL RECORDS ARE _____ .
9. When LABEL RECORDS ARE STANDARD is specified, header and trailer labels will be _____ on input files and _____ on output files.
10. The BLOCK CONTAINS clause is used only for _____ .
11. Write an FD entry for an input sales file on a disk with 100-position records and standard labels.
12. Make any necessary corrections to the following DATA DIVISION entries:

```
DATA DIVISION.
FILE-SECTION
FD   SALES FILE.
     LABELS ARE OMITTED.
```

Solutions
1. It defines and describes fields, records, and files in storage.
2. The FILE SECTION and the WORKING-STORAGE SECTION.
3. It defines and describes all data areas that are part of input or output.
4. 30; alphabetic character; special characters (except -) or blanks
5. must
6. FD
7. LABEL RECORD(S); RECORD CONTAINS; BLOCK CONTAINS

8. OMITTED

9. checked; created

10. blocked disk files

11. ```
FD SALES-FILE
    LABEL RECORDS ARE STANDARD
    RECORD CONTAINS 100 CHARACTERS.
```

12. No hyphen between FILE and SECTION.

Periods are required after all section names.

SALES-FILE may not have an embedded blank and must not be followed by a period (since the FD contains at least one clause).

The LABEL clause should read LABEL RECORDS ARE OMITTED (assuming that it does not have any labels).

**Corrected Entry**
```
DATA DIVISION.
FILE SECTION.
FD   SALES-FILE
        LABEL RECORDS ARE OMITTED.
```

## RECORD DESCRIPTION ENTRIES

### Defining a Record

A *record* is a unit of information consisting of related data items within a file. Most often, a file consists of records that all have the same length and format. We call these **fixed-length records**. An inventory disk file, for example, may have records each with the following format:

A record, then, is a specific unit of data within a file. We have seen that one file is defined for each form of input and one file is defined for each form of output that the program processes. For each type of data within the file, we define one record format.

Most often, each disk file has only one record format. The one file type that commonly has numerous record formats is a print file. Consider the Printer Spacing Chart in Figure 3.1. There would be *three* record formats for the print file because there are three types

**Figure 3.1** Printer Spacing Chart with heading, detail, and total lines.

```
        H   6   MONTHLY TRANSACTION REPORT
        D   8   X─────────────X   X────X   999.99
             9   (CUSTOMER NAME)   (CUSTOMER NO.) (TRANSACTION AMT)
        T   16   THE FINAL TOTAL OF ALL TRANSACTION AMOUNTS IS 99999.99
```
```

of lines: (1) a heading record or line (denoted as an H line in the left margin); (2) a record or line containing detail or transaction data (denoted as a D line); (3) a record or line containing a final total (denoted as a T line). We will see later on that these individual formats are typically described in the WORKING-STORAGE SECTION.

Level Numbers

After a file is described by an FD, the **record description** entries for each record format within the file follow. The record description specifies the format of a record. Record description entries indicate (1) the items or fields to appear in the record; (2) the order in which the fields appear; and (3) how these fields are related to one another.

Just as the file-name is specified on the FD level, a record-name is coded on the *01 level*. Consider the following illustrations:

Example 1 A transaction disk file with only one record format may have the following entries:

```
FD   TRANSACTION-FILE
     LABEL RECORDS ARE OMITTED
     RECORD CONTAINS 80 CHARACTERS.
01   TRANSACTION-REC-IN.
     :} Entries to be discussed
```

In summary, each FD must be followed by record description entries for the file. Records are defined on the 01 level. We now indicate what fields are contained in each record of the file and how the fields are organized.

Data is grouped in COBOL using the concept of a *level*. Records are considered the *highest level of data* in a file and are coded on the 01 level. A record consists of fields, where a **field** is a group of consecutive storage positions reserved for an item of data. A field of data within the record is coded on a level *subordinate to* 01, that is, 02, 03, and so on. Any **level number** between 02 and 49 may be used to describe fields within a record.

Example 2 Consider the following input record layout:

Employee Record (input)

NAME	ANNUAL SALARY	JOB DESCRIPTION

The record description entries following the FD may be as follows:

```
01   EMPLOYEE-REC-IN.
     05   NAME-IN
     05   ANNUAL-SALARY-IN
     05   JOB-DESCRIPTION-IN
```

The name of the record, EMPLOYEE-REC-IN, is coded on the 01 level in Area A. All fields within the record are coded on any level between 02 and 49, anywhere in Area B. By specifying these fields on the 05 level, we indicate that:

1. All fields on the 05 level are *subordinate to,* or part of, the 01-level entry.
2. All fields that are coded on the same level, 05 in this example, are *independent* items; that is, they are *not* subordinate to, or related to, one another.

Thus NAME-IN, ANNUAL-SALARY-IN, and JOB-DESCRIPTION-IN are fields within EMPLOYEE-REC-IN, and each is independent of the others.

We use 05 rather than 02 to define fields within a record in case we need to add additional levels between 01 and the level specified. That is, if NAME-IN and ANNUAL-SALARY-IN are later to be accessed together, they can be made subordinate to a field called MAJOR. We could easily modify our coding as follows, without changing the level numbers for NAME-IN and ANNUAL-SALARY-IN:

```
01    EMPLOYEE-REC-IN.
        03    MAJOR-IN
            05    NAME-IN
            05    ANNUAL-SALARY-IN
        03    JOB-DESCRIPTION-IN
```

In general, we will use 05 as the first level of fields that are subdivisions of 01. We use the suffix -IN to indicate that these are input fields within an input record.

Although COBOL 85 permits the use of Area A for level numbers, we recommend you denote fields within a record by indenting, that is, using Area B for all levels except 01.

Let us redefine the preceding input:

Employee Record (input)

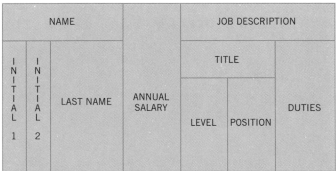

In this case, all fields are *not* independent of one another, as in the preceding input layout. Here, some fields are subordinate to, or contained within, other fields in a record. INITIAL1-IN, INITIAL2-IN, and LAST-NAME-IN, for example, would be fields within NAME-IN, which itself is contained within a record. INITIAL1-IN, INITIAL2-IN, and LAST-NAME-IN, then, would be coded on a level subordinate to NAME-IN. If NAME-IN were specified on level 05, INITIAL1-IN, INITIAL2-IN, and LAST-NAME-IN could each be specified on either level 06 or level 07, and so forth. To allow for possible insertions later on, we will use 10 for the level subordinate to 05.

Example 3   The record description for the preceding redefined input is as follows:

```
01    EMPLOYEE-REC-IN.
        05    NAME-IN
            10    INITIAL1-IN
            10    INITIAL2-IN
            10    LAST-NAME-IN
        05    ANNUAL-SALARY-IN
        05    JOB-DESCRIPTION-IN
            10    JOB-TITLE-IN
                15    LEVEL-IN
                15    JOB-POSITION-IN
            10    DUTIES-IN
```

There are three major fields within the record: NAME-IN, ANNUAL-SALARY-IN, and JOB-DESCRIPTION-IN, all coded on the 05 level. The NAME-IN field is further subdivided into level 10 items called INITIAL1-IN, INITIAL2-IN, and LAST-NAME-IN. Similarly, JOB-TITLE-IN and

DUTIES-IN are subdivisions of JOB-DESCRIPTION-IN. JOB-TITLE-IN is further subdivided into LEVEL-IN and JOB-POSITION-IN.

Names used to define fields, like the names of records and files, must conform to the rules for establishing user-defined data-names.

Specifying the Order of Fields in a Record

The order in which fields are placed within the record is crucial. If NAME-IN is the first item specified within EMPLOYEE-REC-IN, this implies that NAME-IN is the first data field in the record. The relationships among data elements in a program are described in Figure 3.2.

Coding Guidelines for Record Description Entries

We code all fields in Area B and code the highest level of organization, which is the record level, in Area A. We also indent subordinate levels. Although this indentation is not required by the compiler, it does make the lines easier to read. Using this method, the fact that INITIAL1-IN, INITIAL2-IN, and LAST-NAME-IN are contained within NAME-IN is quite clear.

Level numbers may vary from 02 to 49 for fields of data. As we have seen, level numbers need not be consecutive. As a matter of style, we will use 05, 10, 15, and so on, as level numbers so that other level numbers can be inserted later on if the need arises. The following, however, are also valid entries:

```
01  REC-A-OUT.
    03  DATE-OF-HIRE-OUT
        07  MONTH-OUT
        07  YEAR-OUT
    03  NAME-OUT
```

Figure 3.2 The relationships among SELECT, FD, 01, and fields.

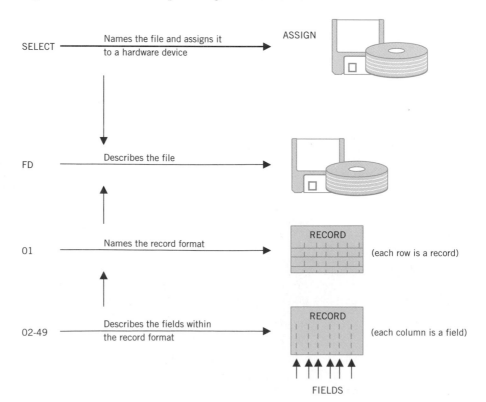

MONTH-OUT and YEAR-OUT on the 07 level are contained within DATE-OF-HIRE-OUT on the 03 level. MONTH-OUT and YEAR-OUT must have the same level number because they are independent fields. Although consecutive level numbers can be used, we will avoid them because they make it difficult to insert fields later on if it becomes necessary.

Invalid Use of Level Numbers

Look at the following illustration, which is not valid:

```
01  SALES-REC-IN.
    02  NAME-IN
    03  LAST-NAME-IN
    05  FIRST-NAME-IN  ◄──── Inaccurate level number
    02  AMOUNT-IN
```

This record description is *not* correct. It implies that FIRST-NAME-IN, as an 05-level item, is contained in LAST-NAME-IN, an 03-level item. To indicate that LAST-NAME-IN and FIRST-NAME-IN are *independent* subdivisions of NAME-IN, they both must be coded on the same level. To place them both on either the 03 or 04 or 05 level would be accurate. Using indentation in the preceding example would have helped to discover the error.

Fields May Be Defined as Either Elementary or Group Items

A field that is *not* further subdivided is called an **elementary item**. A field that is further subdivided is called a **group item**. In Example 3, NAME-IN is a group item that is subdivided into three elementary items, INITIAL1-IN, INITIAL2-IN, and LAST-NAME-IN. ANNUAL-SALARY-IN, on the same level as NAME-IN, is an elementary item since it is not further subdivided.

All elementary items must be additionally described with a PICTURE clause that indicates the *size* and *type* of the field. A group item, because it is subdivided, needs no further specification and ends with a period. Thus we have, for example:

```
01  ACCOUNT-REC-IN.
    05  CUSTOMER-NAME-IN.
        10  LAST-NAME-IN          (PICTURE CLAUSE)
        10  FIRST-NAME-IN         (PICTURE CLAUSE)
    05  TRANSACTION-NUMBER-IN     (PICTURE CLAUSE)
    05  DATE-OF-TRANSACTION-IN.
        10  MONTH-IN              (PICTURE CLAUSE)
        10  YEAR-IN               (PICTURE CLAUSE)
```

Note that there is a period at the end of each group item in this illustration. Each elementary item requires further description with a PICTURE clause. We treat the record entry, on the 01 level, as a group item, since it is, in fact, a data element that is further subdivided.

SELF-TEST

1. All records are coded on the ___(no.)___ level.
2. Levels ___(no.)___ to ___(no.)___ may be used to represent fields within a record.
3. An 03-level item may be subordinate to an ___(no.)___ or ___(no.)___-level item.
4. What, if anything, is wrong with the following user-defined data-names?
   (a) CUSTOMER NAME   (b) TAX%   (c) DATA
5. What is the difference between an elementary item and a group item?
6. The level number 01 is coded in Area _____ ; level numbers 02–49 are coded in Area _____ .
7. Write record description entries for the following insofar as you are able.

TRANSACTION RECORD

	LOCATION			PRODUCT DESCRIPTION		
				NO. OF ITEM		ITEM NAME
INVOICE NUMBER	WAREHOUSE	CITY	JOB LOT	SIZE	MODEL	

Solutions

1. 01

2. 02; 49

3. 02; 01

4. (a) No embedded blanks allowed (CUSTOMER-NAME would be okay).
   (b) No special characters other than the hyphen are permitted—% is not valid.
   (c) DATA is a COBOL reserved word.

5. An elementary item is one that is not further subdivided and a group item is one that is further subdivided.

6. A; B

7.
```
01  TRANSACTION-REC-IN.
    05  INVOICE-NO-IN               (PICTURE required)
    05  LOCATION-IN.
        10  WAREHOUSE-IN            (PICTURE required)
        10  CITY-IN                (PICTURE required)
        10  JOB-LOT-IN             (PICTURE required)
    05  PRODUCT-DESCRIPTION-IN.
        10  NO-OF-ITEM-IN.
            15  SIZE-IN            (PICTURE required)
            15  MODEL-IN           (PICTURE required)
        10  ITEM-NAME-IN           (PICTURE required)
```

Note: Periods follow group items only. Elementary items will contain PICTURE clauses as specified in the next section.

PICTURE (PIC) Clauses

Group items are defined by a level number and a name, which is followed by a period. Elementary items or fields *not* further subdivided must be described with a **PICTURE** (or **PIC**, for short) clause.

FUNCTIONS OF THE PICTURE CLAUSE

1. To specify the *type* of data contained within an elementary item.

2. To indicate the *size* of the field.

Types of Data Fields

There are *three* types of data fields:

TYPES OF DATA FIELDS

1. **Alphabetic**
   A field that may contain only letters or blanks is classified as alphabetic. A name or item description field could be alphabetic.

2. **Alphanumeric**
A field that may contain *any* character is considered alphanumeric. An address field, for example, would be alphanumeric, since it may contain letters, digits, blanks, and/or special characters.

3. **Numeric**
Any signed or unsigned field that will contain only digits is considered numeric. We typically define as numeric only those fields to be used in arithmetic operations.

To denote the type of data within an elementary field, a PICTURE or PIC clause will contain the following:

CHARACTERS USED IN PICTURE CLAUSES

A for alphabetic

X for alphanumeric

9 for numeric

─────────── DEBUGGING TIP ───────────

Note that data entered into a field should be consistent with the data type specified in the PIC clause to ensure that errors do not occur. That is, if you define a field with a PIC of 9's it must contain numeric characters to be processed correctly. If it does not, errors are likely to occur. Use a PIC of 9's only for fields used in arithmetic operations. Remember that a space is *not* a valid character in a numeric field.

Size of Data Fields

We denote the *size* of the field by the *number* of A's, X's, or 9's used in the PICTURE. For example, consider the following:

```
05  AMT-OUT  PICTURE IS 99999.
```

AMT-OUT is an elementary item consisting of *five positions of numeric data.*
Consider the following entry:

```
05  CODE-IN   PICTURE XXXX.
```

CODE-IN defines a four-position storage area that will contain alphanumeric data, which means that it can contain any character. Consider the following entries:

```
01  CUST-REC-IN.
    05  CUST-ID-IN    PICTURE XXXX.
    05  AMT-IN        PICTURE 99999.
```

CUST-ID-IN is the first data field specified. This means that the first four positions of the record represent the field called CUST-ID-IN. AMT-IN, as the second entry specified, would be describing the next field of data, or positions 5–9 of the record.

If a field is numeric, its PICTURE clause will contain 9's; if a field is alphabetic, its PICTURE clause will contain only A's; if a field may contain any character or combination of digits, letters, and special symbols, it is defined with a PICTURE of X's. Numeric fields may contain a maximum of 18 digits. Thus a PICTURE clause with 20 9's, for example, is typically invalid unless the compiler permits an increased size as an enhancement to the standard.

The following defines a 10-position alphanumeric field:

```
05  NAME-IN  PICTURE IS X(10).
```

Rather than coding 10 X's, we may use *parentheses* to designate the size of the field. The word IS in the PICTURE clause is optional, as in all COBOL statements, and may always be omitted. A period will follow each PICTURE clause in the FILE SECTION. Because the abbreviation PIC may be used in place of PICTURE, the preceding field can be defined as:

```
05  NAME-IN  PIC X(10).
```

Guidelines

(1)   We recommend that you use X's rather than A's in PIC clauses because an X is applicable to any nonnumeric field. Since nonnumeric fields are all represented the same way internally in the computer, we will follow the convention of designating nonnumeric items (e.g., NAME-IN, ADDRESS-IN) with a PICTURE of X's, avoiding the use of A's entirely. We use 9's for numeric fields that will be used in arithmetic operations.

(2)   X(nn) or 9(nn) format.   Some organizations prefer a format whereby all PIC clauses are specified as X(nn) or 9(nn), where nn indicates the number of characters. In this way it is easier to read the record description entries because they are all properly aligned as in the following:

```
01  INVENTORY-REC-IN.
    05  ITEM-IN    PIC X(14).
    05  AMT-IN     PIC 9(05).
    05  CODE-IN    PIC X(02).
```

In this text, we will align PIC clauses for ease of reading.

Format of PIC Clauses

Group items are those fields that are further subdivided; they do not have PICTURE clauses. Elementary items require a PICTURE clause, which denotes the size of a field and the type of data it will contain.

Consider the following record layout for an output disk record:

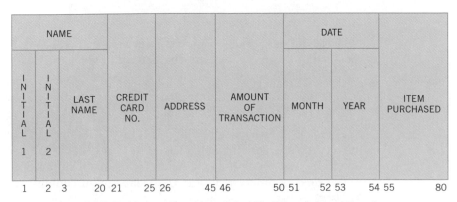

Credit Card Account Record in an Output File (Alternate Record Format)

Its record description entry could appear as follows:

```
01  CREDIT-CARD-ACCT-OUT.
    05  NAME-OUT.
        10  INIT1-OUT           PICTURE X.
        10  INIT2-OUT           PICTURE X.
        10  LAST-NAME-OUT       PICTURE X(18).
    05  CREDIT-CARD-NO-OUT      PICTURE X(5).
    05  ADDRESS-OUT             PICTURE X(20).
    05  AMT-OF-TRANS-OUT        PICTURE 9(5).
    05  DATE-OF-TRANS-OUT.
        10  MONTH-OUT           PICTURE 99.
        10  YEAR-OUT            PICTURE 99.
    05  ITEM-PURCHASED-OUT      PICTURE X(26).
```

A PICTURE clause may appear *anywhere* on the line following the data-name. All A's, X's, or 9's in a PICTURE clause should appear consecutively with no spaces between these characters. Similarly, if parentheses are used to denote the size of a field, no spaces should appear within the parentheses. The following entries may cause syntax errors unless your compiler includes an enhancement to override format requirements:

```
            ↓
PICTURE A  (25)    ⎫
                   ⎬  These entries are invalid because
                   ⎭  of spacing errors denoted by the arrows
PICTURE X(  15  )
          ↑  ↑
```

The PICTURE clauses in a record description entry should, in total, add up to the number of characters in the record. Thus, if CREDIT-CARD-ACCT-OUT is a disk record consisting of 80 characters, all PICTURE clauses on the elementary level would total 80 positions of storage.

Allotting Space for Unused Areas in Record Description Entries

Examine the following record layout:

SAMPLE RECORD LAYOUT FOR AN INPUT EMPLOYEE RECORD	
Field	**Positions in Record**
EMPLOYEE-NAME-IN	1-25
Not used	26-30
HOURS-WORKED-IN	31-35
Not used	36-80

Record positions 26–30 and 36–80 may contain data, but it is not pertinent to the processing of our program. These areas, however, must be defined in the record description entry. Note that the following is *not correct coding* for this sample layout:

```
01  EMPLOYEE-REC-IN.
    05  EMPLOYEE-NAME-IN      PICTURE X(25).
    05  HOURS-WORKED-IN       PICTURE 9(5).
```

The preceding record description entries cause two major errors:

1. The computer will assume that HOURS-WORKED-IN *immediately follows* EMPLOYEE-NAME-IN, since it is the next designated field. A READ instruction, then, would place record positions 26–30, not 31–35, in the storage area called HOURS-WORKED-IN.

2. The PICTURE clauses should account for 80 positions of storage. Instead, only 30 positions have been defined.

The preceding could be coded correctly as:

```
01  EMPLOYEE-REC-IN.
    05  EMPLOYEE-NAME-IN      PIC X(25).
    05  UNUSED1               PIC X(5).
    05  HOURS-WORKED-IN       PIC 9(5).
    05  UNUSED2               PIC X(45).
```

Instead of creating data-names such as UNUSED1 and UNUSED2 in the preceding, we may omit a field-name entirely with COBOL 85. Our record description entry could be coded, then, as:

```
01  EMPLOYEE-REC-IN.
    05  EMPLOYEE-NAME-IN      PIC X(25).
    05                        PIC X(5).
    05  HOURS-WORKED-IN       PIC 9(5).
    05                        PIC X(45).
```

With COBOL 74, we must use the COBOL reserved word FILLER in place of a blank field-name:

```
01  EMPLOYEE-REC-IN.
    05  EMPLOYEE-NAME-IN      PIC X(25).
    05  FILLER                PIC X(5).
    05  HOURS-WORKED-IN       PIC 9(5).
    05  FILLER                PIC X(45).
```

COBOL 85 permits either a blank field-name or the word FILLER. Blank field-names are preferable.

A blank field-name or the word FILLER with an appropriate PICTURE clause designates an area set aside for some part of a record that will *not* be individually referenced in the PROCEDURE DIVISION. To say: MOVE FILLER TO OUT-AREA, for example, is invalid because the word FILLER indicates that the field will not be accessed in this program.

As we have seen, a record- or a file-name must *never* be used more than once in the DATA DIVISION, but field-names need not be unique. Except for the COBOL reserved word FILLER, we will keep all other data-names unique for now; that is, we will *not* use the same name for different fields. We will see in Chapter 6 that the same data-name may, however, be used to define several fields if it is properly qualified.

The Use of the Implied Decimal Point in PIC Clauses

Suppose a five-position input amount field, with contents 10000, is to be interpreted as 100.00. We want the computer to "assume" that a decimal point exists. When any calculations are performed on the amount field, the computer is to consider the data as having three integer positions and two decimal positions. Its PICTURE clause, then, is:

```
05  AMT-IN    PICTURE 999V99.
```

The symbol V denotes an implied decimal point, which does *not* occupy a storage position. Thus, the field AMT-IN is five positions. If 38726 is read into the storage area, it will be interpreted as 387.26 when the program is executed. All arithmetic operations will function properly with decimal alignment when we specify the PIC as 999V99. A PICTURE of 9(3)V99 or 9(3)V9(2) could be used as well.

Summary of Record Description Entries

For *every* record format in a file, an 01-level entry and its corresponding field descriptions must be included. All record formats within an FD are described before the next FD is defined. The DATA DIVISION in Figure 3.3 indicates the sequence in which entries are coded.

Figure 3.3 Sample DATA DIVISION entries.

```
                    DATA DIVISION.
                    FILE SECTION.
                    FD  ACCOUNTS-RECEIVABLE-FILE
                        LABEL RECORDS ARE OMITTED
                        RECORD CONTAINS 80 CHARACTERS.
                 *
                    01  DEBIT-REC-IN.
                        05  CUSTOMER-NAME-IN    PIC X(20).
                        05  ADDRESS-IN          PIC X(15).
                        05  AMT-OF-DEBIT-IN     PIC 999V99.
Use FILLER here ──▶     05                      PIC X(39).
for COBOL 74            05  CODE-IN             PIC X.
                    FD  OUTPUT-FILE
                        LABEL RECORDS ARE STANDARD
                        RECORD CONTAINS 25 CHARACTERS.
                 *
                    01  REC-OUT.
                        05  NAME-OUT            PIC X(20).
                        05  AMT-OF-TRANS-OUT    PIC 999V99.
```

Characters in the COBOL Character Set

All fields consist of individual units of data called **characters**. The characters permitted in a COBOL program are collectively referred to as the **COBOL character set**. These include letters (both uppercase and lowercase), digits (0–9), and special symbols such as a dollar sign ($) or a percent sign (%). The full set of these characters appears in Appendix A.

TYPES OF DATA

Variable and Constant Data

Thus far, we have discussed the organization of data as it appears in a COBOL program. Input and output files have records that are described by record formats. Each record has fields classified as group items or elementary items.

By defining files, records, and fields and assigning corresponding user-defined data-names in the DATA DIVISION, we reserve storage for data. The File Description entries, as illustrated in the previous section, reserve storage for the records in the input and output files. The area described by the File Description entries is said to contain **variable data**.

The contents of data fields in the input area is variable because it changes with each READ instruction. After input fields are processed, the results are placed in the output area, which is defined by another FD. Since the output depends on the input, the contents of output fields is also variable. The contents of the fields containing variable data, then, is not known until the program is actually executed.

When we define a data field with a data-name, we do not know anything about its contents. AMT-IN, for example, is the name of a data field within PAYROLL-REC-IN; the contents of AMT-IN, however, is variable. It depends on the input record being processed, and thus changes with each run of the program. Any field within an input or output record is said to contain variable data.

A **constant**, on the other hand, is a form of data required for processing that is *not* dependent on the input to the system. A constant, as opposed to variable data, is coded directly in the program. Suppose, for example, we wish to multiply each amount field of every input record by .05, a fixed tax rate. The tax rate, .05, unlike each inputted amount field, is *not* a variable but remains fixed in the program. We call .05 a *constant,* since it is a form of data required for processing that is not dependent on the input to the system.

Similarly, suppose we wish to check input records and print the message 'INVALID RECORD' if the data is erroneous. The message 'INVALID RECORD' will be part of the output line, but is *not* entered as input to the system. It is a constant with a fixed value that is required for processing.

A constant may be defined directly in the PROCEDURE DIVISION of a COBOL program. The PROCEDURE DIVISION entry to multiply AMT-IN by a tax of .05 and place the result in an output field called TAX-AMT-OUT is as follows:

```
               MULTIPLY AMT-IN BY .05
                  GIVING TAX-AMT-OUT
```

The two data fields, AMT-IN and TAX-AMT-OUT, are described in the DATA DIVISION. The constant .05 is defined directly in the MULTIPLY statement, so it need *not* be described in the DATA DIVISION. A constant may also be defined in the WORKING-STORAGE SECTION of the DATA DIVISION with a **VALUE clause** as follows:

```
WORKING-STORAGE SECTION.
01  TAX-RATE    PICTURE V99    VALUE .05.
```

Thus we may define TAX-RATE in the WORKING-STORAGE SECTION and give it a VALUE of .05. In this way, we may multiply AMT-IN by TAX-RATE in the PROCEDURE DIVISION:

```
MULTIPLY AMT-IN BY TAX-RATE
   GIVING TAX-AMT-OUT
```

We discuss WORKING-STORAGE in detail in the next section.

Three types of constants may be defined in a COBOL program: numeric literals, nonnumeric literals, and figurative constants. Each type will be discussed here in detail. (The word "literal" and the word "constant" are used interchangeably.)

TYPES OF CONSTANTS

Numeric Literal

A **numeric literal** is a constant used primarily for arithmetic operations. The number .05 in the preceding example is a numeric literal. The rules for forming numeric literals are as follows:

RULES FOR FORMING NUMERIC LITERALS

1. 1 to 18 digits.

2. A + or − sign may be used, but it must appear to the *left* of the number.

3. A decimal point is permitted *within* the literal. The decimal point, however, may not be the rightmost character of the literal.

A plus or minus sign is *not* required within the literal, but it *may* be included to the left of the number. That is, +16 and −12 are valid numeric literals but 16+ and 12− are not. If no sign is used, the number is assumed positive. Since a decimal point may not appear as the rightmost character in a numeric literal, 18.2 is a valid literal but 16. is not; however, 16.0 is valid.

The following are valid numeric literals that may be used in the PROCEDURE DIVISION of a COBOL program:

VALID NUMERIC LITERALS

+15.8	.05
−387.58	−.97
42	

Suppose we wish to add 10.3 to a field, TOTAL-OUT, defined within an output record in the DATA DIVISION. The following is a valid instruction:

```
ADD 10.3 TO TOTAL-OUT
```

The following are *not* valid numeric literals for the reasons noted:

INVALID NUMERIC LITERALS

Literal	Reason It Is Invalid
1,000	Commas are *not* permitted.
15.	A decimal point is not valid as the rightmost character.
$100.00	Dollar signs are not permitted.
17.45−	Plus or minus signs, if used, must appear to the left of the number.

A numeric literal, then, is a constant that may be used in the PROCEDURE DIVISION of a COBOL program. Numeric literals are numeric constants that can be used for arithmetic operations. The preceding rules must be employed when defining a numeric literal.

Representing Decimal Data in Storage

Suppose we have an output field defined in a disk record as follows:

```
01  REC-OUT.
    05  AMT-OUT PIC 99V99.
```

If we wish to move a constant to AMT-OUT in the PROCEDURE DIVISION, the constant would actually include the decimal point as in the following:

```
MOVE 21.50 TO AMT-OUT
```

Thus a decimal point is implied but not included on magnetic media such as disk in order to save storage; a decimal point must, however, actually be included in a numeric constant when decimal alignment is required.

Nonnumeric Literal

A **nonnumeric** or **alphanumeric literal** is a constant that is used in the PROCEDURE DIVISION for all operations *except* arithmetic. The following are rules for defining a nonnumeric or alphanumeric literal:

RULES FOR FORMING NONNUMERIC LITERALS

1. The literal must be enclosed in quotation marks.

2. From 1 to 160 characters, including spaces, may be used. (Only 120 characters are permitted for COBOL 74.) Many compilers include enhancements that permit longer nonnumeric literals than specified in the standard.

3. Any character permitted in the COBOL character set may be used except the quotation mark. (To use a quotation mark in a nonnumeric literal, the COBOL reserved word QUOTE must precede and follow the literal—see Chapter 6.)

As noted, the COBOL character set includes those characters that are permitted within a COBOL program. Appendix A lists these characters.

In this text, we use a single quotation mark or apostrophe to delimit nonnumeric literals. Some compilers, however, use double quotation marks (''). Others permit either single or double quotes to delimit a nonnumeric literal. Check your COBOL manual. On all systems there are commands that enable you to change the specification for a nonnumeric literal from an apostrophe (single quote) to a quotation mark (double quotes) or from double quotes to an apostrophe.

The following are valid nonnumeric literals:

VALID NONNUMERIC LITERALS

'CODE'	'INPUT'
'ABC 123'	'$100.00'
'1,000'	'MESSAGE'

Moving any of these literals to a print area and then writing the print record results in the printing of the characters *within* the quotation marks; that is CODE, ABC 123, 1,000, and so on will print if the preceding literals are moved to a print area. Note that a nonnumeric literal may contain *all* numbers. '123' is a valid nonnumeric literal, but it is not the same as the numeric literal 123. The literal 123 (1) is the only type of literal permitted in an arithmetic operation and (2) should be the type of literal moved to a field with a PIC of 9's.

Suppose we wish to move the message 'INVALID RECORD' to an output field, MESSAGE-FIELD-OUT, before we write an output record. The following is a valid COBOL instruction:

```
MOVE 'INVALID RECORD' TO MESSAGE-FIELD-OUT
```

'INVALID RECORD' is a nonnumeric literal. It is a value specified in the PROCEDURE DIVISION and does *not* appear in the DATA DIVISION. MESSAGE-FIELD-OUT is a data-name. It could not be a nonnumeric literal, since it is not enclosed in quotation marks. All data-names, such as MESSAGE-FIELD-OUT, would be defined in the DATA DIVISION.

In summary, a nonnumeric literal is any constant defined directly in a source program that is not used for arithmetic operations. Any character may be used to form a nonnumeric literal. That is, once the string of characters is enclosed within quotes, the computer does *not* check to determine if a reserved word is being used. Thus 'DATA' and 'MOVE' are valid nonnumeric literals.

Figurative Constant

A **figurative constant** is a COBOL reserved word that has special significance to the compiler. In this section we discuss the two most frequently used figurative constants: ZEROS and SPACES.

The figurative constant ZEROS is a COBOL reserved word meaning all zeros. Consider the following instruction:

```
MOVE ZEROS TO TOTAL-OUT
```

This operation results in the field called TOTAL-OUT being filled with all zeros. ZERO, ZEROES, and ZEROS may be used interchangeably in the PROCEDURE DIVISION of a COBOL program. ZEROS can be moved to both numeric and alphanumeric fields.

SPACES is a figurative constant meaning all blanks. Consider the following instruction:

```
                         MOVE SPACES TO CODE-OUT
```

This results in blanks being placed in every position of the field CODE-OUT. SPACES may be used interchangeably with the figurative constant SPACE. SPACES should be moved only to alphanumeric or alphabetic fields.

In summary, three types of constants may be specified in the PROCEDURE DIVISION: a numeric literal, a nonnumeric literal, and a figurative constant. Fields that contain variable data must be described in the DATA DIVISION and may be accessed in the PROCEDURE DIVISION.

In future discussions of PROCEDURE DIVISION entries, the use of constants will become clearer. Right now, you should be able to recognize literals and to distinguish them from the names used to define data fields. The specific formats of ADD and MOVE statements, in which these literals were illustrated, are discussed more fully later.

The following is a review of COBOL language elements:

COBOL LANGUAGE ELEMENTS

I. Words
  A. Reserved
  B. User-defined
II. Constants or Literals
  A. Nonnumeric
  B. Numeric
  C. Figurative constants

THE WORKING-STORAGE SECTION OF THE DATA DIVISION

INTRODUCTION

Any field necessary for processing that is not part of an input or output file may be defined in the WORKING-STORAGE SECTION of the DATA DIVISION. Such a field may also be established with a constant as its value. The following summarizes the rules for using WORKING-STORAGE:

RULES FOR USING THE WORKING-STORAGE SECTION

1. The WORKING-STORAGE SECTION follows the FILE SECTION.

2. WORKING-STORAGE SECTION is coded on a line by itself beginning in Area A and ending with a period.

3. A group item that will be subdivided into individual storage areas as needed may then be defined. All necessary fields can be described within this 01-level entry:

```
WORKING-STORAGE SECTION.
01  WS-STORED-AREAS.
    05  ARE-THERE-MORE-RECORDS      PIC X(3).
    05  WS-GROSS-AMT                PIC 999V99.
        :
        :
```

4. Names associated with group and elementary items must conform to the rules for forming data-names. WS- is frequently used as a prefix to denote fields as WORKING-STORAGE entries.

5. Each elementary item must contain a PIC clause.

6. Each elementary item may contain an initial value, if desired:

```
WORKING-STORAGE SECTION.
01  WS-STORED-AREAS.
    05  ARE-THERE-MORE-RECORDS   PIC X(3)    VALUE 'YES'.
    05  WS-GROSS-AMT             PIC 999V99  VALUE ZERO.
```

VALUE clauses for initializing fields may *only* be used in the WORKING-STORAGE SECTION, *not* in the FILE SECTION. Either figurative constants or literals may be used in VALUE clauses.

USES OF WORKING-STORAGE

We will provide some examples of how the WORKING-STORAGE SECTION is used. The actual PROCEDURE DIVISION entries that operate on WORKING-STORAGE fields will be explained as we proceed through the text.

Example 1
Storing Intermediate
Results

Consider the following input and output layouts:

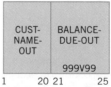

Input Record Layout: CUSTOMER-IN

CUST-NAME-IN	UNIT-PRICE-IN	QUANTITY-IN	DISCOUNT-AMT-IN
	9V99	99	999V99

1   20 21   23 24   25 26   30

Output Record Layout: BILLING-OUT

CUST-NAME-OUT	BALANCE-DUE-OUT
	999V99

1   20 21   25

Note: BALANCE-DUE-OUT is equal to UNIT-PRICE-IN × QUANTITY-IN − DISCOUNT-AMT-IN

Using the basic arithmetic verbs that will be discussed in detail later on, we would code the following to obtain the output BALANCE-DUE field:

```
MULTIPLY UNIT-PRICE-IN BY
    QUANTITY-IN GIVING WS-GROSS-AMT
SUBTRACT DISCOUNT-AMT-IN FROM WS-GROSS-AMT
    GIVING BALANCE-DUE-OUT
```

UNIT-PRICE-IN, QUANTITY-IN, and DISCOUNT-AMT-IN are input fields defined for the CUSTOMER-IN file. BALANCE-DUE-OUT is a field in the BILLING-OUT file. WS-GROSS-AMT, however, is an **intermediate result field** necessary for calculating BALANCE-DUE-OUT; it is not part of either an input or an output record. As an intermediate result, it is stored in a work area defined with an appropriate PICTURE clause in WORKING-STORAGE. It could be defined as follows:

```
WORKING-STORAGE SECTION.
01  WS-WORK-AREAS.
    05  WS-GROSS-AMT              PIC 9(3)V99.
***********************************************************************
*  any other work areas necessary for processing will               *
*  be placed here                                                    *
***********************************************************************
```

Example 2
Storing Counters

Suppose we wish to count the number of input records contained within a file and store that number in a **counter field**. The following program excerpt could be used:

COBOL 74

```
100-MAIN-MODULE.
    MOVE ZERO TO WS-COUNTER.
    READ INVENTORY-FILE
        AT END MOVE 'NO ' TO ARE-THERE-MORE-RECORDS.
    PERFORM 200-COUNT-THE-RECORDS
        UNTIL ARE-THERE-MORE-RECORDS = 'NO '.
    PERFORM 300-PRINT-TOTAL.
       :
       :
200-COUNT-THE-RECORDS.
    ADD 1 TO WS-COUNTER.
    READ INVENTORY-FILE
        AT END MOVE 'NO ' TO ARE-THERE-MORE-RECORDS.
```

COBOL 85

```
100-MAIN-MODULE.
    MOVE ZERO TO WS-COUNTER
    PERFORM UNTIL ARE-THERE-MORE-RECORDS = 'NO '
        READ INVENTORY-FILE
            AT END
                MOVE 'NO ' TO ARE-THERE-MORE-RECORDS
            NOT AT END
                ADD 1 TO WS-COUNTER
        END-READ
    END-PERFORM
    PERFORM 300-PRINT-TOTAL
       :
       :
```

WS-COUNTER could be a field defined in WORKING-STORAGE. It is incremented by one each time a record is read; hence, after all records have been read, it will contain a sum equal to the total number of records read as input. WS-COUNTER would be defined as part of WS-WORK-AREAS in WORKING-STORAGE:

```
WORKING-STORAGE SECTION.
01  WS-WORK-AREAS.
    05  WS-GROSS-AMT              PIC 9(5)V99.
    05  WS-COUNTER                PIC 9(3).
```

Example 3
Using an End-of-File
Indicator: A Review

We have been using the data-name ARE-THERE-MORE-RECORDS as an *end-of-file indicator*. ARE-THERE-MORE-RECORDS is initialized at 'YES'. During program execution, when an AT END condition is reached, 'NO ' is moved to ARE-THERE-MORE-RECORDS. Thus, ARE-THERE-MORE-RECORDS contains a 'YES' as long as there are still records to process. We perform a standard calculation or process routine on all records until ARE-THERE-MORE-RECORDS = 'NO ', that is, until an AT END condition occurs, at which point 'NO ' is moved to ARE-THERE-MORE-RECORDS. ARE-THERE-MORE-RECORDS would be an elementary work area in WORKING-STORAGE:

```
WORKING-STORAGE SECTION.
01  WS-WORK-AREAS.
    05  WS-GROSS-AMT              PIC 9(5)V99.
    05  WS-COUNTER                PIC 9(3).
    05  ARE-THERE-MORE-RECORDS    PIC X(3).
```

Other user-defined names besides ARE-THERE-MORE-RECORDS would serve just as well. EOF or WS-EOF could be used as a field-name, where EOF is an abbreviation for *end of file*. In fact, any identifier can be coded as a user-defined data-name. Suppose we define EOF as follows:

```
01  WS-WORK-AREAS.
       :
       :
    05  EOF                       PIC X.
```

In our PROCEDURE DIVISION we could indicate an end-of-file condition when EOF = 'Y' for 'YES'. Consider the following:

<table>
<tr><td align="center">COBOL 74</td><td align="center">COBOL 85</td></tr>
</table>

```
PROCEDURE DIVISION.                    PROCEDURE DIVISION.
100-MAIN-MODULE.                       100-MAIN-MODULE.
      :                                      :
      :                                      :
    MOVE 'N' TO EOF.                       MOVE 'N' TO EOF
    READ INFILE                            PERFORM UNTIL EOF = 'Y'
        AT END MOVE 'Y' TO EOF.                READ INFILE
    PERFORM 200-PROCESS-RTN                        AT END
        UNTIL EOF = 'Y'.                                   MOVE 'Y' TO EOF
      :                                            NOT AT END
      :                                                    PERFORM 200-PROCESS-RTN
200-PROCESS-RTN.                               END-READ
      :                                    END-PERFORM
      :                                      :
    READ INFILE                              :
        AT END MOVE 'Y' TO EOF.        200-PROCESS-RTN.
                                             :
                                             :
```

 Interactive Processing.   When input is entered from a keyboard, it is stored in WORK-ING-STORAGE, not in the FILE SECTION:

```
WORKING-STORAGE SECTION.
01  LAST-NAME      PIC X(20).
      :
      :
PROCEDURE DIVISION.
      :
      :
    ACCEPT LAST-NAME
```

The ACCEPT verb inputs data from a keyboard into WORKING-STORAGE. Similarly, to display data on a screen, we code DISPLAY data-name, where data-name is also a WORK-ING-STORAGE entry. Chapters 5 and 6 discuss interactive processing in more detail.

VALUE CLAUSES FOR WORKING-STORAGE ENTRIES

The Purpose of VALUE Clauses

An area that is specified in the DATA DIVISION typically has an undefined value when a program begins execution. Thus, unless the programmer moves an initial value into a field, it cannot be assumed that the field will contain specific contents, such as blanks or zeros.

Elementary items in the WORKING-STORAGE SECTION may be given initial contents by a VALUE clause. If a WORKING-STORAGE field is given a VALUE, there will be no need to move a literal or a figurative constant into it in the PROCEDURE DIVISION.

To ensure that output records or fields specified in the FILE SECTION contain blanks when program execution begins, we MOVE SPACES to these areas in the PROCEDURE DIVISION before any processing is performed. When fields are defined in the WORKING-STORAGE SECTION, however, we have the added flexibility of being able to initialize these areas by using a VALUE clause:

Examples
```
WORKING-STORAGE SECTION.
01  WS-WORK-AREAS.
    05  WS-TOTAL              PIC 999    VALUE ZEROS.
    05  WS-CONSTANT-1         PIC XXXX   VALUE SPACES.
```

We align VALUE clauses as well as PIC clauses to make programs easier to read.

As an enhancement, some compilers allow a VALUE clause on the group level if all items are to be initialized with the same value:

```
01  WS-WORK-AREAS            VALUE ZEROS.
    05  WS-COUNTER           PIC 999.
    05  WS-AMT               PIC 9(5).
```

A VALUE clause is *not required* for any WORKING-STORAGE item. If it is omitted, however, no assumption can be made about the initial contents of the field. Where no VALUE clause has been coded, use a MOVE instruction in the PROCEDURE DIVISION to obtain an initial value in the field.

DEBUGGING TIP

It is best to initialize fields in WORKING-STORAGE with VALUE clauses rather than with MOVE statements in the PROCEDURE DIVISION. You are more apt to remember to initialize when defining the fields themselves.

Four entries, then, can be used to define independent or elementary items in the WORKING-STORAGE SECTION. We will always use the first three, but it is recommended that you use the fourth as well:

ITEMS IN WORKING-STORAGE

1. Level 01, coded in Area A, may be used to define a group of independent or elementary items. These independent elementary items would be coded on a level subordinate to 01 in Area B.

2. A user-defined data-name or identifier defines each field. Frequently, we use the prefix WS- to denote WORKING-STORAGE entries.

3. The size of a field and its data type are defined by the PIC clause.

4. An initial value may be stored in the field by a VALUE clause defined on the elementary level. VALUE clauses may also be used on the group level for initializing a series of fields.

Literals and Figurative Constants in VALUE Clauses

The VALUE clause, which is a literal or a figurative constant, must be the same data type as the PICTURE clause. If the PICTURE denotes a numeric field, for example, the value must be a numeric literal or the figurative constant ZERO.

Example 1
```
WORKING-STORAGE SECTION.
01  WS-WORK-AREAS.
    05  WS-SOC-SEC-TAX-RATE      PIC V9999      VALUE .0765.
    05  WS-CONSTANT-1            PIC 9(5)       VALUE 07600.
    05  WS-TOTAL                 PIC 9999       VALUE ZERO.
```

Remember that to code 05 WS-SOC-SEC-TAX-RATE PICTURE V9999 VALUE .0765 is the same as coding MOVE .0765 TO WS-SOC-TAX-RATE before processing data, where WS-SOC-SEC-TAX-RATE has no VALUE clause.

If a field contains an alphanumeric or alphabetic PICTURE clause, a VALUE clause, if used, must contain a nonnumeric literal or a figurative constant:

Example 2
```
************************************************************************
*    alpha fields must have values enclosed in quotes                 *
************************************************************************
WORKING-STORAGE SECTION.
01  WS-WORK-AREAS.
    05  WS-DATE                       PIC X(5)   VALUE 'APRIL'.
    05  WS-NAME                       PIC XXX    VALUE SPACES.
    05  ARE-THERE-MORE-RECORDS        PIC XXX    VALUE 'YES'.
```

PICTURE type and literal type should match when using VALUE clauses:

Incorrect Coding
```
05  WS-TOTAL          PICTURE 9(5)      VALUE SPACES.  ◄──── SPACES is not valid in a
                                                             numeric field
```

The above will result in a syntax error. Digits 0–9, decimal points, and plus or minus signs are the only characters that may be used in a numeric literal. To clear a numeric field, we fill it with zeros, not blanks. The above entry should read:

Corrected Entry

```
05  WS-TOTAL         PICTURE 9(5)     VALUE ZERO.
```

VALUE clauses for initializing fields may *not* be used in the FILE SECTION of the DATA DIVISION. Only WORKING-STORAGE entries may have VALUE clauses for this purpose.

We have seen that we can initialize WS-TOTAL by (1) moving zeros to it in the PROCEDURE DIVISION before processing any data or by (2) using a VALUE clause of ZERO in WORKING-STORAGE. If the contents of WS-TOTAL is changed during execution, the initial value of zero will be replaced:

```
WORKING-STORAGE SECTION.
01  WS-WORK-AREAS.
    05  WS-TOTAL      PIC 9(5)    VALUE ZERO.
    :
    :
PROCEDURE DIVISION.
    :
    :
    ADD AMT-IN TO WS-TOTAL
```

After the ADD instruction is executed the first time, WS-TOTAL will contain the value of AMT-IN and *not* zero. If, however, we did not initialize WS-TOTAL at ZERO, the contents of WS-TOTAL after the ADD would be unpredictable. It may even cause a program interrupt if the field has nonnumeric characters such as blanks. We cannot assume a value of zero in a field that has not been initialized.

——————————— DEBUGGING TIP ———

Note: Failure to initialize a field used in an arithmetic operation is a frequent cause of program interrupts. Be sure to use a VALUE of ZEROS to initialize all numeric fields prior to processing.

We may use a WORKING-STORAGE entry defined with a VALUE in place of a literal in the PROCEDURE DIVISION. Consider the following coding:

```
IF  CODE-IN = ZERO
    MOVE 'CR' TO CREDIT-AREA-OUT
```

The above is the same as:

```
IF  CODE-IN = ZERO
    MOVE WS-CREDIT TO CREDIT-AREA-OUT
```

where WS-CREDIT is an independent item in WORKING-STORAGE defined as follows:

```
05  WS-CREDIT      PICTURE XX     VALUE 'CR'.
```

——————————— DEBUGGING TIP ———

The programmer decides whether to use a WORKING-STORAGE data item to store a constant in a work area or to code the constant as a literal in the PROCEDURE DIVISION. As a general rule, however, any literal that will be used more than once in the PROCEDURE DIVISION should be given an assigned storage area and a data-name in WORKING-STORAGE. It is more efficient to use this data-name several times in the program than to redefine the same literal again and again in the PROCEDURE DIVISION.

Continuation of Nonnumeric Literals in VALUE Clauses from One Line to the Next

Recall that numeric literals and numeric fields may not exceed 18 digits in length. Similarly, the VALUE and PICTURE clauses of a numeric item in the WORKING-STORAGE SECTION may not exceed 18 digits.

A nonnumeric literal, however, may contain up to 160 characters for COBOL 85 or 120 characters for COBOL 74. Similarly, a nonnumeric literal in a VALUE clause, like any other nonnumeric literal, is enclosed in quotes and contains a maximum of 160 characters (COBOL 85) or 120 characters (COBOL 74).

Since the VALUE clause for an alphanumeric field in the WORKING-STORAGE SECTION may contain as many as 160 (or 120) characters, it is sometimes necessary to continue the VALUE from one line of the coding sheet to the next line. The continuation of nonnumeric literals to two or more lines conforms to the following rules:

RULES FOR CONTINUATION OF LITERALS FROM ONE LINE TO THE NEXT

1. Begin the literal in the VALUE clause with a quotation mark.

2. Continue the literal until position 72, the end of the line, is reached. Do *not* end with a quotation mark on this line.

3. Place a hyphen on the *next line* in the position marked Cont. for continuation (position 7 on the coding sheet).

4. Continue the literal in any position beginning in Area B of the second line. Begin with a quotation mark.

5. End the literal with a quotation mark.

The same rules may be applied to the continuation of nonnumeric literals defined in the PROCEDURE DIVISION.

Examples 1. The following illustrates the continuation of a literal to a second line:

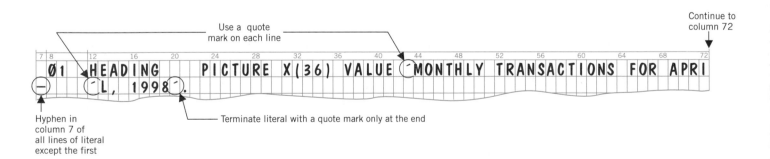

2. The following illustrates the continuation of a nonnumeric literal to three lines:

To reduce the risk of erroneous coding, we recommend that you avoid continuing literals from one line to another. Subdivide literals into separate fields:

```
01   COLUMN-HDGS.
     05       PIC X(22) VALUE '   NAME      TRANSACTION '.
     05       PIC X(28) VALUE 'NUMBER    DATE OF TRANSACTION'.
     05       PIC X(28) VALUE '   AMOUNT    INVOICE NUMBER'.
     05       PIC X(22) VALUE '    ITEM DESCRIPTION '.
```

COBOL 85: SUMMARY OF DATA DIVISION FEATURES

1. The entire DATA DIVISION is itself optional. This means that file specifications may be copied from a library, eliminating the need for FDs in some user programs.

2. The LABEL RECORDS clause is optional. The reading or writing of label records can be left entirely to the operating system. If the clause is omitted, LABEL RECORDS are assumed to be STANDARD.

3. The BLOCK CONTAINS clause may be deleted for blocked records if blocking is handled by the operating system.

4. The word FILLER is optional in record descriptions. The following is acceptable:

```
01   EMPLOYEE-OUTPUT-REC.
     05                      PIC X(6).
     05   NAME-OUT           PIC X(10).
     05                      PIC X(30).
     05   ADDRESS-OUT        PIC X(14).
```

1. The LABEL RECORDS clause will be phased out entirely.

2. VALUE clauses will be permitted in the FILE SECTION for defining initial contents of fields.

3. The way nonnumeric literals are continued will change. The hyphen in the continuation column (7) will be eliminated. Instead, you will add a – on the line being continued.

```
MOVE   'PART 1 OF LITERAL' –
       'PART 2 OF LITERAL' TO ABC.
```

4. As noted previously, rules for Margins A and B will become guidelines rather than requirements.

5. Commas and dollar signs will be permissible in numeric literals. Thus, $1,000.00 would be a valid numeric literal.

CHAPTER SUMMARY
A. Data Organization
1. **File**—The major classification of data for a specific business use or application.
2. **Record**—Data within a file that contains a unit of information.
3. **Field**—A group of consecutive positions reserved for an item of data.

Note: Files, records, and fields are all defined with data-names.

B. Types of Data
1. **Variable Data**—Data that varies with each run.
2. **Constant or Literal**—Data that is defined within the program; it is *not* entered as input to the system.

        a. Numeric Literal—A constant that may be used in the PROCEDURE
           DIVISION for arithmetic operations.

        b. Nonnumeric Literal—A constant that may be used in the PROCEDURE DIVISION for all
           operations except arithmetic.

        c. Figurative Constant—A COBOL reserved word with special significance to the compiler (e.g., ZERO or ZEROES or ZEROS; SPACE or SPACES).

C. The FILE SECTION

  1. FD Entries

        a. FD is coded in Area A.

        b. The file-name, which is typically coded in Area B, must be the same name that is used in the SELECT statement.

        c. Clauses: LABEL RECORDS ARE $\left\{ \begin{array}{l} \text{OMITTED} \\ \text{STANDARD} \end{array} \right\}$
                RECORD CONTAINS integer CHARACTERS
                BLOCK CONTAINS integer RECORDS.

      All clauses are optional for COBOL 85. The LABEL RECORDS clause is required for COBOL 74.

        d. After any clauses have been specified, a single period ends the FD.

  2. Record Description Entries

        a. Record-names are coded on the 01 level.

        b. Field-names are coded on levels 02–49. We will use 05, 10, 15, and so on to allow for insertions if they become necessary.

        c. Level 01 is coded in Area A. All other levels are coded in Area B for COBOL 74, although Area A can be used for COBOL 85.

        d. Items with higher level numbers are considered subordinate to, or contained within, items with lower level numbers. We indent subordinate items for the sake of clarity.

        e. Group items are further subdivided; elementary items are not.

        f. Only elementary items have PICTURE or PIC clauses to describe the data:

           X—alphanumeric
           A—alphabetic
           9—numeric
           V—implied decimal position (used only with numeric fields)

        g. A period must follow a PICTURE clause in an elementary item; a period directly follows a group item name.

        h. Fields must be defined in the DATA DIVISION in the same sequence as they appear in the record being described.

        i. FILLER is a COBOL reserved word used to define areas within a record that will not be referenced individually during processing. With COBOL 85, a blank field-name can be used instead of the word FILLER.

D. The WORKING-STORAGE SECTION

  1. Used for storing intermediate results, counters, end-of-file indicators, and interactive data to be accepted as input or displayed.

  2. VALUE clauses may be used to initialize fields.

KEY TERMS

Alphanumeric literal	Figurative constant	Numeric literal
BLOCK CONTAINS	FILE SECTION	PICTURE (PIC)
Blocking	FILLER	Record
Characters	Fixed-length record	RECORD CONTAINS
COBOL character set	Group item	Record description
Constant	Header label	Reserved word
Counter field	Identifier	Trailer label
DATA DIVISION	Intermediate result field	Update procedure
Data-name	LABEL RECORDS	VALUE clause
Elementary item	Level number	Variable data
FD (File Description)	Master file	WORKING-STORAGE
Field	Nonnumeric literal	SECTION

CHAPTER SELF-TEST

1. The contents of fields defined within input and output records is (fixed, variable).

2. A constant may be used directly in the _____ DIVISION as part of an instruction, or defined in the _____ SECTION.

3. Fields whose names appear in PROCEDURE DIVISION statements must be defined in the _____ DIVISION.

4. What, if anything, is wrong with the following numeric literals?
   (a) 123.
   (b) 15.8 −
   (c) 1,000,000.00
   (d) $38.90
   (e) 58

5. What, if anything, is wrong with the following nonnumeric literals?
   (a) 'THIS IS 'CODE-1'.'
   (b) 'INPUT'
   (c) 'ZERO'
   (d) '123'
   (e) '   '

6. The literal '   ', if printed, would result in the printing of _____ .

7. Two examples of figurative constants are _____ and _____ .

8. Consider the following instruction: MOVE '1' TO FLD1. '1' is a _____ . FLD1 is a _____ and must be defined in the _____ DIVISION.

9. To print 'ZEROS' results in the printing of _____ . To print ZEROS results in the printing of _____ . ZEROS is called a _____ .

10. A PICTURE clause must be used in conjunction with each _____ item in a record description.

11. A PICTURE clause specifies the _____ and the _____ of a data field.

12. The characters that may be included in an alphabetic field are _____ .

13. The characters that may be included in an alphanumeric field are _____ .

14. The characters that may be included in a numeric data field are _____ .

15. An alphanumeric PICTURE clause contains _____ ; an alphabetic PICTURE clause contains _____ ; a numeric PICTURE clause contains _____ .

What, if anything, is wrong with the following entries (16–18)? Consider each separately:

16. 01 TRANSACTION-REC.
        05 DATE-OF-SALE PICTURE 9999.
            10 MONTH PICTURE 99.
            10 YEAR   PICTURE 99.

17. 03 FIELDA PICTURE XX.

18. 04 FIELDB PICTURE X (22).

19. The sum of the X's, A's, or 9's in all the PICTURE clauses in a record description should, in total, equal _____ .

20. The COBOL reserved word _____ can be used to denote an area of a record that will not be used for processing.

21. A PICTURE clause of 9V9 indicates a __(no.)__ -position numeric data field.

22. If a three-position tax field is to be interpreted as a number with no integers, just decimal places, its PICTURE clause should be _____ .

23. The _____ SECTION of the DATA DIVISION usually follows the FILE SECTION.

24. WORKING-STORAGE entries may contain _____ clauses to indicate the initial contents of fields.

25. Is the use of level numbers in the following correct? Explain your answer.

```
01  IN-REC.
    05  NAME-IN.
        07  LAST-NAME          PIC X(10).
        07  FIRST-NAME         PIC X(10).
        07  MIDDLE-NAME        PIC X(10).
    05  ADDRESS-IN.
        10  STREET             PIC X(10).
        10  CITY               PIC X(10).
        10  STATE              PIC X(10).
```

Solutions

1. variable

2. PROCEDURE; WORKING-STORAGE

3. DATA

4. (a) A decimal point may not be the last character.
   (b) A minus sign must be to the left of the number.
   (c) Commas are not permitted.
   (d) A dollar sign is not permitted.
   (e) Nothing is wrong.

5. (a) Quotation marks may not be used within a nonnumeric literal.
   (b) Nothing is wrong.
   (c) Nothing is wrong.
   (d) Nothing is wrong.
   (e) Nothing is wrong.

6. two blanks or spaces

7. ZERO, ZEROES, ZEROS; SPACE, SPACES

8. nonnumeric literal (enclosed in quotes); data-name (not enclosed in quotes); DATA

9. the word ZEROS; a zero value (all 0's); figurative constant

10. elementary

11. size; type

12. letters and blanks

13. any characters in the COBOL character set (letters, digits, and special symbols)

14. digits, and a plus or minus sign

15. X's; A's; 9's

16. Group items, such as DATE-OF-SALE, should not have PICTURE clauses.

17. Okay

18. Should be: 04 FIELDB PICTURE X(22). There is no space between X and (.

19. the number of positions in the record

20. FILLER

21. two (the V does not occupy a storage position)

22. V999.

23. WORKING-STORAGE

24. VALUE

25. Yes, although it is somewhat unusual. All level 07 items are contained within NAME-IN, and all level 10 items are contained within ADDRESS-IN. Thus, the same level number need not be used throughout for elementary items. In the first case, LAST-NAME with a level of 07 is an elementary item, and in the second case, STREET with a level number of 10 is also an elementary item.

PRACTICE PROGRAM Consider the following input and output layouts, hierarchy chart, pseudocode, and PROCEDURE DIVISION for a program that reads in customer records, each with three amount fields, and calculates a total price. Write the first three divisions for the program. Both files are on disk, with standard labels.

TRANSACTION-FILE Record Layout			
Field	**Size**	**Type**	**No. of Decimal Positions (if Numeric)**
CUST-NO-IN	5	Alphanumeric	
AMT1-IN	5	Numeric	0
AMT2-IN	5	Numeric	0
AMT3-IN	5	Numeric	0

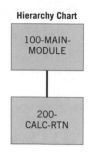

Hierarchy Chart

100-MAIN-MODULE

200-CALC-RTN

TOTAL-FILE Record Layout			
Field	**Size**	**Type**	**No. of Decimal Positions (if Numeric)**
CUST-NO-OUT	5	Alphanumeric	
TOTAL-OUT	6	Numeric	0

Note: Only fields used in arithmetic operations will be defined as numeric.

Pseudocode
START
    Open Files
    PERFORM UNTIL no more records (Are-There-More-Records = 'NO ')
        READ a Record
            AT END Move 'NO ' to Are-There-More-Records
            NOT AT END
                Move Input Customer Number to Output Customer Number
                Add Three Amount Fields and Place Sum in Output Area
                Write Output Record
        END-READ
        END-PERFORM
        End-of-Job Operations
STOP

Procedure Division

<table>
<tr><th>COBOL 74</th><th>COBOL 85</th></tr>
</table>

```
100-MAIN-MODULE.                          100-MAIN-MODULE.
    OPEN INPUT TRANSACTION-FILE               OPEN INPUT  TRANSACTION-FILE
         OUTPUT TOTAL-FILE.                        OUTPUT TOTAL-FILE
    READ TRANSACTION-FILE                     PERFORM UNTIL ARE-THERE-MORE-RECORDS = 'NO '
        AT END MOVE 'NO ' TO ARE-THERE-MORE-RECORDS.    READ TRANSACTION-FILE
    PERFORM 200-CALC-RTN                              AT END
        UNTIL ARE-THERE-MORE-RECORDS = 'NO '.                 MOVE 'NO ' TO ARE-THERE-MORE-RECORDS
    CLOSE TRANSACTION-FILE                            NOT AT END
          TOTAL-FILE.                                     PERFORM 200-CALC-RTN
    STOP RUN.                                     END-READ
200-CALC-RTN.                                 END-PERFORM
    MOVE CUST-NO-IN TO CUST-NO-OUT.           CLOSE TRANSACTION-FILE
    ADD AMT1-IN AMT2-IN AMT3-IN                     TOTAL-FILE
       GIVING TOTAL-OUT.                       STOP RUN.
    WRITE TOTAL-REC-OUT.                   200-CALC-RTN.
    READ TRANSACTION-FILE                     MOVE CUST-NO-IN TO CUST-NO-OUT
        AT END MOVE 'NO ' TO ARE-THERE-MORE-RECORDS.    ADD AMT1-IN  AMT2-IN  AMT3-IN
                                                       GIVING TOTAL-OUT
                                              WRITE-TOTAL-REC-OUT.
```

Note: *COBOL 74 statements end with a period. Only the* last *statement in each paragraph of a COBOL 85 program ends with a period.*

Solution   The first three divisions of the Practice Program are:

```
IDENTIFICATION DIVISION.
PROGRAM-ID. CHAPTER3.
AUTHOR. NANCY STERN.
ENVIRONMENT DIVISION.
CONFIGURATION SECTION.
SOURCE-COMPUTER. VAX.
OBJECT-COMPUTER. VAX.
INPUT-OUTPUT SECTION.
FILE-CONTROL.
     SELECT  TRANSACTION-FILE ASSIGN TO DISK1.
     SELECT  TOTAL-FILE      ASSIGN TO DISK2.
DATA DIVISION.
FILE SECTION.
FD  TRANSACTION-FILE
    LABEL RECORDS ARE STANDARD
    RECORD CONTAINS 20 CHARACTERS.
01  TRANSACTION-REC.
    05  CUST-NO-IN              PIC X(5).
    05  AMT1-IN                 PIC 9(5).
    05  AMT2-IN                 PIC 9(5).
    05  AMT3-IN                 PIC 9(5).
FD  TOTAL-FILE
    LABEL RECORDS ARE STANDARD
    RECORD CONTAINS 11 CHARACTERS.
01  TOTAL-REC-OUT.
    05  CUST-NO-OUT             PIC X(5).
    05  TOTAL-OUT               PIC 9(6).
WORKING-STORAGE SECTION.
01  ARE-THERE-MORE-RECORDS      PIC XXX   VALUE 'YES'.
```

REVIEW QUESTIONS

I. True-False Questions

_____ 1. A file is a collection of records each of which consists of a collection of fields.

_____ 2. PICTURE clauses are not specified on the group level; they are used to describe elementary fields only.

_____ 3. Numeric literals may contain as many as 30 characters.

_____ 4. Numeric literals may include a + or − sign but not a comma or dollar sign.

_____ 5. A data-name or identifier may not exceed 30 characters.

_____ 6. MOVE SPACES TO CODE-OUT is valid regardless of the size of CODE-OUT, as long as CODE-OUT is a nonnumeric field.

_____ 7. The order in which fields are specified in a record description is not significant.

_____ 8. Levels 03, 08, 75 may be used to define fields within records.

_____ 9. Fields not part of input or output, but necessary for processing, are coded in the WORKING-STORAGE SECTION, which follows the FILE SECTION in the DATA DIVISION.

_____ 10. Record-names are defined in the ENVIRONMENT DIVISION.

II. General Questions

1. Make necessary corrections to the following data-names:
   - (a) CUSTOMER NAME
   - (b) AMOUNT-
   - (c) INVOICE-NO.
   - (d) PROCEDURE
   - (e) TAX-%
   - (f) QUANTITY-OF-PRODUCT-ABC-ON-HAND
   - (g) AMT-OF-SALES

2. Make necessary corrections to the following numeric literals:
   - (a) 123
   - (b) 123.
   - (c) 123.0
   - (d) $100.00
   - (e) 1,000
   - (f) 100.7-
   - (g) +54
   - (h) -1.3

3. Make necessary corrections to the following nonnumeric literals:
   - (a) '$1000.00'
   - (b) 'DATA'
   - (c) 'ISN'T IT LOVERLY?'
   - (d) 'TAX % = '

For Questions 4–7, state the contents of FIELDA, which has a PIC X(6), after the MOVE operation.

4. MOVE 'ABC' TO FIELDA.

5. MOVE ABC TO FIELDA.

6. MOVE 'SPACES' TO FIELDA.

7. MOVE SPACES TO FIELDA.

8. Which of the following entries should be coded in Area A?
   (a) FD (b) FILE SECTION (c) 01 (d) 03 (e) LABEL RECORDS ARE OMITTED

9. Consider the following pictorial description of a record called PURCHASE-ORDER. Code the record description entries for it:

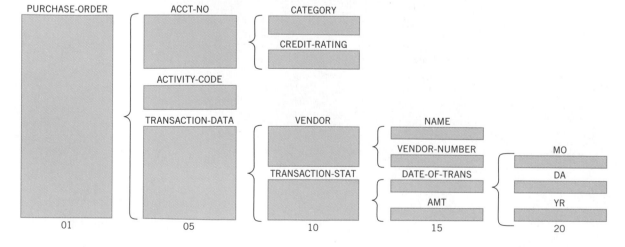

DEBUGGING EXERCISE

Correct the following DATA DIVISION entries:

```
DATA DIVISION.
FILE-SECTION.
FD   SALES FILE.
01   INPUT.
     05   TRANS.NO                PICTURE 9999.
     05   TRANSACTION-NAME        PICTURE 20X.
     05   ADDRESS
          10   NUMBER             PICTURE XXXX.
          10   STREET             PICTURE A(15).
          10   CITY               PICTURE AAA.
     05   CREDIT-RATING           PICTURE XX.
          10   CREDIT-CODE        PICTURE X.
          10   LIMIT OF PURCHASE  PICTURE X.
     05   UNIT-PRICE              PICTURE 99.9.
     05   QTY-PURCHASED           PICTURE 9(5).
     05   DISCOUNT-%              PICTURE V99.
```

PROGRAMMING ASSIGNMENTS

For Assignments 1–3 indicate which elements in the specified programs are (a) files, (b) records, (c) fields, (d) numeric literals, (e) nonnumeric literals, and (f) figurative constants.

1. See Figure 1.9 in Chapter 1.
2. See Figure 1.14 in Chapter 1.
3. See Figure 1.15 in Chapter 1.

For Assignments 4–7, write the FD and record description entries. (Assume that these disk files have standard labels.)

4. Inventory Record

LOCATION				PART NO.	PART NAME	REORDER LEVEL	UNIT COST	TOTAL SALES 2 MOS. AGO 999V99	TOTAL SALES LAST MO 999V99
STATE (Alphabetic)	WAREHOUSE				Alphanumeric		999V99		
	FLOOR	BIN	CITY (Alphabetic)						

```
1        3 4     5 6   7 8       11 12    16 17       25 26       29 30       34 35       39 40       44
```

BALANCE ON HAND	QTY. SOLD	TOTAL COST	BIN CAPACITY	DESCRIPTION OF PART
		99999V99		Alphanumeric

```
45             50 51      55 56     62 63      67 68                                      100
```

(Unless otherwise noted, fields are numeric)

5. Purchase Record

Item Description	Field Type	Field Size	Positions to Right of Decimal Point
Name of item	Alphabetic	20	—
Date of order (month, day, year)	Numeric	6	0
Purchase order number	Alphanumeric	5	—
Inventory group	Alphanumeric	10	—
Number of units	Numeric	5	0
Cost per unit	Numeric	4	0
Freight charge	Numeric	4	0
Tax percent	Numeric	2	2

6. Student Record

STUDENT NAME			EMPLOYER		COURSE				GRADES				
I N I T I A L 1	I N I T I A L 2	LAST NAME	NAME	ADDRESS	NAME	CLASS		APTITUDE TEST SCORE	FINAL SCORE			FINAL GRADE	
						SECTION	ROOM		DATE	SCORE			

1   2   3   20 21   40 41   50 51   60 61   63 64   66 67   69 70   75 76   78   79   80

7. Figure 3.4 shows the input and output layouts for a program to create a master customer disk file (CUSTOMER-MASTER) from a customer transaction disk file (CUSTOMER-TRANS). Code the first three divisions of this program after reviewing the following pseudocode and PROCEDURE DIVISION entries.

Notes:

1. If sales exceed $100.00, allow 3% discount. If sales are $100.00 or less, allow 2% discount.
2. Discount Amount = Sales × Discount %.
3. New Amount = Sales − Discount Amount.

The pseudocode on the next page was used to plan the program. It may be helpful in evaluating the logic.

Figure 3.4   Input and output layouts for Programming Assignment 7.

CUSTOMER-TRANS Record Layout			
Field	Size	Type	No. of Decimal Positions (if Numeric)
IDENT-IN	5	Alphanumeric	
SALES-IN	5	Numeric	2

CUSTOMER-MASTER Record Layout			
Field	Size	Type	No. of Decimal Positions (if Numeric)
IDENT-OUT	5	Alphanumeric	
SALES-AMT-OUT	5	Numeric	2
DISCOUNT-PERCENT-OUT	2	Numeric	2
NET-OUT	5	Numeric	2

Pseudocode

```
START
        Open the Files
        Clear the Output Area
        PERFORM UNTIL no more records (Are-There-More-Records = 'NO ')
                READ a Record
                        AT END Move 'NO ' to Are-There-More-Records
                        NOT AT END
                                Move Input to Output
                                Calculate Discount Amount
                                Calculate Net
                                Write a Record
                END-READ
                END-PERFORM
                End-of-Job Operations
STOP
```

The following are the PROCEDURE DIVISION entries to produce the required results:

COBOL 85

```
PROCEDURE DIVISION.
100-MAIN-MODULE.
    OPEN INPUT  CUSTOMER-TRANS
         OUTPUT CUSTOMER-MASTER
    MOVE SPACES TO MASTER-REC
    PERFORM UNTIL ARE-THERE-MORE-RECORDS = 'NO '
        READ CUSTOMER-TRANS
            AT END
                    MOVE 'NO ' TO ARE-THERE-MORE-RECORDS
            NOT AT END
                    PERFORM 200-PROCESS-DATA
        END-READ
    END-PERFORM
    CLOSE CUSTOMER-TRANS
          CUSTOMER-MASTER
    STOP RUN.
200-PROCESS-DATA.
    MOVE IDENT-IN TO IDENT-OUT
    MOVE SALES-IN TO SALES-AMT-OUT
    IF   SALES-IN > 100.00
        MOVE .03 TO DISCOUNT-PERCENT-OUT
    ELSE
        MOVE .02 TO DISCOUNT-PERCENT-OUT
    END-IF
    MULTIPLY SALES-IN BY DISCOUNT-PERCENT-OUT GIVING WS-DISCOUNT-AMT
    SUBTRACT WS-DISCOUNT-AMT FROM SALES-IN GIVING NET-OUT
    WRITE MASTER-REC.
```

COBOL 74 Substitutions

```
100-MAIN-MODULE.
    OPEN INPUT  CUSTOMER-TRANS
         OUTPUT CUSTOMER-MASTER.
    MOVE SPACES TO MASTER-REC.
    READ CUSTOMER-TRANS
        AT END MOVE 'NO ' TO
            ARE-THERE-MORE-RECORDS.
    PERFORM 200-PROCESS-DATA
        UNTIL ARE-THERE-MORE-RECORDS
            = 'NO '.
    CLOSE CUSTOMER-TRANS
          CUSTOMER-MASTER.
    STOP RUN.
```

```
◄────── READ CUSTOMER-TRANS
               AT END MOVE 'NO ' TO
                   ARE-THERE-MORE-RECORDS.
```

Note: The END-IF *scope terminator is used with COBOL 85 only; COBOL 74 users omit this scope terminator and end the preceding line with a period.*

CHAPTER 4

Coding Complete COBOL Programs: The PROCEDURE DIVISION

OBJECTIVES

To familiarize you with the methods used to

1. Access input and output files.
2. Read data from an input file.
3. Perform simple move operations.
4. Write information onto an output file.
5. Accomplish end-of-job operations.
6. Execute paragraphs from a main module and then return control to that main module.

CONTENTS

A REVIEW OF THE FIRST THREE DIVISIONS

Thus far, three of the four divisions of a COBOL program have been discussed in detail. The PROCEDURE DIVISION, the last to be studied, is unquestionably the most significant. The **PROCEDURE DIVISION** contains all the instructions that the computer will execute.

The IDENTIFICATION and ENVIRONMENT DIVISIONs supply information about the nature of the program and the specific equipment and files that will be used. The FILE SECTION of the DATA DIVISION defines, in detail, the input and output records. The WORKING-STORAGE SECTION of the DATA DIVISION is used for defining any areas not part of input and output files but nonetheless required for processing; these include work areas such as counters and end-of-file indicators. The instructions in the PROCEDURE DIVISION, however, actually read and process the data and produce the output information. Since all instructions are written in the PROCEDURE DIVISION, the majority of chapters in this book will focus on this division.

In this chapter, we will consider simple instructions that access files, read data, move fields from one area to another, produce output, and accomplish end-of-job functions. Knowledge of these types of instructions will enable you to write elementary COBOL programs *in their entirety*. The PROCEDURE DIVISION instructions we focus on illustrate the structured, top-down approach to writing COBOL programs.

THE FORMAT OF THE PROCEDURE DIVISION

PARAGRAPHS THAT SERVE AS MODULES

Defining Paragraphs

The PROCEDURE DIVISION is divided into **paragraphs.** Each paragraph is an independent **module** or **routine** that includes a series of instructions designed to perform a specific set of operations. As noted, we use the terms paragraph, module, and routine interchangeably.

Paragraph-names, like the PROCEDURE DIVISION entry itself, are coded in Area A. All other entries in the PROCEDURE DIVISION are coded in Area B. Paragraph-names, like the PROCEDURE DIVISION entry, end with periods and are coded on lines by themselves.

Rules for Forming Paragraph-Names

Rules for forming paragraph-names are the same as rules for forming data-names except that a paragraph-name may have all digits. Paragraph-names must be unique, meaning that two paragraphs may *not* have the same name. Similarly, a data-name cannot also serve as a paragraph-name.

Coding Guidelines

We will use descriptive paragraph-names along with a numeric prefix such as 200-PROCESS-RTN to identify the type of paragraph. A paragraph with a prefix of 200- is located after paragraph 100-XXX and before paragraph 300-YYY.

STATEMENTS WITHIN PARAGRAPHS

Each paragraph in a COBOL program consists of **statements**, where a statement begins with a verb such as READ, MOVE, or WRITE, or a condition such as IF A = B .... As noted, all COBOL statements are coded in Area B whereas paragraph-names are coded in Area A. Statements that end with a period are called **sentences**.

With COBOL 85, only the last statement in a paragraph ends with a period. With COBOL 74, we typically end each statement with a period.

Coding Guidelines

Although statements can be written across the coding sheet in paragraph form, we recommend that each statement be coded on an individual line as in Figure 4.1. This makes programs much easier to read and debug.

THE SEQUENCE OF INSTRUCTIONS IN A PROGRAM

Instructions are typically executed in **sequence** unless a PERFORM statement is encountered. A PERFORM UNTIL ... END-PERFORM is a loop that repeatedly executes the included statements until the condition specified in the UNTIL clause is met. A PERFORM paragraph-name is an instruction that temporarily transfers control to another paragraph.

In the COBOL 85 version of Figure 4.1, for example, the OPEN is executed first. Then, in sequence, the in-line PERFORM UNTIL ... END-PERFORM loop is executed UNTIL ARE-THERE-MORE-RECORDS = 'NO '. In this loop, for each record that is successfully read, 200-PROCESS-RTN is executed as a simple PERFORM. When there are no more records,

Figure 4.1 The preferred way to code PROCEDURE DIVISION entries.

COBOL 74

```
PROCEDURE DIVISION.
100-MAIN-MODULE.
    OPEN INPUT INVENTORY-FILE
        OUTPUT PAYMENT-FILE.
    READ INVENTORY-FILE
        AT END MOVE 'NO ' TO ARE-THERE-MORE-RECORDS.
    PERFORM 200-PROCESS-RTN
        UNTIL ARE-THERE-MORE-RECORDS = 'NO '.
    CLOSE INVENTORY-FILE
        PAYMENT-FILE.
    STOP RUN.
```

COBOL 85

```
PROCEDURE DIVISION.
100-MAIN-MODULE.
    OPEN INPUT INVENTORY FILE
        OUTPUT PAYMENT-FILE
    PERFORM UNTIL ARE-THERE-MORE-RECORDS = 'NO '
        READ INVENTORY-FILE
            AT END
                MOVE 'NO ' TO
                    ARE-THERE-MORE-RECORDS
            NOT AT END
                PERFORM 200-PROCESS-RTN
        END-READ
    END-PERFORM
    CLOSE INVENTORY-FILE
        PAYMENT-FILE
    STOP RUN.
```

'NO ' is moved to ARE-THERE-MORE-RECORDS by the READ ... AT END and the PERFORM UNTIL ... END-PERFORM is terminated. Then, in sequence, the CLOSE and STOP RUN instructions are executed.

Let us begin by discussing the instructions in the paragraph labeled 100-MAIN-MODULE. These instructions are usually included in most batch programs. The only changes that will be necessary will be in the data- and paragraph-names used; it also may be necessary to add some functions to our main module in more complex programs. After this main module has been explained in detail, we will discuss sample entries that can be coded in 200-PROCESS-RTN, which is executed from the PERFORM statement in 100-MAIN-MODULE. We will discuss interactive programs in the next chapter.

THE TOP-DOWN APPROACH FOR CODING PARAGRAPHS

You may recall that well-designed programs are written using a top-down approach. This means that the **main module** is coded first and that subsequent modules are coded from the major level to the detail level. That is, you should code the more general paragraphs first and end with the most detailed ones. This will help ensure that the program is properly designed and well organized. Think of the main module as an outline of a term paper. It is best to write the major paragraphs of a paper first (I, II, III, A, B, C, etc.) and leave minor levels for later on (1, a, etc.). This top-down approach is useful when writing programs as well.

STATEMENTS TYPICALLY CODED IN THE MAIN MODULE OF BATCH PROGRAMS

OPEN STATEMENT

The Instruction Format: A Review

The OPEN statement accesses the files in a program and indicates which are input and which are output. It has the following instruction format:

Format

$$
\text{OPEN} \left\{ \begin{array}{ll} \underline{\text{INPUT}} & \text{file-name-1} \ldots \\ \underline{\text{OUTPUT}} & \text{file-name-2} \ldots \end{array} \right\}
$$

The following rules will help you interpret instruction formats in general:

A REVIEW OF INSTRUCTION FORMAT SPECIFICATIONS

1. Uppercase words are COBOL reserved words.

2. Underlined words are required in the statement or option specified.

3. Lowercase entries are user-defined words.

4. Braces { } denote that one of the enclosed items is required.

5. Brackets [ ] denote that the enclosed item is optional.

6. Punctuation, when included in the format, is required.

7. The use of three dots or ellipses (. . .) indicates that additional entries of the same type (a file-name in this case) may be repeated if desired.

These rules are repeated on the inside of the front cover of this text for ease of reference.

Standard COBOL reference manuals use the same instruction formats as specified here. As you become familiar with the meaning of these instruction formats, it will be easier for you to consult a reference manual for additional information. Sometimes we simplify an instruction format by including only those options pertinent to our discussion or only those most frequently used.

The preceding specifications tell us the following about an OPEN statement:

1. Because the word OPEN is a COBOL reserved word, it is in uppercase; because it is also required in the statement, it is underlined.
2. Either the {INPUT file-name-1 . . .} or {OUTPUT file-name-2 . . .} clause must be used since they are in braces. Most frequently, they are both used.

If the first clause is used, the underlined word INPUT is required. The file-name, which appears as a lowercase entry, is user-defined. The dots or ellipses mean that any number of input files may be included. Similarly, if the {OUTPUT file-name-2 . . .} clause is used, the word OUTPUT is required. The output file-names are also user-defined. Thus, if we have both input *and* output files to process, which is usually the case in batch processing, we would include both an INPUT and an OUTPUT clause in the OPEN statement.

The Purpose of the OPEN Statement

Before an input or output file can be read or written, it must first be accessed with the use of an OPEN statement.

Recall that for every SELECT statement in the ENVIRONMENT DIVISION, a file-name is defined and a device or implementor-name is assigned.

Example

```
SELECT PAYROLL-FILE
    ASSIGN TO DISK 'EMP.DAT'.
SELECT PAYCHECKS-OUT
    ASSIGN TO PRINTER.
```

We use the SELECT statement to assign a file on a disk drive to the file-name PAYROLL-FILE. That is, PAYROLL-FILE will be found on the disk in a file called EMP.DAT. The file-name PAY-CHECKS-OUT is assigned to a device called PRINTER here.

Files that are defined in SELECT statements must be described in FD entries. The OPEN statement, however, actually tells the computer which files will be *input* and which will be *output*. Consider the following:

```
OPEN INPUT PAYROLL-FILE
    OUTPUT PAYCHECKS-OUT
```

This statement informs the computer that the storage positions assigned to PAYROLL-FILE will serve as an input area and the storage positions assigned to PAYCHECKS-OUT will serve as an output area. The data from PAYROLL-FILE will be read by the computer, and the information in PAYCHECKS-OUT will be produced as output by the computer.

An OPEN statement, then, designates files as either input or output. It also accesses the specific devices. Since PAYROLL-FILE, for example, is an input disk file in the program, the OPEN statement accesses the specific disk drive to determine if it is ready to read data. If not, execution would be suspended until the operator makes the device and the file ready.

Suppose your input or output file is on a floppy disk. The assign clause would include a device name such as 'A:SALES1':

```
SELECT SALES-FILE ASSIGN TO DISK 'A:SALES1'.
```

Be sure the disk is in the floppy drive before you begin executing the program.

In addition to distinguishing input files from output files and accessing specified devices, an OPEN statement performs certain checking functions. If label records for an input disk file are indicated as STANDARD, an OPEN statement checks the header label to determine if the correct file has been accessed. If label records for an output disk file were designated as STANDARD, the OPEN statement creates the header label. The actual header information is frequently entered using an operating system command that is separate from the program. In summary, three basic functions are performed by the OPEN statement:

FUNCTIONS OF THE OPEN STATEMENT

1. Indicates which files will be input and which will be output.

2. Makes the files available for processing.

3. Performs header label routines if label records are STANDARD.

Programs are often written using several input and output files. An update program, for example, takes an OLD-MASTER-IN file and a file of transaction or change records called TRANS-FILE and uses them to create a NEW-MASTER-OUT. In addition, a printed file of errors called ERR-LIST may also be produced. The OPEN statement for such a program can be coded as:

```
OPEN INPUT    OLD-MASTER-IN
              TRANS-FILE
      OUTPUT  NEW-MASTER-OUT
              ERR-LIST
```

In this case, there are two input files and two output files.

── DEBUGGING TIP ──

Although the OPEN statement can be written across the coding form, it is far better to put each clause on a separate line, as shown above, for ease of reading and debugging.

All input files follow the COBOL reserved word INPUT and, similarly, all output files follow the COBOL word OUTPUT. The word INPUT should not be repeated for each incoming file. The word OUTPUT should also be omitted after the first output file is coded. The preceding OPEN statement may also be written as four distinct statements:

```
OPEN INPUT OLD-MASTER-IN
OPEN INPUT TRANS-FILE
OPEN OUTPUT NEW-MASTER-OUT
OPEN OUTPUT ERR-LIST
```

When separate OPEN statements are used, the word INPUT or OUTPUT must be included for each file that is opened. This method is preferable when files are to be opened at different points throughout the program; that is, if a program processes one entire file before it accesses the next, the files should be opened separately. Unless such periodic intervals are required for the opening of files, however, it is considered inefficient to code an independent OPEN sentence for each file.

The order in which files are opened is *not* significant. The only restriction is that a file must be opened before it may be read or written; a file must be *accessed* before it may be *processed*. Since the OPEN statement accesses the files, it is generally one of the first instructions coded in the PROCEDURE DIVISION.

Coding Guidelines for the OPEN Statement

1. Each file to be opened should appear on a separate line. This makes it easier to read the statement and makes debugging easier as well. If each file is opened on a separate line and an OPEN error occurs, it is easier to pinpoint the file that caused the error because the computer will print the erroneous line number when an error occurs.

2. Indent each line within an OPEN statement as illustrated. This makes a program more readable. For the OPEN statement, we typically indent so that the words INPUT and OUTPUT are aligned. For other entries we indent four spaces.

DEBUGGING TIP

For output disk files, the ASSIGN clause of a SELECT statement often specifies the name of the file as it will be saved by the computer's operating system. Suppose, for example, that the SELECT for an output disk file is coded as SELECT SALES-FILE ASSIGN TO DISK 'DATA100'. The computer will save the file on disk as DATA100. If a DATA100 file already exists on the disk, it will be erased. To minimize the risk of erasing existing files, be sure you specify an implementor-name in the ASSIGN clause of a SELECT statement that is unique.

PERFORM UNTIL ... END-PERFORM STATEMENT: A STRUCTURED PROGRAMMING TECHNIQUE

The basic instruction format of the **PERFORM UNTIL ... END-PERFORM** statement is as follows:

Format

```
        PERFORM
            UNTIL condition-1
            :
        [END-PERFORM]*
```

*COBOL 85 only.

A PERFORM UNTIL ... END-PERFORM is called an in-line PERFORM and is used only with COBOL 85. The PERFORM UNTIL ... END-PERFORM statement is critical for implementing the *structured programming technique*. First, it executes the statements within the PERFORM UNTIL ... END-PERFORM loop. This sequence of instructions is executed repeatedly until the condition specified in the UNTIL clause is met. When the condition is met, control returns to the statement *directly following* the END-PERFORM.

Example

```
PERFORM UNTIL ARE-THERE-MORE-RECORDS = 'NO '
    READ ...
        AT END ...
        NOT AT END PERFORM 200-PROCESS-RTN
    END-READ
END-PERFORM
```

The instructions in the in-line PERFORM UNTIL ... END-PERFORM loop will be executed repeatedly until ARE-THERE-MORE-RECORDS = 'NO ', where ARE-THERE-MORE-RECORDS is a user-defined WORKING-STORAGE area that serves as an end-of-file indicator. It is initialized at 'YES' and will contain the value 'NO ' only when an AT END condition is met. Hence, the PERFORM UNTIL ... END-PERFORM loop is really indicating that the instructions within the loop are to be executed until there are no more records to process, at which point control will return to the statement *following* the END-PERFORM in the main module.

The condition used to terminate the PERFORM UNTIL ... END-PERFORM should be one that is eventually reached within the loop. To say PERFORM UNTIL ARE-THERE-MORE-RECORDS = 'NO ' ... END-PERFORM implies that within the loop there will be an instruction that at some point moves 'NO ' to ARE-THERE-MORE-RECORDS. The READ ... AT END MOVE 'NO ' TO ARE-THERE-MORE-RECORDS is the instruction that changes the value of ARE-THERE-MORE-RECORDS. In order for the in-line PERFORM UNTIL ... END-PERFORM loop to be executed properly, this READ must be an instruction within it. If it were not included, an error would occur. We use the data-name ARE-THERE-MORE-RECORDS for an end-of-file indicator, but any user-defined data-name would be valid.

The following sequence of instructions is typical of those that appear in most batch programs in COBOL 85:

```
PROCEDURE DIVISION.
100-MAIN-MODULE.
     OPEN ...
     PERFORM UNTIL ARE-THERE-MORE-RECORDS = 'NO '
             READ ...
                 AT END
                         MOVE 'NO ' TO ARE-THERE-MORE-RECORDS
                 NOT AT END
                         PERFORM 200-PROCESS-RTN
             END-READ
     END-PERFORM
     CLOSE ...
     STOP RUN.
200-PROCESS-RTN.
     :
     :
```

READ STATEMENT

Typically, after an input file has been opened, the PERFORM UNTIL ... END-PERFORM loop, which begins with a READ, is executed. A **READ** statement transmits data from the input device, assigned in the ENVIRONMENT DIVISION, to the input storage area, defined in the FILE SECTION of the DATA DIVISION. The following is a partial instruction format for a READ statement:

Format

> READ file-name-1
>   AT END statement-1 ...
>   [NOT AT END statement-2 ...]*
> [END-READ]*

*COBOL 85 only.

The file-name specified in the READ statement appears in three previous places in the program:

1. The SELECT statement, indicating the file-name and the device or implementor-name assigned to the file. If a file is stored on a disk, for example, a READ operation transmits data from the disk to the input area.
2. The FD entry, describing the file and its format.
3. The OPEN statement, accessing the file and activating the device.

The primary function of the READ statement is to transmit *one data record* to the input area reserved for that file. That is, each time a READ statement is executed, *one record* is read into primary storage—not the entire file.

The READ statement has, however, several other functions. Like the OPEN statement, it performs certain checks. It checks the length of each input record to ensure that it corresponds to the length specified in a RECORD CONTAINS clause in the DATA DIVISION, if specified. If a discrepancy exists, an error message prints, and a program interrupt occurs resulting in a run-time error.

The READ statement will also use the BLOCK CONTAINS clause, if specified, to perform a check on the blocking factor. Although the primary function of the READ instruction is the transmission of data, these checking routines are essential for proper execution of the program.

The **AT END** clause in the READ statement tests to determine if there is any more input. An AT END clause of the READ statement tells the computer what to do if there is no more data to be read. In our programs, the READ instruction generally begins with the following form:

```
READ file-name
    AT END
            MOVE 'NO ' TO ARE-THERE-MORE-RECORDS
    ...
```

The clause MOVE 'NO ' TO ARE-THERE-MORE-RECORDS is executed only when there are no more input records to process. The field called ARE-THERE-MORE-RECORDS is a WORK-ING-STORAGE item that always contains a 'YES' except when an end-of-file condition occurs, at which point a 'NO ' will be moved to the field. The AT END clause in a READ statement is ignored entirely if there are more records to process. Thus, only when there are no more records to read is the AT END clause executed.

With COBOL 85, when a record is successfully read, the NOT AT END clause, which processes the record, is executed. We typically use a simple PERFORM statement in conjunction with the NOT AT END clause to process each record read:

In-line
PERFORM
```
┌ PERFORM UNTIL ...
│       READ file-name
│           AT END
│                   MOVE 'NO ' TO ARE-THERE-MORE-RECORDS
│           NOT AT END
│                   PERFORM paragraph-name ◄─── Simple PERFORM
│       END-READ
│           :
│           :
└ END-PERFORM
```

For each record read, the paragraph named in the simple PERFORM is executed and control returns to the initial PERFORM UNTIL ... END-PERFORM loop, which is repeated until there are no more records.

The END-READ is a scope terminator that delimits, or sets the end point for, the READ.

All COBOL 85 programs have the format specified above with the READ ... END-READ within an in-line PERFORM UNTIL ... END-PERFORM loop.

─────── DEBUGGING TIP ───────

Code the AT END and NOT AT END clauses on separate lines and indent them for readability. If an error occurs, you will be able to more easily identify the problem because the line number of the error is specified.

The main module of a COBOL 74 program is different from the main module of a COBOL 85 program for two reasons:

1. COBOL 74 does not have a standard in-line PERFORM UNTIL ... END-PERFORM loop.

2. COBOL 74 does not have a READ ... NOT AT END ... clause or an END-READ scope terminator.

As a result, we need to structure COBOL 74 programs a little differently. The basic format is as follows:

```
PROCEDURE DIVISION.
100-MAIN-MODULE.
    OPEN ...
    READ ...                                          ◄——Initial READ
        AT END MOVE 'NO ' TO ARE-THERE-MORE-RECORDS.
    PERFORM 200-PROCESS-RTN
        UNTIL ARE-THERE-MORE-RECORDS = 'NO '.
    CLOSE ...
    STOP RUN.
200-PROCESS-RTN.
    .
    .
    .
    READ ...                                          ◄——Process paragraphs typically
        AT END MOVE 'NO ' TO ARE-THERE-MORE-RECORDS.    end with a READ
```

In COBOL 74 programs, we begin with a priming READ that inputs the first record. Then we PERFORM 200-PROCESS-RTN, which processes the first input record read in the main module. As the last step in 200-PROCESS-RTN, we read the next record. If the next record has been successfully read, then 200-PROCESS-RTN, which is under the control of the PERFORM in the main module, is repeated. If there is no next record, the AT END clause of the READ in 200-PROCESS-RTN is executed and 'NO ' is moved to ARE-THERE-MORE-RECORDS. Since ARE-THERE-MORE-RECORDS will equal 'NO ', 200-PROCESS-RTN will no longer be executed. Since it is executed from the PERFORM ... UNTIL in the main module, it is terminated when ARE-THERE-MORE-RECORDS = 'NO ' in 200-PROCESS-RTN.

With COBOL 74, after a file is opened and an input record is successfully read, the PERFORM 200-PROCESS-RTN statement transfers control to a paragraph, where each record is processed.

HOW COBOL 74 INSTRUCTIONS ARE EXECUTED IN 200-PROCESS-RTN

1. The first input record is processed in 200-PROCESS-RTN.

2. The next input record is read at the end of 200-PROCESS-RTN.

3. A test is then made by the PERFORM to see if ARE-THERE-MORE-RECORDS = 'NO '. It will only be a 'NO ' if the AT END condition has been met.

4. If there are more records to process, the field called ARE-THERE-MORE-RECORDS will not equal 'NO ' and 200-PROCESS-RTN will be executed again. That is, the next input record will be processed.

5. This sequence continues until there are no more input records to process, at which point ARE-THERE-MORE-RECORDS will be set equal to 'NO ' when the AT END clause of the READ is executed. When ARE-THERE-MORE-RECORDS = 'NO ', control returns to the statement following the PERFORM in the main module, in this case the CLOSE statement.

If there are 10 input records to process, the *eleventh* attempt to read a record is the one that causes an AT END condition to be executed. The very last record, therefore, is processed in the usual way—it does *not* cause an AT END condition to be executed; it is the *next* READ that results in an AT END condition.

The standard PERFORM ... UNTIL, which is *not* an in-line PERFORM, is coded within the first paragraph labeled 100-MAIN-MODULE, which is the main routine. 200-PROCESS-RTN is a separate module, executed repeatedly from 100-MAIN-MODULE, that processes the input data until an AT END condition occurs.

The PERFORM statement causes all instructions within the named paragraph to be executed. Consider the following:

```
      PERFORM 100-RTN1
          UNTIL ARE-THERE-MORE-RECORDS = 'NO '.
                  :
                  :
  100-RTN1.
                  :
                  :
  200-RTN2.
```

The instructions within 100-RTN1 will be executed by the PERFORM. The range of the PERFORM includes all instructions within the named paragraph until another paragraph-name is reached or until there are no more instructions. Within 100-RTN1 there should be a statement that includes: READ ... AT END MOVE 'NO ' TO ARE-THERE-MORE-RECORDS.

Every PERFORM UNTIL includes a conditional test. That is, a condition must be met for control to return to the statement following the PERFORM. Note that the test is made *initially* even before the named paragraph or in-line instructions are executed for the first time. The condition specified in the PERFORM UNTIL is tested again each time the named paragraph or in-line instructions have been executed in their entirety. Thus, if the condition is met when the PERFORM UNTIL is first encountered, the named paragraph or in-line instructions will be executed 0, or *no*, times.

MORE ON PERFORM STATEMENTS

The Simple PERFORM

To execute a paragraph like 200-RTN1 *only once* we could code a simple PERFORM as follows:

```
  100-MAIN-MODULE.
      :
      :
      PERFORM 200-RTN1
```

In our COBOL 85 programs, we have a simple PERFORM as part of the READ ... NOT AT END clause:

Example
```
  100-MAIN-MODULE.
      :
      :
      READ ...
          AT END
              MOVE 'NO ' TO ARE-THERE-MORE-RECORDS
          NOT AT END
              PERFORM 200-RTN1
      END-READ
```

Instructions within 200-RTN1 would be executed once and control would return to the statement following the PERFORM in 100-MAIN-MODULE.

Simple PERFORMs are coded so that a series of steps can be executed in a separate module.

A Summary of PERFORMs

Note that with COBOL 74 and COBOL 85 we may have the following:

PERFORM paragraph-name UNTIL condition

Here, control transfers to the named paragraph and is repeated until the specified condition is met.

With COBOL 85 we may *also* have an in-line PERFORM UNTIL:

PERFORM UNTIL condition
    :
END-PERFORM

where there is no named paragraph. Here, the instructions in the loop are coded *in-line* between the PERFORM UNTIL ... END-PERFORM.

With COBOL 74 and COBOL 85, we can also have a simple PERFORM, either as a statement by itself or as part of another statement such as the READ:

PERFORM paragraph-name

where the named paragraph is executed once and control returns to the statement following the PERFORM.

SELF-TEST

1. The PROCEDURE DIVISION is divided into _____ each of which contains _____ .
2. Statements are executed in the order _____ unless a _____ occurs.
3. Before a file may be read, it must be _____ .
4. The in-line PERFORM UNTIL ... END-PERFORM executes _____ . When the condition specified is met, control returns to the _____ .
5. In the statement PERFORM ... UNTIL EOF = 1, EOF should be initialized at _____ . Write the required WORKING-STORAGE entries for defining and initializing EOF.
6. In a COBOL 85 PERFORM UNTIL ... END-PERFORM in-line main processing loop, the first instruction within the loop is typically a _____ statement.
7. The basic format for a READ within a PERFORM UNTIL loop for COBOL 85 is _____ .
8. The NOT AT END clause of a READ statement in COBOL 85 is executed when _____ .
9. Typically the NOT AT END clause in COBOL 85 includes a _____ statement.
10. In COBOL 85, END-PERFORM and END-READ are called _____ because they terminate the range of the PERFORM and READ statements, respectively.

Solutions

1. modules, routines or paragraphs; sentences or instructions or statements
2. in which they appear; PERFORM
3. opened
4. all the instructions within the PERFORM UNTIL ... END-PERFORM loop; statement directly following the PERFORM UNTIL ... END-PERFORM loop
5. 0—Actually any other value but 1:

```
WORKING-STORAGE SECTION.
01  WS-STORED-AREAS.
    05  EOF         PIC 9     VALUE 0.
```

6. READ
7. READ ...
       AT END ...
       NOT AT END ...
   END-READ
8. a record has been successfully read
9. PERFORM
10. scope terminators

END-OF-JOB PROCESSING: THE CLOSE AND STOP RUN STATEMENTS

Let us continue with the main module of Figure 4.1 on page 102 before focusing on the instructions to be included in 200-PROCESS-RTN.

200-PROCESS-RTN will be performed until ARE-THERE-MORE-RECORDS = 'NO '. At that point, control will return to the instruction directly following the PERFORM 200-PROCESS-RTN in the main module. After all records have been processed, we will execute end-of-job functions. This usually includes releasing all files and terminating the processing. It may contain other procedures as well, such as printing totals.

There are *two* statements that are typically a part of every end-of-job routine. We first CLOSE all files to indicate that they are no longer needed for processing, and we terminate execution of the program with a STOP RUN.

CLOSE Statement

As we have seen, files must be accessed or activated by an OPEN statement before data may be read or written. Similarly, a **CLOSE** statement is coded at the end of the job after all records have been processed to release these files and deactivate the devices. The format of the CLOSE is:

Format

> CLOSE   file-name-1 . . .

All files that have been opened at the beginning of the program are closed at the end of a program. The CLOSE statement, like the OPEN, will perform additional functions. When creating disk records, for example, the CLOSE will create trailer labels.

Note that a CLOSE statement, unlike an OPEN, does *not* specify which files are input and which are output. We say, for example, OPEN INPUT PAYROLL-FILE OUTPUT PAY-CHECKS to access the files, but to release them, we simply say CLOSE PAYROLL-FILE PAYCHECKS. Distinguishing between input and output files is essential *before* processing begins, but serves no real purpose when the job is being terminated.

Guidelines: Using Separate Lines Rather Than Commas to Set Clauses Apart

You could use commas to separate file-names, but we recommend that you use separate lines instead for ease of reading and debugging. As noted, when an error occurs, the computer will print the line number that caused the error. If each file is closed on a separate line and a CLOSE error occurs, it is very easy to pinpoint the file that caused the error. Indent the file-names for readability.

Using Separate CLOSE Statements

As with an OPEN statement, the following two routines are equivalent:

```
1. CLOSE PAYROLL-FILE            2. CLOSE PAYROLL-FILE
         PAYCHECKS                  CLOSE PAYCHECKS
         ERR-LIST                   CLOSE ERR-LIST
```

Unless files are closed at different points in the program, the second method, with separate CLOSE instructions, is inefficient.

STOP RUN Statement

The **STOP RUN** instruction tells the computer to terminate the program. All programs should include a STOP RUN statement to end the run. The STOP RUN is usually the last instruction in the main module.

With COBOL 85, when a STOP RUN statement is executed, it will close any files that are still opened. Thus, with COBOL 85, a CLOSE statement is unnecessary. We recommend you use it, however, for documentation and debugging purposes.

In summary, we have discussed the following main module in detail:

COBOL 85

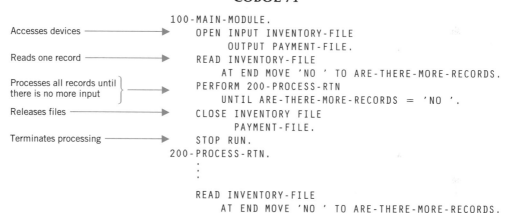

```
100-MAIN-MODULE.
    OPEN INPUT INVENTORY-FILE                          ◄──── Accesses devices
         OUTPUT PAYMENT-FILE
    PERFORM UNTIL ARE-THERE-MORE-RECORDS = 'NO '
        READ INVENTORY-FILE
            AT END
                    MOVE 'NO ' TO ARE-THERE-MORE-RECORDS     Processes all
                NOT AT END                                   records until there
                    PERFORM 200-PROCESS-RTN                  is no more input
        END-READ
    END-PERFORM
    CLOSE INVENTORY-FILE                               ◄──── Releases files
          PAYMENT-FILE
    STOP RUN.                                          ◄──── Terminates processing
200-PROCESS-RTN.
    :
    :
```

COBOL 74

```
                                      100-MAIN-MODULE.
Accesses devices  ──────►                 OPEN INPUT INVENTORY-FILE
                                               OUTPUT PAYMENT-FILE.
Reads one record  ──────►                 READ INVENTORY-FILE
                                               AT END MOVE 'NO ' TO ARE-THERE-MORE-RECORDS.
Processes all records until               PERFORM 200-PROCESS-RTN
there is no more input    ──────►              UNTIL ARE-THERE-MORE-RECORDS = 'NO '.
Releases files  ──────►                   CLOSE INVENTORY FILE
                                               PAYMENT-FILE.
Terminates processing  ──────►            STOP RUN.
                                      200-PROCESS-RTN.
                                          :
                                          :

                                          READ INVENTORY-FILE
                                              AT END MOVE 'NO ' TO ARE-THERE-MORE-RECORDS.
```

Note: END-READ is a COBOL 85 scope terminator. With COBOL 74, the READ . . . AT END is followed by a period and not a scope terminator.

─── DEBUGGING TIP ───

Be sure you remember to code a STOP RUN as the last statement in the main module. If you forget, then 200-PROCESS-RTN, as the next paragraph in sequence, will be executed erroneously after files have been closed.

STATEMENTS TYPICALLY CODED FOR PROCESSING INPUT RECORDS AND PRODUCING OUTPUT RECORDS

The instructions specified at 200-PROCESS-RTN process each input record. With COBOL 85, 200-PROCESS-RTN is executed as part of the PERFORM UNTIL ... END-PERFORM loop in the main module. That is, the READ within the PERFORM UNTIL ... END-PERFORM includes a NOT AT END PERFORM 200-PROCESS-RTN, which processes each record read.

Note that using a top-down modular approach, a paragraph named 200-(module-name) should follow one named 100-(module-name).

For now, we concentrate on two processing instructions: the MOVE and the WRITE. In order to produce output, we must store data in an output area so that when we use a WRITE instruction, there will be some outgoing information generated. We could use arithmetic operations or MOVE statements to store output data. Here, we focus on the MOVE statement.

Simplified MOVE Statement

A simple MOVE statement has the following basic instruction format:

Format

> MOVE   identifier-1   TO   identifier-2

Fields in main memory may be moved to other fields with the use of the MOVE instruction. The word "identifier" means "data-name".

Sample Problem

Consider the following input and output formats for a program that is to produce output name and address disk records from an input accounts receivable disk file.

Input Master ACCOUNTS-RECEIVABLE-FILE Record Layout		
Field	**Size**	**Type**
NAME-IN	15	Alphanumeric
ADDRESS-IN	25	Alphanumeric
BALANCE-DUE-IN	5	Alphanumeric
CREDIT-HISTORY-IN	35	Alphanumeric
Unused	20	Alphanumeric

Output NAME-AND-ADDRESS-FILE Record Layout		
Field	**Size**	**Type**
NAME-OUT	15	Alphanumeric
ADDRESS-OUT	25	Alphanumeric

The first three divisions of the program conform to the rules of the last three chapters. Figure 4.2 illustrates the coding of these divisions. Note that ENVIRONMENT DIVISION entries are computer- and compiler-dependent.

Figure 4.2   IDENTIFICATION, ENVIRONMENT, and DATA DIVISIONs for Sample Problem.

```
IDENTIFICATION DIVSION.
PROGRAM-ID. SAMPLE.
*
ENVIRONMENT DIVISION.
INPUT-OUTPUT SECTION.
FILE-CONTROL.
    SELECT ACCOUNTS-RECEIVABLE-FILE
        ASSIGN TO DISK1.
    SELECT NAME-AND-ADDRESS-FILE
        ASSIGN TO DISK2.
*
DATA DIVISION.
FILE SECTION.
FD  ACCOUNTS-RECEIVABLE-FILE
    LABEL RECORDS ARE STANDARD.
01  INPUT-REC.
    05  NAME-IN              PIC X(15).
    05  ADDRESS-IN           PIC X(25).
    05  BALANCE-DUE-IN       PIC X(5).
    05  CREDIT-HISTORY-IN    PIC X(35).
```

Figure 4.2 (continued)

The word FILLER is optional ⟶
with COBOL 85 but required
with COBOL 74

```
        05                          PIC X(20).
FD  NAME-AND-ADDRESS-FILE
        LABEL RECORDS ARE STANDARD.
01  OUTPUT-REC.
        05  NAME-OUT                PIC X(15).
        05  ADDRESS-OUT             PIC X(25).
WORKING-STORAGE SECTION.
01  WS-STORED-AREAS.
        05  ARE-THERE-MORE-RECORDS  PIC XXX   VALUE 'YES'.
```

We may include the following coding in the PROCEDURE DIVISION:

COBOL 85

```
PROCEDURE DIVISION.
100-MAIN-MODULE.
    OPEN INPUT ACCOUNTS-RECEIVABLE-FILE
         OUTPUT NAME-AND-ADDRESS-FILE
    PERFORM UNTIL ARE-THERE-MORE-RECORDS = 'NO '
        READ ACCOUNTS-RECEIVABLE-FILE
            AT END
                MOVE 'NO ' TO ARE-THERE-MORE-RECORDS
            NOT AT END
                PERFORM 200-PROCESS-RTN
        END-READ
    END-PERFORM
    CLOSE ACCOUNTS-RECEIVABLE-FILE
          NAME-AND-ADDRESS-FILE
    STOP RUN.
200-PROCESS-RTN.
    MOVE NAME-IN TO NAME-OUT
    MOVE ADDRESS-IN TO ADDRESS-OUT
        .
        .
        .
```

Will begin by moving
the first record's data

COBOL 74 Substitutions

```
READ ACCOUNTS-RECEIVABLE-FILE
    AT END MOVE 'NO ' TO ARE-THERE-MORE-RECORDS.
PERFORM 200-PROCESS-RTN
    UNTIL ARE-THERE-MORE-RECORDS = 'NO '.
```

```
READ ACCOUNTS-RECEIVABLE-FILE                    ⟶
    AT END MOVE 'NO ' TO ARE-THERE-MORE-RECORDS.
```

Recall that the END-PERFORM and END-READ are for COBOL 85 only; with COBOL 74, the READ ... AT END statement, as do all statements, ends with a period.

Assuming the PIC clause of an output field is the same as the PIC clause of the corresponding input field, a MOVE operation *duplicates* or copies input data to the output area. That is, the input field still retains its value. Note that the technique of using the same base name for different fields while altering only the prefix or suffix is considered good programming form. The distinction between NAME-IN and ADDRESS-IN, as input fields, and NAME-OUT and ADDRESS-OUT, as the same fields for the output, is clear.

Recall that 200-PROCESS-RTN is a *separate* module executed under the control of the PERFORM statement. To complete 200-PROCESS-RTN, we will WRITE the record stored at the output area.

For COBOL 74, the 200-PROCESS-RTN paragraph ends with a READ.

WRITE Statement

The **WRITE** instruction takes data in the output area defined in the DATA DIVISION and transmits it to the device specified in the ENVIRONMENT DIVISION. A simple WRITE statement has the following format:

Format

> WRITE   record-name-1

Note that although *files* are *read*, we *write records*. The record-name appears on the

01 level and is generally subdivided into fields. The record description specifies the *format* of the output. With each WRITE instruction, we tell the computer to write data that is in the output area.

Thus, in our example, the appropriate instruction is WRITE OUTPUT-REC, *not* WRITE NAME-AND-ADDRESS-FILE. When we *write* or produce information, we use the 01 *record-name*; when we read from a file, we use the FD or file-name.

We may now code the PROCEDURE DIVISION for our sample program in its entirety, keeping in mind that after a complete record has been processed and an output record created, we want to read another input record:

COBOL 85

```
PROCEDURE DIVISION.
100-MAIN-MODULE.
    OPEN INPUT ACCOUNTS-RECEIVABLE-FILE
         OUTPUT NAME-AND-ADDRESS-FILE
    PERFORM UNTIL ARE-THERE-MORE-RECORDS = 'NO '
        READ ACCOUNTS-RECEIVABLE-FILE
            AT END
                MOVE 'NO ' TO ARE-THERE-MORE-RECORDS
            NOT AT END
                PERFORM 200-PROCESS-RTN
        END-READ
    END-PERFORM
    CLOSE ACCOUNTS-RECEIVABLE-FILE
          NAME-AND-ADDRESS-FILE
    STOP RUN.
200-PROCESS-RTN.
    MOVE NAME-IN TO NAME-OUT
    MOVE ADDRESS-IN TO ADDRESS-OUT
    WRITE OUTPUT-REC.
```

COBOL 74 Substitutions

```
READ ACCOUNTS-RECEIVABLE-FILE
    AT END MOVE 'NO ' TO ARE-THERE-MORE-RECORDS.
PERFORM 200-PROCESS-RTN
    UNTIL ARE-THERE-MORE-RECORDS = 'NO '.
```

```
READ ACCOUNTS-RECEIVABLE-FILE
    AT END MOVE 'NO ' TO ARE-THERE-MORE-RECORDS.
```

Note that each clause is coded on a separate line for readability and ease of debugging. Note, too, that the END-READ scope terminator, as well as the END-PERFORM that delimits the in-line PERFORM loop, are COBOL 85 options. With COBOL 74, the AT END clause of the READ statement, along with all other statements, ends with a period.

LOOKING AHEAD

The following is a brief introduction to two classes of verbs—arithmetic and conditional. We explain the formats, options, and rules for using these verbs in Chapters 7 and 8. We merely introduce them here so that you can begin to write more advanced programs. Once you begin using these verbs, questions may occur to you, mainly because we have not yet explained them fully. If you follow the basic instruction format rules provided here, you will be able to code simple but complete COBOL programs.

The four basic arithmetic verbs have the following simple formats:

Formats

$$\underline{ADD} \begin{Bmatrix} \text{identifier-1} \\ \text{literal-1} \end{Bmatrix} \cdots \underline{TO} \text{ identifier-2}$$

$$\underline{SUBTRACT} \begin{Bmatrix} \text{identifier-1} \\ \text{literal-1} \end{Bmatrix} \underline{FROM} \text{ identifier-2}$$

$$\underline{MULTIPLY} \begin{Bmatrix} \text{identifier-1} \\ \text{literal-1} \end{Bmatrix} \underline{BY} \text{ identifier-2}$$

$$\underline{DIVIDE} \begin{Bmatrix} \text{identifier-1} \\ \text{literal-1} \end{Bmatrix} \underline{INTO} \text{ identifier-2}$$

Examples
```
ADD AMT1-IN AMT2-IN TO WS-TOTAL
SUBTRACT 100 FROM SALARY
MULTIPLY .0765 BY SALARY
```

Using the above format, the result field is always the last field or identifier; the result field can never be a literal. Note that GIVING may be used with these verbs (e.g., SUBTRACT 100 FROM SALARY GIVING SALARY-OUT). There are many other options of these four arithmetic verbs that we will discuss in Chapter 7.

The basic instruction format for a conditional is as follows:

Format

> IF   (condition)
>
>   (statement-1) . . .
>
> [ELSE
>
>   (statement-2) . . .]
>
> [END-IF]*

*COBOL 85 only. COBOL 74 IF statements end with a period instead of an END-IF scope terminator.

The simple conditions that can be tested are as follows:

$$(\text{identifier-1}) \begin{Bmatrix} = \text{ (or IS EQUAL TO)} \\ < \text{ (or IS LESS THAN)} \\ > \text{ (or IS GREATER THAN)} \end{Bmatrix} \begin{Bmatrix} \text{identifier-2} \\ \text{literal-1} \end{Bmatrix}$$

Note that the ELSE clause is optional. Numerous statements can follow each IF or ELSE clause. An END-IF scope terminator is used with COBOL 85.

Examples

Coding	Explanation

1. IF   AMT-IN IS GREATER THAN ZERO
        ADD AMT-IN TO WS-TOTAL
    END-IF
	If the contents of the input field AMT-IN is greater than zero, add AMT-IN to a total.

2. IF   AMT1-IN > AMT2-IN
        ADD AMT1-IN TO WS-TOTAL1
    ELSE
        ADD AMT1-IN TO WS-TOTAL2
    END-IF
	If AMT1-IN exceeds AMT2-IN, add AMT1-IN to a field called WS-TOTAL1; otherwise (if AMT1-IN is *not* greater than AMT2-IN), ADD AMT1-IN to WS-TOTAL2.

COBOL 74 ends with a period after the last clause instead of an END-IF. Conditional statements are discussed in depth in Chapter 8.

REVIEW OF COMMENTS IN COBOL

You will find that as programs become more complex, comments are helpful as reminders and explanations of the processing being performed. The following is the method that may be used for inserting comments in a COBOL program:

> **COMMENTS IN COBOL**
>
> An asterisk (*) in column 7 (the continuation position) of any line makes the entire line a comment. Use comments freely to document your program and to make it easier to understand.

Sometimes programmers enter their comments in lowercase letters to set them apart even more clearly from actual instructions.

We recommend that you use comments in the IDENTIFICATION DIVISION to describe the program and that comments be used to describe each module in the PROCEDURE

DIVISION. As your programs become more complex, you may want to add comments in other places as well. For very long programs, code a line with just a / in column 7 after each division; this causes the next division to begin on a new page of the source listing.

Coding Guidelines for PROCEDURE DIVISION Entries

1. Each clause should be on a separate line and indented for readability. For example:

```
READ ...
     AT END ...
     NOT AT END ...
END-READ
```

2. Each paragraph-name should begin with a sequence number that helps to pinpoint the location of the paragraph; a descriptive name should follow this number (e.g., 100-MAIN-MODULE, 200-PROCESS-RTN).

3. The last statement in a paragraph should always end with a period.

─────────── COBOL 9x CHANGES ───────────

You will be able to code comments on a line with an instruction. *> will be used to add a comment to a line. After *> appears, characters to the end of the line will not be compiled.

CHAPTER SUMMARY   Most programs illustrated or assigned as homework in this text will use the following structure (lowercase entries are user-defined names):

COBOL 85

```
PROCEDURE DIVISION.
paragraph-name-1.
     OPEN INPUT  file-name-1
          OUTPUT file-name-2
     PERFORM UNTIL ARE-THERE-MORE-RECORDS = 'NO '
          READ file-name-1
               AT END
                    MOVE 'NO ' TO ARE-THERE-MORE-RECORDS
               NOT AT END
                    PERFORM paragraph-name-2
          END-READ
     END-PERFORM
     CLOSE file-name-1
           file-name-2
     STOP RUN.
paragraph-name-2.
          :
          :
     WRITE ...
```

Main module

Processing steps for each record

COBOL 74 Substitutions

```
READ file-name-1
     AT END MOVE 'NO ' TO
          ARE-THERE-MORE-RECORDS.
PERFORM paragraph-name-2
     UNTIL ARE-THERE-MORE-RECORDS
          = 'NO '.
```

```
READ file-name-1
     AT END MOVE 'NO ' TO
          ARE-THERE-MORE-RECORDS.
```

A. Paragraph-names are coded in Area A and end with a period. Rules for forming paragraph-names are the same as for data-names except that a paragraph-name can have all digits. We use a prefix such as 100-, 200-, 300-, along with a descriptive name such as HEADING-RTN or MAIN-MODULE. A paragraph with a prefix of 200- is located after a paragraph with prefix 100- and before a paragraph with prefix 300-.

B. All statements are coded in Area B; we recommend coding one statement per line.

C. Instructions are executed in the order in which they appear unless a PERFORM statement executes a loop or transfers control.

D. When the main module's in-line PERFORM UNTIL ... END-PERFORM is encountered, the loop specified is executed repeatedly until there are no more input records.

KEY TERMS

AT END	OPEN	Sentence
CLOSE	Paragraph	Sequence
END-PERFORM	PERFORM UNTIL	Statement
Main module	PROCEDURE DIVISION	STOP RUN
Module	READ	WRITE
MOVE	Routine	

CHAPTER SELF-TEST

1. Assume that the statement READ PAY-FILE ... is coded in a program. PAY-FILE appears in a _____ statement of the ENVIRONMENT DIVISION, an _____ entry of the DATA DIVISION, and _____ statements of the PROCEDURE DIVISION.

2. With every READ statement for sequential files, a(n) _____ clause is used that tells the computer what to do if there is no more input data.

3. Unlike READ statements in which the _____-name is specified, a WRITE statement specifies the _____-name.

4. What is wrong with the following?
   (a) WRITE REC-1
           AT END MOVE 1 TO EOF
   (b) PRINT REC-2

5. When using a MOVE to obtain *exactly* the same data at the output area that appears in the input area, the _____ clause of both fields should be identical.

6. The instruction used to execute a loop or transfer control from the main module to some other part of the program is a _____ instruction.

7. If PERFORM 500-STEP-5 is a statement in the program, 500-STEP-5 is a _____ that must appear somewhere in the program in Area _____ .

8. The statement CLOSE INPUT ACCTS-PAYABLE (is, is not) valid.

9. What is the purpose of a STOP RUN?

10. If PERFORM UNTIL END-OF-FILE = 'YES' ... END-PERFORM is coded in the main module, the first instruction following the PERFORM is typically _____ .

Solutions

1. SELECT; FD; OPEN, CLOSE, and READ

2. AT END

3. file; record

4. (a) The AT END clause is specified only with a READ statement.
   (b) A WRITE instruction should be used, not PRINT.

5. PICTURE or PIC

6. PERFORM

7. paragraph-name; A

8. is not (INPUT or OUTPUT is *not* specified with CLOSE statements.)

9. A STOP RUN is used to terminate the job. (With COBOL 85, STOP RUN also closes the files.)

10. READ file-name
        AT END MOVE 'YES' TO END-OF-FILE
        NOT AT END ...
    END-READ

PRACTICE PROGRAM

From this point on, each chapter includes one practice program with a suggested solution provided to assist you in reviewing the material in the chapter. First plan and code the practice program on your own. Then check your solution against the one illustrated. A problem definition is provided that includes (1) a systems flowchart, which is an overview of the input and output, (2) record layout forms (we use different types to familiarize you with them), and (3) Printer Spacing Charts, if printed output is required.

Write a program to write an output salary disk from input master employee disk records. The problem definition is as follows:

Systems Flowchart

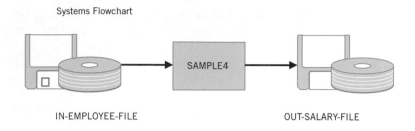

IN-EMPLOYEE-FILE   OUT-SALARY-FILE

IN-EMPLOYEE-FILE Record Layout		
Field*	Size	Type
EMPLOYEE NAME	20	Alphanumeric
SALARY	5	Alphanumeric
NO. OF DEPENDENTS	1	Alphanumeric
FICA (Soc. Sec. Tax)	5	Alphanumeric
STATE TAX	6	Alphanumeric
FEDERAL TAX	6	Alphanumeric
Unused	37	Alphanumeric

OUT-SALARY-FILE Record Layout		
Field*	Size	Type
EMPLOYEE NAME	20	Alphanumeric
SALARY	5	Alphanumeric

*Note: These are *not* COBOL field-names.

Figure 4.3 illustrates the pseudocode for a COBOL 85 version of this program. Both pseudocode and flowcharts as planning tools will be discussed in detail in the next chapter. Look at the pseudocode planning tool first to see if you understand the logic and then try to write the program yourself. Compare your coding with the solution in Figure 4.4.

Figure 4.3 Pseudocode for the Practice Program.

Pseudocode
START
     Open the Files
     Clear the Output Area
     PERFORM UNTIL no more records (ARE-THERE-MORE-RECORDS = 'NO ')
          Move Input Fields to the Output Area
          Write the Output Record
     END-PERFORM
     Close the Files
STOP

Figure 4.4 Solution to the Practice Program.

COBOL 85

```
IDENTIFICATION DIVISION.
PROGRAM-ID. SAMPLE.
************************************************
*   sample  - updates a file with employee   *
*             names and salaries             *
************************************************
ENVIRONMENT DIVISION.
CONFIGURATION SECTION.
SOURCE-COMPUTER. VAX-6410.
OBJECT-COMPUTER. VAX-6410.
INPUT-OUTPUT SECTION.
FILE-CONTROL.
    SELECT IN-EMPLOYEE-FILE ASSIGN TO DATA4E.
    SELECT OUT-SALARY-FILE  ASSIGN TO DATA4S.
*
DATA DIVISION.
FILE SECTION.
FD  IN-EMPLOYEE-FILE
    LABEL RECORDS ARE STANDARD.
01  IN-EMPLOYEE-REC.
    05  IN-EMPLOYEE-NAME        PIC X(20).
    05  IN-SALARY               PIC X(5).
    05  IN-NO-OF-DEPENDENTS     PIC X(1).
    05  IN-FICA                 PIC X(5).
    05  IN-STATE-TAX            PIC X(6).
    05  IN-FED-TAX              PIC X(6).
    05                          PIC X(37).
FD  OUT-SALARY-FILE
    LABEL RECORDS ARE STANDARD.
01  OUT-SALARY-REC.
    05  OUT-EMPLOYEE-NAME       PIC X(20).
    05  OUT-SALARY              PIC X(5).
WORKING-STORAGE SECTION.
01  WS-WORK-AREAS.
    05  ARE-THERE-MORE-RECORDS  PIC X(3)  VALUE 'YES'.
*
PROCEDURE DIVISION.
*************************************************************
*  100-main-module - controls opening and closing files   *
*                    and direction of program logic;      *
*                    returns control to operating system  *
*************************************************************
100-MAIN-MODULE.
    OPEN INPUT  IN-EMPLOYEE-FILE
         OUTPUT OUT-SALARY-FILE
    MOVE SPACES TO OUT-SALARY-REC
    PERFORM UNTIL ARE-THERE-MORE-RECORDS = 'NO '
      READ IN-EMPLOYEE-FILE
        AT END
           MOVE 'NO ' TO ARE-THERE-MORE-RECORDS
        NOT AT END
           PERFORM 200-PROCESS-RTN
      END-READ
    END-PERFORM
    CLOSE IN-EMPLOYEE-FILE
          OUT-SALARY-FILE
    STOP RUN.
```

The word FILLER is optional with COBOL 85 but required with COBOL 74

COBOL 74 Substitutions

```
READ IN-EMPLOYEE-FILE
  AT END MOVE 'NO ' TO
     ARE-THERE-MORE-RECORDS.
PERFORM 200-PROCESS-RTN
  UNTIL ARE-THERE-MORE-RECORDS
     = 'NO '.
```

Figure 4.4 Solution to the Practice Program (continued).

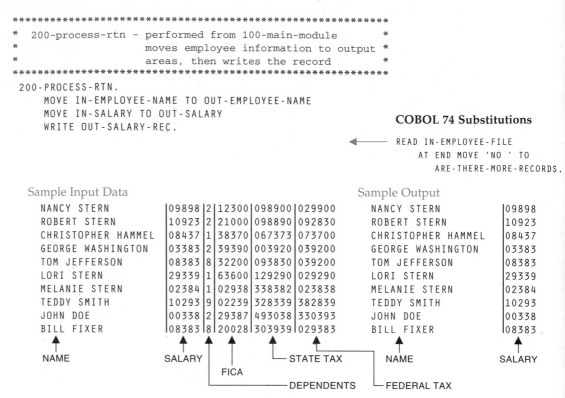

```
*****************************************************************
*  200-process-rtn - performed from 100-main-module         *
*                    moves employee information to output   *
*                    areas, then writes the record          *
*****************************************************************
200-PROCESS-RTN.
    MOVE IN-EMPLOYEE-NAME TO OUT-EMPLOYEE-NAME
    MOVE IN-SALARY TO OUT-SALARY
    WRITE OUT-SALARY-REC.
```

COBOL 74 Substitutions

```
READ IN-EMPLOYEE-FILE
    AT END MOVE 'NO ' TO
        ARE-THERE-MORE-RECORDS.
```

REVIEW QUESTIONS

I. True-False Questions

_____ 1. Files must be opened before they can be read.

_____ 2. A simple PERFORM, such as PERFORM 300-CHECK-RTN, will execute the named paragraph once and return control to the statement following the PERFORM.

_____ 3. COBOL paragraph-names end with a period.

_____ 4. Each module in a COBOL program is identified by a paragraph-name.

_____ 5. A PERFORM UNTIL ... will be executed repeatedly until the condition specified is met.

_____ 6. Consider the following statement: PERFORM ... UNTIL ARE-THERE-MORE-RECORDS = 'NO '. The data-name ARE-THERE-MORE-RECORDS must be defined in the FILE SECTION.

_____ 7. Suppose EOF were initialized at 1. It would be correct to use the following as an end-of-file test: READ FILE-IN AT END MOVE 0 TO EOF.

_____ 8. The READ ... AT END ... NOT AT END ... should end with an END-READ scope terminator.

_____ 9. The last instruction to be executed in a program should be a STOP RUN.

_____ 10. A paragraph-name may consist of all numbers, but it is best to use meaningful words to help identify the purpose of the paragraph.

II. General Questions

1. Indicate the DIVISION in which each of the following is coded and state its purpose.
   (a) DATE-COMPILED
   (b) WORKING-STORAGE SECTION
   (c) paragraph-name
   (d) CONFIGURATION SECTION
   (e) FD
   (f) level numbers
   (g) LABEL RECORDS
   (h) FILE SECTION
   (i) SELECT
   (j) AUTHOR
   (k) STOP RUN

(l) AT END clause
(m)VALUE
(n) PICTURE
(o) FILE-CONTROL
(p) OPEN

2. When the computer encounters a READ instruction in the PROCEDURE DIVISION, how does it know which of its input units to activate?

3. Indicate the reasons why we OPEN and CLOSE files.

4. Indicate when we assign VALUE clauses to data-names.

5. State which of the following, if any, are invalid paragraph-names:
   (a) INPUT-RTN
   (b) MOVE
   (c) 123
   (d) %-RTN

6. If a READ statement is used for a sequential file, what clause is required? Why? Why do we use a NOT AT END clause with a READ?

III. Interpreting Instruction Formats

Use the instruction formats in this book or in your reference manual to determine if the following instructions have the correct syntax.

```
1. READ INFILE-1, INFILE-2
       AT END MOVE 'NO ' TO MORE-RECORDS
   END-READ.

2. OPEN FILE-1 FILE-2 AND FILE-3.

3. WRITE REC-A
       AT END MOVE 0 TO EOF.

4. READ FILE-1
       AT  END MOVE 1 TO EOF
                WRITE FINAL-LINE
   END-READ.

5. CLOSE INPUT IN-FILE
        OUTPUT OUT-FILE.
```

DEBUGGING EXERCISES

Beginning in this chapter, we will illustrate common programming mistakes and ask you to identify and correct them.

Consider the following PROCEDURE DIVISION coding:

```
PROCEDURE DIVISION.
100-MAIN-MODULE.
    OPEN SALES-FILE
          PRINT-FILE
    PERFORM 200-PROCESS-RTN
        UNTIL ARE-THERE-MORE-RECORDS = 'NO '
    CLOSE SALES-FILE
          PRINT-FILE
    STOP RUN.
200-PROCESS-RTN
    READ SALES-FILE
        AT END MOVE 'NO ' TO ARE-THERE-MORE-RECORDS
    END-READ
    MOVE SALES-FILE TO PRINT-FILE
    WRITE PRINT-FILE.
```

1. The OPEN statement will result in a syntax error. Indicate why.

2. The MOVE statement will result in a syntax error. Indicate why.

3. The WRITE statement will result in a syntax error. Indicate why.

4. This programming excerpt does not follow the appropriate structured format. In fact, it will result in a logic error when the last record has been processed. Indicate why.

5. The CLOSE statement does not have commas separating the files. Will this result in a syntax error? Explain your answer.

6. Indicate how you can determine what device SALES-FILE uses.

7. Suppose the READ statement was coded as READ SALES-FILE with no AT END clause. Would this cause an error? Explain your answer.

8. The line that contains the paragraph-name called 200-PROCESS-RTN will be listed as a syntax error. Why?

PROGRAMMING ASSIGNMENTS

The following notes apply to all Programming Assignments in this and subsequent chapters.

1. Each of the following assignments specifies a particular form of input, such as disk, as well as a particular form of output such as a printed report or disk. Your instructor may choose to modify these device assignments to make more effective use of the computer facilities at your school or installation.

   A program assignment that specifies 80-position disk records as input could easily be modified to indicate other input instead. Only the SELECT statement and possibly the LABEL RECORDS clause would need to be altered.

2. The first two or three Programming Assignments in each chapter will be specified in traditional problem definition form. Any additional assignments will be specified in narrative form to familiarize you with an alternative method for designating programming specifications.

3. A sample data set for Problem 2 of each chapter is provided in Appendix B. Your instructor may require you to use the data set provided. For all other programs you will need to create your own input data files or obtain them from your instructor. You can create data files using your computer's text editor. Or, you can write a COBOL program that creates a disk file.

4. For Programming Assignments 1 through 3, if printed output is required, a Printer Spacing Chart will be included with the problem definition. For additional programming assignments where printed output is required, you should create your own Printer Spacing Chart. There are blank Printer Spacing Charts at the end of the text.

5. When output is created on disk, you will need to learn how to print these files so that you can check them when debugging the program. You may code DISPLAY record-name prior to each WRITE record-name to view each disk record on the screen before actually creating it. Or you may use an operating system command such as PRINT or TYPE file-name to print or display the entire output file after it has been created. Ask your instructor or a computer aide how to print files for your system.

6. The Programming Assignments are arranged in increasing order of difficulty, with the last ones considered to be the most difficult.

7. For all Programming Assignments, use your own field-names unless specific COBOL field-names have been provided.

1. The chain Video Trap: Movies for Less needs to create two mailing lists for each customer record on file. One mailing will be for video rentals and the other for video sales. Each customer record has the following format:

CUSTOMER Record Layout		
Field	**Size**	**Type**
CUSTOMER NAME	20	Alphanumeric
STREET ADDRESS	20	Alphanumeric
CITY	10	Alphanumeric
STATE	3	Alphanumeric
ZIP CODE	5	Alphanumeric

a. Print two mailing labels per individual, stacked one on top of the other. For example:

```
--------------------------------------
TOM CRUISE
1 MAIN ST.
MIAMI, FL 33431
--------------------------------------
TOM CRUISE
1 MAIN ST.
MIAMI, FL 33431
```

b. Now assume that the printer contains perforated stick-on labels that can be printed side by side. Write a program to produce a mailing list as follows:

```
-----------------------------------------------------------------------
TOM CRUISE                              TOM CRUISE
1 MAIN ST.                              1 MAIN ST.
MIAMI, FL 33431                         MIAMI, FL 33431
-----------------------------------------------------------------------
BILLY JOEL                              BILLY JOEL
26 FIFTH AVE.                           26 FIFTH AVE.
NEW YORK, NY 10158                      NEW YORK, NY 10158
```

2. Write a program to print all information from payroll records for employees of the International Cherry Machine Company (ICM). The problem definition is shown in Figure 4.5.

Figure 4.5 Problem definition for Programming Assignment 2.

Systems Flowchart

PAYROLL-MASTER
80-position records
standard labels

CH 4-2
PROGRAM

PAYROLL-LIST

PAYROLL-MASTER Record Layout		
Field	**Size**	**Type**
EMPLOYEE NO.	5	Alphanumeric
EMPLOYEE NAME	20	Alphanumeric
LOCATION CODE:		
TERRITORY NO.	2	Alphanumeric
OFFICE NO.	2	Alphanumeric
ANNUAL SALARY	6	Alphanumeric
SOCIAL SECURITY NO.	9	Alphanumeric
NO. OF DEPENDENTS	2	Alphanumeric
JOB CLASSIFICATION CODE	2	Alphanumeric
Unused	32	Alphanumeric

Figure 4.5 (continued)

PAYROLL-LIST Printer Spacing Chart

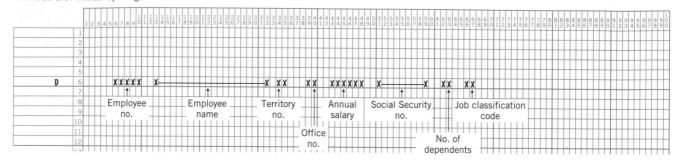

3. The Light-Em-Up Utility Company has master disk records, each of which will be used to create an electric bill record to be stored on an ELEC-BILL-FILE and a gas bill record to be stored on a GAS-BILL-FILE. The problem definition is shown in Figure 4.6. Note that for each input record, the program will create two disk records, one on the ELEC-BILL-FILE and one on the GAS-BILL-FILE.

Figure 4.6 Problem definition for Programming Assignment 3.

Systems Flowchart

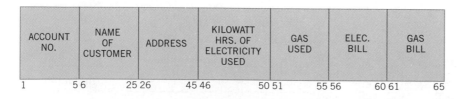

ACCOUNT-MASTER Record Layout (Alternate Format)

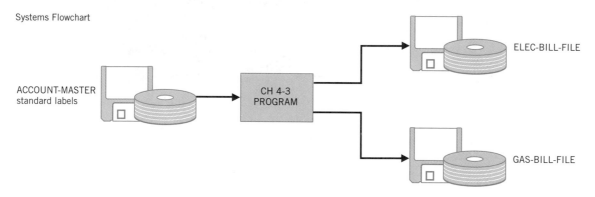

4. The Video Trap has one input file containing data on video tapes for rent and one input file containing data on video tapes for sale. Create a single master file where each record contains data from each file. The following represents records with a different type of record layout:

RENTAL-FILE Record Layout (Alternate Format)

ITEM NO	VIDEO NAME	NO. OF RENTAL TAPES IN STOCK
1 3 4	20 21	23

SALES-FILE Record Layout (Alternate Format)

ITEM NO	VIDEO NAME	NO. OF TAPES FOR SALE
1 3 4	20 21	23

Both files have exactly the same item numbers in the same sequence. Create a master file as follows:

MASTER-FILE Record Layout (Alternate Format)

ITEM NO	VIDEO NAME	NO. OF RENTAL TAPES IN STOCK	NO. OF TAPES FOR SALE
1 3 4	20 21	23 24	26

Assume that when you read Record 1 from the RENTAL-FILE and then Record 1 from the SALES-FILE, they both will have the same item number and video name.

5. Using the RENTAL-FILE and SALES-FILE specified in Assignment 4, write a program to create a merged file that contains a rental record followed by a sales record.

6. Redo Assignment 5, placing all rental records on a master file followed by all sales records.

7. Write a program to create a master sequential disk file from transaction disk records. Note: Use the format for arithmetic operations discussed on page 116.

   Notes:
   a. Total = Amount 1 + Amount 2.
   b. Amount due = Total − Amount of discount.

   Input ACCOUNT-TRANS

   ```
   1-5    ACCT-NO-IN
   6-25   CUST-NAME-IN
   26-30  AMT1-IN 999V99
   31-35  AMT2-IN 999V99
   36-40  DISCOUNT-AMT-IN 999V99
   ```

   Output ACCOUNT-MASTER

   ```
   1-5    ACCT-NO-OUT
   6-25   CUST-NAME-OUT
   26-31  TOTAL-OUT 9999V99
   32-37  AMT-DUE-OUT 9999V99
   38-40  FILLER
   ```

8. Write a program for the Pass-Em State College bursar to compute for each semester the tuition for each student. If a student is taking 12 credits or less, tuition is $525 per credit. If a student is taking more than 12 credits, the total tuition is $6300. Note: Use the format for arithmetic and conditional operations discussed on pages 116 and 117.

   Input: Disk File

   1–20 Student name
   21–22 Number of credits
   23–80 Not used
   (standard labels)

   Output: Print File

   1–20 Student name
   41–42 Number of credits
   63–66 Tuition

9. **Maintenance Program.**   Modify the Practice Program in this chapter as follows. Instead of creating an output salary disk, print each employee's name and a new salary. Each employee's new salary is calculated by adding $700 to his or her salary in the input master employee disk record. Note: Use the format for arithmetic operations discussed on page 116.

UNIT II
Designing Structured Programs

CHAPTER 5

Designing and Debugging Batch and Interactive COBOL Programs

■ **OBJECTIVES**

To familiarize you with

1. The way structured programs should be designed.
2. Pseudocode and flowcharts as planning tools used to map out the logic in a structured program.
3. Hierarchy or structure charts as planning tools used to illustrate the relationships among modules in a top-down program.
4. The logical control structures of sequence, selection, iteration, and case.
5. Techniques used to make programs easier to code, debug, maintain, and modify.
6. Interactive processing.

■ **CONTENTS**

WHAT MAKES A WELL-DESIGNED PROGRAM?

Many programming texts teach the instruction formats and coding rules necessary for writing programs without ever fully explaining the way programs should be designed. In this chapter, you will learn how to construct or design a program so that you can create structures that are easy to understand, debug, maintain, and modify.

We use the term *program design* to mean the development of a program so that its elements fit together logically and in an integrated way. In Chapter 1, we discussed several program design techniques. We review them here.

PROGRAM LOGIC SHOULD BE MAPPED OUT USING A PLANNING TOOL

If programs are systematically planned before they are coded, they will be better designed. Planning tools such as pseudocode, flowcharts, and hierarchy charts help programmers map out program logic. Just as architects prepare blueprints before buildings are constructed, so, too, should programmers use planning tools before a program is coded. The planning process minimizes logic errors by helping the programmer determine how all instructions will interrelate when the program is actually coded.

PROGRAMS SHOULD BE STRUCTURED

Well-designed, structured programs are those that have a series of logical constructs, where the *order* in which instructions are executed *is standardized.* In structured programs, each set of instructions that performs a specific function is defined in a **module** or program segment. A module is also called a routine or, in COBOL, a paragraph. It consists of a series of related statements. Each module is executed in its entirety from specific places in a program. In the program in Chapter 1, for example, there were two modules or paragraphs, one labeled 100-MAIN-MODULE and one labeled 200-WAGE-ROUTINE (see Figure 1.9 on page 19).

In COBOL, modules are executed using a PERFORM statement, which allows control to pass temporarily to a different module and then return to the original one from which the PERFORM was executed. A simple PERFORM (without an UNTIL clause) results in the following sequence of operations:

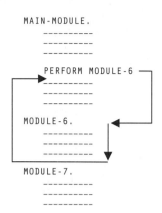

```
                    MAIN-MODULE.
                    ----------
                    ----------
                    ----------
                → PERFORM MODULE-6 ┐
                    ----------
                    ----------
                    ----------
                MODULE-6.        ←
                    ----------
                    ----------
                    ----------    ▼
                MODULE-7.
                    ----------
                    ----------
                    ----------
```

After MODULE-6 is executed from the main module, control returns to the statement following the PERFORM in MAIN-MODULE.

An unconditional branch to different routines, called a GO TO in most languages, is *avoided entirely* in a well-designed structured program.

This modular technique, combined with the use of PERFORM statements for executing modules, makes structured programs easier to code, debug, maintain, and modify.

PROGRAMS SHOULD USE A TOP-DOWN APPROACH

In summary, well-designed programs use structured techniques for coding and executing modules or program segments. These modules should also be coded in a *hierarchical order*, with main modules written first followed by secondary modules that include the detailed code. The coding of modules in a hierarchical manner is called **top-down programming.**

Top-down programming is analogous to the technique of outlining a paper before it is actually written. First, each topic in a paper is sketched out until the organization is clear; only then are the details filled in. Similarly, the main module of a top-down program is coded first, with the details for each subordinate module left for later. This top-down approach is sometimes called **stepwise refinement.**

PROGRAMS SHOULD BE MODULAR

Each well-defined unit or program segment should be written as a module and executed with a PERFORM. Subordinate modules can be written after the main structure or overall logic has been mapped out.

Consider a program that is to execute a sequence of steps if two fields are equal, and a different sequence of steps if the fields are not equal. We could code the instructions as:

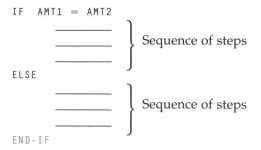

```
IF   AMT1  =  AMT2
        _____  ⎫
        _____  ⎬ Sequence of steps
        _____  ⎭
    ELSE
        _____  ⎫
        _____  ⎬ Sequence of steps
        _____  ⎭
    END-IF
```

A modular approach is preferable, where each sequence of steps is performed in a separate paragraph:

```
IF  AMT1 = AMT2
    PERFORM 100-EQUAL-RTN
ELSE
    PERFORM 200-UNEQUAL-RTN
END-IF
```

In this way, the main module focuses on the primary issue of whether the two fields are equal. Later on, in subordinate modules 100-EQUAL-RTN and 200-UNEQUAL-RTN, we focus on the detailed instructions to be executed depending on whether the fields are equal. Note that END-IF is a scope terminator used with COBOL 85 IF statements, as we will see in Chapter 8.

DESIGNING PROGRAMS BEFORE CODING THEM

HOW PROGRAMS ARE DESIGNED

Most students believe, quite understandably, that learning the rules of a programming language is all that is needed to write well-designed programs. It is, of course, true that you must learn programming rules, or *syntax*, before instructions can be coded. But knowledge of a programming language's rules will not guarantee that programs will be designed properly. It is possible for elements of a program to be coded correctly and yet the entire set of procedures might be poorly designed so that they do not work properly or efficiently. In addition to learning syntax, then, programmers must learn how to *design a program* so that it functions effectively *as an integrated whole*. That is, programmers must know the techniques used to structure programs as well as the programming rules.

Learning syntax, then, is only one step in the process of developing programs. The syntax you learn is language-specific, meaning that each programming language has *its own particular rules*. Knowing COBOL's syntax will be of only minimal value in learning Pascal's syntax, for example, although many other languages do share common features.

But the *techniques* for developing well-designed programs are *applicable to all languages*. That is, the logical control structures for designing a COBOL program are very similar to those in all languages. Once you know how to design programs efficiently and effectively, you need only learn the syntax rules of a specific language to implement these design elements.

In this chapter, we will focus on the *logical control structures* used to design a program. We will be illustrating them throughout the text, and you will use them in the COBOL programs that you will code. This discussion, then, is meant as an introduction to logical control structures and will be reinforced and reviewed in later chapters.

Logical control structures refer to the different ways in which instructions may be executed. Most instructions are executed in the sequence in which they appear in the program. Sometimes, however, different sequences of instructions are executed depending on the outcome of a test that the computer performs. Still other times, a series of instructions might be executed repeatedly from different points in a program.

We will illustrate these logical control structures using the two most common structured program planning tools—pseudocode and the flowchart. Both of these planning tools are language independent. That is, they help plan the logic to be used in *any program* regardless of the language in which the program will be coded. Thus, they afford us the benefit of illustrating the control structures in a general or theoretical way, without being dependent on any specific language rules. Once you understand how to plan the logical control structure of a program using pseudocode and flowcharts, you need only learn the specific language's rules to write the program. Programmers typically plan a program using either pseudocode or a flowchart; we discuss both tools in their entirety.

We will also show you how to plan a program using a *hierarchy chart*, which is a different type of planning tool. This tool is not intended to map out logical control structures but to illustrate the top-down approach to programming. More about hierarchy charts later on. For now, we will focus on pseudocode and flowcharts and how they illustrate the ways in which a structured program can be designed.

PSEUDOCODE AND FLOWCHARTS

Two tools for planning the logic to be used in a program are **pseudocode** and **flowcharts**. Pseudocode is a set of statements that specifies the instructions and logical control structures that will be used in a program. A flowchart is a diagram or pictorial representation of the instructions and logical control structures that will be used in a program.

Pseudocode and flowcharts are planning tools that should be prepared *before* the program is coded. They map out and then verify the logic to be incorporated in the program. Usually a program is planned with *either* pseudocode or a flowchart.

Pseudocode

Flowcharts have been used as planning tools for four decades. Structured programming, on the other hand, is a more recently developed technique. When structured programming became the preferred method for designing programs, flowchart symbols had to be modified to accurately depict a structured design. Many programmers and managers found that these modifications made flowcharts difficult to use as a planning tool. As a result, flowcharts are less widely used in many organizations, having been replaced by other tools that more clearly depict the logic in a *structured program*. Pseudocode is one such tool. In our programs, we will focus on pseudocode rather than flowcharts as our primary planning tool.

Pseudocode has been designed *specifically* for representing the logic in a structured program. No symbols are used as in a flowchart; rather, a series of logical control terms define the structure. Each processing or input/output step is denoted by a line or group of lines of pseudocode. The pseudocode need not indicate *all* the processing details; abbreviations are permissible. You need not follow any language rules when using pseudocode; it is a language-independent tool. We will see that logical control constructs are more easily specified using pseudocode because they closely resemble those in COBOL.

Pseudocode is read in sequence unless a logical control structure is encountered. The pseudocode for a program that reads in two numbers, adds them, and prints the total is as follows:

```
START
    Read Amt1, Amt2
    Compute Total = Amt1 + Amt2
    Write Total
STOP
```

The START and STOP delineate the beginning and end points of the program module. The words such as "Read Amt1, Amt2" are used to convey a message and need not be written precisely as shown. Thus, "Input Amt1, Amt2" would be acceptable. Similarly, "Let Total = Amt1 + Amt2" could be used rather than "Compute Total = Amt1 + Amt2" for the second instruction.

To illustrate the pseudocode for an in-line PERFORM that prints output, we would have the following:

```
PERFORM
     Write 'Amt1 = ', Amt1
     Write 'Amt2 = ', Amt2
     Write 'Amt1 + Amt2 = ', Total
END-PERFORM
```

This is called an in-line PERFORM since all instructions appear directly after the word PERFORM and are terminated with an END-PERFORM. We have already seen that COBOL 85 permits in-line PERFORMs with END-PERFORM scope terminators:

In-Line PERFORMs (COBOL 85)

Example 1
```
PERFORM
     WRITE RECORD-1
     WRITE RECORD-2
     WRITE RECORD-3
END-PERFORM
```

Example 2
```
PERFORM UNTIL ARE-THERE-MORE-RECORDS = 'NO '
     READ IN-FILE
          AT END
                    MOVE 'NO ' TO ARE-THERE-MORE RECORDS
          NOT AT END
                    MOVE IN-REC TO OUT-REC
                    WRITE OUT-REC
     END-READ
END-PERFORM
```

Thus, instructions to be executed within a PERFORM can be coded *in place* with pseudocode (and also in COBOL 85 as shown in the two examples above).

Alternatively, we can code a pseudocode that would include the following simple PERFORM statement:

MAIN-MODULE
START
    Read Amt1, Amt2
    Compute Total = Amt1 + Amt2
    PERFORM Print-Module
STOP

PRINT-MODULE
    Write 'AMT1 = ', Amt1
    Write 'AMT2 = ', Amt2
    Write 'AMT1 + AMT2 = ', Total

Throughout this text we will be illustrating both types of COBOL PERFORMs—in-line PERFORM ... END-PERFORMs and simple PERFORMs where the statements to be executed appear in separate modules. Both are permissible with COBOL 85 but only the latter is permissible with COBOL 74. We recommend you use simple PERFORMs for lengthy modules. The more advanced logical control structures that are part of most structured programs will be illustrated in the next section.

Flowcharts

The following symbols are the ones most frequently used in program flowcharts:

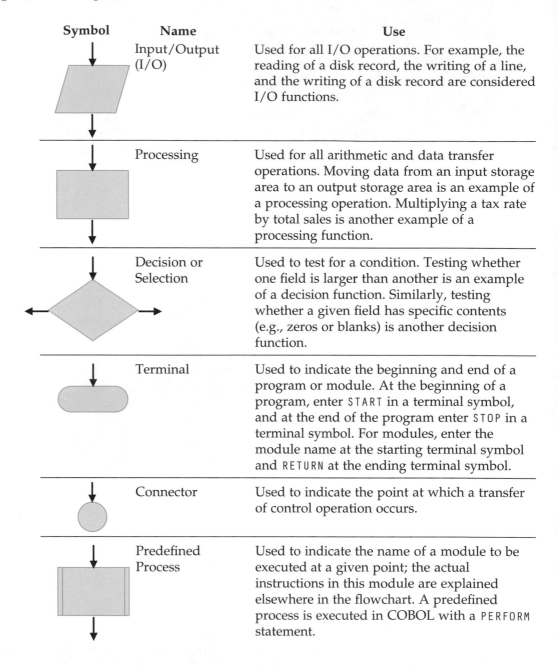

Symbol	Name	Use
	Input/Output (I/O)	Used for all I/O operations. For example, the reading of a disk record, the writing of a line, and the writing of a disk record are considered I/O functions.
	Processing	Used for all arithmetic and data transfer operations. Moving data from an input storage area to an output storage area is an example of a processing operation. Multiplying a tax rate by total sales is another example of a processing function.
	Decision or Selection	Used to test for a condition. Testing whether one field is larger than another is an example of a decision function. Similarly, testing whether a given field has specific contents (e.g., zeros or blanks) is another decision function.
	Terminal	Used to indicate the beginning and end of a program or module. At the beginning of a program, enter START in a terminal symbol, and at the end of the program enter STOP in a terminal symbol. For modules, enter the module name at the starting terminal symbol and RETURN at the ending terminal symbol.
	Connector	Used to indicate the point at which a transfer of control operation occurs.
	Predefined Process	Used to indicate the name of a module to be executed at a given point; the actual instructions in this module are explained elsewhere in the flowchart. A predefined process is executed in COBOL with a PERFORM statement.

FLOWCHARTING CONVENTIONS

1. Each symbol denotes a type of operation.

2. A note is written inside each symbol to indicate the specific function to be performed.

3. The symbols are connected by flowlines.

4. Flowcharts are drawn and read from top to bottom unless a specific condition is met that alters the path.

5. A sequence of operations is performed until a terminal symbol designates the sequence's end or the end of the program.

6. Sometimes several steps or statements are combined in a single processing symbol for ease of reading.

Consider the following simple flowchart:

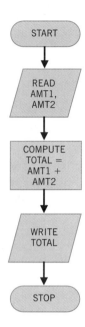

This sequence of instructions is called a *module.* The beginning and end of a module are designated with terminal symbols that are labeled START and STOP respectively. The first instruction or statement is READ AMT1, AMT2 meaning "read into storage a value for a field called AMT1 and a value for a field called AMT2." This is an input operation and is coded in an input/output or I/O symbol. The words used in the symbol need not be precisely as written, as with pseudocode. For example, INPUT AMT1, AMT2 would also be acceptable. Because a flowchart is a planning tool that is language-independent, you need not follow any language's specific syntax rules when drawing the flowchart.

When coded and executed, the first instruction in the sequence will read into primary storage or main memory a value for AMT1 and a value for AMT2, where AMT1 and AMT2 are field-names or symbolic addresses:

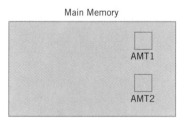

The next instruction in the illustrated flowchart module computes TOTAL as the sum of AMT1 and AMT2; it is described in a processing symbol. All arithmetic operations are considered processing operations.

In the program, AMT1 and AMT2 will be added and the result placed in a field called TOTAL. Suppose 10 is entered as input for AMT1 and 15 is entered as input for AMT2. Main memory would have the following contents in the fields defined in this program:

Main Memory

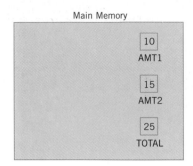

The next instruction, WRITE TOTAL, is an output operation that will print the contents of the field called TOTAL. It is also coded in an I/O symbol.

The flowchart is read from top to bottom. Since there is no need to repeat instructions or to test for any conditions, this simple flowchart indicates that two numbers will be read, added together, and the sum printed.

Specific instructions or statements are coded in each of the following flowchart symbols: input/output, processing, and decision. Terminal symbols indicate the beginning and end points of each module. A predefined process is drawn as a single step within the sequence; it indicates that another module is to be executed at that point. The steps within the named module are specified in detail in a separate sequence.

Suppose we wish to print not only TOTAL but a series of headings and other data. We can include each of these processing steps in our module or sequence but that would mean our main module would include numerous details. It would be better to include a predefined process in which we say PERFORM PRINT-MODULE; in this way, the print details could be left to the subordinate module called PRINT-MODULE. The following illustrates how we would draw a flowchart symbol to indicate that a predefined process called PRINT-MODULE is to be executed at a specific point:

In a COBOL program we can execute such a PRINT-MODULE by coding PERFORM PRINT-MODULE. PRINT-MODULE, then, would be defined in detail in a separate sequence:

The term PRINT-MODULE itself can identify the entire sequence, as in the preceding, or replace the word ENTRY in the terminal symbol.

Most programs make use of additional logical control structures, which will be explained in the next section.

THE FOUR LOGICAL CONTROL STRUCTURES

Structured programs use logical control structures to specify the order in which instructions are executed. These structures are the same for all languages. Thus, if you learn how to use them in COBOL, it will make learning to program in other languages much easier. These structures are used to form the logical design in a program. The four logical control structures are:

LOGICAL CONTROL STRUCTURES	
1. Sequence.	3. Iteration.
2. Selection.	4. Case Structure.

Sequence

When instructions are to be executed in the order in which they appear, we call this a **sequence.** The first pseudocode and first flowchart in the preceding section illustrated a module executed as a sequence, one instruction after the other. If all data is to be processed step-by-step in some fixed way, we use a sequence to depict the logic. That is, when instructions are executed in order *regardless of any existing condition,* we code them as a sequence. As another example, the following instructions would represent a sequence. The ellipses (dots) just mean that each statement has other components:

Pseudocode	**Flowchart**

START

    .
    .

       ADD ...
       WRITE ...

STOP

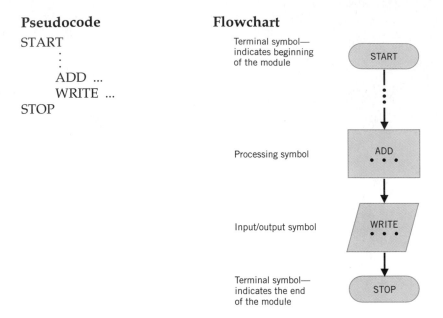

The preceding sequence or set of instructions would always be executed in the order in which it appears, that is, from top to bottom.

Beginning and Ending Modules

All modules or sequences in a pseudocode and a program flowchart should be clearly delineated. The pseudocode uses START and STOP as code words to delimit a sequence or module, particularly the main module. Similarly, to denote the beginning and end of a module or sequence in a flowchart, we use a terminal symbol with START and STOP as the delimiters.

    Each instruction in a structured program is executed in sequence unless another logical control structure is specified. We now consider these other structures.

Selection

Selection is a logical control construct that executes instructions *depending on the existence of a condition*. It is sometimes called an **IF-THEN-ELSE** logical control structure. In COBOL, for example, we can code an IF-THEN-ELSE structure as follows:

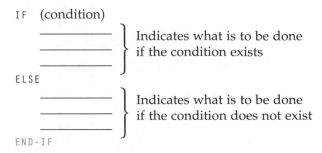

Example The following COBOL program excerpt illustrates the IF-THEN-ELSE logical control structure:

COBOL 74	**COBOL 85**

```
IF  AMT IS LESS THAN ZERO
        ADD 1 TO ERR-COUNTER
    ELSE
        WRITE NEW-RECORD.
```

```
IF  AMT IS LESS THAN ZERO
        ADD 1 TO ERR-COUNTER
    ELSE
        WRITE NEW-RECORD
    END-IF
```

The general pseudocode format for the IF-THEN-ELSE logical control structure along with the specific pseudocode for the preceding example are as follows:

Pseudocode Format for a Selection	**Example**
IF condition	IF Amt is Less Than Zero
THEN	THEN
_____	Add 1 to Error Counter
_____	ELSE
_____	Write a New Record
ELSE	END-IF
_____	
_____	
_____	
END-IF	

In pseudocode, the word IF is followed by the condition to be tested, the word THEN is followed by the statements to be executed if the condition exists, the word ELSE is followed by the statements to be executed if the condition does not exist, and the word END-IF ends the selection process. All coded entries except the words IF, THEN, ELSE, and END-IF are *indented* on a separate line so that the structure of the selection is highlighted. We capitalize only the logical control terms IF, THEN, ELSE, and END-IF, which also helps to highlight the structure.

We will see later that a COBOL 85 program can look *just like pseudocode.* That is, the word THEN may be used to indicate which statements to execute if the condition exists. Similarly, END-IF can be used to mark the end of the IF statement itself—but only with COBOL 85. Thus the pseudocode for the preceding example with IF-THEN-ELSE-END-IF resembles a COBOL 85 program excerpt.

The flowchart format for an IF-THEN-ELSE logical control structure along with the specific flowchart excerpt for the preceding example are as follows:

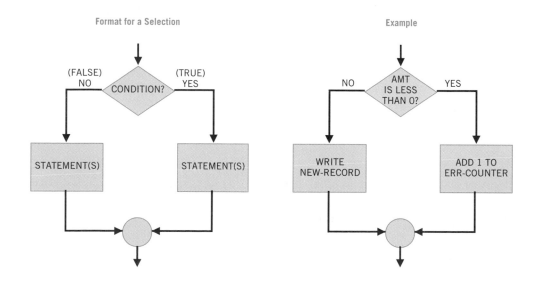

If the condition is true (or exists), we execute the statement or statements on the right. If the condition does not exist (or is false), we execute the statement or statements on the left. In either case, the flow returns to the circle or connector, where the next instruction, in sequence, is executed.

Here we present the general form for IF-THEN-ELSE and focus on the pseudocode and flowchart techniques that illustrate this logical control structure. The precise details for coding COBOL programs using IF-THEN-ELSE are discussed in Chapter 8.

Iteration

In our sample programs in Unit I, we illustrated a logical control structure in the main module referred to as the in-line PERFORM UNTIL ... END-PERFORM. This instruction enables us to execute a series of steps in the main module repeatedly until a specific condition exists or is met. The structure that makes use of the PERFORM UNTIL is called iteration. **Iteration** or **looping** is a logical control structure used for specifying the repeated execution of a series of steps. Consider the following type of iteration for COBOL 85:

```
PERFORM UNTIL

PERFORM
    UNTIL ARE-THERE-MORE-RECORDS = 'NO '
    :
    :

END-PERFORM
```

This means that the statements within the PERFORM UNTIL ... END-PERFORM loop are executed *repeatedly* until the field labeled ARE-THERE-MORE-RECORDS is equal to 'NO '. This type of iteration can be illustrated as:

Format of a PERFORM UNTIL ... END-PERFORM Loop or Iteration

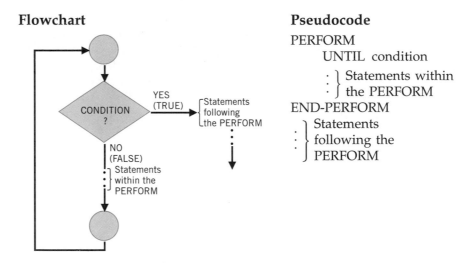

Flowchart

Pseudocode

PERFORM
      UNTIL condition
        · } Statements within
        · } the PERFORM
END-PERFORM
   · } Statements
   · } following the
   · } PERFORM

A PERFORM UNTIL ... END-PERFORM loop can be illustrated in-line as follows:

Pseudocode

PERFORM
      UNTIL Are-There-More-Records = 'NO '
      READ a Record
         AT END
             Move 'NO ' to Are-There-More-Records
         NOT AT END
             · } Process
             · } the record
      END-READ
END-PERFORM
Close the files
Stop the Run

Flowchart

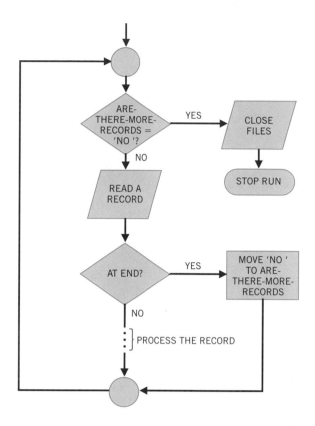

The same result can be achieved by coding a standard PERFORM paragraph-name UNTIL condition, where a *paragraph* is executed repeatedly until the condition specified is achieved. The paragraph would include the statements that could alternatively be included within an in-line PERFORM UNTIL ... END-PERFORM:

Pseudocode

MAIN-MODULE
PERFORM Paragraph-1
    UNTIL Are-There-More-Records = 'NO '
Close the files
Stop the Run

PARAGRAPH -1
READ a record
    AT END
        Move 'NO ' to Are-There-More-Records
    NOT AT END
        : } Process
        : } the record
END-READ

Flowchart

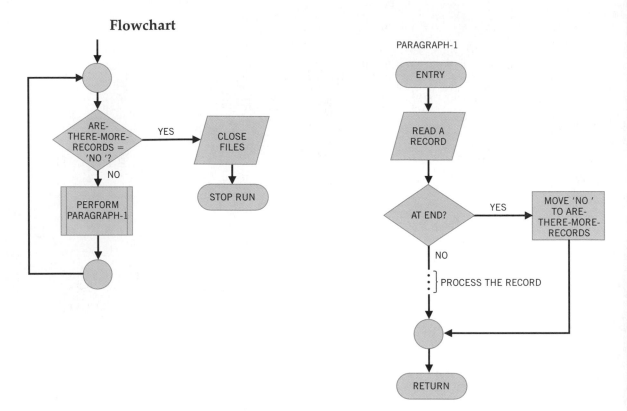

A Simple PERFORM

Finally, an in-line PERFORM UNTIL ... END-PERFORM can have a simple PERFORM within it to be executed for each successful READ. This is the way we have coded most of our programs thus far:

Pseudocode

```
PERFORM
    UNTIL Are-There-More-Records = 'NO '
    READ a Record
        AT END
            Move 'NO ' to Are-There-More-Records
        NOT AT END
            PERFORM 200-Calc-Rtn  ◄─── Simple PERFORM
    END-READ
END-PERFORM
Close the files
Stop the run
```

In-line
PERFORM
UNTIL ...
END-PERFORM
loop

200-CALC-RTN

. ⎫ Process
. ⎭ the record

Flowchart

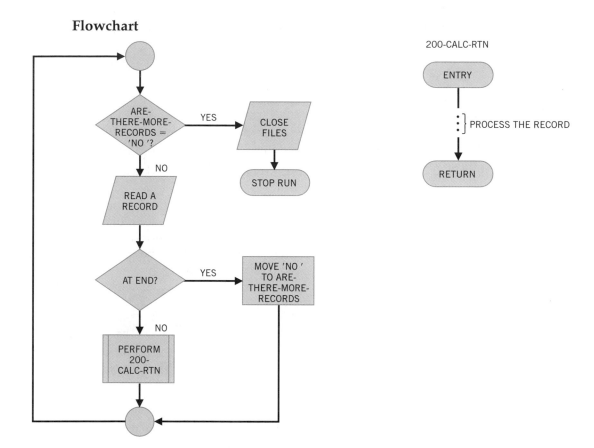

We will see later that other formats of the PERFORM, such as PERFORM ... TIMES and PERFORM ... VARYING, can also be used in COBOL for iteration.

The Infinite Loop: An Error to Be Avoided

Let us again consider the PERFORM UNTIL in which a series of steps is executed as part of an iteration:

In-line PERFORM UNTIL   **Standard** PERFORM UNTIL

PERFORM UNTIL condition   PERFORM paragraph UNTIL condition

   ⋮   ⋮

END-PERFORM   <u>paragraph</u>

                                                                 ⋮

Keep in mind that the series of steps executed is under the control of the PERFORM and will be executed repeatedly until a specified condition exists or is true. The condition being tested must at some point be true for the PERFORM UNTIL to terminate properly. PERFORM UNTIL ARE-THERE-MORE-RECORDS = 'NO ' ... END-PERFORM means that the statements within the in-line PERFORM UNTIL loop must contain an instruction that, at some point, causes the contents of the field ARE-THERE-MORE-RECORDS to be changed to 'NO '. If the field ARE-THERE-MORE-RECORDS is never changed to 'NO ', then the PERFORM UNTIL... END-PERFORM will be executed repeatedly without any programmed termination. This error is called an **infinite loop.** We avoid infinite loops by ensuring that the field tested in the UNTIL clause of a PERFORM is changed within the loop that is being executed.

Consider the following pseudocode excerpt:

Move Zero to Total
PERFORM UNTIL Total = 10
         ⋮
    Add 1 to Total
END-PERFORM

If the instruction ADD 1 TO TOTAL were omitted from the PERFORM UNTIL... END-PER-FORM iteration, then the sequence of instructions would result in an infinite loop because TOTAL would never equal 10.

Case Structure

The **case structure** is a special logical control structure used when there are numerous paths to be followed depending on the contents of a given field. For example, if a coded field is equal to 1, we want to perform a print routine; if it is equal to 2, we want to perform a total routine, and so on. With the case structure, then, we wish to perform one of several possible procedures depending on some condition.

Consider the following menu that may be displayed to determine a course of action:

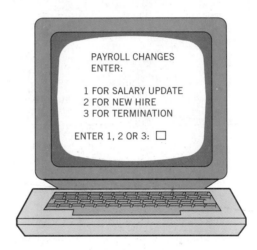

PAYROLL CHANGES
ENTER:

1 FOR SALARY UPDATE
2 FOR NEW HIRE
3 FOR TERMINATION

ENTER 1, 2 OR 3: ☐

The procedure or module to be executed depends on the entry made by a user.

The pseudocode for a case structure can be illustrated as follows:

Pseudocode

EVALUATE Update-Code
    WHEN 1
        PERFORM Update
    WHEN 2
        PERFORM New-Hire
    WHEN 3
        PERFORM Terminate
    WHEN OTHER
        PERFORM Error
END-EVALUATE

UPDATE
  ⋮
NEW-HIRE
  ⋮
TERMINATE
  ⋮
ERROR
  ⋮

One of these modules will be executed depending on the contents of Update-Code

Using in-line PERFORMs, the pseudocode for the same case structure would be:

```
EVALUATE Update-Code
        WHEN 1
                PERFORM
                    ⋮                      } Salary Update Procedure
                END-PERFORM
        WHEN 2
                PERFORM
                    ⋮                      } New Hire Procedure
                END-PERFORM
        WHEN 3
                PERFORM
                    ⋮                      } Terminate Procedure
                END-PERFORM
        WHEN OTHER
                PERFORM
                    ⋮                      } Error Procedure
                END-PERFORM
END-EVALUATE
```

The flowchart for this case structure is as follows:

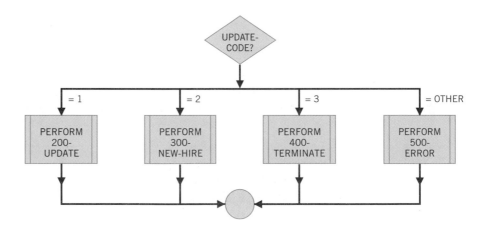

We use a case structure in place of a series of simple conditions. As we will see in Chapters 8 and 11, the best way to code the case structure with COBOL 85 is by using the EVALUATE verb:

```
EVALUATE UPDATE-CODE
    WHEN 1
        PERFORM 200-UPDATE
    WHEN 2
        PERFORM 300-NEW-HIRE
    WHEN 3
        PERFORM 400-TERMINATE
    WHEN OTHER
        PERFORM 500-ERROR
END-EVALUATE
```

If additional valid values need to be added, it is a simple task to add the appropriate clauses. EVALUATE is part of COBOL 85 but not part of COBOL 74; most 1974 compilers, however, include it as an enhancement. END-EVALUATE is a COBOL 85 scope terminator.

 Interactive Processing. The case structure is an important construct for processing menus interactively and for helping to validate data so that errors are minimized.

With the use of the case structure or `EVALUATE` statement, you can perform different routines depending on the contents of a field. You can also determine if a field has invalid contents with the use of the `WHEN OTHER` clause. In the preceding, we perform the appropriate procedure depending on the contents of the `UPDATE-CODE` entered; if the code is invalid with a value other than 1, 2, or 3, an error message would be printed.

The following are pseudocode rules:

PSEUDOCODE RULES

1. Pseudocode is written and read from top to bottom.

2. The logical control structure of pseudocode is defined with the use of key terms such as PERFORM UNTIL . . . END-PERFORM, IF-THEN-ELSE . . . END-IF, and EVALUATE . . . END-EVALUATE.

3. The operations to be executed within a PERFORM, IF-THEN-ELSE, or EVALUATE can be coded in-line or in a separate module.

Let us review the following rules of flowcharting:

FLOWCHART RULES

1. A flowchart is drawn and read from top to bottom unless a specific condition alters the path.

2. The symbol itself denotes the type of operation such as input/output or processing.

3. An explanatory note within the symbol describes the *specific* operation to be performed such as read a record or add amount to total.

ILLUSTRATING LOGICAL CONTROL STRUCTURES USING PSEUDOCODE AND FLOWCHARTS

EXAMPLE 1

Let us consider a program that reads disk records and prints the data contained in them.

The following is the pseudocode for Example 1 that uses an in-line `PERFORM`:

```
START
        Housekeeping Operations
        PERFORM UNTIL no more records (Are-There-More-Records = 'NO ')
                READ a record
                        AT END
                                Move 'NO ' to Are-There-More-Records
                        NOT AT END
                                Move Input Data to the Print Area
                                Write a Line
                END-READ
        END-PERFORM
        End-of-Job Operations
STOP
```

A more structured, modular version of the pseudocode for Example 1 is:

MAIN-MODULE
START
    Housekeeping Operations
    PERFORM UNTIL no more records (Are-There-More-Records = 'NO ')
        READ a record
            AT END
                Move 'NO ' to Are-There-More Records
            NOT AT END
                PERFORM Process-Data
        END-READ
    END-PERFORM
    End-of-Job Operations
STOP

PROCESS-DATA
    Move Input Data to the Print Area
    Write a Line

We will continue to illustrate both in-line PERFORMs and simple PERFORMs in both pseudocode and COBOL 85. We recommend you use PERFORM paragraph-name for detailed or complex sets of instructions, but where just a few operations need to be specified, the in-line PERFORM may suffice.

The actual words used in a pseudocode need not follow any specific rules. We can say "Housekeeping Operations" to mean any initializing steps, or we can say "Open Files." Similarly, we can say "PERFORM UNTIL no more records" or "PERFORM UNTIL ARE-THERE-MORE-RECORDS = 'NO '''. As a rule, however, the logical control words such as PERFORM UNTIL ... END-PERFORM are capitalized. This highlights the control structures in a pseudocode.

The degree of detail used in a pseudocode can vary. Only the logical control structures such as PERFORM UNTIL ... END-PERFORM, IF ... THEN ... ELSE ... END-IF, EVALUATE ... END-EVALUATE need to be precisely defined. The actual instructions themselves may be abbreviated. For example, Move and Write instructions within a PERFORM UNTIL structure might be abbreviated as "Process the data". You will find that the more detailed a pseudocode becomes, the closer it is to COBOL. We will be fairly detailed in our illustrations.

See Figure 5.1 for the flowchart and COBOL program excerpt for Example 1.

Note that there are two separate sequences or modules defined in the flowchart and program. These two modules are labeled 100-MAIN-MODULE and 200-PROCESS-DATA. Both modules begin and end with terminal symbols. The main module, which is labeled 100-MAIN-MODULE, includes the logical control structures of selection and iteration. In this instance, selection is illustrated with the use of a READ ... AT END. The AT END clause functions like an IF (no more records) ... statement; that is, we will treat this clause as a simple conditional test. Iteration is accomplished with a PERFORM UNTIL ... END-PERFORM. The main module has the following operations:

INSTRUCTIONS IN THE 100-MAIN-MODULE
(Labeled 1–6 in the flowchart in Figure 5.1)

1. Files are opened or prepared for processing.

2. The end-of-file indicator field called ARE-THERE-MORE-RECORDS is initialized with a value of 'YES' and changed to 'NO ' only after the last input record has been read and processed. Thus, ARE-THERE-MORE-RECORDS is 'YES' throughout the entire program except when there are no more records to process. This technique of using meaningful names, such as ARE-THERE-MORE-RECORDS, 'YES', and 'NO ', makes programs easier to code, debug, and modify.

Figure 5.1 Flowchart and COBOL instructions for Example 1.

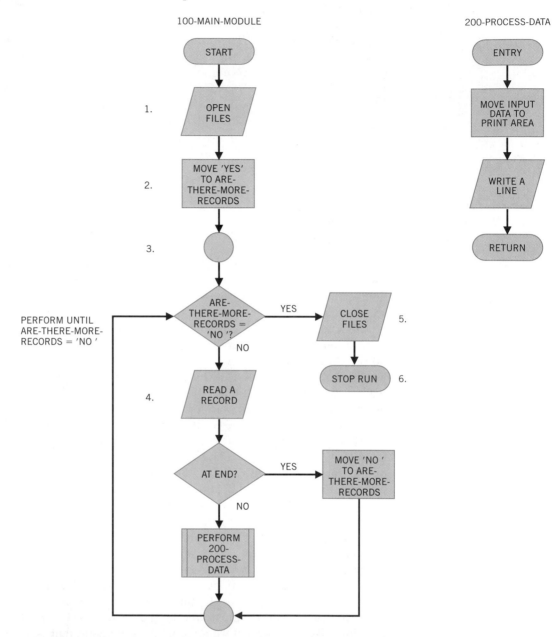

COBOL Instructions

COBOL 85

```
100-MAIN-MODULE.
    OPEN INPUT SALES-FILE
        OUTPUT PRINT-FILE
    MOVE 'YES' TO ARE-THERE-MORE-RECORDS
    PERFORM UNTIL ARE-THERE-MORE-RECORDS = 'NO '
        READ SALES-FILE
            AT END
                    MOVE 'NO ' TO ARE-THERE-MORE-RECORDS
            NOT AT END
                    PERFORM 200-PROCESS-DATA
        END-READ
    END-PERFORM
```

COBOL 74 Substitutions

```
READ SALES-FILE
    AT END MOVE 'NO ' TO ARE-THERE-MORE-RECORDS.
PERFORM 200-PROCESS-DATA
    UNTIL ARE-THERE-MORE-RECORDS = 'NO '.
```

(continued on next page)

Figure 5.1   (continued)

```
                          CLOSE SALES-FILE
                                PRINT-FILE
                          STOP RUN.
                    200-PROCESS-DATA.
                          MOVE IN-REC TO PRINT-REC
                          WRITE PRINT-REC.
```

COBOL 74 Substitutions

```
READ SALES-FILE
    AT END MOVE 'NO ' TO ARE-THERE-MORE-RECORDS.
```

3. A PERFORM loop is executed UNTIL ARE-THERE-MORE-RECORDS = 'NO '.

4. A record is read. If a record cannot be read because there is no more input, an AT END condition will be met, and 'NO ' will be moved to ARE-THERE-MORE-RECORDS. If the AT END condition is NOT met (NOT AT END), a process paragraph is performed. Thus a decision symbol is used to illustrate a READ ... AT END instruction:

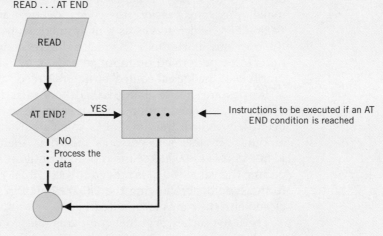

READ ... AT END

5. After all records have been processed, files are closed or deactivated.

6. The job is terminated by a STOP RUN instruction.

200-PROCESS-DATA contains the sequence of steps that will be executed if there are more records to process. This module, then, performs the required operations for each input record. At 200-PROCESS-DATA, we have the following steps:

INSTRUCTIONS AT 200-PROCESS-DATA

1. The input data is moved from the input area to the print area.

2. A line is written.

3. The sequence of steps at 200-PROCESS-DATA is executed under the control of PERFORM UNTIL ... END-PERFORM in 100-MAIN-MODULE. It is repeated until an AT END condition occurs in the main module. When an AT END occurs, 'NO ' is moved to the field called ARE-THERE-MORE-RECORDS. The PERFORM UNTIL ... END-PERFORM iteration is then terminated, files are closed, and the program is terminated.

The flowchart and pseudocode for Example 1 are shown here to help you understand how a full program uses the logical control structure of iteration with a PERFORM UNTIL . . . END-PERFORM and the logical control structure of selection with a READ . . . AT END.

Typically, programmers plan the logic to be used in a program with *either* pseudocode or a flowchart. Your instructor or computer center may require that you use one or the other. If not, we recommend you use pseudocode. We use pseudocode from Chapter 6 on.

EXAMPLE 2

Consider now the pseudocode, flowchart, and corresponding COBOL 85 program excerpt in Figure 5.2.

The pseudocode and flowchart depict the logic used to print salary checks for all salespeople in a company. The salary is dependent on how much sales the salesperson generated. If a salesperson has made more than $100 in sales, the commission is 10% or .10 of sales, which is added to the person's salary. If a salesperson has made $100 or less in sales, then the commission is only 5% or .05 of sales.

Here, again, there are two sequences: one labeled 100-MAIN-PARAGRAPH and the other 200-PROCESS-DATA-PARAGRAPH. Selecting paragraph-names that are meaningful will make programs easier to code, debug, and modify. Note that 100-MAIN-PARAGRAPH, which serves as a main module, has the very same set of instructions as the previous illustration. The major difference in this pseudocode is the actual operations to be performed on input records in 200-PROCESS-DATA-PARAGRAPH. This paragraph uses the logical control structure called *selection* in two different ways.

If sales are greater than $100, 10% of sales is used to determine the commission; otherwise, the commission is 5% of sales. After the percentage or commission rate has been determined, the amount is calculated, and a check is written with name and amount. Another salesperson's record is then read, and the module called 200-PROCESS-DATA-PARAGRAPH is repeated until an AT END condition exists. When AT END occurs, the value 'NO ' is moved to ARE-THERE-MORE-RECORDS and control is returned to the statement following the END-PERFORM in 100-MAIN-PARAGRAPH, where files are closed and the run is terminated.

The flowchart excerpt that compares sales to 100.00 uses a standard IF-THEN-ELSE or selection logical control structure. Recall that it has the following general format:

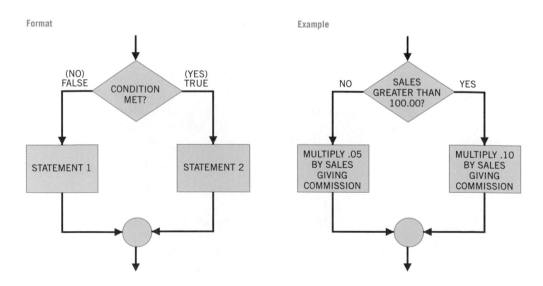

Figure 5.2 Pseudocode, flowchart, and COBOL 85 coding for Example 2.

Pseudocode

100-MAIN-PARAGRAPH
START
    Housekeeping Operations
    Clear the Output Area
    PERFORM UNTIL no more records (Are-There-More-Records = 'NO ')
        READ a record
            AT END
                Move 'NO ' to Are-There-More-Records
            NOT AT END
                PERFORM 200-Process-Data-Paragraph
        END-READ
    END-PERFORM
    End-of-Job Operations
STOP

200-PROCESS-DATA-PARAGRAPH
    IF Sales > 100.00 THEN
        MULTIPLY 10% By Sales Giving Commission
    ELSE
        Multiply 5% by Sales Giving Commission
    END-IF
    Calculate Check Amount as Salary + Commission
    Write a Check

COBOL Instructions

```
100-MAIN-PARAGRAPH.
    OPEN INPUT SALES-FILE
         OUTPUT CHECK-FILE
    MOVE 'YES' TO ARE-THERE-MORE-RECORDS
    MOVE SPACES TO CHECK-REC
    PERFORM UNTIL ARE-THERE-MORE-RECORDS = 'NO '
        READ SALES-FILE
            AT END
                    MOVE 'NO ' TO ARE-THERE-MORE-RECORDS
            NOT AT END
                    PERFORM 200-PROCESS-DATA-PARAGRAPH
        END-READ
    END-PERFORM
    CLOSE SALES-FILE
          CHECK-FILE
    STOP RUN.
200-PROCESS-DATA-PARAGRAPH.
    IF SALES-IN IS GREATER THAN 100.00
        MULTIPLY .10 BY SALES-IN GIVING WS-COMMISSION
    ELSE
        MULTIPLY .05 BY SALES-IN GIVING WS-COMMISSION
    END-IF
    COMPUTE AMT-OUT = SALARY-IN + WS-COMMISSION
    MOVE NAME-IN TO NAME-OUT
    WRITE CHECK-REC.
```

(continued on next page)

Figure 5.2 (continued)

Flowchart

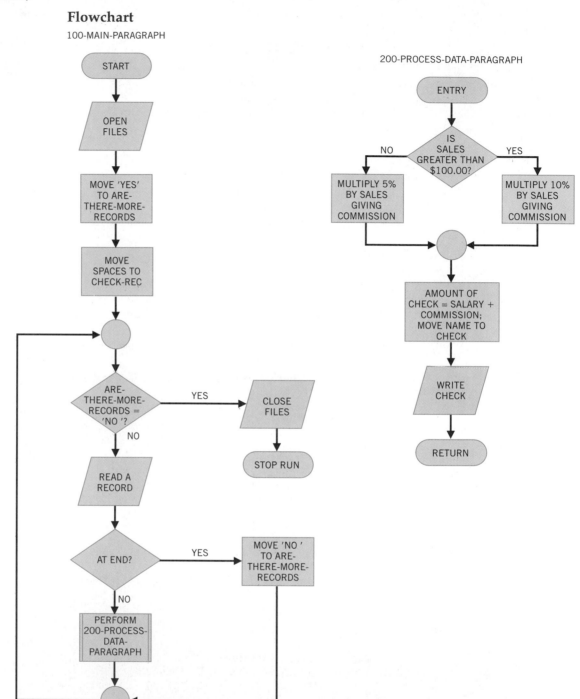

Pseudocode and flowcharts are illustrated in this section to help you understand the logical control structures of sequence, iteration, selection, and case as used in a full program. We will be depicting the logic for the Practice Programs at the end of each chapter with pseudocode.

HIERARCHY CHARTS FOR TOP-DOWN PROGRAMMING

Pseudocode and flowcharts are used to plan a program so that the structured design concept is implemented properly and efficiently. But what about the other major component of well-designed programs—the top-down approach? We need a tool that will illustrate the top-down relationships among modules in a structured program.

The planning tool best used for illustrating a *top-down approach* to a program is a **hierarchy** or **structure chart.** A hierarchy or structure chart provides a graphic method for segmenting a program into modules. Its main purpose is to provide a visual or graphic overview of the relationships among modules in a program. With a hierarchy chart, an entire set of procedures can be segmented into a series of related tasks.

Thus, before writing a program you will need to plan the logic in two ways: (1) with pseudocode (or a flowchart) to illustrate the logical structure, that is, how instructions are actually executed, and (2) with a hierarchy chart to illustrate how modules should relate to one another in a top-down fashion.

In COBOL, the concept of top-down or hierarchical programming is accomplished by coding main modules first, with minor ones detailed later. These modules are said to be coded hierarchically.

A main module is subdivided into its components, which are considered subordinate modules. Think of a top-down design as an outline of a paper. Begin by sketching the main subject areas and components, then focus on the minor details only after the main organization has been defined.

Note the following about hierarchy charts:

HIERARCHY CHARTS

1. A hierarchy chart represents program modules as rectangular boxes and illustrates the interrelationships among these modules with the use of connected lines.

2. A module is a well-defined program segment that performs a specific function. A module may be a heading routine, an error-checking routine, a calculation routine, and so forth.

The following example illustrates the relationships of modules in a hierarchy chart. In practice, we would use meaningful names for modules. The letters A through H are used here as paragraph-names for the sake of brevity and to highlight the concepts being illustrated.

Example of a Hierarchy Chart

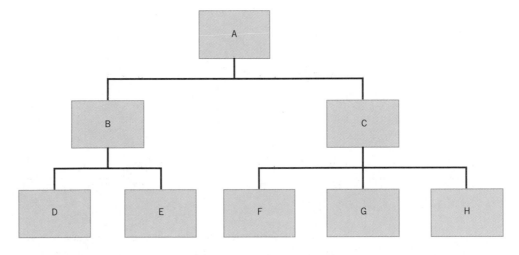

The letters A through H represent paragraph-names that are executed with the use of a PERFORM as follows:

```
A.
    :
    PERFORM B.
    :
    PERFORM C.
    :
B.
    :
    PERFORM D.
    :
    PERFORM E.
    :
C.
    :
    PERFORM F.
    :
    PERFORM G.
    :
    PERFORM H.
```

The hierarchy chart only illustrates modules executed from other modules. Unlike pseudocode or a flowchart, actual instructions are *not* depicted. Each block or box in a hierarchy chart represents a module. If a module calls for another module, this is depicted in a separate box. Consider the following section of the preceding hierarchy chart:

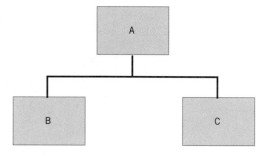

From this excerpt, we see that modules B and C are executed from module A.

Note that a module that is executed by a PERFORM can itself have a PERFORM in it. Module D, for example, is performed from Module B, which itself is executed from the main module, Module A.

Consider the following excerpt:

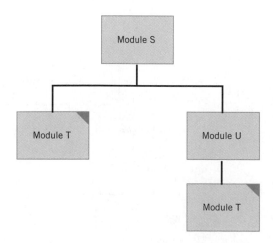

This excerpt shows that Module T is executed from both Module S and Module U. To highlight the fact that Module T is executed from more than one point in the program, we use a corner cut in both boxes labeled Module T.

In summary, the hierarchy chart illustrates how modules relate to one another, which modules are subordinate to others, and whether or not a module is executed from more than one point in the program. This structure chart makes it easier to keep track of the logic in a program. Moreover, if a module must be modified at some later date, the hierarchy chart will tell you how the change might affect the entire program. It does not consider the actual instructions within each module, just the relationships among them. The actual sequence of instructions is depicted in pseudocode or a flowchart, which would supplement a hierarchy chart as a program planning tool. A hierarchy chart is sometimes called a **Visual Table of Contents (VTOC)** because it provides a graphic overview of a program.

Consider the COBOL program in Figure 5.3, which calculates wages for each employ-

Figure 5.3 Sample payroll program—COBOL 85.

COBOL 85

```
100-MAIN-MODULE.
    OPEN INPUT PAYROLL
        OUTPUT PRINT-REPORT
    PERFORM 200-INITIALIZE-RTN
    PERFORM 300-HEADING-RTN
    PERFORM UNTIL ARE-THERE-MORE-RECORDS = 'NO '
        READ PAYROLL
            AT END
                MOVE 'NO ' TO ARE-THERE-MORE-RECORDS
            NOT AT END
                PERFORM 400-COMPUTE-WAGES
        END-READ
    END-PERFORM
    CLOSE PAYROLL
        PRINT-REPORT
    STOP RUN.
200-INITIALIZE-RTN.
    MOVE 'YES' TO ARE-THERE-MORE-RECORDS
    MOVE 1 TO WS-PAGE-CT.
300-HEADING-RTN.
    WRITE PRINT-REC FROM HEADING1
        AFTER PAGE
    WRITE PRINT-REC FROM HEADING2
        AFTER ADVANCING 2 LINES
    ADD 1 TO WS-PAGE-CT
    MOVE 0 TO WS-LINE-CT.
```

COBOL 74 Substitutions

```
PERFORM 350-READ-PAYROLL-REC.
PERFORM 400-COMPUTE-WAGES
    UNTIL ARE-THERE-MORE-RECORDS = 'NO '.
```

```
350-READ-PAYROLL-REC.
    READ PAYROLL
        AT END MOVE 'NO ' TO ARE-THERE-MORE-RECORDS.
```

```
PERFORM 350-READ-PAYROLL-REC.           ⟶
```

```
400-COMPUTE-WAGES.
    IF HOURS-IN > 40
        PERFORM 500-OVERTIME-RTN
    ELSE
        COMPUTE WAGES-OUT = HOURS-IN * RATE-IN
    END-IF
    PERFORM 600-WRITE-RTN.

500-OVERTIME-RTN.
    COMPUTE WAGES-OUT = 40 * RATE-IN +
        (HOURS-IN - 40) * RATE-IN * 1.5.
600-WRITE-RTN.
    IF WS-LINE-CT = 25
        PERFORM 300-HEADING-RTN
    END-IF
    WRITE PRINT-REC FROM DETAIL-REC
        AFTER ADVANCING 2 LINES
    ADD 1 TO WS-LINE-CT.
```

Note: END-PERFORM, END-READ, *and* END-IF *are used with COBOL 85 only.*

ee, where overtime is calculated as time-and-a-half. The program prints 25 lines on a page, after which a new page with headings is generated.

The hierarchy chart or VTOC for this COBOL 85 payroll program is illustrated in Figure 5.4. Although you may not be entirely familiar with all the specific instructions in Figure 5.3, you can see that the hierarchy chart provides a visual overview of the relationships among modules. Modules marked with a black corner cut are performed from more than one point in the program.

Note that when a subordinate module such as 500-OVERTIME-RTN is executed in its entirety, control then returns to the next highest module, 400-COMPUTE-WAGES in this instance. 400-COMPUTE-WAGES is executed repeatedly until ARE-THERE-MORE-RECORDS = 'NO ', at which time control returns to 100-MAIN-MODULE. Because logical control is depicted in this hierarchical fashion in a hierarchy or structure chart, it is referred to as a *top-down* tool.

In summary, then, a hierarchy chart has the following advantages:

ADVANTAGES OF A HIERARCHY OR STRUCTURE CHART

1. It helps programmers, systems analysts, and users see how modules interrelate.

2. It helps programmers debug and modify programs.

3. It helps programming managers assess the efficiency of programs.

Thus the hierarchy chart, like a pseudocode and flowchart, is both a design and documentation tool.

You can see that a hierarchy chart is *not* designed to highlight individual instructions; pseudocode and flowcharts serve that purpose. Rather, a hierarchy chart provides an overview of the interrelationships among modules. It also serves as a kind of table of contents, helping users and programmers locate modules in a program. This is why the term "visual table of contents" (VTOC) is sometimes used.

From this point on, each chapter in the text will illustrate program logic with pseudocode and a hierarchy chart. Examine these planning tools and be sure you understand the logic and the relationships among modules before you look at the programs.

Figure 5.4 Hierarchy chart for sample payroll program.

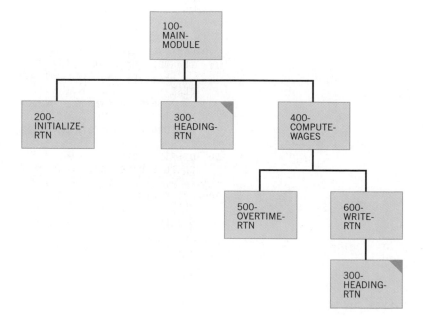

When you design your own programs, we recommend that you begin by writing a pseudocode (or drawing a flowchart) and drawing a hierarchy chart. You will find that these tools are extremely helpful in mapping out the logic to be used in your program. Although our early programs have relatively simple logical control constructs, the habitual use of program planning tools will be extremely helpful later on when you write more complex programs. When a pseudocode or a flowchart is written correctly, it is relatively easy to convert it to a program, assuming you know the syntax or rules of the programming language. You may also find that these planning tools will help you spot potential logic errors that, if coded in a program, may produce erroneous results.

NAMING MODULES OR PARAGRAPHS

As previously noted, a module or set of related instructions is equivalent to a paragraph. We have been using module or paragraph-names such as 100-MAIN-MODULE and 200-PROCESS-DATA without really reviewing why those names were selected. Recall that paragraph-names can be a combination of letters, digits, and hyphens up to 30 characters.

We will use a standard method for naming paragraphs in all programs. First, we will choose a meaningful name, one that describes the module. Names such as MAIN-MODULE, PROCESS-DATA, and ERROR-ROUTINE are descriptive in that they provide the reader with some idea of the type of instructions within the module.

In our examples, we also use 100-, 200-, and so on as prefixes to these descriptive names. Module-names are given prefixes that provide information on their location. That is, module 100- precedes module 200-, which precedes module 300-, and so forth. You will find that in very large programs that require several pages for listing, this type of numbering makes it much easier to locate a module during debugging or program modification. The numeric prefixes we use begin with 100-, then increase by intervals of 100 (200-, 300-, etc.). This convention is easy to follow and allows for possible insertions later on.

MODULARIZING PROGRAMS

We have seen that top-down programs are written with main units or modules planned and coded first, followed by more detailed ones. Structure or hierarchy charts illustrate the relationships among these modules. Statements that together achieve a given task should be coded as a module. Consider the following:

```
100-MAIN-MODULE.
    PERFORM 200-INITIALIZE-RTN
    PERFORM UNTIL ARE-THERE-MORE-RECORDS = 'NO '
        READ ...
            AT END
                MOVE 'NO ' TO ARE-THERE-MORE-RECORDS
            NOT AT END
                PERFORM 300-PROCESS-RTN
        END-READ
    END-PERFORM
    PERFORM 400-END-OF-JOB-RTN
    STOP RUN.
```

200-INITIALIZE-RTN would OPEN all files and perform any other operations required prior to the processing of data. These instructions could have been coded directly in 100-MAIN-MODULE, but because they are really a related set of instructions we treat them as a separate unit. We encourage this type of modularity especially for complex programs or when standard initializing procedures are required by an organization.

Similarly, 400-END-OF-JOB-RTN would CLOSE all files but might also include other procedures such as the printing of final totals. Here, again, such statements represent a unit and should be modularized.

Most programmers use initializing and end-of-job procedures as modules rather than including the individual instructions in the main module. In this way, the main module provides a "bird's eye" view of the entire structure in the program. This modularization eliminates the need to include detailed coding until after the structure has been fully developed. We will use initializing and end-of-job modules extensively beginning with Chapter 9 where we discuss all options of the PERFORM in full detail.

A REVIEW OF TWO CODING GUIDELINES

CODE EACH CLAUSE ON A SEPARATE LINE

In general, we code COBOL programs with *one clause per line*.

Examples

```
1. READ INVENTORY
       AT END MOVE 'NO ' TO ARE-THERE-MORE-RECORDS
   END-READ
2. PERFORM 100-CALC-RTN
       UNTIL ARE-THERE-MORE-RECORDS = 'NO '
```

Words and clauses can be separated with any number of blank spaces. Therefore, we can be as generous as we wish in our use of coding lines. Coding one clause per line makes programs easier to read and debug. If an error occurs, the compiler lists the erroneous line number. Having only one clause on each line helps to isolate the error.

INDENT CLAUSES WITHIN A STATEMENT

In addition to coding one clause per line, we also *indent* clauses. Indentation makes programs easier to read. In general, we will indent four spaces on each line. On some systems, you can use the Tab key to indent four spaces.

Examples

```
1. SELECT INVENTORY
       ASSIGN TO DISK1.
2. READ SALES-FILE
       AT END
           MOVE 'NO ' TO ARE-THERE-MORE-RECORDS
       :
       :
```

Sometimes we indent more than four spaces for the sake of alignment:

Example

```
OPEN INPUT   INVENTORY
     OUTPUT  PRINTOUT
```

To align the words INPUT and OUTPUT and the file-names we indented more than four spaces on the second line.

Suppose we want to add 1 to TOTAL *and* read a record if AMT1 = 100:

```
IF  AMT1 = 100
    ADD 1 TO TOTAL
    READ INFILE
        AT END MOVE 'NO ' TO ARE-THERE-MORE-RECORDS
    END-READ
END-IF
```

Notice the use of indentation here. We actually indent *twice* on the fourth line to help clarify that the AT END clause is part of a READ, which itself is part of an IF statement.

The END-READ and END-IF are in color because they are permitted with COBOL 85 only. NOT AT END is a READ clause that can be omitted, as in the above.

As you proceed through this text, you will see how indentation is used to clarify the logic. You should use this technique in your programs as well. Note, however, that indentation does not affect the program logic at all. It is simply a tool that helps people *read* the program.

─────────────── DEBUGGING TIP FOR COBOL 85 USERS ───────────────

COBOL 85 programmers should always use scope terminators with the READ and IF statements, as well as others we will discuss. When scope terminators are coded, periods are not used to end statements except for the last statement in a paragraph. Scope terminators ensure that all clauses within a statement will be associated with the appropriate instruction, thereby minimizing logic errors.

AN INTRODUCTION TO INTERACTIVE PROCESSING

Interactive Processing. COBOL was originally developed to process files of data and is still widely used for that purpose. Many organizations, however, are using COBOL for interactive processing—where the user enters data using a keyboard of a PC or terminal, and output is displayed on the monitor at the user's desk. We use the ACCEPT verb for entering input from a keyboard and the DISPLAY verb for displaying output on a screen.

The instruction ACCEPT *identifier* enables the user to enter input data directly from a keyboard rather than from a disk file. The identifier is likely to be a WORKING-STORAGE entry. When input is entered using the ACCEPT verb, there is no need to establish a file.

To enter as input a DISCOUNT-AMT, for example, you can code:

```
ACCEPT DISCOUNT-AMT
```

The format for the input is determined by the PIC clause for DISCOUNT-AMT.

Example 1
```
WORKING-STORAGE SECTION.
01   DISCOUNT-AMT        PIC 9(3).
```

Using a keyboard, the user would enter three integers into DISCOUNT-AMT.

Example 2
```
WORKING-STORAGE SECTION.
01   DISCOUNT-AMT        PIC 99V99.
```

Here, the user would enter four numbers that will be interpreted by the computer as a dollars-and-cents amount. That is, data entered as 1234 will be stored as 12ₐ34.

To create an accounts receivable file interactively from data entered at a keyboard, we code:

```
IDENTIFICATION DIVISION.
PROGRAM-ID.  CREATE.
ENVIRONMENT DIVISION.
INPUT-OUTPUT SECTION.
FILE-CONTROL.
    SELECT ACCOUNTS-RECEIVABLE-FILE
        ASSIGN TO DISK1.
DATA DIVISION.
FILE SECTION.
FD  ACCOUNTS-RECEIVABLE-FILE
    LABEL RECORDS ARE STANDARD.
01  ACCOUNTS-RECEIVABLE-REC.
    05   AR-NAME         PIC X(20).
    05   AR-ADDRESS      PIC X(20).
    05   AR-BAL-DUE      PIC X(6).
```

```
          PROCEDURE DIVISION.
          100-MAIN.
              OPEN OUTPUT ACCOUNTS-RECEIVABLE-FILE
              PERFORM 200-PROCESS-RTN
                  UNTIL AR-NAME = 'END'
              CLOSE ACCOUNTS-RECEIVABLE-FILE
              STOP RUN.
          **********************************************************
          *  when user enters 'end' for ar-name the program terminates  *
          **********************************************************
          200-PROCESS-RTN.
              ACCEPT AR-NAME
              IF  AR-NAME NOT = 'END'
                  ACCEPT AR-ADDRESS
                  ACCEPT AR-BAL-DUE
                  WRITE-ACCOUNTS-RECEIVABLE-REC
              END-IF.
```

Only the output file, `ACCOUNTS-RECEIVABLE-FILE`, is defined with a `SELECT` statement. When the user enters a name of `'END'`, the program terminates.

The `DISPLAY`, which displays output on a screen, has the following basic format:

$$\underline{DISPLAY} \left\{ \begin{array}{l} \text{identifier-1} \\ \text{literal-1} \end{array} \right\} \dots$$

The format indicates that you can display fields or literals or some combination of the two.

Examples

1. To prompt for input at a keyboard:

```
DISPLAY 'ENTER NAME'
ACCEPT NAME
```

2. To display a message:

```
READ IN-FILE
    AT END DISPLAY 'END OF FILE'
END-READ
```

3. To display a result:

```
DISPLAY RECORD-COUNTER
```

4. To display a literal along with a result:

```
DISPLAY 'NO. OF RECORDS IS ', RECORD-COUNTER
```

Commas may be used to separate displayed data for ease of reading, but they are not required. To ensure that the message and result do not collide (e.g., `'NO. OF RECORDS IS100'`), always leave a space at the end of the literal.

We will discuss `ACCEPT`s and `DISPLAY`s in more detail throughout the text. We introduce these topics here for PC users who want to focus on interactive processing early on.

Let us modify our preceding program to prompt for input and to prompt the user to specify when there is no more data. We also use a `MORE-RECS` indicator here to determine when there is no more data to be entered.

```
          100-MAIN.
              OPEN OUTPUT ACCOUNTS-RECEIVABLE-FILE
              MOVE 'Y' TO MORE-RECS
              PERFORM 200-PROCESS-RTN
                  UNTIL MORE-RECS = 'N'
              CLOSE ACCOUNTS-RECEIVABLE-FILE
```

```
      STOP RUN.
200-PROCESS-RTN.
   DISPLAY 'ENTER NAME'
   ACCEPT AR-NAME
   DISPLAY 'ENTER ADDRESS'
   ACCEPT AR-ADDRESS
   DISPLAY 'ENTER BALANCE DUE'
   ACCEPT AR-BAL-DUE
   WRITE ACCOUNTS-RECEIVABLE-REC
   DISPLAY 'IS THERE MORE INPUT (Y/N)?'
   ACCEPT MORE-RECS.
```

This version requires a WORKING-STORAGE entry:

```
WORKING-STORAGE SECTION.
01  MORE-RECS   PIC X.
```

After each set of input is entered, the user responds to 'IS THERE MORE INPUT (Y/N)?' with a 'Y' or 'N'. 'Y' is entered to indicate that there is more input and 'N' is entered to indicate that there is no more input.

DEBUGGING PROGRAMS

After you design a program using the planning tools discussed in this chapter, you are ready to code it. Programs can be coded first on coding sheets or they can be keyed directly on a computer using a COBOL text editor or even a standard word processor. COBOL margin rules must be followed, however, regardless of the method used for entering the program.

Programs must be fully tested to ensure that there are no errors. The process of eliminating errors from a program is called debugging. In this section, we discuss the types of errors that can occur in a program and the methods used to fix them.

SYNTAX ERRORS

After a program has been planned and coded, it is keyed into a computer. The programmer should then desk check it for typographical errors and for logic errors. Then it is ready to be compiled or translated into machine language. During this translation or compilation process, the compiler will list any violations in programming rules that may have occurred. These rule violations are called **syntax errors;** they must be corrected before the program can be executed. Note that logic errors are not detected by the computer during the compilation; they can be discovered only during actual execution of the program.

Examples of syntax errors are:

1.   Attempting to add two fields using the verb AD instead of ADD.
2.   Attempting to read from a file that has not been opened.
3.   Using a field in the PROCEDURE DIVISION that has not been defined in the DATA DIVISION.

Such syntax errors are quite common even in programs written by experienced programmers.

Each compiler has its own set of **diagnostic** or error **messages.** These will be printed or displayed along with your source program listing.

Sometimes it takes practice to become accustomed to the concise format of a diagnostic message. Consult your computer's specifications manual for a listing of common diagnostics. Note that although the messages illustrated in this section may not conform exactly to those for your compiler, the general format is the same. Thus, experience with diagnostics of one compiler will help you understand diagnostics of other compilers.

Some compilers print diagnostics on the line following the error. Others print them at the end of the source listing. When diagnostics appear at the end of a source listing, they typically have the following format:

> Line No.   Error Code   Error Message

Line No. refers to the sequence number assigned to each line of a source program. This line number is assigned by the compiler and printed on the source program listing.

Error Code is a code number assigned to the specific message in the COBOL manual. If you look up the Error Code in your manual, it will provide further clarification about the type of error that has occurred.

The printed Error Message is a concise description of the syntax error. After debugging a few programs, you will become familiar with these messages.

The following are sample IBM diagnostics:

Sample Diagnostics		
Line No.	**Error Code**	**Error Message**
18	1KF2041-C	NO OPEN CLAUSE FOUND FOR FILE
25	1KF0651-W	PERIOD MISSING IN PRECEDING STATEMENT
29	1KF5531-E	FIGURATIVE CONSTANT IS NOT ALLOWED AS RECEIVING FIELD
30	1KF4011-C	SYNTAX REQUIRES A DATA-NAME FOUND 'DATA'

Suppose we accidentally omit the period at the end of the following line:

```
05   ARE-THERE-MORE-RECORDS          PIC X(3)     VALUE 'YES'
```

Each reference to the identifier ARE-THERE-MORE-RECORDS will cause a diagnostic or syntax error to print. On some computers, errors will print at the end of the source listing as follows:

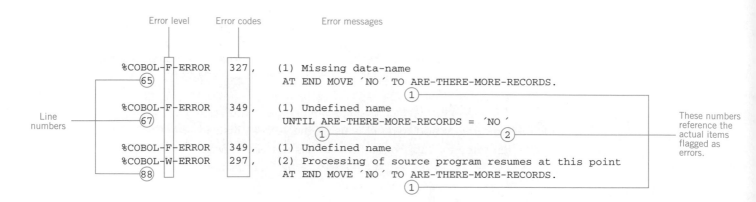

See our *Getting Started with RM/COBOL-85* and *Getting Started with Micro Focus Personal COBOL* manuals for a discussion of how errors are displayed with these PC compilers.

Sometimes errors detected by the compiler may have been triggered by a mistake several lines earlier. Thus, if the error is not readily found, examine the lines directly preceding the ones specified in the error message.

The Error Code accompanying all diagnostics contains, as the last character, usually a W or 0 for warning, a C or 1 for conditional, or an E (or F) or 2 for execution (or fatal) error. These letters or numbers indicate the *severity* of the error. The execution of the program may be terminated depending on the level of severity of errors.

W-Level or Level-0 Errors

Minor-level errors, sometimes called warning, observation, W-level, or level-0 messages, are merely warnings to the programmer. To move a five-position alphanumeric field to a three-position alphanumeric field, for example, may result in the following warning message:

```
DESTINATION FIELD DOES NOT ACCEPT THE WHOLE SENDING FIELD IN MOVE
```

To MOVE a larger field to a smaller one is *not* necessarily incorrect. The compiler is merely indicating that truncation will occur. If truncation occurs as a result of a programming oversight, it should be corrected. If, however, the programmer chooses to truncate a field, no changes are necessary. A program with only warning-level errors is still executable after it has been compiled. When you finalize your program, you should change source code that produces even warning messages.

C-Level or Level-1 Errors

Intermediate-level errors are conditional errors, usually called C-level, where the compiler must make an assumption about what a coded statement means. The compiler then makes the necessary change so that the program is executable. This assumption is called a **default.** If the default is what the programmer wants, execution will proceed normally. Consider the following C-level diagnostic:

```
0072 C-UNKNOWN NAME
FIRST NAME DEFINED IS ASSUMED
```

which applies to the following statement on line 72 (0072):

```
0072    MOVE NAME-IN TO NAME-OUT OF REC-OUT
```

Suppose NAME-IN is an identifier that defines two different fields, one in the FILE SECTION and one in WORKING-STORAGE. The compiler does not know which NAME-IN is being referenced on line 0072. It will *assume* you mean the first NAME-IN field specified in the DATA DIVISION. If, in fact, the first NAME-IN field designated in the DATA DIVISION is the required one, the statement need not be corrected for execution to continue properly. If, however, the NAME-IN field required is *not* the first one, then the program must be corrected before execution can begin. In any case, all C-level diagnostics should eventually be corrected before the program is considered fully debugged.

E- (or F-) Level or Level-2 Errors

Major-level errors, called **execution** or *fatal* **errors**, will prevent program execution. The following are examples of major-level errors:

MAJOR-LEVEL ERRORS

```
FILE SECTION OUT OF SEQUENCE
UNDEFINED IDENTIFIER
INVALID LITERAL: $100.00
INVALID IDENTIFIER: DISCOUNT-%
```

Note that a single typographical error, such as omitting a hyphen in a user-defined word or a reserved word (e.g., FILE-CONTROL), could generate numerous error messages. One advantage of this situation is that a single "fix" can often eliminate many errors.

Do not be surprised when you review your first few compilations and see error messages that are difficult to understand. It takes practice to be able to fully interpret syntax errors. Initially, you may need some help, but eventually the meaning of compiler-generated messages will become clearer to you.

LOGIC ERRORS

Syntax errors are detected by the compiler and, except for warnings, they should all be corrected before you run the program. Even after a program has been compiled so that it has no syntax errors, however, it is not yet fully debugged. The program must be executed with test data to ensure that there are no logic errors. Recall that a logic error may result from a mistake in the sequencing of instructions as well as from an improperly coded instruction that does not accomplish what was desired.

Some logic errors result in a **program interrupt**. These are called run-time errors and must be corrected before execution can continue. Other logic errors result in erroneous output. These will be detected only if the test data is complete and the program is carefully checked by the programmer.

Suppose a program has been written to be run on a regularly scheduled basis. If a programmer has not carefully debugged the program, logic errors that may occasionally result in erroneous output could go undetected until after the program is operational. Correcting such errors after a program is being used on a regular basis is very difficult. The programmer may no longer be completely familiar with all aspects of the program and is likely to make changes that may compound the original problem or create other ones. Moreover, if the company is using the program for scheduled runs, the time it takes to correct errors will be costly and probably create backlogs.

In short, all logic errors should be found *before* a program becomes operational, which means that the program should be carefully debugged during the testing stage. We will focus on two methods for detecting logic errors.

Designing Test Data That Is Comprehensive and Realistic

Programs must be tested with input **test data** to ensure that they will run properly. Because debugging depends on complete and well-designed test data, the preparation of this test data is an important responsibility of the programmer. If the test data is not complete, the program will not be fully debugged and the possibility will exist that logic errors or erroneous output may occur later on during regular production runs.

We will see in Chapter 11 that when a program tests to see if specific conditions are met, test data must include values that will meet each condition as well as values that will not. This ensures that the program works properly in all situations.

After the test data is prepared, perform a *structured walkthrough* to determine what results the computer *should produce* if the program is working properly. Then run the program with the test data and compare the computer-produced results with those of the walkthrough. If your structured walkthrough produced the same results as the computer, the program is correct and may be considered debugged. If not, you must find the source of the error, correct it, then recompile and rerun the program.

Checking for Logic Errors Using the DISPLAY Statement

In their eagerness to complete a program, programmers sometimes spend too little time testing their programs. If the first few lines of output in a test run look perfect, some programmers assume that subsequent output will also look correct. If a specific type of test data is handled properly by a program, some programmers assume that all types of test data will be processed properly. Such assumptions could, in the end, prove incorrect and costly.

To make debugging easier, it is possible to examine the contents of certain fields at various checkpoints in the program using a DISPLAY statement. This is usually done after the fields have been altered. In this way, the programmer can easily spot a logic error by manually performing the necessary operations on the data and comparing the results with the computer-produced output that is displayed. When a discrepancy is found, the logic error must have occurred *after the previous checkpoint.*

As we saw in the previous section, the DISPLAY statement prints the contents of the specified fields on either the printer or a screen, depending on the computer system. We can use this DISPLAY statement not only for interactive processing but for debugging programs as well.

Example   Suppose your program adds to a total. When you check your program for logic errors, you find that the final total is incorrect. The following DISPLAYs, which are typically included during the debugging phase, will print *each input amount* and *the total* as it is being accumulated:

```
200-CALC-RTN.
     :
     :
     ADD AMT-IN TO TOTAL
     DISPLAY AMT-IN
     DISPLAY TOTAL.
```

In this way, you can check each addition to help isolate the error.

The DISPLAY statements used for debugging should be placed at key locations in the program to test the outcome of specific arithmetic or logic instructions. During the run, the DISPLAY statements will display on a screen the contents of the named fields.

In the preceding example, you can check each addition by displaying the resulting field after each calculation. To ensure proper execution, you should step through the program manually, comparing your intermediate results with the displayed items.

The DISPLAY statement, then, can be used for debugging purposes to view on a screen intermediate results at crucial checkpoints in the program. If you are displaying a series of fields, it might be helpful to view the field-name as a literal along with the data. A DISPLAY can include literals along with the contents of fields.

Examples
```
DISPLAY 'INPUT AMT = ', AMT-IN
DISPLAY 'TOTAL = ', TOTAL
```

To say DISPLAY *identifier* will produce output on the computer center's standard display device, which is usually a screen.

Another use for the DISPLAY when debugging a program is to show the contents of records that are produced as output on a disk to verify that they are correct. After the program has been fully debugged, DISPLAY statements inserted for debugging purposes are then removed.

In summary, the DISPLAY statement is used for both debugging and interactive processing. One last point on debugging: Keep in mind that the more planning and desk-checking that is done, the fewer errors there will be and the less need to debug a program.

CHAPTER SUMMARY   I. Program Design
    A. Logical Control Structures
        The full range of logical control structures is as follows:
        1. Sequence

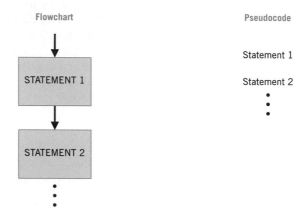

        2. IF-THEN-ELSE or Selection

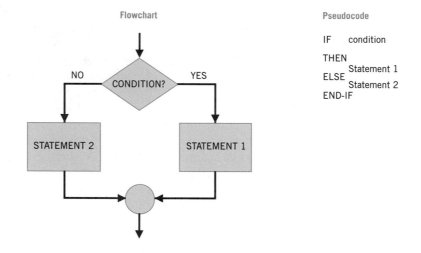

        3. Iteration Using a PERFORM UNTIL . . . END-PERFORM loop

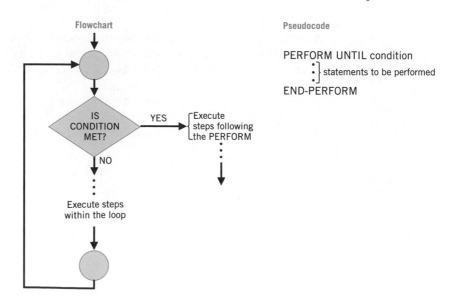

The flowchart processing symbol with two parallel bars is used to denote a predefined function, which is a module to be executed under the control of a `PERFORM` statement. That is, when the condition is met, control is passed to the named module and then returns to the point directly following the `PERFORM`.
4. Case Structure
This logical control structure is used when there are numerous paths to be followed depending on the contents of a given field.

Example

if `MARITAL-STATUS` = "D" execute `DIVORCE-MODULE`
if `MARITAL-STATUS` = "S" execute `SINGLE-MODULE`
if `MARITAL-STATUS` = "M" execute `MARRIED-MODULE`
otherwise execute `OTHER-MODULE`

Chapters 8 and 11 discuss in detail how this structure is implemented.
B. Program Planning Tools
1. To structure a program, use pseudocode or a flowchart.
2. To illustrate the top-down approach showing how modules interrelate, use a hierarchy chart.
C. Naming Modules
Use descriptive names along with numeric prefixes that help locate the paragraphs quickly (`200-PRINT-HEADING`, `500-PRINT-FINAL-TOTAL`).
D. A Well-Designed Program Uses:
1. Structured programming techniques.
2. A modularized organization.
3. A top-down approach.
Code main modules first, followed by minor ones.
4. Meaningful names for fields and paragraphs.
5. One clause per line and indented clauses within a statement.
II. Interactive Processing
A. You can use `ACCEPT` to input data from a keyboard.
B. You can use `DISPLAY` to output information to a screen.
III. Debugging
A. Correct all syntax errors or *rule* violations that are listed by the compiler.
B. Test your program carefully with test data that includes all possible values that the program might encounter during a normal production run.

KEY TERMS

Case structure	Iteration	Stepwise refinement
Default	Logical control structure	Structure chart
Diagnostic message	Looping	Syntax error
Execution error	Module	Test data
Flowchart	Program interrupt	Top-down programming
Hierarchy chart	Pseudocode	Visual Table of Contents
IF-THEN-ELSE	Selection	(VTOC)
Infinite loop	Sequence	

CHAPTER SELF-TEST

True-False Questions

_____ 1. In general, programs that are first planned with a pseudocode or flowchart take less time to code and debug.

_____ 2. Programmers should write a pseudocode and draw a flowchart before coding a program.

_____ 3. To ensure that pseudocodes are correct, it is best to write them after you have coded the program.

_____ 4. Programs without syntax errors will always run properly.

_____ 5. The terms "top-down" and "structured" are used synonymously in this chapter.

_____ 6. The terms "module" and "paragraph" may be used synonymously in COBOL.

_____ 7. Pseudocode for a COBOL program should generally be the same as for a Pascal program.

_____ 8. The syntax for COBOL and Pascal are, in general, the same.

_____ 9. A hierarchy chart can illustrate how the logical control structure of selection is used in a program.

_____ 10. The four logical control structures used in well-designed programs are sequence, selection, iteration, and case.

Fill in the Blanks

1. The program planning tool specifically designed for depicting the logic in a structured program is _____ .

2. The program planning tool specifically designed for depicting the top-down approach used in a structured program is the _____ .

3. If instructions are executed step-by-step without any change in control, we call this a _____ .

4. Another name for selection, when used in pseudocode or in a COBOL program, is _____ .

5. Iteration, or the repeated execution of a module, is accomplished using a _____ statement.

6. The flowchart symbol for performing a module is called _____ .

7. Paragraph- or module-names should consist of two components: the first or prefix is used for _____ ; the second is used for _____ .

8. The pseudocode structure for a selection begins with the word _____ and ends with the scope terminator _____ .

9. An iteration in pseudocode can be coded as an in-line PERFORM UNTIL . . . END-PERFORM or as a separate _____ .

10. Another name for a hierarchy chart is _____ .

Solutions: True-False

1. T
2. F—Usually they use one _or_ the other.
3. F—A pseudocode is not very useful as a planning tool if it is drawn after a program has been coded.
4. F—They may have logic errors as well.
5. F—"Top-down" refers to the hierarchical representation of modules; "structured" refers to the fact that a program uses the modular approach.
6. T—Routine is also a synonym.
7. T—Pseudocode and flowcharts are language-independent.
8. F—Syntax is language-dependent.
9. F—A hierarchy chart illustrates the relationships among modules.
10. T

Solutions: Fill in the Blanks

1. pseudocode (Flowcharts were not originally developed for structured programs.)
2. hierarchy or structure chart
3. sequence
4. IF-THEN-ELSE
5. PERFORM UNTIL . . . END-PERFORM
6. a predefined process
7. numbering modules to help locate them in a large program (100-, 200-, etc.); describing the nature of the module (ERROR-ROUTINE, TOTAL-ROUTINE, etc.)
8. IF; END-IF
9. module
10. structure chart or visual table of contents (VTOC)

PRACTICE PROGRAM 1

Consider a program to determine the overall effect on a university budget if faculty are given salary increases as follows:

6.2% for full professors (Rank = FP)
8.1% for associate professors (Rank = AS)

8.3% for assistant professors (Rank = AP)
10.2% for instructors (Rank = IP)

Read in a file of faculty records and print a payroll report. The input and output formats are as follows:

Input Format

Faculty Payroll Record Layout			
Field	Size	Type	No. of Decimal Positions (if Numeric)
Employee No.	3	Alphanumeric	
Last Name	20	Alphanumeric	
First Name	10	Alphanumeric	
Rank	2	Alphanumeric	
Salary	7	Numeric	2

Output Format

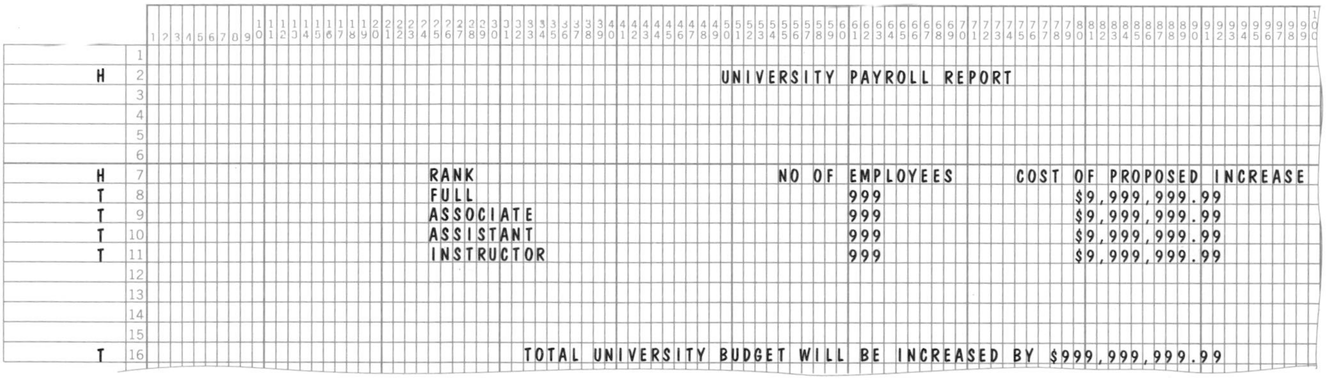

The pseudocode is illustrated in Figure 5.5 and the program in Figure 5.6. The hierarchy chart is in Figure 5.7. Do not be overly concerned about instructions that we have not yet discussed in detail. The purpose of these illustrations is to familiarize you with the structure of a program.

Figure 5.5 Pseudocode for Practice Program 1.

Pseudocode

MAIN-MODULE
START
    Housekeeping Operations
    PERFORM UNTIL no more records (Are-There-More-Records = 'NO ')
        READ a record
            AT END
                Move 'NO ' to Are-There-More-Records
            NOT AT END
                PERFORM Calc-Rtn
        END-READ
        END-PERFORM
        PERFORM Final-Rtn
        End-of-Job Operations
STOP

Figure 5.5 (continued)

CALC-RTN
    IF   Rank = 'FP'
    THEN
        Calculate Increase and Add to Professor Total
        Add 1 to Professor Counter
    END-IF
    IF   Rank = 'AS'
    THEN
        Calculate Increase and Add to Associate Professor Total
        Add 1 to Associate Professor Counter
    END-IF
    IF   Rank = 'AP'
    THEN
        Calculate Increase and Add to Assistant Professor Total
        Add 1 to Assistant Professor Counter
    END-IF
    IF   Rank = 'IP'
    THEN
        Calculate Increase and Add to Instructor Total
        Add 1 to Instructor Counter
    END-IF

FINAL-RTN
    Write Headings
    Move Professor Data to Total Line
    Write Output Line
    Move Associate Professor Data to Total Line
    Write Output Line
    Move Assistant Professor Data to Total Line
    Write Output Line
    Move Instructor Data to Total Line
    Write Output Line
    Add all Totals
    Write a Final Total Line

Figure 5.6 Practice Program 1.

```
                              COBOL 85
        IDENTIFICATION DIVISION.
        PROGRAM-ID. SAMPLE.
        AUTHOR. NANCY STERN.
        ****************************************************************
        *  sample     - determines the effect of salary increases for  *
        *               the university - the cost for each rank of      *
        *               employee will be calculated and added to totals *
        ****************************************************************
        *
        ENVIRONMENT DIVISION.
        INPUT-OUTPUT SECTION.
        FILE-CONTROL.
           SELECT IN-EMPLOYEE-FILE ASSIGN TO DISK 'DATA5'.
           SELECT OUT-REPORT-FILE  ASSIGN TO PRINTER.
        *
        DATA DIVISION.
        FILE SECTION.
        FD  IN-EMPLOYEE-FILE
            LABEL RECORDS ARE STANDARD.
        01  IN-EMPLOYEE-REC.
            05  IN-EMPLOYEE-NO        PIC X(3).
            05  IN-EMPLOYEE-LAST-NAME PIC X(20).
```

Figure 5.6 (continued)

```
                              05  IN-EMPLOYEE-FIRST-NAME PIC X(10).
                              05  IN-RANK                PIC XX.
                              05  IN-SALARY              PIC 9(5)V99.
                          FD  OUT-REPORT-FILE
                              LABEL RECORDS ARE OMITTED.
                          01  OUT-REPORT-REC             PIC X(132).
                          WORKING-STORAGE SECTION.
                          01  WS-WORK-AREAS.
                              05  ARE-THERE-MORE-RECORDS PIC X(3)       VALUE 'YES'.
                              05  WS-PROFESSOR-CTR       PIC 9(3)       VALUE ZEROS.
                              05  WS-ASSOCIATE-CTR       PIC 9(3)       VALUE ZEROS.
                              05  WS-ASSISTANT-CTR       PIC 9(3)       VALUE ZEROS.
                              05  WS-INSTRUCTOR-CTR      PIC 9(3)       VALUE ZEROS.
                              05  WS-PROFESSOR-COST      PIC 9(7)V99    VALUE ZEROS.
                              05  WS-ASSOCIATE-COST      PIC 9(7)V99    VALUE ZEROS.
                              05  WS-ASSISTANT-COST      PIC 9(7)V99    VALUE ZEROS.
                              05  WS-INSTRUCTOR-COST     PIC 9(7)V99    VALUE ZEROS.
                              05  WS-TOTAL-COST          PIC 9(9)V99    VALUE ZEROS.
                              05  NEW-SAL                PIC 9(7)V99    VALUE ZEROS.
                          01  HL-HEADER-1.
```

COBOL 74 Substitutions

Replace blank field-names with the word FILLER ⟶

```
                              05                         PIC X(49)      VALUE SPACES.
                              05                         PIC X(25)
                                  VALUE 'UNIVERSITY PAYROLL REPORT'.
                              05                         PIC X(58)      VALUE SPACES.
                          01  HL-HEADER-2.
                              05                         PIC X(24)      VALUE SPACES.
                              05                         PIC X(30)
                                  VALUE 'RANK'.
                              05                         PIC X(20)
                                  VALUE 'NO OF EMPLOYEES'.
                              05                         PIC X(25)
                                  VALUE 'COST OF PROPOSED INCREASE'.
                              05                         PIC X(33)      VALUE SPACES.
                          01  TL-TOTAL-LINE.
                              05                         PIC X(24)      VALUE SPACES.
                              05  TL-RANK                PIC X(10).
                              05                         PIC X(26)      VALUE SPACES.
                              05  TL-NO-OF-EMPLOYEES     PIC 9(3).
                              05                         PIC X(16)      VALUE SPACES.
                              05  TL-COST                PIC $Z,ZZZ,ZZ9.99.
                              05                         PIC X(41)      VALUE SPACES.
                          01  TL-FINAL-TOTAL-LINE.
                              05                         PIC X(32)      VALUE SPACES.
                              05                         PIC X(46)
                                  VALUE 'TOTAL UNIVERSITY BUDGET WILL BE INCREASED BY '.
                              05  TL-TOTAL-COST          PIC $ZZZ,ZZZ,ZZ9.99.
                              05                         PIC X(39)      VALUE SPACES.
                          *
                          PROCEDURE DIVISION.
                          *************************************************************
                          *  100-main-module - controls the opening and closing of *
                          *                    files & direction of program logic; *
                          *                    returns control to operating system *
                          *************************************************************
                          100-MAIN-MODULE.
                              OPEN INPUT  IN-EMPLOYEE-FILE
                                  OUTPUT OUT-REPORT-FILE
                              PERFORM UNTIL ARE-THERE-MORE-RECORDS = 'NO '
                                  READ IN-EMPLOYEE-FILE
                                      AT END
                                          MOVE 'NO ' TO ARE-THERE-MORE-RECORDS
                                      NOT AT END
                                          PERFORM 200-CALC-RTN
                                  END-READ
                              END-PERFORM
```

```
READ IN-EMPLOYEE-FILE
    AT END MOVE 'NO ' TO ARE-THERE-MORE-RECORDS.
PERFORM 200-CALC-RTN
    UNTIL ARE-THERE-MORE-RECORDS = 'NO '.
```

Figure 5.6   (continued)

```
                    PERFORM 300-FINAL-RTN
                    CLOSE IN-EMPLOYEE-FILE
                          OUT-REPORT-FILE
                    STOP RUN.
           ********************************************************
           *   200-calc-rtn - performed from 100-main-module.  *
           *                  determines rank of employee       *
           *                  calculates salary increase        *
           ********************************************************
            200-CALC-RTN.
                IF  IN-RANK = 'FP'
                    MULTIPLY IN-SALARY BY .062 GIVING NEW-SAL
                    ADD NEW-SAL TO WS-PROFESSOR-COST
                    ADD 1 TO WS-PROFESSOR-CTR
                END-IF
                IF  IN-RANK = 'AS'
                    MULTIPLY  IN-SALARY BY .081 GIVING NEW-SAL
                    ADD NEW-SAL TO WS-ASSOCIATE-COST
                    ADD 1 TO WS-ASSOCIATE-CTR
                END-IF
                IF  IN-RANK = 'AP'
                    MULTIPLY IN-SALARY BY .083 GIVING NEW-SAL
                    ADD NEW-SAL TO WS-ASSISTANT-COST
                    ADD 1 TO WS-ASSISTANT-CTR
                END-IF
                IF  IN-RANK = 'IP'
                    MULTIPLY IN-SALARY BY .102 GIVING NEW-SAL
                    ADD NEW-SAL TO WS-INSTRUCTOR-COST
                    ADD 1 TO WS-INSTRUCTOR-CTR
                END-IF.
```

COBOL 74 Substitutions

```
READ IN-EMPLOYEE-FILE                              ⎫
    AT END MOVE 'NO ' TO ARE-THERE-MORE-RECORDS.   ⎬
                                                   ⎭
           ***********************************************************
           *   300-final-rtn - performed from 100-main-module        *
           *                   prints page and column headings       *
           *                   calculates and prints total for ranks *
           ***********************************************************
            300-FINAL-RTN.
                WRITE OUT-REPORT-REC FROM HL-HEADER-1
                    AFTER ADVANCING PAGE
                WRITE OUT-REPORT-REC FROM HL-HEADER-2
                    AFTER ADVANCING 5 LINES
                MOVE 'FULL' TO TL-RANK
                MOVE WS-PROFESSOR-CTR TO TL-NO-OF-EMPLOYEES
                MOVE WS-PROFESSOR-COST TO TL-COST
                WRITE OUT-REPORT-REC FROM TL-TOTAL-LINE
                    AFTER ADVANCING 1 LINE
                MOVE 'ASSOCIATE' TO TL-RANK
                MOVE WS-ASSOCIATE-CTR TO TL-NO-OF-EMPLOYEES
                MOVE WS-ASSOCIATE-COST TO TL-COST
                WRITE OUT-REPORT-REC FROM TL-TOTAL-LINE
                    AFTER ADVANCING 1 LINE
                MOVE 'ASSISTANT' TO TL-RANK
                MOVE WS-ASSISTANT-CTR TO TL-NO-OF-EMPLOYEES
                MOVE WS-ASSISTANT-COST TO TL-COST
                WRITE OUT-REPORT-REC FROM TL-TOTAL-LINE
                    AFTER ADVANCING 1 LINE
                MOVE 'INSTRUCTOR' TO TL-RANK
                MOVE WS-INSTRUCTOR-CTR TO TL-NO-OF-EMPLOYEES
                MOVE WS-INSTRUCTOR-COST TO TL-COST
                WRITE OUT-REPORT-REC FROM TL-TOTAL-LINE
                    AFTER ADVANCING 1 LINE
```

Figure 5.6 (continued)

```
                        ADD WS-PROFESSOR-COST, WS-ASSOCIATE-COST,
                            WS-ASSISTANT-COST, WS-INSTRUCTOR-COST
                                GIVING WS-TOTAL-COST
                        MOVE WS-TOTAL-COST TO TL-TOTAL-COST
                        WRITE OUT-REPORT-REC FROM TL-FINAL-TOTAL-LINE
                                AFTER ADVANCING 5 LINES.
```

Note: END-PERFORM, END-READ, *and* END-IF *are used with COBOL 85 only.*

B. Sample Input Data

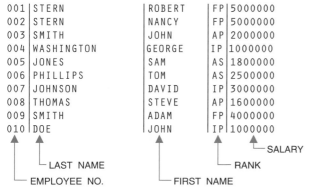

```
001 STERN          ROBERT      FP 5000000
002 STERN          NANCY       FP 5000000
003 SMITH          JOHN        AP 2000000
004 WASHINGTON     GEORGE      IP 1000000
005 JONES          SAM         AS 1800000
006 PHILLIPS       TOM         AS 2500000
007 JOHNSON        DAVID       IP 3000000
008 THOMAS         STEVE       AP 1600000
009 SMITH          ADAM        FP 4000000
010 DOE            JOHN        IP 1000000
```
                                        └─ SALARY
        └─ LAST NAME   └─ RANK
└─ EMPLOYEE NO.   └─ FIRST NAME

C. Sample Output

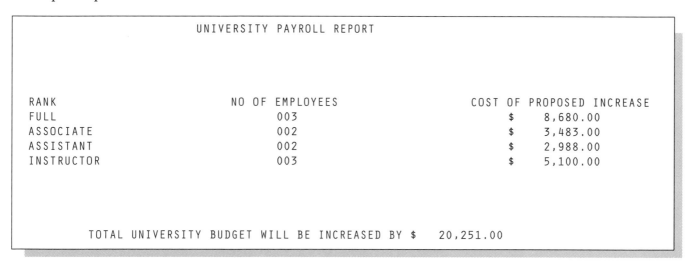

```
                        UNIVERSITY PAYROLL REPORT



RANK                        NO OF EMPLOYEES              COST OF PROPOSED INCREASE
FULL                             003                        $        8,680.00
ASSOCIATE                        002                        $        3,483.00
ASSISTANT                        002                        $        2,988.00
INSTRUCTOR                       003                        $        5,100.00




        TOTAL UNIVERSITY BUDGET WILL BE INCREASED BY $      20,251.00
```

Figure 5.7 Hierarchy chart for Practice Program 1.

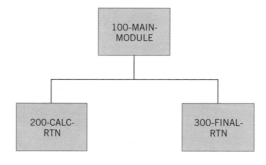

PRACTICE PROGRAM 2

Read in records with the following fields.

Name
Sex (M = Male, F = Female)
Color of eyes (1 = Blue, 2 = Brown, 3 = Other)
Color of hair (1 = Brown, 2 = Blonde, 3 = Other)

Write a pseudocode and draw a flowchart to print the names of all (1) blue-eyed, blonde males and (2) all brown-eyed, brown-haired (brunette) females. See Figure 5.8 for a suggested solution.

Figure 5.8   Pseudocode and flowchart for Practice Program 2.

Pseudocode (With two modules and two in-line PERFORMs)

MAIN-MODULE
START
            Housekeeping Operations
            PERFORM UNTIL no more records (Are-There-More-Records = 'NO ')
                        READ a record
                                    AT END
                                                Move 'NO ' to Are-There-More-Records
                                    NOT AT END
                                                PERFORM Process-Rtn
                        END-READ
            END-PERFORM
            End-of-Job Operations
STOP

PROCESS-RTN
            IF   Sex = 'M'
            THEN
                        PERFORM
                                    IF   Eyes = 1
                                    THEN
                                                IF   Hair = 2
                                                THEN
                                                            Move Name to Print
                                                            Write a Line
                                                END-IF
                                    END-IF
                        END-PERFORM
            ELSE
                        PERFORM
                                    IF   Eyes = 2
                                    THEN
                                                IF   Hair = 1
                                                THEN
                                                            Move Name to Print
                                                            Write a Line
                                                END-IF
                                    END-IF
                        END-PERFORM
            END-IF

Figure 5.8 (continued)

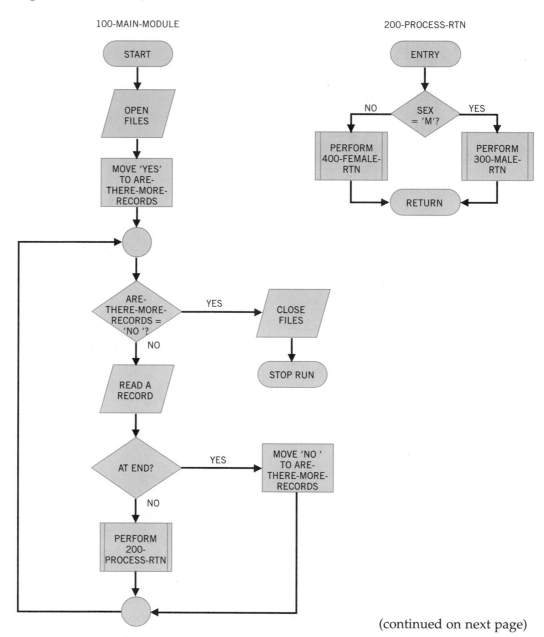

(continued on next page)

Figure 5.8 (continued)

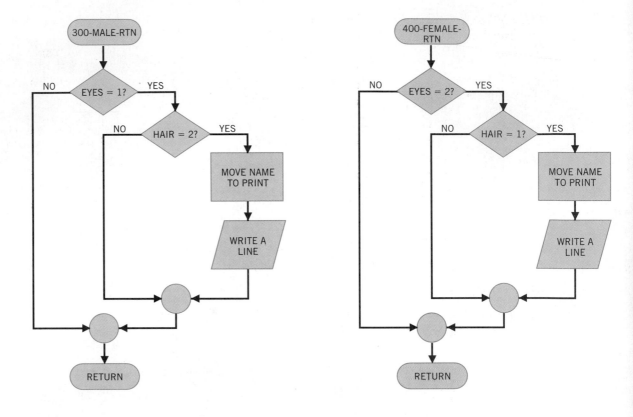

REVIEW QUESTIONS

I. Fill in the Blanks

1. A flowchart is used for analyzing the _____ in a program.
2. Different symbols in a flowchart are used to denote different _____ .
3. An input/output symbol is coded as _____ .
4. A processing symbol is coded as _____ .
5. All flowchart symbols have notes within them indicating the specific _____ to be performed.
6. Pseudocodes have been used with increasing frequency in place of _____ for representing the logical flow to be used in a program.
7. A hierarchy chart is used for depicting the _____ in a program.
8. A decision symbol corresponds to the logical control structure of _____ .
9. The last word written in an IF sequence in a pseudocode is _____ .
10. What two verbs are used for interactive input/output? How do they differ from READ and WRITE?
11. (T or F) Most logic errors are detected by the compiler and listed as diagnostic messages.
12. (T or F) You can use a DISPLAY for debugging purposes to view output data to be created on disk.
13. (T or F) Testing a program with one or two sample input records is usually sufficient.

II. General Questions

1. Indicate in each case whether the pseudocode and flowchart accomplish the same thing:

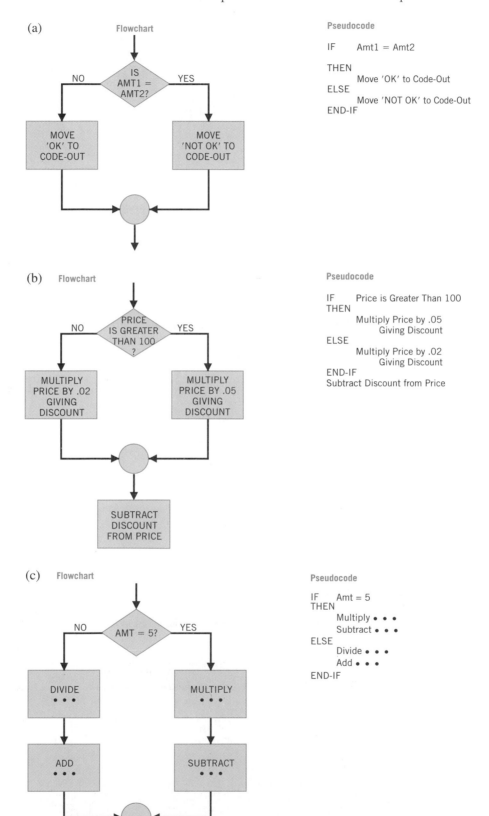

(a)   **Flowchart**

Pseudocode

```
IF      Amt1 = Amt2

THEN
        Move 'OK' to Code-Out
ELSE
        Move 'NOT OK' to Code-Out
END-IF
```

(b)   **Flowchart**

Pseudocode

```
IF      Price is Greater Than 100
THEN
        Multiply Price by .05
                Giving Discount
ELSE
        Multiply Price by .02
                Giving Discount
END-IF
Subtract Discount from Price
```

(c)   **Flowchart**

Pseudocode

```
IF      Amt = 5
THEN
        Multiply • • •
        Subtract • • •
ELSE
        Divide • • •
        Add • • •
END-IF
```

2. Is the following selection permitted in a structured flowchart? Explain your answer.

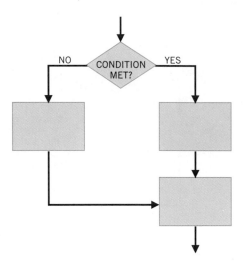

3. Write a pseudocode and draw a flowchart to accomplish each of the following:
    (a) Add 1 to MINOR if a field called AGE is 17 or less.
    (b) Add 1 to LARGE if SIZE-IN is greater than 500; add 1 to SMALL if SIZE-IN is less than or equal to 500.
    (c) If the value of a field called HOURS-WORKED is anything but 40, perform a routine called 200-ERROR-RTN.
    (d) Read in an exam grade. If the grade is 60 or greater, print the word PASS; otherwise print the word FAIL.

4. What is the meaning of each of the following when used in a Format Statement?
    (a) [ ]
    (b) { }
    (c) uppercase words
    (d) lowercase words
    (e) underlined words
    (f) ellipses (...)

PROGRAMMING ASSIGNMENTS

1. Consider the pseudocode in Figure 5.9.

    With the following input records, what will be the contents of TOTAL at the end of all operations?

Record No.	Contents of Record Position 18	Contents of Record Position 19
1	1	2
2	1	3
3	1	2
4	1	0
5	(blank)	(blank)
6	(blank)	1
7	1	(blank)
8	1	2
9	1	2
10	(blank)	2

2. Draw a flowchart for the program logic depicted in Question 1.

Figure 5.9 Pseudocode for Programming Assignment 1.

```
START
      Open all files
      Set Total to 0
      Set Are-There-More-Records to 'YES'
      PERFORM UNTIL Are-There-More-Records = 'NO '
            READ a record
                  AT END
                              Move 'NO ' to Are-There-More-Records
                  NOT AT END
                              PERFORM 200-Calc-Rtn
            END-READ
      END-PERFORM
      Move Total to print area
      Print Total
      Close all files
STOP


200-CALC-RTN
      IF position 18 = 1
      THEN
            IF position 19 NOT = 2
            THEN
                  Add 2 to Total
            END-IF
      ELSE
            IF position 19 = 2
            THEN
                  Add 1 to Total
            END-IF
      END-IF
```

3. Use the pseudocode in Figure 5.10 to answer the following questions.
   (a) A disk-1 record is written after reading how many input records? Explain.
   (b) The pseudocode indicates that a record is printed after reading how many input records? Explain.
   (c) The pseudocode indicates that a disk-2 record is written after reading how many input records? Explain.

4. Draw a flowchart equivalent to the pseudocode in Figure 5.10.

5–9. Although flowcharts, pseudocode, and hierarchy charts should be drawn before a program is written, go back to Chapter 4 and write a pseudocode and draw a hierarchy chart for each of the Programming Assignments numbered 1–5.

10. **Interactive Processing.** Write a program to create an inventory file interactively, prompting the user for input (i.e., you should code DISPLAY 'ENTER PART-NO' before ACCEPT PART-NO). For purposes of this Programming Assignment, assume that UNIT-PRICE is an integer field (i.e., there are no decimal positions). The format for the inventory records is as follows:

INVENTORY Record Layout		
Field	**Size**	**Type**
PART-NO	5	Alphanumeric
PART-DESCRIPTION	15	Alphanumeric
QTY-ON-HAND	5	Alphanumeric
UNIT-PRICE	5	Alphanumeric

Figure 5.10 Pseudocode for Programming Assignment 3.

```
START
      Open all files
      Set Are-There-More-Records to 'YES'
      Set Counter-3 to 10
      Set Counter-2 to 20
      Set Counter-1 to 5
      PERFORM UNTIL no more records
            READ a record
                  AT END
                              Move 'NO ' to Are-There-More-Records
                  NOT AT END
                              PERFORM 200-Calc-Rtn
            END-READ
      END-PERFORM
      Close all files
STOP

200-CALC-RTN
      Subtract 1 from Counter-1
      IF Counter-1 = 0
      THEN
            Write a disk-1 record
            Subtract 1 from Counter-2
            IF Counter-2 = 0
            THEN
                  PERFORM 300-Print-Rtn
            END-IF
            Set Counter-3 to 5
      END-IF

300-PRINT-RTN
      Print a record
      Subtract 1 from Counter-3
      IF Counter-3 = 0
      THEN
            Write a disk-2 record
            Set Counter-3 to 10
            Set Counter-2 to 20
      ELSE
            Set Counter-2 to 20
      END-IF
```

11. Maintenance Program.   Modify Practice Program 1 in this chapter so that the following salary increases are used for determining the overall effect on the budget:

   4.3% for full professors
   4.8% for associate professors
   5.2% for assistant professors
   5.7% for instructors

In addition, print the total number of faculty.

CHAPTER 6

Moving Data, Printing Information, and Displaying Output Interactively

INTRODUCTION

The **MOVE** statement has the following components:

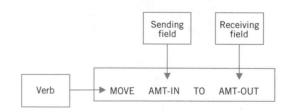

Every COBOL statement in the PROCEDURE DIVISION, like every English sentence, must contain a verb. A COBOL statement usually starts with a verb. In the preceding, MOVE is the verb. The identifier or data-name AMT-IN is called the **sending field.** The contents of AMT-IN will be transmitted or copied to the second field, AMT-OUT, as a result of the MOVE operation. AMT-OUT is called the **receiving field.** The contents of AMT-OUT will be replaced by the contents of AMT-IN when the MOVE operation is executed. AMT-IN will remain unchanged.

The MOVE statement, like all COBOL imperative statements, appears in the PROCEDURE DIVISION. AMT-IN and AMT-OUT are identifiers defined in the DATA DIVISION. You will recall that elementary items in the DATA DIVISION require PICTURE or PIC clauses to indicate (1) the type of data in the field (numeric, alphanumeric, or alphabetic) and (2) the size of the field. To perform a MOVE operation that replaces the contents of AMT-OUT with the *very same contents* as AMT-IN, the PICTURE clauses of both fields must be identical.

Example 1

```
                        MOVE TAX-IN TO TAX-OUT

    TAX-IN  PICTURE  999            TAX-OUT  PICTURE  999
            CONTENTS 123                     CONTENTS 456
```

When MOVE TAX-IN TO TAX-OUT is executed, the contents of TAX-OUT will be replaced by 123, the contents of TAX-IN. This will occur only if TAX-IN and TAX-OUT have identical PIC clauses (in this case, 999). The original contents of the receiving field, TAX-OUT in this example, is replaced during the MOVE operation.

Note also that in a MOVE operation, the contents of the sending field, TAX-IN in this case, is duplicated or copied at the receiving field, TAX-OUT. Thus, at the end of the MOVE operation, both fields will have *the same contents*. The contents of TAX-IN remains unchanged after the MOVE.

Example 2

```
                        MOVE CODE-IN TO CODE-OUT

    CODE-IN  PICTURE  XXXX           CODE-OUT  PICTURE  XXXX
             CONTENTS ABCD                     CONTENTS EFGH
```

After MOVE CODE-IN TO CODE-OUT is executed, CODE-OUT has ABCD as its contents and CODE-IN also remains with ABCD. Since the fields have the same PICTURE clauses, they will have identical contents after the MOVE operation.

THE INSTRUCTION FORMATS OF THE MOVE STATEMENT

We have thus far discussed one instruction format of the MOVE statement:

Format 1

```
                    MOVE identifier-1 TO identifier-2
```

Identifier-1 and identifier-2 are data-names that are defined in the DATA DIVISION. To obtain in identifier-2 the same contents as in identifier-1, the PICTURE clauses of both fields must be the same.

A second form of the MOVE statement is as follows:

Format 2

```
                    MOVE literal-1 TO identifier -2
```

Recall that there are two kinds of literals: numeric and nonnumeric. The rules for forming these literals are as follows:

REVIEW OF LITERALS

Numeric Literals

1. 1 to 18 digits.

2. Decimal point (optional, but it may not be the rightmost character).

3. Sign (optional, but if included it must be the leftmost character).

Nonnumeric or Alphanumeric Literals

1. 1 to 160 characters for COBOL 85 (120 is the upper limit for COBOL 74).

2. Any characters may be used (except the quote mark or apostrophe).

3. The literal is enclosed in single quotes or apostrophes in this text. Some compilers use double quotes to delimit literals.

The following are examples of MOVE statements where a literal is moved to a data-name or identifier:

Example 1
```
05   DEPT-OUT                      PIC 999.
     :
     :
MOVE 123 TO DEPT-OUT      ◄————A numeric literal is moved
```

Example 2
```
05   CLASSIFICATION-OUT      PIC X(5).
     :
     :
MOVE 'CODE1' TO CLASSIFICATION-OUT   ◄————A nonnumeric literal is moved
```

(Your compiler may require double quotes rather than single quotes for nonnumeric literals. Many compilers permit either.)

Although identifiers are defined in the DATA DIVISION, literals may be defined directly in the PROCEDURE DIVISION. Assuming an appropriate PICTURE clause in the receiving field, the exact contents or value of the literal will be moved to the receiving field. Keep in mind that the receiving field of any MOVE instruction must *always* be an identifier, never a literal.

In Example 1, 123 is a numeric literal. It must be a literal and not an identifier because it contains all numbers; identifiers must have at least one alphabetic character. To move a numeric literal to a field, the field should have the same data type as the literal. Thus, in Example 1, the receiving field, DEPT-OUT, should be numeric. To obtain exactly 123 in DEPT-OUT, DEPT-OUT should have a PIC of 999.

In Example 2, 'CODE1' is a nonnumeric literal. We know that it is not an identifier because it is enclosed in quotation marks. To move a nonnumeric literal to a field, the field must have the same format as the literal. Thus, CLASSIFICATION-OUT must have a PIC of X's to indicate that it is alphanumeric. To obtain exactly 'CODE1' as the contents of CLASSIFICATION-OUT, CLASSIFICATION-OUT must have a PIC clause of X(5).

To say MOVE 123 TO ADDRESS-OUT would be poor form if ADDRESS-OUT had a PICTURE of XXX, because the literal does *not* have the same format as the receiving field. If ADDRESS-OUT has a PICTURE of X(3), the literal to be moved to it should be nonnumeric. Thus, we should code: MOVE '123' TO ADDRESS-OUT.

The MOVE statement can also move a figurative constant to an identifier. Recall that a figurative constant is a COBOL reserved word, such as SPACE (or SPACES) or ZERO (or ZEROS or ZEROES), that represents a specific value.

The following examples illustrate the use of figurative constants in a MOVE statement:

Example 3

> MOVE ZEROS TO TOTAL-OUT

ZEROS is a figurative constant meaning all 0's. Since 0 is a valid numeric character and also a valid alphanumeric character, TOTAL-OUT may have a PIC of 9's or a PIC of X's. In either case, TOTAL-OUT will be filled with all zeros. When moving ZEROS to a receiving field, a zero will be placed in every position of that field regardless of its size.

Example 4

> MOVE SPACES TO HEADING1

SPACES is a figurative constant meaning all blanks. Since blanks are not valid numeric characters, the PICTURE clause of HEADING1 must specify X's, indicating an alphanumeric field, or A's, indicating an alphabetic field. Again, the size of HEADING1 is not relevant since blanks will be placed in every position.

─────────── DEBUGGING TIP ───────────

1. Nonnumeric literals, not numeric literals, should be moved to alphanumeric fields. The receiving field determines how the move is performed.
2. As noted previously, we typically use X's in a PICTURE clause of nonnumeric fields and avoid the use of A's.

SELF-TEST   Use the following statement to answer Questions 1–5.

> MOVE NAME-IN TO NAME-OUT

1. MOVE is called the _____ . NAME-IN is called the _____ . NAME-OUT is called the _____ .
2. Assume NAME-IN has contents of SAM and NAME-OUT has contents of MAX; assume also that the fields have the same PICTURE clauses. At the end of the MOVE operation, NAME-OUT will have _____ as its contents and NAME-IN will contain _____ .
3. In a MOVE operation, the sending field may be a(n) _____ or a(n) _____ or a(n) _____ .
4. What are the two kinds of literals that may serve as a sending field in a MOVE operation?
5. The receiving field in a MOVE operation is always a(n) _____ .

Use the following statement to answer Questions 6 and 7.

> MOVE A12 TO FIELD3

6. A12 must be a(n) _____ and not a nonnumeric literal because it is not _____ .
7. If the identifier A12 has contents of 453, _____ will be moved to FIELD3 and A12 will have _____ as its contents at the end of the operation.

Use the following statement to answer Questions 8–11.

> MOVE 'AB1' TO FIELD6

8. The sending field is a _____ .
9. The sending field cannot be an identifier because it is _____ .
10. To obtain exactly AB1 in FIELD6, the PICTURE clause of the receiving field should be _____ .
11. 'AB1' (is, is not) defined in the DATA DIVISION.

12. In the statement MOVE 12384 TO SAM, the sending field must be a numeric literal and not a data-name because it _____ .

13. In the statement MOVE SPACES TO HEADING-OUT, SPACES is a _____ , and HEADING-OUT would have a(n) _____ PICTURE clause. The contents of HEADING-OUT will be replaced with _____ at the end of the operation.

14. In the statement MOVE ZEROS TO TOTAL-OUT, TOTAL-OUT may have a(n) _____ PICTURE clause. After the MOVE, TOTAL-OUT will contain _____ .

15. In the statement MOVE 'SPACES' TO CODE-OUT, where CODE-OUT has a PICTURE OF X(6), 'SPA-CES' is a _____ . The contents of CODE-OUT will be _____ at the end of the operation.

Solutions
1. verb or operation; sending field; receiving field
2. SAM; SAM (*Note:* The contents of a sending field remains unchanged.)
3. literal; identifier (data-name); figurative constant
4. Numeric and nonnumeric (or alphanumeric) literals
5. identifier or data-name
6. identifier; enclosed in quotation marks
7. 453; 453
8. nonnumeric literal
9. enclosed in quotation marks
10. XXX or X(3)
11. is not (Literals appearing in the PROCEDURE DIVISION need not be defined elsewhere in the program.)
12. contains no alphabetic character
13. figurative constant; alphanumeric or alphabetic; blanks or spaces
14. alphanumeric or numeric; 0's (*Note:* ZERO is a valid numeric and alphanumeric character.)
15. nonnumeric literal (it is enclosed in quotes); the word SPACES

NUMERIC MOVE

We will divide our discussion of the MOVE statement into two parts: numeric MOVEs and nonnumeric MOVEs. We discuss numeric moves in this section. A numeric MOVE is one in which a numeric field or literal is moved to a numeric receiving field.

WHEN SENDING AND RECEIVING FIELDS HAVE THE SAME PIC CLAUSES

We have seen that if the PIC clauses of both fields are identical, the contents of identifier-2 will be replaced with the contents of identifier-1 and the sending field will be unchanged.

WHEN SENDING AND RECEIVING FIELDS HAVE DIFFERENT PIC CLAUSES

Sometimes we may need to move one numeric field to another, where the sizes of the two fields differ. You might want to move a smaller field to a larger one to perform an arithmetic operation on it; or you may want to move a work area with precision of three decimal places (V999) to an output area that requires precision of only two decimal places (V99). In both cases, the MOVE operation will *not* produce the same contents in the receiving field as in the sending field, since the sizes of the two fields differ. We will see that in no case is any data of the original receiving field retained after the MOVE. We will also see that decimal alignment is always maintained.

Two rules apply in numeric MOVE operations—one for the movement of the integer portion of a number, and one for the movement of the decimal or fractional portion. Let us focus first on the rule for integer moves:

Moving Integer Portions of Numeric Fields

> **RULE 1: MOVING INTEGER PORTIONS OF NUMERIC FIELDS**
>
> When moving an integer sending field or an integer *portion* of a numeric sending field to a numeric receiving field, movement is from *right* to *left*. All nonfilled **high-order** (leftmost) integer positions of the receiving field are replaced with zeros.

Example 1
**The Receiving Field
Has More Integer
Positions Than The
Sending Field**

Operation: `MOVE AMT-IN TO AMT-OUT`

```
AMT-IN   PICTURE  999          AMT-OUT   PICTURE  9(4)
            CONTENTS 123                    CONTENTS 4567
```

According to Rule 1, movement is from right to left:

(a) The 3 in `AMT-IN` replaces the 7 in `AMT-OUT`.

(b) The 2 in `AMT-IN` replaces the 6 in `AMT-OUT`.

(c) The 1 in `AMT-IN` replaces the 5 in `AMT-OUT`.

and all nonfilled high-order positions are filled with zeros:

(d) 0 replaces the 4 in `AMT-OUT`.

Thus we obtain 0123 in `AMT-OUT`:

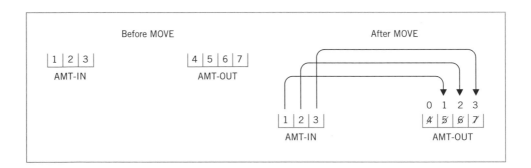

As noted, no portion of the original contents of the receiving field is retained after any `MOVE` is performed.

Avoiding Truncation

In numeric `MOVE` operations be sure that the receiving field has at least as many integer positions as the sending field. If the receiving field has more integer positions than the sending field, its high-order positions will be replaced with zeros. If, however, the receiving field has fewer integer positions than the sending field, you may inadvertently **truncate** or cut off the most significant digits.

Example 2
**An Illustration of
Truncation**

Operation: `MOVE TAKE-HOME-PAY TO AMT-OF-CHECK`

```
TAKE-HOME-PAY  PICTURE  9(4)     AMT-OF-CHECK  PICTURE  999
                  CONTENTS 1000                  CONTENTS 999
```

In this example, the receiving field has only three positions. Since movement of integer positions is from right to left, 000 will be placed in `AMT-OF-CHECK`. The high-order 1 is truncated, which will undoubtedly upset the check's recipient:

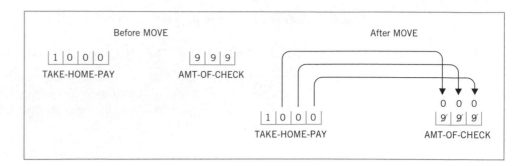

If a sending field has more integer positions than a receiving field, most compilers will print a warning-level syntax error during compilation. This will not, however, affect execution of the program, so the program could be run with this error in it. The software developer must ensure that the receiving field has at least as many integer positions as the sending field.

Moving Decimal Portions of Numeric Fields

The rule for moving decimal positions of numeric fields is as follows:

RULE 2: MOVING DECIMAL PORTIONS OF NUMERIC FIELDS

When moving a decimal portion of a numeric sending field to the decimal portion of a numeric receiving field, movement is from *left* to *right*, beginning at the implied decimal point. **Low-order** (rightmost) nonfilled decimal positions of the receiving field are replaced with zeros.

Example 3
The Receiving Field Has More Decimal Positions Than The Sending Field

Operation: MOVE COST-IN TO COST-OUT

COST-IN   PICTURE   99V99   COST-OUT   PICTURE   99V999
          CONTENTS 12ᴧ34   CONTENTS 56ᴧ789

The integer portion of COST-IN replaces the integer portion of COST-OUT, according to Rule 1. The decimal portion of each field initially contains the following:

According to Rule 2, movement is from the implied decimal point on and is from left to right:

   (a) The 3 of COST-IN replaces the 7 of COST-OUT.
   (b) The 4 of COST-IN replaces the 8 of COST-OUT.

Low-order nonfilled decimal positions of the receiving field are replaced with zeros:

   (c) 0 replaces the 9 of COST-OUT.

Thus we have the following in the receiving field after the MOVE:

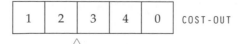

Note that decimal alignment will always be maintained in a numeric MOVE.

Example 4
The Receiving Field
Has Fewer Decimal
Positions Than The
Sending Field

Operation: MOVE DISCOUNT-IN TO DISCOUNT-OUT

DISCOUNT-IN   PICTURE   V99   DISCOUNT-OUT   PICTURE   V9
                CONTENTS ∧12   CONTENTS ∧3

Movement from the implied decimal point on is from left to right. Thus the 1 of DISCOUNT-IN replaces the 3 of DISCOUNT-OUT. The operation is terminated at this point since DISCOUNT-OUT has only one decimal position. The result, then, in DISCOUNT-OUT is ∧1.

Example 5
The Sending Field Has
More Integer and
Decimal Positions
Than the Receiving
Field

Operation: MOVE QTY-IN TO QTY-OUT

QTY-IN   PICTURE   999V9   QTY-OUT   PICTURE   99
            CONTENTS 123∧4   CONTENTS 00

Since integer movement is from right to left, the 3 of QTY-IN replaces the low-order or rightmost 0, and the 2 of QTY-IN replaces the high-order or leftmost zero. Since there are no more integer positions in the receiving field, the integer portion of the move is terminated. The operation itself is complete at this point, since there are no decimal positions in QTY-OUT. Thus the contents of QTY-OUT is 23 after the MOVE:

MOVING NUMERIC LITERALS TO NUMERIC FIELDS

Numeric literals are moved to fields in exactly the same manner as numeric fields are moved. The same rules for moving integer and decimal portions of one field to another apply.

Example 6
The Sending Field Is a
Numeric Literal with
Integers Only

Operation: MOVE 123 TO LEVEL-NO-OUT

05   LEVEL-NO-OUT   PICTURE 9(4).

Since there are only integers in this example, movement is from right to left and nonfilled high-order positions of the receiving field are replaced with zeros. Thus we obtain 0123 in LEVEL-NO-OUT. Treat the literal 123 as if it were LEVEL-NO-IN with a PICTURE of 999, contents 123, and proceed as if MOVE LEVEL-NO-IN TO LEVEL-NO-OUT is performed.

Example 7
The Sending Field Is a
Numeric Literal with a
Decimal Component

Operation: MOVE 12.34 TO PRICE-OUT

05   PRICE-OUT   PICTURE 99V999.

Note that the numeric literal is coded with a decimal point where intended, but the decimal point is only implied in PRICE-OUT. The integers in the sending field are transmitted, so that 12 is moved to the integer positions of PRICE-OUT. Movement from the implied decimal point on is from left to right, the result being 34 in the first two decimal positions of PRICE-OUT. Nonfilled low-order decimal positions of PRICE-OUT are replaced with zeros. Thus PRICE-OUT will contain 12∧340. Note again that the result is the same as if we had performed the operation MOVE PRICE-IN TO PRICE-OUT, where PRICE-IN had a PICTURE of 99V99, and contents 12∧34.

The numeric MOVE operation functions exactly the same whether the sending field is a literal or an identifier. Treat a numeric literal as if it were a field in storage, and proceed according to the two rules specified in this section.

MOVING SIGNED NUMBERS: AN INTRODUCTION

If a numeric field can have negative contents, then it must have an S in its PIC clause. If we code MOVE −123 TO AMT1, for example, then AMT1 should be defined with a PIC S9(3). An S should be included in the PIC clause of a numeric field whenever the sign of the number is to be retained. We discuss signed numbers in more detail in the next chapter.

SELF-TEST   Use the following statement to complete Questions 1–4.

MOVE TAX TO TOTAL

	TAX		**TOTAL**	
	PICTURE	*Contents*	PICTURE	*Contents (after* MOVE*)*
1.	99V99	10ᴧ35	999V999	_____
2.	9(4)	1234	999	_____
3.	99V99	02ᴧ34	9V9	_____
4.	9V9	1ᴧ2	_____	ᴧ20

5. The specific questions from the preceding group that might give undesirable results are _____ .

6. The operation MOVE 12.487 TO WORK-AREA is performed. To obtain the *exact* digits of the literal in the field called WORK-AREA, its PICTURE clause must be _____ .

7. In a numeric MOVE operation, there (are, are not) instances when some significant portion of the data in the receiving field is retained and not replaced with something else.

Solutions

1. 010ᴧ350
2. 234
3. 2ᴧ3
4. V99
5. 2 and 4—Truncation of the high-order or most significant integer occurs.
6. 99V999
7. are *not* (*Note: All* positions of the receiving field are replaced either with data from the sending field or with zeros.)

NONNUMERIC OR ALPHANUMERIC MOVE

BASIC RULES

Recall that we separated the MOVE operation into two categories: *numeric* MOVE, discussed in the previous section, and *nonnumeric* or alphanumeric MOVE, which we will discuss here. By a nonnumeric MOVE operation, we mean:

NONNUMERIC MOVE

1. Moving an alphanumeric or alphabetic field, defined by a PICTURE of X's or A's, to another alphanumeric or alphabetic field.

2. Moving a nonnumeric literal to an alphanumeric or alphabetic field.

3. Moving a numeric field or numeric literal to an alphanumeric field or to any group item.

When the receiving field has a PICTURE of X's or A's, or is a group item, the move is treated as a nonnumeric move. There is only one rule for such moves:

RULE FOR NONNUMERIC MOVE

In a nonnumeric move, data is transmitted from the sending field to the receiving field from *left* to *right*. Low-order or rightmost positions of the receiving field that are not replaced with sending field characters are filled with spaces.

Example 1
The Receiving Field Is Larger Than the Sending Field

Operation: MOVE NAME-IN TO NAME-OUT

NAME-IN   PICTURE XXX   NAME-OUT   PICTURE X(5)
          CONTENTS ABC   CONTENTS DEFGH

According to the rule, data is transmitted from left to right. Thus,

(a) The A of NAME-IN replaces the D of NAME-OUT.
(b) The B of NAME-IN replaces the E of NAME-OUT.
(c) The C of NAME-IN replaces the F of NAME-OUT.

Low-order positions of NAME-OUT are replaced with spaces. Thus,

(d) A blank replaces the G of NAME-OUT.
(e) A blank replaces the H of NAME-OUT.

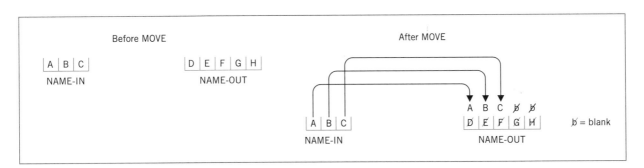

NAME-OUT will contain ABCℬℬ after the MOVE, where ℬ represents a blank. Again, no portion of the receiving field is retained after the move.

The effect of this operation would have been the same if the following were performed: MOVE 'ABC' TO NAME-OUT.

Example 2
The Receiving Field Is Smaller Than the Sending Field

Operation: MOVE CODE-IN TO CODE-OUT

CODE-IN   PICTURE X(4)   CODE-OUT   PICTURE XXX
          CONTENTS NAME   CONTENTS (BLANKS)

In this case

(a) The N of CODE-IN replaces the leftmost blank of CODE-OUT.
(b) The A of CODE-IN replaces the middle blank of CODE-OUT.
(c) The M of CODE-IN replaces the rightmost blank of CODE-OUT.

The operation is terminated at this point, since the entire receiving field is filled. The result would have been the same if the following were performed: MOVE 'NAME' TO CODE-OUT. In either case, truncation occurs, but with nonnumeric MOVEs it is the rightmost characters that are truncated. As in the case of numeric moves, truncation will be avoided if the receiving field is at least as large as the sending field. Here, again, a warning level syntax error will alert the programmer to the fact that a sending field is larger than a receiving field, but program execution will continue.

Example 3
The Sending Field Is
Numeric Integer and
the Receiving Field
Is Nonnumeric

Operation: MOVE UNIT-IN TO UNIT-OUT

UNIT-IN	PICTURE	999	UNIT-OUT	PICTURE	XXXX
	CONTENTS	321		CONTENTS	DCBA

Note that although UNIT-IN is a numeric integer field, this operation is considered to be an *alphanumeric* MOVE because the receiving field is alphanumeric. It is always the receiving field that determines the type of move.

(a) The 3 of UNIT-IN replaces the D of UNIT-OUT.
(b) The 2 of UNIT-IN replaces the C of UNIT-OUT.
(c) The 1 of UNIT-IN replaces the B of UNIT-OUT.
(d) A space replaces the A of UNIT-OUT.

UNIT-OUT will contain 321ƀ after the MOVE, where ƀ represents a blank. If UNIT-OUT had a PIC 9(4), the results would have been different. That is, 0321 would be stored in UNIT-OUT. We recommend that you avoid mixing data types when performing a MOVE operation. Note that attempting to move a numeric field that has a V in its PIC clause to a nonnumeric field results in a syntax error.

Moving Literals or Figurative Constants to Nonnumeric Fields

Literals or figurative constants can also be moved to nonnumeric fields:

Example 4
The Sending Field Is a
Nonnumeric Literal

Operation: MOVE 'ABC' TO CODE-OUT

05 CODE-OUT PICTURE X(5).

The result will be ABCƀƀ in CODE-OUT.

Example 5
The Sending Field Is a
Figurative Constant

Operation: MOVE SPACES TO NAME-OUT

05 NAME-OUT PICTURE X(5).

Regardless of the size of NAME-OUT, it will contain all blanks after the MOVE.

As a rule, do not move alphanumeric fields to numeric fields. The move will be performed by the computer, but the results could cause a program interrupt or termination of the job if the receiving field is used later on in an arithmetic operation and it does not contain numeric data.

A GROUP MOVE IS CONSIDERED A NONNUMERIC MOVE

All group items, even those with numeric subfields, *are treated as alphanumeric fields*. Consider the following:

Example

Suppose we want to represent January 1998 as 0198 in DATE-OUT, which has been defined as a group item:

```
05  DATE-OUT.
    10  MONTH-OUT   PICTURE 99.
    10  YEAR-OUT    PICTURE 99.
```

Because MONTH-OUT and YEAR-OUT are numeric fields, MOVE 1 TO MONTH-OUT and MOVE 98 TO YEAR-OUT would result in 0198 in DATE-OUT. If, however, the programmer attempts to move data into

Figure 6.1   Permissible MOVE operations.

Sending Field	Receiving Field			
	Numeric	**Alphabetic**	**Alphanumeric**	**Group item**
Numeric	√	x	√*	√
Alphabetic	x	√	√	√
Alphanumeric	x	√	√	√
ZEROS ⎱ Figurative	√	x	√	√
SPACES ⎰ constants	x	√	√	√
Group item	x	√	√	√

*Numeric integer fields can be moved to alphanumeric fields but numeric fields with a V in the PIC clause cannot be moved to alphanumeric fields.

DATE-OUT, DATE-OUT will be treated as an alphanumeric field because it is a group item. The statement MOVE '198' TO DATE-OUT would erroneously result in 198Ƅ in DATE-OUT, *not* 0198 as it would if the month and year were moved separately.

We typically initialize a record with a group MOVE. Consider the following:

The word FILLER must be used here with COBOL 74

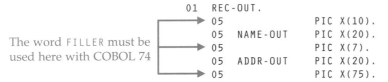

```
01  REC-OUT.
    05              PIC X(10).
    05  NAME-OUT    PIC X(20).
    05              PIC X(7).
    05  ADDR-OUT    PIC X(20).
    05              PIC X(75).
```

We could clear the entire output area with the following group MOVE instruction: MOVE SPACES TO REC-OUT.

Figure 6.1 is a chart outlining the various MOVE operations. A check (√) denotes that the move is permissible; an x denotes that it is not.

Sending fields are of six types: numeric, alphabetic, alphanumeric, the figurative constant ZEROS, the figurative constant SPACES, and group item. Numeric, alphabetic, and alphanumeric sending fields can be either identifiers *or* literals. A numeric field is moved in the same manner as a numeric literal. The receiving fields refer only to identifiers that can be numeric, alphabetic, alphanumeric, and group fields. A literal or figurative constant cannot serve as a receiving field. Note that when mixed data types appear, the MOVE operation is always performed in the format of the receiving field. We recommend that you avoid mixing data types in MOVE operations.

SELF-TEST

1. In a nonnumeric move, data is transmitted from (left, right) to (left, right).

2. In a nonnumeric move, if the receiving field is larger than the sending field, (right-, left-) most positions are replaced with _____ .

Use the following statement to complete Questions 3–5.

```
MOVE CODE-IN TO CODE-OUT
```

	CODE-IN		**CODE-OUT**	
	PICTURE	*Contents*	PICTURE	*Contents (after MOVE)*
3.	X(4)	AB12	X(6)	_____
4.	X(4)	AB12	X(3)	_____
5.	XXX	ABC	_____	AB

6. Suppose TOTAL-OUT has a PIC of X(5) and we code MOVE '0' TO TOTAL-OUT. What would the contents of TOTAL-OUT be at the end of the MOVE? Would this be the same as moving ZEROS to TOTAL-OUT?

OTHER OPTIONS OF THE MOVE STATEMENT

QUALIFICATION OF NAMES

If the same name is used to define fields in different records or group items, indicate which record or group item is to be accessed by qualifying the identifier with the word OF or IN. If AMT is both an input and an output field, we cannot code ADD AMT TO TOTAL, since AMT is the name of two different fields and it is unclear which is to be added. We could say instead ADD AMT OF IN-REC TO TOTAL.

When more than one field in storage has the same name, we qualify the name in the PROCEDURE DIVISION as follows:

Format

$$\text{identifier-1} \left\{ \begin{matrix} \underline{\text{OF}} \\ \underline{\text{IN}} \end{matrix} \right\} \left\{ \begin{matrix} \text{record-name-1} \\ \text{group-item-name-1} \end{matrix} \right\}$$

Example

    ADD AMT OF IN-REC TO TOTAL

The words OF and IN may be used interchangeably to qualify a name.

A field-name may be qualified by using OF or IN with the name of either a record or group item of which the field is a part. Consider the following:

    01 REC-IN.
        05 CODE-IN.
            10 GENDER   PIC X.
            10 MARITAL-STATUS PIC X.

If the identifier GENDER defines more than one field in the DATA DIVISION, the GENDER field may be accessed as GENDER OF REC-IN or GENDER OF CODE-IN. Both REC-IN and CODE-IN serve to uniquely identify the GENDER field referenced.

Coding Guidelines

Coding the same identifier to define several fields in separate records is frequently considered a useful programming tool. Many people believe that qualification of names makes PROCEDURE DIVISION entries easier to understand for someone reading the program, and easier to debug.

On the other hand, most installations prefer software developers to use unique names with descriptive prefixes or suffixes to define data. To say, for example, MOVE AMT-IN TO AMT-OUT, where AMT-IN is an input field and AMT-OUT is an output field, is often considered better form than saying MOVE AMT OF IN-REC TO AMT OF OUT-REC. We recommend that you use prefixes or suffixes rather than qualify names in the PROCEDURE DIVISION.

PERFORMING MULTIPLE MOVES WITH A SINGLE STATEMENT

The full instruction format for a MOVE statement is as follows:

Full Format for the MOVE Instruction

$$\underline{\text{MOVE}} \left\{ \begin{matrix} \text{identifier-1} \\ \text{literal-1} \end{matrix} \right\} \underline{\text{TO}} \text{ identifier-2} \dots$$

A Review of Instruction Format Rules

The braces { } mean that either of the two elements may be used as a sending field. The receiving field must be a data-name or identifier. Uppercase words like MOVE and TO are reserved words. Because they are underlined, they are required in the statement. The ellipses or dots at the end of the statement mean that one sending field can be moved to numerous receiving fields.

Example

```
MOVE 'ABC' TO CODE-1
               CODE-2
               CODE-3
```

If CODE-1, CODE-2, and CODE-3 each has a PIC of X(3), then the literal ABC will be transmitted to all three fields. Recall that the commas in this example are for readability only; they do not affect the compilation.

One way of initializing a series of fields to zero at the beginning of a procedure is to use a multiple move:

```
MOVE ZEROS TO WS-AMT
               WS-TOTAL
               WS-COUNTER
```

REFERENCE MODIFICATION: ACCESSING SEGMENTS OF A FIELD USING COBOL 85

It is possible to reference a portion of an elementary item with COBOL 85. Consider the following:

```
MOVE 'TOM CRUISE' TO NAME-IN
MOVE NAME-IN (5:6) TO NAME-OUT
```

The first digit in parentheses indicates the start of the MOVE. Thus, movement begins with the fifth position of NAME-IN. The second digit in parentheses indicates the length of the MOVE. Thus, positions 5–10 of NAME-IN are moved to NAME-OUT. In this way, 'CRUISE' will be moved to NAME-OUT.

Suppose we READ or ACCEPT a telephone number with an area code so that '516-555-1212' is entered in TELEPHONE-NO. To extract just the area code, we could write MOVE TELEPHONE-NO (1:3) TO AREA-CODE.

Note that defining a field as a group item with elementary subfields is, in general, preferable, but sometimes reference modification can be useful.

PRINTING OUTPUT

FEATURES OF PRINTED OUTPUT

Files that are maintained by computer must be printed or displayed in order to be accessed by users. *Output* that is *displayed* on a screen is useful for answering inquiries about the status of a file or for quick, interactive results. *Printed reports*, on the other hand, are formal documents that provide users with the information they need to perform their jobs effectively. Because computer-produced displays and reports are to be read by people, they must be clear, neat, and easy to understand. Whereas conciseness and efficiency are the overriding considerations for designing disk files, clarity is the primary concern when designing displayed output and printed reports.

Several characteristics, not applicable to disk output, must be considered when designing and preparing reports:

Use of Edit Symbols

A disk record may, for example, have two amount fields with the following data: 00450 and 3872658. Although these fields are appropriate in disk files, the printed report should contain this information in *edited form* to make it more meaningful to the user. For example, $450.00 and $38,726.58 are better methods of presenting the data. **Edit symbols** are used to make data fields clearer, neater, and more readable.

Spacing of Forms

The lines on printed output must be properly spaced for ease of reading. Some lines might be single-spaced, others double-spaced, and so on. Moreover, printed output must have margins at both the top and bottom of each page. This requires the computer to be programmed to sense the end of a page and then to transmit the next line of information to a new page.

Alignment of Information

Reports do not have fields of information adjacent to one another as is the practice with disk. Printed output is more easily interpreted when fields are spaced evenly across the page. We have seen how the Printer Spacing Chart is used for planning the output design so that detail lines and heading lines are properly spaced for readability. There is a set of Printer Spacing Charts at the back of the book that you can use to plan your output.

Printing Headings, Total Lines, and Footings

We typically establish a print area as 80, 100, or 132 characters per line depending on the printer used. Three types of headings may appear on each page of a report:

1. *Report heading*—includes a title for the report, date, etc. This heading may appear once at the beginning of the report or on each page.
2. *Page heading*—appears on each page and may include page numbers, distribution list, etc. Often a single heading on each page serves both as a report and page heading.
3. *Column heading*—identifies the fields that will print on subsequent lines.

Figure 6.2 is a **Printer Spacing Chart** that illustrates the three types of headings. The first heading, a report heading, supplies the report name; the second heading, a page heading, supplies a page number and date; the third heading, a column heading, describes the fields to be printed. The headings are neatly spaced across the form, as noted in the Printer Spacing Chart. All headings are printed on each page, since continuous forms are separated after they are generated.

Figure 6.2 Printer Spacing Chart that illustrates a report heading, a page heading, and column headings.

Total lines and footings may also appear at the end of a page or report. Page footings appear at the end of each page, and report footings appear at the end of the report.

The Printer Spacing Chart

The Printer Spacing Chart helps ensure that (1) headings appear properly spaced across the page and (2) fields are properly aligned under column headings and are evenly spaced across the page.

In most of our examples, the Printer Spacing Chart is subdivided into 132 print positions. The headings are spaced evenly across the page. From the numbered positions, the programmer can determine in which print positions he or she should place the literals and which positions should be left blank. If you use an 80 position or 100 position printer, you would cut the Printer Spacing Chart so that it includes only the number of positions you need.

In our illustration in Figure 6.2, note that, for the first heading line, print positions 1–56 will be left blank as will print positions 77–132. The literal 'MONTHLY TRANSAC-TIONS' will be placed in the area between. On the Printer Spacing Chart, X's indicate where alphanumeric data will be placed and 9's indicate where numeric data will be placed. Twenty X's under the column heading CUSTOMER NAME, for example, denote that the field contains 20 nonnumeric characters. Edit symbols can be used on the Printer Spacing Chart as well. The H's in the left margin designate the lines as headings; the D designates the line as a detail or data line. If total lines were included, they would be designated with a T. If end-of-page or end-of-report footings were to print, designate these lines with an F for footing.

Because printed information has characteristics different from other output, we study the printed report as a separate topic.

THE EDITING FUNCTION

The following editing functions will be discussed:

EDITING FUNCTIONS

1. Printing of decimal points where decimal alignment is implied.

2. Suppression of leading zeros.

3. Printing of dollar signs and commas.

4. Printing of asterisks for check protection.

5. Printing of plus or minus signs.

6. Printing of debit or credit symbols for accounting applications.

7. Printing of spaces or zeros as separators within fields.

The first six editing functions just described may only be performed on *numeric* fields that have PICTURE clauses consisting of 9's. The last editing function, the printing of zeros or spaces as separators, may be performed on *any* type of field.

All **editing** is accomplished by moving an elementary item to a **report-item**, which is a field that contains appropriate edit symbols. An elementary item, you will recall, is a field with a PIC clause; that is, it is a data item that is not further subdivided. A *report-item* is an elementary item that has the appropriate PIC clause to perform editing functions. Note that it is the PIC clause of the receiving field, the report-item, that determines the editing to be performed. The operation of editing is accomplished by moving a numeric sending field to a receiving field that has edit symbols in its PIC clause.

As in *all* MOVE operations, the sending field remains unchanged after the data has been transmitted to the report-item. The report-item itself may be defined as part of the output record or in a WORKING-STORAGE area that will be moved to the output area before printing. We will see later on that it is best to define output record formats in WORKING-STORAGE.

We will see in the next chapter that the GIVING option of the arithmetic verbs (ADD, SUBTRACT, MULTIPLY, DIVIDE) permits the receiving field to be a report-item. Thus, if ADD AMT1 AMT2 GIVING RESULT is coded, RESULT may be a report-item that includes edit symbols.

AMT1 and AMT2 must be strictly numeric because they are part of the arithmetic operation. If RESULT is a report-item, it could not be used in any arithmetic operation other than as a receiving field.

Thus, we can accomplish editing by (1) moving a field to a report-item or (2) performing an arithmetic operation where the result is a report-item.

Printing Decimal Points

As indicated in previous illustrations, a field such as TAX, with PICTURE 99V99 and contents of $12_\wedge 35$, should print as 12.35 when edited. It is through editing that the implied decimal point will be replaced with an actual decimal point. That is, printing TAX as is would result in output of 1235 since implied decimal points do not print.

The appropriate report-item that will print a decimal point will have a PICTURE of 99.99. The decimal point, which would not appear in the PICTURE clause of a numeric item, is part of a report-item. It instructs the computer to place an actual decimal point where it is implied in the sending field. The sending field in this instance should have a PICTURE of 99V99.

A sending field with PICTURE 99V99 takes *four* storage positions, since implied decimal points do not use storage, whereas the corresponding report-item takes *five* positions, since a real decimal point does, in fact, use one position. The number 12.35, when printed, uses five print positions.

Suppressing Leading Zeros

Nonsignificant or leading zeros are zeros appearing in the leftmost positions of a field and having no significant value. For example, 00387 has two leading zeros. Nonsignificant zeros should generally be omitted when printing. That is, 00387 should print as ƀƀ387, since the two numbers are numerically equivalent and the latter is easier to read. (The ƀ represents a blank.) The operation to perform this type of editing is called **suppression of leading zeros**. Note that the number 10000 has *no* leading zeros. Thus we would not want to suppress the printing of any zeros in 10000.

The edit symbol [Z] is used to suppress leading zeros and to replace them with blanks or spaces. WS-TOTAL, with a PICTURE of 999, might be edited by moving it to TOTAL-OUT, with a PICTURE of ZZZ.

Each Z represents one storage position that may accept data from a sending field. In addition, any nonsignificant zeros encountered in the sending field will be replaced with blanks. Thus, the following are examples of how WS-TOTAL will print depending on its initial value:

038 will print as ƀ38
003 will print as ƀƀ3
000 will print as ƀƀƀ

Any number that does not have leading zeros, such as 108, will print as is.

When suppressing leading zeros, the sending field must be defined as numeric. The receiving field should accept the *same number of integers* as are in the sending field. PICTURE ZZZ is a three-position storage area that may accept three integers and will suppress all leading zeros.

Often it is desirable to suppress only some leading zeros. Consider the case where the contents of four sending fields denoting Charitable Deductions are 0020, 4325, 0003, and 0000, respectively. The output may be as follows.

```
                              SAMPLE OUTPUT

                                               DEDUCTIONS
           NAME                  SALARY         FOR CHARITY

           P.  NEWMAN            13872               20
           B.  STREISAND         40873             4325
           B.  REYNOLDS          10287                3
           T.  SELLECK           25382
```

All leading zeros for the Deductions field are suppressed. The PICTURE clause for the report-item is ZZZZ or Z(4).

As may be evident from this illustration, it is sometimes inadvisable to leave fields completely blank when a zero balance is implied. Users who are skeptical about the accuracy of computer output tend to regard blank fields suspiciously. Perhaps T. SELLECK did, in fact, make a contribution, but the computer, through machine malfunction, failed to indicate it. Or, the field may have been left blank and is to be supplied later.

For these reasons, it is sometimes good practice to print a *single* zero when a zero balance exists. In this way, the report will leave no doubt about the charitable inclinations of T. SELLECK.

Thus, if the four-position charity field has contents 0000, we want it to print as ⸴⸴⸴0. That is, we want only the three leftmost positions of the field to be zero suppressed and the rightmost position to print *without* suppressing the zero. The PICTURE clause of the report-item, then, would be ZZZ9. Z's indicate numeric characters to be zero suppressed, and 9's indicate numeric characters to be printed without zero suppression. Hence 0000 will print as ⸴⸴⸴0 if the report-item PICTURE clause is ZZZ9 or Z(3)9.

The combined use of Z's and 9's in a report-item requires that all Z's *precede* any 9's. Zeros may be suppressed only if they precede significant digits.

We can combine the two editing functions thus far discussed so that we zero suppress *and* place decimal points in the edited field. The following examples will clarify both types of editing. We are assuming edited results are obtained by the operation: MOVE SENDING-FIELD TO REPORT-ITEM. Edited results may also be obtained by using the GIVING option of an arithmetic statement or by using the COMPUTE statement.

Examples of Decimal Point Insertion with Zero Suppression			
Sending-Field		**Report-Item**	
PICTURE	*Contents*	PICTURE	*Edited Results*
1. 99V99	02ᴧ38	ZZ.99	⸴2.38
2. 99V99	00ᴧ03	ZZ.99	⸴⸴.03
3. 99V99	00ᴧ05	Z9.99	⸴0.05

Since numeric positions to the right of a decimal point have significance even when they are zero, we will *not* perform zero suppression on these quantities. That is, .01 should *not* be edited to read .1, since the two numbers are not numerically equivalent.

There is one exception to this rule. COBOL allows you to use a report-item with PICTURE ZZ.ZZ. This will suppress zeros to the right of the decimal point *only if the entire field is zero,* in which case all spaces will print. Thus 00ᴧ03 prints as ⸴⸴.03 but

$00_\wedge00$ prints as five blanks. Because this PICTURE clause may be confusing, we will not, in general, use it.

Be Sure to Size the Report-Item Correctly

The number of Z's representing integers in the report-item should be equal to the number of integers or 9's in the sending field. Including too many Z's or two few Z's may produce either a syntax error or incorrect results, depending on the compiler being used.

If the sending field has decimal positions, however, we may truncate them if desired by including only integer Z's in the report-item. Similarly, an integer-only sending field may be made to print as a dollars and cents field by using .99 or .ZZ in the report-item. The following illustrates these points:

Examples of Decimal Point Insertion and Truncation of Decimal Digits			
Sending-Field		**Report-Item**	
PICTURE	*Contents*	PICTURE	*Contents*
1. 9(3)V99	$008_\wedge27$	Z(3)	ƀƀ8
2. 9(3)	027	Z(3).99	ƀ27.00
3. 9(3)	018	Z(3).ZZ	ƀ18.00
4. 9(3)	000	Z(3).ZZ	ƀƀƀƀƀƀ

In all instances, the number of Z's to the left of the decimal point must equal the number of integer 9's in the sending field.

Printing Dollar Signs and Commas

Dollar signs and commas are editing symbols frequently used in conjunction with the suppression of leading zeros and the printing of decimal points, since many numeric quantities often appear on printed reports as dollars and cents figures. The dollar sign and comma are placed in the positions in which they are desired, as in the case with decimal points. The following examples illustrate this point:

Examples of Dollar Sign and Comma Insertion

	Sending-Field		**Report-Item**	
	PICTURE	*Contents*	PICTURE	*Edited Results*
1.	9(4)V99	$3812_\wedge34$	$9,999.99	$ 3 , 8 1 2 . 3 4
2.	99V99	$05_\wedge00$	$ZZ.99	$ 5 . 0 0
3.	999V99	$000_\wedge05$	$ZZZ.99	$. 0 5
4.	9(4)V99	$0003_\wedge82$	$Z,ZZZ.99	$ 3 . 8 2

In Example 1, the sending field uses six storage positions, whereas the receiving field uses nine. Dollar signs, commas, and decimal points each use one position of storage. When defining the print record in the DATA DIVISION, nine positions must be included in the report-item for this example. Editing typically results in the use of more storage positions for a report-item to be printed than if the data were printed without editing.

Examples 2 through 4 illustrate zero suppression with dollar sign and comma insertion. In Examples 2 and 3, leading zeros are replaced with spaces. Thus, there are blanks between the dollar sign and the first significant digit. Example 4 indicates that the zero suppression character Z will also eliminate or suppress leading commas. Note that the result of the edit was *not* $, 3.82 , but $ 3.82 . Thus, a comma will be appropriately suppressed if no significant digit precedes it. In Example 4, *four* spaces will appear between the dollar sign and the first significant digit, three for the suppressed zeros and one for the suppressed comma.

Recall that the report-item must allow for the same number of integer positions as the sending field, but it can include *additional decimal positions* if desired. AMT-IN, with PICTURE 99 and contents 40, may be edited by moving it to AMT-OUT, with PICTURE $ZZ.99. In this case, the two decimal places are filled with zeros. The result, then, in AMT-OUT will be $40.00.

Printing Asterisks (*) for Check Protection

The suppression of zeros, with the use of Z, in conjunction with the printing of dollar signs may, at times, prove unwise. Suppose we are using the computer to print checks. To print $ .05, as in Example 3, would be inadvisable since the blanks between the dollar sign and the decimal point may easily be filled in by a dishonest person. Using a typewriter, someone could collect $999.05 on what should be a $.05 check.

To prevent such occurrences, a **check protection symbol,** the asterisk (*), is used in place of blanks when leading zeros are to be suppressed. Using a report-item with check protection *'s, Example 3 would print as $***.05. In this way, it would be more difficult to tamper with the intended figure.

To print an asterisk in place of a blank when zero suppression is to be performed, use an *✱* instead of a *Z* in each position. Asterisks are zero-suppression characters that replace each nonsignificant zero and comma with * instead of a space.

Examples of Zero Suppression with Asterisk Insertion			
Sending-Field		**Report-Item**	
PICTURE	*Contents*	PICTURE	*Edited Results*
1. 9(3)V99	123∧45	$***.99	$123.45
2. 9(3)V99	012∧34	$***.99	$*12.34
3. 9(5)V99	00234∧56	$**,***.99	$***234.56

The asterisk is used most often for the printing of checks or when there is some concern that resultant amount fields might be tampered with. Under other conditions, the use of Z's for normal zero suppression is sufficient.

Printing Plus or Minus Signs

A PIC of 9's is used to define an unsigned numeric field that will contain positive numbers. A PIC clause with a leading S defines a field that is signed. PIC S99, for example, defines a two-digit signed field. To store −120 in a numeric field, for example, the PIC clause should be S9(3).

Printing Minus Signs.   Unless the computer is instructed to do otherwise, all numeric quantities will print without a sign. When reports are printed, we interpret the absence of a sign as an indication of a positive number.

If we wish to print a minus sign when a number is negative, we must use an editing symbol. As noted, the PICTURE clause of a numeric sending field must contain an S if it can have negative contents. Without the S, the field will be considered unsigned.

To print a minus sign for a negative sending field, we use the edit symbol *−* . This minus sign may be placed *either* to the right *or* to the left of the report-item. A minus sign will print in the corresponding position *only if* the sending field is negative.

In the examples that follow, the sign of a number in a sending field is indicated by placing it above the low-order or rightmost position of the number. The computer uses the rightmost position for storing the sign along with the low-order digit. (We discuss this in more detail in Chapter 7.) Consider the following:

Examples of Minus Sign Insertion			
Sending-Field		**Report-Item**	
PICTURE	*Contents**	PICTURE	*Edited Results*
1. S999	12$\bar{3}$	−999	−123
2. S999	12$\bar{3}$	999−	123−
3. 999	123	−999	⌿123
4. S999	12$\overset{+}{3}$	−999	⌿123
5. S99V99	02$_\wedge$3$\bar{4}$	ZZ.99−	⌿2.34−

*The sign of the number may be stored along with the rightmost digit (see Chapter 7).

Examples 1 and 2 illustrate that if the sending field is negative, the edited results print with the minus sign. Examples 1 and 2 also illustrate that the minus sign within a report-item may print to the right or the left of a field. Examples 3 and 4 illustrate that *no* sign will print if the sending field is signed positive or unsigned. Example 5 illustrates the use of the minus sign in conjunction with other editing symbols such as the Z.

Printing Either a Minus or Plus Sign. There are occasions when a sign is required for *both* positive and negative quantities. That is, we may want a + sign to print when the field is unsigned or signed positive, and a − sign to print when the field is signed negative. The edit symbol ⊟ would not be used because it generates the minus sign only if the quantity is negative and omits a sign for all other quantities.

To print either a plus sign *or* a minus sign for *all* values, the edit symbol ⊞ is used. To edit a sending field by moving it to a report-item with a + in its PICTURE clause will instruct the computer to always generate a sign. A + sign will be generated for positive or unsigned quantities, and a − sign will be generated for negative quantities. Once again, the sending field should have an S in its PIC clause for it to be interpreted as a signed number.

Like the minus sign, the plus sign may be made to appear either to the left or to the right of a field. Consider the following examples:

Examples of Plus or Minus Sign Insertion			
Sending-Field		**Report-Item**	
PICTURE	*Contents*	PICTURE	*Contents*
1. S999	12$\overset{+}{3}$	+999	+123
2. S999	12$\overset{+}{3}$	999+	123+
3. S999	12$\bar{3}$	+999	−123
4. S9999V99	0387$_\wedge$2$\bar{5}$	+Z,ZZZ.99	−⌿⌿387.25

Printing Debit and Credit Symbols for Accounting Applications

For most applications, a plus or minus sign to indicate positive or negative quantities is sufficient. For accounting applications, however, a minus sign often indicates either a debit or a credit to a particular account.

The edit symbols ⎮DB⎮, for debit, or ⎮CR⎮, for credit, may be used in place of the minus sign. If an amount is to be *debited* to an account *when it is negative*, DB will be used. If a quantity is to be *credited* to an account *when it is negative*, CR will be used. Here again, the sending field should have an S in its PIC clause for it to be interpreted as a signed number.

The DB and CR symbols must always be specified to the *right* of the report-item. Unlike the minus sign itself, these symbols may *not* be used to the left of a field. If the amount is negative and CR or DB is used, then either CR or DB will print, respectively. If the field is unsigned or signed positive, neither CR nor DB will print.

Whereas a minus sign uses *one* storage position, CR and DB each use *two* positions. The following examples illustrate the use of CR and DB:

Examples of CR or DB Insertion			
Sending-Field		**Report-Item**	
PICTURE	Contents	PICTURE	Contents
1. S999	$12\bar{3}$	999CR	123CR
2. S999	$12\bar{3}$	999DB	123DB
3. S999	$12\overset{+}{3}$	999CR	123ƀƀ
4. S999	$12\overset{+}{3}$	999DB	123ƀƀ

Printing Spaces, Zeros, or Slashes as Separators within Fields

Suppose the first nine positions of an input record contain a Social Security number. If the field is printed without editing, it might appear as: 080749263. For ease of reading, a better representation might be 080 74 9263. Spaces between the numbers would add clarity.

Any field, whether nonnumeric or numeric, may be edited by placing blanks as separators within the field. The edit symbol $\boxed{B}$ in a PICTURE clause of a report-item will cause a space to be inserted in the corresponding position.

Zeros and slashes may also be inserted into fields for editing purposes. The edit symbol $\boxed{0}$ or $\boxed{/}$ in the PICTURE clause of a report-item will cause a 0 or / to be inserted in the corresponding position of the receiving field without loss of characters from the sending field.

The following illustrates the use of spaces, zeros, or slashes in a report-item:

Examples of Blanks, Zeros, and Slashes as Separators				
	Sending-Field		**Report-Item**	
Identifier	PICTURE	Contents	PICTURE	Edited Results
SSNO	9(9)	089743456	999BB99BB9999	089 74 3456
NAME	X(10)	PASMITHƀƀƀ	XBXBX(8)	P A SMITH
QTY-IN-100S	999	153	99900	15300
DATE-IN	9(6)	010598	99/99/99	01/05/98

Note, again, that spaces, zeros, or slashes can print as separators within *any type of field*. For all other editing operations discussed here, only *elementary* numeric items may be used. Recall that group items, even if they are subdivided into numeric fields, are treated as alphanumeric items by the computer. Thus, to obtain a valid numeric edit, only *elementary items* may be used.

──────── DEBUGGING TIPS ────────

Editing may be performed in two ways: (1) by *moving* a sending field to a report-item; or (2) by performing an arithmetic operation and placing the result in a report-item. It is the PICTURE clause of the report-item itself that determines what type of editing is to be performed.

The following, however, results in an error if TOTAL-OUT is a report-item:

Invalid

```
ADD WS-TOTAL TO TOTAL-OUT
```

The computer performs ADD instructions, and any other arithmetic operations, on numeric fields only. TOTAL-OUT, as a report-item, is *not* a numeric field. To use TOTAL-OUT as a report-item, it must follow the word GIVING in an ADD or other arithmetic operation.

Table 6.1 reviews edit operations.

—————————————————————DEBUGGING TIPS—————

1. A VALUE clause may be shorter but not longer than the corresponding PIC clause.
2. Do not use VALUE clauses with report-items.

De-editing

Using COBOL 85 you may *de-edit* a report-item by moving it to a numeric field. The following, for example, is permitted:

```
01  REC-A.
    05  AMT-EDITED          PIC $ZZ,ZZZ.99
    :
    :
01  REC-B.
    05  AMT-UNEDITED         PIC 9(5)V99.
    :
    :
    MOVE AMT-EDITED TO AMT-UNEDITED
```

Here, again, the receiving field must be large enough to accept the number of digits that are transmitted by the sending field.

Table 6.1

Review of Edit Operations			
Sending Field		**Report-Item**	
PICTURE	Contents	PICTURE	Edited Results
1. 9(6)	123456	$ZZZ,ZZZ.99	$123,456.00
2. 9999V99	0012∧34	$Z,ZZZ.99	$ 12.34
3. 9(5)V99	00001∧23	$**,***.99	$*****1.23
4. S9(6)	01234$\bar{5}$	+Z(6)	− 12345
5. S9(6)	12345$\overset{+}{6}$	−Z(6)	123456
6. S9999V99	1234∧5$\overset{+}{6}$	+Z(4).99	+ 1234.56
7. S999	12$\bar{3}$	ZZZ−	123−
8. 9(6)	123456	99BBBB9999	12 3456
9. S99	0$\bar{5}$	$ZZ.99DB	$ 5.00DB
10. 999	123	999000	123000
11. S99V99	12∧3$\bar{4}$	$ZZ.99CR	$12.34CR

Interactive Processing. When accepting input interactively, it is best to enable users to key in the data in standard decimal form. That is, if a dollars-and-cents AMT field is to be entered, users are less likely to make mistakes if they can include the actual decimal point. But if the field is entered with a decimal point it cannot be used in an arithmetic operation. De-editing is useful in this instance:

```
01  AMT-IN      PIC 999.99.
01  WS-AMT      PIC 999V99.
    :
    :
    DISPLAY 'ENTER AN AMOUNT FIELD'
    ACCEPT AMT-IN
    MOVE AMT-IN TO WS-AMT
```

In this way, the user can enter the amount with the decimal point (e.g., 123.45), which can then be moved to a field with an implied decimal point so that arithmetic can be performed.

SELF-TEST

1. All editing must be performed on _____ fields except editing using _____ .
2. To say MULTIPLY UNITS BY QTY GIVING TOTAL (is, is not) correct if TOTAL is a report-item.
3. What is a report-item?
4. How many storage positions must be allotted for a report-item with PICTURE $*,***.99?
5. Will an error occur if you move a field with PIC 9(4) to a report-item with PIC ZZZ? Explain.
6. Suppose NAME-FIELD with a PICTURE X(15) is part of an input record, where the first two positions of the field contain a first initial and a second initial. To edit this field so that a space appears between INITIAL1 and INITIAL2, and another space between INITIAL2 and LAST-NAME, what is the PIC clause of the report-item?

For Questions 7 through 20, fill in the edited results.

	Sending-Field PICTURE	Contents	Receiving-Field PICTURE	Edited Results
7.	9(6)	000123	ZZZ,999	
8.	9(6)	123456	ZZZ,999.99	
9.	9(4)V99	0000ˬ78	$Z,ZZ9.99	
10.	S9(4)V99	0000ˬ78̅⁺	$Z,ZZZ.99CR	
11.	S9(4)V99	0000ˬ7̄8̄	$Z,ZZZ.99CR	
12.	S9(6)	12345̄6̄	-999,999	
13.	9(6)	123456	-999,999	
14.	S999	12̄3̄⁺	-999	
15.	999	123	+999	
16.	S999	12̄3̄⁺	+999	
17.	S999	12̄3̄	-999	
18.	9(6)	000092	Z(6)00	
19.	X(6)	123456	XXXBBXXX	
20.	9(4)V99	0012ˬ34	$*,***.99	

Solutions

1. elementary numeric; zeros, blanks, or slashes as field separators
2. is
3. A report-item is a field to be printed that contains edit symbols.
4. Nine
5. Yes—A report-item must accept the same number of integers as appear in the sending field.
6. XBXBX(13)
7. ᵇᵇᵇᵇ123
8. 123,456.00
9. $ 0.78
10. $ .78
11. $ .78CR

12. −123,456
13. ⊘123,456
14. ⊘123
15. +123
16. +123
17. −123
18. ⊘⊘⊘⊘9200
19. 123   456
20. $∗∗∗12.34

EDITING USING FLOATING STRINGS

Examine the following sample output:

CUSTOMER NAME	QTY SOLD	AMT
J. SMITH	5,000	$38,725.67
A. JONES	− 2	$ 3.00CR

Note that the dollar sign of AMT and the minus sign of QTY SOLD for A. JONES are separated from the actual numeric data by numerous spaces. This is because the report-item must contain enough positions to accommodate the entire sending field. If the sending field has many nonsignificant zeros (e.g., 00003∧00), numerous blank positions will appear between the dollar sign and the first significant digit, or the sign and the first significant digit.

With the use of **floating strings,** a leading edit character such as a plus sign, minus sign, or dollar sign may appear in the position *directly* preceding the first significant digit. A dollar sign or a plus or a minus sign may be made to "float" with the field. That is, a floating string will cause suppression of leading zeros (and commas) and, *at the same time,* force the respective floating character to appear in the position *adjacent to the first significant digit.*

With the proper use of floating strings in PICTURE clauses of report-items, the following sample output may be obtained:

	Sending-Field Contents	Report-Item Edited Results
1.	00004∧00	$4.00
2.	038̄7	−387
3.	000005	+5

You will note that in this sample output the dollar sign, minus sign, or plus sign always appears in the position *directly* preceding the first significant digit. Only these three edit symbols may be made to float in this way.

To perform a floating-string edit operation, two steps are necessary:

1.   Create the report-item PICTURE clause as in the previous section. Use the floating character of +, −, or $ in conjunction with Z's.

2.   Then replace all Z's with the corresponding floating character.

Example 1   05 WS-TOTAL   PICTURE 9(4)V99.

Problem: Edit WS-TOTAL by moving it to a report-item called TOTAL-OUT that has a floating dollar sign. Describe the PICTURE clause of TOTAL-OUT.

First, create the PICTURE clause of the report-item as usual: $Z,ZZZ.99.

Then, replace all Z's with the floating character, a dollar sign: $$, $$$. 99. This should be the PICTURE clause for TOTAL-OUT.

Note that there are *five* dollar signs in the report-item. The four rightmost dollar signs are zero suppression symbols. They cause suppression of leading zeros and commas and place the dollar sign in the position adjacent to the first significant digit. The leftmost dollar sign indicates to the computer that $ will be the first character to print. In total, there should be one more dollar sign than integer positions to be edited. *Four* integer positions are edited using *five* dollar signs. In general, n characters may be edited using a floating string of $n + 1$ characters. The extra floating character is needed in case the sending field has all significant positions; that is, the receiving field must have one additional position in which to place the floating character.

Example 2   05 WS-TAX   PICTURE S9(4).

Problem: Edit WS-TAX using a report-item called TAX-OUT that has a floating minus sign.

First, create the PICTURE clause of the report-item according to the rules of the last section, using a minus sign and zero suppression: -ZZZZ.

Then, replace all Z's with the appropriate floating character: – – – – –.

Thus, TAX-OUT will have a PICTURE of – – – – – or – (5).

a. $00\overline{32}$ will print as -32 and   b. $048\overline{7}$ will print as -487

Example 3   QTY-OUT has a PICTURE clause of + + +99.

Problem: Determine the PICTURE clause of the sending field, QTY-IN.

Note that the + will float but not completely. That is, the two rightmost digits always print even if they are leading zeros.

Three plus signs indicate a floating-string report-item that will accept *two* integers. The leftmost plus sign does *not* serve as a zero suppression character and is *never* replaced with integer data. Two digits will be accepted by three plus signs, and two digits will be accepted by two 9's. Thus, the sending field should have a PICTURE of S9(4). Consider the following examples:

a. $038\overline{2}$ will print as -382 and   b. $000\overset{+}{2}$ will print as $+02$

A floating-string character may be used in conjunction with other edit symbols such as 9's, decimal points, and commas, but it must be the leftmost character in the PICTURE clause of the report-item.

We may *not* use *two* floating-string characters in one report-item. If a dollar sign is to float, then a sign may not be placed in the leftmost position of the field. You will recall, however, that signs may also appear in the rightmost position of a report-item. Thus, $$, $$$ .99– is a valid PICTURE clause, but $$, – – – .99 or something similar, is not valid. Only *one* character can float.

BLANK WHEN ZERO OPTION

We may want spaces to print when a sending field consists entirely of zeros. With the use of complex editing, you may find, however, that $.00, −0, or a + or − sign by itself will print. This may detract from the clarity of a report. In such cases, the COBOL expression **BLANK WHEN ZERO** may be used along with the PIC clause for the report-item.

Example   05 QTY-OUT   PICTURE + + +.

This report-item will accept *two* characters of data, as in the following examples:

a. $0\overset{+}{3}$ will print as $+3$ and   b. 00 will print as $+$

To eliminate the printing of + for a zero sending field as in the last case, the BLANK WHEN ZERO option may be added:

Table 6.2

Editing Using Floating Strings and the BLANK WHEN ZERO Option			
Sending-Field		**Report-Item**	
PICTURE	Contents	PICTURE	Edited Results
1. S999V99	012ᴧ34̅	$$$$.99−	$12.34−
2. S999	123̅	− − − −	123
3. S999	005̅	− − − −	−5
4. 99	37	+ + +	+37
5. S99	05̅	+ + +	−5
6. S99	05	+ + +	+5
7. 999	000	+ + + +	+
8. 999V99	000ᴧ00	$$$$.99	$.00
9. 999V99	000ᴧ00	$$$$.99 BLANK WHEN ZERO	

```
05   QTY-OUT   PICTURE + + + BLANK WHEN ZERO.
```

When using the BLANK WHEN ZERO option with a report-item, the normal rules of editing will be followed, depending on the edit symbols in the PICTURE clause. If the sending field is zero, however, spaces will print. We do not use BLANK WHEN ZERO with the * edit symbol.

Table 6.2 reviews the rules for using floating strings and the BLANK WHEN ZERO option.

DEFINING PRINT RECORDS IN WORKING-STORAGE

EACH RECORD FORMAT SHOULD BE ESTABLISHED AS A SEPARATE AREA IN WORKING-STORAGE

Since printed output typically includes lines containing headings, data, error messages, final totals, footings, and so on, each type of output line would be defined as a separate 01-level record in the WORKING-STORAGE SECTION.

In WORKING-STORAGE each record can be treated independently, established with appropriate VALUEs, and printed by moving the WORKING-STORAGE record to PRINT-REC and writing the PRINT-REC:

```
FD   PRINT-FILE
        LABEL RECORDS ARE OMITTED.
01   PRINT-REC            PIC X(132).
WORKING-STORAGE SECTION.
************************************************************
*   note: each 01 occupies a separate area of storage     *
************************************************************
01   HEADING-1.
     05                   PIC X(56)   VALUE SPACES.
     05                   PIC X(20)   VALUE 'MONTHLY TRANSACTIONS'.
     05                   PIC X(56)   VALUE SPACES.
01   HEADING-2.
     05                   PIC X(10)   VALUE SPACES.
     05                   PIC X(6)    VALUE 'PAGE'.
     05   HL-PAGE         PIC 99      VALUE 0.
     05                   PIC X(82)   VALUE SPACES.
     05   HL-DATE         PIC X(8).
     05                   PIC X(24)   VALUE SPACES.
01   HEADING-3.
     05                   PIC X(6)    VALUE SPACES.
     05                   PIC X(13)   VALUE 'CUSTOMER NAME'.
```

←Even fields with actual VALUEs can have a field name that is blank or FILLER

The word FILLER in place of a blank field name is optional with COBOL 85 but is required with COBOL 74

```
        05                      PIC X(17)   VALUE SPACES.
        05                      PIC X(14)   VALUE 'TRANSACTION NO'.
        05                      PIC X(6)    VALUE SPACES.
        05                      PIC X(18)   VALUE 'AMT OF TRANSACTION'.
        05                      PIC XX      VALUE SPACES.
        05                      PIC X(13)   VALUE 'DATE OF TRANS'.
        05                      PIC X(7)    VALUE SPACES.
        05                      PIC X(10)   VALUE 'SHIPPED TO'.
        05                      PIC X(10)   VALUE SPACES.
        05                      PIC X(10)   VALUE 'INVOICE NO'.
        05                      PIC X(6)    VALUE SPACES.
    01  DETAIL-LINE.
        05                      PICTURE X(6)    VALUE SPACES.
        05  DL-NAME             PICTURE X(20).
        05                      PICTURE X(10)   VALUE SPACES.
        05  DL-TRANS-NO         PICTURE X(5).
        05                      PICTURE X(15)   VALUE SPACES.
        05  DL-AMT-OF-TRANS     PICTURE $$,$$$.99.
        05                      PICTURE X(11)   VALUE SPACES.
        05  DL-DATE             PICTURE X(5).
        05                      PICTURE X(15)   VALUE SPACES.
        05  DL-DESTINATION      PICTURE X(10).
        05                      PICTURE X(10)   VALUE SPACES.
        05  DL-INV-NO           PICTURE X(5).
        05                      PICTURE X(11)   VALUE SPACES.
*
    PROCEDURE DIVISION.
        :
        :
        MOVE HEADING-1 TO PRINT-REC
        WRITE PRINT-REC
          :
          :
        MOVE HEADING-2 TO PRINT-REC
        WRITE PRINT-REC
          :
          :
        MOVE HEADING-3 TO PRINT-REC
        WRITE PRINT-REC
          :
          :
        MOVE DETAIL-LINE TO PRINT-REC
        WRITE PRINT-REC
          :
          :
```

Since none of the fields within HEADING-1 and HEADING-3 will be accessed in the PROCEDURE DIVISION, it is customary to leave the field names blank (COBOL 85) or call them all FILLER (COBOL 74), even though some have nonnumeric literals as VALUE clauses. We will leave them blank from this point on. The word FILLER itself is optional if you are using a COBOL 85 compiler. If a field in a heading contains variable data like a page number, we typically define the field with a prefix such as HL-, where HL means *h*eading *l*ine. HL-PAGE and HL-DATE in HEADING-2 are defined this way. We will discuss page numbers and dates in more detail later on.

Note that the DETAIL-LINE contains edit symbols in the field called DL-AMT-OF-TRANS. Input fields or work areas will be moved to that area of the detail line. We use DL- as a prefix for all fields so that they are clearly designated as part of the detail line.

THE WRITE ... FROM STATEMENT

As noted, we use the WORKING-STORAGE SECTION to store records to be printed because a separate area is established for each record and all constants and blanks may be preassigned with VALUE clauses. The data stored in WORKING-STORAGE must, however, be transmitted to the print area and then printed. We can use a **WRITE** (FILE SECTION record) **FROM** (WORKING-STORAGE record) to accomplish this instead of a MOVE and WRITE:

Example   WRITE PRINT-REC FROM HEADING-1

instead of

MOVE HEADING-1 TO PRINT-REC
WRITE PRINT-REC

THE JUSTIFIED RIGHT OPTION

If a **JUSTIFIED RIGHT** option is specified as part of the PIC clause of an alphanumeric field, then a MOVE will right-justify the contents into the field. That is, JUSTIFIED RIGHT can be used to override the normal rules for alphanumeric moves in which data is left-justified in a field. Consider the following:

```
01  HEADING-1.
    05  HL-LITERAL-1      PIC X(76)      JUSTIFIED RIGHT.
    05                    PIC X(56)      VALUE SPACES.
    :
    :
    MOVE 'MONTHLY TRANSACTIONS' TO HL-LITERAL-1
```

The literal 'MONTHLY TRANSACTIONS' will be placed in positions 57–76, *not* 1–20. This is called right-justification.

The use of JUSTIFIED RIGHT can reduce coding by eliminating the need for extra FILLER areas, but it requires the use of a MOVE in the PROCEDURE DIVISION to actually achieve right-justification of data.

THE ADVANCING OPTION FOR SPACING FORMS

Advancing the Paper a Fixed Number of Lines

When a file has been assigned to a printer, a simple WRITE statement will print *one line* of information. After the WRITE instruction, the paper will be advanced *one line* so that *single spacing* results. Single spacing, however, is ordinarily not sufficient for most printing applications. Many programs require double or triple spacing between lines.

We may obtain any number of blank lines between each print line by using an **AFTER ADVANCING** or **BEFORE ADVANCING** option with WRITE instructions for a print file. The format for this WRITE statement is:

Format
```
       WRITE   record-name-1   [FROM   identifier-1]

       [ {AFTER }              {integer-1  }  [LINE  ] ]
       [ {BEFORE}   ADVANCING  {identifier-2}  [LINES ] ]
```

For ease of reading, code the WRITE ... FROM ... on one line and the ADVANCING option indented on the next. The integer, if used, must be nonnegative; similarly, identifier-2, if used, may contain any positive integer.

Typically, the paper can be spaced a maximum of 100 lines. Check your manual for the upper limit on this option for the compiler you are using.

If a line is to print *after* the paper is spaced, use the AFTER ADVANCING option. WRITE PRINT-REC FROM DETAIL-REC AFTER ADVANCING 2 LINES will space two lines and *then* print. That is, after the paper advances two lines, printing will occur. If a line is to print *before* spacing occurs, use the BEFORE ADVANCING option. WRITE PRINT-REC FROM HEAD-ING-REC BEFORE ADVANCING 3 LINES will print and then advance the paper three lines.

The words ADVANCING, LINES, and LINE are not underlined in the instruction format, indicating that they are optional. Hence, the following two statements produce the same results:

```
1.  WRITE PRINT-REC FROM DETAIL-REC
        AFTER ADVANCING 2 LINES
2.  WRITE PRINT-REC FROM DETAIL-REC
        AFTER 2
```

In general, the first WRITE statement is preferred because it is clearer.

Overprinting

The BEFORE ADVANCING option should not be used in the same program as the AFTER ADVANCING option unless overprinting on the same line is desired. That is, consider the following:

```
WRITE PRINT-REC FROM HEADING-REC-1
    AFTER ADVANCING 2 LINES
    :
WRITE PRINT-REC FROM HEADING-REC-2
    BEFORE ADVANCING 2 LINES
```

The first WRITE statement causes two lines to be spaced and then HEADING-REC-1 to be printed. The subsequent WRITE instruction prints *first* and then spaces the form. This means that HEADING-REC-2 will print *on the same line* as HEADING-REC-1. This over-printing would, in general, be incorrect unless you wished to use it for underlining a heading; that is, the first WRITE would print the heading and the second would print the underline. As a rule, to avoid any problems associated with printing two records on the same line, use *either* the BEFORE ADVANCING or the AFTER ADVANCING option in a particular program, but not both. To achieve overprinting or underlining, the second WRITE can be coded as WRITE ... AFTER ADVANCING 0 LINES.

Note, also, that once the ADVANCING option is used for a print file, it should be specified for *all* WRITE statements for that file. Thus, if single spacing is sufficient for the entire report, you may use a simple WRITE statement with no ADVANCING clause. If single spacing is not sufficient, the ADVANCING option should be used with *all* WRITE statements for the print file. In general, we will use the ADVANCING option when writing print records.

Advancing the Paper to a New Page

It is best to print headings at the top of each page and to print a fixed number of lines per page. We will consider the most common method for advancing the paper to a new page.

The PAGE Option

The word **PAGE** used after the word ADVANCING will cause the paper to skip to a new form. Thus, to advance the paper to the top of a new page and print a heading, we can code the following:

```
WRITE PRINT-REC FROM HEADING-REC
    AFTER ADVANCING PAGE
```

HEADING-REC is a record described with appropriate VALUE clauses in the WORKING-STORAGE SECTION.

We can expand the instruction format of the WRITE statement to include *all* options of the ADVANCING clause thus far discussed:

Format—Expanded Version

$$
\text{WRITE} \quad \text{record-name-1} \quad [\text{FROM} \quad \text{identifier-1}]
$$

$$
\left\{ \begin{matrix} \underline{\text{AFTER}} \\ \underline{\text{BEFORE}} \end{matrix} \right\} \quad \text{ADVANCING} \quad \left\{ \begin{matrix} \text{PAGE} \\ \text{identifier-2} \\ \text{integer-1} \end{matrix} \right\} \left[\begin{matrix} \text{LINE} \\ \text{LINES} \end{matrix} \right]
$$

End-of-Page Control—With the Use of a Programmed Line Counter

To ensure that a fixed number of lines print on each page, an end-of-page control routine must be coded. Using a programmed **line counter,** the programmer can control the precise number of lines to be printed per page:

PROGRAMMED LINE COUNTER

1. Determine the number of lines to be printed.

2. Establish a WORKING-STORAGE line-counter field initialized at zero.

3. After each WRITE statement, increment the WORKING-STORAGE line-counter field by one. In this way, the number in the line-counter field will be equal to the number of lines actually printed.

4. Before each WRITE statement, test the line-counter field to see if it equals or exceeds the desired number of lines to be printed per page. If it does, print a heading on the top of a new page and reinitialize the line counter at zero. If the line counter is still less than the desired number of lines per page, continue with the program.

The programmed line counter should be used for all programs where the possibility exists that more than one page of printing will be required. Without such a procedure, the printer will simply print one line after another, paying no attention to page delineations, or perforations on continuous forms. A **continuous form** has all pages connected, with perforations at the end of each page for separating the sheets. Nonimpact printers use individual sheets of paper, but line printers and some character printers use continuous forms. In any case, a line-counter routine is needed to indicate a new page, where headings should be printed first.

Regardless of whether you use continuous forms or individual sheets, you can use a programmed line counter that is incremented by one after a line is written. The procedure should begin by testing to see if the desired number of lines have already been printed (e.g., 50). If so, you can instruct the computer to print a heading on a new page:

Line Counting for Single-Spaced Reports

```
300-PRINT-RTN.
    IF  LINE-COUNT >= 50
        PERFORM 600-HEADING-RTN
    END-IF
    WRITE PRINT-REC FROM DETAIL-REC
        AFTER ADVANCING 1 LINE
    ADD 1 TO LINE-COUNT.
    :
    :
600-HEADING-RTN.
    WRITE PRINT-REC FROM HEADING-REC
        AFTER ADVANCING PAGE
    MOVE ZEROS TO LINE-COUNT.
```

LINE-COUNT must be a WORKING-STORAGE item initialized at zero.

To obtain double spacing instead of single spacing, change the first few lines as follows:

Line Counting for Double-Spaced Reports

```
300-PRINT-RTN.
    IF  LINE-COUNT >= 25
        PERFORM 600-HEADING-RTN
    END-IF
    WRITE PRINT-REC FROM DETAIL-REC
        AFTER ADVANCING 2 LINES
    ADD 1 TO LINE-COUNT.
```

Figure 6.3 Pseudocode for the line-counter routine.

```
IF Line Counter >= 25
THEN
    PERFORM Heading-Rtn
END-IF
Write an Output Line
Add 1 to Line Counter
```

Both routines assume that a page consists of 50 lines. In the first case, we actually print 50 records, one per line. In the second, we print 25 double-spaced records. Thus, in the second routine, we have 25 print records and 25 blank lines. The pseudocode for the latter procedure is illustrated in Figure 6.3.

─────────────── DEBUGGING TIPS ───────────────

Test `LINE-COUNT` prior to writing, because you want to print headings only when there is more output to be generated. If we test `LINE-COUNT` at the end of our `300-PRINT-RTN` and it happens that we reached the end of a page *at the same time* that the last input record was processed, then we will end our report with a heading followed by *no* data. That would be inappropriate unless there are totals to print.

To avoid any potential problems where the number of lines to print may vary depending on the printer or length of paper used, we recommend that you establish a `LINE-LIMIT` field and initialize it with a value equal to the desired number of lines. Then all line-counter routines should compare `LINE-COUNT` to `LINE-LIMIT`. If a change is necessary in the number of lines to print, only the literal moved to that `LINE-LIMIT` needs to be modified; that is, all line-counter routines will be unaffected:

```
MOVE 50 TO LINE-LIMIT
 :
 :
IF  LINE-COUNT >= LINE-LIMIT
    PERFORM 600-HEADING-RTN
END-IF
```

Setting `LINE-LIMIT` to an initial value enables you to change `LINE-LIMIT` any time a form or the number of print lines on a form changes, *without having to modify line-counter routines.*

Note that you should test to see if `LINE-COUNT` is greater than or equal to `LINE-LIMIT` rather than just equal to `LINE-LIMIT`. Suppose `LINE-LIMIT` = 50. If `LINE-COUNT` were 49 previously and you added 2 to it after double-spacing, it would be 51; performing a heading routine that tests to see if `LINE-COUNT` precisely equals `LINE-LIMIT` would not produce the desired result because `LINE-COUNT` could exceed `LINE-LIMIT`. To obtain headings on a new page when a `LINE-COUNT` equals, *or exceeds*, the page limit, use a >= test, rather than an = test, when making the comparison.

SELF-TEST

1. To space the paper two lines and then print a line, the `WRITE` statement would be coded as _____ .

2. Write a COBOL statement to print a `WORKING-STORAGE` record called `TOTAL-LINE` and then advance the form two lines. `PRINT-REC` is defined in the `FILE SECTION`.

3. What, if anything, is wrong with the following statement?

```
WRITE PRINT-REC
    AFTER ADVANCING TWO LINES
```

4. Code a routine to write `PRINT-REC` from `DETAIL-REC` and space two lines; perform a `HEADING-RTN` if 30 lines have already been printed.

5. To skip to a new page, use the phrase AFTER ADVANCING _____ .

Solutions

1. WRITE ... AFTER ADVANCING 2 LINES
2. WRITE PRINT-REC FROM TOTAL-LINE
       BEFORE ADVANCING 2 LINES
3. Use the integer 2, unless TWO has been defined as a field with a value of 2.
4. IF LINE-CT >= 30
       PERFORM 500-HEADING-RTN
   END-IF
   WRITE PRINT-REC FROM DETAIL-REC
       BEFORE ADVANCING 2 LINES
   ADD 1 TO LINE-CT
5. PAGE

PRINTING PAGE NUMBERS

Often, when printing headings, a page number is required as part of either a report or page heading. Consider the following WORKING-STORAGE record:

```
01  HEADING-LINE.
    05              PIC X(60) VALUE SPACES.
    05              PIC X(20) VALUE 'SALARY CHANGES'.
    05              PIC X(8)  VALUE 'PAGE NO'.
    05  HL-PAGE-CT  PIC ZZZZ.
    05              PIC X(40) VALUE SPACES.
```

The word FILLER is optional as a data-name with COBOL 85 but required with COBOL 74

We use the prefix HL- for fields within the *Heading Line.*

A WORKING-STORAGE numeric item defined as WS-PAGE-CT PICTURE 9999 VALUE 0001 is established for actually counting pages. The following 500-HEADING-RTN will print a page number on each page:

```
500-HEADING-RTN.
    MOVE WS-PAGE-CT TO HL-PAGE-CT
    WRITE PRINT-REC FROM HEADING-LINE
        AFTER ADVANCING PAGE
    ADD 1 TO WS-PAGE-CT
    MOVE ZEROS TO LINE-CT.
```

500-HEADING-RTN should be performed initially, after the files are opened in the main module. To execute 500-HEADING-RTN again after the end of a page has been reached, we code our 300-PROCESS-RTN as follows:

```
300-PROCESS-RTN.
    :
    :
    IF  LINE-CT >= 25
        PERFORM 500-HEADING-RTN
    END-IF
    WRITE PRINT-REC FROM DETAIL-REC
        AFTER ADVANCING 2 LINES
    ADD 1 TO LINE-CT.
```

Each time through 500-HEADING-RTN, the page counter, WS-PAGE-CT, is incremented by 1. Before each record is printed, WS-PAGE-CT is moved to the report-item HL-PAGE-CT. Thus, a correct page number will appear on each form with leading zeros suppressed. Note that the following is *not* correct:

Invalid: ADD 1 TO HL-PAGE-CT

HL-PAGE-CT is a report-item containing edit symbols that cause zero suppression. Only *numeric* items may be used in arithmetic operations. HL-PAGE-CT, as a report-item, is not a numeric field and cannot be part of an ADD operation. Hence, a separate field, referred to in this case as `WS-PAGE-CT`, *must* be established in `WORKING-STORAGE` as a numeric field. It is incremented to reflect the actual page number. To suppress leading zeros in the page number, we then move `WS-PAGE-CT` to the report-item `HL-PAGE-CT`, which is defined as part of `HEADING-LINE`.

The `ADD` and `IF` statements will be discussed in greater detail in the next two chapters. Note that `END-IF` is a COBOL 85 scope terminator.

PRINTING THE DATE OF THE RUN

Accepting DATE

The computer stores the current date in a field that can be accessed with the COBOL reserved word **DATE**. DATE stores the run date as a six-digit field consisting of the following elements in the order specified:

DATE
Two-digit year (e.g., 98 for 1998)
Two-digit month (e.g., 02 for February)
Two-digit day (e.g., 01–31)

Suppose, for example, that 980223 is stored in `DATE`. This represents February 23, 1998. We will establish a `WORKING-STORAGE` entry as follows:

```
01   WS-DATE.
     05   RUN-YEAR        PIC 99.
     05   RUN-MONTH       PIC 99.
     05   RUN-DAY         PIC 99.
```

To obtain the current date in `WS-DATE`, we code:

```
                    ACCEPT WS-DATE FROM DATE
```

With this **ACCEPT** statement, there is no need to enter a date as input. The `ACCEPT` statement will move the date in the yymmdd format into the field called `WS-DATE`. (yy = the two-digit year; mm = the month number, dd = the day of the month.) `RUN-YEAR` will contain the two-digit year, `RUN-MONTH` will contain the two-digit month, and `RUN-DAY` will contain the two-digit day.

The format for obtaining the date in a program, then, is as follows:

Format

```
          ACCEPT   identifier-1   FROM DATE
```

The identifier must consist of six numeric characters.

After the `ACCEPT` statement is executed, the identifier will contain the run date as yymmdd (year, month, day). But this date format is not very user-friendly. We would normally want to print this in a more readable form, perhaps as mo/day/yr.

Printing the date as month/day/year could be accomplished with the following coding:

```
WORKING-STORAGE SECTION.
01   WS-DATE.
     05   RUN-YEAR        PIC 99.
     05   RUN-MONTH       PIC 99.
     05   RUN-DAY         PIC 99.
01   HEADING-REC.
       :
       :
```

The word FILLER is optional as a data-name with COBOL 85 but required with COBOL 74

```
       05  DATE-OF-RUN.
           10  MO-OUT    PIC 99.
           10            PIC X     VALUE '/'.
           10  DAY-OUT   PIC 99.
           10            PIC X     VALUE '/'.
           10  YEAR-OUT  PIC 99.
              ⋮
              ⋮
   PROCEDURE DIVISION.
              ⋮
              ⋮
       ACCEPT WS-DATE FROM DATE
       MOVE RUN-MONTH TO MO-OUT
       MOVE RUN-DAY TO DAY-OUT
       MOVE RUN-YEAR TO YEAR-OUT
       WRITE PRINT-REC FROM HEADING-REC
           AFTER ADVANCING PAGE.
```

The date is reformatted and printed with /'s separating month, day, year

If DATE contained 980223, the heading would print with a run date of 02/23/98.

With many compilers, the identifier following the word ACCEPT must be an *elementary numeric item with integer value*. In such a case WS-DATE would need to be defined with PIC 9(6) and then redefined as a group-item using a REDEFINES clause. We use a **REDEFINES** clause as follows:

```
   01  STORED-AREAS.
       05  WS-DATE    PIC 9(6).
       05  WS-DATE-X  REDEFINES  WS-DATE.
           10  RUN-YEAR   PIC 99.
           10  RUN-MONTH  PIC 99.
           10  RUN-DAY    PIC 99.
```

In this way, WS-DATE and WS-DATE-X use the same six positions of storage, but describe those positions in two different ways. Most compilers, however, have an enhancement that allows the original identifier, WS-DATE, to specify a group item.

Accessing the Day of the Week and Time Using COBOL 85

With COBOL 85, we can also obtain a numeric representation for the day of the week, where 1 represents Monday, 2 represents Tuesday, and so on. To obtain a digit 1 to 7 for Monday through Sunday, respectively, we code:

```
               ACCEPT identifier FROM DAY-OF-WEEK
```

We can also code:

```
               ACCEPT identifier FROM TIME
```

where the identifier should have a PIC 9(8). The time will be stored in the identifier as hhmmsscc, where:

hh = hour (01–24)
mm = minute (01–60)
ss = second (01–60)
cc = hundredths of second (01–99)

For example, 02153000 would be 30 seconds past 2:15 A.M.

Finally, we can code:

```
               ACCEPT identifier FROM DAY
```

where identifier should have a PIC 9(5). The day will be stored as yyddd, where ddd is a day number from 001–365 (001–366 in leap years). This value is commonly referred to as a **Julian Date**. 98002, then would be equivalent to a date of January 2, 1998 (the second day of the year).

Julian date is very useful for calculations, e.g., for determining accounts that are 30, 60, or 90 days past due. Subtracting 90 from a Julian date of purchase of 98190, for example, tells us that if a payment was made after 98100, then the account is *not* past due. The next chapter includes intrinsic date functions that enable the programmer to change the format for different types of dates.

WEB SITE

Until recently, COBOL programs have typically stored dates in mmddyy format, with yy being a two-digit year that assumed a twentieth-century date. That is, 010298 was assumed to be January 2, 1998. With the new century on the horizon, processing dates will become a big problem. Depending on the application, a two-digit date of 01 could mean 1901 (e.g., a person's year of birth) or 2001 (e.g., a year in a transaction).

This millenium change is likely to require extensive modifications to the billions of lines of existing COBOL code.

Our Web site (http://www.wiley.com/cobol/) as well as the Web sites http://www.flexus.com/cobol.html and http://www.year2000.com contain some interesting information about this and other problems. These Web sites also point to several shareware programs that can be used to solve the two-digit date problem.

PRINTING QUOTATION MARKS

As noted, nonnumeric literals are enclosed in quotation marks (''), or apostrophes ('), depending on the computer system. Thus, the quotation mark (or apostrophe) itself cannot actually be part of a nonnumeric literal.

To print a quotation mark, then, we would use the COBOL figurative constant QUOTE. Suppose we wish to print a heading such as:

```
ITEM DESCRIPTION: 'SPECIAL'
```

This heading, which is to include quotation marks, is defined as:

The word FILLER is optional as a data-name with COBOL 85 but is required with COBOL 74

```
01   HEADING-1.
     05            PIC X(19)   VALUE SPACES.
     05            PIC X(18)   VALUE 'ITEM DESCRIPTION: '.
     05            PIC X       VALUE QUOTE.
     05            PIC X(7)    VALUE 'SPECIAL'.
     05            PIC X       VALUE QUOTE.
     05            PIC X(86)   VALUE SPACES.
```

The word QUOTE can be used to print a quotation mark as shown here; it cannot, however, be used to delimit a literal. Thus, MOVE QUOTE SPECIAL QUOTE... is not permissible.

CODING GUIDELINES FOR DESIGNING REPORTS

1. Include a heading that identifies the report.

2. Include the date and the page number in the report heading or on a separate page heading.

3. Include column headings for identifying fields to be printed.

4. Place the most significant fields where they are most visible.

5. Edit numeric fields for readability.

6. Include totals at the end of the report or at the end of a page.

7. Use *'s to identify the level of a total.

   Example

   ```
   DEPT TOTAL IS $33,266.25*
        :
        :
   FINAL TOTAL IS $167,267.53**
   ```

8. Include page footings at the end of each page and report footings at the end of the report, if desired.

THE READ ... INTO STATEMENT IN PLACE OF USING READ AND MOVE STATEMENTS

In our introduction to the WORKING-STORAGE SECTION, we noted that WORKING-STORAGE is sometimes used for storing input records as well as output records. Suppose the first input record contains information to be saved, such as the number of records to be processed. After it is read, such a record must be moved from the input area to WORKING-STORAGE. If it is not, the next READ will replace the first record's data with that of the second record. We could READ the first record and then MOVE it to WORKING-STORAGE. Or we could combine a READ and MOVE with a single statement:

```
READ file-name
     INTO (WORKING-STORAGE-record-area)
     AT END       (imperative statement ...)
     NOT AT END (imperative statement ...)
END-READ
```

Example

COBOL 85

```
FD IN-TRANS
       :
       :
WORKING-STORAGE SECTION.
01  CONTROL-RECORD-1.
       :
       :
PROCEDURE DIVISION.
       :
       :
```

COBOL 74 Substitutions

```
READ IN-TRANS INTO CONTROL-RECORD-1
    AT END MOVE 'NO ' TO ARE-THERE-MORE-RECORDS.
PERFORM 200-PROCESS-RTN
    UNTIL ARE-THERE-MORE-RECORDS = 'NO '.
```

```
PERFORM UNTIL ARE-THERE-MORE-RECORDS = 'NO '
    READ IN-TRANS INTO CONTROL-RECORD-1
        AT END
            MOVE 'NO ' TO ARE-THERE-MORE-RECORDS
        NOT AT END
            PERFORM 200-PROCESS-RTN
    END-READ
END-PERFORM
```

The **READ ... INTO** is very similar to the WRITE ... FROM. Both have uses in addition to those discussed here; we will consider these later on. Use the END-READ scope terminator with the READ ... INTO if you are using a COBOL 85 compiler.

─────────────── DEBUGGING TIP ───────────────

Some organizations have programmers describe *all* input and output records in WORKING-STORAGE and use READ ... INTO and WRITE ... FROM for input/output operations. In this way, you always know to look for record descriptions in WORKING-STORAGE.

CLEARING FIELDS USING THE INITIALIZE STATEMENT (COBOL 85)

With COBOL 85, a series of elementary items contained within a group item can all be initialized with the **INITIALIZE** verb. Numeric items will be initialized at zero, and nonnumeric items will be initialized with blanks:

```
01   WS-REC-1.
     05               PIC X(19).
     05    NAME       PIC X(20).
     05               PIC X(15).
     05    AMT-1      PIC 9(5)V99.
     05               PIC X(15).
     05    AMT-2      PIC 9(5)V99.
     05               PIC X(15).
     05    TOTAL      PIC 9(6)V99.
     05               PIC X(26).
       .
       .
     PROCEDURE DIVISION.
       .
       .
       INITIALIZE WS-REC-1
```

The word FILLER is optional with COBOL 85 but required with COBOL 74

The above will set AMT-1, AMT-2, and TOTAL to zeros and will set all the other fields to spaces.

INTERACTIVE OUTPUT THAT IS DISPLAYED ON A SCREEN

Interactive Processing. In interactive processing, output information is often displayed on a screen. As with printed output, screen displays must be clear, concise, and informative. Output should include headings and be neatly aligned, spaced, and edited.

Displayed output can typically be viewed in an 80-column × 24-row form. A screen layout sheet, similar to a Printer Spacing Chart, is used to plan the output design so that data is properly aligned and spaced for readability. See Figure 6.4.

Output can be positioned on a screen using LINE and COLUMN or POSITION numbers along with the DISPLAY:

Figure 6.4 Screen layout sheet.

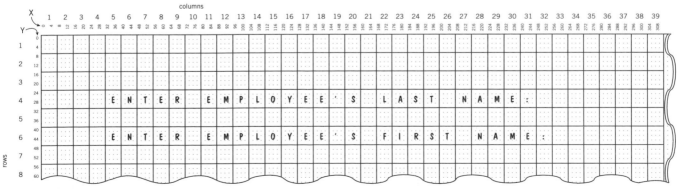

Example

```
DISPLAY 'ENTER CODE'
    LINE 2 {POSITION 10}
           {COLUMN 10  }
```

Use COLUMN for Micro Focus COBOL, VAX, and IBM AS/400 compilers. Use POSITION for the Ryan McFarland compiler.

If input is also entered interactively with the ACCEPT verb, then the input, as well as the output, can be positioned on the screen.

Example

```
200-REQUEST-FOR-EMPLOYEE-INFORMATION.
    DISPLAY 'ENTER EMPLOYEE'S LAST NAME:'
        LINE 4 COLUMN 5
    ACCEPT E-LAST-NAME
        LINE 4 COLUMN 35
    DISPLAY 'ENTER EMPLOYEE'S FIRST NAME:'
        LINE 6 COLUMN 5
    ACCEPT E-FIRST-NAME
        LINE 6 COLUMN 35.
```

The screen display would appear as follows:

```
Position 5 ─────┐                        ┌───────── Position 35
                ▼                        ▼
Line 4 ───────► ENTER EMPLOYEE'S LAST NAME:   BROWN
Line 6 ───────► ENTER EMPLOYEE'S FIRST NAME:  CHARLES
```

Using LINE and COLUMN (or POSITION), you can design your interactive screen displays any way you like. Without the LINE clause, the default would be the next sequential line. Without the COLUMN or POSITION clause, the default would be column 1 of the next line.

THE SCREEN SECTION FOR DEFINING SCREEN LAYOUTS USING PCs

Interactive Processing.   Because the need for interactive processing is greatest with microcomputers, PC versions of COBOL tend to have the most advanced features. PC versions of COBOL usually have a SCREEN SECTION as the last one in the DATA DIVISION for defining screen layouts.[1] They also have enhancements to the ACCEPT and DISPLAY verbs that are very helpful for solving some of the problems we have described.

We will discuss some of the elements of the SCREEN SECTION that are common to many compilers. Keep in mind that because this section is not part of the standard, the available options will differ, depending on both the COBOL compiler and the hardware you are using. Most of the options presented here are available in one form or another. We focus on RM/COBOL-85 and Micro Focus COBOL for illustrating the SCREEN SECTION, because (1) they are so popular and (2) student editions of these compilers are available with this text.

The SCREEN SECTION of the DATA DIVISION describes the format of a screen so that (1) the DISPLAY statement can more dynamically display literals and data and (2) the ACCEPT statement can enter data in a more user-friendly way.

The following are some of the features that can be provided by a SCREEN SECTION:

Highlighted display—in boldface (dual intensity) or blinking.
Reverse video—the background and foreground colors are reversed.
Underlining.
Color display—compiler dependent.

---

[1]See Stern, Stern, and Janossy, *Getting Started with RM/COBOL-85* and *Getting Started with Micro Focus Personal COBOL*, which are available with this text.

Sounding a bell to signal that input is to be entered.
Clearing the screen after each interaction.
Designating the specific positions in which data is to be entered on a screen.

As noted, many microcomputer versions of COBOL, like Micro Focus COBOL and RM/COBOL-85, include a SCREEN SECTION of the DATA DIVISION for screen design. This section follows the FILE and WORKING-STORAGE SECTIONs. The DISPLAY statement in the PROCEDURE DIVISION causes the screen to be displayed according to the specifications in the SCREEN SECTION; similarly, the ACCEPT statement enables users to enter input according to the same SCREEN SECTION specifications.

The SCREEN SECTION, like the other sections of the DATA DIVISION, consists of group items that themselves are subdivided into elementary items. Consider the following, in which the date is generated by the computer and a name is entered by the user:

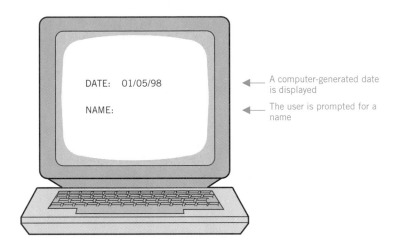

The SCREEN SECTION elements that will enable the literals to print and the user to enter the date on the same line is as follows:

```
SCREEN SECTION.
01   SCREEN-1.
     05   BLANK SCREEN.
     05   LINE 1 COLUMN 1     VALUE 'DATE:'.
     05   COLUMN 8    PIC X(8)  FROM STORED-DATE.   ◀──STORED-DATE is a field already
     05   LINE 3 COLUMN 1     VALUE 'NAME:'.                stored in the DATA DIVISION.
     05   COLUMN 8    PIC X(20) TO NAME-IN.
                                    ▲
                                    └──────────────── The name is typed in columns 8-27.
                                                       It will be transmitted to a NAME-IN
                                                       field in the DATA DIVISION.
```

To obtain the computer-generated date and then to have the computer prompt for name, we code:

```
DISPLAY SCREEN-1
ACCEPT  SCREEN-1
```

Let us consider the SCREEN-1 entries in the SCREEN SECTION.

1.   The first entry within SCREEN-1 clears the screen.
2.   The following two entries refer to LINE 1:

```
05   LINE 1 COLUMN 1     VALUE 'DATE:'.
05   COLUMN 8    PIC X(8)  FROM STORED-DATE.
```

Since the line beginning with COLUMN 8 does not have a LINE number, it is assumed by the computer that column 8 refers to LINE 1 specified in the previous entry.

STORED-DATE is a DATA DIVISION entry that must already have a value before we DISPLAY SCREEN-1. That is, we can read input with a date field that is moved to STORED-DATE, or we can move a value into STORED-DATE before displaying SCREEN-1.

3. The next entry prompts the user for a name on LINE 3:

   ```
   05   LINE 3 COLUMN 1   VALUE 'NAME:'.
   ```

4. The last entry will accept a 20-character field beginning in screen position 8 and move it to a predefined DATA DIVISION entry called NAME-IN:

   ```
   05   COLUMN 8    PIC X(20) TO NAME-IN.
   ```

   Since no line number appears here, the computer assumes that the data will be entered on LINE 3, as specified in the previous entry. NAME-IN is a field defined in either the FILE or WORKING-STORAGE SECTION.

In summary, we design screen formats using the SCREEN SECTION. Then we can display literals and any stored data with a DISPLAY statement. To enable a user to key in data, follow the DISPLAY screen-name statement with an ACCEPT screen-name statement. Thus, a single 01 screen item in the SCREEN SECTION can both DISPLAY and ACCEPT data.

The general form of a screen group item is as follows:

$$\text{level-number}\quad \text{screen-name}\quad [\text{AUTO}]\quad [\text{SECURE}]\quad [\text{REQUIRED}]\quad \begin{bmatrix} \text{EMPTY-CHECK}^2 \\ \text{FULL}^3 \end{bmatrix}.$$

1. Level-number ranges from 01-49.
2. Screen-name conforms to the rules for COBOL user-defined words.
3. AUTO—When an input field has been keyed in its entirety by a user, the AUTO clause enables the cursor to skip automatically to the next field to be entered as input. Without the AUTO clause, the computer would wait for the user to press the Enter key.

   Consider the following:

   ```
   ENTER ACCT NO:
   ENTER AMT OF PURCHASE:
   ```

   ```
   01   SCREEN1 AUTO.
        05   LINE 1 COLUMN 1          VALUE 'ENTER ACCT NO:'
        05   LINE 1 COLUMN 15    PIC 9(5)  TO ACCT-IN AUTO.
        05   LINE 3 ...
             ⋮
   ```

   AUTO means that when five integers are entered for ACCT NO, the cursor will *automatically* move to line 3. Without the AUTO clause, the cursor would not move until the user presses the Enter key.

4. SECURE—With this clause, keyed data would *not be displayed*. This clause is used for security reasons. If a password or user identification is to be accepted, for example, the SECURE clause should be used.

   Typically, asterisks (*) or pound signs (#) will appear in the data entry field in place of the actual data that is entered.

5. REQUIRED—This clause means that the corresponding entries to be accepted *must be keyed* before the cursor will move to the next field to be entered as input. Pressing Enter without keying in REQUIRED data will not bypass this entry; it must be keyed before the program can continue.

---

[2]Micro Focus COBOL option.
[3]RM/COBOL-85 option.

6. FULL (RM/COBOL-85) or EMPTY-CHECK (Micro Focus)—This clause means that the *entire* field must be filled. Pressing the Enter key will have no effect until the entry is complete. Thus, if the field has PIC 9(5), five digits must be entered; 123 would not be acceptable but 00123 would be okay.

When these options are specified, they apply to all elements in the group item. We will see that they can be specified on the elementary level instead, when they are applicable to some, but not all, screen entries.

Some entries for an elementary screen item for both RM/COBOL-85 and Micro Focus COBOL are:

```
level-number  [screen-name]
    [BLANK SCREEN]
    [LINE NUMBER IS [PLUS]  integer-1]
    [COLUMN NUMBER IS [PLUS]  integer-2]
    [BLANK LINE]
    [BELL]
    [UNDERLINE]
    [REVERSE-VIDEO]
    [HIGHLIGHT]
    [BLINK]
    [VALUE IS  literal-1]
```

$$
\left[
\begin{array}{l}
\left\{\begin{array}{l} \underline{PICTURE} \\ \underline{PIC} \end{array}\right\} \ IS \quad \text{picture-string} \\
\left\{\begin{array}{l}
\left[\ \underline{FROM} \quad \left\{\begin{array}{l} \text{identifier-1} \\ \text{literal-2} \end{array}\right\}\ \right] \\
[\underline{TO} \quad \text{identifier-2}] \\
[\underline{USING} \quad \text{identifier-3}]
\end{array}\right\}
\end{array}
\right]
$$

```
    [BLANK WHEN ZERO]
    [JUSTIFIED RIGHT]
    [AUTO]
    [SECURE]
    [REQUIRED]
    [FULL] (RM/COBOL-85) or [EMPTY-CHECK] (Micro Focus)
```

Level-number and *screen-name* are subject to the same rules as in the group screen description.

1. BLANK SCREEN will clear the screen and position the cursor at the home or first position.
2. LINE and COLUMN specify the screen location of elements to be either displayed or accepted.
3. BELL causes a beep to sound when an ACCEPT is executed. This signals the user that data is to be entered.

    The next three options refer to *displayed data* only.
4. UNDERLINE underlines items that are displayed.
5. REVERSE-VIDEO causes items to be displayed with the foreground and background colors reversed.
6. BLINK causes a displayed item to blink.
7. VALUE is used for literals to be displayed.
8. PIC clauses are used for data fields to be displayed. We use the phrase FROM (data-name) with a PIC clause where the data-name indicates the DATA DIVISION field or record that contains the data to be displayed. PIC clauses are also used to accept data items. We use a PIC clause along with the phrase TO (data-name) to indicate where in the DATA DIVISION we wish to store the accepted entry.
9. BLANK WHEN ZERO displays a blank for a field that has a value of 0.
10. JUSTIFIED RIGHT—right justifies the item.

11. The last four entries (AUTO, SECURE, REQUIRED, and FULL) have the same meaning as specified with group items.

Example

```
SCREEN SECTION.
01  PASSWORD-SCREEN.
    05  BLANK SCREEN.
    05  LINE 5 COLUMN 18      PIC X(10) TO USER-PASSWORD
                SECURE BELL AUTO.
    05  LINE 10 COLUMN 10         VALUE
                    'ENTER PASSWORD ABOVE'.
    05  LINE 15 COLUMN 18      PIC X(25) TO USER-NAME.
    05  LINE 20 COLUMN 10         VALUE
                    'ENTER NAME ABOVE'.
PROCEDURE DIVISION.
100-SIGN-ON.
*GIVES THE PROMPTS
    DISPLAY PASSWORD-SCREEN
*ACCEPTS PASSWORD AND NAME
    ACCEPT PASSWORD-SCREEN
    :
    :
```

Additional coding here
to test user entries
for validity

Additional RM/COBOL-85 and Micro Focus COBOL Enhancements

RM/COBOL-85 also includes the following control options that can be used with the DISPLAY or ACCEPT verbs:

LOW	Low intensity
HIGH	Extra brightness
REVERSED	Dark characters on a light background
BLINK	Displayed characters blink on and off
LINE	integer-1
POSITION	integer-2
ERASE	Erases or clears entire screen
ERASE EOL	Erases or clears to the end of the line
ERASE EOS	Erases or clears to the end of the screen

Example

```
DISPLAY 'THIS IS IT!' REVERSED LINE 2 POSITION 15 ERASE EOS
```

Colors

If you have a color monitor, you can specify a foreground color and/or a background color that can be used at any level in the screen definition. If they are specified on a group level, they apply to all fields in the group. If no colors are selected, the default colors are displayed (e.g., black for background and white for foreground).

Colors are specified as follows:

Micro Focus COBOL
```
FOREGROUND-COLOR IS integer
BACKGROUND-COLOR IS integer
```

RM/COBOL-85
```
FOREGROUND IS color
BACKGROUND IS color
```

The colors that can be selected are as follows:

Micro Focus COBOL		RM/COBOL-85
0	=	BLACK
1	=	BLUE
2	=	GREEN
3	=	CYAN
4	=	RED
5	=	MAGENTA
6	=	BROWN
7	=	WHITE

──────── COBOL 9x CHANGES ────────

1. You will be able to perform arithmetic operations on report-items. That is, the following will be valid:

```
05  TOTAL-OUT   PIC $Z,ZZZ.99.
     ⋮
ADD AMT-IN TO TOTAL-OUT
```

2. You will be able to combine nonnumeric literals in a MOVE statement.

   Long nonnumeric literals may require more than one line; if so, the continuation column (column 7) must be coded with a -.

   To define a column heading that extends beyond one line, we can use a VALUE clause as follows:

```
01  COLUMN-HDGS    PICTURE X(100)  VALUE '  NAME      TRANSACTION N
-   'UMBER   DATE OF TRANSACTION     AMOUNT     INVOICE NUMBER
-   'ITEM DESCRIPTION '.
```

   Alternatively, we could code:

```
01  COLUMN-HDGS    PIC X(100).
     ⋮
    MOVE '  NAME    TRANSACTION NUMBER   DATE OF TRANSACTION     A
-        'MOUNT    INVOICE NUMBER    ITEM DESCRIPTION '
         TO COLUMN-HDGS
```

   Both versions require the use of a - in the continuation column. With COBOL 9x, you will be able to combine or concatenate literals in a MOVE statement instead:

```
01  COLUMN-HDGS    PIC X(100).
     ⋮
    MOVE '  NAME    TRANSACTION'
      & ' NUMBER    DATE OF TRANSACTION'
      & '   AMOUNT     INVOICE'
      & ' NUMBER     ITEM DESCRIPTION '
         TO COLUMN-HDGS
```

3. As in the current standard, the INITIALIZE statement initializes numeric fields at zero and nonnumeric fields with spaces; if a field contains a VALUE clause, the current INITIALIZE will change the VALUE to zero or spaces depending on the PIC clause. With COBOL 9x, the VALUE will override the INITIALIZE.

CHAPTER SUMMARY A. Numeric Move—Sending and receiving fields are both numeric.

Rules
1. Integer portion.
   a. Movement is from right to left.
   b. Nonfilled high-order positions are replaced with zeros.
   c. Truncation of high-order digits occurs if the receiving field is not large enough to hold the results.
2. Decimal portion.
   a. Decimal alignment is maintained.
   b. Movement is from left to right, beginning at the decimal point.
   c. Nonfilled low-order positions are replaced with zeros.

B. Nonnumeric Move—Receiving field is nonnumeric.

Rules
1. Movement is from left to right.
2. Low-order nonfilled positions are replaced with spaces.
3. Truncation of low-order characters occurs if the receiving field is not large enough to hold the results.

C. The format of the *receiving* field determines the type of MOVE operation that is performed—either numeric or nonnumeric.

D. A field-name may be qualified by using OF or IN with the name of a record or group item of which the field is a part.

E. Editing—Table 6.3 reviews edit symbols used in a PICTURE clause.

F. Rules for printing output.
1. The AFTER or BEFORE ADVANCING option should be used with each WRITE instruction to indicate the spacing of the form. AFTER ADVANCING 1, 2, or 3 lines, for example, will

Table 6.3

Characters That May Be Used in a PICTURE Clause	
Symbol	**Meaning**
X	Alphanumeric field
9	Numeric field
A	Alphabetic field
V	Assumed decimal point; used only in numeric fields
S	Operational sign; used only in numeric fields
Z	Zero suppression character
.	Decimal point
+	Plus sign
−	Minus sign
$	Dollar sign
,	Comma
CR	Credit symbol
DB	Debit symbol
*	Check protection symbol
B	Field separator—space insertion character
0	Zero insertion character
/	Slash insertion character

Edit Symbols: Z through /

cause zero, one, or two blank lines, respectively, to appear before the next record is written.

2. Records defining all printed output including heading and detail lines should be established in WORKING-STORAGE so that VALUE clauses can be used. These records must be moved to the print area defined in the FILE SECTION. A WRITE ... FROM instruction may be used in place of a MOVE and a WRITE to print these lines.

3. Use a Printer Spacing Chart to determine the print positions to be used.

4. After each record is printed, a test for the end of a form should be performed. If the desired number of lines have been printed, code WRITE (print record) FROM (heading record) AFTER ADVANCING PAGE.

5. The appropriate editing symbols should be specified in the PICTURE clauses of report-items within the detail record.

G. Output can be displayed in exact screen positions. Using the SCREEN SECTION, screen displays can be made more user-friendly.

KEY TERMS

ACCEPT	Floating string	READ ... INTO
AFTER ADVANCING	High-order position	Receiving field
BEFORE ADVANCING	INITIALIZE	REDEFINES
BLANK WHEN ZERO	Julian Date	Report-item
Check protection symbol	JUSTIFIED RIGHT	Sending field
(*)	Line counter	Suppression of leading
Continuous forms	Low-order position	zeros
DATE	MOVE	Truncation
Edit symbol	PAGE	WRITE ... FROM
Editing	Printer Spacing Chart	

CHAPTER SELF-TEST

1. (T or F) In a nonnumeric move, high-order nonfilled positions are replaced with spaces.

2. Indicate the result in each of the following cases:

MOVE TAX TO TOTAL

	TAX		**TOTAL**	
PIC	*Contents*	PIC		*Contents (after MOVE)*
(a) 9(3)	123	9(4)		
(b) V99	$_\wedge$67	V9(3)		
(c) V99	$_\wedge$53	9(2)		
(d) 9(2)	67	9V9		
(e) 9(3)V9(3)	123$_\wedge$123	9(4)V99		

3. Indicate the result in each of the following cases:

MOVE CODE-1 OF IN-REC TO CODE-1 OF OUT-REC

	IN-REC		**OUT-REC**	
	CODE-1		**CODE-1**	
PIC	*Contents*	PIC		*Contents (after MOVE)*
(a) X(4)	ZZYY	X(5)		
(b) X(4)	ABCD	X(3)		

4. (T or F) A numeric MOVE always maintains decimal alignment.

5. (T or F) Two files may be given the same file-names as long as the names are qualified when used in the PROCEDURE DIVISION.

6. (T or F) VALUE clauses may be used in the FILE SECTION to initialize fields.

For Questions 7 through 16, fill in the missing column:

	Sending-Field		**Report-Item**	
	PICTURE	**Contents**	**PICTURE**	**Edited Results**
7.	999V99	000$_\wedge$05	$$$$.99	
8.	S999V99	000$_\wedge$0$\bar{5}$	$$$$.99 −	

	Sending-Field		Report-Item	
	PICTURE	**Contents**	**PICTURE**	**Edited Results**
9.	9999V99	0026ᴧ54		ƀƀ26.54 +
10.	S999	00$\bar{2}$	+ + + +	
11.	S99		− − −	− 4
12.	999V99	000ᴧ00	$$$$.99	
13.	999V99	000ᴧ00	$$$$.99 BLANK WHEN ZERO	
14.	9(3)	008	Z(3).99	
15.	9(5)	00123	$ZZ,ZZZ.ZZ	
16.	9(4)	0002	Z,Z99	

17. What types of headings may appear on a printed report?

18. (T or F) Print records are typically 132, 100, or 80 characters long.

19. One reason that records to be printed are described in the WORKING-STORAGE SECTION is because this section allows the use of _____ clauses.

20. Assume print records are described in the WORKING-STORAGE SECTION with appropriate VAL-UE clauses. Code a sample record description entry in the FILE SECTION for the print file.

21. Indicate how you might obtain underlining of headings by using the ADVANCING option.

22. What tools are used for aligning the data to be printed or displayed?

23. To print a heading on a new page, we might code the following:

```
WRITE PRINT-REC FROM HEADING-REC
     AFTER ADVANCING _____
```

24. To obtain the date stored by the system, we may code ACCEPT DATE-IN FROM _____ .

25. (T or F) Printing a literal such as END OF REPORT on the last page would be an example of a report footing.

Solutions

1. F—*Low-order* nonfilled positions are replaced with spaces.

2. (a) 0123;   (b) ᴧ670;   (c) 00;   (d) 7ᴧ0;   (e) 0123ᴧ12

3. (a) ZZYYƀ;   (b) ABC

4. T

5. F—File-names (as well as record-names) must be unique; only names that define fields may be qualified.

6. F

7. $.05

8. $.05 −

9. ZZZZ.99 +

10. − 2

11. 0$\bar{4}$

12. $.00

13. (7 blanks)

14. ƀƀ8.00

15. $ 123.00

16. ƀƀƀ02

17. Report headings; page headings; column headings

18. T

19. VALUE

20. 01 PRINT-REC PICTURE X(132). (No field descriptions are necessary.)

21. The following may be used as an example:

```
01  HDG1.
    05            PIC X(56)   VALUE SPACES.
    05            PIC X(76)
        VALUE 'MONTHLY SALES REPORT'.
```

```
01  HDG2.
    05              PIC X(56)    VALUE SPACES.
    05              PIC X(76)
        VALUE '_____'.
            :
            :
    WRITE PRINT-REC FROM HDG1 AFTER ADVANCING 2 LINES
    WRITE PRINT-REC FROM HDG2 BEFORE ADVANCING 2 LINES.
```

Note: The word FILLER is required in place of a blank data-name with COBOL 74.

22. The Printer Spacing Chart and the Screen Layout Sheet
23. PAGE
24. DATE
25. T

PRACTICE PROGRAM

Using the following problem definition, print all fields for each input record on a single line. The Printer Spacing Chart indicates how each output record is to be spaced. For readability, place a / between month, day, and year of the date. Also print headings at the top of each page of the report. Use WORKING-STORAGE with VALUE clauses for describing output lines. Figure 6.5 presents the pseudocode. Figure 6.6 shows the solution, and Figure 6.7 illustrates the hierarchy chart. The planning tools will become more useful as the logic in our programs becomes more complex.

Systems Flowchart

PURCHASE-TRANS
32-position records
standard labels

SAMPLE PROGRAM

PURCHASE-REPORT

PURCHASE-TRANS Record Layout			
Field	**Size**	**Type**	**No. of Decimal Positions (if Numeric)**
Customer No.	5	Alphanumeric	
Customer Name	20	Alphanumeric	
Amount of Purchase	7	Numeric	2

PURCHASE-REPORT Printer Spacing Chart

Figure 6.5 Pseudocode for the Practice Program.

MAIN-MODULE
START
    Open the files
    Accept the date and move to output area
    PERFORM Hdg-Rtn

Figure 6.5 (continued)

```
                PERFORM UNTIL there is no more data
                    READ a Record
                        AT END Move 'NO ' to Are-There-More-Records
                        NOT AT END PERFORM Report-Rtn
                    END-READ
                END-PERFORM
                Close the files
            STOP
```

<u>HDG-RTN</u>
```
                Write Headings
                Initialize Line Counter
                Add 1 to Page Counter
```

<u>REPORT-RTN</u>
```
                IF Line Counter >= 25
                THEN
                    PERFORM Hdg-Rtn
                END-IF
                Move input to output areas
                Write a detail line
                Add 1 to Line Counter
```

Figure 6.6 Solution to the Practice Program.

COBOL 85

```
IDENTIFICATION DIVISION.
PROGRAM-ID. CH0601.
ENVIRONMENT DIVISION.
INPUT-OUTPUT SECTION.
FILE-CONTROL.
    SELECT PURCHASE-TRANS   ASSIGN TO CH6.
    SELECT PURCHASE-REPORT ASSIGN TO PRINTER.
DATA DIVISION.
FILE SECTION.
FD  PURCHASE-TRANS
    LABEL RECORDS ARE STANDARD
    RECORD CONTAINS 32 CHARACTERS.
01  TRANS-REC-IN.
    05  CUST-NO-IN                  PIC X(5).
    05  CUST-NAME-IN                PIC X(20).
    05  AMT-OF-PUR-IN               PIC 9(5)V99.
FD  PURCHASE-REPORT
    LABEL RECORDS ARE OMITTED
    RECORD CONTAINS 132 CHARACTERS.
01  PRINT-REC                       PIC X(132).
WORKING-STORAGE SECTION.
01  WORK-AREAS.
    05  ARE-THERE-MORE-RECORDS      PIC XXX
                VALUE 'YES'.
    05  WS-DATE.
        10  WS-YEAR                 PIC 99.
        10  WS-MONTH                PIC 99.
        10  WS-DAY                  PIC 99.
    05  WS-PAGE-CT                  PIC 99
                VALUE ZERO.
    05  WS-LINE-CT                  PIC 99
                VALUE ZERO.
01  HDR1-OUT.
    05                              PIC X(40)
                VALUE SPACES.
    05                              PIC X(20)
```

COBOL 74 Substitutions

For COBOL 74, FILLER must be used instead of a blank field name

Figure 6.6   (continued)

```
                                          VALUE 'PURCHASE REPORT'.
                 05   DATE-OUT.
                     10   MONTH-OUT              PIC 99.
                     10                          PIC X
                             VALUE '/'.
                     10   DAY-OUT                PIC 99.
                     10                          PIC X
                             VALUE '/'.
                     10   YEAR-OUT               PIC 99.
                 05                              PIC X(2)
                         VALUE SPACES.
                 05                              PIC X(5)
                         VALUE 'PAGE'.
                 05   PAGE-OUT                   PIC Z9.
                 05                              PIC X(55)
                         VALUE SPACES.
            01   HDR2-OUT.
                 05                              PIC X(10)
                         VALUE SPACES.
                 05                              PIC X(27)
                         VALUE 'CUSTOMER NO   CUSTOMER NAME'.
                 05                              PIC X(13)
                         VALUE SPACES.
                 05                              PIC X(82)
                         VALUE 'AMOUNT OF PURCHASE'.
            01   DETAIL-REC-OUT.
                 05                              PIC X(13)
                         VALUE SPACES.
                 05   CUST-NO-OUT                PIC X(5).
                 05                              PIC X(6)
                         VALUE SPACES.
                 05   CUST-NAME-OUT              PIC X(20).
                 05                              PIC X(11)
                         VALUE SPACES.
                 05   AMT-OF-PUR-OUT             PIC Z(5).99.
                 05                              PIC X(69)
                         VALUE SPACES.
            PROCEDURE DIVISION.
       ****************************************************
       *     all program logic is controlled by the       *
       *                main-module                        *
       ****************************************************
            100-MAIN-MODULE.
                OPEN INPUT  PURCHASE-TRANS
                     OUTPUT PURCHASE-REPORT
                ACCEPT WS-DATE FROM DATE
                MOVE WS-MONTH TO MONTH-OUT
                MOVE WS-DAY TO DAY-OUT
                MOVE WS-YEAR TO YEAR-OUT
                PERFORM 200-HDG-RTN
                PERFORM UNTIL ARE-THERE-MORE-RECORDS = 'NO '
                    READ PURCHASE-TRANS
                        AT END
                            MOVE 'NO ' TO ARE-THERE-MORE-RECORDS
                        NOT AT END
                            PERFORM 300-REPORT-RTN
                    END-READ
                END-PERFORM
                CLOSE PURCHASE-TRANS
                      PURCHASE-REPORT
                STOP RUN.
       ****************************************************
       *   200-hdg-rtn is executed once from the main module *
       *        and then again after 25 detail lines print   *
       ****************************************************
            200-HDG-RTN.
                ADD 1 TO WS-PAGE-CT
```

COBOL 74 Substitutions

```
READ PURCHASE-TRANS
    AT END MOVE 'NO ' TO ARE-THERE-MORE-RECORDS.
PERFORM 300-REPORT-RTN
    UNTIL ARE-THERE-MORE-RECORDS = 'NO '.
```

Figure 6.6   (continued)

```
                                      MOVE WS-PAGE-CT TO PAGE-OUT
                                      WRITE PRINT-REC FROM HDR1-OUT
                                          AFTER ADVANCING PAGE
                                      WRITE PRINT-REC FROM HDR2-OUT
                                          AFTER ADVANCING 2 LINES
                                      MOVE ZEROS TO WS-LINE-CT.
                              *************************************************************
                              *    300-report-rtn is executed from the main-module   *
                              *       until all input records have been processed      *
                              *************************************************************
                               300-REPORT-RTN.
                                   IF WS-LINE-CT >= 25
                                          PERFORM 200-HDG-RTN
                                   END-IF
                                   MOVE SPACES TO DETAIL-REC-OUT
                                   MOVE CUST-NO-IN TO CUST-NO-OUT
                                   MOVE CUST-NAME-IN TO CUST-NAME-OUT
                                   MOVE AMT-OF-PUR-IN TO AMT-OF-PUR-OUT
                                   WRITE PRINT-REC FROM DETAIL-REC-OUT
                                          AFTER ADVANCING 2 LINES
                                   ADD 1 TO WS-LINE-CT.
```

COBOL 74 Substitutions

```
READ PURCHASE-TRANS                                    ──────────►
    AT END MOVE 'NO ' TO ARE-THERE-MORE-RECORDS.
```

Figure 6.7   Hierarchy chart for the Practice Program.

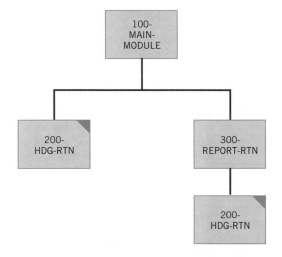

Sample Input

```
    12345 │CHARLES NEWTON,INC. │0031500
    23456 │HARWOOD ASSOCIATES  │5187975
    34567 │LEMON AUTOMOTIVE    │0950000
    54321 │BISTRO BROTHERS     │0134565
       ↑         ↑                  ↑
CUSTOMER NO.  CUSTOMER NAME    AMOUNT OF PURCHASE
```

Sample Output

```
                              PURCHASE REPORT      12/19/98   PAGE 1

    CUSTOMER NO    CUSTOMER NAME           AMOUNT OF PURCHASE

       12345       CHARLES NEWTON,INC.          315.00

       23456       HARWOOD ASSOCIATES         51879.75
```

| 34567 | LEMON AUTOMOTIVE | 9500.00 |
| 54321 | BISTRO BROTHERS | 1345.65 |

REVIEW QUESTIONS

I. True-False Questions

_____ 1. Elementary numeric items within a group item are treated as nonnumeric fields.

_____ 2. Group items, although they contain elementary numeric items, are treated as nonnumeric fields.

_____ 3. XYZ∅∅ will be moved to a three-position alphanumeric field as Z∅∅.

_____ 4. 66200 will be moved to a numeric field with PIC 9(3) as 200.

_____ 5. 92.17 will be moved to a field with a PICTURE of 999V999 as 092∧017.

_____ 6. The statement MOVE ZEROS TO FLD1 is only valid if FLD1 is numeric.

_____ 7. The following is a valid MOVE: MOVE FILLER TO DETAIL-LINE.

_____ 8. Blanks in a numeric field are valid characters.

_____ 9. Data is always left-justified in a field.

_____ 10. The following is a valid MOVE: MOVE SPACES TO DETAIL-LINE.

II. General Questions

For Questions 1–7, determine the contents of the receiving field:

Sending Field		Receiving Field	
PICTURE	Contents	PICTURE	Contents (after MOVE)
1. 99V99	12∧34	9(3)V9(3)	
2. 9V99	7∧89	9V9	
3. 999V9	678∧9	99V99	
4. 99	56	XXX	
5. XX	AB	XXX	
6. X(4)	CODE	XXX	
7. XXX	124	999	

8. Consider the following:

```
05   ITEM-1.
     10   ITEM-1A   PIC 99.
     10   ITEM-1B   PIC 99.
```

What is the difference between MOVE 0 TO ITEM-1 and MOVE ZERO TO ITEM-1?

For Questions 9 and 10, determine the contents of UNIT-PRICE if the operation performed is:

```
MOVE 13.579 TO UNIT-PRICE
```

UNIT-PRICE

PICTURE	Contents (after MOVE)
9. 999V9(4)	
10. 99V9	

For Questions 11 through 25, fill in the missing entries:

Sending-Field		Report-Item	
PICTURE	Contents	PICTURE	Contents
11. 999	467	$ZZZ.99	
12. S99V99	00∧98̄	$ZZ.99+	
13. S99V99	00∧89⁺	$ZZ.99−	
14. S999	005⁺	$ZZZ.99CR	
15. S999	005⁺	$ZZZ.99DB	

16.	S99V99	00∧05̄⁺	$**.99−
17.	9(4)	1357	$*,***.99
18.	XXXX	CRDB	XXBBXX
19.	999V99	135∧79	$$$$.99
20.	999V99	000∧09	$$$$.99
21.	S9(5)	00567̄	+ + + + +
22.	S99	00̄⁺	+ + +
23.	S99	00̄⁺	− − −
24.	9999V99	0009∧88	$9.88
25.	V9999V99	0009∧88	$ 9.88

INTERPRETING INSTRUCTION FORMATS

Based on the instruction format for the MOVE statement described in this chapter, indicate what, if anything, is wrong with the following:

1. MOVE 'ABC', AMT1 TO AMT-OUT

2. MOVE 1 TO AMT1 AND AMT2

3. MOVE AMT2 TO 123

DEBUGGING EXERCISES

Consider the following DATA DIVISION entries:

```
01  IN-REC.
    05  AMT1        PIC 9(4)V99.
    05  AMT2        PIC 9(5)V99.
    05  AMT3        PIC 9(3)V99.
    05  AMT4        PIC 9(3).
    05  AMT5        PIC 9(3).
      .
      .
01  OUT-REC.
    05  AMT1-OUT    PIC $(4).99.
    05              PIC X(10).
    05  AMT2-OUT    PIC ZZ,ZZZ.
    05              PIC X(10).
    05  AMT3-OUT    PIC ZZZZ.99
    05              PIC X(10).
    05  AMT4-OUT    PIC Z(3).ZZ.
    05              PIC X(10).
    05  AMT5-OUT    PIC -999.
    05              PIC X(10).
    05  TOTAL1      PIC $(5).99.
    05              PIC X(10).
    05  TOTAL2      PIC Z(5).99.
    05              PIC X(26).
```

1. Before moving the amount fields of IN-REC to the corresponding amount fields of OUT-REC, is it necessary to MOVE SPACES TO OUT-REC? Explain your answer.

2. Should OUT-REC be defined within the FILE SECTION or the WORKING-STORAGE SECTION? Explain your answer.

3. Indicate which of the following would result in a syntax error and explain why.
   (a) MOVE AMT1 TO AMT1-OUT
   (b) MOVE AMT2 TO AMT2-OUT
   (c) MOVE AMT3 TO AMT3-OUT
   (d) MOVE AMT4 TO AMT4-OUT
   (e) MOVE AMT5 TO AMT5-OUT

4. Suppose OUT-REC is defined in the WORKING-STORAGE SECTION and we add the following field:

   05 AMT6   PIC $(5).99 VALUE ZERO.

   Will this specification result in a syntax error? Explain your answer.

PROGRAMMING ASSIGNMENTS

For each assignment, plan the program first with pseudocode or a flowchart and a hierarchy chart. Remember that programs are not complete until they have been tested or debugged. Use WORKING-STORAGE for describing print records. Use VALUE clauses for describing literals in print records. Edit all numeric fields and print headings as appropriate.

1. Write a program to print data using the following problem definition:

Systems Flowchart

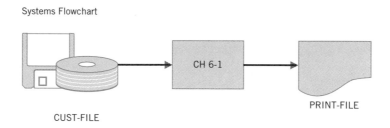

CUST-FILE

CH 6-1

PRINT-FILE

CUST-FILE **Record Layout**			
Field	**Size**	**Type**	**No. of Decimal Positions (if Numeric)**
Initial1	1	Alphanumeric	
Initial2	1	Alphanumeric	
Last Name	10	Alphanumeric	
Month of Transaction	2	Alphanumeric	
Year of Transaction	2	Alphanumeric	
Transaction Amount	6	Numeric	0

PRINT-FILE Printer Spacing Chart

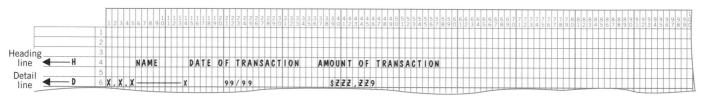

Heading line — H
Detail line — D

```
        NAME      DATE OF TRANSACTION   AMOUNT OF TRANSACTION
      X.X.X------X      99/99                $ZZZ,ZZ9
```

Sample Input Data

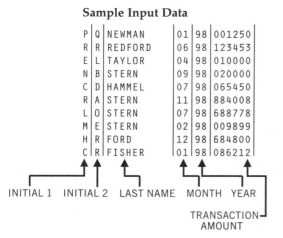

P	Q	NEWMAN	01	98	001250
R	R	REDFORD	06	98	123453
E	L	TAYLOR	04	98	010000
N	B	STERN	09	98	020000
C	D	HAMMEL	07	98	065450
R	A	STERN	11	98	884008
L	O	STERN	07	98	688778
M	E	STERN	02	98	009899
H	R	FORD	12	98	684800
C	R	FISHER	01	98	086212

INITIAL 1 INITIAL 2 LAST NAME MONTH YEAR
TRANSACTION AMOUNT

Sample Output

```
   NAME        DATE OF TRANSACTION   AMOUNT OF TRANSACTION

P.Q.NEWMAN          01/98               $   1,250
R.R.REDFORD         06/98               $123,453
E.L.TAYLOR          04/98               $  10,000
N.B.STERN           09/98               $  20,000
C.D.HAMMEL          07/98               $  65,450
R.A.STERN           11/98               $884,008
L.O.STERN           07/98               $688,778
M.E.STERN           02/98               $   9,899
H.R.FORD            12/98               $684,800
C.R.FISHER          01/98               $  86,212
```

Figure 6.8 Problem definition for Programming Assignment 2.

Systems Flowchart

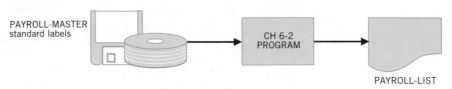

PAYROLL-MASTER
standard labels

CH 6-2
PROGRAM

PAYROLL-LIST

PAYROLL-MASTER Record Layout		
Field	**Size**	**Type**
Employee No.	5	Alphanumeric
Employee Name	20	Alphanumeric
Territory No.	2	Alphanumeric
Office No.	2	Alphanumeric
Annual Salary	6	Alphanumeric
Social Security No.	9	Alphanumeric
Unused	36	Alphanumeric

PAYROLL-LIST Printer Spacing Chart

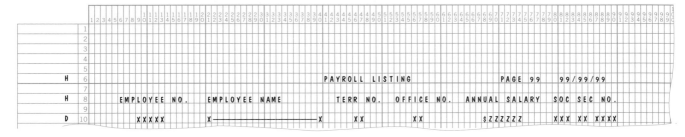

2. Write a program to print data from a payroll disk file. The problem definition is shown in Figure 6.8.

3. Write a program to print a mailing list from a name and address file. The problem definition is shown in Figure 6.9.

Figure 6.9 Problem definition for Programming Assignment 3.

Systems Flowchart

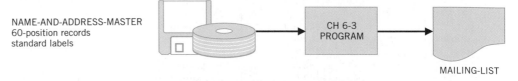

NAME-AND-ADDRESS-MASTER
60-position records
standard labels

CH 6-3
PROGRAM

MAILING-LIST

NAME-AND-ADDRESS-MASTER Record Layout (Alternate Format)

CUSTOMER NAME	ADDRESS		
	STREET	CITY STATE ZIP	

1   20 21   40 41   60

Figure 6.9   (continued)

MAILING-LIST Printer Spacing Chart

Notes:

a. Each input record generates three output lines.

b. Leave one blank line after each set of three lines is printed.

4. **Interactive Processing.**   Redo Programming Assignment 3 accepting name and address from a keyboard. If you have a PC compiler, use the SCREEN SECTION to enhance the quality of the displayed output.

5. The following is a file of data records containing information on subscribers to a magazine. The record format is as follows:

Record Position	Field
1–20	Customer name
21–40	Street address
41–60	City, State, and Zip
61–62	Number of labels needed

Write a program that prints the required number of mailing labels in the following format:

Name
Street address
City, State Zip

If positions 61–62 indicate 05, for example, you will perform a print module 5 times. *Hint:* PERFORM 300-PRINT-RTN NO-OF-LABELS TIMES, where NO-OF-LABELS is an input field.

6. **Interactive Processing.**   Redo Programming Assignment 5 so that users can enter the customer name, address, and number of copies from a PC or terminal keyboard. Do not forget to prompt for input. Display a mailing label on the screen and ask the user to verify that it is correct before printing. Include instructions such as the following:

```
DISPLAY 'IS LABEL OK (Y/N)?'
ACCEPT REPLY
IF REPLY = 'Y'
    PERFORM 300-PRINT-RTN
        NO-OF-LABELS TIMES
END-IF
```

If you have a PC compiler, use the SCREEN SECTION to enhance the quality of the displayed output.

7. **Maintenance Program.**   Modify the Practice Program in this chapter to print the total amount of all purchases for all customers at the end of the report.

CHAPTER 7

Computing in COBOL: The Arithmetic Verbs and Intrinsic Functions

■ **OBJECTIVES**

To familiarize you with
1. The ways in which arithmetic may be performed in COBOL.
2. The formats and options available with the arithmetic verbs.

■ **CONTENTS**

THE BASIC ARITHMETIC VERBS

All the basic arithmetic operations of ADD, SUBTRACT, MULTIPLY, and DIVIDE require that the fields operated on (1) have numeric PICTURE clauses and (2) actually have numeric data when the program is executed.

ADD Statement

A simple **ADD** statement has the following two instruction formats:

Format 1
(ADD ... TO)

$$\text{ADD} \begin{Bmatrix} \text{identifier-1} \\ \text{literal-1} \end{Bmatrix} \dots \text{ TO } \text{identifier-2} \dots$$

Format 2
(ADD ... GIVING)

$$\text{ADD} \begin{Bmatrix} \text{identifier-1} \\ \text{literal-1} \end{Bmatrix} \dots \text{ GIVING } \text{identifier-2} \dots$$

Examples 1–4

```
1. ADD DEPOSIT TO BALANCE
2. ADD 15.80 TO TAX
3. ADD 40, OVERTIME-HOURS
      GIVING TOTAL-HOURS
4. ADD AMT1
      AMT2
      GIVING TOTAL-AMT
```

Fields Used in an ADD

As noted, the specified fields or **operands** that are added should be numeric when used in an ADD statement. Thus, in Examples 1 through 4, all literals are numeric, and it is assumed that all data-names or identifiers, when specified in the DATA DIVISION, have numeric PICTURE clauses.

A comma can be used anywhere in an instruction, as in Example 3, as long as at least one space follows it. We recommend that you omit commas, however, because they are added characters that can cause errors. You should separate entries instead by placing them on individual lines, as in Example 4. This will reduce the risk of errors and help identify any syntax errors that may occur, because syntax errors are specified by line numbers.

The Resultant Field in an ADD

The result, or sum, of an ADD operation is always placed in the last field mentioned. The *only* field that is altered as a result of the ADD operation is this last field, which is the one directly following the word TO, when using Format 1, or GIVING, when using Format 2. Thus, in Example 1, the sum of DEPOSIT and BALANCE is placed in BALANCE. DEPOSIT remains unchanged.

In all cases, *the resultant field must be an identifier or data-name,* not a literal. The statement ADD HOURS-WORKED TO 40, for example, is incorrect because 40, which immediately follows the word TO, would be the resultant field, and resultant fields may not be literals.

When using the TO format in an ADD statement, *all* the data-names and literals are added together, and the result is placed in the last field specified:

Example 5
```
ADD HOURS-WORKED TO WEEKLY-HOURS
```

The fields HOURS-WORKED and WEEKLY-HOURS are added together. The sum is placed in WEEKLY-HOURS; HOURS-WORKED remains unchanged.

When using the GIVING format, all fields and literals *preceding* the word GIVING are added together and the sum is placed in the field *following* the word GIVING. Thus, when using the GIVING format, the last data field is *not* part of the ADD operation. Because it is not part of the arithmetic operation, it can be a report-item with edit symbols.

Example 6
```
ADD HOURS-WORKED
    WEEKLY-HOURS
    GIVING TOTAL-HOURS
```

The same addition is performed as in Example 5: HOURS-WORKED and WEEKLY-HOURS are summed. In this case, however, the result is placed in TOTAL-HOURS. The original contents of TOTAL-HOURS do not in any way affect the arithmetic operation. TOTAL-HOURS may contain a decimal point and a dollar sign if it is to be printed.

Keep in mind that the data-names specified in any arithmetic statement must be defined in the DATA DIVISION, either in an input or output area of the FILE SECTION, or in the WORKING-STORAGE SECTION.

The COBOL words TO and GIVING may be used in the same ADD operation for COBOL 85 users. To say ADD TAX TO NET GIVING TOTAL, then, is correct if you are using a COBOL 85 compiler. With COBOL 74 you may code ADD TAX TO NET, in which case the result is placed in NET; or you may code ADD TAX NET GIVING TOTAL, in which case the result is placed in TOTAL.

Thus, Format 2 for the ADD instruction with COBOL 85 is:

$$ \text{ADD} \begin{Bmatrix} \text{identifier-1} \\ \text{literal-1} \end{Bmatrix} \ldots \text{TO} \begin{Bmatrix} \text{identifier-2} \\ \text{literal-2} \end{Bmatrix} $$

$$ \underline{\text{GIVING}} \text{ identifier-3} \ldots $$

As noted, commas followed by at least one space may be used to separate operands, but they are optional. Thus ADD HOURS-WORKED, WEEKLY-HOURS GIVING TOTAL-HOURS is correct.

Deciding Whether to Use the TO or GIVING Format

Use the GIVING format with the ADD statement when the contents of operands are to be retained. When you will no longer need the original contents of an operand after the addition, the TO format may be used. Let us review some rules for interpreting instruction formats that will help in evaluating Formats 1 and 2 of the ADD statement just specified:

INTERPRETING FORMATS

1. Underlined words are required.

2. Uppercase words are COBOL reserved words.

3. The word "identifier" means a field or record defined in the DATA DIVISION.

4. The braces { } mean that one of the enclosed words is required.

5. The ellipses or dots (. . .) indicate that *two or more fields or literals* may be specified.

Adding More Than Two Fields

As you can see from the instruction formats, you are not restricted to two operands when using an ADD operation.

Example 7
```
ADD AMT1
    AMT2
    AMT3
    GIVING AMT4
```

	AMT1	AMT2	AMT3	AMT4
Before the ADD:	2	4	6	15
After the ADD:	2	4	6	12

Note that the original contents of AMT4, the resultant field, are destroyed and have no effect on the ADD operation. The three operands AMT1, AMT2, and AMT3 are unchanged.

Example 8
```
ADD AMT1
    AMT2
    AMT3
    TO AMT4
```

	AMT1	AMT2	AMT3	AMT4
Before the ADD:	2	4	6	15
After the ADD:	2	4	6	27

AMT1, AMT2, and AMT3 are added to the original contents of AMT4. The result here, too, is placed in AMT4; the other three fields remain the same.

Producing More Than One Sum

It is also possible to perform *several* ADD operations with a single statement, using the TO format. That is, the following is a valid statement:

```
ADD AMT1 AMT2 TO TOTAL1
                TOTAL2
```

This results in the same series of operations as:

```
ADD AMT1 AMT2 TO TOTAL1
ADD AMT1 AMT2 TO TOTAL2
```

The rules specified thus far for addition are as follows:

RULES FOR ADDITION

1. All literals and fields that are part of the addition must be numeric. After the word GIVING, however, the field may be a report-item.

2. The resultant field, following the word TO or the word GIVING, must be a data-name, not a literal.

3. When using the TO format, the data-name following the word TO is the receiving field. This receiving field is part of the ADD; that is, its initial contents are summed along with the other fields. The receiving field must be numeric when using this format.

4. When using the GIVING format, the data-name following the word GIVING is the receiving field. It will contain the sum, but its original contents will not be part of the ADD. It may be either a numeric field or a report-item.

5. The words TO and GIVING may be specified in the same statement if you are using a COBOL 85 compiler.

SELF-TEST   Indicate the errors, if any, in Statements 1 and 2.

1. ADD '12' TO TOTAL
2. ADD TAX TO TOTAL
       GIVING AMT
3. If ADD 1 15 3 TO COUNTER is performed and COUNTER is initialized at 10, the sum of __(no.)__ will be placed in _____ at the end of the operation.
4. Without using the word TO, write a statement equivalent to the one in Question 3.
5. If ADD 1 15 3 GIVING COUNTER is performed, __(no.)__ will be the result in _____ .

Solutions
1. '12' is not a numeric literal.
2. For COBOL 85, the statement is okay; for COBOL 74, the words TO and GIVING may not appear in the same ADD statement.
3. 29; COUNTER
4. ADD 1 15 3 COUNTER GIVING WS-AREA1. In this case, the result is placed in WS-AREA1 and COUNTER remains unchanged. The arithmetic is, however, the same as in the previous problem. ADD 1 15 3 COUNTER GIVING COUNTER is also correct.
5. 19; COUNTER

SUBTRACT STATEMENT

The **SUBTRACT** operation has the following two instruction formats:

Format 1

$$\text{\underline{SUBTRACT}} \quad \begin{Bmatrix} \text{identifier-1} \\ \text{literal-1} \end{Bmatrix} \quad \dots \quad \text{\underline{FROM}} \quad \text{identifier-2} \dots$$

Format 2

$$\text{SUBRACT} \begin{Bmatrix} \text{identifier-1} \\ \text{literal-1} \end{Bmatrix} \dots \text{FROM} \begin{Bmatrix} \text{identifier-2} \\ \text{literal-2} \end{Bmatrix}$$

$$\text{GIVING identifier-3} \dots$$

Rules for Interpreting the Instruction Format
1. Notice the placement of ellipses or dots in Format 1. The first set after identifier-1 means that two or more operands may be subtracted from identifier-2. In addition, operands may be subtracted from identifier-3, identifier-4, and so on.
2. With Format 2, any number of identifiers can follow the word SUBTRACT or the word GIVING, but after the word FROM only one identifier or literal is permitted.

Examples 1–4
1. SUBTRACT CHECK-AMOUNT FROM BALANCE
2. SUBTRACT CHECK-AMOUNT SERVICE-CHARGE
    FROM OLD-BALANCE GIVING NEW-BALANCE
3. SUBTRACT TAX FROM GROSS-PAY-IN
    GIVING NET-PAY-OUT
4. SUBTRACT TAX FICA INSUR-PREM
    FROM GROSS-PAY-IN GIVING NET-PAY-OUT

The rules for a SUBTRACT are similar to those for an ADD:

RULES FOR SUBTRACTION

1. All literals and data-names that are part of the subtraction must be numeric; the field specified after the word GIVING, however, may be a report-item.

2. The receiving field, which is the one that will hold the result, must be a data-name and *not* a literal.
   The following statement is incorrect: SUBTRACT TAX FROM 100.00. If you want to subtract a quantity from a literal (e.g., 100.00), you *must* use the GIVING format: SUBTRACT TAX FROM 100.00 GIVING NET.

3. All fields and literals preceding the word FROM will be added together and the sum subtracted from the field following the word FROM. The result, or difference, will be placed in this same field if no GIVING option is used. All other fields will remain unchanged.

4. When using the GIVING option, the operation performed is the same as in Rule 3, but the result, or difference, is placed in the field following the word GIVING. The initial contents of the resultant field after the word GIVING do *not* take part in the arithmetic operation.

Example 5
SUBTRACT 15.40 TAX TOTAL
    FROM AMT

	TAX	TOTAL	AMT
Before the SUBTRACT:	30∧00	10∧00	100∧00
After the SUBTRACT:	30∧00	10∧00	044∧60

Example 6
SUBTRACT 15.40 TAX TOTAL
    FROM AMT GIVING NET

	TAX	TOTAL	AMT	NET
Before the SUBTRACT:	30ʌ00	10ʌ00	100ʌ00	87ʌ00
After the SUBTRACT:	30ʌ00	10ʌ00	100ʌ00	44ʌ60

Examples 5 and 6 produce the same result but in different storage areas. In Example 6, the original contents of NET are replaced with the result and do *not* affect the calculation.

Deciding Which Format to Use

As a rule, when the contents of an operand are not needed after the SUBTRACT operation, Format 1 may be used. When the contents of all operands are to be retained, use Format 2.

As in ADD operations, all commas are optional. A space must, however, follow each comma.

As noted, it is possible to perform several SUBTRACT operations with a single statement using Format 1. That is, the following is a valid statement:

```
SUBTRACT AMT1 AMT2 AMT3
     FROM TOTAL1
          TOTAL2
          TOTAL3
```

The preceding results in the same series of operations as:

```
SUBTRACT AMT1 AMT2 AMT3 FROM TOTAL1
SUBTRACT AMT1 AMT2 AMT3 FROM TOTAL2
SUBTRACT AMT1 AMT2 AMT3 FROM TOTAL3
```

SELF-TEST

1. In the operation SUBTRACT 1500 FROM GROSS GIVING NET, the result, or difference, is placed in _____ . What happens to the original contents of GROSS? If GROSS has an original value of 8500, and NET has an original value of 2000, the result in NET would be _____ .

What is wrong with Statements 2 and 3?

2. SUBTRACT $23.00 FROM AMOUNT

3. SUBTRACT AMT FROM 900.00

4. Change the statement in Question 3 to make it valid.

5. Use one SUBTRACT statement to subtract three fields (TAX, CREDIT, DISCOUNT) from TOTAL and place the answer in WS-AMT.

Solutions

1. NET; it remains unchanged; 7000 (The original 2000 in NET does not enter into the calculation.)

2. $23.00 is an invalid numeric literal—numeric literals may not contain dollar signs.

3. The resultant field of a SUBTRACT operation may not be a literal.

4. SUBTRACT AMT FROM 900.00 GIVING TOTAL

5. SUBTRACT TAX CREDIT DISCOUNT FROM TOTAL GIVING WS-AMT

MULTIPLY AND DIVIDE STATEMENTS

Basic Instruction Format

Because of their similarities, the MULTIPLY and DIVIDE statements are discussed together.

The **MULTIPLY** statement has the following instruction formats:

Format 1

$$\text{MULTIPLY} \quad \left\{ \begin{array}{l} \text{identifier-1} \\ \text{literal-1} \end{array} \right\} \quad \text{BY identifier-2} \ldots$$

Format 2

$$
\text{MULTIPLY} \left\{ \begin{matrix} \text{identifier-1} \\ \text{literal-1} \end{matrix} \right\} \underline{\text{BY}} \left\{ \begin{matrix} \text{identifier-2} \\ \text{literal-2} \end{matrix} \right\}
$$

$$
\underline{\text{GIVING}} \text{ identifier-3} \ldots
$$

Examples

```
1. MULTIPLY HOURS-WORKED BY HOURLY-RATE
2. MULTIPLY QTY BY PRICE
3. MULTIPLY 2000 BY NO-OF-EXEMPTIONS
      GIVING EXEMPTION-AMT
4. MULTIPLY 60 BY HOURS
      GIVING MINUTES
```

The **DIVIDE** statement has the following instruction formats:

Format 1

$$
\underline{\text{DIVIDE}} \left\{ \begin{matrix} \text{identifier-1} \\ \text{literal-1} \end{matrix} \right\} \underline{\text{INTO}} \text{ identifier-2} \ldots
$$

Format 2

$$
\underline{\text{DIVIDE}} \left\{ \begin{matrix} \text{identifier-1} \\ \text{literal-1} \end{matrix} \right\} \underline{\text{INTO}} \left\{ \begin{matrix} \text{identifier-2} \\ \text{literal-2} \end{matrix} \right\}
$$

$$
\underline{\text{GIVING}} \text{ identifier-3} \ldots
$$

Format 3

$$
\underline{\text{DIVIDE}} \left\{ \begin{matrix} \text{identifier-1} \\ \text{literal-1} \end{matrix} \right\} \underline{\text{BY}} \left\{ \begin{matrix} \text{identifier-2} \\ \text{literal-2} \end{matrix} \right\}
$$

$$
\underline{\text{GIVING}} \text{ identifier-3} \ldots
$$

Either the word INTO *or* BY may be used with a DIVIDE statement. The GIVING clause is optional with INTO but required with BY.

Examples

```
1. DIVIDE MINUTES BY 60        3. DIVIDE 12 INTO ANN-SAL-IN
      GIVING HOURS                   GIVING MONTHLY-SAL-OUT
2. DIVIDE 60 INTO MINUTES      4. DIVIDE ANN-SAL-IN BY 12
      GIVING HOURS                   GIVING MONTHLY-SAL-OUT
```

Note that Examples 1 and 2 produce the same results, as do Examples 3 and 4. All arithmetic statements may have a GIVING clause. When the contents of the operands are to be retained during an arithmetic operation, use the GIVING option. If operands need not be retained and are large enough to store the answer, the GIVING option is not required. In either case, the resultant field must always be a data-name or identifier and *never* a literal.

All arithmetic operations can have more than one resultant field. Although ADD and SUBTRACT instructions can operate on numerous fields, the MULTIPLY and DIVIDE instructions are limited in the number of operations performed. For example, suppose we wish to obtain the product of PRICE × QTY × DISCOUNT. *Two* operations would be used to obtain the desired product: (1) MULTIPLY PRICE BY QTY GIVING WS-AMT. The result, or product, is placed in WS-AMT. Then, (2) MULTIPLY WS-AMT BY DISCOUNT. The product of the three numbers is now in DISCOUNT. Hence, with each MULTIPLY or DIVIDE statement specified, *only two operands* can be multiplied or divided. Always make sure the receiving field is large enough to store the result.

Note that one operand can be multiplied by numerous fields. That is, MULTIPLY AMT BY WS-TOTAL1, WS-TOTAL2 is valid.

The preposition used with the MULTIPLY verb is always BY. To say MULTIPLY PRICE TIMES QTY GIVING WS-AMT is incorrect. In the DIVIDE operation, the preposition is either BY or INTO. To say DIVIDE QTY INTO WS-TOTAL places in the resultant field, WS-TOTAL, the quotient of WS-TOTAL divided by QTY.

Note that the following two statements produce the same results:

```
1.  DIVIDE 3 INTO GRADES      2.  DIVIDE 3 INTO GRADES
        GIVING GRADES
```

Examples of Arithmetic Operations

Let us now illustrate some arithmetic operations. Assume that all fields used in the following examples have the proper numeric PICTURE clauses. Keep in mind that the solution indicated for each example is only *one* method for solving the problem.

Example 1 Celsius temperatures are to be converted to Fahrenheit temperatures according to the following formula:

FAHRENHEIT = (9 / 5) CELSIUS + 32

CELSIUS is a field in the input area, and FAHRENHEIT is a field in the output area. Both have numeric PICTURE clauses in the DATA DIVISION.

One solution may be specified as follows:

```
MULTIPLY 9 BY CELSIUS
DIVIDE 5 INTO CELSIUS
ADD 32
    CELSIUS
    GIVING FAHRENHEIT
```

If CELSIUS had an initial value of 20, its contents at the end of the operation would be 36 [i.e., $(9 * \text{CELSIUS}) / 5$] and FAHRENHEIT would be equal to 68 (36 + 32).

You may have realized that 9/5 CELSIUS = 1.8 CELSIUS. Thus, the preceding solution may be reduced to two steps:

```
MULTIPLY 1.8 BY CELSIUS
ADD 32
    CELSIUS
    GIVING FAHRENHEIT
```

Example 2 Compute the average of three fields: EXAM1, EXAM2, EXAM3. Place the answer in AVERAGE, and do not alter the contents of the three fields.

One solution may be specified as follows:

```
ADD EXAM1 EXAM2 EXAM3
    GIVING AVERAGE
DIVIDE 3 INTO AVERAGE
```

Example 3 Find C = A² + B² where A, B, and C are fields defined in the DATA DIVISION.

Solution

```
MULTIPLY A BY A
MULTIPLY B BY B
ADD A B
    GIVING C
```

Note that to multiply A by itself places A $\times$ A or A² in the field called A.

Observe that the following is *not* a correct solution:

```
ADD A TO B
MULTIPLY B BY B
    GIVING C
```

The initial ADD operation places in B the sum of A + B. The multiplication would then result in the product of $(A + B) \times (A + B)$, which is $(A + B)^2$, *not* $A^2 + B^2$. If A = 2 and B = 3, the result in C should be $2^2 + 3^2 = 4 + 9 = 13$. However, the preceding coding places the value 25 in C, which is $(2 + 3)^2$.

Use of the REMAINDER Clause in the DIVIDE Operation

When performing a division operation, the result will be placed in the receiving field according to the PIC specifications of that field. Consider the following:

Example 4

```
DIVIDE 130 BY 40
    GIVING WS-TOTAL
```

WS-TOTAL has a PICTURE of 99. After the operation is performed, 03 is placed in WS-TOTAL:

$$
\begin{array}{r}
3 \longleftarrow \text{Quotient} \\
40\overline{)130} \\
-120 \\
\hline
10 \longleftarrow \text{Remainder}
\end{array}
$$

It is sometimes useful to store the remainder of a division operation either for additional processing or simply because you need to know if there is a remainder. The DIVIDE can be used for these purposes by including a **REMAINDER** clause.

Additional Instruction Formats for the DIVIDE Statement

Format 4

$$
\underline{DIVIDE} \begin{Bmatrix} \text{identifier-1} \\ \text{literal-1} \end{Bmatrix} \underline{INTO} \begin{Bmatrix} \text{identifier-2} \\ \text{literal-2} \end{Bmatrix} \underline{GIVING} \text{ identifier-3}
$$
$$
\underline{REMAINDER} \text{ identifier-4}
$$

Format 5

$$
\underline{DIVIDE} \begin{Bmatrix} \text{identifier-1} \\ \text{literal-1} \end{Bmatrix} \underline{BY} \begin{Bmatrix} \text{identifier-2} \\ \text{literal-2} \end{Bmatrix} \underline{GIVING} \text{ identifier-3}
$$
$$
\underline{REMAINDER} \text{ identifier-4}
$$

To retain the remainder for future processing in the preceding example, we have:

```
WORKING-STORAGE SECTION.
01  WORK-AREAS.
    05  WS-REMAINDER     PIC 99.
    05  WS-TOTAL         PIC 99.
        :
        :
*
PROCEDURE DIVISION.
    :
    :
    DIVIDE 130 BY 40
        GIVING WS-TOTAL            ◄──WS-TOTAL will = 03
            REMAINDER WS-REMAINDER ◄──WS-REMAINDER will = 10
```

The use of the REMAINDER clause is optional; including it does *not change*, in any way, the results of the original divide operation. We may use the REMAINDER clause, for example, to determine if a DIVIDE operation produces a quotient with no remainder at all. That is, we could test the REMAINDER field to see if it is zero. Table 7.1 summarizes the arithmetic operations we have discussed.

Table 7.1

	Summary of How Arithmetic Operations Are Performed			
	Value *After* Execution of the Statement			
Arithmetic Statement	A	B	C	D
1. ADD A TO B	A	A + B		
2. ADD A B C TO D	A	B	C	A + B + C + D
3. ADD A B C GIVING D	A	B	C	A + B + C
4. ADD A TO B C	A	A + B	A + C	
5. SUBTRACT A FROM B	A	B − A		
6. SUBTRACT A B FROM C	A	B	C − (A + B)	
7. SUBTRACT A B FROM C GIVING D	A	B	C	C − (A + B)
8. MULTIPLY A BY B	A	A × B		
9. MULTIPLY A BY B GIVING C	A	B	A × B	
10. DIVIDE A INTO B	A	B/A		
11. DIVIDE A INTO B GIVING C	A	B	B/A	
12. DIVIDE A BY B GIVING C	A	B	A/B	
13. DIVIDE A INTO B GIVING C REMAINDER D (Assume C and D are integers)	A	B	$\left(\begin{array}{c}\text{INTEGER VALUE}\\ \text{OF B/A}\end{array}\right)$	$\left(\begin{array}{c}\text{INTEGER}\\ \text{REMAINDER}\end{array}\right)$

SELF-TEST   1. DISTANCE is the distance traveled in a specific car trip, and GAS is the number of gallons of gas used. Calculate the average gas mileage and place it in a field called AVERAGE.

2. Using MULTIPLY and DIVIDE verbs, compute: (C / B + E / F) × S.

What, if anything, is wrong with the following three statements?

```
3. DIVIDE  −35 INTO A
4. MULTIPLY A TIMES B
        GIVING C
5. MULTIPLY A BY B BY C
        GIVING D
```

Solutions
```
1. DIVIDE DISTANCE BY GAS
        GIVING AVERAGE
2. DIVIDE B INTO C
   DIVIDE F INTO E
   ADD C
       E
       GIVING WS-HOLD-AREA
   MULTIPLY WS-HOLD-AREA BY S
       GIVING ANS
```

3. Nothing wrong (Negative numbers may be used as literals but the field called A should have an S in its PIC clause.)

4. The preposition must be BY in the MULTIPLY operation.

5. Only two operands may be multiplied together with one MULTIPLY verb.

OPTIONS AVAILABLE WITH ARITHMETIC VERBS

ROUNDED Option

Consider the following example:

```
ADD AMT1
    AMT2
    GIVING AMT3
```

AMT1		AMT2		AMT3		
PICTURE	*Contents*	PICTURE	*Contents*	PICTURE	*Contents After* ADD	12.857
99V999	12ᴧ857	99V999	25ᴧ142	99V99	37ᴧ99	+25.142
						37.99**9̸**

Performing arithmetic operations on fields that have different numbers of decimal positions is not uncommon in programming. In the preceding example, two fields, each with three decimal positions, are added together, and the resultant field contains only two decimal places. The computer adds the two fields AMT1 and AMT2, with the sum 37ᴧ999 placed in an accumulator. It attempts to move this result to AMT3, a field with only two decimal positions. The effect is the same as coding MOVE 37.999 TO AMT3. The low-order decimal position is truncated. Thus, AMT3 is replaced with 37ᴧ99.

A more desirable result would be 38ᴧ00 since 38 is closer to the sum of 37.999 than is 37.99. Generally, we consider results more accurate if they are *rounded* to the nearest decimal position.

To obtain rounded results, the **ROUNDED** option may be specified with any arithmetic statement. In all cases, it directly follows the resultant data-name. The following examples serve as illustrations:

Examples 1–6
```
1. ADD AMT1 TO AMT2 ROUNDED        5. ADD AMT1
2. SUBTRACT DISCOUNT FROM TOTAL           AMT2
      ROUNDED                             GIVING TOTAL1 ROUNDED
3. MULTIPLY QTY BY PRICE ROUNDED   6. ADD AMT1
4. DIVIDE UNITS-OF-ITEM INTO TOTAL        AMT2
      ROUNDED                             GIVING TOTAL1 ROUNDED
                                                 TOTAL2 ROUNDED
```

If AMT1 and AMT2 had contents of 12.8576 and 25.142 in Examples 5 and 6, and TOTAL1 had a PIC of 99V99, the result would be rounded to 38ᴧ00.

How Rounding Is Accomplished

ROUNDED is optional with all arithmetic operations. If the ROUNDED option is not specified, truncation of decimal positions will occur if the resultant field cannot accommodate all the decimal positions in the answer. With the ROUNDED option, the computer will always round the result to the PICTURE specification of the receiving field. Consider the following example:

Example 7
```
SUBTRACT DISCOUNT FROM TOTAL
    GIVING AMT
```

DISCOUNT		TOTAL		AMT	
PICTURE	*Contents*	PICTURE	*Contents*	PICTURE	*Contents*
99V99	87ᴧ23	99V99	99ᴧ98	99	12

In this case, 87.23 is subtracted from 99.98 and the result, 12.75, is placed in an accumulator. The computer moves this result to AMT. Since AMT has no decimal positions, truncation occurs and 12 is placed in AMT.

Now consider the following SUBTRACT operation:

```
SUBTRACT DISCOUNT FROM TOTAL
    GIVING AMT ROUNDED
```

In this case, 12.75 is rounded to the PICTURE specification of the receiving field; that is, rounding to the nearest integer position will occur. 12.75 rounded to the nearest integer is 13, which is placed in AMT. In practice, .5 is added to 12.75 producing 13.25, which is then truncated to an integer:

$$
\begin{array}{r}
12.75 \\
+\ \ .5 \\
\hline
13.2\cancel{5}
\end{array}
$$

If ROUNDED and REMAINDER are to be used in the same DIVIDE statement, ROUNDED must appear first:

Format

> DIVIDE   ...
>   [ROUNDED] [REMAINDER identifier]

ON SIZE ERROR Option

Consider the following:

```
ADD AMT1 AMT2 TO AMT3
```

Before the operation, the fields contain the following:

AMT1		AMT2		AMT3	
PICTURE	Contents	PICTURE	Contents	PICTURE	Contents
999	800	999	150	999	050

The computer will add 800, 150, and 050 in an accumulator. It will attempt to place the sum, 1000, into AMT3, which is a three-position field. The effect would be the same as coding MOVE 1000 TO AMT3. Since numeric MOVE operations move integer data from right to left, 000 will be placed in AMT3. In this case, the resultant field is not large enough to store the accumulated sum. We say that an **overflow** or size error condition has occurred.

Note that an overflow condition will produce erroneous results. The computer will not generally stop or abort the run because of a size error condition; instead, it will truncate high-order or leftmost positions of the field. In our example, 000 will be placed in AMT3.

Avoiding Size Errors

The best way to avoid a size error condition is to be absolutely certain that the receiving field is large enough to accommodate any possible result. Sometimes, however, the programmer forgets to account for the rare occasion when an overflow might occur. COBOL has a built-in solution. Use an **ON SIZE ERROR** clause with any arithmetic operation as follows:

Format

> arithmetic statement
>   [ON SIZE ERROR imperative statement . . .]

The word ON is optional; hence it is not underlined. By an **imperative statement,** we mean any COBOL statement that gives a direct command and does not perform a test.

Statements beginning with the COBOL word IF are conditional statements and are not considered imperative. This concept will become clearer in the next chapter when we discuss conditional statements.

Coding Guideline

Since ON SIZE ERROR is a separate clause, we place it on a separate line for ease of reading and debugging.

Examples 1–2

```
1. ADD AMT1 AMT2 TO AMT3 GIVING TOTAL-OUT
       ON SIZE ERROR MOVE ZERO TO TOTAL-OUT
   END-ADD
2. DIVIDE 60 INTO MINUTES GIVING HOURS
       ON SIZE ERROR MOVE 'INVALID DIVIDE' TO ERROR-MESSAGE
   END-DIVIDE
```

How ON SIZE ERROR Works

The computer performs the arithmetic and ignores the SIZE ERROR clause if there is no size error condition. If a size error occurs, the computer does *not* perform the arithmetic but instead executes the statement(s) in the SIZE ERROR clause. In Example 1, the computer will move zeros to TOTAL-OUT if it does not contain enough integer positions to accommodate the sum of AMT1, AMT2, and AMT3. If TOTAL-OUT is large enough for the result, zeros will *not* be moved to it and execution will continue with the next sentence.

Dividing by Zero Causes a SIZE ERROR

A size error, then, is a condition in which the receiving field does not have enough *integer* positions to hold the result of an arithmetic operation. In a divide, the size error condition has additional significance. If an attempt is made to *divide by zero*, a size error condition will occur. This is because division by zero yields a result of infinity, which makes it impossible to define a sufficiently large receiving field.
  Consider the following:

Example 3

```
DIVIDE QTY INTO TOTAL
    ON SIZE ERROR MOVE ZERO TO TOTAL
END-DIVIDE
```

Assume that the fields contain the following data before the operation:

QTY		TOTAL	
PICTURE	Contents	PICTURE	Contents
9999	0000	99	10

A size error occurs during the DIVIDE operation because QTY = 0. When the SIZE ERROR clause is executed, TOTAL is set equal to 0. If a SIZE ERROR clause were not specified, the computer would attempt to divide by zero. The result of such a division would be unpredictable or may even cause a program interrupt. When you specify ON SIZE ERROR, the computer will make certain that the divisor is *not* zero before attempting to DIVIDE. You will see in the next chapter that you may also avoid errors by coding:

```
IF  QTY IS NOT ZERO
    DIVIDE QTY INTO TOTAL
ELSE
    MOVE 0 TO TOTAL
END-IF
```

If the ON SIZE ERROR option is employed along with the ROUNDED option, the word ROUNDED always precedes ON SIZE ERROR:

Format

> arithmetic statement
> [ROUNDED] [ON SIZE ERROR imperative statement . . .]

When using a REMAINDER in a DIVIDE operation, we would have the following sequence of clauses:

Format

> DIVIDE . . . [ROUNDED] [REMAINDER identifier]
> [ON SIZE ERROR imperative statement . . .]
> [END-DIVIDE]*

*COBOL 85 only.

When using a separate clause such as ON SIZE ERROR, use a scope terminator with COBOL 85 to delimit or end the arithmetic operation. END-ADD, END-SUBTRACT, END-MULTIPLY, and END-DIVIDE are all permissible scope terminators. For COBOL 74, each statement ends with a period instead of a scope terminator.

If you use an ON SIZE ERROR clause and do not use a scope terminator, a period must be placed at the end of the statement to designate the end of the clause. Consider the following example:

Example

```
    ADD A TO B
        ON SIZE ERROR MOVE 0 TO B
    PERFORM 400-WRITE-RTN.
300-HEADING-RTN.
    :
    :
```

Because of the alignment, you might assume that the PERFORM is a statement separate from the ADD. Actually the PERFORM is part of the ON SIZE ERROR clause. That is, if there is a size error, 0 is moved to B *and* 400-WRITE-RTN is executed. Because there is no END-ADD scope terminator, the computer assumes that for size errors, all statements *up to the period* are to be executed. This means that 400-WRITE-RTN is *only* executed in case of a size error.

To avoid any problems, always end an arithmetic statement that has an ON SIZE ERROR clause with a scope terminator (COBOL 85) or a period (COBOL 74).

NOT ON SIZE ERROR CLAUSE

With COBOL 85, another permissible test that may be used with any arithmetic operation is NOT ON SIZE ERROR:

Example

```
ADD AMT1 AMT2
        GIVING TOTAL-AMT
    NOT ON SIZE ERROR
        PERFORM 300-WRITE-RTN
END-ADD
```

300-WRITE-RTN is executed only if the ADD operation results in a valid addition, that is, only if TOTAL-AMT is large enough to hold the sum of AMT1 and AMT2.

With COBOL 85, *both* ON SIZE ERROR *and* NOT ON SIZE ERROR can be specified with any arithmetic operation. These clauses are similar to the AT END and NOT AT END with a READ.

DETERMINING THE SIZE OF RECEIVING FIELDS

When performing arithmetic, you must make certain that the receiving field is large enough to accommodate the result. In an ADD, determine the largest quantity that can be stored in each field and manually perform an addition. Use the result to determine how large the receiving field should be. With a subtract, manually subtract the smallest possible number from the largest possible number to determine how large to make the receiving field.

As a general rule, the number of integer positions in the receiving field of a MULTIPLY operation should be equal to the *sum* of the integers of the fields being multiplied. Suppose we code MULTIPLY QTY BY PRICE GIVING TOTAL. If QTY has a PIC of 99 and PRICE has a PIC of 999, then to ensure that TOTAL is large enough to accommodate the result it should have a PIC of 9(5), which is the sum of the two integers in QTY plus the three integers in PRICE. The number of decimal positions in the receiving field will depend on the decimal precision desired in the result.

For DIVIDE operations, the PIC clause of the quotient or receiving field is dependent on the type of divide. Consider the following:

```
DIVIDE TOTAL-PRICE BY QTY
    GIVING UNIT-COST
```

If TOTAL-PRICE and QTY have PIC 9, the receiving field may have PIC 9V99 or 9V9, to allow for decimal values (e.g., 3/6 = .5). But suppose TOTAL-PRICE has PIC 9V9 and contents of 9∧0, and QTY has the same PIC clause with contents of .1. The result of the divide is 9/.1, which is equal to 90. Hence UNIT-COST would need a PIC of 99. As a rule, determine the range of values that the fields can have and code the PIC clause of the receiving field accordingly.

Examples to Help Determine the Size of a Resultant Field

Arithmetic Operation	Example		A General Rule-of-Thumb
1. Addition of two operands	999 +999 1998	PIC 9(3) PIC 9(3) PIC 9(4)	Resultant field should be one position larger than the largest field being added.
2. Subtraction (assuming positive numbers)	999 − 1 998	PIC 9(3) PIC 9 PIC 9(3)	Resultant field should be as large as the minuend (field being subtracted from) if a smaller number is subtracted from a larger number.
3. Multiplication	999 ×999 998001	PIC S9(3) PIC S9(3) PIC S9(6)	Resultant field size should equal the sum of the lengths of the operands being multiplied.
4. Division	9990 .1 ⟌ 999	Dividend: PIC 9(3) Divisor: PIC V9 Quotient (result): PIC 9(4)	To be safe, the resultant field size should equal the sum of the number of digits in the divisor and dividend.

SELF-TEST   Fill in the dashes for Questions 1–4:

		A		B		C		D	
	PIC	Contents	PIC	Contents	PIC	Contents	PIC	Contents
1. SUBTRACT A B FROM C GIVING D	99V9	12∧3	99V9	45∧6	999V9	156∧8	999	—
2. DIVIDE A INTO B GIVING C	9V9	5∧1	9V9	8∧0	9	—		
3. DIVIDE A INTO B GIVING C ROUNDED	9V9	5∧1	9V9	8∧0	9	—		
4. DIVIDE A INTO B GIVING C ROUNDED REMAINDER D	99	20	99	50	99	—	99	—

5. Under what conditions might an ON SIZE ERROR condition occur?
6. The word ROUNDED (precedes, follows) the ON SIZE ERROR clause in an arithmetic statement.
7. DIVIDE 0 INTO A GIVING B (will, will not) result in an ON SIZE ERROR condition.
8. DIVIDE 0 BY A GIVING B (will, will not) result in an ON SIZE ERROR condition if A = 2.
9. ADD 50, 60 TO FLDA ON SIZE ERROR MOVE 1 TO COUNT results in _____ if FLDA has a PICTURE of 99.
10. ADD 50, 60 TO FLDA ON SIZE ERROR MOVE 1 TO COUNT results in _____ if FLDA has a PICTURE of 999.

Solutions
1. 098
2. 1
3. 2
4. C = 03, D = 10 (*Note:* D is calculated as follows: 50/20 = 2 with a remainder of 10. Rounding of the quotient to 3 occurs afterward.)
5. When the resultant field does not have enough integer positions to hold the entire result or when an attempt is made to divide by zero.
6. precedes
7. will
8. will not (0 divided by any positive number = 0)
9. COUNT = 1, because FLDA is not large enough to be incremented by 110
10. 110 added to FLDA (assuming that the result is less than 1000, i.e., assuming FLDA had contents less than 890 before the ADD operation)

THE COMPUTE STATEMENT

BASIC FORMAT

Most business applications operate on large volumes of input and output and require comparatively few numeric calculations. For this type of processing, the four arithmetic verbs just discussed may be adequate. If complex or extensive arithmetic operations are required in a program, however, the use of the four arithmetic verbs may prove cumbersome. The COMPUTE verb provides another method of performing arithmetic.

The COMPUTE statement uses arithmetic symbols rather than arithmetic verbs. The following symbols may be used in a COMPUTE statement:

SYMBOLS USED IN A COMPUTE

Symbol	Meaning
+	ADD
−	SUBTRACT
*	MULTIPLY
/	DIVIDE
**	exponentiation (there is no corresponding COBOL verb)

The following examples illustrate the use of the COMPUTE verb:

Examples 1–3

1. COMPUTE TAX = .05 * AMT
2. COMPUTE DAILY-SALES = QTY * UNIT-PRICE / 5
3. COMPUTE NET = AMT - .05 * AMT

Note that the COMPUTE statement has a data-name or identifier to the left of, or preceding, the equal sign. The value computed in the arithmetic expression to the right of the equal sign *is placed in* the field preceding the equal sign.

Thus, if AMT = 200 in Example 1, TAX will be set to .05 × 200, or 10, at the end of the operation. The original contents of TAX, before the COMPUTE is executed, are not retained. The fields specified to the right of the equal sign remain unchanged.

Example 4   COMPUTE TOTAL = AMT1 + AMT2 − AMT3

	Contents before operation	Contents after operation
TOTAL	100	95
AMT1	80	80
AMT2	20	20
AMT3	5	5

AMT1, AMT2, and AMT3 remain unchanged after the COMPUTE. TOTAL is set equal to the result of AMT1 + AMT2 − AMT3. The previous contents of TOTAL do not affect the operation. 95 is moved to TOTAL.

The fields specified after the equal sign in a COMPUTE statement may be numeric literals or data-names with numeric PIC clauses.

The COMPUTE statement may include more than one operation. In Example 2, both multiplication and division operations are performed. The following two statements are equivalent to the single COMPUTE statement in Example 2:

```
MULTIPLY QTY BY UNIT-PRICE
    GIVING DAILY-SALES
DIVIDE 5 INTO DAILY-SALES
```

The COMPUTE statement has the advantage of performing more than one arithmetic operation with a single verb. For this reason, it is often less cumbersome to use COMPUTE statements to code complex arithmetic.

Thus ADD, SUBTRACT, MULTIPLY, and DIVIDE correspond to the arithmetic symbols +, −, *, and /, respectively. In addition, we may raise a number to a power with the use of the arithmetic symbol ** in a COMPUTE statement. No COBOL verb corresponds to this operation. Thus COMPUTE B = A ** 2 is the same as multiplying A by A and placing the result in B. A ** 2 is expressed mathematically as A^2. A ** 3 is the same as A^3 or A $\times$ A $\times$ A. To find B^4 and place the results in C, we could code: COMPUTE C = B ** 4.

Spacing Rules with a COMPUTE

On most systems, you must follow precise spacing rules when using the COMPUTE statement. That is, the equal sign as well as the arithmetic symbols must be *preceded and followed* by a space. Thus, to calculate A = B + C + D^2 and place the result in A, use the following COMPUTE statement:

```
COMPUTE A = B + C + D ** 2
```

So far, we have used arithmetic expressions to the right of the equal sign. We may also have literals or data-names as the *only* entry to the right of the equal sign. To say COMPUTE AMT1 = 10.3 is the same as saying MOVE 10.3 TO AMT1. Similarly, to say COMPUTE AMT2 = AMT3 places the contents of AMT3 in the field called AMT2. This is the same as saying MOVE AMT3 TO AMT2. Thus, in a COMPUTE statement, we may have one of the following three entries after the equal sign:

1. An arithmetic expression. For example:

```
COMPUTE SALARY = HRS * RATE
```

2. A literal. For example:

```
COMPUTE TAX = .05
```

3. A data-name or identifier. For example:

```
COMPUTE AMT-OUT = AMT-IN
```

The ROUNDED and ON SIZE ERROR options may also be used with the COMPUTE. The rules governing the use of these clauses in ADD, SUBTRACT, MULTIPLY, and DIVIDE operations apply to COMPUTE statements as well.

To round the results in a COMPUTE statement to the specifications of the receiving field, we use the ROUNDED option directly following the receiving field. If we need to test for a size error condition we may use the ON SIZE ERROR clause as the last one in the statement. The instruction format for the COMPUTE follows:

Format

$$
\text{COMPUTE identifier-1 [ROUNDED]} \ldots = \left\{ \begin{array}{l} \text{arithmetic expression-1} \\ \text{literal-1} \\ \text{identifier-2} \end{array} \right\}
$$

[ON SIZE ERROR imperative statement]
[END-COMPUTE]*

*COBOL 85 only.

Example 5
The COMPUTE with and without rounding

a. COMPUTE A = B + C + D
b. COMPUTE A ROUNDED = B + C + D

B		C		D	
PICTURE	Contents	PICTURE	Contents	PICTURE	Contents
9V99	1$_\wedge$05	9V99	2$_\wedge$10	9V99	6$_\wedge$84

	Result in A	
	PICTURE	Contents
Example 5(a)—without rounding	99V9	09$_\wedge$9
Example 5(b)—with rounding	99V9	10$_\wedge$0

With COBOL 85, NOT ON SIZE ERROR may also be used with a COMPUTE statement. If it is used, then it would be the last clause in the statement.

END-COMPUTE may be used as a scope terminator to mark the end of a COMPUTE statement. We recommend you use END-COMPUTE if you use ON SIZE ERROR or NOT ON SIZE ERROR.

Example 6 `COMPUTE AMT1 = 105 - 3`

This COMPUTE statement would result in an overflow condition if AMT1 has a PICTURE of 99. The computed result should be 102. However, placing 102 in AMT1, a two-position numeric field, results in the truncation of the most significant digit, the hundreds position. Thus 02 will be placed in AMT1. To protect against this type of truncation of high-order integer positions, we use an ON SIZE ERROR test as follows:

```
COMPUTE AMT1  =  105  -  3
    ON SIZE ERROR PERFORM 500-ERR-RTN
END-COMPUTE
```

Use END-COMPUTE with COBOL 85 only. For COBOL 74, end the ON SIZE ERROR clause with a period.

In summary, the primary advantage of a COMPUTE statement is that several arithmetic operations may be performed with one instruction. The data-name preceding the equal sign is made equal to the literal, identifier, or arithmetic expression to the right of the equal sign. Thus, ADD 1 TO TOTAL is equivalent to COMPUTE TOTAL = TOTAL + 1.

A COMPUTE statement often requires less coding than if the arithmetic verbs such as ADD or SUBTRACT were used. The expression $C = A^2 + B^2$, for example, is more easily coded with only one COMPUTE statement:

```
COMPUTE C = A ** 2 + B ** 2
```

There is no COBOL arithmetic symbol to perform a square root operation. Mathematically, however, the square root of any number is that number raised to the ½ or .5 power. $\sqrt{25} = 25^{.5} = 5$. Thus, the square root of any number will be represented as the number raised to the .5 power. To calculate $C = \sqrt{A}$ in COBOL, we code COMPUTE C = A ** .5.

COBOL 85 users who have compilers with the Intrinsic Function Extension can use a function to calculate square roots. See the final section of this chapter.

ORDER OF EVALUATION

The order in which arithmetic operations are performed will affect the results in a COMPUTE statement. Consider the following example:

Example 7 `COMPUTE UNIT-PRICE-OUT = AMT1-IN + AMT2-IN / QTY-IN`

Depending on the order of evaluation of arithmetic operations, one of the following would be the mathematical equivalent of the preceding:

a. $UNIT\text{-}PRICE\text{-}OUT = \dfrac{AMT1\text{-}IN + AMT2\text{-}IN}{QTY\text{-}IN}$

b. $UNIT\text{-}PRICE\text{-}OUT = AMT1\text{-}IN + \dfrac{AMT2\text{-}IN}{QTY\text{-}IN}$

Note that (a) and (b) are *not* identical. If AMT1-IN = 3, AMT2-IN = 6, and QTY-IN = 3, the result of the COMPUTE statement evaluated according to the formula in (a) is 3 [(3 + 6) / 3] but according to the formula in (b) is 5 [3 + (6 / 3)].

The hierarchy of arithmetic operations is as follows:

> ### THE SEQUENCE IN WHICH OPERATIONS ARE PERFORMED IN A COMPUTE STATEMENT
>
> 1. **
>
> 2. * or / (whichever appears first from left to right)
>
> 3. + or − (whichever appears first from left to right)
>
> 4. The use of parentheses overrides rules 1–3. That is, operations within parentheses are performed first.

Without parentheses, exponentiation operations are performed first. Multiplication and division operations follow any exponentiation and precede addition or subtraction operations. If there are two or more multiplication or division operations, they are evaluated from left to right in the expression. Addition and subtraction are evaluated last, also from left to right.

Thus, in Example 7, `COMPUTE UNIT-PRICE-OUT = AMT1-IN + AMT2-IN / QTY-IN` is calculated as follows:

1. `AMT2-IN / QTY-IN`
2. `AMT1-IN + (AMT2-IN / QTY-IN)`

The result, then, is that (b) is the mathematical equivalent of the original `COMPUTE` statement. To divide `QTY-IN` into the sum of `AMT1-IN` plus `AMT2-IN`, we code:

```
COMPUTE UNIT-PRICE-OUT = (AMT1-IN + AMT2-IN) / QTY-IN
```

As another example, `COMPUTE A = C + D ** 2` results in the following order of evaluation:

1. `D ** 2`   Exponentiation is performed first
2. `C + (D ** 2)`   Addition is performed next

The result, then, is $A = C + D^2$, *not* $A = (C + D)^2$.

The statement, `COMPUTE S = T * D + E / F`, results in the following order of evaluation:

1. `T * D`   Multiplication is performed first
2. `E / F`   Division is performed next
3. `(T * D) + (E / F)`   Addition is performed last

The result, then, is: $S = T \times D + \dfrac{E}{F}$

We may alter the standard order of evaluation in a `COMPUTE` statement with the use of parentheses because operations within parentheses are always evaluated first.

Suppose we wish to compute `AVERAGE-SALES` by adding `DAYTIME-SALES` and `EVENING-SALES` and dividing the sum by two. The instruction `COMPUTE AVERAGE-SALES = DAYTIME-SALES + EVENING-SALES / 2` is *not* correct. The result of this operation is to compute `AVERAGE-SALES` by adding `DAYTIME-SALES` and one half of `EVENING-SALES`. To divide the sum of `DAYTIME-SALES` and `EVENING-SALES` by two, we must use parentheses to override the standard hierarchy rules:

```
COMPUTE AVERAGE-SALES = (DAYTIME-SALES + EVENING-SALES) / 2
```

All operations within parentheses are evaluated first. Thus we have:

1. `(DAYTIME-SALES + EVENING-SALES)`

2. `(DAYTIME-SALES + EVENING-SALES) / 2`

The following provides additional examples of the hierarchy rules:

Operation	Order of Evaluation
A / B + C	Divide A by B and add C.
A / (B + C)	Add B and C and divide A by the sum.
A + B * C	Multiply B by C and add A.
A * B / C	Multiply A by B and divide the result by C.

Example 8 We wish to obtain `NET = GROSS - DISCOUNT`, where `DISCOUNT = GROSS × .03`:

```
COMPUTE NET = GROSS - (.03 * GROSS)
```

In this example, the parentheses are not really needed, since the standard hierarchy rules produce the correct results. Including parentheses for clarity, however, is not incorrect. The following would also be correct: `COMPUTE NET = GROSS - .03 * GROSS`.

A simpler method of obtaining the correct result is:

```
COMPUTE NET = .97 * GROSS
```
or
```
MULTIPLY GROSS BY .97 GIVING NET
```

COMPARING COMPUTE TO ARITHMETIC VERBS

As we have seen, any calculation can be performed using *either* the four arithmetic verbs or the `COMPUTE`. Exponentiation, which has no corresponding verb, is more easily handled with a `COMPUTE` but can be accomplished with a `MULTIPLY` statement as well.

On pages 248 and 249 we provided three examples using the four arithmetic verbs. Alternatively, we can code these with the `COMPUTE` as:

1. Calculate Fahrenheit temperature using Celsius temperature:

   ```
   COMPUTE FAHRENHEIT = 9 / 5 * CELSIUS + 32
   ```

2. Calculate the average of three exams:

   ```
   COMPUTE AVERAGE = (EXAM1 + EXAM2 + EXAM3) / 3
   ```

3. Calculate C as $A^2 + B^2$:

   ```
   COMPUTE C = A ** 2 + B ** 2
   ```

One rule of thumb is: If one arithmetic statement will do the job, use it; if it takes more than one, use a `COMPUTE`.

A Potential Source of Errors When Using a COMPUTE

The way in which a `COMPUTE` performs its arithmetic operations varies from compiler to compiler. Consider the following, where `AMT-OUT` has `PIC 9(3)`:

```
COMPUTE AMT-OUT ROUNDED = (AMT-IN + 2.55) * 3.6
```

With some compilers, *each arithmetic operation* (in this case, the addition and multiplication) would be rounded to three integer positions (the size of `AMT-OUT`), whereas other compilers round to three integers only at the end. This means that separate runs of a program that uses this `COMPUTE` could produce different results if different compilers are used. This is one reason why some programmers use arithmetic verbs instead of the `COMPUTE`.

USE OF SIGNED NUMBERS IN ARITHMETIC OPERATIONS

THE USE OF S IN PIC CLAUSES FOR FIELDS THAT CAN BE NEGATIVE

In our illustrations, we have assumed that numbers used in calculations are *positive* and that results of calculations produce positive numbers. If, however, a number may be negative or if a calculation may produce negative results, we must use an S in the PICTURE clause of the field as noted in Chapter 6. Thus AMT1 with a PIC of S9(3) is a field that may have positive or negative contents. The S, like an implied decimal point, does not use a storage position; that is, S9(3) represents a *three-position* signed field. If AMT1 with a PIC of S9(3) has an initial value of 010 and we subtract 15 from it, the result will be −5. But if we had defined AMT1 with a PIC of 9(3), then the result would have been incorrectly retained without the sign as 5.

In summary, if a field used in an arithmetic operation may contain a negative number, use an S in the PICTURE clause. Without an S in the PICTURE clause, the field will always be considered an unsigned or positive number.

You have seen in Chapter 6 that *printing a negative number* requires a minus sign in the PICTURE clause of the receiving field. Suppose AMT1-IN has contents of −123. To print −123 correctly when we move AMT1-IN TO AMT1-OUT, AMT1-IN should have a PIC of S9(3) and AMT1-OUT should have a PICTURE of −9(3).

RULES FOR PERFORMING ARITHMETIC WITH SIGNED NUMBERS

The following are rules for performing arithmetic using signed numbers:

I. Multiplication

$$\begin{array}{r} \text{Multiplicand} \\ \times\ \text{Multiplier} \\ \hline \text{Product} \end{array}$$

A. Product is + if multiplicand and multiplier have the same sign.
B. Product is − if multiplicand and multiplier have different signs.

Examples

$$\begin{array}{r} 1.\quad +\ 5 \\ \times\ -\ 3 \\ \hline -15 \end{array} \qquad \begin{array}{r} 2.\quad -\ 3 \\ \times\ -\ 2 \\ \hline +\ 6 \end{array}$$

II. Division

$$\text{Divisor}\ \overline{\big)\ \text{Dividend}} \quad \overset{\text{Quotient}}{}$$

A. Quotient is + if dividend and divisor have the same sign.
B. Quotient is − if dividend and divisor have different signs.

Examples

$$1.\quad -3\ \overline{\big)\ -6} \quad\overset{2}{} \qquad 2.\quad -1\ \overline{\big)\ 5} \quad\overset{-5}{}$$

III. Addition
A. If signs of the fields being added are the same, add and use the sign.

Examples

$$\begin{array}{r} 1.\quad +\ 15 \\ +\ 10 \\ +\ 20 \\ \hline +\ 45 \end{array} \qquad \begin{array}{r} 2.\quad -\ 15 \\ -\ 10 \\ -\ 20 \\ \hline -\ 45 \end{array}$$

B. If signs of the fields being added are different, add all + numbers, and add all − numbers separately. Then subtract the smaller total from the larger total and use the sign of the larger.

Examples

1. + 15
    + 10
    − 15
    − 5

2. + 25
    − 20
    + 5

IV. Subtraction

Minuend
− Subtrahend
Difference

Change the sign of the subtrahend and proceed as in addition.

Examples

1. $15 - 5 = 15 + (-5) = +10$

2. $-3 - (+2) = -3 + (-2) = -5$

ENTERING SIGNED NUMBERS

Suppose we establish an input field, with one integer, as PIC S9. This is a *one-position field*. How do we enter or key −1, for example, into a one-position field?

The way in which a signed number is entered as input varies from computer to computer. One common method is as follows:

	Negative Numbers		Positive Numbers
Value	**How It Is Entered**	**Value**	**How It Is Entered**
−0	}	+1	A
−1	J	+2	B
−2	K	+3	C
−3	L	+4	D
−4	M	+5	E
−5	N	+6	F
−6	O	+7	G
−7	P	+8	H
−8	Q	+9	I
−9	R		

Thus, to enter −5 in a one-position field, we would key in the *letter N*. The contents of a numeric field with PIC S9 and a value of N will be treated as containing −5.

If a field has two or more integers, a negative value is represented with a letter J–R that is typically entered as the *rightmost* or low-order *digit*. −12, for example, would be entered as 1K; −228 would be entered as 22Q. This convention is a holdover from the old punched card days where negative numbers 1–9 were represented as J–R to save space on a card.

To enter a sign as a *separate character*, use the following clause after the PIC clause in the DATA DIVISION:

$$\text{SIGN IS} \begin{Bmatrix} \text{TRAILING} \\ \text{LEADING} \end{Bmatrix} \text{SEPARATE}$$

That is, to enter −1234 in a field with PIC S9(4), code the field as 05 AMT PIC S9(4) SIGN IS LEADING SEPARATE. Similarly, to enter 1234− in a field, code it as 05 AMT PIC S9(4) SIGN IS TRAILING SEPARATE. Note, however, that these SIGN clauses make AMT a five-position field.

Finally, note that to change the sign of a field we could code either:

1. MOVE −B TO STORE or

2. MULTIPLY B BY −1 GIVING STORE

IMPROVING PROGRAM EFFICIENCY WITH THE USAGE CLAUSE

FORMAT

There are many ways in which numeric data can be stored internally within the computer. The specific method for storing numeric data affects the type of processing that can be performed as well as the program's efficiency.

The **USAGE clause** specifies the form in which data is stored within the computer. The format for the USAGE clause is:

Format

$$[\underline{USAGE} \ IS] \begin{Bmatrix} \underline{DISPLAY} \\ \underline{COMPUTATIONAL} \\ \underline{COMP} \\ \underline{PACKED-DECIMAL}* \end{Bmatrix}$$

*Available with COBOL 85 only.

PACKED-DECIMAL is only available for COBOL 85 users, but many computers permit a similar clause for all their compilers:

$$[\underline{USAGE} \ IS] \begin{Bmatrix} \underline{COMPUTATIONAL-3} \\ \underline{COMP-3} \end{Bmatrix}$$

We have not included all the options that can be used with a USAGE clause, only the most common ones. The *COBOL Syntax Reference Guide* that accompanies this text has a complete list of options available.

Example

The USAGE clause may be used with a group item or an elementary item. If it is used with a group item, then it refers to *all* elements within the group:

```
01   TABLE-X USAGE IS COMPUTATIONAL.
     05   ITEM-X        PIC S9(10).
     05   ITEM-Y        PIC S9(5).
     :
     :
```

USAGE IS DISPLAY

The USAGE IS DISPLAY clause means that the standard data format is used to represent a field. That is, a single position of storage will be used to *store one character of data*. The clause USAGE IS DISPLAY stores *one character per storage position*, which is the default. Thus, unless the programmer specifies otherwise, data is always stored in DISPLAY mode.

USAGE IS PACKED-DECIMAL (COBOL 85) OR COMPUTATIONAL-3 (COMP-3)—A COMMON ENHANCEMENT

PACKED-DECIMAL means that each digit is represented as compactly or concisely as is possible given the computer's configuration. Thus, each implementor determines the precise effect of the USAGE IS PACKED-DECIMAL clause. Typically, it is used to conserve storage space when defining numeric WORKING-STORAGE items because it enables numeric fields to be stored as compactly as possible.

On many computers, PACKED-DECIMAL (COBOL 85) or COMPUTATIONAL-3 enables the computer to store *two digits* in each storage position, except for the rightmost position, which holds the sign. Suppose you move 1258738 into a WS-AMT field defined with PIC 9(7). In DISPLAY mode, which is the default, this field will use *seven storage positions.* If you define the field with PIC 9(7) USAGE IS PACKED-DECIMAL, it will, however, use only four positions:

| 12 | 58 | 73 | 8+ | ◄————The rightmost position contains a digit and a sign

We can save a significant amount of storage by using the USAGE IS PACKED-DECIMAL clause for numeric WORKING-STORAGE entries. It is also widely used for concisely storing numeric data on disk.

Similarly, tables are frequently defined as PACKED-DECIMAL fields. We use an OCCURS to define a table. Consider the following table consisting of 1000 entries:

Example
```
01  TABLE-1 USAGE IS PACKED-DECIMAL.
    05  ENTRIES OCCURS 1000 TIMES      PIC 9(5).
```

Each of the ENTRIES fields will use three storage positions instead of five. For example, 12345 can be stored as: | 1 2 | 3 4 | 5 + | rather than: | 1 | 2 | 3 | 4 | 5 |. Since there are 1000 ENTRIES, this USAGE clause can save thousands of storage positions. We discuss this in more detail in Chapter 12.

The PACKED-DECIMAL (COBOL 85) or COMPUTATIONAL-3 (COMP-3) option should *not* be used for printing output because packed-decimal data is not readable. Since each storage position does *not* contain an actual character, printing it will produce unreadable output. To print packed-decimal data, it must first be *moved* to a numeric field in character (PIC 9 or PIC 9 USAGE IS DISPLAY) form or to a report-item.

Input disk fields may also be defined using this PACKED-DECIMAL (or COMP-3) clause if the data was originally produced in packed-decimal form.

The computer automatically converts from packed to unpacked form and vice versa. Thus, moving a packed numeric field to an unpacked numeric field will automatically unpack the sending field into the receiving field.

In summary, COMPUTATIONAL-3 or COMP-3 is not part of the standard but it is widely used. PACKED-DECIMAL is available with COBOL 85.

USAGE IS COMPUTATIONAL (COMP)

USAGE IS COMPUTATIONAL or COMP stores data in the form in which the computer actually does its computation. Usually this form is *binary.* Thus, defining WORKING-STORAGE entries in binary format is desirable when many repetitive arithmetic computations must be performed. Similarly, for some applications, it is more efficient to produce binary output, so that when the data is read in again at a later date, conversion to binary will not be necessary.

Subscripts and counters are typically generated in binary form on many computers. To avoid compiler-generated conversions of fields such as subscripts from binary to decimal, you should define them with USAGE IS COMP or COMPUTATIONAL.

 COBOL 85 permits the USAGE IS BINARY clause as well to specifically represent data in binary form.

INTRINSIC FUNCTIONS (COBOL 85)

 Many programming languages have built-in or **intrinsic functions**. Thus far, 42 functions have been approved for COBOL 85; more may be forthcoming in the new standard. These functions were approved in 1989 as extensions to the standard and many compilers have incorporated them.

Example 1   Let us consider first a function to calculate the square root of a number. To calculate the square root of X and place the result in Y, we may code:

```
COMPUTE Y = FUNCTION SQRT (X)
```

The word `FUNCTION` is required, followed by the specific intrinsic function, in this case the square root or `SQRT` function. The field or argument to be operated on is enclosed in parentheses. Arguments can be identifiers or literals. We use the `COMPUTE` instruction to return to the field called Y the value of the square root of X.

Example 2   Suppose we want to convert an alphanumeric field called `NAME-IN` to all uppercase letters. There is an intrinsic function for this as well:

```
MOVE FUNCTION UPPER-CASE (NAME-IN) TO NAME-OUT
```

`UPPER-CASE` is an intrinsic function that is used to move to `NAME-OUT` the uppercase equivalent of whatever value is in `NAME-IN`. Characters that are not letters will be moved as is, and lowercase letters will be converted to uppercase. John O'Connor 3rd, for example, will be returned to `NAME-OUT` as JOHN O'CONNOR 3RD.

We have divided the 42 intrinsic functions that have already been approved into several categories: calendar functions, numerical analysis and statistical functions, trigonometric functions, financial functions, and character and string functions.

CALENDAR FUNCTIONS

1. `CURRENT-DATE`—If you code `MOVE FUNCTION CURRENT-DATE TO CURRENT-DATE-AND-TIME`, the latter should contain 21 characters and have the following components:

```
01  CURRENT-DATE-AND-TIME.
    03  THIS-DATE.
        05  CURRENT-YEAR    PIC 9999.
        05  CURRENT-MONTH   PIC 99.
        05  CURRENT-DAY     PIC 99.
    03  THIS-TIME.
        05  HRS             PIC 99.
        05  MINUTES         PIC 99.
        05  SECONDS         PIC 99.
        05  HUNDREDTHS      PIC 99.
        05  OFFSET-VALUE    PIC X.
        05  OFFSET-HOUR     PIC 99.
        05  OFFSET-MINUTE   PIC 99.
```

2. `WHEN-COMPILED`—This calendar function returns the same 21 characters of date and time information indicating when the program was compiled.

3. `INTEGER-OF-DATE`—This is another calendar function that returns the number of days since January 1, 1601. The starting date of January 1, 1601 was chosen somewhat arbitrarily as a base from which integer values for more recent dates could be calculated. This numeric value is often used to determine the days that have elapsed from one date to another:

```
COMPUTE NUMBER-OF-DAYS-SINCE-LAST-PURCHASE =
    FUNCTION INTEGER-OF-DATE (THIS-DATE)
    - FUNCTION INTEGER-OF-DATE (PURCHASE-DATE)
```

or

```
SUBTRACT FUNCTION INTEGER-OF-DATE (PURCHASE-DATE)
    FROM FUNCTION INTEGER-OF-DATE (THIS-DATE)
        GIVING NUMBER-OF-DAYS-SINCE-LAST-PURCHASE
```

The `INTEGER-OF-DATE` function assumes that the argument or date field is in yyyymmdd format (e.g., January 1, 1998 would be 19980101). Note that any starting date that would precede all dates in typical records could have been used in place of January 1, 1601.

4. DAY-OF-INTEGER—Julian dates are in yyddd format, where ddd is a number from 1 to 366 specifying the day of the year. Now there is a function that can be used to calculate Julian date. To obtain a Julian date from a calendar date in yyyymmdd format, we may use the DAY-OF-INTEGER function:

```
COMPUTE JULIAN-DATE = FUNCTION DAY-OF-INTEGER (FUNCTION INTEGER-OF-DATE
                      (THIS-DATE))
```

DAY-OF-INTEGER requires an integer date as the argument. Such a date may be obtained using the INTEGER-OF-DATE function. In the preceding, we used nested FUNCTIONs to obtain a Julian date.

5. INTEGER-OF-DAY—This function converts a date in Julian date format (yyddd) to an integer.

6. DATE-OF-INTEGER—This is the opposite of DAY-OF-INTEGER. It converts an integer date, typically calculated using the INTEGER-OF-DATE function, to a Julian date (yyddd) format.

Calendar functions that begin INTEGER-OF- convert dates to integer format. Calendar functions that have the word DATE in them refer to calendar dates; those with the word DAY in them refer to Julian dates. In summary, we have the following calendar functions:

CURRENT-DATE—returns 21 characters of day and time information
WHEN-COMPILED—returns 21 characters of compile date and time information
INTEGER-OF-DATE—converts a yyyymmdd calendar date to an integer
INTEGER-OF-DAY—converts a Julian yyddd date into an integer
DATE-OF-INTEGER—converts an integer date to yyyymmdd calendar format
DAY-OF-INTEGER—converts an integer to Julian yyddd date format

NUMERICAL ANALYSIS FUNCTIONS

In all cases, the arguments can be identifiers or literals:

1. INTEGER—returns the largest integer that does not exceed the argument value. For example, FUNCTION INTEGER (3.1) is returned as 3, which is the largest integer value that does not exceed 3.1. But FUNCTION INTEGER (−4.3) is returned as −5 because −4 would exceed −4.3:

    Any negative value with a nonzero decimal component has LESS value than just the negative integer (e.g., −4.0 is greater than −4.3). Thus, COMPUTE INTEGER-OUT = FUNCTION INTEGER (3.1) results in 3 being moved to INTEGER-OUT, and COMPUTE INTEGER-OUT = FUNCTION (−4.3) results in −5 being moved or returned to INTEGER-OUT.

2. INTEGER-PART—returns the integer portion of the argument. For example, FUNCTION INTEGER-PART (3.1) is returned as 3, FUNCTION INTEGER-PART (−4.3) is returned as −4. That is, COMPUTE INTEGER-OUT = FUNCTION INTEGER-PART (−4.3) results in −4 being moved to INTEGER-OUT.

3. MAX—returns the largest value in a list of arguments. For example, FUNCTION MAX (A, B, C) will return the largest value of A, B, or C. Similarly, FUNCTION MAX (SALES-AMT-ARRAY (ALL)) will return the largest array value in SALES-AMT-ARRAY. The reserved word ALL can be used to indicate all the elements in an array.

4. MIN—returns the smallest value in a list of arguments. MOVE FUNCTION MIN (4, 5.2, 1.6) TO SMALLEST results in 1.6 being moved to SMALLEST.

5. MEAN—returns the average of all values in a list of arguments.

6. NUMVAL—returns the pure numeric value in a simple edited report item. For example, MOVE FUNCTION NUMVAL (E-AMT1) TO AMT1, where E-AMT1 contains $1,234.56 and AMT1 has a PIC 9(4)V99, will return 1234∧56 to AMT1. The edited report item must include only "simple" editing, such as commas, dollar signs and decimal points.

7. NUMVAL-C—returns the pure numeric value in an edited report item that can be more complex (e.g., one with floating characters).

8. MIDRANGE—returns the average between the lowest and highest values in a list of arguments.

9. MEDIAN—returns the middle value from a list of arguments. If there are an even number of arguments, the median is the average of the two middle values.

10. FACTORIAL—returns the factorial of a number. For example, COMPUTE N-OUT = FUNCTION FACTORIAL (5) returns 120 to N-OUT (e.g., $5 \times 4 \times 3 \times 2 \times 1 = 120$).

11. REM—returns the remainder obtained when argument 1 is divided by argument 2.

12. MOD—returns the greatest integer value of the remainder obtained when argument 1 is divided by argument 2.

13. ORDMAX—returns the position of the maximum value in a list. For example, MOVE FUNCTION ORDMAX (2,7,9,11,5) TO NUM-OUT results in 4 being moved to NUM-OUT since the fourth value in the list is the largest.

14. ORDMIN—returns the position of the minimum value in a list.

15. RANGE—returns the difference between the largest value and the smallest value in a list.

16. SUM—returns the sum of values in a list.

17. SQRT—returns the square root of an argument.

18. LOG—returns the natural logarithm of a number.

19. LOG10—returns the logarithm to base 10 of a number.

20. STANDARD-DEVIATION—returns the standard deviation.

21. VARIANCE—returns the variance.

22. RANDOM—returns a random number. This function can be coded without an argument (e.g., COMPUTE X = FUNCTION RANDOM) or with an argument that is a seed value (e.g., COMPUTE X = FUNCTION RANDOM (Y)). The latter would be used to obtain the same sequence of random numbers.

TRIGONOMETRIC FUNCTIONS

SIN, COS, and TAN functions have arguments that are in radians, while ASIN, ACOS, and ATAN functions have arguments that are sines, cosines, and tangents, respectively, and return radian values:

1. ACOS—returns the arc cosine of an argument

2. ASIN—returns the arc sine of an argument

3. COS—returns the cosine of an argument

4. ATAN—returns the arc tangent of an argument

5. SIN—returns the sine of an argument

6. TAN—returns the tangent of an argument

FINANCIAL FUNCTIONS

1. ANNUITY—requires two arguments to determine the value of an investment over a period of time. The first argument is the interest per period expressed as a decimal number. The second argument is the number of periods to be calculated.

COMPUTE MONTHLY-INCOME = 50000 * FUNCTION ANNUITY (0.01, 240), for example, determines the monthly income to be earned on an initial investment of $50,000 at an annual rate of 12% (.01 monthly) over a period of 20 years (240 months).

2. PRESENT-VALUE—requires two arguments to calculate the amount to be invested today to obtain some desired future value. The first argument is the interest per period expressed as a decimal value and the second argument is the "future value" amount at the end of the period. COMPUTE CURRENT-VALUE = FUNCTION PRESENT-VALUE (.12, 50000), for example, calculates the current value of a future investment to be worth $50,000 invested at an annual rate of 12%.

STRING FUNCTIONS

1. LOWER-CASE—returns in lowercase alphabetic mode the value of an argument.
2. UPPER-CASE—returns in uppercase alphabetic mode the value of an argument.
3. LENGTH—returns the length or number of positions in an argument.
4. ORD—returns the ASCII code for a character. For example, MOVE FUNCTION ORD ('$') TO ASCII-OUT returns a value of 38 because the $ is equivalent to an ASCII code of 38.
5. CHAR—returns the character equivalent of an ASCII code. For example, MOVE FUNCTION CHAR (38) TO CHAR-OUT returns a $ to CHAR-OUT.
6. REVERSE—returns the value of an argument in reverse order. For example, MOVE FUNCTION REVERSE (FIELD-1) TO FIELD-2 where FIELD-1 has contents '123abc', results in 'cba321' in FIELD-2.

Note that relative positions can be used with many of these functions. We may code, for example, MOVE FUNCTION UPPER-CASE (NAME-IN (1:5)) TO NAME-OUT to move in uppercase mode the first five characters of NAME-IN to NAME-OUT.

--- COBOL 9x CHANGES ---

1. Spaces around arithmetic operators such as *, /, +, −, and ** will no longer be required.
2. The COMPUTE statement will yield the same results regardless of the compiler used by making the precision or number of decimal places in each intermediate calculation fixed.

CHAPTER SUMMARY (The *COBOL Syntax Reference Guide* that accompanies this text has the full format for each arithmetic instruction.)

A. The ADD, SUBTRACT, MULTIPLY, and DIVIDE verbs all have a GIVING format. With this GIVING format, the receiving field is *not* part of the arithmetic and can be a report-item.

B. A COMPUTE can be used for performing multiplication, division, addition, subtraction, exponentiation, or a combination of these.

C. The COMPUTE can save coding if used in place of the ADD, SUBTRACT, MULTIPLY, and DIVIDE verbs:

OPERATIONS

+	Addition	/	Division
−	Subtraction	**	Exponentiation
*	Multiplication		

D. If several operations are performed with one COMPUTE statement, the order of evaluation is as follows:
1. **
2. * or / in sequence left to right

3. + or − in sequence left to right

4. Parentheses ( ) override normal hierarchy rules

E. The `ROUNDED` and `ON SIZE ERROR` options can be used with the four arithmetic verbs and with the `COMPUTE`.

F. With COBOL 85, `NOT ON SIZE ERROR` can be used as well. With COBOL 85, when using `ON SIZE ERROR` or `NOT ON SIZE ERROR` with any arithmetic verb, use a scope terminator (`END-ADD`, `END-SUBTRACT`, `END-MULTIPLY`, `END-DIVIDE`, `END-COMPUTE`). With COBOL 74, be sure the `ON SIZE ERROR` clause ends with a period.

G. `USAGE` Clause

1. Specifies how data is to be stored internally.

2. Options available:

a. `USAGE IS DISPLAY`

(1) Data is stored in standard character form.

(2) If the clause is omitted, display mode is assumed.

(3) Used for printing output or reading in data in standard form.

b. `USAGE IS` $\left\{\begin{array}{l}\underline{\text{PACKED-DECIMAL}}\\ \underline{\text{COMPUTATIONAL-3}}\\ \underline{\text{COMP-3}}\end{array}\right\}$

(1) Stores numeric data in a concise format.

(2) Increases efficiency by reducing the number of positions needed to store numbers.

(3) `PACKED-DECIMAL` is only available for COBOL 85 users and `COMPUTATIONAL-3` or `COMP-3` is widely available for both COBOL 85 and 74 users.

c. `USAGE IS COMPUTATIONAL`

(1) Stores numeric data in the form in which the computer actually does its computation.

(2) Typically, this form is binary.

(3) Used for defining subscripts and counters.

H. Intrinsic functions have been added as an extension to COBOL 85. They include calendar, numerical analysis, statistical, trigonometric, financial, character, and string functions.

KEY TERMS

ADD	MULTIPLY	REMAINDER
COMPUTE	ON SIZE ERROR	ROUNDED
DIVIDE	Operand	SUBTRACT
Imperative statement	Overflow	USAGE clause
Intrinsic function		

CHAPTER SELF-TEST   Indicate what, if anything, is wrong with the following arithmetic statements (1–5):

1. `ADD AMT1 TO AMT1-OUT, AMT2-OUT`

2. `ADD AMT1 TO AMT2`
   `     GIVING TOTAL`

3. `MULTIPLY A BY B BY C`

4. `DIVIDE AMT BY 5`
   `     REMAINDER REM-1`

5. `SUBTRACT AMT1 AMT2 FROM AMT3 AMT4`

6. The word directly following the verb `COMPUTE` must be a(n) _____ .

7. What, if anything, is wrong with the following `COMPUTE` statements?
   (a) `COMPUTE TOTAL = AMT1 + AMT2 ROUNDED`
   (b) `COMPUTE AMT-OUT = 10.5`
   (c) `COMPUTE OVERTIME-PAY = (HOURS − 40.) * 1.5`
   (d) `COMPUTE E = A * B /* C + D`
   (e) `COMPUTE X + Y = A`
   (f) `COMPUTE 3.14 = PI`

8. Do the following pairs of operations perform the same function?
   (a) `COMPUTE SUM-1 = 0`
   `     MOVE ZEROS TO SUM-1`
   (b) `COMPUTE AMT = AMT − 2`
   `     SUBTRACT 2 FROM AMT`

```
(c) COMPUTE X = A * B - C * D
    COMPUTE X = (A * B) - (C * D)
(d) COMPUTE Y = A - B * C - D
    COMPUTE Y = (A - B) * (C - D)
```

9. Using a COMPUTE statement, find the average of EXAM1, EXAM2, and EXAM3.

10. Using a COMPUTE statement, find total wages = rate × 40 + (1.5 × rate × overtime hours). *Two* fields are supplied: RATE and HRS-WORKED. Overtime hours are hours worked in excess of 40 hours. (Assume everyone works at least 40 hours.)

Solutions

1. Okay.

2. TO and GIVING in the same statement are permissible using COBOL 85; ADD AMT1 AMT2 GIVING C is acceptable with all compilers.

3. Cannot have two multiply operations as specified:

```
MULTIPLY A BY B
    GIVING Q
MULTIPLY Q BY C
```

4. The GIVING clause must be used when a REMAINDER is specified:

```
DIVIDE AMT BY 5
    GIVING STORE-IT
    REMAINDER REM-1
```

5. Okay.

6. identifier

7. (a) ROUNDED follows the receiving field:
   COMPUTE TOTAL ROUNDED = AMT1 + AMT2
   (b) Okay.
   (c) 40. is not a valid numeric literal; numeric literals may not end with a decimal point.
   (d) /* may not appear together; each symbol must be preceded by and followed by an identifier or a numeric literal.
   (e) Arithmetic expressions must follow the equal sign and not precede it: COMPUTE A = X + Y.
   (f) Identifiers, not literals, must follow the word COMPUTE: COMPUTE PI = 3.14.

8. (a) Same.
   (b) Same.
   (c) Same.
   (d) In the first statement, the order of evaluation is A − (B × C) − D; in the second statement, the order is (A − B) × (C − D); thus, these two are not equivalent.

9. COMPUTE AVERAGE = (EXAM1 + EXAM2 + EXAM3) / 3

10. COMPUTE WAGES = RATE * 40 + 1.5 * RATE * (HRS-WORKED − 40)

PRACTICE PROGRAM

Round all the results and stop the run on a size error condition.

Write a program to print out each student's average. The problem definition is as follows:

Notes:

a. STUDENT-MASTER is a sequential disk file.

b. Each student's average should be rounded to the nearest integer (e.g., 89.5 = 90).

Systems Flowchart

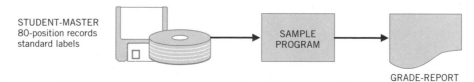

STUDENT-MASTER
80-position records
standard labels

SAMPLE
PROGRAM

GRADE-REPORT

STUDENT-MASTER Record Layout			
Field	**Size**	**Type**	**No. of Decimal Positions (if Numeric)**
ID-NO-IN	5	Alphanumeric	
STUDENT-NAME-IN	20	Alphanumeric	
EXAM1	3	Numeric	0
EXAM2	3	Numeric	0
EXAM3	3	Numeric	0
EXAM4	3	Numeric	0
Unused	43	Alphanumeric	

GRADE-REPORT Printer Spacing Chart

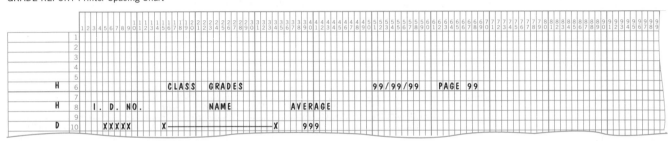

Figure 7.1 illustrates the pseudocode and hierarchy chart. Figure 7.2 shows the solution along with sample input and output.

Figure 7.1   Pseudocode and hierarchy chart for the Practice Program.

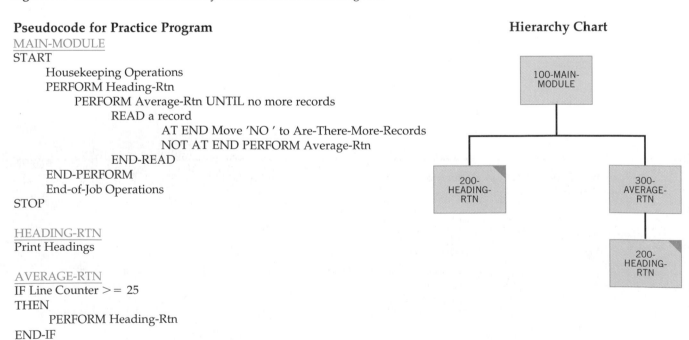

Pseudocode for Practice Program

MAIN-MODULE
START
    Housekeeping Operations
    PERFORM Heading-Rtn
        PERFORM Average-Rtn UNTIL no more records
            READ a record
                AT END Move 'NO ' to Are-There-More-Records
                NOT AT END PERFORM Average-Rtn
            END-READ
        END-PERFORM
    End-of-Job Operations
STOP

HEADING-RTN
Print Headings

AVERAGE-RTN
IF Line Counter >= 25
THEN
      PERFORM Heading-Rtn
END-IF
Move input fields to output
Calculate average
Write detail line
Add 1 to Line Counter

Hierarchy Chart

Figure 7.2   Solution to the Practice Program.

COBOL 85

```
IDENTIFICATION DIVISION.
PROGRAM-ID. CHAPTER7.
***********************************************************
*    this program reads in student records each with    *
*         four exams and prints detail lines with        *
*         each student's average                         *
***********************************************************
ENVIRONMENT DIVISION.
INPUT-OUTPUT SECTION.
FILE-CONTROL.
    SELECT STUDENT-MASTER ASSIGN TO DISK 'DATA1'.
    SELECT GRADE-REPORT   ASSIGN TO PRINTER.
DATA DIVISION.
FILE SECTION.
FD  STUDENT-MASTER
    LABEL RECORDS ARE STANDARD
    RECORD CONTAINS 80 CHARACTERS.
01  STUDENT-REC.
    05  ID-NO-IN                    PIC X(5).
    05  STUDENT-NAME-IN             PIC X(20).
    05  EXAM1                       PIC 999.
    05  EXAM2                       PIC 999.
    05  EXAM3                       PIC 999.
    05  EXAM4                       PIC 999.
    05                              PIC X(43).
FD  GRADE-REPORT
    LABEL RECORDS ARE OMITTED
    RECORD CONTAINS 132 CHARACTERS.
01  REPORT-REC                      PIC X(132).
WORKING-STORAGE SECTION.
01  LINE-CT                         PIC 99      VALUE 0.
01  ARE-THERE-MORE-RECORDS          PIC XXX     VALUE 'YES'.
01  WS-DATE.
    05  WS-YEAR                     PIC XX.
    05  WS-MONTH                    PIC XX.
    05  WS-DAY                      PIC XX.
01  DETAIL-LINE.
    05                              PIC X(4)    VALUE SPACES.
    05  ID-NO-OUT                   PIC X(5).
    05                              PIC X(5)    VALUE SPACES.
    05  STUDENT-NAME-OUT            PIC X(20).
    05                              PIC X(4)    VALUE SPACES.
    05  AVERAGE                     PIC 999.
    05                              PIC X(91)   VALUE SPACES.
01  HDR-1.
    05                              PIC X(15)   VALUE SPACES.
    05                              PIC X(13)
        VALUE 'CLASS GRADES'.
    05                              PIC X(22)   VALUE SPACES.
    05  DATE-OUT.
        10 MONTH-OUT                PIC XX.
        10                          PIC X       VALUE '/'.
        10 DAY-OUT                  PIC XX.
        10                          PIC X       VALUE '/'.
        10 YEAR-OUT                 PIC XX.
    05                              PIC X(11).
    05                              PIC X(5)    VALUE 'PAGE'.
    05  PAGE-NO                     PIC 99      VALUE ZERO.
    05                              PIC X(56)   VALUE SPACES.
01  HDR-2.
    05                              PIC X(2)    VALUE SPACES.
    05                              PIC X(20)
        VALUE 'I. D. NO.'.
    05                              PIC X(110)
        VALUE 'NAME            AVERAGE'.
```

COBOL 74 Substitutions

The word FILLER is optional as a data-name with COBOL 85 but is required with COBOL 74.

Figure 7.2 (continued)

```
                        PROCEDURE DIVISION.
                        ***********************************************************
                        *      program logic is controlled from the        *
                        *          main module                             *
                        ***********************************************************
                        100-MAIN-MODULE.
                            OPEN INPUT  STUDENT-MASTER
                                 OUTPUT GRADE-REPORT
                            ACCEPT WS-DATE FROM DATE
                            MOVE WS-MONTH TO MONTH-OUT
                            MOVE WS-DAY TO DAY-OUT
                            MOVE WS-YEAR TO YEAR-OUT
                            PERFORM 200-HEADING-RTN
                            PERFORM UNTIL ARE-THERE-MORE-RECORDS = 'NO '
                                READ STUDENT-MASTER
                                    AT END
                                        MOVE 'NO ' TO ARE-THERE-MORE-RECORDS
                                    NOT AT END
                                        PERFORM 300-AVERAGE-RTN
                                END-READ
                            END-PERFORM
                            CLOSE STUDENT-MASTER
                                  GRADE-REPORT
                            STOP RUN.
                        ***********************************************************
                        *      headings are printed from 200-heading-rtn    *
                        ***********************************************************
                        200-HEADING-RTN.
                            ADD 1 TO PAGE-NO
                            WRITE REPORT-REC FROM HDR-1
                                AFTER ADVANCING PAGE
                            WRITE REPORT-REC FROM HDR-2
                                AFTER ADVANCING 2 LINES
                            MOVE 0 TO LINE-CT.
                        ***********************************************************
                        *   each student's average is calculated and printed *
                        *    at 300-average-rtn                             *
                        ***********************************************************
                        300-AVERAGE-RTN.
                            IF LINE-CT >= 25
                                PERFORM 200-HEADING-RTN
                            END-IF
                            MOVE ID-NO-IN TO ID-NO-OUT
                            MOVE STUDENT-NAME-IN TO STUDENT-NAME-OUT
                            ADD EXAM1 EXAM2 EXAM3 EXAM4
                                GIVING AVERAGE
                            DIVIDE 4 INTO AVERAGE ROUNDED
                                ON SIZE ERROR STOP RUN
                            END-DIVIDE
                            WRITE REPORT-REC FROM DETAIL-LINE
                                AFTER ADVANCING 2 LINES
                            ADD 1 TO LINE-CT.
```

COBOL 74 Substitutions

```
READ STUDENT-MASTER
    AT END MOVE 'NO ' TO
        ARE-THERE-MORE-RECORDS.
PERFORM 300-AVERAGE-RTN
    UNTIL ARE-THERE-MORE-RECORDS = 'NO '.
```

```
READ STUDENT-MASTER
    AT END MOVE 'NO ' TO ARE-THERE-MORE-RECORDS.
```

Note: Use END-IF and END-DIVIDE with COBOL 85 only. Otherwise omit them and end preceding lines with a period.

Figure 7.2 (continued)

Input STUDENT-MASTER

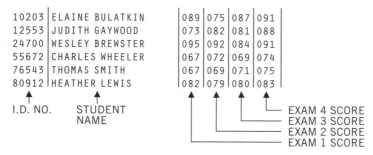

```
10203 ELAINE BULATKIN      089 075 087 091
12553 JUDITH GAYWOOD       073 082 081 088
24700 WESLEY BREWSTER      095 092 084 091
55672 CHARLES WHEELER      067 072 069 074
76543 THOMAS SMITH         067 069 071 075
80912 HEATHER LEWIS        082 079 080 083
```

I.D. NO.   STUDENT NAME

EXAM 4 SCORE
EXAM 3 SCORE
EXAM 2 SCORE
EXAM 1 SCORE

Sample Output

```
              CLASS   GRADES              12/31/98   PAGE 01

     I. D. NO.              NAME          AVERAGE

       10203        ELAINE BULATKIN         086

       12553        JUDITH GAYWOOD          081

       24700        WESLEY BREWSTER         091

       55672        CHARLES WHEELER         071

       76543        THOMAS SMITH            071

       80912        HEATHER LEWIS           081
```

REVIEW QUESTIONS

I. True-False Questions

The following are valid instructions (1–5):

_____ 1. ADD A TO B, C, D

_____ 2. ADD A, B GIVING C, D

_____ 3. COMPUTE A = A + 1

_____ 4. MULTIPLY A BY B BY C

_____ 5. SUBTRACT A FROM 150

_____ 6. Unless parentheses are used, ** will always be performed first in a COMPUTE statement.

_____ 7. Anything that can be coded with a COMPUTE statement can be coded instead with the four arithmetic verbs.

_____ 8. The DIVIDE operation can produce a remainder as well as a quotient.

_____ 9. The last field mentioned in all arithmetic operations except the COMPUTE is always the receiving field.

_____ 10. If both the ROUNDED and ON SIZE ERROR options are used, the ROUNDED always appears first.

II. General Questions

Fill in the missing columns (1–3).

COBOL Statement	Result in	Result if A = 3, B = 2, X = 5 (PIC of each is 99V99)
1. ADD A B GIVING X		

2. ADD A B TO X
    ON SIZE ERROR
    MOVE ZERO TO X		

3. `DIVIDE A INTO B ROUNDED`

4. Write a routine to calculate the number of miles traveled. There are two input fields, `MPG`, for miles per gallon, and `GAS`, for the number of gallons of gas used.

5. Write a routine to find $Y = (A + B)^2 / X$.

Determine what, if anything, is wrong with the following statements (6–10):

6. `SUBTRACT A FROM 87.3 GIVING B`

7. `ADD A, 10.98, B TO 100.3`

8. `ADD AMT. TO TOTAL GIVING TAX`

9. `DIVIDE A BY B AND MULTIPLY B BY C`

10. `COMPUTE X = Y + Z ROUNDED`

11. Determine the most economical quantity to be stocked for each product that a manufacturing company has in its inventory. This quantity, called the *economic order quantity*, is calculated as follows:

$$\text{Economic order quantity} = \sqrt{\frac{2RS}{I}} \text{ where R, S, and I are input fields.}$$

R = total yearly production requirement
S = setup cost per order
I = inventory carrying cost per unit

Write the program excerpt to calculate the economic order quantity.

12. Use a `COMPUTE` statement to add one to A.

13. Read in as input the length and width of a lawn. Write a program excerpt to calculate the amount and cost of the grass seed needed. One pound of grass seed costs $2.50 and can plant 1000 square feet.

14. Using the instruction formats for the `SUBTRACT` statement, indicate whether the following is correct:

```
SUBTRACT AMT1 FROM AMT2, AMT3
    GIVING AMT4
```

Write a single statement to carry out the following operations (15–20):

(a) Using the `COMPUTE` verb
(b) Using the four arithmetic verbs

15. Add the values of `OVERTIME-HOURS` and `HOURS`, with the sum replacing the value of `HOURS`.

16. Determine the number of feet in X inches, placing the quotient in `FEET` and the remainder in `INCHES`.

17. Add the values of `FRI`, `SAT`, and `SUN`, and place the sum in `WEEK-END`.

18. Add the values of `AMT1`, `AMT2`, and `AMT3` to `TOTAL`.

19. Decrease the value of `AMT-X` by 47.5.

20. Divide the `TOTAL-TUITION` by 15 to determine `TUITION-PER-CREDIT`.

DEBUGGING EXERCISES

Consider the following arithmetic statements:

```
1      ADD AMT1 TO FIN-TOT
2      ADD AMT1 TO AMT2 GIVING AMT3
3      COMPUTE AVERAGE = AMT1 + AMT2 / 2
4      COMPUTE AMT4 = AMT1 + AMT2 ROUNDED
5      MULTIPLY AMT1 BY AMT2
6      DIVIDE AMT1 BY 2
7      MULTIPLY AMT4 TIMES AMT3
```

1. Which statements will produce syntax errors? Correct these.

2. On line 3, will a correct average of `AMT1` and `AMT2` be computed? If your answer is no, make whatever changes you think are necessary to obtain the correct results.

3. For line 5, suppose the PIC clause of AMT1 is 99V99. AMT2 has a PIC clause of 9(4)V99. Under what conditions will a logic error result? What can you do to prevent such an error?

4. Assume that all the syntax and logic errors have been corrected on lines 1 through 7 and that the preceding steps are executed in sequence. What will be the results in the following fields: AMT1; AMT2; AMT3; AMT4; AVERAGE?

PROGRAMMING ASSIGNMENTS

1. Write a program to create a salary disk file from an employee disk file. The problem definition is as follows.

Systems Flowchart

IN-EMPLOYEE-FILE → CHAPT 7-1 → OUT-SALARY-FILE

IN-EMPLOYEE-FILE Record Layout			
Field	Size	Type	No. of Decimal Positions (if Numeric)
Employee Name	15	Alphanumeric	
Hours Worked	3	Numeric	0
Rate	3	Numeric	2

OUT-SALARY-FILE Record Layout			
Field	Size	Type	No. of Decimal Positions (if Numeric)
Employee Name	15	Alphanumeric	
Gross Pay	6	Numeric	2
F.I.C.A.	5	Numeric	2
Net Pay	6	Numeric	2

SAMPLE INPUT DATA

```
P NEWMAN    050 525
R REDFORD   040 810
E TAYLOR    035 925
N STERN     070 615
K ROGERS    032 785
R STERN     012 345
C HAMMEL    157 577
M STERN     070 654
L STERN     100 987
S SMITH     097 667
```
NAME   HOURS RATE

LISTING OF DISK RECORDS CREATED FROM SAMPLE INPUT

```
P NEWMAN     026250    02008    024242
R REDFORD    032400    02479    029921
E TAYLOR     032375    02477    029898
N STERN      043050    03293    039757
K ROGERS     025120    01922    023198
R STERN      004140    00317    003823
C HAMMEL     090589    06930    083659
M STERN      045780    03502    042278
L STERN      098700    07551    091149
S SMITH      064699    04949    059750
```
NAME   GROSS PAY   FICA   NET PAY

(a) Gross pay = Hours worked × Rate
(b) F.I.C.A. (Social Security and Medicare taxes) = 7.65% of Gross pay
(c) Net pay = Gross pay − F.I.C.A.

Note: For purposes of this assignment, we are assuming that no employee has Gross Pay greater than $62,700. (If Gross Pay were greater than $62,700, a different formula would be used for F.I.C.A. calculations.)

2. Write a program to print out payroll information for each employee. The problem definition is shown in Figure 7.3.

Notes:

a. Each employee's salary is to be increased by 7%.
b. The union dues have increased by 4%.
c. The insurance has increased by 3%.
d. The amounts for dues and insurance are to be printed with actual decimal points.

Figure 7.3 Problem definition for Programming Assignment 2.

Systems Flowchart

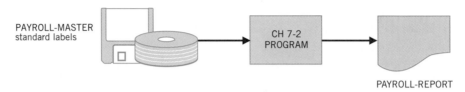

PAYROLL-MASTER
standard labels

CH 7-2
PROGRAM

PAYROLL-REPORT

PAYROLL-MASTER **Record Layout**			
Field	**Size**	**Type**	**No. of Decimal Positions (if Numeric)**
Employee No.	5	Alphanumeric	
Employee Name	20	Alphanumeric	
Unused	4	Alphanumeric	
Annual Salary	6	Numeric	0
Unused	13	Alphanumeric	
Union Dues	5	Numeric	2
Insurance	5	Numeric	2
Unused	22	Alphanumeric	

PAYROLL-REPORT Printer Spacing Chart

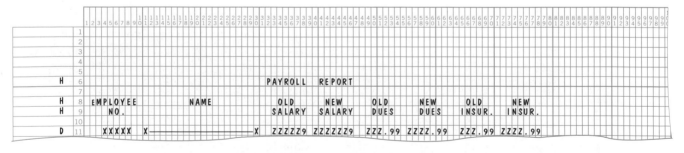

```
                                              PAYROLL  REPORT

EMPLOYEE          NAME          OLD       NEW      OLD      NEW      OLD       NEW
   NO.                         SALARY    SALARY   DUES     DUES    INSUR.    INSUR.

   XXXXX  X----------------X  ZZZZZ9   ZZZZZZ9  ZZZ.99  ZZZZ.99  ZZZ.99  ZZZZ.99
```

3. **Interactive Processing.** For each customer loan approved at Dollars-And-Sense Bank, display a line indicating the monthly payment for that customer. Enter the following information from the keyboard:

CUSTOMER NAME:
AMT OF LOAN (PRINCIPAL):
YEARLY INTEREST RATE:
LENGTH OF LOAN (IN YEARS):

Note: Interest rate is to be entered with an implied decimal point (e.g., 9% is entered as 0900).

The monthly payment on an *N*-year loan with a principal of *P* at a yearly interest rate of *R* is:

$$\text{Monthly Payment} = P * (R/12) - \left(P * \frac{(R/12)}{1 - (1 + R/12)^{12*N}} \right)$$

Example   What are the monthly payments on a twenty-year loan of $20,000 at 12%?

$P = 20000$
$R = .12$
$N = 20$ years

$$
\begin{aligned}
\text{Monthly payment} &= 20000 * (.12/12) - (20000 * (.12/12)/(1 - (1.01)^{240})) \\
&= 20000 * (.01) - (20000 * .01/(1 - (1.01)^{240})) \\
&= 200 - (-20.22) \\
&= 220.22
\end{aligned}
$$

Round monthly payments to the nearest penny.

Design the interactive screen displays yourself.

4. Your company has a fleet of taxis and you wish to determine the energy efficiency of each taxi in the fleet as well as that of the entire fleet. Input consists of records with the following format:

   1–10 Vehicle identification
   11–20 Vehicle description
   21–24 Miles traveled
   25–28 No. of gallons of gas used (99V99)

   Print a report that indicates the miles per gallon for each taxi and for the fleet as a whole.

5. Input records have the following format:

   1–3   Stock Code
   4–20   Stock Name
   21–25 Price Per Share (999V99)
   26–35 Latest Earnings Per Share

   For each record read, print Stock Code, Stock Name, Price Per Share, Latest Earnings, and P/E Ratio edited and spaced neatly across the page.

   P/E Ratio is the Price Per Earnings and is calculated as Price Per Share divided by Latest Earnings Per Share.

6. Write a program that will input a file of records each consisting of an item number (2 digits), item description (20 characters), and an item cost (99V99). Print the item's description and the price at which it should be sold, assuming a 30% profit margin. The formula for calculating selling price is:

$$\text{Selling Price} = \left(\frac{1}{1 - \text{Profit Margin}} \right) * \text{Cost}$$

7. The Pass-Em State College has a student file with the following data:

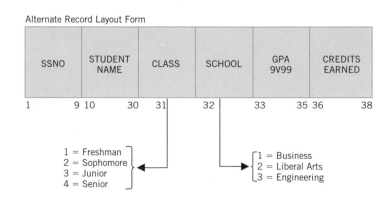

Print the average GPA for all students at the college.

8. **Interactive Processing.** Write an interactive program for a bank. Users will enter on a PC or terminal a customer name, principal amount to be invested (P_0), rate of interest (R), and number of years that the principal will be invested (N). Display the user's name and the value of the investment after N years. The formula is:

Principal after N years $= P_0 (1 + R)^N$

Do not forget to include prompts before accepting input.

9. **Maintenance Program.** Modify the Practice Program in this chapter to print the overall class average at the end of the report.

CHAPTER 8

Decision Making Using the
IF and EVALUATE Statements

OBJECTIVES

To familiarize you with
1. The use of IF statements for selection.
2. The variety of formats and options available with the conditional statement.
3. The use of the EVALUATE statement with COBOL 85.

CONTENTS

SELECTION USING A SIMPLE IF STATEMENT

A REVIEW OF LOGICAL CONTROL STRUCTURES

Thus far we have learned the syntax rules for numerous COBOL instructions. The pseudocode and flowchart excerpts for executing a *sequence of instructions* are as follows:

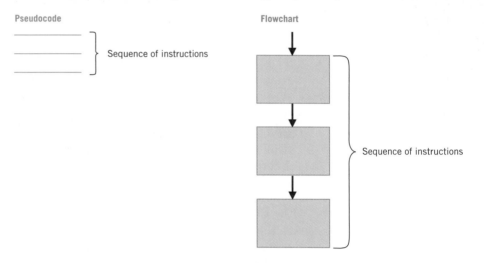

But a *sequence* is only one method for executing instructions. In this chapter we will focus on some instructions that enable the computer to make decisions that affect the order in which statements are executed. Such instructions are referred to as *logical control structures*.

The full range of logical control structures used in any program, regardless of the programming language, is as follows:

LOGICAL CONTROL STRUCTURES

1. Sequence

2. Selection (IF-THEN-ELSE)

3. Iteration (PERFORM)

4. Case (EVALUATE)

In this chapter we focus first on the IF-THEN-ELSE structure, which permits us to execute one or more instructions depending on the contents of fields. The IF-THEN-ELSE structure is coded in COBOL with the IF statement. Then we focus on the case structure, which is coded in COBOL 85 with the EVALUATE verb. In the next chapter, we will consider iteration in detail, focusing on the PERFORM statement and its options.

BASIC CONDITIONAL STATEMENTS

The Instruction Format for an IF Statement

A **conditional statement** is one that performs operations depending on the existence of some condition. In COBOL, such statements generally begin with the word IF and are called IF-THEN-ELSE or selection structures.

The basic instruction format for IF statements is as follows:

Format

> IF   condition-1
> [THEN]*
>   imperative statement-1 . . .
> [ELSE
>   imperative statement-2 . . .]
> [END-IF]*

*The words THEN and END-IF are COBOL 85 options.

An **imperative statement,** as opposed to a conditional statement, is one that performs an operation regardless of any existing conditions. ADD AMT-IN TO AMT-OUT and MOVE NAME-IN TO NAME-OUT are examples of imperative statements that do not test for conditions but simply perform operations. We say that COBOL statements are divided into two broad categories: (1) **imperative**, which perform operations, and (2) **conditional**, which test for the existence of one or more conditions. Another way to say that "a condition exists" is to say that "a condition is met" or "a condition is true."

The pseudocode and flowchart excerpts that correspond to an IF-THEN-ELSE selection structure are as follows:

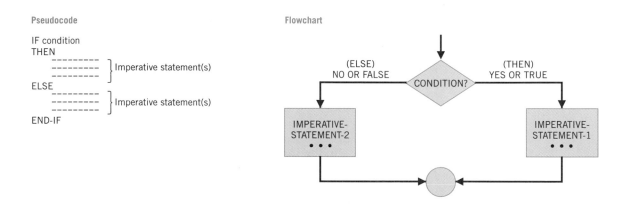

A condition may test for a specific relation. A **simple condition** may be a single relational test of the following form:

SIMPLE RELATIONAL CONDITIONS
1. IF identifier-1 IS EQUAL TO identifier-2
2. IF identifier-1 IS LESS THAN identifier-2
3. IF identifier-1 IS GREATER THAN identifier-2

These three tests are considered simple relational conditions.

An illustration of a simple conditional is as follows:

```
IF  AMT1 IS EQUAL TO AMT2
    DIVIDE QTY INTO TOTAL
ELSE
    ADD UNIT-PRICE TO FINAL-TOTAL
END-IF *
```

There are two possible results of the test performed by the preceding statement:

1. AMT1 is equal to AMT2   or   2. AMT1 is not equal to AMT2

Explanation

1. If AMT1 is equal to AMT2, the DIVIDE operation is performed and the second part of the statement, beginning with the ELSE clause, is ignored. Then the program will continue executing with the next statement, disregarding the clause that begins with the word ELSE.
2. If the two fields are not equal, then the DIVIDE operation is *not executed.* Only the ELSE portion of the statement, the ADD operation, is executed.
    In either case, the program continues executing with the next statement.

Thus, by using the word IF, we test the initial condition and perform the instruction specified. By using ELSE, we can perform an operation if the initial condition is not met or is "false."

We have adopted the convention of coding END-IF in color to highlight the fact that it is a COBOL 85 feature. COBOL 74 users should omit the END-IF and terminate the IF sentence by placing a period on the previous line. When you use a scope terminator with COBOL 85 (such as END-IF, END-READ, END-ADD, etc.), a period at the end of the line is optional except for the last statement in a paragraph. We only use periods at the end of a paragraph.

The word THEN is permitted with COBOL 85 to make the IF statement totally consistent with structured programming terminology and pseudocode. That is, with the THEN and END-IF, COBOL 85 conforms completely to the IF-THEN-ELSE logical control structure.

Interpreting Instruction Formats

ELSE Is Optional

The ELSE clause in the instruction format is bracketed with [ ], which means that it is optional. If some operation is required *only if* a condition exists and nothing different need be done if the condition does not exist, the entire ELSE clause may be omitted.

Example of an IF Statement Without an ELSE Clause

```
MOVE NAME-IN TO NAME-OUT
MOVE AMOUNT-IN TO AMOUNT-OUT
IF  AMOUNT-IN IS EQUAL TO ZEROS
    MOVE 'NO TRANSACTIONS THIS MONTH' TO OUT-AREA
END-IF
WRITE PRINT-REC.
```

In this case, the message 'NO TRANSACTIONS THIS MONTH' is printed only if AMOUNT-IN is zero. If AMOUNT-IN is not zero, we continue with the next statement without performing any operation. The ELSE clause is unnecessary in this instance.

---

*All scope terminators are in color to highlight the fact that they are COBOL 85 features. COBOL 74 users should end IF sentences with a period and not use scope terminators.

More Than One Operation Can Be Performed When a Condition Exists

The instruction format includes dots or ellipses (...) after the imperative statements indicating that more than one operation may be executed for each condition. The following will perform two MOVE operations if AMT1 is equal to AMT2, and two ADD operations if AMT1 is not equal to AMT2:

```
IF  AMT1 IS EQUAL TO AMT2
    MOVE NAME-IN TO NAME-OUT
    MOVE DESCRIPTION-IN TO DESCRIPTION-OUT
ELSE
    ADD AMT1 TO TOTAL1
    ADD AMT2 TO TOTAL2
END-IF
```

When you use scope terminators with COBOL 85, periods are optional at the end of statements except for the last one in each paragraph. With COBOL 74, every IF statement must end with a period.

The difference between a statement and a sentence is as follows:

Statement   A combination of COBOL words, literals, and separators that begins with a COBOL verb such as ADD, READ, PERFORM, or the word IF.

Sentence   One or more statements that end with a period.

--- DEBUGGING TIP ---

Omitting the scope terminator is permitted for all versions of COBOL as long as the IF sentence ends with a period. We recommend, however, that you use scope terminators with COBOL 85 and omit periods except for the last statement in a paragraph.

Coding Guidelines

Indenting

We indent statements within the IF instruction to make programs easier to read and debug. We use the following coding style for conditionals:

```
IF   condition
THEN
        imperative statement
          :
ELSE
        imperative statement
          :
END-IF
```

The technique of indenting and coding each statement on a separate line makes reading the program easier, but it does not affect compilation or execution. Suppose you determine that an error occurred on the (IF condition) line. It will be easier to determine the cause of error if that line contained a single statement than if it were coded as follows:

```
IF AMT1 IS EQUAL TO AMT2 ADD 5 TO TOTAL ELSE ADD 10 TO TOTAL
```

In this statement, the exact clause that caused an error would be more difficult to determine.

Using Relational Operators in Place of Words

The following symbols for simple relational conditions are valid within a COBOL statement:

RELATIONAL OPERATORS

Symbol	Meaning
<	IS LESS THAN
>	IS GREATER THAN
=	IS EQUAL TO
<=	IS LESS THAN OR EQUAL TO
>=	IS GREATER THAN OR EQUAL TO

COBOL 85 only { <= , >=

A COBOL conditional, then, may have the following form:

a) IF AMT1 > AMT2 ...   or   b) IF AMT1 IS GREATER THAN AMT2 ...

Most COBOL compilers require a blank on each side of the symbols <, >, =, <=, >=.

Example 1
```
IF  AMT1 <= ZERO
    MOVE 'NOT POSITIVE' TO CODE-OUT
END-IF
```

With COBOL 85, a conditional can also compare a field to an arithmetic expression:

Example 2
```
IF  AMT1 = AMT2 + 500
    PERFORM 100-A-OK
END-IF
```

Using COBOL 74, or indeed any COBOL compiler, we could code the preceding as:

Example 1
```
IF  AMT1 < ZERO OR AMT1 = ZERO
    MOVE 'NOT POSITIVE' TO CODE-OUT.
```

Example 2
```
ADD 500 TO AMT2.
IF  AMT1 = AMT2
    PERFORM 100-A-OK.
```

Do Not Mix Field Types in a Comparison

Keep in mind that conditional statements must use fields with the same data types to obtain proper results. In the statement, IF CODE-IN = '123' MOVE NAME-IN TO NAME-OUT, CODE-IN should be a nonnumeric field, since it is compared to a nonnumeric literal. As in MOVE operations, the literal should have the same format as the data item. If CODE-OUT has a PICTURE of 9's, the following conditional would be appropriate:

```
IF CODE-OUT = 123 MOVE AMT-IN TO AMT-OUT.
```

Similarly, to ensure correct results, fields that are compared to one another should have the same data types, whether numeric or nonnumeric. Thus, in the statement, IF CTR1 = CTR2 ADD AMT1 TO TOTAL, *both* CTR1 and CTR2 should be either numeric or nonnumeric.

Numeric Fields Should Not Contain Blanks

Suppose we code IF AMT-IN IS EQUAL TO 10 ADD 1 TO COUNTER. If AMT-IN were a field defined as numeric, but actually contained all blanks, the instruction would result in a **data exception error**, which causes a program interrupt. This error will occur because *blanks are not valid numeric characters*. Be certain, then, that if a field is defined as numeric, it actually contains numbers. We will discuss this again in Chapter 11 when we consider data validation techniques.

PLANNING CONDITIONAL STATEMENTS WITH PSEUDOCODE AND FLOWCHARTS

Recall that ELSE clauses are optional in an IF statement. The pseudocode and flowchart that correspond to a simple condition without an ELSE clause are as follows:

General Format

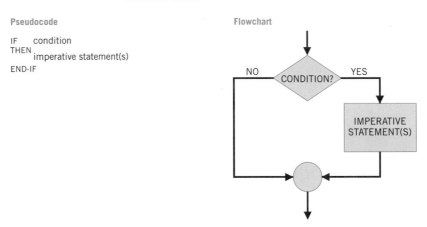

Pseudocode

```
IF    condition
THEN
      imperative statement(s)
END-IF
```

Flowchart

The following indicates the processing if multiple statements are to be executed when a condition is true:

Example

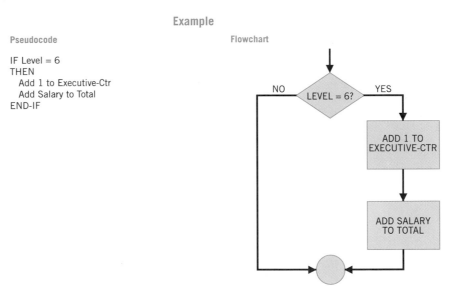

Pseudocode

```
IF Level = 6
THEN
    Add 1 to Executive-Ctr
    Add Salary to Total
END-IF
```

Flowchart

HOW COMPARISONS ARE PERFORMED

When comparing numeric fields, the following are all considered equal:

   012   12.00   12   +12

Numeric comparisons are performed in COBOL *algebraically*. Although 12.00 does not have the same internal configuration as 012, their numeric values are known to be equal.

Similarly, when comparing nonnumeric fields, the following are considered equivalent:

   ABC   ABCб (б denotes a blank position)   ABCбб

Low-order or rightmost blanks do not affect the comparison. Only significant or non-blank positions are compared, from left to right. Note, however, that бABC is *not* equal to ABCб since A is not equal to б.

ASCII AND EBCDIC COLLATING SEQUENCES

When performing an alphanumeric comparison, the hierarchy of the comparison, called the **collating sequence,** depends on the computer being used.

The two types of internal codes that are most commonly used for representing data are **EBCDIC,** for IBM and IBM-compatible mainframes, and **ASCII,** used on most micros and many minis and mainframes. The collating sequences for these differ somewhat. EBCDIC is pronounced eb-cee-dick and ASCII is pronounced ass-key. Characters are compared to one another in EBCDIC and ASCII as follows:

	COLLATING SEQUENCES	
	EBCDIC	ASCII
Low	Special characters	Special characters
	a-z	0-9
▼	A-Z	A-Z
High	0-9	a-z

On both ASCII and EBCDIC computers a numeric comparison or an alphabetic comparison will be performed properly. That is, 012 < 022 < 042, and so on, on both types of computers. Similarly, all computers will be able to determine if data is arranged alphabetically using uppercase letters, because A is considered less than B, which is less than C, and so on. Thus, ABCD < BBCD < XBCD, and so on. Lowercase letters are also compared properly.

Note, however, that on ASCII computers uppercase letters are less than lowercase letters whereas the reverse is true with EBCDIC computers. Suppose you are performing an alphabetic sequence check. SMITH is considered < Smith on ASCII computers but on EBCDIC computers Smith < SMITH. Note, too, that SAM < Stu on ASCII computers but Stu < SAM on EBCDIC computers. Mixing uppercase and lowercase letters, then, could produce different results in a comparison, depending on whether you are using an ASCII or EBCDIC computer.

Similarly, if alphanumeric fields are being compared where there may be a *mix of letters and digits*, the results of the comparison will differ, depending on whether you are running the program on an EBCDIC or an ASCII computer. On EBCDIC machines, letters are all less than numbers; on ASCII machines, numbers are less than letters.

Consider the following comparison:

```
IF  ADDRESS-IN < '100 MAIN ST'
    ADD 1 TO TOTAL
END-IF
```

If ADDRESS-IN has a value of 'ROUTE 109', the result of the comparison will *differ* depending on whether you are using an ASCII or EBCDIC computer. On EBCDIC computers, 'ROUTE 109' is less than '100 MAIN ST' because the first character, R, compares "less than" the number 1; hence 1 *would be added to* TOTAL. On ASCII computers the reverse is true; that is, letters are "greater than" numbers so that 1 *would not be added to* TOTAL.

These differences are worth mentioning, but not worth dwelling on since alphanumeric comparisons of these types are not usually required in programs. For comparisons of fields containing *either* all numbers, all uppercase letters, or all lowercase letters, both ASCII and EBCDIC computers will produce exactly the same results. In addition, you can usually tell the computer which collating sequence you prefer, regardless of the internal code, with an operating system command.

─────── DEBUGGING TIP ───────

Do not mix upper- and lowercase letters when entering data in fields. This reduces the risk that comparisons might give problematic results. If, for example, we compare `NAME-IN` to `'PAUL'` and we inadvertently entered the name as 'Paul' or 'paul' or with any lowercase letter, the comparison would result in an unequal condition. As a convention, we recommend you use uppercase letters in all input fields as well as in instructions. Use lowercase letters only for comments.

ENDING CONDITIONAL SENTENCES WITH A PERIOD OR AN END-IF SCOPE TERMINATOR (COBOL 85)

If an `END-IF` is not used in an `IF` statement, the placement of periods can affect the logic. Consider the following:

```
IF  PRICE1 IS LESS THAN PRICE2
    ADD PRICE1 TO TOTAL
    MOVE 2 TO ITEM1
ELSE
    ADD PRICE2 TO TOTAL.◄────Note the period
MOVE 0 TO ITEM2.
```

Because the statement `ADD PRICE2 TO TOTAL` ends with a period, the last statement, `MOVE 0 TO ITEM2`, is *always executed* regardless of the comparison.

The preceding program excerpt may be written as pseudocode and flowcharted as follows:

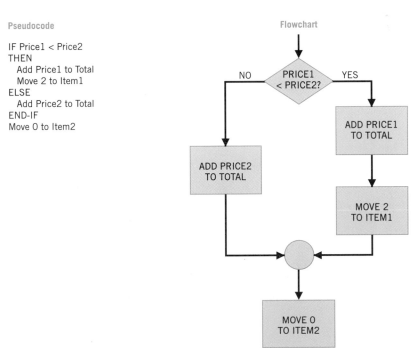

Pseudocode

```
IF Price1 < Price2
THEN
    Add Price1 to Total
    Move 2 to Item1
ELSE
    Add Price2 to Total
END-IF
Move 0 to Item2
```

If a period were accidentally omitted after `ADD PRICE2 TO TOTAL`, then `MOVE 0 TO ITEM2` would be considered *part of the `ELSE` clause* and would *not* be executed if `PRICE1` were less than `PRICE2`. The placement of the period, then, can significantly affect the logic.

To definitively specify the boundaries of an IF with COBOL 74, you would use a period to end the IF sentence. With COBOL 85, you should use END-IF as a scope terminator:

```
IF  PRICE1 < PRICE2
THEN
      ADD PRICE1 TO TOTAL
      MOVE 2 TO ITEM1
ELSE
      ADD PRICE2 TO TOTAL
END-IF
MOVE 0 TO ITEM2.
```

The END-IF marks the boundary of the IF statement without the need for periods. A period is optional after END-IF. If you use scope terminators to delimit instructions as you should, then all periods except for the last one in the paragraph can be omitted. The word THEN is optional in an IF statement.

With the END-IF, COBOL 85 even more closely resembles pseudocode, which uses IF-THEN-ELSE-END-IF for selection.

If you are using an ELSE clause, *never* place a period before the ELSE.

THE CONTINUE OR NEXT SENTENCE CLAUSE

There are times when you might want to execute a series of steps only if a certain condition does *not* exist. The COBOL expression CONTINUE (COBOL 85) or NEXT SENTENCE (COBOL 74) will enable you (1) to avoid performing any operation if a condition exists and (2) to execute instructions only if the ELSE condition is met.

Example 1   Consider the following pseudocode and flowchart:

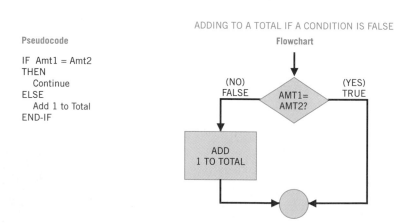

Pseudocode

```
IF  Amt1 = Amt2
THEN
     Continue
ELSE
     Add 1 to Total
END-IF
```

ADDING TO A TOTAL IF A CONDITION IS FALSE
Flowchart

This may be coded in COBOL as follows:

COBOL 74

```
IF  AMT1 = AMT2
     NEXT SENTENCE
ELSE
     ADD 1 TO TOTAL.
```

COBOL 85

```
IF AMT1 = AMT2
     CONTINUE
ELSE
     ADD 1 TO TOTAL
END-IF
```

If AMT1 is equal to AMT2, *no* operation will be performed and the computer will continue execution with the next sentence, which follows the period in COBOL 74. In COBOL 85, the computer will continue execution with the statement following the END-IF. If AMT1 is not equal to AMT2, 1 is added to TOTAL and then the next statement will be executed.

With COBOL 85, NEXT SENTENCE may not be used if END-IF is included as a scope terminator. We recommend that you always use the END-IF scope terminator. You may code the preceding in a different way:

```
IF  AMT1 NOT = AMT2
     ADD 1 TO TOTAL
END-IF
```

We discuss the use of NOT in a conditional later on.

Example 2   Note that the following two statements produce identical results:

     A. COBOL 74 or 85   *B. Preferred Method with COBOL 85*

```
IF  TOTAL1 IS EQUAL TO TOTAL2        IF  TOTAL1 IS EQUAL TO TOTAL2
     ADD 1 TO COUNTER                     ADD 1 TO COUNTER
ELSE                                 END-IF
     NEXT SENTENCE.
```

The phrase ELSE NEXT SENTENCE in statement (A) is unnecessary and can be omitted. If TOTAL1 is not equal to TOTAL2, the computer will proceed to the next sentence anyway. Thus, with a simple IF, the ELSE clause is used only when a specific operation is required if a condition does *not* exist.

Note that the following is invalid:

Invalid Coding—COBOL 74   **Invalid Coding—COBOL 85**

```
IF  A IS EQUAL TO B                   IF  A IS EQUAL TO B
    ADD A TO TOTAL                        ADD A TO TOTAL
    NEXT SENTENCE  →    If NEXT SENTENCE (COBOL 74)  ←  CONTINUE
ELSE                    or CONTINUE (COBOL 85) is    ELSE
    ADD 1 TO CTR.      coded, it must be the only       ADD 1 TO CTR
                       imperative statement following  END-IF
                       the condition
```

CONTINUE or NEXT SENTENCE must be the *only* clause following a condition, since it indicates that no action is to be performed. To correct the preceding, we code:

Corrected Coding

```
IF  A IS EQUAL TO B
    ADD A TO TOTAL
ELSE
    ADD 1 TO CTR
END-IF
```

SELF-TEST   What is wrong with the following statements (1–6)?

```
1. IF  A IS LESS THAN B              4. IF  A IS LESS THEN B
       GO TO CONTINUE                       MOVE 2 TO CODE1
   ELSE                              END-IF
       ADD 1 TO XX
   END-IF

2. IF  A IS EQUAL TO '127'           5. IF  C = D
       ADD A TO B                           MOVE 0 TO COUNTER.
   END-IF                            ELSE
                                            MOVE 100 TO COUNTER
                                        END-IF

3. IF  A EQUALS B                    6. IF  C = D
       MOVE 1 TO A                          MOVE 0 TO COUNTER
   END-IF                            ELSE
                                            NEXT SENTENCE.
```

7. Will the following pair of statements cause the same instructions to be executed?

(a) ```
IF A IS EQUAL TO C
    MOVE 1 TO C
ELSE
    NEXT SENTENCE.
```

(b) ```
IF  A IS EQUAL TO C
    MOVE 1 TO C
END-IF
```

8. Code the following routine:

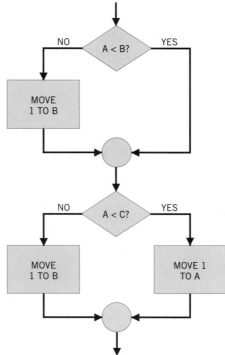

9. Write a routine to move the smallest of three numbers A, B, and C to a field called PRINT-SMALL.

10. Indicate the difference between the following two routines:

(a) ```
IF A IS EQUAL TO B
    ADD C TO D
    MOVE E TO TOTAL.
```

(b) ```
IF  A IS EQUAL TO B
    ADD C TO D.
    MOVE E TO TOTAL.
```

Solutions

1. You cannot say: GO TO CONTINUE.

2. Since A is compared to a nonnumeric literal, it should be an alphanumeric field. But A is *added* to another field, which implies that it is numeric. Hence a data type mismatch exists. Although this may, in fact, produce the correct results (depending on the contents of A), it is inadvisable to make a comparison where one field or literal is nonnumeric and the other is numeric.

3. This should be: IF A IS EQUAL TO B ....

4. When the words GREATER and LESS are used, the COBOL word that follows is THAN and not THEN.

5. There should be no period after MOVE 0 TO COUNTER.

6. ELSE NEXT SENTENCE, although not incorrect, is unnecessary. Note that END-IF cannot be used with NEXT SENTENCE (unless your compiler has an enhancement that permits it) but can always be used with CONTINUE.

7. Yes.

8. ```
IF A IS LESS THAN B
    CONTINUE
ELSE
    MOVE 1 TO B
END-IF
IF A IS LESS THAN C
    MOVE 1 TO A
```
```

```
    ELSE
        MOVE 1 TO B
    END-IF
 9. MOVE A TO PRINT-SMALL
    IF  B IS LESS THAN PRINT-SMALL
        MOVE B TO PRINT-SMALL
    END-IF
    IF  C IS LESS THAN PRINT-SMALL
        MOVE C TO PRINT-SMALL
    END-IF
```

(*Note:* This is *not* the only way to write this routine.)

10. They are different because of the placement of the periods. In (a), MOVE E TO TOTAL is per-formed only if A = B. In (b), however, a period follows ADD C TO D. Thus, if A is equal to B, only one imperative statement is executed. Then, regardless of whether A equals B, E is moved to TOTAL. The indenting included in both (a) and (b) does not affect the execution—the place-ment of the period is the critical factor. To avoid mistakes, use END-IF with COBOL 85.

SELECTION USING OTHER OPTIONS OF THE IF STATEMENT

NESTED CONDITIONAL

A **nested conditional** is a conditional in which an IF statement itself can contain addi-tional IF clauses. Consider the following:

```
IF  condition-1
    statement-1
ELSE
    IF  condition-2
        statement-2
    ELSE
        statement-3
    END-IF
END-IF
```
⎫
⎬ With COBOL 85 only—the END-IF delimits each IF clause
⎭

This is an example of a nested conditional. Because complex nesting of conditions can sometimes be confusing, we recommend that nested conditionals always be *balanced* by having each IF clause paired with an ELSE, as shown in the following:

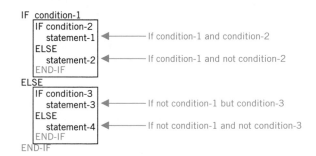

In our nested conditionals, each END-IF scope terminator will be paired with the preceding IF except for the last END-IF, which is paired with the first IF.

We will see later on that the use of END-IF to delimit each IF clause reduces the risk of errors. That is, it can sometimes make a logical difference in the meaning of the full statement.

Example 1

Without Scope Terminators
(COBOL 74 or 85)

```
IF   AMT  =  6
     IF   TAX  =  10
          PERFORM 200-RTN-2
     ELSE
          PERFORM 300-RTN-3
ELSE
     PERFORM 100-RTN-1.
```

With Scope Terminators
(Preferred Method with COBOL 85)

```
IF   AMT  =  6
     IF   TAX  =  10
          PERFORM 200-RTN-2
     ELSE
          PERFORM 300-RTN-3
     END-IF◄──────Used to delimit inner IF
ELSE
     PERFORM 100-RTN-1
END-IF◄────────────Used to delimit outer IF;
                   period is optional unless this
                   is the last instruction in a
                   paragraph
```

This example conforms to the original format specified for an IF instruction, but statement-1 is a conditional, not an imperative statement. This makes Example 1 a *nested conditional*. The tests performed are:

1. If AMT is not equal to 6, the last ELSE, PERFORM 100-RTN-1, is executed.
2. If AMT = 6, the second condition (which corresponds to statement-1) is tested as follows:
   (a) (if AMT = 6) and TAX = 10, 200-RTN-2 is performed.
   (b) (If AMT = 6) and TAX is not equal to 10, 300-RTN-3 is performed.

This procedure may also be written in terms of a decision table:

Decision Table for Example 1		
Condition 1	**Condition 2**	**Action**
AMT = 6	TAX = 10	PERFORM 200-RTN-2
AMT = 6	TAX ≠ 10	PERFORM 300-RTN-3
AMT ≠ 6	TAX = anything	PERFORM 100-RTN-1

Decision tables list the various conditions that may occur and the actions to be performed. Decision tables are frequently prepared by systems analysts and programmers to map out or chart complex logic that requires execution of different modules depending on the results of numerous tests.

A nested conditional is really a shortcut method of writing a series of conditionals. The nested conditional in Example 1 may also be coded as follows:

```
500-CALC-RTN.
     IF   AMT IS NOT EQUAL TO 6
          PERFORM 100-RTN-1
     END-IF
     IF   TAX IS EQUAL TO 10 AND AMT = 6
          PERFORM 200-RTN-2
     END-IF
     IF   TAX NOT = 10 AND AMT = 6
          PERFORM 300-RTN-3
     END-IF
```

See the next section for a discussion of AND and NOT in a conditional.

A nested conditional is used in COBOL for the following reasons: (1) it minimizes coding effort where numerous conditions are to be tested; and (2) it tests conditions just as they appear in a decision table.

Example 2   Consider the following decision table:

Condition	Condition	Action
A = B	C = D	PERFORM 100-RTN-A
A = B	C ≠ D	PERFORM 200-RTN-B
A ≠ B	anything	PERFORM 300-RTN-C

We could code this decision table as a nested conditional. To help clarify the sentence, parentheses or scope terminators (for COBOL 85) may be used as follows:

Using Parentheses
(COBOL 74 or 85)

```
IF  A = B
   (IF  C = D
        PERFORM 100-RTN-A
    ELSE
        PERFORM 200-RTN-B)
ELSE
    PERFORM 300-RTN-C.
```

Using Scope Terminators
(Preferred Method with COBOL 85)

```
IF  A = B
    IF  C = D
        PERFORM 100-RTN-A
    ELSE
        PERFORM 200-RTN-B
    END-IF
ELSE
        PERFORM 300-RTN-C
END-IF
```

The indenting of clauses helps to clarify the relationships between statements and should be consistently employed when coding nested conditionals. This will not only help in reading the statement, but it will make it easier to debug your program as well. Parentheses may be included for clarification.

Thus, the general format for an IF is:

Format

$$
\text{IF condition-1}
$$

```
    IF  condition-1
    [THEN]*
        ⎧ statement-1 ...   ⎫
        ⎨ NEXT SENTENCE     ⎬
        ⎩ CONTINUE*         ⎭

        ⎡ ELSE statement-2 ... [END-IF]* ⎤
        ⎨ ELSE NEXT SENTENCE             ⎬
        ⎣ END-IF*                        ⎦
```

*END-IF should be used to delimit each IF clause when using COBOL 85. THEN and CONTINUE are COBOL 85 options.

In a nested conditional, statements 1 and 2 above can themselves be conditional statements.

Because END-IFs are not used with COBOL 74, ELSE NEXT SENTENCE is sometimes required for proper pairing of ELSE clauses with IF statements. Consider the following:

Condition 1	Condition 2	Action
A = 5	B < 20	MOVE 30 TO C
A = 5	B >= 20	do nothing
A ≠ 5	B = anything	MOVE 25 TO D

The procedure for this decision table sequence is:

```
           IF   A = 5
                IF   B < 20
                     MOVE 30 TO C
                ELSE
                     NEXT SENTENCE
           ELSE
                MOVE 25 TO D.
```

This clause is required for proper pairing of clauses →

If ELSE NEXT SENTENCE is *not* included, then 25 is moved to D if A = 5 and B >= 20, and no action is taken if A ≠ 5. This would *not* be the same as what is represented in the decision table.

With COBOL 85, END-IFs can be used to eliminate the need for pairing ELSE clauses with IF statements and for coding clauses such as ELSE NEXT SENTENCE. Indeed, END-IF, in general, reduces the risk of logic errors:

COBOL 85
```
IF   A = 5
     IF   B < 20
          MOVE 30 TO C
     END-IF
ELSE
     MOVE 25 TO D
END-IF
```

──────────────────────────DEBUGGING TIPS──────

1. With COBOL 85, use END-IF for each IF clause to reduce errors and to eliminate the need for pairing.
2. Avoid the use of NEXT SENTENCE with an END-IF scope terminator in COBOL 85. Note that:

```
IF   A = B
     NEXT SENTENCE
ELSE
     ⋮
```

could be coded as:

```
IF   A NOT = B
     ⋮
```

We will see later on in this chapter that the EVALUATE verb is often used in place of nested conditionals.

COMPOUND CONDITIONAL

We have seen that selection and iteration structures provide programs with a great deal of logical control capability. The **compound conditional** offers even greater flexibility for selection and enables the IF statement to be used for more complex problems. With the compound conditional, the programmer can test for several conditions with one statement.

OR in a Compound Conditional

To perform an operation or a series of operations if *any one of several conditions exists*, use a compound conditional with conditions separated by OR. This means that if *any one of several conditions* exists, the imperative statement(s) specified will be executed.

Examples
```
1. IF   AMT1 = AMT2 OR AMT2 > AMT3
          PERFORM 500-TOTAL-RTN
     END-IF
2. IF   AMT1 < AMT3 OR AMT1 = AMT4
          ADD AMT1 TO TOTAL
     ELSE
          PERFORM 600-ERR-RTN
     END-IF
```

By using OR in a compound conditional, *any* of the conditions specified causes execution of the statement(s). If none of the conditions is met, the computer executes either the ELSE clause, if coded, or the next sentence. Any number of conditions separated by ORs may be coded in a single statement.

In the second example, the paragraph 600-ERR-RTN is executed only if AMT1 is greater than or equal to AMT3 *and* AMT1 is not equal to AMT4. If *either* AMT1 is less than AMT3, or AMT1 is equal to AMT4, AMT1 will be added to TOTAL and then the next sentence will be executed.

Limitations on a Compound Conditional

Using the preceding instruction format, note that the following is invalid:

Invalid Syntax   ⌐—— Will cause a syntax error
                                             ▼
```
IF   A IS EQUAL TO B OR  IF  B IS EQUAL TO C
      PERFORM 500-PARA-5
END-IF
```

With compound conditionals, the word IF is coded only once.

Implied Operands

In compound conditionals, it is not always necessary to specify both operands for each condition. To say IF TOTAL = 7 OR 8 PERFORM 500-PRINT-RTN tests two simple conditions: (1) TOTAL = 7 and (2) TOTAL = 8. Since the identifier TOTAL is omitted from the second condition test, we say that it is an *implied operand.* For most compilers, a compound conditional statement with an implied operand is valid; that is, both operands need not be included for each condition. The preceding statement can also be coded as:

```
IF   TOTAL = 7 OR TOTAL = 8
      PERFORM 500-PRINT-RTN
END-IF
```

The following use of an implied operand, however, is *not* valid:

Invalid Use of an Implied Operand

```
IF TOTAL-1 OR TOTAL-2 = 7 ...
```

A *full condition* must be specified following the word IF. In a conditional such as IF condition-1 OR condition-2 . . ., condition-1 must include a *full test,* but subsequent conditions can have implied operands, where the first operand of the next condition is the one that is implied. In the clause IF TOTAL = 7 OR 8, for example, the compiler assumes you mean to compare TOTAL to 8 as well as to 7.

Not Greater Than or Equal To Is Equivalent to Less Than

Note that the following two routines produce identical results:

```
1.  IF  AMT-IN IS GREATER THAN 5 OR EQUAL TO 5
         PERFORM 100-STEP1
```

```
        ELSE
            PERFORM 200-STEP2
        END-IF
    2.  IF  AMT-IN IS LESS THAN 5
            PERFORM 200-STEP2
        ELSE
            PERFORM 100-STEP1
        END-IF
```

That is, if AMT-IN is not greater than or equal to 5 it must be less than 5.

With COBOL 85 compilers, the first routine above can be coded as IF AMT-IN >= 5 .... That is, >= and <= are permitted in compound conditionals with COBOL 85.

AND in a Compound Conditional

If a statement or statements are to be executed only when *all* of several conditions are met, use the word AND in the compound conditional. Thus, either AND or OR (or both) can be used in a compound conditional:

Format

$$
\text{IF} \quad \text{condition-1} \left\{ \begin{matrix} \underline{OR} \\ \underline{AND} \end{matrix} \right\} \quad \text{condition-2} \ldots
$$

$$
[\text{THEN}]^*
$$

$$
\left\{ \begin{matrix} \text{statement-1} \ldots \\ \underline{NEXT} \ \underline{SENTENCE} \\ \underline{CONTINUE}^* \end{matrix} \right\}
$$

$$
\left\{ \begin{matrix} \underline{ELSE} \ \text{statement-2} \ldots \ [\text{END-IF}]^* \\ \underline{ELSE} \ \underline{NEXT} \ \underline{SENTENCE} \\ \underline{END-IF}^* \end{matrix} \right\}
$$

*THEN, CONTINUE, and END-IF are COBOL 85 features.

All conditions must be met when AND is used in a compound condition. The ELSE clause is executed if *any one* of the stated conditions is not met.

Example Suppose we want to perform 400-PRINT-RTN if all the following conditions are met:

```
AMT1 = AMTA; AMT2 = AMTB; AMT3 = AMTC
```

If one or more of these conditions are *not* met, 500-ERR-RTN should be performed. We may use a compound conditional for this:

```
IF  AMT1 IS EQUAL TO AMTA
        AND  AMT2 IS EQUAL TO AMTB
            AND AMT3 IS EQUAL TO AMTC
    PERFORM 400-PRINT-RTN
ELSE
    PERFORM 500-ERR-RTN
END-IF
```

If all the conditions are met, 400-PRINT-RTN is executed. If any condition is *not* met, 500-ERR-RTN is executed.

Using AND and OR in the Same Statement

Introduction

There are times when *both* the AND and OR are required within the same compound conditional.

Example Write a routine to perform 700-PRINT-RTN if AMT is between 10 and 20, inclusive of the end points (i.e., including 10 and 20).

The best way to code this, using COBOL 85, is:

```
IF AMT >= 10 AND AMT <= 20
    PERFORM 700-PRINT-RTN
END-IF
```

With COBOL 74, we cannot code AMT >= 10 AND AMT <= 20.
Only <, >, and = are permitted in each conditional.

You might have considered coding the compound conditional as follows:

```
IF  AMT = 10 OR AMT = 11 OR AMT = 12 ... OR AMT = 20
    PERFORM 700-PRINT-RTN
END-IF
```

This statement, however, will function properly *only if* AMT *is an integer.* The number 10.3, for instance, is between 10 and 20, but it will not pass the preceding tests. For a similar reason, we cannot say: IF AMT > 9 AND AMT < 21 PERFORM 700-PRINT-RTN. If AMT is 9.8, it is *not* between 10 and 20, but it passes both tests. Thus, we want to perform 700-PRINT-RTN if:

(1) AMT = 10, |or| (2) AMT > 10 AND AMT < 20, |or| (3) AMT = 20

We could code the compound conditional as follows:

```
IF  AMT IS EQUAL TO 10
    OR  AMT IS GREATER THAN 10 AND AMT IS LESS THAN 20
    OR  AMT IS EQUAL TO 20
        PERFORM 700-PRINT-RTN
END-IF
```

Order of Evaluation of Compound Conditionals

When using both AND and OR in the same compound conditional as in the preceding example, the order of evaluation of each condition is critical. For example, look at the following:

```
IF  A = B OR C = D AND E = F
    PERFORM 600-PARA-1
END-IF
```

Suppose A = 2, B = 2, C = 3, D = 4, E = 5, and F = 6. Depending on the order in which these conditions are evaluated, 600-PARA-1 may or may not be executed. Suppose the statement is evaluated as follows:

Order of Evaluation: Possibility 1

(a) IF A = B OR C = D |and| (b) E = F

If this is the order of evaluation, there are two ways that 600-PARA-1 will be executed: (1) A = B and E = F, or (2) C = D and E = F. That is, E and F must be equal *and* either A must be equal to B or C must be equal to D. Since E does not equal F, 600-PARA-1 will not be executed if this order of evaluation is correct.

Suppose, however, that the preceding instruction is evaluated as follows:

Order of Evaluation: Possibility 2

(a) IF A = B |or| (b) C = D AND E = F

If this is the order of evaluation, there are two ways that 600-PARA-1 will be executed: (1) A = B, or (2) C = D and E = F. That is, either A and B are equal *or* C must equal D and E must equal F. Because the first condition, A = B, is met, the PERFORM will occur if this order of evaluation is correct.

Hence, if the second order of evaluation is the one actually used by the computer, 600-PARA-1 is executed; but if the first is used, the paragraph is not executed. Only one of these evaluations is correct. Now that the importance of the order of evaluation is clear, we will consider the hierarchy rules:

> ## HIERARCHY RULES FOR COMPOUND CONDITIONALS
>
> 1. Conditions surrounding the word AND are evaluated first.
>
> 2. Conditions surrounding the word OR are evaluated last.
>
> 3. When there are several AND or OR connectors, the AND conditions are evaluated first, as they appear in the statement, from left to right. Then the OR conditions are evaluated, also from left to right.
>
> 4. To override Rules 1–3, use parentheses around conditions you want to be evaluated first.

Using these hierarchy rules and the preceding example, the conditions will be evaluated as follows:

   (a) IF C = D AND E = F or (b) A = B

With A = 2, B = 2, C = 3, D = 4, E = 5, and F = 6, 600-PARA-1 will be executed because A = B. To change the order so that the evaluation is performed as in Possibility 1 above, code the condition as follows:

```
IF (A = B OR C = D) AND E = F
    PERFORM 600-PARA-1
END-IF
```

In this case, 600-PARA-1 will *not* be executed.

Examples

As in a previous example, we want to print AMT if it is between 10 and 20, inclusive. This is often written mathematically as $10 \le AMT \le 20$; if 10 is less than or equal to AMT and, at the same time, AMT is less than or equal to 20, then we wish to print AMT.

With COBOL 85, we code the instruction as follows:

```
IF  AMT <= 20 AND AMT >= 10
    PERFORM 700-PRINT-RTN
END-IF
```

Let us determine if the following statement also results in the proper test:

```
IF  AMT < 20 OR AMT = 20 AND AMT = 10 OR AMT > 10
    PERFORM 700-PRINT-RTN
END-IF
```

Using the hierarchy rules for evaluating compound conditionals, the first conditions tested are those surrounding the word AND. Then, from left to right, those surrounding the OR expressions are evaluated. Thus, we have:

    1. IF AMT = 20 AND AMT = 10

or 2. AMT < 20

or 3. AMT > 10

The compound conditional test in (1) is always false because the value for AMT can never equal 10 and, at the same time, be equal to 20. Since the first expression tested will never be true, it can be eliminated from the statement, which then reduces to:

```
IF  AMT < 20 OR AMT > 10
    PERFORM 700-PRINT-RTN
END-IF
```

Obviously, this is *not* the solution to the original problem. In fact, using the preceding conditional, *all* values for AMT will cause 700-PRINT-RTN to be executed. If AMT were, in fact, greater than 20, it would cause 700-PRINT-RTN to be performed since it passes the test: AMT > 10. (Any number > 10 passes this test.) If AMT were less than 10, it would cause 700-PRINT-RTN to be executed since it passes the test: AMT < 20. (Any number < 20 passes this test.)

The original statement would be correct if we could change the order of evaluation. We want the comparisons performed according to the following hierarchy:

1. IF AMT < 20 OR AMT = 20

and 2. AMT = 10 OR AMT > 10

To change the normal order of evaluation, place parentheses around the conditions you want to be evaluated first, as a unit. *Parentheses override the other hierarchy rules*—all conditions within parentheses are evaluated together. Thus, the following statement is correct:

```
IF  (AMT < 20 OR AMT = 20)
    AND (AMT = 10 OR AMT > 10)
    PERFORM 700-PRINT-RTN
END-IF
```

When in doubt about the normal sequence of evaluation, use parentheses. Even when they are not necessary, as in IF (A = B AND C = D) OR (E = F) ..., they ensure that the statements are performed in the proper sequence. Moreover, they help the user better understand the logic of a program.

SIGN AND CLASS TESTS

In addition to simple and compound conditionals, there are various specialized tests that can be performed with the IF statement.

Sign Test

We can test whether a field is POSITIVE, NEGATIVE, or ZERO with a **sign test**.

Example
```
IF  AMT IS POSITIVE
    PERFORM 200-CALC-RTN
END-IF
```

We can also test to see if AMT IS NEGATIVE or ZERO.

Designating Fields as Signed Negative or Positive: A Review

To test a field for its sign implies that the field may have a negative value. As noted in Chapters 6 and 7, a numeric field will be considered unsigned or positive by the computer unless there is an S in its PICTURE clause. This S, like the implied decimal point V, does not occupy a storage position. Thus 05 AMT1 PIC 99 is a two-position *unsigned* field and 05 AMT2 PIC S99 is a two-position *signed* field, unless SIGN IS LEADING SEPARATE or TRAILING SEPARATE is specified (which would make it a three-position signed field).

If you move −12 to AMT1, AMT1 will contain 12 because it is unsigned. Moving −12 to AMT2 will result in −12 in AMT2, since AMT2 allows for a sign. Use S in a PIC clause of a numeric field that may have negative contents.

On most computers, the phrase IF A IS EQUAL TO ZERO is the same as IF A IS ZERO. If a numeric field contains an amount less than zero, it is considered negative. If it has an amount greater than zero, then it is considered positive.

−382 is negative   382 is positive   +382 is positive

0 is neither negative nor positive in this context, unless it is indicated as −0 or +0, respectively.

Example Suppose we want to compute the distance of AMT from zero, regardless of its sign. For instance, if AMT = 2, its distance from zero is 2. If AMT = −2, its distance from zero is also 2, since we do not consider the sign. We call this quantity the *absolute value* of AMT, denoted mathematically as |AMT|. It is formulated as follows:

If AMT is greater than or equal to 0, then |AMT| = AMT.

If AMT is less than 0, then |AMT| = −AMT = −1 × AMT.

In other words, if AMT is greater than or equal to zero, the absolute value of AMT is simply the value of AMT. If AMT is less than zero, the absolute value of AMT is equal to −1 times the value of AMT, which will be a positive number. Let us find the absolute value of AMT:

```
MOVE ZERO TO ABS-A
IF  AMT IS POSITIVE
    MOVE AMT TO ABS-A
END-IF
IF  AMT IS NEGATIVE
    MULTIPLY −1 BY AMT GIVING ABS-A
END-IF
```

The clause IF AMT IS NEGATIVE is equivalent to saying IF AMT < 0, and IF AMT IS POSITIVE is the same as IF AMT > 0. If AMT is 0, the contents of ABS-A remains unchanged; that is, it contains zero.

We could also code MOVE AMT TO ABS-A, where ABS-A is an unsigned field.

Class Test

We can test for the type of data in a field by coding IF identifier-1 IS NUMERIC or IF identifier-1 IS ALPHABETIC.

If the ELSE option is executed with the NUMERIC **class test,** then either the field contains alphabetic data (only letters and/or spaces) or it contains alphanumeric data, meaning any possible characters. Suppose we code the following:

```
IF  AMT-IN IS NUMERIC
    PERFORM 300-CALC-RTN
ELSE
    PERFORM 400-ERROR-RTN
END-IF
```

If the field contains 123AB, for example, the ELSE clause will be executed since the contents of the field are not strictly numeric.

Using Class Tests for Validating Data

A class test is a useful tool for minimizing program errors. Suppose we wish to add AMT-IN to TOTAL, where AMT-IN is an input field. Since input is always subject to data-entry errors, it is possible that the field might be entered erroneously with nonnumeric data or spaces. In such a case, ADD AMT-IN TO TOTAL can cause the computer to abort the run.

The following test may be used to minimize such errors:

```
IF  AMT-IN IS NUMERIC
    ADD AMT-IN TO TOTAL
ELSE
    PERFORM 500-ERR-RTN
END-IF
```

It is good practice to validate the AMT-IN field, as in the preceding, before we perform arithmetic. As noted, periods are optional when using END-IF for COBOL 85 unless you are at the end of a paragraph.

ALPHABETIC Class with COBOL 85

When COBOL was originally developed, most computers were unable to represent lowercase letters. Thus, only uppercase letters were used.

When computers began to have internal codes for lowercase letters, the use of the ALPHABETIC class test became ambiguous. Some COBOL compilers considered both 'abc' and 'ABC' to be ALPHABETIC, for example, whereas others considered only 'ABC' to be ALPHABETIC.

COBOL 85 has eliminated this ambiguity by specifying that any letter—either uppercase or lowercase, or any blank—is considered ALPHABETIC. Moreover, two new *class tests* have been added: ALPHABETIC-UPPER and ALPHABETIC-LOWER. Thus the three alphabetic class tests for COBOL 85 are:

Alphabetic Class Tests

Reserved Word	Meaning
ALPHABETIC	A–Z, a–z, and blank
ALPHABETIC-UPPER	A–Z and blank
ALPHABETIC-LOWER	a–z and blank

Example

```
IF NAME-IN IS ALPHABETIC-LOWER
THEN
     PERFORM 600-LOWER-CASE-RTN
END-IF
```

NEGATING CONDITIONALS

Negating Simple Conditionals

All simple relational, class, or sign tests may be coded using a **negated conditional**. The full format for conditionals, including a negated conditional, is as follows:

Format

```
                              ⎧ ⎧ GREATER THAN (>)                         ⎫ ⎫
                              ⎪ ⎪ LESS THAN (<)                            ⎪ ⎪
                              ⎪ ⎨ EQUAL TO (=)                identifier-2 ⎬ ⎪
                              ⎪ ⎪ LESS THAN OR EQUAL TO (<=)*             ⎪ ⎪
                              ⎪ ⎩ GREATER THAN OR EQUAL TO (>=)*          ⎭ ⎪
                              ⎪                                             ⎪
   IF identifier-1 IS [NOT]  ⎨ ⎧ NUMERIC                ⎫                  ⎬
                              ⎪ ⎪ POSITIVE               ⎪                  ⎪
                              ⎪ ⎪ NEGATIVE               ⎪                  ⎪
                              ⎪ ⎨ ZERO                   ⎬                  ⎪
                              ⎪ ⎪ ALPHABETIC             ⎪                  ⎪
                              ⎪ ⎪ ALPHABETIC-UPPER*      ⎪                  ⎪
                              ⎩ ⎩ ALPHABETIC-LOWER*      ⎭                  ⎭

   [THEN]*
   ⎧ statement-1 ...  ⎫
   ⎨ NEXT SENTENCE    ⎬
   ⎩ CONTINUE*        ⎭

   ⎧ ELSE statement-2 ... [END-IF]* ⎫
   ⎨ ELSE NEXT SENTENCE             ⎬
   ⎩ END-IF*                        ⎭
```

*Options with COBOL 85 only.

Examples   The following two statements are equivalent:

```
1.  IF  AMT1 IS EQUAL TO AMT2        2.  IF  AMT1 IS NOT EQUAL TO AMT2
        PERFORM 100-EQUAL-RTN               PERFORM 200-NOT-EQUAL-RTN
    ELSE                                ELSE
        PERFORM 200-NOT-EQUAL-RTN           PERFORM 100-EQUAL-RTN
    END-IF                              END-IF
```

NOT NEGATIVE Is Not Equal to POSITIVE

To say, however, IF AMT1 IS NOT NEGATIVE, is *not* the same as saying AMT1 IS POSITIVE. If AMT1 is zero, it is *neither*. Thus, the following two statements are *not* equivalent if AMT1 = 0:

```
1.  IF  AMT1 IS NEGATIVE             2.  IF  AMT1 IS NOT POSITIVE
        PERFORM 100-NEG-RTN                 PERFORM 100-NEG-RTN
    ELSE                                ELSE
        PERFORM 200-ADD-RTN                 PERFORM 200-ADD-RTN
    END-IF                              END-IF
```

Suppose AMT1 is equal to 0. In statement (1), 200-ADD-RTN is executed; in statement (2), 100-NEG-RTN is executed. Similarly, to say IF CODE-IN IS NOT ALPHABETIC, is *not* the same as saying IF CODE-IN IS NUMERIC. If CODE-IN is alphanumeric, containing combinations of letters, digits, and special characters, then it is neither ALPHABETIC nor NUMERIC. Thus, the following two statements are *not* equivalent:

```
1.  IF  CODE-X IS NOT ALPHABETIC     2.  IF  CODE-X IS NUMERIC
        PERFORM 100-RTN1                    PERFORM 100-RTN1
    ELSE                                ELSE
        PERFORM 200-RTN2                    PERFORM 200-RTN2
    END-IF                              END-IF
```

Negating Compound Conditionals

Negating compound conditionals can cause a logic error. The following example will explain the error and how it can be avoided:

Example   The following is a routine to perform 200-MARRIED-RTN if MARITAL-CODE is not equal to 'S' (single) or 'D' (divorced); otherwise 100-UNMARRIED-RTN is performed:

```
IF  MARITAL-CODE IS EQUAL TO 'S'
        OR MARITAL-CODE IS EQUAL TO 'D'
    PERFORM 100-UNMARRIED-RTN
ELSE
    PERFORM 200-MARRIED-RTN
END-IF
```

But suppose we want to use negated conditionals. On first thought, you may decide simply to negate each simple condition:

```
IF  MARITAL-CODE IS NOT EQUAL TO 'S'
        OR MARITAL-CODE IS NOT EQUAL TO 'D'
    PERFORM 200-MARRIED-RTN
ELSE
    PERFORM 100-UNMARRIED-RTN
END-IF
```

An evaluation of this statement will show that the preceding is *not* correct. As coded, one of two conditions must exist for 200-MARRIED-RTN to be executed:

     a. MARITAL-CODE IS NOT EQUAL TO 'S'

      |or| b. MARITAL-CODE IS NOT EQUAL TO 'D'

Suppose MARITAL-CODE is 'M' (for married); 200-MARRIED-RTN will be executed, which is what we want. If MARITAL-CODE is 'S', however, we wish 100-UNMARRIED-RTN to be executed. In the preceding conditional, condition (a) is *not met* since MARITAL-CODE does equal 'S'. However, condition (b) *is met* since MARITAL-CODE *is not equal to* 'D', but is equal to 'S'. Only one condition needs to be satisfied for 200-MARRIED-RTN to be executed, and since condition (b) is satisfied, 200-MARRIED-RTN will be executed *instead of* 100-UNMARRIED-RTN, which is really the procedure we should execute.

Similarly, suppose MARITAL-CODE is 'D'. We want 100-UNMARRIED-RTN to be executed, but note again that 200-MARRIED-RTN is executed. Condition (a) is satisfied, because MARITAL-CODE is not equal to 'S' (it is equal to 'D'). Since only one condition needs to be satisfied, 200-MARRIED-RTN is executed. In fact, you can now see that the statement as coded will *always* cause 200-MARRIED-RTN to be executed, regardless of the contents of MARITAL-CODE.

The "moral" of this illustration is a lesson in Boolean algebra, called DeMorgan's Rule, which is: When negating conditions separated by OR: IF NOT (CONDITION1 OR CONDITION2...), the stated conditions become: IF NOT CONDITION1 **AND** NOT CONDITION2 **AND** .... Hence, the IF statement could be coded as IF NOT (MARITAL-CODE = 'S' OR MARITAL-CODE = 'D') or as:

```
IF   MARITAL-CODE IS NOT EQUAL TO 'S'
         AND MARITAL-CODE IS NOT EQUAL TO 'D'
      PERFORM 200-MARRIED-RTN
ELSE
      PERFORM 100-UNMARRIED-RTN
END-IF
```

We negate AND statements using a similar rule: IF NOT (A = B AND C = D) ... can be coded IF A NOT = B OR C NOT = D ....

The hierarchy rules for statements that include negated conditionals, then, are:

HIERARCHY RULES

1. NOT is evaluated first.

2. AND (from left to right if more than one) is evaluated next.

3. OR (from left to right if more than one) is evaluated last.

CONDITION-NAMES

A **condition-name** is a user-defined word established in the DATA DIVISION that gives a name to a specific value that an identifier can assume. An 88-level entry coded in the DATA DIVISION is a condition-name that denotes a possible value for an identifier. Consider the following example:

```
05  MARITAL-STATUS      PICTURE X.
```

Suppose that an 'S' in the field called MARITAL-STATUS denotes that the person is single. We may use a condition-name SINGLE to indicate this value:

```
05  MARITAL-STATUS      PICTURE X.
    88  SINGLE            VALUE 'S'.
```

When the field called MARITAL-STATUS is equal to 'S', we will call that condition SINGLE. The 88-level item is not the name of a *field* but the name of a *condition*; it refers specifically to the elementary item *directly preceding it*. SINGLE is a condition-name applied to the field called MARITAL-STATUS, since MARITAL-STATUS directly precedes the 88-level item. The condition SINGLE exists or is "true" if MARITAL-STATUS = 'S'.

A condition-name is always coded on the 88 level and has only a VALUE clause associated with it. Since a condition-name is *not* the name of a field, it will *not* contain a PICTURE clause.

The following is the format for 88-level items:

Format

```
88 condition-name VALUE literal.
```

The condition-name must be unique and its VALUE must be a literal consistent with the data type of the field preceding it:

```
05   CODE-IN              PIC XX.
     88  STATUS-OK        VALUE '12'.
```

For readability, we indent each 88-level item to clarify its relationship to the data-name directly preceding it.

Any elementary item on level numbers 01–49 in the FILE or WORKING-STORAGE SECTIONs may have a condition-name associated with it.

Condition-names are defined in the DATA DIVISION to simplify processing in the PROCEDURE DIVISION. A condition-name is an alternate method of expressing a simple relational test in the PROCEDURE DIVISION. Consider the following DATA DIVISION entries:

```
05   MARITAL-STATUS       PIC X.
     88  DIVORCED         VALUE 'D'.
```

We may use *either* of the following tests in the PROCEDURE DIVISION:

```
IF   MARITAL-STATUS IS EQUAL TO 'D'        or    IF   DIVORCED
     PERFORM 600-DIVORCE-RTN                          PERFORM 600-DIVORCE-RTN
END-IF                                           END-IF
```

The condition-name DIVORCED will test to determine if MARITAL-STATUS does, in fact, have a value of 'D'.

You may code as many 88-level items for a field as you wish:

```
05   MARITAL-STATUS       PIC X.
     88  DIVORCED         VALUE 'D'.
     88  MARRIED          VALUE 'M'.
        :
```

Condition-names may be used in the PROCEDURE DIVISION to make programs easier to read and debug. They may refer to fields with or without VALUE clauses.

88-level items can also specify multiple values. If a field called STATUS-1 can have values 1, 2, 3, or 4, we can code:

```
01   STATUS-1 PIC 9.
     88  VALID-STATUS     VALUE 1 THRU 4.
```

THRU is a COBOL reserved word. VALID-STATUS is a condition that is met if STATUS-1 has any of the values 1, 2, 3, or 4.

If a MARITAL-STATUS field can have a value S, M, D, or W, we can code:

```
01   MARITAL-STATUS  PIC X.
     88  VALID-MARITAL-STATUS    VALUE 'S' 'M' 'D' 'W'.
```

VALID-MARITAL-STATUS is a condition that is met if MARITAL-STATUS has a value of 'S' or 'M' or 'D' or 'W'.

VALUE ALL may be used to specify repeated entries for a literal:

```
01   CODE-1          PIC X(5).
     88  CODE-ON     VALUE ALL 'A'.
```

If CODE-1 = 'AAAAA' then the condition CODE-ON will be met.

VALUE ALL could also be used to initialize the field itself:

```
05   LITERAL-1      PIC X(10)    VALUE ALL 'AB'.
```

LITERAL-1 will contain ABABABABAB.

Condition-names are frequently used for indicating when an AT END condition has been reached, as in the following:

Example
```
05   ARE-THERE-MORE-RECORDS          PIC X(3)  VALUE 'YES'.
     88  THERE-ARE-NO-MORE-RECORDS               VALUE 'NO '.
        :
```

```
IF  THERE-ARE-NO-MORE-RECORDS
    PERFORM 900-END-OF-JOB-RTN
END-IF
```

Using the condition-name THERE-ARE-NO-MORE-RECORDS may be more meaningful than comparing ARE-THERE-MORE-RECORDS to 'NO '.

THE COBOL 85 EVALUATE STATEMENT: USING THE CASE STRUCTURE AS AN ALTERNATIVE TO SELECTION

With COBOL 85 we use the **EVALUATE** verb to implement the **case structure,** which is a logical control construct described in Chapter 5. This verb can test for a series of conditions and is often used instead of IF statements.

Suppose an input field called YEARS-IN-COLLEGE-IN is used to determine the type of processing to be performed. With COBOL 74, we could code the following:

```
IF  YEARS-IN-COLLEGE-IN = 1
    PERFORM 300-FRESHMAN-RTN.
IF  YEARS-IN-COLLEGE-IN = 2
    PERFORM 400-SOPHOMORE-RTN.
IF  YEARS-IN-COLLEGE-IN = 3
    PERFORM 500-JUNIOR-RTN.
IF  YEARS-IN-COLLEGE-IN = 4
    PERFORM 600-SENIOR-RTN.
```

To ensure correct processing, we must add a fifth condition to perform an error routine if the input field is invalid:

```
IF  YEARS-IN-COLLEGE-IN IS NOT = 1 AND NOT = 2
        AND NOT = 3 AND NOT = 4
    PERFORM 700-ERR-RTN.
```

With COBOL 85, we could use simple IF statements as in the preceding, ending each IF with an END-IF instead of a period. Alternatively, we could use the EVALUATE verb, which enables the series of cases to be coded more clearly and efficiently, and in a more structured form. We could code:

```
EVALUATE YEARS-IN-COLLEGE-IN
    WHEN 1     PERFORM 300-FRESHMAN-RTN
    WHEN 2     PERFORM 400-SOPHOMORE-RTN
    WHEN 3     PERFORM 500-JUNIOR-RTN
    WHEN 4     PERFORM 600-SENIOR-RTN
    WHEN OTHER PERFORM 700-ERR-RTN
END-EVALUATE
```

The WHEN OTHER clause is executed when YEARS-IN-COLLEGE-IN is not 1, 2, 3, or 4. The EVALUATE verb has the following instruction format:

Format

EVALUATE $\begin{Bmatrix} \text{identifier-1} \\ \text{expression-1} \end{Bmatrix}$

    WHEN condition-1   imperative-statement-1 . . .

    [WHEN OTHER   imperative-statement-2]

[END-EVALUATE]

Note that we can EVALUATE an identifier or an expression such as TRUE. Another way to code the preceding EVALUATE, then, is:

```
EVALUATE TRUE
    WHEN YEARS-IN-COLLEGE-IN = 1  PERFORM 300-FRESHMAN-RTN
    WHEN YEARS-IN-COLLEGE-IN = 2  PERFORM 400-SOPHOMORE-RTN
```

```
          WHEN YEARS-IN-COLLEGE-IN = 3   PERFORM 500-JUNIOR-RTN
          WHEN YEARS-IN-COLLEGE-IN = 4   PERFORM 600-SENIOR-RTN
          WHEN OTHER                     PERFORM 700-ERR-RTN
     END-EVALUATE
```

Condition-1 in the Format can be a value that identifier-1 may assume or it can be a condition-name associated with identifier-1 when EVALUATE TRUE is used.

An EVALUATE is not only easier to code than a series of IF statements, it is more efficient as well. Once a condition in an EVALUATE is met, there is no need for the computer to test other conditions in the statement. Thus, after a condition in a WHEN is met and the corresponding imperative statements are executed, execution continues with the statement following END-EVALUATE.

Nested conditionals are executed in a similar manner. Once an IF condition is met and its imperative statements are executed, all the ELSE clauses are bypassed and execution continues after the END-IF. With simple conditionals, on the other hand, each statement is executed independently. This means that in the preceding, if we use five IF statements in place of an EVALUATE, each is executed in sequence *even if the first condition is met*. This is why an EVALUATE (or even a nested conditional) is more efficient than a series of simple conditionals.

The full instruction format for the EVALUATE includes additional options. We discuss this statement again in numerous chapters beginning with Chapter 11.

CHAPTER SUMMARY

A. Simple Relational for Selection
1. Relations

$$\text{IF}\quad \text{identifier-1}\left\{\begin{array}{l}\left\{\begin{array}{l}\text{IS EQUAL TO}\\=\end{array}\right\}\\\left\{\begin{array}{l}\text{IS LESS THAN}\\<\end{array}\right\}\\\left\{\begin{array}{l}\text{IS GREATER THAN}\\>\end{array}\right\}\\\left\{\begin{array}{l}\text{IS LESS THAN OR EQUAL TO}\\<=\end{array}\right\}^*\\\left\{\begin{array}{l}\text{IS GREATER THAN OR EQUAL TO}\\>=\end{array}\right\}^*\end{array}\right\}\text{identifier-2}$$

*COBOL 85 only.

2. If the condition exists, all statements are executed up to (a) the ELSE clause or (b) the END-IF (COBOL 85) or the period if there is no ELSE clause.
3. If the condition does not exist, the statements after the word ELSE, if coded, are executed, or (if there is no ELSE clause) processing continues after the END-IF or with the next sentence.
4. Comparisons are algebraic or logical:
   (1) Numeric: 12.0 = 12.00 = 12 = +12
   (2) Nonnumeric: ABC = ABC$\not b$ = ABC$\not b\not b$
5. Collating sequences (EBCDIC and ASCII) are the same with regard to A–Z, 0–9, and a–z. They differ when upper- and lowercase letters are compared or when letters and digits are compared. With ASCII, lowercase letters are greater than uppercase letters; with EBCDIC, lowercase letters are less than uppercase letters. With EBCDIC, letters are less than numbers. With ASCII, numbers are less than letters.

B. Other Types of IF Statements
1. Compound Condition
   a. Format

   IF condition-1 <u>OR</u> condition-2 ...
   IF condition-1 <u>AND</u> condition-2 ...

b. Hierarchy
   (1) If ORs and ANDs are used in the same sentence, ANDs are evaluated first from left to right, followed by ORs.
   (2) Parentheses can be used to override hierarchy rules.
2. Other Tests
   a. Sign test

$$\text{\underline{IF}} \quad \text{identifier-1} \quad \text{IS} \quad \left\{ \begin{array}{l} \underline{\text{POSITIVE}} \\ \underline{\text{NEGATIVE}} \\ \underline{\text{ZERO}} \end{array} \right\} \cdots$$

Identifier-1 must have an S in its PIC clause if it is to store numeric data with a negative value.
   b. Class Test

$$\text{\underline{IF}} \quad \text{identifier-1} \quad \text{IS} \quad \left\{ \begin{array}{l} \underline{\text{NUMERIC}} \\ \underline{\text{ALPHABETIC}} \end{array} \right\} \cdots$$

   c. Negated Conditionals
      (1) Any test can be preceded with a NOT to test the negative of a conditional.
      (2) IF NOT (A = B OR A = C) is the same as IF A NOT = B **AND** A NOT = C.
C. Condition-Names
   1. Coded on the 88-level directly following the field to which it relates. For example:

```
05   CODE-IN              PIC X.
     88   OK-CODE          VALUE '6'.
```

   2. A condition-name specifies a condition in the PROCEDURE DIVISION. For example:

```
IF   OK-CODE
     PERFORM 200-OK-RTN
END-IF
```

D. The COBOL 85 EVALUATE statement is often used as an alternative to nested IFs or a series of IF statements.

KEY TERMS

ASCII code	Conditional statement	Imperative statement
Case structure	Condition-name	Negated conditional
Class test	Data exception error	Nested conditional
Collating sequence	EBCDIC code	Sign test
Compound conditional	EVALUATE	Simple condition

CHAPTER SELF-TEST What, if anything, is wrong with the following entries (1–5)? Correct all errors.

```
1. IF   A = B OR IF A = C
        PERFORM 100-RTN-X
   END-IF

2. IF   B = 3 OR 4
        PERFORM 100-RTN-X
   END-IF

3. IF   C < A + B
        PERFORM 500-STEP-5
   END-IF

4. IF   A < 21 OR A = 21 AND A = 5 OR A > 5
        PERFORM 100-RTN-1
   END-IF

5. IF   A IS NOT EQUAL TO 3 OR
        A IS NOT EQUAL TO 4
        PERFORM 600-RTN-X
   END-IF
```

6. The hierarchy rule for evaluating compound conditionals states that conditions surrounding the word _____ are evaluated first, followed by conditions surrounding the word _____ .

7. Indicate whether the following two statements are equivalent.
   (a) ```
   IF   AMT < 3 OR AMT > 4
           PERFORM 700-ERR-RTN
    END-IF
   ```
   (b) ```
   IF   AMT IS NOT EQUAL TO 3 AND
           AMT IS NOT EQUAL TO 4
           PERFORM 700-ERR-RTN
    END-IF
   ```

8. Write a single statement to PERFORM 500-PARA-5 if A is between 3 and 13, *inclusive of the end points.* Code this two ways: (1) using an IF and (2) using an EVALUATE.

9. Write a single statement to execute 500-PARA-5 if A is between 3 and 13, *exclusive of the end points.* Code this two ways: (1) using an IF and (2) using an EVALUATE.

10. Write a single statement to perform 300-PARA-3 if the following conditions are all met; otherwise perform 200-PARA-2: (a) A = B; (b) C = D; (c) E = F.

Solutions

1. The word IF should appear only once in the statement:

```
IF   A = B OR A = C
        PERFORM 100-RTN-X
END-IF
```

2. Nothing wrong—implied operands are permitted. The statement is the same as:

```
IF B = 3 OR B = 4
        PERFORM 100-RTN-X
END-IF
```

3. This is okay for COBOL 85. For COBOL 74, each element in a condition must be an identifier or a literal; A + B as an arithmetic expression would not be permitted. For COBOL 74, the following would be valid:

```
ADD A TO B.
IF   C < B
        PERFORM 500-STEP-5.
```

4. Parentheses must be used to make the statement logical: IF (A < 21 OR A = 21) AND (A = 5 OR A > 5) PERFORM 100-RTN-1. Without the parentheses, the statement reduces to: IF A < 21 OR A > 5 PERFORM 100-RTN-1. This is because the clause A = 21 AND A = 5 is a compound condition that cannot be met. Note that with COBOL 85 we can code IF A <= 21 AND A >= 5 ....

5. A branch to 600-RTN-X will always occur. This should read:

```
IF   A IS NOT EQUAL TO 3 AND
            A IS NOT EQUAL TO 4
        PERFORM 600-RTN-X
END-IF
```

6. AND; OR

7. Only if AMT is an integer field.

8. (1) ```
   IF   A <= 13 AND A >= 3
           PERFORM 500-PARA-5
    END-IF
   ```

   With COBOL 74, you need to code IF A = 13 OR A < 13 AND A > 3 OR A = 3 PERFORM 500-PARA-5. (Note that there is no need for parentheses, but including them would be okay.)

   (2) ```
   EVALUATE TRUE
         WHEN A <= 13 AND >= 3
                 PERFORM 500-PARA-5
    END-EVALUATE
   ```

```
9. (1) IF  A > 3 AND A < 13
           PERFORM 500-PARA-5
       END-IF
   (2) EVALUATE TRUE
           WHEN A > 3 AND < 13
               PERFORM 500-PARA-5
       END-EVALUATE
10. IF  A = B AND C = D AND E = F
           PERFORM 300-PARA-3
       ELSE
           PERFORM 200-PARA-2
       END-IF
```

PRACTICE PROGRAM

Write a program to create a master customer file. The problem definition is as follows:

Systems Flowchart

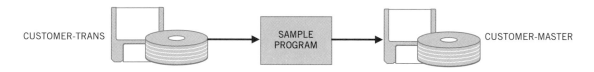

CUSTOMER-TRANS → SAMPLE PROGRAM → CUSTOMER-MASTER

CUSTOMER-TRANS Record Layout			
Field	Size	Type	No. of Decimal Positions (if Numeric)
Identifying Data	35	Alphanumeric	
Sales Amount	5	Numeric	2

CUSTOMER-MASTER Record Layout			
Field	Size	Type	No. of Decimal Positions (if Numeric)
Identifying Data	35	Alphanumeric	
Sales Amount	5	Numeric	2
Discount Percent	2	Numeric	2
Discount Amount	5	Numeric	2
Net Amount	5	Numeric	2

Notes:

a. If sales exceed $500.00, allow 5% discount.
   If sales are between $100.00 and $500.00, inclusive of the end points, allow 2% discount.
   If sales are less than $100.00, allow 1% discount.

b. Discount amount = Sales × Discount %.

c. Net amount = Sales − Discount amount.

The pseudocode and hierarchy chart that describe the logic of this program are in Figure 8.1. The solution along with sample input and output is shown in Figure 8.2.

Figure 8.1 Pseudocode and hierarchy chart for the Practice Program.

Pseudocode

<u>MAIN-MODULE</u>

START

    Housekeeping Operations

    Clear output area

    PERFORM UNTIL no more input (Are-There-More-Records = 'NO ')

        Read a Record

            AT END Move 'NO ' to Are-There-More-Records

            NOT AT END PERFORM Calc-Rtn

        END-READ

    END-PERFORM

    End-of-Job Operations

STOP

<u>CALC-RTN</u>

    Move identifying data and sales amount

            to output area

    IF   Sales Amt > 500.00

    THEN

        Discount Percent = .05

    END-IF

    IF   Sales Amt is between 100 and 500 inclusive

    THEN

        Discount Percent = .02

    END-IF

    IF   Sales Amt < 100

    THEN

        Discount Percent = .01

    END-IF

    Multiply Sales Amt by Discount Percent

        Giving Discount Amt

    Subtract Discount Amt from Sales Amt

        Giving Net

    Write the output record

Hierarchy Chart

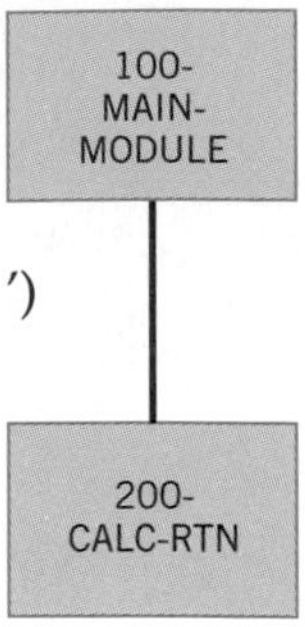

Figure 8.2 Solution to the Practice Program.

COBOL 85

```
IDENTIFICATION DIVISION.
PROGRAM-ID. CHAPTER8.
*********************************************************
*     program calculates a discount on sales           *
*********************************************************
ENVIRONMENT DIVISION.
INPUT-OUTPUT SECTION.
FILE-CONTROL.
    SELECT CUSTOMER-TRANS  ASSIGN TO DISK1.
    SELECT CUSTOMER-MASTER ASSIGN TO DISK2.
DATA DIVISION.
FILE SECTION.
FD  CUSTOMER-TRANS
    LABEL RECORDS ARE STANDARD.
01  TRANS-REC.
    05  IDENT-IN                        PIC X(35).
    05  SALES-AMT-IN                    PIC 999V99.
```

Figure 8.2 (continued)

```
                                    FD  CUSTOMER-MASTER
                                        LABEL RECORDS ARE STANDARD.
                                    01  MASTER-REC.
                                        05  IDENT-OUT                PIC X(35).
                                        05  SALES-AMT-OUT            PIC 999V99.
                                        05  DISC-PERCENT-OUT         PIC V99.
                                        05  DISC-AMT-OUT             PIC 999V99.
                                        05  NET-AMT-OUT              PIC 999V99.
                                    WORKING-STORAGE SECTION.
                                    01  ARE-THERE-MORE-RECORDS       PIC XXX  VALUE 'YES'.
                                        88 NO-MORE-RECORDS                    VALUE 'NO '.
                                    PROCEDURE DIVISION.
                                    **********************************************************
                                    *    main module controls overall program logic       *
                                    **********************************************************
                                    100-MAIN-MODULE.
                                        OPEN INPUT  CUSTOMER-TRANS
                                             OUTPUT CUSTOMER-MASTER
                                        MOVE SPACES TO MASTER-REC
```

COBOL 74 Substitutions

```
READ CUSTOMER-TRANS
    AT END MOVE 'NO ' TO ARE-THERE-MORE-RECORDS.
PERFORM 200-CALC-RTN
    UNTIL NO-MORE-RECORDS.
```

```
                                        PERFORM UNTIL ARE-THERE-MORE-RECORDS = 'NO '
                                            READ CUSTOMER-TRANS
                                                AT END
                                                    MOVE 'NO ' TO ARE-THERE-MORE-RECORDS
                                                NOT AT END
                                                    PERFORM 200-CALC-RTN
                                            END-READ
                                        END-PERFORM
                                        CLOSE CUSTOMER-TRANS
                                              CUSTOMER-MASTER
                                        STOP RUN.
                                    **********************************************************
                                    *    performed from 100-main-module, this routine     *
                                    *    calculates a discount and net amount for          *
                                    *    each transaction                                  *
                                    **********************************************************
                                    200-CALC-RTN.
                                        MOVE IDENT-IN TO IDENT-OUT
                                        MOVE SALES-AMT-IN TO SALES-AMT-OUT
                                        IF  SALES-AMT-IN > 500.00
                                            MOVE .05 TO DISC-PERCENT-OUT
```

```
IF  SALES-AMT-IN = 100.00 OR
    SALES-AMT-IN > 100.00 AND < 500.00 OR
    SALES-AMT-IN = 500.00
        MOVE .02 TO DISC-PERCENT-OUT.
```

```
                                        END-IF
                                        IF  SALES-AMT-IN >= 100.00 AND <= 500.00
                                            MOVE .02 TO DISC-PERCENT-OUT
                                        END-IF
                                        IF SALES-AMT-IN < 100.00
                                            MOVE .01 TO DISC-PERCENT-OUT
                                        END-IF
                                    **********************************************************
                                    *    note that end-if, <=, and >= are used with       *
                                    *    cobol 85 only                                     *
                                    **********************************************************
                                        MULTIPLY SALES-AMT-IN BY DISC-PERCENT-OUT
                                            GIVING DISC-AMT-OUT
                                        SUBTRACT DISC-AMT-OUT FROM SALES-AMT-IN
                                            GIVING NET-AMT-OUT
                                        WRITE MASTER-REC.
```

```
READ CUSTOMER-TRANS
    AT END MOVE 'NO ' TO
        ARE-THERE-MORE-RECORDS.
```

Figure 8.2   (continued)

Sample Input CUSTOMER-TRANS

```
SHODDE CONSTRUCTION COMPANY     |75057|
REDTAPE OFFICE SUPPLIES         |09110|
LEMON AUTOMOTIVE                |10095|
GOODTIME CHARLIE CATERERS       |10000|
FRISBY COLLEGE                  |07265|
SWINDLER'S DEPARTMENT STORE     |93689|
```

IDENTIFYING DATA ⟶   ⟵ SALES AMOUNT

Sample Output CUSTOMER-MASTER

```
SHODDE CONSTRUCTION COMPANY     |75057|05|03752|71305|
REDTAPE OFFICE SUPPLIES         |09110|01|00091|09019|
LEMON AUTOMOTIVE                |10095|02|00201|09894|
GOODTIME CHARLIE CATERERS       |10000|02|00200|09800|
FRISBY COLLEGE                  |07265|01|00072|07193|
SWINDLER'S DEPARTMENT STORE     |93689|05|04684|89005|
```

IDENTIFYING DATA   NET AMOUNT

SALES AMOUNT   DISCOUNT AMOUNT

DISCOUNT PERCENT

REVIEW QUESTIONS

I. True-False Questions

_____ 1. In a compound conditional, statements surrounding the word AND are evaluated first.

_____ 2. With COBOL 85, <= and >= can be used in relational tests.

_____ 3. The clause IF A IS POSITIVE is the opposite of the clause IF A IS NEGATIVE, and the clause IF A IS NUMERIC is the opposite of the clause IF A IS ALPHABETIC.

_____ 4. Numbers are considered greater than uppercase letters in both EBCDIC and ASCII.

_____ 5. Fields being compared in an IF statement must always be the same size.

_____ 6. On most computers, at least one space must precede and follow every symbol such as <, >, and =.

_____ 7. Comparing numeric fields to nonnumeric literals can cause erroneous results.

_____ 8. The class test is frequently used before an arithmetic operation to ensure that a field designated as numeric actually contains numeric data.

_____ 9. The hierarchy of operations in a compound conditional can be overridden by parentheses.

_____ 10. Using a conditional, ABC = ABCb = bABC.

II. General Questions

State whether AMT1 is equal to, greater than, or less than AMT2 (1–4).

	AMT1	PIC	AMT2	PIC
1.	012	9(3)	12	9(2)
2.	12∧0	9(2)V9	12	9(2)
3.	ABC	X(3)	ABCb	X(4)
4.	43	99	+43	S9(2)

5. Write a routine for determining FICA (Social Security and Medicare taxes) where a field called SALARY is read in as input. Assume FICA is equal to 7.65% of SALARY up to $62,700. SALARY in excess of $62,700 is taxed at 1.45% for Medicare only.

6. Find the largest of four numbers A, B, C, and D and place it in the field called HOLD-IT.

Are the following groups of statements equivalent (7–9)?

```
7. (a) IF  A = B
          ADD C TO D
```

```
        ELSE
            ADD E TO F
        END-IF
        PERFORM 600-PRINT-RTN.
    (b) IF   A = B
            ADD C TO D
            PERFORM 600-PRINT-RTN
        ELSE
            ADD E TO F
        END-IF
```

8. (a)
```
    IF   A IS POSITIVE
            PERFORM 600-RTN-X
        ELSE
            PERFORM 700-RTN-Y
        END-IF
```
    (b)
```
    IF   A IS NOT NEGATIVE
            PERFORM 600-RTN-X
        ELSE
            PERFORM 700-RTN-Y
        END-IF
```

9. (a)
```
    IF   DISCOUNT IS GREATER THAN TOTAL
            PERFORM 500-ERR-RTN
        ELSE
            SUBTRACT DISCOUNT FROM TOTAL
        END-IF
```
    (b)
```
    IF   TOTAL > DISCOUNT OR TOTAL = DISCOUNT
            CONTINUE
        ELSE
            PERFORM 500-ERR-RTN
        END-IF
        SUBTRACT DISCOUNT FROM TOTAL
```

What, if anything, is wrong with the following statements (10–11)?

10.
```
    IF   A IS NOT EQUAL TO B OR
            A IS NOT EQUAL TO C
            PERFORM 400-RTN-4
        END-IF
```

11.
```
    IF   A = 3 OR IF   A = 4
            PERFORM 200-PRINT-RTN
        END-IF
```

12. Doughnuts cost 25¢ each if a customer purchases less than a dozen. The doughnuts are 18¢ if 12 or more are purchased. Write a program excerpt using the EVALUATE verb to read in the number of doughnuts purchased and calculate the total price.

13. **Interactive Processing.**   Write a program excerpt to determine and display the concert ticket price for each purchase order. The ticket price depends on whether or not the request is for (1) a weekend and (2) orchestra seats. The following table shows the various prices for different combinations of requests.

Weekend	Yes	Yes	No	No
Orchestra	Yes	No	Yes	No
Price	$48	$36	$44	$24

Input from a keyboard is as follows:

```
CUST NO:
CUST NAME:
REQUEST WEEKEND (Y/N):
REQUEST ORCHESTRA (Y/N):
```

14. Write a program excerpt to read in a file of exam grades and print the percent of students who received a grade of 85 or better. Code this two ways: (1) using an IF and (2) using an EVALUATE.

15. Write a program excerpt to prepare a multiplication table as follows:

Number	2X	3X	4X	5X	...	10X
1	2	3	4	5	...	10
2	4	6	8	10	...	20
.	.	.	.	.		.
.	.	.	.	.		.
.	.	.	.	.		.
10	20	30	40	50		100

16. Consider the following conditional:

```
IF  XX NOT = ZERO
    AND ZZ = 1
    AND XX NOT = 1
    OR XX NOT = 2
    PERFORM 900-FINISH
END-IF
```

Indicate whether 900-FINISH will be performed if XX and ZZ contain the following:

	XX	ZZ			XX	ZZ
(a)	0	0		(e)	1	0
(b)	0	1		(f)	1	1
(c)	0	2		(g)	1	2
(d)	0	3		(h)	1	3

17. Write a program excerpt to determine whether a field called FLDA, with a PIC 99, contains an odd or even number.

    Hint: You may use the DIVIDE ... REMAINDER for this, or some other technique.

DEBUGGING EXERCISES

1. Consider the following coding:

```
    :
    :
    PERFORM UNTIL NO-MORE-RECORDS
        READ TRANS-FILE
            AT END
                MOVE 'NO ' TO ARE-THERE-MORE-RECORDS
            NOT AT END
                PERFORM 200-CALC-RTN
        END-READ
    END-PERFORM
    :
    :
200-CALC-RTN.
    IF  AMT1 = 5400
        ADD AMT2 TO TOTAL
    ELSE
        ADD 1 TO ERR-CT
    WRITE OUT-REC FROM DETAIL-REC.
```

Under what conditions is a record written?
(*Hint:* The punctuation is more critical here than the indentations.)

2. The following coding will result in a syntax error. Explain why.

```
IF  AMT1 = AMT2
    ADD AMT3 TO TOTAL.
ELSE
    ADD AMT4 TO TOTAL.
```

3. Consider the following specifications:

```
01  REC-1.
    05  A       PIC X.
    05  B       PIC 9.
    05  C       PIC 9.
```

(a) The following coding will result in a syntax error. Explain why.

```
IF  A IS POSITIVE
    PERFORM 900-GO-TO-IT.
```

(b) Consider the following:

```
IF  A NOT EQUAL TO 6 OR
    A NOT EQUAL TO 7
    PERFORM 800-RTN-X.
```

Will a syntax error result? Explain your answer. Under what condition will 800-RTN-X be performed?

(c) Suppose that REC-1 was not initialized and you included the following coding in the PROCEDURE DIVISION:

```
IF  B = 6
    PERFORM 500-RTN5.
```

Under what conditions, if any, will a syntax error occur? Under what conditions, if any, would a program interrupt occur?

PROGRAMMING ASSIGNMENTS

Because of the importance of conditional statements, an extended list of programming assignments has been included here. We recommend that you begin by planning your logic with a pseudocode and a hierarchy chart for each program before coding it.

1. Write a program for a rental car company that prints the amount owed by each customer. The amount owed depends on the miles driven, the number of days the car was rented, and the type of car rented. Toyotas rent at $26 per day and 18¢ per mile. Oldsmobiles rent at $32 per day and 22¢ per mile. Cadillacs rent for $43 per day and 28¢ per mile. The first 100 miles are free regardless of the car rented.

   The format of the input is as follows:

CUSTOMER Record Layout			
Field	Size	Type	No. of Decimal Positions (if Numeric)
Customer Last Name	20	Alphanumeric	
First Initial	1	Alphanumeric	
Type of Car	1	Alphanumeric: 1 = Toyota 2 = Oldsmobile 3 = Cadillac	
Miles Driven	5	Numeric	0
No. of Days Rented	3	Numeric	0

2. Write a program to list all employees who meet all of the following conditions:
   a. Annual salary is at least $20,000.
   b. Job classification code is 02.
   c. Territory number is 01.
   The problem definition is shown in Figure 8.3.

Figure 8.3 Problem definition for Programming Assignment 2.

Systems Flowchart

PAYROLL-MASTER Record Layout (Alternate Layout Form)

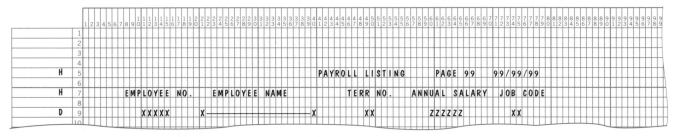

PAYROLL-LIST Printer Spacing Chart

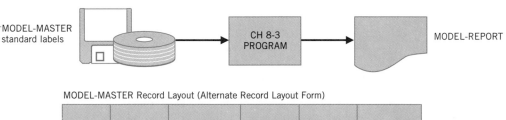

Figure 8.4 Problem definition for Programming Assignment 3.

Systems Flowchart

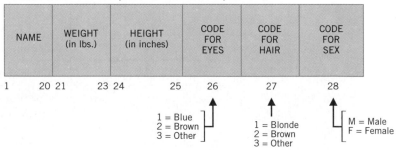

MODEL-MASTER Record Layout (Alternate Record Layout Form)

MODEL-REPORT Printer Spacing Chart

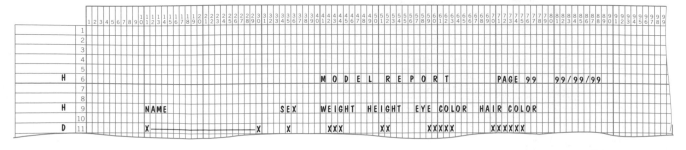

3. Write a program for the Electra Modeling Agency. The problem definition is shown in Figure 8.4. Output is a printed report with the names of all:

   a. Blonde hair, blue-eyed males over 6 feet tall and weighing between 185 and 200 pounds.

   b. Brown hair, brown-eyed females between 5 feet 2 inches and 5 feet 6 inches and weighing between 110 and 125 pounds.

   All other combinations should *not* be printed. For each record printed, include the actual colors for eyes and hair.

4. **Interactive Processing.** Write a program to create a sequential disk file from data entered on a keyboard or terminal.

   Input:
   Employee number
   Employee name
   Hours worked
   Rate

   Output (standard labels):

   1–5 Employee number   32–37 Tax 9999V99
   6–25 Employee name   38–50 Not used
   26–31 Gross pay 9999V99

   Notes:

   a. Calculating gross pay

      Gross pay = Regular hours × Rate + Overtime hours × 1.5 × Rate

      Overtime hours are those hours exceeding 40.

   b. Calculating tax
      The tax is computed as follows:

Gross Pay	Tax
Less than 150.00	0
Between 150.00 and 500.00 inclusive	5% of Gross pay greater than 150.00
Over 500.00	$25.00 + 10% of the Gross pay over 500.00

   c. Rate should be entered with a decimal point (e.g., 22.50). De-edit rate so that it can be used in arithmetic operations.

5. Pass-Em State College has a student file with the following data:

STUDENT **Record Layout**			
Field	Size	Type	No. of Decimal Positions (if Numeric)
Social Security No.	9	Alphanumeric	
Student Name	21	Alphanumeric	
Class Code	1	Alphanumeric: 1 = Freshman 2 = Sophomore 3 = Junior 4 = Senior	
School Code	1	Alphanumeric: 1 = Business 2 = Liberal Arts 3 = Engineering	
GPA	3	Numeric	2
Credits Earned	3	Numeric	0

Print summary data as follows:
a. The percentage of students with a GPA of:
1) less than 2.0.
2) between 2.0 and 3.0 (inclusive).
3) greater than 3.0.
b. The percentage of students with GPAs greater than 3.0 who are:
1) Business majors.
2) Liberal Arts majors.
3) Engineering majors.
c. The percentage of students who have earned more than 100 credits and have GPAs less than 2.00.
d. The percentage of students with GPAs greater than 3.0 who are:
1) Freshmen.
2) Sophomores.
3) Juniors.
4) Seniors.

6. **Interactive Processing.** Write a program to summarize accident records to obtain the following information:
a. The percentage of drivers under 25.
b. The percentage of drivers who are female.
c. The percentage of drivers from New York.
There is one disk record for each driver involved in an accident in the past year:

1–4	Driver number	7–10 Birth date (month and year)
5–6	State code (01 for New York)	11 Sex (M for male, F for female)
(standard labels)		

Results should be displayed on a screen as follows:

```
% OF DRIVERS UNDER 25         99.99
% OF DRIVERS WHO ARE FEMALE   99.99
% OF DRIVERS FROM NY          99.99
```

7. The Animal Lover's pet store sells cats, dogs, birds, and tropical fish. Management would like to know which pets are the most profitable. Input consists of the following type of record, each of which is created when a sale is made:

```
  1   Pet Type (1 = Cat, 2 = Dog, 3 = Bird, 4 = Fish)
2–6   Amount of Sale (999V99)
7–11  Net Cost of Pet to the Store (999V99)
```

The report should have the following format:

```
PET        TOTAL NO. SOLD      TOTAL SALES      TOTAL PROFIT

CATS
DOGS
BIRDS
FISH
```

8. Write a program to print out patient name and diagnosis for each input medical record. Figure 8.5 illustrates the input record layout.

Notes:

a. Output is a printed report with the heading DIAGNOSIS REPORT, a date, and page number.
b. Assume that all patients have at least one symptom.
c. If the patient has lung infection and temperature, the diagnosis is PNEUMONIA.
d. If the patient has a combination of two or more symptoms (except the combination of lung infection and temperature), the diagnosis is COLD.
e. If the patient has any single symptom, the diagnosis is OK.

9. The International Cherry Machine (ICM) Company encourages its employees to enroll in college courses. It offers them a 70% rebate on the first $800 of tuition, a 50% rebate on the next $500, and a 30% rebate on the next $300. Write a program that inputs Employee Name and Tuition and prints, for each employee, the Name and Rebate Amount.

Figure 8.5   Input record layout for Programming Assignment 8.

Field	Size	Type	No. of Decimal Positions (if Numeric)
MEDICAL-FILE **Record Layout**			
PATIENT-NAME	20	Alphanumeric	
LUNG-INFECTION	1	Numeric: 1 = present 0 = absent	0
TEMPERATURE	1	Numeric: 1 = high 0 = normal	0
SNIFFLES	1	Numeric: 1 = present 0 = absent	0
SORE-THROAT	1	Numeric: 1 = present 0 = absent	0

10. **Interactive Processing.**   The LENDER Bank offers mortgages on homes valued up to $500,000. The required down payment is calculated as follows:

    4% of the first $60,000 borrowed
    8% of the next $30,000 borrowed
    10% of the rest

    The amount borrowed cannot exceed 50% of the value of the house.

    Write a program to accept input from a keyboard that specifies for each borrower the amount that he or she wishes to borrow along with the price at which the house is valued. Display (1) a message that indicates if the amount the user wishes to borrow is acceptable (no more than 50% of the value) and (2) the required down payment if the amount to be borrowed is acceptable.

11. **Maintenance Program.**   Modify the Practice Program in this chapter as follows. Every time a record is created on the master customer file, print the contents (edited) of that record as well.

CHAPTER 9

Iteration: Beyond the Basic PERFORM

■ **OBJECTIVES**

To familiarize you with

1. The simple PERFORM.
2. How PERFORM statements are used for iteration.
3. The various options available with the PERFORM statement.

■ **CONTENTS**

THE SIMPLE PERFORM REVIEWED

THE BASIC FORMATS

In this section, we will review the simple **PERFORM** statement, which is used for executing a specified routine *from one or more points in a program.* This topic was introduced in Chapter 4 but will be discussed in more detail here. Later on in this chapter, we will review how other options of the PERFORM are used for iteration or looping. There are two formats of the basic PERFORM:

1. PERFORM Paragraph-Name
The format for this version of the basic PERFORM is:

Format

> PERFORM [paragraph-name-1]

The PERFORM paragraph-name statement will:

1.   Execute all instructions in the named paragraph.
2.   Transfer control to the next instruction in sequence, after the PERFORM paragraph-name.

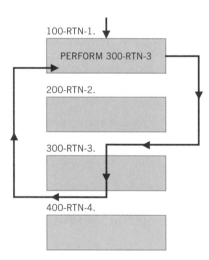

If you look at a reference manual you will find that this format for a PERFORM uses the word "procedure-name" rather than paragraph-name. Because all paragraph-names are also procedure-names, we will use the terms interchangeably for now. In Chapter 14, we will consider procedure-names in more detail.

A simple PERFORM paragraph-name statement is used whenever a series of instructions in a particular paragraph is to be executed from different points in the program. An example of this is the printing of a heading at the top of each new page. Most often, a printed report consists of more than a single page. Let us review the following program excerpt, which uses a PERFORM to print headings on each new page from various points in the program:

Example 1
```
PROCEDURE DIVISION.
100-MAIN-MODULE.
    :
    :
    PERFORM 400-HEADING-RTN
    :
    :
200-CALC-RTN.
    :
    :
```

```
        IF  LINE-CTR >= 25
            PERFORM 400-HEADING-RTN
        END-IF
        WRITE PRINT-REC FROM DETAIL-REC
        ADD 1 TO LINE-CTR.
            :
    300-ERR-RTN.
            :
        IF  LINE-CTR >= 25
            PERFORM 400-HEADING-RTN
        END-IF
        WRITE PRINT-REC FROM ERROR-REC
        ADD 1 TO LINE-CTR.
            :
    400-HEADING-RTN.
            :
```

After a line is printed, we add one to a line counter. When 25 lines have printed on a page, we print headings on a new page. (Recall that to print a heading on a new page, code WRITE PRINT-REC FROM HEADING-REC AFTER ADVANCING PAGE.)

2. In-Line PERFORM

```
PERFORM
    . ⎱ Statements to
    . ⎰ be executed
END-PERFORM
```

An **in-line PERFORM** begins with the word PERFORM, is followed by statements to be executed, and ends with an END-PERFORM **scope terminator**. All instructions within the PERFORM . . . END-PERFORM are executed in sequence. Periods are optional after any scope terminator except at the end of a paragraph, when they are required.

In-line PERFORMs are best used when there are only a few imperative statements to be executed. When a PERFORM requires execution of numerous instructions that may include additional logical control constructs, it is best to modularize the program with PERFORMs that execute a separate paragraph or module.

Just as there are two basic PERFORMs, there are two alternatives for coding a PERFORM with pseudocode:

Pseudocode for an In-line PERFORM	**Pseudocode for PERFORM Paragraph-name**
PERFORM	PERFORM Paragraph
. ⎧ Statements	:
. ⎨ to be performed	PARAGRAPH
. ⎩ go here	: {Statements to be performed go here
END-PERFORM	

With an in-line PERFORM . . . END-PERFORM structure, the pseudocode omits mention of a paragraph-name entirely. The sequence of steps to be performed is indented in the pseudocode to make it easier to read. With a pseudocode for PERFORM paragraph-name, the statements to be executed are in a separate module.

Suppose you code PERFORM 200-PROCESS-RTN. When this instruction is encountered, the computer will execute all statements in 200-PROCESS-RTN until it reaches a new paragraph-name, or the end of the program if there is no new paragraph-name found.

MODULARIZING PROGRAMS USING PERFORM STATEMENTS

As noted in Chapter 5, well-designed programs should be modular. This means that each set of related instructions should be written as a separate routine or **module** rather than coded line-by-line. Consider the following two program excerpts. They execute the same series of instructions, but the second is better designed because it includes the modular approach:

Version 1: Nonmodular Approach	Version 2: Modular Approach

```
IF  AMT1-IN < AMT2-IN
    ADD AMT1-IN TO TOTAL-1
    ADD AMT2-IN TO TOTAL-2
    ADD 1 TO OK-REC-CTR
ELSE
    ADD AMT2-IN TO TOTAL-3
    ADD 1 TO ERR-REC-CTR
END-IF
```

```
    IF  AMT1-IN < AMT2-IN
        PERFORM 300-OK-RTN
    ELSE
        PERFORM 400-ERR-RTN
    END-IF
     :
300-OK-RTN.
    ADD AMT1-IN TO TOTAL-1
    ADD AMT2-IN TO TOTAL-2
    ADD 1 TO OK-REC-CTR.
400-ERR-RTN.
    ADD AMT2-IN TO TOTAL-3
    ADD 1 TO ERR-REC-CTR.
```

The IF sentence in version 2 uses a *top-down, modular approach.* That is, if there are numerous instructions within the IF, the details for processing correct and incorrect records should be left for subordinate modules. This makes the program easier to design because the programmer can begin by focusing on the major elements and leave minor considerations for later. We recommend that you use this top-down approach when there are numerous instructions within an IF. When a top-down approach is employed throughout the program, the main module is best coded as:

COBOL 85

COBOL 74 Substitutions

```
READ ...
    AT END MOVE 'NO ' TO ARE-THERE-MORE-RECORDS.
PERFORM 200-PROCESS-RTN
    UNTIL ARE-THERE-MORE-RECORDS = 'NO '.
```

```
100-MAIN-MODULE.
    PERFORM 500-INITIALIZATION-RTN
    PERFORM 400-HEADING-RTN
    PERFORM UNTIL ARE-THERE-MORE-RECORDS = 'NO '
        READ ...
            AT END
                MOVE 'NO ' TO ARE-THERE-MORE-RECORDS
            NOT AT END
                PERFORM 200-PROCESS-RTN
        END-READ
    END-PERFORM
    PERFORM 900-END-OF-JOB-RTN
    STOP RUN.
     :
500-INITIALIZATION-RTN.
    OPEN ...
    (initialize fields)
     :
900-END-OF-JOB-RTN.
    (print any final totals)
    CLOSE ...
```

By coding 100-MAIN-MODULE with a series of PERFORMs, the details for initializations, headings, and end-of-job procedures are left for subordinate modules.

NESTED PERFORM: A PERFORM WITHIN A PERFORM

PERFORM statements are permitted within the range of a PERFORM statement. This is called a **nested PERFORM**. To say PERFORM 200-PARA-1 is permissible even if 200-PARA-1 has a PERFORM statement as one of its instructions. The following is a valid structure:

```
    PERFORM 200-PARAGRAPH
     :
200-PARAGRAPH.
     :
    PERFORM 500-PARAGRAPH  ◄——Nested PERFORM
```

Similarly, in-line PERFORMs in COBOL 85 can include nested in-line PERFORMs or PER-FORMs with paragraph-names:

```
PERFORM
    .
    .
    PERFORM
        .
        .
    END-PERFORM
    .
    .
END-PERFORM
```

or

```
PERFORM
    .
    .
    PERFORM 300-PARAGRAPH
    .
    .
END-PERFORM
```

Our main modules have been including an in-line PERFORM UNTIL . . . END-PERFORM with a nested PERFORM paragraph-name:

```
       PERFORM UNTIL ARE-THERE-MORE-RECORDS = 'NO '
In-line PERFORM UNTIL      READ ...
                               AT END
                                   MOVE 'NO ' TO ARE-THERE-MORE-RECORDS
                               NOT AT END
PERFORM paragraph-name             PERFORM 200-PROCESS-RTN
                           END-READ
       END-PERFORM
```

EXECUTING A GROUP OF PARAGRAPHS WITH A SIMPLE PERFORM

The following is an expanded format for the PERFORM paragraph-name statement:

Format 1

$$\underline{\text{PERFORM}} \quad \text{paragraph-name-1} \quad \left[\left\{ \begin{array}{c} \underline{\text{THROUGH}} \\ \underline{\text{THRU}} \end{array} \right\} \text{paragraph-name-2} \right]$$

The PERFORM paragraph-name executes all statements beginning at paragraph-name-1 until the *end* of paragraph-name-2 is reached. Control is then transferred to the statement directly following the PERFORM. The following schematic illustrates how the PERFORM . . . THRU may be used:

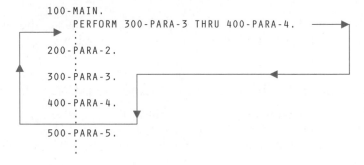

```
100-MAIN.
        PERFORM 300-PARA-3 THRU 400-PARA-4.
    .
200-PARA-2.
    .
300-PARA-3.
    .
400-PARA-4.
    .
500-PARA-5.
    .
```

There are times when a PERFORM . . . THRU . . . statement may be the best method for coding a procedure, but, in general, it should be avoided because it increases the risk of logical control errors.

THE USE AND MISUSE OF GO TO STATEMENTS

The format for a GO TO is:

Format

> GO TO   paragraph-name-1

Unlike the PERFORM, which returns control to the statement following the PERFORM, the GO TO permanently transfers control to another paragraph. Figure 9.1 illustrates the distinction between a PERFORM and a GO TO.

Why Well-Designed Programs Avoid the Use of GO TOs

In structured, top-down programming, we use one main routine followed by a series of subordinate routines. All paragraphs are executed from the main routine or from subordinate routines using PERFORM statements. In this way, the overall logical structure of the program is easy to follow. Because a GO TO permanently transfers control to another paragraph, its use makes it difficult to achieve the same level of control. Moreover, the risk of logic errors is much greater with GO TOs than with PERFORMs. We focus, then, on structured, GO TO-less coding so that programs will be easier to read, debug, and modify.

There are, however, times when a GO TO is permissible. If you use the THRU option of the PERFORM statement, a GO TO may appear *within the paragraphs being performed*. If, in Figure 9.1, we had PERFORM PARA-8 THRU PARA-9 coded in PARA-2, a GO TO PARA-9 within PARA-8 would be permitted. But it is best to avoid both the THRU and the GO TO, where possible.

Figure 9.1 The distinction between a PERFORM and a GO TO.

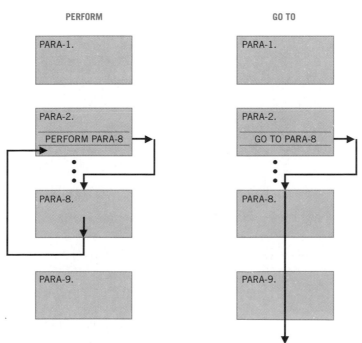

THE EXIT STATEMENT

Consider the following program excerpt, which is designed to process only those amount fields that are valid, or numeric:

```
300-VALIDATION-RTN.
    IF  AMT IS NOT NUMERIC
        GO TO 400-VALIDATION-RTN-EXIT
    END-IF
    ADD 1 TO TOTAL-COUNT
    ADD AMT TO TOTAL
    IF  AMT IS GREATER THAN 50
        ADD 1 TO OVER-50-CLUB
    END-IF.
400-VALIDATION-RTN-EXIT.
    EXIT.
```

To execute this routine properly, the PERFORM statement should read:

```
PERFORM 300-VALIDATION-RTN
    THRU 400-VALIDATION-RTN-EXIT
```

EXIT is a COBOL reserved word that performs *no operation*. It is used to allow execution to pass over other statements or to transfer control back to the statement following the original PERFORM. It is used, when necessary, as an end point in a paragraph being performed. In the preceding example, we used the paragraph called 400-VALIDATION-RTN-EXIT to avoid processing incorrect data the same way we process valid data. A GO TO is permitted within 300-VALIDATION-RTN since it causes a branch to 400-VALIDATION-RTN-EXIT, which is still within the range of the paragraphs being performed. We use the name 400-VALIDATION-RTN-EXIT for documentation purposes, but *any* paragraph-name could be used.

With COBOL 85, EXIT can be used *in addition to* other statements within a paragraph; with COBOL 74, EXIT must be the only word in the paragraph.

A preferred way to code 300-VALIDATION-RTN is as follows:

A More Modular Approach

```
300-VALIDATION-RTN.
    IF  AMT IS NUMERIC
        PERFORM 400-PROCESS-REC
    END-IF
        .
        .
400-PROCESS-REC.
    ADD 1 TO TOTAL-COUNT
    ADD AMT TO TOTAL
    IF  AMT IS GREATER THAN 50
        ADD 1 TO OVER-50-CLUB
    END-IF
```

The preceding is not only more modular, it avoids the use of EXITs and GO TOs entirely, which makes the program more structured and less prone to errors.

DEBUGGING TIP

Although a PERFORM paragraph-name THRU . . . is permitted to execute a series of paragraphs and GO TOs can be used within these paragraphs, we recommend you avoid THRU, GO TO, and EXIT entirely. They complicate logical control constructs and make programs more difficult to debug, maintain, and modify.

ITERATION USING OTHER TYPES OF PERFORMS

PERFORM UNTIL ...: A Review

As noted, one type of logical control structure is a sequence where instructions are executed in the order in which they appear. A second type of logical control structure is the IF-THEN-ELSE or selection structure in which different instructions are executed depending on whether a condition is true or false. We have also seen in Chapter 5 that the third type of logical structure called **iteration** or **looping** means that a series of instructions in-line or in a different module can be executed repeatedly. Iteration may be performed in COBOL using a **PERFORM UNTIL** ... statement.

The format of a PERFORM UNTIL ... is:

Format 2

$$\underline{\text{PERFORM}} \quad [\text{paragraph-name-1}] \quad \left[\left\{ \begin{array}{l} \underline{\text{THROUGH}} \\ \underline{\text{THRU}} \end{array} \right\} \text{paragraph-name-2} \right]$$

$$\underline{\text{UNTIL}} \quad \text{condition-1}$$

With COBOL 85, if an in-line PERFORM is used, no paragraph-name is coded and the statements within the PERFORM end with an END-PERFORM scope terminator.

Any simple or compound condition can be specified in a PERFORM UNTIL .... As with a simple PERFORM, COBOL 85 permits an in-line PERFORM UNTIL ..., which has END-PERFORM as a scope terminator:

Examples

```
1. PERFORM 600-ERROR-CHECK1
       THRU 800-ERROR-CHECK3 UNTIL X = 2
2. PERFORM 200-VALIDITY-CHECK
       UNTIL X > 7
3. PERFORM 800-PRINT-RTN
       UNTIL A = B OR A = C
4. PERFORM UNTIL A > B AND A > C
       WRITE PRINT-REC FROM ERROR-LINE
           AFTER ADVANCING 2 LINES
       ADD 1 TO A
   END-PERFORM
```

In-line PERFORM with COBOL 85

The contents of the identifiers used in the UNTIL clause should be changed within the paragraph(s) or series of instructions being performed. To say PERFORM 600-PRINT-RTN UNTIL X = 5, for example, implies that X will change somewhere within 600-PRINT-RTN. If X remains as 3, for example, then 600-PRINT-RTN will be performed indefinitely or until a program interrupt occurs.

For COBOL 85, an in-line PERFORM UNTIL ... is permitted, as in Example 4. With an in-line PERFORM there must be *no* periods between the PERFORM and END-PERFORM. When using scope terminators like END-PERFORM in a COBOL 85 program, the only periods required are those at the end of a paragraph.

A PERFORM UNTIL (Condition) Tests for the Condition First

If the condition indicated in the UNTIL clause is met at the time of execution, then the named paragraph(s) or series of instructions will be executed 0, or no, times. If PERFORM 600-PROCESS-RTN UNTIL X = 3 is executed and X equals 3 initially, then 600-PROCESS-RTN will not be performed at all. This condition does *not* imply that an error has occurred. Keep in mind, then, that the condition in a PERFORM UNTIL ... is tested *before* the named paragraph is executed even once.

Coding a Loop with a PERFORM

PERFORM UNTIL ... is a type of iteration used for programming a loop, which is a sequence of steps that is executed repeatedly until a condition exists. You have thus far been using the PERFORM UNTIL ... to transfer control to another paragraph until there are no more records to process. In this section, we will see that the PERFORM UNTIL ... is also used for other types of loops.

Suppose we want to print five mailing labels for each input record. The pseudocode excerpt for this problem is as follows:

Pseudocode
PERFORM UNTIL no more records (Are-There-More-Records = 'No ')
    READ a Record
        AT END
            Move 'NO ' to Are-There-More-Records
       NOT AT END
           PERFORM Calc-Rtn
    END-READ
END-PERFORM

CALC-RTN
    Move Zeros to Counter1
    Move Input to Output Area
    PERFORM Write-Rtn UNTIL Counter1 = 5

WRITE-RTN
    Write the Mailing Label (3 lines)
    Add 1 to Counter1

The following coding illustrates the COBOL instructions to perform the required operation:

COBOL 85

```
PROCEDURE DIVISION.
100-MAIN-MODULE.
    OPEN INPUT IN-FILE
         OUTPUT PRINT-FILE
    PERFORM UNTIL ARE-THERE-MORE-RECORDS = 'NO '
        READ IN-FILE
            AT END
                MOVE 'NO ' TO ARE-THERE-MORE-RECORDS
            NOT AT END
                PERFORM 200-CALC-RTN
        END-READ
    END-PERFORM
    CLOSE IN-FILE
          PRINT-FILE
    STOP RUN.
200-CALC-RTN.
    MOVE ZEROS TO COUNTER1
    MOVE NAME TO WS-NAME OF MAIL-LINE-1
    MOVE ST-ADDR TO WS-ADDR OF MAIL-LINE-2
    MOVE CITY-STATE-ZIP TO WS-CITY OF MAIL-LINE-3
    PERFORM 300-WRITE-RTN
        UNTIL COUNTER1 = 5.
300-WRITE-RTN.
    WRITE PRINT-REC FROM MAIL-LINE-1
    WRITE PRINT-REC FROM MAIL-LINE-2
    WRITE PRINT-REC FROM MAIL-LINE-3
    ADD 1 TO COUNTER1.
```

COBOL 74 Substitutions

```
READ IN-FILE
    AT END MOVE 'NO ' TO ARE-THERE-MORE-RECORDS.
PERFORM 200-CALC-RTN
    UNTIL ARE-THERE-MORE-RECORDS = 'NO '.
```

```
READ IN-FILE
    AT END MOVE 'NO ' TO ARE-THERE-MORE-RECORDS.
```

Note that 200-CALC-RTN, which is performed from 100-MAIN-MODULE, has its own PERFORM statement. This is another example of a nested PERFORM. We will first discuss the 200-CALC-RTN and 300-WRITE-RTN modules.

200-CALC-RTN and 300-WRITE-RTN Modules

Each time 200-CALC-RTN is executed, COUNTER1 is set to zero. We call this *initializing* COUNTER1 at zero. Data in the input area is then moved to WORKING-STORAGE in preparation for printing. Since COUNTER1 was initialized at zero, it is not equal to 5 at this point; thus, PERFORM 300-WRITE-RTN will be executed from 200-CALC-RTN.

300-WRITE-RTN begins by printing three output lines, or one mailing label. After a mailing label is written, one is added to COUNTER1. Thus, COUNTER1 is equal to 1 after three lines (or the first mailing label) is printed. Since COUNTER1 is not yet equal to 5, 300-WRITE-RTN is executed again. The second three-line mailing label is printed, and 1 is added to COUNTER1, giving COUNTER1 a value of 2. This process is repeated until a fifth label is printed and COUNTER1 contains a value of 5. At that point, COUNTER1 is compared to 5. COUNTER1 now equals 5 and we have printed exactly 5 labels. For COBOL 85, control returns to 200-CALC-RTN and then immediately to the PERFORM UNTIL in 100-MAIN-MODULE, which causes another input record to be read. (For COBOL 74, control returns to the statement within 200-CALC-RTN after the PERFORM, which is a READ.) If there are more records to process, 200-CALC-RTN is executed again and COUNTER1 is initialized at zero each time.

Since COUNTER1 begins at zero, the steps at 300-WRITE-RTN will be repeated five times for each input record, that is, UNTIL COUNTER1 = 5. Each execution of this series of steps is called one *iteration*. Note that COUNTER1 would be defined in the WORKING-STORAGE SECTION. Using an in-line PERFORM with COBOL 85, we could code the preceding as:

```
200-CALC-RTN.
    :
    :
    PERFORM UNTIL COUNTER1 = 5
        WRITE PRINT-REC FROM MAIL-LINE-1
        WRITE PRINT-REC FROM MAIL-LINE-2
        WRITE PRINT-REC FROM MAIL-LINE-3
        ADD 1 TO COUNTER1
    END-PERFORM.
```

Iteration as illustrated by the PERFORM within 200-CALC-RTN in the original program is called a *loop*, which means that the sequence of steps at 300-WRITE-RTN is repeated until the condition specified is met. The loop should:

1. Be preceded by an instruction that initializes the field to be tested (e.g., MOVE 0 TO COUNTER1).
2. Include a PERFORM UNTIL . . . that is executed repeatedly UNTIL the field to be tested reaches the desired value (e.g., PERFORM UNTIL COUNTER1 = 5 or PERFORM UNTIL COUNTER1 >= 5).
3. Include, as one of the instructions within the PERFORM UNTIL . . ., a statement that increases (or decreases) the value of the field being tested (e.g., ADD 1 TO COUNTER1).

The contents of the counter is used to control the number of times that the loop is performed.

Common Errors to Avoid

Consider the following program excerpt and see if you can find the logic error that results:

Problem: To add the amount fields of 10 input records to a TOTAL.

LOOPING: WITH AN ERROR

COBOL 74

```
    MOVE 0 TO COUNTER-A.
    READ IN-FILE
        AT END MOVE 'NO ' TO ARE-THERE-MORE-RECORDS.
    PERFORM 400-ADD-RTN
        UNTIL COUNTER-A >= 10.
    WRITE TOTAL-REC.
        :
400-ADD-RTN.
    ADD AMT TO TOTAL.
    READ IN-FILE
        AT END MOVE 'NO ' TO ARE-THERE-MORE-RECORDS.
```

COBOL 85

```
    MOVE 0 TO COUNTER-A
    PERFORM UNTIL COUNTER-A >= 10
        READ IN-FILE
            AT END
                MOVE 'NO ' TO ARE-THERE-MORE-RECORDS
            NOT AT END
                PERFORM 400-ADD-RTN
        END-READ
    END-PERFORM
    WRITE TOTAL-REC
        :
400-ADD-RTN.
    ADD AMT TO TOTAL.
```

An error will occur because 400-ADD-RTN does not include an instruction that increments COUNTER-A. Thus, COUNTER-A is initialized at 0 and *will remain at zero*. Each time 400-ADD-RTN is executed, a test is performed to determine if COUNTER-A is greater than or equal to 10. Since 400-ADD-RTN does not include ADD 1 TO COUNTER-A, the PERFORM statement will cause 400-ADD-RTN to be executed over and over again. This type of error is called an **infinite loop.** What will happen on a mainframe is that the computer's built-in clock will sense that 400-ADD-RTN is being executed more times than would normally be required by any program and will then, after a fixed period of time, automatically terminate the job. With PCs, the program will remain in an infinite loop until it is manually terminated by the programmer by pressing (1) the Escape key, (2) the Ctrl + Break keys, or (3) some other set of interrupt keys.

Corrected Program Excerpt

The correct coding for 400-ADD-RTN is:

```
400-ADD-RTN.
    ADD AMT TO TOTAL
    ADD 1 TO COUNTER-A.
        :
```

The ADD may be placed anywhere in the paragraph because COUNTER-A is compared to 10 initially and then again each time 400-ADD-RTN has been executed in its entirety.

─── DEBUGGING TIP ───

Some programmers prefer to initialize a counter at 1 and then use a PERFORM UNTIL COUNTER $>$ a specified value, rather than UNTIL COUNTER $=$ a specified value. Consider the following two routines, which both execute a module 10 times.

Alternative 1
```
    MOVE 0 TO COUNTER
    PERFORM 200-DO-IT-10-TIMES
        UNTIL COUNTER = 10
        :
200-DO-IT-10-TIMES.
        :
    ADD 1 TO COUNTER.
```

Alternative 2
```
    MOVE 1 TO COUNTER
    PERFORM 200-DO-IT-10-TIMES
        UNTIL COUNTER > 10
        :
```

```
200-DO-IT-10-TIMES.
       .
       .
       ADD 1 TO COUNTER.
```

ADD 1 TO COUNTER can be coded *anywhere* in 200-DO-IT-10-TIMES because the test comparing COUNTER to 10 is made initially, before the paragraph is even executed, and then again at the end of each iteration.

You can use either of the preceding techniques for looping, but we suggest that you consistently use Alternative 2. In general, testing for ">" or ">=" rather than "=" is less prone to infinite loops. It sometimes happens that you inadvertently exceed some value in a field. Fewer errors are apt to occur if a loop is terminated by testing for ">" or ">=" some value rather than just "=" to some value.

PERFORM TIMES

We have thus far focused on the PERFORM UNTIL ... as the main type of iteration that is used for looping. We can also program a loop by instructing the computer to execute a sequence of steps a *fixed number of times.* The following is an alternative to the preceding coding:

COBOL 74

```
PERFORM 400-ADD-RTN 10 TIMES.
WRITE TOTAL-REC.
    .
    .
400-ADD-RTN.
    READ IN-FILE
        AT END DISPLAY 'FEWER THAN 10 RECORDS ARE AVAILABLE',
            STOP RUN.
    ADD AMT TO TOTAL.
```

COBOL 85

```
PERFORM 10 TIMES
    READ IN-FILE
        AT END
            DISPLAY
                'FEWER THAN 10 RECORDS ARE AVAILABLE'
            STOP RUN
        NOT AT END
            ADD AMT TO TOTAL
    END-READ
END-PERFORM
WRITE TOTAL-REC
```

With a PERFORM TIMES, it is *not* necessary to establish a counter that must be incremented each time through the loop.

The format for a **PERFORM TIMES** is:

Format 3

$$
\text{PERFORM } [(\text{paragraph-name-1})] \left[\begin{Bmatrix} \text{THROUGH} \\ \text{THRU} \end{Bmatrix} \text{paragraph-name-2} \right]
$$
$$
\begin{Bmatrix} \text{integer-1} \\ \text{identifier-1} \end{Bmatrix} \underline{\text{TIMES}}
$$

With COBOL 85, if an in-line PERFORM is used, no paragraph-name is coded and the statements within the PERFORM end with an END-PERFORM scope terminator.

Example 1   A program creates department store credit cards. Each customer is issued two cards:

```
PERFORM 400-CREDIT-CARD-RTN 2 TIMES
```

Example 2   Each customer indicates the number of credit cards desired. This data is entered in a field called NO-OF-COPIES in a disk record. The following excerpt describes the disk record and the PERFORM statement that prints the desired number of credit cards:

```
01  IN-REC.
    05  NAME            PICTURE X(20).
```

```
05  NO-OF-COPIES      PICTURE 9.
   :
PERFORM 600-CREDIT-CARD-RTN
   NO-OF-COPIES TIMES
```

When using the TIMES format (PERFORM paragraph-name-1 identifier-1 TIMES): (1) the identifier must be specified in the DATA DIVISION; (2) it must have a *numeric* PICTURE clause; and (3) it must contain only integers or zeros. To say PERFORM 100-RTN-1 COPY-IT TIMES is valid if COPY-IT has a numeric PICTURE clause and integer or zero contents. If COPY-IT has zero as its value, then 100-RTN-1 will be performed 0, or *no*, times.

With all versions of COBOL, the word preceding TIMES may be either an integer or an identifier, but with COBOL 85 it can also be *an arithmetic expression*. To say PERFORM 100-PARA-1 B+1 TIMES, for example, is valid with COBOL 85. Also with COBOL 85 you may use an in-line PERFORM TIMES that ends with an END-PERFORM scope terminator.

The THRU clause is optional with any PERFORM paragraph-name statement. The statement PERFORM 100-RTN1 THRU 800-RTN8 5 TIMES, then, is correct.

When using the *integer* option with the PERFORM TIMES format, only the actual number is acceptable. We may *not* say PERFORM RTN-1 FIVE TIMES unless FIVE is a field defined in the DATA DIVISION with a VALUE of 5. Typically, the integer itself is used: PERFORM 100-RTN1 5 TIMES.

EXAMPLES OF LOOPS

In this section we illustrate how loops can be executed with different options of the PERFORM.

Example 1   Sum the odd numbers from 1 through 99 (TOTAL = 1 + 3 + ... 99). First write the pseudocode. Then try to code the program and compare your results with the following, which uses a PERFORM UNTIL:

Pseudocode	**COBOL Program Excerpt**
Move 1 to Num	`MOVE 1 TO NUM`
Move 0 to Total	`MOVE 0 TO TOTAL`
PERFORM UNTIL Num > 99	`PERFORM 200-ADD-NOS`
Add Num to Total	`    UNTIL NUM > 99`
Add 2 to Num	`WRITE TOTAL-REC.`
END-PERFORM	`   :`
Write Total-Rec	`200-ADD-NOS.`
:	`    ADD NUM TO TOTAL`
	`    ADD 2 TO NUM.`

Using a PERFORM TIMES option for this, we have:

```
MOVE 1 TO NUM
MOVE 0 TO TOTAL
PERFORM 200-ADD-NOS 50 TIMES
WRITE TOTAL-REC.
   :
200-ADD-NOS.
    ADD NUM TO TOTAL
    ADD 2 TO NUM.
```

Or, with COBOL 85, we could use an in-line PERFORM:

```
MOVE 1 TO NUM
MOVE 0 TO TOTAL
PERFORM 50 TIMES
    ADD NUM TO TOTAL
    ADD 2 TO NUM
END-PERFORM
WRITE TOTAL-REC.
```

Example 2 Sum the even integers from 2 through 100 $(2 + 4 + \ldots 100)$. First plan the program with a pseudocode and compare your results to the one that follows. Then write the instructions and compare yours to the program excerpt that follows. Remember that your program may differ slightly and still be correct, so test it to be sure.

Pseudocode	COBOL Program Excerpt
Move 2 to Num	`MOVE 2 TO NUM`
Move 0 to Total	`MOVE 0 TO TOTAL`
PERFORM UNTIL Num > 100	`PERFORM 200-ADD-EVEN`
Add Num to Total	`    UNTIL NUM > 100`
Add 2 to Num	`WRITE ANSWER-REC.`
END-PERFORM	
Write Answer-Rec	`200-ADD-EVEN.`
	`ADD NUM TO TOTAL`
	`ADD 2 TO NUM.`

Example 3 Each record has a value N. Find N!, called "N factorial." $N! = N \times (N-1) \times (N-2) \times \ldots \times 1$. For example, $5! = 5 \times 4 \times 3 \times 2 \times 1 = 120$; $3! = 3 \times 2 \times 1 = 6$. Use a `PERFORM UNTIL ...` statement. Assume N is greater than or equal to 1.

COBOL 85

```
100-MAIN-MODULE.
      :
      :
      PERFORM UNTIL ARE-THERE-MORE-RECORDS = 'NO '
          READ INPUT-FILE
              AT END
                  MOVE 'NO ' TO
                      ARE-THERE-MORE-RECORDS
              NOT AT END
                  PERFORM 200-CALC-RTN
          END-READ
      END-PERFORM
      :
      :
  200-CALC-RTN.
      MOVE N TO M
              PRODUCT
      PERFORM 300-FACT-RTN
          UNTIL M = 1
      MOVE PRODUCT TO FACTORIAL OF DETAIL-REC
      WRITE PRINT-REC FROM DETAIL-REC.

  300-FACT-RTN.
      SUBTRACT 1 FROM M
      MULTIPLY M BY PRODUCT.
```

COBOL 74 Substitutions

```
READ INPUT-FILE
    AT END MOVE 'NO ' TO ARE-THERE-MORE-RECORDS.
PERFORM 200-CALC-RTN
    UNTIL ARE-THERE-MORE-RECORDS = 'NO '.
```

```
READ INPUT-FILE
    AT END MOVE 'NO ' TO ARE-THERE-MORE-RECORDS.
```

M and `PRODUCT` are defined in `WORKING-STORAGE`. M has the same `PICTURE` as N, and `PRODUCT` is defined with a `PICTURE` that is large enough to hold the result. We use M, which initially contains the value of N but then varies in the program from N to $(N - 1)$ to $(N - 2)$, and so on. Note that we could also have coded `PERFORM 300-FACT-RTN UNTIL M = 2` instead of `M = 1`, since when $M = 1$ we simply multiply the `PRODUCT` by 1, which does not change its value.

As previously noted, in a `PERFORM UNTIL ...` the condition specified is tested *before* the paragraph to be performed is executed. This means that if the condition tested in `200-CALC-RTN` is met initially, the named paragraph is simply not executed at all. Thus, in the preceding, if N had an initial value of 1, then `300-FACT-RTN` would not be executed at all because N is moved to M. The 1 initially moved to `PRODUCT` would print as the correct answer $(1! = 1)$.

Nested PERFORMs: Loops within Loops

Suppose we wish to read in 50 records as five groups of 10 records. The amount fields of each group of 10 input records are to be added and a total printed. Thus *five* totals will print. That is, we wish to execute a routine five times that adds 10 amounts and reads 10 records. The following coding can be used:

COBOL 74

```
100-MAIN-MODULE
    OPEN INPUT SALES-FILE
        OUTPUT PRINT-FILE.
    READ SALES-FILE
        AT END MOVE 'NO ' TO ARE-THERE-MORE-RECORDS.
    PERFORM 200-MAJOR-RTN 5 TIMES.
    CLOSE SALES-FILE
        PRINT-FILE.
    STOP RUN.
200-MAJOR-RTN.
    PERFORM 300-ADD-RTN 10 TIMES.
    MOVE TOTAL TO EDITED-TOTAL-OUT.
    MOVE ZEROS TO TOTAL.
    WRITE PRINT-OUT FROM TOTAL-REC.
300-ADD-RTN.
    ADD AMT TO TOTAL.
    READ SALES-FILE
        AT END MOVE 'NO ' TO ARE-THERE-MORE-RECORDS.
```

COBOL 85

```
100-MAIN-MODULE.
    OPEN INPUT SALES-FILE
        OUTPUT PRINT-FILE
    PERFORM 5 TIMES
        PERFORM 10 TIMES
            READ SALES-FILE
                AT END
                    MOVE 'NO ' TO
                        ARE-THERE-MORE-RECORDS
                NOT AT END
                    ADD AMT TO TOTAL
            END-READ
        END-PERFORM
        PERFORM 200-MAJOR-RTN
    END-PERFORM
    CLOSE SALES-FILE
        PRINT-FILE
    STOP RUN.
200-MAJOR-RTN.
    MOVE TOTAL TO EDITED-TOTAL-OUT
    MOVE ZEROS TO TOTAL
    WRITE PRINT-OUT FROM TOTAL-REC.
```

──────── DEBUGGING TIPS ────────

Use `PERFORM TIMES` rather than `PERFORM UNTIL` if you know in advance the specific number of times a paragraph is to be executed. If the number of times a paragraph is to be executed is variable, use a `PERFORM UNTIL`.

It is also best to use a `PERFORM UNTIL` if the number of times a paragraph is being executed needs to be used for output.

Example

Print a 9s multiplication table for 9 × 1 through 9 × 12:

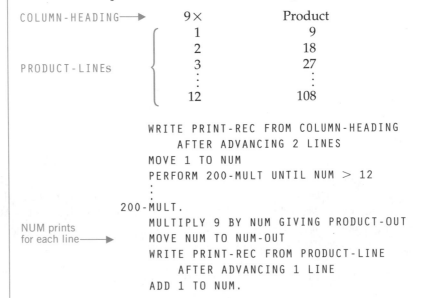

COLUMN-HEADING →	9×	Product
	1	9
	2	18
PRODUCT-LINEs	3	27
	⋮	⋮
	12	108

```
    WRITE PRINT-REC FROM COLUMN-HEADING
        AFTER ADVANCING 2 LINES
    MOVE 1 TO NUM
    PERFORM 200-MULT UNTIL NUM > 12
    ⋮
200-MULT.
    MULTIPLY 9 BY NUM GIVING PRODUCT-OUT
    MOVE NUM TO NUM-OUT
    WRITE PRINT-REC FROM PRODUCT-LINE
        AFTER ADVANCING 1 LINE
    ADD 1 TO NUM.
```

NUM prints for each line →

PERFORM VARYING

The last format for a PERFORM statement is the most comprehensive:

Format 4

$$
\begin{array}{l}
\underline{\text{PERFORM}} \quad [\text{paragraph-name-1}] \quad \left[\left\{ \begin{array}{l} \underline{\text{THROUGH}} \\ \underline{\text{THRU}} \end{array} \right\} \text{paragraph-name-2} \right] \\[2em]
\underline{\text{VARYING}} \quad \text{identifier-1} \quad \underline{\text{FROM}} \quad \left\{ \begin{array}{l} \text{identifier-2} \\ \text{integer-1} \end{array} \right\} \quad \underline{\text{BY}} \quad \left\{ \begin{array}{l} \text{identifier-3} \\ \text{integer-2} \end{array} \right\} \\[2em]
\underline{\text{UNTIL}} \quad \text{condition-1}
\end{array}
$$

With COBOL 85, if an in-line PERFORM is used, no paragraph-name is coded, and the statements within the PERFORM end with an END-PERFORM scope terminator.

Suppose we wish to sum all odd-numbered integers from 1 through 1001. We could use the **PERFORM VARYING** format as follows:

```
200-CALC-RTN.
    PERFORM 300-ADD-RTN VARYING INTEGER1 FROM 1
        BY 2 UNTIL INTEGER1 > 1001
    :
300-ADD-RTN.
    ADD INTEGER1 TO ODD-CTR.
```

The PERFORM VARYING:

1. Initializes INTEGER1 at 1.
2. Tests to see if INTEGER1 > 1001.
3. If INTEGER1 does not exceed 1001: (a) 300-ADD-RTN is performed; (b) 2 is added to INTEGER1; and (c) steps 2 and 3 are repeated.
4. When INTEGER1 exceeds 1001, execution continues with the instruction following the PERFORM.

Using an in-line PERFORM (with COBOL 85) for the above, we have:

```
200-CALC-RTN.
    PERFORM VARYING INTEGER1 FROM 1 BY 2
            UNTIL INTEGER1 > 1001
        ADD INTEGER1 TO ODD-CTR
    END-PERFORM
    :
```

Examples   The following two examples execute 300-PROCESS-RTN 20 TIMES.

```
1. PERFORM 300-PROCESS-RTN
        VARYING CTR FROM 0 BY 1 UNTIL CTR = 20
2. PERFORM 300-PROCESS-RTN
        VARYING CTR FROM 1 BY 1 UNTIL
            CTR IS GREATER THAN 20
```

CTR controls the number of times 300-PROCESS-RTN is performed in both examples. In Example 1, CTR begins at 0 and 300-PROCESS-RTN is executed until CTR = 20, or 20 times. In Example 2, CTR begins at 1 and 300-PROCESS-RTN is executed until CTR > 20, which is again 20 times. In either case, CTR should *not* be modified within the PERFORM VARYING loop.

Identifier-1 (CTR in the preceding examples) must be defined in the DATA DIVISION, usually in WORKING-STORAGE, and have a PIC clause large enough to hold the maximum value that it can assume. For these examples, CTR should have a PIC of 99.

If CTR had a PIC of 9, a syntax error may not occur, but a logic error would most certainly result because CTR is not large enough to hold an upper limit of 20.

It is not necessary to use a VALUE clause to initialize CTR since CTR will *automatically* be initialized with the PERFORM VARYING statement.

Other examples of the PERFORM VARYING option are as follows:

Examples

```
3. PERFORM 100-RTN1
        VARYING DATEX FROM 1900 BY 10
            UNTIL DATEX > 1990

4. PERFORM 200-RTN2
        VARYING COUNTER FROM 10 BY −1
            UNTIL COUNTER < 1
```

Notice in Example 4 that the counter or loop control field can be *decreased*, rather than increased, each time through the loop. This would be the same as coding:

```
PERFORM 200-RTN2
    VARYING COUNTER FROM 0 BY 1
        UNTIL COUNTER = 10
```

or

```
PERFORM 200-RTN2
    VARYING COUNTER FROM 1 BY 1
        UNTIL COUNTER > 10
```

USING NESTED PERFORM VARYING STATEMENTS

Figure 9.2 illustrates how a PERFORM VARYING statement can be used to print the class average on a final exam for each of 10 classes. For simplicity, we are assuming that each class has exactly 20 students and that each student took every exam. Thus exactly 200 records will be read; we also assume that the first 20 records are for Class 1, the next 20 are for Class 2, and so on. If exactly 200 records are read and processed, an AT END condition should not be reached. Because we know exactly how many input records are being read, we do not need a priming READ for COBOL 74 and can use the same procedure for all versions of COBOL.

This program illustrates nested PERFORM VARYING loops, or a PERFORM VARYING within a PERFORM VARYING. The basic rules for the execution of a nested PERFORM VARYING are as follows:

RULES FOR USING A NESTED PERFORM VARYING

1. The *innermost* PERFORM VARYING loop is executed *first*.

2. The *next outer* PERFORM VARYING loop in sequence is then executed.

In Figure 9.2 the *innermost* or minor loop is controlled by:

```
PERFORM 300-CALC-RTN
    VARYING STUDENT-CTR FROM 1 BY 1 UNTIL STUDENT-CTR > 20
```

The outermost or major loop is controlled by:

```
PERFORM 200-MAJOR-RTN
    VARYING CLASS-CTR FROM 1 BY 1 UNTIL CLASS-CTR > 10
```

We thus have the following sequence of values for CLASS-CTR and STUDENT-CTR in this program:

Figure 9.2   Example of a nested PERFORM VARYING loop.

```
          WORKING-STORAGE SECTION.
          01  WORK-AREAS.
              05  CLASS-TOTAL             PIC 9(4).
              05  CLASS-CTR               PIC 99.
              05  STUDENT-CTR             PIC 99.
              05  ARE-THERE-MORE-RECORDS  PIC X(3)   VALUE 'YES'.
                  88  NO-MORE-RECORDS                VALUE 'NO '.
          01  OUT-REC.
              05                          PIC X(14)  VALUE SPACES.
              05                          PIC X(22)
                                   VALUE  'THE AVERAGE FOR CLASS '.
              05  CLASS-NUMBER            PIC 99.
              05                          PIC XXX    VALUE 'IS '.
              05  CLASS-AVERAGE           PIC 999.99.
              05                          PIC X(85)  VALUE SPACES.
          PROCEDURE DIVISION.
          ******************************************************************
          *              the main module controls all processing          *
          ******************************************************************
          100-MAIN-MODULE.
              OPEN INPUT STUDENT-FILE
                   OUTPUT PRINT-FILE
              PERFORM 200-MAJOR-RTN
                  VARYING CLASS-CTR FROM 1 BY 1 UNTIL CLASS-CTR > 10
              CLOSE STUDENT-FILE
                    PRINT-FILE
              STOP RUN.
          ******************************************************************
          *    this is the major or outer loop that is executed 10 times   *
          ******************************************************************
          200-MAJOR-RTN.
              MOVE ZEROS TO CLASS-TOTAL
              PERFORM 300-CALC-RTN
                  VARYING STUDENT-CTR FROM 1 BY 1 UNTIL STUDENT-CTR > 20
              PERFORM 400-WRITE-RTN.
          ******************************************************************
          * this is the minor or inner loop that is executed 20 times for  *
          * each class                                                     *
          ******************************************************************
          300-CALC-RTN.
              READ STUDENT-FILE
                  AT END MOVE 'NO ' TO ARE-THERE-MORE-RECORDS
              END-READ
              ADD GRADE TO CLASS-TOTAL.
          ******************************************************************
          * each write instruction prints one class average. this routine  *
          * is executed 10 times, one for each class                       *
          ******************************************************************
          400-WRITE-RTN.
              MOVE CLASS-CTR TO CLASS-NUMBER
              DIVIDE CLASS-TOTAL BY 20
                  GIVING CLASS-AVERAGE
              WRITE PRINT-REC FROM OUT-REC.
```

Use
FILLER
for
COBOL 74

Number of Times Through 300-CALC-RTN		CLASS-CTR	STUDENT-CTR
	1	1	1
	2	1	2
	3	1	3
Student records 1–20 for Class 1 are read and processed here	.	.	.
	.	.	.
	.	.	.
	20	1	20
	21	2	1
	.	2	2
	.	2	3
Student records 21–40 for Class 2 are read and processed here	.	.	.
	.	.	.
	.	.	.
	40	2	20
	41	3	1
	.	3	2
	.	3	3
Student records 41–60 for Class 3 are read and processed here	.	.	.
	.	.	.
	.	.	.
	60	3	20
	.	.	.
	.	.	.
	.	.	.
	181	10	1
	.	10	2
Student records 181–200 for Class 10 are read and processed here	.	10	3
	.	.	.
	.	.	.
	.	.	.
	200	10	20

The first time through 300-CALC-RTN, CLASS-CTR is 1 and STUDENT-CTR is 1. After 300-CALC-RTN has been executed once, the computer increments STUDENT-CTR by 1 since the innermost loop is:

```
PERFORM 300-CALC-RTN
    VARYING STUDENT-CTR FROM 1 BY 1 UNTIL STUDENT-CTR > 20
```

Stepping through the logic of a program using sample data as we have here is an example of a *structured walkthrough*.

When nested PERFORM ... VARYING statements are used in a program, it is often possible to combine them into a single statement using a PERFORM ... VARYING ... AFTER option. We could replace the preceding nested PERFORM routines with the following:

```
100-MAIN-MODULE.
    OPEN INPUT STUDENT-FILE
         OUTPUT PRINT-FILE
    MOVE ZEROS TO CLASS-TOTAL
    PERFORM
         VARYING CLASS-CTR FROM 1 BY 1 UNTIL CLASS-CTR > 10
             AFTER STUDENT-CTR FROM 1 BY 1 UNTIL
                 STUDENT-CTR > 20
       READ STUDENT-FILE
           AT END MOVE 'NO ' TO ARE-THERE-MORE-RECORDS
       END-READ
       ADD GRADE TO TOTAL
       IF STUDENT-CTR = 20
           PERFORM 400-WRITE-RTN
           MOVE ZEROS TO CLASS-TOTAL
       END-IF
    END-PERFORM
    CLOSE STUDENT-FILE
          PRINT-FILE
    STOP RUN.
400-WRITE-RTN.
    :
    :
```

The PERFORM ... VARYING ... AFTER is used extensively when processing some types of tables, as we will see in Chapter 12.

Example   Suppose a company has 25 salespeople, each of whom works Monday through Saturday. A sales record is created for each salesperson per day that contains the total sales he or she transacted that day. Suppose records are in sequence by salesperson as follows:

SALESPERSON NO (1–25)	DAY NO (1–6)	SALES AMT 9999V99
1 2	3 4	9

SALESPERSON	DAY
1	1
:	:
1	6
2	1
:	:
2	6
:	:
25	1
:	:
25	6

Suppose we want to print each salesperson's weekly sales total:

```
                  WEEKLY SALES

SALESPERSON NO            TOTAL
           1          $ZZ,ZZ9.99
           :              :
          25          $ZZ,ZZ9.99
```

We will read in 150 records and print 25 weekly salesperson totals.

The major PERFORM would use a PERFORM VARYING SALESPERSON-CTR ... because we want to print a salesperson number along with a total weekly sales for that salesperson:

```
PERFORM 200-PRINT-RTN
    VARYING SALESPERSON-CTR
        FROM 1 BY 1 UNTIL SALESPERSON-CTR > 25
```

The minor PERFORM could just say PERFORM 400-ADD-SALES-AMTS 6 TIMES. There is no need for a day counter since we do not print the day number. That is, we print only the total weekly sales for each salesperson.

The program would be as follows:

```
100-MAIN.
    OPEN INPUT  SALES-FILE
         OUTPUT PRINT-FILE
    PERFORM 200-PRINT-RTN
        VARYING SALESPERSON-CTR
            FROM 1 BY 1 UNTIL SALESPERSON-CTR > 25
    CLOSE SALES-FILE
          PRINT-FILE
    STOP RUN.
200-PRINT-RTN.
    PERFORM 300-ADD-SALES-AMTS 6 TIMES
    MOVE SALESPERSON-CTR TO SALESPERSON-OUT
    MOVE TOTAL TO TOTAL-OUT
    WRITE PRINT-REC FROM SALESPERSON-LINE
        AFTER ADVANCING 2 LINES
    MOVE 0 TO TOTAL.
300-ADD-SALES-AMTS.
    READ SALES-FILE
        AT END MOVE 'NO ' TO MORE-RECS
    END-READ
    ADD SALES-AMT TO TOTAL.
```

Note that the READ is performed at the *minor* level so that exactly 25 × 6 (150) records are read. Note, too, that an AT END condition would not be reached since we read precisely 150 records.

THE PERFORM WITH TEST AFTER OPTION (COBOL 85)

The type of iteration using a PERFORM UNTIL is similar to a DO WHILE in other languages. With this structure, a test for the condition is made *first*, even before the sequence of steps within the PERFORM is executed. If the condition is *not* met initially, then the instructions to be PERFORMed are executed at least once. If the condition is met initially, then the instructions to be PERFORMed are *not executed at all*.

Most languages also have an iteration structure that executes the instructions to be PERFORMed *even before the test is made*. Pascal, for example, uses the Repeat Until structure. This ensures that the sequence of steps to be performed is executed *at least once*. With versions of COBOL prior to COBOL 85, there was no convenient way of executing the instructions to be PERFORMed at least once *before* testing the condition.

With COBOL 85, a PERFORM UNTIL can be made equivalent to a Repeat Until with the use of a TEST AFTER clause. This means we instruct the computer to test for the condition in the PERFORM UNTIL *after* the instructions are executed. The format for the WITH TEST clause is:

Format

> PERFORM [paragraph-name-1]
>
> [WITH TEST { BEFORE / AFTER }] UNTIL condition-1

With COBOL 85, if an in-line PERFORM is used, no paragraph-name is coded, and the statements within the PERFORM end with an END-PERFORM scope terminator.

Suppose we have a program that prints mailing labels for customers. Each customer record has a name and address and a field called NO-OF-LABELS. Suppose we always want to print at least one mailing label even if the NO-OF-LABELS field is entered as a number less than one:

```
PERFORM WITH TEST AFTER
        UNTIL NO-OF-LABELS < 1
    PERFORM 500-WRITE-A-MAILING-LABEL
    SUBTRACT 1 FROM NO-OF-LABELS
END-PERFORM
```

The WITH TEST AFTER clause can also be used with the VARYING option of the PER-
FORM. The format is: PERFORM WITH TEST AFTER VARYING . . . .

Note that PERFORM UNTIL (with no WITH TEST clause) and PERFORM WITH TEST BEFORE
UNTIL accomplish the same thing.

CHAPTER SUMMARY   A. Formats of the PERFORM Statement
1. Simple PERFORM statements: (1) In-line PERFORM: PERFORM . . . END-PERFORM and
   (2) PERFORM paragraph-name-1 [THRU paragraph-name-2]
   a. Cause execution of the instructions at the named paragraph(s).
   b. After execution of the instructions within either the PERFORM . . . END-PERFORM or the
      PERFORM paragraph-name, control is transferred to the statement directly following
      the PERFORM.
2. The PERFORM UNTIL statement
   a. The identifier(s) used in the UNTIL clause must be altered within the paragraph(s)
      being performed; otherwise, the paragraphs will be performed indefinitely.
   b. If the condition in the UNTIL clause is met at the time of execution, then the named
      paragraph(s) will not be executed at all. With COBOL 85, the WITH TEST AFTER clause
      can be used to test the condition *after* the paragraph has been executed once.
3. The PERFORM TIMES statement
   A numeric identifier or an integer can precede the word TIMES; with COBOL 85, an
   arithmetic expression can be used as well.
4. The PERFORM VARYING statement
   a. The counter or loop control field must be defined in the DATA DIVISION, typically in
      WORKING-STORAGE. An initial VALUE for the loop control field is not required.
   b. The PERFORM VARYING automatically does the following:
      (1) Initializes the counter with the value specified in the FROM clause.
      (2) Tests the counter for the condition specified in the UNTIL clause.
      (3) Continues with the statement directly following the PERFORM if the condition spec-
          ified in the UNTIL clause is satisfied.
      (4) Executes the named paragraph(s) if the condition specified in the UNTIL clause is
          not met.
      (5) After execution of the named paragraph(s), increases (or decreases) the counter by
          the value of the integer or identifier specified in the VARYING clause.
   B. Additional Considerations
1. The THRU option can be included with all versions of the PERFORM but we recommend
   that you avoid this option.
2. PERFORM statements within PERFORM statements are permissible. These are called nested
   PERFORMs.
3. EXIT is a reserved word that can be used to indicate the end point of paragraph(s) being
   performed. EXIT must be the only entry in a paragraph when it is used with COBOL 74.
4. In-line PERFORMs are permitted in COBOL 85 with all PERFORM options; with in-line
   PERFORMs it is not necessary to code separate paragraphs. The PERFORM is terminated
   with an END-PERFORM.

KEY TERMS

EXIT	Looping	PERFORM TIMES
GO TO	Module	PERFORM UNTIL
In-line PERFORM	Nested PERFORM	PERFORM VARYING
Infinite loop	PERFORM	Scope terminator
Iteration		

CHAPTER SELF-TEST

1. After instructions executed by a PERFORM paragraph-name statement are run, control returns to _____ .

2. Suppose X = 0 when PERFORM 200-PROCESS-RTN X TIMES is executed. How many times will 200-PROCESS-RTN be performed?

3. PERFORM 300-PRINT-RTN ITEMX TIMES is valid only if ITEMX has contents of _____ or _____ .

4. How many times will the paragraph named 400-PROCESS-RTN be executed by the following PERFORM statements?
   (a) PERFORM   400-PROCESS-RTN
          VARYING X FROM 1 BY 1 UNTIL X = 10
   (b) PERFORM   400-PROCESS-RTN
          VARYING X FROM 1 BY 1 UNTIL X > 10
   (c) PERFORM   400-PROCESS-RTN
          VARYING X FROM 0 BY 1 UNTIL X = 10

5. Write a PERFORM routine to add A to B five times using (a) the TIMES option, (b) the UNTIL option, (c) the VARYING option.

What, if anything, is wrong with the following routines (Questions 6–8)?

6.   PERFORM 300-ADD-RTN
                 VARYING A FROM 1 BY 1 UNTIL A > 20.
      :
   300-ADD-RTN.
       ADD C TO B
       ADD 1 TO A.

7.   PERFORM 600-TEST-IT 8 TIMES.
      :
   600-TEST-IT.
       IF A = B GO TO 700-ADD-IT.
       ADD A TO B.
   700-ADD-IT.
       ADD 5 TO B.

8.   PERFORM 800-PROCESS-RTN
                 UNTIL CTR = 8.
      :
   800-PROCESS-RTN.
       ADD A TO B
       ADD 1 TO CTR
       IF CTR = 8
           STOP RUN.

9. Using the TIMES option of the PERFORM statement, restate the following:

        MOVE 0 TO X1
        PERFORM 700-LOOP UNTIL X1 = 10.
       :
   700-LOOP.
       :
       ADD 1 TO X1.

10. Using the VARYING option of the PERFORM statement, write a routine to sum all even numbers from 2 through 100.

Solutions

1. the statement directly following the PERFORM

2. no (0) times

3. an integer; 0

4. 9 times; 10 times; 10 times

5. (a)   PERFORM 200-ADD-RTN 5 TIMES.
           :
       200-ADD-RTN.
           ADD A TO B.

```
(b)      MOVE 1 TO CTR
         PERFORM 200-ADD-RTN UNTIL CTR > 5.
         :
         :
    200-ADD-RTN
         ADD A TO B
         ADD 1 TO CTR.

(c)      PERFORM 200-ADD-RTN VARYING N FROM 1 BY 1
              UNTIL N > 5.
         :
         :
    200-ADD-RTN.
         ADD A TO B.
```

6. A, the identifier in the PERFORM statement, should *not* be changed in 300-ADD-RTN. It is incremented automatically by the PERFORM VARYING statement.

7. 600-TEST-IT, a paragraph executed by a PERFORM statement, should not have a GO TO that transfers control outside its range. The following is valid:

```
         PERFORM 600-TEST-IT 8 TIMES.
         :
         :
    600-TEST-IT.
         IF  A = B
              ADD 5 TO B
         ELSE
              ADD A TO B
         END-IF.
```

8. A PERFORM statement will automatically compare CTR to 8; thus the last conditional in 800-PROCESS-RTN is not only unnecessary, it is incorrect.

9. PERFORM 700-LOOP 10 TIMES.

10.
```
         PERFORM 900-SUM-RTN
              VARYING X FROM 2 BY 2
                   UNTIL X IS GREATER THAN 100.
         :
         :
    900-SUM-RTN.
         ADD X TO EVEN-SUM.
```

PRACTICE PROGRAM

Write a program to compute compound interest from disk records with the following format:

1–5 Account number	
6–25 Depositor's name	
26–30 Principal	P_0
31–32 Interest rate (V99)	r
33–34 Period of investment (in years)	n
35–80 Not used	
(standard labels)	

For each record read, print the input data and a table showing n new balances for years 1–n, where n is the number of years of investment. The principal after n years of investment is determined by the following formula:

$$P_n = P_0 (1 + r)^n$$

r = interest rate expressed as a decimal number (e.g., 7% = .07)

n = years of investment

P_0 = initial principal amount

P_n = principal compounded after n years of investment

Also print the accrued interest on each detail line indicating the interest earned through the year specified on that line.

The Printer Spacing Chart is in Figure 9.3. The pseudocode and hierarchy chart are in Figure 9.4. The program with sample input and output appears in Figure 9.5.

Figure 9.3 Printer Spacing Chart for the Practice Program.

PRINT-FILE Printer Spacing Chart

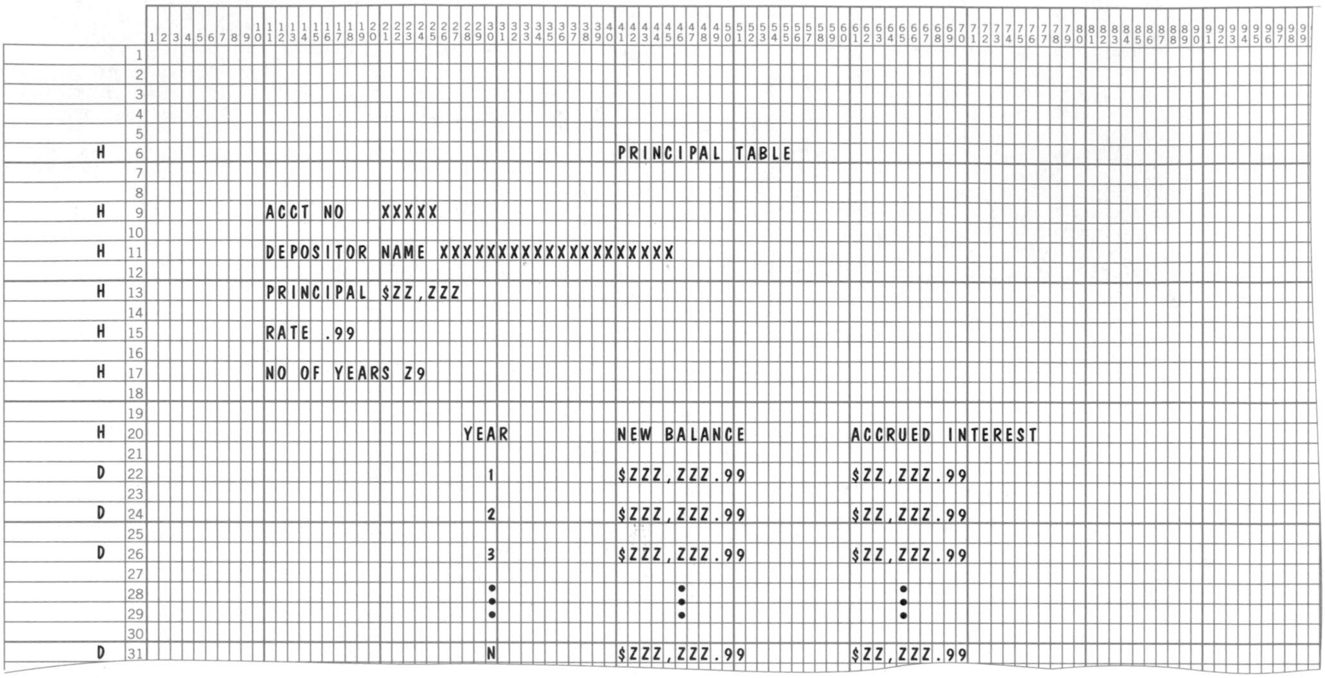

Figure 9.4 Pseudocode and hierarchy chart for the Practice Program.

Pseudocode

MAIN-MODULE
START
    PERFORM Initialization-Rtn
    PERFORM UNTIL there is no more data
        READ a Record
           AT END
                Move 'NO ' to Are-There-More-Records
           NOT AT END
                PERFORM Calc-Rtn
        END-READ
        END-PERFORM
        PERFORM Termination-Rtn
STOP

INITIALIZATION-RTN
    Open the files

CALC-RTN
    PERFORM Hdr-Module
    PERFORM Compute-Interest VARYING Year FROM 1 BY 1
        UNTIL Year > Period of Investment

COMPUTE-INTEREST
    Move Year to Year Out
    Compute New Balance
    Compute Accrued Interest
    Write a Line

HDR-MODULE
    Print Headings

TERMINATION-RTN
    Close the files

Figure 9.4   (continued)

Hierarchy Chart

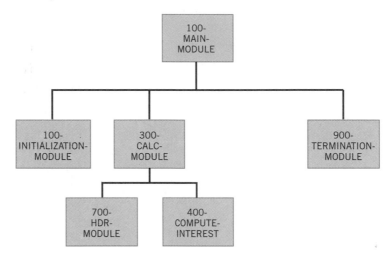

Figure 9.5   Solution and sample input and output for the Practice Program.

COBOL 85

```
IDENTIFICATION DIVISION.
PROGRAM-ID. CHAPTER9.
ENVIRONMENT DIVISION.
INPUT-OUTPUT SECTION.
FILE-CONTROL.
    SELECT ACCT-FILE  ASSIGN TO DISK 'C09PP.DAT'.
    SELECT PRINT-FILE ASSIGN TO PRINTER 'C09PP.RPT'.
DATA DIVISION.
FILE SECTION.
FD  ACCT-FILE
    LABEL RECORDS ARE STANDARD
    RECORD CONTAINS 34 CHARACTERS.
01  DISK-REC.
    05  ACCT-NO-IN              PIC X(5).
    05  NAME-IN                 PIC X(20).
    05  PRIN-IN                 PIC 9(5).
    05  RATE-IN                 PIC V99.
    05  PERIOD-OF-INV-IN        PIC 99.
FD  PRINT-FILE
    LABEL RECORDS ARE OMITTED
    RECORD CONTAINS 80 CHARACTERS.
01  PRINT-REC                   PIC X(80).
WORKING-STORAGE SECTION.
01  ARE-THERE-MORE-RECORDS      PIC XXX
        VALUE 'YES'.
01  WS-NEW-BALANCE              PIC 9(6)V99.
01  YEAR                        PIC 99.
01  HDR-1.
    05                          PIC X(40)
        VALUE SPACES.
    05                          PIC X(40)
        VALUE 'PRINCIPAL TABLE'.
01  HDR-2.
    05                          PIC X(10)
        VALUE SPACES.
    05                          PIC X(10)
        VALUE 'ACCT NO'.
    05  ACCT-OUT                PIC 9(5).
01  HDR-3.
    05                          PIC X(10)
        VALUE SPACES.
    05                          PIC X(15)
        VALUE 'DEPOSITOR NAME'.
```

COBOL 74 Substitutions

For COBOL 74, FILLER must be used
instead of a blank field name

Figure 9.5   (continued)

```
                                          05    NAME-OUT                          PIC X(20).
                                      01  HDR-4.
                                          05                                      PIC X(10)
                                              VALUE SPACES.
                                          05                                      PIC X(10)
                                              VALUE 'PRINCIPAL'.
                                          05    PRINCIPAL-OUT                     PIC $ZZ,ZZZ.
                                      01  HDR-5.
                                          05                                      PIC X(10)
                                              VALUE SPACES.
                                          05                                      PIC X(5)
                                              VALUE 'RATE'.
                                          05    RATE-OUT                          PIC .99.
                                      01  HDR-6.
                                          05                                      PIC X(10)
                                              VALUE SPACES.
                                          05                                      PIC X(12)
                                              VALUE 'NO OF YEARS'.
                                          05    PERIOD-OUT                        PIC Z9.
                                      01  COLUMN-HEADINGS.
                                          05                                      PIC X(27)
                                              VALUE SPACES.
                                          05                                      PIC X(13)
                                              VALUE 'YEAR'.
                                          05                                      PIC X(20)
                                              VALUE 'NEW BALANCE'.
                                          05                                      PIC X(20)
                                              VALUE 'ACCRUED INTEREST'.
                                      01  DETAIL-LINE.
                                          05                                      PIC X(28)
                                              VALUE SPACES.
                                          05    YEAR-OUT                          PIC Z9.
                                          05                                      PIC X(10)
                                              VALUE SPACES.
                                          05    NEW-BALANCE-OUT                   PIC $ZZZ,ZZZ.99.
                                          05                                      PIC X(9)
                                              VALUE SPACES.
                                          05    ACCRUED-INTEREST-OUT              PIC $ZZ,ZZZ.99.
                                      PROCEDURE DIVISION.
                                      100-MAIN-MODULE.
                                          PERFORM 100-INITIALIZATION-MODULE
                                        ⌈ PERFORM UNTIL ARE-THERE-MORE-RECORDS = 'NO '
                                        |     READ ACCT-FILE
                                        |         AT END
                                        |             MOVE 'NO ' TO ARE-THERE-MORE-RECORDS
                                        ⟨         NOT AT END
                                        |             PERFORM 300-CALC-MODULE
                                        |     END-READ
                                        ⌊ END-PERFORM
                                          PERFORM 900-TERMINATION-MODULE
                                          STOP RUN.
                                      100-INITIALIZATION-MODULE.
                                          OPEN INPUT  ACCT-FILE
                                               OUTPUT PRINT-FILE.
```

COBOL 74 Substitutions

```
    PERFORM 300-CALC-MODULE
        UNTIL ARE-THERE-MORE-RECORDS = 'NO '.
```

```
    PERFORM 600-READ-MODULE.    ⟶
```

```
                                      300-CALC-MODULE.
                                          PERFORM 700-HDR-MODULE
                                          PERFORM 400-COMPUTE-INTEREST VARYING
                                              YEAR FROM 1 BY 1 UNTIL YEAR > PERIOD-OF-INV-IN.
```

```
    PERFORM 600-READ-MODULE.    ⟶
```

```
                                      400-COMPUTE-INTEREST.
                                          MOVE YEAR TO YEAR-OUT
                                          COMPUTE WS-NEW-BALANCE = PRIN-IN * (1 + RATE-IN)
                                                                    ** YEAR
                                          MOVE WS-NEW-BALANCE TO NEW-BALANCE-OUT
                                          SUBTRACT PRIN-IN FROM WS-NEW-BALANCE
```

Figure 9.5 (continued)

```
                                                    GIVING ACCRUED-INTEREST-OUT
                                              WRITE PRINT-REC FROM DETAIL-LINE
                                                    AFTER ADVANCING 2 LINES.
600-READ-MODULE.
    READ ACCT-FILE
        AT END MOVE 'NO ' TO ARE-THERE-MORE-RECORDS.
                                              700-HDR-MODULE.
                                                  WRITE PRINT-REC FROM HDR-1
                                                       AFTER ADVANCING PAGE
                                                  MOVE ACCT-NO-IN TO ACCT-OUT
                                                  MOVE NAME-IN TO NAME-OUT
                                                  MOVE PRIN-IN TO PRINCIPAL-OUT
                                                  MOVE RATE-IN TO RATE-OUT
                                                  MOVE PERIOD-OF-INV-IN TO PERIOD-OUT
                                                  WRITE PRINT-REC FROM HDR-2
                                                       AFTER ADVANCING 3 LINES
                                                  WRITE PRINT-REC FROM HDR-3
                                                       AFTER ADVANCING 2 LINES
                                                  WRITE PRINT-REC FROM HDR-4
                                                       AFTER ADVANCING 2 LINES
                                                  WRITE PRINT-REC FROM HDR-5
                                                       AFTER ADVANCING 2 LINES
                                                  WRITE PRINT-REC FROM HDR-6
                                                       AFTER ADVANCING 2 LINES
                                                  WRITE PRINT-REC FROM COLUMN-HEADINGS
                                                       AFTER ADVANCING 2 LINES.
                                              900-TERMINATION-MODULE.
                                                  CLOSE ACCT-FILE
                                                       PRINT-FILE.
```

Sample Input Data

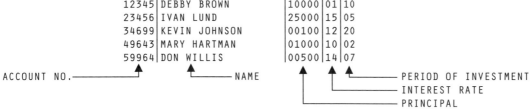

```
12345 DEBBY BROWN      10000 01 10
23456 IVAN LUND        25000 15 05
34699 KEVIN JOHNSON    00100 12 20
49643 MARY HARTMAN     01000 10 02
59964 DON WILLIS       00500 14 07
```

ACCOUNT NO. —————— —————— NAME —— PERIOD OF INVESTMENT
                                   —— INTEREST RATE
                                   —— PRINCIPAL

Sample Output

```
                      PRINCIPAL TABLE

          ACCT NO   12345
          DEPOSITOR NAME DEBBY BROWN
          PRINCIPAL $10,000
          RATE .01
          NO OF YEARS 10

               YEAR         NEW BALANCE        ACCRUED INTEREST
                 1        $ 10,100.00        $     100.00
                 2        $ 10,201.00        $     201.00
                 3        $ 10,303.01        $     303.01
                 4        $ 10,406.04        $     406.04
                 5        $ 10,510.10        $     510.10
                 6        $ 10,615.20        $     615.20
                 7        $ 10,721.35        $     721.35
                 8        $ 10,828.56        $     828.56
                 9        $ 10,936.85        $     936.85
                10        $ 11,046.22        $   1,046.22
```

Figure 9.5 (continued)

```
                          PRINCIPAL TABLE


ACCT NO   23456
DEPOSITOR NAME IVAN LUND
PRINCIPAL $25,000
RATE .15
NO OF YEARS 5


          YEAR          NEW BALANCE          ACCRUED INTEREST
           1            $ 28,750.00          $  3,750.00
           2            $ 33,062.50          $  8,062.50
           3            $ 38,021.87          $ 13,021.87
           4            $ 43,725.15          $ 18,725.15
           5            $ 50,283.92          $ 25,283.92
```

```
                          PRINCIPAL TABLE


ACCT NO   34699
DEPOSITOR NAME KEVIN JOHNSON
PRINCIPAL $    100
RATE .12
NO OF YEARS 20


          YEAR          NEW BALANCE          ACCRUED INTEREST
           1            $     112.00         $      12.00
           2            $     125.44         $      25.44
           3            $     140.49         $      40.49
           4            $     157.35         $      57.35
           5            $     176.23         $      76.23
           6            $     197.38         $      97.38
           7            $     221.06         $     121.06
           8            $     247.59         $     147.59
           9            $     277.30         $     177.30
          10            $     310.58         $     210.58
          11            $     347.85         $     247.85
          12            $     389.59         $     289.59
          13            $     436.34         $     336.34
          14            $     488.71         $     388.71
          15            $     547.35         $     447.35
          16            $     613.03         $     513.03
          17            $     686.60         $     586.60
          18            $     768.99         $     668.99
          19            $     861.27         $     761.27
          20            $     964.62         $     864.62
```

```
                          PRINCIPAL TABLE


ACCT NO   49643
DEPOSITOR NAME MARY HARTMAN
PRINCIPAL $ 1,000
RATE .10
NO OF YEARS 2


          YEAR          NEW BALANCE          ACCRUED INTEREST
           1            $  1,100.00          $     100.00
           2            $  1,210.00          $     210.00
```

Figure 9.5   (continued)

```
                          PRINCIPAL TABLE

    ACCT NO   59964
    DEPOSITOR NAME DON WILLIS
    PRINCIPAL $    500
    RATE .14
    NO OF YEARS   7

              YEAR         NEW BALANCE         ACCRUED INTEREST
               1        $      570.00        $       70.00
               2        $      649.80        $      149.80
               3        $      740.77        $      240.77
               4        $      844.48        $      344.48
               5        $      962.70        $      462.70
               6        $    1,097.48        $      597.48
               7        $    1,251.13        $      751.13
```

REVIEW QUESTIONS

I. True-False
Questions

_____   1. A PERFORM paragraph-name statement permanently transfers control to some other section of a program.

_____   2. In-line PERFORMs are permitted with COBOL 85 as long as they end with END-PERFORM.

_____   3. GO TO statements are generally avoided in structured programs.

_____   4. EXIT is a COBOL reserved word that performs no operation.

_____   5. Using a PERFORM UNTIL option, the condition is tested before the paragraph is executed even once.

_____   6. PERFORM 400-LOOP-RTN N TIMES is only valid if N is defined as numeric.

_____   7. Using PERFORM 400-LOOP-RTN N TIMES, N should not be altered within 400-LOOP-RTN.

_____   8. It is valid to say PERFORM 400-LOOP-RTN N TIMES, where N = 0.

_____   9. The PERFORM and GO TO statements will cause identical branching.

_____ 10. If several paragraphs are to be executed by a PERFORM statement, we may use the THRU option.

II. General Questions

1. Using a PERFORM statement with a TIMES option, write a routine to find N factorial, where N is the data item. Recall that N factorial = $N \times (N - 1) \times (N - 2) \times \ldots \times 1$; e.g., 5 factorial = $5 \times 4 \times 3 \times 2 \times 1 = 120$.

2. Rewrite the following routine using (a) a PERFORM statement with a TIMES option and (b) a PERFORM with a VARYING option:

```
        MOVE ZEROS TO COUNTER
        PERFORM 400-LOOP-RTN
            UNTIL COUNTER = 20.
          .
          .
    400-LOOP-RTN.
        READ SALES-FILE
            AT END MOVE 'NO ' TO ARE-THERE-MORE-RECORDS
        END-READ
        ADD QTY OF SALES-REC TO TOTAL
        ADD 1 TO COUNTER.
```

3. Write two routines, one with a PERFORM ... TIMES and one with a PERFORM UNTIL ... to sum all odd integers from 1 to 1001, exclusive of 1001.

4. Write a routine to sum all odd integers between 1 and 99 inclusive.

5. Write a routine to calculate the number of minutes in a 24-hour day using the PERFORM ... TIMES option.

DEBUGGING EXERCISES

1. Consider the following coding:

```
PERFORM 400-ADD-RTN
    VARYING X FROM 1 BY 1 UNTIL X > 50.
    :
400-ADD-RTN.
    READ AMT-FILE
        AT END MOVE 'NO ' TO ARE-THERE-MORE-RECORDS
    END-READ
    ADD AMT TO TOTAL
    ADD 1 TO X.
```

(a) How many times is AMT added to TOTAL?

(b) Is the logic in the program excerpt correct? Explain your answer.

(c) What will happen if there are only 14 input records? Explain your answer.

(d) Correct the coding so that it adds amounts from 50 input records and prints an error message if there are fewer than 50 records.

2. Consider the following program excerpt:

```
    :
PERFORM 200-CALC-RTN
    UNTIL NO-MORE-RECORDS
    :
200-CALC-RTN.
    READ SALES-FILE
        AT END MOVE 'NO ' TO ARE-THERE-MORE-RECORDS
    END-READ
    MOVE 0 TO COUNTER
    PERFORM 300-LOOP-RTN
        UNTIL COUNTER = 5
    MOVE TOTAL TO TOTAL-OUT
    MOVE TOTAL-REC TO PRINT-REC
    WRITE PRINT-REC.
300-LOOP-RTN.
    ADD AMT1 AMT2 GIVING AMT3
    MULTIPLY 1.08 BY AMT3 GIVING GROSS
    SUBTRACT DISCOUNT FROM GROSS
        GIVING TOTAL.
```

(a) This coding will result in a program interrupt. Indicate why. What changes should be made to correct the coding?

(b) Suppose COUNTER is initialized in WORKING-STORAGE with a VALUE of 0. Would it be correct to eliminate the MOVE 0 TO COUNTER instruction from 200-CALC-RTN? Explain your answer.

(c) Code the three arithmetic statements in 300-LOOP-RTN with a single COMPUTE statement.

PROGRAMMING ASSIGNMENTS

1. *Interactive Processing.* Write a program to display a temperature conversion table on a screen. Compute and print the Fahrenheit equivalents of all Celsius temperatures at 10-degree intervals from 0 to 150 degrees. The conversion formula is Celsius = 5/9 (Fahrenheit − 32).

2. Write a program to produce a bonus report. See the problem definition in Figure 9.6.

Notes:

a. The payroll records have been sorted into ascending sequence by office number within territory number. There are three territories, two offices within each territory, and 10 employees within each office. We have, therefore, 60 records (3 × 2 × 10). Thus, all employees within office 01 within territory 01 will appear before employee records for office 02 within territory 01, and so on.

b. Only employees who were hired before 1994 are entitled to a 10% bonus.

Figure 9.6 Problem definition for Programming Assignment 2.

Systems Flowchart

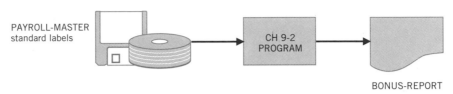

PAYROLL-MASTER
standard labels

CH 9-2
PROGRAM

BONUS-REPORT

PAYROLL-MASTER **Record Layout**			
Field	**Size**	**Type**	**No. of Decimal Positions (if Numeric)**
EMPLOYEE-NO	5	Alphanumeric	
EMPLOYEE-NAME	20	Alphanumeric	
TERRITORY-NO	2	Alphanumeric	
OFFICE-NO	2	Alphanumeric	
ANNUAL-SALARY	6	Numeric	0
Unused	29	Alphanumeric	
DATE-HIRED	6	Format: mmddyy	
Unused	10	Alphanumeric	

BONUS-REPORT Printer Spacing Chart

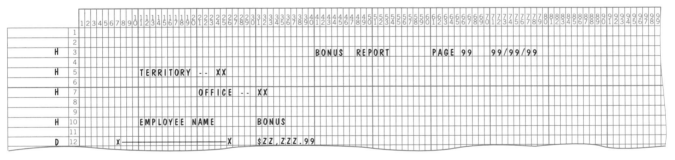

c. Print the names of all employees and their bonuses. Print a separate page for each office within each territory. Use a nested PERFORM to achieve page breaks for each office within each territory.

3. The problem definition for this program appears in Figure 9.7.

   Given the initial cost of an item, print a table indicating the item's anticipated cost over a 10-year span taking inflation into account. Assume the inflation rate for the first 5 years is projected at 8% and the inflation rate for the next 5 years is projected at 6%. Be sure to accumulate the effects of inflation.

```
ITEM-COST: $1.00
YEAR 1      1.08   (1 X 1.08)
YEAR 2      1.08²  (1.08 X 1.08)
  :
YEAR 5      1.08⁵
YEAR 6      1.08⁵  X 1.06
  :
YEAR 10     1.08⁵  X 1.06⁵
```

Figure 9.7 Problem definition for Programming Assignment 3.

Systems Flowchart

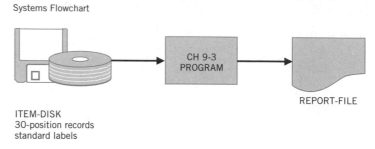

ITEM-DISK
30-position records
standard labels

REPORT-FILE

ITEM-DISK Record Layout			
Field	**Size**	**Type**	**No. of Decimal Positions (if Numeric)**
ITEM-NO	5	Alphanumeric	
ITEM-DESCRIPTION	20	Alphanumeric	
ITEM-COST	5	Numeric	2

REPORT-FILE Printer Spacing Chart

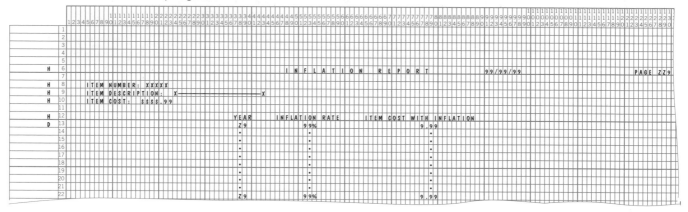

4. Write a program to compute class averages for an input disk file with the following format.

Record 1 for group:

1–5 Class number
6–7 Number of students in class
8–10 Not used

Remainder of records for group:

1–5 Class number
6–8 Exam grade (999)
9–10 Not used

Print: Class number and class average for each class. The average should be rounded to the nearest integer. The disk has standard labels.

5. Write a program to print one line from a variable number of input records, where the first record of each group indicates the total number of records in the group. Each group of records pertains to a single salesperson and consists of all sales that person transacted during the month. The output is a printed report with each line consisting of a salesperson name and the accumulated amount for the total number of records in the group. The problem definition appears in Figure 9.8. Use a READ . . . INTO to define the two input record layouts in WORKING-STORAGE.

6. The We-Sell-Low Store has twenty-five salespeople. For each day of the week (Mon–Sat), a record is created that includes:

SALES Record Layout			
Field	Size	Type	No. of Decimal Positions (if Numeric)
DAY-OF-WEEK (1 = Mon 2 = Tue ⋮ 6 = Sat)	1	Alphanumeric	
SALESPERSON-NUMBER	2	Alphanumeric	
TOTAL-AMOUNT-SOLD	7	Numeric	2

The records are in sequence by Day of Week (1–6) and within day of week, by salesperson number (1–25). (Continued on the next page.)

Figure 9.8 Problem definition for Programming Assignment 5.

Systems Flowchart

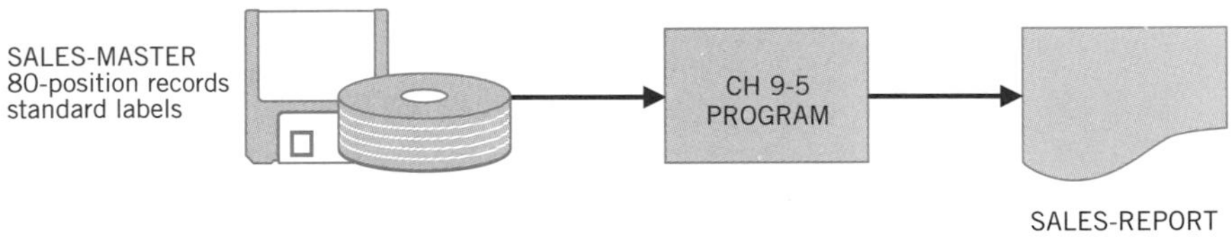

SALES-MASTER
80-position records
standard labels

CH 9-5 PROGRAM

SALES-REPORT

SALES-MASTER Header Record Layout (First record for each salesperson)			
Field	Size	Type	No. of Decimal Positions (if Numeric)
Salesperson No.	5	Alphanumeric	
Salesperson Name	20	Alphanumeric	
No. of Records in Group	3	Numeric	0

SALES-MASTER Sales Record Layout (Each record represents a salesperson's sales)			
Field	Size	Type	No. of Decimal Positions (if Numeric)
Salesperson No.	5	Alphanumeric	
Salesperson Name	20	Alphanumeric	
Sales Amount	5	Numeric	2

SALES-REPORT Printer Spacing Chart

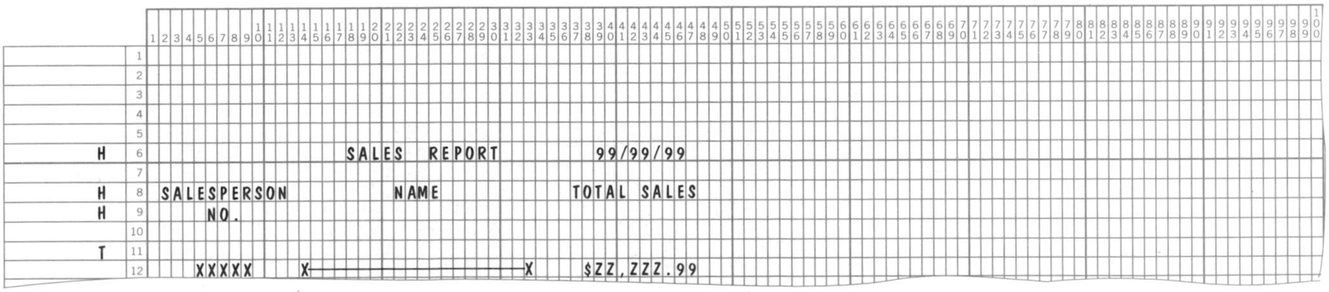

Print a report indicating the total amount sold for each day:

```
DAY               TOTAL SALES

MON                 $99,999.99
TUE                 $99,999.99
:                        :
:                        :
SAT                 $99,999.99

 TOTAL WEEKLY SALES $999,999.99
```

7. Print a depreciation table using the straight-line method of depreciation.

The Internal Revenue Service permits a tax write-off depending on the expected life of an asset. The amount to be depreciated or written off may be deducted from taxable income. For this reason, depreciation schedules are prepared by companies for many of their assets. In this way, each year's write-off or depreciation is simply obtained from the table entry for that year. The asset's value at any given time is referred to as its *book value*. This is equal to its initial value minus the accumulated depreciation.

At the end of the anticipated useful life of an asset, its value should depreciate to the *salvage* or *scrap value*. We call this REM-VAL for remaining value. Suppose, for example, that the useful life of an item such as an automobile is considered to be 5 years. If the car is estimated to have a value of $2,000 at the end of 5 years, that amount is referred to as the salvage or remaining value.

There are numerous ways of spreading depreciation over the life of an asset. Your program should use the method referred to as *straight-line depreciation*, which means that an amount equal to the original cost (purchase price) of an asset minus its salvage value may be written off each year of the asset's depreciable or useful life.

To prepare a depreciation table for a given asset using the straight-line method, use the problem definition shown in Figure 9.9. Beginning with the current period, calculate depreciation as follows:

Depreciation = (Purchase Price − Remaining Value) / Useful Life

Print a depreciation table indicating yearly depreciation values. If, for example, an asset were expected to last for 6 years, one-sixth of the asset would be depreciated each year. This is because with straight-line depreciation the amount of depreciation is the same for each period. There would thus be 6 yearly depreciation figures printed out in the depreciation table.

Tables are produced indicating the amount of depreciation or write-off each year from the current date to the end of the useful life of the asset.

Suppose a piece of equipment has a purchase price of $11,000 and a salvage value of $1,000. We wish to produce a 3-year table of depreciation. Thus, there will be three yearly figures to be calculated.

The depreciation is calculated as follows:

$$\frac{\text{Price} - \text{Salvage Value}}{\text{Number of Periods}} = \frac{11000 - 1000}{3} = 3333.33$$

The depreciation per year for each of 3 years is 3333.33. Using straight-line depreciation, the rate is the same each year.

For each Item Description, Cost, and Number of Years entered, print a depreciation table.

Figure 9.9   Problem definition for Programming Assignment 7.

Input Record Layout (Alternate Layout Form)

ITEM DESCRIPTION	COST 999V99	NO. OF YEARS TO DEPRECIATE
1 20	21 25	26 27

Figure 9.9   (continued)

Sample Input

FLOOR PADS	010ₐ00	05

Sample Output

```
ITEM FLOOR PADS
COST 10
YEAR   DEPRECIATION TO DATE   REMAINING VALUE
1              2                    8
2              4                    6
3              6                    4
4              8                    2
5             10                    0
```

8. **Interactive Processing.**   Write a program to enable users to enter:

> Name
> Street Address
> City, State, and Zip

on three lines of a screen. Prompt the user for the number of mailing labels needed:

```
DISPLAY 'ENTER NO. OF MAILING LABELS'
ACCEPT NO-OF-LABELS
```

Display all accepted input on the screen again, asking the user to verify that it is correct (e.g., 'IS THE DATA CORRECT (Y/N)?'). If the user responds by keying Y for 'yes' (upper- or lowercase Y should be acceptable), then print the required mailing labels on the printer. If you are using a PC, make the interactive screen display as interesting as possible (e.g., use different colors, highlighting, etc.).

9. **Maintenance Program.**   Modify the Practice Program in this chapter so that the interest earned each year appears on each detail line printed.

   Hint: For the first year, subtract the initial principal amount from the new balance at the end of the first year. Thereafter, subtract the previous year's balance from the new balance at the end of the corresponding year.

UNIT III
Writing High-Level COBOL Programs

CHAPTER 10

Control Break Processing

![bar] **OBJECTIVES**

To familiarize you with

1. The main types of computer-generated reports.
2. The techniques used for efficient printing of group reports and control totals.
3. Control break processing and control break printing.

![bar] **CONTENTS**

AN INTRODUCTION TO CONTROL BREAK PROCESSING

TYPES OF REPORTS: A SYSTEMS OVERVIEW

Printed reports fall into three major categories:

Detail or Transaction Reports

Detail or **transaction reports** are those that include one or more lines of output for *each* input record read. Customer bills generated from a master accounts receivable file would be an example of a transaction or detail report. Similarly, payroll checks generated from a master payroll file would be a detail report. Finally, a listing of each part number stocked by a company would be a detail report. Transaction or detail output is produced when information for each input record is required.

Because detail reports generate output for each input record read, they can take a relatively long time to produce. Printing 300,000 checks from a file of 300,000 records, for example, could take several hours.

Exception Reports

Sometimes users ask for detail reports when, in fact, other types of output would be more useful. Suppose an insurance agent, for example, has requested a listing of all clients and their last payment date. When asked by a systems analyst why the detail report is necessary, the agent responds that all clients who have not made a payment within the last 90 days must be contacted. An experienced computer professional would suggest an alternative type of output, one that lists *only* those clients who meet the criterion the insurance agent has set. A listing of only those clients who have not made a payment within 90 days would save the time and effort necessary to print out *all* clients, but more importantly it would make the insurance agent's job easier. Rather than having to sift through numerous pages of a listing, the agent would have a list of only those people to be contacted. Sometimes less output can be more useful than too much output!

A listing of those clients with overdue balances is called an **exception report**, which is any printout of individual records that meet (or fail to meet) certain criteria. Other examples of exception reports are a list of employees who are 65 years old or older, and a list of part numbers in stock with a quantity on hand below some minimum value.

Summary Reports

As the name suggests, a **summary** or **group report** summarizes rather than itemizes. Often summaries or totals can provide more comprehensive and meaningful information for the user than a detail or exception report.

As a rule, either exception reports or summary reports should be generated instead of detail reports if they can serve the user's purpose. Detail reports take a long time to produce, they tend to be voluminous, and they often require some summarizing anyway before they are meaningful to the operating staff or to managers.

Displayed Output: A Systems Overview

Interactive Processing. When output is required as responses to inquiries and where printed copies are not needed, displayed output is often used. The output is generated on a screen very quickly and there is no need to produce pages of paper, which can be costly and burdensome to store. While detail and summary reports generally appear in printed form, it is not unusual for a short exception report to be displayed on a monitor.

Keep in mind that displayed output must be clear, concise, and informative just like printed output. When we use a DISPLAY verb to generate output on a screen, there is no need to establish an output file for output that will be displayed.

This chapter considers a type of summary procedure called **control break process-ing.** With this type of processing, control fields are used to indicate when totals are to print.

AN EXAMPLE OF A CONTROL BREAK PROCEDURE

Consider the problem definition in Figure 10.1. A disk file consists of sales records, each with three input fields: a salesperson's department number, the salesperson's number, and the amount of sales accrued by that salesperson for the week. The input file is in sequence by the department number, so all records pertaining to salespeople in DEPT 01 are followed by all records pertaining to salespeople in DEPT 02, and so on. (Later on, we will see that files can always be sorted into the desired sequence if they were originally created in some other order.)

There may be numerous salesperson records for DEPT 01, DEPT 02, and so on. That is, there may be several records with the same department number, depending on the actual number of salespeople within a given department. The output is a report that prints not only each salesperson's amount of sales but also *every department's total sales amount.*

For this problem, *detail printing* is required; that is, each input record containing a salesperson's total amount of sales is to be printed. Computer professionals would recommend such detail printing only if the user must see data from each input record.

Figure 10.1 Problem definition for sample control break procedure.

Systems Flowchart

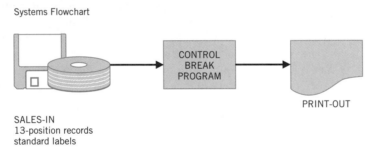

SALES-IN
13-position records
standard labels

SALES-IN **Record Layout**			
Field	**Size**	**Type**	**No. of Decimal Positions (if Numeric)**
DEPT-IN	2	Alphanumeric	
SLSNO-IN	5	Alphanumeric	
AMT-OF-SALES-IN	6	Numeric	2

PRINT-OUT Printer Spacing Chart

```
H   6                              MONTHLY STATUS REPORT        PAGE 99
H   8        DEPT      SALESPERSON NO     AMT OF SALES
D  10        XX          XXXXX             $9,999.99
D  12        XX          XXXXX             $9,999.99
T  14                                            TOTAL FOR DEPT IS $99,999.99
D  16        XX          XXXXX             $9,999.99
```

Figure 10.1 (continued)

Sample Input Data

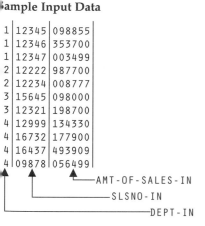

Sample Output

```
                                  MONTHLY STATUS REPORT          PAGE 01

      DEPT      SALESPERSON NO    AMT OF SALES

      01         12345              $988.55

      01         12346            $3,537.00

      01         12347               $34.99

                                            TOTAL FOR DEPT IS   $4,560.54

      02         12222            $9,877.00

      02         12234               $87.77

                                            TOTAL FOR DEPT IS   $9,964.77

      03         15645              $980.00

      03         12321            $1,987.00

                                            TOTAL FOR DEPT IS   $2,967.00

      04         12999            $1,343.30

      04         16732            $1,779.00

      04         16437            $4,939.09

      04         09878              $564.99
                                            TOTAL FOR DEPT IS   $8,626.38
```

In addition to this detail printing, *summary lines* indicating *department totals* will also print. Thus, in this example, *group printing* is also required, where a total line is written for each department.

After all salesperson records for DEPT 01 have been read and printed, a total for DEPT 01 will print. Similarly, after all records for DEPT 02 have been read and printed, a total for DEPT 02 will print, and so on. This type of processing requires the file of input records to be *in sequence by department number*. All salesperson records for DEPT 01 must be entered first, followed by salesperson records for DEPT 02, and so on. Unless records are sorted into department number sequence, it would not be possible, using this procedure, to accumulate a total and print it at the end of a group.

Detail lines print in the usual way, after each input record is read and processed. In addition, after each input record is read, the amount of sales in that record is added to a DEPT total. This department total will be printed whenever a change in DEPT occurs. Since a change in DEPT triggers the printing of a department total, we call DEPT the **control field.**

Thus, all salesperson records for DEPT 01 will be read and printed, and a DEPT total will be accumulated. This processing continues until a salesperson record is read that contains a DEPT different from the previous one. When a record with a different DEPT is read, then the total for the previous department will be printed. Thus, the first input record pertaining to a salesperson in DEPT 02 will cause a total for DEPT 01 to print. Since totals are printed *after* a change occurs in DEPT, which is the control field, we call this type of group processing *control break processing*. Consider the following illustration:

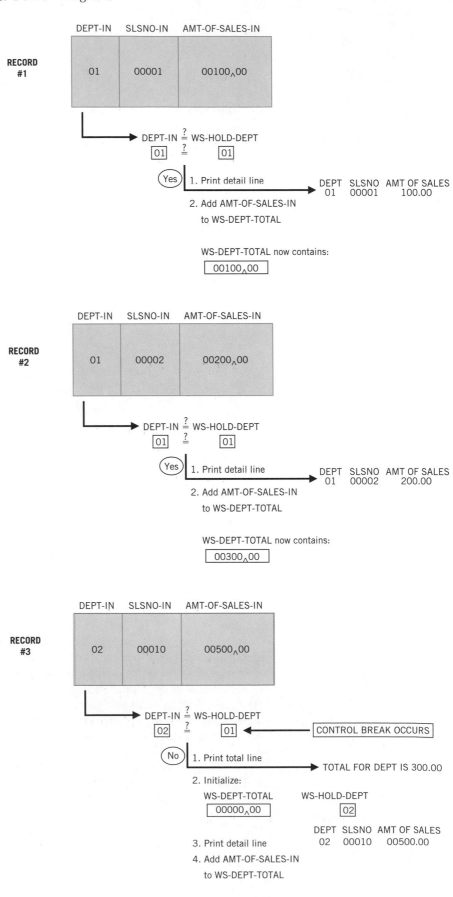

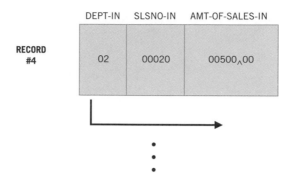

This section has focused on definitions related to control break processing and on an actual illustration of the output produced by a control break procedure. In the next section, we focus on ways to code this procedure. You may wish to examine Figure 10.2 for the pseudocode planning tool used to prepare the program. Recall that the program is designed at the planning stage with *either* a flowchart *or* a pseudocode. Study the pseudocode carefully so that you understand the structure to be used in the programs. The program that will perform the above control break procedure is shown in Figure 10.3 and will be discussed in detail in the next section, along with the hierarchy chart in Figure 10.4.

Figure 10.2   Pseudocode for sample control break procedure.

MAIN-MODULE
START
    Open the Files
    PERFORM Heading-Rtn
    PERFORM UNTIL no more records
        READ a Record
            AT END
                Move 'NO ' to Are-There-More-Records
            NOT AT END
                PERFORM Detail-Rtn
        END-READ
    END-PERFORM
    PERFORM End-Of-Job-Rtn
STOP

DETAIL-RTN
    EVALUATE TRUE
        WHEN First-Record = 'YES'
            Move Dept No to Hold Area
            Move 'NO ' to First-Record
        WHEN there is a change in Dept No
            PERFORM Control-Break-Rtn
    END-EVALUATE
    IF Line Counter > 25
    THEN
        PERFORM Heading-Rtn
    END-IF
    Move Input Data to Detail Line
    Write a Record
    Add 1 to Line Counter
    Add Amt to Dept Total

CONTROL-BREAK-RTN
    Move Dept Total to Output
    Write Summary Line
    Add 1 to Line Counter
    Initialize Dept Total
    Store Dept No

HEADING-RTN
    Write Headings
    Initialize Line Counter

END-OF-JOB-RTN
    Write last Dept Total
    Close Files

Figure 10.3 Program for sample control break procedure.

COBOL 85

```
IDENTIFICATION DIVISION.
PROGRAM-ID. SAMPLE.
****************************************************************
*   The program creates a departmental sales report using a   *
*      control break procedure.  Comments are printed in       *
*      lowercase to set them apart from the program            *
*      instructions.                                           *
****************************************************************
ENVIRONMENT DIVISION.
INPUT-OUTPUT SECTION.
FILE-CONTROL.
     SELECT SALES-IN  ASSIGN TO DATA103.
     SELECT PRINT-OUT ASSIGN TO PRINTER.
*
DATA DIVISION.
FILE SECTION.
FD  SALES-IN
    LABEL RECORDS ARE STANDARD.
01  SALES-REC-IN.
     05  DEPT-IN                 PIC XX.
     05  SLSNO-IN                PIC X(5).
     05  AMT-OF-SALES-IN         PIC 9(4)V99.
FD  PRINT-OUT
    LABEL RECORDS ARE OMITTED.
01  PRINT-REC                    PIC X(132).
WORKING-STORAGE SECTION.
01  WORK-AREAS.
     05  ARE-THERE-MORE-RECORDS  PIC X(3)      VALUE 'YES'.
     05  FIRST-RECORD            PIC X(3)      VALUE 'YES'.
     05  WS-HOLD-DEPT            PIC XX        VALUE ZEROS.
     05  WS-DEPT-TOTAL           PIC 9(5)V99   VALUE ZEROS.
     05  WS-LINE-CT              PIC 99        VALUE ZEROS.
     05  WS-PAGE-CT              PIC 99        VALUE ZEROS.
01  HEADING-1.
     05                          PIC X(49)     VALUE SPACES.
     05                          PIC X(21)
        VALUE 'MONTHLY STATUS REPORT'.
     05                          PIC X(9)      VALUE SPACES.
     05                          PIC X(5)      VALUE 'PAGE'.
     05  HL-PAGE-NO-OUT          PIC 99.
     05                          PIC X(46)     VALUE SPACES.
01  HEADING-2.
     05                          PIC X(10)     VALUE SPACES.
     05                          PIC X(10)     VALUE 'DEPT'.
     05                          PIC X(20)
        VALUE 'SALESPERSON NO'.
     05                          PIC X(12)
        VALUE 'AMT OF SALES'.
     05                          PIC X(80)     VALUE SPACES.

01  DETAIL-LINE.
     05                          PIC X(11)     VALUE SPACES.
     05  DL-DEPT-OUT             PIC XX.
     05                          PIC X(9)      VALUE SPACES.
     05  DL-SLSNO-OUT            PIC X(5).
     05                          PIC X(14)     VALUE SPACES.
     05  DL-AMT-OF-SALES-OUT     PIC $$,$$$.99.
     05                          PIC X(82)     VALUE SPACES.
01  GROUP-REC.
     05                          PIC X(60)     VALUE SPACES.
     05                          PIC X(18)
        VALUE 'TOTAL FOR DEPT IS '.
     05  DEPT-TOTAL-OUT          PIC $$$,$$$.99.
     05                          PIC X(44)     VALUE SPACES.
*
```

COBOL 74 Substitutions

For COBOL 74, FILLER must be used instead of a blank field name

Figure 10.3 (continued)

COBOL 74 Substitutions

```
PERFORM 200-DETAIL-RTN
    UNTIL ARE-THERE-MORE-RECORDS = 'NO '.
```

```
IF  DEPT-IN NOT = WS-HOLD-DEPT
    PERFORM 300-CONTROL-BREAK.
```

```
READ SALES-IN
    AT END MOVE 'NO ' TO ARE-THERE-MORE-RECORDS.
```

```
PROCEDURE DIVISION.
*********************************************
*   Controls direction of program logic.   *
*********************************************
100-MAIN-MODULE.
    PERFORM 500-INITIALIZATION-RTN
    PERFORM 400-HEADING-RTN
    PERFORM UNTIL ARE-THERE-MORE-RECORDS = 'NO '
        READ SALES-IN
            AT END
                MOVE 'NO ' TO ARE-THERE-MORE-RECORDS
            NOT AT END
                PERFORM 200-DETAIL-RTN
        END-READ
    END-PERFORM
    PERFORM 600-END-OF-JOB-RTN
    STOP RUN.
*****************************************************************
*  Performed from 100-main-module. Controls department         *
*  break and pagination. The first instruction moves the       *
*  first record's Dept No to the hold area.                    *
*****************************************************************
200-DETAIL-RTN.
    EVALUATE TRUE
        WHEN FIRST-RECORD ='YES'
            MOVE DEPT-IN TO WS-HOLD-DEPT
            MOVE 'NO ' TO FIRST-RECORD
        WHEN DEPT-IN NOT = WS-HOLD-DEPT
            PERFORM 300-CONTROL-BREAK
    END-EVALUATE
    IF WS-LINE-CT > 25
        PERFORM 400-HEADING-RTN
    END-IF
    MOVE DEPT-IN TO DL-DEPT-OUT
    MOVE SLSNO-IN TO DL-SLSNO-OUT
    MOVE AMT-OF-SALES-IN TO DL-AMT-OF-SALES-OUT
    WRITE PRINT-REC FROM DETAIL-LINE
        AFTER ADVANCING 2 LINES
    ADD 1 TO WS-LINE-CT
    ADD AMT-OF-SALES-IN TO WS-DEPT-TOTAL.



*********************************************************
*   Performed from 200-detail-rtn, prints               *
*   department totals, resets control fields & totals.  *
*********************************************************
300-CONTROL-BREAK.
    MOVE WS-DEPT-TOTAL TO DEPT-TOTAL-OUT
    WRITE PRINT-REC FROM GROUP-REC
        AFTER ADVANCING 2 LINES
    ADD 1 TO WS-LINE-CT
    MOVE ZEROS TO WS-DEPT-TOTAL
    MOVE DEPT-IN TO WS-HOLD-DEPT.
*************************************************
*   Performed from 100-main-module 200-detail-rtn  *
*   Prints out headings and resets line counter.   *
*************************************************
400-HEADING-RTN.
    ADD 1 TO WS-PAGE-CT
    MOVE WS-PAGE-CT TO HL-PAGE-NO-OUT
    WRITE PRINT-REC FROM HEADING-1
        AFTER ADVANCING PAGE
    WRITE PRINT-REC FROM HEADING-2
        AFTER ADVANCING 2 LINES
    MOVE ZEROS TO WS-LINE-CT.
```

Figure 10.3 (continued)

```
************************************************
*  Performed from 100-main-module. Opens files.  *
************************************************
500-INITIALIZATION-RTN.
      OPEN INPUT  SALES-IN
            OUTPUT PRINT-OUT.
```

COBOL 74 Substitutions

```
READ SALES-IN
    AT END MOVE 'NO ' TO ARE-THERE-MORE-RECORDS.
MOVE DEPT-IN TO WS-HOLD-DEPT.
```

```
*****************************************************************
*  Performed from 100-main-module, performs end-of-job  *
*  functions and closes files                           *
*****************************************************************
600-END-OF-JOB-RTN.
*****************************************************************
*  The following 2 instructions force the printing of   *
*  the last control total after an at end has occurred  *
*****************************************************************
      MOVE WS-DEPT-TOTAL TO DEPT-TOTAL-OUT
      WRITE PRINT-REC FROM GROUP-REC
            AFTER ADVANCING 2 LINES
      CLOSE SALES-IN
            PRINT-OUT.
```

Figure 10.4 Hierarchy chart for sample control break procedure.

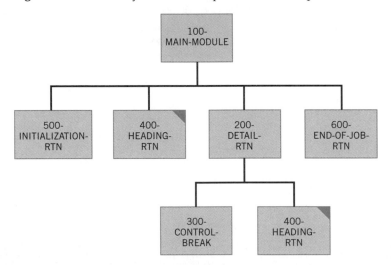

DEBUGGING TIP

Note that a control break procedure is used if records are in sequence by a control field and the number of records in each control field is variable. If we know in advance the number of records in each control field, you may use a PERFORM ... TIMES or a PERFORM ... VARYING instead. In Figure 10.3, if there were always 20 salespeople in each department, we could code the following:

```
200-DETAIL-RTN.
      PERFORM 250-READ-ADD-AND-PRINT 20 TIMES
      PERFORM 300-CONTROL-BREAK.
```

250-READ-ADD-AND-PRINT would read each record, print the record, and add the sales amount to WS-DEPT-TOTAL. 300-CONTROL-BREAK would appear as in Figure 10.3.

PROGRAM REQUIREMENTS FOR CONTROL BREAK PROCESSING

A SINGLE-LEVEL CONTROL BREAK

For each record read for the problem just outlined, we perform two functions:

1. Print a detail line, with the salesperson's number, department number, and amount of sales.
2. Add AMT-OF-SALES-IN to a department total called WS-DEPT-TOTAL.

In addition, a total line ("TOTAL FOR DEPT IS $ZZ,ZZZ.ZZ") will print only *after the first record with the next DEPT is read.* When this total prints, we reinitialize WS-DEPT-TOTAL by setting it back to zero and then process the new input record as in steps 1 and 2 above.

Control break processing depends on whether the current record's DEPT-IN is equal to the one in the hold area called WS-HOLD-DEPT. If they are equal, then detail processing is performed. If they are not equal, then a control break occurs before the current record is processed. This procedure works fine for all records *except* the first one, because for the first record, DEPT-IN will not equal WS-DEPT-HOLD and a control break will occur initially before any records have been processed—unless we modify the coding. The EVALUATE in 200-DETAIL-RTN is used to avoid an initial control break when the first record is read. That is, we establish a WORKING-STORAGE entry called FIRST-RECORD with an initial value of 'YES'. The first time through 200-DETAIL-RTN when DEPT-IN is not equal to WS-HOLD-DEPT but FIRST-RECORD is equal to 'YES', special processing is performed: WS-HOLD-DEPT is set equal to the first record's DEPT-IN, FIRST-RECORD is set to 'NO ', and a control break is avoided. With FIRST-RECORD now at 'NO ', the first WHEN in the EVALUATE will not be executed again. We use this procedure just for the first record to ensure that a control break does not occur initially. FIRST-RECORD is called a flag. Its initial value of 'YES' alerts us to the fact that the first record read needs special handling. This is called a *single-level control break* because we have only one field, DEPT-IN, that triggers the printing of totals.

A Modular, Top-Down MAIN MODULE

The first set of instructions to be executed could be part of an *initialization routine* that is performed *from the main module:*

Pseudocode Excerpt

```
MAIN-MODULE
    PERFORM Initialize-Rtn
    PERFORM Heading-Rtn
    PERFORM UNTIL there is no more input
        READ a Record
            AT END Move 'NO ' to Are-There-More-Records
            NOT AT END PERFORM Detail-Rtn
        END-READ
    END-PERFORM
    :
    :
```

COBOL 85 Program Excerpt

```
100-MAIN-MODULE.
    PERFORM 500-INITIALIZATION-RTN
    PERFORM 400-HEADING-RTN
    PERFORM UNTIL ARE-THERE-MORE-RECORDS
                    = 'NO '
        READ SALES-IN
            AT END
                MOVE 'NO ' TO
                    ARE-THERE-MORE-RECORDS
            NOT AT END
                PERFORM 200-DETAIL-RTN
        END-READ
    END-PERFORM
    :
    :
500-INITIALIZATION-RTN.
    OPEN INPUT  SALES-IN
         OUTPUT PRINT-OUT
```

This modularization makes a program easier to code and modify. The main module is subdivided into subordinate modules that perform initialization functions, heading functions, calculations, and end-of-job procedures. You would begin coding the program with the above three PERFORMs in the main module. Later, after the logic of the program has been mapped out, you could fill in the details in each of these subordinate routines. This top-down approach helps you focus on the program's *design and structure*. Programs written this way are easier to debug. To code the required statements in the main module rather than in a separate paragraph is still correct, but we will focus on this more modular approach.

Remember, pseudocode and COBOL 85 can include either in-line PERFORMs or standard PERFORMs coded as separate modules. We recommend you use the latter if more than a few instructions are required within the PERFORM.

200-DETAIL-RTN

The processing of input records at 200-DETAIL-RTN depends on whether there is a change in control fields, which we call a control break. As noted, for the first record processed, we need to move the DEPT-IN to WS-HOLD-DEPT to initialize it. Then for all subsequent records at 200-DETAIL-RTN we test to see if there is a control break by comparing each DEPT-IN read as input to the department number stored in WS-HOLD-DEPT. We accomplish this with a single EVALUATE statement:

```
EVALUATE TRUE
    WHEN FIRST-RECORD = 'YES'
        MOVE DEPT-IN TO WS-HOLD-DEPT
        MOVE 'NO ' TO FIRST-RECORD
    WHEN DEPT-IN NOT = WS-HOLD-DEPT
        PERFORM 300-CONTROL-BREAK
END-EVALUATE
```

The EVALUATE statement, then, enables us to accomplish two things. First, we use it to determine if the record being processed is the first one and, if so, we initialize WS-HOLD-DEPT with that record's DEPT-IN control field.

To determine if a record is the first one to be processed, we create a special field called FIRST-RECORD, which we initialize at 'YES'. When the EVALUATE is first performed for our initial record it has a value of 'YES' to indicate that no previous record has been processed. We move the DEPT-IN control field to WS-HOLD-DEPT and turn "off" the FIRST-RECORD "flag" or "indicator" field by moving 'NO ' to it. For all subsequent passes through 200-DETAIL-RTN, the EVALUATE will bypass this first record procedure since the condition tested, FIRST-RECORD = 'YES', is false.

We use the EVALUATE also to determine if there is an actual control break.

The first time through the EVALUATE in 200-DETAIL-RTN, WS-HOLD-DEPT and DEPT-IN will be equal because we just moved DEPT-IN to WS-HOLD-DEPT in the main module. For all subsequent passes through 200-DETAIL-RTN, WS-HOLD-DEPT will contain the DEPT-IN of the previous record read. When WS-HOLD-DEPT and DEPT-IN are equal, there is no control break and we perform the following steps:

1. Move input data to a detail line and print, and increment the line counter:

Program Excerpt

```
200-DETAIL-RTN.
    :
    :
    IF  WS-LINE-CT > 25
        PERFORM 400-HEADING-RTN
    END-IF
    MOVE DEPT-IN TO DL-DEPT-OUT
    MOVE SLSNO-IN TO DL-SLSNO-OUT
    MOVE AMT-OF-SALES-IN TO DL-AMT-OF-SALES-OUT
    WRITE PRINT-REC FROM DETAIL-LINE
        AFTER ADVANCING 2 LINES
    ADD 1 TO WS-LINE-CT
    :
    :
```

2. Accumulate a WS-DEPT-TOTAL:

Program Excerpt

```
ADD AMT-OF-SALES-IN TO WS-DEPT-TOTAL.
```

We continue processing input records in this way from the PERFORM UNTIL ... END-PERFORM in the main module until the DEPT-IN on an input record differs from the previous department number stored at WS-HOLD-DEPT. When they are different, a *control break* has occurred. Thus, each time DEPT-IN is not equal to WS-HOLD-DEPT we will perform the 300-CONTROL-BREAK procedure (from 200-DETAIL-RTN), where we print the accumulated department total.

300-CONTROL-BREAK prints a total for the *previous* department. After the total is printed and then reinitialized at zero, we continue by processing the *current* record, which involves (1) printing a detail line and (2) adding AMT-OF-SALES-IN to WS-DEPT-TOTAL.

The full procedure at 200-DETAIL-RTN is as follows:

COBOL 85 Program Excerpt

```
200-DETAIL-RTN.
    EVALUATE TRUE
        WHEN FIRST-RECORD = 'YES'
            MOVE DEPT-IN TO WS-HOLD-DEPT
            MOVE 'NO ' TO FIRST-RECORD
        WHEN DEPT-IN NOT = WS-HOLD-DEPT
            PERFORM 300-CONTROL-BREAK
    END-EVALUATE
    IF  WS-LINE-CT > 25
        PERFORM 400-HEADING-RTN
    END-IF
    MOVE DEPT-IN TO DL-DEPT-OUT
    MOVE SLSNO-IN TO DL-SLSNO-OUT
    MOVE AMT-OF-SALES-IN TO DL-AMT-OF-SALES-OUT
    WRITE PRINT-REC FROM DETAIL-LINE
        AFTER ADVANCING 2 LINES
    ADD 1 TO WS-LINE-CT
    ADD AMT-OF-SALES-IN TO WS-DEPT-TOTAL.
```

If there is a change in DEPT-IN, then 300-CONTROL-BREAK is performed. Regardless of whether a control break procedure is executed or not, the current record is printed and its amount is added to WS-DEPT-TOTAL.

Note that the full program in Figure 10.3 also checks for page overflow with a line-count procedure at 200-DETAIL-RTN. When a field called WS-LINE-CT exceeds 25, we print headings on a new page and reinitialize WS-LINE-CT at zero.

300-CONTROL-BREAK

In the 300-CONTROL-BREAK module we print a summary line after a record is read that has a different department number than the one stored at WS-HOLD-DEPT.

300-CONTROL-BREAK is performed when an input record's DEPT-IN, the control field, differs from the one stored at WS-HOLD-DEPT. As we have seen, WS-HOLD-DEPT contains the previous DEPT-IN. When there is a change in DEPT-IN, we must:

1. Print a line with the department total accumulated for the previous DEPT-IN control group, which is stored in WS-DEPT-TOTAL.

2. Reinitialize WS-DEPT-TOTAL, the control total, so that the next department's total begins at zero before any amounts for the new control group have been accumulated.

3. Move the current DEPT-IN to WS-HOLD-DEPT so that we can compare succeeding input records to this new DEPT-IN control field.

4. Return to 200-DETAIL-RTN and process the current record by printing a detail line and adding the amount to the control total.

Consider the following 300-CONTROL-BREAK routine:

Program Excerpt

```
300-CONTROL-BREAK.
    MOVE WS-DEPT-TOTAL TO DEPT-TOTAL-OUT
    WRITE PRINT-REC FROM GROUP-REC
        AFTER ADVANCING 2 LINES
    ADD 1 TO WS-LINE-CT
    MOVE ZEROS TO WS-DEPT-TOTAL
    MOVE DEPT-IN TO WS-HOLD-DEPT.
```

Since 300-CONTROL-BREAK is performed from 200-DETAIL-RTN, processing continues with the next instruction at 200-DETAIL-RTN. The detail line is then printed and the current amount added to the new total, which has been reset to 0 in the control break module.

Thus far we have seen how 200-DETAIL-RTN is executed. FIRST-RECORD is equal to 'YES' only for the first record in order to move the first DEPT-IN to WS-HOLD-DEPT. After that, when a record is read with the same DEPT-IN as the previous one, we print it and add AMT-OF-SALES-IN to WS-DEPT-TOTAL.

When a change in DEPT-IN occurs, DEPT-IN and WS-HOLD-DEPT will be different and 300-CONTROL-BREAK will be executed. At 300-CONTROL-BREAK, we print a total line, reinitialize WS-DEPT-TOTAL at zero, and store the current DEPT-IN at WS-HOLD-DEPT. We then return to 200-DETAIL-RTN, where we print the current input record and add its amount to a new WS-DEPT-TOTAL. What remains is the processing of the *very last control total* when an end-of-file condition is reached.

Forcing a Control Break When There Are No More Records

Control break printing of totals occurs when a record with a *new* control field is read. The total for the last group of records, then, will have been accumulated when ARE-THERE-MORE-RECORDS is equal to 'NO ', but a control total will not have been printed since there is no subsequent record to trigger a change. Consider the following:

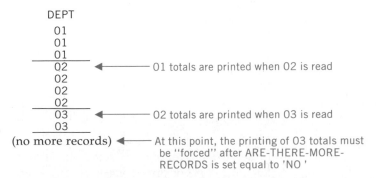

We need to include a procedure to print the 03 totals. In the main module, after 200-DETAIL-RTN has been repeatedly executed and ARE-THERE-MORE-RECORDS is equal to 'NO ', we must return to the statement following the in-line PERFORM UNTIL . . . END-PERFORM and force a printing of this final total:

COBOL 85 Program Excerpt

```
PROCEDURE DIVISION.
100-MAIN-MODULE.
    PERFORM 500-INITIALIZATION-RTN
    PERFORM 400-HEADING-RTN
```

COBOL 74 Substitution

```
PERFORM 200-DETAIL-RTN
   UNTIL ARE-THERE-MORE-RECORDS = 'NO '.
```

```
       { PERFORM UNTIL ARE-THERE-MORE-RECORDS = 'NO '
       {     READ SALES-IN
       {         AT END
       {             MOVE 'NO ' TO ARE-THERE-MORE-RECORDS
       {         NOT AT END
       {             PERFORM 200-DETAIL-RTN
       {     END-READ
       { END-PERFORM
         PERFORM 600-END-OF-JOB-RTN
         STOP RUN.
             :
             :
  600-END-OF-JOB-RTN.
         MOVE WS-DEPT-TOTAL TO DEPT-TOTAL-OUT
         WRITE PRINT-REC FROM GROUP-REC
             AFTER ADVANCING 2 LINES
         CLOSE SALES-IN
               PRINT-OUT.
```

The full program for a single-level control break procedure with detail printing appeared in Figure 10.3. Included in the program is a line-counting procedure that ensures that a maximum of 26 detail lines will print on any given page. After 26 detail lines have printed, 400-HEADING-RTN is performed. Twenty-six detail lines print per page because (1) WS-LINE-CT is initialized at *zero* and (2) a test is made to determine if WS-LINE-CT is *greater than* 25 after a line is printed and 1 is added to WS-LINE-CT.

The hierarchy chart for this program is shown in Figure 10.4. Notice that in the hierarchy chart 400-HEADING-RTN has a corner cut, indicating that it is executed from more than one point in the program.

Thus, the main module is now subdivided into individual modules, each with a specific function. With this organization, the overall structure of the program can be outlined in the main module with all the details left for subordinate modules. This is called *top-down programming*.

REFINEMENTS TO IMPROVE THE QUALITY OF A CONTROL BREAK REPORT

The refinements discussed in this section are illustrated in Figure 10.5, a single-level control break program that incorporates some additional features.

Printing a Final Total

Sometimes, control break processing also requires the printing of a *summary line* containing a final total. This would be printed *after* the last control total is written.

Figure 10.5 Control break program with refinements.

COBOL 85

```
IDENTIFICATION DIVISION.
PROGRAM-ID. SAMPLE.
*****************************************************************
*  This program uses lowercase letters for comments to         *
*       distinguish them from program logic. Program creates   *
*       a departmental sales report using a control break.     *
*****************************************************************
ENVIRONMENT DIVISION.
INPUT-OUTPUT SECTION.
FILE-CONTROL.
    SELECT SALES-IN  ASSIGN TO DATA105.
    SELECT PRINT-OUT ASSIGN TO PRINTER.
*
DATA DIVISION.
FILE SECTION.
```

Figure 10.5 (continued)

```
                                 FD  SALES-IN
                                     LABEL RECORDS ARE STANDARD.
                                 01  SALES-REC-IN.
                                     05  DEPT-IN                PIC XX.
                                     05  SLSNO-IN               PIC X(5).
                                     05  AMT-OF-SALES-IN        PIC 9(4)V99.
                                 FD  PRINT-OUT
                                     LABEL RECORDS ARE OMITTED.
                                 01  PRINT-REC                  PIC X(132).
                                 WORKING-STORAGE SECTION.
                                 01  WORK-AREAS.
                                     05  ARE-THERE-MORE-RECORDS  PIC X(3)    VALUE 'YES'.
                                         88  MORE-RECORDS                    VALUE 'YES'.
                                         88  NO-MORE-RECORDS                 VALUE 'NO '.
                                     05  FIRST-RECORD            PIC X(3)    VALUE 'YES'.
                                     05  WS-HOLD-DEPT            PIC XX      VALUE ZEROS.
                                     05  WS-DEPT-TOTAL           PIC 9(5)V99 VALUE ZEROS.
                                     05  WS-FINAL-TOTAL          PIC 9(6)V99 VALUE ZEROS.
                                     05  WS-LINE-CT              PIC 99      VALUE ZEROS.
                                     05  WS-PAGE-CT              PIC 99      VALUE ZEROS.
```

COBOL 74 Substitutions

For COBOL 74, FILLER must be used instead of a blank field name

```
                                 01  HEADING-1.
                                     05                         PIC X(49)   VALUE SPACES.
                                     05                         PIC X(21)
                                         VALUE 'MONTHLY STATUS REPORT'.
                                     05                         PIC X(9)    VALUE SPACES.
                                     05                         PIC X(5)    VALUE 'PAGE'.
                                     05  HL-PAGE-NO-OUT         PIC 99.
                                     05                         PIC X(46)   VALUE SPACES.
                                 01  HEADING-2.
                                     05                         PIC X(10)   VALUE SPACES.
                                     05                         PIC X(5)    VALUE 'DEPT-'.
                                     05  HL-DEPT-OUT            PIC XX.
                                     05                         PIC X(114)  VALUE SPACES.
                                 01  HEADING-3.
                                     05                         PIC X(17)   VALUE SPACES.
                                     05                         PIC X(14)
                                         VALUE 'SALESPERSON NO'.
                                     05                         PIC X(9)    VALUE SPACES.
                                     05                         PIC X(12)
                                         VALUE 'AMT OF SALES'.
                                     05                         PIC X(80)   VALUE SPACES.
                                 01  DETAIL-LINE.
                                     05                         PIC X(22)   VALUE SPACES.
                                     05  DL-SLSNO-OUT           PIC X(5).
                                     05                         PIC X(14)   VALUE SPACES.
                                     05  DL-AMT-OF-SALES-OUT    PIC $$,$$$.99.
                                     05                         PIC X(82)   VALUE SPACES.
                                 01  DEPT-TOTAL-REC.
                                     05                         PIC X(60)   VALUE SPACES.
                                     05                         PIC X(18)
                                         VALUE 'TOTAL FOR DEPT IS '.
                                     05  DEPT-TOTAL-OUT         PIC $$$,$$$.99.
                                     05                         PIC X(44)   VALUE SPACES.
                                 01  FINAL-TOTAL-REC.
                                     05                         PIC X(39)   VALUE SPACES.
                                     05                         PIC X(25)
                                         VALUE 'THE FINAL TOTAL SALES IS '.
                                     05  FINAL-TOTAL-OUT        PIC $$$$,$$$.99.
                                     05                         PIC XX      VALUE '**'.
                                     05                         PIC X(66)   VALUE SPACES.
                                 01  ERROR-REC.
                                     05                         PIC X(39)   VALUE SPACES.
                                     05                         PIC X(39)
                                         VALUE 'RECORDS OUT OF SEQUENCE--JOB TERMINATED'.
                                     05                         PIC X(54)   VALUE SPACES.
                             *
```

Figure 10.5   (continued)

COBOL 74 Substitutions

```
PERFORM 200-DETAIL-RTN
    UNTIL NO-MORE-RECORDS.
```

```
IF  DEPT-IN NOT = WS-HOLD-DEPT
    PERFORM 300-CONTROL-BREAK.
```

```
READ SALES-IN
    AT END MOVE 'NO ' TO ARE-THERE-MORE-RECORDS.
```

```
PROCEDURE DIVISION.
**********************************************
*  Controls direction of program logic.  *
**********************************************
100-MAIN-MODULE.
    PERFORM 500-INITIALIZATION-RTN
    PERFORM 400-HEADING-RTN
    PERFORM UNTIL NO-MORE-RECORDS
        READ SALES-IN
            AT END
                MOVE 'NO ' TO ARE-THERE-MORE-RECORDS
            NOT AT END
                PERFORM 200-DETAIL-RTN
        END-READ
    END-PERFORM
    PERFORM 600-END-OF-JOB-RTN
    STOP RUN.
**************************************************************
*  Performed from 100-main-module. Controls department  *
*  break and pagination.                                *
**************************************************************
200-DETAIL-RTN.
    EVALUATE TRUE
        WHEN FIRST-RECORD = 'YES'
            MOVE DEPT-IN TO WS-HOLD-DEPT
            MOVE 'NO ' TO FIRST-RECORD
        WHEN DEPT-IN NOT = WS-HOLD-DEPT
            PERFORM 300-CONTROL-BREAK
    END-EVALUATE
    IF WS-LINE-CT > 25
        PERFORM 400-HEADING-RTN
    END-IF
    MOVE SLSNO-IN TO DL-SLSNO-OUT
    MOVE AMT-OF-SALES-IN TO DL-AMT-OF-SALES-OUT
    WRITE PRINT-REC FROM DETAIL-LINE
        AFTER ADVANCING 2 LINES
    ADD 1 TO WS-LINE-CT
    ADD AMT-OF-SALES-IN TO WS-DEPT-TOTAL.

**************************************************************
*  Performed from 200-detail-rtn, 600-end-of-job-rtn.  *
*  Prints department totals, checks for sequence       *
*  error, and zeros ctr.                               *
**************************************************************
300-CONTROL-BREAK.
    MOVE WS-DEPT-TOTAL TO DEPT-TOTAL-OUT
    WRITE PRINT-REC FROM DEPT-TOTAL-REC
        AFTER ADVANCING 2 LINES
    IF  DEPT-IN < WS-HOLD-DEPT
        WRITE PRINT-REC FROM ERROR-REC
            AFTER ADVANCING 2 LINES
        CLOSE SALES-IN PRINT-OUT
        STOP RUN
    END-IF
    ADD WS-DEPT-TOTAL TO WS-FINAL-TOTAL
    IF  MORE-RECORDS
        MOVE ZEROS TO WS-DEPT-TOTAL
        MOVE DEPT-IN TO WS-HOLD-DEPT
        PERFORM 400-HEADING-RTN
    END-IF.
**************************************************************
*  Performed from 100-main-module, 200-detail-rtn,     *
*  300-control-break. Prints out headings after advancing *
*  new page, resets line ctr.                          *
**************************************************************
```

Figure 10.5 (continued)

```
400-HEADING-RTN.
    ADD 1 TO WS-PAGE-CT
    MOVE WS-PAGE-CT TO HL-PAGE-NO-OUT
    MOVE DEPT-IN TO HL-DEPT-OUT
    WRITE PRINT-REC FROM HEADING-1
        AFTER ADVANCING PAGE
    WRITE PRINT-REC FROM HEADING-2
        AFTER ADVANCING 2 LINES
    WRITE PRINT-REC FROM HEADING-3
        AFTER ADVANCING 1 LINES
    MOVE ZEROS TO WS-LINE-CT.
*******************************************************
*   Performed from 100-main-module; opens files     *
*******************************************************
500-INITIALIZATION-RTN.
    OPEN INPUT  SALES-IN
        OUTPUT PRINT-OUT.
```

COBOL 74 Substitutions

```
READ SALES-IN
    AT END MOVE 'NO ' TO ARE-THERE-MORE-RECORDS.
MOVE DEPT-IN TO WS-HOLD-DEPT.
```

```
***********************************************************
*   Performed from 100-main-module, processes last        *
*   control break, prints final totals and closes files   *
***********************************************************
600-END-OF-JOB-RTN.
    PERFORM 300-CONTROL-BREAK
    MOVE WS-FINAL-TOTAL TO FINAL-TOTAL-OUT
    WRITE PRINT-REC FROM FINAL-TOTAL-REC
        AFTER ADVANCING 2 LINES
    CLOSE SALES-IN
        PRINT-OUT.
```

Sample Input Data

```
01 12345 098855
01 12346 353700
01 12347 003499
02 12222 987700
02 12234 008777
03 15645 098000
02 12446 200890
03 12321 198700
04 12999 134330
04 16732 177900
04 16437 493909
04 09878 056499
         └─AMT-OF-SALES-IN
      └─SLSNO-IN
   └─DEPT-IN
```

Sample Output

```
                              MONTHLY STATUS REPORT      PAGE 01

DEPT-01
    SALESPERSON NO    AMT OF SALES

        12345           $988.55

        12346         $3,537.00

        12347           $34.99

                          TOTAL FOR DEPT IS  $4,560.54

                              MONTHLY STATUS REPORT      PAGE 02

DEPT-02
    SALESPERSON NO    AMT OF SALES

        12222         $9,877.00

        12234           $87.77

                          TOTAL FOR DEPT IS  $9,964.77
```

Figure 10.5 (continued)

```
                                      MONTHLY STATUS REPORT        PAGE 03

DEPT-03
        SALESPERSON NO      AMT OF SALES

           15645              $980.00

                                              TOTAL FOR DEPT IS    $980.00

                  RECORDS OUT OF SEQUENCE--JOB TERMINATED
```

Method 1   The final total, which we will call WS-FINAL-TOTAL, may be accumulated by adding AMT-OF-SALES-IN for each record. This may be accomplished by changing the ADD instruction in the 200-DETAIL-RTN of Figure 10.3 to:

```
ADD  AMT-OF-SALES-IN TO WS-DEPT-TOTAL
                        WS-FINAL-TOTAL
```

Method 2   The WS-FINAL-TOTAL may be accumulated, instead, by adding each WS-DEPT-TOTAL to it in 300-CONTROL-BREAK. This means that WS-FINAL-TOTAL would be accumulated, *not* for each detail record, but only when a control break has occurred. This would be accomplished by coding the following before we reinitialize WS-DEPT-TOTAL:

```
300-CONTROL-BREAK.
    .
    .
    ADD WS-DEPT-TOTAL TO WS-FINAL-TOTAL
    MOVE ZEROS TO WS-DEPT-TOTAL
    .
    .
```

The second method is more efficient than the first. Suppose we have 10,000 input records but only 20 department control breaks. If we added AMT-OF-SALES-IN to WS-FINAL-TOTAL for each input record, we would be performing 10,000 additions. If, instead, we added the WS-DEPT-TOTAL to WS-FINAL-TOTAL when each control break occurred, we would be performing the addition only 20 times, once for each control break. Thus, to add WS-DEPT-TOTAL to WS-FINAL-TOTAL at control break time would result in far fewer additions than adding AMT-OF-SALES-IN for each record to WS-FINAL-TOTAL.

Starting a New Page After Each Control Break

It is likely that separate pages of a control break report will be distributed to different users. For example, the pages pertaining to DEPT 01 in the preceding illustration might be transmitted to users in DEPT 01; the pages for DEPT 02 might go to that department, and so on. In this case, it is useful to have *each department's* data begin on a new page. Thus, a control break module would also include a statement to PERFORM the heading routine so that the paper is advanced to a new page when a control break occurs. We would add a PERFORM statement to the 300-CONTROL-BREAK module for printing headings on a new page each time that module is executed.

In this instance, it would be redundant to print the Department Number on each detail line. Rather, it would be better to print it *once* at the beginning of each page as a page heading:

```
                      MONTHLY STATUS REPORT      PAGE 99

         DEPT-99
                      SALESPERSON NO.            AMT OF SALES

                         12345                    $7,326.45
                         18724                    $9,264.55

                            TOTAL FOR DEPT IS    $16,591.00
```

Sequence-Checking or Sorting: To Ensure That Input Data Was Entered in the Correct Sequence

For accurate control break processing, records must be in sequence by the control field. Consider the following sequence error:

```
DEPT
  01
  01
  02  ←── Sequence error—DEPT 02 out of sequence
  01
  01
   .
   .
   .
```

Because it is sometimes possible for sequence errors in the input to occur, it might be useful to check to make certain, after each control break, that the current DEPT-IN is greater than the previous one in WS-HOLD-DEPT. If a current DEPT-IN is less than WS-HOLD-DEPT, then a sequence error has occurred and an error message should be printed. We may also wish to terminate processing in such a case. The software developer along with the user and systems analyst would decide what action to take in case of a sequence error.

One method to ensure that an input file is in the correct sequence is to *sort* it by computer. Computer-sorted files will always be in the correct sequence so that any processing of such files does not require a separate sequence-checking routine. We discuss sorting in detail in Chapter 14.

Once a file has been sorted by a computer, you can be certain that the records in the sorted file are in the correct sequence. Thus, a sequence-checking procedure is only necessary for input files that have been manually sorted (e.g., a file keyed directly onto disk by a data entry operator who is responsible for sorting the file before entering the data).

Executing the Control Break Module from the Main Module After an End-of-File Condition Has Been Met

Consider 600-END-OF-JOB-RTN in Figure 10.3, where we move WS-DEPT-TOTAL TO DEPT-TOTAL-OUT and WRITE the last output line. This MOVE and WRITE could be replaced with the following:

```
PERFORM 300-CONTROL-BREAK
```

Since we wish to "force" a control break at the end of the job, it is best to perform the sequence of steps in the control break routine rather than duplicate the instructions in the end-of-job module. Consider, however, the last statements of the control break procedure, 300-CONTROL-BREAK:

```
ADD 1 TO WS-LINE-CT
MOVE ZEROS TO WS-DEPT-TOTAL
MOVE DEPT-IN TO WS-HOLD-DEPT.
```

Once the last record has been read and processed and an AT END condition has been reached, these instructions are really not necessary. To avoid performing them on an AT END condition, we could code the last sentence of the 300-CONTROL-BREAK module as:

```
IF  ARE-THERE-MORE-RECORDS = 'YES'
    ADD 1 TO WS-LINE-CT
    MOVE ZEROS TO WS-DEPT-TOTAL
    MOVE DEPT-IN TO WS-HOLD-DEPT
END-IF
```

WS-LINE-CT is incremented by one, WS-DEPT-TOTAL is initialized at 0, and the new DEPT-IN is stored *only if* an AT END condition has not been reached. If a condition-name of MORE-RECORDS with a value of 'YES' is included under ARE-THERE-MORE-RECORDS as in Figure 10.5, we can substitute IF MORE-RECORDS for IF ARE-THERE-MORE-RECORDS = 'YES'. If NO-MORE-RECORDS is also used as a condition-name, our main module may be coded with the following:

```
        PERFORM UNTIL NO-MORE-RECORDS
        :
        :
        END-PERFORM
        PERFORM 600-END-OF-JOB-RTN
        :
        :
600-END-OF-JOB-RTN.
        PERFORM 300-CONTROL-BREAK
        :
        :
```

Another reason for testing for more records in 300-CONTROL-BREAK is to print new headings only if an AT END condition has not occurred. Otherwise, the last page of the report would just contain a heading and this would be incorrect.

The full single-level control break program that includes all the preceding refinements is illustrated in Figure 10.5.

SUMMARY OF A SINGLE-LEVEL CONTROL BREAK PROCEDURE

**SUMMARY OF STEPS INVOLVED IN A
SINGLE-LEVEL CONTROL BREAK PROBLEM**

1. For the first record read, move the control field to a hold area in WORKING-STORAGE.

2. For each additional record, as long as the control field is equal to the hold area, execute the detail routine for the input record. This means: Add the appropriate amount to a control total, print the detail record (if desired), and read the next record.

3. If, for a specific record read, the control field is not equal to the hold area:

   Print the control total.
   Initialize the control total field to zero.
   Reinitialize the hold field with the new control field value if ARE-THERE-MORE-RECORDS is not equal to 'NO '.
   Process the detail record as in step 3.
   Print headings on a new page if each control total is to appear on a separate page.

4. After all records have been processed, perform a control break to print the last control group.

SELF-TEST

1. In control break processing, we typically MOVE the control field to _____ after reading the first record (when FIRST-RECORD = 'YES').

2. What processing is performed if an input control field is equal to the control field stored in the hold area?

3. What processing is performed if an input control field is not equal to the control field stored in the hold area?

4. If each control group is to begin on a separate page, we would perform a heading routine at the _____ module.

5. If a final total is required, it is most efficient to accumulate the final total in the _____ module.

6. At the control break module, we must print _____ , initialize _____ at zero, and move _____ .

7. When each individual input record results in the printing of an output line, we call this _____ .

Consider the following output in answering Questions 8–10.

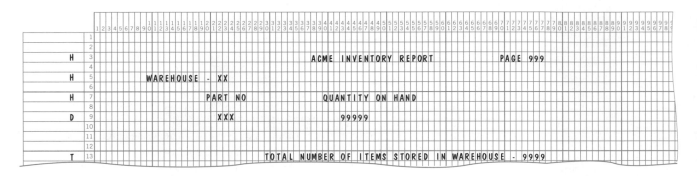

The input consists of 10-character disk records, each with a warehouse field, part number, and quantity on hand. The first three divisions of a COBOL 85 program to meet these requirements appear in Figure 10.6. Use COBOL 85 to code the routines in Questions 8-10.

Figure 10.6 The first three divisions of the program for Questions 8–10.

```
IDENTIFICATION DIVISION.
PROGRAM-ID. FIG106.
*
ENVIRONMENT DIVISION.
INPUT-OUTPUT SECTION.
FILE-CONTROL.
    SELECT INVENTORY-IN ASSIGN TO DISK 'FIG106'.
    SELECT REPORT-OUT ASSIGN TO PRINTER.
*
DATA DIVISION.
FILE SECTION.
FD  INVENTORY-IN
    LABEL RECORDS ARE STANDARD.
01  INV-REC.
    05  WAREHOUSE-IN              PIC XX.
    05  PART-NO-IN                PIC XXX.
    05  QTY-ON-HAND-IN            PIC 9(5).
FD  REPORT-OUT
    LABEL RECORDS ARE OMITTED.
01  REPORT-REC                    PIC X(132).
WORKING-STORAGE SECTION.
01  WS-AREAS.
    05  ARE-THERE-MORE-RECORDS    PIC X(3)    VALUE 'YES'.
        88  NO-MORE-RECORDS                   VALUE 'NO '.
```

Figure 10.6   (continued)

```
                       05   FIRST-RECORD                  PIC X(3)    VALUE 'YES'.
                       05   WS-WH-HOLD                     PIC 99      VALUE ZEROS.
                       05   WS-PART-TOTAL                  PIC 9(4)    VALUE ZEROS.
                       05   WS-LINE-CT                     PIC 99      VALUE ZEROS.
                       05   WS-PAGE-CT                     PIC 999     VALUE ZEROS.
                  01   HEADING-1.
                       05                                  PIC X(37)   VALUE SPACES.
                       05                                  PIC X(21)
                                      VALUE 'ACME INVENTORY REPORT'.
                       05                                  PIC X(11)   VALUE SPACES.
                       05                                  PIC X(5)    VALUE 'PAGE '.
                       05   HL-PAGE-OUT                     PIC ZZZ.
                       05                                  PIC X(55)   VALUE SPACES.
                  01   HEADING-2.
                       05                                  PIC X(9)    VALUE SPACES.
                       05                                  PIC X(12)   VALUE 'WAREHOUSE - '.
                       05   HL-WH-OUT                       PIC XX.
                       05                                  PIC X(109)  VALUE SPACES.
                  01   HEADING-3.
                       05                                  PIC X(19)   VALUE SPACES.
                       05                                  PIC X(20)   VALUE 'PART NO'.
                       05                                  PIC X(83)
                                      VALUE 'QUANTITY ON HAND'.
                  01   DETAIL-LINE.
                       05                                  PIC X(21)   VALUE SPACES.
                       05   DL-PART-NO-OUT                  PIC XXX.
                       05                                  PIC X(18)   VALUE SPACES.
                       05   DL-QTY-ON-HAND-OUT              PIC Z(5).
                       05                                  PIC X(85)   VALUE SPACES.
                  01   TOTAL-LINE.
                       05                                  PIC X(29)   VALUE SPACES.
                       05                                  PIC X(44)
                              VALUE 'TOTAL NUMBER OF ITEMS STORED IN WAREHOUSE - '.
                       05   TL-TOTAL-PARTS-OUT              PIC Z(4).
                       05                                  PIC X(55)   VALUE SPACES.
```

8. Code the main module for the preceding problem definition.

9. Assume that 200-CALC-RTN is a detail routine. Code it.

10. Code the control break routine.

Solutions   1. a hold or WORKING-STORAGE area

2. We add to a control total and print, if detail printing is required.

3. We perform a control break procedure.

4. control break

5. control break

6. the control total; the control total; the input control field to the hold area

7. detail or transaction printing

8. 100-MAIN-MODULE.
```
      OPEN INPUT INVENTORY-IN
           OUTPUT REPORT-OUT
      PERFORM UNTIL NO-MORE-RECORDS
         READ INVENTORY-IN
             AT END
                 MOVE 'NO ' TO ARE-THERE-MORE-RECORDS
             NOT AT END
                 PERFORM 200-CALC-RTN
         END-READ
```

```
                          END-PERFORM
This could be            PERFORM 300-CONTROL-MODULE
coded in an              CLOSE INVENTORY-IN
end-of-job routine              REPORT-IN
                         STOP RUN.
```

9. 200-CALC-RTN.

```
        EVALUATE TRUE
            WHEN FIRST-RECORD = 'YES'
                MOVE DEPT-IN TO WS-HOLD-DEPT
                MOVE WAREHOUSE-IN TO WS-WH-HOLD
                PERFORM 400-HEADING-RTN
                MOVE 'NO ' TO FIRST-RECORD
            WHEN DEPT-IN NOT = WS-HOLD-DEPT
                PERFORM 300-CONTROL-BREAK
        END-EVALUATE
        IF WS-LINE-CT > 25
            PERFORM 400-HEADING-ROUTINE
        END-IF
        MOVE PART-NO-IN TO DL-PART-NO-OUT
        MOVE QTY-ON-HAND-IN TO DL-QTY-ON-HAND-OUT
        WRITE REPORT-REC FROM DETAIL-LINE
            AFTER ADVANCING 2 LINES
        ADD 1 TO WS-PART-TOTAL
        ADD 1 TO WS-LINE-CT.
```

10. 300-CONTROL-MODULE.

```
        MOVE WS-PART-TOTAL TO TL-TOTAL-PARTS-OUT
        WRITE REPORT-REC FROM TOTAL-LINE
            AFTER ADVANCING 4 LINES
        IF  ARE-THERE-MORE-RECORDS IS NOT EQUAL TO 'NO '
            MOVE WAREHOUSE-IN TO WS-WH-HOLD
            MOVE 0 TO WS-PART-TOTAL
            PERFORM 400-HEADING-ROUTINE
        END-IF.
```

MULTIPLE-LEVEL CONTROL BREAKS

You will recall that in order to perform control break processing, a file must be in sequence by the control field. Suppose we require *two* fields as control fields. Consider the following transaction or detail input file:

TRANS-FILE **Record Layout**			
Field	**Size**	**Type**	**No. of Decimal Positions (if Numeric)**
DEPT-IN	2	Alphanumeric	
SLSNO-IN	3	Alphanumeric	
AMT-OF-TRANS-IN	5	Numeric	2

Each time a salesperson makes a sale, a record is created that indicates the department (DEPT-IN), salesperson number (SLSNO-IN), and the amount of the transaction (AMT-OF-TRANS-IN). In this instance, unlike the previous illustration, if a given salesperson has made numerous sales in a given period, there will be *more than one record for that salesperson*. That is, if salesperson 1 in DEPT 01 made three sales, there would be three input records for that salesperson; if salesperson 2 in DEPT 02 made four sales, there would be four records for that salesperson, and so on.

The difference between this input and the input used in the previous example is that in this instance each salesperson is assigned to a specific department and may have numerous records, one for each sale. The input file is sorted so that all salesperson records for DEPT 01 appear first, followed by all salesperson records for DEPT 02, and so on. In addition, all records for the first SLSNO-IN within each DEPT-IN appear *first*, followed by all records for the second SLSNO-IN in that DEPT-IN, and so on. Thus, the following input is a sample of what you might expect:

DEPT-IN	SLSNO-IN		AMT-OF-TRANS-IN
01	004		127.23
01	004	In	100.14
01	006	sequence	027.45
01	006	within	052.23
01	006	DEPT 01	126.27
01	008		223.28
02	003		111.14
02	003	In	027.23
02	003	sequence	119.26
02	005	within	600.45
02	018	DEPT 02	427.33
03	014		100.26

We have, then, *two control fields:* SLSNO-IN is the minor control field and DEPT-IN is the major control field. Records are in sequence by SLSNO-IN within DEPT-IN. Note that for a given SLSNO-IN within a DEPT-IN, there may be numerous transaction records.

Suppose we wish to print a department report as indicated in the Printer Spacing Chart in Figure 10.7.

We accumulate the total amount of sales for each salesperson before printing a line. Thus, if SLSNO-IN 001 in DEPT-IN 01 has made three sales entered in three separate input records, we would print *one* line after all three records have been read and totaled.

No detail printing is required here; rather, the program results in *group printing* of salesperson totals and department totals. The printing of a SLSNO-IN total line is performed after all records for a given SLSNO-IN have been processed. Moreover, printing of a DEPT-IN total and headings for the next DEPT-IN are printed when a DEPT-IN break has occurred.

In our main module, we begin by performing an initialization routine that will open the files and accept a date. Since the second heading line includes a literal 'DEPT' with the actual DEPT number, we *must* print headings *after* the first record is read. We do this in the detail routine. The first instruction in the detail routine tests for FIRST-RECORD. In addition to moving the control fields to hold areas, we print headings when FIRST-RECORD = 'YES'. In the first control break procedure in Figure 10.3, we were able to print a heading *before* the READ, since we did not need the first record's DEPT-IN to print as part of the heading.

First examine the planning tools used to prepare this program. The pseudocode is in Figure 10.8, the hierarchy chart is in Figure 10.9, and the program is in Figure 10.10. For this program we would use a *double-level control break* procedure. We need *two* hold areas for comparison purposes, one for DEPT-IN and one for SLSNO-IN.

Figure 10.7 Printer Spacing Chart for a double-level control break procedure.

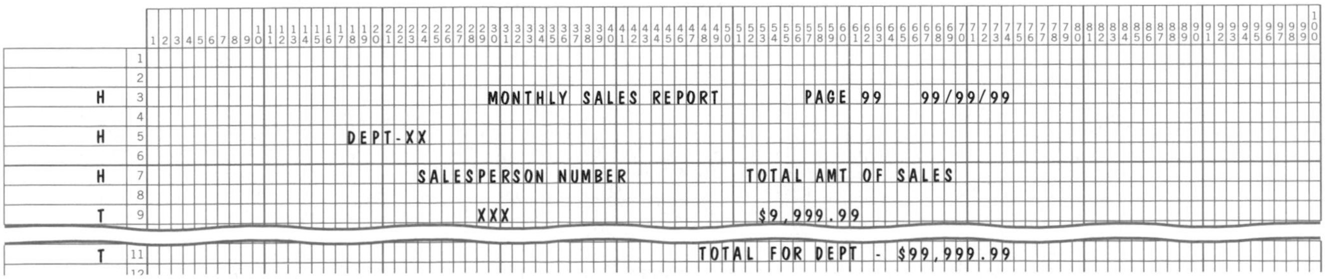

Figure 10.8 Pseudocode for a double-level control break procedure.

MAIN-MODULE
START
    PERFORM Initialize-Rtn
    PERFORM UNTIL there are no more records
        READ a Record
            AT END
                Move 'NO ' to Are-There-More-Records
            NOT AT END
                PERFORM Detail-Rtn
        END-READ
    END-PERFORM
    PERFORM Dept-Control-Break
    PERFORM End-of-Job-Rtn
STOP

INITIALIZE-RTN
    Open the Files
    Accept a Date

DETAIL-RTN
    EVALUATE TRUE
        WHEN First-Record = 'YES'
            Move Slsno-In to Hold Area
            Move Dept-No to Hold Area
            PERFORM Heading-Rtn
            Move 'NO ' to First-Record
        WHEN there is a Dept-No change
            PERFORM Dept-Control-Break
        WHEN there is a Slsno-In change
            PERFORM Sales-Control-Break
    END-EVALUATE
    Add Amt to a Total

HEADING RTN
    Write the Headings

DEPT-CONTROL-BREAK
    PERFORM Sales-Control-Break
    Move Dept-No Total to Output Area
    Write a Record
    Initialize Dept-No Total
    Store Dept-No
    PERFORM Heading-Rtn

SALES-CONTROL-BREAK
    Move Slsno-In Total to Output Area
    Write a Record
    Add Slsno-In Total to Dept-No Total
    Initialize Slsno-In Total
    Store Slsno-In

END-OF-JOB-RTN
    End-of-Job Operations

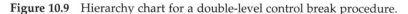

Figure 10.9 Hierarchy chart for a double-level control break procedure.

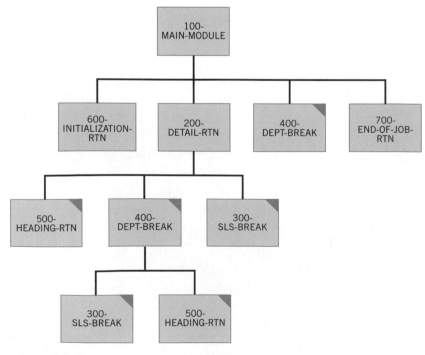

Note: A corner cut is made in the 300-SLS-BREAK, 400-DEPT-BREAK, and 500-HEADING-RTN procedures because they are each performed from two different modules.

Figure 10.10 A double-level control break program.

COBOL 85

```
IDENTIFICATION DIVISION.
PROGRAM-ID. SAMPLE.
**************************************************
*  this program creates a monthly sales report  *
*  by using a double-level control break         *
**************************************************
ENVIRONMENT DIVISION.
INPUT-OUTPUT SECTION.
FILE-CONTROL.
    SELECT TRANS-FILE-IN   ASSIGN TO DATA1010.
    SELECT REPORT-FILE-OUT ASSIGN TO PRINTER.
*
DATA DIVISION.
FILE SECTION.
FD  TRANS-FILE-IN
    LABEL RECORDS ARE STANDARD.
01  TRANS-REC-IN.
    05   DEPT-IN                  PIC XX.
    05   SLSNO-IN                 PIC X(3).
    05   AMT-OF-TRANS-IN          PIC 9(3)V99.
FD  REPORT-FILE-OUT              LABEL RECORDS ARE OMITTED.
01  REPORT-REC-OUT               PIC X(132).
WORKING-STORAGE SECTION.
01  WS-WORK-AREAS.
    05   WS-HOLD-DEPT             PIC XX        VALUE ZEROS.
    05   WS-HOLD-SLSNO            PIC X(3)      VALUE ZEROS.
    05   ARE-THERE-MORE-RECORDS PIC X(3)       VALUE 'YES'.
        88   MORE-RECORDS                       VALUE 'YES'.
        88   NO-MORE-RECORDS                    VALUE 'NO '.
    05   FIRST-RECORD            PIC X(3)       VALUE 'YES'.
    05   WS-SLS-TOTAL            PIC 9(4)V99    VALUE ZEROS.
    05   WS-DEPT-TOTAL           PIC 9(5)V99    VALUE ZEROS.
    05   WS-PAGE-CTR             PIC 99         VALUE ZEROS.
01  WS-DATE.
    05   WS-YR                   PIC 99.
    05   WS-MO                   PIC 99.
    05   WS-DAY                  PIC 99.
01  HL-HEADING1.
    05                           PIC X(29)      VALUE SPACES.
    05                           PIC X(20)
         VALUE 'MONTHLY SALES REPORT'.
    05                           PIC X(7)       VALUE SPACES.
    05                           PIC X(5)       VALUE 'PAGE '.
    05   HL-PAGE                 PIC Z9.
    05                           PIC X(3)       VALUE SPACES.
    05   HL-DATE.
        10   HL-MO               PIC 99.
        10                       PIC X          VALUE '/'.
        10   HL-DAY              PIC 99.
        10                       PIC X          VALUE '/'.
        10   HL-YR               PIC 99.
    05                           PIC X(58)      VALUE SPACES.
01  HL-HEADING2.
    05                           PIC X(17)      VALUE SPACES.
    05                           PIC X(5)       VALUE 'DEPT-'.
    05   HL-DEPT                 PIC XX.
    05                           PIC X(108)     VALUE SPACES.
01  HL-HEADING3.
    05                           PIC X(12)      VALUE SPACES.
    05                           PIC X(19)
         VALUE 'SALESPERSON NUMBER '.
    05                           PIC X(10)      VALUE SPACES.
    05                           PIC X(18)
         VALUE 'TOTAL AMT OF SALES'.
    05                           PIC X(73)      VALUE SPACES.
01  DL-SLS-LINE.
    05                           PIC X(28)      VALUE SPACES.
    05   DL-SLSNO                PIC X(3).
```

COBOL 74 Substitutions
Note: The word FILLER must be used in place of a blank field name with COBOL 74

385

Figure 10.10 (continued)

```
                                    05                          PIC X(21)      VALUE SPACES.
                                    05  DL-SLS-TOTAL            PIC $$,$$$.99.
                                    05                          PIC X(71)      VALUE SPACES.
                                01  DL-DEPT-LINE.
                                    05                          PIC X(47)      VALUE SPACES.
                                    05                          PIC X(17)
                                      VALUE 'TOTAL FOR DEPT - '.
                                    05  DL-DEPT-TOTAL           PIC $$$,$$$.99.
                                    05                          PIC X(58)      VALUE SPACES.
                                *
                                    PROCEDURE DIVISION.
                                ********************************************
                                *   controls direction of program logic  *
                                ********************************************
                                100-MAIN-MODULE.
                                    PERFORM 600-INITIALIZATION-RTN
                                    PERFORM UNTIL NO-MORE-RECORDS
                                        READ TRANS-FILE-IN
                                           AT END
                                               MOVE 'NO ' TO ARE-THERE-MORE-RECORDS
                                           NOT AT END
                                               PERFORM 200-DETAIL-RTN
                                        END-READ
                                    END-PERFORM
                                    PERFORM 400-DEPT-BREAK
                                    PERFORM 700-END-OF-JOB-RTN
                                    STOP RUN.
                                *****************************************************************
                                *   performed from 100-main-module, tests for dept and slsno   *
                                *   breaks. adds transaction amount to ws-sls-total.            *
                                *****************************************************************
                                200-DETAIL-RTN.
                                    EVALUATE TRUE
                                        WHEN FIRST-RECORD = 'YES'
                                            MOVE SLSNO-IN TO WS-HOLD-SLSNO
                                            MOVE DEPT-IN TO WS-HOLD-DEPT
                                            PERFORM 500-HEADING-RTN
                                            MOVE 'NO ' TO FIRST-RECORD
                                        WHEN DEPT-IN NOT = WS-HOLD-DEPT
                                            PERFORM 400-DEPT-BREAK
                                        WHEN SLSNO-IN NOT = WS-HOLD-SLSNO
                                            PERFORM 300-SLS-BREAK
                                    END-EVALUATE
                                    ADD AMT-OF-TRANS-IN TO WS-SLS-TOTAL.
                                ******************************************************
                                *   performed from 200-detail-rtn and 400-dept-break *
                                *   performs slsno break                              *
                                ******************************************************
                                300-SLS-BREAK.
                                    MOVE WS-SLS-TOTAL TO DL-SLS-TOTAL
                                    MOVE WS-HOLD-SLSNO TO DL-SLSNO
                                    WRITE REPORT-REC-OUT FROM DL-SLS-LINE
                                        AFTER ADVANCING 2 LINES
                                    ADD  WS-SLS-TOTAL TO WS-DEPT-TOTAL
                                    IF  MORE-RECORDS
                                        MOVE ZERO TO WS-SLS-TOTAL
                                        MOVE SLSNO-IN TO WS-HOLD-SLSNO
                                    END-IF.
                                ***********************************************************
                                *   performed from 100-main-module and 200-detail-rtn*
                                *   performs department break.                        *
                                ***********************************************************
                                400-DEPT-BREAK.
                                    PERFORM 300-SLS-BREAK
                                    MOVE WS-DEPT-TOTAL TO DL-DEPT-TOTAL
                                    WRITE REPORT-REC-OUT FROM DL-DEPT-LINE
                                        AFTER ADVANCING 2 LINES
                                    IF  MORE-RECORDS
                                        MOVE ZEROS TO WS-DEPT-TOTAL
```

COBOL 74 Substitutions

```
PERFORM 500-HEADING-RTN.
PERFORM 200-DETAIL-RTN
    UNTIL NO-MORE-RECORDS.
```

```
IF  DEPT-IN NOT EQUAL WS-HOLD-DEPT
    PERFORM 400-DEPT-BREAK.
IF  SLSNO-IN NOT EQUAL WS-HOLD-SLSNO
    PERFORM 300-SLS-BREAK.
ADD AMT-OF-TRANS-IN TO WS-SLS-TOTAL.
READ TRANS-FILE-IN
    AT END MOVE 'NO ' TO ARE-THERE-MORE-RECORDS.
```

Figure 10.10 (continued)

```
                                   MOVE DEPT-IN TO WS-HOLD-DEPT
                                   PERFORM 500-HEADING-RTN
                             END-IF.
                        *************************************************************
                        *   performed from 100-main-module and 400-dept-break.    *
                        *   prints out report headings after advancing new page   *
                        *************************************************************
                          500-HEADING-RTN.
                              ADD 1 TO WS-PAGE-CTR
                              MOVE WS-PAGE-CTR TO HL-PAGE
                              MOVE WS-HOLD-DEPT TO HL-DEPT
                              WRITE REPORT-REC-OUT FROM HL-HEADING1
                                  AFTER ADVANCING PAGE
                              WRITE REPORT-REC-OUT FROM HL-HEADING2
                                  AFTER ADVANCING 2 LINES.
                        ************************************************************
                        *   performed from 100-main-module. opens the files      *
                        *   gets the current date from the operating system.      *
                        ************************************************************
                          600-INITIALIZATION-RTN.
                              OPEN INPUT   TRANS-FILE-IN
                                   OUTPUT REPORT-FILE-OUT
                              ACCEPT WS-DATE FROM DATE
                              MOVE WS-YR TO HL-YR
                              MOVE WS-MO TO HL-MO
                              MOVE WS-DAY TO HL-DAY.
```

COBOL 74 Substitutions

```
READ TRANS-FILE-IN
    AT END MOVE 'NO ' TO
        ARE-THERE-MORE-RECORDS.
MOVE SLSNO-IN TO WS-HOLD-SLSNO.
MOVE DEPT-IN TO WS-HOLD-DEPT.
```

```
                        ************************************************************
                        *   performed from 100-main-module.  closes files   *
                        ************************************************************
                          700-END-OF-JOB-RTN.
                              CLOSE TRANS-FILE-IN
                                    REPORT-FILE-OUT.
```

Sample Input Data

```
01 001 34555
01 001 54434
01 002 65544
01 003 76353
02 001 09377
02 001 92838
02 002 09374
02 002 09383
         AMT-OF-TRANS-IN
       SLSNO-IN
     DEPT-IN
```

Sample Output

```
                    MONTHLY SALES REPORT          PAGE   1     01/29/98

        DEPT-01

        SALESPERSON NUMBER            TOTAL AMT OF SALES

                001                        $889.89

                002                        $655.44

                003                        $763.53

                                      TOTAL FOR DEPT -   $2,308.86
                    MONTHLY SALES REPORT          PAGE   2     01/29/98

        DEPT-02

        SALESPERSON NUMBER            TOTAL AMT OF SALES

                001                       $1,022.15

                002                        $187.57

                                      TOTAL FOR DEPT -   $1,209.72
```

Let us begin by considering the main and initialization modules:

Program Excerpt

```
100-MAIN-MODULE.
    PERFORM 600-INITIALIZATION-RTN
    PERFORM UNTIL NO-MORE-RECORDS
        READ TRANS-FILE-IN
            AT END
                MOVE 'NO ' TO ARE-THERE-MORE-RECORDS
            NOT AT END
                PERFORM 200-DETAIL-RTN
        END-READ
    END-PERFORM
    :
    :
600-INITIALIZATION-RTN.
    OPEN INPUT  TRANS-FILE-IN
         OUTPUT REPORT-FILE-OUT
    ACCEPT WS-DATE FROM DATE
    :
    :
```

At 200-DETAIL-RTN we begin with an EVALUATE. For the first record processed, FIRST-RECORD will be equal to 'YES'; then we must move the department number and the salesperson number to a hold area and set FIRST-RECORD to 'NO '. The EVALUATE can also be used to compare the major and minor control fields to their respective hold areas. If there is no change in either DEPT-IN or SLSNO-IN, we add the AMT-OF-TRANS-IN to a WS-SLS-TOTAL . Since there is no detail printing required, there is no WRITE in 200-DETAIL-RTN.

Program Excerpt

```
200-DETAIL-RTN.
    EVALUATE TRUE
        WHEN FIRST-RECORD = 'YES'
            MOVE SLSNO-IN TO WS-HOLD-SLSNO
            MOVE DEPT-IN TO WS-HOLD-DEPT
            PERFORM 500-HEADING-RTN
            MOVE 'NO ' TO FIRST-RECORD
        WHEN DEPT-IN NOT = WS-HOLD-DEPT
            PERFORM 400-DEPT-BREAK
        WHEN SLSNO-IN NOT = WS-HOLD-SLSNO
            PERFORM 300-SLS-BREAK
    END-EVALUATE
    ADD AMT-OF-TRANS-IN TO WS-SLS-TOTAL.
```

Top-down programs begin by developing the overall logic, leaving all details until later on. We will fill in the major-level (or department change) procedure and the minor-level (or salesperson-number change) procedure *after* the main structure is defined. Similarly, in top-down fashion we code the 400-DEPT-BREAK before the 300-SLS-BREAK since DEPT-IN is the major control field.

A major control break routine should begin by forcing a minor control break. That is, the first thing we do when there is a change in DEPT-IN is to process the *last salesperson's total for the previous department*. The assumption here is that each salesperson works for only one department. Thus, the first instruction at 400-DEPT-BREAK would be to PERFORM 300-SLS-BREAK. This not only prints the previous salesperson's total, but it adds that salesperson's total to the department total, initializes WS-SLS-TOTAL at zero, and moves the new SLSNO-IN to WS-HOLD-SLSNO.

After executing 300-SLS-BREAK from 400-DEPT-BREAK, we need to perform the following steps:

1. Print the WS-DEPT-TOTAL.
2. Reinitialize the WS-DEPT-TOTAL at 0.
3. Move DEPT-IN to WS-HOLD-DEPT.

4. Print a heading on a new page.

Thus, 400-DEPT-BREAK would be coded as follows:

Program Excerpt

```
400-DEPT-BREAK.
    PERFORM 300-SLS-BREAK
    MOVE WS-DEPT-TOTAL TO DL-DEPT-TOTAL
    WRITE REPORT-REC-OUT FROM DL-DEPT-LINE AFTER
        ADVANCING 2 LINES
    IF  MORE-RECORDS
        MOVE ZEROS TO WS-DEPT-TOTAL
        MOVE DEPT-IN TO WS-HOLD-DEPT
        PERFORM 500-HEADING-RTN
    END-IF.
```

When there is a change in DEPT-IN, this is considered a *major control break*. Note that we test for a major control break in the EVALUATE statement in 200-DETAIL-RTN *before* we test for a minor control break. Once a condition is met, such as a change in the major control field, the EVALUATE does not continue testing for additional WHEN conditions. This means that the major-level control routine must begin by forcing a minor-level control-break.

Recall that the last statement in 400-DEPT-BREAK ensures that we store the new DEPT-IN and print a heading in all instances *except* after an AT END condition. This is required because 400-DEPT-BREAK will be executed (1) from 200-DETAIL-RTN and (2) from the main module, after all records have been processed, when we must force a break.

Keep in mind that in top-down programs, major procedures are coded before minor ones. The hierarchy chart in Figure 10.9 shows the relationships among these modules.

The last WHEN condition tested in the EVALUATE is the minor-level control break. This test is performed only if FIRST-RECORD is not equal to 'YES' (for all records except the first) and if there is no major control break. When a change in SLSNO-IN occurs even *without* a change in DEPT-IN, this would force a *minor control break* called 300-SLS-BREAK. Thus, when SLSNO-IN is not equal to WS-HOLD-SLSNO (or when a department break has occurred) we do the following:

1. Print the total for the previous SLSNO-IN.
2. Add that total to a WS-DEPT-TOTAL.
3. Initialize the WS-SLS-TOTAL field at zero.
4. Move the new SLSNO-IN to WS-HOLD-SLSNO.

This would be performed as follows:

Program Excerpt

```
300-SLS-BREAK.
    MOVE WS-SLS-TOTAL TO DL-SLS-TOTAL
    MOVE WS-HOLD-SLSNO TO DL-SLSNO
    WRITE REPORT-REC-OUT FROM DL-SLS-LINE
        AFTER ADVANCING 2 LINES
    ADD WS-SLS-TOTAL TO WS-DEPT-TOTAL
    IF  MORE-RECORDS
        MOVE ZERO TO WS-SLS-TOTAL
        MOVE SLSNO-IN TO WS-HOLD-SLSNO
    END-IF.
```

Here, too, the program excerpt tests for more records in 300-SLS-BREAK because we want to avoid moving SLSNO-IN after an AT END condition has been met.

After all records have been read and processed and an AT END condition occurs, control returns to the main module, where an end-of-job routine is executed. As with single-level control break processing, we must *force a break* at this point so that we print the last SLSNO-IN total *and* the last DEPT-IN total. To accomplish this, we perform 400-DEPT-BREAK from the main module after all records have been processed.

In 400-DEPT-BREAK and 300-SLS-BREAK, there are instructions that are to be executed under normal conditions (when there are still records to process), but not on an AT END condition. These instructions are preceded with an IF MORE-RECORDS clause to ensure that they are not executed when an AT END condition occurs:

```
300-SLS-BREAK.
     :
     :
    IF  MORE-RECORDS
        MOVE ZERO TO WS-SLS-TOTAL
        MOVE SLSNO-IN TO WS-HOLD-SLSNO
    END-IF.
400-DEPT-BREAK.
     :
     :
    IF  MORE-RECORDS
        MOVE ZEROS TO WS-DEPT-TOTAL
        MOVE DEPT-IN TO WS-HOLD-DEPT
        PERFORM 500-HEADING-RTN
    END-IF.
```

The full pseudocode and hierarchy chart for this double-level control break procedure are illustrated in Figures 10.8 and 10.9, respectively. The complete program is shown in Figure 10.10.

Note that a program may have any number of control fields. The processing is essentially the same, with major-level control breaks forcing minor-level control breaks.

DEBUGGING TIPS

When programs start to get complex with numerous procedures, programmers sometimes lose sight of the relationships among modules. This is where hierarchy charts can be helpful.

Note, too, that the PIC clause for the control field in the input record must be exactly the same as the PIC clause for the hold area that stores a control field. If they are not the same, the comparison performed to test for a control break could result in errors.

CHAPTER SUMMARY   The following is a COBOL 85 PROCEDURE DIVISION shell that indicates the processing to be performed for any number of control breaks within a program:

```
100-MAIN-MODULE.
    OPEN INPUT INFILE
         OUTPUT OUTFILE
    PERFORM UNTIL NO-MORE-RECORDS
        READ INFILE
            AT END
                MOVE 'NO ' TO ARE-THERE-MORE-RECORDS
            NOT AT END
                PERFORM 200-DETAIL-RTN
        END-READ
    END-PERFORM
    PERFORM (major control break, which forces all other breaks)
    [PERFORM final total routine, if needed]
    CLOSE INFILE
          OUTFILE
    STOP RUN.
200-DETAIL-RTN.
    EVALUATE TRUE
        WHEN FIRST-RECORD = 'YES'
            MOVE (major control field to major hold)
            MOVE (intermediate control field to intermediate hold)
            MOVE (minor control field to minor hold)
            PERFORM 600-HEADING-RTN
            MOVE 'NO ' TO FIRST-RECORD
```

Can be performed in an → initialization routine

Can be performed in an → end-of-job routine

```
           WHEN (major control field) IS NOT EQUAL TO
                   (major control field hold)
               PERFORM (major control break)
           WHEN (intermediate control field) IS NOT EQUAL TO
                   (intermediate control field hold)
               PERFORM (intermediate control break)
           WHEN (minor control field) IS NOT EQUAL TO
                   (minor control field hold)
               PERFORM (minor control break)
       END-EVALUATE
       ADD (to minor total).
       [MOVE and WRITE, if detail printing is required]
300-MAJOR-BREAK.
       PERFORM 400-INTERMEDIATE-BREAK
       MOVE (totals to output) and WRITE (major total line)
       [ADD major total to final total, if final total needed]
       IF  THERE-ARE-MORE-RECORDS
           MOVE 0 TO (major total)
           MOVE (major control field to major hold)
           PERFORM 600-HEADING-RTN
       END-IF.
400-INTERMEDIATE-BREAK.
       PERFORM 500-MINOR-BREAK
       MOVE (totals to output) and WRITE (intermediate total line)
       ADD (intermediate total to major total)
       IF  THERE-ARE-MORE-RECORDS
           MOVE 0 TO (intermediate total)
           MOVE (intermediate control field to intermediate hold area)
       END-IF.
600-HEADING-RTN.
           .
           .
           .
```

Control Break Routines:

> Higher-level breaks force lower-level breaks.
> Appropriate control total line is printed.
> Appropriate control field is initialized.
> Appropriate control total is initialized.

In a control break program, all input records must be in sequence by minor control fields within intermediate control fields within major control fields. If the records are not already in this order, then the file must be *sorted* into the required sequence before it can be processed.

KEY TERMS	Control break processing	Exception report	Summary report
	Control field	Group report	Transaction report
	Detail report		

CHAPTER SELF-TEST   Consider the following problem definition. Each input record includes (1) a warehouse number where the item is stocked and (2) the value of that item's stock on hand.

INVENTORY-FILE **Record Layout**			
Field	**Size**	**Type**	**No. of Decimal Positions (if Numeric)**
WH-NO	2	Alphanumeric	
ITEM-NO	3	Alphanumeric	
QTY-ON-HAND	4	Numeric	0
UNIT-PRICE	5	Numeric	2
TOTAL-VALUE	9	Numeric	2

SUMMARY-LISTING Layout

```
                                          WAREHOUSE REPORT    99/99/99   PAGE 99
     WAREHOUSE NO.    TOTAL NO. OF ITEMS STORED      TOTAL VALUE OF INVENTORY
          XX               Z,ZZZ                    $ZZZ,ZZZ,ZZZ.99
```

1. If the output report consists of each warehouse's total value of inventory, we would call this a _____ report.

2. To print warehouse totals using the format described in this chapter, input data must be in sequence by _____ .

3. Write the main module for this problem.

4. Assuming that you have labeled the detail module 200-DETAIL-RTN, code that module.

5. Assuming that you have labeled the control break module 300-CONTROL-BREAK, code that module.

6. Suppose you have the following sentence in the control break module:

```
300-CONTROL-BREAK.
    :
    IF   THERE-ARE-MORE-RECORDS
        MOVE WH-NO TO WS-WH-HOLD
    END-IF.
```

THERE-ARE-MORE-RECORDS is a condition-name equivalent to the condition IF ARE-THERE-MORE-RECORDS = 'YES'. Why should we check this condition before we move WH-NO to WS-WH-HOLD?

7. Suppose a control break procedure also requires printing of a final total inventory value. We could code the following in 200-DETAIL-RTN:

```
200-DETAIL-RTN.
    :
    ADD TOTAL-VALUE TO WS-WH-TOTAL
                       WS-FINAL-TOTAL
```

Indicate a more efficient way to obtain a final total and explain why it is more efficient.

8. If multiple control breaks are used in a program, the routine for producing the major-level control break would always begin by performing _____ .

9. (T or F) When a double-level control break is used, input data must be in sequence by major fields within minor fields.

10. (T or F) Records must be in sequence by the control field in order for control break processing to be performed correctly.

Solutions

1. control break, group, or summary

2. warehouse number

3. ```
   100-MAIN-MODULE.
       PERFORM 500-INITIALIZATION-RTN
   ```
   ```

COBOL 74 Substitutions

```
MOVE WH-NO TO WS-WH-HOLD.
PERFORM 200-DETAIL-RTN
    UNTIL THERE-ARE-NO-MORE-RECORDS.
```

```
        PERFORM UNTIL THERE-ARE-NO-MORE-RECORDS
            READ-INVENTORY-FILE
                AT END
                    MOVE 'NO ' TO ARE-THERE-MORE-RECORDS
                NOT AT END
                    PERFORM 200-DETAIL-RTN
            END-READ
        END-PERFORM
        PERFORM 600-END-OF-JOB-RTN
        STOP RUN.
    500-INITIALIZATION-RTN.
        OPEN INPUT  INVENTORY-FILE
             OUTPUT SUMMARY-LISTING
        PERFORM 400-HEADING-RTN.
```

```
READ INVENTORY-FILE
    AT END MOVE 'NO ' TO
    ARE-THERE-MORE-RECORDS.
```

$\longrightarrow$

```
    600-END-OF-JOB-RTN.
        PERFORM 300-CONTROL-BREAK
        CLOSE INVENTORY-FILE
              SUMMARY-LISTING.
```

4.
```
    200-DETAIL-RTN.
        EVALUATE TRUE
            WHEN FIRST-RECORD = 'YES'
                MOVE WH-NO TO WS-WH-HOLD
                MOVE 'NO ' TO FIRST-RECORD
            WHEN WH-NO NOT = WS-WH-HOLD
                PERFORM 300-CONTROL-BREAK
        END-EVALUATE
        ADD 1 TO WS-TOTAL-ITEMS
        ADD TOTAL-VALUE TO WS-WH-TOTAL.
```

```
IF  WH-NO IS NOT EQUAL TO
        WS-WH-HOLD
    PERFORM 300-CONTROL-BREAK.
```

```
READ INVENTORY-FILE
    AT END MOVE 'NO ' TO
    ARE-THERE-MORE-RECORDS.
```

$\longrightarrow$

5.
```
    300-CONTROL-BREAK.
        MOVE WS-WH-HOLD TO WH-OUT
        MOVE WS-WH-TOTAL TO TOTAL-OUT
        MOVE WS-TOTAL-ITEMS TO ITEMS-OUT
        WRITE PRINT-REC FROM WH-REC
            AFTER ADVANCING 2 LINES
        IF  THERE-ARE-MORE-RECORDS
            MOVE WH-NO TO WS-WH-HOLD
            MOVE 0 TO WS-TOTAL-ITEMS
            MOVE 0 TO WS-WH-TOTAL
        END-IF.
```

6. At the end of the job, when `THERE-ARE-NO-MORE-RECORDS` (`ARE-THERE-MORE-RECORDS` = `'NO '`), the input record and its fields are no longer available for processing. If we perform `300-CONTROL-BREAK` from `600-END-OF-JOB-RTN` after `THERE-ARE-NO-MORE-RECORDS`, the `MOVE WH-NO TO WS-WH-HOLD` instruction is unnecessary and might even cause a program interrupt.

7. In `300-CONTROL-BREAK`, start with the following instruction:

```
300-CONTROL-BREAK.
    ADD WS-WH-TOTAL TO WS-FINAL-TOTAL
```

Suppose there are 10,000 input records but only 20 warehouses. Adding `TOTAL-VALUE` to `WS-FINAL-TOTAL` in `200-DETAIL-RTN` will perform 10,000 additions, but adding `WS-WH-TOTAL` and `WS-FINAL-TOTAL` at `300-CONTROL-BREAK` will perform only 20 additions. This could save considerable computer time.

8. a minor-level control break

9. F—Sorting is by minor fields within major fields.

10. T

PRACTICE PROGRAM

Consider the following problem definition:

Systems Flowchart

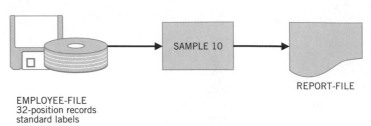

EMPLOYEE-FILE
32-position records
standard labels

SAMPLE 10

REPORT-FILE

EMPLOYEE-FILE **Record Layout**			
Field	**Size**	**Type**	**No. of Decimal Positions (if Numeric)**
IN-DEPT	2	Alphanumeric	
IN-TERR	2	Alphanumeric	
IN-EMPLOYEE-NO	3	Alphanumeric	
IN-EMPLOYEE-NAME	20	Alphanumeric	
IN-ANNUAL-SALARY	5	Numeric	0

REPORT-FILE Printer Spacing Chart

```
           1111111111222222222233333333334444444444555555555566666666667777777777888888888899999999
  1234567890123456789012345678901234567890123456789012345678901234567890123456789012345678901234567889
 1
 2
H 3                      ALPHA DEPARTMENT STORE     PAGE 999
 4
H 5                         PAYROLL FOR THE WEEK OF 99/99/99
 6
H 7      DEPARTMENT - XX
 8
H 9      TERRITORY - XX
10
H11          EMPLOYEE NUMBER          EMPLOYEE NAME          ANNUAL SALARY
12
D13                   XXX          X------------X   $$$,$$$.99
14
D15                   XXX          X------------X   $$$,$$$.99
16
17
T18                   TOTAL SALARY FOR TERRITORY IS    $$$$,$$$.99
19
20
T21                        TOTAL SALARY FOR DEPARTMENT IS $$,$$$,$$$.99
22
23
T24                        TOTAL OF ALL SALARIES IS $$$,$$$,$$$.99
25
F26      END OF REPORT
```

Sample Input Data

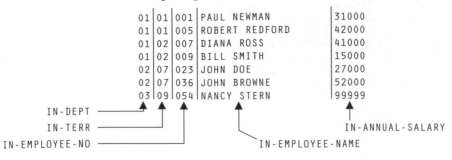

```
01 01 001 PAUL NEWMAN          31000
01 01 005 ROBERT REDFORD       42000
01 02 007 DIANA ROSS           41000
01 02 009 BILL SMITH           15000
02 07 023 JOHN DOE             27000
02 07 036 JOHN BROWNE          52000
03 09 054 NANCY STERN          99999
```

IN-DEPT
IN-TERR
IN-EMPLOYEE-NO
IN-EMPLOYEE-NAME
IN-ANNUAL-SALARY

Sample Output

```
              A L P H A  D E P A R T M E N T  S T O R E    PAGE    1

                     PAYROLL FOR THE WEEK OF 01/29/98

 DEPARTMENT - 01

 TERRITORY - 01

     EMPLOYEE NUMBER          EMPLOYEE NAME          ANNUAL SALARY

           001              PAUL NEWMAN               $31,000.00

           005              ROBERT REDFORD            $42,000.00

            TOTAL SALARY FOR TERRITORY IS    $73,000.00
```

```
              A L P H A  D E P A R T M E N T  S T O R E    PAGE    2

                     PAYROLL FOR THE WEEK OF 01/29/98

 DEPARTMENT - 01

 TERRITORY - 02

     EMPLOYEE NUMBER          EMPLOYEE NAME          ANNUAL SALARY

           007              DIANA ROSS                $41,000.00

           009              BILL SMITH                $15,000.00

            TOTAL SALARY FOR TERRITORY IS    $56,000.00

               TOTAL SALARY FOR DEPARTMENT IS $129,000.00
```

```
              A L P H A  D E P A R T M E N T  S T O R E    PAGE    3

                     PAYROLL FOR THE WEEK OF 01/29/98

 DEPARTMENT - 02

 TERRITORY - 07

     EMPLOYEE NUMBER          EMPLOYEE NAME          ANNUAL SALARY

           023              JOHN DOE                  $27,000.00

           036              JOHN BROWNE               $52,000.00

            TOTAL SALARY FOR TERRITORY IS    $79,000.00

               TOTAL SALARY FOR DEPARTMENT IS  $79,000.00
```

```
          A L P H A   D E P A R T M E N T   S T O R E     PAGE   4

                  PAYROLL FOR THE WEEK OF 01/29/98

     DEPARTMENT - 03

     TERRITORY - 09

          EMPLOYEE NUMBER        EMPLOYEE NAME        ANNUAL SALARY

               054             NANCY STERN             $99,999.00

                    TOTAL SALARY FOR TERRITORY IS    $99,999.00

                         TOTAL SALARY FOR DEPARTMENT IS  $99,999.00

                              TOTAL OF ALL SALARIES IS    $307,999.00

     END OF REPORT
```

Write a program to produce the double-level control break printing described above. Figure 10.11 illustrates the pseudocode and hierarchy chart, and Figure 10.12 shows the program.

Figure 10.11   Pseudocode and hierarchy chart for the Practice Program.

Pseudocode

MAIN-MODULE
    PERFORM Initialize-Rtn
    PERFORM Date-Rtn
    PERFORM UNTIL no more records
        READ a Record
            AT END
                Move 'NO ' to Are-There-More-Records
            NOT AT END
                PERFORM Calc-Rtn
        END-READ
    END-PERFORM
    PERFORM Dept-Break
    PERFORM Total-Rtn
    PERFORM End-of-Job

INITIALIZE-RTN
    Open the Files

DATE-RTN
    Accept Date

HEADING-RTN
    Write the Headings
    Initialize Line Counter

CALC-RTN
    EVALUATE TRUE
        WHEN First-Record = 'YES'
            Move Control Fields to Hold Areas

TERR-BREAK
    Add Terr Total to Dept Total
    Print Terr Total
    Initialize Terr Hold Area, Terr Total

DEPT-BREAK
    PERFORM Terr-Break
    Add Dept Total to Final Total
    Write Dept Total
    Initialize Dept Hold Area, Dept Total

TOTAL-RTN
    Write Final Total

END-OF-JOB
    End-of-Job Operations

Figure 10.11   (continued)

PERFORM Heading-Rtn
Move 'NO ' to First-Record
When Dept Break
PERFORM Dept-Break
WHEN Terr Break
PERFORM Terr-Break
END-EVALUATE
IF   end of page
THEN
PERFORM Heading-Rtn
END-IF
Write Detail Record
Add Amt to Terr Total

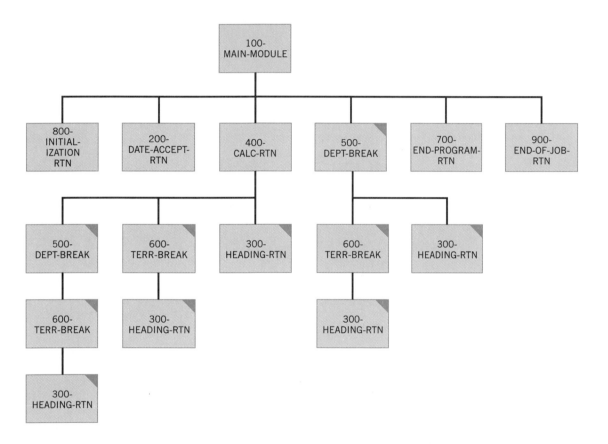

Figure 10.12   Solution to the Practice Program.

COBOL 85

```
IDENTIFICATION DIVISION.
PROGRAM-ID. SAMPLE.
**********************************************************
*  sample          -  this is an example of a double-level  *
*                     control break. the major field is     *
*                     dept and the minor field is terr       *
**********************************************************
ENVIRONMENT DIVISION.
INPUT-OUTPUT SECTION.
FILE-CONTROL.
```

Figure 10.12   (continued)

```
                                        SELECT IN-EMPLOYEE-FILE ASSIGN TO DATA1012.
                                        SELECT OUT-REPORT-FILE  ASSIGN TO PRINTER.
                                   *
                                   DATA DIVISION.
                                   FILE SECTION.
                                   FD  IN-EMPLOYEE-FILE
                                       LABEL RECORDS ARE STANDARD.
                                   01  IN-EMPLOYEE-REC.
                                       05  IN-DEPT              PIC XX.
                                       05  IN-TERR              PIC XX.
                                       05  IN-EMPLOYEE-NO       PIC X(3).
                                       05  IN-EMPLOYEE-NAME     PIC X(20).
                                       05  IN-ANNUAL-SALARY     PIC 9(5).
                                   FD  OUT-REPORT-FILE
                                       LABEL RECORDS ARE OMITTED.
                                   01  OUT-REPORT-REC           PIC X(132).
                                   WORKING-STORAGE SECTION.
                                   01  WS-WORK-AREAS.
                                       05  ARE-THERE-MORE-RECORDS PIC X(3)     VALUE 'YES'.
                                           88  MORE-RECORDS                    VALUE 'YES'.
                                           88  NO-MORE-RECORDS                 VALUE 'NO '.
                                       05  FIRST-RECORD         PIC X(3)     VALUE 'YES'.
                                       05  WS-LINE-CTR          PIC 99       VALUE ZEROS.
                                       05  WS-PAGE-CTR          PIC 999      VALUE ZEROS.
                                       05  WS-DEPT-SALARY       PIC 9(7)V99  VALUE ZEROS.
                                       05  WS-TERR-SALARY       PIC 9(6)V99  VALUE ZEROS.
                                       05  WS-DEPT-HOLD         PIC XX       VALUE ZEROS.
                                       05  WS-TERR-HOLD         PIC XX       VALUE ZEROS.
                                       05  WS-TOTAL-SALARY      PIC 9(8)V99  VALUE ZEROS.
                                       05  WS-T-DATE.
                                           10  WS-IN-YR         PIC XX.
                                           10  WS-IN-MO         PIC XX.
                                           10  WS-IN-DAY        PIC XX.
                                   01  HL-HEADING1.
                                       05                       PIC X(23)    VALUE SPACES.
                                       05                       PIC X(44)
                                           VALUE 'A L P H A   D E P A R T M E N T   S T O R E'.
                                       05                       PIC X(5)
                                           VALUE 'PAGE '.
                                       05  HL-OUT-PAGE          PIC ZZ9.
                                       05                       PIC X(57)    VALUE SPACES.
                                    01  HL-HEADING2.
                                       05                       PIC X(29)    VALUE SPACES.
                                       05                       PIC X(24)
                                           VALUE 'PAYROLL FOR THE WEEK OF'.
                                       05  HL-TODAYS-DATE.
                                           10  HL-OUT-MO        PIC XX.
                                           10                   PIC X        VALUE '/'.
                                           10  HL-OUT DAY       PIC XX.
                                           10                   PIC X        VALUE '/'.
                                           10  HL-OUT-YR        PIC XX.
                                       05                       PIC X(71)    VALUE SPACES.
                                    01  HL-HEADING3.
                                       05                       PIC X(17)    VALUE SPACES.
                                       05                       PIC X(15)
                                           VALUE 'EMPLOYEE NUMBER'.
                                       05                       PIC X(9)     VALUE SPACES.
                                       05                       PIC X(13)
                                           VALUE 'EMPLOYEE NAME'.
                                       05                       PIC X(8)     VALUE SPACES.
                                       05                       PIC X(13)
                                           VALUE 'ANNUAL SALARY'.
                                       05                       PIC X(57)    VALUE SPACES.
                                    01  DL-SALARY-LINE.
                                       05                       PIC X(28)    VALUE SPACES.
                                       05  DL-OUT-EMPLOYEE-NO   PIC X(3).
                                       05                       PIC X(10)    VALUE SPACES.
```

COBOL 74 Substitutions

For COBOL 74, FILLER must be used instead of a blank field name

Figure 10.12 (continued)

```
                          05  DL-OUT-EMPLOYEE-NAME    PIC X(20).
                          05                          PIC XX          VALUE SPACES.
                          05  DL-OUT-ANNUAL-SALARY    PIC $$$,$$$.99.
                          05                          PIC X(59)       VALUE SPACES.
                      01  DL-TERRITORY-TOTAL-LINE.
                          05                          PIC X(28)       VALUE SPACES.
                          05                          PIC X(34)
                            VALUE 'TOTAL SALARY FOR TERRITORY IS '.
                          05  DL-OUT-TERR-SALARY      PIC $$$$,$$$.99.
                          05                          PIC X(59)       VALUE SPACES.
                      01  DL-DEPARTMENT-TOTAL-LINE.
                          05                          PIC X(37)       VALUE SPACES.
                          05                          PIC X(31)
                            VALUE 'TOTAL SALARY FOR DEPARTMENT IS '.
                          05  DL-OUT-DEPT-SALARY      PIC $$,$$$,$$$.99.
                          05                          PIC X(51)       VALUE SPACES.
                      01  DL-FINAL-TOTAL-LINE.
                          05                          PIC X(40)       VALUE SPACES.
                          05                          PIC X(25)
                            VALUE 'TOTAL OF ALL SALARIES IS '.
                          05  DL-OUT-TOT-ANN-SALARY   PIC $$$,$$$,$$$.99.
                          05                          PIC X(53)       VALUE SPACES.
                      01  DL-DEPT-HEADING.
                          05                          PIC X(14)       VALUE SPACES.
                          05                          PIC X(13)
                            VALUE 'DEPARTMENT - '.
                          05  DL-OUT-DEPT             PIC XX.
                          05                          PIC X(103)      VALUE SPACES.
                      01  DL-TERR-HEADING.
                          05                          PIC X(14)       VALUE SPACES.
                          05                          PIC X(12)
                            VALUE 'TERRITORY - '.
                          05  DL-OUT-TERR             PIC XX.
                          05                          PIC X(104)      VALUE SPACES.
                      01  HL-HEADING-FINAL.
                          05                          PIC X(9)        VALUE SPACES.
                          05                          PIC X(13)
                            VALUE 'END OF REPORT'.
                          05                          PIC X(110)      VALUE SPACES.
                      *
                      PROCEDURE DIVISION.
                      *******************************************************
                      *  100-main-module - controls direction of program logic *
                      *******************************************************
                      100-MAIN-MODULE.
                          PERFORM 800-INITIALIZATION-RTN
                          PERFORM 200-DATE-ACCEPT-RTN
                          PERFORM UNTIL NO-MORE-RECORDS
                            READ IN-EMPLOYEE-FILE
                                AT END
                                    MOVE 'NO ' TO ARE-THERE-MORE-RECORDS
                                NOT AT END
                                    PERFORM 400-CALC-RTN
                            END-READ
                          END-PERFORM
                          PERFORM 500-DEPT-BREAK
                          PERFORM 700-END-PROGRAM-RTN
                          PERFORM 900-END-OF-JOB-RTN
                          STOP RUN.
                      *******************************************************
                      *  200-date-accept-rtn - performed from 100-main-module.  *
                      *      gets the current date from the operating system.   *
                      *******************************************************
                      200-DATE-ACCEPT-RTN
                          ACCEPT WS-T-DATE FROM DATE
                          MOVE WS-IN-MO TO HL-OUT-MO
```

COBOL 74 Substitutions

```
PERFORM 300-HEADING-RTN.
PERFORM 400-CALC-RTN
    UNTIL NO-MORE-RECORDS.
```

Figure 10.12   (continued)

```
                                 MOVE WS-IN-YR TO HL-OUT-YR
                                 MOVE WS-IN-DAY TO HL-OUT-DAY.
                        **********************************************************
                        *   300-heading-rtn - performed from                     *
                        *                     400-calc-rtn 500-dept-break and     *
                        *                     600-terr-break, prints the headings *
                        *                     on a new page.                      *
                        **********************************************************
                         300-HEADING-RTN.
                             ADD 1 TO WS-PAGE-CTR
                             MOVE WS-PAGE-CTR TO HL-OUT-PAGE
                             MOVE WS-TERR-HOLD TO DL-OUT-TERR
                             MOVE WS-DEPT-HOLD TO DL-OUT-DEPT
                             MOVE 0 TO WS-LINE-CTR
                             WRITE OUT-REPORT-REC FROM HL-HEADING1
                                 AFTER ADVANCING PAGE
                             WRITE OUT-REPORT-REC FROM HL-HEADING2
                                 AFTER ADVANCING 2 LINES
                             WRITE OUT-REPORT-REC FROM DL-DEPT-HEADING
                                 AFTER ADVANCING 2 LINES
                             WRITE OUT-REPORT-REC FROM DL-TERR-HEADING
                                 AFTER ADVANCING 2 LINES
                             WRITE OUT-REPORT-REC FROM HL-HEADING3
                                 AFTER ADVANCING 2 LINES.
                        *****************************************************
                        *   400-calc-rtn - performed from 100-main-module   *
                        *                  controls terr and dept breaks     *
                        *                  prints out employee information   *
                        *****************************************************
                         400-CALC-RTN.
                             EVALUATE TRUE
                                 WHEN FIRST-RECORD = 'YES'
                                     MOVE IN-DEPT TO WS-DEPT-HOLD
                                     MOVE IN-TERR TO WS-TERR-HOLD
                                     PERFORM 300-HEADING-RTN
                                     MOVE 'NO ' TO FIRST-RECORD
                                 WHEN IN-DEPT NOT = WS-DEPT-HOLD
                                     PERFORM 500-DEPT-BREAK
                                 WHEN IN-TERR NOT = WS-TERR-HOLD
                                     PERFORM 600-TERR-BREAK
                             END-EVALUATE
                             IF WS-LINE-CTR IS GREATER THAN 25
                                 PERFORM 300-HEADING-RTN
                             END-IF
                             MOVE IN-EMPLOYEE-NO TO DL-OUT-EMPLOYEE-NO
                             MOVE IN-EMPLOYEE-NAME TO DL-OUT-EMPLOYEE-NAME
                             MOVE IN-ANNUAL-SALARY TO DL-OUT-ANNUAL-SALARY
                             WRITE OUT-REPORT-REC FROM DL-SALARY-LINE
                                 AFTER ADVANCING 2 LINES
                             ADD IN-ANNUAL-SALARY TO WS-TERR-SALARY
                             ADD 1 TO WS-LINE-CTR.


                        **********************************************************
                        *   500-dept-break - performed from 100-main-module and  *
                        *                    400-calc-rtn. forces a terr break then *
                        *                    prints dept totals                  *
                        **********************************************************
                         500-DEPT-BREAK.
                             PERFORM 600-TERR-BREAK
                             ADD WS-DEPT-SALARY TO WS-TOTAL-SALARY
                             MOVE WS-DEPT-SALARY TO DL-OUT-DEPT-SALARY
                             WRITE OUT-REPORT-REC FROM DL-DEPARTMENT-TOTAL-LINE
                                 AFTER ADVANCING 3 LINES
                             ADD 1 TO WS-LINE-CTR
```

COBOL 74 Substitutions

```
IF  IN-DEPT NOT EQUAL TO WS-DEPT-HOLD
    PERFORM 500-DEPT-BREAK.
IF  IN-TERR NOT EQUAL TO WS-TERR-HOLD
    PERFORM 600-TERR-BREAK.
```

```
READ IN-EMPLOYEE-FILE
    AT END MOVE 'NO ' TO
        ARE-THERE-MORE-RECORDS.
```

Figure 10.12   (continued)

```
        IF  MORE-RECORDS
            MOVE ZEROS TO WS-DEPT-SALARY
            MOVE IN-DEPT TO WS-DEPT-HOLD
            PERFORM 300-HEADING-RTN
        END-IF.
*********************************************************
*   600-terr-break - performed from 400-calc-rtn and   *
*                    500-dept-break. controls terr     *
*                    break and prints terr totals      *
*********************************************************
    600-TERR-BREAK.
        ADD WS-TERR-SALARY TO WS-DEPT-SALARY
        MOVE WS-TERR-SALARY TO DL-OUT-TERR-SALARY
        WRITE OUT-REPORT-REC FROM DL-TERRITORY-TOTAL-LINE
            AFTER ADVANCING 3 LINES
        ADD 1 TO WS-LINE-CTR
        IF  MORE-RECORDS
            MOVE IN-TERR TO WS-TERR-HOLD
            MOVE ZEROS TO WS-TERR-SALARY
        END-IF
        IF MORE-RECORDS AND IN-DEPT IS EQUAL TO WS-DEPT-HOLD
                PERFORM 300-HEADING-RTN
        END-IF.
***********************************************************
*   700-end-program-rtn - performed from 100-main-module  *
*                         prints total of all salaries    *
***********************************************************
    700-END-PROGRAM-RTN.
        MOVE WS-TOTAL-SALARY TO DL-OUT-TOT-ANN-SALARY
        WRITE OUT-REPORT-REC FROM DL-FINAL-TOTAL-LINE
            AFTER ADVANCING 3 LINES
        WRITE OUT-REPORT-REC FROM HL-HEADING-FINAL
            AFTER ADVANCING 2 LINES.
***********************************************************
*   800-initialization-rtn - performed from 100-main-module *
*                            controls opening of files      *
***********************************************************
    800-INITIALIZATION-RTN.
        OPEN INPUT   IN-EMPLOYEE-FILE
             OUTPUT OUT-REPORT-FILE.
```

COBOL 74 Substitutions

```
READ IN-EMPLOYEE-FILE
    AT END MOVE 'NO ' TO
        ARE-THERE-MORE-RECORDS.
MOVE IN-DEPT TO WS-DEPT-HOLD.
MOVE IN-TERR TO WS-TERR-HOLD.
```

```
***********************************************************
*   900-end-of-job-rtn - performed from 100-main-module  *
*                        closes the files                *
***********************************************************
    900-END-OF-JOB-RTN.
        CLOSE IN-EMPLOYEE-FILE
              OUT-REPORT-FILE.
```

REVIEW QUESTIONS

True-False
Questions

_____ 1. In order to execute a control break program, input data must be in sequence by the control fields.

_____ 2. In the main module of a control break program, we always perform a heading routine before reading the first record.

_____ 3. Before a detail or calculation routine is executed from them a in module of a control break program, the control fields must be moved to hold areas in WORKING-STORAGE.

_____ 4. If there are numerous control breaks to be performed, major level breaks should force minor level breaks.

_____ 5. After a control break has occurred, the hold field should be initialized to zero.

_____ 6. The detail module of a control break program always has a WRITE statement.

_____ 7. One method for minimizing errors in a control break program is to perform a sequence-checking routine where you check that the control fields have been sorted properly.

_____ 8. The control break module must always clear the total fields to zero.

_____ 9. The control break module typically includes a WRITE statement.

_____ 10. A maximum of two levels of control breaks are permitted in a control break program.

DEBUGGING EXERCISES

Consider the following coding:

```
PROCEDURE DIVISION.
100-MAIN-MODULE.
    OPEN INPUT  TRANS-FILE
         OUTPUT PRINT-FILE
    PERFORM UNTIL THERE-ARE-NO-MORE-RECORDS
        READ TRANS-FILE
            AT END
                MOVE 'NO ' TO ARE-THERE-MORE-RECORDS
            NOT AT END
                MOVE ACCT-NO-IN TO WS-HOLD-ACCT
                PERFORM 200-DETAIL-RUN
        END-READ
    END-PERFORM
    CLOSE TRANS-FILE
          PRINT-FILE
    STOP RUN.
200-DETAIL-RTN.
    PERFORM 300-ADD-IT-UP
        UNTIL ACCT-NO IS NOT EQUAL TO WS-HOLD-ACCT OR
            THERE-ARE-NO-MORE-RECORDS
    MOVE WS-HOLD-ACCT TO ACCT-OUT
    MOVE WS-TOTAL TO TOTAL-OUT
    WRITE PRINT-REC FROM OUT-REC
    :
    :
300-ADD-IT-UP.
    ADD AMT TO WS-TOTAL
    READ TRANS-FILE
        AT END MOVE 'NO ' TO ARE-THERE-MORE-RECORDS
    END-READ.
```

1. Is the overall logical structure correct?

2. After executing the in-line PERFORM UNTIL . . . in the main module, should there be a PERFORM to print the last control group? Explain your answer.

3. There are two instructions missing from 200-DETAIL-RTN that will result in logic errors. Insert them.

4. Suppose 200-DETAIL-RTN had a READ as its last instruction. How would this affect processing?

5. Suppose we omitted the MOVE ACCT-NO-IN TO WS-HOLD-ACCT statement from the main module. Would this have any substantial effect on the processing? Explain your answer.

PROGRAMMING ASSIGNMENTS

1. Write a program to print a sales total from disk records for each of five transaction days. The problem definition is shown in Figure 10.13.

   Notes:

   a. There is a disk record for each sale made by a salesperson; thus there are an undetermined number of input records.

   b. Records are in sequence by day number, which ranges from 1 to 5 (Mon–Fri).

Figure 10.13 Problem definition for Programming Assignment 1.

Systems Flowchart

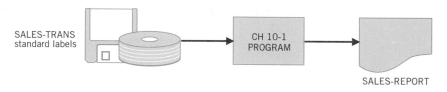

SALES-TRANS
standard labels

CH 10-1
PROGRAM

SALES-REPORT

SALES-TRANS Record Layout			
Field	Size	Type	No. of Decimal Positions (if Numeric)
DAY-NO	1	Alphanumeric	
SALESPERSON-NO	3	Alphanumeric	
SALES-AMOUNT	5	Numeric	2

SALES-REPORT Printer Spacing Chart

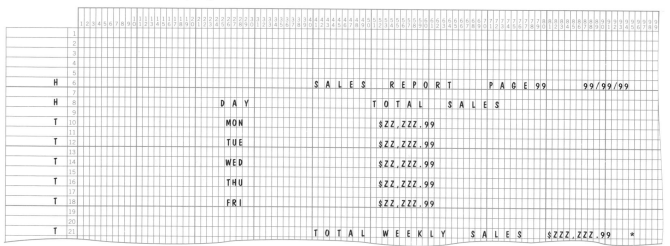

2. Write a program to print total salaries by territory number. The problem definition is shown in Figure 10.14.

   Notes:

   a. The input records are in sequence by territory number.

   b. Print the total salaries for each territory. At the end of the report, print the total salaries for the entire company.

   c. There are nine territories: 01–09.

Figure 10.14 Problem definition for Programming Assignment 2.

Systems Flowchart

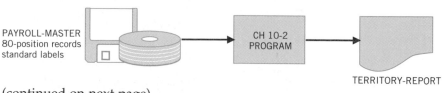

PAYROLL-MASTER
80-position records
standard labels

CH 10-2
PROGRAM

TERRITORY-REPORT

(continued on next page)

Figure 10.14   (continued)

PAYROLL-MASTER Record Layout			
Field	**Size**	**Type**	**No. of Decimal Positions (if Numeric)**
EMPLOYEE-NO	5	Alphanumeric	
EMPLOYEE-NAME	20	Alphanumeric	
TERRITORY-NO	2	Alphanumeric	
Unused	2	Alphanumeric	
ANNUAL-SALARY	6	Numeric	0
Unused	45	Alphanumeric	

TERRITORY-REPORT Printer Spacing Chart

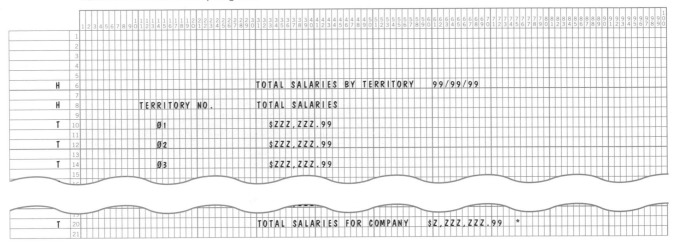

```
H  6                              TOTAL SALARIES BY TERRITORY    99/99/99
H  8        TERRITORY NO.         TOTAL SALARIES
T 10             01                   $ZZZ,ZZZ.99
T 12             02                   $ZZZ,ZZZ.99
T 14             03                   $ZZZ,ZZZ.99
T 20                              TOTAL SALARIES FOR COMPANY  $Z,ZZZ,ZZZ.99  *
```

3. Write a program to print a population total for each state. The problem definition is shown in Figure 10.15. Records are in sequence by county within state.

Figure 10.15   Problem definition for Programming Assignment 3.

Systems Flowchart

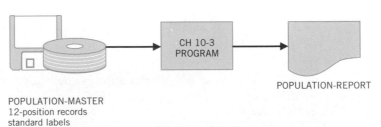

POPULATION-MASTER
12-position records
standard labels

CH 10-3
PROGRAM

POPULATION-REPORT

POPULATION-MASTER Record Layout			
Field	**Size**	**Type**	**No. of Decimal Positions (if Numeric)**
STATE-NO	2	Alphanumeric	
COUNTY-NO	2	Alphanumeric	
DISTRICT-NO	2	Alphanumeric	
POPULATION	6	Numeric	0

Figure 10.15 (continued)

POPULATION-REPORT Printer Spacing Chart

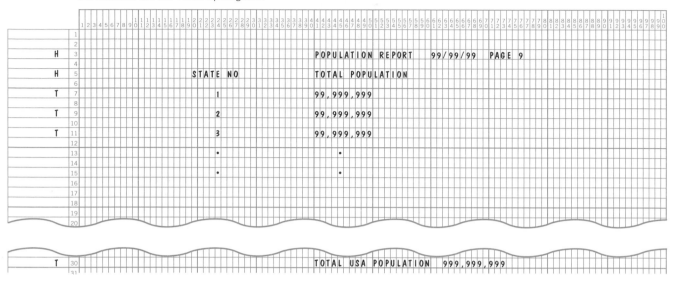

4. Pass-Em State College has student records with the following format:

Alternate Record Layout Form

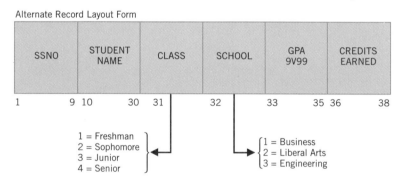

SSNO	STUDENT NAME	CLASS	SCHOOL	GPA 9V99	CREDITS EARNED
1 9	10 30	31	32	33 35	36 38

CLASS:
1 = Freshman
2 = Sophomore
3 = Junior
4 = Senior

SCHOOL:
1 = Business
2 = Liberal Arts
3 = Engineering

Assume records are in sequence by class within school.

Print a summary report of the average GPA for each class within each school. Print each school's statistics on a separate page:

Example:

```
SCHOOL: BUSINESS

   CLASS          AVERAGE GPA

FRESHMAN             9.99
SOPHOMORE            9.99
JUNIOR               9.99
SENIOR               9.99
```

5. The Bon Voyage Travel Agency has a client file with the following data:

Alternate Record Layout Form

BOOKING TYPE	CLIENT NO	CLIENT NAME	CLIENT ADDRESS	COST OF TRIP 99999V99
1	2 4	5 20	21 40	41 47

1 = Cruise
2 = Air-Independent
3 = Air-Tour
4 = Other

The data is in sequence by booking type. Print the average cost of a trip for each booking type.

6. **Interactive Processing.** Write a program to ACCEPT transaction data interactively, where all sales transactions for DEPT 01 are followed by sales transactions for DEPT 02, and so on. Print each department's total sales. Design the dialog between the user and the computer yourself.

7. **Maintenance Program.** Modify the Practice Program in this chapter so that every time a total salary is printed, the average salary is also printed for the corresponding territory or department. In addition, print the average salary for the entire company at the end of the report.

CHAPTER 11

Data Validation

▉ OBJECTIVES

To familiarize you with

1. The types of input errors that may occur.
2. The techniques used to validate input data.
3. The actions that can be taken when input errors are detected.

▉ CONTENTS

AVOIDING LOGIC ERRORS BY VALIDATING INPUT

Everyone is aware of horror stories resulting from computer errors. Newspapers often provide accounts of people who erroneously receive computerized bills or checks for absurd amounts. Although the blame is usually placed on the computer itself, such errors almost always occur because of either *program errors* or *input errors*. Debugging a program means eliminating all types of errors.

In Chapter 5 we discussed in detail program errors and methods used to eliminate them. Program errors fall into two categories: syntax errors and logic errors. Syntax errors are listed by the compiler and must typically be corrected before a program can be executed. These consist primarily of rule violations.

Logic errors are more difficult to find. These may result from using the wrong instruction or the wrong sequence of instructions. Logic errors also include run-time errors, which cause program interrupts. Attempting to divide by zero, for example, will cause a run-time error. To eliminate logic errors, the programmer must develop comprehensive test data that includes all conditions and types of data tested for in the program. The programmer must also be very careful to manually check computer-produced results for accuracy.

--- DEBUGGING TIPS ---

1. For every IF statement in a program, be sure your test data includes multiple instances when the condition is met and multiple instances when the condition is not met.

2. If you use a line counter to determine when a new page is to print, be sure you include enough test data to print several pages. The line counter routine could, for example, work for page 2 but might not properly change the counter, so that page 3 is not printed correctly.

3. If you have ON SIZE ERROR routines, be sure your test data includes instances that would produce size errors.

4. If logic errors occur that are difficult to find, insert DISPLAY statements at various places in your program during test runs to see what intermediate results are being produced. This will help isolate the errors. Remember to eliminate these DISPLAY statements after the program has been fully debugged.

5. When producing disk output, always get a copy of the resulting file and check it for accuracy. You can use a DISPLAY prior to the WRITE to view the output on the screen, or you can use an operating system command such as PRINT or TYPE to obtain a printout of the file after the program has been executed.

6. Pay particular attention to loop counts so that a series of instructions is performed the exact number of times that is required. Often, looping is performed one time more or less than desired. This can happen if counters are set to 0 initially (when they should be set to 1) and if the test for terminating the loop is not consistent with the initial counter value. Setting a counter to 0 initially, for example, and then testing for COUNTER > 5 will result in *six* executions of the loop, when only five may be required.

It is sometimes a good idea to use "real" or "live" input for test data or to have someone else prepare the test data. This is because programmers may fail to see some obvious omissions in their programs. If a program has omissions, it is likely the test data will have similar omissions. For example, if a programmer forgot to include an error procedure for a given condition, he or she is apt to forget to include data to test for that error. Using "real" or "live" input or having another person prepare test data will minimize this type of bias.

Many compilers, especially those for PCs, have an interactive debugger that enables a program to be executed line by line so that you can watch the program as it steps through the logic. *Getting Started with RM/COBOL-85* and *Getting Started with Micro Focus Personal COBOL*, both available with this text, provide information on two popular PC debuggers.

In this chapter, we focus on methods used to minimize the risk that errors in input will result in inaccurate output.

WHY INPUT TO A BUSINESS SYSTEM MUST BE VALIDATED

Most often input for regular production runs is prepared by a data entry operator who keys it in from documents, such as sales slips and payroll forms. This input can be stored as files on disk, to be processed in batch mode, or it can be entered using a keyboard, to be processed interactively.

Because input to a business system is often voluminous, the risks of data entry or input errors are great. Steps must be taken to identify and correct these errors so they are not processed by the computer. Typically, the systems analyst, the programmer, and the user decide on what corrective action to take. Each program within the system should always include *error control procedures* to find input errors. We will consider techniques used to validate data, that is, to determine if input fields have been entered properly. **Data validation** techniques, which are part of all well-designed programs, should include (1) routines that identify the various types of input errors that may occur and (2) error modules that print each specific error that has occurred. A printout of errors identifies problems that have been detected and need to be corrected.

SOME CONSEQUENCES OF INVALID INPUT

Inaccurate Output

If a data entry operator enters a salary field for a payroll record as 43265 instead of 41265, the result will be inaccurate output. It would be extremely difficult for a program itself to find such an error. We must rely on the employees within the payroll department to double-check for such errors when records are created or updated.

Programs, then, cannot entirely eliminate all errors that will result in inaccurate output. They can, however, prevent many errors from being processed by making certain that the input is in the correct format and that it is *reasonable.* Thus, a salary field can be checked to ensure that it is numeric using a NUMERIC class test. It can also be checked to make certain that it falls within a normal range. For example, 25000 to 125000 may be reasonable limits for a given company's employee salaries and a program could check to make certain that each salary falls within that range. In this way, a salary entered as 257311 would be easily identified as an error.

Data validation procedures minimize the risk of an incorrectly entered field being processed. Finding these mistakes reduces the possibility of producing inaccurate output and improves the reliability of the program.

Logic Errors Resulting from Erroneous Input

One important component of data validation, then, is to detect input errors that might produce incorrect output. Sometimes, however, an input error can result in a program interrupt, which means that the program cannot run at all with the given input. If, for example, a numeric field to be used in an arithmetic operation contains spaces, the arithmetic operation will result in a program interrupt. This is just one illustration of the type of logic or run-time error that may occur if input is not valid.

Murphy's Law is one adage with which professional programmers are very familiar: if it is possible for something to go wrong, eventually it *will* go wrong. It is not unusual, for example, for programs that have been tested, debugged, and run regularly on a scheduled production basis to begin to produce errors. This situation will eventually arise if the programmer has not anticipated *every conceivable type of input error;* after a while, someone will enter input in an incorrect format and a program interrupt or erroneous output will result.

Note that input errors are the cause of more programming problems than any other type of error. Validation procedures that can detect such errors will minimize the risk of processing errors and improve the overall reliability of computer-produced output.

DATA VALIDATION TECHNIQUES

In this section, we will focus on the programming methods that may be used to identify input errors.

Testing Fields to Ensure a Correct Format

The Class Test. Before actually processing input data, a program should first ensure that all input fields have the correct format. If an input field has a PIC of 9's, the programmer should make certain that the field does, in fact, have numeric data. Consider the following: ADD AMT-IN TO WS-TOTAL. If the AMT-IN field were erroneously entered as blanks or contained nonnumeric data, this could result in a program interrupt or it could produce erroneous output.

The following program excerpt will minimize the risk of errors caused by fields that should contain numeric data but do not:

```
IF  AMT-IN IS NOT NUMERIC
    PERFORM 500-ERR-RTN
ELSE
    ADD AMT-IN TO WS-TOTAL
END-IF
```

You will recall from Chapter 8 that the test for numeric data is called a **class test.** We review the instruction format for the class test here:

Format for Class Test

$$\underline{\text{IF}} \text{ identifier-1 } \text{ IS } \left\{ \begin{array}{l} \underline{\text{NUMERIC}} \\ \underline{\text{ALPHABETIC}} \end{array} \right\} \text{ THEN* statement-1 } \ldots$$

$$[\underline{\text{ELSE}} \text{ statement-2} \ldots]$$

$$\text{END-IF*}$$

*Optional with COBOL 85.

Use the NUMERIC class test to ensure that a field to be used in arithmetic has numeric value. If a field is to be alphabetic, you could similarly use the ALPHABETIC class test.

Remember that an alphanumeric field, which can contain both letters and digits, is neither NUMERIC nor ALPHABETIC. Hence, NOT NUMERIC is *not* the same as ALPHABETIC, and NOT ALPHABETIC is different from NUMERIC.

The Sign Test. If a numeric field is to have either positive or negative values, we may include a **sign test** to validate input data:

Format for Sign Test

$$
\text{IF} \quad \text{identifier-1} \quad \text{IS} \quad \begin{Bmatrix} \underline{POSITIVE} \\ \underline{NEGATIVE} \\ \underline{ZERO} \end{Bmatrix} \quad \text{THEN* statement-1} \ldots
$$

[ELSE statement-2 ...]

END-IF*

*Optional with COBOL 85.

Use the class and sign tests to ensure that input data has the correct format. Note, however, that the identifier must have an S in its PIC clause when using the sign test. Without the S, the field will always be considered positive. An unsigned zero, however, is neither positive nor negative.

Checking for Missing Data

One main source of error occurs when input fields are missing data. If key fields must contain data, they should be checked before processing continues:

```
IF  SOC-SEC-NO = SPACES
    PERFORM 900-ERR-RTN
END-IF
```

Alternatively, we could use a class test to determine if SOC-SEC-NO contains non-numeric data:

```
IF  SOC-SEC-NO IS NOT NUMERIC
    PERFORM 900-ERR-RTN
END-IF
```

The INSPECT Statement: Tallying and Replacing Specific Characters with Other Characters to Minimize Errors

The **INSPECT** statement may be used for replacing a specific character in a field with another character. It can also be used for counting the number of occurrences of a given character.

As noted, spaces or blanks in a numeric field will cause a program interrupt if an arithmetic or a comparison operation is performed on the field. The INSPECT statement can be used to replace all spaces with zeros in numeric fields, or in an entire record. Because the INSPECT statement can substitute one character for another, it is useful in validity checking routines.

An INSPECT statement also may be used for error control purposes. We may, for example, use the INSPECT to determine the number of erroneous characters that have been entered; we may wish to stop the run if the number of errors exceeds a predetermined value.

Although the INSPECT is commonly used for validity checking, it also has wider applicability. We will, therefore, consider this statement in its entirety. The two main functions of the INSPECT statement follow:

APPLICATIONS OF THE INSPECT STATEMENT

1. To count the number of occurrences of a given character in a field.

2. To replace specific occurrences of a given character with another character.

There are two basic formats of the INSPECT statement. Format 1 may be used to perform the first function just specified, that is, to count the number of times a given character occurs:

Format 1

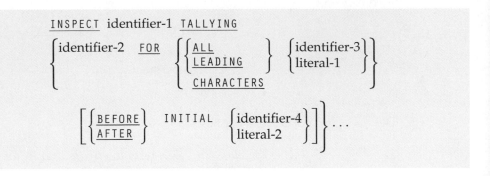

Examples

```
INSPECT ITEM-1 TALLYING CTR1 FOR ALL SPACES
INSPECT ITEM-2 TALLYING CTR2 FOR CHARACTERS
          BEFORE INITIAL SPACE
INSPECT ITEM-3 TALLYING CTR3 FOR LEADING ZEROS
```

Items	Resulting Contents
ITEM-1 = ƀƀƀ67ƀ	CTR1 = 4
ITEM-2 = 01787ƀ	CTR2 = 5
ITEM-3 = 007800	CTR3 = 2

This format of the INSPECT statement will *always* count the number of occurrences of identifier-3 or literal-1. Literal-1 must be a single character or a figurative constant. ZERO, SPACE, 3, and 'X' are all valid entries for literal-1. The tallied count is placed in identifier-2, which is usually established as an elementary item in the WORKING-STORAGE SECTION. This count field is *not* automatically set to zero when the INSPECT is executed; thus the programmer must move 0 to the count field prior to each INSPECT instruction.

Example 1

```
MOVE 0 TO CTRA
INSPECT ITEM-A TALLYING CTRA FOR ALL SPACES
IF  CTRA > 0
    PERFORM 800-ERR-RTN
END-IF
```

An error routine is performed if *any* spaces exist in ITEM-A.

Example 2   Suppose entries in a text field are separated by commas. If there are three entries, for example, there will be two commas. 'TOM, DICK, HARRY' in a field has two commas and three names. To determine the number of names or text entries, we could code:

```
MOVE 0 TO COUNT1
INSPECT TEXT-1
    TALLYING COUNT1 FOR ALL ','
ADD 1, COUNT1 GIVING NO-OF-NAMES
```

The BEFORE or AFTER INITIAL clause in Format 1 is an optional entry. If included, the count will be made according to the condition specified.

Statement	Meaning
`INSPECT ITEM-B TALLYING CTRB` `    FOR ALL '5' BEFORE INITIAL SPACE`	Count the number of occurrences of the digit 5 until the first space is encountered.
`INSPECT ITEM-C TALLYING CTRC` `    FOR ALL '5' AFTER INITIAL SPACE`	Count the number of occurrences of the digit 5 after the first space.

One of the following three clauses is required when using Format 1:

CLAUSES FOLLOWING FOR IN THE INSPECT STATEMENT

1. ALL $\begin{Bmatrix} \text{identifier-3} \\ \text{literal-1} \end{Bmatrix}$

2. LEADING $\begin{Bmatrix} \text{identifier-3} \\ \text{literal-1} \end{Bmatrix}$

3. CHARACTERS

1. If ALL is specified, *every* occurrence of the specified character in the field will be counted.

Examples

	ITEM-F		Resulting Value
	Before	*After*	
INSPECT ITEM-F TALLYING CTRF FOR ALL ZEROS	102050	102050	CTRF = 3
INSPECT ITEM-F TALLYING CTRG FOR ALL ZEROS BEFORE INITIAL 2	102050	102050	CTRG = 1

2. If LEADING is specified, all occurrences of the specified character *preceding any other character* will be tallied.

Examples

	ITEM-C		Resulting Value of CTRH
	Before	*After*	
INSPECT ITEM-C TALLYING CTRH FOR LEADING 9	99129	99129	2
INSPECT ITEM-C TALLYING CTRH FOR LEADING SPACE BEFORE INITIAL 2	ᵇᵇ12ᵇ	ᵇᵇ12ᵇ	2

3. If CHARACTERS is specified, *all characters* within the field will be tallied. This option may be used to determine the size of a field.

Example

	ITEM-D		Resulting Value of CTRQ
	Before	*After*	
INSPECT ITEM-D TALLYING CTRQ FOR CHARACTERS AFTER INITIAL 2	12349	12349	3

Format 2 of the INSPECT statement will replace specified occurrences of a given character with another character. It will *not* tally the number of occurrences of any character.

Format 2

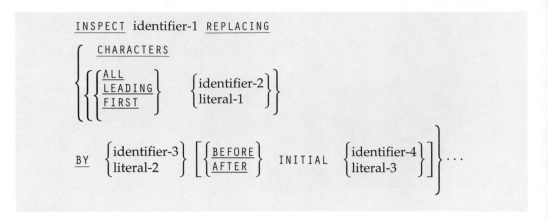

As in Format 1, literals must be single characters or figurative constants consistent with the type of field being inspected.

ALL, LEADING, and CHARACTERS have the same meaning as previously noted. If FIRST is specified in Format 2, then the first occurrence of literal-1 will be replaced by literal-2. That is, a single character replacement will occur if literal-1 is present in the field.

Examples

	Field Inspected	
	Before	*After*
INSPECT DATE-IN REPLACING ALL '-' BY '/'	10-25-98	10/25/98
INSPECT SSNO REPLACING ALL SPACES BY '-'	080 62 7731	080-62-7731
INSPECT PHONE-NO REPLACING ALL SPACES BY '-'	217 555 3321	217-555-3321
INSPECT ITEM-E REPLACING LEADING '1' BY '2'	112111	222111
INSPECT ITEM-E REPLACING CHARACTERS BY '3'		
BEFORE INITIAL '2'	112111	332111
INSPECT ITEM-E REPLACING FIRST 'X' BY 'Y'	ABCXYZ	ABCYYZ

No counting operation is performed with Format 2. When using this format, rules for inserting characters in fields apply. Assume, for example, that we are inspecting a numeric field that has a PICTURE of 9's. We cannot replace a digit with an 'A' because 'A' is not a valid numeric character.

The last three examples may seem to produce strange results, but often application areas have unique requirements for how data should be processed.

Interactive Processing.   When entering data interactively using a PC or terminal, special care must be taken for accepting input. If a field with PIC 9(3)V99 is accepted as input, the data entered should consist of exactly five digits (the decimal point is assumed). If, for example, 123.45 or $10000 is entered, the value stored may be incorrect. The INSPECT statement can be used (1) for alerting the user that symbols such as . or $ have been entered and (2) for eliminating such symbols.

In summary, a primary use of the INSPECT statement is to replace spaces in a numeric field with zeros, but it has other uses as well. There are more advanced formats of the INSPECT that we will not discuss in this text.

SELF-TEST
1. The two major functions of the INSPECT statement are _____ and _____ .

2. (T or F) Literals in an INSPECT statement must be single characters or figurative constants.

For the following statements, fill in the missing columns:

| | FLDX | | | |
Statement	Before	After	Value of CTR1
3. INSPECT FLDX TALLYING CTR1 FOR ALL ZEROS	10050		
4. INSPECT FLDX REPLACING ALL ZEROS BY SPACES	10050		
5. INSPECT FLDX TALLYING CTR1 FOR LEADING ZEROS	00057		
6. INSPECT FLDX TALLYING CTR1 FOR CHARACTERS BEFORE INITIAL '9'	00579		

Solutions
1. to replace certain characters with other characters; to count the number of occurrences of a given character in a field
2. T

	FLDX	CTR1
3.	10050	3
4.	1ᵇᵇ5ᵇ	(Not used)
5.	00057	3
6.	00579	4

Note that each of the following tests should be performed only after it has been verified that the numeric fields contain data of the correct type.

Testing for Reasonableness

As we have seen, routines in a program can *minimize* the risk of errors going undetected, but they cannot be expected to detect *all* errors. Many of these routines include tests to determine if data is reasonable. Thus, although we may not be able to guarantee the validity of a salary field entered as 35000, for example, we can certainly flag as a probable error a salary field with a value of 998325. **Tests for reasonableness** include the following:

Range Tests. One way to validate data is to make certain that fields pass a **range test;** that is, the value contained in a particular field should fall within pre-established guidelines. If a valid account number contains codes from 00001 to 85432 and also from 87001 to 89005, we may include a range test as part of our validity check:

<u>COBOL 85</u>
```
IF (ACCOUNT-NO-IN > 00000 AND < 85433)
    OR (ACCOUNT-NO-IN > 87000 AND < 89006)
        CONTINUE
ELSE
    PERFORM 600-ERR-RTN
END-IF
```

<u>COBOL 74</u>
```
IF (ACCOUNT-NO-IN > 00000 AND < 85433)
    OR (ACCOUNT-NO-IN > 87000 AND < 89006)
        NEXT SENTENCE
ELSE
    PERFORM 600-ERR-RTN.
```

Note: For COBOL 85, NEXT SENTENCE cannot be used with END-IF unless your compiler has an enhancement that permits it.

Limit Tests.   When a field is not to exceed a given value we can perform a **limit test,** which is simply a range test without a lower bound. For example, a manager may establish a rule that the quantity on hand for any part must not exceed 980 units. The program should make certain that this limit is not exceeded:

```
IF  QTY-ON-HAND-IN > 980
    PERFORM 700-ERR-RTN
END-IF
```

Limit tests are important if a PERFORM statement is to be executed a fixed number of times depending on the contents of an input field. Suppose we wish to perform 600-WRITE-A-MAILING-LABEL a variable number of times depending on the contents of an input field called NO-OF-COPIES-IN. In addition, assume that the maximum number of copies has been set at 6. Since NO-OF-COPIES-IN must be less than 7, we should include a *limit test* before performing 600-WRITE-A-MAILING-LABEL:

```
        MOVE 0 TO WS-COUNTER.
        IF  NO-OF-COPIES-IN IS POSITIVE AND < 7
            PERFORM 600-WRITE-A-MAILING-LABEL
                UNTIL WS-COUNTER = NO-OF-COPIES-IN
        ELSE
            PERFORM 800-ERR-RTN
        END-IF
            .
            .
            .
600-WRITE-A-MAILING-LABEL.
            .
            .
        ADD 1 TO WS-COUNTER.
```

The PERFORM could also have been coded as PERFORM 600-WRITE-A-MAILING-LABEL NO-OF-COPIES-IN TIMES. In this way, no WS-COUNTER would be needed and 600-WRITE-A-MAILING-LABEL would not need to ADD 1 TO WS-COUNTER.

With a range test, both ends of an identifier are compared, but with a limit test the comparison is in only one direction. To test that AMT1 is > 7 and < 25 is a *range test* but to test that AMT2 is > 250 is a *limit test.*

Condition-Names: Checking Coded Fields for Valid Contents

Coded fields are frequently used in input records to minimize keystrokes for data entry operators and to keep the input record format shorter and therefore less prone to errors. Thus, a field used to indicate an individual's marital status is *not* likely to be keyed as "SINGLE," "MARRIED," "DIVORCED," and so on. Rather, MARITAL-STATUS might be a one-position field that will be *coded* with a 1 to denote single, 2 for married, 3 for divorced, and so on. To make the coded field more easily understood, we may use instead 'M' for married, 'S' for single, and 'D' for divorced.

Programs should make certain that the contents of coded fields are valid. Condition-names are frequently used to facilitate the coding of error control procedures in a program.

We may use several condition-names along with one field:

```
05  GRADE                 PIC X.
    88  EXCELLENT          VALUE 'A'.
    88  GOOD               VALUE 'B'.
    88  FAIR               VALUE 'C'.
    88  POOR               VALUE 'D'.
    88  FAILING            VALUE 'F'.
```

Assuming that the above VALUEs are the only valid ones, a PROCEDURE DIVISION test may be as follows:

COBOL 85
```
IF  EXCELLENT OR GOOD OR FAIR OR POOR OR FAILING
    CONTINUE
ELSE
    PERFORM 600-ERROR-RTN
END-IF
```

<u>COBOL 74</u>
```
IF EXCELLENT OR GOOD OR FAIR OR POOR OR FAILING
    NEXT SENTENCE
ELSE
    PERFORM 600-ERROR-RTN.
```

We may also say: `IF NOT FAILING PERFORM 400-PASS-RTN`, if we can be sure that the condition `NOT FAILING` guarantees an entry from A through D only. But if `GRADE` contained a 'G' it would be processed improperly in `400-PASS-RTN` and not recognized as an error. The following might be better:

```
05   GRADE                    PIC X.
     88 CREDIT-GIVEN          VALUES 'A', 'B', 'C', 'D'.
     88 NO-CREDIT             VALUE 'F'.
     :
     :
```

<table>
<tr><td><u>COBOL 85</u></td><td><u>COBOL 74</u></td></tr>
<tr><td><pre>IF CREDIT-GIVEN OR NO-CREDIT
    CONTINUE
ELSE
    PERFORM 600-ERROR-RTN
END-IF</pre></td><td><pre>IF CREDIT-GIVEN OR NO-CREDIT
    NEXT SENTENCE
ELSE
    PERFORM 600-ERROR-RTN.</pre></td></tr>
</table>

A condition-name may contain a `VALUE` clause that specifies a range of values. The word `THRU` is used to indicate this range, as in the following:

```
05   GRADE      PIC X.
     88  VALID-CODE    VALUE 'A' THRU 'D', 'F'.
     :
IF  NOT VALID-CODE
    PERFORM 600-ERROR-RTN
END-IF
```

Consider another example:

```
05   DATE-OF-TRANS.
     10   MONTH-OF-TRANS    PIC 99.
     10   DAY-OF-TRANS      PIC 99.
     10   YEAR-OF-TRANS     PIC 99.
          88  VALID-YEAR        VALUE 97 THRU 99.   ← Tests for a
                                                      range of values
```

The condition-name `VALID-YEAR` is "turned on" if `YEAR-OF-TRANS`, the field directly preceding it, has any value from 97 to 99 inclusive of the end points 97 and 99. Similarly, the statement `IF NOT VALID-YEAR PERFORM 600-ERR-RTN` will cause `600-ERR-RTN` to be performed if `YEAR-OF-TRANS` is less than 97 or greater than 99.

In summary, condition-names are frequently used in the `DATA DIVISION` in conjunction with data validation routines.

Sequence Checking

Frequently, input records are entered in sequence by some control or **key field.** A Social Security number may be a key field for a payroll file, a customer number may be a key field for an accounts receivable file, and so on. A key field may also be a control field if it is used to signal a control break, as in the previous chapter.

If the keyed input data is intended to be in sequence, the actual order in which records are entered should be **sequence checked.** Sometimes records are to be in **ascending,** or increasing, **sequence,** where the first record has a key field less than the next record, and so on; sometimes records are to be in **descending,** or decreasing, **sequence.**

For many types of procedures, such as control break processing, input records must be in sequence by the key or control field. If input is sequenced manually by a user or data entry operator, it is advisable to make certain, after each control break, that the current `DEPT-IN` is greater than or equal to the previous one stored in a hold area. We may wish to terminate processing if a sequence error occurs.

The following routine may be used for ensuring that an inventory file is in ascending PART-NO sequence, assuming that part numbers are numeric and that each input record has a unique part number (i.e., no two records have the same part number):

COBOL 85

```
PROCEDURE DIVISION.
100-MAIN-MODULE.
    PERFORM 500-INITIALIZATION-RTN
    MOVE 0 TO WS-HOLD-PART
    PERFORM UNTIL ARE-THERE-MORE-RECORDS = 'NO '
        READ INVENTORY-FILE
            AT END
                MOVE 'NO ' TO ARE-THERE-MORE-RECORDS
            NOT AT END
                PERFORM 200-SEQUENCE-CHECK
        END-READ
    END-PERFORM
        :
    PERFORM 600-END-OF-JOB-RTN
    STOP RUN.
200-SEQUENCE-CHECK.
    IF  PART-NO > WS-HOLD-PART
        MOVE PART-NO TO WS-HOLD-PART
    ELSE
        PERFORM 500-ERR-RTN
    END-IF.
```

COBOL 74 Substitutions

```
READ INVENTORY-FILE
    AT END MOVE 'NO ' TO ARE-THERE-MORE-RECORDS.
PERFORM 200-SEQUENCE-CHECK
    UNTIL ARE-THERE-MORE-RECORDS = 'NO '.
```

```
READ INVENTORY-FILE
    AT END MOVE 'NO ' TO ARE-THERE-MORE-RECORDS.
```

Systems analysts, programmers, and users work together to determine the actions to be taken in case an input error, such as a sequence error, occurs.

TYPICAL VALIDITY CHECKS

1. Determine if numeric data fields do, in fact, contain numeric data. The *class test* is as follows: IF identifier IS NUMERIC ...

2. Determine if alphabetic data fields do, in fact, contain alphabetic data. The *class test* is as follows: IF identifier IS ALPHABETIC ...

3. Determine if data is missing. This can be accomplished with the following test: IF identifier IS EQUAL TO SPACES ...

4. Use the INSPECT statement to replace all spaces with zeros in numeric fields.

   After a field has been verified to ensure that it contains the appropriate type of data (e.g., numeric or alphabetic), you may need to further validate data as follows:

5. Determine if the value of a field falls within an established range; this is called a *range test*.

   Example: The value of a PART-NO field may be between 001 and 215, 287 and 336, or 415 and 555.

6. Determine if the value in a field does not exceed an established limit; this is called a *limit test*.

   Example: The value in a SALARY field is within the required limit if it is less than 95,000, for example. That is, if $95,000 is the highest salary paid, no salary should be greater than $95,000.

7. Determine if specified fields contain valid codes or values. Use *condition-names* to help document such routines.

Example

```
05    MODEL-CAR             PIC 9.
      88  COUPE             VALUE 1.
      88  SEDAN             VALUE 2.
      88  CONVERTIBLE       VALUE 3.
       :
       :
```

COBOL 85
```
IF   COUPE OR SEDAN OR CONVERTIBLE
     CONTINUE
ELSE
     PERFORM 800-ERROR-RTN
END-IF
```

or

```
IF   NOT COUPE AND NOT SEDAN AND NOT CONVERTIBLE
     PERFORM 800-ERROR-RTN
END-IF
```

COBOL 74
```
IF   COUPE OR SEDAN OR CONVERTIBLE
     NEXT SENTENCE
ELSE
     PERFORM 800-ERROR-RTN.
```

8. Determine, where necessary, if input records are in sequence, either ascending or descending, based on the control or key field.

Using the EVALUATE Verb for Data Validation (COBOL 85)

The EVALUATE statement is commonly used with COBOL 85 for data validation:

```
EVALUATE MODEL-CAR
     WHEN 1           PERFORM 200-COUPE-RTN
     WHEN 2           PERFORM 300-SEDAN-RTN
     WHEN 3           PERFORM 400-CONVERTIBLE-RTN
     WHEN OTHER       PERFORM 800-ERROR-RTN
END-EVALUATE
```

Here, again, the EVALUATE should be preceded by a test that ensures that the data is of the proper type or class. Often, programs have separate routines that verify that all data is of the appropriate type. Additional data validation procedures would only be performed on fields that contain data of the proper type. If type verification is not performed separately, then each EVALUATE or other data validation statement would need to be preceded by a class test:

```
IF MODEL-CAR IS NOT NUMERIC
     PERFORM 800-ERROR-RTN
ELSE
     EVALUATE
       :
     END-EVALUATE
END-IF
```

From this point on, we will assume that class tests have been performed on fields being EVALUATEd.

We may also use a THRU clause with the EVALUATE. Suppose you wish to print class grades based on a student's average. The following is valid:

```
EVALUATE AVERAGE
    WHEN 90 THRU 100
        MOVE 'A' TO GRADE
    WHEN 80 THRU 89
        MOVE 'B' TO GRADE
    WHEN 70 THRU 79
        MOVE 'C' TO GRADE
    WHEN 60 THRU 69
        MOVE 'D' TO GRADE
    WHEN 0 THRU 59
        MOVE 'F' TO GRADE
    WHEN OTHER
        PERFORM 700-ERR-RTN
END-EVALUATE
```

We can also code this as:

```
EVALUATE TRUE
    WHEN AVERAGE >= 90 AND <= 100
        MOVE 'A' TO GRADE
    WHEN AVERAGE >= 80 AND <= 89
        MOVE 'B' TO GRADE
    WHEN AVERAGE >= 70 AND <= 79
        MOVE 'C' TO GRADE
    WHEN AVERAGE >= 60 AND <= 69
        MOVE 'D' TO GRADE
    WHEN AVERAGE >= 0 AND <= 59
        MOVE 'F' TO GRADE
    WHEN OTHER
        PERFORM 700-ERR-RTN
END-EVALUATE
```

We can use the EVALUATE in conjunction with condition-names as well:

```
EVALUATE TRUE
    WHEN EXCELLENT PERFORM 500-A-RTN
    WHEN GOOD       PERFORM 600-B-RTN
END-EVALUATE
```

In this instance, GRADE would have condition-names associated with it as follows:

```
05  GRADE                PIC X.
    88  EXCELLENT         VALUE 'A'.
    88  GOOD             VALUE 'B'.
```

Note that to say EVALUATE GRADE WHEN EXCELLENT ... will result in a syntax error. You must say EVALUATE GRADE WHEN 1 ... or EVALUATE TRUE WHEN EXCELLENT ....

Expanding the Format

The EVALUATE statement can be coded in numerous ways. The following are the three most common:

1. EVALUATE identifier
        WHEN value(s) PERFORM ...
        :

Example

```
EVALUATE AGE
    WHEN 0 THRU 19  PERFORM 400-MINOR-RTN
    WHEN 20 THRU 99 PERFORM 500-ADULT-RTN
END-EVALUATE
```

2. EVALUATE TRUE
      WHEN condition PERFORM ...

<table>
<tr><td>Example</td><td>

```
EVALUATE TRUE
    WHEN AGE >= 0 AND <= 19
        PERFORM 400-MINOR-RTN
    WHEN AGE >= 20 AND <= 99
        PERFORM 500-ADULT-RTN
END-EVALUATE
```

</td></tr>
</table>

3. EVALUATE condition
        WHEN TRUE   PERFORM ...
        WHEN FALSE PERFORM ...

TRUE and FALSE are COBOL reserved words that mean "if the condition is met" and "if the condition is not met," respectively.

<table>
<tr><td>Example</td><td>

```
EVALUATE AGE <= 19
    WHEN TRUE  PERFORM 400-MINOR-RTN
    WHEN FALSE PERFORM 500-ADULT-RTN
END-EVALUATE
```

</td></tr>
</table>

Alternatively:

```
EVALUATE TRUE
    WHEN AGE <= 19 PERFORM 400-MINOR-RTN
    WHEN OTHER       PERFORM 500-ADULT-RTN
END-EVALUATE
```

Note, however, that the following is incorrect:

<table>
<tr><td>Invalid</td><td>

```
EVALUATE AGE
    WHEN <= 19 PERFORM 400-MINOR-RTN
END-EVALUATE
```

</td></tr>
</table>

When evaluating an *identifier,* the WHEN clause must specify precise values—for example, WHEN 1, WHEN 0 THRU 10, and so on. We could also code EVALUATE TRUE WHEN identifier >= 1 AND <= 20 ....

In summary, the EVALUATE verb can be used to test the results of a series of conditions. It has numerous applications and is often used for validating data. That is, with the EVALUATE you test for all the valid entries in a field and then include a WHEN OTHER clause to determine if there is an invalid value in the field.

OTHER METHODS FOR VALIDATING DATA

Use of Control Listings for Manual Validation of Input

Computer errors commonly result from erroneous input, but they can also result from an intentional attempt to sabotage or defraud a company.

One major method for minimizing the risk of undetected errors is to print a **control listing** or **audit trail** that includes (1) the identifying data or key fields in each input record, (2) any errors encountered, and (3) totals of amounts accumulated for groups of input records processed. Typically, an individual in the user organization is charged with the task of checking this control listing to make certain that the processing was performed correctly. Figure 11.1 illustrates a Printer Spacing Chart that describes a sample control listing or audit trail. Most organizations require a control listing when output is to be produced on magnetic media such as disk, since the output is not visually readable.

Figure 11.1 Printer Spacing Chart for a sample control listing.

		CONTROL LISTING	99/99/99	

```
         1111111111222222222233333333334444444444555555555566666666667777777777888888888899999999
123456789012345678901234567890123456789012345678901234567890123456789012345678901234567890123456789

H  6                              CONTROL LISTING      99/99/99

H  9        CUSTOMER NO      CUSTOMER NAME    TOTAL SALES      ERROR MESSAGE
                                                                  (IF ANY)
D 11           XXXXX       X-----------X    $ZZ,ZZZ.99   X-----------------X

T 15                                        TOTAL RECORDS PROCESSED   ZZ,ZZ9
T 16                                        TOTAL ERRORS              ZZ,ZZ9
```

Verification as a Means of Validating Input

Interactive Processing. One way to minimize keying errors when input is entered interactively is to verify that data has been keyed in properly using a **verification procedure**. After all data for a record has been keyed, we can DISPLAY the fields entered for that record along with a message that says 'IS DATA CORRECT (Y/N)?'. We use the ACCEPT verb to input the response. If it is a 'Y' we continue, if it is an 'N' we give the user an opportunity to rekey the data.

A second way to minimize keying errors is by using a rekeying or verification procedure, which checks to see that the data originally keyed is the same as the data being keyed the second time. If it is not, then the operator who is verifying the data must find each error and correct it.

A verification procedure is very labor intensive since it doubles data entry time, but it will detect approximately 90% of all data entry errors. Although this process minimizes mistakes, 10% of input errors still go undetected. A combination of manual checking and programmed controls is needed to find most or all input errors.

WHAT TO DO IF INPUT ERRORS OCCUR

Various types of procedures may be employed when input errors are detected. The systems analyst, programmer or software developer, and user work closely together to establish the most productive course of action to be followed when errors occur. We consider several procedures, any one of which may be used in a program.

PRINT AN ERROR RECORD CONTAINING THE KEY FIELD, THE CONTENTS OF THE ERRONEOUS FIELD, AND AN ERROR MESSAGE

Errors should always be clearly displayed with an appropriate message. The key field that identifies each erroneous record should also be included:

Example	Soc Sec No	Employee Name	Error
	080-65-2113	BROWN JOSEPH	SALARY FIELD IS BLANK
	092-11-7844	LOPEZ MARIA	MARITAL STATUS FIELD IS INVALID (= 'Q')

In addition, a count should be maintained of the number of occurrences of each specific type of error. A user would be responsible for correcting all errors that have occurred. This user relies on the count field to determine if any major programming or systems problem exists. That is, if the count of a specific type of error is excessive, there may be a program error, or a data entry operator may be making a particular mistake repeatedly.

STOP THE RUN

If a major error occurs, it may be best simply to stop the run. This procedure is followed when data integrity is the primary consideration and errors must be kept to an absolute minimum. Usually, there is an employee in the user department responsible for checking the data; he or she would need to correct the error and arrange for the job to be restarted.

If your program is to terminate because of an error, remember to close all files before stopping and to display or print a message explaining why the job is being stopped. (With COBOL 85, a `STOP RUN` automatically closes all files.)

PARTIALLY PROCESS OR BYPASS ERRONEOUS RECORDS

Once an error is detected, the program could either (1) proceed to the next record, bypassing the erroneous record entirely, or (2) process some portion of the erroneous record. This, again, is a function of user needs.

Sometimes, for example, an erroneously entered numeric field is replaced with zeros in the output area; sometimes the erroneous input is simply ignored.

STOP THE RUN IF THE NUMBER OF ERRORS EXCEEDS A PREDETERMINED LIMIT

Often we wish to continue processing even if errors occur, but if such errors become excessive, we can stop the run. Consider the following error routine:

```
700-ERR-RTN.
    WRITE PRINT-REC FROM ERR-LINE
    ADD 1 TO WS-SEQUENCE-ERRORS
    IF  WS-SEQUENCE-ERRORS > 25
        MOVE 'JOB TERMINATED: SEQUENCE ERRORS EXCEED 25' TO PRINT-REC
        WRITE PRINT-REC
        CLOSE INFILE
              OUTFILE
        STOP RUN
    END-IF.
```

USE SWITCHES

Suppose we perform multiple validity tests on each record. After all tests, we wish to process valid records only, that is, records without any errors. We may use a **switch** or flag for this purpose. We create a field called `ERR-SWITCH` initialized at `'N'` for no errors. If any error occurs, we move `'Y'` to `ERR-SWITCH` in each error routine to indicate that `'YES'` an error has occurred.

After all validity tests, we test `ERR-SWITCH`. If it contains a `'Y'`, then an error has occurred and we proceed accordingly. If `ERR-SWITCH` is an `'N'`, then no error has occurred. Before processing each new record, be sure to reinitialize `ERR-SWITCH` at `'N'` indicating no errors.

The field called `ERR-SWITCH` is actually a one-position field that will contain either an `'N'` or a `'Y'`. We may use condition-names to clarify this for documentation purposes:

```
01  ERR-SWITCH                PIC X.
    88  ERROR-HAS-OCCURRED     VALUE 'Y'.
    88  NO-ERROR-HAS-OCCURRED  VALUE 'N'.
        :
        :
300-VALIDITY-TESTS.
        :
        :
    IF  ERROR-HAS-OCCURRED
        MOVE 'N' TO ERR-SWITCH
    ELSE
```

```
            PERFORM 500-OK-ROUTINE
    END-IF.
```

or

```
    IF  NO-ERROR-HAS-OCCURRED
            PERFORM 500-OK-ROUTINE
    ELSE
            MOVE 'N' TO ERR-SWITCH
    END-IF.
```

Typically, we use one 88-level condition-name. That is, we would code *either* IF ERROR-HAS-OCCURRED . . . *or* IF NO-ERROR-HAS-OCCURRED . . . so there is usually no need for both condition-names.

PRINT TOTALS

Print a Count of All Records and a Count of All Errors

Programs should provide a count of records processed as well as a count of errors that have occurred. To determine the number of records processed, we ADD 1 TO WS-TOTAL-RECORDS each time we read a record and print the contents of WS-TOTAL-RECORDS at the end of the job. In most cases, a user is responsible for counting the number of records to be entered before processing begins. This person later compares the manually tabulated total to the total number of records processed and counted by the computer. The totals should match. If they do not match, records may have been misplaced or lost. The user must then find the discrepancy and correct the problem.

Print a Batch Total

If large groups of input records are processed during each run, a single count of all records may be insufficient to track down missing records. In this case, we might include **batch totals,** where we print a count of all records within specific groups or batches of records. Suppose we process transactions by TRANS-NO. We may include batch totals as follows:

```
          TOTAL RECORDS PROCESSED              1131
          RECORDS WITH TRANS-NO 001-082          48
          RECORDS WITH TRANS-NO 083-115          53
          RECORDS WITH TRANS-NO 116-246         387
          RECORDS WITH TRANS-NO 247-383         226
          RECORDS WITH TRANS-NO 384-452         417
```

Each individual total is called a *batch total.* A user manually determines the records to be processed in each batch before the data has been entered as input. The manual batch totals should match the computer-produced ones. If not, the user can track down the record or records that were not processed in the specific batch.

The program itself can be used to compare the manual batch totals to the computed ones. To do this, the manual batch totals are entered *along with the input,* either interactively or on a separate control record.

WHEN DATA SHOULD BE VALIDATED

All programs to be run on a regularly scheduled basis should include data validation techniques designed to minimize errors. From this point on in the text, we will consider such techniques when discussing program excerpts. But Practice Programs at the end of each chapter will focus on illustrating the specific topics discussed in the chapter and, in the interest of brevity, will *not* focus on data validation techniques. The set of Review Questions at the end of each subsequent chapter, however, will ask you to modify the Practice Program to include the appropriate data validation routines and to produce a control listing specifying the errors encountered.

COBOL 9x CHANGES

1. The restrictions on the INSPECT statement limiting the AFTER/BEFORE items to one-character literals or fields in the REPLACING clause will be eliminated.

2. A VALIDATE statement has been introduced to check the format of data fields and to see that the contents of such fields fall within established ranges or have acceptable contents as defined by DATA DIVISION VALUEs. This VALIDATE statement has great potential because it will help programmers minimize the risk of undetected input errors.

UNDERSTANDING PROGRAM INTERRUPTS

During program testing, logic errors sometimes occur that cause a program to terminate. Such a termination is called a **program interrupt.** Each time a program interrupt occurs, the computer prints a brief message that specifies the type of error that caused it. The following is a list of common program interrupts and typical reasons why they occur.

COMMON PROGRAM INTERRUPTS

Interrupt	Cause
DATA EXCEPTION	1. You may be performing an arithmetic operation on a field that contains blanks or other nonnumeric characters.
	2. You may be attempting to use a numeric field in a comparison and it contains blanks or other nonnumeric characters.
	3. You may have failed to initialize a subscript or index.
DIVIDE EXCEPTION	You may be attempting to divide by 0. (On some systems, an attempt to divide by 0 will *not* cause an interrupt but will produce unpredictable results.)
ADDRESSING ERROR	1. You may have placed (or left) an incorrect value in a subscript or index so that a table look-up exceeds the number of entries in the table. See Chapter 12.
	2. You may have coded nested PERFORMs (or GO TOs) improperly. This error will also occur if there is an improper exit from a paragraph being performed.
OPERATION ERROR	You may be attempting to access a file with a READ or WRITE before opening it.
SPECIFICATION ERROR	You may be attempting to access either an input area after an AT END condition or an output area directly after a WRITE.

CHAPTER SUMMARY
A. Types of Program Errors
    1. Syntax errors—correct them before executing the program.
    2. Logic errors—use comprehensive test data to find them.
B. Validating Data to Minimize Errors
    1. Error control procedures can minimize errors but not eliminate them entirely.
    2. Types of error control procedures
        a. Range tests—to ensure that data falls within a pre-established range.
        b. Limit tests—to ensure that data does not exceed a pre-established limit.
        c. Format tests—to ensure, for example, that numeric fields do, in fact, contain numeric data.
        d. Tests for missing data—to ensure that all critical fields contain nonzero or nonblank data.
        e. Sequence checks—to ensure that data is in the correct sequence.
    3. INSPECT Statement
        a. Used to replace invalid characters with valid ones.
        b. Used to count the occurrences of invalid characters.
    4. Use condition-names to specify given values that identifiers may assume.
    5. Use the EVALUATE verb to test for conditions if you are using COBOL 85.
    6. Verify input data.
        a. Verification can be performed by displaying all data entered and asking the data entry operator to verify that it is correct.
        b. Data keyed in may be rechecked through a rekeying or verification procedure. If the rekeying produces different entries than the initial data entry, the reason for each discrepancy must be determined and corrective action taken.
C. How to Handle Input Errors
    1. If critical errors occur, stop the run.
    2. Fill erroneous fields with spaces or zeros.
    3. Count the occurrences of errors and stop the run if the number of errors is considered excessive.
    4. Print control listings or audit trails to be checked by the user department.
        a. A control listing contains the key field and other identifying data for every record created, updated, or changed.
        b. The control listing also indicates the total number of records processed and any errors encountered.

KEY TERMS

Ascending sequence	Descending sequence	Range test
Audit trail	INSPECT	Sequence checking
Batch total	Key field	Sign test
Class test	Limit test	Switch
Coded field	Murphy's Law	Test for reasonableness
Control listing	Program interrupt	Verification procedure
Data validation		

CHAPTER SELF-TEST

1. A _____ procedure is the process of rekeying input to ensure that it was entered correctly the first time.

2. The _____ statement is used to replace erroneous characters in an input field with other characters.

3. A _____ is the name assigned to a value of the field directly preceding it in the DATA DIVISION.

4. The sign test IF A IS NEGATIVE will produce correct results only if A has a(n) _____ in its PICTURE clause.

5. (T or F) A programmer should always stop a run if an input error is detected.

6. A count of all records within specific groups is referred to as a _____ total.

7. The _____ verb is used in COBOL 85 for the case structure.

8. (T or F) Condition-names can be used in an EVALUATE statement as part of a WHEN clause.

Solutions
1. verification
2. `INSPECT`
3. condition-name
4. `S`
5. F—Some errors can be handled by zeroing out erroneous fields, for example.
6. batch
7. `EVALUATE`
8. T

PRACTICE PROGRAM

Consider the following problem definition:

Systems Flowchart

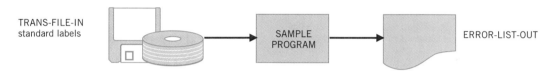

TRANS-FILE-IN
standard labels

SAMPLE PROGRAM

ERROR-LIST-OUT

TRANS-FILE-IN **Record Layout**			
Field	**Size**	**Type**	**No. of Decimal Positions (if Numeric)**
Social Security No. (numeric)	9	Numeric	0
Employee Name (nonblank)	20	Alphanumeric	
Employee Address (nonblank)	20	Alphanumeric	
Transaction Code (1–9)	1	Numeric	0
Annual Salary (Range: 15000–87000)	5	Numeric	0
Marital Status (M, S, D, or W)	1	Alphanumeric	
Level (1–6)	1	Numeric	0
Department (10, 20, or 25)	2	Numeric	0

Note: Validation criteria are indicated under each field-name.

ERROR-LIST-OUT Printer Spacing Chart

```
                                          LISTING OF TRANSACTION ERRORS      PAGE 99        99/99/99
              NAME                                     ERROR MESSAGE                        VALUE IN ERROR FIELD
           X              X              X                              X         X                         X
```

Sample Input Data

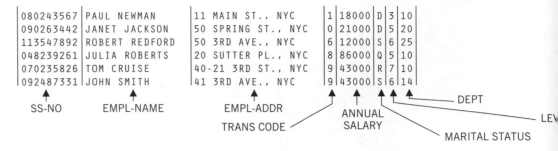

```
080243567 PAUL NEWMAN      11 MAIN ST., NYC    1 18000 D 3 10
090263442 JANET JACKSON    50 SPRING ST., NYC  0 21000 D 5 20
113547892 ROBERT REDFORD   50 3RD AVE., NYC    6 12000 S 6 25
048239261 JULIA ROBERTS    20 SUTTER PL., NYC  8 86000 Q 5 10
070235826 TOM CRUISE       40-21 3RD ST., NYC  9 43000 R 7 10
092487331 JOHN SMITH       41 3RD AVE., NYC    9 43000 S 6 14
```

SS-NO   EMPL-NAME   EMPL-ADDR   TRANS CODE   ANNUAL SALARY   MARITAL STATUS   LEV   DEPT

Sample Output

```
         LISTING OF TRANSACTION ERRORS      PAGE  1      01/29/98
    NAME                         ERROR MESSAGE                  VALUE IN ERROR FIELD

    PAUL NEWMAN                  A-OK                           0

    JANET JACKSON                TRANS CODE IS INVALID          0

    ROBERT REDFORD               SALARY IS INVALID              12000

    JULIA ROBERTS                MARITAL STATUS IS INVALID      Q

    TOM CRUISE                   MARITAL STATUS IS INVALID      R

    TOM CRUISE                   LEVEL IS INVALID               7

    JOHN SMITH                   DEPT IS INVALID                14
```

Figure 11.2 illustrates the hierarchy chart and pseudocode. Figure 11.3 shows a suggested solution.

Figure 11.2   Hierarchy chart and pseudocode for the Practice Program.

Hierarchy Chart

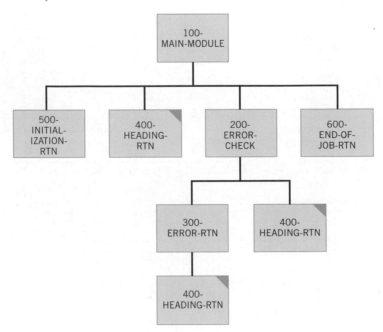

Figure 11.2 (continued)

Pseudocode

MAIN-MODULE
START
    PERFORM Initialize-Rtn
    PERFORM Heading-Rtn
    PERFORM UNTIL no more records
        READ a Record
            AT END
                Move 'NO ' to Are-There-More-Records
            NOT AT END
                PERFORM Error-Check
        END-READ
    END-PERFORM
    PERFORM End-Of-Job-Rtn
STOP

INITIALIZE-RTN
    Open the Files
    Read and Store Date

HEADING-RTN
    Write Headings
    Initialize Line Counter

ERROR-CHECK
    Move Name to Output Area
    IF   Social Security Number is not numeric
    THEN
        PERFORM Err-Rtn
    END-IF
    IF   Name is blank
    THEN
        PERFORM Err-Rtn
    END-IF
    IF   Address is blank
    THEN
        PERFORM Err-Rtn
    END-IF
    IF   Code is erroneous
    THEN
        PERFORM Err-Rtn
    END-IF

IF   Salary is not within required range
THEN
        PERFORM Err-Rtn
END-IF
IF   Marital-status is erroneous
THEN
        PERFORM Err-Rtn
END-IF
IF   Level is erroneous
THEN
        PERFORM Err-Rtn
END-IF
IF   Dept is erroneous
THEN
        PERFORM Err-Rtn
END-IF
IF   page overflow
THEN
        PERFORM Heading-Rtn
END-IF
IF   no errors
THEN
        Write 'A-OK' line
END-IF

ERR-RTN
    IF page overflow
    THEN
        PERFORM Heading-Rtn
    END-IF
    Write Error Record
    Increment Line Counter
    Increment Error Counter

END-OF-JOB-RTN
    End-of-Job Operations

Figure 11.3 Solution to the Practice Program.

COBOL 85

```
IDENTIFICATION DIVISION.
PROGRAM-ID. SAMPLE.
***************************************************
*   validates transaction file and prints errors   *
***************************************************
ENVIRONMENT DIVISION.
INPUT-OUTPUT SECTION.
FILE-CONTROL.
    SELECT TRANS-FILE-IN  ASSIGN TO INVALID1.
```

Figure 11.3 (continued)

```
                                SELECT ERROR-LIST-OUT ASSIGN TO PRINTER.
                        *
                        DATA DIVISION.
                        FILE SECTION.
                        FD   TRANS-FILE-IN
                             LABEL RECORDS ARE STANDARD.
                        01   TRANS-REC-IN.
                             05   SS-NO-IN                    PIC 9(9).
                             05   NAME-IN                     PIC X(20).
                             05   EMPL-ADDR-IN                PIC X(20).
                             05   TRANS-CODE-IN               PIC 9.
                                  88  VALID-CODE-IN                     VALUE 1 THRU 9.
                             05   ANNUAL-SALARY-IN            PIC 9(5).
                                  88  ACCEPTABLE-SALARY-RANGE-IN VALUE 15000 THRU 87000.
                             05   MARITAL-STATUS-IN           PIC X.
                                  88  MARRIED                           VALUE 'M'.
                                  88  SINGLE                            VALUE 'S'.
                                  88  DIVORCED                          VALUE 'D'.
                                  88  WIDOWED                           VALUE 'W'.
                             05   LEVEL-IN                    PIC 9.
                                  88  ACCEPTABLE-LEVEL-IN               VALUE 1 THRU 6.
                             05   DEPT-IN                     PIC 99.
                             05                               PIC X(41).
                        FD   ERROR-LIST-OUT
                             LABEL RECORDS OMITTED.
                        01   ERROR-REC-OUT                    PIC X(132).
                        WORKING-STORAGE SECTION.
                        01   WS-AREAS.
                             05   ARE-THERE-MORE-RECORDS      PIC X(3)     VALUE 'YES'.
                                  88  NO-MORE-RECORDS                      VALUE 'NO '.
                             05   WS-LINE-CT                  PIC 99       VALUE ZEROS.
                             05   WS-DATE                     PIC 9(6).
                             05   WS-DATE-X REDEFINES WS-DATE.
                                  10   WS-YR                  PIC 99.
                                  10   WS-MO                  PIC 99.
                                  10   WS-DA                  PIC 99.
                             05   WS-ERROR-CT                 PIC 9        VALUE ZERO.
                             05   WS-PAGE-CT                  PIC 99       VALUE ZEROS.
                        01   HL-HEADING-1.
                             05                               PIC X(19)    VALUE SPACES.
                             05                               PIC X(35)
                                  VALUE 'LISTING OF TRANSACTION ERRORS'.
                             05                               PIC X(5)     VALUE 'PAGE '.
                             05   HL-PAGE-NO                  PIC Z9.
                             05                               PIC X(10)    VALUE SPACES.
                             05   HL-DATE.
                                  10   HL-MO                  PIC 99.
                                  10                          PIC X        VALUE '/'.
                                  10   HL-DA                  PIC 99.
                                  10                          PIC X        VALUE '/'.
                                  10   HL-YR                  PIC 99.
                             05                               PIC X(53)    VALUE SPACES.
                        01   HL-HEADER-2.
                             05                               PIC X(9)     VALUE SPACES.
                             05                               PIC X(30)    VALUE 'NAME'.
                             05                               PIC X(35)
                                  VALUE 'ERROR MESSAGE'.
                             05                               PIC X(58)
                                  VALUE 'VALUE IN ERROR FIELD'.
                        01   DL-DETAIL-LINE.
                             05                               PIC X(9)     VALUE SPACES.
                             05   DL-NAME                     PIC X(20).
                             05                               PIC X(10)    VALUE SPACES.
                             05   DL-ERROR-MESSAGE            PIC X(25).
                             05                               PIC X(10)    VALUE SPACES.
```

COBOL 74 Substitutions

For COBOL 74, use FILLER instead of a blank field name

Figure 11.3   (continued)

```
                           05   DL-FIELD-IN-ERROR              PIC X(20).
                           05                                  PIC X(38)   VALUE SPACES.
                      *
                       PROCEDURE DIVISION.
                       ********************************************
                      *  controls direction of program logic   *
                      *  and reads the first record.            *
                       ********************************************
                       100-MAIN-MODULE.
                           PERFORM 500-INITIALIZATION-RTN
                           PERFORM 400-HEADING-RTN
                           PERFORM UNTIL NO-MORE-RECORDS
                               READ TRANS-FILE-IN
                                   AT END
                                       MOVE 'NO ' TO ARE-THERE-MORE-RECORDS
                                   NOT AT END
                                       PERFORM 200-ERROR-CHECK
                               END-READ
                           END-PERFORM
                           PERFORM 600-END-OF-JOB-RTN
                           STOP RUN.
                       ****************************************************************
                      *  performed from 100-main-module; tests input data for errors  *
                       ****************************************************************
                       200-ERROR-CHECK.
                           MOVE NAME-IN TO DL-NAME
                           IF  SS-NO-IN NOT NUMERIC
                               MOVE SS-NO-IN TO DL-FIELD-IN-ERROR
                               MOVE 'SS NO IS INVALID' TO DL-ERROR-MESSAGE
                               PERFORM 300-ERROR-RTN
                           END-IF
                           IF  NAME-IN = SPACES
                               MOVE NAME-IN TO DL-FIELD-IN-ERROR
                               MOVE 'NAME IS INVALID' TO DL-ERROR-MESSAGE
                               PERFORM 300-ERROR-RTN
                           END-IF
                           IF  EMPL-ADDR-IN = SPACES
                               MOVE EMPL-ADDR-IN TO DL-FIELD-IN-ERROR
                               MOVE 'ADDRESS IS INVALID' TO DL-ERROR-MESSAGE
                               PERFORM 300-ERROR-RTN
                           END-IF
                           IF  NOT VALID-CODE-IN
                               MOVE TRANS-CODE-IN TO DL-FIELD-IN-ERROR
                               MOVE 'TRANS CODE IS INVALID' TO DL-ERROR-MESSAGE
                               PERFORM 300-ERROR-RTN
                           END-IF
                           IF  NOT ACCEPTABLE-SALARY-RANGE-IN
                               MOVE ANNUAL-SALARY-IN TO DL-FIELD-IN-ERROR
                               MOVE 'SALARY IS INVALID' TO DL-ERROR-MESSAGE
                               PERFORM 300-ERROR-RTN
                           END-IF
                           IF  NOT MARRIED AND NOT SINGLE AND NOT DIVORCED AND NOT WIDOWED
                               MOVE MARITAL-STATUS-IN TO DL-FIELD-IN-ERROR
                               MOVE 'MARITAL STATUS IS INVALID' TO DL-ERROR-MESSAGE
                               PERFORM 300-ERROR-RTN
                           END-IF
                           IF  NOT ACCEPTABLE-LEVEL-IN
                               MOVE LEVEL-IN TO DL-FIELD-IN-ERROR
                               MOVE 'LEVEL IS INVALID' TO DL-ERROR-MESSAGE
                               PERFORM 300-ERROR-RTN
                           END-IF
                           IF  DEPT-IN NOT = 10 AND NOT = 20 AND NOT = 25
                               MOVE DEPT-IN TO DL-FIELD-IN-ERROR
                               MOVE 'DEPT IS INVALID' TO DL-ERROR-MESSAGE
                               PERFORM 300-ERROR-RTN
```

COBOL 74 Substitutions

```
READ TRANS-FILE-IN
    AT END MOVE 'NO ' TO
        ARE-THERE-MORE-RECORDS.
PERFORM 200-ERROR-CHECK
    UNTIL NO-MORE-RECORDS.
```

Figure 11.3   (continued)

```
                                          END-IF
                                          IF  WS-LINE-CT > 25
                                              PERFORM 400-HEADING-RTN
                                          END-IF
                                          IF  WS-ERROR-CT = ZERO
                                              MOVE WS-ERROR-CT TO DL-FIELD-IN-ERROR
                                              MOVE 'A-OK' TO DL-ERROR-MESSAGE
                                              WRITE ERROR-REC-OUT FROM DL-DETAIL-LINE
                                                  AFTER ADVANCING 2 LINES
                                              ADD 1 TO WS-LINE-CT
                                          ELSE
                                              MOVE ZEROS TO WS-ERROR-CT
                                          END-IF.
```

COBOL 74 Substitutions

```
READ TRANS-FILE-IN
    AT END MOVE 'NO ' TO
        ARE-THERE-MORE-RECORDS.
```

```
                     ******************************************************************
                     *  performed from 200-error-check, prints the error messages  *
                     *                                  when errors occur.          *
                     ******************************************************************
                      300-ERROR-RTN.
                          IF  WS-LINE-CT > 25
                              PERFORM 400-HEADING-RTN
                          END-IF
                          WRITE ERROR-REC-OUT FROM DL-DETAIL-LINE
                              AFTER ADVANCING 2 LINES
                          ADD 1 TO WS-LINE-CT
                          ADD 1 TO WS-ERROR-CT.
                     ********************************************************************
                     *  performed from 100-main-module, 200-error-check, 300-error-rtn  *
                     *  prints out headings after new page, zeros out line ctr.         *
                     ********************************************************************
                      400-HEADING-RTN.
                          ADD 1 TO WS-PAGE-CT
                          MOVE WS-PAGE-CT TO HL-PAGE-NO
                          WRITE ERROR-REC-OUT FROM HL-HEADING-1
                              AFTER ADVANCING PAGE
                          WRITE ERROR-REC-OUT FROM HL-HEADER-2
                              AFTER ADVANCING 1 LINES
                          MOVE ZEROS TO WS-LINE-CT.
                     ***********************************************************
                     *  performed from 100-main-module. opens the files,  *
                     *  reads in the current date                         *
                     ***********************************************************
                      500-INITIALIZATION-RTN.
                          OPEN INPUT  TRANS-FILE-IN
                               OUTPUT ERROR-LIST-OUT
                          ACCEPT WS-DATE FROM DATE
                          MOVE WS-MO TO HL-MO
                          MOVE WS-DA TO HL-DA
                          MOVE WS-YR TO HL-YR.
                     ***********************************************
                     *  performed from 100-main-module, closes files  *
                     ***********************************************
                      600-END-OF-JOB-RTN.
                          CLOSE TRANS-FILE-IN
                                ERROR-LIST-OUT.
```

REVIEW QUESTIONS

True-False
Questions

_____   1. Most logic errors are detected by the compiler and listed as diagnostic messages.

_____   2. Control listings are considered optional and, in fact, are rarely produced by a program.

3. Consider the following:

```
05  FLDX        PIC 9.
    88  X-ON    VALUE 1.
```

_____   The condition FLDX = 1 may be referred to as X-ON.

_____   4. In Question 3, we could code a PROCEDURE DIVISION entry as follows:

```
IF  X-ON  =  1
    PERFORM 200-X-RTN.
```

_____   5. A program interrupt will cause the computer to terminate a run.

_____   6. Data verification is rarely used to minimize errors, since it only eliminates a small percentage of data entry mistakes.

_____   7. If a field IS NOT ALPHABETIC, then it must be NUMERIC.

_____   8. If a field IS NOT POSITIVE, then it must be NEGATIVE.

_____   9. An INSPECT statement can be used both to replace one character with another and to count the number of occurrences of a character.

_____   10. To reduce the number of characters in an input record, we frequently use coded fields.

DEBUGGING EXERCISES

Consider the following program excerpt:

COBOL 85

```
01  REC-IN.
    05  ACCT-NO        PIC X(5).
    05  SALARY         PIC 9(4).
    05  AMT2           PIC 9(3).
    05  STATUS-CODE    PIC 9.
PROCEDURE DIVISION.
100-MAIN-MODULE.
    OPEN INPUT  TRANS-FILE
         OUTPUT PRINT-FILE
    PERFORM UNTIL ARE-THERE-MORE-RECORDS = 'NO '
        READ TRANS-FILE
            AT END
                MOVE 'NO ' TO
                    ARE-THERE-MORE-RECORDS
            NOT AT END
                PERFORM 200-EDIT-CHECK
        END-READ
    END-PERFORM
    PERFORM 600-PRINT-TOTALS
    CLOSE TRANS-FILE PRINT-FILE
    STOP RUN.
200-EDIT-CHECK.
    IF  SALARY IS NOT > 5000 OR < 98000
        PERFORM 300-SALARY-ERROR
    END-IF
    IF  AMT2 IS NEGATIVE
        PERFORM 400-AMT2-ERROR
    END-IF
    IF  STATUS-CODE > 5 AND SALARY NOT < 86000
        PERFORM 500-ERROR-IN-STATUS
    END-IF
*******************************************************
*   an error switch is set at each error routine   *
*******************************************************
    IF  ERR-SWITCH = 0
        WRITE PRINT-REC FROM OK-REC
    ELSE
        WRITE PRINT-REC FROM ERR-REC
    END-IF

    ADD 1 TO COUNT-OF-RECORDS.
```

COBOL 74 Substitutions

```
READ TRANS-FILE
    AT END MOVE 'NO ' TO ARE-THERE-MORE-RECORDS.
PERFORM 200-EDIT-CHECK
    UNTIL THERE-ARE-NO-MORE-RECORDS.
```

```
READ TRANS-FILE
    AT END MOVE 'NO ' TO ARE-THERE-MORE-RECORDS.
```  ⟶

1. A syntax error occurs on the line in which AMT2 is tested for a negative quantity. Find and correct the error.

2. Is ADD 1 TO COUNT-OF-RECORDS in the correct place? Explain your answer.

3. When the program is executed, 300-SALARY-ERROR is always performed even when the SALARY is within the correct range. Find and correct the error.

4. When an error occurs, all subsequent records are similarly printed as errors. Find and correct this error.

PROGRAMMING ASSIGNMENTS

1. Consider the following input data with the format shown:

CUSTOMER Record Layout			
Field	Size	Type	No. of Decimal Positions (if Numeric)
CUST-NO	3	Numeric	0
CUST-NAME	27	Alphanumeric	
MAXIMUM-CREDIT-ALLOWED	5	Numeric	0
CREDIT-RATING	2	Alphanumeric	
TOTAL-BALANCE-DUE	5	Numeric	0

Write a program to verify that:
a. CUST NOs range from 101–972 and that records are in sequence by CUST NO.
b. CUST NAME is not blank.
c. TOTAL BALANCE DUE does not exceed the maximum credit allowed.
d. CREDIT RATING is either EX (excellent), VG (very good), G (good), or A (acceptable).

Print an error listing that includes any records with erroneous data along with an appropriate error message. At the end of the report, list the total number of records processed and the total number of each type of error. Prepare a Printer Spacing Chart that describes what the report will look like before writing the program.

2. Write a program to validate payroll records for missing data. See the problem definition in Figure 11.4.

Notes:

a. Perform a validity routine to ensure that:
   1. All fields except Employee Name are numeric.
   2. Employee Name is not missing.
   3. Annual Salary is not greater than $125,000.
b. Include the date and page number in the heading.

3. Write a program to read in data with the following format:

CUSTOMER Record Layout			
Field	Size	Type	No. of Decimal Positions (if Numeric)
CUST-NO	4	Numeric	0
CUST-NAME	26	Alphanumeric	
STORE-NO	1	Numeric	0
SALESPERSON-NO	3	Numeric	0
SALES-AMT	5	Numeric	2
DATE-OF-TRANS	6	Format: mmddyy	

Figure 11.4 Problem definition for Programming Assignment 2.

Systems Flowchart

PAYROLL-MASTER
80-position records
standard labels

CH 11-2
PROGRAM

PAYROLL-LIST

PAYROLL-MASTER **Record Layout**			
Field	**Size**	**Type**	**No. of Decimal Positions (if Numeric)**
EMPLOYEE-NO	5	Numeric	0
EMPLOYEE-NAME	20	Alphanumeric	
TERRITORY-NO	2	Numeric	0
OFFICE-NO	2	Numeric	0
SALARY	6	Numeric	0
SOCIAL-SECURITY-NO	9	Numeric	0
NO-OF-DEPENDENTS	2	Numeric	0
JOB-CLASSIFICATION-CODE	2	Numeric	0
UNION-DUES	5	Numeric	0
INSURANCE	5	Numeric	0
Unused	22	Alphanumeric	

PAYROLL-LIST Printer Spacing Chart

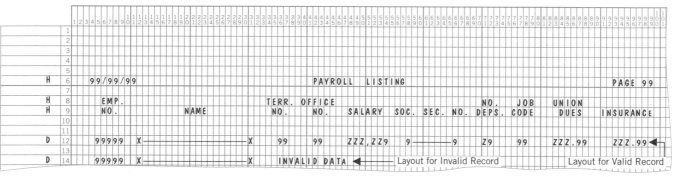

The program should check to ensure that:

a. CUST NO is within the range 101–9621.

b. CUST NAME is nonblank.

c. STORE NO is 1–4.

d. SALESPERSON NO is not blank and salesperson numbers and store numbers are consistent:

STORE NO	SALESPERSON NO
1	001–087
2	088–192
3	193–254

e. SALES AMT is numeric and has a maximum value of $150.00.

f. The date of the transaction is a valid date and is within a year of the date of the run.

(continued on next page)

Print any errors, along with an appropriate error message. Print the total number of records processed and the total of each type of error. Prepare a Printer Spacing Chart before writing the program.

4. For Pass-Em State College, read in student records with the following format:

Student Record (Alternate Record Layout Form)

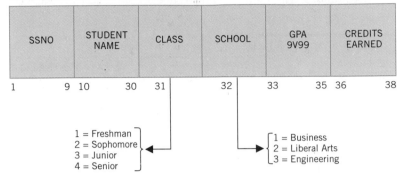

Print an error listing with a corresponding error message for:
a. missing or invalid SSNOs (not numeric).
b. missing names.
c. missing or invalid classes (1–4 are the only acceptable values).
d. missing or invalid schools (1–3 are the only acceptable values).
e. missing or invalid GPAs (0.00–4.00 are the only acceptable values).
f. missing or invalid credits earned. Valid credits earned include:

CLASS	CREDITS EARNED
1	0–30
2	31–59
3	60–92
4	93 +

Credits Earned should not exceed 160.

5. **Interactive Processing.** Write a program to accept data as specified in Programming Assignment 3 above, but assume that the data is entered interactively. Validate the data as indicated in Assignment 3, but add steps to ensure that keyed data that is entered in an improper form is processed correctly (e.g., 9,621 in CUST NO or $263.22 in SALES AMT).

6. **Maintenance Program.** Modify the Practice Program in this chapter so that the validity check on salary ensures instead that annual salaries and department numbers are consistent with new guidelines recently established:

Department	Annual Salary
10	$40,000–$90,000
20	$20,000–$39,999
25	$15,000–$19,999

CHAPTER 12

Array Processing and Table Handling

▮ OBJECTIVES

To familiarize you with

1. How to establish a series of items using an OCCURS clause.
2. How to access and manipulate data stored in an array or table.
3. The rules for using an OCCURS clause in the DATA DIVISION.
4. The use of a SEARCH or SEARCH ALL for a table look-up.

▮ CONTENTS

AN INTRODUCTION TO SINGLE-LEVEL OCCURS CLAUSES

WHY OCCURS CLAUSES ARE USED

We use an **OCCURS clause** in COBOL to indicate the repeated occurrence of fields with the same format. Some of the uses of an OCCURS clause include:

SOME USES OF OCCURS

1. Defining a series of input or output fields, each with the same format.

2. Defining a series of totals in WORKING-STORAGE to which amounts are added; after all data is accumulated, the totals can be printed.

3. Defining a table in WORKING-STORAGE to be accessed by each input record. With a **table,** we use the contents of some input field to "look up" the required data in the table.

Using an OCCURS to Define a Series of Input Fields Each with the Same Format

Defining Fields with an OCCURS Clause

Example Suppose we have one 72-character input record that consists of 24 hourly temperature fields. Each field is three positions long and indicates the temperature for a given city at a particular hour. Using traditional methods, coding the input record with 24 independent hourly fields would prove cumbersome:

```
01   TEMP-REC.
     05   ONE-AM           PIC S9(3).  ⎫
     05   TWO-AM           PIC S9(3).  ⎬ 24 entries
      :                     :          ⎪
     05   MIDNIGHT         PIC S9(3).  ⎭
```

We use the S in the PIC clause for cities in which the temperature might fall below zero.

Moreover, to obtain an average daily temperature would also require a great deal of coding:

```
COMPUTE AVG-TEMP = (ONE-AM + TWO-AM + ... + MIDNIGHT) / 24
```

The ellipses or dots (. . .) mean that the programmer would need to code all 24 entries.

The 24 temperature fields have exactly the same format, that is, three integer positions. Since the format or PIC clause for each of the 24 fields is identical, we could use an OCCURS clause to define the fields. We call the entire 72-position area an **array** that is divided into 24 three-position fields.

With an OCCURS clause, we specify the number of items being defined in the array and the PIC clause of each as follows:

```
01   TEMP-REC.
     05   TEMPERATURE   OCCURS 24 TIMES          PIC S9(3).
```

The OCCURS clause, then, defines 24 three-position numeric fields. Thus, TEMPERATURE is an array that refers to 72 positions or bytes of storage, or 24 three-byte fields. With one OCCURS clause, we define the 72 bytes as 24 fields each three positions long. See Figure 12.1 for an illustration.

Defining a Subscript

Collectively, these 24 fields within the array are called TEMPERATURE, which is the identifier used to access them in the PROCEDURE DIVISION. We would use the identifier TEMPERATURE along with a **subscript** that indicates which of the 24 fields we wish to access. To refer to an item defined by an OCCURS clause, we code the identifier, TEMPERATURE in our example, followed by the subscript, which is in parentheses. The subscript indicates the specific TEMPERATURE desired. Thus, to print the 2 A.M. temperature we code:

```
MOVE TEMPERATURE (2) TO TEMP-OUT
WRITE PRINT-REC FROM OUT-REC
```

Similarly, to display the 11 P.M. temperature on a screen we code:

```
DISPLAY TEMPERATURE (23)
```

Figure 12.1   Storing 24 three-position numeric fields in an array.

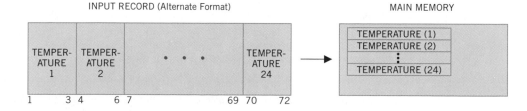

The relationship between OCCURS clauses and subscripts is as follows:

SUMMARY OF OCCURS AND SUBSCRIPTS

1. An OCCURS clause is defined in the DATA DIVISION to indicate the repeated occurrence of items in an array that have the same format.

2. A subscript is used in the PROCEDURE DIVISION to indicate which specific item within the array we wish to access.

We use a subscript, along with the identifier that is defined with an OCCURS, to refer to an item within an array. In the preceding example, the subscript can have any value from 1 through 24. The following, however, have invalid subscripts:

Invalid

```
MOVE TEMPERATURE (0) TO TEMP-OUT
MOVE TEMPERATURE (25) TO TEMP-OUT
```

Since there is no zero element or twenty-fifth element in the array, the subscript cannot take on the values 0 or 25; only the integer values 1 through 24 are valid.

Coding Rules for Subscripts

With many compilers, the coding of a subscript in the PROCEDURE DIVISION requires precise spacing. Other compilers may include enhancements that enable you to use any spacing you want. To be sure your program will run on any computer, there must be at least one space between the identifier and the left parenthesis that precedes the subscript. Similarly, the subscript must be enclosed in parentheses *with no spaces within the parentheses.*

Example
```
ADD TEMPERATURE (22) TO TOTAL
```

The following might result in syntax errors unless the compiler has enhancements that permit more flexible spacing:

Invalid Spacing	Reason
`ADD TEMPERATURE(22) TO TOTAL`	One space is typically required between the word TEMPERATURE and the left parenthesis.
`ADD TEMPERATURE ( 22 ) TO TOTAL`	No spaces are permitted after the left parenthesis or before the right parenthesis.

A Subscript May Be an Integer or an Identifier

Thus far, we have considered subscripts that are numeric literals. A subscript, however, may also be a data-name with a numeric PICTURE clause. Suppose SUB, an abbreviation for subscript, were defined in the WORKING-STORAGE section as follows:

```
01   WORK-AREAS.
     05   SUB PIC 99 VALUE 01.
```

We could move the first field of TEMPERATURE to TEMP-OUT as follows:

```
MOVE TEMPERATURE (SUB) TO TEMP-OUT
```

Subscripts, then, identify items defined with OCCURS clauses and can be either integers or data-names that have a numeric PICTURE clause and an integer value. Using a data-name as a subscript enables us to vary the contents of the subscript so that we can process a series of items with a single routine.

Let us return to our initial TEMPERATURE array. To determine the average daily temperature, we can use numeric literals as subscripts, but to do so would not reduce the coding at all:

```
COMPUTE AVG-TEMP = (TEMPERATURE (1) + ... + TEMPERATURE (24)) / 24
```

It is better to write a routine that adds one temperature at a time to a total. We would vary the contents of a subscript called SUB from 1 to 24 so that all 24 temperatures are added. We define SUB as a WORKING-STORAGE entry with PIC 99. The following is the pseudocode for this problem:

Pseudocode Excerpt

Initialize a Total-Temperature field
PERFORM UNTIL all Temperatures are added
    Add Temperatures to Total-Temperature
END-PERFORM
Compute Average-Temperature = Total-Temperature / 24

The program excerpt could be coded with a standard PERFORM or an in-line PERFORM:

Program Excerpt: With a Standard PERFORM (COBOL 85 and 74)

```
    MOVE 1 TO SUB
    MOVE ZEROS TO TOTAL-TEMP
    PERFORM 500-ADD-RTN
        UNTIL SUB > 24
    COMPUTE AVG-TEMP = TOTAL-TEMP / 24
        :
500-ADD-RTN.
    ADD TEMPERATURE (SUB) TO TOTAL-TEMP
    ADD 1 TO SUB.
```

Program Excerpt: With an In-line PERFORM (COBOL 85)

```
    MOVE 1 TO SUB
    MOVE ZEROS TO TOTAL-TEMP
    PERFORM UNTIL SUB > 24
        ADD TEMPERATURE (SUB) TO TOTAL-TEMP
        ADD 1 TO SUB
    END-PERFORM
    COMPUTE AVG-TEMP = TOTAL-TEMP / 24
```

Alternatively, a subscript can be used as the field to be varied in a PERFORM ... VARYING statement. The PERFORM ... VARYING statement (1) initializes SUB at 1, (2) adds each TEMPERATURE within the array, and (3) increments SUB until it has processed all 24 temperatures:

Program Excerpt: With a Standard PERFORM (COBOL 85 and 74)

```
    MOVE ZEROS TO TOTAL-TEMP
    PERFORM 500-ADD-RTN
        VARYING SUB FROM 1 BY 1
            UNTIL SUB > 24
    COMPUTE AVG-TEMP = TOTAL-TEMP / 24
        :
500-ADD-RTN.
    ADD TEMPERATURE (SUB) TO TOTAL-TEMP.
```

Program Excerpt: With an In-line PERFORM (COBOL 85)

```
    MOVE ZEROS TO TOTAL-TEMP
    PERFORM VARYING SUB
            FROM 1 BY 1 UNTIL SUB > 24
        ADD TEMPERATURE (SUB) TO TOTAL-TEMP
    END-PERFORM
    COMPUTE AVG-TEMP = TOTAL-TEMP / 24
```

Similarly, the PERFORM ... TIMES could be used instead.

When using the UNTIL or TIMES option of the PERFORM, the subscript *must be initialized prior to the* PERFORM; it must also be incremented within the routine or loop to be performed.

We will use the PERFORM ... VARYING in most of our illustrations. It is the most suitable option for accessing subscripted entries since it initializes, increments, and tests the subscript used in the procedure.

Relative Subscripting with COBOL 85

A subscript can be either (1) a data-name with numeric, integer value, or (2) a numeric literal with integer value. With COBOL 85, a subscript can also have a relative value, that is, a data-name or integer to which another data-name or integer is subtracted or added. We call this a **relative subscript**. Thus, the following is an acceptable way with COBOL 85 to find the total of the last 12 hourly (P.M.) temperatures:

Example

```
PERFORM VARYING SUB FROM 1 BY 1 UNTIL SUB > 12
    ADD TEMPERATURE (SUB + 12) TO TOTAL-PM-TEMP
END-PERFORM
```

─────────── DEBUGGING TIP ───────────

Be sure the PIC clause of the subscript includes enough 9's to hold all possible values for the subscript. If a subscript to be used with an array containing 100 elements has a PIC 99 rather than 9(3), a processing error is likely to occur. Also ensure that the contents of the subscript is always greater than or equal to 1 and less than or equal to the maximum number of elements in the array.

When the PERFORM ... VARYING is used, the subscript must be large enough to store a value that is one more than the upper subscript limit. For example, if the subscript varies from 1 to 9, we need a PIC of 99 to allow for the number 10 (SUB > 9) to exit the loop.

SELF-TEST   Consider the following for Questions 1 through 5:

```
01  IN-REC.
    05   AMT1        PIC 9(5).
    05   AMT2        PIC 9(5).
    05   AMT3        PIC 9(5).
    05   AMT4        PIC 9(5).
    05   AMT5        PIC 9(5).
```

1. An OCCURS clause could be used in place of defining each AMT field separately because _____ .

2. (T or F) Suppose AMT2 and AMT4 had PIC 9(3). An OCCURS clause could not be used to define all the AMT fields.

3. Recode the fields within IN-REC using an OCCURS clause.

4. To access any of the five items defined with the OCCURS clause, we must use a _____ in the PROCEDURE DIVISION.

5. Code a routine to determine the total of all five AMT fields. Assume that a field called SUB has been defined in WORKING-STORAGE to serve as a subscript.

Solutions   1. all AMTs have the same format or PIC clause
               2. T
               3.
```
   01   IN-REC.
        05   AMT OCCURS 5 TIMES        PIC 9(5).
```
               4. subscript
               5.

COBOL 74 or 85	COBOL 85 (With an In-line PERFORM)
MOVE ZEROS TO TOTAL	MOVE ZEROS TO TOTAL
PERFORM 500-TOTAL-RTN	PERFORM VARYING SUB
VARYING SUB FROM 1 BY 1	FROM 1 BY 1 UNTIL SUB > 5
UNTIL SUB > 5	ADD AMT (SUB) TO TOTAL
⋮	END-PERFORM
500-TOTAL-RTN.	⋮
ADD AMT (SUB) TO TOTAL.	

Using an OCCURS in WORKING-STORAGE for Storing Totals

Thus far, we have seen that an OCCURS clause may be used as part of an input record to indicate the repeated occurrence of incoming fields. Similarly, an OCCURS may be used as part of an output record to define a series of fields. An OCCURS clause may be used to define fields either in the FILE SECTION or in WORKING-STORAGE.

Suppose, for example, that input consists of the following description for records transacted during the previous year:

```
01   IN-REC.
     05   TRANS-NO-IN                PIC 9(5).
     05   DATE-OF-TRANS-IN.
          10   MONTH-IN              PIC 99.
          10   DAY-NO-IN             PIC 99.
          10   YR-IN                 PIC 99.
     05   AMT-IN                     PIC 9(3)V99.
```

Since there is no item that is repeated, we do not need to use the OCCURS clause within this input record. Suppose we wish to establish an array in WORKING-STORAGE that consists of 12 monthly totals for all transaction records for the previous year:

```
WORKING-STORAGE SECTION.
01   TOTALS.
     05   MO-TOT OCCURS 12 TIMES     PIC 9(5)V99.
```

We would define 12 MO-TOT fields in WORKING-STORAGE to store the total of all transaction amounts for months 01–12 respectively. Each IN-REC read will include an AMT-IN and a MONTH-IN number. We will add the AMT-IN to a MO-TOT field determined by the contents of the MONTH-IN entered within DATE-OF-TRANS-IN. If MONTH-IN = 2, for example, we will add the AMT-IN to the second MO-TOT or MO-TOT (2).

Note that we must initialize the MO-TOT fields to zero at the beginning of the program before any AMT-IN fields are added to them. One way to initialize the 12 MO-TOT fields is as follows:

Program Excerpt:
Standard PERFORM (COBOL 85 and 74)

```
PERFORM 500-INIT-RTN
     VARYING SUB1 FROM 1
          BY 1 UNTIL SUB1 > 12
     :
500-INIT-RTN.
     MOVE ZEROS TO MO-TOT (SUB1).
```

Program Excerpt:
In-Line PERFORM (COBOL 85)

```
PERFORM VARYING SUB1 FROM 1
          BY 1 UNTIL SUB1 > 12
     MOVE ZEROS TO MO-TOT (SUB1)
END-PERFORM
     :
```

With COBOL 85, the best method for setting the MO-TOT fields to zero is by coding INITIALIZE TOTALS. Alternatively, with COBOL 85 compilers (and some COBOL 74 enhanced compilers) we can use the following to set all the MO-TOT fields to zero with one statement: MOVE ZEROS TO TOTALS.

With COBOL 85, we can also use a VALUE clause with MO-TOT:

```
05   MO-TOT OCCURS 12 TIMES         PIC 9(5)V99     VALUE ZEROS.
```

─── DEBUGGING TIP ───

Code MOVE ZEROS TO TOTALS, *not* MOVE 0 TO TOTALS. On some computers, the latter will move only one zero to the leftmost position in the TOTALS array. This is because TOTALS, as a group item, is treated as an alphanumeric field. If a single character is moved to an alphanumeric field, that character is moved to the high-order position and remaining positions are filled with blanks.

For improved efficiency, TOTALS should be defined as a PACKED-DECIMAL field. If it is, then each MO-TOT must be set to zero using a PERFORM, or TOTALS could be set to zero by coding INITIALIZE TOTALS. That is, if TOTALS is defined as PACKED-DECIMAL, MOVE ZEROS TO TOTALS should *not* be used.

The following pseudocode illustrates how we can accumulate the total transaction amounts for months 01–12:

Pseudocode

MAIN-MODULE

    PERFORM Initialize-Rtn

    PERFORM UNTIL there is no more data

        READ a Record

            AT END

                Move 'NO ' to Are-There-More-Records

            NOT AT END

                Add the Input Amount to the Corresponding Monthly Total

        END-READ

    END-PERFORM

    ⋮

INITIALIZE-RTN

    Open the Files

    Initialize the Array

The corresponding program excerpt is as follows:

COBOL 85

```
PROCEDURE DIVISION.
100-MAIN-MODULE.
    PERFORM 500-INITIALIZATION-RTN
    PERFORM UNTIL THERE-ARE-NO-MORE-RECORDS
        READ INFILE
            AT END
                MOVE 'NO ' TO ARE-THERE-MORE-RECORDS
            NOT AT END
                ADD AMT-IN TO MO-TOT (MONTH-IN)
        END-READ
    END-PERFORM
    :
500-INITIALIZATION-RTN.
    OPEN INPUT  INFILE
         OUTPUT PRINT-FILE
    MOVE ZEROS TO TOTALS.
```

COBOL 74 Substitutions

```
PERFORM 200-CALC-RTN
    UNTIL THERE-ARE-NO-MORE-RECORDS.
:
200-CALC-RTN.
    ADD AMT-IN TO MO-TOT (MONTH-IN).
    READ INFILE
        AT END MOVE 'NO ' TO ARE-THERE-MORE-RECORDS.
```

```
READ INFILE
    AT END MOVE 'NO ' TO ARE-THERE-MORE-RECORDS.
```

A subscript called MONTH-IN determines the MO-TOT to which the contents of the input field AMT-IN is to be added. In this case, this subscript is also an *input field*. As noted previously, subscripts can be data-names defined in either the FILE SECTION or the WORKING-STORAGE SECTION. If MONTH-IN is 3, for example, we would add AMT-IN to the third MO-TOT. Coding ADD AMT-IN TO MO-TOT (MONTH-IN) will add an amount to a month total indicated by the month number entered as input.

Performing an initialization routine from the main module results in a more modularized top-down program. All the details such as opening files and setting fields to zero are left for a minor module.

Validating Input Data

You should use input fields as subscripts only if you are sure they have valid values. In this case, MONTH-IN should only vary from 1 to 12. If MONTH-IN were erroneously entered with a value that was less than 01 or greater than 12, the program would not run properly. To minimize such errors, 200-CALC-RTN should include a validity check before adding to a total, as follows:

Pseudocode Excerpt

```
PERFORM UNTIL there is no more data
        READ a Record
                AT END
                        Move 'NO ' to
                                Are-There-More-Records
                NOT  AT  END
                        PERFORM Calc-Rtn
        END-READ
END-PERFORM
⋮
```

CALC-RTN

```
IF the Input Month field is valid
THEN
        Add the Input Amount to
                the corresponding
                        Monthly Total
ELSE
        Write an Error Message
END-IF
```

Program Excerpt (COBOL 85)

```
PERFORM UNTIL ARE-THERE-MORE-RECORDS
        = 'NO '
        READ INFILE
                AT END
                        MOVE 'NO ' TO
                                ARE-THERE-MORE-RECORDS
                NOT AT END
                        PERFORM 200-CALC-RTN
        END-READ
END-PERFORM
        :
        :
200-CALC-RTN.
IF  MONTH-IN > 0 AND < 13
        ADD AMT-IN TO MO-TOT (MONTH-IN)
ELSE
        PERFORM 400-ERR-RTN
END-IF.
```

From the pseudocode you can see that the module will read each record and, if it contains a valid MONTH-IN, AMT-IN will be added to the appropriate MO-TOT. After all the input has been processed, control will return to the main module where we will print out the monthly totals. The monthly totals are to print in sequence from 1 to 12.

In the previous example, we used the NOT AT END clause of the READ to add the amount to the appropriate monthly total. Since only a single imperative statement was required, we did not need a 200-CALC-RTN. In this excerpt, we need to validate the input data before adding it; this requires a compound IF statement that is best coded in a separate module.

The pseudocode for this entire program is as follows:

Pseudocode

MAIN-MODULE

```
START
        PERFORM Initialization-Rtn
        PERFORM UNTIL there is no more data
                READ a Record
                        AT END
                                Move 'NO ' to Are-There-More-Records
                        NOT AT END
                                PERFORM Calc-Rtn
                END-READ
        END-PERFORM
        PERFORM Print-Rtn UNTIL the entire Array is printed
        PERFORM End-of-Job-Rtn
STOP
```

INITIALIZATION-RTN

```
        Open the Files
        Initialize the Array
```

CALC-RTN

```
        IF the Input Month field is valid
        THEN
```

           Add the Input Amount to the corresponding Monthly Total
ELSE
           Write an Error Message
END-IF

PRINT-RTN
    Move Each Array Entry from 1 to 12 to the Output Area
    Write a Line

END-OF-JOB-RTN
    End-of-Job-Operations

We can use a PERFORM 300-PRINT-RTN VARYING ... statement, with a subscript varying from 1 to 12, to print the array:

COBOL 85

```
PROCEDURE DIVISION.
*************************************************************
*  this module controls reading of input and printing      *
*  of 12 total lines                                        *
*************************************************************
100-MAIN-MODULE.
    PERFORM 500-INITIALIZATION-RTN
    PERFORM UNTIL ARE-THERE-MORE-RECORDS = 'NO '
        READ INFILE
            AT END
                MOVE 'NO ' TO ARE-THERE-MORE-RECORDS
            NOT AT END
                PERFORM 200-CALC-RTN
        END-READ
    END-PERFORM
    PERFORM 300-PRINT-RTN VARYING SUB FROM 1 BY 1
        UNTIL SUB > 12
    PERFORM 600-END-OF-JOB-RTN
    STOP RUN.
*************************************************************
*  this module processes input by adding the input amount  *
*  to the corresponding monthly total. it is performed      *
*  from 100-main-module.                                    *
*************************************************************
200-CALC-RTN.
    IF  MONTH-IN > 0 AND < 13
        ADD AMT-IN TO MO-TOT (MONTH-IN)
    ELSE
        PERFORM 400-ERR-RTN
    END-IF.


*************************************************************
*  this module prints the 12 monthly totals in order. it   *
*  is performed from 100-main-module.                       *
*************************************************************
300-PRINT-RTN.
    MOVE MO-TOT (SUB) TO MO-TOT-OUT
    WRITE PR-REC FROM MO-TOT-LINE
        AFTER ADVANCING 2 LINES.
*************************************************************
*  this module prints an error if the input month is not   *
*  between 01 and 12. it is performed from 200-calc-rtn.    *
*************************************************************
400-ERR-RTN.
    WRITE PR-REC FROM ERR-LINE
        AFTER ADVANCING 2 LINES.
```

COBOL 74 Substitutions

```
PERFORM 200-CALC-RTN
    UNTIL ARE-THERE-MORE-RECORDS = 'NO '.
```

```
READ INFILE
    AT END MOVE 'NO ' TO ARE-THERE-MORE-RECORDS.
```

```
****************************************************************
*    this module opens the files and initializes the array.  *
*    it is performed from 100-main-module.                   *
****************************************************************
   500-INITIALIZATION-RTN.
       OPEN INPUT  INFILE
              OUTPUT PRINT-FILE
       INITIALIZE TOTALS.

****************************************************************
*    this module closes the files. it is                     *
*    performed from 100-main-module.                         *
****************************************************************
   600-END-OF-JOB-RTN.
       CLOSE INFILE
              PRINT-FILE.
```

COBOL 74 Substitutions

```
MOVE ZEROS TO TOTALS.
READ INFILE
    AT END MOVE 'NO ' TO ARE-THERE-MORE-RECORDS.
```

Thus, the WORKING-STORAGE array called MO-TOT is accessed in two ways:

1. Using MONTH-IN as a subscript
   For each record read, the input field called MONTH-IN is used to specify to which MO-TOT the AMT-IN is to be added. Data need not be entered in any specific sequence; the contents of MONTH-IN determines which MO-TOT is used in the addition.

2. Using a WORKING-STORAGE entry called SUB as a subscript
   After all input has been read and processed, a subscript called SUB is varied from 1 to 12 to print out the contents of the MO-TOTs in consecutive order.

Note that if the data was entered in sequence by month number, then a control break procedure could be used in place of array processing.

RULES FOR USE OF THE OCCURS CLAUSE

Levels 02–49

An OCCURS clause may be used on levels 02–49 only. That is, the OCCURS is not valid for the 01 level since it must be used for defining fields, not records.

Suppose we wish to read 15 input records with the same format. It is *not* valid to code the following:

```
01  IN-REC OCCURS 15 TIMES.
```

To indicate 15 occurrences of IN-REC, we read and process 15 records:

```
PERFORM 15 TIMES
    READ INFILE
        AT END
            MOVE 'NO ' TO ARE-THERE-MORE-RECORDS
        NOT AT END
            PERFORM 200-PROCESS-RTN
    END-READ
END-PERFORM
```

To read or write a specific number of records, the PROCEDURE DIVISION would include a module that is executed the required number of times. The DATA DIVISION would simply include the record format as in previous programs. OCCURS is used for repeated occurrences of fields, then, *not* records.

In the preceding example, we read and process 15 records. We are assuming that there are precisely 15 records to be entered as input. Validity tests could be added to this procedure to ensure that this is the case.

Defining Elementary or Group Items with an OCCURS Clause

Thus far, we have focused on OCCURS clauses that define elementary items:

Example
```
WORKING-STORAGE SECTION.
01  TOTALS.
    05  MO-TOT OCCURS 12 TIMES  PIC 9(5)V99.
```

The 05-level item defined by an OCCURS has a PIC clause, making the 12 MO-TOT fields elementary items. Thus, TOTALS is an 84-byte array (12 × 7) consisting of 12 elementary items:

TOTALS

99999V99	99999V99	· · ·	99999V99
MO-TOT (1)	MO-TOT (2)		MO-TOT (12)

The identifier used with an OCCURS clause may be a group item as well:

```
01  TAX-TABLE.
    05  GROUP-X OCCURS 20 TIMES.
        10  CITY                PIC X(6).
        10  TAX-RATE            PIC V999.
```

In this instance, CITY and TAX-RATE each occur 20 times within a group item called GROUP-X:

TAX-TABLE

GROUP-X (1)		GROUP-X (2)			GROUP-X (20)	
CITY (1)	TAX-RATE (1)	CITY (2)	TAX-RATE (2)	• • •	CITY (20)	TAX-RATE (20)

Similarly, to print out 20 tax rates, we could have the following print record:

```
01  TAX-LINE.
    05                          PIC X(12).
    :
    05  ENTRIES OCCURS 20 TIMES.
        10  TAX-RATE-OUT        PIC .999.
        10                      PIC X(2).
```

We want the decimal point to print, so we use .999 as the PIC clause for TAX-RATE-OUT. The blank field-name that occurs 20 times will ensure that there are two spaces between each printed tax rate. Use the word FILLER in place of blank field-names with COBOL 74.

Accessing a WORKING-STORAGE Area Defined by an OCCURS Clause

Example 1
Consider again the array consisting of monthly totals that was defined previously:

```
WORKING-STORAGE SECTION.
01  TOTALS.
    05  MO-TOT OCCURS 12 TIMES  PIC 9(5)V99.
```

Suppose all the data has been read from the transaction records and added to the corresponding array entry. Now we wish to write a routine to find the year-end final total, that is, the sum of all monthly totals. The structured pseudocode for this procedure is as follows:

Pseudocode Excerpt

> Clear Yearly Total Area
> PERFORM Add-Rtn UNTIL all Array Elements
>   have been added
> Move Yearly Total to Output
> Write a Record with the Yearly Total

ADD-RTN
>   Add each Array Element to a Yearly Total

The program excerpt for this procedure is as follows:

```
*****************************************************************
*   this procedure calculates a yearly total from monthly   *
*   totals stored in an array                               *
*****************************************************************
 200-YEARLY-TOTAL-RTN.
     MOVE ZEROS TO WS-YEARLY-TOTAL
     PERFORM 300-ADD-RTN
         VARYING SUB FROM 1 BY 1 UNTIL SUB > 12
     MOVE WS-YEARLY-TOTAL TO TOTAL-OUT
     WRITE PRINT-REC FROM TOTAL-LINE
         AFTER ADVANCING 2 LINES.
 300-ADD-RTN.
     ADD MO-TOT (SUB) TO WS-YEARLY-TOTAL.
```

This procedure could also be coded with a PERFORM ... UNTIL or a PERFORM ... TIMES. In all cases, an in-line PERFORM can be used with COBOL 85.

Example 2 Using the same array, find the number of months in which the monthly total exceeded $10,000. The pseudocode and program excerpt for this procedure are as follows:

Pseudocode Excerpt

>   Initialize a Counter
>   PERFORM Test-Rtn UNTIL entire Array
>   is processed
>   Print the value in the Counter

TEST-RTN
>   IF   a Monthly Total exceeds $10,000
>   THEN
>   Add 1 to the Counter
>   END-IF

Program Excerpt

```
***********************************************
*   this procedure determines number of     *
*   mos with totals in excess of $10,000    *
***********************************************
 500-OVER-10000-RTN.
     MOVE ZEROS TO WS-CTR
     PERFORM 600-TEST-RTN
         VARYING SUB
             FROM 1 BY 1 UNTIL SUB > 12
     MOVE WS-CTR TO CTR-OUT
     WRITE PRINT-REC FROM CTR-LINE
         AFTER ADVANCING 2 LINES.
 600-TEST-RTN.
     IF  MO-TOT (SUB) > 10000
         ADD 1 TO WS-CTR
     END-IF.
```

 Interactive Processing.   We could display the result on a screen rather than printing it by substituting the following for the preceding WRITE statement:

```
DISPLAY 'THE NO. OF MONTHS WITH TOTALS > 10,000 IS ', CTR-OUT.
```

PROCESSING DATA STORED IN AN ARRAY

USING OCCURS WITH VALUE AND REDEFINES CLAUSES

Sometimes we want to initialize elements in a table or an array with specific values. We have seen that with COBOL 85 you can use a VALUE clause to set an entire array to zero:

```
01  ARRAY-1    VALUE ZERO.
    05  TOTALS    OCCURS 50 TIMES    PIC 9(5).
```

The VALUE clause can be coded instead on the OCCURS level with COBOL 85:

```
01  ARRAY-1.
    05  TOTALS    OCCURS 50 TIMES    PIC 9(5)    VALUE    ZERO.
```

COBOL 85

But suppose we have an array where we want to set each element to a different value. Because COBOL 85 permits VALUE clauses to be used in conjunction with an OCCURS entry, a data-name called MONTH-NAMES could be coded as follows:

```
01  MONTH-NAMES
        VALUE 'JANFEBMARAPRMAYJUNJULAUGSEPOCTNOVDEC'.
    05  MONTH OCCURS 12 TIMES      PIC XXX.
```

In this instance, a 36-character array is established that consists of 12 three-position fields, the first containing JAN, the second containing FEB, . . . and the twelfth containing DEC.

COBOL 74

With COBOL 74, we cannot use a VALUE clause with an entry defined by an OCCURS clause. Instead, we can define the 36-position storage area as one field with a VALUE of JANFEBMARAPRMAYJUNJULAUGSEPOCTNOVDEC. We can then *redefine* that storage area into 12 separate array elements using an OCCURS. As a result, each array element will have a different value:

```
01  MONTH-NAMES.
    05  STRING-1            PIC X(36) VALUE
          'JANFEBMARAPRMAYJUNJULAUGSEPOCTNOVDEC'.
    05  MONTH REDEFINES STRING-1 OCCURS 12 TIMES PIC XXX.
```

The first 05 field, STRING-1, establishes a 36-position constant that contains a three-character abbreviation for each of the 12 months of the year. MONTH then redefines STRING-1 and enables each three-character abbreviation for months 1 through 12 to be accessed separately using a subscript.

In either case, MONTH (SUB) contains a three-character month abbreviation. If we move MONTH (4), for example, to an output area, APR would print, which is an abbreviation for the fourth month. In this way, each abbreviation for a month can be accessed by using the corresponding subscript, as in the following:

JAN	FEB	MAR	APR	MAY	JUN	JUL	AUG	SEP	OCT	NOV	DEC
MONTH (1)	MONTH (2)	MONTH (3)	MONTH (4)	MONTH (5)	MONTH (6)	MONTH (7)	MONTH (8)	MONTH (9)	MONTH (10)	MONTH (11)	MONTH (12)

To print the appropriate three-character abbreviation for each month, we may use the following routine with any version of COBOL:

```
        :
        :
    PERFORM PRINT-TABLE
        VARYING SUB FROM 1 BY 1 UNTIL SUB  > 12
        :
    PRINT-TABLE.
        MOVE MONTH (SUB) TO MONTH-OUT
        :
        WRITE PRINT-REC FROM PRINT-OUT
            AFTER ADVANCING 2 LINES.
```

Similarly, to define an array with five entries valued at 0102030405, we would have:

COBOL 85	COBOL 74

`01  ARRAY-1 VALUE '0102030405'.`
`    05  TOTALS-1  OCCURS 5 TIMES PIC 99.`
	`01  ARRAY-1.`
	`    05  TOTALS-1  OCCURS 5 TIMES PIC 99.`
	`    05  TOTALS-1A REDEFINES`
	`            TOTALS-1  PIC 9(10)`
	`            VALUE 0102030405.`

With COBOL 85, ARRAY-1 has an alphanumeric value because it is a group item.

Although it is permissible with COBOL 85 to define a field with a VALUE and then redefine it as an array, we cannot do the reverse. That is, once an entry has been defined by an OCCURS clause, it may *not* be redefined. Thus the following is invalid:

Invalid

```
05  ITEM-X  OCCURS 4 TIMES     PIC S999.
05  ITEM-Y  REDEFINES ITEM-X   PIC X(12).◄——Cannot redefine an array
```

Regardless of the compiler, you can always define a field and *then redefine* it with an OCCURS clause. In addition, the first field, which is defined without an OCCURS, may have a VALUE clause that is used to establish a constant, if it is in the WORKING-STORAGE SECTION. With COBOL 85, VALUE clauses can be used in conjunction with OCCURS entries.

PRINTING DATA STORED IN AN ARRAY

At the beginning of this chapter, we discussed a program that processed 24 hourly temperatures for a given city for a particular day. We used a PIC S9(3) so that any city's temperatures could be defined even if the temperature fell below zero. The input record, then, should be defined as:

```
01  TEMP-REC.
    05  TEMPERATURE OCCURS 24 TIMES    PIC S9(3).
```

We could have several such records, each containing temperatures for a different day. Suppose that we want to print out on one line the 24 hourly temperature values in each input record.

Pseudocode Excerpt

MAIN-MODULE
START
    PERFORM Initialization-Rtn
    PERFORM UNTIL there is no more data
        READ a Record
            AT END
                Move 'NO ' to Are-There-More-Records
            NOT AT END
                PERFORM Process-Rtn
        END-READ
    END-PERFORM
    ⋮
STOP

PROCESS-RTN
    PERFORM Move-Rtn UNTIL the entire Input Array
        has been processed
    Write an Output Record

MOVE-RTN
    Move Input Array Entry to Output Area

We can also use the OCCURS clause in an output record, as illustrated in the following program excerpt:

COBOL 85

```
DATA DIVISION.
FILE SECTION.
FD  TEMP-FILE
```

COBOL 74 Substitutions

For COBOL 74, FILLER must be used
instead of a blank field name

```
                              LABEL RECORDS ARE OMITTED.
                          01  TEMP-REC.
                              05  TEMPERATURE OCCURS 24 TIMES     PIC S9(3).
                          FD  PRINT-FILE
                              LABEL RECORDS ARE OMITTED.
                          01  PRINT-REC                           PIC X(132).
                          WORKING-STORAGE SECTION.
                          01  OUT-RECORD.
                              05                                  PIC X.
                              05  AMT-OUT OCCURS 24 TIMES.
                                  10  TEMP-OUT                    PIC -ZZ9.
                                  10                              PIC X.
                              05                                  PIC X(11).
                          01  WORK-AREAS.
                              05  SUB                             PIC 99.
                                   :
                          *
                          PROCEDURE DIVISION.
                          **********************************************************
                          *   this module controls reading of input and printing  *
                          *   of temperatures                                      *
                          **********************************************************
                          100-MAIN-MODULE.
                              PERFORM 400-INITIALIZATION-RTN
                              PERFORM UNTIL THERE-ARE-NO-MORE-RECORDS
                                  READ TEMP-FILE
                                      AT END
                                          MOVE 'NO ' TO ARE-THERE-MORE-RECORDS
                                      NOT AT END
                                          PERFORM 200-PROCESS-RTN
                                  END-READ
                              END-PERFORM
                              PERFORM 500-END-OF-JOB-RTN
                              STOP RUN.
                          **********************************************************
                          *   this module processes each input record. it is      *
                          *   performed from 100-main-module.                      *
                          **********************************************************
                          200-PROCESS-RTN.
                              PERFORM 300-MOVE-RTN
                                  VARYING SUB FROM 1 BY 1 UNTIL SUB > 24
                              WRITE PRINT-REC FROM OUT-RECORD
                                  AFTER ADVANCING 2 LINES.

                          **********************************************************
                          *   this module moves the 24 temperatures from each      *
                          *   record to an output area. it is performed from       *
                          *   200-process-rtn.                                     *
                          **********************************************************
                          300-MOVE-RTN.
                              MOVE TEMPERATURE (SUB) TO TEMP-OUT (SUB).
                          400-INITIALIZATION-RTN.
                              OPEN INPUT  TEMP-FILE
                                   OUTPUT PRINT-FILE
                              MOVE SPACES TO OUT-RECORD.

                          500-END-OF-JOB-RTN.
                              CLOSE TEMP-FILE
                                    PRINT-FILE.
```

```
PERFORM 200-PROCESS-RTN
    UNTIL THERE-ARE-NO-MORE-RECORDS.
```

```
READ TEMP-FILE
    AT END MOVE 'NO ' TO ARE-THERE-MORE-RECORDS.
```

```
READ TEMP-FILE
    AT END MOVE 'NO ' TO ARE-THERE-MORE-RECORDS.
```

AMT-OUT is a group item that consists of two elementary items: TEMP-OUT and a blank field-name or a FILLER. The second field is a separator, which is necessary so that there is a single blank between each temperature for readability. The layout for the print positions of OUT-RECORD, then, is as follows:

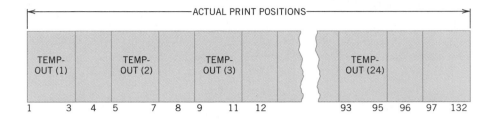

The preceding is a full program that reads records each with 24 hourly temperatures and prints all 24 temperatures for each record on a single line. The program has two arrays, one for storing 24 hourly temperatures per input record and one for storing the same temperatures along with separator fields in the output area.

Suppose we wish to read in the same series of 24 hourly temperatures and print the highest temperature for each day. The input would be the same. The OUT-RECORD and description for HIGHEST-TEMP in WORKING-STORAGE would be:

```
WORKING-STORAGE SECTION.
01  OUT-RECORD.
    05              PIC X(48)
        VALUE ' HIGHEST TEMPERATURE FOR THE DAY IS '.
    05  HIGHEST     PIC -9(3).
    05              PIC X(80)      VALUE SPACES.
01  HIGHEST-TEMP    PIC S9(3).
```

The MAIN-MODULE of the PROCEDURE DIVISION would be the same as the preceding. Assume that the input temperature record has been read into the TEMPERATURE array. 200-PROCESS-RTN and 300-MOVE-RTN would be as follows:

```
200-PROCESS-RTN.
    MOVE -999 TO HIGHEST-TEMP
    PERFORM 300-MOVE-RTN
        VARYING SUB FROM 1 BY 1 UNTIL SUB > 24
    MOVE HIGHEST-TEMP TO HIGHEST
    WRITE PRINT-REC FROM OUT-RECORD
        AFTER ADVANCING 2 LINES.
300-MOVE-RTN.
    IF  TEMPERATURE (SUB) > HIGHEST-TEMP
        MOVE TEMPERATURE (SUB) TO HIGHEST-TEMP
    END-IF.
```

Note that this program handles temperatures that could fall below zero degrees because the PIC for the temperatures contains an S. We initialize HIGHEST-TEMP at -999, a negative number so low that the first TEMPERATURE (SUB) will surely exceed it and be moved to it as the first "real" entry. Alternatively, we could MOVE TEMPERATURE (1) TO HIGHEST-TEMP initially and PERFORM 300-MOVE-RTN VARYING SUB FROM 2 BY 1 UNTIL SUB > 24. The edited field, HIGHEST, contains a minus sign that will print only if HIGHEST-TEMP happens to be negative.

If we wanted to print the number of hours in a day when the temperature dipped below 40 degrees, we would code our OUT-RECORD as:

```
01  OUT-RECORD.
    05              PIC X(49)
        VALUE ' THE NUMBER OF HOURS WHEN TEMPERATURE WAS < 40 IS '.
    05  CTR         PIC 99         VALUE ZEROS.
    05              PIC X(81)      VALUE SPACES.
```

200-PROCESS-RTN and 300-MOVE-RTN would be as follows:

```
200-PROCESS-RTN.
    PERFORM 300-MOVE-RTN
        VARYING SUB FROM 1 BY 1 UNTIL SUB > 24
```

```
        WRITE PRINT-REC FROM OUT-RECORD
            AFTER ADVANCING 2 LINES.
    300-MOVE-RTN.
        IF  TEMPERATURE (SUB) < 40
            ADD 1 TO CTR
        END-IF.
```

Printing Subscripted Variables in a Variety of Ways

Consider the TEMP-FILE described in the preceding section. Suppose we wish to print 24 lines of output, each with an hourly temperature. The TEMP-OUT-RECORD-1 would appear as follows:

```
01  TEMP-OUT-RECORD-1.
    05                  PIC X(50).
    05  TEMP-OUT        PIC -ZZ9.
    05                  PIC X(78).
```

The routine for printing 24 lines would be as follows, using an in-line PERFORM:

```
MOVE SPACES TO TEMP-OUT-RECORD-1
PERFORM     VARYING SUB FROM 1 BY 1
                UNTIL SUB > 24
    MOVE TEMPERATURE (SUB) TO TEMP-OUT
    WRITE PRINT-REC FROM TEMP-OUT-RECORD-1
END-PERFORM.
```

Suppose, instead, that we want to print 12 lines of output, each with an A.M. temperature and a P.M. temperature. The output record would appear as follows:

```
01  TEMP-OUT-RECORD-2.
    05                  PIC X(20).
    05  AM-OUT          PIC -ZZ9.
    05                  PIC X(20).
    05  PM-OUT          PIC -ZZ9.
    05                  PIC X(84).
     :
     :
    MOVE SPACES TO TEMP-OUT-RECORD-2
    PERFORM 400-EACH-LINE-RTN
            VARYING AM-SUB FROM 1 BY 1
                UNTIL AM-SUB > 12.
     :
     :
400-EACH-LINE-RTN.
    MOVE TEMPERATURE (AM-SUB) TO AM-OUT
    ADD 12 AM-SUB GIVING PM-SUB
    MOVE TEMPERATURE (PM-SUB) TO PM-OUT
    WRITE PRINT-REC FROM TEMP-OUT-RECORD-2.
```

Since COBOL 85 permits relative addressing with subscripts, we could replace lines 2 and 3 in 400-EACH-LINE-RTN with MOVE TEMPERATURE (AM-SUB + 12) TO PM-OUT.

Suppose we wish to print two lines of output, the first with 12 A.M. temperatures and the second with 12 P.M. temperatures. The output record would appear as follows:

```
01  TEMP-OUT-RECORD-3.
    05                      PIC X(30).
    05  ENTRIES OCCURS 12 TIMES.
        10 TEMP-OUT         PIC -ZZ9.
        10                  PIC XX.
    05                      PIC X(30).
     :
     :
    MOVE SPACES TO TEMP-OUT-RECORD-3
    MOVE 1 TO SUB1
    PERFORM 600-PRINT-RTN 2 TIMES.
     :
     :
600-PRINT-RTN.
    PERFORM 700-LINE-RTN
            VARYING SUB2 FROM 1 BY 1
                UNTIL SUB2 > 12
```

```
        WRITE PRINT-REC FROM TEMP-OUT-RECORD-3.
    700-LINE-RTN.
        MOVE TEMPERATURE (SUB1) TO TEMP-OUT (SUB2)
        ADD 1 TO SUB1.
```

SUB1, used for subscripting TEMPERATURE, varies from 1 to 24 within 700-LINE-RTN, and SUB2, used for subscripting TEMP-OUT, varies from 1 to 12 within 600-PRINT-RTN, which is executed two times, once for each output line. See Figure 12.2 for sample output layouts and the full program.

Figure 12.2   (a) Printing subscripted variables in a variety of ways. (b) The corresponding COBOL 85 program.

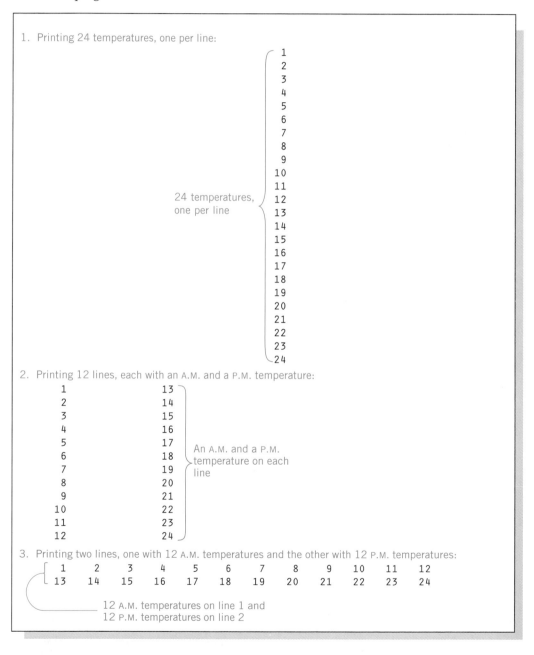

```
IDENTIFICATION DIVISION.
PROGRAM-ID.  TEMP.
ENVIRONMENT DIVISION.
INPUT-OUTPUT SECTION.
FILE-CONTROL.
```

Figure 12.2 (continued)

```
                              SELECT TEMP-FILE ASSIGN TO DISK 'TEMP1.DAT'.
                              SELECT PRINT-FILE ASSIGN TO PRINTER.
           DATA DIVISION.
           FILE SECTION.
           FD  TEMP-FILE
               LABEL RECORDS ARE STANDARD.
           01  TEMP-REC.
               05  TEMPERATURE OCCURS 24 TIMES PIC S999.
           FD  PRINT-FILE
               LABEL RECORDS ARE OMITTED.
           01  PRINT-REC                     PIC X(132).
           WORKING-STORAGE SECTION.
           01  STORED-AREAS.
               05  ARE-THERE-MORE-RECS       PIC X(3)    VALUE 'YES'.
               05  SUB                       PIC 99.
               05  AM-SUB                    PIC 99.
               05  PM-SUB                    PIC 99.
               05  SUB1                      PIC 99.
               05  SUB2                      PIC 99.
           01  TEMP-OUT-RECORD-1.
               05                            PIC X(50).
               05  TEMPERATURE-OUT           PIC -ZZ9.
               05                            PIC X(78).
           01  TEMP-OUT-RECORD-2.
               05                            PIC X(05).
               05  AM-OUT                    PIC -ZZ9.
               05                            PIC X(20).
               05  PM-OUT                    PIC -ZZ9.
               05                            PIC X(69).
           01  TEMP-OUT-RECORD-3.
               05                            PIC X(10).
               05  ENTRIES OCCURS 12 TIMES.
                   10  TEMP-OUT              PIC -ZZ9.
                   10                        PIC XX.
               05                            PIC X(50).
           PROCEDURE DIVISION.
           100-MAIN.
               OPEN INPUT TEMP-FILE
                    OUTPUT PRINT-FILE
               READ TEMP-FILE
                    AT END MOVE 'NO ' TO ARE-THERE-MORE-RECS
               END-READ
               PERFORM 200-ONE-TEMP-PER-LINE
               PERFORM 300-AM-AND-PM-TEMP-PER-LINE
               PERFORM 500-TWELVE-TEMPS-PER-LINE
               CLOSE TEMP-FILE
                     PRINT-FILE
               STOP RUN.
           *************************************************************
           *  The following routine prints 24 temperatures        *
           *         one per line                                  *
           *************************************************************
           200-ONE-TEMP-PER-LINE.
               MOVE SPACES TO TEMP-OUT-RECORD-1
               PERFORM VARYING SUB FROM 1 BY 1
                       UNTIL SUB > 24
                   MOVE TEMPERATURE (SUB) TO TEMPERATURE-OUT
                   WRITE PRINT-REC FROM TEMP-OUT-RECORD-1
               END-PERFORM.
           *************************************************************
           *  The following routine prints one AM and one PM      *
           *         temperature per line - 12 lines print        *
           *************************************************************
           300-AM-AND-PM-TEMP-PER-LINE.
               MOVE SPACES TO TEMP-OUT-RECORD-2
               PERFORM 400-EACH-LINE-RTN
```

Figure 12.2   (continued)

```
             VARYING AM-SUB FROM 1 BY 1 UNTIL AM-SUB > 12.
   400-EACH-LINE-RTN.
       MOVE TEMPERATURE (AM-SUB) TO AM-OUT
       ADD  12 AM-SUB GIVING PM-SUB
       MOVE TEMPERATURE (PM-SUB) TO PM-OUT
       WRITE PRINT-REC FROM TEMP-OUT-RECORD-2.
   ************************************************************
   *   The following routine prints 12 AM temperatures       *
   *        on one line and 12 PM temperatures on a          *
   *        second line. it also uses an in-line PERFORM     *
   ************************************************************
   500-TWELVE-TEMPS-PER-LINE.
       MOVE SPACES TO TEMP-OUT-RECORD-3
       MOVE 1 TO SUB1
       PERFORM 600-PRINT-RTN 2 TIMES.
   600-PRINT-RTN.
       PERFORM    VARYING SUB2 FROM 1 BY 1 UNTIL SUB2 > 12
           MOVE TEMPERATURE (SUB1) TO TEMP-OUT (SUB2)
           ADD 1 TO SUB1
       END-PERFORM
       WRITE PRINT-REC FROM TEMP-OUT-RECORD-3.
```

SELF-TEST

1. What, if anything, is wrong with the following?

   ```
   01   TOTALS OCCURS 50 TIMES.
        05   SUB-TOT              PIC 9(5).
   ```

2. Indicate the difference between the following:
   ```
   (a) 01   TOTAL1.
           05   STATE.
               10   STATE-NAME OCCURS 50 TIMES      PIC X(10).
               10   STATE-POP  OCCURS 50 TIMES      PIC 9(10).
   (b) 01   TOTAL2.
           05   STATE OCCURS 50 TIMES.
               10   STATE-NAME         PIC X(10).
               10   STATE-POP          PIC 9(10).
   ```

3. Suppose the following area is stored in WORKING-STORAGE. It contains the combination of the numbers of the two horses that won the daily double each day for the last year. Assume that last year was not a leap year (i.e., there were 365 rather than 366 days). The data is stored in sequence from January 1 through December 31.

   ```
   01   TOTALS.
        05   DAILY-DOUBLE OCCURS 365 TIMES          PIC 99.
   ```

   Thus, if DAILY-DOUBLE (1) = 45, then horses 4 and 5 won the daily double on January 1. Print the combination of numbers that won the daily double on February 2. (Note that a "real world" application would need to handle leap years as well.)

4. For Question 3, indicate the number of times the winning combination was 25.

5. Consider the following total area in WORKING-STORAGE:

   ```
   01   TOTALS.
        05   DOW-JONES OCCURS 365 TIMES          PIC 9(4)V9.
   ```

   For ease of processing, this total area lists the Dow-Jones industrial average for 365 days from January 1 through December 31 of a given year, including weekends and national holidays. Assume that the year in question was not a leap year. Print the number of days on which the Dow-Jones industrial average fell below 5400.

6. Write a routine to print four temperature lines, each with six hourly temperatures. Code the TEMP-OUT-RECORD first.

Solutions

1. Cannot use OCCURS on the 01 level.

2. The first total area, TOTAL1, defines *two* arrays:

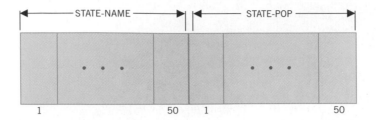

The second total area defines a *single* array with two elementary items:

The first has a string of 50 state names followed by a string of 50 population figures. The second has each state name adjacent to its corresponding population figure.

3.
```
MOVE DAILY-DOUBLE (33) TO NUM-OUT OF PRINT-REC
WRITE PRINT-REC
    AFTER ADVANCING 2 LINES.
```

Note: February 2 is the 33rd day of the year (31 days in January plus 2 in February).

4.
```
    MOVE 0 TO WIN-25
    PERFORM 500-CHECK-RTN
        VARYING SUB FROM 1 BY 1 UNTIL SUB > 365
    MOVE WIN-25 TO NUM-OUT OF PRINT-REC
    WRITE PRINT-REC
        AFTER ADVANCING 2 LINES.
    :
    :
500-CHECK-RTN.
    IF  DAILY-DOUBLE (SUB) = 25
        ADD 1 TO WIN-25
    END-IF.
```

5.
```
    MOVE 0 TO UNDER-5400
    PERFORM 600-LOW-DOW
        VARYING SUB FROM 1 BY 1 UNTIL SUB > 365
    MOVE UNDER-5400 TO NUM-OUT OF PRINT-REC
    WRITE PRINT-REC
        AFTER ADVANCING 2 LINES.
    :
    :
600-LOW-DOW.
    IF  DOW-JONES < 5400
        ADD 1 TO UNDER-5400
    END-IF.
```

6.
```
WORKING-STORAGE SECTION.
01  TEMP-OUT-RECORD
    05                      PIC X(45).
    05  ENTRIES OCCURS 6 TIMES.
        10 TEMP-OUT         PIC -ZZ9.
        10                  PIC XXX.
    05                      PIC X(45).
01  SUB-IN                  PIC 99.
01  SUB-OUT                 PIC 99.
    :
    :
    MOVE SPACES TO TEMP-OUT-RECORD
```

```
         MOVE 1 TO SUB-IN
         PERFORM 500-PRINT-RTN 4 TIMES.
           :
           :
   500-PRINT-RTN.
         PERFORM 600-EACH-LINE-RTN
                VARYING SUB-OUT FROM 1 BY 1
                     UNTIL SUB-OUT > 6
         WRITE OUT-RECORD FROM TEMP-OUT-RECORD.
   600-EACH-LINE-RTN.
         MOVE TEMPERATURE (SUB-IN)
                TO TEMP-OUT (SUB-OUT)
         ADD 1 TO SUB-IN.
```

USING AN OCCURS CLAUSE FOR TABLE HANDLING

DEFINING A TABLE

Thus far, we have focused on the use of an OCCURS clause to:

1. Indicate the repeated occurrence of either input or output fields within the FILE SECTION or WORKING-STORAGE.
2. Store arrays or total areas within WORKING-STORAGE.

In this section, we will focus on the use of an OCCURS clause to store table data. As we will see, tables and arrays are stored in exactly the same way; they are, however, used for different purposes.

A *table* is a list of stored fields that are looked up or referenced by the program. Tables are used in conjunction with table look-ups, where a **table look-up** is a procedure that finds a specific entry in the table.

Thus, an array stores data or totals to be outputted, whereas a table is used for looking up or referencing data.

Why Tables Are Used

Suppose that a mail-order company ships items to customers throughout the United States. A program is required that (1) reads customer input data containing billing information and (2) produces output in the form of bills. Since each county within the United States has a different local tax structure, a procedure must be established for calculating sales tax. Two techniques may be employed:

1. The actual sales tax rate may be entered as part of each input record.
    Entering the sales tax rate in each input record would be very inefficient. First, sales tax rates occasionally change; each time there is a change to a tax rate in a county, *all* input records for that county would need to be changed. Second, recording the sales tax rate for each input record means extra keying. That is, if 1000 input records all pertain to a single county, we would be entering the *same* sales tax rate 1000 times. This results in additional labor and added risk of input errors.
2. The sales tax rates may be entered and stored in a *table*, which can be referenced using a table "look-up."
    This is a far more efficient and effective method for storing tax rate data than the first method. Input to the program would consist of *two files*. The table file with sales tax rates corresponding to each county is entered as the first file and stored in WORKING-STORAGE. Then the input transaction file is read; for each input transaction record, we would find or "look up" the sales tax rate in the table that corresponds to the county specified in the input record.

Suppose there are 1000 tax rates and 10,000 customer records. To include a sales tax rate in each input record would require 10,000 additional fields to be entered as input. It is better to (1) enter and store the 1000 sales tax rates as a table and (2) look up the appropriate rate in the table for each input customer record.

— DEBUGGING TIP —

The table data is typically entered as a file and stored in a WORKING-STORAGE entry using an OCCURS clause. It could be established instead in WORKING-STORAGE directly as a fixed set of values; however, if the sales tax rates are likely to change over time, it is much better to enter them as input. In this way, changes to tax rates can be made to the input file without the need for modifying the program. Wherever possible, use input to enter variable data, and establish constants only when the data is expected to remain unchanged.

STORING THE TABLE IN WORKING-STORAGE

Storing the sales tax data in a table file rather than in each transaction record is more efficient, not only because it minimizes data entry operations, but also because the sales tax rates can be more easily maintained, or *updated*, in a separate table, as needed. That is, if there is a change to a specific tax rate we need only alter the single table entry pertaining to that rate. If the sales tax rate appeared in the input transaction customer file, we would need to revise all records affected by that sales tax change.

To store a table, we must associate a tax rate with each specific tax district. We may use the zip code to identify each tax district.

Assume that a sales tax rate for each zip code is stored in a sales tax table:

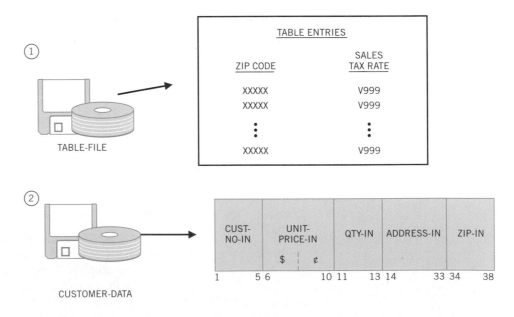

The table file is read first, with zip codes and tax rates stored in WORKING-STORAGE. Then the input customer file is read. The zip code from each customer record is compared to the zip code on the table until a match is found. The sales tax rate corresponding to a specific zip code is used to calculate a total price to be printed as follows:

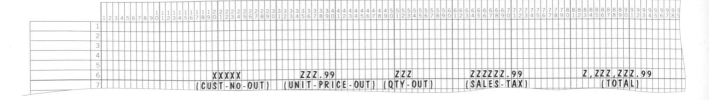

The `TABLE-FILE` consists of table entries, where each table entry is a group item subdivided into a zip code field and its corresponding sales tax rate. The **table argument** is the table entry field that is used to locate the desired element. Here, the table argument is the table's zip code field. The element to be looked up is called the **table function**. In this case, the table function is the table's sales tax rate. The input field in each transaction record that is used for finding a match is called the **search argument**. We compare the search argument to the table argument to find the table function. Consider the following example:

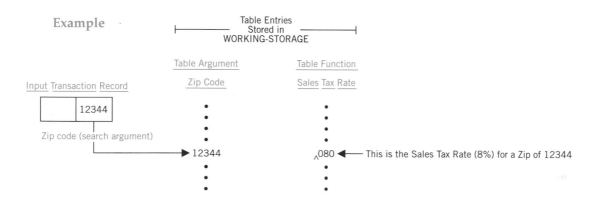

In this example, a zip code of 12344 is in the input transaction record. This is the search argument. We use this search argument to find the corresponding table argument, which is the zip code of 12344 in the table. The table function is the sales tax rate corresponding to that zip code, which is 8% or $_\wedge$080.

After the table is read in and stored in `WORKING-STORAGE`, we enter input transaction records. For each transaction record, we search the table to find the table argument that matches the transaction record's zip code, or search argument. When a match is found between the input transaction zip code (the search argument), and the table's zip code (the table argument), we know the table function or sales tax rate is the corresponding table entry. That is, if the fifth table argument is a zip code of 12344, then the sales tax rate we want is also the fifth entry in the table.

The COBOL program to produce the desired customer bills may be divided into two basic modules: (1) reading and storing the table and (2) processing each input record, which includes a *table look-up*.

Suppose this transaction file has customers from 1000 zip code locations. We would have, then, 1000 table records on disk with the following format:

TABLE-FILE Record Layout			
Field	Size	Type	No. of Decimal Positions (if Numeric)
T-ZIPCODE	5	Alphanumeric	
T-TAX-RATE	3	Numeric	3

See Figure 12.3 for a partial pseudocode and hierarchy chart for this problem.

The `TABLE-FILE` could be coded as follows:

```
FD  TABLE-FILE
    LABEL RECORDS ARE STANDARD.
01  TABLE-REC.
    05  T-ZIPCODE           PIC X(5).
    05  T-TAX-RATE          PIC V999.
```

Figure 12.3 Partial pseudocode and hierarchy chart for sample table-handling routine.

Pseudocode

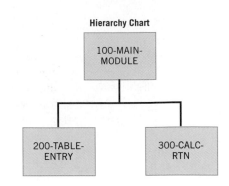

Hierarchy Chart

MAIN-MODULE
START
    Open the Files
    PERFORM Table-Entry UNTIL Table is Loaded
    PERFORM UNTIL there is no more data
        READ a Transaction Record
            AT END
                Move 'NO ' to Are-There-More-Records
            NOT AT END
                PERFORM Calc-Rtn
        END-READ
    END-PERFORM
    End-of-Job Operations
STOP

TABLE-ENTRY
    Read a Table Record
    Move Table Data to Storage

CALC-RTN
    Move Input Fields to Detail Line
    Search Table
        IF   a match is found
        THEN
            Compute Sales Tax using table function
        ELSE
          Move 0 to Sales Tax
        END-IF
    Compute Total
    Write Detail Line

Note that we do *not* indicate in the FILE SECTION the number of table records that will be processed. That is, we do not use an OCCURS to denote the repeated occurrence of 1000 table records. Instead, in the PROCEDURE DIVISION we will perform the 200-TABLE-ENTRY module 1000 times.

Since table data must be stored before we begin processing the input customer file, we need a WORKING-STORAGE area to hold the 1000 table entries:

```
WORKING-STORAGE SECTION.
01   SALES-TAX-TABLE.
     05   TABLE-ENTRIES OCCURS 1000 TIMES.
          10   WS-ZIPCODE              PIC X(5).
          10   WS-TAX-RATE             PIC V999.
01   X1                               PIC 9(4).   ◄─── Will be used initially as a subscript
```

Because the word TABLE is a COBOL reserved word, it should not be used in a program as an identifier unless it has a prefix or suffix.

The WORKING-STORAGE table stores the 1000 entries as follows:

How the Table Data is Stored in WORKING-STORAGE

TABLE-ENTRIES (1)		TABLE-ENTRIES (2)		• • •	TABLE-ENTRIES (1000)	
WS-ZIPCODE (1)	WS-TAX-RATE (1)	WS-ZIPCODE (2)	WS-TAX-RATE (2)	• • •	WS-ZIPCODE (1000)	WS-TAX-RATE (1000)

The main input file will contain customer billing or transaction data used to produce an output file of bills:

```
FD  CUST-FILE
    LABEL RECORDS ARE STANDARD.
01  CUST-REC.
    05  CUST-NO-IN           PIC X(5).
    05  UNIT-PRICE-IN        PIC 9(3)V99.
    05  QTY-IN               PIC 9(3).
    05  ADDRESS-IN           PIC X(20).
    05  ZIP-IN               PIC X(5).
FD  CUST-BILL
    LABEL RECORDS ARE OMITTED.
01  BILLING-REC              PIC X(132).
WORKING-STORAGE SECTION.
    :
    :
01  DETAIL-LINE.
    05                       PIC X(19)    VALUE SPACES.
    05  DL-CUST-NO-OUT       PIC X(5).
    05                       PIC X(10)    VALUE SPACES.
    05  DL-UNIT-PRICE-OUT    PIC 999.99.
    05                       PIC X(10)    VALUE SPACES.
    05  DL-QTY-OUT           PIC ZZ9.
    05                       PIC X(10)    VALUE SPACES.
    05  DL-SALES-TAX         PIC Z(6).99.
    05                       PIC X(10)    VALUE SPACES.
    05  DL-TOTAL             PIC Z,ZZZ,ZZZ.99.
    05                       PIC X(38)    VALUE SPACES.
```

Use the word FILLER in place of blank data-names with COBOL 74

100-MAIN-MODULE would include references to both the 200-TABLE-ENTRY and 300-CALC-RTN modules:

Program Excerpt (COBOL 85)

```
PROCEDURE DIVISION.
***************************************************************
*   this module controls reading and storing of table        *
*   records and then reading and processing of               *
*   transaction records                                       *
***************************************************************
100-MAIN-MODULE.
    OPEN INPUT   TABLE-FILE
                 CUST-FILE
         OUTPUT  CUST-BILL
    PERFORM 200-TABLE-ENTRY
        VARYING X1 FROM 1 BY 1
            UNTIL X1 > 1000
    PERFORM UNTIL THERE-ARE-NO-MORE-RECORDS
        READ CUST-FILE
            AT END
                MOVE 'NO ' TO ARE-THERE-MORE-RECORDS
            NOT AT END
                PERFORM 300-CALC-RTN
        END-READ           .
    END-PERFORM
    CLOSE TABLE-FILE
          CUST-FILE
          CUST-BILL
    STOP RUN.
```

COBOL 74 Substitutions

```
READ CUST-FILE
    AT END MOVE 'NO ' TO ARE-THERE-MORE-RECORDS.
PERFORM 300-CALC-RTN
    UNTIL THERE-ARE-NO-MORE-RECORDS.
```

Consider the PERFORM 200-TABLE-ENTRY statement. When X1 exceeds 1000, that is, when it is 1001, 200-TABLE-ENTRY has been performed 1000 times and control returns to the main module. Since X1, as a subscript, will vary from 1 to 1001, it must be defined as a *four-position numeric field*.

An initial READ is *not* necessary for processing the TABLE-FILE because we know precisely how many table records are to be read. Since 1000 table entries are to be read and stored, we execute the `200-TABLE-ENTRY` routine 1000 times by varying the subscript from 1 to 1001. The `200-TABLE-ENTRY` module could be coded as follows:

```
**********************************************************
*  this module reads each table record and stores the    *
*  table data in working-storage. it is performed         *
*  from 100-main-module.                                  *
**********************************************************
 200-TABLE-ENTRY.
     READ TABLE-FILE
         AT END DISPLAY 'NOT ENOUGH TABLE RECORDS'
                   CLOSE TABLE-FILE, CUST-FILE, CUST-BILL
                   STOP RUN
     END-READ
     MOVE T-ZIPCODE TO WS-ZIPCODE (X1)
     MOVE T-TAX-RATE TO WS-TAX-RATE (X1).
```

We could also have included the two `MOVE` statements as part of a `NOT AT END` clause. In this instance, it does not matter because an `AT END` condition results in a `STOP RUN`.

Subscripts must be used when referencing the table entries `WS-ZIPCODE` and `WS-TAX-RATE` in the `PROCEDURE DIVISION`. Recall that `WS-ZIPCODE` will be the table argument and `WS-TAX-RATE` the table function. We use a subscript name of `X1` here for reasons that will become clear in the next section.

A `READ ... INTO` instruction is better suited for loading tables because it can be used to load a table directly:

```
 200-TABLE-ENTRY
     READ TABLE-FILE INTO TABLE-ENTRIES (X1)
         AT END DISPLAY 'NOT ENOUGH TABLE RECORDS'
                   CLOSE TABLE-FILE, CUST-FILE, CUST-BILL
                   STOP RUN
     END-READ.
```

DEBUGGING TIP

Any time input records need to be saved for future processing, use a `READ ... INTO` to store the data in `WORKING-STORAGE`.

Validating Data

For this program, 1000 table records are to be read and stored. If an error has occurred and there are fewer than 1000 table records, the `AT END` is executed and the run terminates. If an error has occurred and there are more than 1000 table records, we would only process the first 1000. For validating purposes, we may want to ensure that there are precisely 1000 table records. We can code the following:

COBOL 85

```
          PERFORM 200-TABLE-ENTRY.
            :
            :
          200-TABLE-ENTRY.
             PERFORM VARYING X1 FROM 1 BY 1
                       UNTIL X1 > 1000 OR MORE-TABLE-RECS = 'NO '
                  READ TABLE-FILE
                      AT END
                          MOVE 'NO ' TO MORE-TABLE-RECS
                      NOT AT END
                          PERFORM 250-TABLE-LOAD
                  END-READ
             END-PERFORM
             IF  X1 NOT > 1000
                  DISPLAY 'TOO FEW RECORDS IN THE FILE'
             END-IF
             IF  MORE-TABLE-RECS NOT = 'NO '
```

COBOL 74 Substitutions

```
READ TABLE-FILE
    AT END MOVE 'NO ' TO MORE-TABLE-RECS.
PERFORM 250-TABLE-LOAD
    VARYING X1 FROM 1 BY 1
        UNTIL X1 > 1000 OR MORE-TABLE-RECS
              = 'NO '.
```

```
                              DISPLAY 'TOO MANY RECORDS IN THE FILE'
                          END-IF.
                      250-TABLE-LOAD.
                          MOVE T-ZIPCODE TO WS-ZIPCODE (X1)
                          MOVE T-TAX-RATE TO WS-TAX-RATE (X1).
```

COBOL 74 Substitutions

```
READ TABLE-FILE                    ⎫
    AT END MOVE 'NO ' TO MORE-TABLE-RECS. ⎬ ⟶
```

The DISPLAY verb is used, as shown here, to print brief messages to the operator on a screen.

Sometimes we have a variable number of table entries but we know that the number will not exceed a specific value. If, in the preceding, there are *at most* 1000 table entries, but there could be fewer, we replace the first IF in 200-TABLE-ENTRY with:

```
200-TABLE-ENTRY.
     :
     :
     IF  X1 NOT > 1000
         SUBTRACT 1 FROM X1
         DISPLAY 'THERE ARE ', X1, 'TABLE RECORDS'
         MOVE X1 TO NUMBER-OF-ENTRIES
     END-IF
     :
     :
```

We need to subtract 1 from X1 because the PERFORM ... VARYING increments X1 each time a READ is performed—even when the AT END condition is reached and no record is available for processing.

With this procedure, when we process the table we use NO-OF-ENTRIES, not 1000, to control the maximum number of times we access the table. Suppose we want to know the number of zip codes that have a tax rate of 10%. We would code:

```
PERFORM 300-ADD
        VARYING X1 FROM 1 BY 1
              UNTIL X1 > NO-OF-ENTRIES
DISPLAY 'THE NO. OF ZIP CODES WITH 10% TAX IS ', CTR
     :
     :
300-ADD.
     IF  WS-TAX-RATE (X1) = .10
         ADD 1 TO CTR
     END-IF.
```

LOOKING UP DATA IN A TABLE: FINDING A MATCH

After the table entries have been stored in WORKING-STORAGE, we read customer billing data and produce bills. To find the sales tax rate or table function for each CUST-NO-IN, however, we must look up the zip code in the table (table argument) until it matches the zip code in the customer record (search argument). When a match is found between the table argument and the search argument, the corresponding sales tax rate (the table function) with the same subscript as the table's zip code will be used for calculating the sales tax.

Consider again the following partial pseudocode for this 300-CALC-RTN procedure:

Pseudocode

<u>MAIN-MODULE</u>
     :
     :
     PERFORM UNTIL there is no more input
         READ a Record
             AT END
                 MOVE 'NO ' to Are-There-More-Records
             NOT AT END
                 PERFORM Calc-Rtn

```
                        END-READ
                        END-PERFORM
                            ⋮

        CALC-RTN
                Move Input Fields to Detail Line
                Search Table  ◄──────────────In this section we use a
                    IF   a match is found        PERFORM to search the table
                THEN
                        Compute Sales Tax using table function
                ELSE
                        Move 0 to Sales Tax
                END-IF
                Compute Total
                Write Detail Line
```

In the next section we discuss how a table is searched using a SEARCH verb. In Figure 12.4 we use a PERFORM ... UNTIL to search the table. We are assuming that the table has precisely 1000 entries.

Figure 12.4   Using a PERFORM ... UNTIL to search a table.

COBOL 85

```
IDENTIFICATION DIVISION.
PROGRAM-ID.  TABLE1.
ENVIRONMENT DIVISION.
INPUT-OUTPUT SECTION.
FILE-CONTROL.
    SELECT TABLE-FILE ASSIGN TO DISK 'T1'.
    SELECT CUST-FILE ASSIGN TO DISK 'C1'.
    SELECT CUST-BILL ASSIGN TO PRINTER.
DATA DIVISION.
FILE SECTION.
FD  TABLE-FILE
    LABEL RECORDS ARE STANDARD.
01  TABLE-REC.
    05  T-ZIPCODE            PIC X(5).
    05  T-TAX-RATE           PIC V999.
FD  CUST-FILE
    LABEL RECORDS ARE STANDARD.
01  CUST-REC.
    05  CUST-NO-IN           PIC X(5).
    05  UNIT-PRICE-IN        PIC 9(3)V99.
    05  QTY-IN               PIC 9(3).
    05  ADDRESS-IN           PIC X(20).
    05  ZIP-IN               PIC X(5).
FD  CUST-BILL
    LABEL RECORDS ARE OMITTED.
01  BILLING-REC              PIC X(132).
WORKING-STORAGE SECTION.
01  STORED-AREAS.
    05  ARE-THERE-MORE-RECS PIC XXX      VALUE 'YES'.
        88 THERE-ARE-NO-MORE-RECS        VALUE 'NO '.
    05  X1                   PIC 9(4).
    05  MORE-TABLE-RECS      PIC X(3)    VALUE 'YES'.
    05  WS-SALES-TAX         PIC 9(6)V99 VALUE ZEROS.
01  SALES-TAX-TABLE.
    05  TABLE-ENTRIES  OCCURS 1000 TIMES.
        10  WS-ZIPCODE       PIC X(5).
        10  WS-TAX-RATE      PIC V999.
```

Figure 12.4 (continued)

COBOL 74 Substitutions

For COBOL 74, FILLER must be used
instead of a blank field name

```
READ CUST-FILE
    AT END MOVE 'NO ' TO ARE-THERE-MORE-RECS.
PERFORM 300-CALC-RTN
    UNTIL THERE-ARE-NO-MORE-RECS.
```

```
READ TABLE-FILE
    AT END MOVE 'NO ' TO MORE-TABLE-RECS.
PERFORM 250-LOAD-THE-TABLE
    VARYING X1 FROM 1 BY 1
        UNTIL X1 > 1000 OR MORE-TABLE-RECS
            = 'NO '.
```

```
READ TABLE-FILE
    AT END MOVE 'NO ' TO MORE-TABLE-RECS.
```

```
01  DETAIL-LINE.
    05                          PIC X(18)    VALUE SPACES.
    05  DL-CUST-NO-OUT          PIC X(5).
    05                          PIC X(10)    VALUE SPACES.
    05  DL-UNIT-PRICE-OUT       PIC 999.99.
    05                          PIC X(10)    VALUE SPACES.
    05  DL-QTY-OUT              PIC ZZ9.
    05                          PIC X(10)    VALUE SPACES.
    05  DL-SALES-TAX            PIC Z(6).99.
    05                          PIC X(10)    VALUE SPACES.
    05  DL-TOTAL                PIC Z,ZZZ,ZZZ.99.
    05                          PIC X(38)    VALUE SPACES.
PROCEDURE DIVISION.
100-MAIN-MODULE.
    OPEN INPUT  TABLE-FILE
                CUST-FILE
         OUTPUT CUST-BILL
    PERFORM 200-TABLE-ENTRY
    PERFORM UNTIL THERE-ARE-NO-MORE-RECS
        READ CUST-FILE
            AT END
                MOVE 'NO ' TO ARE-THERE-MORE-RECS
            NOT AT END
                PERFORM 300-CALC-RTN
        END-READ
    END-PERFORM
    CLOSE TABLE-FILE
          CUST-FILE
          CUST-BILL
    STOP RUN.
200-TABLE-ENTRY.
    PERFORM VARYING X1 FROM 1 BY 1
            UNTIL X1 > 1000 OR MORE-TABLE-RECS = 'NO '
        READ TABLE-FILE
            AT END
                MOVE 'NO ' TO MORE-TABLE-RECS
            NOT AT END
                PERFORM 250-LOAD-THE-TABLE
        END-READ
    END-PERFORM
    IF X1 NOT > 1000
        DISPLAY 'TOO FEW RECORDS IN THE FILE'
        CLOSE TABLE-FILE
              CUST-FILE
              CUST-BILL
        STOP RUN
    END-IF.
250-LOAD-THE-TABLE.
    MOVE T-ZIPCODE TO WS-ZIPCODE (X1)
    MOVE T-TAX-RATE TO WS-TAX-RATE (X1).

300-CALC-RTN.
    MOVE CUST-NO-IN TO DL-CUST-NO-OUT
    MOVE UNIT-PRICE-IN TO DL-UNIT-PRICE-OUT
    MOVE QTY-IN TO DL-QTY-OUT
    MOVE 1 TO X1
    PERFORM 400-INCREMENT-SUBSCRIPT
            UNTIL ZIP-IN = WS-ZIPCODE (X1)
                    OR X1 > 1000
    IF X1 <= 1000
        COMPUTE WS-SALES-TAX ROUNDED = WS-TAX-RATE (X1)
            * UNIT-PRICE-IN * QTY-IN
    ELSE
        MOVE 0 TO WS-SALES-TAX
    END-IF
```

Figure 12.4   (continued)

```
                                        MOVE WS-SALES-TAX TO DL-SALES-TAX
                                        COMPUTE DL-TOTAL = UNIT-PRICE-IN * QTY-IN
                                            + WS-SALES-TAX
COBOL 74 Substitutions                  WRITE BILLING-REC FROM DETAIL-LINE
                                            AFTER ADVANCING 2 LINES.
READ CUST-FILE
    AT END MOVE 'NO ' TO ARE-THERE-MORE-RECS.
                                   400-INCREMENT-SUBSCRIPT.
                                        ADD 1 TO X1.
```

USE OF THE SEARCH STATEMENT FOR TABLE AND ARRAY PROCESSING

FORMAT OF THE SEARCH STATEMENT

The best method for searching a table is with the use of a **SEARCH** statement.
A basic format of the SEARCH is as follows:

Format

$$
\begin{aligned}
&\underline{\text{SEARCH}} \text{ identifier-1} \\
&\quad [\text{AT } \underline{\text{END}} \text{ imperative-statement-1}] \\
\\
&\underline{\text{WHEN}} \text{ condition-1 } \left\{ \begin{array}{l} \text{imperative-statement-2} \\ \underline{\text{NEXT}} \ \underline{\text{SENTENCE}} \end{array} \right\} \ldots \\
\\
&[\underline{\text{END-SEARCH}}]^*
\end{aligned}
$$

*COBOL 85 only. If END-SEARCH is used, NEXT SENTENCE must be replaced with CONTINUE unless your
COBOL 85 compiler has an enhancement.

Example
Using a SEARCH, we can replace 300-CALC-RTN and 400-INCREMENT-INDEX in Figure 12.4 with
the following:

```
300-CALC-RTN.
    MOVE CUST-NO-IN TO DL-CUST-NO-OUT
    MOVE UNIT-PRICE-IN TO DL-UNIT-PRICE-OUT
    MOVE QTY-IN TO DL-QTY-OUT
****************************************************************
    SET X1 TO 1
    SEARCH TABLE-ENTRIES
        AT END MOVE 0 TO WS-SALES-TAX
        WHEN ZIP-IN = WS-ZIPCODE (X1)
            COMPUTE WS-SALES-TAX = WS-TAX-RATE (X1)
                * UNIT-PRICE-IN * QTY-IN
    END-SEARCH
****************************************************************
    MOVE WS-SALES-TAX TO DL-SALES-TAX
    COMPUTE DL-TOTAL = UNIT-PRICE-IN * QTY-IN * WS-SALES-TAX
    WRITE BILLING-REC FROM DETAIL-LINE
        AFTER ADVANCING 2 LINES.
```

The identifier used with the SEARCH verb is the table entry name specified on the OCCURS level,
not on the 01 level. The WHEN clause indicates what action is to be taken when the condition
specified is actually met. This condition compares an input field or search argument (ZIP-IN in
this example) with a table argument (WS-ZIPCODE (X1) in this example). Additional comparisons
between search and table arguments can be made using other WHEN clauses. [Note the ellipses
(...) in the instruction format.] We use END-SEARCH as a scope terminator with COBOL 85. Note,
however, that the NEXT SENTENCE clause cannot be used with an END-SEARCH scope terminator
unless your compiler has an enhancement that permits it. A period is optional after END-SEARCH
unless the END-SEARCH is the last entry in the paragraph.

Using the SEARCH ... AT END for Data Validation

With the SEARCH statement, the AT END clause specifies what should be done if the table has been completely searched and *no match is found.* That is, suppose the ZIP-IN field does not match any WS-ZIPCODE field in the table; such a condition will cause the AT END clause to be executed if it is specified. Since it is possible for input errors to occur, we strongly recommend that you always use this optional clause. Without it, the "no match" condition would simply cause the program to continue with the next sentence. This could produce incorrect results or even cause a program interrupt.

To use a SEARCH statement, two additional entries are required: the INDEXED BY clause along with OCCURS, and the SET statement in the PROCEDURE DIVISION.

THE INDEXED BY CLAUSE AND THE SEARCH STATEMENT

When using a SEARCH statement, table entries must be specified with an **index** rather than a subscript. An index is similar to a subscript, but it is defined *along with* the table entries *as part* of the OCCURS description:

```
01   SALES-TAX-TABLE.
     05   TABLE-ENTRIES OCCURS 1000 TIMES    INDEXED BY X1.
          10   WS-ZIPCODE                PIC 9(5).
          10   WS-TAX-RATE               PIC V999.
```

As noted, the index, X1 in this illustration, functions like a subscript. Note, however, that unlike a subscript, an index is not defined separately in WORKING-STORAGE. It is defined with an **INDEXED BY** clause along with the OCCURS. The compiler *automatically* provides an appropriate PICTURE clause, in this case 9999, since there are 1000 entries in the table.

The SEARCH statement will perform a table look-up. TABLE-ENTRIES, the identifier used with the OCCURS and INDEXED BY clauses, is the item designated with the SEARCH as well. The 01-level entry, SALES-TAX-TABLE, could *not* be used with the SEARCH.

The table will be searched and the index *automatically* incremented until the condition specified in the WHEN clause is satisfied or until an AT END condition is met. The AT END indicates that the table has been completely searched without the condition being met; that is, no match has been found between an input field (search argument) and a table entry (table argument). Frequently, we code the AT END as: SEARCH ... AT END PERFORM 500-ERR-RTN WHEN .... Note that the programmer must initialize an index before each SEARCH to start a table look-up at the first entry.

How an Index Differs From a Subscript

The difference between a subscript and an index is worth noting because indexes are processed more efficiently than subscripts by the computer. As we have seen, a subscript is a field that refers to the number of the table entry we want to reference. Consider the following:

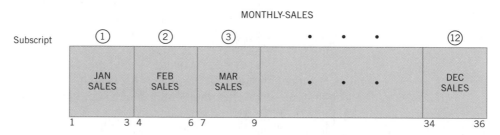

An index for MONTHLY-SALES can be established with an INDEXED BY clause on the OCCURS level. Like a subscript, the index will, in effect, vary from 1 to 12. Internally, however, the computer uses displacement values to actually access indexed table entries. The first table entry has a displacement of zero bytes from the start of the table, the second has a displacement of three bytes from the start of the table, and so on, with the last table entry having a displacement of 33 bytes from the start of the table:

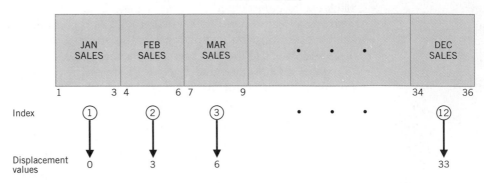

MONTHLY-SALES

The displacement values used by an index depend on the number of bytes in each table entry, which is three in our example.

To the programmer, it may not seem to make a difference whether we use a subscript or an index to access a table entry. The only difference is that a subscript is a separate WORKING-STORAGE entry, while the index is defined by an INDEXED BY clause on the OCCURS level. Both can have values from 1 to 12 in this example. An index, however, is processed more efficiently than a subscript. When you define an index, the computer sets up an internal storage area called an index register, which uses the displacement values determined by the index to access table addresses. This is faster than working with subscripts. We recommend, therefore, that you use indexes and SEARCH statements for table look-ups.

Because an index refers to a displacement and not just an occurrence value, its contents cannot be modified with a MOVE, ADD, or SUBTRACT like a subscript can. To change the contents of an index, then, we use either (1) a PERFORM ... VARYING, which can vary the values in either subscripts or indexes, or (2) a SET statement, which can move, add, or subtract values in an index.

MODIFYING THE CONTENTS OF AN INDEX

The SET Statement

As noted, a *subscript* is a field defined separately in WORKING-STORAGE to access specific entries in an array. Its contents may be changed with the use of a PERFORM ... VARYING and with a MOVE, ADD, or SUBTRACT statement.

As we have seen, an index is also used in a table look-up, but it is defined with an INDEXED BY clause that follows a table's OCCURS clause. The index *must* be specified if a SEARCH is used to perform the table look-up. It can be modified with a PERFORM ... VARYING too. Thus, loading the table with a 200-TABLE-ENTRY routine as described previously is still correct.

Although a PERFORM ... VARYING may be used with an index, we may *not* modify the contents of an index with a MOVE, ADD, or SUBTRACT statement. Instead, we must use a **SET** statement to alter the contents of an index with *any instruction other than the* PERFORM ... VARYING.

Basic Format

$$\text{SET} \quad \text{index-name-1} \quad \begin{Bmatrix} \underline{TO} \\ \underline{UP} \ \underline{BY} \\ \underline{DOWN} \ \underline{BY} \end{Bmatrix} \quad \text{integer-1}$$

Examples

Statement	Meaning
1. `SET X1 TO 1`	Move 1 to the `X1` index.
2. `SET X1 UP BY 1`	Add 1 to the `X1` index.
3. `SET X1 DOWN BY 1`	Subtract 1 from the `X1` index.

Initializing an Index Before Using the SEARCH

A `SEARCH` statement does not automatically initialize the index at 1 because sometimes we may want to begin searching a table at some point other than the beginning. Initializing an index at 1 must be performed by a `SET` statement prior to the `SEARCH` if we want to begin each table look-up with the first entry:

```
SET X1 TO 1
SEARCH TABLE-ENTRIES
    AT END MOVE 0 TO WS-SALES-TAX
    WHEN ZIP-IN = WS-ZIPCODE (X1)
        COMPUTE WS-SALES-TAX = WS-TAX-RATE (X1) * UNIT-PRICE-IN * QTY-IN
END-SEARCH
MOVE WS-SALES-TAX TO DL-SALES-TAX
COMPUTE DL-TOTAL = UNIT-PRICE-IN * QTY-IN + WS-SALES-TAX
WRITE BILLING-REC FROM DETAIL-LINE
    AFTER ADVANCING 2 LINES.
```

The following summarizes the differences between subscripts and indexes:

DIFFERENCES BETWEEN SUBSCRIPTS AND INDEXES

Subscript	Index
Represents an occurrence of an array or table element	Represents a displacement from the first address in the array or table
Defined in a separate `WORKING-STORAGE` entry	Defined along with the `OCCURS` for the array or table
To change the value of `SUB`, a subscript, use a `PERFORM ... VARYING` or any of the following:	To change the value of `X1`, an index, use a `PERFORM ... VARYING` or any of the following:

`MOVE 1 TO SUB`
`ADD 1 TO SUB`
`SUBTRACT 1 FROM SUB`
	`SET X1 TO 1`
	`SET X1 UP BY 1`
	`SET X1 DOWN BY 1`

An index can be used to reference an element only in the table or array for which it was defined. To establish an index, code `INDEXED BY` along with the `OCCURS` entry. Both indexes and subscripts can be accessed using the `PERFORM ... VARYING` to increment or decrement values.

— DEBUGGING TIP —

We recommend that you use `INDEXED BY` and `SEARCH` for table look-ups. Remember to `SET X1 TO 1` before a `SEARCH` when you want to begin searching at the first table entry.

Note that once you have established an index you can use it not only for searching a table but for loading data into it. Using an in-line `PERFORM` (with COBOL 85), we have:

```
200-TABLE-ENTRY.
    PERFORM VARYING X1 FROM 1 BY 1
            UNTIL X1 > 1000
        READ TABLE-FILE
            AT END
```

```
                              MOVE 'NO ' TO MORE-TABLE-RECS
                   NOT AT END
                         MOVE TABLE-ENTRIES-IN
                            TO WS-TABLE-ENTRIES (X1)
               END-READ
           END-PERFORM
              .
              .
```

Hence, once an INDEXED BY clause has been added to a table or array, the index can be used for loading data into the table or array as well as for searching the table or array.

Example Consider the following table and assume that it has already been loaded:

```
01  INVENTORY-TABLE.
    05  PARTS OCCURS 100 TIMES INDEXED BY X1.
        10  PART-NO              PIC 9(3).
        10  ITEM-DESCRIPTION     PIC X(20).
        10  UNIT-PRICE           PIC 9(3)V99.
```

Suppose we want to display the item description for PART-NO 126. We could code:

```
SET X1 TO 1
SEARCH PARTS
    AT END PERFORM 400-NO-MATCH-RTN
    WHEN PART-NO (X1) = 126
        DISPLAY ITEM-DESCRIPTION (X1)
END-SEARCH
```

USING TWO WHEN CLAUSES
FOR AN EARLY EXIT FROM A SEARCH

As you can see from the Format for the SEARCH, multiple WHEN clauses are permitted. Let us consider an example.

Suppose the preceding INVENTORY-TABLE consists of 100 PARTS, where the PART-NOs are in sequence but are not necessarily consecutive. That is, the first entry may be for PART-NO 001, the second for PART-NO 003, the third for PART-NO 008, and so on. The PART-NOs may not be consecutive because some parts may no longer be stocked, while newer ones with different numbers may have been added.

Interactive Processing. If we enter a PART-NO-IN interactively as input and wish to determine its UNIT-PRICE, we can code:

```
ACCEPT PART-NO-IN
SET X1 TO 1
SEARCH  PARTS
    AT END DISPLAY 'NO MATCH'
    WHEN PART-NO-IN = PART-NO (X1)
        DISPLAY 'THE UNIT-PRICE IS ', UNIT-PRICE (X1)
END-SEARCH
```

Since the table is in sequence by PART-NO we could save computer time by exiting the SEARCH procedure as soon as a PART-NO (X1) > PART-NO-IN. Suppose PART-NO-IN is 006, for example, and PART-NO (1) = 001, PART-NO (2) = 003, and PART-NO (3) = 008. We would know after the third comparison that there is no match. Using the preceding routine, the computer would search through all 100 entries before indicating 'NO MATCH'. For more efficient processing, we could use two WHEN clauses instead:

```
ACCEPT PART-NO-IN
SET  X1 TO 1
SEARCH  PARTS
    WHEN PART-NO-IN = PART-NO (X1)
        DISPLAY 'THE UNIT PRICE IS ', UNIT-PRICE (X1)
```

```
         WHEN PART-NO-IN < PART-NO (X1)
             DISPLAY 'NO MATCH'
  END-SEARCH
```

With two WHEN clauses, the computer begins by performing the first comparison. Only if the condition in the first WHEN is not met does it test the second WHEN. That is, only if there is no match will a test be made to see if the search should be terminated and 'NO MATCH' displayed. There is no need for an AT END clause here because 'NO MATCH' will be displayed at some point (assuming that the last PART-NO (X1) contains all 9s). It will be displayed either when the end of the table is reached or as soon as a PART-NO-IN is less than some PART-NO (X1).

Later on in this chapter, we will see that a type of search called a binary search is best used in place of two WHEN clauses for searching a sequential table.

When PART-NOs Do Not Need to Be Stored

Keep in mind that the PART-NO itself must be stored in the preceding examples because, although there are 100 of them, they are not consecutive.

If there were 100 PART-NOs and they varied consecutively from 1 to 100, we would not need to store the PART-NO. We would know, for example, that UNIT-PRICE (5) referred to PART-NO 005 and that ITEM-DESCRIPTION (10) referred to the description for PART-NO 10.

Interactive Processing. To determine the unit price for a PART-NO where the part numbers vary from 1 to 100, we could code:

```
ACCEPT PART-NO-IN
DISPLAY 'THE UNIT PRICE IS ', UNIT-PRICE (PART-NO-IN).
```

We could use the PART-NO-IN as a subscript and eliminate the need for a SEARCH entirely. This type of table is called a **direct-referenced table**. In this example, INVENTORY-TABLE could only be a direct-referenced table if PART-NOs varied consecutively from 1 to 100.

SEARCHING FOR MULTIPLE MATCHES

Sometimes we may want to search for multiple matches in a table. In such instances, it is better to use a PERFORM rather than a SEARCH statement for processing the entire table, because we want to continue processing the table even after a match is found. The SEARCH ... WHEN looks up data from the table until a match is found, at which point the program continues with the next sentence. A PERFORM ... VARYING can be used to process an entire table even after a match is found. Suppose we want to know the item descriptions for all parts with a unit price greater than 100.00. We could code:

```
      PERFORM 500-UNIT-PRICE-TEST
           VARYING X1 FROM 1 BY 1
               UNTIL X1 > 100.
  :
  500-UNIT-PRICE-TEST.
      IF  UNIT-PRICE (X1) > 100.00
          DISPLAY ITEM-DESCRIPTION (X1), ' HAS A UNIT PRICE > $100 '
      END-IF
```

INTERNAL VS EXTERNAL TABLES

Thus far we have focused on tables that are entered as input from secondary storage devices such as disk before transaction records are entered. We read in tables in this way when their contents are likely to change periodically. When tables are stored on secondary storage devices, their contents can be changed as the need arises without having to make modifications to the program accessing the table. Such tables are called **external tables**.

If the contents of a table is fixed, that is, not likely to change, we can define it with VALUE clauses directly in the WORKING-STORAGE section. In this way, we need not read it in each time. Consider the MONTH-NAMES entry we defined previously:

```
01   MONTH-NAMES VALUE 'JANFEBMARAPRMAYJUNJULAUGSEPOCTNOVDEC'.
     05   MONTH OCCURS 12 TIMES       PIC XXX.
```

The subscripted variables MONTH(1) through MONTH(12) can be used for accessing JAN through DEC respectively without the need for loading in a table with the 12 month names. This is called an **internal table** since it is actually part of the program. We store month names in an internal table because the values are not likely to change.

With COBOL 74, a REDEFINES clause would be necessary to define the table:

```
01   MONTH-NAMES.
     05   STRING-1                              PIC X(36)
          VALUE 'JANFEBMARAPRMAYJUNJULAUGSEPOCTNOVDEC'.
     05   MONTH REDEFINES STRING-1 OCCURS 12 TIMES   PIC XXX.
```

--- DEBUGGING TIP ---

If table entries are expected to remain fixed, define them directly in the program using an internal table. When table data changes periodically, as is most often the case, use an external table.

LOOKING UP TABLE DATA FOR ACCUMULATING TOTALS

We have illustrated how to add values to an array and how to look up data in a table. In this section, we combine both techniques.

Suppose a store has 25 charge-account customers each with his or her own customer number (CUST-NO). We want to read in transaction records and print the accumulated BAL-DUE for each customer. If the CUST-NOs vary from 1 to 25, we need only store 25 BAL-DUEs in an array:

```
01   CUST-ARRAY       VALUE ZERO.
     05   BAL-DUE OCCURS 25 TIMES   PIC 9(4)V99.
```

This would be another illustration of a direct-referenced array, where BAL-DUE (CUST-NO-IN) can be used to access specific balances. The CUST-NOs need not be stored because they vary from 1 to 25.

The procedure to add to the appropriate BAL-DUE would be:

COBOL 85

```
100-MAIN-MODULE.
     OPEN INPUT CUST-FILE
          OUTPUT PRINT-FILE
     PERFORM UNTIL NO-MORE-RECS
          READ CUST-FILE
               AT END
                    MOVE 'NO ' TO MORE-RECS
               NOT AT END
                    PERFORM 200-ADD-TO-BAL
          END-READ
     END-PERFORM
     PERFORM 300-PRINT-RTN
          VARYING SUB FROM 1 BY 1 UNTIL SUB > 25
     CLOSE CUST-FILE
          PRINT-FILE
     STOP RUN.
200-ADD-TO-BAL.
     IF  CUST-NO-IN > 0 AND < 26
```

COBOL 74 Substitutions

```
READ CUST-FILE
     AT END MOVE 'NO ' TO MORE-RECS.
PERFORM 200-ADD-TO-BAL
     UNTIL NO-MORE-RECS.
```

```
                                  ADD AMT-IN TO BAL-DUE (CUST-NO-IN)
                              ELSE
COBOL 74 Substitutions            DISPLAY 'ERROR IN CUST NO ', CUST-NO
                              END-IF.
READ CUST-FILE
    AT END MOVE 'NO ' TO MORE-RECS.
```

CUST-ARRAY is a *direct-referenced* array because BAL-DUE (1) refers to the first CUST-NO, BAL-DUE (2) refers to the second CUST-NO, and so on. This type of direct-referenced array is valid only if CUST-NOs vary consecutively from 1 to 25.

Suppose, however, that the CUST-NOs for the 25 customers are not consecutive. That is, you may have 25 customers but their numbers might be 01, 07, 15, and so on. For this, you will need to *store* the CUST-NOs as well as accumulate the total BAL-DUE for each customer. The 200-ADD-TO-BAL procedure could use a SEARCH in order to find a specific CUST-NO and add to the corresponding BAL-DUE:

```
01  CUST-ARRAY                  VALUE ZEROS.
    05  ENTRIES OCCURS 25 TIMES INDEXED BY X1.
        10  T-CUST-NO     PIC 99.
        10  BAL-DUE       PIC 9(4)V99.
    :
    :
200-ADD-TO-BAL.
    SET X1 TO 1
    SEARCH ENTRIES
            AT END DISPLAY 'THERE ARE MORE THAN 25 CUSTOMER NOS'
            STOP RUN
        WHEN T-CUST-NO (X1) = CUST-NO-IN      ◄——— a match is found
            ADD AMT-IN TO BAL-DUE (X1)
        WHEN T-CUST-NO (X1) = ZEROS           ◄——— a new customer must
            MOVE CUST-NO-IN TO T-CUST-NO (X1)      be added to the table
            MOVE AMT-IN TO BAL-DUE (X1)
    END-SEARCH.
```

The SEARCH has two WHEN clauses. If a customer number already appears in the array, an existing T-CUST-NO (X1) will equal the CUST-NO-IN. Then we simply add AMT-IN to the corresponding BAL-DUE (X1). If the CUST-NO-IN does not match an existing T-CUST-NO in the table, then the first T-CUST-NO with a zero will be replaced with the CUST-NO-IN and the AMT-IN will become the BAL-DUE for that customer. If 25 customer numbers are already stored in the array and a customer number is entered as input that does not match any of them, then an error message will be displayed.

Example

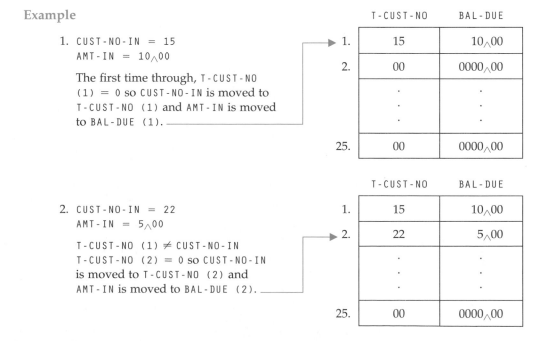

1. CUST-NO-IN = 15
   AMT-IN = 10∧00

   The first time through, T-CUST-NO (1) = 0 so CUST-NO-IN is moved to T-CUST-NO (1) and AMT-IN is moved to BAL-DUE (1). ————

	T-CUST-NO	BAL-DUE
1.	15	10∧00
2.	00	0000∧00
.	.	.
.	.	.
.	.	.
25.	00	0000∧00

2. CUST-NO-IN = 22
   AMT-IN = 5∧00

   T-CUST-NO (1) ≠ CUST-NO-IN
   T-CUST-NO (2) = 0 so CUST-NO-IN is moved to T-CUST-NO (2) and AMT-IN is moved to BAL-DUE (2). ————

	T-CUST-NO	BAL-DUE
1.	15	10∧00
2.	22	5∧00
.	.	.
.	.	.
.	.	.
25.	00	0000∧00

3. CUST-NO-IN = 15
   AMT-IN = 20∧00

   T-CUST-NO (1) = CUST-NO-IN so
   AMT-IN is *added to* BAL-DUE (1).

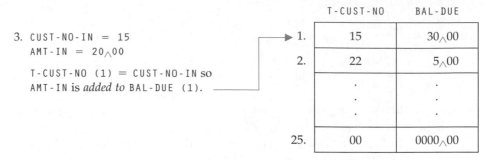

	T-CUST-NO	BAL-DUE
1.	15	30∧00
2.	22	5∧00
.	.	.
.	.	.
.	.	.
25.	00	0000∧00

This illustration shows how to process nonconsecutive customer numbers that must be stored along with the accumulated balances. It also shows how to use two separate WHEN clauses in a SEARCH.

See Figure 12.5 for the full program. Note that the program will not print CUST-NOs in sequence unless they were entered in sequence.

Figure 12.5 Searching a table when customer numbers are not consecutive.

COBOL 85

```
IDENTIFICATION DIVISION.
PROGRAM-ID.  ARRAY1.
******************************************************************
*    This program assumes that there are 25 CUST-NOs, but       *
*       they do not necessarily vary from 1 - 25.               *
*       Commented entries explain how to change the program     *
*       for a direct-referenced table - where CUST-NO           *
*       is a number from 01-25.                                 *
******************************************************************
ENVIRONMENT DIVISION.
INPUT-OUTPUT SECTION.
FILE-CONTROL.
     SELECT CUST-FILE ASSIGN TO DISK 'C1.DAT'.
     SELECT PRINT-FILE ASSIGN TO PRINTER.
DATA DIVISION.
FILE SECTION.
FD  CUST-FILE
     LABEL RECORDS ARE STANDARD.
01  CUST-REC.
     05 CUST-NO-IN       PIC 99.
     05 AMT-IN           PIC 999V99.
FD  PRINT-FILE
     LABEL RECORDS ARE OMITTED.
01  PRINT-REC           PIC X(132).
WORKING-STORAGE SECTION.
01  STORED-AREAS.
     05  MORE-RECS       PIC XXX      VALUE 'YES'.
01  CUST-ARRAY                        VALUE ZEROS.
     05  ENTRIES  OCCURS 25 TIMES INDEXED BY X1.
          10  T-CUST-NO  PIC 99.
          10  BAL-DUE    PIC 9(4)V99.
******************************************************************
*   For direct-referenced tables, there is no need to store     *
*      T-CUST-NO - instead you add to BAL-DUE (CUST-NO-IN)       *
******************************************************************
01  DETAIL-REC.
     05                  PIC X(20)   VALUE SPACES.
     05  CUST-NO-OUT     PIC 99.
     05                  PIC X(10)   VALUE SPACES.
     05  BAL-DUE-OUT     PIC $Z,ZZZ.99.
     05                  PIC X(91)   VALUE SPACES.
```

COBOL 74 Substitutions

For COBOL 74, FILLER must be
used instead of a blank field name

Figure 12.5 (continued)

```
                                   PROCEDURE DIVISION.
                                   100-MAIN.
                                       OPEN INPUT  CUST-FILE
                                            OUTPUT PRINT-FILE
                                       PERFORM UNTIL MORE-RECS = 'NO '
                                           READ CUST-FILE
                                               AT END
                                                   MOVE 'NO ' TO MORE-RECS
                                               NOT AT END
                                                   PERFORM 200-ADD-TO-BAL
                                           END-READ
                                       END-PERFORM
                                       PERFORM 300-PRINT-RTN
                                           VARYING X1 FROM 1 BY 1 UNTIL X1 > 25
                                       CLOSE CUST-FILE
                                             PRINT-FILE
                                       STOP RUN.
                                   200-ADD-TO-BAL.
                                       SET X1 TO 1
                                       SEARCH ENTRIES
                                           AT END DISPLAY 'THERE ARE MORE THAN 25 CUSTOMERS'
                                                   STOP RUN
                                           WHEN T-CUST-NO (X1) = CUST-NO-IN
                                               ADD AMT-IN TO BAL-DUE (X1)
                                           WHEN T-CUST-NO (X1) = ZEROS
                                               MOVE CUST-NO-IN TO T-CUST-NO (X1)
                                               MOVE AMT-IN TO BAL-DUE (X1)
                                       END-SEARCH.
```

COBOL 74 Substitutions

```
READ CUST-FILE
    AT END MOVE 'NO ' TO MORE-RECS.
PERFORM 200-ADD-TO-BAL
    UNTIL MORE-RECS = 'NO '.
```

```
READ CUST-FILE
    AT END MOVE 'NO ' TO MORE-RECS.
```

```
                                   ************************************************************
                                   *  For direct-referenced tables, replace set and search   *
                                   *     above with:  ADD AMT-IN TO BAL-DUE (CUST-NO-IN)      *
                                   *     To minimize errors first ensure that CUST-NO-IN      *
                                   *     is between 1 and 25.                                 *
                                   ************************************************************
                                   300-PRINT-RTN.
                                       IF T-CUST-NO (X1) = ZEROS
                                           SET X1 TO 25        ←——————— This enables you to exit the print routine
                                       ELSE
                                           MOVE T-CUST-NO (X1) TO CUST-NO-OUT
                                           MOVE BAL-DUE (X1) TO BAL-DUE-OUT
                                           WRITE PRINT-REC FROM DETAIL-REC
                                               AFTER ADVANCING 2 LINES
                                       END-IF.
                                   ************************************************************
                                   *  For direct-referenced tables, omit the IF - print      *
                                   *     all 25 BAL-DUE totals                                *
                                   ************************************************************
```

SELF-TEST

1. Suppose an entire table has been searched using a SEARCH statement and the specific condition being tested has not been reached. What will happen?

2. If a SEARCH statement is used in the PROCEDURE DIVISION, then the OCCURS clause entry must also include a(n) _____ clause.

3. Suppose the following entry has been coded:

```
01  TABLE-X.
    05  CTRS OCCURS 100 TIMES INDEXED BY X1.
        10  FLD1    PIC 999.
        10  FLD2    PIC 9.
```

Write a statement to initialize the index at 1.

4. For Question 3, write a `SEARCH` statement to look up the table entries in `CTRS` until `FLD1` = 123, at which time `300-PROCESS-TABLE-DATA` is to be performed.

5. (T or F) The condition coded in a `WHEN` clause usually compares a table argument to a search argument.

Consider the following problem definition for Questions 6 through 9:

Note:

The table contains the delivery charge for each weight category.
Entries are in sequence by WEIGHT-MAX.

Example
00500	100∧25
⋮	
87320	125∧33
99999	150∧75

The first table entry indicates that the delivery charge for an item under 500 pounds is $100.25. The last table entry indicates that the delivery charge for an item that weighs between 87320 and 99999 is $150.75

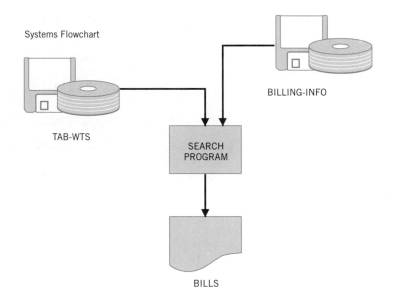

Systems Flowchart

TAB-WTS

BILLING-INFO

SEARCH PROGRAM

BILLS

TAB-WTS **Record Layout (20 entries)**			
Field	**Size**	**Type**	**No. of Decimal Positions (if Numeric)**
WEIGHT-MAX	5	Numeric	0
DELIVERY-CHARGE	5	Numeric	2

BILLING-INFO **Record Layout**			
Field	**Size**	**Type**	**No. of Decimal Positions (if Numeric)**
CUST-NO-IN	5	Alphanumeric	
AMT-IN	5	Numeric	2
WEIGHT-MAILED	5	Numeric	0

BILLS Printer Spacing Chart

		CUSTOMER NO	AMT OF SALES	DELIVERY CHARGE	TOTAL
H	6	CUSTOMER NO	AMT OF SALES	DELIVERY CHARGE	TOTAL
D	8	XXXXX	$ZZZ.99	$ZZZ.99	$$,$$$.99

6. Code the WORKING-STORAGE table area. Assume that a SEARCH will be used.

7. Code the 100-MAIN-MODULE for this program.

8. Code the 200-TABLE-ENTRY routine for this program.

9. Code the 300-CALC-RTN using a SEARCH for the table look-up.

10. Indicate what, if anything, is wrong with the following.

```
01   TABLE-1.
     05   ENTRY-X OCCURS 20 TIMES   PIC 9(4)   INDEXED BY X1.
     :
     :
     SEARCH TABLE-1 ...
```

11. Consider the following:

```
01   INVENTORY-TABLE.
     05   PARTS OCCURS 100 TIMES
               INDEXED BY X1.
          10   PART-NO          PIC 999.
          10   UNIT-PRICE       PIC 9(3)V99.
```

Suppose there are exactly 100 PART-NOs with values 001–100. Do we need to store PART-NO?

Solutions

1. The statement in the AT END clause will be executed if the clause has been included; if it has not, the next statement after the SEARCH ... END-SEARCH statement will be executed. We recommend that you always use an AT END clause with the SEARCH statement.

2. INDEXED BY

3. SET X1 TO 1

4.
```
SEARCH CTRS
     AT END PERFORM 500-ERR-RTN
     WHEN FLD1 (X1) = 123
          PERFORM 300-PROCESS-TABLE-DATA
END-SEARCH*
```

5. T

6.
```
WORKING-STORAGE SECTION.
01   WEIGHT-TABLE.
     05   STORED-ENTRIES OCCURS 20 TIMES INDEXED BY X1.
          10   T-WEIGHT-MAX         PIC 9(5).
          10   T-DELIVERY-CHARGE    PIC 9(3)V99.
```

7.
```
PROCEDURE DIVISION.
100-MAIN-MODULE.
     PERFORM 400-INITIALIZATION-RTN
     PERFORM 200-TABLE-ENTRY
          VARYING X1 FROM 1 BY 1 UNTIL X1 > 20
     PERFORM UNTIL THERE-ARE-NO-MORE-RECORDS
          READ BILLING-INFO
               AT END
                    MOVE 'NO ' TO ARE-THERE-MORE-RECORDS
               NOT AT END
                    PERFORM 300-CALC-RTN
          END-READ
     END-PERFORM
```

COBOL 74 Substitutions

```
READ BILLING-INFO
     AT END MOVE 'NO ' TO
          ARE-THERE-MORE-RECORDS.
PERFORM 300-CALC-RTN
     UNTIL THERE-ARE-NO-MORE-RECORDS.
```

```
                    PERFORM 500-END-OF-JOB-RTN
                    STOP RUN.
         8. 200-TABLE-ENTRY.
                    READ TAB-WTS AT END
                         DISPLAY 'NOT ENOUGH TABLE RECORDS'
                         CLOSE TAB-WTS
                               BILLING-INFO
                               BILLS
                         STOP RUN
                    END-READ*
                    MOVE WEIGHT-MAX TO T-WEIGHT-MAX (X1)
                    MOVE DELIVERY-CHARGE TO T-DELIVERY-CHARGE (X1).
         9. 300-CALC-RTN.
                    MOVE CUST-NO-IN TO CUST-NO-OUT
                    MOVE AMT-IN TO AMT-OF-SALES
                    SET X1 TO 1
                    SEARCH STORED-ENTRIES
                        AT END MOVE 0 TO DELIVERY-CHARGE-OUT
                               MOVE AMT-IN TO TOTAL
                        WHEN WEIGHT-MAILED <= T-WEIGHT-MAX (X1)
                             MOVE T-DELIVERY-CHARGE (X1) TO DELIVERY-CHARGE-OUT
                             COMPUTE TOTAL = AMT-IN + T-DELIVERY-CHARGE (X1)
                    END-SEARCH*
                    WRITE PRINT-REC FROM BILL-REC
                         AFTER ADVANCING 2 LINES.
```

COBOL 74 Substitutions

```
READ BILLING-INFO        ⎫
    AT END MOVE 'NO ' TO  ⎬  ⟶
        ARE-THERE-MORE-RECORDS. ⎭
```

10. SEARCH must be used in conjunction with the identifier ENTRY-X, *not* TABLE-1.

11. No. We could establish a direct-referenced table without PART-NO where UNIT-PRICE (1) refers to PART-NO 001, UNIT-PRICE (2) refers to PART-NO 002; and so on.

THE SEARCH ... VARYING OPTION FOR PROCESSING PARALLEL TABLES

The following is an alternative way of processing tables. If the customer numbers in Figure 12.5 were not consecutive but we knew in advance what they are, we could store them in a separate table:

```
01  CUST-NO-TABLE
        VALUE '0106080911151821242628313437454851545656586164677478'.
    05  EACH-CUST-NO OCCURS 25 TIMES
            INDEXED BY X1   PIC X(2).
```

Then we can store the balances due in a separate array:

```
01  CUST-ARRAY           VALUE ZEROS.
    05  BAL-DUE OCCURS 25 TIMES
            INDEXED BY X2 PIC 9(4)V99.
```

These would be **parallel tables** with CUST-NO-TABLE storing 25 customer numbers and CUST-ARRAY storing the corresponding BAL-DUE for each:

---

*Use END-READ and END-SEARCH with COBOL 85; otherwise end READ and SEARCH statements with a period.

CUST-NO-TABLE   CUST-ARRAY

When we read CUST-NO-IN, we search CUST-NO-TABLE to determine which entry to add to in CUST-ARRAY. We can use the SEARCH ... VARYING option for processing parallel arrays:

```
SET X1, X2 TO 1
SEARCH EACH-CUST-NO   VARYING X2
       AT END PERFORM 300-ERR-RTN
    WHEN CUST-NO-IN = EACH-CUST-NO (X1)
    ADD AMT-IN TO BAL-DUE (X2)
END-SEARCH
```

This technique enables us to enter CUST-NOs into one table and store BAL-DUEs in a corresponding parallel table. Since the CUST-NOs are not consecutive, a direct-referenced CUST-ARRAY cannot be used. Note, too, that the output report would be in sequence only if the CUST-NOs entered as input are in sequence.

We use X2, the index of the parallel table, in the SEARCH ... VARYING, not the index of CUST-NO-TABLE. The SEARCH ... VARYING has the following format:

Format

$$
\underline{\text{SEARCH}} \text{ identifier-1} \quad \underline{\text{VARYING}} \quad \begin{Bmatrix} \text{identifier-2} \\ \text{index-name-1} \end{Bmatrix}
$$

[AT \underline{END} imperative-statement-1]

$$
\begin{Bmatrix} \underline{\text{WHEN}} & \text{condition-1} & \begin{Bmatrix} \text{imperative-statement-2} \\ \underline{\text{NEXT}} \ \underline{\text{SENTENCE}} \end{Bmatrix} \end{Bmatrix} \dots
$$

[END-SEARCH]*

*COBOL 85 only. The NEXT SENTENCE clause is not permitted with the END-SEARCH unless your compiler has an enhancement that allows it.

THE SEARCH ALL STATEMENT

DEFINITION OF A SERIAL SEARCH

Thus far, we have discussed the method of table look-up called a **serial search**:

SERIAL SEARCH

1. The first entry in the table is searched.

2. If the condition is met, the table look-up is completed.

3. If the condition is not met, the index or subscript is incremented by one, and the next entry is searched.

4. This procedure is continued until a match is found or the table has been completely searched.

A sequential or serial search, as described here, is best used when either:

1. The entries in a table are *not* in either ascending or descending sequence; that is, they are arranged randomly; or,

2. Table entries are organized so that the first values are the ones encountered most frequently; in this way, access time is minimized because you are apt to end the search after the first few comparisons.

In many instances, however, the table entries are arranged in some numeric sequence. In a DISCOUNT-TABLE, for example, the table entries are apt to be in ascending sequence by customer number:

	DISCOUNT-TABLE	
	T-CUSTOMER-NO	T-DISCOUNT-PCT
Ascending	0100	2.0
sequence	0200	1.0
	0400	5.0
	⋮	⋮

The table contains the discount percentage to which each customer is entitled. Note that although the customer numbers are in sequence, they are not necessarily consecutive, so we must store the T-CUSTOMER-NO as well as the T-DISCOUNT-PCT.

We could code the table as follows:

```
01  TABLE-1.
    05  DISCOUNT-TABLE OCCURS 50 TIMES INDEXED BY X1.
        10  T-CUSTOMER-NO        PIC 9(4).
        10  T-DISCOUNT-PCT       PIC V999.
```

In this table, a discount of 2.0%, for example, is stored as ∧020.

In cases where the entries in a table are in some sequence, a serial search may be inefficient. For example, it would be time-consuming to begin at the first table entry when searching for the T-DISCOUNT-PCT for customer number 9000. Since the table is in sequence, we know that customer number 9000 is somewhere near the end of the table; hence, beginning with the first entry and proceeding in sequence would waste time.

DEFINITION OF A BINARY SEARCH

When table entries are arranged in sequence by some field, such as T-CUSTOMER-NO, the most efficient type of look-up is a **binary search.** The following is the way the computer performs a binary search:

ALTERNATIVE METHOD FOR TABLE LOOK-UP: BINARY SEARCH

1. Begin by comparing CUST-NO of the input customer record to the *middle table argument* for T-CUSTOMER-NO. In this instance, that would be the twenty-fifth entry in the table.

2. Since T-CUSTOMER-NOs are in sequence, if CUST-NO-IN > T-CUSTOMER-NO (25)—which is the middle entry in our table—we have eliminated the need for searching the first half of the table.

    In such a case, we compare CUST-NO-IN to T-CUSTOMER-NO (37), the middle table argument of the second half of the table (rounding down), and continue our comparison in this way.

3. If CUST-NO-IN < T-CUSTOMER-NO (25), however, we compare CUST-NO-IN to T-CUSTOMER-NO (12); that is, we divide the top half of the table into two segments and continue our comparison in this way.

4. The binary search is complete either (1) when a match has been found, that is, CUST-NO-IN = T-CUSTOMER-NO (X1), or (2) when the table has been completely searched and no match has been found.

On average, a binary search on a table that is in sequence by some field takes fewer comparisons to find a match than does a serial search.

Example   Suppose CUST-NO-IN = 5000

DISCOUNT-TABLE

Table entry number	T-CUSTOMER-NO (*Table argument*)	T-DISCOUNT-PCT (*Table function*)	
1.	0100	2.0	
2.	0200	1.0	
3.	0400	5.0	
4.	0500	3.1	
25. (1st comparison)	4300	4.3 (>)	
31. (3rd comparison)	4890	8.4 (>)	
34. (4th comparison)	5000	5.6 (=)	← match
37. (2nd comparison)	5310	2.4 (<)	
50.	9940	7.1	

CUST-NO-IN matches T-CUSTOMER-NO when the thirty-fourth entry of the table is compared. If a serial search were used, 34 comparisons would be required. The binary search method, however, requires only four comparisons in this instance. In general, for tables with 50 or more entries in sequence by some field, a binary search will save time.

This alternative method for table look-ups is called a binary search because each comparison eliminates one half the entries under consideration; that is, each comparison reduces the entries to be searched by a factor of two.

A binary search is preferable to a serial search in the following instances:

> **USES OF A BINARY SEARCH**
>
> 1. When table entries are arranged in sequence by some table field—either ascending or descending sequence.
>
> 2. When tables with a large number of sequential entries (e.g., 50 or more) are to be looked up or searched.

For small tables or those in which entries are *not* arranged in a sequence, the standard serial search look-up method previously described is used. For large tables in which entries are arranged in a specific sequence, the binary search is most efficient. It is difficult to define a "large" table explicitly, but let us say that any table containing more than 50 entries that are in some sequence could benefit from the use of a binary search.

FORMAT OF THE SEARCH ALL STATEMENT

The **SEARCH ALL** statement is used to perform a binary search. The format of the SEARCH ALL is very similar to that of the SEARCH.

Basic Format

```
SEARCH ALL  identifier-1
     [AT END  imperative-statement-1]

     WHEN  { data-name-1       { IS EQUAL TO }  { identifier-2          }
           {                   { IS =        }  { literal-1             }
           {                                    { arithmetic-expression-1 }
           { condition-name-1

     [ AND { data-name-2       { IS EQUAL TO }  { identifier-3          }
           {                   { IS =        }  { literal-2             }
           {                                    { arithmetic-expression-2 }
           { condition-name-2                                            ]

     ...

           { imperative-statement-2 }
           { NEXT SENTENCE          }

     [END-SEARCH]*
```

*COBOL 85 only. NEXT SENTENCE cannot be used with END-SEARCH unless your compiler has an enhancement that permits it.

A SET statement is *not* necessary with the SEARCH ALL, since the computer sets the index to the appropriate point initially when each binary search begins.

Example
```
SEARCH ALL DISCOUNT-TABLE
     AT END PERFORM 500-ERR-RTN
     WHEN T-CUSTOMER-NO (X1) = CUST-NO-IN
```

```
       MULTIPLY AMT-OF-PURCHASE-IN BY T-DISCOUNT-PCT (X1)
              GIVING DISCOUNT-AMT-OUT
END-SEARCH
```

Note that there are a number of limitations placed on the use of a binary search using a SEARCH ALL. First, binary searches can be used only with WHEN clauses that test for *equal* conditions between a table argument and a search argument. That is, the syntax for a SEARCH ALL requires the WHEN to use = (not <, >, <=, or >=) as the relational test.

This means that you must use a serial search when the look-up checks for a range of entries rather than a single match, even if the table is in sequence. Suppose we want to find a UNIT-PRICE that is <= 100.00, where table entries are in sequence by UNIT-PRICE:

UNIT-PRICE

Using a serial search, the first entry would be <= 100.00 and the search would be completed. If a binary search were permitted, the middle entry, 25, meets the condition (e.g., UNIT-PRICE (25) < 100.00) so this search would also be completed after the first test. A binary search, then, would produce a different match than a serial search.

Because we are using a less than (<) test, going to the midpoint of the table with a SEARCH ALL does not really help when testing for a "less than" condition. It tells us that UNIT-PRICE (25) < 100.00, but UNIT-PRICE (1) could also be < 100.00, as could UNIT-PRICE (2), and so on. In summary, a binary search cannot be used for anything but tests for equality (e.g., WHEN search argument = table argument).

The following summarizes the major limitations to a SEARCH ALL:

LIMITATIONS OF THE SEARCH ALL

1. The condition following the word WHEN can test only for *equality:*

   Valid: WHEN T-CUSTOMER-NO (X1) = CUST-NO-IN
   Invalid: WHEN T-WEIGHT-MAX (X1) $\boxed{<}$ WEIGHT-MAILED

2. If the condition following the word WHEN is a compound conditional:
   a. Each part of the conditional can only consist of a relational test that involves an equal condition.
   b. The only compound condition permitted is with ANDs, not ORs.

   Valid: WHEN S-AMT (X1) = AMT1 AND TAX-AMT (X1) = AMT2
   Invalid: WHEN SALES-AMT (X1) = AMT3 $\boxed{OR}$ AMT4 = AMT5

3. Only one WHEN clause can be used with a SEARCH ALL.

4. The VARYING option may not be used with the SEARCH ALL.

5. The OCCURS item and its index, which define the table argument, must appear to the left of the equal sign.

   Valid: WHEN S-AMT (X1) = AMT1...
   Invalid: WHEN AMT1 = S-AMT (X1)...

ASCENDING OR DESCENDING KEY
WITH THE SEARCH ALL STATEMENT

To use the SEARCH ALL statement, we must indicate which table entry will serve as the *key field*. That is, we specify the table entry that will be in sequence so that the binary search can be used to compare against that field. We must indicate whether that KEY is ASCENDING or DESCENDING:

KEY FIELD

ASCENDING KEY   Entries are in sequence and increasing in value.

DESCENDING KEY   Entries are in sequence and decreasing in value.

The ASCENDING or DESCENDING KEY is specified along with the OCCURS and INDEXED BY clauses of a table entry when a SEARCH ALL is to be used, as shown in the following format:

Format

> (level-number 02–49) identifier-1 <u>OCCURS</u> integer-1 TIMES
>
> $\left\{ \begin{array}{l} \underline{ASCENDING} \\ \underline{DESCENDING} \end{array} \right\}$ KEY IS data-name-2
>
> <u>INDEXED</u> BY index-name-1

Example

```
01  TABLE-1.
    05  DISCOUNT-TABLE OCCURS 50 TIMES
            ASCENDING KEY T-CUSTOMER-NO
            INDEXED BY X1.
        10  T-CUSTOMER-NO          PIC 9(4).
        10  T-DISCOUNT-PCT         PIC V999.
```

The identifier used in the ASCENDING KEY clause must be an entry within the table. If entries in the table decrease in value, then DESCENDING KEY would be used. In either case, the ASCENDING or DESCENDING KEY clause *must* be included and it must appear *before* the INDEXED BY clause.

In this example, T-CUSTOMER-NO increases in value as we move through the table; hence, T-CUSTOMER-NO is used with an ASCENDING KEY clause.

--- DEBUGGING TIP ---

The table must be in sequence by the KEY field to perform a valid binary search. If you code ASCENDING KEY IS PART-NO, the computer will *not* check that part numbers are correctly sequenced but will assume that this is so. If the part numbers are *not* in sequence in the table, a binary search will give unpredictable results.

For best results, the KEY entries or table arguments should be unique; that is, no two table arguments (such as T-CUSTOMER-NO) should have the same value. If it happens, however, that two table arguments defined in an ASCENDING or DESCENDING KEY clause have identical values and one of them is to be accessed, it is difficult to predict which one the computer will use for the look-up with a SEARCH ALL. With a serial SEARCH, the first entry, in sequence, will be the one that is designated as a match.

Differences Between the SEARCH and the SEARCH ALL

SEARCH	SEARCH ALL
Performs a serial search	Performs a binary search
Table entries need not be in any sequence	Tables entries must be in sequence by the table argument or even the table function. The field that is in sequence is specified in an ASCENDING or DESCENDING KEY clause as part of the OCCURS entry
Requires a SET statement prior to the SEARCH to specify the starting point for the look-up	Does not need a SET prior to the SEARCH ALL
Can include any relational test with the WHEN clause (<, >, =, <=, >=) or any compound conditional	Can only have a single = condition tested with the WHEN clause
May include multiple WHEN clauses	May only have one WHEN clause

With COBOL 85 we recommend you use the END-SEARCH scope terminator with either the SEARCH or SEARCH ALL statement and avoid using the NEXT SENTENCE clause unless your compiler permits it.

—————— COBOL 9x CHANGES ——————

1. With the new standard, you can assign every occurrence of an element in a table the same initial value using a single VALUE clause.
2. The INDEXED BY and KEY phrases are permitted in any sequence with an OCCURS. With previous standards, INDEXED BY must follow the KEY clause.
3. You can use the SORT verb to sort table entries as well as files. This means that you will be able to sort a table and then use a binary search, which could save a considerable amount of processing time, depending on the size of the table and the number of searches performed.

MULTIPLE-LEVEL OCCURS CLAUSE

When describing an area of storage, more than one level of OCCURS may be used. As many as seven levels of OCCURS are permitted with COBOL 85, and as many as three levels are permitted with COBOL 74.

Like a single-level OCCURS, multiple levels of OCCURS may be used for (1) accumulating totals in an *array* or (2) storing a *table* for "look-up" purposes. We will look first at multiple-level arrays and then at multiple-level tables.

DEFINING A DOUBLE-LEVEL OR TWO-DIMENSIONAL ARRAY

Suppose we wish to establish in storage an array of hourly temperature readings for Los Angeles or any other city *during a given week*. Once the array is established, we will use it to perform various calculations. The array consists of 7 × 24 temperature readings; that is, there are 24 hourly temperature readings for each of 7 days. The array is represented as follows:

TEMPERATURE-ARRAY

DAY 1 (SUN)				DAY 2 (MON)					DAY 7 (SAT)			
1-AM-TEMP	2-AM-TEMP	...	MIDNIGHT-TEMP	1-AM-TEMP	2-AM-TEMP	...	MIDNIGHT-TEMP	...	1-AM-TEMP	2-AM-TEMP	...	MIDNIGHT-TEMP

To define this array in WORKING-STORAGE with a *single*-level OCCURS would require the following coding:

```
01   TEMPERATURE-ARRAY.
     05   DAY-IN-WEEK OCCURS 7 TIMES.
          10   1-AM-TEMP              PIC S9(3).
          10   2-AM-TEMP              PIC S9(3).
             .
             .
             .
          10   11-PM-TEMP             PIC S9(3).
          10   MIDNIGHT               PIC S9(3).
```

The ellipses or dots (...) indicate that 24 elementary items must be coded, which would be rather cumbersome. Instead, we could use a *double-level* OCCURS to define the array as follows:

```
01   TEMPERATURE-ARRAY.
     05   DAY-IN-WEEK OCCURS 7 TIMES.
          10   HOUR OCCURS 24 TIMES.
               15   TEMP             PIC S9(3).
```

The following illustration shows how this array can be visualized in storage:

Hour / Day-in-Week	1 A.M.	2 A.M.	3 A.M.	4 A.M.	...	11 P.M.	12 MID.	
Day 1 (Sun)					...			
Day 2 (Mon)					...			
Day 3 (Tue)					...			
Day 4 (Wed)					...			7 ROWS
Day 5 (Thu)					...			
Day 6 (Fri)					...			
Day 7 (Sat)					...			

TEMPERATURE-ARRAY

24 COLUMNS

For each DAY-IN-WEEK, we have 24 HOUR figures, each of which will consist of a TEMP (average or mean temperature for that hour) that is three integers long. Thus, this array defines a storage area of 504 positions ($7 \times 24 \times 3$). This *two-dimensional array* is established as follows:

1. The array will have 7 *rows* as indicated by the first OCCURS clause:

   ```
   05   DAY-IN-WEEK OCCURS 7 TIMES.
   ```

2. Within this array, each row will have 24 *columns*, as indicated by the second OCCURS clause:

   ```
   10   HOUR OCCURS 24 TIMES.
   ```

3. Each of the *elements* in this 7×24 array will be large enough to hold three integers, as indicated by the subordinate entry:

```
15  TEMP      PIC S9(3).
```

To access any of the temperature figures, we use the data-name on the *lowest* OCCURS *level* or any data-name subordinate to it. Either TEMP or HOUR could be used to access the temperatures. Because HOUR contains only one elementary item, TEMP and HOUR refer to the same area of storage. Thus, the array could also have been defined as follows:

Alternative Coding

```
01  TEMPERATURE-ARRAY.
    05  DAY-IN-WEEK OCCURS 7 TIMES.
        10  HOUR    OCCURS 24 TIMES        PIC S9(3).
```

We have added the PIC clause to the second OCCURS level data-name, thereby eliminating the reference to the data-name TEMP.

We will use the entry TEMP throughout, however, since it is clearer. Note that we could *not* use DAY-IN-WEEK for accessing a single field in the array, since each DAY-IN-WEEK actually refers to 24 temperatures.

Using Subscripts with Double-Level OCCURS Entries

Since TEMP is defined with two OCCURS, we must use *two* subscripts to access any hourly temperature. The first subscript specified refers to the first or *major*-level OCCURS clause, which, in this example, defines the DAY-IN-WEEK. The second subscript refers to the second or *minor* OCCURS level, which, in this example, defines the HOUR. Thus, TEMP (1, 6) refers to the temperature for Sunday (the first row) at 6 A.M. (the sixth column in the array). Assuming there is data in the array, we can display the temperature for Tuesday at noon with the following instruction:

```
DISPLAY 'TEMPERATURE FOR TUESDAY AT NOON IS ', TEMP (3, 12)
```

The first subscript can vary from 1 to 7 since there are seven rows, one for each day. The second subscript varies from 1 to 24, since there are 24 columns, one for each hour of the day. The following subscripts are *not* valid:

Invalid Subscripts

TEMP (8, 4) The first subscript can vary from 1 through 7.
TEMP (6, 25) The second subscript can vary from 1 through 24.

A pictorial representation of the table with its subscripts follows:

Day-in-Week \ Hour	1 A.M.	2 A.M.	3 A.M.	4 A.M.	...	11 P.M.	12 MID.
Day 1 (Sun)	(1,1)	(1,2)	(1,3)	(1,4)	...	(1,23)	(1, 24)
Day 2 (Mon)	(2,1)	(2,2)	(2,3)	(2,4)	...	(2,23)	(2,24)
Day 3 (Tue)	(3,1)	(3,2)	(3,3)	(3,4)	...	(3,23)	(3, 24)
Day 4 (Wed)	(4,1)	(4,2)	(4,3)	(4,4)	...	(4,23)	(4, 24)
Day 5 (Thu)	(5,1)	(5,2)	(5,3)	(5,4)	...	(5,23)	(5, 24)
Day 6 (Fri)	(6,1)	(6,2)	(6,3)	(6,4)	...	(6,23)	(6, 24)
Day 7 (Sat)	(7,1)	(7,2)	(7,3)	(7,4)	...	(7,23)	(7, 24)

The following are rules for using a double-level OCCURS:

> ### RULES FOR USING A DOUBLE-LEVEL OCCURS
>
> 1. If an item is defined by a *double-level* OCCURS clause, it must be accessed by *two* subscripts.
>
> 2. The first subscript refers to the higher-level OCCURS; the second subscript refers to the lower-level OCCURS.
>
> 3. The subscripts must be enclosed in parentheses.
>
> 4. Subscripts may consist of positive integers or data-names with positive integer contents.
>
> 5. On most systems, the left parenthesis must be preceded by at least one space; similarly, the right parenthesis must be followed by a period, if it is the end of a sentence, or at least one space. The first subscript within parentheses is followed by a comma and a space.

ACCESSING A DOUBLE-LEVEL OR TWO-DIMENSIONAL ARRAY

Example 1 Suppose we wish to print an average temperature for the entire week. We need to add all the array entries to a total and divide by 168 (7 × 24). We can use *nested* PERFORMs for this purpose. The first PERFORM varies the major subscript, which we call DAY-SUB, and the second PERFORM varies the minor subscript, which we call HOUR-SUB:

```
600-AVERAGE-RTN.
    MOVE 0 TO TOTAL
    PERFORM 700-LOOP-ON-DAYS
        VARYING DAY-SUB FROM 1 BY 1 UNTIL DAY-SUB > 7
    COMPUTE WEEKLY-AVERAGE = TOTAL / 168
    WRITE PRINT-REC FROM OUT-REC
        AFTER ADVANCING 2 LINES.
700-LOOP-ON-DAYS.
    PERFORM 800-LOOP-ON-HOURS
        VARYING HOUR-SUB FROM 1 BY 1 UNTIL HOUR-SUB > 24.
800-LOOP-ON-HOURS.
    ADD TEMP (DAY-SUB, HOUR-SUB) TO TOTAL.
```

Using in-line PERFORMs with COBOL 85, we could code the above as:

```
800-AVERAGE-RTN.
    MOVE 0 TO TOTAL
    PERFORM VARYING DAY-SUB FROM 1 BY 1 UNTIL DAY-SUB > 7
        PERFORM VARYING HOUR-SUB FROM 1 BY 1 UNTIL HOUR-SUB > 24
            ADD TEMP (DAY-SUB, HOUR-SUB) TO TOTAL
        END-PERFORM
    END-PERFORM
    COMPUTE WEEKLY-AVERAGE = TOTAL / 168
    WRITE PRINT-REC FROM OUT-REC
        AFTER ADVANCING 2 LINES.
```

The PERFORM ... VARYING with the AFTER Option

The following expanded format for the PERFORM ... VARYING will result in nested PERFORMs *without the need for two separate* PERFORM ... VARYING *statements*:

Expanded Format

$$
\underline{\text{PERFORM}} \text{ procedure-name-1} \left[\left\{ \begin{array}{l} \underline{\text{THROUGH}} \\ \underline{\text{THRU}} \end{array} \right\} \text{procedure-name-2} \right]
$$

$$
\left[\text{WITH } \underline{\text{TEST}} \left\{ \begin{array}{l} \underline{\text{BEFORE}} \\ \underline{\text{AFTER}} \end{array} \right\} \right]
$$

$$
\underline{\text{VARYING}} \left\{ \begin{array}{l} \text{identifier-2} \\ \text{index-name-1} \end{array} \right\} \underline{\text{FROM}} \left\{ \begin{array}{l} \text{identifier-3} \\ \text{index-name-2} \\ \text{literal-1} \end{array} \right\}
$$

$$
\underline{\text{BY}} \left\{ \begin{array}{l} \text{identifier-4} \\ \text{literal-2} \end{array} \right\} \underline{\text{UNTIL}} \text{ condition-1}
$$

$$
\underline{\text{AFTER}} \left\{ \begin{array}{l} \text{identifier-5} \\ \text{index-name-3} \end{array} \right\} \underline{\text{FROM}} \left\{ \begin{array}{l} \text{identifier-6} \\ \text{index-name-4} \\ \text{literal-3} \end{array} \right\}
$$

$$
\underline{\text{BY}} \left\{ \begin{array}{l} \text{identifier-7} \\ \text{literal-4} \end{array} \right\} \underline{\text{UNTIL}} \text{ condition-2} \dots
$$

This format is particularly useful for processing multiple-level arrays and tables. The PERFORM ... VARYING varies the *major subscript*, and the AFTER clause varies the *minor subscript*. Note, however, that the AFTER clause requires a procedure-name-1 following the word PERFORM. Thus, we can simplify the preceding nested PERFORM as follows:

Alternative Coding

```
600-AVERAGE-RTN.
    MOVE 0 TO TOTAL
    PERFORM 700-LOOP1
        VARYING DAY-SUB FROM 1 BY 1 UNTIL DAY-SUB > 7
            AFTER HOUR-SUB FROM 1 BY 1 UNTIL HOUR-SUB > 24
    COMPUTE WEEKLY-AVERAGE = TOTAL / 168
    WRITE PRINT-REC FROM OUT-REC
        AFTER ADVANCING 2 LINES.
700-LOOP1.
    ADD TEMP (DAY-SUB, HOUR-SUB) TO TOTAL.
```

The sequence of values that these subscripts take on is (1, 1), (1, 2) ... (1, 24), (2, 1), (2, 2) ... (2, 24) ... (7, 1) ... (7, 24). That is, with the PERFORM ... VARYING ... AFTER, DAY-SUB is initialized at 1 and HOUR-SUB is varied from 1 to 24. Then DAY-SUB is incremented to 2 and HOUR-SUB is varied again from 1 to 24. This continues until HOUR-SUB is varied from 1 to 24 with DAY-SUB at 7.

Example 2

Interactive Processing. Suppose we want to enable users to make inquiries from the TEMPERATURE-ARRAY:

```
WORKING-STORAGE SECTION.
01  WS-DAY              PIC 9.
01  WS-HOUR             PIC 99.
    :
    :
    DISPLAY 'ENTER DAY OF WEEK (1 = SUN,...7 = SAT)'
    ACCEPT WS-DAY
    DISPLAY 'ENTER HOUR (1 = 1 A.M.,...24 = MIDNIGHT)'
    ACCEPT WS-HOUR
    DISPLAY 'THE TEMPERATURE IS ', TEMP (WS-DAY, WS-HOUR).
```

Example 3   Consider the following double-level array and assume that data has been read into it:

```
01  POPULATION-ARRAY.
    05  STATE OCCURS 50 TIMES.
        10  COUNTY OCCURS 10 TIMES.
            15  POPULATION  PIC 9(10).
```

This array defines 500 fields of data or 5000 characters. Each of the 50 states is divided into 10 counties, each with a 10-character POPULATION. We have arbitrarily selected 10 counties per state, each with a POPULATION of 9(10), *for illustration purposes only.* In reality, the number of counties per state varies from state to state, and counties will have populations that have fewer than 10 digits.

A pictorial representation of the array is as follows:

State \ County	County 1	County 2	POPULATION-ARRAY . . .	County 10
1 (Alabama)	(1,1)	(1,2)	. . .	(1,10)
2 (Alaska)	(2,1)	(2,2)	. . .	(2,10)
. . .	. . .	. . .	. . . . . .	. . .
50 (Wyoming)	(50,1)	(50,2)	. . .	(50,10)

Note: The numbers in parentheses represent the subscripts for each entry.

Suppose we wish to accumulate a total United States population. We will add all 10 counties for each of 50 states. We access elements in the array by using the lowest level item, POPULATION. POPULATION must be accessed using *two* subscripts. The first defines the major level, STATE, and the second defines the minor level, COUNTY. POPULATION (5, 10) refers to the population for STATE 5, COUNTY 10. The first subscript varies from 1 to 50; the second varies from 1 to 10.

To perform the required addition, we will first accumulate all COUNTY figures for STATE 1. Thus, the second or minor subscript will vary from 1 to 10. After 10 additions for STATE 1 are performed, we will accumulate the 10 COUNTY figures for STATE 2. That is, we will increment the major subscript to 2 and then add COUNTY (2, 1), COUNTY (2, 2), ... COUNTY (2, 10) before we add the figures for STATE 3.

Using PERFORM ... VARYING ... AFTER

Using the AFTER option of the PERFORM VARYING, we can simplify coding as follows:

Alternative Coding

```
        PERFORM 700-USA-TOT.
            :
            :
700-USA-TOT.
    PERFORM 800-ADD-POP
        VARYING STATE-SUB FROM 1 BY 1 UNTIL STATE-SUB > 50
        AFTER COUNTY-SUB FROM 1 BY 1 UNTIL COUNTY-SUB > 10
    PERFORM 1000-PRINT-TOTAL.
800-ADD-POP.
    ADD POPULATION (STATE-SUB, COUNTY-SUB) TO TOTAL1.
```

The following illustrates how this procedure could be coded using an in-line PERFORM:

```
PERFORM VARYING STATE-SUB FROM 1 BY 1
                UNTIL STATE-SUB > 50
    AFTER COUNTY-SUB FROM 1 BY 1
                UNTIL COUNTY-SUB > 10
        ADD POPULATION (STATE-SUB, COUNTY-SUB) TO TOTAL1
END-PERFORM
```

We vary the minor subscript first, holding the major subscript constant. That is, when the major subscript is equal to 1, denoting STATE 1, all counties within that STATE are summed. Thus, we set STATE-SUB equal to 1 and vary COUNTY-SUB from 1 to 10. STATE-SUB is then set to 2, and we again vary COUNTY-SUB from 1 to 10, and so on.

USING A DOUBLE-LEVEL OR TWO-DIMENSIONAL ARRAY FOR ACCUMULATING TOTALS

Suppose a company has 10 departments (numbered 1–10) and five salespeople (numbered 1–5) within each department. We wish to accumulate the total amount of sales for each salesperson within each department:

```
01   DEPT-TOTALS.
     05   DEPT OCCURS 10 TIMES.
          10   SALESPERSON OCCURS 5 TIMES.
               15   TOTAL-SALES          PIC 9(5)V99.
```

Before adding any data to a total area, we must ensure that the total area is initialized at zero. To initialize an entire array at zero, we could code the following with COBOL 85: MOVE ZEROS TO DEPT-TOTALS. Alternatively, with COBOL 85 we can code:

```
01   DEPT-TOTALS    VALUE ZEROS.
```

If your compiler permits you to reference DEPT-TOTALS in the PROCEDURE DIVISION, moving ZEROS to DEPT-TOTALS replaces all fields with 0; note, however, that MOVE 0 TO DEPT-TOTALS only moves a 0 to the leftmost position in the array. This is because DEPT-TOTALS, as a group item, is treated as an alphanumeric field; if you move a single 0 to an alphanumeric field, the 0 is placed in the leftmost position; all other positions are replaced with blanks.

With COBOL 74, however, you may not reference the 01 array entry itself. In such a case, you must code a full initializing routine prior to adding to TOTAL-SALES. We will use either nested PERFORMs or a PERFORM with the AFTER option in our illustrations:

```
        PERFORM 700-INITIALIZE-RTN
            VARYING X1 FROM 1 BY 1 UNTIL X1 > 10
                AFTER X2 FROM 1 BY 1 UNTIL X2 > 5
                  .
                  .
        700-INITIALIZE-RTN.
            MOVE 0 TO TOTAL-SALES (X1, X2).
```

This routine, which initializes each TOTAL-SALES field separately, will run on all computers; COBOL 85 compilers, however, will allow you to code MOVE ZEROS TO DEPT-TOTALS. The most efficient method for establishing DEPT-TOTALS is to define it as PACKED-DECIMAL, which saves space. Initializing DEPT-TOTALS with COBOL 85 is best accomplished by coding INITIALIZE DEPT-TOTALS.

Assume an input record has been created each time a salesperson makes a sale. Each input record contains a department number called DEPT-IN, a salesperson number called SALESPERSON-NO-IN, and an amount of sales called AMT-IN. There may be numerous input records for a salesperson if he or she made more than one sale. The coding to accumulate the totals after the array has been initialized at zero is as follows:

COBOL 85

COBOL 74 Substitutions

```
READ SALES-FILE
    AT END MOVE 'NO ' TO ARE-THERE-MORE-RECORDS.
PERFORM 200-ADD-RTN
    UNTIL ARE-THERE-MORE-RECORDS = 'NO '.
```

```
PERFORM UNTIL ARE-THERE-MORE-RECORDS = 'NO '
    READ SALES-FILE
        AT END
            MOVE 'NO ' TO ARE-THERE-MORE-RECORDS
        NOT AT END
            PERFORM 200-ADD-RTN
    END-READ
END-PERFORM
```

```
                                        :
                          200-ADD-RTN.
                              ADD AMT-IN TO TOTAL-SALES (DEPT-IN, SALESPERSON-NO-IN).
```

COBOL 74 Substitutions

```
READ SALES-FILE                                 }
    AT END MOVE 'NO ' TO ARE-THERE-MORE-RECORDS.}  ⟶
```

As indicated previously, input fields may be used as subscripts. For correct processing, a validation procedure should be used to ensure that (1) DEPT-IN is an integer between 1 and 10 and (2) SALESPERSON-NO-IN is an integer between 1 and 5. We should also check that AMT-IN is numeric:

```
200-ADD-RTN.
    IF AMT-IN IS NUMERIC
        AND (DEPT-IN > 0 AND < 11)
        AND (SALESPERSON-NO-IN > 0 AND < 6)
        ADD AMT-IN TO TOTAL-SALES (DEPT-IN, SALESPERSON-NO-IN)
    ELSE
        DISPLAY 'ERROR'
    END-IF.
```

At the end of the job, we wish to print 10 pages of output. Each page will contain five lines, one for each salesperson in a given department. The full PROCEDURE DIVISION is as follows:

COBOL 85

```
PROCEDURE DIVISION.
100-MAIN-MODULE.
    OPEN INPUT SALES-FILE
         OUTPUT PRINT-FILE
    INITIALIZE DEPT-TOTALS
    PERFORM UNTIL ARE-THERE-MORE-RECORDS = 'NO '
        READ SALES-FILE
            AT END
                MOVE 'NO ' TO ARE-THERE-MORE-RECORDS
            NOT AT END
                PERFORM 200-ADD-RTN
        END-READ
    END-PERFORM
    PERFORM 300-PRINT-RTN
        VARYING X1 FROM 1 BY 1 UNTIL X1 > 10
    CLOSE SALES-FILE
          PRINT-FILE
    STOP RUN.
200-ADD-RTN.
*****************************************************************
* note: amt-in, dept-in, salesperson-no-in are input fields *
*****************************************************************
    IF  AMT-IN IS NUMERIC
        AND (DEPT-IN > 0 AND < 11)
        AND (SALESPERSON-NO-IN > 0 AND < 6)
        ADD AMT-IN TO TOTAL-SALES (DEPT-IN,
            SALESPERSON-NO-IN)
    ELSE
        DISPLAY 'ERROR'
    END-IF.
```

COBOL 74 Substitutions

```
MOVE ZEROS TO DEPT-TOTALS.
READ SALES-FILE
    AT END MOVE 'NO ' TO ARE-THERE-MORE-RECORDS.
PERFORM 200-ADD-RTN
    UNTIL ARE-THERE-MORE-RECORDS = 'NO '.
```

```
READ SALES-FILE                                 }
    AT END MOVE 'NO ' TO ARE-THERE-MORE-RECORDS.}  ⟶
```

```
300-PRINT-RTN.
    MOVE X1 TO DEPT-NO-ON-HDG-LINE
    WRITE PRINT-REC FROM HDG-LINE
        AFTER ADVANCING PAGE
    PERFORM 400-LINE-PRINT
        VARYING X2 FROM 1 BY 1 UNTIL X2 > 5.
400-LINE-PRINT.
    MOVE X2 TO SALESPERSON-NO-OUT
    MOVE TOTAL-SALES (X1, X2) TO TOTAL-OUT
    WRITE PRINT-REC FROM SALES-LINE-REC
        AFTER ADVANCING 2 LINES.
```

In this illustration, we assume that the values for DEPT-IN vary from 1–10 and the values for SALESPERSON-NO-IN vary from 1–5. If either or both of these fields have values other than 1–10 or 1–5 consecutively, then the numbers themselves must be stored along with the TOTAL-SALES.

The input consists of transaction records for the previous year, each with the following format:

SALES-FILE **Record Layout**			
Field	**Size**	**Type**	**No. of Decimal Positions (if Numeric)**
SALESPERSON-NO-IN	2	Numeric	0
SALES-AMT-IN	3	Numeric	0
DATE-OF-TRANS	6	Format: mmddyy	

The full program for printing monthly sales totals that uses procedures discussed in this section appears in Figure 12.6.

Figure 12.6 Program to print monthly sales totals.

COBOL 85

```
IDENTIFICATION DIVISION.
PROGRAM-ID.  FIG126.
ENVIRONMENT DIVISION.
INPUT-OUTPUT SECTION.
FILE-CONTROL.
     SELECT SALES-FILE  ASSIGN TO DISK 'S1.DAT'.
     SELECT REPORT-FILE ASSIGN TO PRINTER.
DATA DIVISION.
FILE SECTION.
FD   SALES-FILE
     LABEL RECORDS ARE STANDARD.
01   SALES-REC.
     05   SALESPERSON-NO-IN       PIC 99.
     05   SALES-AMT-IN            PIC 999.
     05   DATE-OF-TRANS.
          10   MONTH-IN           PIC 99.
          10   DAY-IN             PIC 99.
          10   YEAR-IN            PIC 99.
FD   REPORT-FILE
     LABEL RECORDS ARE OMITTED.
01   PRINT-REC                    PIC X(132).
WORKING-STORAGE SECTION.
01   MORE-RECS                    PIC X(3)   VALUE 'YES'.
01   COMPANY-SALES-ARRAY.
     05   SALESPERSON  OCCURS 25 TIMES.
          10   MONTH-AMT OCCURS 12 TIMES  PIC 9(4).
01   HEADING-REC.
     05                           PIC X(30)
               VALUE SPACES.
     05                           PIC X(102)
               VALUE 'ANNUAL SALES REPORT'.
01   COLUMN-HEADING.
     05                           PIC X(43)
               VALUE '  S1   S2   S3   S4   S5   S6   S7   S8     '.
     05                           PIC X(39)
               VALUE 'S9   S10  S11  S12  S13  S14  S15  S16 '.
     05                           PIC X(50)
               VALUE 'S17  S18  S19  S20  S21  S22  S23  S24  S25'.
```

COBOL 74 Substitutions

For COBOL 74, FILLER must be used instead of a blank field name

Figure 12.6 (continued)

```
                                01  SALES-LINE.
                                    05                        PIC X.
                                    05  ITEMX OCCURS 25 TIMES.
                                        10  SALES-ITEM        PIC ZZZ9.
                                        10                    PIC X.
                                    05                        PIC X(6).
                                01  SUB1                      PIC 99.
                                01  SUB2                      PIC 99.
                                PROCEDURE DIVISION.
                                100-MAIN.
                                    OPEN INPUT  SALES-FILE
                                         OUTPUT REPORT-FILE
                                    WRITE PRINT-REC FROM HEADING-REC
                                        AFTER ADVANCING PAGE
                                    WRITE PRINT-REC FROM COLUMN-HEADING
                                        AFTER ADVANCING 3 LINES
                                    MOVE ZEROS TO COMPANY-SALES-ARRAY
                                    PERFORM UNTIL MORE-RECS = 'NO '
                                        READ SALES-FILE
                                            AT END
                                                MOVE 'NO ' TO MORE-RECS
                                            NOT AT END
                                                PERFORM 200-CALC-RTN
                                        END-READ
                                    END-PERFORM
                                    PERFORM 800-WRITE-RTN
                                        VARYING SUB2 FROM 1 BY 1 UNTIL SUB2 > 12
                                    CLOSE SALES-FILE
                                          REPORT-FILE
                                    STOP RUN.
                                200-CALC-RTN.
                                    IF MONTH-IN > 0 AND < 13
                                        AND SALESPERSON-NO-IN > 0 AND < 26
                                            ADD SALES-AMT-IN TO
                                                MONTH-AMT (SALESPERSON-NO-IN, MONTH-IN)
                                    ELSE
                                        DISPLAY 'ERROR ', SALES-REC
                                    END-IF.

                                800-WRITE-RTN.
                                    MOVE SPACES TO SALES-LINE
                                    PERFORM 900-MOVE-RTN
                                        VARYING SUB1 FROM 1 BY 1 UNTIL SUB1 > 25
                                    WRITE PRINT-REC FROM SALES-LINE
                                        AFTER ADVANCING 2 LINES.
                                900-MOVE-RTN.
                                    MOVE MONTH-AMT (SUB1, SUB2) TO SALES-ITEM (SUB1).
```

COBOL 74 Substitutions

```
READ SALES-FILE
    AT END MOVE 'NO ' TO MORE-RECS.
PERFORM 200-CALC-RTN
    UNTIL MORE-RECS = 'NO '.
```

```
READ SALES-FILE
    AT END MOVE 'NO ' TO MORE-RECS.
```

PERFORMING A LOOK-UP USING A DOUBLE-LEVEL OCCURS

We will use a double-level OCCURS entry to define a table and then use a SEARCH to perform a table look-up.

Example   Assume that the following table has been loaded into storage:

```
01  INVENTORY-TABLE.
    05  WAREHOUSE OCCURS 50 TIMES.
        10  ITEM-X OCCURS 100 TIMES.
            15  PART-NO        PIC 9(4).
            15  UNIT-PRICE     PIC 999V99.
```

There are 50 warehouses, and each stores 100 items. Each warehouse stocks its own inventory, which is different from the inventory at other warehouses. This means that a specific PART-NO will appear *only once* in the table. There are 5000 table records, each with a warehouse number, part number, and unit price. The first table record refers to warehouse 1, part number 1; the next to warehouse 1, part number 2; the 101st to warehouse 2, part number 1, and so on.

Suppose that input transaction records have the following format:

```
1-4  PART-NO-IN
5-6  QTY-ORDERED
```

For each PART-NO-IN in a transaction record, we need to look up the corresponding PART-NO in the table and find its UNIT-PRICE. We store the unit price for each part in the table and *not* in the transaction record for the following reasons:

1. If each input transaction record contained a unit price, we would be keying unit price each time a part was ordered. This would increase both keying costs and the risk of input errors.

2. Changes to unit prices can be more easily made to a relatively small number of table entries than to a large number of input transaction records.

We store prices in an external table, which is in a file and is loaded in, rather than in an internal table, which is established with VALUE clauses. External tables are used for this type of application because the table elements themselves are likely to change with some frequency. That is, because we anticipate that unit prices may change, we establish the INVENTORY-TABLE as an external table that can be changed, when needed, by a separate program. If we defined it as an internal table with VALUE clauses, we would need to modify and recompile our look-up program each time a change to unit price occurred.

The output from this program will be a printed transaction report. Each time a PART-NO is ordered, we will print the PART-NO and the TOTAL-AMT of the transaction, where TOTAL-AMT = QTY-ORDERED (from the transaction record) $\times$ UNIT-PRICE (from the table). Since we will use a SEARCH, the table we have described must include the appropriate INDEXED BY clauses with each OCCURS level item:

```
01  INVENTORY-TABLE.
    05  WAREHOUSE OCCURS 50 TIMES INDEXED BY X1.
        10  ITEM-X OCCURS 100 TIMES INDEXED BY X2.
            15  PART-NO          PIC 9(4).
            15  UNIT-PRICE       PIC 999V99.
```

The Identifier Used with the SEARCH Refers to the Lowest-Level OCCURS Entry

To SEARCH the table, we code SEARCH ITEM-X ... because ITEM-X is the *lowest-level OCCURS entry*. *Note that* SEARCH ITEM-X *increments the lowest-level index only*. Hence if X1 is set to 1 initially, the SEARCH will perform a look-up on items in warehouse 1 only, that is (1, 1) through (1, 100). To search *all* warehouses, the SEARCH itself must be executed from a PERFORM ... VARYING that increments the major index, X1.

The routine would then appear as follows:

```
MOVE 'NO ' TO MATCH-FOUND
PERFORM 500-SEARCH-IT
    VARYING X1 FROM 1 BY 1
        UNTIL X1 > 50 OR MATCH-FOUND = 'YES'
IF  MATCH-FOUND = 'YES'
    WRITE OUT-REC FROM TRANS-REC-OUT
        AFTER ADVANCING 2 LINES
ELSE
    PERFORM 600-NO-MATCH-ERR
END-IF.
    :
500-SEARCH-IT.
    SET X2 TO 1
    SEARCH ITEM-X    ◄——— Use lowest-level OCCURS level here
        WHEN PART-NO-IN = PART-NO (X1, X2)
            MULTIPLY UNIT-PRICE (X1, X2) BY QTY-ORDERED
                GIVING TOTAL-AMT
            MOVE 'YES' TO MATCH-FOUND  ◄——— Enables 500-SEARCH-IT to be
    END-SEARCH.                               terminated properly when a
                                              match is found
```

MATCH-FOUND is a field that is initialized at 'NO ' and changed to 'YES' only when the corresponding PART-NO in the table is found. We terminate 500-SEARCH-IT when a match is found (MATCH-FOUND = 'YES') or the entire table has been searched (X1 >

50). 600-NO-MATCH-ERR would be executed only if no match existed between the PART-NO-IN and a table entry.

The full program for this example appears in Figure 12.7.

Figure 12.7 Program to search a double-level table.

COBOL 85

```
IDENTIFICATION DIVISION.
PROGRAM-ID. FIG127.
*
ENVIRONMENT DIVISION.
INPUT-OUTPUT SECTION.
FILE-CONTROL.
    SELECT INVENTORY-TABLE-IN ASSIGN TO DISK1.
    SELECT TRANSACTION-FILE ASSIGN TO DISK2.
    SELECT REPORT-OUT ASSIGN TO PRINTER.
*
DATA DIVISION.
FILE SECTION.
FD  INVENTORY-TABLE-IN
    LABEL RECORDS ARE STANDARD.
01  INVENTORY-TABLE-REC.
    05  T-WAREHOUSE-NO           PIC 99.
    05  T-PART-NO                PIC 9999.
    05  T-UNIT-PRICE             PIC 999V99.
FD  TRANSACTION-FILE
    LABEL RECORDS ARE STANDARD.
01  TRANSACTION-REC.
    05  PART-NO-IN               PIC 9999.
    05  QTY-ORDERED              PIC 99.
    05                           PIC X(14).
FD  REPORT-OUT
    LABEL RECORDS ARE OMITTED.
01  OUT-REC                      PIC X(132).
WORKING-STORAGE SECTION.
01  WS-AREAS.
    05  ARE-THERE-MORE-RECORDS   PIC X(3)  VALUE 'YES'.
        88  NO-MORE-RECORDS                VALUE 'NO '.
    05  MATCH-FOUND              PIC X(3)  VALUE 'NO '.
01  INVENTORY-TABLE.
    05  WAREHOUSE OCCURS 50 TIMES INDEXED BY X1.
        10  ITEM-X OCCURS 100 TIMES INDEXED BY X2.
            15  PART-NO          PIC 9(4).
            15  UNIT-PRICE       PIC 999V99.
01  TRANS-REC-OUT.
    05                           PIC X(9)  VALUE SPACES.
    05  PART-NO-OUT              PIC 9(4).
    05                           PIC X(5)  VALUE SPACES.
    05  QTY-OUT                  PIC 999.
    05                           PIC X(5)  VALUE SPACES.
    05  TOTAL-AMT                PIC $ZZZ,ZZZ.99.
    05                           PIC X(95) VALUE SPACES.
01  ERR-REC.
    05                           PIC X(9)  VALUE SPACES.
    05  ERR-PART                 PIC 9(4).
    05                           PIC X(5)  VALUE SPACES.
    05                           PIC X(114)
               VALUE 'PART NUMBER IS NOT IN TABLE'.
01  HEADING-1.
    05                           PIC X(12) VALUE SPACES.
    05                           PIC X(120)
               VALUE 'INVENTORY REPORT'.
```

COBOL 74 Substitutions

For COBOL 74, FILLER must be used instead of a blank field name

Figure 12.7   (continued)

```
01   HEADING-2.
     05                              PIC X(18)
                     VALUE '        PART NO'.
     05                              PIC X(9)  VALUE 'QTY'.
     05                              PIC X(105)
                     VALUE 'TOTAL AMT'.
*
PROCEDURE DIVISION.
100-MAIN-MODULE.
     PERFORM 700-INITIALIZATION-RTN
     PERFORM 200-TABLE-LOAD
         VARYING X1 FROM 1 BY 1 UNTIL X1 > 50
     MOVE 'YES' TO ARE-THERE-MORE-RECORDS
     PERFORM UNTIL NO-MORE-RECORDS
         READ TRANSACTION-FILE
             AT END
                 MOVE 'NO ' TO ARE-THERE-MORE-RECORDS
             NOT AT END
                 PERFORM 400-CALC-RTN
         END-READ
     END-PERFORM
     PERFORM 800-END-OF-JOB-RTN
     STOP RUN.
200-TABLE-LOAD.
     PERFORM 300-LOAD-IT
         VARYING X2 FROM 1 BY 1 UNTIL X2 > 100.
300-LOAD-IT.
     READ INVENTORY-TABLE-IN
         AT END MOVE 'NO ' TO ARE-THERE-MORE-RECORDS
     END-READ
     IF  T-WAREHOUSE-NO NOT EQUAL TO X1
         DISPLAY 'TABLE IS NOT IN SEQUENCE'
         CLOSE INVENTORY-TABLE-IN
               TRANSACTION-FILE
               REPORT-OUT
         STOP RUN
     END-IF
     MOVE T-PART-NO TO PART-NO (X1, X2)
     MOVE T-UNIT-PRICE TO UNIT-PRICE (X1, X2).
400-CALC-RTN.
     MOVE PART-NO-IN TO PART-NO-OUT
     MOVE QTY-ORDERED TO QTY-OUT
     MOVE 'NO ' TO MATCH-FOUND
     PERFORM 500-SEARCH-IT
         VARYING X1 FROM 1 BY 1 UNTIL X1 > 50
                             OR MATCH-FOUND = 'YES'
     IF MATCH-FOUND = 'YES'
         WRITE OUT-REC FROM TRANS-REC-OUT
             AFTER ADVANCING 2 LINES
     ELSE
         PERFORM 600-NO-MATCH-ERR
     END-IF.

500-SEARCH-IT.
     SET X2 TO 1
     SEARCH ITEM-X
         WHEN PART-NO-IN = PART-NO (X1, X2)
             MULTIPLY UNIT-PRICE (X1, X2) BY QTY-ORDERED
                 GIVING TOTAL-AMT
             MOVE 'YES' TO MATCH-FOUND
     END-SEARCH.
600-NO-MATCH-ERR.
     MOVE PART-NO-IN TO ERR-PART
     WRITE OUT-REC FROM ERR-REC
```

COBOL 74 Substitutions

```
READ TRANSACTION-FILE
    AT END MOVE 'NO ' TO ARE-THERE-MORE-RECORDS.
PERFORM 400-CALC-RTN
    UNTIL NO-MORE-RECORDS.
```

```
READ TRANSACTION-FILE
    AT END MOVE 'NO ' TO ARE-THERE-MORE-RECORDS.
```

Figure 12.7 (continued)

```
                                  AFTER ADVANCING 2 LINES.
                    700-INITIALIZATION-RTN.
                        OPEN INPUT INVENTORY-TABLE-IN
                                  TRANSACTION-FILE
                             OUTPUT REPORT-OUT
                        WRITE OUT-REC FROM HEADING-1 AFTER ADVANCING PAGE
                        WRITE OUT-REC FROM HEADING-2 AFTER ADVANCING 2 LINES.
                    800-END-OF-JOB-RTN.
                        CLOSE INVENTORY-TABLE-IN
                              TRANSACTION-FILE
                              REPORT-OUT.
```

Note: Use scope terminators with COBOL 85 only.
Otherwise omit them and end preceding lines with a period.

Alternatively, we could use a PERFORM ... VARYING ... AFTER for searching the table. The following COBOL 85 excerpt uses an in-line PERFORM:

```
400-CALC-RTN.
    MOVE PART-NO-IN TO PART-NO-OUT
    MOVE QTY-ORDERED TO QTY-OUT
    MOVE 'NO ' TO MATCH-FOUND
    PERFORM
        VARYING X1 FROM 1 BY 1
            UNTIL X1 > 50 OR MATCH-FOUND = 'YES'
        AFTER X2 FROM 1 BY 1
            UNTIL X2 > 100 OR MATCH-FOUND = 'YES'
                IF PART-NO-IN = PART-NO (X1, X2)
                    MULTIPLY UNIT-PRICE (X1, X2) BY QTY-ORDERED
                        GIVING TOTAL-AMT
                    MOVE 'YES' TO MATCH-FOUND
                END-IF
    END-PERFORM
    IF MATCH-FOUND = 'YES'
        WRITE OUT-REC FROM TRANS-REC-OUT
            AFTER ADVANCING 2 LINES
    ELSE
        PERFORM 600-NO-MATCH-ERR
    END-IF.
```

Using the PERFORM ... VARYING ... AFTER, there is no need for the SEARCH in 500-SEARCH-IT.

As noted, arrays and tables can use up to seven levels for COBOL 85 and three levels for COBOL 74. We have explained double-level arrays and tables in some detail.

For more information on multiple-level arrays and tables, you may download a full chapter—with self-tests—from our Web site.

———— WEB SITE ————

Go to www.wiley.com/cobol/ to access the Stern COBOL home page. One of the supplements includes more information on multiple-level arrays that can be downloaded.

CHAPTER SUMMARY A. OCCURS clauses are used in the DATA DIVISION to specify the repeated occurrence of items with the same format.
   1. OCCURS clauses may be written on levels 02–49.
   2. An OCCURS clause may specify an elementary or group item.
B. Use an OCCURS clause to define arrays and tables.
   1. Array: An area used for storing data or totals.
   2. Table: A set of fields used in a table look-up.

C. Use of the SEARCH statement for table handling:
    1. The identifier used with the SEARCH verb is the one specified on the OCCURS level.
    2. The AT END clause specifies what is to be done if the table has been searched and the required condition has not been met.
    3. The WHEN clause indicates what to do when the condition is met.
    4. When using a SEARCH statement, table entries are specified with the use of an index, rather than a subscript.
        a. The index is defined along with the OCCURS. For example:

```
01  UNIT-PRICE-TABLE.
    05 STORED-ENTRIES OCCURS 500 TIMES INDEXED BY X1.
```

        b. An index cannot be modified with a MOVE, ADD, or SUBTRACT statement. Use a SET statement when altering the contents of an index, or use the PERFORM ... VARYING.
        c. SET the index to 1 before using a SEARCH.
        d. Use a PERFORM ... VARYING to load the table.
D. The SEARCH ALL statement—uses and limitations.
    1. Used to perform a binary search.
    2. Can test only an equal condition.
    3. If using a compound condition: (a) each part can only test an equal condition and (b) only ANDs are permitted.
    4. Only one WHEN clause can be used.
    5. The ASCENDING or DESCENDING KEY is specified along with the OCCURS and INDEXED BY clauses of a table entry.
E. Multiple-level OCCURS
    1. May be used for an array or a table.
    2. The lowest-level OCCURS data-name or an item subordinate to it is used to access an entry in the array or the table.
    3. If we use a SEARCH for accessing a multiple-level table, INDEXED BY must be used on all OCCURS levels.
    4. The identifier used with the SEARCH statement should typically be the one on the lowest OCCURS level. Only the index on the same level as the OCCURS level will be incremented by the SEARCH. That is, SEARCH TABLE-1, for example, will only vary the index specified with TABLE-1. Consider the following:

```
05  TABLE-1 OCCURS 10 TIMES INDEXED BY X2.
```

    X2 is the only index incremented in the search regardless of whether TABLE-1 is subordinate to an OCCURS or contains another level of OCCURS.
F. COBOL 85 permits seven levels of OCCURS; COBOL 74 permits three levels.

KEY TERMS

Array	OCCURS clause	SET
Binary search	Parallel table	Subscript
Direct-referenced table	Relative subscript	Table
External table	SEARCH	Table argument
Index	SEARCH ALL	Table function
INDEXED BY	Search argument	Table look-up
Internal table	Serial search	

CHAPTER SELF-TEST

1. (T or F) The following is a valid entry:

```
01  IN-REC OCCURS 50 TIMES.
```

2. (T or F) A subscript may be either a data-name or an integer.

3. If we store totals in WORKING-STORAGE, they must always be _____ before we add to them.

4. (T or F) An item defined by an OCCURS may be a group item that is further divided into elementary items.

Consider the following for Questions 5 and 6:

```
01   EX1          VALUE 'MONTUEWEDTHUFRISATSUN'.
     05   EACH-DAY OCCURS 7 TIMES PIC X(3).
     :
     :
```

5. (T or F) The preceding entries are valid.

6. If we DISPLAY EACH-DAY (3), _____ will print.

7. (T or F) The identifier used with the SEARCH verb is the table-entry specified on the 01 level.

8. When using a SEARCH statement, table entries must be specified with the use of a(n) _____ , rather than a subscript.

9. (T or F) A SEARCH statement automatically initializes the index at 1.

10. The SEARCH ALL statement is used to perform a (binary/serial) search.

11. What, if anything, is wrong with the following SEARCH?

```
SEARCH STORED-ENTRIES
    AT END DISPLAY 'NO ENTRY FOUND'
    WHEN WS-ITEM-NO (X1) = ITEM-NO-IN
        NEXT SENTENCE.
COMPUTE PRICE = QTY * WS-UNIT-PR (X1).
```

12. A serial search of a table begins with the (first/middle/last) entry in the table whereas a binary search of a table begins with the (first/middle/last) entry.

13. (T or F) A SET statement is not necessary with the SEARCH ALL statement.

14. (T or F) The following is a valid SEARCH ALL statement:

```
SEARCH ALL WEIGHT-TABLE
    AT END PERFORM 600-ERR-RTN
    WHEN WS-MAX-WEIGHT (X1) < WEIGHT-IN
        MULTIPLY WEIGHT-IN BY WS-RATE (X1)
            GIVING SHIPPING-COST
END-SEARCH*
```

15. The SEARCH ALL statement requires that a(n) _____ clause be specified along with the OCCURS and INDEXED BY clauses of a table entry.

Using the following TEMPERATURE-ARRAY, code the solutions to Questions 16–20:

```
01   TEMPERATURE-ARRAY.
     05   DAY-IN-WEEK OCCURS 7 TIMES.
          10   HOUR OCCURS 24 TIMES.
               15   TEMP            PIC S9(3).
```

16. Find the average temperature for Sunday (Day 1).

17. Find the day of the week and the hour when the temperature was highest. Also indicate what the highest temperature was.

18. Find the number of days when the temperature fell below 32° at any hour. Could a PERFORM ... VARYING ... AFTER be used?

19. Print the average hourly temperatures for each day of the week.

20. Define a COMPANY-SALES-ARRAY that contains a name and 12 monthly amounts for each of 25 salespersons.

Solutions

1. F—The OCCURS clause may not be used on the 01 level.

2. T

3. initialized (set to zero)

4. T

---

*Use the END-SEARCH scope terminator with COBOL 85; otherwise end the SEARCH statement with a period.

5. T

6. `WED`

7. F—It is the name specified on the `OCCURS` level.

8. index

9. F—The index must be initialized with a `SET` statement prior to the `SEARCH`.

10. binary

11. This procedure will not function properly if an `AT END` condition is reached. In that case, an error message will be displayed and processing will continue with the next sentence—the `COMPUTE`. To remedy this situation, we could code the `COMPUTE` as the imperative statement specified with the `WHEN` clause. Note that `END-SEARCH` cannot be used here because the `NEXT SENTENCE` clause has been coded.

12. first; middle

13. T—The index is automatically set at the appropriate point when a binary search is performed.

14. F—The `SEARCH ALL` can only test an equal condition.

15. `ASCENDING` or `DESCENDING KEY`

16.
```
    MOVE 0 TO TOTAL
    PERFORM 500-SUNDAY-AVERAGE
        VARYING X2 FROM 1 BY 1 UNTIL X2 > 24
    COMPUTE AVERAGE = TOTAL / 24
    DISPLAY 'AVERAGE TEMPERATURE FOR SUNDAY WAS ', AVERAGE
      :
500-SUNDAY-AVERAGE.
    ADD TEMP (1, X2) TO TOTAL.
```

With COBOL 85, we can use an in-line `PERFORM` instead:

```
MOVE 0 TO TOTAL
PERFORM VARYING X2 FROM 1 BY 1
        UNTIL X2 > 24
    ADD TEMP (1, X2) TO TOTAL
END-PERFORM
COMPUTE AVERAGE = TOTAL / 24
DISPLAY 'AVERAGE TEMPERATURE FOR SUNDAY WAS ', AVERAGE.
```

17.
```
    MOVE 0 TO HOLD-IT, STORE1, STORE2
    PERFORM 200-MAJOR-LOOP
        VARYING X1 FROM 1 BY 1 UNTIL X1 > 7
    DISPLAY 'HIGHEST TEMPERATURE WAS ', HOLD-IT
    DISPLAY 'DAY OF WEEK OF HIGHEST TEMPERATURE WAS ', STORE1
    IF  STORE2 < 12
        DISPLAY 'HOUR OF HIGHEST TEMPERATURE WAS ', STORE2, 'A.M.'
    ELSE IF STORE2 > 12 AND < 24
        SUBTRACT 12 FROM STORE2
        DISPLAY 'HOUR OF HIGHEST TEMPERATURE WAS ', STORE2, 'P.M.'
    ELSE IF STORE2 = 12
        DISPLAY 'HOUR OF HIGHEST TEMPERATURE WAS NOON'
    ELSE
        DISPLAY 'HOUR OF HIGHEST TEMPERATURE WAS MIDNIGHT'
      :
200-MAJOR-LOOP.
    PERFORM 300-MINOR-LOOP
        VARYING X2 FROM 1 BY 1 UNTIL X2 > 24.
300-MINOR-LOOP.
    IF  TEMP (X1, X2) > HOLD-IT
        MOVE TEMP (X1, X2) TO HOLD-IT
        MOVE X1 TO STORE1
        MOVE X2 TO STORE2
    END-IF.
```

We could replace the first PERFORM with the following and eliminate 200-MAJOR-LOOP entirely:

```
PERFORM 300-MINOR-LOOP
    VARYING X1 FROM 1 BY 1 UNTIL X1 > 7
        AFTER X2 FROM 1 BY 1 UNTIL X2 > 24
```

With COBOL 85, we could code the following in WORKING-STORAGE:

```
01  DAYS  VALUE 'SUNMONTUEWEDTHUFRISAT'.
    05  DAY-OF-THE-WEEK  OCCURS 7 TIMES  PIC X(3).
```

The second DISPLAY would then change as follows:

```
DISPLAY 'DAY OF WEEK OF HIGHEST TEMPERATURE WAS ',
    DAY-OF-THE-WEEK (STORE1)
```

For COBOL 74, the WORKING-STORAGE entry would require a REDEFINES:

```
01  DAYS.
    05  DAY-VALUE                      PIC X(21)
            VALUE 'SUNMONTUEWEDTHUFRISAT'.
    05  DAY-OF-THE-WEEK REDEFINES DAY-VALUE
            OCCURS 7 TIMES             PIC X(3).
```

18.
```
    MOVE 0 TO COUNTER
    PERFORM 200-MAJOR-LOOP
        VARYING X1 FROM 1 BY 1 UNTIL X1 > 7
    DISPLAY 'NUMBER OF DAYS WHEN TEMPERATURE < 32 WAS ',
        COUNTER
        :
200-MAJOR-LOOP.
    MOVE 'NO ' TO FOUND
    PERFORM 300-MINOR-LOOP
        VARYING X2 FROM 1 BY 1 UNTIL X2 > 24 OR
            FOUND = 'YES'.
300-MINOR-LOOP.
    IF  TEMP (X1, X2) < 32
        ADD 1 TO COUNTER
        MOVE 'YES' TO FOUND
    END-IF.
```

We use a field called FOUND to terminate processing of 300-MINOR-LOOP when we find an hour in any day when the temperature falls below 32°. Because FOUND has one value ('NO ') when no match has been found, and another value ('YES') when a match occurs, we call this field a switch or flag. Once we find a temperature lower than 32, we need not check the rest of the hours during that day.

A PERFORM ... VARYING ... AFTER could *not* be used because 200-MAJOR-LOOP has an operation to be performed *in addition to* varying the minor subscript. That is, PERFORM ... VARYING ... AFTER is used when you want to process all array elements together; when you need to stop, print, or MOVE 'NO ' TO FOUND before or after a row in an array is processed, then this option cannot be used.

19. *Note:* Use 01 DAYS established for Question 3 if an abbreviation for the day (SUN ... SAT) is to print rather than the day number.

```
    PERFORM 500-PRINT-RTN
        VARYING X1 FROM 1 BY 1 UNTIL X1 > 7
        :
500-PRINT-RTN.
    MOVE 0 TO TOTAL
    PERFORM 600-MINOR-LOOP
        VARYING X2 FROM 1 BY 1 UNTIL X2 > 24
    MOVE DAY-OF-THE-WEEK (X1) TO DAY-OUT
    COMPUTE AVERAGE-OUT = TOTAL / 24
    WRITE PRINT-REC FROM OUT-REC
        AFTER ADVANCING 2 LINES.
```

```
600-MINOR-LOOP.
    ADD TEMP (X1, X2) TO TOTAL.
```

20.
```
01  COMPANY-SALES-ARRAY.
    05  SALESPERSON OCCURS 25 TIMES.
        10  NAME                       PIC X(20).
        10  MONTHLY-AMT OCCURS 12 TIMES   PIC 9(4).
```

PRACTICE PROGRAM   Consider the problem definition in Figure 12.8. We have a personnel file at a university and we want to print a report identifying each employee's full title, department name, and campus name, not just the codes. We need to use table look-ups to find the appropriate items from separate title, department, and campus tables.

Suppose the university has five campuses identified as:

Code	Campus
1	Upstate
2	Downstate
3	City
4	Melville
5	Huntington

Figure 12.8   Problem definition for the Practice Program.

Systems Flowchart

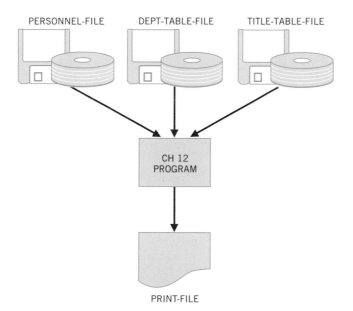

PERSONNEL-FILE **Record Layout**			
Field	**Size**	**Type**	**No. of Decimal Positions (if Numeric)**
SSNO-IN	9	Alphanumeric	
NAME-IN	20	Alphanumeric	
SALARY-IN	6	Numeric	0
CAMPUS-CODE-IN	1	Alphanumeric	
DEPT-CODE-IN	2	Alphanumeric	
TITLE-CODE-IN	3	Alphanumeric	

Figure 12.8 (continued)

DEPT-TABLE-FILE Record Layout		
Field	**Size**	**Type**
T-DEPT-NO	2	Alphanumeric
T-DEPT-NAME	10	Alphanumeric

TITLE-TABLE-FILE Record Layout		
Field	**Size**	**Type**
T-TITLE-CODE	3	Alphanumeric
T-TITLE-NAME	10	Alphanumeric

PRINT-FILE Printer Spacing Chart

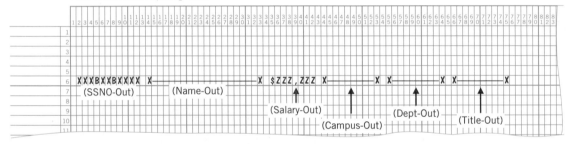

TITLE-TABLE-FILE

Records 1–25

```
001PRESIDENT
002VICE PRES
003PROVOST
005COMPTROL
008DEAN ART
009DEAN SCI
011DEAN ENG
012DEAN BUS
015COMP OPER
020PROGRAMMER
040SYS ANAL
060DATA ENTRY
066ASST DEAN
075SECRETARY
150ADMIN
190SR ADMIN
193SR PROGR
195SR ANALYST
200PROFESSOR
202ASSOC P
203ASST PR
205INSTRUCTOR
207LECTURER
209PSYCHOLOG
210AFFIRM ACT
```

Records 26–50

```
213ADM OFF
215CHAPLAIN
220COUNSELOR
230COOK
234DOCTOR
236CLERK
237SR CLERK
240REGISTRAR
241ASST REG
243CHAIRPER
245PLANT
255TECHNICIAN
257LIBRARIAN
259SR LIBR
260ASST LIB
265BOOKSTORE
267SUPERVISOR
268COACH
270SR COACH
276LAWYER
278RES LIFE
287ALUMNI DIR
288FIN AIDE O
290CUSTODIAN
293ENGINEER
```

DEPT-TABLE-FILE

Data

```
01MATH
04ENGLISH
06FRENCH
07SPANISH
08GEOLOGY
09BIOLOGY
11GEOGRAPHY
13HISTORY
14PHILOSOPHY
15COMP SCI
18ART
20MUSIC
22RUSSIAN
24ENGRG
26CHEMISTRY
27PSYCHOLOGY
28EDUCATION
30READING
31PHYS ED
33GERMAN
36ECONOMICS
36SOCIOLOGY
37HEALTH
39ACCOUNTING
40MANAGEMENT
```

Sample PERSONNEL-FILE Data

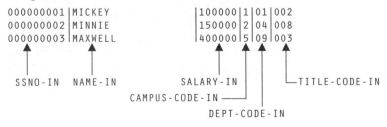

Figure 12.8 (continued)

Sample Output

```
000 00 0001 MICKEY          $100,000 UPSTATE     MATH     VICE PRES
000 00 0002 MINNIE          $150,000 DOWNSTATE   ENGLISH  DEAN ARTS
000 00 0003 MAXWELL         $400,000 HUNTINGTON  BIOLOGY  PROVOST
```

Since the five campuses and their codes are not likely to change, we can store them as an internal table, that is, entered with VALUEs rather than as variable data. Since the campus codes vary consecutively from 1 to 5, we need not store the codes themselves in the internal table, which can be a direct-referenced table:

```
01  CAMPUS-TABLE.
    05  CAMPUS-NAMES                    PIC X(50)
        VALUE 'UPSTATE   DOWNSTATE CITY      MELVILLE  HUNTINGTON'.
    05  EACH-CAMPUS REDEFINES CAMPUS-NAMES
            OCCURS 5 TIMES PIC X(10).
```

Department codes have changed over time so that while there are 25 departments, they range in number from 01–96. The numbers are not consecutive so we cannot establish this as a direct-referenced table. Moreover, since changes occur in department names and department numbers, we need to create a DEPT-TABLE as an external table:

```
01  DEPT-TABLE.
    05  DEPT-ENTRIES OCCURS 25 TIMES INDEXED BY X1.
        10  DEPT-NO      PIC XX.
        10  DEPT-NAME    PIC X(10).
```

We will enter data into DEPT-TABLE using a PERFORM ... VARYING. We will use a SEARCH to determine department names since our table is really too small to benefit from a SEARCH ... ALL, even if the data is in sequence by T-DEPT-NO.

There are 50 TITLE codes ranging from 001-986. They are not consecutive so we establish a table that stores the TITLE-NO along with the TITLE-NAME. The table will be accessed with a SEARCH ... ALL because we will enter the data in TITLE-CODE sequence and the table is large enough to benefit from a binary search.

```
01  TITLE-TABLE.
    05  TITLE-ENTRIES OCCURS 50 TIMES
        ASCENDING KEY IS TITLE-NO INDEXED BY X2.
        10  TITLE-NO      PIC X(3).
        10  TITLE-NAME    PIC X(10).
```

In this program, then, we will use three different methods for establishing tables and looking up data from them.

Figure 12.9 contains the pseudocode and the hierarchy chart. The full COBOL 85 program that processes all three tables appears in Figure 12.10.

Figure 12.9 Pseudocode and hierarchy chart for the Practice Program.

Pseudocode

MAIN-MODULE
START
    Open the files
    PERFORM Load-Dept-Table UNTIL Dept Table is loaded
    PERFORM Load-Title-Table UNTIL Title Table is loaded
    PERFORM UNTIL no more Personnel Records
        READ a Personnel Record
            AT END
                Move 'NO ' to More-Recs

Figure 12.9   (continued)

```
                              NOT AT END
                                     PERFORM Process-Rtn
                         END-READ
                         END-PERFORM
                         Close the files
          STOP


     LOAD-DEPT-TABLE
                    Read a Dept Table Record
                    Load the Dept Table Entry


     LOAD-TITLE-TABLE
                    Read a Title Table Entry
                    Load the Title Table Entry


     PROCESS-RTN
                    Move input data to output areas
                    Move Campus Name from direct-referenced
                       internal table to output area
                    Search Dept Table
                         IF a match is found
                         THEN
                                Move Dept Name to output area
                         ELSE
                                Move X's to Dept-Out
                         END-IF
                    Search Title Table
                         IF a match is found
                         THEN
                                Move Title Name to output area
                         ELSE
                                Move X's to Title-Out
                         END-IF
                    Write an output line
```

Hierarchy Chart

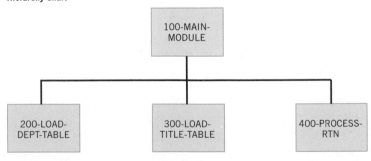

Figure 12.10   COBOL 85 solution to the Practice Program.

```
IDENTIFICATION DIVISION.
PROGRAM-ID. CH12.
ENVIRONMENT DIVISION.
INPUT-OUTPUT SECTION.
FILE-CONTROL.
     SELECT PERSONNEL-FILE    ASSIGN TO DISK 'CH12.DAT'.
     SELECT DEPT-TABLE-FILE   ASSIGN TO DISK 'CH12T1.DAT'.
     SELECT TITLE-TABLE-FILE  ASSIGN TO DISK 'CH12T2.DAT'.
     SELECT PRINT-FILE        ASSIGN TO PRINTER.
```

Figure 12.10 (continued)

```
                DATA DIVISION.
                FILE SECTION.
                FD  PERSONNEL-FILE
                    LABEL RECORDS ARE STANDARD.
                01  PERSONNEL-REC.
                    05  SSNO-IN            PIC X(9).
                    05  NAME-IN            PIC X(20).
                    05  SALARY-IN          PIC 9(6).
                    05  CAMPUS-CODE-IN     PIC X.
                    05  DEPT-CODE-IN       PIC XX.
                    05  TITLE-CODE-IN      PIC XXX.
                FD  DEPT-TABLE-FILE
                    LABEL RECORDS ARE STANDARD.
                01  DEPT-REC.
                    05  T-DEPT-NO          PIC XX.
                    05  T-DEPT-NAME        PIC X(10).
                FD  TITLE-TABLE-FILE
                    LABEL RECORDS ARE STANDARD.
                01  TITLE-REC.
                    05  T-TITLE-CODE       PIC XXX.
                    05  T-TITLE-NAME       PIC X(10).
                FD  PRINT-FILE
                    LABEL RECORDS ARE OMITTED.
                01  PRINT-REC              PIC X(132).
                WORKING-STORAGE SECTION.
                01  STORED-AREAS.
                    05  MORE-RECS          PIC X(3)          VALUE 'YES'.
                ***********************************************************************
                *   The Campus Table consists of 5 10-position names and will be   *
                *     accessed as a direct-referenced table.  EACH-CAMPUS          *
                *     subscripted by the CAMPUS-CODE-IN will provide the name.      *
                ***********************************************************************
                01  CAMPUS-TABLE.
                    05  CAMPUS-NAMES       PIC X(50)
                    VALUE 'UPSTATE   DOWNSTATE CITY      MELVILLE   HUNTINGTON'.
                    05  EACH-CAMPUS REDEFINES CAMPUS-NAMES
                            OCCURS 5 TIMES PIC X(10).
                ***********************************************************************
                *   The Dept Table will be accessed by a SEARCH.  Even if the      *
                *     table is entered in Dept No sequence, there would be no       *
                *     real benefit to using a SEARCH ALL since there are only       *
                *     25 entries.                                                    *
                ***********************************************************************
                01  DEPT-TABLE.
                    05  DEPT-ENTRIES OCCURS 25 TIMES INDEXED BY X1.
                        10  DEPT-NO        PIC XX.
                        10  DEPT-NAME      PIC X(10).
                ***********************************************************************
                *   The Title Table will be accessed by a SEARCH ALL.  To use a    *
                *     binary search the entries must be in sequence by a key        *
                *     field and the table should be relatively large.               *
                ***********************************************************************
                01  TITLE-TABLE.
                    05  TITLE-ENTRIES OCCURS 50 TIMES
                            ASCENDING KEY IS TITLE-NO INDEXED BY X2.
                        10  TITLE-NO       PIC XXX.
                        10  TITLE-NAME     PIC X(10).
                01  DETAIL-REC.
                    05                     PIC X(1)  VALUE SPACES.
                    05  SSNO-OUT           PIC 999B99B9999.
                    05                     PIC X(1)  VALUE SPACES.
                    05  NAME-OUT           PIC X(20).
                    05                     PIC X(1)  VALUE SPACES.
                    05  SALARY-OUT         PIC $ZZZ,ZZZ.
                    05                     PIC X(1)  VALUE SPACES.
                    05  CAMPUS-OUT         PIC X(10).
```

Figure 12.10   (continued)

```
                                05                        PIC X(1)  VALUE SPACES.
                                05   DEPT-OUT             PIC X(10).
                                05                        PIC X(1)  VALUE SPACES.
                                05   TITLE-OUT            PIC X(10).
                                05                        PIC X(59) VALUE SPACES.
                        PROCEDURE DIVISION.
                        100-MAIN-MODULE.
                            OPEN INPUT   PERSONNEL-FILE
                                         DEPT-TABLE-FILE
                                         TITLE-TABLE-FILE
                                 OUTPUT  PRINT-FILE
                            PERFORM 200-LOAD-DEPT-TABLE
                            PERFORM 300-LOAD-TITLE-TABLE
                            PERFORM UNTIL MORE-RECS = 'NO '
                                READ PERSONNEL-FILE
                                    AT END
                                        MOVE 'NO ' TO MORE-RECS
                                    NOT AT END
                                        PERFORM 400-PROCESS-RTN
                                END-READ
                            END-PERFORM
                            CLOSE PERSONNEL-FILE
                                  DEPT-TABLE-FILE
                                  TITLE-TABLE-FILE
                                  PRINT-FILE
                            STOP RUN.
                        200-LOAD-DEPT-TABLE.
                            PERFORM VARYING X1 FROM 1 BY 1
                                        UNTIL X1 > 25
                                READ DEPT-TABLE-FILE
                                    AT END DISPLAY 'NOT ENOUGH DEPT TABLE RECORDS'
                                            STOP RUN
                                END-READ
                                MOVE DEPT-REC TO DEPT-ENTRIES (X1)
                            END-PERFORM.
                        300-LOAD-TITLE-TABLE.
                            PERFORM VARYING X2 FROM 1 BY 1
                                        UNTIL X2 > 50
                                READ TITLE-TABLE-FILE
                                    AT END DISPLAY 'NOT ENOUGH TITLE TABLE RECORDS'
                                            STOP RUN
                                END-READ
                                MOVE TITLE-REC TO TITLE-ENTRIES (X2)
                                IF X2 > 1 THEN
                                    IF TITLE-NO (X2) <= TITLE-NO (X2 - 1)
                                        DISPLAY 'TITLE RECORDS ARE NOT IN SEQUENCE'
                                        STOP RUN
                                    END-IF
                                END-IF
                            END-PERFORM.
                        400-PROCESS-RTN.
                            MOVE SPACES TO DETAIL-REC
                            MOVE SSNO-IN TO SSNO-OUT
                            MOVE NAME-IN TO NAME-OUT
                            MOVE SALARY-IN TO SALARY-OUT
                            IF CAMPUS-CODE-IN >= 1 AND <= 5
                                MOVE EACH-CAMPUS (CAMPUS-CODE-IN) TO CAMPUS-OUT
                            END-IF
                            SET X1 TO 1
                            SEARCH DEPT-ENTRIES
                                AT END MOVE 'XXXXXXXXXX' TO DEPT-OUT
                                WHEN DEPT-CODE-IN = DEPT-NO (X1)
                                    MOVE DEPT-NAME (X1) TO DEPT-OUT
                            END-SEARCH
```

Figure 12.10 (continued)

```
SEARCH ALL TITLE-ENTRIES
    AT END MOVE 'XXXXXXXXXX' TO TITLE-OUT
    WHEN TITLE-NO (X2) = TITLE-CODE-IN
        MOVE TITLE-NAME (X2) TO TITLE-OUT
END-SEARCH
WRITE PRINT-REC FROM DETAIL-REC
    AFTER ADVANCING 2 LINES.
```

Note that since the campuses are fixed and not likely to change over time we have stored them in an internal table that is coded directly in the program. But if many programs access these values it is best to code them and store them in a library. The entries can then be called and copied into each program as needed. If the file that contains CAMPUS-TABLE is called CAMPUS, we can code:

```
COPY CAMPUS
```

in place of the CAMPUS-TABLE entries. Chapter 16 discusses the COPY statement in more detail.

REVIEW QUESTIONS

I. True-False Questions

_____ 1. If an input record contained 10 group items, each with a three-digit elementary item followed by a four-digit elementary item, then an OCCURS clause could be used to define the input fields.

_____ 2. An input field may not be used as a subscript.

_____ 3. An OCCURS clause may not be used on the 01 level.

_____ 4. An OCCURS clause may only be used to define entries in the FILE SECTION.

_____ 5. Data can be either moved or added to an array.

_____ 6. After a WHEN condition has been met in a SEARCH, the index contains the number of the element that resulted in a match.

_____ 7. When the SEARCH ALL statement is used, the table must be in either ASCENDING or DESCENDING sequence.

_____ 8. SEARCH ALL is used for a binary search.

_____ 9. An index used in a SEARCH may be initialized by a MOVE statement.

_____ 10. A binary search is always preferable to a serial search.

II. General Questions

1. An input record consists of 15 group items, each with a 3-digit PART-NO and associated 3-digit QUANTITY-ON-HAND. Use an OCCURS clause to define the input.

2. Print the quantity on hand for PART-NO 126.

3. Find the average quantity on hand for the 15 parts.

4. Assume there are 50 input records, each with fields described as in Question 1. Code the WORKING-STORAGE entry to store these part numbers and their corresponding quantities on hand.

5. Write a routine to load the 50 input records into the WORKING-STORAGE entry.

6. Assume that the array described in Question 5 has been stored. Write a routine to find the average quantity for all parts stored in WORKING-STORAGE.

7. Indicate the differences between a SEARCH and a SEARCH ALL.

8. Consider the following table in storage:

```
01  POPULATION-TABLE.
    05  STATE-POP OCCURS 50 TIMES PIC 9(8).
```

Find both the largest and the smallest state population figures.

9. Using the table in Question 8, write a routine to print the total number of states that have populations smaller than 2,250,000.

10. Using the population table defined in Question 8, print the state number of each state with a population in excess of 2,250,000 people.

Consider the following table in storage for Questions 11 and 12:

```
01  POPULATION-TABLE.
    05  STATE-FACTS OCCURS 50 TIMES.
        10  STATE-NAME      PIC X(14).
        10  STATE-POP       PIC 9(10).
```

11. Write a routine to print the name of the state with the largest population.

12. Write a routine to print the population for Wyoming.

III. Validating Data

Modify the Practice Program so that it includes coding to (1) test for all errors and (2) print a control listing of totals (records processed, errors encountered, batch totals).

DEBUGGING EXERCISES

1. Consider the following:

```
WORKING-STORAGE SECTION.
01  STORED-AREAS.
    05  ARE-THERE-MORE-RECORDS  PIC X(3)        VALUE 'YES'.
        88  THERE-ARE-NO-MORE-RECORDS           VALUE 'NO '.
    05  SUB1                    PIC 9.
01  TABLE-IN.
    05  ENTRIES OCCURS 20 TIMES.
        10  CUST-NO             PIC 999.
        10  DISCT               PIC V99.
*
PROCEDURE DIVISION.
100-MAIN-MODULE.
    PERFORM 400-INITIALIZATION-RTN
    PERFORM 200-TABLE-ENTRY
        VARYING SUB1 FROM 1 BY 1 UNTIL SUB1 > 20
    PERFORM 300-CALC-RTN
        UNTIL THERE-ARE-NO-MORE-RECORDS
    PERFORM 500-END-OF-JOB-RTN.
200-TABLE-ENTRY.
    READ TABLE-FILE
        AT END MOVE 'NO ' TO ARE-THERE-MORE-RECORDS
    END-READ
    MOVE T-CUST-NO TO CUST-NO (SUB1)
    MOVE T-DISCT TO DISCT (SUB1).
```

There are two major logic errors in this program excerpt.
a. After the table has been loaded, you find that 300-CALC-RTN is not performed. That is, the run is terminated after the table is loaded. Find the error and correct it.
b. After receiving an obscure interrupt message you DISPLAY TABLE-IN entries and find that only the last nine have been loaded. Find the error and correct it.

2. Consider the following 700-SEARCH-RTN excerpt (not part of Exercise 1 above):

```
21      700-SEARCH-RTN.
22          SEARCH INV-ENTRIES
23              AT END MOVE 0 TO QTY-OUT
24              WHEN PART-NO-IN = T-PART-NO (X1)
25                  NEXT SENTENCE.
26          MOVE T-QTY-ON-HAND (X1) TO QTY-OUT
27          MOVE PART-NO-IN TO PART-OUT
28          WRITE PRINT-REC FROM DETAIL-REC.
```

a. A program interrupt will occur the first or second time through 700-SEARCH-RTN. Find and correct the error.

b. A program interrupt will occur if there is no match between PART-NO-IN and T-PART-NO. Find and correct the error.

c. Suppose INV-ENTRIES is defined as follows:

```
01   INV-ENTRIES.
     05   TAB1 OCCURS 30 TIMES.
          10   T-PART-NO        PIC 9(3).
          10   T-QTY-ON-HAND    PIC 9(4).
```

This will cause two syntax errors on lines 22 and 24. Find and correct these errors.

PROGRAMMING ASSIGNMENTS

1. Write a program to print total sales for each salesperson. The problem definition is shown in Figure 12.11. (Continued on the next page.)

Figure 12.11 Problem definition for Programming Assignment 1.

Systems Flowchart

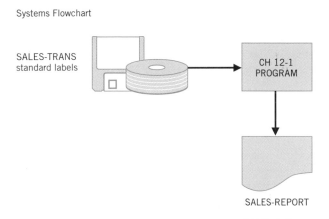

SALES-TRANS
standard labels

CH 12-1
PROGRAM

SALES-REPORT

SALES-TRANS Record Layout			
Field	**Size**	**Type**	**No. of Decimal Positions (if Numeric)**
SALESPERSON-NO	2	Alphanumeric	
SALESPERSON-NAME	20	Alphanumeric	
AMT-OF-SALES	5	Numeric	2

SALES-REPORT Printer Spacing Chart

```
                          TOTAL SALES FOR EACH SALESPERSON      99/99/99
H  6
H  8      SALESPERSON NO.    SALESPERSON NAME          TOTAL SALES
T 10           01           X-------------X        $ZZ,ZZZ.99
                             .                     .           .
                             .                     .           .
                             .                     .           .
                             .                     .           .
                             .                     .           .
                             .                     .           .
                             .                     .           .
T 18           20           X-------------X        $ZZ,ZZZ.99

T 22                                          TOTAL COMPANY SALES   $$,$$$,$$$.99 *
```

Notes:

a. There are 20 salespeople, numbered 1 to 20.

b. Each sale that is made is used to create one input disk record; thus, there may be numerous input records for each salesperson if he or she made more than one sale.

c. Input records are not in sequence. (If they were, you could use a control break procedure.)

d. Print the total sales figure for each salesperson; note that although the number of input records is variable, the output will consist of 20 totals.

e. All total fields should be edited.

2. Consider the problem definition in Figure 12.12.

Notes:

a. Monthly take-home pay is to be computed for each employee of Company ABC. A tax table must be read into main storage from 20 table records which are read before the SALARY-FILE.

Example

Taxable Income	Federal Tax	State Tax
09800	.040	.010
12000	.080	.020

The state tax is 1% and the federal tax is 4% for taxable income less than or equal to 9800; for a taxable income between 9801 and 12000 (inclusive), the state tax is 2% and the federal tax is 8%, and so on.

Figure 12.12 Problem definition for Programming Assignment 2.

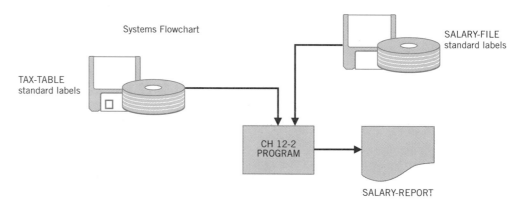

    b. After the table is read and stored, read a salary file. Monthly take-home pay is computed as follows.

      (1) Standard deduction = 10% of the first $10,000 of annual salary

      (2) Dependent deduction = 2000 × number of dependents

      (3) FICA (Social Security and Medicare taxes):

        (a) Social Security tax = 6.2% of the first $62,700 of annual salary.

        (b) Medicare tax = 1.45% of each annual salary, regardless of the amount earned.

      (4) Taxable income = Annual salary − standard deduction − dependent deduction

      (5) Find the tax for the taxable income using the tax table.

      (6) Annual take-home pay = Annual salary − (state tax % × taxable income) − (federal tax % × taxable income) − FICA

      (7) Monthly take-home pay = Annual take-home pay / 12

      (8) Print each employee's name and the corresponding monthly take-home pay (edited).

3. The Bon Voyage Travel Agency has a client file with the following data:

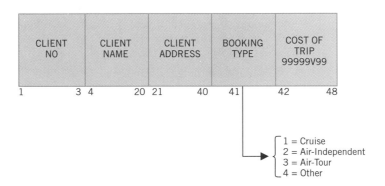

    Data is in sequence by CLIENT NO. Print the average cost of a trip for each booking type. Use arrays.

4. Consider the problem definition in Figure 12.13. (Continued on the next page.)

Notes:

    a. There are 90 table entries, one for each vehicle class.

    b. After the table is read and stored, read in the transaction file.

Figure 12.13 Problem definition for Programming Assignment 4.

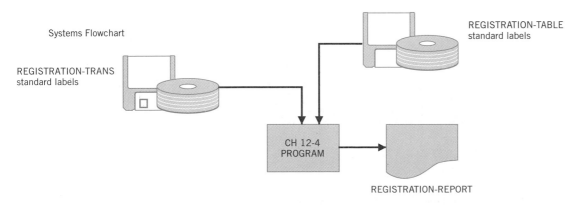

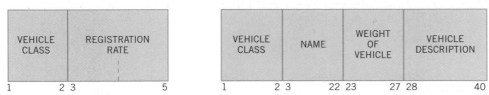

Figure 12.13 (continued)

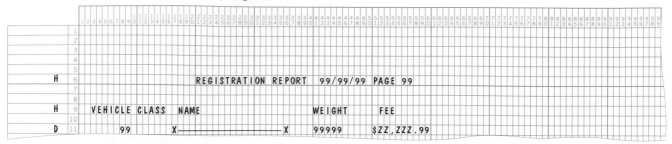

REGISTRATION-REPORT Printer Spacing Chart

H 6		REGISTRATION REPORT 99/99/99 PAGE 99
H 9	VEHICLE CLASS NAME	WEIGHT FEE
D 11	99 X————X	99999 $ZZ,ZZZ.99

c. For each transaction record, the vehicle class must be found in the table to obtain the corresponding registration rate.

d. Registration Fee = Vehicle Weight × Registration Rate (from the table).

5. Consider the problem definition in Figure 12.14.

Notes:

a. Input table entries are entered first. There are 250 table entries.

b. Create an output disk containing product number, unit price, quantity, total amount, and customer name for each transaction inventory record. Total amount = Unit price × Quantity.

c. For each transaction inventory record, the product number must be found in the table to obtain the corresponding unit price.

Figure 12.14 Problem definition for Programming Assignment 5.

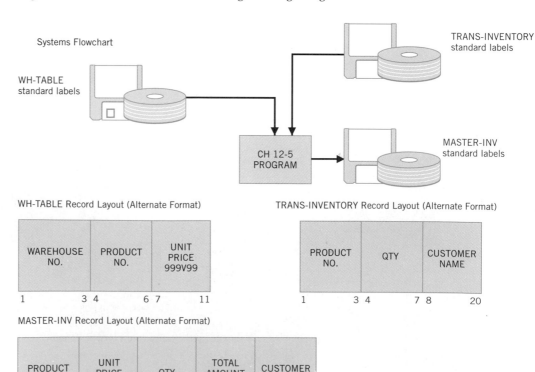

Systems Flowchart

WH-TABLE
standard labels

TRANS-INVENTORY
standard labels

CH 12-5
PROGRAM

MASTER-INV
standard labels

WH-TABLE Record Layout (Alternate Format)

WAREHOUSE NO.	PRODUCT NO.	UNIT PRICE 999V99
1 3	4 6	7 11

TRANS-INVENTORY Record Layout (Alternate Format)

PRODUCT NO.	QTY	CUSTOMER NAME
1 3	4 7	8 20

MASTER-INV Record Layout (Alternate Format)

PRODUCT NO.	UNIT PRICE 999V99	QTY	TOTAL AMOUNT 99999V99	CUSTOMER NAME
1 3	4 8	9 12	13 19	20 32

6. Write a program to read in employee records with the following format:

Employee Record (Alternate Record Layout)

SSNO	EMPLOYEE NAME	ANNUAL SALARY	JOB CLASSIFICATION

1   9 10   30 31   36   37

Records are in sequence by SSNO. Job Classifications vary from 1 to 9.
Print a report that lists the average annual salary for each job classification.

7. Consider the following input data format:

Student Record (Alternate Record Layout)

SSNO	STUDENT NAME	SCHOOL (1-4)	MAJOR	GPA 9V99

1   9 10   30   31   32   34 35   37

Print a detail report that includes the above fields for each student per line. SCHOOL and MAJOR are in coded form in the input record to save space. When printing, you will need to look up the actual SCHOOL and MAJOR from tables and print them:

```
SCHOOL CODE        ACTUAL SCHOOL
1                  LIBERAL ARTS
2                  BUSINESS
3                  ENGINEERING
4                  EDUCATION


MAJOR CODE         ACTUAL MAJOR
QMT                QUANTITATIVE METHODS   ⎫
FIN                FINANCE                ⎪
MKT                MARKETING               ⎬ Business
CIS                COMPUTER INFORMATION SYSTEMS ⎪
MAN                MANAGEMENT             ⎭
PHY                PHYSICS                ⎫
BIO                BIOLOGY                ⎪
HIS                HISTORY                ⎪
FRL                FOREIGN LANGUAGE        ⎬ Liberal Arts
ENG                ENGLISH                ⎪
ECO                ECONOMICS              ⎭
EEN                ELECTRICAL ENGINEERING ⎫
MEN                MECHANICAL ENGINEERING  ⎬ Engineering
CEN                CIVIL ENGINEERING      ⎭
ELE                ELEMENTARY EDUCATION   ⎫
SEE                SECONDARY EDUCATION     ⎬ Education
SPE                SPECIAL EDUCATION      ⎭
```

Be sure that the MAJOR code is consistent with the SCHOOL code; if not, print an error message. Should the tables be stored as internal or external tables? Explain your answer.

8. **Interactive Processing.** Load in as a table a file that contains each student's Social Security number, the number of credits completed, and his or her GPA. There are 500 students. Then, enable users to enter a SSNO interactively on a keyboard, the number of courses taken this semester, and the grades for each course. Have the computer display the new GPA. At this school, all courses are three credits, and A = 4, B = 3, C = 2, D = 1, and F = 0.

Example: A student currently has a 3.0 GPA with 90 credits. This semester the student took four courses and received two A's, one B, and one C:

```
A × 6 credits = 4 × 6        =  24
B × 3 credits = 3 × 3        =   9
C × 3 credits = 2 × 3        =   6
                                39
```

For previous credits: $(90 \times 3.0) = 270$

$$\text{Total} = 309$$

Divide 309 by total credits taken (102) = 3.03
The new GPA displayed for this student should thus be 3.03.

9. Maintenance Program.   Modify the Practice Program in this chapter as follows:
   a. Add a heading routine to print a heading at the top of each page that includes the date and page number.
   b. At the end of the report, print (1) the number of personnel records processed, (2) the number of records where there was an unsuccessful search of the Dept Table, and (3) the number of records where there was an unsuccessful search of the Title Table.

UNIT IV
File Maintenance

CHAPTER 13

Sequential File Processing

SYSTEMS OVERVIEW OF SEQUENTIAL FILE PROCESSING

MASTER FILES

This unit will focus on **master file** processing where a master file is the major collection of data pertaining to a specific application. Companies will have master files in application areas such as payroll, accounts receivable, accounts payable, production, sales, and inventory.

In most companies, a master file will be stored on a magnetic disk. The features of magnetic media such as disk that make it ideally suited for storing master file data include the following:

1. Disks can store billions of characters.
2. Disk drives can read and write data very quickly.
3. Disk records can be any size.

Although tapes were once used for storing files, most companies today use disks because disks have greater versatility. A tape is more often used for backing up a file in case the original disk file becomes unusable.

One main reason why tapes are not as prevalent as disks for master file processing is that tapes *can be accessed only sequentially*, which makes them somewhat limited in applicability. Disk files, however, can be organized for either sequential *or* random access. If a master file is *always* processed sequentially, it may be stored on either disk or tape. But if a file needs to be read, or processed, randomly, or in some sequence that cannot be predetermined, then it would be stored on disk and organized for *random access*. An airline reservation system, for example, in which clerks check on flight availability for customers would most often need to access a master file randomly.

In this chapter, we focus on **sequential file processing** procedures used for handling *master files*. Although either disk or tape can be used for sequential files, we will focus on sequential disks. In Chapter 15 we discuss randomly accessible files, which are typically stored on disk.

TYPICAL MASTER FILE PROCEDURES: A SYSTEMS OVERVIEW

When a business system is computerized, the systems analyst and programmer decide whether the master file is to be organized for sequential processing or for random processing. Sequential organization is used for files that are always processed in some sequence. If a file needs to be accessed randomly, it *must* have a method of organization that permits random access. Regardless of whether a disk is created to be accessed randomly or sequentially, the procedures that would need to be performed include:

Designing a Master File

The following are elements to consider when designing a master file:

1. The first field or fields should be **key fields** that uniquely identify the record.

2. Where possible, key fields should consist of numbers (e.g., Social Security Number rather than Employee Name, Part Number rather than Part Description, etc.).

3. Secondary key fields (e.g., Name) should follow primary key fields in a record.

4. Fields should appear in a master file in order of importance (e.g., Employee Name and Address before Birth Date, etc.).

5. Be sure that fields are large enough to accommodate the data (e.g., a 10-position Last Name field, for example, is not likely to be large enough).

6. Use coded fields where possible to save space (e.g., codes are used for Marital Status, Insurance Plan Option, etc.).

Creating a Master File

When a new system is implemented, or used for the first time, a master file must be initially created. This procedure can be performed by entering all master file data using a keyboard or other data entry device. The data is then usually recorded on a disk, which becomes the new master file. Creating a master file is a one-time procedure. That is, once the master file is created, changes to it are made by a different procedure.

The primary objective of a program that creates a master file is ensuring *data integrity*. A master file is only useful if it contains valid and reliable data; hence, a creation program must be designed so that it minimizes input errors. Chapter 11 focused on some data validation techniques used to minimize the risk of errors when creating a master file.

When a master file is created, a *control listing* or *audit trail* is also produced that prints the data stored on the new master file, as well as whatever control totals are necessary. This control listing should be checked or verified by users.

Creating a Transaction File

After a master file is created, a separate procedure is used to make changes to it. Change records are stored in a file referred to as a **transaction file**, which is also typically stored on disk. Changes to an accounts receivable master file, for example, may consist of sales records and credit records. Changes to a payroll master file may consist of name changes, salary changes, and so on. Such change records would be stored in a transaction file, usually on disk. File design considerations, as specified for master files, should be applied to the transaction file as well. Also, the transaction file should be validated to ensure data integrity. Just as with master file creation, validating transaction data will minimize the risk of errors.

Updating a Master File

The process of making a master file current is referred to as **updating**. The master file is updated by incorporating the changes from the transaction records. This chapter emphasizes techniques used for performing *sequential updates* for master files. Sequential updates process transaction records that are stored *in sequence in a file*, rather than entered randomly and processed interactively. We call this **batch processing**.

 Interactive Processing. Chapter 15 illustrates techniques for performing *random access updates* where the transaction records do not need to be in sequence nor processed in batch mode. In fact, transaction records are often entered interactively using a keyboard or point-of-sale device and the master file updated immediately as the transactions occur.

Reporting from a Master File

The purpose of maintaining a master file is to store data that will provide users with meaningful output. Output in the form of reports are frequently *scheduled*, which means they are prepared on a regular basis. Sales reports, customer bills, and payroll checks are examples of output from master files that are prepared on a regularly scheduled basis.

Reports can also be prepared *on demand*. That is, they are requested and produced whenever the need arises. If a manager or customer inquires about the status of a specific record, for example, we call the response *on demand output*.

The preparation of regularly scheduled reports using detail printing, exception printing, and group printing techniques has already been considered in Chapters 6 and 10. *On demand or interactive output* is often provided by files that are designed to be accessed randomly. We discuss this in Chapter 15.

Using the data validation techniques discussed in Chapter 11, you should be able to write programs to create a master file and a transaction file from input data and to validate the data according to the system's specifications.

SEQUENTIAL FILE UPDATING—CREATING A NEW MASTER FILE

THE FILES USED

Master files that have been designed and created for sequential processing can be updated by reading in the master file along with a transaction file and creating a new master file. This means that the sequential update procedure uses *three* files. Most often, a fourth print file that produces a control listing or audit trail is created as well for printing all changes made, any errors found, and totals. Keep in mind that any program you write to update a master file should create a control listing that specifies all changes made to the master. The systems flowchart in Figure 13.1 summarizes the files used in an update procedure.

Later in this chapter we will see that disks can also be updated using another method where the records to be updated on the master file are *rewritten in place*. This means that only two files would be needed—an input transaction file and a master file that is read from and written onto. For now, however, we focus on the traditional method of updating sequential files where there are two input disk files and one output disk file, because this method provides for better control. That is, at the end of the update procedure, there will be an old master and a new master; should something happen to the new master, it can be recreated from the old. A control listing or audit trail should also be created for validating the changes made.

Figure 13.1 Systems flowchart for a sequential update procedure.

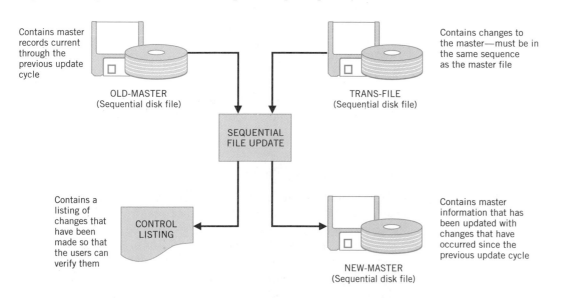

Contains master records current through the previous update cycle

OLD-MASTER
(Sequential disk file)

Contains changes to the master—must be in the same sequence as the master file

TRANS-FILE
(Sequential disk file)

SEQUENTIAL FILE UPDATE

Contains a listing of changes that have been made so that the users can verify them

CONTROL LISTING

Contains master information that has been updated with changes that have occurred since the previous update cycle

NEW-MASTER
(Sequential disk file)

Input Master File

The input master file is current through the previous updating period. That is, if updates are performed weekly, the input master file is the file that was created the previous week as the master. We call this file OLD-MASTER because it does not contain changes that have occurred since the previous update.

Input Transaction File

The transaction file contains data to be used for updating the master file that we call OLD-MASTER. The input transaction file contains all changes that have occurred since OLD-MASTER was created. We call this file TRANS-FILE.

Output Master File

The output master file becomes the new master as a result of the updating procedure. The output master file will integrate data from the OLD-MASTER and the TRANS-FILE. We call this file NEW-MASTER. Note that for the next week's update run, this NEW-MASTER becomes OLD-MASTER.

In our illustration, we assume that all files—the input and output master and the transaction—are on disk, but, as noted previously, they could have been stored on tape as well.

Control Listing or Audit Trail

Recall that a print file or *control listing* is usually created during a sequential file update. This print file would list (1) changes made to the master file, (2) errors encountered during processing, and (3) totals to be used for control and checking purposes. The following is a sample control listing:

```
                          CONTROL LISTING - MASTER FILE UPDATE        99/99/99   PAGE 99

              -------MASTER-------      TRANS      NEW MASTER
              ACCOUNT NO     AMOUNT      AMOUNT     AMOUNT           MESSAGE

              XXXXX        9999.99      9999.99    9999.99        ⎡ MASTER UPDATED            ⎤
                                                                 ⎨ NEW ACCOUNT               ⎬
                                                                 ⎣ ERROR IN TRANSACTION AMOUNT ⎦

     NO. OF TRANSACTION RECORDS PROCESSED      9,999

     NO. OF ERRORS                             9,999

     NO. OF NEW ACCOUNTS                       9,999

     TOTAL OF TRANSACTION AMOUNTS         ZZ,ZZZ,ZZZ.99
```

Since you are already familiar with the techniques for creating print files, we will omit the control listing procedure from some of our sequential update illustrations for the sake of simplicity.

THE ORDERING OF RECORDS FOR SEQUENTIAL UPDATES

OLD-MASTER contains master information that was complete and current through the previous updating cycle. The TRANS-FILE contains transactions or changes that have occurred since the previous updating cycle. These transactions or changes must be incorporated into the master file to make it current. The NEW-MASTER will include all OLD-MASTER data in addition to the changes stored on the TRANS-FILE that have occurred since the last update. The NEW-MASTER will be on the same medium (e.g., disk) as the OLD-MASTER, since the current NEW-MASTER becomes the OLD-MASTER for the next update cycle.

In a sequential master file, all records are in sequence by a key field, such as account number, Social Security number, or part number, depending on the type of master file. This key field uniquely identifies each master record. We compare the key field in the master to the same key field in the transaction file to determine if the master record is to be updated; this comparison requires both files to be in sequence by the key field.

THE PROCEDURES USED FOR SEQUENTIAL UPDATES

Let us consider the updating of a sequential master accounts receivable file. The key field used to identify records in the master file is account number, called M-ACCT-NO, for master account number. All records in the OLD-MASTER accounts receivable file are in sequence by M-ACCT-NO.

The transaction file contains all transactions to be posted to the master file that have occurred since the previous update. This transaction file also has an account number as a key field, called T-ACCT-NO for transaction account number. Records in the TRANS-FILE are in sequence by T-ACCT-NO.

The formats for the two input files are:

OLD-MASTER-REC	TRANS-REC
(in sequence by M-ACCT-NO)	(in sequence by T-ACCT-NO)

```
1-5     M-ACCT-NO              1-5     T-ACCT-NO
6-11    AMOUNT-DUE 9999V99     6-11    AMT-TRANS-IN-CURRENT-PER   9999V99
12-100  FILLER                 12-100  FILLER
```

Each transaction record contains the *total* amount transacted during the current period for a specific master record. Hence, there will be *one transaction record* for each master record to be updated. The next section describes the processing required if there were multiple transactions permitted for a given master record.

NEW-MASTER becomes the current master accounts receivable file after the update procedure. It must have the same format as the OLD-MASTER. We will name the fields as follows:

```
NEW-MASTER-REC
  1-5     ACCT-NO-OUT
  6-11    AMOUNT-DUE-OUT
  12-100  FILLER
```

The FILLERs may contain additional data used in other programs or for purposes not related to this update. The word FILLER may be replaced with a blank field-name with COBOL 85.

Keep in mind that records within OLD-MASTER are in sequence by M-ACCT-NO and that records within TRANS-FILE are in sequence by T-ACCT-NO. Records must be in sequence by key field so that when we compare key fields we can determine if a given master record is to be updated. The NEW-MASTER file will also be created in account number sequence.

Figure 13.2 shows the pseudocode for this program; Figure 13.3 is the hierarchy chart. Examine these carefully before looking at the program in Figure 13.4.

For COBOL 74, 200-COMP-RTN would be replaced with the following nested conditional:

```
200-COMP-RTN.
    IF T-ACCT-NO = M-ACCT-NO
        PERFORM 300-REGULAR-UPDATE
    ELSE
        IF T-ACCT-NO < M-ACCT-NO
            PERFORM 400-NEW-ACCOUNT
        ELSE
            PERFORM 500-NO-UPDATE.
```

Figure 13.2   Pseudocode for sample update program.

MAIN-MODULE
START
      PERFORM Initialize-Rtn
      PERFORM Read-Master
      PERFORM Read-Trans
      PERFORM Comp-Rtn UNTIL no more input
      PERFORM End-of-Job-Rtn
      Stop Run
STOP

COMP-RTN
      EVALUATE TRUE
            WHEN T-Acct-No = M-Acct-No
                  PERFORM Regular-Update
            WHEN T-Acct-No < M-Acct-No
                  PERFORM New-Account
            WHEN OTHER
                  PERFORM No-Update
      END-EVALUATE

REGULAR-UPDATE
      Update and Write the Master Record
      PERFORM Read-Master
      PERFORM Read-Trans

NEW-ACCOUNT
      Write a New Master Record from a Transaction Record
      PERFORM Read-Trans

NO-UPDATE
      Write a New Master Record from an Old Master Record
      PERFORM Read-Master

READ-MASTER
      Read a Master Record

READ-TRANS
      Read a Transaction Record

INITIALIZE-RTN
      Open the Files

END-OF-JOB-RTN
      Close the Files

Figure 13.3   Hierarchy chart for sample update program.

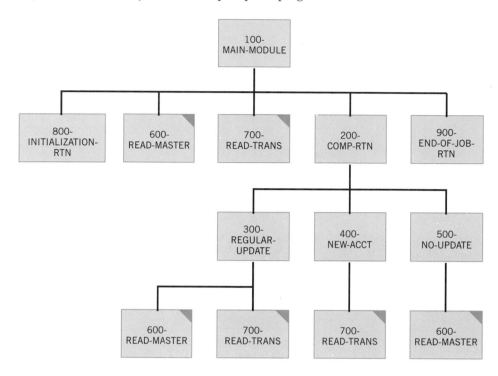

Figure 13.4   Sample update program.

```
IDENTIFICATION DIVISION.
PROGRAM-ID. SAMPLE.
***********************************************************
*     sample      -  program updates the old-master    *
*                    file with a transaction file      *
*                    and creates a new-master file.    *
*                    a control listing is typically    *
*                    created as well. We omit it       *
*                    here for the sake of simplicity.  *
***********************************************************
ENVIRONMENT DIVISION.
INPUT-OUTPUT SECTION.
FILE-CONTROL.
    SELECT OLD-MASTER ASSIGN TO DATA13O.
    SELECT TRANS-FILE ASSIGN TO DATA13T.
    SELECT NEW-MASTER ASSIGN TO DATA13N.
*
DATA DIVISION.
FILE SECTION.
FD  OLD-MASTER
    LABEL RECORDS ARE STANDARD.
01  OLD-MASTER-REC.
    05  M-ACCT-NO                 PIC X(5).
    05  AMOUNT-DUE                PIC 9(4)V99.
    05                            PIC X(89).
FD  TRANS-FILE
    LABEL RECORDS ARE STANDARD.
01  TRANS-REC.
    05  T-ACCT-NO                 PIC X(5).
    05  AMT-TRANS-IN-CURRENT-PER  PIC 9(4)V99.
    05                            PIC X(89).
FD  NEW-MASTER
    LABEL RECORDS ARE STANDARD.
```

Figure 13.4   (continued)

```
01  NEW-MASTER-REC.
    05   ACCT-NO-OUT                PIC X(5).
    05   AMOUNT-DUE-OUT             PIC 9(4)V99.
    05                              PIC X(89).
*
PROCEDURE DIVISION.
*********************************************
*  controls direction of program logic  *
*********************************************
100-MAIN-MODULE.
    PERFORM 800-INITIALIZATION-RTN
    PERFORM 600-READ-MASTER
    PERFORM 700-READ-TRANS
    PERFORM 200-COMP-RTN
        UNTIL M-ACCT-NO = HIGH-VALUES
                 AND
              T-ACCT-NO = HIGH-VALUES
    PERFORM 900-END-OF-JOB-RTN
    STOP RUN.
**************************************************************
*  performed from 100-main-module. compares the account    *
*  numbers from both files to determine the action to be    *
*  taken.                                                   *
**************************************************************
200-COMP-RTN.
    EVALUATE TRUE
        WHEN T-ACCT-NO = M-ACCT-NO
            PERFORM 300-REGULAR-UPDATE
        WHEN T-ACCT < M-ACCT-NO
            PERFORM 400-NEW-ACCOUNT
        WHEN OTHER
            PERFORM 500-NO-UPDATE
    END-EVALUATE.
**************************************************************
*  performed from 200-comp-rtn. combines old-master and    *
*  transaction file to create new-master records           *
**************************************************************
300-REGULAR-UPDATE.
    MOVE OLD-MASTER-REC TO NEW-MASTER-REC
    COMPUTE AMOUNT-DUE-OUT = AMT-TRANS-IN-CURRENT-PER + AMOUNT-DUE
    WRITE NEW-MASTER-REC
    PERFORM 600-READ-MASTER
    PERFORM 700-READ-TRANS.
**************************************************************
*  performed from 200-comp-rtn. adds new account to new-master *
*  from transaction file                                      *
**************************************************************
400-NEW-ACCOUNT.
    MOVE SPACES TO NEW-MASTER-REC
    MOVE T-ACCT-NO TO ACCT-NO-OUT
    MOVE AMT-TRANS-IN-CURRENT-PER TO AMOUNT-DUE-OUT
    WRITE NEW-MASTER-REC
    PERFORM 700-READ-TRANS.
**************************************************************
*  performed from 200-comp-rtn. copies the old-master to new-master  *
**************************************************************
500-NO-UPDATE.
    WRITE NEW-MASTER-REC FROM OLD-MASTER-REC
    PERFORM 600-READ-MASTER.
**************************************************************
*  performed from 100-main-module 300-regular-update       *
*  and 500-no-update. reads old-master file                *
**************************************************************
600-READ-MASTER.
    READ OLD-MASTER
```

Figure 13.4 (continued)

```
                AT END MOVE HIGH-VALUES TO M-ACCT-NO
           END-READ.
   ************************************************************
   *   performed from 100-main-module 300-regular-update   *
   *   and 400-new-account. reads transaction file         *
   ************************************************************
       700-READ-TRANS.
           READ TRANS-FILE
                AT END MOVE HIGH-VALUES TO T-ACCT-NO
           END-READ.
   ********************************************************
   *   performed from 100-main-module. opens files   *
   ********************************************************
       800-INITIALIZATION-RTN.
           OPEN INPUT   OLD-MASTER
                        TRANS-FILE
                OUTPUT NEW-MASTER.
   ********************************************************
   *   performed from 100-main-module. closes files   *
   ********************************************************
       900-END-OF-JOB-RTN.
           CLOSE OLD-MASTER
                 TRANS-FILE
                 NEW-MASTER.
```

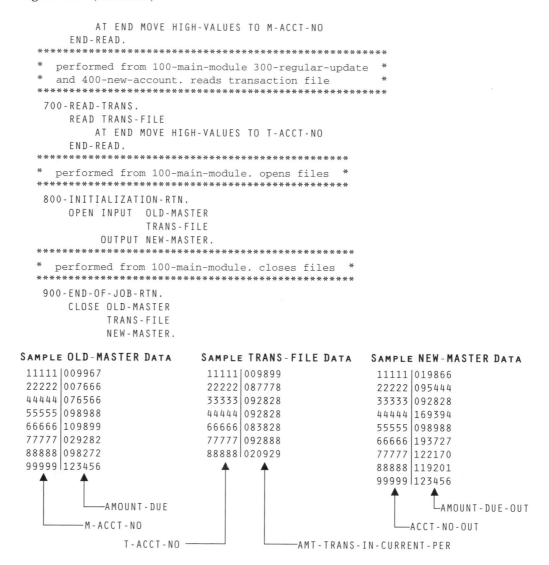

The Main Module

The main module at 100-MAIN-MODULE performs an initialization routine that opens all files. Then a record is read from both the master and the transaction file. 200-COMP-RTN is performed until all records are processed. At that point, an end-of-job routine is executed from the main module; this routine closes the files. Then the run is terminated. The significance of the COBOL reserved word HIGH-VALUES in the PERFORM statement will be discussed later in this section.

How Input Transaction and Master Records are Processed

Initially, a record is obtained from both the OLD-MASTER and the TRANS-FILE in read modules executed from the main module. 200-COMP-RTN then compares the account numbers, M-ACCT-NO of OLD-MASTER-REC and T-ACCT-NO of TRANS-REC. Since both files are in sequence by their respective account numbers, a comparison of M-ACCT-NO to T-ACCT-NO will determine the next module to be executed. Three possible conditions may be met when comparing M-ACCT-NO to T-ACCT-NO:

T-ACCT-NO IS EQUAL TO M-ACCT-NO

If the account numbers are equal, this means that a transaction record exists with the same account number that is on the master file. If this condition is met, we perform 300-REGULAR-UPDATE where OLD-MASTER-REC is updated. That is, the transaction data is posted to the master record, which means that the NEW-MASTER-REC will contain the previous AMOUNT-DUE from the old master record plus the AMT-TRANS-IN-CURRENT-PER of the transaction record. After a NEW-MASTER-REC is written, another record from both OLD-MASTER and TRANS-FILE must be read. Here, again, we are assuming that a master record can be updated with at most one transaction record.

T-ACCT-NO IS GREATER THAN M-ACCT-NO

If T-ACCT-NO IS > M-ACCT-NO, this means that M-ACCT-NO < T-ACCT-NO. In that case, there is a master record with an account number *less than* the account number on the transaction file. If this condition occurs in our program, then the last ELSE in 200-COMP-RTN will be executed. Since both files are in sequence by account number, this condition means that a master record exists for which there is *no corresponding transaction record*. That is, the master record has had no activity or changes during the current update cycle and should be written onto the NEW-MASTER file *as is*. We call this procedure 500-NO-UPDATE.

At 500-NO-UPDATE, we write the NEW-MASTER-REC from the OLD-MASTER-REC and read another record from OLD-MASTER. Since we have not yet processed the last transaction record that caused T-ACCT-NO to compare greater than the M-ACCT-NO of the OLD-MASTER, we should *not* read another transaction record at the 500-NO-UPDATE procedure. Consider the following example that illustrates the processing to be performed if M-ACCT-NO IS < T-ACCT-NO, which is the same as T-ACCT-NO > M-ACCT-NO:

```
M-ACCT-NO       T-ACCT-NO

00001           00001   ◄——     Update master record
00002           00003   ◄——     00002 is written to the NEW-MASTER as
                                is; the next master record is read;
                                T-ACCT-NO 00003 has not yet been
                                processed
```

T-ACCT-NO IS LESS THAN M-ACCT-NO

Since both files are in sequence by account number, this condition would mean that a transaction record exists for which there is no corresponding master record. Depending on the type of update procedure being performed, this could mean either (1) a new account is to be processed from the TRANS-FILE or (2) an error has occurred; that is, the T-ACCT-NO is wrong. In our illustration, we will assume that when a T-ACCT-NO is less than an M-ACCT-NO, this is a *new account*; but first let us consider in more detail the two ways to process transaction data if T-ACCT-NO is less than M-ACCT-NO:

Create a New Account If T-ACCT-NO < M-ACCT-NO. As noted, for some applications a transaction record with no corresponding master record means a new account. We call this procedure 400-NEW-ACCOUNT in our program. In this instance, a new master record is created entirely from the transaction record. Then the next transaction record is read. We do *not* read another record from OLD-MASTER at this time, since we have not yet processed the master record that compared greater than T-ACCT-NO. The other possibility is to:

Specify an Error Condition If T-ACCT-NO < M-ACCT-NO. For some applications, all account numbers on the transaction file *must* have corresponding master records with the same account numbers. For these applications, new accounts are handled by a different program and are *not* part of the update procedure.

Thus, if T-ACCT-NO is less than M-ACCT-NO, an error routine should be executed, which we could have labeled 400-ERROR-RTN. The error routine would usually print out on the control listing the transaction record that has a nonmatching account number; then the next transaction record would be read.

Illustrating the Update Procedure with Examples

In our program, a master and a transaction record are read from the main module. Then 200-COMP-RTN is executed, where the account numbers are compared. Based on the comparison, either 300-REGULAR-UPDATE, 500-NO-UPDATE, or 400-NEW-ACCOUNT will be executed. 200-COMP-RTN is then repeated until there are no more records to process. The following examples illustrate the routines to be performed depending on the account numbers read and stored in the input areas:

M-ACCT-NO	T-ACCT-NO	CONDITION	ACTION
00001	00001	T-ACCT-NO = M-ACCT-NO	300-REGULAR-UPDATE
00002	00004	T-ACCT-NO > M-ACCT-NO	500-NO-UPDATE
00003	00004	T-ACCT-NO > M-ACCT-NO	500-NO-UPDATE
00005	00004	T-ACCT-NO < M-ACCT-NO	400-NEW-ACCOUNT
00005	00005	T-ACCT-NO = M-ACCT-NO	300-REGULAR-UPDATE

Remember that this update procedure assumes that there is no more than a *single transaction record for each master record*. Later on we will consider the procedures used when there may be multiple transaction records with the same account number that are to update a single master record.

Review again the pseudocode in Figure 13.2, the hierarchy chart in Figure 13.3, and the program in Figure 13.4. Recall that we have not included the procedures to print a control listing for the sake of simplicity, but your update programs should include such listings. Note, too, that transaction records should include codes that explicitly define them as updates, new accounts, or perhaps even records to be deleted. These codes reduce the risk of errors. We will discuss using transaction codes in update procedures in the next section.

One element in the program requires further clarification: the use of HIGH-VALUES in the master and transaction account number fields when an AT END condition is reached.

The Use of HIGH-VALUES for End-of-File Conditions

With two input files, you cannot assume that both will reach AT END conditions at the same time. It is likely that we will run out of records from one file before the other has been completely read. First, an AT END condition for the TRANS-FILE may occur *before* we have reached the end of the OLD-MASTER file. Or, we may run out of OLD-MASTER records before we reach the end of the TRANS-FILE. We must account for both possibilities in our program.

The COBOL reserved word **HIGH-VALUES** is used in the 600-READ-MASTER and 700-READ-TRANS procedures. Consider first 600-READ-MASTER. When the OLD-MASTER file has reached the end, there may be additional transaction records to process. Hence, we would not want to automatically terminate all processing at an OLD-MASTER end-of-file condition; instead, we want to continue processing transaction records as new accounts. To accomplish this, we place HIGH-VALUES in M-ACCT-NO of OLD-MASTER-REC when an AT END condition occurs for that file. HIGH-VALUES refers to the largest value in the computer's collating sequence. This is a character consisting of "all bits on" in a single storage position. All bits on, in either EBCDIC or ASCII, represents a nonstandard, nonprintable character used to specify the highest value in the computer's collating sequence.

HIGH-VALUES in M-ACCT-NO ensures that subsequent attempts to compare the T-ACCT-NO of new transaction records to this M-ACCT-NO will always result in a "less than" condition. Suppose we reach an AT END condition for OLD-MASTER first. The 400-NEW-ACCOUNT routine would be executed until there are no more transaction records, because M-ACCT-NO contains HIGH-VALUES, which is the computer's highest possible value. T-ACCT-NO will always compare "less than" M-ACCT-NO if M-ACCT-NO has HIGH-VALUES in it.

Now consider 700-READ-TRANS. We may reach an AT END condition for TRANS-FILE while there are still OLD-MASTER records left to process. In this case, we would continue processing OLD-MASTER records at 500-NO-UPDATE until we have read and processed the master file in its entirety. Hence, at 700-READ-TRANS, we move HIGH-VALUES to T-ACCT-NO on an AT END condition. HIGH-VALUES in T-ACCT-NO is a way of ensuring that the field will compare higher, or greater than, M-ACCT-NO. In this way, 500-NO-UPDATE will continue to be executed for the remaining master records. Any remaining OLD-MASTER records will be read and processed using this 500-NO-UPDATE sequence. This procedure will be repeated until an AT END condition at OLD-MASTER is reached.

Thus, we continue to process records at 200-COMP-RTN even if one of the two input files has reached an AT END condition. Only when *both* AT END *conditions* have been reached would control return to the main module where the program is terminated. To accomplish this, the main module executes 200-COMP-RTN with the following statement:

```
PERFORM 200-COMP-RTN UNTIL
    M-ACCT-NO = HIGH-VALUES
        AND
    T-ACCT-NO = HIGH-VALUES
```

HIGH-VALUES is a figurative constant that may be used only with fields that are defined as *alphanumeric*. Thus M-ACCT-NO, T-ACCT-NO, and ACCT-NO-OUT must be defined with a PIC of Xs rather than 9s even though they typically contain numeric data. This does not affect the processing, since 9s are required only if a field is to be used in an arithmetic operation.

It may have occurred to you that moving 99999 to M-ACCT-NO or T-ACCT-NO on an end-of-file condition would produce the same results as moving HIGH-VALUES. That is, a trailer record of 9s in an account number field will always compare higher than any other number. This use of 9s in the key field is only possible, however, if the key field could not have a valid value of 9s. That is, if an account number of 99999 is a possible entry, moving 99999 to an account number when an end-of-file condition is reached could produce erroneous results.

In summary, HIGH-VALUES means "all bits on," which is *not* a printable character and which has a nonnumeric value greater than all 9s. Using it on an end-of-file condition will ensure correct file handling regardless of the actual values that the account numbers can assume. This is because an incoming account number will always compare "less than" HIGH-VALUES.

— DEBUGGING TIP —

When testing a program that creates a disk file as output, you should examine the output records to make sure that they are correct. You can do this by coding DISPLAY record-name just prior to writing the record. This will display the record on the screen so you can see what it looks like before it is written to disk. Most computer systems also have an *operating system command* such as PRINT or TYPE file-name that will print or display the entire file that was created as output after the program has been executed in its entirety. Keep in mind that an update program is not fully debugged until all files have been checked for accuracy.

SELF-TEST

1. What do we call the major collection of data pertaining to a specific application?
2. Changes to be made to a master file are placed in a separate file called a _____ file.
3. In a sequential update procedure, we use three files called _____ , _____ , and _____ .
4. (T or F) In a sequential update procedure, all files must be in sequence by the same key field.
5. In a sequential update procedure, the key field in the transaction file is compared to the key field in the _____ .

6. In Question 5, if the key fields are equal, a _____ procedure is performed. Describe this procedure.

7. In Question 5, if the transaction key field is greater than the master key field, a _____ procedure is performed. Describe this procedure.

8. In Question 5, if the transaction key field is less than the master key field, a _____ procedure is performed. Describe this procedure.

9. The statement `READ TRANS-FILE AT END MOVE HIGH-VALUES TO T-ACCT-NO ...` moves _____ if there are no more records in `TRANS-FILE`. To contain `HIGH-VALUES`, `T-ACCT-NO` must be defined with a `PIC` of _____ .

10. (T or F) Disk files can be created for either sequential or random access.

Solutions

1. A master file

2. transaction

3. the old master file—current through the previous updating cycle; the transaction file; the new master file—which incorporates the old master data along with the transaction data

4. T

5. old master file

6. regular update; transaction data is added to the master data, a new master record is written, and records from the old master file and the transaction file are read.

7. no update; a new master record is created directly from the old master record and a record from the old master file is read.

8. new account or error; if it is a new account, move transaction data to the new master and write; if it is an error, an error message is printed. In either case, a transaction record is then read.

9. a value of all bits on to the `T-ACCT-NO` field. (Any subsequent comparison of `T-ACCT-NO` to an actual `M-ACCT-NO` will cause a ">" condition); Xs because `HIGH-VALUES` is a nonnumeric figurative constant

10. T

VALIDITY CHECKING IN UPDATE PROCEDURES

Because updating results in changes to master files, data entry errors must be kept to an absolute minimum. Numerous data validation techniques should be incorporated in update programs to minimize errors. Let us consider some common validity checking routines.

CHECKING FOR NEW ACCOUNTS

You will recall that there are two ways we can process a transaction if `T-ACCT-NO` is less than `M-ACCT-NO`, that is, if there is a transaction record for which there is no corresponding master record. For some applications, transaction records should always have corresponding master records; in this case, if `T-ACCT-NO` < `M-ACCT-NO`, we treat this as an error.

For other applications, if `T-ACCT-NO` < `M-ACCT-NO`, the transaction record could be a new account to be added to the `NEW-MASTER` file. To simply add this transaction record to the new master file, however, without any additional checking could result in an error, since the possibility exists that `T-ACCT-NO` was coded incorrectly and that the transaction record is, in fact, *not* a new account.

To verify that a `TRANS-REC` is a new account, we usually include a *coded field* in the `TRANS-REC` itself that definitively specifies the record as a new account. A more complete format for `TRANS-REC` would be as follows:

TRANS-REC
```
    1-5    T-ACCT-NO
    6-11   AMT-TRANS-IN-CURRENT-PER 9999V99
   12-99   FILLER
   100     CODE-IN (1 = NEW-ACCT; 2 = REGULAR-UPDATE)
```

Thus, if T-ACCT-NO IS LESS THAN M-ACCT-NO, we would process the transaction record as a new account *only if* it also contains a 1 in CODE-IN. The procedure at 400-NEW-ACCOUNT in our sample update, then, could be modified to *validate* the data being entered:

Pseudocode Excerpt

NEW-ACCOUNT

    EVALUATE TRUE

        WHEN Code-In = 1

            Add a new record

        WHEN OTHER

            PERFORM Error-Rtn

    END-EVALUATE

    PERFORM Read-Trans

ERROR-RTN

    Write an error line

READ-TRANS

    Read a transaction record

Program Excerpt

```
400-NEW-ACCOUNT.
    EVALUATE TRUE
        WHEN CODE-IN = 1
            MOVE SPACES TO NEW-MASTER-REC
            MOVE T-ACCT-NO TO ACCT-NO-OUT
            MOVE AMT-TRANS-IN-CURRENT-PER
                TO AMOUNT-DUE-OUT
            WRITE NEW-MASTER-REC
        WHEN OTHER
            PERFORM 800-ERROR-RTN
    END-EVALUATE
    PERFORM 700-READ-TRANS.
```

Similarly, CODE-IN may be used to validate transaction data processed at 300-REGULAR-UPDATE:

Pseudocode Excerpt

REGULAR-UPDATE

    EVALUATE TRUE

        WHEN regular update

            Update and write the record

        WHEN OTHER

            PERFORM Error-Rtn

    END-EVALUATE

    PERFORM Read-Master

    PERFORM Read-Trans

ERROR-RTN

    Write an error line

READ-MASTER

    Read a master record

READ-TRANS

    Read a transaction record

Program Excerpt

```
300-REGULAR-UPDATE.
    EVALUATE TRUE
        WHEN CODE-IN = 2
            MOVE OLD-MASTER-REC
                TO NEW-MASTER-REC
            COMPUTE AMOUNT-DUE-OUT =
                AMT-TRANS-IN-CURRENT-PER
                    + AMOUNT-DUE
            WRITE NEW-MASTER-REC
        WHEN OTHER
            PERFORM 800-ERROR-RTN
    END-EVALUATE
    PERFORM 600-READ-MASTER
    PERFORM 700-READ-TRANS.
```

It is better still to establish CODE-IN in the DATA DIVISION with condition-names as follows:

```
05  CODE-IN        PIC 9.
    88  NEW-ACCT            VALUE 1.
    88  UPDATE-CODE         VALUE 2.
```

Then, in 400-NEW-ACCOUNT, the conditional could be replaced by EVALUATE TRUE WHEN NEW-ACCT .... Similarly, in 300-REGULAR-UPDATE, the conditional could be replaced with EVALUATE TRUE WHEN UPDATE-CODE ....

The Practice Program at the end of this chapter illustrates an update that uses coded transaction records.

CHECKING FOR DELETE CODES AND DELETING RECORDS FROM A SEQUENTIAL MASTER FILE

One type of update function not considered in our previous illustrations is that of *deleting master records*. Since accounts may need to be deleted if customers give up their charge privileges or have not paid their bills, there must be some provision for eliminating specific records from the master file during an update. We may use the technique of a coded transaction field as described earlier to accomplish this. We could add a code of '3' to indicate that a record is to be deleted:

TRANS-REC
```
  1-5    T-ACCT-NO
  6-11   AMT-TRANS-IN-CURRENT-PER 9999V99
 12-99   FILLER
100      CODE-IN (1 = NEW-ACCT; 2 = UPDATE-CODE; 3 = DELETE-THE-RECORD)
```

The procedure at 300-REGULAR-UPDATE might be revised as follows:

Pseudocode Excerpt

REGULAR-UPDATE
    EVALUATE TRUE
        WHEN regular update
            Update and write the record
        WHEN delete code
            CONTINUE
        WHEN OTHER
            PERFORM Error-Rtn
    END-EVALUATE
    PERFORM Read-Master
    PERFORM Read-Trans.

ERROR-RTN
    Write an error line

READ-MASTER
    Read a master record

READ-TRANS
    Read a transaction record

Program Excerpt

```
300-REGULAR-UPDATE.
    EVALUATE TRUE
        WHEN UPDATE-CODE
            MOVE OLD-MASTER-REC
                TO NEW-MASTER-REC
            COMPUTE AMOUNT-DUE-OUT =
                AMT-TRANS-IN-CURRENT-PER
                    + AMOUNT-DUE
            WRITE NEW-MASTER-REC
        WHEN DELETE-THE-RECORD
            CONTINUE
        WHEN OTHER
            PERFORM 800-ERROR-RTN
    END-EVALUATE
    PERFORM 600-READ-MASTER
    PERFORM 700-READ-TRANS.
```

See the Practice Program in Figure 13.9 at the end of this chapter for a full illustration of how transaction codes are used.

The following is a summary of how transaction records with transaction codes can be processed:

	SUMMARY
	HOW TRANSACTION RECORDS ARE PROCESSED
A. T-KEY = M-KEY	1. Delete the master record if T-CODE indicates deletion.
	2. Change or update the master record if T-CODE indicates update.
	3. Process the transaction record as an error if T-CODE indicates new record.
B. T-KEY < M-KEY	1. Add the transaction record to the master file if T-CODE indicates a new record.
	2. Process the transaction record as an error if T-CODE does not indicate a new record.
C. T-KEY > M-KEY	Rewrite the master record as is.

CHECKING FOR SEQUENCE ERRORS

As noted, in an update program, the sequence of the records in the transaction and master files is critical. If one or more records in the transaction or master file is not in the correct sequence, the entire production run could produce erroneous results. The SORT verb in COBOL is described in detail in the next chapter. It is used to sort both the master and transaction files prior to updating.

UPDATE PROCEDURES WITH MULTIPLE TRANSACTION RECORDS FOR EACH MASTER RECORD

We have thus far focused on an update procedure in which a *single transaction record* is used to update the contents of a master record. For some applications, a single transaction record may be all that is required. For example, in a SALES file, we may use a single transaction record that indicates a salesperson's total sales for the current period to update his or her corresponding master record as in the preceding example.

For other applications, there may be a need to process more than one change for each master record during each update cycle. For example, a master accounts receivable file may be updated with transaction records where a single transaction record is created for *each purchase or credit* charged to a customer. If a customer has purchased 12 items during the current updating cycle, then there will be 12 transaction records for that one master customer record. This requires a different type of updating from the kind previously discussed, one that permits the processing of multiple transactions per master.

The update procedure described in Figure 13.4 is suitable only if *one transaction per master* is permitted. If more than one transaction had the same account number as a master record, the second transaction would be handled incorrectly. Since an equal condition between the key fields in TRANS-REC and OLD-MASTER-REC causes a NEW-MASTER-REC to be written and a new TRANS-REC and MASTER-REC to be read, the processing would *not* be performed properly if multiple transaction records per master record were permissible.

The pseudocode for updating a file where multiple transactions per master record are permitted is in Figure 13.5, and the program is illustrated in Figure 13.6.

Figure 13.5 Pseudocode for sample update program where multiple transactions per master record are permitted.

```
MAIN-MODULE
START
        PERFORM Initialize-Rtn
        PERFORM Comp-Rtn
            UNTIL no more input
        PERFORM End-of-Job-Rtn
        Stop Run
STOP

INITIALIZE-RTN
        Open the files
        PERFORM Read-Master
        PERFORM Read-Trans

COMP-RTN
EVALUATE
        WHEN   T-Acct-No = M-Acct-No
               PERFORM Regular-Update
```

Figure 13.5   (continued)

```
              WHEN   T-Acct-No < M-Acct-No
                        PERFORM New-Account
              WHEN   Other
                        PERFORM No-Update
         END-EVALUATE

         REGULAR-UPDATE
              Move old master record to new master record
              PERFORM Add-And-Read
                   UNTIL T-Acct-No ≠ M-Acct-No
              Write a new master record
              PERFORM Read-Master

         NEW-ACCOUNT
              Add a new record to the master file
              PERFORM Read-Trans

         NO-UPDATE
              Write a new master record from old master record
              PERFORM Read-Master

         ADD-AND-READ
              Add transaction amount to new master record
              PERFORM Read-Trans

         READ-MASTER
              Read a Master Record

         READ-TRANS
              Read a Transaction Record

         END-OF-JOB-RTN
              Close the files
```

Figure 13.6   Sample update program where multiple transactions per master record are permitted.

```
          IDENTIFICATION DIVISION.
          PROGRAM-ID. SAMPLE.
          ******************************************************
          *    sample        -  program updates an old-master*
          *                     file with a transaction file *
          *                     and creates a new-master file*
          *   multiple transactions per master are permitted  *
          *   a control listing print file is typically       *
          *   created here as well. we omit it for            *
          *   the sake of simplicity.                         *
          ******************************************************
          ENVIRONMENT DIVISION.
          INPUT-OUTPUT SECTION.
          FILE-CONTROL.
              SELECT OLD-MASTER-IN  ASSIGN TO DATA13O.
              SELECT TRANS-FILE-IN  ASSIGN TO DATA136T.
              SELECT NEW-MASTER-OUT ASSIGN TO DATA136N.
          *
          DATA DIVISION.
          FILE SECTION.
```

Figure 13.6 (continued)

```
    FD  OLD-MASTER-IN
        LABEL RECORDS ARE STANDARD.
    01  OLD-MASTER-REC-IN.
        05  M-ACCT-NO-IN            PIC X(5).
        05  AMOUNT-DUE-IN           PIC 9(4)V99.
        05                          PIC X(89).
    FD  TRANS-FILE-IN
        LABEL RECORDS ARE STANDARD.
    01  TRANS-REC-IN.
        05  T-ACCT-NO-IN            PIC X(5).
        05  AMT-TRANS-IN            PIC 9(4)V99.
        05                          PIC X(89).
    FD  NEW-MASTER-OUT
        LABEL RECORDS ARE STANDARD.
    01  NEW-MASTER-REC-OUT.
        05  ACCT-NO-OUT             PIC X(5).
        05  AMOUNT-DUE-OUT          PIC 9(4)V99.
        05                          PIC X(89).
    *
    PROCEDURE DIVISION.
    ************************************************
    *   controls the direction of program logic  *
    ************************************************
    100-MAIN-MODULE.
        PERFORM 800-INITIALIZATION-RTN
        PERFORM 200-COMP-RTN
            UNTIL M-ACCT-NO-IN = HIGH-VALUES
                            AND
                  T-ACCT-NO-IN = HIGH-VALUES
        PERFORM 900-END-OF-JOB-RTN
        STOP RUN.
    **********************************************************************
    *   performed from 100-main-module. compares the account numbers  *
    *   to determine the appropriate procedure to be performed        *
    **********************************************************************
    200-COMP-RTN.
        EVALUATE TRUE
            WHEN T-ACCT-NO-IN = M-ACCT-NO-IN
                PERFORM 300-REGULAR-UPDATE
            WHEN T-ACCT-NO-IN < M-ACCT-NO-IN
                PERFORM 400-NEW-ACCOUNT
            WHEN OTHER
                PERFORM 500-NO-UPDATE
        END-EVALUATE.

    ******************************************************************
    *   performed from 200-comp-rtn. combines the old-master and  *
    *   transaction records to create the new-master record.      *
    ******************************************************************
    300-REGULAR-UPDATE.
        MOVE OLD-MASTER-REC-IN TO NEW-MASTER-REC-OUT
        PERFORM 550-ADD-AND-READ-TRANS
            UNTIL T-ACCT-NO-IN NOT = M-ACCT-NO-IN
        WRITE NEW-MASTER-REC-OUT
        PERFORM 600-READ-MASTER.

    ********************************************************
    *   performed from 200-comp-rtn. adds a new account  *
    *   to new-master from the transaction file.         *
    ********************************************************
    400-NEW-ACCOUNT.
        MOVE SPACES TO NEW-MASTER-REC-OUT
        MOVE T-ACCT-NO-IN TO ACCT-NO-OUT
        MOVE AMT-TRANS-IN TO AMOUNT-DUE-OUT
        WRITE NEW-MASTER-REC-OUT
        PERFORM 700-READ-TRANS.
```

Figure 13.6   (continued)

```
*********************************************************************
*   performed from 200-comp-rtn. copies the old-master record   *
*   to the new-master file.                                     *
*********************************************************************
    500-NO-UPDATE.
        WRITE NEW-MASTER-REC-OUT FROM OLD-MASTER-REC-IN
        PERFORM 600-READ-MASTER.
*********************************************************************
*   performed from 300-regular-update. adds the transaction amount *
*   to the amount due.                                          *
*********************************************************************
    550-ADD-AND-READ-TRANS.
        ADD AMT-TRANS-IN TO AMOUNT-DUE-OUT
        PERFORM 700-READ-TRANS.
*********************************************************************
*   performed from 800-initialization-rtn, 300-regular-update *
*   and 500-no-update. reads the old-master file.             *
*********************************************************************
    600-READ-MASTER.
        READ OLD-MASTER-IN
            AT END MOVE HIGH-VALUES TO M-ACCT-NO-IN
        END-READ.
*********************************************************************
*  performed from 800-initialization-rtn, 300-regular-update,  *
*  400-new-account, and 550-add-and-read-trans. reads the next *
*  record from the transaction file.                           *
*********************************************************************
    700-READ-TRANS.
        READ TRANS-FILE-IN
            AT END MOVE HIGH-VALUES TO T-ACCT-NO-IN
        END-READ.
*************************************************
*   performed from 100-main-module.            *
*   opens files and performs initial read     *
*************************************************
    800-INITIALIZATION-RTN.
        OPEN INPUT   OLD-MASTER-IN
                     TRANS-FILE-IN
             OUTPUT  NEW-MASTER-OUT
        PERFORM 600-READ-MASTER
        PERFORM 700-READ-TRANS.
*****************************************************
*   performed from 100-main-module. closes files  *
*****************************************************
    900-END-OF-JOB-RTN.
        CLOSE OLD-MASTER-IN
              TRANS-FILE-IN
              NEW-MASTER-OUT.
```

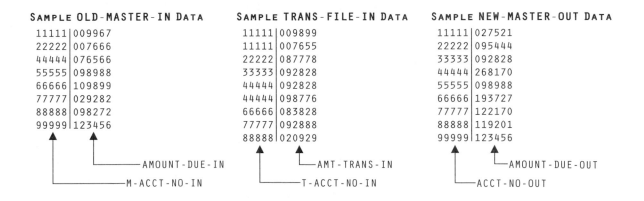

SAMPLE OLD-MASTER-IN Data	SAMPLE TRANS-FILE-IN Data	SAMPLE NEW-MASTER-OUT Data
11111 009967	11111 009899	11111 027521
22222 007666	11111 007655	22222 095444
44444 076566	22222 087778	33333 092828
55555 098988	33333 092828	44444 268170
66666 109899	44444 092828	55555 098988
77777 029282	44444 098776	66666 193727
88888 098272	66666 083828	77777 122170
99999 123456	77777 092888	88888 119201
	88888 020929	99999 123456

For COBOL 74, 200-COMP-RTN can be replaced with the following nested conditional:

```
200-COMP-RTN.
    IF  T-ACCT-NO-IN = M-ACCT-NO-IN
        PERFORM 300-REGULAR-UPDATE
    ELSE
        IF  T-ACCT-NO-IN < M-ACCT-NO-IN
            PERFORM 400-NEW-ACCOUNT
        ELSE
            PERFORM 500-NO-UPDATE.
```

Note that the program in Figure 13.6 does not handle records that need to be deleted.

SEQUENTIAL FILE UPDATING—REWRITING RECORDS ON A DISK

THE REWRITE STATEMENT FOR A DISK FILE OPENED AS I-O

As we have noted, both disk and tape can be organized sequentially and both can use sequential update procedures like the ones described in this chapter.

Disks, however, unlike tape, can serve as *both input and output during the same run*. Thus, it is possible to read a disk record, make changes *directly to the same record*, and rewrite it or update it in place. With this capability of disks, we need use only two files:

Open as	Name of File
I-O	MASTER-FILE
INPUT	TRANS-FILE

A disk file, then, can be opened as I-O, which means records from the disk will be accessed, read, changed, and rewritten. Consider the following systems flowchart:

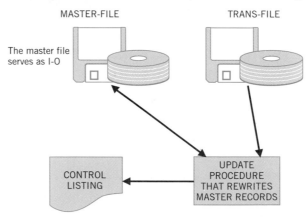

We read each disk record in sequence; when a record is to be updated, we make the changes directly to the MASTER-FILE record and **REWRITE** it.

The program in Figure 13.7 provides an alternative method for updating sequential files, one that uses a master disk file as I-O and then REWRITEs records in place. This program assumes that transaction records with no corresponding master record are to be treated as errors.

For COBOL 74, we could replace the EVALUATE in 200-UPDATE-RTN with the following:

```
IF M-CUST-NO = T-CUST-NO
    ADD T-AMT TO BAL-DUE
    DISPLAY T-CUST-NO, ' AMOUNT OF TRANSACTION ', T-AMT,
            ' BALANCE DUE  ', BAL-DUE
    REWRITE MASTER-REC
ELSE
    IF M-CUST-NO > T-CUST-NO
        DISPLAY T-CUST-NO, ' NOT ON MASTER FILE'.
```

Figure 13.7 Sample program to update a sequential disk file using the disk as I-0.

```
IDENTIFICATION DIVISION.
PROGRAM-ID.     SAMPLE.
****************************************************************
* sample - updates a master file with a transaction file. *
* the transaction file may contain one or more records    *
* per master.  master records are rewritten in place.     *
****************************************************************
ENVIRONMENT DIVISION.
INPUT-OUTPUT SECTION.
FILE-CONTROL.
    SELECT TRANS-FILE ASSIGN TO DATA13A.
    SELECT MASTER-FILE ASSIGN TO DATA13B.
DATA DIVISION.
FILE SECTION.
FD  TRANS-FILE
    LABEL RECORDS ARE STANDARD.
01  TRANS-REC.
    05  T-CUST-NO             PIC X(5).
    05  T-AMT                 PIC 999V99.
    05                        PIC X(90).
FD  MASTER-FILE
    LABEL RECORDS ARE STANDARD.
01  MASTER-REC.
    05  M-CUST-NO             PIC X(5).
    05  BAL-DUE               PIC 9(6)V99.
    05                        PIC X(89).
WORKING-STORAGE SECTION.
01  WORK-AREA.
    05  ARE-THERE-MORE-RECORDS PIC X(3)    VALUE 'YES'.
        88  NO-MORE-RECORDS               VALUE 'NO '.
PROCEDURE DIVISION.
*****************************************************************
*  100-main-rtn  - opens the files, controls the program logic, *
*                  and closes the files.                        *
*****************************************************************
100-MAIN-RTN.
    OPEN INPUT TRANS-FILE
         I-O   MASTER-FILE
    PERFORM 400-READ-TRANS
    PERFORM 200-UPDATE-RTN
         UNTIL NO-MORE-RECORDS
    CLOSE TRANS-FILE
          MASTER-FILE
    STOP RUN.
*****************************************************************
* 200-update-rtn  - compares the customer number of the master  *
*                   file to that of the transaction file and    *
*                   processes the records accordingly           *
*****************************************************************
200-UPDATE-RTN.
    PERFORM 300-READ-MASTER
            UNTIL M-CUST-NO = T-CUST-NO
                  OR
                  M-CUST-NO > T-CUST-NO
                  OR
                  M-CUST-NO = HIGH-VALUES
    EVALUATE TRUE
        WHEN M-CUST-NO = T-CUST-NO
            ADD T-AMT TO BAL-DUE
            DISPLAY T-CUST-NO, ' AMOUNT OF TRANSACTION ', T-AMT,
                    ' BALANCE DUE ', BAL-DUE
            REWRITE MASTER-REC
        WHEN M-CUST-NO > T-CUST-NO
            DISPLAY T-CUST-NO, ' NOT ON MASTER-FILE'
    END-EVALUATE
    PERFORM 400-READ-TRANS.
```

Figure 13.7   (continued)

```
***********************************************************************
* 300-read-master   -reads the next record from the master file  *
*                      performed from 200-update-rtn             *
***********************************************************************
 300-READ-MASTER.
     READ MASTER-FILE
         AT END MOVE HIGH-VALUES TO M-CUST-NO
     END-READ.
*************************************************
* 400-read-trans   -reads the transaction file  *
*                    performed from 100-main-rtn *
*                    and 200-update-rtn.         *
*************************************************
 400-READ-TRANS.
     READ TRANS-FILE
         AT END MOVE 'NO ' TO ARE-THERE-MORE-RECORDS
     END-READ.
```

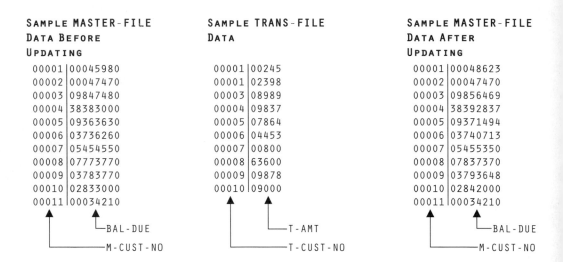

SAMPLE MASTER-FILE DATA BEFORE UPDATING	SAMPLE TRANS-FILE DATA	SAMPLE MASTER-FILE DATA AFTER UPDATING
00001|00045980	00001|00245	00001|00048623
00002|00047470	00001|02398	00002|00047470
00003|09847480	00003|08989	00003|09856469
00004|38383000	00004|09837	00004|38392837
00005|09363630	00005|07864	00005|09371494
00006|03736260	00006|04453	00006|03740713
00007|05454550	00007|00800	00007|05455350
00008|07773770	00008|63600	00008|07837370
00009|03783770	00009|09878	00009|03793648
00010|02833000	00010|09000	00010|02842000
00011|00034210		00011|00034210

Note that the REWRITE statement replaces the master disk record, currently in storage, that was accessed by the preceding READ statement.

Updating Sequential Disks in Place Requires Creation of a Backup Disk in a Separate Procedure

Accessing a disk as I-O and rewriting records eliminates the need for creating a new master file, but some caution must be exercised when using this procedure. Since the master disk file is itself updated, there is no old master available for backup purposes. This means that if the master file gets lost, stolen, or damaged, there is no way of conveniently recreating it. Thus, master files that are to be rewritten should be recreated or copied before an update procedure.

When performing a sequential update using an input old master that is separate from an output new master, as in the previous section, we always have the old master as backup in case we cannot use the new master. However, since there is no backup when we *rewrite* a master disk, we must create a duplicate copy of the master before each update procedure is performed. This duplicate is a *backup copy*, which can be stored on tape or disk. Backup copies should always be kept in a safe location separate from the master, in case something happens to the new master and it must be recreated.

In summary, the primary advantage of using a REWRITE statement for a disk file opened as I-O is that records can be updated in place without the need for creating an entirely new master file. A disadvantage of using a REWRITE is that a backup version of the updated master disk must be created in a *separate procedure* in case the master becomes unusable.

USING AN ACTIVITY-STATUS FIELD FOR DESIGNATING RECORDS TO BE DELETED

When we created a NEW-MASTER file in an update procedure, as in Figure 13.4, we were able to physically delete master records by not writing them onto the new master. If a sequential disk file is to be updated by rewriting records directly on it, we need a *different procedure for deleting records*. One common technique is to begin each record with a one-character activity-status code that *precedes* the key field.

The activity-status code would have a specific value for active records, and the code would have a different value if a record is to be deactivated. For example:

```
01  MASTER-REC.
    05  ACTIVITY-STATUS    PIC X.
        88  ACTIVE              VALUE LOW-VALUES.
        88  INACTIVE            VALUE HIGH-VALUES.
    05  M-CUST-NO         PIC X(5).
        :
```

HIGH-VALUES represents the highest value in a collating sequence, and LOW-VALUES represents the lowest value. We can use these figurative constants to distinguish active records from inactive ones, but, in fact, any two values could have been used (e.g., 1 for ACTIVE, 2 for INACTIVE).

When the master records are written, they are created with the ACTIVE value, which is LOW-VALUES in ACTIVITY-STATUS in our example. An INACTIVE code of HIGH-VALUES would be moved to ACTIVITY-STATUS only if a transaction record indicated that the corresponding master record was to be deleted.

An activity-status field can be used to designate records to be deleted with *any* type of update, as an alternative to physically deleting master records from the file. Many organizations prefer to keep inactive records in the file so that they can be (1) reactivated later on if necessary or (2) used for some sort of analysis. For these reasons, most database management systems as well as many COBOL programs use an activity-status code to designate records as inactive rather than physically deleting them.

To report from a master file that has an activity-status field, we must include the following clause before printing a record:

```
IF  ACTIVITY-STATUS = LOW-VALUES
    PERFORM 500-PRINT-RTN
END-IF
```

or

```
IF  ACTIVE
    PERFORM 500-PRINT-RTN
END-IF
```

You should test the activity-status field before any type of processing to ensure that only active records are processed.

Thus, when a sequential disk file may have records that are to be deleted, we may use an activity-status code field as follows:

**CODED FIELDS TO DESIGNATE RECORDS
AS ACTIVE OR INACTIVE**

1. Include an ACTIVITY-STATUS code as the first position in the record.

2. Set the ACTIVITY-STATUS code to a value designating the record as active.

3. Change the ACTIVITY-STATUS code to a value designating the record as inactive only if it is to be deleted.

4. Before printing or other processing, check first to see if the record is active.

Note that there is a difference between records that have been deactivated and records that have been physically deleted from a file; inactive records are still in the file. This means that inactive records could easily be reactivated if the need arose or if the records were incorrectly deactivated. Moreover, a list of inactive records could easily be obtained if records were deactivated with an ACTIVITY-STATUS code. On the other hand, if a record has been physically deleted, it would be more difficult to keep track of inactive records.

Files updated as I-O *must* use an activity status code to deactivate records while updates that create entirely new master files could either delete inactive records or use an ACTIVITY-STATUS code to designate records as inactive.

But having inactive records on the file, as opposed to deleting such records, could eventually result in less efficient processing. When processing time increases greatly because of a large number of inactive records on a file, it is time to perform a file "cleanup," where only the active records on a file are recreated onto a new master file:

```
        OPEN INPUT OLD-MASTER
             OUTPUT NEW-MASTER
        PERFORM 300-READ-MASTER
        PERFORM 200-CLEAN-UP
             UNTIL NO-MORE-RECORDS
        PERFORM 400-END-OF-JOB.
   200-CLEAN-UP.
        IF  ACTIVITY-STATUS = LOW-VALUES
             WRITE NEW-REC FROM OLD-REC
        END-IF
        PERFORM 300-READ-MASTER.
```

THE EXTEND OPTION FOR ADDING RECORDS TO THE END OF A SEQUENTIAL FILE

In this section we have focused on how an I-O disk file can be updated with a transaction file (see Figure 13.7). This is an alternative to using an input master and an input transaction file to create an entirely new master file, as in Figure 13.4.

Figure 13.7 illustrated how the update procedure with a REWRITE is performed on a disk opened as I-O. In this program, records were rewritten in place using the REWRITE verb. We also illustrated how records could be deactivated instead of deleted with the use of an ACTIVITY-STATUS code. Deactivating records serves a purpose similar to deleting records, which was performed as part of the sequential update program in Figure 13.4.

But we have not considered in our REWRITE program the technique used to add new records to a master file. In Figure 13.4, where an input master and an output master were used, if a transaction record existed for which there was no corresponding master, we were able to add it to the NEW-MASTER *in its proper sequence*. This is not, however, possible when rewriting records onto a disk opened as I-O. Suppose the first two master disk records have CUST-NO 00001 and 00006. If a transaction record with a T-CUST-NO of 00003 is read and it is a new account, there is *no physical space* to insert it in its proper place on the master file. Thus, when a file is opened as I-O we can rewrite records and deactivate records, but *we cannot add records* so that they are physically located in their correct place in sequence.

It is, however, possible to write a separate program or separate procedure to add records to the *end of a sequential disk (or tape) file* if you use the following OPEN statement:

OPEN EXTEND file-name

When the **OPEN EXTEND** statement is executed, the disk is positioned at the *end* of the file, immediately after the last record. A WRITE statement, then, will add records to the *end of this file*. If all records to be added have key fields in sequence that are greater than those currently on the master, then the entire file will be in the correct order. If the records that are added are not in sequence, the file must be sorted before it is processed again. Thus, if a T-CUST-NO of 00003 is added to the end of the file, the file will need to be sorted after records have been added so that it is in proper sequence by CUST-NO. We discuss the SORT instruction in the next chapter.

In summary, to add records to the end of an existing file we must use a separate program or a separate procedure in which the file is opened in the EXTEND mode. The following illustrates how a *single* update program could use *two separate transaction files*—one with change records and one with new account records to be added to the end of the file. Both transaction files could update an existing master disk in separate routines within the same program. Note that a transaction file of *change records* updates the master disk in I-O mode and a transaction file of *new records* updates the master disk in EXTEND mode. This means that the master must be opened, first in I-O mode, then closed, then opened again in EXTEND mode:

COBOL 85

```
100-MAIN-MODULE.
    OPEN INPUT TRANS-CHANGE  ◄───This is a file of changes to
         I-O MASTER-FILE              be made to the master
    PERFORM UNTIL ARE-THERE-MORE-RECORDS = 'NO '
        READ TRANS-CHANGE
            AT END
                MOVE 'NO ' TO ARE-THERE-MORE-RECORDS
            NOT AT END
                PERFORM 200-UPDATE-RTN
        END-READ
    END-PERFORM
    CLOSE MASTER-FILE
          TRANS-CHANGE
    OPEN INPUT TRANS-NEW  ◄───This is a file of new records
         EXTEND MASTER-FILE
    MOVE 'YES' TO ARE-THERE-MORE-RECORDS
    PERFORM UNTIL ARE-THERE-MORE-RECORDS = 'NO '
        READ TRANS-NEW
            AT END
                MOVE 'NO ' TO ARE-THERE-MORE-RECORDS
            NOT AT END
                PERFORM 300-ADD-RECORDS
        END-READ
    END-PERFORM
    CLOSE TRANS-NEW
          MASTER-FILE
    STOP RUN.
200-UPDATE-RTN.
***************************************************
*   this routine is the same as in figure 13.7.   *
***************************************************
300-ADD-RECORDS.
    WRITE MASTER-REC FROM TRANS-REC.
```

COBOL 74 Substitutions

```
READ TRANS-CHANGE
    AT END MOVE 'NO ' TO
        ARE-THERE-MORE-RECORDS.
PERFORM 200-UPDATE-RTN
    UNTIL ARE-THERE-MORE-RECORDS
        = 'NO '.
```

```
READ TRANS-NEW
    AT END MOVE 'NO ' TO
        ARE-THERE-MORE-RECORDS.
PERFORM 300-ADD-RECORDS
    UNTIL ARE-THERE-MORE-RECORDS
        = 'NO '.
```

```
READ TRANS-NEW
    AT END MOVE 'NO ' TO
        ARE-THERE-MORE-RECORDS.
```

The shaded excerpts *excluding* 200-UPDATE-RTN could be an entirely *separate program* that just adds transaction records to the end of an existing sequential disk file. If the key fields of these new records begin with a number greater than the last key field on the master, the file will still be in sequence by the key field. For example, if we add CUST-NO 775, 780, and 782 to a file that has CUST-NO 772 as its last entry, we still have a sequential file. But if the key fields of the new records contain numbers such as 026, 045, and 587, the master file will need to be sorted before it is processed again.

The following is a chart of permissible input/output statements depending on how a sequential file was opened:

	OPEN MODE			
Statement	INPUT	OUTPUT	I-O	EXTEND
READ	X		X	
WRITE		X		X
REWRITE			X	

SUMMARY: UPDATING A MASTER DISK IN PLACE

- Open the file as I-O.
- Read a master record to be updated, make changes, and then REWRITE the record in place.
- Instead of deleting master records, establish each record with an activity code that indicates either an active record or an inactive record (e.g., 1 in CODE-X for active or 2 in CODE-X for inactive). All master records are initially active (1 in CODE-X) unless the transaction record indicates that the master should be deactivated. To deactivate the master record, change the activity code: e.g., MOVE 2 TO CODE-X.

To add records to the end of an existing sequential master file in a separate program or procedure:

- Open the file as EXTEND. If the file was already opened as I-O for updating, it must be closed and then reopened.
- WRITE the new records to the end of the file.
- The file will need to be sorted if the added records are not in sequence.

A REVIEW OF SEQUENTIAL UPDATE PROCEDURES

	Update Where a New Master is Created	*Update Where We Rewrite to a Master*
Total number of files	3	2
Number of master files	2 (OLD-MASTER-INPUT NEW-MASTER-OUTPUT)	1 (MASTER-I-O)
How records are updated	WRITE NEW-MASTER-REC FROM OLD-MASTER-REC	REWRITE MASTER-REC

	Update Where a New Master is Created	*Update Where We Rewrite to a Master*
How records are deleted	(a) `NEW-MASTER-REC` is *not* written or (b) an activity-status code field is set equal to an "inactive" status and the record is written	An activity-status code field *must* be set to an "inactive" status before the record is rewritten
How new records are created	`WRITE NEW-MASTER-REC FROM TRANS-REC` when the master's key field is greater than the transaction's key field	Transaction records to be written to the master can only be written to the end of the file in a separate program or procedure. The master file must be opened in `EXTEND` mode.

CHAPTER SUMMARY A. Sequential updating by creating a new master.
Use three files: an incoming master file, a transaction file with change records, and a new output master file that will incorporate all the changes. The techniques used are as follows:
1. All files to be processed must be in sequence by the same key field.
2. A record is read from each file and specified routines are performed depending on whether or not the key fields match.
3. The transaction record could have a coded field to determine:
   a. What type of update is required.
   b. If the master record is to be deleted.
   c. If the transaction is a new account.
4. The end-of-job test for each file must be processed individually. By moving `HIGH-VALUES` to the key field of the file that ends first, we can be assured that the other file will always compare low and hence will continue to be processed. The job is terminated only after both input files have been processed. `HIGH-VALUES` can only be moved to a key field that has been defined as alphanumeric.

B. Sequential updating by rewriting a disk.
As an alternative to the preceding, records on a sequential disk can also be updated by *rewriting them* in place, if the disk file is opened as `I-O`. A backup file should always be created in this case.

C. Records can be added to the end of a disk file if we code `OPEN EXTEND` file-name.

KEY TERMS
Batch processing
`HIGH-VALUES`
Key field
Master file
`OPEN EXTEND`
`REWRITE`
Sequential file processing
Transaction file
Updating

CHAPTER SELF-TEST
1. What do we call the process of making a file of data current?
2. (T or F) A disk file may be processed sequentially or randomly.
3. (T or F) Files must be in sequence by key field to perform a sequential update.
4. The three files used to update a sequential master disk file are _____ , _____ , and _____ .
5. Suppose `EMPLOYEE-NO` is a field in a payroll record. Write a routine to make certain that the payroll file is in `EMPLOYEE-NO` sequence.

6. Assume the following statement is executed:

```
MOVE HIGH-VALUES TO PART-NO OF TRANS-REC.
```

Suppose the following is then executed:

```
IF  PART-NO OF MASTER-REC < PART-NO
        OF TRANS-REC
    PERFORM 500-MASTER-RTN
ELSE
    PERFORM 600-UPDATE
END-IF.
```

Because PART-NO of TRANS-REC contains HIGH-VALUES, the IF statement causes the _____ routine to be executed.

7. If a disk file is opened as I-O, disk records to be updated can be changed directly on the file with the use of a _____ statement.

8. To add records to the end of a disk file, open the file with the following statement: _____ .

9. (T or F) It is possible to have a single update program that permits both (1) only one transaction per master and (2) multiple transactions per master.

10. (T or F) If a disk is opened in I-O mode, then we cannot add records to the end of it.

Solutions

1. An update procedure

2. T

3. T

4. a transaction file; the old master file; the new master file

5. **COBOL 85**

```
05  EMPLOYEE-NO-HOLD    PIC 9(5)
      VALUE ZERO.
     :
PERFORM UNTIL ARE-THERE-MORE-RECORDS = 'NO '
    READ PAYROLL-FILE
        AT END
            MOVE 'NO ' TO ARE-THERE-MORE-RECORDS
        NOT AT END
            PERFORM 800-SEQ-CHECK
    END-READ
END-PERFORM
     :
800-SEQ-CHECK.
    IF  EMPLOYEE-NO < EMPLOYEE-NO-HOLD
        PERFORM 900-ERR-RTN
    ELSE
        MOVE EMPLOYEE-NO TO
                EMPLOYEE-NO-HOLD
    END-IF.
```

COBOL 74 Substitutions

```
READ PAYROLL-FILE
    AT END MOVE 'NO ' TO
        ARE-THERE-MORE-RECORDS.
PERFORM 800-SEQ-CHECK
    UNTIL ARE-THERE-MORE-RECORDS
        = 'NO '.
```

```
READ PAYROLL-FILE
    AT END MOVE 'NO ' TO
        ARE-THERE-MORE-RECORDS.
```

6. 500-MASTER-RTN—The comparison will always result in a 'less than' condition.

7. REWRITE

8. OPEN EXTEND file-name

9. T

10. T

PRACTICE PROGRAM The problem definition for this practice program is shown in Figure 13.8. Figure 13.9 illustrates the pseudocode, hierarchy chart, and program. Note that for this program we assume one transaction record per master, at most.

Figure 13.8 Problem definition for the Practice Program.

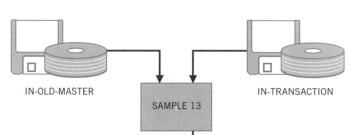

Systems Flowchart

IN-OLD-MASTER Record Layout			
Field	**Size**	**Type**	**No. of Decimal Positions (if Numeric)**
IN-OLD-PART-NO	5	Alphanumeric	
IN-OLD-QTY-ON-HAND	5	Numeric (signed)	0

IN-TRANSACTION Record Layout			
Field	**Size**	**Type**	**No. of Decimal Positions (if Numeric)**
IN-TRANS-PART-NO	5	Alphanumeric	
IN-TRANS-QTY	5	Numeric	0
IN-TRANS-CODE*	1	Numeric	0

*Code of 1 = Delete the master record
Code of 2 = Add a new master record
Code of 3 = Update the master record

OUT-NEW-MASTER Record Layout			
Field	**Size**	**Type**	**No. of Decimal Positions (if Numeric)**
OUT-MAS-PART-NO	5	Alphanumeric	
OUT-MAS-QTY-ON-HAND*	5	Numeric (signed)	0

*If OUT-MAS-QTY-ON-HAND falls below zero, display a message indicating that OUT-MAS-PART-NO is to be reordered. For example:

```
DISPLAY 'REORDER, QUANTITY FELL BELOW ZERO'
DISPLAY 'PART NUMBER ', OUT-MAS-PART-NO
```

Figure 13.8   (continued)

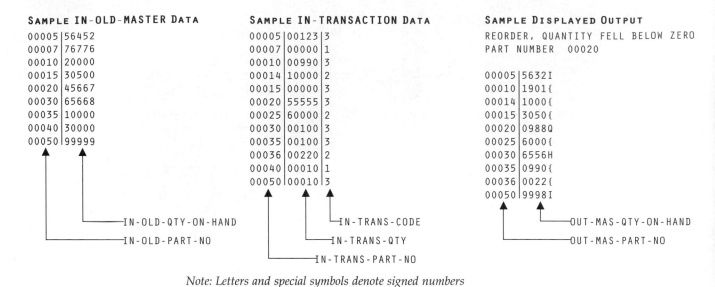

SAMPLE **IN-OLD-MASTER** DATA

```
00005|56452
00007|76776
00010|20000
00015|30500
00020|45667
00030|65668
00035|10000
00040|30000
00050|99999
```

────────────IN-OLD-QTY-ON-HAND
────────────IN-OLD-PART-NO

SAMPLE **IN-TRANSACTION** DATA

```
00005|00123|3
00007|00000|1
00010|00990|3
00014|10000|2
00015|00000|3
00020|55555|3
00025|60000|2
00030|00100|3
00035|00100|3
00036|00220|2
00040|00010|1
00050|00010|3
```

────────IN-TRANS-CODE
────────IN-TRANS-QTY
────────IN-TRANS-PART-NO

SAMPLE **DISPLAYED** OUTPUT

REORDER, QUANTITY FELL BELOW ZERO
PART NUMBER   00020

```
00005|5632I
00010|1901{
00014|1000{
00015|3050{
00020|0988Q
00025|6000{
00030|6556H
00035|0990{
00036|0022{
00050|9998I
```

────────OUT-MAS-QTY-ON-HAND
────────OUT-MAS-PART-NO

Note: Letters and special symbols denote signed numbers
(I = +9, { = + 0, Q = −8, H = +8). See page 263.

Figure 13.9   Pseudocode, hierarchy chart, and solution to the Practice Program.

Pseudocode

MAIN-MODULE
START
    PERFORM Initialization-Rtn
    PERFORM Update-Rtn UNTIL no more data
    PERFORM End-of-Job-Rtn
    Stop the Run
STOP

INITIALIZATION-RTN
    Open the Files
    PERFORM Read-Master
    PERFORM Read-Trans

UPDATE-RTN
EVALUATE
    WHEN   In-Old-Part-No = In-Trans-Part-No
           PERFORM Update-Test
    WHEN   In-Old-Part-No > In-Trans-Part-No
           PERFORM Add-Rtn
    WHEN   Other
           PERFORM Write-Old-Rec
END-EVALUATE

UPDATE-TEST
EVALUATE
    WHEN   delete code
           Continue
    WHEN   add-a-record code
           PERFORM Error-Rtn
    WHEN   Other
           PERFORM Update-the-Record
END-EVALUATE

Figure 13.9 (continued)

PERFORM Read-Master
PERFORM Read-Trans

ADD-RTN
    IF   add-a-record code
    THEN
        Write a Master-Record from a Transaction Record
    ELSE
        Write an Error Line
    END-IF
    PERFORM Read-Trans

WRITE-OLD-REC
    Write a New Master Record from Old Master Record
    PERFORM Read-Master

ERROR-RTN
    Write an Error Line

UPDATE-THE-RECORD
    Update the record
    IF   Qty-on-hand < 0
    THEN
        PRINT reorder message
    END-IF

READ-MASTER
    Read a Master Record

READ-TRANS
    Read a Transaction Record

END-OF-JOB-RTN
    Close the files

Hierarchy Chart

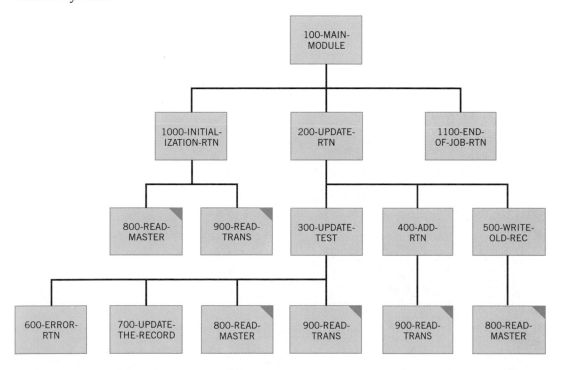

Figure 13.9 (continued)

Program

```
IDENTIFICATION DIVISION.
PROGRAM-ID.  SAMPLE.
AUTHOR. NANCY STERN.
********************************************************************
*  the program updates a master file with a coded transaction   *
*     file, comments are printed with lowercase letters to       *
*     distinguish them from instructions                         *
********************************************************************
ENVIRONMENT DIVISION.
INPUT-OUTPUT SECTION.
FILE-CONTROL.
    SELECT IN-OLD-MASTER  ASSIGN TO DATA13O.
    SELECT IN-TRANSACTION ASSIGN TO DATA13T.
    SELECT OUT-NEW-MASTER ASSIGN TO DATA13N.
DATA DIVISION.
FILE SECTION.
FD   IN-OLD-MASTER
     LABEL RECORDS ARE STANDARD.
01   IN-OLD-REC.
     05  IN-OLD-PART-NO            PIC X(5).
     05  IN-OLD-QTY-ON-HAND        PIC S9(5).
FD   IN-TRANSACTION
     LABEL RECORDS ARE STANDARD.
01   IN-TRANS-REC.
     05   IN-TRANS-PART-NO         PIC X(5).
     05   IN-TRANS-QTY             PIC 9(5).
     05   IN-TRANS-CODE            PIC 9.
         88   DELETE-THE-RECORD                 VALUE 1.
         88   ADD-THE-RECORD                    VALUE 2.
         88   UPDATE-THE-RECORD                 VALUE 3.
FD   OUT-NEW-MASTER
     LABEL RECORDS ARE STANDARD.
01   OUT-NEW-REC.
     05   OUT-MAS-PART-NO          PIC X(5).
     05   OUT-MAS-QTY-ON-HAND      PIC S9(5).
*
PROCEDURE DIVISION.
*************************************************
*  controls the direction of program logic.   *
*************************************************
100-MAIN-MODULE.
    PERFORM 1000-INITIALIZATION-RTN
    PERFORM 200-UPDATE-RTN
        UNTIL IN-OLD-PART-NO = HIGH-VALUES
            AND IN-TRANS-PART-NO = HIGH-VALUES
    PERFORM 1100-END-OF-JOB-RTN
    STOP RUN.
************************************************************
*  performed from 100-main-module. determines input record  *
*  processing path by comparing the master and transaction  *
*  part numbers.                                             *
************************************************************
200-UPDATE-RTN.
    EVALUATE TRUE
        WHEN IN-OLD-PART-NO = IN-TRANS-PART-NO
            PERFORM 300-UPDATE-TEST
        WHEN IN-OLD-PART-NO > IN-TRANS-PART-NO
            PERFORM 400-ADD-RTN
        WHEN OTHER
            PERFORM 500-WRITE-OLD-REC
    END-EVALUATE.
```

Figure 13.9 (continued)

```
*******************************************************************
*  performed from 200-update-rtn, determines transaction code   *
*  and performs appropriate action.                             *
*******************************************************************
   300-UPDATE-TEST.
       EVALUATE TRUE
           WHEN DELETE-THE-RECORD
                CONTINUE
           WHEN ADD-THE-RECORD
                PERFORM 600-ERROR-RTN
           WHEN OTHER
                PERFORM 700-UPDATE-THE-RECORD
       END-EVALUATE
       PERFORM 800-READ-MASTER
       PERFORM 900-READ-TRANS.
***************************************************************
*  performed from 200-update-rtn, adds new transaction to *
*  master file, reads next transaction record.           *
***************************************************************
   400-ADD-RTN.
       IF  ADD-THE-RECORD
           MOVE IN-TRANS-PART-NO TO OUT-MAS-PART-NO
           MOVE IN-TRANS-QTY TO OUT-MAS-QTY-ON-HAND
           WRITE OUT-NEW-REC
       ELSE
           DISPLAY 'ERROR IN CODE, SHOULD BE EQUAL TO 2  ',
                    IN-TRANS-PART-NO
       END-IF
       PERFORM 900-READ-TRANS.
*************************************************************
*  performed from 200-update-rtn and 300-update-test,  *
*  writes old master record to new master file.        *
*************************************************************
   500-WRITE-OLD-REC.
       MOVE IN-OLD-PART-NO TO OUT-MAS-PART-NO
       MOVE IN-OLD-QTY-ON-HAND TO OUT-MAS-QTY-ON-HAND
       WRITE OUT-NEW-REC
       PERFORM 800-READ-MASTER.
*************************************************************
*  performed from 300-update-test, displays error message  *
*************************************************************
   600-ERROR-RTN.
       DISPLAY 'ERROR IN CODE, SHOULD NOT EQUAL 2 ', IN-TRANS-PART-NO.
*****************************************************************************
*  performed from 300-update-test, updates transaction record with  *
*  master record, displays a message if a quantity error occurs.    *
*****************************************************************************
   700-UPDATE-THE-RECORD.
       MOVE IN-TRANS-PART-NO TO OUT-MAS-PART-NO
       COMPUTE OUT-MAS-QTY-ON-HAND = IN-OLD-QTY-ON-HAND - IN-TRANS-QTY
       WRITE OUT-NEW-REC
       IF  OUT-MAS-QTY-ON-HAND IS LESS THAN ZERO
           DISPLAY 'REORDER, QUANTITY FELL BELOW ZERO'
           DISPLAY 'PART NUMBER  ', OUT-MAS-PART-NO
       END-IF.
*********************************************************
*  performed from 300-update-test, 500-write-old-rec, *
*  1000-initialization-rtn.   reads master file       *
*********************************************************
   800-READ-MASTER.
       READ IN-OLD-MASTER
           AT END MOVE HIGH-VALUES TO IN-OLD-PART-NO
       END-READ.
```

Figure 13.9   (continued)

```
***********************************************************
*   performed from 300-update-test, 400-add-rtn,      *
*   1000-initialization-rtn. reads transaction file   *
***********************************************************
    900-READ-TRANS.
        READ IN-TRANSACTION
            AT END MOVE HIGH-VALUES TO IN-TRANS-PART-NO
        END-READ.
***************************************************************************
*   performed from 100-main-module, opens files, performs initial reads *
***************************************************************************
    1000-INITIALIZATION-RTN.
        OPEN INPUT   IN-OLD-MASTER
                     IN-TRANSACTION
             OUTPUT  OUT-NEW-MASTER
        PERFORM 800-READ-MASTER
        PERFORM 900-READ-TRANS.
***********************************************************
*   performed from 100-main-module, closes files         *
***********************************************************
    1100-END-OF-JOB-RTN.
        CLOSE IN-OLD-MASTER
              IN-TRANSACTION
              OUT-NEW-MASTER.
```

REVIEW QUESTIONS

I. True-False
   Questions

_____ 1. Updating is the process of making a file current.

_____ 2. Disk files can only be processed sequentially.

_____ 3. Records on a disk can be any length.

_____ 4. The nested conditional or the EVALUATE (COBOL 85) is used in a sequential update because both of these make it possible to test three separate conditions in a single statement.

_____ 5. When the master file has been completely read and processed during an update procedure, the program should be terminated.

_____ 6. A transaction record with no corresponding master record always means an error.

_____ 7. A REWRITE statement may be used with a file that is opened as an OUTPUT file.

_____ 8. A REWRITE statement may be used with a disk master file.

_____ 9. A file opened as I-O can be read from and written onto.

_____ 10. If a file is opened as EXTEND, it is possible to add records to the end of it.

II. General Questions

1. In an update, describe three different ways that a transaction record might be processed if it is "less than" a master record.

Define the following (2–4):

2. "On demand" output.

3. Key field.

4. Sequential file processing.

III. Validating Data

Modify the Practice Program so that it includes coding to (1) test for all errors and (2) print a control listing of totals (records processed, errors encountered, batch totals).

DEBUGGING EXERCISES   Consider the following procedure in which there can be multiple transaction records per master file. This procedure is somewhat different from the one coded in the chapter, but that does not necessarily make it wrong.

```
100-MAIN-MODULE.
    OPEN INPUT TRANS-FILE
               MASTER-FILE
         OUTPUT MASTER-OUT
                  PRINT-FILE
    READ TRANS-FILE
        AT END MOVE 'NO ' TO RECORDS1
    END-READ
    READ MASTER-FILE
        AT END MOVE 'NO ' TO RECORDS2
    END-READ
    PERFORM 200-COMP-RTN
        UNTIL RECORDS1-OVER AND RECORDS2-OVER
    CLOSE TRANS-FILE
          MASTER-FILE
          MASTER-OUT
          PRINT-FILE
    STOP RUN.
200-COMP-RTN.
    IF ACCT-TRANS = ACCT-MASTER
       PERFORM 300-EQUAL-RTN
    END-IF
    IF ACCT-TRANS < ACCT-MASTER
       PERFORM 400-TRANS-LESS-RTN
    END-IF
    IF ACCT-TRANS > ACCT-MASTER
       PERFORM 500-TRANS-GREATER-RTN
    END-IF.
300-EQUAL-RTN.
    ADD TRANS-AMT TO MASTER-AMT
    READ TRANS-FILE
        AT END MOVE 'NO ' TO RECORDS1
    END-READ.
400-TRANS-LESS-RTN.
    MOVE TRANS-NO TO TRANS-ERR
    WRITE PRINT-REC FROM ERR-REC
    READ TRANS-FILE
        AT END MOVE 'NO ' TO RECORDS1
    END-READ.
500-TRANS-GREATER-RTN.
    WRITE MASTER-REC-OUT FROM MASTER-REC-IN
    READ MASTER-FILE
        AT END MOVE 'NO ' TO RECORDS2
    END-READ.
```

(1) Will this sequence of steps produce the correct results for a multiple transaction update procedure? Explain your answer.

(2) How does the basic logic in this problem differ from the logic used for multiple transaction updates illustrated in the chapter?

(3) This program does not use HIGH-VALUES. Will that cause a logic error? Explain your answer.

(4) Could 300-EQUAL-RTN be eliminated entirely by coding 200-COMP-RTN as follows:

```
200-COMP-RTN.
    IF  ACCT-TRANS = ACCT-MASTER
        ADD TRANS-AMT TO MASTER-AMT
        READ TRANS-FILE AT END
            MOVE 'NO ' TO RECORDS1
        END-READ
    END-IF.
```

PROGRAMMING ASSIGNMENTS

1. Write a program to update a master sales file. The problem definition is shown in Figure 13.10.

Figure 13.10 Problem definition for Programming Assignment 1.

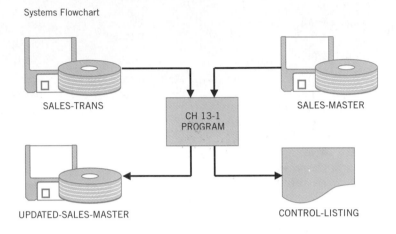

Systems Flowchart

SALES-TRANS → CH 13-1 PROGRAM → SALES-MASTER

UPDATED-SALES-MASTER ← CH 13-1 PROGRAM → CONTROL-LISTING

SALES-TRANS Record Layout			
Field	**Size**	**Type**	**No. of Decimal Positions (if Numeric)**
SALESPERSON-NO	5	Alphanumeric	
SALES	6	Numeric	2
COMMISSION	6	Numeric	2

SALES-MASTER Record Layout (same layout for UPDATED-SALES-MASTER)			
Field	**Size**	**Type**	**No. of Decimal Positions (if Numeric)**
SALESPERSON-NO	5	Alphanumeric	
FILLER	32	Alphanumeric	
YEAR-TO-DATE-FIGURES:			
SALES	6	Numeric	2
COMMISSION	6	Numeric	2
FILLER	6	Alphanumeric	
CURRENT-PERIOD-FIGURES:			
SALES	6	Numeric	2
COMMISSION	6	Numeric	2
FILLER	3	Alphanumeric	

Figure 13.10 (continued)

CONTROL-LISTING Printer Spacing Chart

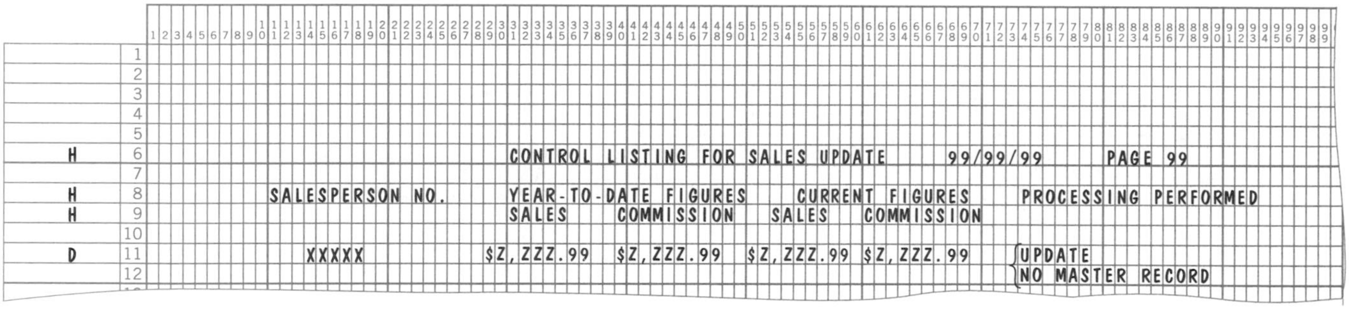

Notes:

a. SALES-MASTER and UPDATED-SALES-MASTER are sequential disk files.

b. For a transaction record that has a corresponding master record (match on salesperson number), add the transaction figures for sales and commission to the corresponding year-to-date figures and the current period figures.

c. For a transaction record that has no corresponding master record, print the transaction record. Do not put the transaction record on the master file.

d. Both files are in salesperson number sequence. Only one transaction per master is permitted.

e. Create a new SALES-MASTER file.

2. Write a program to update a payroll file using the problem definition in Figure 13.11.

Figure 13.11 Problem definition for Programming Assignment 2.

Systems Flowchart

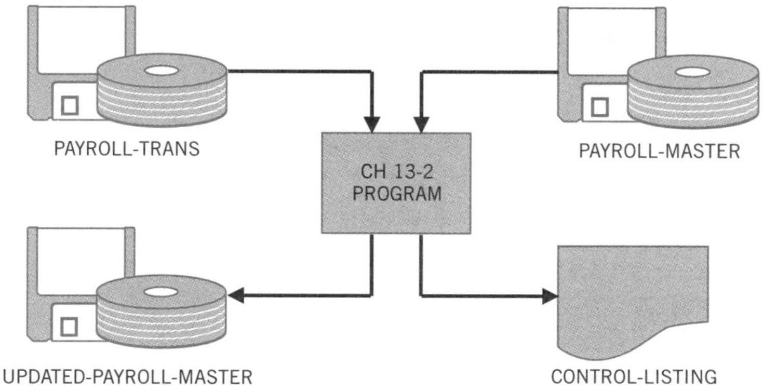

PAYROLL-MASTER **Record Layout** (same layout for PAYROLL-TRANS and UPDATED-PAYROLL-MASTER)			
Field	**Size**	**Type**	**No. of Decimal Positions (if Numeric)**
EMPLOYEE-NO	5	Alphanumeric	
FILLER	24	Alphanumeric	
ANNUAL-SALARY	6	Numeric	0
FILLER	45	Alphanumeric	

Figure 13.11 (continued)

CONTROL-LISTING Printer Spacing Chart

D	6	CONTROL LISTING FOR PAYROLL UPDATE 99/99/99 PAGE 99
H	8	EMPLOYEE NO. PREVIOUS ANNUAL SALARY NEW ANNUAL SALARY ACTION TAKEN
H	10	XXXXX $ZZZ,ZZZ.99 $ZZZ,ZZZ.99 {RECORD UPDATED / NEW RECORD ADDED

Notes:

a. Assume both files are in employee number sequence.

b. For master records with no corresponding transaction records (no match on employee number), create an output record from the input master record.

c. For transaction records with no corresponding master records, create an output record from the input transaction record.

d. For a master record with a corresponding transaction record, take the annual salary from the transaction record and all other data from the master record.

e. Print all updated records for control purposes.

3. Redo Programming Assignment 1 assuming that there may be numerous transactions per master.

4. Redo Programming Assignment 2 assuming that the PAYROLL-TRANS file has the following record description:

```
 1-5  EMPLOYEE-NO-IN
 6-25 EMPLOYEE-NAME-IN
26-27 TERRITORY-NO-IN
28-29 OFFICE-NO-IN
30-35 ANNUAL-SALARY-IN
   36 CODE-X-IN (1 = Delete master; 2 = Add a new record; 3 = Change Name;
                 4 = Change Territory;  5 = Change Office;  6 = Change Salary)
```

PAYROLL-MASTER has the same format for positions 1–35. Update the master assuming that numerous changes per master are possible.

5. Redo Programming Assignment 4 using a REWRITE procedure to update the master file. Assume that records with CODE-X-IN = 2 are errors, since additions get added to the file in a separate procedure.

6. There are two input files, one called MASTER-DEPOSITORS-FILE and the other called WEEKLY-TRANSACTION-FILE, each in sequence by account number and both with the same format:

```
FD  MASTER-DEPOSITORS-FILE
    :
01  MASTER-REC.
    05  ACCT-NO1        PIC 9(5).
    05  OTHER-DATA1     PIC X(70).
FD  WEEKLY-TRANSACTION-FILE
    :
01  TRANS-REC.
    05  ACCT-NO2        PIC 9(5).
    05  OTHER-DATA2     PIC X(70).
```

Each record from the WEEKLY-TRANSACTION-FILE must match a record on the MASTER-DEPOS-ITORS-FILE, although there may be MASTER-REC records with no corresponding TRANS-REC records. Moreover, there may be more than one TRANS-REC record for a given MASTER-REC record.

The output is a merged file that has records from both files in sequence by account number. For an account number with matching records from both files, the MASTER-REC is followed by all TRANS-REC records with the same number.

Example

MASTER-REC	TRANS-REC	MASTER-OUT-REC
00120	00120	00120 M
00124	00120	00120 T
00125	00125	00120 T
00127	00126	00124 M
		00125 M
		00125 T
		00127 M [00126 T is to be printed as an error]

$$M = \text{MASTER-REC record}$$
$$T = \text{TRANS-REC record}$$

Note: Print all merged records in the output file for control purposes.

7. Redo Programming Assignment 1 by opening the master file as I-O and rewriting records.

8. Interactive Processing. Write a program that adds records interactively to the end of a master sequential disk file. The file, with the following format, should be opened in EXTEND mode:

```
1-5    ACCT-NO
6-10   BAL-DUE (999V99)
```

Make sure that the records being added are in sequence and have ACCT-NOs greater than the last one on the current master file.

9. Maintenance Program. Modify the Practice Program in this chapter to allow for multiple transaction records per master.

CHAPTER 14

Sorting and Merging

■ OBJECTIVES

To familiarize you with

1. How files may be sorted within a COBOL program.
2. How to process a file during a SORT procedure before it is actually sorted.
3. How to process a file during a SORT procedure after it is sorted but before it is created as output.
4. How to use the MERGE verb for merging files.

■ CONTENTS

THE SORT FEATURE: AN OVERVIEW

FORMAT OF THE SORT STATEMENT

Records in files frequently must be sorted into specific sequences for updating, answering inquiries, or generating reports. A master payroll file, for example, might be updated in Social Security number sequence while paychecks produced from the file may be needed in alphabetic order. *Sorting* is a common procedure used for arranging records into a specific order so that sequential processing can be performed.

There are two techniques used for sorting files processed by COBOL programs. One is to use either a utility or a database management system's sort program. These sort programs are completely separate from, or external to, the COBOL program and would be executed first if records needed to be in a sequence other than the sequence in which they were created. For these types of sort programs, you would simply indicate which key fields to sort on.

As an alternative, COBOL has a SORT verb, which enables you to sort a file as part of a COBOL program. Often, a COBOL program will SORT a file prior to processing it.

A simplified format for the **SORT** statement in COBOL is as follows:

Simplified Format

$$
\begin{array}{l}
\underline{\text{SORT}}\ \text{file-name-1} \\[4pt]
\left\{ \text{ON}\ \left\{ \begin{array}{l} \underline{\text{DESCENDING}} \\ \underline{\text{ASCENDING}} \end{array} \right\}\ \text{KEY data-name-1} \right\}\ \dots \\[4pt]
\underline{\text{USING}}\ \text{file-name-2} \\
\underline{\text{GIVING}}\ \text{file-name-3}
\end{array}
$$

ASCENDING OR DESCENDING KEY

The programmer must specify whether the key field is to be an ASCENDING KEY or a DESCENDING KEY, depending on which sequence is required:

(1) ASCENDING: From lowest to highest.
(2) DESCENDING: From highest to lowest.

Sorting a file into ascending CUST-NO sequence, for example, where CUST-NO is defined with PIC 9(3) would result in the following order: 001, 002, 003, and so on. The SORT can also be performed on nonconsecutive key fields. That is, records 009, 016, and 152 are sorted into their proper sequence even though they are not consecutive. Suppose several records had the same CUST-NO; *all* CUST-NO 01 records would precede records with CUST-NO 02, and so on, if ascending sequence were specified.

A file can also be sorted into descending sequence where a key field of 99, for example, precedes 98, and so on.

Records may be sorted using either numeric or nonnumeric key fields. Ascending sequence used with an alphabetic field will cause sorting from A–Z, and descending sequence will cause sorting from Z–A.

Collating Sequence

As indicated in Chapter 8, the two major codes used for representing data in a computer are **EBCDIC** (an abbreviation for Extended Binary Coded Decimal Interchange Code), primarily used on mainframes, and **ASCII** (an abbreviation for American Standard Code for Information Interchange), widely used on PCs.

The sequencing of characters from lowest to highest, which is referred to as the **collating sequence**, is somewhat different in EBCDIC and ASCII:

	EBCDIC	ASCII
Lowest	ƀ	ƀ
	Special characters	Special characters
	Lowercase letters a-z	Integers 0-9
	Uppercase letters A-Z	Special characters
	Integers 0-9	Uppercase letters A-Z
Highest		Lowercase letters a-z

We have not included the collating sequence for the individual special characters here because we rarely sort on special characters. See Appendix A for the collating sequence of all characters.

Basic numeric sorting and basic alphabetic sorting are performed the same way in EBCDIC and ASCII. These codes are, however, not the same when alphanumeric fields containing both letters and digits or special characters are sorted. Letters are considered "less than" numbers in EBCDIC, and letters are considered "greater than" numbers in ASCII. Moreover, lowercase letters are considered "less than" uppercase letters in EBCDIC and "greater than" uppercase letters in ASCII.

Thus, an ASCII computer could sort data into a different sequence than an EBCDIC computer if an alphanumeric field is being sorted or if a combination of upper- and lowercase letters is used. "Box 891" will appear before "111 Main St." in an address field on EBCDIC computers, for example, but will appear *after* it on ASCII computers. Similarly, "abc" is less than "ABC" on EBCDIC computers whereas the reverse is true of ASCII computers.

Sequencing Records with More Than One SORT Key

The SORT verb may be used to sequence records *with more than one key field*. Suppose that we wish to sort a payroll file so that it is in ascending alphabetic sequence by name, within each level, for each office. That is:

Office number is the major sort field.
Level number is the intermediate sort field.
Name is the minor sort field.

Thus for Office 1, we want the following sequence:

```
OFFICE-NO     LEVEL-NO          NAME
    1             1         ADAMS, J. R.
    1             1         BROCK, P. T.
    1             1         LEE, S.
    1             2         ARTHUR, Q. C.
    1             2         SHAH, J.
    1             3         RAMIREZ, A. P.
    ⋮             ⋮            ⋮
```

For Office Number 1, Level 1, all entries are in uppercase alphabetic order. These are followed by Office Number 1, Level 2 entries, in alphabetic order, and so on.

We may use a *single* SORT procedure to perform this sequencing. The first KEY field indicated is the *major* field to be sorted, the next KEY fields represent *intermediate* sort fields, followed by *minor* sort fields.

The following is a SORT statement that sorts records into ascending alphabetic NAME sequence within LEVEL-NO within OFFICE-NO:

```
SORT SORT-FILE
    ON ASCENDING KEY OFFICE-NO
    ON ASCENDING KEY LEVEL-NO
    ON ASCENDING KEY NAME
        USING PAYROLL-FILE-IN
        GIVING SORTED-PAYROLL-FILE-OUT
```

Because all key fields are independent, some key fields can be sorted in ASCENDING sequence and others in DESCENDING sequence. Note too that the words ON and KEY were *not* underlined in the instruction format, which means that they are optional words. If all key fields are to be sorted in ascending sequence, as in the preceding, we can condense the coding by using the phrase ON ASCENDING KEY only once. For example:

```
SORT SORT-FILE
    ON ASCENDING KEY MAJOR-KEY
                     INTERMEDIATE-KEY
                     MINOR-KEY
    ⋮
```

With COBOL 74, if two or more records have the same value in the sort field (e.g., DEPT 01 in two or more records), you cannot predict which will appear first in the sorted file. With COBOL 85 you can request the computer to put such records into the sort file *in the same order* that they appeared in the original input file. We add the WITH DUPLICATES IN ORDER clause to accomplish this:

```
SORT ...
    ON ASCENDING KEY ...
    WITH DUPLICATES IN ORDER
        USING ...
        GIVING ...
```

This means that if both the 106th record and the 428th record in the input file, for example, had DEPT-NO 1 where DEPT-NO is the sort field, then record 106 would appear first in the sorted file. This is called the first in, first out (**FIFO**) principle.

CODING A SIMPLE SORT PROCEDURE WITH THE USING AND GIVING OPTIONS

There are three major files used in a sort:

FILES USED IN A SORT

1. Input file: File of unsorted input records.

2. Work or sort file: File used to store records temporarily during the sorting process.

3. Output file: File of sorted output records.

All these files would be defined in the ENVIRONMENT DIVISION using standard ASSIGN clauses, which are system dependent. Note, however, that a sort file is usually assigned to a special work device, indicated as SYSWORK in the following:

```
SELECT UNSORTED-MASTER-FILE ASSIGN TO DISK1.
SELECT SORT-FILE ASSIGN TO SYSWORK.
SELECT SORTED-MASTER-FILE ASSIGN TO DISK2.
```

Your system may use SYSWORK or some other special name in the ASSIGN clause for the work or sort file. The SORT-FILE is actually assigned to a temporary work area that is used during processing but not saved. Only the unsorted disk file and the sorted output disk file are assigned standard file-names so that they can be permanently stored.

FDs are used in the DATA DIVISION to define and describe the input and output files in the usual way. The sort or work file is described with an SD entry (which is an abbreviation for *sort file description*). The only difference between SD and FD entries is that an SD must *not* have a LABEL RECORDS clause. Note, too, that the field(s) specified as the KEY field(s) for sorting purposes must be defined *as part of the sort record format*.

In the following, the field to be sorted is S-DEPT-NO within the SD file called SORT-FILE:

```
DATA DIVISION.
FILE SECTION.
FD  UNSORTED-MASTER-FILE
    LABEL RECORDS ARE STANDARD.
01  UNSORTED-REC                      PIC X(80).
**********************************************************
SD  SORT-FILE.         ◄──────────────────────────────────  Note that SORT-FILE is defined with
01  SORT-REC.                                                an SD and has no LABEL RECORDS
    05  S-DEPT-NO                     PIC XX.                clause
    05  FILLER                        PIC X(78).
**********************************************************
FD  SORTED-MASTER-FILE
    LABEL RECORDS ARE STANDARD.
01  SORTED-REC                        PIC X(80).
```

The SORT procedure would then be coded as follows:

```
SORT  SORT-FILE
    ON ASCENDING KEY S-DEPT-NO   ◄────────  Defined within the SD file
    USING UNSORTED-MASTER-FILE
    GIVING SORTED-MASTER-FILE
STOP RUN.
```

The only field descriptions required in the SORT record format are the ones used for sorting purposes. In this instance, only the S-DEPT-NO must be defined as part of the SD, since that is the only key field to be used for sorting.

In summary, the SORTED-MASTER-FILE would contain records with the same format as UNSORTED-MASTER-FILE, but the records would be placed in the sorted master file in department number sequence.

A SORT procedure can also *precede* an update or control break procedure *within the same program*. That is, where a file must be in a specific sequence, we can sort it first and then proceed with the required processing. In this case, the file defined in the GIVING clause would be opened as input, after it has been created as a sorted file:

```
PROCEDURE DIVISION.
100-MAIN-MODULE.
    SORT SORT-FILE
        ON ASCENDING KEY TERR
            USING UNSORTED-MASTER-FILE
            GIVING SORTED-MASTER-FILE
    OPEN INPUT SORTED-MASTER-FILE
         OUTPUT CONTROL-REPORT
    PERFORM UNTIL ARE-THERE-MORE-RECORDS = 'NO '
        READ SORTED-MASTER-FILE
            AT END
                MOVE 'NO ' TO ARE-THERE-MORE-RECORDS
            NOT AT END
                PERFORM 200-PROCESS-RTN
        END-READ
    END-PERFORM
        :
        :
```

Standard processing { (bracket spanning from OPEN INPUT to END-PERFORM)

SELF-TEST

1. Suppose we want EMPLOYEE-FILE records in alphabetic order by NAME within DISTRICT within TERRITORY, all in ascending sequence. The output file is called SORTED-EMPLOYEE-FILE. Complete the following SORT statement:

   ```
   SORT  WORK-FILE ...
   ```

2. How many files are required in a SORT routine? Describe these files.

3. The work or sort file is defined as an _____ in the DATA DIVISION.

4. Suppose we have an FD called NET-FILE-IN, an SD called NET-FILE, and an FD called

NET-FILE-OUT. We want NET-FILE-OUT sorted into ascending DEPT-NO sequence. Code the PROCEDURE DIVISION entry.

5. In Question 4, DEPT-NO must be a field defined within the (SD/FD) file.

Solutions

1. ON ASCENDING KEY TERRITORY
   ON ASCENDING KEY DISTRICT
   ON ASCENDING KEY NAME
       USING EMPLOYEE-FILE
       GIVING SORTED-EMPLOYEE-FILE

2. three; input—unsorted; work or sort file—temporary; output—sorted

3. SD

4. SORT   NET-FILE
       ON ASCENDING KEY DEPT-NO
           USING NET-FILE-IN
           GIVING NET-FILE-OUT

5. SD

PROCESSING DATA BEFORE AND/OR AFTER SORTING

Consider the following SORT statement:

```
SORT   SORT-FILE
    ON ASCENDING KEY TERR
        USING IN-FILE
        GIVING SORTED-MSTR
```

This statement performs the following operations:

1. Opens IN-FILE and SORTED-MSTR.
2. Moves IN-FILE records to the SORT-FILE.
3. Sorts SORT-FILE into ascending sequence by TERR, which is a field defined as part of the SD SORT-FILE record.
4. Moves the sorted SORT-FILE to the output file called SORTED-MSTR.
5. Closes IN-FILE and SORTED-MSTR after all records have been processed.

The SORT statement can, however, be used in conjunction with procedures that process records *before they are sorted* and/or process records *after they are sorted*.

INPUT PROCEDURE

In this section, we focus on the use of the SORT statement to perform some processing of incoming records just before they are sorted. This is accomplished with an **INPUT PROCEDURE** clause *in place of* the USING clause.

Expanded Format

SORT file-name-1

$\left\{ \text{ON} \left\{ \begin{array}{l} \underline{\text{ASCENDING}} \\ \underline{\text{DESCENDING}} \end{array} \right\} \text{KEY data-name-1} \ldots \right\} \ldots$

$\left\{ \begin{array}{l} \underline{\text{INPUT}} \ \underline{\text{PROCEDURE}} \ \text{IS procedure-name-1} \left[\left\{ \begin{array}{l} \underline{\text{THRU}} \\ \underline{\text{THROUGH}} \end{array} \right\} \text{procedure-name-2} \right] \\ \underline{\text{USING}} \ \text{file-name-2} \ldots \end{array} \right\}$

$\underline{\text{GIVING}}$ file-name-3

The INPUT PROCEDURE processes data from the incoming file *prior* to sorting. We may wish to use an INPUT PROCEDURE, for example, to perform the following operations prior to sorting: (1) validate data in the input records, (2) eliminate records with blank fields, (3) remove unneeded fields from the input records, and (4) count input records.

Example 1 We will code a SORT routine that eliminates records with a quantity field equal to zero *before sorting*. The test for zero quantity will be performed in an INPUT PROCEDURE. Consider the first three DIVISIONs of the COBOL program:

```
IDENTIFICATION DIVISION.
PROGRAM-ID. SORT-IT.
*
ENVIRONMENT DIVISION.
INPUT-OUTPUT SECTION.
FILE-CONTROL.
    SELECT IN-FILE ASSIGN TO DISK 'DISK1'.
    SELECT SORT-FILE ASSIGN TO DISK 'WORK1'.
    SELECT SORTED-MSTR ASSIGN TO DISK 'DISK2'.
*
DATA DIVISION.
FILE SECTION.
FD  IN-FILE
    LABEL RECORDS ARE STANDARD.
01  IN-REC.
    05              PIC X(25).
    05  QTY         PIC 9(5).  ◄──Needed for INPUT PROCEDURE section
    05              PIC X(70).
SD  SORT-FILE.
01  SORT-REC.
    05  TERR        PIC X(5).  ◄──Needed for ASCENDING KEY clause
    05              PIC X(95).
FD  SORTED-MSTR
    LABEL RECORDS ARE STANDARD.
01  SORTED-MSTR-REC PIC X(100).
```

INPUT PROCEDUREs are coded in an easier and more structured way with COBOL 85. We discuss here techniques used for both COBOL 85 and COBOL 74.

With COBOL 85, procedure-names used with INPUT PROCEDURE can be regular paragraphs. Thus, we can code:

```
100-MAIN-MODULE.
    SORT  SORT-FILE
            ON ASCENDING KEY TERR
                INPUT PROCEDURE 200-TEST-IT
                GIVING SORTED-MSTR
    STOP RUN.
200-TEST-IT.
    OPEN INPUT IN-FILE
    PERFORM UNTIL ARE-THERE-MORE-RECORDS = 'NO '
        READ IN-FILE
            AT END
                MOVE 'NO ' TO ARE-THERE-MORE-RECORDS
            NOT AT END
                PERFORM 300-PROCESS-RTN
        END-READ
    END-PERFORM
    CLOSE IN-FILE.
300-PROCESS-RTN.
    IF  QTY = ZEROS
        CONTINUE
    ELSE
        MOVE IN-REC TO SORT-REC
        RELEASE SORT-REC    ◄────────Writes the record onto the sort file
    END-IF.
```

The 200-TEST-IT paragraph must:

1. Open the input file. (With a USING option instead of the INPUT PROCEDURE, the input file is automatically opened by the SORT verb.)
2. Perform some processing of input records until there is no more data.
3. Close the input file.

The processing performed at 200-TEST-IT may be executed with an in-line PERFORM. In 300-PROCESS-RTN, for all records with a nonzero QTY, the input fields are moved to the sort record. We do not WRITE records to be sorted; instead, we **RELEASE** them for sorting purposes. We must release records to the sort file in an INPUT PROCEDURE. With a USING option, this is done for us automatically.

Note that the RELEASE verb is followed by a record-name, just like the WRITE statement. Note, too, that RELEASE SORT-REC FROM IN-REC can be substituted for:

```
MOVE IN-REC TO SORT-REC
RELEASE SORT-REC
```

That is, the RELEASE verb functions just like a WRITE but is used to output sort records.

For COBOL 85 users, you can skip the following section, which applies only to COBOL 74 users.

With COBOL 74, the coding is more complex because the procedure-name of an INPUT PROCEDURE must be a section-name and not a paragraph-name. A **section** is a series of PROCEDURE DIVISION paragraphs that is treated as a single entity or unit. Rules for forming section-names are the same as rules for forming paragraph-names. The word SECTION, however, follows a section-name (e.g., A000-ERROR SECTION). The end of a section is recognized when another section-name is encountered, or when the end of the program is reached.

The INPUT PROCEDURE identifies a separate section in which the test for zero will be performed:

```
            SORT  SORT-FILE
               ON ASCENDING KEY TERR
               INPUT PROCEDURE A000-TEST-IT  ◄──── This must be a section
               GIVING SORTED-MSTR.                 with COBOL 74
            STOP RUN.
         A000-TEST-IT SECTION.
         A100-PARA-1.
              ⋮
              ⋮
```

In this section we code the instructions that eliminate records with a zero quantity field

A section-name must conform to the rules for forming paragraph-names. The COBOL reserved word SECTION follows the actual section-name. In the preceding, A000-TEST-IT SECTION will be executed first, *before the input file is sorted*. Then the input file will be sorted in the main module, producing a sorted file called SORTED-MSTR. After the sorted records have been created as output, the STOP RUN is executed, terminating the program run.

More About Sections and Naming Conventions

A procedure may be a paragraph or section in the PROCEDURE DIVISION. In all programs thus far, we have used paragraphs as procedures. In this chapter we discuss sections *that can consist of one or more paragraphs*. The PROCEDURE DIVISION, then, can be divided into individual paragraphs or into sections, where each section contains one or more paragraphs.

With COBOL 74, the clause INPUT PROCEDURE IS procedure-name-1 *must refer to a section*. With COBOL 85, this INPUT PROCEDURE may reference either a section or a paragraph. With COBOL 85, using a paragraph-name as in Example 1 results in less complex programs that are better structured.

Naming Procedures

When a program is subdivided into sections, we will use a more detailed numbering convention for prefixes of paragraphs. This convention will highlight the fact that specific paragraphs are located within particular sections. A `SECTION` named `A000` or with a prefix of `A000-` will be followed by a paragraph with a prefix of `A100-`, `A200-`, and so on, with the letter `A` designating the first `SECTION`.

Example

```
PROCEDURE DIVISION.
A000 SECTION.
A100-PARA-1.
        :
A200-PARA-2.
        :

B000 SECTION.
B100-PARA-1.
        :
B200-PARA-2.
        :
```

The `A000 SECTION` has paragraphs with prefixes of `A100`, `A200`, and so on. Similarly, a section called `A000-REARRANGE SECTION` can be followed by a paragraph called `A100-HSKPG-RTN`, then an `A200-PROCESS-RTN` paragraph, and so on.

Another naming convention is to use four digits, with no letters, as a numeric prefix. Sections could have prefixes `0000-`, `1000-`, `2000-`, and so on. Paragraphs within section `0000-` would have a prefix of `0100-`, `0200-`, and so on. These are just two of the conventions you could adopt for prefixes of procedure names.

As noted, in our example we wish to sort only those input records that have a non-zero quantity. For COBOL 74, the coding required within the section specified by the `INPUT PROCEDURE` section-name includes the following instructions:

```
        :
SORT    SORT-FILE
        ON ASCENDING KEY TERR
        INPUT PROCEDURE  A000-TEST-IT
        GIVING SORTED-MSTR.
STOP RUN.
A000-TEST-IT SECTION.
A100-PARA-1.  ◄───────────────────  ⎰On many systems, a paragraph-name must
                                     ⎱follow a section-name
    OPEN INPUT IN-FILE.
    READ IN-FILE
        AT END MOVE 'NO ' TO ARE-THERE-MORE-RECORDS.
    PERFORM A200-TEST-RTN
        UNTIL THERE-ARE-NO-MORE-RECORDS.
    CLOSE IN-FILE.
    GO TO A300-TEST-IT-EXIT.
A200-TEST-RTN.
    IF  QTY = ZEROS
        NEXT SENTENCE
    ELSE
        MOVE IN-REC TO SORT-REC
        RELEASE SORT-REC.  ◄──── Writes the record onto the sort file
    READ IN-FILE
        AT END MOVE 'NO ' TO ARE-THERE-MORE-RECORDS.
A300-TEST-IT-EXIT.  ⎰The last coded statement in the section must
    EXIT.  ◄────────⎱be the last statement executed
```

The first paragraph within `A000-TEST-IT SECTION` functions like a main module. It opens the input file, performs an initial read, continually executes a paragraph that processes records until there is no more input, and closes the input file after all records have been processed.

A200-TEST-RTN within A000-TEST-IT SECTION is the paragraph that processes input records. Records with nonzero quantities are released to the sort file in this paragraph.

Keep in mind that when using an INPUT PROCEDURE with COBOL 74 we divide our program into sections:

1. The first section in the PROCEDURE DIVISION contains the SORT instruction, any processing to be performed before or after the SORT verb is executed, and a STOP RUN.

2. The second section begins with the main module of the INPUT PROCEDURE. It opens the input file, reads the first record, and then performs a process routine (in a separate paragraph within this second section) until there is no more data.

3. After the separate paragraph is executed until ARE-THERE-MORE-RECORDS = 'NO ', control returns to the main module of the second section (A100-PARA-1 above). The input file is then closed. In order for this section to be terminated, control must pass to the *last statement* within the section. This means that a GO TO is required. We code GO TO A300-TEST-IT-EXIT as the last sentence. Since no operations are required in this last paragraph, EXIT is coded, which passes control back to the SORT statement, where the file is then sorted.

Regardless of whether you are using COBOL 85 or COBOL 74, an INPUT PROCEDURE opens the input file, processes input records, and releases them to the sort file. After all input records are processed, the input file is closed. The format for the RELEASE is:

Format

$$\underline{\text{RELEASE}} \text{ sort-record-name-1}$$
$$[\underline{\text{FROM}} \text{ identifier-1}]$$

The RELEASE is the verb used to write records to a sort file.

Examples

```
MOVE IN-REC TO SORT-REC
RELEASE SORT-REC.
```
or
```
RELEASE SORT-REC FROM IN-REC.  ◄——Functions like a
                                    WRITE ... FROM
```

INPUT PROCEDURE SUMMARY (COBOL 85)

1. The INPUT PROCEDURE of the SORT should refer to a paragraph-name but it could refer to a section-name.

   Example
   ```
   100-MAIN-MODULE.
       SORT WORK-FILE
           INPUT PROCEDURE 200-PRIOR-TO-SORT-MAIN-MODULE
           GIVING SORT-FILE
       STOP RUN.
   200-PRIOR-TO-SORT-MAIN-MODULE.
       ⋮
   ```

2. In the paragraph specified in the INPUT PROCEDURE:
   a. OPEN the input file.
   b. PERFORM a paragraph that will read and process input records until there is no more data.
   c. After all records have been processed, close the input file.

d. After the last sentence in the INPUT PROCEDURE paragraph is executed, control will then return to the SORT.

Example

```
200-PRIOR-TO-SORT-MAIN-MODULE.
    OPEN INPUT IN-FILE
    PERFORM UNTIL NO-MORE-RECS
        READ IN-FILE
            AT END
                MOVE 'NO ' TO MORE-RECS
            NOT AT END
                PERFORM 300-PROCESS-INPUT-RECS
        END-READ
    END-PERFORM
    CLOSE IN-FILE.
```

3. At the paragraph that processes input records prior to sorting:
   a. Perform any operations on input that are required.
   b. MOVE input data to the sort record.
   c. RELEASE each sort record, which makes it available for sorting.
   d. Continue to read input until there is no more data.

Example

```
300-PROCESS-INPUT-RECS.
    :                          {Process input records
    MOVE IN-REC TO SORT-REC }  Can be coded as:
    RELEASE SORT-REC.       }  RELEASE SORT-REC FROM IN-REC
```

INPUT PROCEDURE SUMMARY: COBOL 74

1. The entire program should consist of sections. Each section is followed by a paragraph-name. The INPUT PROCEDURE of the SORT refers to a section-name followed by a paragraph-name.

Example

```
A100-MAIN SECTION.    {Start the program with a section-name
A100-MAIN-MODULE.     {followed by a paragraph-name
    SORT WORK-FILE
        INPUT PROCEDURE A200-PRIOR-TO-SORT
        GIVING SORTED-FILE.
    STOP RUN.
A200-PRIOR-TO-SORT SECTION.              {Section-names are
A200-PRIOR-TO-SORT-MAIN-MODULE.          {followed by paragraph-
    :                                    {names
```

2. In the main paragraph of the section specified in the INPUT PROCEDURE:
   a. OPEN the input file.
   b. READ an initial record from the input file.
   c. PERFORM a paragraph within the INPUT PROCEDURE section that will process input records, release them to the sort file, and continue to read records until there is no more data.
   d. After all records have been processed CLOSE the input file.
   e. With COBOL 74, in order for the INPUT PROCEDURE to be terminated, the last statement in the last paragraph of the section must be executed. We must use a GO TO for branching to the paragraph that contains this last statement.

Example

```
A200-PRIOR-TO-SORT SECTION.
A200-PRIOR-TO-SORT-MAIN-MODULE.
    OPEN INPUT IN-FILE.
    READ IN-FILE
        AT END MOVE 'NO ' TO MORE-RECS.
    PERFORM A200-PROCESS-INPUT-RECS
        UNTIL NO-MORE-RECS.
    CLOSE IN-FILE.
    GO TO A200-END-OF-SECTION.
```

3. At the paragraph within the INPUT PROCEDURE section that processes input records prior to sorting:
   a. Perform any operations on input that are required.
   b. MOVE input data to the sort record.
   c. RELEASE each sort record, which writes the record to the sort file. This RELEASE makes the record available for sorting. RELEASE ... FROM ... can be used in place of a MOVE and RELEASE.
   d. Continue to read and process input until there is no more data.

Example

```
A200-PROCESS-INPUT-RECS.
    :                        {Process input records
    MOVE IN-REC TO SORT-REC. ⎫ Can be coded as:
    RELEASE SORT-REC.        ⎭ RELEASE SORT-REC FROM IN-REC
    READ IN-FILE
        AT END MOVE 'NO ' TO MORE-RECS.
```

4. As noted, the paragraph located physically at the end of the INPUT PROCEDURE section must be the last one executed with COBOL 74. Hence a GO TO in the section's main module is required to transfer control to this last paragraph. If no processing is required, code an EXIT statement as the only entry in this last paragraph of the section.

Example

```
A100-MAIN SECTION.
A100-MAIN-MODULE.
    SORT WORK-FILE
        INPUT PROCEDURE A200-PRIOR-TO-SORT
        GIVING SORTED-FILE.
    STOP RUN.
A200-PRIOR-TO-SORT SECTION.
A200-PRIOR-TO-SORT-MAIN-MODULE.
    :
    :
    GO TO A200-END-OF-SECTION.
A200-PROCESS-INPUT-RECS.
    :
    :
A200-END-OF-SECTION.
    EXIT. ◄——Must be the only entry in the paragraph
              for COBOL 74
```

Figure 14.1 illustrates both a full COBOL 85 program with an INPUT PROCEDURE and a full COBOL 74 program with an INPUT PROCEDURE. The INPUT PROCEDURE increases each employee's salary by 10% before sorting the file into alphabetic sequence by name.

Note that some enhanced versions of COBOL 74 are like COBOL 85 in that they permit you to use paragraph-names in place of section-names in an INPUT PROCEDURE.

Figure 14.1 Sample Problem using an INPUT PROCEDURE (COBOL 85 and COBOL 74).

The first three DIVISIONS

```
IDENTIFICATION DIVISION.
PROGRAM-ID. SORTPROG.
ENVIRONMENT DIVISION.
INPUT-OUTPUT SECTION.
FILE-CONTROL.
    SELECT SAL-FILE    ASSIGN TO DISK1.
    SELECT WORK-FILE    ASSIGN TO DISC.
    SELECT SORTED-FILE ASSIGN TO DISK2.
DATA DIVISION.
FILE SECTION.
FD  SAL-FILE
    LABEL RECORDS ARE STANDARD.
01  SAL-REC                    PIC X(28).
SD  WORK-FILE.
01  SORT-REC.
    05  S-DEPT-NO              PIC XX.
    05  S-NAME                 PIC X(20).
    05  S-SALARY               PIC 9(6).
FD  SORTED-FILE
    LABEL RECORDS ARE STANDARD.
01  SORTED-REC                 PIC X(28).
WORKING-STORAGE SECTION.
01  MORE-RECS                  PIC X(3)    VALUE 'YES'.
    88 NO-MORE-RECS                        VALUE 'NO '.
```

COBOL 85

```
PROCEDURE DIVISION.
100-MAIN-MODULE.
    SORT WORK-FILE
        ASCENDING KEY S-NAME
        INPUT PROCEDURE
            200-SALARY-INCREASE
        GIVING SORTED-FILE
    STOP RUN.
200-SALARY-INCREASE.
    OPEN INPUT SAL-FILE
    PERFORM UNTIL NO-MORE-RECS
        READ SAL-FILE
            AT END
                MOVE 'NO ' TO MORE-RECS
            NOT AT END
                PERFORM 300-SALARY-UPDATE
        END-READ
    END-PERFORM
    CLOSE SAL-FILE.
300-SALARY-UPDATE.
    MOVE SAL-REC TO SORT-REC
    COMPUTE S-SALARY =
        S-SALARY * 1.10
    RELEASE SORT-REC.
```

COBOL 74

```
PROCEDURE DIVISION.
A000-MAIN SECTION.
A000-MAIN-MODULE.
    SORT WORK-FILE
        ASCENDING KEY S-NAME
        INPUT PROCEDURE
            A100-SALARY
        GIVING SORTED-FILE.
    STOP RUN.
A100-SALARY SECTION.
A100-SALARY-INCREASE.
    OPEN INPUT SAL-FILE.
    READ SAL-FILE
        AT END
            MOVE 'NO ' TO MORE-RECS.
    PERFORM A100-SALARY-UPDATE
        UNTIL NO-MORE-RECS.
    CLOSE SAL-FILE.
    GO TO A100-END-OF-SECTION.
A100-SALARY-UPDATE.
    MOVE SAL-REC TO SORT-REC.
    COMPUTE S-SALARY =
        S-SALARY * 1.10.
    RELEASE SORT-REC.
    READ SAL-FILE
        AT END
            MOVE 'NO ' TO MORE-RECS.
A100-END-OF-SECTION.
    EXIT.
```

This not only makes programming easier but it eliminates the need for GO TOs.

Note, too, that we never OPEN or CLOSE the sort file-name specified in the SD. It is always opened and closed automatically, as are files specified with USING or GIVING. Only the input file processed in an INPUT PROCEDURE needs to be opened and closed by the program. In the next section, we will see that output files processed in an OUTPUT PROCEDURE must also be opened and closed by the programmer.

SELF-TEST The following illustrates the problem definition for a program that is to sort a disk file. Note that the format of the sorted file called SORTED-FILE will be *different* from that of the incoming UNSORTED-FILE:

UNSORTED-FILE Record Layout (Input)		
Field	**Size**	**Type**
PART-NO-IN	5	Alphanumeric
QTY-IN	5	Alphanumeric
DEPT-IN	2	Alphanumeric

SORTED-FILE Record Layout (Output)		
Field	**Size**	**Type**
DEPT-OUT	2	Alphanumeric
PART-NO-OUT	5	Alphanumeric
QTY-OUT	5	Alphanumeric

Notes
1. Sort into Department Number Sequence.
2. Sorted output will have a different format than input.

Consider the following FILE SECTION:

```
DATA DIVISION.
FILE SECTION.
FD  UNSORTED-FILE
    LABEL RECORDS ARE STANDARD.
01  REC-1.
    05  PART-NO-IN          PIC X(5).
    05  QTY-IN              PIC X(5).
    05  DEPT-IN             PIC X(2).
SD  SORT-FILE.
01  SORT-REC.
    05  S-DEPT              PIC X(2).
    05  S-PART-NO           PIC X(5).
    05  S-QTY               PIC X(5).
FD  SORTED-FILE
    LABEL RECORDS ARE STANDARD.
01  REC-2                   PIC X(12).
```

1. (T or F) It would be possible, although inefficient, to (1) first sort the input and produce a sorted master, and (2) then code a separate module to read from the sorted master, moving the data in a rearranged format to a new sorted master.
2. (T or F) It would be more efficient to use an INPUT PROCEDURE for this problem.
3. Code the SORT statement.
4. Code the INPUT PROCEDURE SECTION assuming that you are using a COBOL 85 compiler.
5. Code the INPUT PROCEDURE SECTION assuming that you are using a COBOL 74 compiler.

Solutions

1. T
2. T
3.
```
SORT  SORT-FILE
    ON ASCENDING KEY S-DEPT
    INPUT PROCEDURE A000-REARRANGE
    GIVING SORTED-FILE
STOP RUN.
        ⋮
        ⋮
```

```
4. A000-REARRANGE.
      OPEN INPUT UNSORTED-FILE
      PERFORM UNTIL NO-MORE-RECORDS
           READ UNSORTED-FILE
                AT END
                     MOVE 'NO ' TO ARE-THERE-MORE-RECORDS
                NOT AT END
                     PERFORM A200-PROCESS-RTN
           END-READ
      END-PERFORM
      CLOSE UNSORTED-FILE.
   A200-PROCESS-RTN.
      MOVE PART-NO-IN TO S-PART-NO
      MOVE QTY-IN TO S-QTY
      MOVE DEPT-IN TO S-DEPT
      RELEASE SORT-REC.
5. A000-REARRANGE SECTION.
   A100-PARA-1.
      OPEN INPUT UNSORTED-FILE.
      READ UNSORTED-FILE
           AT END MOVE 'NO ' TO ARE-THERE-MORE-RECORDS.
      PERFORM A200-PROCESS-RTN
           UNTIL NO-MORE-RECORDS.
      CLOSE UNSORTED-FILE.
      GO TO A300-END-OF-SECTION.
   A200-PROCESS-RTN.
      MOVE PART-NO-IN TO S-PART-NO.
      MOVE QTY-IN TO S-QTY.
      MOVE DEPT-IN TO S-DEPT.
      RELEASE SORT-REC.
      READ UNSORTED-FILE
           AT END MOVE 'NO ' TO ARE-THERE-MORE-RECORDS.
   A300-END-OF-SECTION.
      EXIT.
```

OUTPUT PROCEDURE

After records have been sorted, they are placed in the sort file in the sequence required. If the GIVING option is used, then the sorted records are automatically written onto the output file after they are sorted.

We may, however, wish to process the sorted records *prior* to, or perhaps even instead of, placing them in the output file. We would then use an OUTPUT PROCEDURE instead of the GIVING option. This OUTPUT PROCEDURE is very similar to the INPUT PROCEDURE. The full format for the SORT, including both INPUT and OUTPUT PROCEDURE options, is as follows:

Full Format for SORT Statement

$$
\text{SORT file-name-1} \left\{ \text{ON} \left\{ \frac{\text{DESCENDING}}{\text{ASCENDING}} \right\} \text{KEY data-name-1} \ldots \right\} \ldots
$$

$$
\left\{ \begin{array}{l} \underline{\text{INPUT}} \ \underline{\text{PROCEDURE}} \ \text{IS procedure-name-1} \left[\left\{ \frac{\text{THROUGH}}{\text{THRU}} \right\} \text{procedure-name-2} \right] \\ \underline{\text{USING}} \ \text{file-name-2} \ldots \end{array} \right\}
$$

$$
\left\{ \begin{array}{l} \underline{\text{OUTPUT}} \ \underline{\text{PROCEDURE}} \ \text{IS procedure-name-3} \left[\left\{ \frac{\text{THROUGH}}{\text{THRU}} \right\} \text{procedure-name-4} \right] \\ \underline{\text{GIVING}} \ \text{file-name-3} \ldots * \end{array} \right\}
$$

*With COBOL 85 the word GIVING can be followed by more than one file-name, which means that we can create multiple copies of the sorted file.

As indicated, an INPUT PROCEDURE, if used, is processed prior to sorting. When the SORT verb is encountered, control goes to the INPUT PROCEDURE. When the INPUT PROCEDURE is complete, the file is then sorted. An **OUTPUT PROCEDURE** processes all sorted records *in the sort file* and handles the transfer of these records to the output file.

In an INPUT PROCEDURE we RELEASE records to a sort file rather than writing them. In an OUTPUT PROCEDURE we **RETURN** records from the sort file rather than reading them. The format for the RETURN is as follows:

Format

$$\underline{\text{RETURN}} \text{ sort-file-name-1}$$
$$\text{AT } \underline{\text{END}} \text{ imperative statement-1}$$
$$[\underline{\text{NOT}} \text{ AT } \underline{\text{END}} \text{ imperative statement-2}]^*$$
$$[\underline{\text{END-RETURN}}]^*$$

*Valid with COBOL 85 only.

The following provides a summary of OUTPUT PROCEDURE coding rules for both COBOL 85 and COBOL 74.

OUTPUT PROCEDURE SUMMARY: COBOL 85

1. The OUTPUT PROCEDURE of the SORT should refer to a paragraph-name, but it could refer to a section-name.

    Example
    ```
    100-MAIN-MODULE.
         SORT WORK-FILE
             USING IN-FILE
             OUTPUT PROCEDURE 200-AFTER-SORT-MAIN-MODULE
         STOP RUN.
    200-AFTER-SORT-MAIN-MODULE.
         ⋮
    ```

2. In the paragraph specified in the OUTPUT PROCEDURE:
    a. OPEN the output file.
    b. PERFORM a paragraph that will RETURN (which is like a READ) and process records from the sort file until there is no more data.
    c. After all records have been processed, CLOSE the output file.
    d. When the OUTPUT PROCEDURE paragraph has been fully executed, control will then return to the SORT.

    Example
    ```
    200-AFTER-SORT-MAIN-MODULE.
        OPEN OUTPUT SORTED-FILE
        PERFORM UNTIL NO-MORE-RECS
            RETURN WORK-FILE
                AT END
                    MOVE 'NO ' TO MORE-RECS
                NOT AT END
                    PERFORM 300-PROCESS-SORT-RECS
            END-RETURN
        END-PERFORM
        CLOSE SORTED-FILE.
    ```

3. At the paragraph that processes the sort records after they have been sorted but before they are created as output:
   a. Perform any operations on the work or sort records.
   b. MOVE the work or sort record to the output area.
   c. WRITE each sort record to the output file. (A WRITE ... FROM can be used in place of a MOVE and WRITE.)

Example

```
300-PROCESS-SORT-RECS.
    :                        {Process records in the sort file
    WRITE SORTED-REC FROM WORK-REC.
```

OUTPUT PROCEDURE SUMMARY: COBOL 74

1. The entire program should consist of sections. The OUTPUT PROCEDURE should refer to a section-name followed by a paragraph-name.

Example

```
A100-MAIN SECTION.          {Start the program with a section-
A100-MAIN-MODULE.           {name followed by a paragraph-name
    SORT WORK-FILE
        USING IN-FILE
        OUTPUT PROCEDURE A200-AFTER-SORT.
    STOP RUN.
A200-AFTER-SORT SECTION.
A200-AFTER-SORT-MAIN-MODULE.  ◄——Section-names are
    :                             followed by paragraph-
                                  names
```

2. In the main module of the section specified in the OUTPUT PROCEDURE:
   a. OPEN the output file.
   b. RETURN an initial record from the sort-file—the RETURN functions like a READ.
   c. PERFORM a paragraph within the section that will process records from the sort file and continue to process them until there is no more data.
   d. After all records have been processed, CLOSE the output file.
   e. Code a GO TO, branching to the paragraph located physically at the end of the section.

Example

```
A200-AFTER-SORT SECTION.
A200-AFTER-SORT-MAIN-MODULE.
    OPEN OUTPUT SORTED-FILE.
    RETURN WORK-FILE
        AT END MOVE 'NO ' TO MORE-RECS.
    PERFORM A200-PROCESS-SORT-RECS
        UNTIL NO-MORE-RECS.
    CLOSE SORTED-FILE.
    GO TO A200-END-OF-SECTION.
```

3. At the paragraph that processes sort records after sorting:
   a. Perform any operations on work or sort records.
   b. Move the sort record to the output area.
   c. WRITE each sorted record to the output file.
   d. Continue to RETURN sort file records until there is no more data.

Example

```
A200-PROCESS-SORT-RECS.
    :                    {Process records in the sort file
    :
    WRITE SORTED-REC FROM WORK-REC.
    RETURN WORK-FILE
        AT END MOVE 'NO ' TO MORE-RECS.
```

4. The paragraph located physically at the end of the OUTPUT PROCEDURE section must be the last one executed. Hence a GO TO in the section's main module is required to transfer control to this last paragraph. If no processing is required, code an EXIT statement as the only entry in this last paragraph.

Example

```
A100-MAIN SECTION.
A100-MAIN-MODULE.
    SORT WORK-FILE
        USING IN-FILE
        OUTPUT PROCEDURE A200-AFTER-SORT.
    STOP RUN.
A200-AFTER-SORT SECTION.
A200-AFTER-SORT-MAIN-MODULE.
    :
    :
    GO TO A200-END-OF-SECTION.
A200-PROCESS-SORT-RECS.
    :
    :
A200-END-OF-SECTION.
    EXIT. ◄———— Must be the only entry in the
                paragraph for COBOL 74
```

Example After a file has been sorted but before it has been placed on the output file, MOVE .02 TO DISCOUNT for all records with AMT-OF-PURCHASE in excess of $500; otherwise there should be no DISCOUNT. The following, which uses sections, is permissible with either COBOL 85 or COBOL 74 but is only advised for COBOL 74 users:

```
IDENTIFICATION DIVISION.
PROGRAM-ID. SORT2.
*
ENVIRONMENT DIVISION.
INPUT-OUTPUT SECTION.
FILE-CONTROL.
    SELECT INPUT-FILE ASSIGN TO DISK 'DISK1'.
    SELECT SORT-FILE ASSIGN TO DISK 'WORK1'.
    SELECT OUTPUT-FILE ASSIGN TO DISK 'DISK2'.
*
DATA DIVISION.
FILE SECTION.
FD  INPUT-FILE
    LABEL RECORDS ARE STANDARD.
01  INPUT-REC                    PIC X(150).
SD  SORT-FILE.
01  SORT-REC.
    05  TRANS-NO                 PIC X(5).
    05  AMT-OF-PURCHASE          PIC 9(5)V99.
    05  DISCOUNT                 PIC V99.
    05  FILLER                   PIC X(136).
FD  OUTPUT-FILE
    LABEL RECORDS ARE STANDARD.
01  OUT-REC                      PIC X(150).
```

```
**********************************************************
*  this sort procedure uses section-names and will       *
*  work with cobol 74 or 85                               *
**********************************************************
WORKING-STORAGE SECTION.
01  STORED-AREAS.
    05  ARE-THERE-MORE-RECORDS      PIC X(3)  VALUE 'YES'.
        88 THERE-ARE-NO-MORE-RECORDS          VALUE 'NO '.
PROCEDURE DIVISION.
A000 SECTION.
A100-MAIN-MODULE.
    SORT SORT-FILE
        ON ASCENDING KEY TRANS-NO
            USING INPUT-FILE
            OUTPUT PROCEDURE B000-CALC-DISCOUNT.
    STOP RUN.
B000-CALC-DISCOUNT SECTION.
B000-MAIN-PARAGRAPH.
    OPEN OUTPUT OUTPUT-FILE.
    RETURN SORT-FILE                        ◄── To access records from the
        AT END MOVE 'NO ' TO ARE-THERE-MORE-RECORDS.   sort file use a RETURN
    PERFORM B200-DISC-RTN
        UNTIL THERE-ARE-NO-MORE-RECORDS.
    CLOSE OUTPUT-FILE.
    GO TO B000-EXIT.
B200-DISC-RTN.
    IF AMT-OF-PURCHASE > 500
        MOVE .02 TO DISCOUNT
    ELSE                                    ── Put sorted records from the
        MOVE .00 TO DISCOUNT.                  sort file into the output file
    WRITE OUT-REC FROM SORT-REC.           ◄──
    RETURN SORT-FILE                        ◄── Functions like a READ
        AT END MOVE 'NO ' TO ARE-THERE-MORE-RECORDS.
B000-EXIT.
    EXIT.
```

Consider the following alternative for COBOL 85 users, which simplifies the coding:

```
**********************************************************************
*      this procedure is valid only with cobol 85 compilers         *
**********************************************************************
PROCEDURE DIVISION.
A000-MAIN-MODULE.
    SORT SORT-FILE
        ON ASCENDING KEY TRANS-NO
        USING INPUT-FILE
        OUTPUT PROCEDURE B000-CALC-DISCOUNT
    STOP RUN.
B000-CALC-DISCOUNT.
    OPEN OUTPUT OUTPUT-FILE
    PERFORM UNTIL THERE-ARE-NO-MORE-RECORDS
        RETURN SORT-FILE
            AT END
                MOVE 'NO ' TO ARE-THERE-MORE-RECORDS
            NOT AT END
                PERFORM C000-DISC-RTN
        END-RETURN
    END-PERFORM
    CLOSE OUTPUT-FILE.
C000-DISC-RTN.
    IF AMT-OF-PURCHASE > 500
        MOVE .02 TO DISCOUNT
    ELSE
        MOVE .00 TO DISCOUNT
    END-IF
    WRITE OUT-REC FROM SORT-REC.
```

Both an INPUT PROCEDURE and an OUTPUT PROCEDURE can be used in a program by combining the preceding examples. We illustrate this in the Practice Program at the end of the chapter.

Recall that the SD file as well as files specified with USING or GIVING are opened and closed automatically. The programmer opens and closes the input file in an INPUT PROCEDURE and the output file in an OUTPUT PROCEDURE.

WHEN TO USE INPUT AND/OR OUTPUT PROCEDURES

Sometimes it is more efficient to process data *before* it is sorted in an INPUT PROCEDURE, whereas other times it is more efficient to process data *after* it is sorted in an OUTPUT PROCEDURE. For instance, suppose we wish to sort a large file into DEPT-NO sequence. Suppose, further, we wish to eliminate from our file all records with a blank PRICE or blank QTY field. We could eliminate the designated records *prior to* sorting in an INPUT PROCEDURE, or we could eliminate the records *after* sorting in an OUTPUT PROCEDURE.

If we expect only a few records to be eliminated during a run, then it really would not matter much whether we sort first and then eliminate those records we do not wish to put on the output file. If, however, there are many records that need to be eliminated, it is more efficient to remove them *before* sorting. In this way, we do not waste computer time sorting numerous records that will then be removed from the sorted file. Thus, in the case where a large number of records will be removed, an INPUT PROCEDURE should be used.

Suppose, however, that we wish to eliminate records with a blank DEPT-NO, which is the key field. In this case, it is more efficient to remove records with a blank DEPT-NO *after* sorting, because we know that after sorting, all blank DEPT-NOs will be at the *beginning* of the file. (A blank is the lowest printable character in a collating sequence and will appear first in a sorted file.)

Keep in mind that you must use either an INPUT or an OUTPUT PROCEDURE if the unsorted and sorted files have different-sized fields or have fields in different order. This is because the input record must be moved to a record with a different format either prior to or after sorting.

Alternatives to INPUT and OUTPUT PROCEDUREs

Suppose you want to count the number of records in a file to be sorted. In this case, it really does not matter when the count is performed. You can use a *separate procedure* prior to sorting to accomplish this. That is, you can open the file, count the records, close the file, and *then* SORT it with a USING and GIVING:

Here, unsorted records are processed in an → independent module prior to using the SORT

```
100-MAIN-MODULE.
    MOVE 0 TO CTR
    OPEN INPUT UNSORTED-MASTER
    PERFORM UNTIL NO-MORE-RECS
        READ UNSORTED-MASTER
            AT END
                MOVE 'NO ' TO MORE-RECS
            NOT AT END
                ADD 1 TO CTR
        END-READ
    END-PERFORM
    DISPLAY 'THE RECORD COUNT IS ', CTR
    CLOSE UNSORTED-MASTER
    SORT WORK-FILE
        ON ASCENDING KEY DEPT-NO
            USING UNSORTED-MASTER
            GIVING SORTED-MASTER
    STOP RUN.
```

Similarly, you could sort first and have the boxed entries follow the SORT. In this case, the count procedure could use either UNSORTED-MASTER or SORTED-MASTER as input.

In the preceding, the procedure to count records and the procedure to sort records are entirely separate. If you want to interrupt the SORT process and count records prior to sorting, but remain under the control of the SORT statement, use an INPUT PROCEDURE. We illustrate both the COBOL 85 and 74 versions:

COBOL 85

```
100-MAIN MODULE.
    SORT WORK-FILE
        ON ASCENDING KEY DEPT-NO
            INPUT PROCEDURE 200-COUNT-RTN
            GIVING SORTED-MASTER
    STOP RUN.
200-COUNT-RTN.
    MOVE 0 TO CTR
    OPEN INPUT UNSORTED-MASTER
    PERFORM UNTIL NO-MORE-RECS
        READ UNSORTED-MASTER
            AT END
                MOVE 'NO ' TO MORE-RECS
            NOT AT END
                PERFORM-300-PROCESS-RTN
        END-READ
    END-PERFORM
    DISPLAY 'THE RECORD COUNT IS ', CTR
    CLOSE UNSORTED-MASTER.
300-PROCESS-RTN.
    ADD 1 TO CTR
    RELEASE WORK-REC
        FROM UNSORTED-REC.
```

COBOL 74

```
A100-MAIN SECTION.
A100-MAIN-MODULE.
    SORT WORK-FILE
        ON ASCENDING KEY DEPT-NO
            INPUT PROCEDURE A200-COUNT
            GIVING SORTED-MASTER.
    STOP RUN.
A200-COUNT SECTION.
A200-MAIN-MODULE.
    MOVE 0 TO CTR.
    OPEN INPUT UNSORTED-MASTER.
    READ UNSORTED-MASTER
        AT END MOVE 'NO ' TO MORE-RECS.
    PERFORM A200-PROCESS-RTN
        UNTIL NO-MORE-RECS.
    DISPLAY 'THE RECORD COUNT IS ', CTR.
    CLOSE UNSORTED-MASTER.
    GO TO A200-END-OF-SECTION.
A200-PROCESS-RTN.
    ADD 1 TO CTR.
    RELEASE WORK-REC
        FROM UNSORTED-REC.
    READ UNSORTED-MASTER
        AT END MOVE 'NO ' TO MORE-RECS.
A200-END-OF-SECTION.
    EXIT.
```

Finally, we could also count records in an OUTPUT PROCEDURE, after sorting but before the records are actually written to the sorted master. We illustrate both the COBOL 85 and 74 versions:

COBOL 85

```
100-MAIN-MODULE.
    SORT WORK-FILE
        ON ASCENDING KEY DEPT-NO
        USING UNSORTED-MASTER
        OUTPUT PROCEDURE 200-COUNT-RTN
    STOP RUN.
200-COUNT-RTN.
    MOVE 0 TO CTR
    OPEN OUTPUT SORTED-MASTER
    PERFORM UNTIL NO-MORE-RECS
        RETURN WORK-FILE
            AT END
                MOVE 'NO ' TO MORE-RECS
            NOT AT END
                PERFORM 300-PROCESS-RTN
        END-RETURN
    END-PERFORM
    DISPLAY 'THE RECORD COUNT IS ', CTR
    CLOSE SORTED-MASTER.
300-PROCESS-RTN.
    ADD 1 TO CTR
    WRITE SORTED-MASTER-REC
        FROM WORK-REC.
```

COBOL 74

```
A100-MAIN SECTION.
A100-MAIN-MODULE.
    SORT WORK-FILE
        ON ASCENDING KEY DEPT-NO
        USING UNSORTED-MASTER
        OUTPUT PROCEDURE A200-COUNT.
    STOP RUN.
A200-COUNT SECTION.
A200-MAIN.
    MOVE 0 TO CTR.
    OPEN OUTPUT SORTED-MASTER.
    RETURN WORK-FILE
        AT END MOVE 'NO ' TO MORE-RECS.
    PERFORM A200-PROCESS-RTN
        UNTIL NO-MORE-RECS.
    DISPLAY 'THE RECORD COUNT IS ', CTR.
    CLOSE SORTED-MASTER.
    GO TO A200-END-OF-SECTION.
A200-PROCESS-RTN.
    ADD 1 TO CTR.
    WRITE SORTED-MASTER-REC
        FROM WORK-REC.
    RETURN WORK-FILE
        AT END MOVE 'NO ' TO MORE-RECS.
A200-END-OF-SECTION.
    EXIT.
```

It is more efficient to use an INPUT or OUTPUT PROCEDURE in this instance, rather than a separate program excerpt, because the unsorted master will be read and processed only once. With the separate routines described initially, the unsorted master is read, records are counted, the file is closed, and the unsorted master must be read again for sorting purposes, which is inefficient. So if files are large, INPUT and OUTPUT PROCEDUREs can save considerable processing time. On the other hand, some software developers find these PROCEDUREs difficult to code. If files are not so large, it might be best to select a programming methodology that will minimize debugging time; this is likely to be a methodology with which the programmer is most comfortable. In other words, select the option you prefer unless there is an overriding reason to use a different one.

Summary

Figure 14.2 provides a summary of the SORT feature and its options. Note that both an INPUT PROCEDURE and an OUTPUT PROCEDURE can be used in a single program. The Practice Program at the end of the chapter illustrates a SORT with both an INPUT PRO-CEDURE and an OUTPUT PROCEDURE.

THE MERGE STATEMENT

COBOL has a MERGE statement that will combine two or more files into a single file. Its format is similar to that of the SORT:

Format

$$
\begin{aligned}
&\underline{MERGE} \text{ file-name-1} \left\{ ON \left\{ \frac{ASCENDING}{DESCENDING} \right\} KEY \text{ data-name-1} \dots \right\} \dots \\
&\underline{USING} \text{ file-name-2 \{file-name-3\}} \dots \\
&\left\{ \begin{array}{l} \underline{OUTPUT} \; \underline{PROCEDURE} \; IS \text{ procedure-name-1} \left[\left\{ \frac{THROUGH}{THRU} \right\} \text{ procedure-name-2} \right] \\ \underline{GIVING} \text{ \{file-name-4\}} \end{array} \right\}
\end{aligned}
$$

File-name-1 is a work file designated as an SD. The key field specified as data-name-1, and any subsequent key fields, are defined within the SD. The first key field indicated in the ASCENDING or DESCENDING KEY clause of the MERGE is the major one, followed by

Figure 14.2 Options of the SORT feature.

SORT OPTIONS: A BRIEF OVERVIEW	
Format	**Result**
1. USING GIVING	File is sorted, no special handling.
2. INPUT PROCEDURE GIVING	Used for processing the unsorted input records before they are sorted. Write records to the sort file with a RELEASE verb. After an INPUT PROCEDURE is completed, the records are automatically sorted.
3. USING OUTPUT PROCEDURE	Used for processing the sorted records before writing them on the output file. Access or read records from the sort file with a RETURN verb.
4. INPUT PROCEDURE OUTPUT PROCEDURE	Used for processing the data both before and after it is sorted.

intermediate and minor key fields. Rules for `ASCENDING/DESCENDING KEY`, `USING`, `GIVING`, and `OUTPUT PROCEDURE` are the same as for the `SORT`.

With the `USING` clause, we indicate the files to be merged. At least two file-names must be included for a merge, but more than two are permitted. Unlike the `SORT`, however, an `INPUT PROCEDURE` may *not* be specified with a `MERGE` statement. That is, using the `MERGE` statement, you may only process records *after* they have been merged, *not* before. The `OUTPUT PROCEDURE` has the same format as with the `SORT`, and the same distinctions between COBOL 85 and COBOL 74 apply.

The **MERGE** statement automatically handles the opening, closing, and input/output (`READ/WRITE` functions) associated with the files. See Figure 14.3 for an illustration of a program with the `MERGE` instruction.

The files to be merged must each be in sequence by the key field. If `ASCENDING KEY` is specified, then the merged output file will have records in increasing order by key field, and if `DESCENDING KEY` is specified, the merged output file will have key fields from high to low.

An `OUTPUT PROCEDURE` for a `MERGE` may be used, for example, to:

1. Flag duplicate records as errors.
   If an `UPSTATE-PAYROLL-FILE` and a `DOWNSTATE-PAYROLL-FILE` are being merged to produce a `MASTER PAYROLL-FILE` in Social Security number sequence, we may use an `OUTPUT PROCEDURE` to ensure that no two records on the merged file have the same Social Security number.

2. Ensure duplicate records.
   If an `UPSTATE-INVENTORY-FILE` and a `DOWNSTATE-INVENTORY-FILE` store the same `PART-NO`s, we may `MERGE` them into a `MASTER-INVENTORY-FILE` and in an

Figure 14.3   Illustration of the `MERGE` instruction.

```
IDENTIFICATION DIVISION.
PROGRAM-ID. MERGE1.
*
ENVIRONMENT DIVISION.
INPUT-OUTPUT SECTION.
FILE-CONTROL.
    SELECT INPUT-FILE-1 ASSIGN TO DISK 'DISK1'.
    SELECT INPUT-FILE-2 ASSIGN TO DISK 'DISK2'.
    SELECT MERGE-THEM ASSIGN TO DISK 'WORK'.
    SELECT OUTPUT-FILE ASSIGN TO DISK 'DISK3'.
*
DATA DIVISION.
FD  INPUT-FILE-1
    LABEL RECORDS ARE STANDARD.
01  IN-REC-1            PIC X(100).
FD  INPUT-FILE-2
    LABEL RECORDS ARE STANDARD.
01  IN-REC-2            PIC X(100).
SD  MERGE-THEM.
01  MERGE-REC.
    05  KEY-FIELD       PIC X(5).
    05  REST-OF-REC     PIC X(95).
FD  OUTPUT-FILE
    LABEL RECORDS ARE STANDARD.
01  OUT-REC            PIC X(100).
*
PROCEDURE DIVISION.
100-MAIN-MODULE.
    MERGE MERGE-THEM
          ON ASCENDING KEY KEY-FIELD
          USING INPUT-FILE-1, INPUT-FILE-2
          GIVING OUTPUT-FILE
    STOP RUN.
```

OUTPUT PROCEDURE check to see that there are always two records for each PART-NO—an UPSTATE and a DOWNSTATE record.

The same rules apply to OUTPUT PROCEDUREs for the MERGE as for the SORT. Section-names are required for COBOL 74 but paragraph-names can be used for COBOL 85.

Example Suppose we want to merge an Upstate and a Downstate payroll file. In addition, in an output procedure, we want to count the number of employees earning more than $100,000. We will print the count after the merge. Figure 14.4 illustrates the full COBOL 85 program that uses paragraph-names as procedure-names.

Figure 14.4 Sample MERGE program.

```
IDENTIFICATION DIVISION.
PROGRAM-ID.  MERGE2.
ENVIRONMENT DIVISION.
INPUT-OUTPUT SECTION.
FILE-CONTROL.
    SELECT DOWNSTATE-PAYROLL-FILE ASSIGN TO DISK 'M1'.
    SELECT UPSTATE-PAYROLL-FILE ASSIGN TO DISK 'M2'.
    SELECT MERGE-FILE ASSIGN TO DISK 'WORK'.
    SELECT MASTER-PAYROLL-FILE ASSIGN TO DISK 'M3'.
DATA DIVISION.
FILE SECTION.
FD  DOWNSTATE-PAYROLL-FILE
    LABEL RECORDS ARE STANDARD.
01  DOWNSTATE-REC.
    05  D-EMP-NO     PIC X(5).
    05  D-EMP-NAME   PIC X(20).
    05  D-SALARY     PIC 9(6).
    05               PIC X(49).
FD  UPSTATE-PAYROLL-FILE
    LABEL RECORDS ARE STANDARD.
01  UPSTATE-REC.
    05  U-EMP-NO     PIC X(5).
    05  U-EMP-NAME   PIC X(20).
    05  U-SALARY     PIC 9(6).
    05               PIC X(49).
SD  MERGE-FILE.
01  MERGE-REC.
    05  M-EMP-NO     PIC X(5).
    05  M-EMP-NAME   PIC X(20).
    05  M-SALARY     PIC 9(6).
    05               PIC X(49).
FD  MASTER-PAYROLL-FILE
    LABEL RECORDS ARE STANDARD.
01  MASTER-REC      PIC X(80).
WORKING-STORAGE SECTION.
01  MORE-RECS       PIC X(3)  VALUE 'YES'.
01  OVER-100000-CTR PIC 9(3)  VALUE ZERO.
PROCEDURE DIVISION.
100-MAIN.
    MERGE MERGE-FILE
        ON ASCENDING KEY M-EMP-NO
        USING DOWNSTATE-PAYROLL-FILE
              UPSTATE-PAYROLL-FILE
        OUTPUT PROCEDURE 200-COUNT
    DISPLAY 'NO OF RECORDS WITH SALARIES > 100,000 = '
            OVER-100000-CTR
    STOP RUN.
200-COUNT.
    OPEN OUTPUT MASTER-PAYROLL-FILE
    PERFORM UNTIL MORE-RECS = 'NO '
        RETURN MERGE-FILE
            AT END
```

Figure 14.4 (continued)

```
                MOVE 'NO ' TO MORE-RECS
            NOT AT END
                PERFORM 300-CALC
        END-RETURN
    END-PERFORM
    CLOSE MASTER-PAYROLL-FILE.
300-CALC.
    IF M-SALARY > 100000
        ADD 1 TO OVER-100000-CTR
    END-IF
    WRITE MASTER-REC FROM MERGE-REC.
```

Note that the elementary items within the two input files need not have been specified since they are not used. Instead, we could have coded 01 DOWNSTATE-REC PIC X(80) and 01 UPSTATE-REC PIC X(80).

CHAPTER SUMMARY A. The SORT is used for sorting records in either ascending or descending order.

1. A program can simply sort a file on key fields:

    SORT   file-name-1

    $$\left\{ \text{ON} \quad \left\{ \begin{array}{l} \underline{\text{ASCENDING}} \\ \underline{\text{DESCENDING}} \end{array} \right\} \quad \text{KEY} \quad \text{data-name-1} \ldots \right\} \ldots$$

    USING   file-name-2
    GIVING file-name-3

    a. File-name-1 is a work or sort file that is described with an SD (sort file description) in the FILE SECTION.
    b. The KEY field(s) to be sorted are data-names defined within the SD or sort file.
    c. Files can be sorted into ascending or descending sequence.
    d. Files can be sorted using more than one key field. The first field specified is the main sort field followed by intermediate and/or minor ones. SORT ... ON ASCENDING KEY DEPT ON DESCENDING KEY NAME ... will sort a file into ascending department number order (01–99) and, within that, into descending NAME order (Z–A). For Dept 01, ZACHARY precedes YOUNG who precedes VICTOR, etc.

2. A program can include an entirely separate routine that processes an unsorted file prior to performing the SORT and/or an entirely separate routine that processes the sorted file after the SORT is executed:

    [can open, read, and process the unsorted file; then close it before sorting]
    SORT ...

        ...
        USING ...
        GIVING ...
    [can open, read, and process the sorted file]
    STOP RUN.

3. An INPUT PROCEDURE that is part of the SORT statement permits processing of the unsorted file just before the sort is performed, yet under the control of the SORT itself:

    SORT file-name-1

        ...
        INPUT PROCEDURE procedure-name-1
        GIVING file-name-2

    a. COBOL 85 uses a paragraph-name when specifying an INPUT PROCEDURE. COBOL 74 uses a section-name. Since the physical end of a section must be reached to terminate the section, an INPUT PROCEDURE for COBOL 74 must end with an EXIT statement.
    b. With COBOL 85 paragraph-names can be substituted for section-names so there is no need for a GO TO to branch to the end of a section.

    c. The clause RELEASE sort-rec FROM unsorted-rec is necessary in an INPUT PROCEDURE to make input records available for sorting.

4. An OUTPUT PROCEDURE that is part of the SORT statement permits processing of the sorted work (or sort) file records before they are written to the sorted file:

SORT file-name-1 ...

$$\left\{\begin{array}{l}\text{USING file-name-2}\\\text{INPUT PROCEDURE procedure-name-1}\end{array}\right\}$$
    OUTPUT PROCEDURE procedure-name-2

    a. As with the INPUT PROCEDURE, the procedure-name specified must be a section-name for standard COBOL 74 but can be either a section- or paragraph-name with COBOL 85 (or enhanced versions of COBOL 74). Using paragraph-names simplifies the coding and eliminates the need for GO TOs.

    b. An OUTPUT PROCEDURE:
      (1) Opens the output file.
      (2) Includes a RETURN sort-file-name AT END ... which is like a READ.
      (3) Processes all records from the sort file before writing them to the sorted-file-name.
      (4) Uses a RETURN in place of a READ for *all* inputting of sort-file records.
      (5) Closes the output sorted-file after all records have been processed.
    c. Both an INPUT and an OUTPUT PROCEDURE can be used in a program.

B. The MERGE statement can be used to merge two or more files. It is very similar to the SORT. It can have a USING and GIVING option or an OUTPUT PROCEDURE in place of the GIVING option. It *cannot*, however, have an INPUT PROCEDURE.

KEY TERMS

ASCII	INPUT PROCEDURE	RETURN
Collating sequence	MERGE	Section
EBCDIC	OUTPUT PROCEDURE	SORT
FIFO (first in, first out)	RELEASE	

CHAPTER SELF-TEST

1. Code a simple SORT to read a file called IN-FILE, sort it into ascending name sequence, and create an output file called OUT-FILE.

2. It is possible to process records before they are sorted by using the _____ option in place of the _____ option.

3. A(n) (unsorted input, sorted output) file is opened in an INPUT PROCEDURE and a(n) (unsorted input, sorted output) file is opened in an OUTPUT PROCEDURE.

4. In place of a WRITE statement in an INPUT PROCEDURE, the _____ verb is used to write records onto the sort or work file.

5. In place of a READ statement in an OUTPUT PROCEDURE, the _____ verb is used to read records from the sort or work file.

6. (T or F) The RELEASE statement uses a file-name, as does the RETURN statement.

7. (T or F) If section-names are used in the PROCEDURE DIVISION, they should be followed by paragraph-names.

8. Code a simple SORT to read a file called IN-PAYROLL, sort it into ascending NAME sequence, and create an output file called OUT-PAYROLL.

9. Write the PROCEDURE DIVISION for a program to sort records into DEPT-NO sequence but, in an INPUT PROCEDURE, to eliminate blank DEPT-NOs before sorting. Use paragraph-names and assume that you are using the COBOL 85 standard.

10. Recode the preceding, eliminating blanks *after sorting in an* OUTPUT PROCEDURE. Assume that you are using the COBOL 85 standard.

Solutions   1. SORT   SORT-FILE ON ASCENDING KEY S-NAME
               USING IN-FILE
               GIVING OUT-FILE.
      (S-NAME is the name field in the SORT-FILE.)

---

2. INPUT PROCEDURE; USING

3. unsorted input (FD); sorted output (FD)

4. RELEASE

5. RETURN

6. F—We RELEASE <u>record</u>-names and RETURN <u>file</u>-names.

7. T

8.
```
SORT SORT-FILE ON ASCENDING KEY NAME
     USING IN-PAYROLL
     GIVING OUT-PAYROLL.
```

9.
```
PROCEDURE DIVISION.
100-MAIN-MODULE.
    SORT SORT-FILE
        ON ASCENDING KEY DEPT-NO
        INPUT PROCEDURE 200-TEST-DEPT
        GIVING SORTED-MSTR
    STOP RUN.
200-TEST-DEPT.
    OPEN INPUT UNSORTED-MSTR
    PERFORM UNTIL THERE-ARE-NO-UNSORTED-RECORDS
        READ UNSORTED-MSTR
            AT END
                MOVE 'NO ' TO ARE-THERE-ANY-UNSORTED-RECORDS
            NOT AT END
                PERFORM 300-ELIM
        END-READ
    END-PERFORM
    CLOSE UNSORTED-MSTR.
300-ELIM.
    IF  DEPT-NO-IN IS NOT EQUAL TO SPACES
        RELEASE SORT-REC FROM IN-REC
    END-IF.
```

10.
```
PROCEDURE DIVISION.
A100-MAIN-MODULE.
    SORT SORT-FILE
        ON ASCENDING KEY DEPT-NO
        USING INFILE
        OUTPUT PROCEDURE B100-PARA-1
    STOP RUN.
*
B100-PARA-1.
    OPEN OUTPUT SORTED-MSTR
    PERFORM UNTIL DEPT-NO NOT = SPACES
                  OR THERE-ARE-NO-MORE-SORTED-RECORDS
        RETURN SORT-FILE
            AT END
                MOVE 'NO ' TO ARE-THERE-MORE-SORTED-RECORDS
            NOT AT END
                CONTINUE
        END-RETURN
    END-PERFORM
    PERFORM UNTIL THERE-ARE-NO-MORE-SORTED-RECORDS
        RETURN SORT-FILE
            AT END
                MOVE 'NO ' TO ARE-THERE-MORE-SORTED-RECORDS
            NOT AT END
                WRITE SORTED-MASTER-REC FROM SORT-REC
        END-RETURN
    END-PERFORM
    CLOSE SORTED-MSTR.
```

PRACTICE PROGRAM The program definition appears in Figure 14.5.

1. Sort the records into `DEPT-IN` sequence within `AREAX-IN` within `TERR-IN`.

2. In an `INPUT PROCEDURE`, count all input records processed. `DISPLAY` the value of the count field in the main module.

3. In an `OUTPUT PROCEDURE`, eliminate all records with a blank territory so that they are not included in the output file.

The pseudocode, hierarchy chart, and program for this problem appear in Figure 14.6.

Note: With the input file illustrated, the count field will be displayed on the screen as 10 because there are 10 input records.

Figure 14.5 Problem definition for the Practice Program.

Systems Flowchart

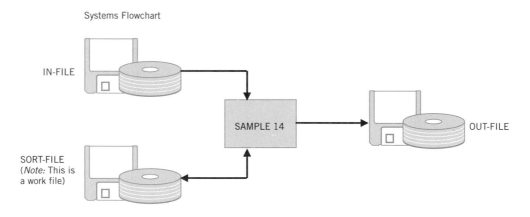

IN-FILE Record Layout*		
Field	**Size**	**Type**
TERR-IN	2	Alphanumeric
AREAX-IN	3	Alphanumeric
DEPT-IN	3	Alphanumeric
LAST-NAME-IN	12	Alphanumeric
FIRST-NAME-IN	8	Alphanumeric

Note: Input field names are not really needed in this program.

SORT-FILE Record Layout		
Field	**Size**	**Type**
TERR	2	Alphanumeric
AREAX	3	Alphanumeric
DEPT	3	Alphanumeric
LAST-NAME	12	Alphanumeric
FIRST-NAME	8	Alphanumeric

Figure 14.5 (continued)

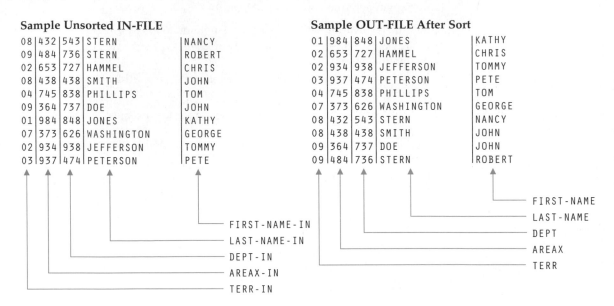

Sample Unsorted IN-FILE

```
08 432 543 STERN        NANCY
09 484 736 STERN        ROBERT
02 653 727 HAMMEL       CHRIS
08 438 438 SMITH        JOHN
04 745 838 PHILLIPS     TOM
09 364 737 DOE          JOHN
01 984 848 JONES        KATHY
07 373 626 WASHINGTON   GEORGE
02 934 938 JEFFERSON    TOMMY
03 937 474 PETERSON     PETE
```

                    FIRST-NAME-IN
                 LAST-NAME-IN
              DEPT-IN
           AREAX-IN
        TERR-IN

Sample OUT-FILE After Sort

```
01 984 848 JONES        KATHY
02 653 727 HAMMEL       CHRIS
02 934 938 JEFFERSON    TOMMY
03 937 474 PETERSON     PETE
04 745 838 PHILLIPS     TOM
07 373 626 WASHINGTON   GEORGE
08 432 543 STERN        NANCY
08 438 438 SMITH        JOHN
09 364 737 DOE          JOHN
09 484 736 STERN        ROBERT
```

                    FIRST-NAME
                 LAST-NAME
              DEPT
           AREAX
        TERR

Figure 14.6 Pseudocode, hierarchy chart, and solution for the Practice Program (COBOL 85 and COBOL 74).

Pseudocode

MAIN-MODULE

START
    Sort File into Terr, Area, Dept Sequence
    INPUT PROCEDURE Count1-Input
    OUTPUT PROCEDURE Elim-Blank-Terr
    Display Counter
STOP

COUNT1-INPUT
    Open the Input file
    PERFORM UNTIL no more input
        READ a Record
            AT END
                Move 'NO ' to Are-There-More-Records
            NOT AT END
                PERFORM Calc-Rtn
        END-READ
    END-PERFORM
    Close the input file

CALC-RTN
    Add 1 to counter
    Release input record for sorting

ELIM-BLANK-TERR
    Open the output file
    Move spaces to Terr
    PERFORM UNTIL no more blank records
        RETURN a Record from the sort file
            AT END
                Move 'NO ' to Are-There-More-Records
            NOT AT END
                Continue
        END-RETURN

Figure 14.6 (continued)

```
            END-PERFORM
            Write an output record from the sort file
            PERFORM UNTIL no more records
                RETURN a Record from the sort file
                    AT END
                        Move 'NO ' to Are-There-More-Records
                    NOT AT END
                        Write an output record from the sort file
                END-RETURN
            END-PERFORM
```

Hierarchy Chart—COBOL 85 version

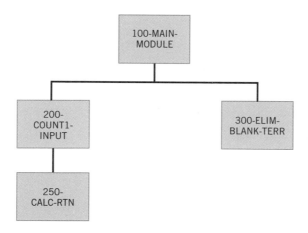

Program—COBOL 85 version

```
IDENTIFICATION DIVISION.
PROGRAM-ID.     SAMPLE.
AUTHOR.         NANCY STERN.
*************************************************************
*    this program sorts a file into terr area dept order   *
*    and also includes an input and output procedure       *
*************************************************************
ENVIRONMENT DIVISION.
INPUT-OUTPUT SECTION.
FILE-CONTROL.
    SELECT IN-FILE ASSIGN TO DISK 'DAT146'.
    SELECT SORT-FILE ASSIGN TO DISK 'SORT1'.
    SELECT OUT-FILE ASSIGN TO DISK 'OUT146'.
*
DATA DIVISION.
FILE SECTION.
FD  IN-FILE
    LABEL RECORDS ARE STANDARD.
01  IN-REC                        PIC X(28).
SD  SORT-FILE.
01  SORT-REC.
    05  TERR                      PIC XX.
    05  AREAX                     PIC XXX.
    05  DEPT                      PIC XXX.
    05  LAST-NAME                 PIC X(12).
    05  FIRST-NAME                PIC X(8).
FD  OUT-FILE
    LABEL RECORDS ARE STANDARD.
01  OUT-REC                       PIC X(28).
WORKING-STORAGE SECTION.
01  STORED-AREAS.
```

Figure 14.6 (continued)

```
     05   ARE-THERE-MORE-RECORDS      PIC X(3) VALUE 'YES'.
          88  NO-MORE-RECORDS                  VALUE 'NO '.
     05   COUNT1                      PIC 999  VALUE ZERO.
 PROCEDURE DIVISION.
 *************************************************************
 *    this is the main module of the program.             *
 *    with cobol 74, separate sections are required       *
 *************************************************************
 100-MAIN-MODULE.
     SORT SORT-FILE
         ASCENDING KEY TERR
             ASCENDING KEY AREAX
                 ASCENDING KEY DEPT
         INPUT PROCEDURE IS 200-COUNT1-INPUT
         OUTPUT PROCEDURE IS 300-ELIM-BLANK-TERR
     DISPLAY COUNT1
     STOP RUN.
 *************************************************************
 *    this is the input procedure                         *
 *************************************************************
 200-COUNT1-INPUT.
 *************************************************************
 *   opens the input file, reads records, counts them     *
 *        and releases them to the sort file              *
 *************************************************************
     OPEN INPUT IN-FILE
     PERFORM UNTIL NO-MORE-RECORDS
         READ IN-FILE
             AT END
                 MOVE 'NO ' TO ARE-THERE-MORE-RECORDS
             NOT AT END
                 PERFORM 250-CALC-RTN
         END-READ
     END-PERFORM
     CLOSE IN-FILE.
 250-CALC-RTN.
     ADD 1 TO COUNT1
     RELEASE SORT-REC FROM IN-REC.
 *************************************************************
 *     this is the output procedure                       *
 *************************************************************
 300-ELIM-BLANK-TERR.
 *************************************************************
 *   opens the output file, returns records from          *
 *   the sort file, eliminates records with blank         *
 *   terr, and writes records to the output file          *
 *************************************************************
     OPEN OUTPUT OUT-FILE
     MOVE 'YES' TO ARE-THERE-MORE-RECORDS
     MOVE SPACES TO TERR
     PERFORM UNTIL TERR IS NOT EQUAL TO SPACES
             OR NO-MORE-RECORDS
         RETURN SORT-FILE
             AT END
                 MOVE 'NO ' TO ARE-THERE-MORE-RECORDS
             NOT AT END
                 CONTINUE
         END-RETURN
     END-PERFORM
     WRITE OUT-REC FROM SORT-REC
     PERFORM UNTIL NO-MORE-RECORDS
         RETURN SORT-FILE
             AT END
                 MOVE 'NO ' TO ARE-THERE-MORE-RECORDS
             NOT AT END
                 WRITE OUT-REC FROM SORT-REC
```

Figure 14.6 (continued)

```
        END-RETURN
    END-PERFORM
    CLOSE OUT-FILE.
```

Hierarchy Chart—COBOL 74 version

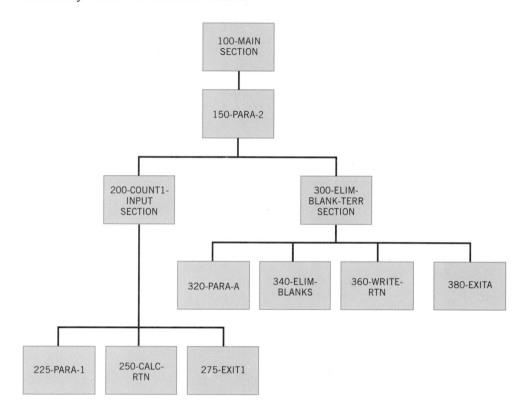

Program—COBOL 74 version

```
IDENTIFICATION DIVISION.
PROGRAM-ID.     SAMPLE.
AUTHOR.         NANCY STERN.
***************************************************************
*    this program sorts a file into terr area dept order     *
*    and also includes an input and output procedure         *
***************************************************************
ENVIRONMENT DIVISION.
INPUT-OUTPUT SECTION.
FILE-CONTROL.
    SELECT IN-FILE ASSIGN TO DISK 'DAT146'.
    SELECT SORT-FILE ASSIGN TO DISK 'SORT1'.
    SELECT OUT-FILE ASSIGN TO DISK 'OUT146'.
*
DATA DIVISION.
FILE SECTION.
FD  IN-FILE
    LABEL RECORDS ARE STANDARD.
01  IN-REC                      PIC X(28).
SD  SORT-FILE
    RECORD CONTAINS 28 CHARACTERS.
01  SORT-REC.
    05  TERR                    PIC XX.
    05  AREAX                   PIC XXX.
    05  DEPT                    PIC XXX.
    05  LAST-NAME               PIC X(12).
```

Figure 14.6   (continued)

```
        05  FIRST-NAME                  PIC X(8).
FD  OUT-FILE
        LABEL RECORDS ARE STANDARD.
01  OUT-REC                             PIC X(28).
WORKING-STORAGE SECTION.
01  STORED AREAS.
        05  ARE-THERE-MORE-RECORDS      PIC X(3) VALUE 'YES'.
            88  NO-MORE-RECORDS                  VALUE 'NO '.
        05  COUNT1                      PIC 999  VALUE ZERO.
*
    PROCEDURE DIVISION.
****************************************************************
*    this is the main module of the program                   *
****************************************************************
    100-MAIN SECTION.
    150-PARA-2.
        SORT SORT-FILE
            ASCENDING KEY TERR
                ASCENDING KEY AREAX
                    ASCENDING KEY DEPT
            INPUT PROCEDURE IS 200-COUNT1-INPUT
            OUTPUT PROCEDURE IS 300-ELIM-BLANK-TERR.
        DISPLAY COUNT1.
        STOP RUN.
****************************************************************
*    this is the input procedure section                      *
****************************************************************
    200-COUNT1-INPUT SECTION.
****************************************************************
*    opens the input file, reads records, counts them         *
*         and releases them to the sort file                  *
****************************************************************
    225-PARA-1.
        OPEN INPUT IN-FILE.
        READ IN-FILE
            AT END MOVE 'NO ' TO ARE-THERE-MORE-RECORDS.
        PERFORM 250-CALC-RTN
            UNTIL NO-MORE-RECORDS.
        CLOSE IN-FILE.
        GO TO 275-EXIT1.
    250-CALC-RTN.
        ADD 1 TO COUNT1.
        RELEASE SORT-REC FROM IN-REC.
        READ IN-FILE
            AT END MOVE 'NO ' TO ARE-THERE-MORE-RECORDS.
    275-EXIT1.
        EXIT.
****************************************************************
*      this is the output procedure section                   *
****************************************************************
    300-ELIM-BLANK-TERR SECTION.
****************************************************************
*    opens the output file, returns records from              *
*    the sort file, eliminates records with blank             *
*    terr, and writes records to the output file              *
****************************************************************
    320-PARA-A.
        OPEN OUTPUT OUT-FILE.
        MOVE 'YES' TO ARE-THERE-MORE-RECORDS.
        RETURN SORT-FILE
            AT END MOVE 'NO ' TO ARE-THERE-MORE-RECORDS.
        PERFORM 340-ELIM-BLANKS
            UNTIL TERR IS NOT EQUAL TO SPACES
                OR NO-MORE-RECORDS.
        PERFORM 360-WRITE-RTN
            UNTIL NO-MORE-RECORDS.
```

Figure 14.6 (continued)

```
      CLOSE OUT-FILE.
      GO TO 380-EXITA.
  340-ELIM-BLANKS.
      RETURN SORT-FILE
          AT END MOVE 'NO ' TO ARE-THERE-MORE-RECORDS.
  360-WRITE-RTN.
      WRITE OUT-REC FROM SORT-REC.
      RETURN SORT-FILE
          AT END MOVE 'NO ' TO ARE-THERE-MORE-RECORDS.
  380-EXITA.
      EXIT.
```

Note: Sections are *not* required with COBOL 85 although they are permissible.

REVIEW QUESTIONS

I. True-False
Questions

_____ 1. If the OUTPUT PROCEDURE is used with the SORT verb, then the INPUT PROCEDURE is required.

_____ 2. RELEASE must be used in an INPUT PROCEDURE.

_____ 3. RETURN must be used in an OUTPUT PROCEDURE.

_____ 4. The RELEASE statement is used in place of the WRITE statement in an INPUT PROCEDURE.

_____ 5. A maximum of three SORT fields are permitted in a single SORT statement.

_____ 6. The only method for sorting a disk file is with the use of the SORT statement in COBOL.

_____ 7. Data may be sorted in either ascending or descending sequence.

_____ 8. With COBOL 85, the procedure-name specified in the INPUT PROCEDURE clause can be a paragraph-name.

_____ 9. If a file is described by an SD, it is not defined in a SELECT clause.

_____ 10. In the EBCDIC collating sequence, a blank has the lowest value.

II. General Questions

Consider the following input:

Store No	Dept No	Salesperson	Amt of Sales
002	01	GONZALES	12500
003	02	BROWN	05873
002	02	CHANG	06275
003	02	ANDREWS	09277
001	01	O'CONNOR	05899
002	02	ADAMS	18733
003	01	FRANKLIN	12358

1. Indicate the sequence in which the records would appear if sorted into Dept No within Store No.

2. Indicate the sequence in which the records would appear if sorted alphabetically, by Salesperson name, within Store No where Store Nos are in descending order.

III. Validating Data

Modify the Practice Program so that it includes coding to (1) test for all errors and (2) print a control listing of totals (records processed, errors encountered, batch totals).

DEBUGGING EXERCISES

Consider the following COBOL 85 program:

```
PROCEDURE DIVISION.
100-MAIN-MODULE.
    SORT SORT-FILE
         ASCENDING KEY S-EMP-NO
         USING MASTER-FILE
         OUTPUT PROCEDURE 200-ADD-TAX
    PERFORM 400-PRINT-RTN.
```

```
200-ADD-TAX SECTION.
    OPEN OUTPUT SORT-FILE, SORTED-MASTER
    PERFORM UNTIL NO-MORE-RECORDS
        RETURN SORT-REC
            AT END
                MOVE 'NO ' TO ARE-THERE-MORE-RECORDS
            NOT AT END
                PERFORM 300-RTN1
        END-RETURN
    END-PERFORM
    CLOSE SORTED-MASTER.
300-RTN1.
    MOVE .10 TO TAX-OUT
    WRITE SORTED-MASTER-REC FROM SORT-REC
    RELEASE SORTED-MASTER-REC.
400-PRINT-RTN.
    MOVE 'YES' TO ARE-THERE-MORE-RECORDS
    OPEN INPUT SORTED-MASTER
              PRINT-FILE
    PERFORM UNTIL NO-MORE-INPUT
        READ SORTED-MASTER
            AT END
                MOVE 'NO ' TO ARE-THERE-MORE-RECORDS
            NOT AT END
                PERFORM 500-PRINT-IT
        END-READ
    END-PERFORM
    CLOSE SORTED-MASTER
          PRINT-FILE.
500-PRINT-IT.
    WRITE PRINT-REC FROM SORTED-MASTER-REC.
```

1. The first OPEN causes an error. Why?
2. There is an error on the RETURN line. What is it?
3. There is an error associated with the RELEASE statement. Find and correct it.
4. After all the preceding errors are corrected, you run the program and obtain all the appropriate results, but a program interrupt occurs. You find that the program is attempting to continue execution even after all records have been processed. Find and correct the error.

PROGRAMMING ASSIGNMENTS

Use the specifications in Figure 14.7 for Programming Assignments 1 through 3.

1. Sort the input file into descending sequence by Territory Number and Office Number, but eliminate, before sorting, all records that have a blank Territory Number, Office Number, or Social Security Number. Print all records that have been eliminated.

2. Interactive Processing.   Sort the input file into ascending sequence by Territory Number, and, after sorting, add $1,000 to the salaries of employees who earn less than $35,000. Display on a screen the names and salaries of all employees who get increases.

3. Sort the input file into ascending Territory Number sequence. Then write a control break program to print a report with the format shown in Figure 14.8.

4. A large corporation with two plants has discovered that some of its employees are on the payrolls of both of its plants. Each plant has a payroll file in Social Security Number sequence. Write a program to merge the two files and to print the names of the "double-dippers"; that is, the employees who are on both files.

5. Merge an upstate transaction file with a downstate transaction file. The format for both files is:

```
1-5    TRANS-NO
6-10   AMT-PURCHASED
```

The transaction numbers should be unique on each file, but it is permissible to have the same transaction number on both files (e.g., 00002 may be on both input files, but there should be

Figure 14.7 Problem definition for Programming Assignments 1–3.

Systems Flowchart

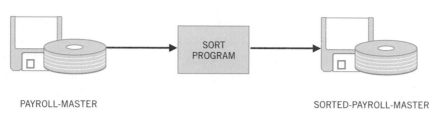

PAYROLL-MASTER   SORTED-PAYROLL-MASTER

PAYROLL-MASTER and SORTED-PAYROLL-MASTER Record Layouts			
Field	Size	Type	No. of Decimal Positions (if Numeric)
EMPLOYEE-NO	5	Alphanumeric	
EMPLOYEE-NAME	20	Alphanumeric	
TERRITORY-NO	2	Alphanumeric	
OFFICE-NO	2	Alphanumeric	
ANNUAL-SALARY	6	Numeric	0
SOCIAL-SECURITY-NO	9	Alphanumeric	
Unused	36	Alphanumeric	

Figure 14.8 Printer Spacing Chart for Programming Assignment 3.

```
       1234567890123456789012345678901234567890...
 H  6              EMPLOYEE SUMMARY REPORT      99/99/99  PAGE 99
 H  8        TERRITORY           TOTAL NO. OF EMPLOYEES
 T 10           XX               Z,ZZ9
   11            .                 .
   12            .                 .
   13            .                 .
 T 16        TOTAL NO. OF EMPLOYEES   ZZ,ZZZ *
```

at most one such record on each). Print a count of transaction numbers that appear on both input files using an OUTPUT PROCEDURE.

6. The SmartBell Telephone Company maintains transaction records of long-distance calls made by its customers. A transaction record with the following format is created for each long-distance call made. The transaction file is in no specific order since a record is automatically created when a call is made. The transaction file format is:

1–10   Caller's telephone number   21–22   Number of minutes of call
11–20   Called telephone number   23–27   Charge (999V99)

A separate master file is maintained with the following format:

1–10	Telephone number	41–60	Street address
11–30	Customer's last name	61–80	City-state-zip
31–40	Customer's first name	81–85	Monthly charge

This master file is in sequence by telephone number.

Create monthly telephone bills for each customer. Design the format of the bills yourself.

7. Write a program to sort a file into STUDENT-NAME sequence within CLASS-NO sequence, where CLASS-NO is not part of the input but is calculated using the NO-OF-CREDITS field:

STUDENT Record Layout			
Field	Size	Type	No. of Decimal Positions (if Numeric)
STUDENT-NO	5	Alphanumeric	
STUDENT-NAME	25	Alphanumeric	
NO-OF-CREDITS	3	Numeric	0

CLASS-NO is calculated as follows:

FRESHMAN (CLASS-NO 1)	NO-OF-CREDITS <= 29
SOPHOMORE (CLASS-NO 2)	NO-OF-CREDITS between 30 and 59
JUNIOR (CLASS-NO 3)	NO-OF-CREDITS between 60 and 89
SENIOR (CLASS-NO 4)	NO-OF-CREDITS 90 or more

Add CLASS-NO to the sorted output records.

8. Maintenance Program.   Modify the Practice Program in this chapter to print all records that have been eliminated because of a blank territory.

CHAPTER 15

Indexed and Relative File Processing

▨ **OBJECTIVES**

To familiarize you with

1. Methods of disk file organization.
2. Random processing of disk files.
3. How to create, update, and access indexed disk files.
4. How to create, update, and access relative files.
5. Methods used for organizing relative files.

▨ **CONTENTS**

SYSTEMS CONSIDERATIONS FOR ORGANIZING DISK FILES

Recall that the term *file* refers to a collection of records to be used for a given application. An accounts receivable file, for example, is the collection of all customer records. We now discuss the major ways in which files can be stored or organized on a disk storage unit.

SEQUENTIAL FILE ORGANIZATION

The simplest type of disk file organization is *sequential*. Sequential files are processed in the same way regardless of the type of magnetic media on which they are stored. Typically, the records to be stored in a sequential file are first sorted into sequence by a key field such as customer number, part number, or employee number. It is then relatively easy to locate a given record. The record with employee number 00986, for example, would be physically located between records with employee numbers 00985 and 00987. To access that record, the computer must read past the first 985 records.

We have already seen in Chapter 13 how a master sequential file can be updated by either (1) creating a new master file using the previous master and the transaction file of changes as input or (2) rewriting master records that have changes.

There are two methods of file organization that enable a disk file to be accessed randomly as well as sequentially. *Indexed files* and *relative files* can be processed both sequentially and randomly. We consider both in this chapter.

INDEXED FILE ORGANIZATION

An **indexed file** is really two files—the data file, which is created in sequence but can be accessed randomly, and the **index** file, which contains the value of each key field and the disk address of the record with that corresponding key field. To access an indexed record randomly, the key field is looked up in the index file to find the disk address of the record; then the record is accessed in the indexed data file directly.

When creating an indexed payroll file, for example, you might specify the Social Security number of each record within the file to be the key field. The computer then establishes the index on the disk, which will contain each record's Social Security number and the record's corresponding disk address.

To access a payroll record randomly, the Social Security number of the desired record is supplied by the user, and the computer "looks up" the address of the corresponding record in the index; it then moves the disk drive's access mechanism to the disk address where the employee record with that Social Security number is located. This is very useful for **interactive processing**, where a user communicates directly with the computer using a keyboard, and the key fields he or she is entering are not ordinarily in sequence.

Once the address of the disk record is obtained from an index, the disk drive's access mechanism can move directly to that address on the disk where the record is located. It is *not* necessary to read sequentially past all the previous records in the file looking for the desired one.

The index on a disk is similar to a book's index, which has unique subjects (keys) and their corresponding page numbers (addresses). There would be two ways to find a topic in the book. You can read the book sequentially, from the beginning, until that topic is found, but this would be very time-consuming and inefficient. The best method would be to look up the topic in the index, find the corresponding page number, and go directly to that page. This is precisely how records can be accessed on a disk file that has an index.

With an indexed file we can access records *either* sequentially or randomly, depending on the user's needs. The term **random access** implies that records are to be processed or accessed in some order other than the one in which they were physically written on the disk.

RELATIVE FILE ORGANIZATION

Relative files also permit random access. A relative file does not use an index to access records randomly. Rather, the key field of each record is used to calculate the record's relative location in the file. When records are created as output in a relative file, the key field is used to compute a disk address where the record is written. When records are randomly accessed from a relative file, the user enters the key field, which is used to determine the physical location of the corresponding record. That record is then accessed directly. With a relative file, therefore, there is no need for an index.

FEATURES OF MAGNETIC DISKS AND DISK DRIVES

Before considering the methods used to process files randomly, we will review here the physical features of disks that make random access possible.

Magnetic disk is a storage medium that can serve as either input to or output from any computer system—from mainframes to micros. The disk has a metal oxide coating that can store hundreds of millions of characters of data, or more. The magnetic disk drive, which can be a hard disk drive or a floppy disk drive on the micro, is used both for recording information onto the disk and for reading information from it at very high speeds.

Most hard disks currently used with larger computers are fixed disks, which cannot be removed from the fixed-head disk drive. They are similar to hard disks for micros.

Another type of magnetic disk for mainframes and minis is a disk pack consisting of a series of removable platters or disks arranged in a vertical stack and connected by a central shaft. The concept is similar to a group of phonograph records stacked on a spindle. The actual number of disks in a pack varies with the unit. We illustrate a disk pack with 11 disks. See Figure 15.1 for a cross-sectional view.

Data may be recorded on *both* sides of each disk. There are, however, only 20 recording surfaces for an 11-disk unit, because the top surface of the first disk and the bottom surface of the last disk do not contain data. These two surfaces tend to collect dust and hence are not viable for storing data. In some organizations, disk packs are being replaced by fixed disks because of the potential for deterioration in data when disks are moved on and off the system.

The disk drive used with an 11-disk pack (with 20 recording surfaces) would have 10 *access arms*, each with its own read/write head for reading and writing data. Figure 15.1 illustrates these read/write heads, each of which reads the bottom surface of one disk and the top surface of the next disk. Multiple read/write mechanisms make it possible to access records without always having to perform sequential reads.

Figure 15.1 How data is accessed from a disk pack.

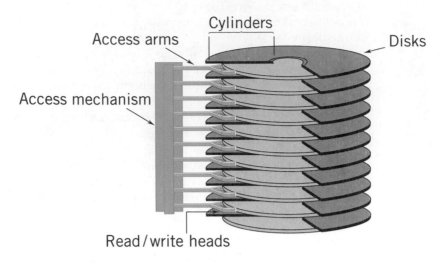

Figure 15.2 Tracks on a disk surface.

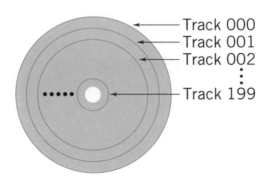

Each disk surface of a hard disk writes data as magnetized bits in concentric circles called **tracks** (see Figure 15.2). The number of tracks varies with the disk. Each track can store thousands of bytes of data or more. Although the surface area of tracks near the center is smaller than the surface area of outermost tracks, all tracks store precisely the same number of bytes. This is because data stored in the innermost tracks is stored more densely.

Individual records on disks can typically be addressed in the following way:

ADDRESSING DISK RECORDS

1. Surface number.

2. Track number.

3. Sector number (for floppy disks) or cylinder number (for larger units).

Floppy disks have only two surfaces—top and bottom. On each surface there are concentric tracks that are segmented into wedge-shaped **sectors**. See Figure 15.3. Larger disk systems use cylinders instead of sectors for addressing disk records.

Figure 15.3 Sectors on a floppy disk.

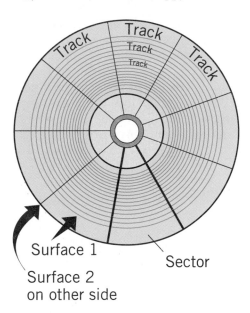

PROCESSING INDEXED DISK FILES

Most disk files that need to be accessed randomly are created using the indexed method of file organization. Along with the data file, an index is created that associates an actual disk address with each key field in the data file. See Figure 15.4.

COBOL 85 is the first version of COBOL that has standardized the processing of indexed files. Hence, we focus primarily on COBOL 85 in this chapter. If you are using a COBOL 74 compiler, you may need to code entries that are slightly different from those discussed here. Most COBOL 74 compilers, however, provide enhancements that are close to or even identical with the features we present here. VSAM, which is IBM's implementation for the processing of indexed files, was one of the first indexed file techniques to incorporate the COBOL 85 features specified here.

Figure 15.4 An index associates an actual disk address with each key field in an indexed data file.

	Data File (e.g., Payroll)			
RECORD	EMPLOYEE NO.	LAST NAME	FIRST NAME	SALARY
1	0004	SMITH	JOHN	022000
2	0007	PHILLIPS	TOM	037000
3	0192	MORALES	PETE	029000
4	0587	AKERS	ALICE	042500
.	.	.	.	.
.	.	.	.	.
.	.	.	.	.

Index File			
RECORD KEY	RECORD LOCATION		
EMPLOYEE NO.	Surface	Track	Sector
0004	1	1	2
0007	1	2	1
0192	2	5	3
0587	2	6	4
.	.	.	.
.	.	.	.
.	.	.	.

CREATING AN INDEXED FILE

Indexed files are created *in sequence*; that is, the indexed file is created by reading each record from an input file, in sequence by the key field, and writing the output indexed disk records *in the same sequence*. Note, however, that once the indexed file is created, it can be accessed randomly.

The indexed file, then, is created in the same manner as a sequential disk file is created, with some very minor differences. See Figure 15.5 for an illustration of a program that creates an indexed file sequentially. There are several new entries in this program that need a brief explanation. We will discuss each in detail.

Figure 15.5   Program that creates an indexed file sequentially.

COBOL 85

```
IDENTIFICATION DIVISION.
PROGRAM-ID. SAMPLE.
**********************************************************
*   this program creates an indexed             *
*   disk from an input file.                     *
**********************************************************
ENVIRONMENT DIVISION.
INPUT-OUTPUT SECTION.
FILE-CONTROL.
    SELECT PAYROLL-FILE-IN ASSIGN TO DISK 'DATA155'.
    SELECT MASTER-FILE-OUT ASSIGN TO DISK 'DISK1'
        ORGANIZATION IS INDEXED
        ACCESS IS SEQUENTIAL
        RECORD KEY IS INDEXED-SSNO-OUT.
*
DATA DIVISION.
FILE SECTION.
FD  PAYROLL-FILE-IN
    LABEL RECORDS ARE STANDARD.
01  PAYROLL-REC-IN.
    05   SSNO-IN                    PIC 9(9).
    05   NAME-IN                    PIC X(20).
    05   SALARY-IN                  PIC 9(5).
FD  MASTER-FILE-OUT
    LABEL RECORDS ARE STANDARD.
01  MASTER-REC-OUT.
    05   INDEXED-SSNO-OUT           PIC 9(9).
    05   INDEXED-NAME-OUT           PIC X(20).
    05   INDEXED-SALARY-OUT         PIC 9(5).
WORKING-STORAGE SECTION.
01  WS-WORK-AREAS.
    05   ARE-THERE-MORE-RECORDS    PIC X(3)    VALUE 'YES'.
         88  NO-MORE-RECORDS                   VALUE 'NO '.
*
PROCEDURE DIVISION.
********************************************
*   controls direction of program logic   *
********************************************
100-MAIN-MODULE.
    PERFORM 300-INITIALIZATION-RTN
    PERFORM UNTIL NO-MORE-RECORDS
        READ PAYROLL-FILE-IN
            AT END
                MOVE 'NO ' TO ARE-THERE-MORE-RECORDS
            NOT AT END
                PERFORM 200-CREATE-RTN
        END-READ
    END-PERFORM
```

Establishes the file as indexed

Indexed files are created in sequence

Specifies the indexed record's key field

COBOL 74 Substitutions

```
PERFORM 200-CREATE-RTN
    UNTIL NO-MORE-RECORDS.
```

Figure 15.5   (continued)

```
        PERFORM 400-END-OF-JOB-RTN
        STOP RUN.
   ************************************************************
   *  performed from 100-main-module. creates new records  *
   *  in master file from payroll file                     *
   ************************************************************
    200-CREATE-RTN.
        MOVE PAYROLL-REC-IN TO MASTER-REC-OUT
        WRITE MASTER-REC-OUT
            INVALID KEY DISPLAY 'INVALID RECORD ', PAYROLL-REC-IN
        END-WRITE.


   ***********************************************
   *  performed from 100-main-module,           *
   *  opens files                               *
   ***********************************************
    300-IALIZATION-RTN.
        OPEN INPUT  PAYROLL-FILE-IN
             OUTPUT MASTER-FILE-OUT.


   ***************************************************
   *  performed from 100-main-module, closes files  *
   ***************************************************
    400-END-OF-JOB-RTN.
        CLOSE PAYROLL-FILE-IN
              MASTER-FILE-OUT.
```

COBOL 74 Substitutions

```
READ PAYROLL-FILE-IN
    AT END MOVE 'NO ' TO
        ARE-THERE-MORE-RECORDS.
```

```
READ PAYROLL-FILE-IN
    AT END MOVE 'NO ' TO
        ARE-THERE-MORE-RECORDS.
```

←—DISPLAY is executed if MASTER-REC-OUT's key field:
1. is not in sequence, or
2. duplicates the key field of a record already on the disk.

The SELECT Statement

When an indexed file is being created, the full SELECT statement is as follows:

CREATING AN INDEXED FILE: SELECT CLAUSE

SELECT file-name-1 ASSIGN TO implementor-name-1
    [ORGANIZATION IS] INDEXED
    [ACCESS MODE IS SEQUENTIAL]
    RECORD KEY IS data-name-1

The implementor-name in the ASSIGN clause is *exactly* the same as for standard sequential disk files.

The ORGANIZATION Clause

The clause ORGANIZATION IS INDEXED indicates that the file is to be created *with an index*. Even though we are creating the file sequentially, we must indicate that this is an indexed file; this instructs the computer to establish an index so that we can randomly access the file later on.

The ACCESS Clause

Since indexed files may be accessed *either sequentially or randomly*, the ACCESS clause is used to denote which method will be used in the specific program. If the ACCESS clause is omitted, the compiler will assume that the file is being processed in SEQUENTIAL mode. Indexed files are always created sequentially; that is, *the input records must be in sequence by key field.* Thus, the ACCESS clause is optional when the file is to be accessed sequentially since ACCESS IS SEQUENTIAL is the default.

The RECORD KEY Clause

The RECORD KEY clause names the *key field within the disk record* that will be used to form the index. This field must be in the same physical location in each indexed record. Usually, it is the first field. It must have a unique value for each record, and it usually has a numeric value as well.

DEBUGGING TIP—GUIDELINES FOR RECORD KEYS

1. COBOL 85 states that the RECORD KEY should be defined with a PIC of X's. Most compilers also allow a PIC of 9's as an enhancement. Regardless of whether the record key is defined with X's or 9's, it is best to use a RECORD KEY that has a numeric value. Fields such as ACCT-NO in an accounts receivable record, SOC-SEC-NO in a payroll record, or PART-NO in an inventory record, for example, are commonly used key fields. Nonnumeric fields such as CUST-NAME, EMPLOYEE-NAME, or PART-DESCRIPTION should not, as a rule, be used as RECORD KEYs since extra blanks might be inserted, upper- and lowercase letters might be mixed, and other characters such as commas might be used that make look-ups from an index difficult. Also, different collating sequences (EBCDIC or ASCII) can cause records to be ordered differently in an indexed file if the record key values are not all numeric.

2. We recommend that key fields be the first fields in a record, for ease of reference.

Note that ACCESS IS SEQUENTIAL is the default, so that the ACCESS clause can be omitted entirely from the SELECT statement when creating an indexed file.

Figure 15.5 illustrates the three additional clauses used in the SELECT statement for creating an indexed file. The only other difference between creating an indexed file and creating a sequential file is in the use of the INVALID KEY clause with the WRITE statement.

The INVALID KEY Clause

Examine the WRITE statement in Figure 15.5, which includes an **INVALID KEY** clause. The INVALID KEY clause is used with a WRITE instruction to test for two possible errors: (1) a key field that is not in sequence or (2) a key field that is the same as one already on the indexed file (on many systems, a blank key field will also be considered an INVALID KEY). If any of these conditions exist, we call this an INVALID KEY *condition.* The computer checks for an INVALID KEY *prior to* writing the record.

Thus, if you use an INVALID KEY clause with the WRITE statement and a record has an erroneous key, *the record is not written* and the statement(s) following INVALID KEY would be executed. Coding WRITE ... INVALID KEY, then, ensures that the key field of the record being written is acceptable, which means it is unique and sequential (and, for many systems, not blank). If, for example, two records have the same Social Security number, or the Social Security numbers are not entered in sequence, the index would not be able to associate the record or key field with a disk address.

The INVALID KEY clause is required when writing records, unless a separate DECLARATIVE SECTION, which we do not discuss here, is coded for handling I/O errors.

The format for the INVALID KEY clause is:

Format

```
WRITE record-name-1  [FROM identifier-1]
        [INVALID KEY imperative-statement-1]
```

With COBOL 85, NOT INVALID KEY imperative-statement and END-WRITE are also options that make it easier to delimit the WRITE statement. Thus with COBOL 85 you may code:

```
WRITE      INDEXED-REC
           INVALID KEY PERFORM 500-ERROR-RTN
           NOT INVALID KEY PERFORM 400-OK-RTN
END-WRITE
```

Interactive Processing.   In Figure 15.5 we created an indexed file from a sequential disk file. Alternatively, we can create an indexed file interactively using data entered from a keyboard. Using the first three DIVISIONs as in Figure 15.5, the PROCEDURE DIVISION is:

```
PROCEDURE DIVISION.
***********************************************
*   Controls direction of program logic   *
***********************************************
100-MAIN-MODULE.
    OPEN OUTPUT MASTER-FILE-OUT
    PERFORM 200-CREATE-RTN
        UNTIL NO-MORE-RECORDS
    CLOSE MASTER-FILE-OUT
    STOP RUN.
200-CREATE-RTN.
    DISPLAY 'ENTER SSNO'
    ACCEPT INDEXED-SSNO-OUT
    DISPLAY 'ENTER NAME'
    ACCEPT INDEXED-NAME-OUT
    DISPLAY 'ENTER SALARY'
    ACCEPT INDEXED-SALARY-OUT
    WRITE MASTER-REC-OUT
        INVALID KEY DISPLAY 'INVALID RECORD ', MASTER-REC-OUT
    END-WRITE
    DISPLAY 'ARE THERE MORE RECORDS (YES/NO)?'
    ACCEPT ARE-THERE-MORE-RECORDS.
```

In summary, creating an indexed file is not significantly different from creating a sequential file. The SELECT statement has an ORGANIZATION IS INDEXED clause, an ACCESS IS SEQUENTIAL clause (optional because SEQUENTIAL access is the default), and a RECORD KEY clause. In the PROCEDURE DIVISION, an INVALID KEY clause is used with the WRITE statement to ensure that only records with valid key fields are created on disk.

DEBUGGING TIP

   Until now, you may have used a text editor to create files for testing purposes. Indexed files, however, *must* be created by a program.

   When you create sequential files, as opposed to indexed files, you can use operating system commands such as TYPE or PRINT to view and check them. Indexed files, however, are created with special control characters that may make them unreadable with these operating system commands, especially on PCs.

   When testing a program that creates an indexed file, then, use a DISPLAY output-indexed-disk-record statement, prior to the WRITE, to view the records on the screen. You can then check that the file was created properly.

UPDATING AN INDEXED FILE RANDOMLY

As we have seen, one main feature of disk processing is that master records can be updated *directly* without having to create a new file. That is, a disk record can be read into storage where changes are made and the changed record can be rewritten back onto the disk in place. This eliminates the need to create an entirely new file. See the

Figure 15.6 Systems flowchart showing an update procedure for an indexed file.

INDEXED
MASTER
DISK FILE

or

Changes are
rewritten back
to the master

Transactions can be saved to
a file or made interactively
using a PC or terminal keyboard

Indexed
File
Update

CONTROL LISTING

This lists all changes made to the
master and any errors. It is used
for checking or control purposes

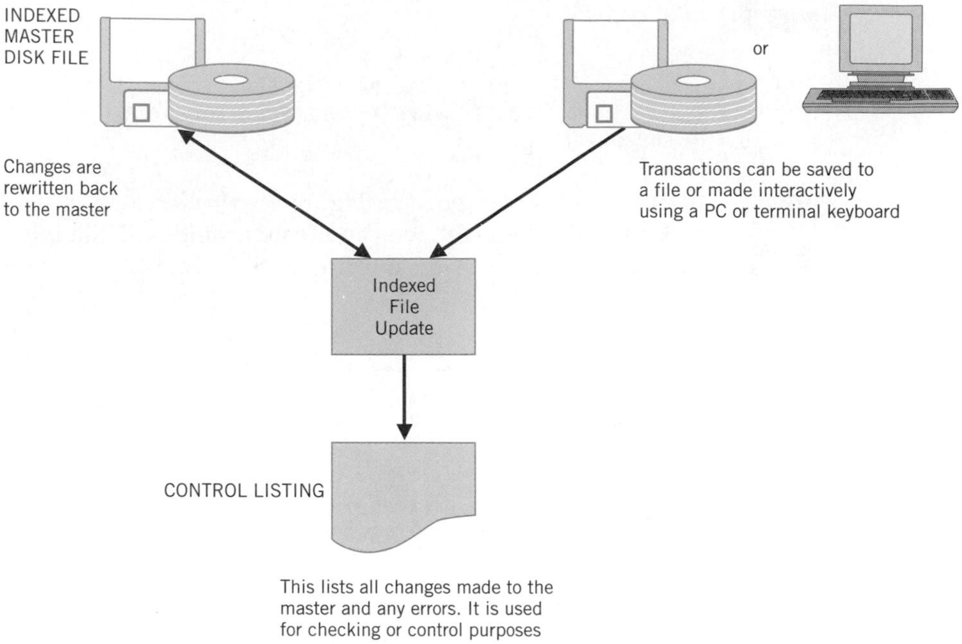

systems flowchart in Figure 15.6, which illustrates an update procedure for an indexed file.

When updating an indexed disk only *two* files are needed—the transaction file and the master disk itself, which serves as *both* input and output. One additional feature of updating indexed files is that changes can be made out of sequence. That is, *since the indexed disk file may be accessed randomly, there is no need to sort the transaction file* before performing an update. Note, however, that a backup procedure should be used to create another copy of the master file in case something happens to the original.

For accessing indexed files *randomly*, we may have either (1) a transaction file, which can be stored on any storage medium (usually disk) or (2) transaction data entered interactively as the change occurs; such changes are usually entered on a keyboard. In either case, the transaction data will specify which disk records we want to read or access for updating purposes. We will assume, first, that the changes are in a transaction file, which will be processed in batch mode. We will also focus on updating an indexed file interactively.

Suppose we wish to update a record with PART-NO 123 on an indexed inventory file that has PART-NO as its record key. We simply enter 123 in the RECORD KEY field of the disk record and instruct the computer to read a record from the indexed file. The computer will then randomly access the corresponding indexed record. In an update procedure, the transaction data contains the PART-NOs of records to be changed or updated on the master file. To find each corresponding master record, we must perform the following:

1. Read the transaction record or accept transaction data from a terminal or PC. (Each record contains a transaction part number called T-PART-NO.)
2. Move the transaction part number, T-PART-NO, to the RECORD KEY of the master file called PART-NO.
    (Move the transaction key field to the indexed record's key field, which is defined within the record description for the indexed file.)
3. When a READ from the indexed file is executed, the computer will look up or access the disk record that has a key field (PART-NO in our illustration) equal to

the value stored in the record key. If no such record is found, an error routine should be performed. The READ and its associated error procedure can be executed with:

```
    MOVE T-PART-NO TO PART-NO
    READ INDEXED-FILE
         INVALID KEY PERFORM 600-ERR-RTN
    END-READ
```

With COBOL 85 we can make this READ even more structured by coding:

```
MOVE T-PART-NO TO PART-NO
READ INDEXED-FILE
     INVALID KEY PERFORM 600-ERR-RTN
     NOT INVALID KEY PERFORM 500-OK-RTN
END-READ
```

The coding requirements for randomly updating an indexed file are:

The SELECT Statement

The SELECT statement for an indexed file that is to be *updated randomly* is as follows:

ACCESSING AN INDEXED FILE RANDOMLY

SELECT file-name-1 ASSIGN TO implementor-name-1
   [ORGANIZATION IS] INDEXED
   ACCESS MODE IS RANDOM
   RECORD KEY IS data-name-1

Example   An indexed file to be updated would have the following SELECT statement:

```
SELECT INDEXED-FILE ASSIGN TO DISK1 ◀——System-dependent implementor-name
     ORGANIZATION IS INDEXED ◀——Index was established when the file was created
     ACCESS MODE IS RANDOM ◀——File will not be accessed sequentially
     RECORD KEY IS PART-NO. ◀——The index is in record key order and keeps track of the
                                 disk address for each record key
```

Opening an Indexed File as I-O

When updating an indexed file, we open it as I-O, for input-output, because it will be read from and written to. That is, (1) it is used as input [I] for reading or accessing disk records, and (2) it is also used as output [O] for rewriting or updating the records read.

The READ Statement

We read in the transaction record, which has the part number to be accessed from the disk. We move the transaction T-PART-NO to PART-NO, and then read the disk. With COBOL 85, we can code:

```
MOVE T-PART-NO TO PART-NO
READ TRANS-FILE
    AT END MOVE 'NO ' TO ARE-THERE-MORE-RECORDS
    NOT AT END
        MOVE T-PART-NO TO PART-NO
        READ INDEXED-FILE
            INVALID KEY PERFORM 600-ERR-RTN
            NOT INVALID KEY PERFORM 500-OK-RTN
        END-READ
END-READ
```

The record read from INDEXED-FILE will have a PART-NO RECORD KEY equal to T-PART-NO, and 500-OK-RTN will be executed; if the indexed file does not contain a record with a RECORD KEY equal to T-PART-NO, 600-ERR-RTN will be executed. With COBOL 74, we would code:

```
MOVE T-PART-NO TO PART-NO.
READ TRANS-FILE
    AT END MOVE 'NO ' TO ARE-THERE-MORE-RECORDS.
MOVE T-PART-NO TO PART-NO.
READ INDEXED-FILE
    INVALID KEY MOVE 'Y' TO ERROR-SWITCH.
IF ERROR-SWITCH = 'Y'
    PERFORM 600-ERR-RTN
ELSE
    PERFORM 500-OK-RTN.
```

Interactive Processing. If the T-PART-NO were entered interactively rather than stored in a file, we would code the following:

```
DISPLAY 'ENTER PART NUMBER'
ACCEPT T-PART-NO  ◄——a WORKING-STORAGE entry
MOVE T-PART-NO TO PART-NO
READ INDEXED-FILE
    INVALID KEY PERFORM 600-ERR-RTN
    NOT INVALID KEY PERFORM 500-OK-RTN
END-READ
```

There Is No AT END Clause When Reading from a Disk Randomly

When reading a disk file randomly, we do not test for an AT END condition because we are not reading the file in sequence; instead, we include an INVALID KEY test. If there is no record in the INDEXED-FILE with a RECORD KEY equal to T-PART-NO, the INVALID KEY clause will be executed. Thus, the computer executes the INVALID KEY option only if the T-PART-NO does not match any of the master disk records. If NOT INVALID KEY is specified (with COBOL 85 only), then this clause will be executed if a match is found.

REWRITE a Disk Record to Update It

Once a master indexed record has been accessed, transaction data is used to update the master record, and we code a REWRITE to change or overlay the existing indexed master record on disk, so that it includes the additional data. Thus, for updating an indexed file, we have the following:

UPDATING AN INDEXED MASTER FILE

1. OPEN the indexed master file as I-O.

2. Read transaction data from a transaction file or accept transaction data from a keyboard.
   Move the key field for the transaction record, which was either read in or accepted as input, to the RECORD KEY of the indexed master file. When a READ (master file) instruction is executed, the computer will find the indexed master file record with that RECORD KEY and transmit it to the master record storage area in the FILE SECTION.

3. When the READ (master file) instruction is executed, the corresponding master record that needs to be updated will be read into main memory.

4. Make the changes to the master record directly by moving transaction data to the master I/O record area.

5. REWRITE the master record.

The format for the REWRITE is as follows:

Format

REWRITE record-name-1   [FROM identifier-1]
        [INVALID KEY imperative-statement-1]
        [NOT INVALID KEY imperative-statement-2]*
    [END-REWRITE]*

*These are optional with COBOL 85 only.

An INVALID KEY will occur on a REWRITE if the programmer has changed the key field of the record. You should always avoid changing a key field of an existing record.

Illustrating a Simple Update Procedure for an Indexed File

Reading from a Transaction File as Input

Example   Assume that a master indexed disk file contains payroll data with Social Security number as its RECORD KEY. Another disk file contains transaction or change records where each record is identified by a Social Security number and has new salary data for that employee. The transaction data, which is not in any sequence, is to be used to change the corresponding master record. An excerpt of the PROCEDURE DIVISION follows:

```
PROCEDURE DIVISION.
100-MAIN-MODULE.
    PERFORM 500-INITIALIZATION-RTN
    PERFORM UNTIL THERE-ARE-NO-MORE-RECORDS
        READ TRANS-IN
            AT END
                MOVE 'NO ' TO ARE-THERE-MORE-RECORDS
            NOT AT END
                PERFORM 200-CALC-RTN
        END-READ
    END-PERFORM
    PERFORM 600-END-OF-JOB-RTN
    STOP RUN.
200-CALC-RTN.
    MOVE T-SOC-SEC-NO TO MASTER-SSNO
    READ MASTER-FILE
        INVALID KEY PERFORM 400-ERROR-RTN
        NOT INVALID KEY PERFORM 300-UPDATE-RTN
    END-READ.
300-UPDATE-RTN.
    MOVE T-SALARY TO MASTER-SALARY
    REWRITE MASTER-REC
        INVALID KEY DISPLAY 'REWRITE ERROR ', MASTER-SSNO
    END-REWRITE.
400-ERROR-RTN.
    DISPLAY 'INVALID RECORD ', MASTER-SSNO.
500-INITIALIZATION-RTN.
    OPEN INPUT TRANS-IN
        I-O MASTER-FILE.
600-END-OF-JOB-RTN.
    CLOSE TRANS-IN
        MASTER-FILE.
```

Handling Invalid Keys with COBOL 74

For COBOL 74, we use the usual priming READ and PERFORM ... UNTIL in place of the in-line PERFORM and READ ... NOT AT END in 100-MAIN-MODULE. Because NOT INVALID KEY cannot be used with COBOL 74, we also code the following for 200-CALC-RTN:

```
200-CALC-RTN.
    MOVE T-SOC-SEC-NO TO MASTER-SSNO.
    READ  MASTER-FILE
        INVALID KEY PERFORM 400-ERROR-RTN.
    IF  WS-ERR-CODE = 0
        PERFORM 300-UPDATE-RTN
    ELSE
        MOVE 0 TO WS-ERR-CODE.
    READ TRANS-IN
        AT END MOVE 'NO ' TO ARE-THERE-MORE-RECORDS.
```

400-ERROR-RTN would need to include an instruction to set WS-ERR-CODE to 1:

```
400-ERROR-RTN.
    DISPLAY 'INVALID RECORD ', MASTER-SSNO.
    MOVE 1 TO WS-ERR-CODE.
```

If we attempt to read an indexed record at 200-CALC-RTN and an INVALID KEY condition results, 400-ERROR-RTN is performed, where an error message is displayed. This means that there is no record on the indexed file with a RECORD KEY equal to the transaction key field. If such an error occurs, 400-ERROR-RTN is executed, but control then returns to 200-CALC-RTN, where processing would continue *as if* there were an indexed record corresponding to the transaction record. To avoid such incorrect processing, we establish a one-position WS-ERR-CODE in WORKING-STORAGE that will contain a 0 when there is no error and a 1 when an error occurs.

You can see that COBOL 85 results in a more structured program and eliminates the need for using error codes.

Accepting Transaction Data from a Keyboard Instead of a Disk File.

When updating records from an indexed file, we often use interactive processing rather than batch processing to access records to be updated:

```
PROCEDURE DIVISION.
100-MAIN-MODULE.
    OPEN I-O MASTER-FILE
    PERFORM 200-CALC-RTN
        UNTIL THERE-ARE-NO-MORE-RECORDS
    PERFORM 600-END-OF-JOB-RTN
    STOP RUN.
200-CALC-RTN.
    DISPLAY 'ENTER SOCIAL SECURITY NO OF RECORD TO BE UPDATED'
    ACCEPT T-SOC-SEC-NO
    MOVE T-SOC-SEC-NO TO MASTER-SSNO
    READ MASTER-FILE
        INVALID KEY PERFORM 400-ERROR-RTN
        NOT INVALID KEY PERFORM 300-UPDATE-RTN
    END-READ
    DISPLAY 'ARE THERE MORE RECORDS TO UPDATE (YES/NO)?'
    ACCEPT ARE-THERE-MORE-RECORDS.
300-UPDATE-RTN.
    DISPLAY 'ENTER NEW SALARY'
    ACCEPT T-SALARY
    MOVE T-SALARY TO MASTER-SALARY
    REWRITE MASTER-REC
        INVALID KEY DISPLAY
            'REWRITE ERROR ', MASTER-SSNO
    END-REWRITE.
```

400-ERR-RTN and 600-END-OF-JOB-RTN are the same as in the previous illustration. Note that there is no SELECT, OPEN, READ, or CLOSE for the transaction data entered interactively.

Additional Features of an Update Procedure

The previous update procedure used transaction data to change or update the salary in a master record. Often other types of update processing are required, such as adding or deleting records or changing other fields. We may use a *coded field* to designate the specific type of updating we want. Types of updating may include:

1. Making other types of changes to existing records. For example, promotions, salary increases, name changes, and transfers might need to be incorporated in existing payroll records. A code may be used to indicate the type of update. The REWRITE verb is used to alter existing records.

2. Creating new records. For example, new hires must be added to a payroll file. There is no need to look up a master disk record when a transaction record has a coded field that designates it as a new hire. Rather, the transaction data should be moved to the master disk area, and a simple WRITE instruction (*not* REWRITE) for a new hire should be used to create the new record.

3. Deleting some existing records. For example, the records of employees who have resigned must be deleted from a payroll file. If a transaction record indicates that a master record is to be deleted, we look up the corresponding indexed master record and code a DELETE statement. The format for the DELETE statement is as follows:

Format

```
DELETE indexed-file-name-1 RECORD
    [INVALID KEY imperative-statement-1]
    [NOT INVALID KEY imperative-statement-2]*
[END-DELETE]*
```

*The NOT INVALID KEY clause and the END-DELETE scope terminator are used only with COBOL 85.

Note that we use the *file-name* with the DELETE verb, but the word RECORD can be specified as well. That is, both the statements DELETE INDEXED-FILE and DELETE INDEXED-FILE RECORD can be used to delete the record in the INDEXED-FILE storage area. Note that the word RECORD is optional with the DELETE statement.

To delete a record from an indexed file, you need not first read the record into storage before executing a DELETE statement. When an audit trail is being created in conjunction with an update, however, you may want to READ the record before a DELETE so that you can print a line indicating the contents of the record being deleted.

With COBOL 74, we need a switch or flag to avoid processing errors when an INVALID KEY has occurred. With COBOL 85, we can code INVALID KEY and NOT INVALID KEY, where NOT INVALID KEY executes all the instructions we need when a "match" occurs, signifying that an indexed record was found.

Suppose we have an indexed inventory file that uses PART-NO as the RECORD KEY. To delete the record for PART-NO 005 where the RECORD KEY is called I-PART-NO, we code one of the following:

1. Using a switch or flag for processing errors with *COBOL 74*:

```
MOVE 0 TO ERR-SWITCH.
MOVE 005 TO I-PART-NO.
READ INVENTORY-FILE
    INVALID KEY DISPLAY 'NO SUCH RECORD'
                MOVE 1 TO ERR-SWITCH.
IF  ERR-SWITCH = 0
    DELETE INVENTORY-FILE RECORD
        INVALID KEY DISPLAY 'DELETE ERROR'.
```

2. Using the NOT INVALID KEY clause with *COBOL 85* to control processing:

```
MOVE 005 TO I-PART-NO
```

```
READ INVENTORY-FILE
    INVALID KEY DISPLAY 'NO SUCH RECORD'
    NOT INVALID KEY
        DELETE INVENTORY-FILE RECORD
            INVALID KEY DISPLAY 'DELETE ERROR'
        END-DELETE
END-READ.
```

Example of a Full Update Procedure

Thus, a single update procedure can include routines for changing existing records, adding new records, or deleting existing records. This is accomplished by using a coded field in the transaction record that specifies whether the corresponding transaction is to be used to change a master record, add a master record, or delete a master record.

Consider an update program where disk transaction records will be used to (1) change existing master records, (2) create new master records, or (3) delete some master records. Because an indexed master file can be accessed randomly, the transaction records need not be in the same sequence as the master records. The transaction record format is as follows:

   1–9   Social Security number
  10–29 Payroll data
    30   Update Code (1-new employee, 2-regular update, 3-separation from company)

The master file format is as follows:

   1–9   Social Security number (RECORD KEY)
  10–29 Payroll data

Figure 15.7 has the hierarchy chart and pseudocode. See Figure 15.8 for a suggested solution.

Figure 15.7   Hierarchy chart and pseudocode for updating an indexed file randomly.

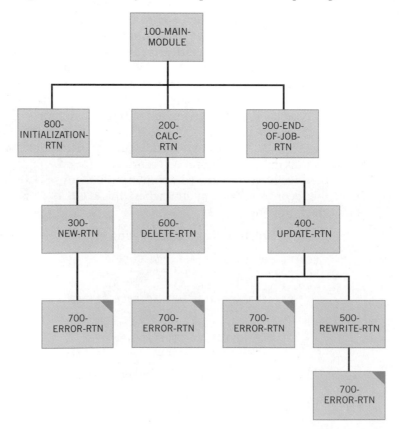

Figure 15.7 (continued)

Pseudocode

MAIN-MODULE
START
    PERFORM Initialization-Rtn
    PERFORM UNTIL there is no more data
        READ a Transaction Record
            AT END
                Move 'NO ' to Are-There-More-Records
            NOT AT END
                PERFORM Calc-Rtn
        END-READ
    END-PERFORM
    PERFORM End-of-Job-Rtn
STOP

INITIALIZATION-RTN
    Open the Files

CALC-RTN
    EVALUATE
        WHEN New Employee
                PERFORM New-Rtn
        WHEN Separation
                PERFORM Delete-Rtn
        WHEN Update
                PERFORM Update-Rtn
        WHEN Other
                Display error message
    END-EVALUATE

NEW-RTN
    Write a New Record

DELETE-RTN
    Delete the Record

UPDATE-RTN
    Read the Corresponding Master Record
    Update and Rewrite the Record

END-OF-JOB-RTN
    End-of-Job Operations

Figure 15.8 Program to update an indexed file randomly.

COBOL 85

```
IDENTIFICATION DIVISION.
PROGRAM-ID. SAMPLE.
****************************************************************
*  this program updates a master file with transactions   *
****************************************************************
ENVIRONMENT DIVISION.
INPUT-OUTPUT SECTION.
FILE-CONTROL.
    SELECT TRANS-FILE-IN  ASSIGN TO DISK 'DATA158'.
    SELECT MASTER-FILE-IO ASSIGN TO DISK 'D158M'
```

Figure 15.8 (continued)

```
                        ORGANIZATION IS INDEXED
                        ACCESS IS RANDOM
                        RECORD KEY IS MASTER-SSNO-IO.
             *
             DATA DIVISION.
             FILE SECTION.
             FD  TRANS-FILE-IN
                 LABEL RECORDS ARE STANDARD.
             01  TRANS-REC-IN.
                 05  TRANS-SSNO-IN           PIC X(9).
                 05  TRANS-PAYROLL-DATA-IN   PIC X(20).
                 05  TRANS-CODE-IN           PIC X.
                     88  NEW-EMPLOYEE                    VALUE '1'.
                     88  UPDATE-EMPLOYEE                 VALUE '2'.
                     88  SEPARATION                      VALUE '3'.
             FD  MASTER-FILE-IO
                 LABEL RECORDS ARE STANDARD.
             01  MASTER-REC-IO.
                 05  MASTER-SSNO-IO          PIC X(9).
                 05  MASTER-DATA-IO          PIC X(20).
             WORKING-STORAGE SECTION.
             01  WORK-AREAS.
                 05  ARE-THERE-MORE-RECORDS  PIC X(3)    VALUE 'YES'.
                     88  NO-MORE-RECORDS                 VALUE 'NO '.
             *
             PROCEDURE DIVISION.
             ********************************************
             *  controls direction of program logic  *
             ********************************************
             100-MAIN-MODULE.
                 PERFORM 800-INITIALIZATION-RTN
                 PERFORM UNTIL NO-MORE-RECORDS
                     READ TRANS-FILE-IN
                         AT END
                             MOVE 'NO ' TO ARE-THERE-MORE-RECORDS
                         NOT AT END
                             PERFORM 200-CALC-RTN
                     END-READ
                 END-PERFORM
                 PERFORM 900-END-OF-JOB-RTN
                 STOP RUN.
             ***************************************************
             *  performed from 100-main-module. determines the  *
             *  type of action required by the transaction file.*
             ***************************************************
             200-CALC-RTN.
                 EVALUATE TRUE
                     WHEN NEW-EMPLOYEE
                         PERFORM 300-NEW-RTN
                     WHEN SEPARATION
                         PERFORM 600-DELETE-RTN
                     WHEN UPDATE-EMPLOYEE
                         PERFORM 400-UPDATE-RTN
                     WHEN OTHER
                         DISPLAY 'ERROR IN CODE'
                 END-EVALUATE.



             ***************************************************
             *  performed from 200-calc-rtn. adds new records  *
             *  to the master file                             *
             ***************************************************
             300-NEW-RTN.
                 MOVE TRANS-SSNO-IN TO MASTER-SSNO-IO
                 MOVE TRANS-PAYROLL-DATA-IN TO MASTER-DATA-IO
                 WRITE MASTER-REC-IO
```

COBOL 74 Substitutions

```
PERFORM 200-CALC-RTN
    UNTIL NO-MORE-RECORDS.
```

COBOL 74 users substitute
nested IFs for the EVALUATE

```
READ TRANS-FILE-IN
    AT END MOVE 'NO ' TO
    ARE-THERE-MORE-RECORDS.
```

Figure 15.8 (continued)

```
                           INVALID KEY PERFORM 700-ERROR-RTN
                      END-WRITE.
              ****************************************************
              *  performed from 200-calc-rtn. reads a master record  *
              *  and tests for errors.                               *
              ****************************************************
              400-UPDATE-RTN.
                  MOVE SPACES TO MASTER-REC-IO
                  MOVE TRANS-SSNO-IN TO MASTER-SSNO-IO
                  READ MASTER-FILE-IO ◄
                      INVALID KEY PERFORM 700-ERROR-RTN
                      NOT INVALID KEY PERFORM 500-REWRITE-RTN
                  END-READ.
              ****************************************************
              *  performed from 400-update-rtn. updates a record on the *
              *  master file with the transaction data and rewrites the *
              *  master record.                                         *
              ****************************************************
              500-REWRITE-RTN.
                  MOVE TRANS-PAYROLL-DATA-IN TO MASTER-DATA-IO
                  REWRITE MASTER-REC-IO ◄
                      INVALID KEY PERFORM 700-ERROR-RTN
                  END-REWRITE.
              ****************************************************
              *  performed from 200-calc-rtn. deletes a record from *
              *  the master file.                                   *
              ****************************************************
              600-DELETE-RTN.
                  MOVE TRANS-SSNO-IN TO MASTER-SSNO-IO
                  DELETE MASTER-FILE-IO ◄
                      INVALID KEY PERFORM 700-ERROR-RTN
                  END-DELETE.
              ****************************************************
              *  performed from 300-new-rtn, 400-update-rtn,       *
              *  500-rewrite-rtn, and 600-delete-rtn.  displays    *
              *  an error message.                                 *
              ****************************************************
              700-ERROR-RTN.
                  DISPLAY 'ERROR ', TRANS-SSNO-IN.
              ****************************************************
              *  performed from 100-main-module. opens files.  *
              ****************************************************
              800-INITIALIZATION-RTN.
                  OPEN INPUT TRANS-FILE-IN
                       I-O   MASTER-FILE-IO. ◄



              ****************************************************
              *  performed from 100-main-module. closes files.    *
              ****************************************************
              900-END-OF-JOB-RTN.
                  CLOSE TRANS-FILE-IN
                        MASTER-FILE-IO.
```

COBOL 74 Substitutions

COBOL 74 users substitute → an error code test

Accesses the master record that corresponds to the Social Security number in the transaction record

Updates the master record with the transaction data

The master record need not be read before it is deleted

When disks are updated directly, they are opened as I-O

```
READ TRANS-FILE-IN
    AT END MOVE 'NO ' TO
ARE-THERE-MORE-RECORDS.
```
→

DEBUGGING TIP—COBOL 85 USERS

Note that with so many INVALID KEY clauses in a program the risk of errors because of misplacement of periods is great. COBOL 85 users should minimize such risks by always including scope terminators and including a period only for the last statement in a paragraph.

The IDENTIFICATION DIVISION of programs updating indexed disk files is the same as previously described. It is the ENVIRONMENT DIVISION that incorporates the clauses necessary for specifying indexed disk files. Since an indexed disk file is typically updated randomly, ORGANIZATION IS INDEXED and ACCESS MODE IS RANDOM would be coded. The RECORD KEY clause is a required entry for all indexed files regardless of whether we are creating, updating, or reading from an indexed file.

The DATA DIVISION for indexed file updating is basically the same as when updating sequential files. Note that disk records generally use standard labels. Typically, the first field within each disk record is the RECORD KEY.

In the PROCEDURE DIVISION for an indexed file update, the transaction file's TRANS-SSNO-IN must be moved to the RECORD KEY field called MASTER-SSNO-IO *before* an indexed record may be accessed randomly. For updates, the READ MASTER-FILE-IO instruction will read into storage a record from the indexed file with the *same* Social Security number as the one that appears in the TRANS-FILE-IN.

Because NOT INVALID KEY cannot be used with COBOL 74, we need to establish an error code field instead:

```
WORKING-STORAGE SECTION.
01  WS-ERROR-CODE                      PIC 9 VALUE ZERO.
    88  NO-ERROR                       VALUE ZERO.
200-CALC-RTN.
    MOVE ZERO TO WS-ERROR-CODE.    ◄──── Sets the error code to "off" each
      :                                   time through 200-CALC-RTN
400-UPDATE-RTN.
      :
    READ MASTER-FILE-IO
        INVALID KEY PERFORM 700-ERROR-RTN.
    IF NO-ERROR
        PERFORM 500-REWRITE-RTN.   ◄──── Rewrites only if record found
      :                                   (error code is off)
600-DELETE-RTN.
    MOVE TRANS-SSNO-IN TO MASTER-SSNO-IO.
    DELETE MASTER-FILE-IO RECORD
        INVALID KEY PERFORM 700-ERROR-RTN.
700-ERROR-RTN.
    DISPLAY 'ERROR ', TRANS-SSNO-IN.
    MOVE 1 TO WS-ERROR-CODE.   ◄──── Sets error code on
```

200-CALC-RTN re-initializes a WS-ERROR-CODE field to 0. We use this error code field at 400-UPDATE-RTN to control processing when an error has occurred. That is, if there was a READ error, we can avoid processing a record that could not be accessed properly. The condition name NO-ERROR means that WS-ERROR-CODE has a zero, that is, there is no error. Only if the condition-name NO-ERROR exists will processing of the desired indexed record continue; if WS-ERROR-CODE is not zero at 400-UPDATE-RTN, then it means we did not find a corresponding indexed record when we performed a READ and we do not, therefore, want to perform 500-REWRITE-RTN.

Interactive Processing. When updating an indexed file, it is likely that the transactions or changes would be entered from a terminal or PC keyboard rather than read from a file. See Figure 15.9 for the program that updates an indexed file interactively.

Figure 15.9 Program to update an indexed file interactively.

```
IDENTIFICATION DIVISION.
PROGRAM-ID.  SAMPLE.
***************************************************************
*   This program updates an indexed file interactively *
***************************************************************
ENVIRONMENT DIVISION.
INPUT-OUTPUT SECTION.
```

Figure 15.9   (continued)

```
      FILE-CONTROL.
          SELECT MASTER-FILE-IO ASSIGN TO DISK 'PAY.IND'
              ORGANIZATION IS INDEXED
              ACCESS IS RANDOM
              RECORD KEY IS MASTER-SSNO-IO.
  *
      DATA DIVISION.
      FILE SECTION.
      FD  MASTER-FILE-IO
          LABEL RECORDS ARE STANDARD.
      01  MASTER-REC-IO.
          05  MASTER-SSNO-IO         PIC X(9).
          05  MASTER-NAME            PIC X(20).
          05  MASTER-SALARY          PIC 9(6).
          05  MASTER-DEPT            PIC 99.
      WORKING-STORAGE SECTION.
      01  WORK-AREAS.
          05  ARE-THERE-MORE-RECORDS PIC X(3)        VALUE 'YES'.
              88  MORE-RECORDS                        VALUE 'YES'.
              88  NO-MORE-RECORDS                     VALUE 'NO '.
          05  TRANS-CODE             PIC 9.
              88  NEW-EMPLOYEE                        VALUE 1.
              88  UPDATE-EMPLOYEE                     VALUE 2.
              88  SEPARATION                          VALUE 3.
          05  ANSWER-1               PIC X.
          05  ANSWER-2               PIC X.
          05  ANSWER-3               PIC X.
  *
      PROCEDURE DIVISION.
      100-MAIN-MODULE.
          PERFORM 800-INITIALIZATION-RTN
          PERFORM 200-CALC-RTN
              UNTIL NO-MORE-RECORDS
          PERFORM 900-END-OF-JOB-RTN
          STOP RUN.
      200-CALC-RTN.
          DISPLAY 'ENTER 1 FOR NEW EMPLOYEE'
          DISPLAY 'ENTER 2 FOR UPDATE THE RECORD'
          DISPLAY 'ENTER 3 FOR DELETE THE RECORD'
          ACCEPT TRANS-CODE
          DISPLAY 'ENTER SOCIAL SECURITY NUMBER'
          ACCEPT MASTER-SSNO-IO
          EVALUATE TRUE
              WHEN NEW-EMPLOYEE     PERFORM 300-NEW-RTN
              WHEN SEPARATION       PERFORM 600-DELETE-RTN
              WHEN UPDATE-EMPLOYEE  PERFORM 400-UPDATE-RTN
              WHEN OTHER            DISPLAY 'ERROR'
          END-EVALUATE
          DISPLAY 'ARE THERE MORE RECORDS (YES/NO)?'
          ACCEPT ARE-THERE-MORE-RECORDS.
      300-NEW-RTN.
          DISPLAY 'ENTER NAME'
          ACCEPT MASTER-NAME
          DISPLAY 'ENTER SALARY'
          ACCEPT MASTER-SALARY
          DISPLAY 'ENTER DEPT NO'
          ACCEPT MASTER-DEPT
          WRITE MASTER-REC-IO
              INVALID KEY DISPLAY 'RECORD IS ALREADY ON THE FILE'
          END-WRITE.
      400-UPDATE-RTN.
          READ MASTER-FILE-IO
              INVALID KEY DISPLAY 'NO MASTER RECORD FOUND'
              NOT INVALID KEY PERFORM 500-OK-RTN
          END-READ.
```

Figure 15.9   (continued)

```
500-OK-RTN.
    DISPLAY 'DO YOU WANT TO CHANGE THE NAME (Y/N)?'
    ACCEPT ANSWER-1
    IF ANSWER-1 = 'Y'
        DISPLAY 'ENTER NEW NAME'
        ACCEPT MASTER-NAME
    END-IF
    DISPLAY 'DO YOU WANT TO CHANGE THE SALARY (Y/N)?'
    ACCEPT ANSWER-2
    IF ANSWER-2 = 'Y'
        DISPLAY 'ENTER NEW SALARY'
        ACCEPT MASTER-SALARY
    END-IF
    DISPLAY 'DO YOU WANT TO CHANGE THE DEPT NO. (Y/N)?'
    ACCEPT ANSWER-3
    IF ANSWER-3 = 'Y'
        DISPLAY 'ENTER NEW DEPT NO'
        ACCEPT MASTER-DEPT
    END-IF
    REWRITE MASTER-REC-IO
        INVALID KEY DISPLAY 'REWRITE ERROR'
    END-REWRITE.
600-DELETE-RTN.
    DELETE MASTER-FILE-IO RECORD
        INVALID KEY DISPLAY 'DELETE ERROR'
    END-DELETE.
800-INITIALIZATION-RTN.
    OPEN I-O MASTER-FILE-IO.
900-END-OF-JOB-RTN.
    CLOSE MASTER-FILE-IO.
```

UPDATING AN INDEXED FILE WITH MULTIPLE TRANSACTION RECORDS FOR EACH MASTER RECORD

In Chapter 13, we illustrated *two separate types* of updates for sequential master files: when (1) only one transaction per master is permitted or when (2) multiple transactions per master are permitted. With indexed master files, the *same procedure* can be used regardless of the number of transactions per master. That is, we can REWRITE the *same* master disk record each time a transaction record is read. Suppose 10 transaction records for a given master record are needed to add 10 amounts to the master's balance due. We simply retrieve the master record 10 times and each time add the corresponding transaction amount to the master record's balance due.

Thus, an indexed file update is exactly *the same* regardless of whether there is only one transaction record per master or there are multiple transactions per master. See Figure 15.8 again.

──────── DEBUGGING TIP ────────

As noted, to test programs that update indexed master files, the indexed master file must first be created. Indexed files cannot be created as test data using a text editor the way sequential files can. Rather, a program is required to create them.

Always precede the test of the update program by running the indexed file creation program first. This ensures that the indexed file used in the update is a "clean" copy. When it is updated, display the changes and check them during debugging. In this way, you always know what the master file contained initially and what it contains after the update.

If you do several tests of the update program without creating a "clean" indexed master file first, the file may contain changes generated from prior test runs and you may not be able to effectively check if the update works properly.

One way to ensure that a clean indexed file is created before each test run of the update program is to code the create routine in a separate program and CALL the program-id entry as the first instruction in the main module of the update program:

Main Update Program	**Called Program**
	IDENTIFICATION DIVISION.
.	PROGRAM-ID. CREATE.
.	
100-MAIN.	.
CALL 'CREATE'	.
.	

Chapter 16 discusses the CALL statement in more detail.

Note, too, that records in an indexed file cannot be viewed with a simple DISPLAY statement. Data in an indexed record must be moved to a standard sequential record and printed with a WRITE instruction or viewed with a DISPLAY instruction.

ACCESSING OR READING FROM AN INDEXED FILE FOR REPORTING PURPOSES

An indexed file may be read from, or accessed, either sequentially or randomly for reporting purposes. We discuss both access methods next.

Printing from an Indexed File Sequentially

Suppose we have an accounts receivable indexed master file that is in ACCT-NO sequence and we want to process records in that sequence. In this case, processing the ACCTS-RECEIVABLE file is *exactly the same* regardless of whether it is an indexed file accessed sequentially or a sequential file.

If we wished to print customer bills from the ACCTS-RECEIVABLE file in ascending alphabetic sequence by NAME, we could *still* use sequential processing even though the file is not initially in sequence by NAME. First, we would *sort* the file into alphabetic sequence by NAME and then print the bills using standard sequential processing techniques:

COBOL 85

```
SORT SORT-FILE
      ON ASCENDING KEY S-NAME
          USING ACCTS-RECEIVABLE
          GIVING AR-SORTED-BY-NAME
OPEN INPUT AR-SORTED-BY-NAME
     OUTPUT PRINT-FILE
PERFORM UNTIL THERE-ARE-NO-MORE-RECORDS
    READ AR-SORTED-BY-NAME
        AT END
            MOVE 'NO ' TO ARE-THERE-MORE-RECORDS
        NOT AT END
            PERFORM 200-PRINT-BILLS
    END-READ
END-PERFORM
CLOSE AR-SORTED-BY-NAME
      PRINT-FILE
STOP RUN.
```

COBOL 74 Substitutions

```
READ AR-SORTED-BY-NAME
    AT END MOVE 'NO ' TO
        ARE-THERE-MORE-RECORDS.
PERFORM 200-PRINT-BILLS
    UNTIL THERE-ARE-NO-MORE-RECORDS.
```

Note that COBOL 85 compilers permit sorting of indexed files with the SORT verb. COBOL 74 compilers might not permit this; if your compiler does not allow sorting of indexed files, a sort utility program would need to be used.

Even though we are not using the index of the ACCTS-RECEIVABLE file in this SORT procedure, the corresponding SELECT statement must have the clauses ORGANIZATION IS INDEXED and RECORD KEY IS ACCT-NO. In all other ways, however, the programs would be the same as if ACCTS-RECEIVABLE were a sequential file.

Figure 15.10 illustrates a program that accesses an indexed file sequentially.

Figure 15.10 Program that accesses an indexed file sequentially.

COBOL 85

```
IDENTIFICATION DIVISION.
PROGRAM-ID. SAMPLE.
************************************************************
*     this program accesses an indexed                    *
*     sequential file sequentially.                       *
************************************************************
ENVIRONMENT DIVISION.
INPUT-OUTPUT SECTION.
FILE-CONTROL.
     SELECT ACCTS-RECEIVABLE ASSIGN TO DISK1
         ORGANIZATION IS INDEXED
         ACCESS IS SEQUENTIAL
         RECORD KEY IS M-CUST-NO-IN.
     SELECT PRINT-OUT ASSIGN TO PRINTER.
*
DATA DIVISION.
FILE SECTION.
FD  ACCTS-RECEIVABLE
    LABEL RECORDS ARE STANDARD.
01  MASTER-REC.
    05  M-CUST-NO-IN              PIC 9(9).
    05  M-NAME-IN                 PIC X(20).
    05  M-SALARY-IN               PIC 9(5).
    05                            PIC X(66).
FD  PRINT-OUT
    LABEL RECORDS ARE OMITTED.
01  PRINT-REC                     PIC X(132).
WORKING-STORAGE SECTION.
01  WORK-AREAS.
    05  ARE-THERE-MORE-RECORDS    PIC X(3)    VALUE 'YES'.
        88  NO-MORE-RECORDS                   VALUE 'NO '.
    05  WS-LINE-CT                PIC 99      VALUE ZEROS.
    05  WS-PAGE-CT                PIC 999     VALUE ZEROS.
01  HDG.
    05                            PIC X(55)   VALUE SPACES.
    05                            PIC X(43)
                        VALUE 'PAYROLL SUMMARY REPORT'.
    05                            PIC X(4)    VALUE 'PAGE'.
    05  PAGE-OUT                  PIC ZZ9.
    05                            PIC X(27)   VALUE SPACES.
01  DETAIL-REC.
    05                            PIC X(9)    VALUE SPACES.
    05  CUST-NO-OUT               PIC 9(9).
    05                            PIC X(10)   VALUE SPACES.
    05  NAME-OUT                  PIC X(20).
    05                            PIC X(10)   VALUE SPACES.
    05  SALARY-OUT                PIC $ZZ,ZZZ.ZZ.
    05                            PIC X(62)   VALUE SPACES.
*
PROCEDURE DIVISION.
100-MAIN-MODULE.
    OPEN INPUT ACCTS-RECEIVABLE
         OUTPUT PRINT-OUT
    PERFORM 300-HDG-RTN
    PERFORM UNTIL NO-MORE-RECORDS
        READ ACCTS-RECEIVABLE
            AT END
                MOVE 'NO ' TO
                    ARE-THERE-MORE-RECORDS
            NOT AT END
                PERFORM 200-CALC-RTN
        END-READ
    END-PERFORM
```

←—This is a typical SELECT statement for an indexed file that is to be accessed sequentially

COBOL 74 Substitutions

For COBOL 74, FILLER must be used instead of a blank field name

```
READ ACCTS-RECEIVABLE
    AT END MOVE 'NO ' TO
        ARE-THERE-MORE-RECORDS.
PERFORM 200-CALC-RTN
    UNTIL NO-MORE-RECORDS.
```

—AT END and NOT AT END are used when an indexed file is accessed sequentially

Figure 15.10 (continued)

```
                              CLOSE ACCTS-RECEIVABLE
                                    PRINT-OUT
                              STOP RUN.
                          200-CALC-RTN.
                              MOVE M-CUST-NO-IN TO CUST-NO-OUT
                              MOVE M-NAME-IN TO NAME-OUT
                              MOVE M-SALARY-IN TO SALARY-OUT
                              IF  WS-LINE-CT > 25
                                  PERFORM 300-HDG-RTN
                              END-IF
                              WRITE PRINT-REC FROM DETAIL-REC
                                    AFTER ADVANCING 2 LINES
                              ADD 1 TO WS-LINE-CT.


                          300-HDG-RTN.
                              ADD 1 TO WS-PAGE-CT
                              MOVE WS-PAGE-CT TO PAGE-OUT
                              WRITE PRINT-REC FROM HDG
                                    AFTER ADVANCING PAGE
                              MOVE ZEROS TO WS-LINE-CT.
```

COBOL 74 Substitutions

```
READ ACCTS-RECEIVABLE
    AT END MOVE 'NO ' TO
        ARE-THERE-MORE-RECORDS.
```

Printing from an Indexed File Randomly When Inquiries Are Made

Indexed files may also be read randomly for printing purposes. Suppose, for example, we have an indexed accounts receivable file and that customers may call a store at any time to inquire about their current balance. Since these inquiries are random, we will need to access the indexed file randomly in order to print a reply to each inquiry. Figure 15.11 illustrates the PROCEDURE DIVISION for a program that makes random inquiries

Figure 15.11 PROCEDURE DIVISION for a program that makes random inquiries about the status of master disk records.

COBOL 85

```
100-MAIN-MODULE.
    OPEN INPUT   QUERY-FILE
                 ACCTS-RECEIVABLE
         OUTPUT PRINT-FILE
    PERFORM UNTIL THERE-ARE-NO-MORE-RECORDS
        READ QUERY-FILE
            AT END
                MOVE 'NO ' TO ARE-THERE-MORE-RECORDS
            NOT AT END
                PERFORM 200-CALC-RTN
        END-READ
    END-PERFORM
    CLOSE QUERY-FILE
          ACCTS-RECEIVABLE
          PRINT-FILE
    STOP RUN.
200-CALC-RTN.
    MOVE Q-ACCT-NO TO ACCT-NO
    READ ACCTS-RECEIVABLE
        INVALID KEY
            DISPLAY 'ERROR ', ACCT-NO
        NOT INVALID KEY
            MOVE BAL-DUE TO BAL-DUE-OUT
            MOVE ACCT-NO TO ACCT-OUT
            WRITE PRINT-REC AFTER ADVANCING 2 LINES
    END-READ.
```

COBOL 74 Substitutions

```
READ QUERY-FILE
    AT END MOVE 'NO ' TO ARE-THERE-MORE-RECORDS.
PERFORM 200-CALC-RTN
    UNTIL THERE-ARE-NO-MORE-RECORDS.
```

```
READ QUERY-FILE
    AT END MOVE 'NO ' TO ARE-THERE-MORE-RECORDS.
```

about the status of master records in an indexed file using a query file as input. The user enters customer account numbers, which are stored on disk, and the computer accesses the corresponding master disk records and prints the balances due for those customers.

Interactive Processing.   Often, inquiries are made interactively from a keyboard as opposed to being stored in a QUERY-FILE that is processed in batch mode. The output would normally be displayed, but it could be printed as in Figure 15.11. Figure 15.12 illustrates the PROCEDURE DIVISION for answering interactive inquiries using COBOL 85.

THE FILE STATUS CLAUSE

Consider the following coding for an indexed file to be created as output:

```
WRITE INDEXED-PAY-REC
      INVALID KEY DISPLAY 'A WRITE ERROR HAS OCCURRED'
END-WRITE
```

If the INVALID KEY clause is executed, we know that a write error occurred, but we do not really know what specifically caused the error. It could be a duplicate key error, a sequence error, or some other error.

The **FILE STATUS** clause can be used with the SELECT statement to determine the exact type of input or output error that has occurred when either reading from or writing to a file.

The SELECT statement for an indexed file could include FILE STATUS as its last clause:

Format

> SELECT ...
>   [FILE STATUS is data-name]

where the data-name specified must appear in WORKING-STORAGE as a *two-position alphanumeric field*.

Example

```
        SELECT INDEXED-PAY-FILE ...
            FILE STATUS IS WS-STATUS.
        :
WORKING-STORAGE SECTION.
01  WS-STATUS          PIC X(2).
```

Figure 15.12   PROCEDURE DIVISION for answering interactive inquiries using COBOL 85.

```
100-MAIN-MODULE.
    OPEN INPUT ACCTS-RECEIVABLE
    PERFORM 200-CALC-RTN
        UNTIL THERE-ARE-NO-MORE-RECORDS
    CLOSE ACCTS-RECEIVABLE
        PRINT-FILE
    STOP RUN.
200-CALC-RTN.
    DISPLAY 'ENTER ACCT NO OF RECORD TO BE ACCESSED'
    ACCEPT ACCT-NO
    READ ACCTS-RECEIVABLE
        INVALID KEY     DISPLAY 'THIS ACCT IS NOT ON THE FILE'
        NOT INVALID KEY DISPLAY 'BALANCE DUE = ', BAL-DUE
    END-READ
    DISPLAY 'ARE THERE MORE QUERIES (YES/NO)?'
    ACCEPT ARE-THERE-MORE-RECORDS.
```

When an input or output operation is performed on INDEXED-PAY-FILE, the operating system will place a value in WS-STATUS, which may be tested by the programmer in the PROCEDURE DIVISION. The result of an I/O operation can thus be more specifically determined.

The following are possible values that may be placed in the FILE STATUS field when an input or output operation is performed. FILE STATUS can be used with *any* type of file; we highlight those values specifically relating to indexed files with an *. Note that if the leftmost character in the FILE STATUS field is a 0, the I/O operation was successfully completed. If it is not zero, then the I/O operation resulted in an error.

Contents of the FILE STATUS field after an input or output operation	Meaning
Successful Completion	
* 00	Successful completion—no error occurred.
04	A READ statement has been successfully completed, but the length of the record does not conform to the File Description specifications.
Unsuccessful Completion	
* 10	A sequential READ statement (READ ... AT END) has been attempted, but there are no more input records.
* 21	A sequence error has occurred—keys are not in the correct order.
* 22	An attempt was made to write a record that would create a duplicate primary record key.
* 23	The required record was not found during a READ.
* 24	A boundary error has occurred—an attempt has been made to write beyond the preestablished boundaries of an indexed file as established by the operating system.
* 30	A permanent data error has occurred (this is a hardware problem.)
34	A boundary error for a sequential file has occurred.
37	A permanent error has occurred because an OPEN statement has been attempted on a file that will not support the mode specified in the OPEN statement (e.g., an indexed file is opened as OUTPUT when ACCESS IS RANDOM has been specified, or a print file is opened as I-0).
41	An OPEN statement has been attempted on a file that is already open.
42	A CLOSE statement has been attempted on a file that has not been opened.
* 43	An attempt has been made to DELETE or REWRITE a record after an unsuccessful READ (e.g., there is no record in storage to delete or rewrite).
9x	Codes of 91–99 are specifically defined by the implementor—consult your user's manual.

The preceding are just some of the values that the FILE STATUS field can contain. As noted, the FILE STATUS clause can be used with *any* type of file, not only indexed files. The * entries, however, are those that apply specifically to indexed files.

Using the FILE STATUS field, we can display a more meaningful message if an input or output error occurs. Consider the following output routine:

```
WRITE INDEXED-PAY-REC
    INVALID KEY PERFORM 500-ERROR-RTN
END-WRITE
IF  WS-STATUS = '00'
    PERFORM 600-OK-RTN
END-IF
    ⋮
```

```
500-ERROR-RTN.
    IF  WS-STATUS = '21'
        DISPLAY 'KEY IS NOT IN SEQUENCE ',
                EMP-NO-RECORD-KEY
    END-IF
    IF  WS-STATUS = '22'
        DISPLAY 'DUPLICATE KEY ',
                EMP-NO-RECORD-KEY
    END-IF
      :
      :
```

Each time an input or output operation is performed on a file with a FILE STATUS clause, the specified data-name will be reset with a new value.

SELF-TEST
1. To access records in an indexed file randomly, we move the transaction record's key field to the _____ .
2. When a record is to be deleted from an indexed file, we use a _____ instruction.
3. The INVALID KEY option can be part of which statements?
4. The INVALID KEY option tests the validity of the _____ KEY.
5. If READ FILE-X INVALID KEY PERFORM 800-ERROR-1 is executed, 800-ERROR-1 will be performed if _____ .
6. (T or F) Indexed files are typically created in sequence by RECORD KEY.
7. If a record is to be added to a disk file, a (WRITE, REWRITE) statement is used.
8. Consider the following input transaction record:

   1   Update Code (1-new account; 2-update account; 3-delete account)
   2–5   Transaction number
   6–80   Transaction data

   Consider the following indexed master disk record:

   1–4   Transaction number
   5–79   Master data

   Write a PROCEDURE DIVISION routine to update the master file with input data. Stop the run if an INVALID KEY condition is encountered.

Solutions
1. RECORD KEY of the indexed record
2. DELETE file-name
3. The READ (where ACCESS IS RANDOM is specified), WRITE, REWRITE, or DELETE
4. RECORD
5. a record with the indicated RECORD KEY cannot be found in FILE-X
6. T
7. WRITE
8. **COBOL 85 Program:**

```
PROCEDURE DIVISION.
100-MAIN-MODULE.
    OPEN INPUT TRANS
              I-O INDEXED-FILE
    PERFORM UNTIL THERE-ARE-NO-MORE-RECORDS
        READ TRANS
            AT END
                MOVE 'NO ' TO ARE-THERE-MORE-RECORDS
            NOT AT END
                PERFORM 200-CALC-RTN
        END-READ
    END-PERFORM
    CLOSE TRANS
          INDEXED-FILE
    STOP RUN.
200-CALC-RTN.
    MOVE TRANS-KEY TO MASTER-KEY
```

COBOL 74 Substitutions

```
READ TRANS
    AT END MOVE 'NO ' TO
        ARE-THERE-MORE-RECORDS.
PERFORM 200-CALC-RTN UNTIL
    THERE-ARE-NO-MORE-RECORDS.
```

COBOL 74 Substitutions

COBOL 74 users
should substitute
nested IFs for
the EVALUATE

```
EVALUATE TRUE
    WHEN CODE-X = 1
        PERFORM 300-NEW-ACCT
    WHEN CODE-X = 2
        PERFORM 400-UPDATE-RTN
    WHEN CODE-X = 3
        PERFORM 500-DELETE-RTN
    WHEN OTHER
        DISPLAY 'ERROR'
END-EVALUATE.
```

```
READ TRANS
    AT END MOVE 'NO ' TO
        ARE-THERE-MORE-RECORDS.
```

```
300-NEW-ACCT.
    MOVE TRANS-DATA TO MASTER-DATA
    WRITE MASTER-REC
        INVALID KEY PERFORM 600-ERR-RTN
    END-WRITE.
400-UPDATE-RTN.
    READ INDEXED-FILE
        INVALID KEY PERFORM 600-ERR-RTN
    END-READ
    MOVE TRANS-DATA TO MASTER-DATA
    REWRITE MASTER-REC
        INVALID KEY PERFORM 600-ERR-RTN
    END-REWRITE.
500-DELETE-RTN.
    DELETE INDEXED-FILE RECORD
        INVALID KEY DISPLAY 'ERROR ON DELETE'
    END-DELETE.
600-ERR-RTN.
    DISPLAY 'ERROR ', TRANS-KEY
    CLOSE TRANS
            INDEXED-FILE
    STOP RUN.
```

— WEB SITE —

There are many more options that can be used with indexed files. These include ALTERNATE RECORD KEY, START, DYNAMIC access, and READ ... NEXT RECORD, all of which can facilitate inquiry into a database. Error control procedures can also be handled in alternate ways. For more information on indexed files, you can access or download a supplement to this chapter. Go to www.wiley.com/cobol/ to access this book's Home Page with directions for downloading supplements.

PROCESSING RELATIVE DISK FILES

WHAT IS A RELATIVE FILE?

We have seen in this chapter how disk files that are organized as INDEXED can be accessed and updated randomly. The relative method of file organization is another technique used when files are to be accessed randomly.

With indexed files, the key fields of records to be accessed are looked up in an index to find the disk address. With relative files, the key field is converted to an actual disk address so that there is no need for an index or for a search to find the location of a record. We begin with the simplest type of relative file where there is a direct one-to-one correlation between the value of the key and its disk location. That is, the key also serves as a relative record number.

Suppose, for example, an Accounts Receivable file is created with records entered in sequence by ACCT-NO. If the ACCT-NOs vary from 0001 to 9999, then the record with

ACCT-NO 0001 can be placed in the first disk location, the record with ACCT-NO 0002 can be placed in the next, and so on. Accessing records randomly from such a relative file is an easy task. To find a record with ACCT-NO 9785, the computer goes directly to the 9785th record location on the disk.

When a key field does not have consecutive values, as is the case with many ACCT-NOs, we can still use the relative method of file organization but we need to convert the key to a disk address using some type of algorithm or mathematical formula.

Relative file organization is best used where each record contains a kind of built-in relative record number. Files with records that have key fields with fairly consecutive values are ideal for using relative organization. CUST-NO, PART-NO, and EMP-NO key fields are often consecutive or nearly consecutive. Since not all files have records with such key fields, however, relative files are not used as often as indexed files.

One advantage of relative files is that the random access of records is very efficient because there is no need to look up the address of a record in an index; we simply convert the key to a disk address and access the record directly.

The field that supplies the key information, such as ACCT-NO above, can also serve as a relative record number or **RELATIVE KEY**. The input/output instructions in the PROCEDURE DIVISION for random or sequential processing of relative files are very similar to those of indexed files. The following is the SELECT statement used to create or access a relative file:

```
SELECT file-name-1 ASSIGN TO implementor-name-1
    [ORGANIZATION IS] RELATIVE
    [                  { SEQUENTIAL [RELATIVE KEY IS data-name-1] } ]
    [ ACCESS IS        { RANDOM                                    } ]
    [                  { DYNAMIC   } RELATIVE KEY IS data-name-1   } ]
    [FILE STATUS IS data-name-2].
```

When ACCESS is SEQUENTIAL, as in the sequential reading of the file, the RELATIVE KEY clause is optional. When ACCESS is RANDOM or DYNAMIC, the RELATIVE KEY clause is required. A RELATIVE KEY must be unique.

If ACCESS IS DYNAMIC is specified, you can access the file both sequentially and randomly in the same program, using appropriate input/output statements. Suppose you wish to update a relative file randomly and, when the update procedure is completed, you wish to print the file in sequence. Use ACCESS IS DYNAMIC for this procedure, because it permits both sequential and random access. Indexed files can also be processed this way.

A FILE STATUS field that specifies input/output conditions may be defined in WORKING-STORAGE and used in exactly the same way as with indexed files, discussed earlier in this chapter.

The FD that defines and describes the relative file is similar to indexed file FDs except that the RELATIVE KEY is *not* part of the record but is a separate WORKING-STORAGE entry:

```
FILE SECTION.
FD   file-name
     LABEL RECORDS ARE STANDARD.
01   record.
       .
       .
WORKING-STORAGE SECTION.
       .
       .
     05   (relative-key-field)      PIC ... .
```

Example

```
SELECT REL-FILE
    ORGANIZATION IS RELATIVE
    ACCESS IS SEQUENTIAL
    RELATIVE KEY IS R-KEY.
        :
FD  REL-FILE
        :
WORKING-STORAGE SECTION.
01  R-KEY                   PIC 9(3).
```

In some relative files, each record's key field is the same as R-KEY, its relative key (e.g., a record with ACCT-NO 5832 is found at the 5,832nd disk location). In other relative files, each record's key field must be converted to R-KEY, its relative key.

CREATING RELATIVE FILES

Relative files are created sequentially, and either the computer or the user can supply the key. When a relative file's SELECT statement includes ACCESS IS SEQUENTIAL, the RELATIVE KEY clause can be omitted. If the RELATIVE KEY clause is omitted, the computer writes the records with keys designated as 1 to n. That is, the first record is placed in relative record location 1 (RELATIVE KEY = 1), the second in relative record location 2 (RELATIVE KEY = 2), and so on.

Suppose the programmer designates CUST-NO as the RELATIVE KEY when creating the file. The record with CUST-NO 001 will be the first record on disk, the record with CUST-NO 002 will be the second record, and so on. If there is no CUST-NO 003, then a blank record will automatically be inserted by the computer. Similarly, suppose a CUST-NO field that also serves as a RELATIVE KEY is entered in sequence as 10, 20, 30, and so on; blank records would be inserted in disk locations 1 to 9, 11 to 19, 21 to 29, ... This allows records to be added later between the records originally created. That is, if a CUST-NO of 09 is inserted in the file later on, there is space available for it so that it will be in the correct sequence.

The following program excerpt writes 10 records with COBOL assigning RELATIVE KEYs 1 to 10 to the records being written:

COBOL 85

```
        SELECT TRANS-FILE ASSIGN TO DISK2.
        SELECT REL-FILE ASSIGN TO DISK1
            ORGANIZATION IS RELATIVE
            ACCESS IS SEQUENTIAL. ◄──No RELATIVE KEY need be specified
                :
        OPEN INPUT TRANS-FILE
            OUTPUT REL-FILE
        PERFORM 10 TIMES
            READ TRANS-FILE
                AT END
                    MOVE 'NO ' TO ARE-THERE-MORE-RECORDS
                NOT AT END
                    PERFORM 200-WRITE-RTN
            END-READ
        END-PERFORM
                :
    200-WRITE.
        WRITE REL-REC FROM TRANS-REC
            INVALID KEY DISPLAY 'ERROR'
        END-WRITE.
*******************************************************************
* The INVALID KEY clause is executed if there is                 *
* insufficient space to store the record or if records           *
* are not in sequence.                                           *
*******************************************************************
```

COBOL 74 Substitutions

```
READ TRANS-FILE
    AT END MOVE 'NO ' TO
        ARE-THERE-MORE-RECORDS.
PERFORM 200-WRITE-RTN 10 TIMES.
```

```
READ TRANS-FILE
    AT END MOVE 'NO ' TO
        ARE-THERE-MORE-RECORDS.
```
──►

In this case there is no need for a RELATIVE KEY clause in the SELECT statement because the computer will assign relative locations to each record.

Often, a transaction file has a field that is to be used as the relative key for the relative file. The following example shows one way the programmer could supply the RELATIVE KEYs when creating a relative file:

COBOL 85

```
            SELECT TRANS-FILE  ASSIGN TO DISK2.
            SELECT REL-FILE    ASSIGN TO DISK1
                ORGANIZATION IS RELATIVE
                ACCESS IS DYNAMIC
                RELATIVE KEY IS WS-ACCT-NO. ←─This must be a WORKING-
        DATA DIVISION.                              STORAGE entry
        FILE SECTION.
        FD  TRANS-FILE
            LABEL RECORDS ARE STANDARD.
        01  TRANS-REC.
            05  ACCT-NO                 PIC 9(5).
            05  REST-OF-REC             PIC X(95).
        FD  REL-FILE
            LABEL RECORDS ARE STANDARD.
        01  REL-REC                     PIC X(100).
        WORKING-STORAGE SECTION.
        01  WORK-AREAS.
            05  ARE-THERE-MORE-RECORDS  PIC X(3)   VALUE 'YES'.
                88  NO-MORE-RECORDS                VALUE 'NO '.
            05  WS-ACCT-NO              PIC 9(5).
        PROCEDURE DIVISION.
        100-MAIN-MODULE.
            OPEN INPUT TRANS-FILE
                OUTPUT REL-FILE
            PERFORM UNTIL NO-MORE-RECORDS
                READ TRANS-FILE
                    AT END
                        MOVE 'NO ' TO ARE-THERE-MORE-RECORDS
                    NOT AT END
                        PERFORM 200-WRITE-RTN
                END-READ
            END-PERFORM
            CLOSE TRANS-FILE
                  REL-FILE
            STOP RUN.
        200-WRITE-RTN.
            MOVE ACCT-NO TO WS-ACCT-NO
            MOVE TRANS-REC TO REL-REC
            WRITE REL-REC
                INVALID KEY DISPLAY 'WRITE ERROR'
            END-WRITE.
```

COBOL 74 Substitutions

```
READ TRANS-FILE
    AT END MOVE 'NO ' TO ARE-THERE-MORE-RECORDS.
PERFORM 200-WRITE-RTN
    UNTIL NO-MORE-RECORDS.
```

```
READ TRANS-FILE
    AT END MOVE 'NO ' TO ARE-THERE-MORE-RECORDS.  }  ──→
```

In the preceding, the input ACCT-NO field also serves as a relative record number or RELATIVE KEY. Later on, we will see that if the ACCT-NO is not generally consecutive or is too long, we can *convert* it to a relative key using different types of procedures or algorithms.

SEQUENTIAL READING OF RELATIVE FILES

The records in relative files may be read sequentially, that is, in the order that they were created. Because a relative file is created in sequence by RELATIVE KEY, a sequential READ reads the records in ascending relative key order.

There is no need to specify a RELATIVE KEY for reading from a relative file sequentially. Consider the following example:

COBOL 85

```
SELECT REL-FILE  ASSIGN TO DISK1
    ORGANIZATION IS RELATIVE
    ACCESS IS SEQUENTIAL. ◄──RELATIVE KEY not needed when
      :                      sequentially reading from the file
      :
OPEN INPUT REL-FILE
    OUTPUT PRINT-FILE
PERFORM UNTIL NO-MORE-RECORDS
    READ REL-FILE
       AT END
           MOVE 'NO ' TO ARE-THERE-MORE-RECORDS
       NOT AT END
           PERFORM 200-CALC-RTN
    END-READ
END-PERFORM
CLOSE REL-FILE
      PRINT-FILE
STOP RUN.
200-CALC-RTN.
    :        (process each record in sequence)
    :
```

COBOL 74 Substitutions

```
READ REL-FILE
    AT END MOVE 'NO ' TO
        ARE-THERE-MORE-RECORDS.
PERFORM 200-CALC-RTN
    UNTIL NO-MORE-RECORDS.
```

```
READ REL-FILE
    AT END MOVE 'NO ' TO
        ARE-THERE-MORE-RECORDS.
```

Note, then, that reading from a relative file sequentially is the same as sequentially reading from either an indexed file or a standard sequential file. (An indexed file, however, must always include the RECORD KEY clause in the SELECT statement even when ACCESS IS SEQUENTIAL.)

RANDOM READING OF RELATIVE FILES

Suppose we wish to find the BAL-DUE for selected customer records in a relative file. Suppose, too, that an inquiry file includes the customer numbers of the specific records sought. These inquiry records are *not* in sequence by relative keys. Assume that the customer number was used as a relative record number or RELATIVE KEY. With COBOL 85, we can code:

```
            SELECT REL-FILE  ASSIGN TO DISK1
                ORGANIZATION IS RELATIVE
                ACCESS IS RANDOM
                RELATIVE KEY IS WS-KEY. ◄──The RELATIVE KEY must be a
                                            WORKING-STORAGE entry
            SELECT QUERY-FILE  ASSIGN TO DISK2.
    DATA DIVISION.
    FILE SECTION.
    FD  QUERY-FILE
        LABEL RECORDS ARE STANDARD.
    01  QUERY-REC.
        05  Q-KEY                 PIC 9(5).
        05                        PIC X(75).
    FD  REL-FILE
        LABEL RECORDS ARE STANDARD.
    01  REL-REC.
        05  CUST-NO               PIC 9(5).
        05  CUST-NAME             PIC X(20).
        05  BAL-DUE               PIC 9(5).
        05                        PIC X(70).
    WORKING-STORAGE SECTION.
    01  STORED-AREAS.
        05  ARE-THERE-MORE-RECORDS  PIC X(3)  VALUE 'YES'.
            88  NO-MORE-RECORDS               VALUE 'NO '.
        05  WS-KEY                PIC 9(5).
    PROCEDURE DIVISION.
    100-MAIN-MODULE.
        OPEN INPUT QUERY-FILE
                   REL-FILE
```

```
        PERFORM UNTIL NO-MORE-RECORDS
            READ QUERY-FILE
                AT END
                    MOVE 'NO ' TO ARE-THERE-MORE-RECORDS
                NOT AT END
                    PERFORM 200-CALC-RTN
            END-READ
        END-PERFORM
        CLOSE QUERY-FILE
     .       REL-FILE
        STOP RUN.
 200-CALC-RTN.
     MOVE Q-KEY TO WS-KEY
     READ REL-FILE
         INVALID KEY DISPLAY 'ERROR - NO RECORD FOUND'
         NOT INVALID KEY DISPLAY CUST-NAME BAL-DUE
     END-READ.
```

The INVALID KEY clause is executed if the *key* on the query file does not match a key on the relative file.

With COBOL 74, the main module includes a priming READ as in all previous cases. In addition, we must use an error switch because the NOT INVALID KEY clause is unavailable:

```
WORKING-STORAGE SECTION.
01  STORED-AREAS.
     :
     :
    05 ERR-SWITCH   PIC 9  VALUE 0.
       88 ERR-SWITCH-OFF   VALUE 0.
     :
     :
 200-CALC-RTN.
     MOVE Q-KEY TO WS-KEY.
     READ REL-FILE
         INVALID KEY
             DISPLAY 'ERROR - NO RECORD FOUND'
             MOVE 1 TO ERR-SWITCH.
     IF  ERR-SWITCH-OFF
         DISPLAY CUST-NAME BAL-DUE
     ELSE
         MOVE 0 TO ERR-SWITCH.
     READ QUERY-FILE
         AT END MOVE 'NO ' TO ARE-THERE-MORE-RECORDS.
```

Interactive Processing.   Instead of using an input QUERY-FILE, we can inquire about each customer's name and balance due using an interactive program:

COBOL 85

```
IDENTIFICATION DIVISION.
PROGRAM-ID.  INQUIRY.
ENVIRONMENT DIVISION.
INPUT-OUTPUT SECTION.
FILE-CONTROL.
    SELECT REL-FILE ASSIGN TO DISK
        ORGANIZATION IS RELATIVE
        ACCESS IS RANDOM
        RELATIVE KEY IS WS-KEY.
DATA DIVISION.
FILE SECTION.
FD  REL-FILE
    LABEL RECORDS ARE STANDARD.
01  REL-REC.
    05  CUST-NO                   PIC 9(5).
    05  CUST-NAME                 PIC X(20).
    05  BAL-DUE                   PIC 9(5).
    05                            PIC X(70).
```

```
WORKING-STORAGE SECTION.
01  STORED-AREAS.
    05  ARE-THERE-MORE-RECORDS  PIC X VALUE 'Y'.
    05  WS-KEY                   PIC 9(5).
PROCEDURE DIVISION.
100-MAIN-MODULE.
    OPEN INPUT REL-FILE
    PERFORM 200-CALC-RTN
        UNTIL ARE-THERE-MORE-RECORDS = 'N' OR 'n'
    CLOSE REL-FILE
    STOP RUN.
200-CALC-RTN.
    DISPLAY 'ENTER CUST NO'
    ACCEPT WS-KEY
    READ REL-FILE
        INVALID KEY DISPLAY 'ERROR - NO RECORD FOUND'
        NOT INVALID KEY DISPLAY CUST-NAME BAL-DUE
    END-READ
    DISPLAY 'ARE THERE MORE INQUIRIES (Y/N)?'
    ACCEPT ARE-THERE-MORE-RECORDS.
```

In the above, the computer assumes a direct conversion from the file's key field to its disk location. That is, the record with CUST-NO 942 is the 942nd record in the file. When the file is accessed randomly, the computer will directly access each record by the CUST-NO relative key. We can also use a conversion procedure to convert a key field to a relative key, as we will discuss later.

RANDOM UPDATING OF RELATIVE FILES

When updating a relative file, you can access each record to be changed and REWRITE it directly. The relative file must be opened as I-O, the required record must be read, changed, and then rewritten for each update.

Suppose we wish to read a transaction file and add the corresponding transaction amounts to records in a relative master accounts receivable file. With COBOL 85, we could code:

```
SELECT TRANS-FILE  ASSIGN TO DISK2.
SELECT REL-FILE    ASSIGN TO DISK1
    ORGANIZATION IS RELATIVE
    ACCESS IS RANDOM
    RELATIVE KEY IS WS-KEY.
DATA DIVISION.
FILE SECTION.
FD  TRANS-FILE
    LABEL RECORDS ARE STANDARD.
01  TRANS-REC.
    05  T-KEY               PIC 9(5).
    05  T-AMT               PIC 999V99.
FD  REL-FILE
    LABEL RECORDS ARE STANDARD.
01  REL-REC.
    05  CUST-NO             PIC 9(5).
    05  CUST-NAME           PIC X(20).
    05  BAL-DUE             PIC 9(5).
    05                      PIC X(70).
WORKING-STORAGE SECTION.
01  STORED-AREAS.
    05  ARE-THERE-MORE-RECORDS PIC X(3)  VALUE 'YES'.
        88  NO-MORE-RECORDS             VALUE 'NO '.
    05  WS-KEY              PIC 9(5).
PROCEDURE DIVISION.
100-MAIN-MODULE.
    OPEN INPUT TRANS-FILE
             I-O REL-FILE
```

```
                    PERFORM UNTIL NO-MORE-RECORDS
                        READ TRANS-FILE
                            AT END
                                MOVE 'NO ' TO ARE-THERE-MORE-RECORDS
                            NOT AT END
                                PERFORM 200-CALC-RTN
                        END-READ
                    END-PERFORM
                    CLOSE TRANS-FILE
                          REL-FILE
                    STOP RUN.
               200-CALC-RTN.
                    MOVE T-KEY TO WS-KEY
                    READ REL-FILE
                        INVALID KEY DISPLAY 'ERROR ', WS-KEY
                        NOT INVALID KEY PERFORM 300-UPDATE-RTN
                    END-READ.
               300-UPDATE-RTN.
                    ADD T-AMT TO BAL-DUE
                    REWRITE REL-REC
                        INVALID KEY DISPLAY 'REWRITE ERROR'
                    END-REWRITE.
```

Using COBOL 74, the main module includes a priming READ as in all previous cases. In addition, we must use an error switch and replace 200-CALC-RTN with:

```
WORKING-STORAGE SECTION.
01   STORED-AREAS.
         :
         :
     05  ERR-SWITCH   PIC 9  VALUE 0.
         88 ERR-SWITCH-OFF    VALUE 0.
         :
         :
200-CALC-RTN.
     MOVE T-KEY TO WS-KEY.
     READ REL-FILE
         INVALID KEY DISPLAY 'ERROR ', WS-KEY
                     MOVE 1 TO ERR-SWITCH.
     IF  ERR-SWITCH-OFF
         PERFORM 300-UPDATE-RTN
     ELSE
         MOVE 0 TO ERR-SWITCH.
     READ TRANS-FILE
         AT END MOVE 'NO ' TO ARE-THERE-MORE-RECORDS.
```

The INVALID KEY clause of the READ statement is executed if the record in the transaction file did not match a corresponding record in the relative file.

Interactive Processing.   We can randomly update a relative file interactively as well:

COBOL 85

```
IDENTIFICATION DIVISION.
PROGRAM-ID.  RUPDATE.
ENVIRONMENT DIVISION.
INPUT-OUTPUT SECTION.
FILE-CONTROL.
    SELECT REL-FILE ASSIGN TO DISK 'DISK1'
        ORGANIZATION IS RELATIVE
        ACCESS IS RANDOM
        RELATIVE KEY IS WS-KEY.
DATA DIVISION.
FILE SECTION.
FD  REL-FILE
    LABEL RECORDS ARE STANDARD.
01  REL-REC.
    05  CUST-NO               PIC 9(5).
    05  CUST-NAME             PIC X(20).
```

```
      05  BAL-DUE                    PIC 9(5).
      05                             PIC X(70).
WORKING-STORAGE SECTION.
01  STORED-AREAS.
      05  ARE-THERE-MORE-RECORDS  PIC X VALUE 'Y'.
      05  WS-KEY                     PIC 9(5).
      05  T-AMT                      PIC 9(5).
PROCEDURE DIVISION.
100-MAIN-MODULE.
      OPEN I-O REL-FILE
      PERFORM 200-CALC-RTN
          UNTIL ARE-THERE-MORE-RECORDS = 'N' OR 'n'
      CLOSE REL-FILE
      STOP RUN.
200-CALC-RTN.
      DISPLAY 'ENTER CUST NO'
      ACCEPT WS-KEY
      READ REL-FILE
          INVALID KEY DISPLAY 'ERROR ', WS-KEY
          NOT INVALID KEY PERFORM 300-UPDATE-RTN
      END-READ
      DISPLAY 'ARE THERE MORE RECORDS (Y/N)?'
      ACCEPT ARE-THERE-MORE-RECORDS.
300-UPDATE-RTN.
      DISPLAY 'ENTER TRANSACTION AMT'
      ACCEPT T-AMT
      ADD T-AMT TO BAL-DUE
      REWRITE REL-REC
          INVALID KEY DISPLAY 'REWRITE ERROR'
      END-REWRITE.
```

The INVALID KEY clause of the REWRITE statement is executed if the key in WS-KEY is outside the file's range. The INVALID KEY clause is required when reading, writing, or rewriting records unless the USE AFTER EXCEPTION procedure, which we do not focus on, is coded for performing input/output error functions. The FILE STATUS specification can also be used in the SELECT statement for determining which specific input/output error occurred when an INVALID KEY condition is met.

To delete relative records from a file, use the DELETE verb as we did with indexed files:

```
MOVE relative-record-number TO working-storage-key
DELETE file-name RECORD
    INVALID KEY imperative-statement
END-DELETE
```

Once deleted, the record is removed from the file and cannot be read again.

SELF-TEST

1. When creating a relative file, ACCESS IS _____ . When using a relative file as input, ACCESS IS either _____ or _____ .

2. RELATIVE KEY is optional when reading or writing a relative file (sequentially, randomly).

3. (T or F) If ACCT-NO is used to calculate a disk address when writing records on a relative file, then ACCT-NO must be moved to a WORKING-STORAGE entry designated as the RELATIVE KEY before a WRITE is executed.

4. (T or F) To read the record with CUST-NO 125 from a relative file, move 125 to the record's CUST-NO key field and execute a READ.

5. (T or F) Relative file organization is the most popular method for organizing a disk file that may be accessed randomly.

Solutions

1. SEQUENTIAL; SEQUENTIAL; RANDOM (or DYNAMIC)

2. sequentially

3. T

4. F—125 must be moved to a WORKING-STORAGE *entry* specified in the RELATIVE KEY clause of the SELECT statement or converted to the WORKING-STORAGE RELATIVE KEY, as described in the next section.
5. F—Indexed file organization is still the most popular.

CONVERTING A KEY FIELD TO A RELATIVE KEY

As noted, a key field such as CUST-NO or PART-NO can often serve as a relative record number or RELATIVE KEY. Sometimes, however, it is impractical to use a key field as a RELATIVE KEY.

Suppose a file has Social Security number as its key or identifying field for each record. It would not be feasible to also use this field as a relative record number or RELATIVE KEY. It would not be practical to place a record with a Social Security number of 977326322 in relative record location 977,326,322. Most files do not have that much space allotted to them, and, even if they did, Social Security numbers as relative record locations would result in more blank areas than areas actually used for records.

Similarly, suppose we have a five-digit TRANS-NO that serves as a key field for records in a transaction file. Although TRANS-NO could vary from 00001 to 99999, suppose there are only 1000 actual transaction numbers. To use TRANS-NO itself as a RELATIVE KEY would be wasteful since it would mean allocating 99999 record locations for a file with only 1000 records.

In such instances, the key field can be converted into a RELATIVE KEY. Methods used to convert or transform a key field into a relative record number are called **hashing**.

Hashing techniques can be fairly complex. We will illustrate a relatively simple one here. We use the following hashing technique to compute a RELATIVE KEY for the preceding TRANS-NO example:

```
DIVIDE TRANS-NO BY 1009
    REMAINDER REL-KEY
```

The REMAINDER from this division will be a number from 0 to 1008 that is a sufficiently large relative record number or RELATIVE KEY. If we add 1 to this REMAINDER, we get a relative record number from 1 to 1009, which is large enough to accommodate a 1000-record file.

This is a rather simplified example, but such a direct conversion from key to disk address can be made. In this way, there is no need to establish an index, and records may be accessed directly, simply by including a formula for the conversion of a key field to a relative key in the program.

The algorithm or conversion procedure, then, is coded:

1. When creating the relative file. Each record's key field is used to calculate the RELATIVE KEY for positioning or writing each record.
2. When accessing the relative file randomly. Again, the inquiry or transaction record's key will need to be converted to a RELATIVE KEY before reading from the relative file randomly.

This type of relative processing requires more programming than when processing indexed files because a conversion procedure is necessary and the hashing technique is sometimes complex. But the random access of relative files is faster than the random access of indexed files because there is no need to look up a record's address from an index.

When creating a relative file, then, it may be necessary to include a routine or algorithm for calculating the disk record's location or RELATIVE KEY. See Figure 15.13 for an illustration of a program that creates a relative file using a hashing algorithm called the **division algorithm method**, which is similar to the one described above.

Figure 15.13 Program that creates a relative file.

COBOL 85

```
IDENTIFICATION DIVISION.
PROGRAM-ID. CREATE.
*****************************************************************
*    this program creates a relative file                      *
*****************************************************************
ENVIRONMENT DIVISION.
INPUT-OUTPUT SECTION.
FILE-CONTROL.
    SELECT TRANS-IN ASSIGN TO DISK1.
    SELECT RELATIVE-FILE ASSIGN TO DISK2
        ORGANIZATION IS RELATIVE
        ACCESS IS SEQUENTIAL
        RELATIVE KEY IS RELATIVE-KEY-STORE.
*
DATA DIVISION.
FILE SECTION.
FD  TRANS-IN
    LABEL RECORDS ARE STANDARD.
01  IN-REC.
    05   TRANS-NO              PIC 9(5).
    05   QTY-ON-HAND           PIC 9(4).
    05   TOTAL-PRICE           PIC 9(5)V99.
    05                         PIC X(64).
FD  RELATIVE-FILE
    LABEL RECORDS ARE STANDARD.
01  DISK-REC-OUT.
    05   DISK-REC-DATA.
        10   D-PART-NO         PIC 9(5).
        10   D-QTY-ON-HAND     PIC 9(4).
        10   D-TOTAL-PRICE     PIC 9(5)V99.
        10                     PIC X(64).
WORKING-STORAGE SECTION.
01  WORK-AREAS.
    05   ARE-THERE-MORE-RECORDS   PIC X(3)  VALUE 'YES'.
        88  NO-MORE-RECORDS                 VALUE 'NO '.
    05   STORE1                   PIC S9(5).
01  RELATIVE-KEY-STORE           PIC 9(5).
*
PROCEDURE DIVISION.
100-MAIN-MODULE.
    OPEN INPUT TRANS-IN
        OUTPUT RELATIVE-FILE
    PERFORM UNTIL NO-MORE-RECORDS
        READ TRANS-IN
            AT END
                MOVE 'NO ' TO ARE-THERE-MORE-RECORDS
            NOT AT END
                PERFORM 200-WRITE-RTN
        END-READ
    END-PERFORM
    CLOSE TRANS-IN
          RELATIVE-FILE
    STOP RUN.
200-WRITE-RTN.
    MOVE IN-REC TO DISK-REC-DATA
*****************************************************************
***   the following is one method for calculating           ***
***   a relative record no.                                  ***
*****************************************************************
    DIVIDE TRANS-NO BY 1009 GIVING STORE1
        REMAINDER RELATIVE-KEY-STORE
```

COBOL 74 Substitutions

For COBOL 74, FILLER must be used instead of a blank field name

```
READ TRANS-IN
    AT END MOVE 'NO ' TO ARE-THERE-MORE-RECORDS.
PERFORM 200-WRITE-RTN
    UNTIL NO-MORE-RECORDS.
```

Figure 15.13 (continued)

```
                                        ADD 1 TO RELATIVE-KEY-STORE
                                        WRITE DISK-REC-OUT
                                            INVALID KEY PERFORM 300-COLLISION
                                        END-WRITE.
```

COBOL 74 Substitutions

```
READ TRANS-IN
    AT END MOVE 'NO ' TO ARE-THERE-MORE-RECORDS.

                                    300-COLLISION.
                                        DISPLAY 'WRITE ERROR ', IN-REC.
```

The same hashing technique or routine is needed for the program that creates the relative file, for the program that updates the file, and for programs that report from it. Since this hashing technique will be used in several programs, it is often written in an independent program or subprogram and called in as needed.

Relative files can be accessed either sequentially or randomly. Sequential access of a relative file means that the records are read and processed in order by key field as with sequential files that are sorted into key field sequence. This is rarely done with relative files because records with sequential key fields do not necessarily follow one another if a hashing technique is used for determining relative keys. When we randomly access a relative file, either (1) another input file (typically a transaction or query file) or (2) transactions entered interactively will indicate which disk records are to be accessed. Thus ACCESS IS RANDOM is the usual method for reading and updating relative files.

Suppose that a master payroll file has been created with Social Security number used to calculate the RELATIVE KEY. To access any payroll record on this file, we read in a transaction field called IN-SSNO, perform the calculations necessary for converting IN-SSNO to a disk address, and store that address in a WORKING-STORAGE field called SSNO-CONVERTED. Note that the RELATIVE KEY would also be defined as SSNO-CONVERTED. When the appropriate value has been moved to SSNO-CONVERTED, we can then execute the following: READ RELATIVE-FILE INVALID KEY .... The READ instruction will move into storage the record with a relative record number specified in SSNO-CONVERTED.

Many of the input/output instructions that apply to indexed files apply to all relative files, even those in which the RELATIVE KEY must be converted to a disk location.

CLAUSES USED TO UPDATE RANDOM-ACCESS FILES

OPEN I-O	Used when a relative file is being updated.
REWRITE	Writes back onto a relative file (you can only use REWRITE when the file is opened as I-O and a record has already been read from it).
INVALID KEY	Is required with relative (and indexed) files for a random READ and any WRITE, DELETE, and REWRITE. The computer will perform the statements following the INVALID KEY if the record cannot be found or if the RELATIVE KEY is blank or not numeric. A NOT INVALID KEY clause may also be used with COBOL 85.
DELETE	Eliminates records from the file.

Several other *randomizing* or hashing *algorithms* for calculating relative file disk addresses are as follows:

RANDOMIZING OR HASHING ALGORITHMS

For transforming a numeric key field to a relative record number:

Algorithm	Explanation	Examples
Folding	Split the key into two or more parts, add the parts, truncate if there are more digits than needed (depending on file size)	1. An `ACCT-NO` key = 0125 a. Split and add each part: 01 + 25 = `RELATIVE KEY` of 26. b. The record would be placed in the 26th disk location. 2. An `ACCT-NO` key = 2341 Split and add: 23 + 41 = `RELATIVE KEY` of 64.

Algorithm	Explanation	Examples
Digit extraction	Extract a digit in a fixed digit position—try to analyze digit distribution before selecting the digit position	1. An `ACCT-NO` key = 0<u>1</u>2<u>5</u>; we may make the `RELATIVE KEY` 15 if we assume that the second and fourth numbers are the most evenly distributed. 2. A `RELATIVE KEY` of 31 may be extracted from an `ACCT-NO` of 2<u>3</u>4<u>1</u>.
Square value truncation	Square the key value and truncate to the number of digits needed	An `ACCT-NO` key = 0125 a. Square the key giving a value of 15625. b. Truncate to three positions; 625 becomes the `RELATIVE KEY`.

In summary, one main difference between a relative file and an indexed file is that relative files may require a calculation for computing the actual address of the disk record. Relative files do not, however, use an index for looking up addresses of disk records.

In general, it is *not efficient* to process relative files sequentially when a `RELATIVE KEY` is computed using a randomizing algorithm. This is because the records that are physically adjacent to one another do not necessarily have their key fields such as `ACCT-NO` or `PART-NO` in sequence. Hence, relative file organization is primarily used for random access only. Note, too, that algorithms for transforming key fields into relative record numbers sometimes place records on a disk in a somewhat haphazard way so that increased disk space is required. Thus, although relative files can be processed rapidly, they do not usually make the most efficient use of disk space.

CHAPTER SUMMARY

I. Indexed File Processing
   A. What Is an Indexed File?
      1. `ENVIRONMENT DIVISION`—`SELECT` clause specifies:
         `ORGANIZATION IS INDEXED`
         `ACCESS IS RANDOM`—For nonsequential updates, inquiries, and so on.
                 `SEQUENTIAL`—For creating an indexed file, reporting from it in sequence, and updating it sequentially.
         `RECORD KEY`—This is the key field in each indexed disk record that is used for establishing the index and for accessing disk records.

The SELECT clause can also specify FILE STATUS IS data-name for indicating whether an input or output operation was completed successfully.

2. DATA DIVISION—LABEL RECORDS are usually STANDARD for all disk files.
3. PROCEDURE DIVISION
   a. Creating an indexed file
      (1) Indexed files are created with an ACCESS IS SEQUENTIAL clause in the ENVIRON-MENT DIVISION.
      (2) The WRITE statement should include the INVALID KEY clause. The statement following INVALID KEY is executed (1) if a record with the same key was already created, (2) if the record is out of sequence or, (3) on many systems, if the key is blank.
   b. Reading from an indexed file—in sequence
      (1) Same as all sequential processing.
      (2) Use READ ... AT END.
   c. Reading from an indexed file—randomly
      (1) ACCESS IS RANDOM in SELECT clause.
      (2) If an indexed record is to be updated, use OPEN I-O.
      (3) Transaction key is moved to the RECORD KEY and READ ... INVALID KEY is used.
      (4) To write updated disk records back onto the disk, use REWRITE.

II. Relative File Processing
   A. What Is a Relative File?
      1. Relative files, like indexed files, can be accessed randomly.
      2. With a relative file, there is no index. Instead, a record's key field such as ACCT-NO is converted to a relative record number or RELATIVE KEY. The conversion can be one-to-one (RELATIVE KEY = record key), or a randomizing algorithm may be used to calculate a relative record number from a record's key field.
      3. The random accessing of a relative file is very fast because there is no need to look up a disk address from an index.
      4. Sequential access of a relative file may be slow because records adjacent to one another in the file do not necessarily have key fields in sequence.
   B. Processing Relative Files
      1. SELECT statement.
         a. Code ORGANIZATION IS RELATIVE
         b. RELATIVE KEY clause
            Uses
            (1) For randomly accessing the file.
            (2) For sequential reads and writes if a conversion is necessary from a record's key field to a RELATIVE KEY.
            (3) The data-name used as the relative record number or RELATIVE KEY is defined in WORKING-STORAGE.
         c. ACCESS can be SEQUENTIAL, RANDOM, or DYNAMIC. DYNAMIC means the file is accessed both randomly and sequentially in the same program.
      2. Processing routines.
         a. Creating a relative file:
            (1) ACCESS IS SEQUENTIAL in the SELECT statement.
            (2) Move the input record's key field to the RELATIVE KEY, which is in WORKING-STORAGE (or convert the input key to a WORKING-STORAGE relative key) and WRITE ... INVALID KEY ....
         b. Accessing a relative file randomly:
            (1) ACCESS IS RANDOM in the SELECT statement.
            (2) Move the transaction record's key field to the RELATIVE KEY, which is in WORKING-STORAGE (or convert) and READ ... INVALID KEY ....
         c. When updating a relative file, open it as I-O, ACCESS IS RANDOM, and use READ, WRITE, REWRITE, or DELETE with INVALID KEY clauses.

KEY TERMS	DELETE	Index	Relative file
	Digit extraction	Indexed file	RELATIVE KEY
	Division algorithm method	Interactive processing	Sector
	FILE STATUS	INVALID KEY	Square value truncation
	Folding	Random access	Track
	Hashing		

CHAPTER SELF-TEST

1. (T or F) An indexed file is usually created in sequence by key field.

2. When writing a record onto disk, a(n) _____ clause should be used with the WRITE to test for a key that is not in sequence or is the same as one already on the indexed file.

3. To update an indexed file, OPEN the file as _____ .

4. To update an indexed record, use a _____ statement.

5. Suppose PART-NO in an inventory file is to be used as the RELATIVE KEY. Write the SELECT statement for the relative file. Include a RELATIVE KEY clause.

6. If a record is written on a relative file with PART-NO 12 and a second record with PART-NO 12 is to be written, an INVALID KEY error (will, will not) occur.

7. The field specified with the RELATIVE KEY clause must be defined in _____ .

8. It is generally faster to access a relative file randomly than an indexed file because _____ .

9. Write a procedure to accept an input T-PART-NO from a terminal or PC keyboard and use it to look up the corresponding relative record and print its QTY-ON-HAND. Assume that T-PART-NO can be used as the RELATIVE KEY.

10. Modify the procedure in Question 9 to enable the operator at the terminal or PC keyboard to change the QTY-ON-HAND.

Solutions

1. T

2. INVALID KEY

3. I-O

4. REWRITE

5.
```
SELECT INV-FILE
     ORGANIZATION IS RELATIVE
     ACCESS IS SEQUENTIAL
     RELATIVE KEY IS WS-PART-NO.
```

6. will

7. WORKING-STORAGE

8. there is no need to look up the address of the record from an index

9. For COBOL 85, we could code:

```
ACCEPT T-PART-NO
MOVE T-PART-NO TO WS-PART-NO
READ INV-FILE
     INVALID KEY DISPLAY 'ERROR'
     NOT INVALID KEY DISPLAY QTY-ON-HAND
END-READ.
```

For COBOL 74, we would code:

```
ACCEPT T-PART-NO.
MOVE T-PART-NO TO WS-PART-NO.
READ INV-FILE
     INVALID KEY DISPLAY 'ERROR'
                 MOVE 'YES' TO ERR-CODE.
IF  ERR-CODE = 'NO '
     DISPLAY QTY-ON-HAND
ELSE
     MOVE 'NO ' TO ERR-CODE.
```

10.
```
DISPLAY 'CHANGE QTY-ON-HAND (Y/N)?'
ACCEPT ANS
IF  ANS = 'Y'
     ACCEPT QTY-ON-HAND
     REWRITE INV-REC
         INVALID KEY DISPLAY 'ERROR'
     END-REWRITE
END-IF.
```

Note: Both Questions 9 and 10 need to be put into the context of a structured program if the procedures are to be repeated.

PRACTICE PROGRAM

Write a program to update a master indexed disk file. The problem definition appears in Figure 15.14.

Figure 15.14 Problem definition for the Practice Program.

Systems Flowchart

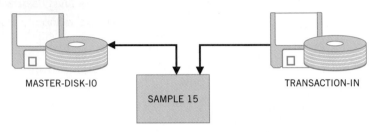

MASTER-DISK-IO   SAMPLE 15   TRANSACTION-IN

MASTER-DISK-IO Record Layout			
Field	Size	Type	No. of Decimal Positions (if Numeric)
MASTER-CUST-NO	5	Alphanumeric	
MASTER-BALANCE-DUE	5	Numeric	2

TRANSACTION-IN Record Layout			
Field	Size	Type	No. of Decimal Positions (if Numeric)
TRANS-CUST-NO-IN	5	Alphanumeric	
TRANS-AMT-IN	5	Numeric	2
TRANS-CODE-IN (1 = Delete Master Record)	1	Alphanumeric	

Notes:

a. Transaction records are used to update the Balance Due in the indexed master file. If a transaction record has the same customer number as the master record, process it; if not, display the transaction record as an error.

b. Master disk records are indexed; transaction records are not in sequence by customer number.

See Figure 15.15 for the pseudocode, hierarchy chart, and solution.

Figure 15.15 Pseudocode, hierarchy chart, and solution for the Practice Program.

Pseudocode

MAIN-MODULE
START
    PERFORM Initialization-Rtn
    PERFORM UNTIL no more data
        READ a Transaction Record
        AT END

Figure 15.15 (continued)

```
                              Move 'NO ' to Are-There-More-Records
                     NOT AT END
                              PERFORM Calc-Rtn
               END-READ
          END-PERFORM
          PERFORM End-of-Job-Rtn
STOP
```

<u>INITIALIZATION-RTN</u>
    Open the files

<u>CALC-RTN</u>
    Move Input Transaction key field to Master key field
    IF Delete Code
    THEN
        PERFORM Delete-Rtn
    ELSE
        Read the Corresponding Master Record
        IF   No Error
        THEN
            PERFORM Update-the-Record
        ELSE
            Display error message
        END-IF
    END-IF

<u>UPDATE-THE-RECORD</u>
    Update the Record
    Rewrite the Record

<u>DELETE-RTN</u>
    Delete the Record

<u>END-OF-JOB-RTN</u>
    Close the files

Hierarchy Chart

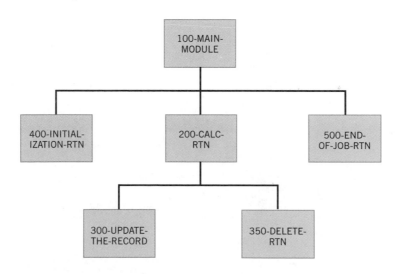

Figure 15.15 (continued)

COBOL 85

```
IDENTIFICATION DIVISION.
PROGRAM-ID.  SAMPLE.
AUTHOR. NANCY STERN.
***********************************************
*  this program updates an indexed file    *
***********************************************
ENVIRONMENT DIVISION.
INPUT-OUTPUT SECTION.
FILE-CONTROL.
    SELECT MASTER-DISK-IO ASSIGN TO DISK 'DATA15'
            ORGANIZATION IS INDEXED
            ACCESS IS RANDOM
            RECORD KEY MASTER-CUST-NO.
    SELECT TRANSACTION-IN ASSIGN TO DISK 'DATA15A'.
*
DATA DIVISION.
FILE SECTION.
FD  MASTER-DISK-IO
    LABEL RECORDS ARE STANDARD.
01  MASTER-REC-IO.
    05  MASTER-CUST-NO          PIC X(5).
    05  MASTER-BALANCE-DUE      PIC 9(3)V99.
FD  TRANSACTION-IN
    LABEL RECORDS ARE STANDARD.
01  TRANS-REC-IN.
    05  TRANS-CUST-NO-IN        PIC X(5).
    05  TRANS-AMT-IN            PIC 9(3)V99.
    05  TRANS-CODE-IN           PIC X.
        88  DELETE-RECORD                   VALUE '1'.
WORKING-STORAGE SECTION.
01  WS-WORK-AREAS.
    05  ARE-THERE-MORE-RECORDS  PIC X(3)    VALUE 'YES'.
        88  NO-MORE-RECORDS                 VALUE 'NO '.
*
PROCEDURE DIVISION.
*******************************************
*  controls direction of program logic  *
*******************************************
100-MAIN-MODULE.
    PERFORM 400-INITIALIZATION-RTN
    PERFORM UNTIL NO-MORE-RECORDS
        READ TRANSACTION-IN
            AT END
                MOVE 'NO ' TO ARE-THERE-MORE-RECORDS
            NOT AT END
                PERFORM 200-CALC-RTN
        END-READ
    END-PERFORM
    PERFORM 500-END-OF-JOB-RTN
    STOP RUN.
***************************************************
*  performed from 100-main-module. reads and    *
*  updates master file.                         *
***************************************************
200-CALC-RTN.
    MOVE TRANS-CUST-NO-IN TO MASTER-CUST-NO
    IF  DELETE-RECORD
        PERFORM 350-DELETE-RTN
    ELSE
        READ MASTER-DISK-IO
            INVALID KEY DISPLAY 'INVALID TRANSACTION RECORD ', TRANS-REC-IN
            NOT INVALID KEY PERFORM 300-UPDATE-THE-RECORD
        END-READ
    END-IF.
```

COBOL 74 Substitutions

```
PERFORM 200-CALC-RTN
    UNTIL NO-MORE-RECORDS.
```

COBOL 74 users must specify an error code because NOT INVALID KEY cannot be used

Figure 15.15   (continued)

COBOL 74 Substitutions

```
PERFORM 450-READ-RTN. ────►
                            300-UPDATE-THE-RECORD.
                                ADD TRANS-AMT-IN TO MASTER-BALANCE-DUE
                                REWRITE MASTER-REC-IO
                                    INVALID KEY DISPLAY 'ERROR IN REWRITE'
                                END-REWRITE.
                            350-DELETE-RTN.
                                DELETE MASTER-DISK-IO RECORD
                                    INVALID KEY DISPLAY 'ERROR IN DELETE FILE'
                                END-DELETE.
                            ********************************************
                            *  performed from 100-main-module.        *
                            *  opens files                            *
                            ********************************************
                            400-INITIALIZATION-RTN.
                                OPEN INPUT TRANSACTION-IN
                                     I-O   MASTER-DISK-IO.

      PERFORM 450-READ-RTN.  ⎫
   450-READ-RTN.             ⎬
      READ TRANSACTION-IN    ⎮  ────►
          AT END MOVE 'NO ' TO
              ARE-THERE-MORE-RECORDS. ⎭
                            **********************************************************
                            *  performed from 100-main-module, closes files  *
                            **********************************************************
                            500-END-OF-JOB-RTN.
                                CLOSE TRANSACTION-IN
                                      MASTER-DISK-IO.
```

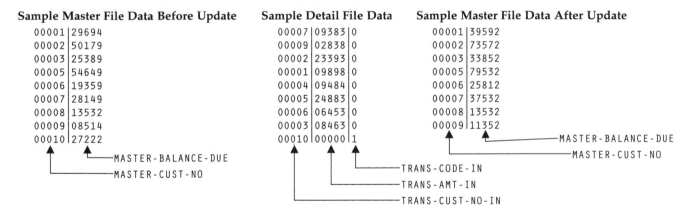

Sample Master File Data Before Update	Sample Detail File Data	Sample Master File Data After Update
00001|29694	00007|09383|0	00001|39592
00002|50179	00009|02838|0	00002|73572
00003|25389	00002|23393|0	00003|33852
00005|54649	00001|09898|0	00005|79532
00006|19359	00004|09484|0	00006|25812
00007|28149	00005|24883|0	00007|37532
00008|13532	00006|06453|0	00008|13532
00009|08514	00003|08463|0	00009|11352
00010|27222	00010|00000|1	

MASTER-BALANCE-DUE
MASTER-CUST-NO

TRANS-CODE-IN
TRANS-AMT-IN
TRANS-CUST-NO-IN

MASTER-BALANCE-DUE
MASTER-CUST-NO

One line will be displayed: `INVALID TRANSACTION RECORD 00004094840`

REVIEW QUESTIONS

I. True-False
Questions

_____   1. An indexed file is usually created with `ACCESS IS RANDOM` but read with `ACCESS IS SEQUENTIAL`.

_____   2. To update an indexed master file with transaction records that are not in sequence by key field, we use the `ACCESS IS RANDOM` clause with the `SELECT` statement for the indexed file.

_____   3. The procedures for updating an indexed file randomly are the same regardless of whether multiple transactions are permitted per master or only a single transaction per master is permitted.

_____   4. The `REWRITE` clause may only be used with an `I-O` file.

_____   5. The `INVALID KEY` clause may be used with `READ`, `WRITE`, or `DELETE` statements.

_____   6. A `RELATIVE KEY` clause is optional when reading from or writing to a relative file sequentially.

_____   7. Relative keys must be unique.

_____   8. The data-name specified with a `RELATIVE KEY` clause must be part of the relative file's record.

_____ 9. Relative keys must be entered sequentially when creating a relative file.

_____ 10. In general, accessing a relative file randomly is faster than accessing an indexed file randomly.

II. General Questions

1. Write the ENVIRONMENT DIVISION entries for the creation of an indexed file called MASTER-INVENTORY-FILE.

2. Write the ENVIRONMENT DIVISION entries for an indexed file called TRANS-FILE that is in transaction number sequence but will be accessed by invoice number.

3. Explain the purpose of the REWRITE statement in a COBOL program.

4. Explain the use of the INVALID KEY option.

5. When is a file opened as I-O?

III. Validating Data

Modify the Practice Program so that it includes appropriate coding to (1) test for all errors and (2) print a control listing of totals (records processed, errors encountered, batch totals).

DEBUGGING EXERCISES

Consider the following coding:

```
PROCEDURE DIVISION.
100-MAIN-MODULE.
    OPEN INPUT TRANS-FILE
              I O INDEX-FILE
    PERFORM UNTIL THERE-ARE-NO-MORE-RECORDS
        READ TRANS-FILE
            AT END
                MOVE 'NO ' TO ARE-THERE-MORE-RECORDS
            NOT AT END
                PERFORM 200-CALC-RTN
        END-READ
    END-PERFORM
    CLOSE TRANS-FILE
          INDEX-FILE
    STOP RUN.
200-CALC-RTN.
    MOVE TRANS-NO TO DISK-TRANS-NO
    READ INDEX-FILE
        AT END MOVE 'NO ' TO ARE-THERE-MORE-INDEXED-RECORDS
    END-READ
    IF  TRANS-CODE = 'X'
        DELETE DISK-TRANS-REC
        REWRITE DISK-TRANS-REC
    END-IF
    MOVE TRANS-AMT TO DISK-AMT
    WRITE DISK-TRANS-REC
        INVALID KEY
            MOVE 'ERROR' TO MSSGE
            WRITE PRINT-REC FROM ERR-REC.
```

1. A syntax error occurs on one of the lines associated with the OPEN statement. Find and correct the error.

2. A syntax error occurs on the lines associated with READ INDEX-FILE. Find and correct the error.

3. You find that the INVALID KEY clause associated with WRITE DISK-TRANS-REC is executed incorrectly. Find and correct the error. The DELETE and REWRITE also cause syntax errors. Find and correct them.

4. After execution of the program, you print INDEX-FILE for checking purposes. You find that records which were to be deleted were not, in fact, deleted. Find and correct the error.

PROGRAMMING ASSIGNMENTS

Code the following programs using an indexed file.

1. Write a program to update a master indexed file. The problem definition is shown in Figure 15.16.

Figure 15.16 Problem definition for Programming Assignment 1.

Systems Flowchart

CUSTOMER-TRANS   CUSTOMER-MASTER (indexed)

CUSTOMER-TRANS Record Layout			
Field	**Size**	**Type**	**No. of Decimal Positions (if Numeric)**
CUSTOMER-NO	5	Alphanumeric	
CUSTOMER-NAME	20	Alphanumeric	
DATE-OF-PURCHASE	4	Date (MM/YY)	
AMT-OF-PURCHASE	5	Numeric	2

CUSTOMER-MASTER Record Layout			
Field	**Size**	**Type**	**No. of Decimal Positions (if Numeric)**
CUSTOMER-NO	5	Alphanumeric	
CUSTOMER-NAME	20	Alphanumeric	
DATE-OF-LAST-PURCHASE	4	Date (MM/YY)	
AMOUNT-OWED	6	Numeric	2

Notes:

a. Customer number is the key field for the indexed master file.
b. If a transaction record exists for which there is no corresponding master, display it as an error.
c. For all transaction records with corresponding master records (these are master records to be updated), add the amount of purchase from the transaction record to the amount owed in the master record and update the date of last purchase.
d. There need not be a transaction record for each master record.
e. Transaction records are not in sequence.

2. Interactive Processing. **Redo Programming Assignment 1 so that transaction data can be entered interactively.**

3. Write a program to create an indexed master payroll file from transaction records. The problem definition is in Figure 15.17 on page 646.

Notes:

a. Employee number is the key field for the master file.
b. Before placing a record on the master file, add 5% to the employee's salary that is in the transaction record.
c. At the end of the run, obtain a printout of all master records.

Figure 15.17 Problem definition for Programming Assignment 3.

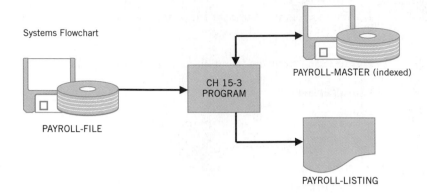

Systems Flowchart

| PAYROLL-FILE | | CH 15-3 PROGRAM | | PAYROLL-MASTER (indexed) |
| PAYROLL-LISTING |

PAYROLL-FILE and PAYROLL-MASTER Record Layout			
Field	Size	Type	No. of Decimal Positions (if Numeric)
EMPLOYEE-NO	5	Alphanumeric	
EMPLOYEE-NAME	20	Alphanumeric	
TERRITORY-NO	2	Alphanumeric	
OFFICE-NO	2	Alphanumeric	
ANNUAL-SALARY	6	Numeric	0
FILLER	45	Alphanumeric	

PAYROLL-LISTING Printer Spacing Chart

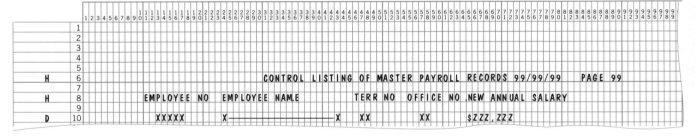

```
H  6                         CONTROL LISTING OF MASTER PAYROLL RECORDS 99/99/99    PAGE 99
H  8        EMPLOYEE NO   EMPLOYEE NAME            TERR NO  OFFICE NO .NEW ANNUAL SALARY
D 10           XXXXX     X----------------X  XX      XX       $ZZZ,ZZZ
```

4. Interactive Processing. Redo Programming Assignment 3 so that transaction data can be entered interactively.

5. Write a program to create an indexed master file from transaction records. The problem definition is shown in Figure 15.18 on page 647.

   Notes:

   a. A table of product numbers and corresponding unit prices is to be created in storage from PRODUCT-MASTER. There are 50 product numbers.
   b. Customer number is the key field for the CUSTOMER-MASTER file.
   c. Amount owed = Quantity purchased × Unit price (from table).
   d. Perform a table look-up using the product number from a PURCHASE-TRANS record to find the corresponding unit price in the PRODUCT-MASTER table.

6. Redo Programming Assignments 1–5 using a relative file instead of an indexed file.

7. Maintenance Program. Redo the Practice Program in this chapter using a relative file instead of an indexed file.

Figure 15.18   Problem definition for Programming Assignment 5.

Systems Flowchart

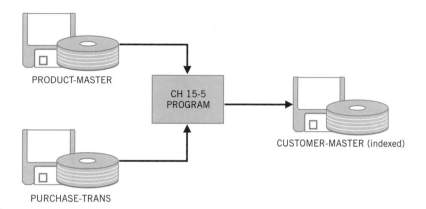

PRODUCT-MASTER

CH 15-5
PROGRAM

CUSTOMER-MASTER (indexed)

PURCHASE-TRANS

PRODUCT-MASTER Record Layout (Alternate Format)

PRODUCT NO.	UNIT PRICE $ ¢
1 5	6 10

PURCHASE-TRANS Record Layout (Alternate Format)

CUSTOMER NO.	CUSTOMER NAME	QUANTITY PURCHASED	PRODUCT NO.
1 5	6 25	26 28	29 33

CUSTOMER-MASTER Record Layout (Alternate Format)

CUSTOMER NO.	AMOUNT OWED	PRODUCT NO.
1 5	6 13	14 18

UNIT V
Advanced Topics

CHAPTER 16

Improving Program Performance Using The COPY, CALL, and Other Statements

■ **OBJECTIVES**

To familiarize you with

1. The COPY statement for copying parts of a program that are stored in a library.
2. The CALL statement for executing called programs as subroutines.
3. Text manipulation with the STRING and UNSTRING statements.

■ **CONTENTS**

COPY STATEMENT

INTRODUCTION

A `COPY` statement is used to bring into a program a series of prewritten COBOL entries that have been stored in a **library**. Copying entries from a library, rather than coding them, has the following benefits: (1) it could save a programmer a considerable amount of coding and debugging time; (2) it promotes program standardization since all programs that copy entries from a library will be using common data-names and/or procedures; (3) it reduces the time it takes to make modifications and reduces duplication of effort; if a change needs to be made to a data entry, it can be made just once in the library without the need to alter individual programs; and (4) library entries are extensively annotated so that they are meaningful to all users; this annotation results in better-documented programs and systems.

Most often, the `COPY` statement is used to copy `FD` and `01` entries that define and describe files and records. In addition, standard *modules* to be used in the `PROCEDURE DIVISION` of several programs may also be stored in a library and copied as needed.

Organizations that have large databases or files that are shared make frequent use of libraries from which entries are copied. Students may also find that file and record description entries for test data for programming assignments have been stored in a library, which may then be copied when needed.

Each computer has its own machine-dependent operating system commands for creating and accessing a library. You will need to check with your computer center for the required entries.

ENTRIES THAT CAN BE COPIED

With the `COPY` statement, you may include prewritten `ENVIRONMENT`, `DATA`, or `PROCEDURE DIVISION` entries in your source programs as follows:

ENVIRONMENT DIVISION

Option 1 (within the `CONFIGURATION SECTION`):

$$\text{SOURCE-COMPUTER. } \underline{\text{COPY}} \text{ text-name } \begin{Bmatrix} \underline{\text{OF}} \\ \underline{\text{IN}} \end{Bmatrix} \text{ library-name.}$$

$$\text{OBJECT-COMPUTER. } \underline{\text{COPY}} \text{ text-name } \begin{Bmatrix} \underline{\text{OF}} \\ \underline{\text{IN}} \end{Bmatrix} \text{ library-name.}$$

$$\text{SPECIAL-NAMES. } \underline{\text{COPY}} \text{ text-name } \begin{Bmatrix} \underline{\text{OF}} \\ \underline{\text{IN}} \end{Bmatrix} \text{ library-name.}$$

Option 2 (within the `INPUT-OUTPUT SECTION`):

$$\text{FILE-CONTROL. } \underline{\text{COPY}} \text{ text-name } \begin{Bmatrix} \underline{\text{OF}} \\ \underline{\text{IN}} \end{Bmatrix} \text{ library-name.}$$

$$\text{I-O-CONTROL. } \underline{\text{COPY}} \text{ text-name } \begin{Bmatrix} \underline{\text{OF}} \\ \underline{\text{IN}} \end{Bmatrix} \text{ library-name.}$$

DATA DIVISION

Option 1 (within the FILE SECTION):

$$FD \text{ file-name } \underline{COPY} \text{ text-name } \begin{Bmatrix} \underline{OF} \\ \underline{IN} \end{Bmatrix} \text{ library-name.}$$

Option 2 (within a File Description entry):

$$01 \text{ data-name } \underline{COPY} \text{ text-name } \begin{Bmatrix} \underline{OF} \\ \underline{IN} \end{Bmatrix} \text{ library-name.}$$

PROCEDURE DIVISION

$$\text{paragraph-name. } \underline{COPY} \text{ text-name } \begin{Bmatrix} \underline{OF} \\ \underline{IN} \end{Bmatrix} \text{ library-name.}$$

The library-name is an external-name. It should be 1 to 8 characters and include letters and digits only.

AN EXAMPLE

Suppose we have created a library entry called CUSTOMER that contains the following:

```
01  CUSTOMER-REC.
    05  CUST-NO          PIC X(5).
    05  CUST-NAME        PIC X(20).
    05  CUST-ADDRESS     PIC X(30).
    05  CUST-BAL-DUE     PIC 9(4)V99.
```

To copy the entries in CUSTOMER into our source program, code the following at the point in the program where you want the entries to appear:

```
COPY CUSTOMER
```

The source listing would appear as follows (we use lowercase letters for the copied library entries to distinguish them from the source program coding):

The numbers are source statement line numbers. The lines that include a C after the line number are the copied statements

```
 1   IDENTIFICATION DIVISION.
 2   PROGRAM-ID. CUST01.
 :   :
10   DATA DIVISION.
11   FD  CUSTFILE
12       LABEL RECORDS ARE STANDARD.
13   COPY CUSTOMER.
14C  01  customer-rec.
15C      05  cust-no          pic x(5).
16C      05  cust-name        pic x(20).
17C      05  cust-address     pic x(30).
18C      05  cust-bal-due     pic 9(4)v99.
```

The C following the source program line numbers indicates that these entries have been copied from a library. Some systems use an L (for library) or another letter to distinguish copied entries from programmer-supplied ones.

As noted, other prewritten program entries besides file and record descriptions can also be copied.

THE FULL FORMAT FOR THE COPY STATEMENT

A COPY statement can be used not only to copy prewritten entries but to make certain changes to them in the source program. The full format for the COPY is:

Format

$$
\underline{COPY} \text{ text-name-1} \left[\left\{ \begin{array}{c} \underline{OF} \\ \underline{IN} \end{array} \right\} \text{library-name-1} \right]
$$

$$
\left[\underline{REPLACING} \left\{ \left\{ \begin{array}{c} ==\text{pseudo-text-1}== \\ \text{identifier-1} \\ \text{literal-1} \\ \text{word-1} \end{array} \right\} \underline{BY} \left\{ \begin{array}{c} ==\text{pseudo-text-2}== \\ \text{identifier-2} \\ \text{literal-2} \\ \text{word-2} \end{array} \right\} \right\} \dots \right]
$$

If the REPLACING clause is omitted from the COPY statement, the library text is copied unchanged.

The REPLACING option allows virtually any library entry to be changed when it is being copied into the user's source program. This includes COBOL entries as well as comments or other elements that would appear as "pseudo-text." Literals and identifiers can also be changed as well as "words" that refer to COBOL reserved words.

Example   Using the library entry called CUSTOMER in the preceding example, suppose we code:

```
COPY CUSTOMER REPLACING CUST-NO BY
        CUST-NUMBER, ==X(5)== BY
                 ==X(6)==.
```

This results in the following changes to the library entry when it is called into the source program:

```
14C  01  customer-rec.
15C      05  cust-number    pic x(6).   ◄──Data-name and PIC clause
16C      05  cust-name      pic x(20).      have been changed
17C      05  cust-address   pic x(30).
18C      05  cust-bal-due   pic 9(4)v99.
```

The REPLACING clause does *not* alter the prewritten entries in the library. That is, the changes are made *to the user's source program only.*

Typically, FDs with long or complex record descriptions are copied into programs, as are SCREEN SECTIONs and even modules or paragraphs that are common to more than one program.

Tables are also often copied. In Chapter 12, we saw that some tables are coded directly in the WORKING-STORAGE SECTION with VALUE clauses. Suppose that records in a student file contain a code (01–10) identifying each student's major. If the school has only 10 majors and these majors are not likely to change, we can code them in a COBOL-85 program as:

```
01  MAJOR-TABLE VALUE 'ART  HIS  ECO  MATH CSC  PHIL BIO  ENGL SOC  PSYCH'.
    05  EACH-MAJOR OCCURS 10 TIMES    PIC X(5).
```

The table would consist of 10 five-position majors, where a major code of 1 would indicate ART, a major code of 2 would indicate HIS (for history), and so on.

It is likely that more than one file makes use of this table for processing student information. An alumni file, a department file, and a personnel file, for example, may all need these table entries. It is best, therefore, to store the data in a library and allow it to be copied into programs that need it. Moreover, since the possibility exists that a change of major codes might occur on rare occasions, you should store the table data in a single location so that any change need only be made once.

SELF-TEST
1. A single series of file or record description entries may be used in several different programs by placing it in a _____ and _____ it when needed.
2. With the _____ statement you can include prewritten entries in your program.
3. (T or F) A user or source program can copy library routines and make changes to the field-names initially specified in the library.
4. (T or F) Using the REPLACING option of the COPY statement, it is possible to alter the field-names stored in the library itself.
5. Two purposes of using library functions are to _____ and to _____ .

Solutions
1. library; copying
2. COPY
3. T
4. F—This option only alters library functions *for the user program*.
5. make coding and debugging easier; increase standardization

---

CALL STATEMENT

WHY USE A CALL STATEMENT?

You will recall that structured programs should consist of a series of independent modules that are executed from the main module.

When programs are properly structured:

1. Each module may be written, compiled, and perhaps even tested independently.
2. The modules may be written in different stages, in a top-down manner. They may even be coded by different programmers.
3. If a specific module needs to be modified, the entire logical flow should still function properly without the need for extensive revision to other parts of the program.

Modules within a program can be viewed as subroutines that are called or executed from the main module. But a program may also CALL or reference independent **subprograms** stored in a library that are *entirely separate* from the main program itself. The main program that references or calls a subprogram is referred to as the **calling program**. The subprogram that is linked and executed within the main program is referred to as the **called program**.

Main (or user or source) program: Calling program
Subprogram: Called program

The called program would need to be compiled, debugged, and catalogued or stored in a library so that it may be called when needed. Typical subprograms that may be used by numerous calling programs include edit routines, error control checks, standard calculations, and summary and total printing. Some programming languages use the term "external subroutines" to refer to these; the term "subprogram" is used in COBOL.

The technique of enabling a main program to call a subprogram has the following advantages:

ADVANTAGES OF CALLING SUBPROGRAMS

1. Avoids duplication of effort.
   When modules need to be included in more than one program, it is best to write them separately and call them into each program as needed.

2. Improves programmer productivity.
   Programmers can "specialize" or code modules that make use of their specific talents or skills.

3. Provides greater flexibility.
   Subprograms may be written in *any* programming language; they are typically written in a language best suited to the specific task required.

4. Changes to the called program can be made without the need to modify the calling program.

5. Results in greater standardization. ´

Since a subprogram is really an independent module that is external to the main program, it may be called in just as one would use a PERFORM to execute an internal module.

Differences between CALL and COPY

The CALL statement is very different from the COPY statement. The COPY brings into a user program separate ENVIRONMENT, DATA, or PROCEDURE DIVISION segments *as is*. The copied entries are compiled and executed together with the source program. The CALL causes *an entire program*, which is already in machine language, to be executed. The calling and called programs are separate, but data may be passed from the called program to the calling program *or* from the calling program to the called program. That is, a called program is stored in compiled form in a library.

When the CALL is performed, data is passed from the calling to the called program (if the calling program has assigned values to fields used in the called program). The entire called program is executed, data is passed from the called program back to the calling program, and control returns to the calling program.

Typically, we COPY ENVIRONMENT and DATA DIVISION entries into a source program and we CALL programs from a library rather than COPY them.

FORMAT OF THE CALL STATEMENT

Figure 16.1 illustrates the relationships between a calling program and called programs.

A subprogram is called into a main program with the CALL statement. The following is the basic format for the CALL statement:

Format

```
CALL literal-1
    [USING identifier-1 ...]
```

Literal-1 is the name of the called program as specified in its PROGRAM-ID statement; it is enclosed in quotes like a nonnumeric literal. Typically, the program name conforms to the rules for forming external-names: 1 to 8 characters, letters and digits only. Literal-1 must also be catalogued as the called or subprogram name. This is performed with operating system commands that are system-dependent.

Figure 16.1 The relationships between a calling program and called programs.

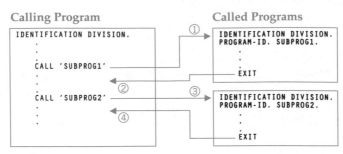

① The program called SUBPROG1 is executed in its entirety
② Control returns to the calling program
③ The program called SUBPROG2 is executed in its entirety
④ Control returns to the calling program

The USING clause of the CALL statement is required if the subprogram performs any operations in which data is to be passed from one program to another. The CALL ... USING identifies fields in the main or calling program that will be either passed to the called program before it is executed, or passed back to the calling program after the called program has been executed. Since the purpose of calling a subprogram is to perform operations or calculations on data, we almost always employ the USING option. See Figure 16.2.

The passing of parameters in Figure 16.2 can be performed in several ways:

1. Suppose the called program needs to operate on two values that have to be passed to it from the calling program. A and B in the calling program can be passed to the called program as X and Y. Then the called program can perform its operations, produce results, and/or pass results back to the calling program as new values for A and B.

Figure 16.2 Passing parameters between a calling program and a called program.

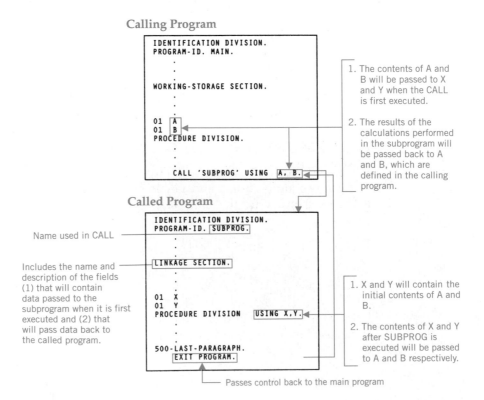

Example   Suppose the called program computes and prints state and federal taxes owed for each individual. The calling program passes a Federal-Taxable-Income value and a State-Taxable-Income value to the called program, where calculations are performed and the actual taxes either printed out or used to replace the taxable income figures in the calling program.

2. Suppose the called program needs to operate on only one value that must be passed to it from the calling program. A from the calling program can be passed to X in the called program as in Figure 16.2. The called program can then perform its calculations, producing a result in Y, which is passed back to the called program as B.

Example   A called program computes a salary increase for employees on level numbers 1 to X, where the value for X is specified in a field called A in the calling program. The salary increase generated as Y in the called program is returned to the calling program as B.

3. Suppose the called program needs no values passed to it from the calling program but produces two results in X and Y that are needed for processing in the calling program.

Example   The called program accepts the date of the run and the time of the run and converts that date and time to a different format needed by the calling program. (The format needed is not one of those available as an intrinsic function.) The computed date and time are stored as X and Y in the called program and passed to the calling program as A and B. There is no need to pass parameters from the calling program because the called program can ACCEPT the computer-generated date and time.

Let us consider the coding requirements of the called program first and then consider the corresponding coding requirements of the calling program.

Called Program Requirements

PROGRAM-ID

The literal used in the CALL statement of the main program to extract a subprogram or routine from a library and execute it must be identical to the called program's PROGRAM-ID. In the calling program, we code CALL $\boxed{\text{'literal-1'}}$ USING ... . In the called program, we code PROGRAM-ID. $\boxed{\text{literal-1.}}$. Note that the literal is enclosed in quotation marks when used in the CALL statement.

LINKAGE SECTION

A **LINKAGE SECTION** must be defined in the called program for identifying those items that (1) will be passed to the called program from the calling program and (2) passed back from the called program to the calling program. The LINKAGE SECTION *of the called program*, then, describes all items to be passed between the two programs.

The LINKAGE SECTION, if used, is coded after the FILE and WORKING-STORAGE SECTIONs of the called program. This section is similar to WORKING-STORAGE except that VALUE clauses for initializing fields are *not* permitted in the LINKAGE SECTION.

PROCEDURE DIVISION USING

The identifiers specified in the USING clause in the PROCEDURE DIVISION entry include all fields defined in the LINKAGE SECTION; these identifiers will be passed from one program to the other. They are passed to and from corresponding identifiers in the CALL ... USING of the main program. See Figure 16.2 again.

EXIT PROGRAM

The *last* executed statement in the *called program* must be the **EXIT PROGRAM**. It signals the computer to return control back to the calling program.

With COBOL 74, EXIT PROGRAM must be the *only* statement in the last paragraph. With COBOL 85, other statements can precede EXIT PROGRAM in the last paragraph.

Note that the subprogram should not have a STOP RUN since program termination should be controlled by the calling program. If the subprogram is ever used independently, as well as used as a called program, it should have a STOP RUN immediately after the EXIT PROGRAM statement.

Calling Program Requirements

We have seen that the called program will include the following PROCEDURE DIVISION entries:

CALLED PROGRAM

```
PROGRAM-ID. PROG1.
    :
    :
PROCEDURE DIVISION USING identifier-1A, identifier-2A, ...
```

Identifier-1A, identifier-2A, ... must be defined in the LINKAGE SECTION of the *called program*.

To execute a subprogram stored in a library, the only statement required in the calling program is the CALL 'literal-1' USING ... statement. The literal specified in the CALL statement of the main program should be the same as in the PROGRAM-ID of the called program, but it is enclosed in quotes in the CALL. The calling program, then, will have the following entry:

```
CALL 'PROG1' USING identifier-1, identifier-2, ...
```

Identifier-1, identifier-2, ... must be defined in the calling program.

When the called program is executed, the contents of identifier-1 of the calling program will be passed to identifier-1A of the called program; the contents of identifier-2 of the calling program will be passed to identifier-2A of the called program, and so on. In this way, initial values, if there are any, may be passed from the calling program to the called program for execution. Then, after execution of the called program, identifier-1A of the called program is passed back to identifier-1 of the calling program, and so on. Thus, resultant data, if there is any, is passed from the called program back to the calling program for subsequent processing.

Data is passed in sequence so that the corresponding items in each statement are made equivalent (e.g., after the called program has been executed, identifier-1A is set equal to identifier-1). The PIC specifications for corresponding items must be the same. Data-names passed from a calling program to a called program may be the same or they may be different, as in our previous illustrations.

As noted, called programs must have a LINKAGE SECTION, the entry PROCEDURE DIVISION USING, and an EXIT PROGRAM at the end of the last module.

EXAMPLES

Example 1   Suppose that a called program is to determine the Social Security and Medicare taxes for each employee. These taxes are commonly referred to as FICA (Federal Insurance Contributions Act) taxes and are based on the employee's annual salary, which is read in by the calling program.

The contents of ANN-SAL, a field in the calling program, must be passed to the called program before the calculation can be made.

Passing data from one program to another is performed with a USING clause. As indicated, the USING clause of both programs indicates fields to be transmitted. Thus, USING defines data passed from calling to called *and* from called to calling. The following will clarify these points:

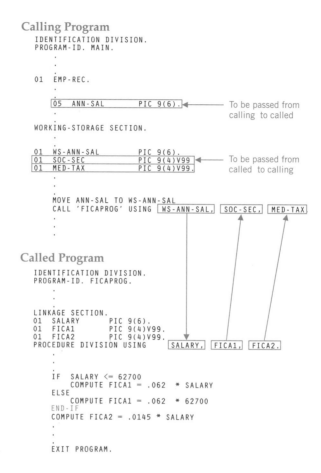

Calling Program

```
IDENTIFICATION DIVISION.
PROGRAM-ID. MAIN.
      .
      .
      .
01  EMP-REC.
      .
      .
     05  ANN-SAL        PIC 9(6).        ← To be passed from
      .                                     calling to called
      .
WORKING-STORAGE SECTION.
      .
      .
01  WS-ANN-SAL        PIC 9(6).
01  SOC-SEC           PIC 9(4)V99.       ← To be passed from
01  MED-TAX           PIC 9(4)V99.          called to calling
      .
      .
     MOVE ANN-SAL TO WS-ANN-SAL
     CALL 'FICAPROG' USING  WS-ANN-SAL,  SOC-SEC,  MED-TAX
      .
      .
      .
```

Called Program

```
IDENTIFICATION DIVISION.
PROGRAM-ID. FICAPROG.
      .
      .
      .
LINKAGE SECTION.
01  SALARY      PIC 9(6).
01  FICA1       PIC 9(4)V99.
01  FICA2       PIC 9(4)V99.
PROCEDURE DIVISION USING    SALARY,  FICA1,  FICA2.

      .
      .
     IF  SALARY <= 62700
          COMPUTE FICA1 = .062 * SALARY
     ELSE
          COMPUTE FICA1 = .062 * 62700
     END-IF
     COMPUTE FICA2 = .0145 * SALARY

      .
      .
     EXIT PROGRAM.
```

Note the following about the *called program*:

1. PROGRAM-ID. name.
   The PROGRAM-ID should be the same as the literal specified in the CALL statement of the calling program except that the literal is enclosed in quotes.

2. LINKAGE SECTION.
   All identifiers to be passed from called program to calling program *and* from calling program to called program must be defined here. The LINKAGE SECTION appears after the WORKING-STORAGE SECTION. Its format is similar to that of WORKING-STORAGE, but VALUE clauses are not permitted.

3. PROCEDURE DIVISION USING . . . .
   Arguments or fields in the CALL are matched by position in the USING, not by location in the LINKAGE SECTION. The identifiers may be the same in both the called and calling programs, but we recommend you use different names.

4. EXIT PROGRAM.
   This must be the last entry in the called program. It must be in a paragraph by itself for COBOL 74. With COBOL 85, other statements can precede it in the last paragraph.

With COBOL 74 you pass 01-level items. With COBOL 85 you can pass parameters *at any level* as long as they are elementary items.

Example 2   Consider the following:

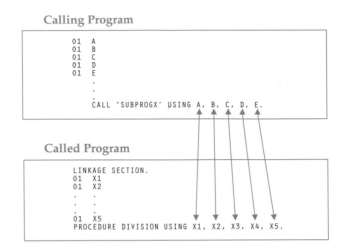

Calling Program

```
    01   A
    01   B
    01   C
    01   D
    01   E
             .
             .
             .
         CALL 'SUBPROGX' USING A, B, C, D, E.
```

Called Program

```
    LINKAGE SECTION.
    01   X1
    01   X2
     .    .
     .    .
     .    .
    01   X5
    PROCEDURE DIVISION USING X1, X2, X3, X4, X5.
```

In the above, before X1, X2, X3, X4, and X5 are used in SUBPROGX, the contents of A, B, C, D, and E, respectively, in the calling program, will be passed to them. That is, A will be transmitted to X1, B will be transmitted to X2, and so on. Correspondingly, after the called program has been executed, the contents of X1 will be passed to A, X2 to B, and so on. That is, the *sequence* of the identifiers in the USING clause determines how data is passed. The sequence of the identifiers as they are defined in the DATA DIVISION is not a factor in parameter passing. Thus, the following would produce the same results as the above:

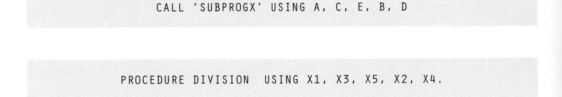

```
CALL 'SUBPROGX' USING A, C, E, B, D
```

```
PROCEDURE DIVISION   USING X1, X3, X5, X2, X4.
```

Note that the PIC clauses of corresponding fields must have the same specifications. That is, the PIC clauses of A and X1 must have the same number of characters as must B and X2, C and X3, D and X4, and E and X5. Moreover, the same names could have been used in both programs.

Passing Data from Called to Calling Programs Only

In Example 2, data is passed in both directions—first, from calling to called and then, after the called program has been executed, the resultant data is passed back. Suppose we wish to do calculations in the calling program that are *not* affected by the initial values of A–E. Then we simply reinitialize X1–X5 in the called program before we perform any calculations.

Example 3   Random numbers are often needed in programs. Most programming languages have predefined functions that generate random numbers. The COBOL 85 Extensions include predefined functions such as a random number generator. See Chapter 7. But if you needed random numbers you might alternatively code a procedure for generating them yourself or CALL in a prewritten procedure. Most such callable procedures enable you to establish the initial value called the *seed*. Moreover, users need to establish the range of random numbers they wish to have generated. Figure 16.3 provides an example of a program that generates a random number.

Figure 16.3 Using a callable procedure to obtain random numbers.

Calling Program

```
IDENTIFICATION DIVISION.
PROGRAM-ID.  CALLING1.
DATA DIVISION.
WORKING-STORAGE SECTION.
01  SEED-Y          PIC 9(10).
01  RANDOM-Y        PIC 9(5).
PROCEDURE DIVISION.
100-MAIN.
*****************************************************************
*      Accepting SEED-Y from TIME results in a relatively      *
*          random start-up number or seed but any fixed        *
*          value for SEED-Y could be used                      *
*****************************************************************
     ACCEPT SEED-Y FROM TIME
*****************************************************************
*    SEED-Y is passed to CALLED1 and RANDOM-Y is passed        *
*          back to CALLING1 as the result                      *
*****************************************************************
     CALL 'CALLED1' USING SEED-Y RANDOM-Y
*****************************************************************
*    RANDOM-Y will be a 5-digit random number - you can        *
*          set it to any size here in the calling program      *
*****************************************************************
     DISPLAY RANDOM-Y
     :
```

Called Program

```
IDENTIFICATION DIVISION.
PROGRAM-ID. CALLED1.
DATA DIVISION.
WORKING-STORAGE SECTION.
01  WS-STORE         PIC 9(10).
*******************************************************************
*  Any numbers for MULTIPLIER, INCREMENT, and MODULUS can be      *
*        selected but the three used here seem to give the        *
*        widest distribution of numbers - that is, the most       *
*        random selection                                         *
*******************************************************************
01  MULTIPLIER       PIC 9(5) VALUE 25173.
01  INCREMENT        PIC 9(5) VALUE 13849.
01  MODULUS          PIC 9(5) VALUE 65536.
LINKAGE SECTION.
01  SEED-X           PIC 9(10).
01  RANDOM-X         PIC 9(5).
PROCEDURE DIVISION USING SEED-X RANDOM-X.
100-MAIN-MODULE.
    MULTIPLY MULTIPLIER BY SEED-X GIVING WS-STORE
    ADD INCREMENT TO WS-STORE
    DIVIDE WS-STORE BY MODULUS GIVING WS-STORE
          REMAINDER SEED-X
    MOVE SEED-X TO RANDOM-X.
200-END.
    EXIT.
```

With COBOL 85, the PROGRAM-ID paragraph in the IDENTIFICATION DIVISION of the called program may have the following INITIAL PROGRAM clause:

PROGRAM-ID. program-name [IS <u>INITIAL</u> PROGRAM].

If this clause is used, the called program will be restored to its initial state each time it is called. This means that all identifiers in WORKING-STORAGE will contain their original values, as specified by their VALUE clauses, before and after each call.

Data items passed *to* a subprogram may have their values protected from modification with the use of the BY CONTENT clause. Consider the following:

```
PROGRAM-ID. CALLING.
   :                                                    ⎫
   CALL 'SUBPROG1'                                      ⎬  calling program
       USING BY CONTENT AMT-1 AMT-2                     ⎭
   :
- - - - - - - - - - - - - - - - - - - - - - - - - - - - - - - - - - - - - - - - - - - - -
PROGRAM-ID. SUBPROG1.                                   ⎫
   :                                                    ⎬  called program
PROCEDURE DIVISION USING AMT-1 AMT-2.                   ⎭
```

Because the BY CONTENT clause is included, the called program *may not change* the value of AMT-1 or AMT-2.

───────────────── DEBUGGING TIP ─────────────────

When testing a program that updates an indexed file, it is best to always begin the test run with a "clean" copy of the initial indexed file. In this way, you can manually determine what the updated file should look like and debug your program accordingly until the actual results obtained are as expected. If you create the initial indexed file and update it in a test run, and then test the program again with the changed file, it is more difficult to know what the initial values were and what the end results should be.

It is, therefore, good practice to include a CALL statement in the update program during the debugging phase that creates a clean copy of the initial indexed file. If this CALL is always executed before an update test run, then you always know what the starting values are in that indexed file. Once the update program is fully debugged, you can remove the CALL statement.

In summary, it is best to CALL programs rather than code the full routines in your program if such routines are needed in different places or if the routines themselves are likely to change.

TEXT MANIPULATION WITH THE STRING AND UNSTRING STATEMENTS

Interactive Processing.   When data is entered interactively, we sometimes need to convert it into a more concise form for processing purposes or for storing it on disk. Similarly, when data is to be displayed, we sometimes need to convert it from a concise form to a more readable form. We can use the STRING and UNSTRING for these purposes.

THE STRING STATEMENT

The Basic Format

A **STRING** statement may be used to combine several fields to form one concise field. This process is called **concatenation**.

For example, consider the following:

```
05  NAME.
    10   LAST-NAME      PIC X(10).
    10   FIRST-NAME     PIC X(10).
    10   MIDDLE-NAME    PIC X(6).
```

Suppose NAME had the following contents:

LAST-NAME	FIRST-NAME	MIDDLE-NAME

E	D	I	S	O	N					T	H	O	M	A	S					A	L	V	A		

1   10 11   20 21   26

We may wish to print the name with only a single blank between each component as: THOMAS ALVA EDISON.

We can use the STRING statement to move, combine, and condense fields. We can also use the STRING to add literals such as 'WAS AN INVENTOR' to the name. The STRING, then, is a very useful instruction for text manipulation.

A simplified format of the STRING statement is:

Simplified Format

$$\underline{STRING} \left\{ \begin{Bmatrix} \text{identifier-1} \\ \text{literal-1} \end{Bmatrix} \right\} \ldots$$

$$\underline{DELIMITED}\ BY \begin{Bmatrix} \text{identifier-2} \\ \text{literal-2} \\ \underline{SIZE} \end{Bmatrix} \Big\} \Big\} \ldots$$

$$\underline{INTO}\ \text{identifier-3}$$
$$[\underline{END-STRING}]*$$

*COBOL 85 only.

With the STRING statement, we can instruct the computer to transmit only significant or nonblank characters in FIRST-NAME, MIDDLE-NAME, and LAST-NAME. Once a blank is reached, we stop transmitting that field:

```
STRING
    FIRST-NAME DELIMITED BY ' '
    MIDDLE-NAME DELIMITED BY ' '
    LAST-NAME DELIMITED BY ' '
    INTO NAME-OUT
```

The delimiter itself would not be placed in the receiving field. Thus for our first example, THOMASALVAEDISON will appear in NAME-OUT using the preceding STRING statement. Note, however, that we can use literals between clauses. Thus we would insert blanks between significant characters as follows:

```
STRING
    FIRST-NAME DELIMITED BY ' '
    ' ' DELIMITED BY SIZE
    MIDDLE-NAME DELIMITED BY ' '
    ' ' DELIMITED BY SIZE
    LAST-NAME DELIMITED BY ' '
    ' ' DELIMITED BY SIZE
    INTO NAME
```
— Places a blank after each field

In this instance the NAME would be displayed as:

THOMAS ALVA EDISON

The delimiter SIZE means that the entire content of the specified literal is transmitted (it could have been a field as well). Each time ' ' DELIMITED BY SIZE is executed, a one-position blank is transmitted. Consider the following record format:

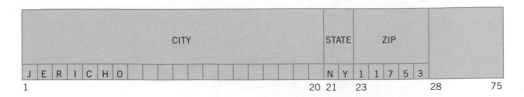

Suppose we wish to print the address. Simply to MOVE the three components and print them would result in:

```
            JERICHO             NY11753
```

There would be thirteen spaces between the CITY and the STATE and no spaces between the STATE and ZIP.

Using a STRING verb, we can place the data in an ADDRESS-OUT field so that it will be more readable when displayed or printed:

```
STRING CITY DELIMITED BY ' '
       ', '   DELIMITED BY SIZE
       STATE  DELIMITED BY SIZE
       ' '    DELIMITED BY SIZE
       ZIP    DELIMITED BY SIZE
       INTO ADDRESS-OUT
DISPLAY ADDRESS-OUT
```

ADDRESS-OUT would then be displayed as:

```
            JERICHO, NY 11753
```

As noted, the delimiter SIZE means that the entire content of the field (or literal) is transmitted. In the preceding, the delimiter for STATE and ZIP can also be SIZE because we will always print two characters for STATE and five characters for ZIP. Note that this coding would *not* be correct if the city consisted of more than one word (e.g., NEW ORLEANS). We could *not* use DELIMITED BY a single space in such instances. It would, however, be possible to delimit by two spaces to catch any two-word cities (e.g., DELIM-ITED BY ' ' where *two spaces* are contained within the quotation marks). In this way, the single space between NEW and ORLEANS would *not* delimit the field; only the two spaces *at the end* of the field would serve as a delimiter.

This STRING option may also be used for changing some of the contents of a field. You will recall that a MOVE operation always replaces the contents of a receiving field, either with significant characters or with spaces or zeros, depending on whether the field is alphanumeric or numeric. With a STRING statement, however, we can change specific characters, leaving the rest of the field intact. In this sense, the character manipulation features of a STRING statement are similar to an INSPECT.

Example

```
01  AGE-OUT        PIC X(12)   VALUE '21 YEARS OLD'.
      :
    STRING '18' DELIMITED BY SIZE
       INTO AGE-OUT
```

The result in AGE-OUT at the end of the STRING operation would be 18 YEARS OLD. In this way, we can make changes to a portion of a field, leaving the rest of the field unaltered. Unlike a MOVE, the STRING does not replace rightmost characters with spaces.

There are numerous additional options available with the STRING, only some of which we will discuss.

OVERFLOW Option

> STRING ...
>   [ON OVERFLOW imperative-statement-1]

The OVERFLOW option specifies the operation(s) to be performed if the receiving field is not large enough to accommodate the result.

The clause NOT ON OVERFLOW is available with COBOL 85, as is an END-STRING scope terminator.

POINTER Option

We may also count the number of characters actually moved in a STRING statement:

> STRING ...
>   [WITH POINTER identifier-1]
>   [ON OVERFLOW ...]

The identifier will specify the number of nonblank characters moved to the receiving field if it is initialized at *one*.

Example   The following moves a FIRST-NAME field to a NAME-OUT field *and* determines the number of significant or nonblank characters in FIRST-NAME:

```
01   WS-COUNT    PIC 99.
  :
  :
     MOVE 1 TO WS-COUNT
     STRING FIRST-NAME DELIMITED BY ' '
         INTO NAME-OUT
         WITH POINTER WS-COUNT
```

When the STRING is performed, WS-COUNT will be increased by one for every character actually moved into NAME-OUT. Thus, if FIRST-NAME IS 'PAUL', for example, WS-COUNT will contain a *five* after the STRING operation. This means that it is ready to reference the fifth position in NAME-OUT. The following uses WS-COUNT to determine *the number of characters actually transmitted* in a STRING:

```
SUBTRACT 1 FROM WS-COUNT
DISPLAY WS-COUNT
```

Since WS-COUNT would contain a five after 'PAUL' is transmitted to NAME-OUT, we must subtract one from it to obtain the length of the move. If we initialized WS-COUNT at zero originally, then it would contain a four after the STRING is performed, but you would need to add one to it for positioning the next data item.

We may also use the POINTER option to move data to a receiving field *beginning at some point other than the first position.* If WS-COUNT in the preceding was initialized at 15, then FIRST-NAME would be moved to NAME-OUT beginning with the *fifteenth* position of NAME-OUT.

Note that we are assuming that FIRST-NAME is a single word (e.g., MARY ANNE would be entered as MARYANNE). If not, we would need to delimit by *two* spaces, not one, where there are at least two spaces at the end of the field.

General Rules for Using the STRING

The following are rules governing the use of the STRING statement:

RULES FOR USING THE STRING STATEMENT

1. The DELIMITED BY clause is required. It can indicate:

   SIZE: The entire sending field is transmitted.

   Literal: The transfer of data is terminated when the specified literal is encountered; the literal itself is not moved.

   Identifier: The transfer of data is terminated when the contents of the identifier is encountered.

2. The receiving field must be an elementary data item with *no* editing symbols or JUSTIFIED RIGHT clause.

3. All literals must be described as nonnumeric.

4. The identifier specified with the POINTER clause must be an elementary numeric item.

5. The STRING statement moves data from left to right just like alphanumeric fields are moved, but a STRING does *not* pad with low-order blanks the way an alphanumeric MOVE does.

THE UNSTRING STATEMENT

The Basic Format

The **UNSTRING** statement may be used to convert keyed data to a more appropriate form for storing it on disk. For example, a program may include a statement that causes the following to be displayed on a screen:

```
ENTER NAME: LAST, FIRST, MIDDLE INITIAL
           : USE COMMAS TO SEPARATE ENTRIES
```

The message to the operator is fairly clear. When the name is entered, it will be stored in an alphanumeric field called NAME-IN. The routine may appear as follows:

```
WORKING-STORAGE SECTION.
01   NAME-IN          PIC X(36).
     :
     DISPLAY 'ENTER NAME: LAST, FIRST, MIDDLE INITIAL'
     DISPLAY '           : USE COMMAS TO SEPARATE ENTRIES'
     ACCEPT NAME-IN
```

Since each name has a variable number of characters, there is no way of knowing how large each individual last name and first name is.

Suppose we wish to store the name in an output disk record as follows:

```
01   PAYROLL-REC.
     05   NAME-OUT.
          10   LAST-NAME       PIC X(20).
          10   FIRST-NAME      PIC X(15).
          10   MIDDLE-INITIAL  PIC X.
```

With an UNSTRING statement, we can instruct the computer to separate the NAME-IN into its components and store them *without* the commas:

```
UNSTRING NAME-IN
     DELIMITED BY ','
          INTO LAST-NAME
               FIRST-NAME
               MIDDLE-INITIAL
```

Suppose NAME-IN is entered as TAFT,WILLIAM,H. NAME-OUT will appear as follows after the UNSTRING:

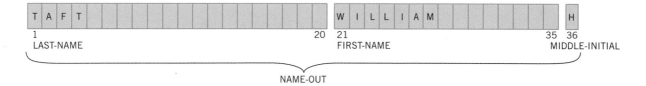

The format for the UNSTRING statement as we have used it is:

Format

> UNSTRING identifier-1
>
> $\left[\underline{\text{DELIMITED}}\text{ BY }[\underline{\text{ALL}}]\begin{Bmatrix}\text{identifier-2}\\\text{literal-1}\end{Bmatrix}\right.$
>
> $\left.\left[\underline{\text{OR}}\text{ }[\underline{\text{ALL}}]\begin{Bmatrix}\text{identifier-3}\\\text{literal-2}\end{Bmatrix}\right]\dots\right]$
>
> <u>INTO</u> identifier-4 . . .
> [END-UNSTRING]*

*COBOL 85 only.

We may use *any* literal, even a blank, as a delimiter. We may also ACCEPT a name from a keyboard and UNSTRING it so that we can use just the last name for looking up a corresponding disk record with last name as a RECORD KEY. When the ALL phrase is included, one or more occurrences of the literal or identifier are treated as just one occurrence.

With the UNSTRING, the programmer can use POINTER and ON OVERFLOW. With COBOL 85, NOT ON OVERFLOW as well as an END-UNSTRING scope terminator can also be used.

General Rules for Using the UNSTRING

SUMMARY
RULES FOR USING THE UNSTRING STATEMENT

1. The sending field must be nonnumeric. The receiving fields may be numeric or nonnumeric.

2. Each literal must be nonnumeric.

3. The [WITH POINTER identifier] and [ON OVERFLOW imperative-statement] clauses may be used in the same way as with the STRING.

Both the STRING and the UNSTRING have numerous options, many of which have not been considered here. Check the *COBOL Syntax Reference Guide* that accompanies this text if you wish additional information on these verbs.

CHAPTER SUMMARY

A. COPY Statement
1. To copy entries stored in a library to a user program.
2. ENVIRONMENT, DATA, and PROCEDURE DIVISION entries may be copied.
3. Most often used for copying standard file and record description entries or modules to be used in the PROCEDURE DIVISION.
4. The format is: COPY text-name $\left\{ \begin{array}{c} \underline{OF} \\ \underline{IN} \end{array} \right\}$ library-name.

B. CALL Statement
1. To call or reference *entire programs* stored in a library.
2. The user program is referred to as the calling program; the program accessed from the library will serve as a subprogram and is referred to as the called program.
3. To pass data from the called program to the calling program.
   a. The CALL statement can include a USING clause that lists the names of the fields in the calling program that are passed to the called program and fields that will be passed back from the called program.
   b. The PROCEDURE DIVISION statement of the called program also includes a USING clause to indicate identifiers specified in this subprogram that will correspond to identifiers in the calling program.
   c. Identifiers in the called and calling programs may be the same or they may be different.
   d. The called program must have a LINKAGE SECTION in which fields to be passed to and from the calling program are defined. This is the last section of the DATA DIVISION.
   e. The called program must end with an EXIT PROGRAM statement. This must be in a separate paragraph only for COBOL 74.

C. The STRING statement joins or concatenates fields or portions of fields into one field. The UNSTRING statement enables processing of a portion of a sending field.

KEY TERMS

CALL	COPY	STRING
Called program	EXIT PROGRAM	Subprogram
Calling program	Library	UNSTRING
Concatenation	LINKAGE SECTION	

CHAPTER SELF-TEST

1. The CALL statement is particularly useful in structured programs because _____ .
2. When using a CALL statement, your program is referred to as the _____ program; the subprogram is referred to as the _____ program.
3. To CALL a program, you code _____ .
4. In Question 3, the literal specified must be the same as _____ .
5. If you include USING with the CALL statement in the calling program, the identifiers specified must be described in the (calling, called) program.
6. The program being called has a _____ SECTION in which data to be passed to the calling program is defined.
7. The PROCEDURE DIVISION entry for the called program includes a _____ clause.
8. The identifiers specified in the USING clause for Question 7 are defined in _____ .
9. The last statement in the called program is _____ .
10. (T or F) The identifiers specified in both the called and calling program must be the same.
11. (T or F) In a STRING or UNSTRING statement, the delimiter specified must be alphanumeric.
12. (T or F) With an UNSTRING statement, the delimiter specified is itself transmitted.

Solutions

1. subprograms being called can be coded and executed as independent programs
2. calling (or main or user); called
3. CALL literal-1
      USING identifier-1 . . .
4. the PROGRAM-ID entry in the called program; the literal is, however, enclosed in quotes.

5. calling

6. LINKAGE

7. USING; e.g., PROCEDURE DIVISION USING identifier . . .

8. the LINKAGE SECTION of the called program

9. EXIT PROGRAM

10. F—They may be different.

11. T

12. F

PRACTICE PROGRAM Consider the problem definition in Figure 16.4. The input consists of an address entered with street, city, state, and zip separated by /. The output requires this address component to be separated into individual fields using the UNSTRING. The UNSTRING routine is called in from a program called UNSTR. The program is illustrated in Figure 16.5.

Figure 16.4 Problem definition for the Practice Program.

Systems Flowchart

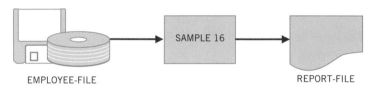

EMPLOYEE-FILE   SAMPLE 16   REPORT-FILE

EMPLOYEE-FILE **Record Layout**		
Field	**Size**	**Type**
SOC-SEC-NO	9	Alphanumeric
EMPLOYEE-NAME	20	Alphanumeric
EMPLOYEE-ADDRESS	50	Alphanumeric

REPORT-FILE Printer Spacing Chart

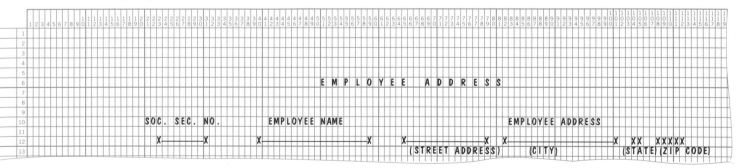

Sample Input Data

```
345234231 TOM CRUISE           165 WEST ST/MIDDLETOWN/NY/10098/
986654543 BURT REYNOLDS        56 EAST AVE/ANYTOWN/NJ/00876/
654898535 JAY LENO             100 NORTH ST/NEW YORK/NY/10000/
876567653 MICHAEL DOUGLAS      1452 WEST MAIN ST/WARYING/CA/90006/
567744544 CHRISTOPHER PLUMMER  77 EAST 63 ST/NEW YORK/NY/00987/
611102388 NICK NOLTE           432 CONCORD RD/HOLLYWOOD/CA/90078/
345443344 BILL MURRAY          98 WARD ST/WESTVILLAGE/VT/09898/
656554566 HARRISON FORD        100 DELLWOOD RD/CENTERTOWN/ND/78776/
```

SOC-SEC-NO   EMPLOYEE-NAME   EMPLOYEE-ADDRESS

Figure 16.4   (continued)

Sample Output

```
                    E M P L O Y E E     A D D R E S S

   SOC. SEC. NO.      EMPLOYEE NAME                    EMPLOYEE ADDRESS

      345234231     TOM CRUISE           165 WEST ST      MIDDLETOWN        NY 10098

      986654543     BURT REYNOLDS        56 EAST AVE      ANYTOWN           NJ 00876

      654898535     JAY LENO             100 NORTH ST     NEW YORK          NY 10000

      876567653     MICHAEL DOUGLAS      1452 WEST MAIN   WARYING           CA 90006

      567744544     CHRISTOPHER PLUMMER  77 EAST 63 ST    NEW YORK          NY 00987

      611102388     NICK NOLTE           432 CONCORD RD   HOLLYWOOD         CA 90078

      345443344     BILL MURRAY          98 WARD ST       WESTVILLAGE       VT 09898

      656554566     HARRISON FORD        100 DELLWOOD RD  CENTERTOWN        ND 78776
```

Figure 16.5   Solution to the Practice Program.

COBOL 85

```
IDENTIFICATION DIVISION.
PROGRAM-ID.  SAMPLE16.
AUTHOR. NANCY STERN.
ENVIRONMENT DIVISION.
INPUT-OUTPUT SECTION.
FILE-CONTROL.
    SELECT EMPLOYEE-FILE ASSIGN TO DISK 'DISK16'.
    SELECT REPORT-FILE   ASSIGN TO PRINTER.
DATA DIVISION.
FILE SECTION.
FD  EMPLOYEE-FILE
    LABEL RECORDS ARE STANDARD.
01  EMPLOYEE-REC.
    05   SOC-SEC-NO              PIC X(9).
    05   EMPLOYEE-NAME           PIC X(20).
    05   EMPLOYEE-ADDRESS        PIC X(50).
FD  REPORT-FILE
    LABEL RECORDS ARE OMITTED.
01  REPORT-REC                   PIC X(132).
WORKING-STORAGE SECTION.
01  WORK-AREAS.
    05   ARE-THERE-MORE-RECORDS  PIC X(3)      VALUE 'YES'.
        88  NO-MORE-RECORDS                    VALUE 'NO '.
01  DATA-TO-BE-SENT-TO-UNSTRING.
    05   EMPLOYEE-ADDRESS-STR    PIC X(50).
    05   DATA-UNSTRING.
        10   STREET-ADDRESS      PIC X(15).
        10   CITY                PIC X(20).
        10   STATE               PIC XX.
        10   ZIP-CODE            PIC X(5).
01  HEADER1.
    05                           PIC X(50)     VALUE SPACES.
    05                           PIC X(32)
        VALUE 'E M P L O Y E E     A D D R E S S'.
    05                           PIC X(50)     VALUE SPACES.
```

COBOL 74 Substitutions

For COBOL 74, FILLER must be used
instead of a blank field name

Figure 16.5   (continued)

```
01   HEADER2.
     05                              PIC X(20)        VALUE SPACES.
     05                              PIC X(34)
       VALUE 'SOC. SEC. NO.         EMPLOYEE NAME'.
     05                              PIC X(28)        VALUE SPACES.
     05                              PIC X(16)
       VALUE 'EMPLOYEE ADDRESS'.
     05                              PIC X(34)        VALUE SPACES.
01   DETAIL-LINE.
     05                              PIC X(22)        VALUE SPACES.
     05   SOC-SEC-NUMBER-OUT         PIC X(9).
     05                              PIC X(8)         VALUE SPACES.
     05   EMPLOYEE-NAME-OUT          PIC X(20).
     05                              PIC X(5)         VALUE SPACES.
     05   STREET-ADDRESS-OUT         PIC X(15).
     05                              PIC XX           VALUE SPACES.
     05   CITY-OUT                   PIC X(20).
     05                              PIC XX           VALUE SPACES.
     05   STATE-OUT                  PIC XX.
     05                              PIC XX           VALUE SPACES.
     05   ZIP-CODE-OUT               PIC X(5).
     05                              PIC X(20)        VALUE SPACES.
PROCEDURE DIVISION.
100-MAIN1.
     OPEN INPUT  EMPLOYEE-FILE
          OUTPUT REPORT-FILE
     PERFORM 300-HEADING-RTN
     PERFORM UNTIL NO-MORE-RECORDS
        READ EMPLOYEE-FILE
           AT END
              MOVE 'NO ' TO ARE-THERE-MORE-RECORDS
           NOT AT END
              PERFORM 200-REPORT-RTN
        END-READ
     END-PERFORM
     CLOSE EMPLOYEE-FILE
           REPORT-FILE
     STOP RUN.
200-REPORT-RTN.
     MOVE EMPLOYEE-ADDRESS TO EMPLOYEE-ADDRESS-STR
     CALL 'UNSTR' USING DATA-TO-BE-SENT-TO-UNSTRING
     MOVE SOC-SEC-NO TO SOC-SEC-NUMBER-OUT
     MOVE EMPLOYEE-NAME TO EMPLOYEE-NAME-OUT
     MOVE STATE TO STATE-OUT
     MOVE CITY TO CITY-OUT
     MOVE ZIP-CODE TO ZIP-CODE-OUT
     MOVE STREET-ADDRESS TO STREET-ADDRESS-OUT
     WRITE REPORT-REC FROM DETAIL-LINE
        AFTER ADVANCING 2 LINES.

300-HEADING-RTN.
     WRITE REPORT-REC FROM HEADER1
        AFTER ADVANCING PAGE
     WRITE REPORT-REC FROM HEADER2
        AFTER ADVANCING 4 LINES.
```

COBOL 74 Substitutions

```
READ EMPLOYEE-FILE
     AT END MOVE 'NO ' TO ARE-THERE-MORE-RECORDS.
PERFORM 200-REPORT-RTN
     UNTIL NO-MORE-RECORDS.
```

```
READ EMPLOYEE-FILE
     AT END MOVE 'NO ' TO ARE-THERE-MORE-RECORDS.
```

UNSTR Source Listing

```
IDENTIFICATION DIVISION.
PROGRAM-ID. UNSTR.
AUTHOR. ROBERT A. STERN.
ENVIRONMENT DIVISION.
DATA DIVISION.
LINKAGE SECTION.
```

Figure 16.5 (continued)

```
01  DATA-SENT-FROM-CALLING-PROG.
    05  EMPLOYEE-ADDR              PIC X(50).
    05  UNSTR-ADDR.
        10  STREET-ADDR           PIC X(15).
        10  CITY-ADDR             PIC X(20).
        10  STATE-ADDR            PIC XX.
        10  ZIP-CODEX             PIC X(5).
PROCEDURE DIVISION USING DATA-SENT-FROM-CALLING-PROG.
100-MAIN-PARA.
    UNSTRING EMPLOYEE-ADDR
            DELIMITED BY '/'
            INTO STREET-ADDR
                 CITY-ADDR
                 STATE-ADDR
                 ZIP-CODEX
    END-UNSTRING.
200-EXIT-PARA.
    EXIT PROGRAM.
```

REVIEW QUESTIONS

I. True-False
Questions

_____ 1. COPY and CALL statements may be used interchangeably in a COBOL program.

_____ 2. In order to CALL or COPY an entry, it must be stored in a library.

_____ 3. A COPY statement enables numerous users to call into their program standardized record description entries.

_____ 4. A COPY statement may not be used for copying PROCEDURE DIVISION entries.

_____ 5. When using a CALL statement, the data-names specified must be identical in both the called and calling program.

_____ 6. When using a CALL statement, the called program is typically referred to as the user program.

_____ 7. A called program must have a LINKAGE SECTION.

_____ 8. All calling programs must end with an EXIT PROGRAM entry.

_____ 9. A called program is not altered when it is accessed by a calling program.

_____ 10. Another term for a called program is a subprogram.

II. General Questions

1. Indicate the differences between the COPY and CALL statements.

2. Code a statement to COPY a record description called INVENTORY-REC from a library.

3. Code the shell of a calling program to access a subroutine called VALIDATE that will place the total number of errors found into a user-defined field called COUNT1.

4. For Question 3, assume that the called program stores the count of errors in a field called SUM-IT. Code the shell of the called program.

III. Validating Data

Modify the Practice Program so that it includes appropriate coding to (1) test for all errors and (2) print a control listing of totals (records processed, errors encountered, batch totals).

DEBUGGING EXERCISES

Suppose SUBPROG is called with a CALL IS SUBPROGR USING X, Y. SUBPROG contains the following:

```
LINKAGE-SECTION.
    :
    05  Q
    05  R
PROCEDURE DIVISION USING X, Y.
    :
    EXIT.
```

(a) The line containing LINKAGE SECTION results in a syntax error. Find the error and correct it.

(b) The PROCEDURE DIVISION entry results in a syntax error. Find and correct it.

(c) The last line results in a syntax error. Find and correct it.

PROGRAMMING ASSIGNMENTS

1. Write a subroutine called INFLTN to calculate the price of an item over a 10-year period taking inflation into account. You may modify the solution to Programming Assignment 3 on page 353 so that it can be used as a subroutine. Write a second program to call in this subroutine and to pass to the calling program all the calculated variables.

2. A subroutine called BENEFITS is used to calculate certain benefits to which an employee is entitled, based on the employee's Job Classification Code. Write a program to call in this subroutine and to pass to the called program the following:

   a. Number of vacation days.
   b. Number of sick days.

(Continued on the next page.)

Figure 16.6 Problem definition for Programming Assignment 2.

Systems Flowchart

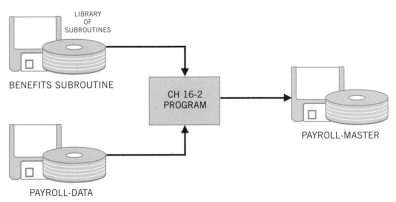

PAYROLL-DATA **Record Layout**			
Field	**Size**	**Type**	**No. of Decimal Positions (if Numeric)**
EMPLOYEE-NO	5	Alphanumeric	
EMPLOYEE-NAME	20	Alphanumeric	
TERRITORY-NO	2	Alphanumeric	
OFFICE-NO	2	Alphanumeric	
ANNUAL-SALARY	6	Numeric	0
SOCIAL-SECURITY-NO	9	Alphanumeric	
NO-OF-DEPENDENTS	2	Numeric	0
JOB-CLASSIFICATION-CODE	2	Alphanumeric	
UNION-DUES	5	Numeric	2
INSURANCE	5	Numeric	2
Unused	22	Alphanumeric	

Figure 16.6 (continued)

PAYROLL-MASTER Record Layout			
Field	**Size**	**Type**	**No. of Decimal Positions (if Numeric)**
EMPLOYEE-NO	5	Alphanumeric	
EMPLOYEE-NAME	20	Alphanumeric	
TERRITORY-NO	2	Alphanumeric	
OFFICE-NO	2	Alphanumeric	
ANNUAL-SALARY	6	Numeric	0
SOCIAL-SECURITY-NO	9	Alphanumeric	
NO-OF-DEPENDENTS	2	Numeric	0
JOB-CLASSIFICATION-CODE	2	Alphanumeric	
UNION-DUES	5	Numeric	2
INSURANCE	5	Numeric	2
SICK-DAYS	3	Numeric	0
VACATION-DAYS	3	Numeric	0
Unused	16	Alphanumeric	

The purpose of the program is to create an indexed master payroll file that adds vacation days and sick days to each employee's record. See the Problem Definition in Figure 16.6.

3. Maintenance Program.   Modify the Practice Program in this chapter to print the following at the end of the report:

   a. The total number of employees.
   b. The total number of employees who live in New York (STATE = NY).

CHAPTER 17

The Report Writer Module

INTRODUCTION

COBOL has a Report Writer Module that greatly facilitates print operations. By including additional DATA DIVISION entries, the Report Writer Module will automatically handle all:

1. Spacing of forms.
2. Skipping to a new page.
3. Testing for end of page.
4. Printing of headings at the top of a page and footings at the bottom of a page.
5. Accumulating of amount fields.
6. Testing for control breaks.
7. Detail and/or summary printing.
8. Printing of totals for control breaks.
9. Printing of a final total when there are no more input records.

The Report Writer Module provides a facility for producing reports by focusing on the physical characteristics of the report rather than specifying the detailed procedures necessary to produce the report. Many new DATA DIVISION entries are required when using this module but there are very few PROCEDURE DIVISION entries.

THE BENEFITS OF THE REPORT WRITER MODULE

FOR DETAIL AND SUMMARY PRINTING

You will recall that many reports in businesses require:

1. *Detail printing* The printing of one or more lines for each input record.
2. *Summary or group printing* The printing of totals or other summary information for groups of records.

The Report Writer Module can be easily used for both detail and/or summary reports.

FOR CONTROL BREAK PROCESSING

One type of summary or group printing uses a **control break** procedure as discussed in Chapter 10. We review control break procedures here.

Consider the output in Figure 17.1. This report has both detail and summary printing. That is, when input records with the same department number are read, the records are printed and the total amount of sales for each salesperson is accumulated. When a change or "break" in the department number occurs, the accumulated total of all amounts of sales is printed as a *control total line*. We call department number a *control field*. Summary printing is performed as a result of the control break that occurs when there is a change in the department number (see line 17 of Figure 17.1).

Note that department is not the only control field in this illustration. A change in *area* also results in a *control break* that produces a control total (see line 31). The area control field, however, is a *higher level control field* than department and is designated with two **'s rather than one. A change in area, therefore, forces a department or minor-level control break. Thus, while reading input records, when a change in the area occurs,

Figure 17.1 Report with both detail and summary printing.

```
                                      MONTHLY SALES REPORT        PAGE   99


     TERRITORY     AREA     DEPARTMENT        SALESPERSON   AMOUNT OF SALES
         1           1          01         A NEWMAN            417.45

         1           1          01         P PETERSON JR       628.14

         1           1          01         D SILVERS           404.55


                                           TOTAL DEPARTMENT 01  $1450.14 *
         1           1          02         J ADAMS             379.23

         1           1          02         B JONES             298.16


                                           TOTAL DEPARTMENT 02   $677.39 *
         1           1          03         A BYRNES            559.26

         1           1          03         F CARLETON          223.68


                                           TOTAL DEPARTMENT 03   $782.94 *
                                                TOTAL AREA 1     $2910.47 **
         1           2          04         A FRANKLIN          627.34

         1           2          04         D ROBERTS           572.26

         1           2          04         S STONE             426.32


                                           TOTAL DEPARTMENT 04  $1625.92 *
         1           2          05         L DANTON            365.22

         1           2          05         R JACKSON           426.22


                                           TOTAL DEPARTMENT 05   $791.44 *
                                                TOTAL AREA 2     $2417.36 **
                                                TOTAL TERRITORY 1  $ 5327.83 ***
```

the total amount of sales for the last department in the area is printed first; then the total amount of sales for the entire area is printed. For area 01, for example, we have three department totals and then an area total that is a higher-level total (see lines 29 and 31 of Figure 17.1).

Territory is the *major control field*. Area and department are control fields subordinate to territory. During the reading of input, when a change in territory occurs, first the corresponding department total is printed, then an area total is printed, and finally a major level territory total is printed. That is, a major territory break forces an intermediate area break, which forces a minor department break (see lines 45, 47, and 49).

The illustration in Figure 17.1 is intended as a review of the control break procedures that can be easily handled using the Report Writer Module. The Practice Program at the end of this chapter illustrates how the Report Writer Module can produce the report in Figure 17.1.

FOR PRINTING HEADINGS AND FOOTINGS

A Report Writer program can designate print lines of the following types:

REPORT HEADING (RH) Prints identifying information about the report *only once*, at the top of the first page of the report.

PAGE HEADING (PH) Prints identifying information at the top of each page. This may include page numbers, column headings, and so on.

CONTROL HEADING (CH) Prints a heading that typically contains new control values when a control break has occurred.

DETAIL (DE) Prints for each input record read.

CONTROL FOOTING (CF) Prints control totals for the previous group of detail records just printed, after a control break has occurred.

PAGE FOOTING (PF) Prints at the end of each page.

REPORT FOOTING (RF) Prints only once, at the end of the report. This may include, for example, an 'End of Report' message.

The printing of each type of print line is controlled by the Report Writer Module. That is, a line designated as a Report Heading is printed at the beginning of a report, a Page Heading line prints at the beginning of each page, and so on.

The Report Writer Module makes it possible for the programmer to specify a report's format in the REPORT SECTION of the DATA DIVISION while reducing the coding needed in the PROCEDURE DIVISION.

THE REPORT SECTION IN THE DATA DIVISION

The DATA DIVISION of a program using the Report Writer Module can consist of three sections that must be coded in the order shown:

1. FILE SECTION
2. WORKING-STORAGE SECTION
3. REPORT SECTION

The REPORT SECTION is specified only when the Report Writer Module is used. We can use this module when complex summary or group printing is required, or it can be used for simple detail printing as well. Lines must be designated as heading, detail, and footing lines, and they will print as appropriate under the control of the Report Writer Module.

Let us consider a sample program using the Report Writer Module that produces a group report, as in Figure 17.2. This is also a control break procedure, but there is only one control field, Customer Number. Thus, this report is not quite as complex as in the previous illustration. A CONTROL FOOTING FINAL line indicating the Final Cost is printed at the end of the report.

The program listing, using the Report Writer Module, appears in Figure 17.3. Note that although the DATA DIVISION tends to be more complex than in previous programs, the Report Writer simplifies the PROCEDURE DIVISION.

The first part of the program is similar to other COBOL programs. That is, the first two divisions, the input File Description and the ARE-THERE-MORE-RECORDS field as specified in WORKING-STORAGE, are all the same. The only change is in FD FILE-OUT, which contains a REPORT IS REPORT-LISTING clause in place of an 01 record description entry.

Figure 17.2 Printer Spacing Chart for sample program that uses the Report Writer Module.

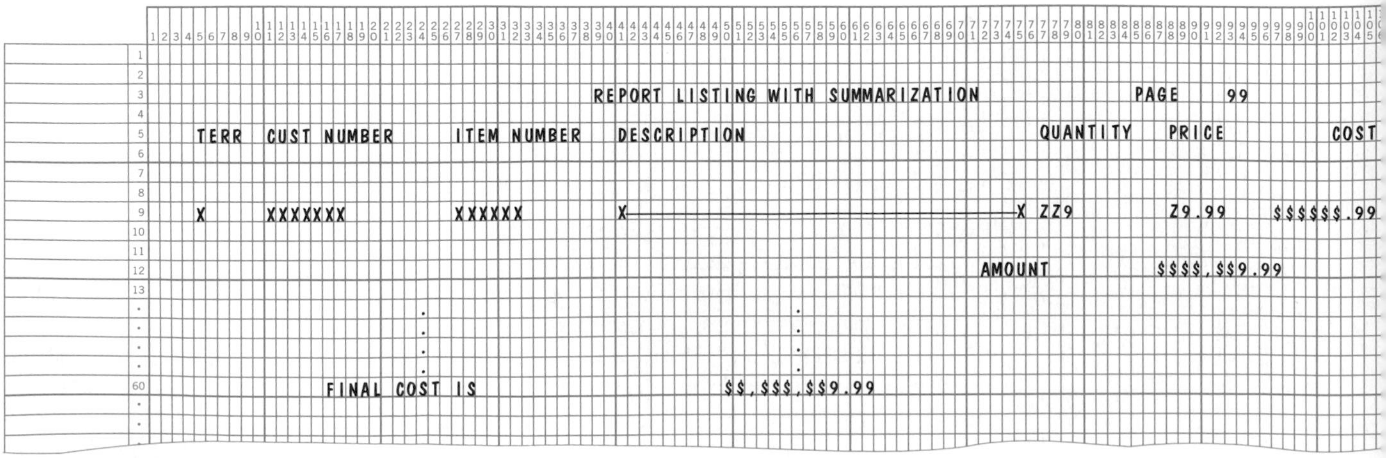

Figure 17.3 Sample program that uses the Report Writer Module.

COBOL 85

```
IDENTIFICATION DIVISION.
PROGRAM-ID.    REPORT-WRITER2.
AUTHOR.        CAROL EISEN.
***************************
*  this is an example of  *
*  report writer feature  *
***************************
ENVIRONMENT DIVISION.
INPUT-OUTPUT SECTION.
FILE-CONTROL.
    SELECT FILE-IN ASSIGN TO DATA17.
    SELECT FILE-OUT ASSIGN TO PRINTER.
*
DATA DIVISION.
FILE SECTION.
FD  FILE-IN
    LABEL RECORDS ARE STANDARD.
01  IN-REC.
    05  TERR                        PIC X.
    05  CUST-NO                     PIC X(7).
    05  ITEM-NO                     PIC X(6).
    05  DESCRIPTION                 PIC X(35).
    05  QTY                         PIC 9(3).
    05  PRICE                       PIC 99V99.
    05  COST                        PIC 9(5)V99.
FD  FILE-OUT
    LABEL RECORDS ARE OMITTED
    REPORT IS REPORT-LISTING.
WORKING-STORAGE SECTION.
01  ARE-THERE-MORE-RECORDS          PIC X(3)  VALUE 'YES'.
    88  NO-MORE-RECORDS                       VALUE 'NO '.
REPORT SECTION.
RD  REPORT-LISTING
    CONTROLS ARE FINAL, CUST-NO
    PAGE LIMIT IS 60 LINES
    HEADING 3
    FIRST DETAIL 9.
01  TYPE IS REPORT HEADING.
    05  LINE NUMBER IS 3.
        10  COLUMN NUMBER IS 39         PIC X(33)
                VALUE 'REPORT LISTING WITH SUMMARIZATION'.
        10  COLUMN NUMBER IS 85         PIC X(4)
                VALUE 'PAGE'.
        10  COLUMN NUMBER IS 92         PIC 99
                SOURCE PAGE-COUNTER.
01  TYPE IS PAGE HEADING.
    05  LINE NUMBER IS 5.
        10  COLUMN NUMBER IS 5          PIC X(4)
                VALUE 'TERR'.
        10  COLUMN NUMBER IS 11         PIC X(11)
                VALUE 'CUST NUMBER'.
        10  COLUMN NUMBER IS 27         PIC X(11)
                VALUE 'ITEM NUMBER'.
        10  COLUMN NUMBER IS 41         PIC X(11)
                VALUE 'DESCRIPTION'.
        10  COLUMN NUMBER IS 77         PIC X(8)
                VALUE 'QUANTITY'.
        10  COLUMN NUMBER IS 88         PIC X(5)
                VALUE 'PRICE'.
        10  COLUMN NUMBER IS 102        PIC X(4)
                VALUE 'COST'.
01  DETAIL-LINE TYPE IS DETAIL.
    05  LINE NUMBER IS PLUS 1.
```

Figure 17.3 (continued)

```
                                         10   COLUMN NUMBER IS 5              PIC X
                                              SOURCE IS TERR.
                                         10   COLUMN NUMBER IS 11 GROUP INDICATE PIC X(7)
                                              SOURCE IS CUST-NO.
                                         10   COLUMN NUMBER IS 27             PIC X(6)
                                              SOURCE IS ITEM-NO.
                                         10   COLUMN NUMBER IS 41             PIC X(35)
                                              SOURCE IS DESCRIPTION.
                                         10   COLUMN NUMBER IS 77             PIC ZZ9
                                              SOURCE IS QTY.
                                         10   COLUMN NUMBER IS 88             PIC Z9.99
                                              SOURCE IS PRICE.
                                         10   COLUMN NUMBER IS 97             PIC $(6).99
                                              SOURCE IS COST.
                            01   TYPE IS CONTROL FOOTING CUST-NO.
                                 05  LINE NUMBER IS PLUS 2.
                                         10   COLUMN NUMBER IS 72             PIC X(6)
                                              VALUE 'AMOUNT'.
                                         10   AMT COLUMN NUMBER IS 87         PIC $$$$,$$9.99
                                              SUM COST.
                            01   TYPE IS CONTROL FOOTING FINAL.
                                 05  LINE NUMBER IS 60.
                                         10   COLUMN NUMBER IS 16             PIC X(13)
                                              VALUE 'FINAL COST IS'.
                                         10   COLUMN NUMBER IS 50             PIC $$,$$$,$$9.99
                                              SUM AMT.
                       *
                       PROCEDURE DIVISION.
                       100-MAIN-MODULE.
                           OPEN INPUT FILE-IN
                                OUTPUT FILE-OUT
                           INITIATE REPORT-LISTING
                           PERFORM UNTIL NO-MORE-RECORDS
                               READ FILE-IN
                                   AT END
                                       MOVE 'NO ' TO ARE-THERE-MORE-RECORDS
                                   NOT AT END
                                       PERFORM 200-CALC-RTN
                               END-READ
                           END-PERFORM
                           TERMINATE REPORT-LISTING
                           CLOSE FILE-IN
                                 FILE-OUT
                           STOP RUN.
                       200-CALC-RTN.
                           GENERATE DETAIL-LINE.
```

COBOL 74 Substitutions

```
READ FILE-IN
     AT END MOVE 'NO ' TO
          ARE-THERE-MORE-RECORDS.
PERFORM 200-CALC-RTN
     UNTIL NO-MORE-RECORDS.
```

```
READ FILE-IN
     AT END MOVE 'NO ' TO
          ARE-THERE-MORE-RECORDS.
```

Sample Input Data

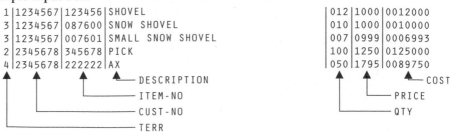

Figure 17.3 (continued)

Sample Output

```
                  REPORT  LISTING  WITH  SUMMARIZATION      PAGE     01
 TERR    CUST NUMBER    ITEM NUMBER    DESCRIPTION          QUANTITY    PRICE       COST

 1       1234567        123456         SHOVEL                  12       10.00     $120.00
 3                      087600         SNOW SHOVEL             10       10.00     $100.00
 3                      007601         SMALL SNOW SHOVEL        7        9.99      $69.93

                                                      AMOUNT           $289.93
 2       2345678        345678         PICK                   100       12.50    $1250.00
 4                      222222         AX                      50       17.95     $897.50

                                                      AMOUNT          $2,147.50

           FINAL COST IS                              $2,437.43
```

The FD for the print file in a program using the Report Writer Module contains a LABEL RECORDS clause and may include a RECORD CONTAINS clause. A REPORT clause is added as in the following:

Format

> FD print-file-name
>   LABEL RECORDS ARE OMITTED
>   [RECORD CONTAINS integer-1 CHARACTERS]
>
> $\left\{ \begin{array}{l} \text{REPORT IS} \\ \text{REPORTS ARE} \end{array} \right\}$ report-name-1 . . .

As noted, the RECORD CONTAINS clause is optional, but if used it should equal the number of characters per print line.

The report-name must conform to the rules for forming data-names. In our program, the report-name is REPORT-LISTING. Each report-name refers to a specific report, *not* just to a specific record format. That is, a report may (and usually does) contain several types of print records or report line formats. Most programs produce only *one report* in a program.

The REPORT clause within the FD entry is added to the LABEL RECORDS and the optional RECORD CONTAINS clauses when the Report Writer Module is used. No 01 entry for a record description follows the FD for this file. Instead, each report-name listed in an FD entry must be further described by an RD entry with the same name, in the **REPORT SECTION** of the DATA DIVISION.

If a WORKING-STORAGE SECTION is required in a program, it follows the FILE SECTION, as illustrated in Figure 17.3. Note that since the Report Writer Module handles all control breaks, page breaks, summations, and reset procedures, our program will use the WORKING-STORAGE SECTION only for the end-of-file indicator.

The REPORT SECTION, which follows the WORKING-STORAGE SECTION, defines all aspects of the printed output. It specifies:

1. The report group type that describes each type of line (e.g., Report Heading, Page Heading, Detail).
2. The line on which each record is to print. This can be specified as an actual line

number (e.g., 3) or a relative line number that relates to a previous line (e.g., PLUS 2).

3. The control fields.
4. The positions within each line where data is to print. Each field can be given a VALUE or can have data passed to it from another field.
5. The fields to be used as summation fields.

With these specifications in the REPORT SECTION, the PROCEDURE DIVISION need not include coding for control break or summary operations.

THE RD ENTRY WITHIN THE REPORT SECTION

The RD entry's name corresponds to the report-name assigned in the FD for the output print file. Thus, in our program, we would have:

```
                        REPORT SECTION.
                        RD   REPORT-LISTING
```

Both the REPORT SECTION header and the RD entry are required.

The RD entry describes the report and, like its counterpart the FD entry in the FILE SECTION, it can have numerous subordinate clauses. The basic format for the *RD* or *Report Description Entry* is as follows:

Format

```
     REPORT SECTION.
     RD report-name-1

        [ {CONTROL IS    }  {{data-name-1} ...        } ]
        [ {CONTROLS ARE  }  {FINAL   [data-name-1] ...} ]

        [                 [LIMIT IS  ]            [LINE ]  ]
        [ PAGE            [LIMITS ARE] integer-1   [LINES]  ]  .
        [        [HEADING integer-2]                      ]
        [        [FIRST DETAIL integer-3]                 ]
        [        [LAST DETAIL integer-4]                  ]
        [        [FOOTING integer-5]                      ]
```

We will discuss these CONTROL and PAGE clauses in depth.

CONTROL Clause

The CONTROL clause specifies the control fields. These fields will be tested against their previous value to determine if a control break has occurred.

Major Control Fields Must be Specified before Minor Ones

The sequence in which the data-names are listed in the CONTROL clause indicates their level in the control hierarchy. Thus, in our illustration, the CONTROL clause must be specified as: CONTROLS ARE FINAL, CUST-NO.

This means that FINAL is the highest control level and CUST-NO is a lower control level. If there were several levels, they would be listed in sequence *with the first being the highest control level*. Thus for Figure 17.1, TERR, a field defined in the input record, is the major control item. AREA-IN is an intermediate control item, and DEPARTMENT is a minor control item. We would code, then, CONTROLS ARE TERR, AREA-IN, DEPARTMENT.

The Report Writer Module automatically tests these control fields when input records are processed. We will see later on that this is accomplished with the `GENERATE` verb in the `PROCEDURE DIVISION`. The highest control level is tested first; if a control break occurs at this level, it automatically forces lower-level control breaks. Consider a date field that consists of `MONTH` and `YEAR` and is used for control breaks. A change in `YEAR` would force a break in `MONTH`, in this instance. A `FINAL` control break occurs *after the last detail line is printed*.

How Lines Are Printed When a Control Break Occurs

The action to be taken when a control break occurs is specified by the programmer. After a control break occurs, we can print a `CONTROL FOOTING` (for the previous control group) and/or a `CONTROL HEADING`. Both are coded on the `01` level in the `REPORT SECTION`. `CONTROL FOOTINGS` (`CF`) print *followed* by `CONTROL HEADINGS` (`CH`). That is, `CONTROL FOOTINGS` typically contain accumulated control totals, so they should print first. Then `CONTROL HEADINGS`, which relate to the *new control fields*, will print *before* any detail or summary lines for these new control fields.

If a major-level control break occurs, the Report Writer Module prints minor-level `CONTROL FOOTINGS` first, followed sequentially by the next level `CONTROL FOOTINGS` until the major-level footings are printed. Then the major-level `CONTROL HEADINGS`, if any, for the next control group are printed, followed by any intermediate and minor-level `CONTROL HEADINGS`. Thus, in the illustration in Figure 17.1, note that a `TERR` control break first results in the printing of a `DEPARTMENT` footing, followed by an `AREA-IN` footing, followed by a `TERR` footing. We have not illustrated multiple-level control breaks in our first Report Writer program in Figure 17.3 because of their complexity.

PAGE LIMIT Clause

The `PAGE LIMIT` clause specifies the layout of a page of the report, indicating actual line numbers on which specific report group types are to print. The `PAGE LIMIT` clause indicates:

1. The number of actual lines that should be used for printing (integer-1). Approximately 60 lines are usually allotted for a page; this would allow for adequate margins at both the top and bottom of the page.
2. The line on which the `PAGE` or first `REPORT HEADING` record may print (integer-2).
3. The line on which the `FIRST DETAIL` record may print (integer-3).
4. The line on which the `LAST DETAIL` record may print (integer-4).
5. The last line on which a `CONTROL FOOTING` record may print (integer-5). Only a `PAGE` or `REPORT FOOTING` can print beyond integer-5.

Our illustration includes the following entries:

```
PAGE LIMIT IS 60 LINES
HEADING 3
FIRST DETAIL 9
```

The entire `PAGE LIMIT` clause is optional, but in order to use any of the subordinate clauses such as `HEADING` or `FIRST DETAIL`, `PAGE LIMIT` must be included. We recommend that you always include this clause. If included, a `PAGE-COUNTER` field is automatically established by the Report Writer Module containing the number of pages generated, and a `LINE-COUNTER` field is also established automatically, containing the number of lines generated on each page. These fields must *not* be defined in the `DATA DIVISION`; they are reserved words used by the Report Writer Module. You can access the `PAGE-COUNTER` field in the report group description entries that follow, to print a page number; similarly, you can access the `LINE-COUNTER` field to print the number of lines that actually appear on a page.

A period must follow the last clause of an RD or report description. The REPORT SECTION coding for our example, thus far, is as follows:

```
REPORT SECTION.
RD   REPORT-LISTING
     CONTROLS ARE FINAL, CUST-NO
     PAGE LIMIT IS 60 LINES
     HEADING 3
     FIRST DETAIL 9.
```

SELF-TEST Consider the following input record:

SALES Record Layout			
Field	**Size**	**Type**	**No. of Decimal Positions (if Numeric)**
DIV	2	Alphanumeric	
DEPT	2	Alphanumeric	
ITEM	2	Alphanumeric	
AMT-OF-SALES	6	Numeric	2

Suppose we wish to print a report like the following:

```
                  SALES REPORT                    PAGE NO. 9999
     DIV        DEPT      ITEM      AMT OF SALES
     XX         XX        XXX       $9999.99
     XX         XX        XXX       $9999.99
                           .
                           .
                           .
                           .
                TOTAL ITEM AMT                     $99999.99*
     XX         XX        XXX       $9999.99
     XX         XX        XXX       $9999.99
                           .
                           .
                           .
                           .
                TOTAL ITEM AMT                     $99999.99*
                TOTAL DEPT AMT                     $99999.99**
     XX         XX        XXX       $9999.99
     XX         XX        XXX       $9999.99
                           .
                           .
                           .
                           .
                  TOTAL ITEM AMT                   $99999.99*
                  TOTAL DEPT AMT                   $99999.99**
                 TOTAL DIV AMT                     $99999.99***
                           .
                           .
                           .
                           .
          FINAL TOTAL                              $999999.99****
```

1. DIV, DEPT, and ITEM are called _____ fields.
2. The first line printed is called a _____ .
3. The printing of a line for each input record is called _____ printing.
4. The printing of total lines for DIV, DEPT, and ITEM is called _____ printing.
5. Each total line is referred to as a _____ .
6. The major-level control item, as specified on the output, is _____ .
7. The intermediate-level control item is _____ , and the minor-level control item is _____ .
8. A change in DEPT results in the printing of ___(no.)___ lines. That is, a DEPT control break also forces a(n) _____ control break.
9. A change in DIV results in the printing of ___(no.)___ lines. That is, a DIV control break causes a _____ line to print, followed by a _____ line and then a _____ line.
10. A _____ prints after all records and control totals, at the end of the job.
11. Assuming the Report Writer Module will be used in this program, code the FD for the preceding output file.
12. (T or F) 01-level record description entries must not follow the above FD entries.
13. The REPORT SECTION must follow the _____ and _____ SECTIONs in the _____ DIVISION.
14. The name following the RD level-indicator is the same as the name following the _____ clause in the _____ SECTION for the output file.
15. Code the RD entry and its clauses for the preceding illustration.

Solutions

1. control
2. Page Heading (it is not a Report Heading, which would appear only on the first page of a report)
3. Detail
4. summary or group
5. CONTROL FOOTING
6. DIV (after FINAL)
7. DEPT; ITEM
8. two; ITEM
9. three; ITEM total or footing; DEPT total or footing; DIV total or footing
10. final total
11. A suggested solution is:

```
FD   OUTPUT-FILE
      LABEL RECORDS ARE OMITTED
      REPORT IS REPORT-OUT.
```

Note: The REPORT clause is required when using the Report Writer Module.
12. T
13. FILE; WORKING-STORAGE; DATA
14. REPORT IS or REPORTS ARE; FILE
15. REPORT SECTION.
```
RD   REPORT-1
      CONTROLS ARE FINAL, DIV, DEPT, ITEM
      PAGE LIMIT IS 60 LINES
      HEADING 2
      FIRST DETAIL 4
      LAST DETAIL 50
      FOOTING 59.
```

Note: Assume that DIV, DEPT, ITEM are the input record description data-names.

CLAUSES USED AT THE GROUP LEVEL
WITHIN A REPORT GROUP DESCRIPTION

The first entry for a report group within the RD is called the *report group description entry*. It is coded on the 01 level.

The report groups within the REPORT SECTION are classified as headings, detail lines, and footings. The printing specifications and the format of each are defined in a series of *report group descriptions*.

> **AN OVERVIEW OF THE FORMAT
> FOR THE REPORT GROUP DESCRIPTION ENTRY**
>
> 01 [data-name-1]
>   TYPE Clause
>   [LINE Clause]
>   [NEXT GROUP Clause]

Data-name-1 is the name of the *report group*. It is a *required* entry *only* when the report group is specifically called for in the PROCEDURE DIVISION. We will see later that *detail report groups* are referenced in the PROCEDURE DIVISION with a GENERATE statement, but that headings and footings need not be identified with a data-name. This is because the Report Writer Module will automatically print them at the appropriate time based on their TYPE.

Headings and footings, then, are given data-names only if a USE BEFORE REPORTING declarative will refer to them; we will *not* discuss this declarative here, but it is a method for interrupting the Report Writer sequence and performing procedures *prior to* printing certain lines of a report. With the Report Writer Module, headings and footings automatically print at predetermined points, so that any record with a TYPE clause indicating a heading and footing need not have a data-name.

We discuss each clause in detail, beginning with the TYPE clause, which is the only required one. *Clauses may be coded in any sequence.* Note, however, that the TYPE clause is typically coded first in an 01-level entry.

Format

```
01  [data-name-1]
        .
        .

                          ⎧ ⎧REPORT HEADING⎫          ⎫
                          ⎪ ⎩RH            ⎭          ⎪
                          ⎪                           ⎪
                          ⎪ ⎧PAGE HEADING⎫            ⎪
                          ⎪ ⎩PH          ⎭            ⎪
                          ⎪                           ⎪
                          ⎪ ⎧CONTROL HEADING⎫ ⎧data-name-2⎫ ⎪
                          ⎪ ⎩CH             ⎭ ⎩FINAL      ⎭ ⎪
                          ⎪                           ⎪
          TYPE IS         ⎨ ⎧DETAIL⎫                  ⎬
                          ⎪ ⎩DE    ⎭                  ⎪
                          ⎪                           ⎪
                          ⎪ ⎧CONTROL FOOTING⎫ ⎧data-name-3⎫ ⎪
                          ⎪ ⎩CF             ⎭ ⎩FINAL      ⎭ ⎪
                          ⎪                           ⎪
                          ⎪ ⎧PAGE FOOTING⎫            ⎪
                          ⎪ ⎩PF          ⎭            ⎪
                          ⎪                           ⎪
                          ⎪ ⎧REPORT FOOTING⎫          ⎪
                          ⎩ ⎩RF            ⎭          ⎭
```

TYPE Clause—Required

The TYPE clause specifies the category of the report group. The time at which each report group is printed within a report is dependent on its type. For example, a REPORT HEADING is printed before a PAGE HEADING, a CONTROL FOOTING is printed when a control break occurs, and so on. There are also established rules for the formation of each report group, which will be considered later on.

Data-name-2 and data-name-3 in the format refer to control fields defined in the CONTROL clause of the RD entry.

Let us consider the report in Figure 17.4, which illustrates the various types of report groups:

Figure 17.4 Sample report that illustrates the various types of report groups.

	MONTH	DAY	DEPT	NO-PURCHASES	TYPE	COST	CUMULATIVE-COST
ⒶACME MANUFACTURING COMPANY QUARTERLY EXPENDITURES REPORT							
ⒷJANUARY EXPENDITURES							
Ⓒ	JANUARY	01	A00	2	A	2.00	
			A02	1	A	1.00	
			A02	2	C	16.00	
Ⓓ	PURCHASES AND COST FOR 1-01			5		$19.00	$19.00
	JANUARY	02	A01	2	B	2.00	
			A04	10	A	10.00	
			A04	10	C	80.00	
	PURCHASES AND COST FOR 1-02			22		$92.00	$111.00
	JANUARY	05	A01	2	B	2.00	
	PURCHASES AND COST FOR 1-05			2		$2.00	$113.00
	JANUARY	08	A01	10	A	10.00	
			A01	8	B	12.48	
			A01	20	C	38.40	
	PURCHASES AND COST FOR 1-08			38		$60.88	$173.88
	JANUARY	13	A00	4	B	6.24	
			A00	1	C	8.00	
	PURCHASES AND COST FOR 1-13			5		$14.24	$188.12
	JANUARY	15	A00	10	D	19.20	
			A02	1	C	8.00	
	PURCHASES AND COST FOR 1-15			11		$27.20	$215.32
	JANUARY	21	A03	10	E	30.00	
			A03	10	F	25.00	
			A03	10	G	50.00	
	PURCHASES AND COST FOR 1-21			30		$105.00	$320.32
	JANUARY	23	A00	5	A	5.00	
	PURCHASES AND COST FOR 1-23			5		$5.00	$325.32
Ⓔ							REPORT-PAGE-01
Ⓕ	END OF REPORT						

1. Ⓐ represents the REPORT HEADING
   A REPORT HEADING, which can be abbreviated as RH, is the title of a report. It is the first item printed on each report. Note that there can be only one 01-level entry categorized as a REPORT HEADING. It appears once—at the top of the first page of the report.

2. Ⓑ represents the PAGE HEADING
   A PAGE HEADING (or PH) indicates a report group that is produced at the beginning of each page. There can be only one 01-level entry categorized as a PAGE HEADING.

3. Ⓒ represents the DETAIL line
   Each DETAIL (or DE) record is described with an 01-level entry. The first detail line of each group indicates the month and day. We call these GROUP INDICATE fields. They print when a control break has occurred. The first time a detail group prints is considered a control break as well.

4. Ⓓ represents the CONTROL FOOTING
   The CONTROL FOOTING (or CF) report group is produced at the *end* of a control group for a given control item. The CONTROL FOOTING is printed when a control break occurs. It prints *prior to* any CONTROL HEADING, which would refer to the next control field's value. There can be only one CONTROL FOOTING per control item. CONTROL FOOTING FINAL is used to print final totals at the end of a report. A CONTROL HEADING could be specified as well. There is no CONTROL HEADING in this report.

5. Ⓔ represents the PAGE FOOTING
   The PAGE FOOTING (or PF) report group is printed at the end of each page. There can be only one 01-level entry designated as a PAGE FOOTING.

6. Ⓕ represents the REPORT FOOTING
   The REPORT FOOTING (or RF) report group is produced at the end of the report. There can be only one REPORT FOOTING.

We must designate the TYPE of a record or report group so that the Report Writer Module can determine when it is to print. Remember that CONTROL FOOTINGs print before their corresponding CONTROL HEADINGs. This is because footings typically print control totals for the *previous group* and CONTROL HEADINGs print information relating to a new control group such as column headings and/or the *new control values*. Also, minor CONTROL FOOTINGs print before intermediate and then major CONTROL FOOTINGs. Note, too, that major CONTROL HEADINGs print before intermediate and minor CONTROL HEADINGs.

In the above, if we chose to print the date for each series of input records on a *separate line* rather than make it a GROUP INDICATE field, then it could be a control heading:

Control heading → JANUARY 01

       . . .
       . . .

Control footing → PURCHASES AND COST FOR 1-01

Control heading → JANUARY 02

       . . .
       . . .

A CONTROL FOOTING need not print at the bottom of a page, and a CONTROL HEADING need not print at the top of a page. That is, a CONTROL HEADING can be programmed to print several lines after the previous CONTROL FOOTING totals by using relative line numbers (e.g., LINE NUMBER PLUS 3). This will be explained in the next section.

LINE Clause

The format of this clause is as follows:

Format

$$
01 \quad [\text{data-name-1}]
$$

$$
\vdots
$$

$$
\left[\underline{\text{LINE}} \text{ NUMBER IS} \begin{Bmatrix} \text{integer-1 [ON \underline{NEXT} \underline{PAGE}]} \\ \underline{\text{PLUS}} \text{ integer-2} \end{Bmatrix} \right]
$$

$$
\vdots
$$

This optional LINE clause specifies either:

1. An actual or absolute line number on which the corresponding report line is to be printed (e.g., LINE 3 or LINE 10), or

2. A line number *relative to* the previous entry or to the previous page (e.g., LINE PLUS 2).

The LINE NUMBER clause can appear on the 01 level or on a level subordinate to it. If *two detail lines* were to print, one on line 5 and one on line 7, a level number subordinate to 01 would be required for each.

Printing Two Detail Lines for Each Input Record

```
01   TYPE IS DETAIL.
     05   LINE NUMBER IS 5.
          10                  ⎫
          :                   ⎬ Fields to print on line 5
                              ⎭
     05   LINE NUMBER IS 7.
          10                  ⎫
          :                   ⎬ Fields to print on line 7
                              ⎭
```

Illustrations

1. Printing on actual Line Numbers.
   Example:

```
01   TYPE IS REPORT HEADING.
     05   LINE NUMBER IS 3.
```

This could also be coded as 01 TYPE IS REPORT HEADING LINE NUMBER IS 3 if there is only one line generated for this report heading.

2. Relative Line Numbering.
   Example:

```
01   DETAIL-LINE TYPE IS DETAIL.
     05   LINE NUMBER IS PLUS 1.
```

This means that detail lines will be single spaced.

We will use the convention of placing the LINE NUMBER clause *on a separate level* within the 01, although it sometimes can be coded along with the TYPE clause on the 01 level. If a specific report group has more than one line that is to print, it *must not have a* LINE *clause* in an 01-level entry. That is, if three lines are to print for an 01 level, they would all be coded on some subordinate level:

```
01   TYPE IS ...
     05   LINE 5.
     :
     05   LINE 7.
     :
     05   LINE 9.
     :
```

For consistency and ease of maintenance, then, *we code all* LINE *clauses on level* 05 *within the* 01 *level*. This is also a more structured way of coding.

The following is a brief review:

RULES

TYPE	Absolute Line Number	Relative Line Number	NEXT PAGE
REPORT HEADING	OK[a]	Line number is relative to HEADING integer specified in RD	X[b]
PAGE HEADING	OK	Line number is relative to HEADING integer-1, or value of LINE-COUNTER, whichever is greater	X
CONTROL HEADING	OK	OK*	OK
DETAIL	OK	OK*	OK
CONTROL FOOTING	OK	OK*	OK
PAGE FOOTING	OK	Line number is relative to FOOTING integer	X
REPORT FOOTING	OK	Line number is relative to FOOTING integer or LINE-COUNTER, whichever is greater	OK

[a]OK—permitted.
[b]X—not permitted.

* The first relative line number on a page for a CONTROL HEADING, DETAIL line, or CONTROL FOOTING prints at the first detail line regardless of its PLUS integer-1 operand.

As noted, a LINE-COUNTER is established by the Report Writer Module and used to control line numbering. The initial value of LINE-COUNTER will be the integer specified in the (HEADING integer) clause of the RD. Thus, if HEADING 10 is specified, LINE-COUNTER begins with a 10.

NEXT GROUP Clause

This clause is most often used in a report group to indicate the line spacing (absolute or relative) to be performed when the last line of the control footing has been printed. The format is as follows:

Format

```
01  [data-name-1]
     ⋮
    [                    ⎧ integer-1        ⎫ ]
    [ NEXT GROUP IS      ⎨ PLUS integer-2   ⎬ ]
    [                    ⎩ NEXT PAGE        ⎭ ]
     ⋮
```

One main use of the NEXT GROUP clause is to provide some extra blank lines between the end of one control group and the start of the next. Another main use is to force a REPORT HEADING report group to print on a separate page before all other report groups. To accomplish this, the following is coded:

```
NEXT GROUP IS NEXT PAGE
```

Other Examples

1. To reinitialize LINE-COUNTER at a new line number after a report group is complete (line 6 for example), the following is coded: NEXT GROUP IS 6.
2. To print a new group on a line that is a fixed number of lines from the previous group, the following is coded: NEXT GROUP IS PLUS 3.

Note that if a CONTROL FOOTING (NEXT GROUP integer-1) or (NEXT GROUP PLUS integer-2) causes a page change, the Report Writer Module will advance the paper to a new page with proper formatting.

We have thus far considered all those items that can be designated on the 01 level. As in the other sections of the DATA DIVISION, we must specify the entries subordinate to the 01 report group description.

SELF-TEST   Consider the report in Figure 17.5.

Figure 17.5 Sample report for the Self-Test.

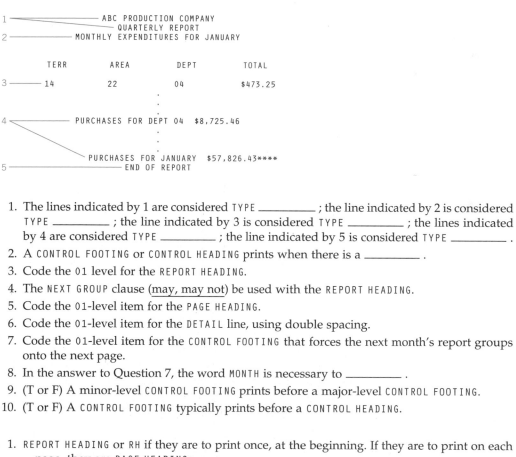

```
1 ─────────────── ABC PRODUCTION COMPANY
                ── QUARTERLY REPORT
2 ───────────── MONTHLY EXPENDITURES FOR JANUARY


      TERR        AREA        DEPT        TOTAL

3 ──── 14          22          04         $473.25
                                   .
                                   .
                                   .
4 ───────── PURCHASES FOR DEPT 04  $8,725.46
                                   .
                                   .
                                   .
            ─ PURCHASES FOR JANUARY  $57,826.43****
5 ───────────── END OF REPORT
```

1. The lines indicated by 1 are considered TYPE _____ ; the line indicated by 2 is considered TYPE _____ ; the line indicated by 3 is considered TYPE _____ ; the lines indicated by 4 are considered TYPE _____ ; the line indicated by 5 is considered TYPE _____ .
2. A CONTROL FOOTING or CONTROL HEADING prints when there is a _____ .
3. Code the 01 level for the REPORT HEADING.
4. The NEXT GROUP clause (may, may not) be used with the REPORT HEADING.
5. Code the 01-level item for the PAGE HEADING.
6. Code the 01-level item for the DETAIL line, using double spacing.
7. Code the 01-level item for the CONTROL FOOTING that forces the next month's report groups onto the next page.
8. In the answer to Question 7, the word MONTH is necessary to _____ .
9. (T or F) A minor-level CONTROL FOOTING prints before a major-level CONTROL FOOTING.
10. (T or F) A CONTROL FOOTING typically prints before a CONTROL HEADING.

Solutions

1. REPORT HEADING or RH if they are to print once, at the beginning. If they are to print on each page, they are PAGE HEADINGs.
   PAGE HEADING or PH—this heading changes when there is a new month—e.g., January to February, so it must be a PAGE HEADING.
   DETAIL LINE or DE
   CONTROL FOOTING or CF
   REPORT FOOTING or RF
2. change in a specific control item (TERRITORY, YEAR, CUSTNO, etc.). The control field is usually an input field.
3. A suggested solution is:

```
01  TYPE IS REPORT HEADING, LINE NUMBER 1.
```

Note: We will not use a data-name after the 01 and before the TYPE unless it is a detail line to be referenced in the PROCEDURE DIVISION.

4. may not
5. 01 TYPE IS PAGE-HEADING, LINE NUMBER IS 5.
6. 01 DETAIL-LINE TYPE IS DETAIL, LINE NUMBER IS PLUS 2.
7. 01 TYPE IS CONTROL FOOTING MONTH, LINE PLUS 3
        NEXT GROUP IS NEXT PAGE.
8. indicate the control item—a change in month (and a change in terr, area, and dept also cause control breaks)
9. T
10. T

CLAUSES USED AT THE ELEMENTARY LEVEL WITHIN A REPORT GROUP DESCRIPTION

As in previous sections of the DATA DIVISION, we describe fields as entries subordinate to the 01 level. The format for fields within an 01 report group is:

Format

$$
\text{level-no [data-name-1]} \left\{ \begin{array}{l} \underline{\text{PICTURE}} \\ \underline{\text{PIC}} \end{array} \right\} \text{ IS character-string}
$$

$$
\left[\underline{\text{LINE}} \text{ NUMBER IS } \left\{ \begin{array}{l} \text{integer-1 [ON } \underline{\text{NEXT PAGE}}] \\ \underline{\text{PLUS}} \text{ integer-2} \end{array} \right\} \right]
$$

$$
[\underline{\text{COLUMN}} \text{ NUMBER IS integer-3}]
$$

$$
\left\{ \begin{array}{l} \underline{\text{SOURCE}} \text{ IS identifier-1} \\ \underline{\text{VALUE}} \text{ IS literal-1} \\ [\underline{\text{SUM}} \quad \{\text{identifier-2}\} \ldots] \\ \quad \left[\underline{\text{RESET}} \text{ ON } \left\{ \begin{array}{l} \text{data-name-2} \\ \underline{\text{FINAL}} \end{array} \right\} \right] \\ [\underline{\text{GROUP}} \text{ INDICATE}]. \end{array} \right\}
$$

For headings and footings that have VALUES, we need not indicate a field-name or FILLER at all. We simply specify (1) the COLUMN in which the field is to print, (2) the field's PIC clause, and (3) its VALUE.

Data-names or identifiers are only required with detail, heading, and footing fields that are to be referenced elsewhere. For example, a data-name called AMT may be specified in the CUST-NO CONTROL FOOTING report group. This data-name may be needed because we will be summing or accumulating or "rolling forward" the AMT field into another, higher-level CONTROL FOOTING.

The REPORT HEADING in Figure 17.3 has the following entries:

```
01  TYPE IS REPORT HEADING.
    05  LINE NUMBER IS 3.
        10  COLUMN NUMBER IS 39        PIC X(33)
                VALUE 'REPORT LISTING WITH SUMMARIZATION'.
        10  COLUMN NUMBER IS 85        PIC X(4)
                VALUE 'PAGE'.
        10  COLUMN NUMBER IS 92        PIC 99
                SOURCE PAGE-COUNTER.
```

PAGE-COUNTER is a COBOL special register that contains the number of the page to be printed.

The following clauses may be used to transmit the content in some named storage area to an individual field in a Heading, Footing, or Detail report group.

The SOURCE Clause

The SOURCE clause specifies that a data item is to be printed from a different field, usually defined in the input area or in WORKING-STORAGE. That is, the SOURCE clause indicates a field that is used as a *source* for this report item. If an input field is designated as DEPT-IN, for example, we can indicate SOURCE IS DEPT-IN in any individual item within a report group. If SOURCE IS TERR for COLUMN 5 of a DETAIL line, then the input TERR field will print beginning in column 5 of that detail line.

The SUM Clause

The SUM clause is used for *automatic summation* of data. SUM is used only on a CONTROL FOOTING line. For example, 10 COLUMN NUMBER IS 50 ... SUM AMT in the CONTROL FOOTING FINAL report group in Figure 17.3 will print the sum of all AMT fields when that CONTROL FOOTING line prints.

Consider the following additional examples:

1. `05   COLUMN 14 PICTURE $ZZ,ZZZ.99 SOURCE IS COST.`

2. `01   TYPE IS CONTROL FOOTING   LINE NUMBER IS PLUS 2.`
   `    05   COLUMN 55 PICTURE $ZZ,ZZZ,ZZZ.99 SUM PRICE.`

Example 1 indicates that beginning at Column 14 of the specified record, the contents of the field called COST should print. COST may be either a FILE or WORKING-STORAGE SECTION item; usually it is an input field.

Example 2 is a CONTROL FOOTING group. In Column 55 of the CONTROL FOOTING report group, the sum of all accumulated PRICE fields will print. That is, PRICE is accumulated until the CONTROL FOOTING report group (of which Example 2 is a part) is to print; then the sum of all PRICE fields is printed, beginning in Column 55.

Thus, the use of SUM in an elementary item defines a summation counter. Each time a DETAIL report group is generated, the field specified (PRICE in the example) is summed.

The RESET Phrase

The RESET phrase may be used only in conjunction with a SUM clause. If the RESET phrase is not included, a SUM counter will be reset immediately after it is printed. The RESET clause is used to *defer the resetting* of a SUM counter to zero until some higher-level control break occurs. Thus, the RESET phrase permits a sum to serve as a running total for higher-level control breaks.

Examples

1. `05   COLUMN 65 PICTURE $$$$9.99 SUM COST`
   `    RESET ON DEPT-NO.`

2. `05   COLUMN 42 PICTURE $ZZZ.99 SUM AMT`
   `    RESET ON MONTH.`

3. `05   COLUMN 85 PICTURE $Z,ZZZ.99 SUM TOTAL`
   `    RESET ON FINAL.`

REVIEW

In our program in Figure 17.3 on pages 679 and 680, we see that there are five report group types that are printed:

Report Heading

```
01   TYPE IS REPORT HEADING.
     05  LINE NUMBER IS 3.
         10   COLUMN NUMBER IS 39              PIC X(33)
              VALUE 'REPORT LISTING WITH SUMMARIZATION'.
         10   COLUMN NUMBER IS 85              PIC X(4)
              VALUE 'PAGE'.
         10   COLUMN NUMBER IS 92              PIC 99
              SOURCE PAGE-COUNTER.
```

a. The Report Heading prints on line number 3.

b. The literal 'REPORT LISTING WITH SUMMARIZATION' begins in column 39.

c. The literal 'PAGE' begins in column 85.

d. The page number prints beginning in column 92. When the COBOL reserved word PAGE-COUNTER, which is a special register, is used as a SOURCE, the actual page number will automatically print.

Page Heading

```
01   TYPE IS PAGE HEADING.
     05  LINE NUMBER IS 5.
         10   COLUMN NUMBER IS 5              PIC X(4)
                 VALUE 'TERR'.
         10   COLUMN NUMBER IS 11             PIC X(11)
                 VALUE 'CUST NUMBER'.
         10   COLUMN NUMBER IS 27             PIC X(11)
                 VALUE 'ITEM NUMBER'.
         10   COLUMN NUMBER IS 41             PIC X(11)
                 VALUE 'DESCRIPTION'.
         10   COLUMN NUMBER IS 77             PIC X(8)
                 VALUE 'QUANTITY'.
         10   COLUMN NUMBER IS 88             PIC X(5)
                 VALUE 'PRICE'.
         10   COLUMN NUMBER IS 102            PIC X(4)
                 VALUE 'COST'.
```

Detail Line

```
01   DETAIL-LINE TYPE IS DETAIL.
     05  LINE NUMBER IS PLUS 1.
         10   COLUMN NUMBER IS 5                         PIC X
                 SOURCE IS TERR.
         10   COLUMN NUMBER IS 11 GROUP INDICATE   PIC X(7)
                 SOURCE IS CUST-NO.
         10   COLUMN NUMBER IS 27                        PIC X(6)
                 SOURCE IS ITEM-NO.
         10   COLUMN NUMBER IS 41                        PIC X(35)
                 SOURCE IS DESCRIPTION.
         10   COLUMN NUMBER IS 77                        PIC ZZ9
                 SOURCE IS QTY.
         10   COLUMN NUMBER IS 88                        PIC Z9.99
                 SOURCE IS PRICE.
         10   COLUMN NUMBER IS 97                        PIC $(6).99
                 SOURCE IS COST.
```

a. "PLUS 1" means that each detail line will print on the line following the previous detail line. That is, these lines will be single-spaced. Note that the *first* detail line on a page will print on the line specified by the FIRST DETAIL clause in the RD entry.

b. The input fields of TERR, CUST-NO, ITEM-NO, DESCRIPTION, QTY, PRICE, and COST will print in their specified columns.

c. The input field CUST-NO is a GROUP INDICATE field. This means that it prints when a change in the CUST-NO control field occurs (or after a page break). The source of a GROUP INDICATE field would typically be a control field.

d. QTY, PRICE, and COST are printed in edited form.

CONTROL FOOTING for Printing Control Totals

```
01   TYPE IS CONTROL FOOTING CUST-NO.
     05   LINE NUMBER IS PLUS 2.
          10   COLUMN NUMBER IS 72              PIC X(6)
                 VALUE 'AMOUNT'.
          10   AMT COLUMN NUMBER IS 87          PIC $$$$,$$9.99
                 SUM COST.
```

a. When there is a change in the CUST-NO control field, this footing will print.

b. LINE NUMBER PLUS 2 results in double spacing.

c. The literal 'AMOUNT' and the sum of all input COST fields will print in the designated columns.

CONTROL FOOTING for Printing the Final Total

```
01   TYPE IS CONTROL FOOTING FINAL.
     05   LINE NUMBER IS 60.
          10   COLUMN NUMBER IS 16             PIC X(13)
                 VALUE 'FINAL COST IS'.
          10   COLUMN NUMBER IS 50             PIC $$,$$$,$$9.99
                 SUM AMT.
```

a. CONTROL FOOTING FINAL prints *after the last control break* at the end of the report. We will see later that this occurs when the TERMINATE statement is executed in the PROCEDURE DIVISION.

b. LINE NUMBER IS 60 in a report group, where a PAGE LIMIT of 60 has been designated in the RD, prints the footing on the bottom or last designated line of the page.

c. The literal 'FINAL COST IS' and the sum of all AMT fields will print. The sum of all AMTs, which themselves are SUMs, will print as a final total. AMT is a sum counter accumulated at the lower-level CONTROL FOOTING for CUST-NO.

PROCEDURE DIVISION STATEMENTS

INITIATE Statement

The INITIATE statement begins the processing of a report. It is usually coded directly after the OPEN statement. It initiates the Report Writer Module. Its format is:

Format

```
                    INITIATE report-name-1 ...
```

The `INITIATE` statement sets all `SUM` and `COUNTER` fields to zero, including `LINE-COUNTER` and `PAGE-COUNTER`.

GENERATE Statement

The `GENERATE` statement is used to produce the report. It usually names a detail report group to be printed after an input record has been read. The format of this statement is:

Format

$$\underline{\text{GENERATE}} \begin{Bmatrix} \text{data-name-1} \\ \text{report-name-1} \end{Bmatrix}$$

We may generate a `DETAIL` report group name (data-name-1 in this format) or an `RD` entry (report-name-1):

1. If the data-name is the `DETAIL` report group name, then the `GENERATE` statement performs all the functions of the Report Writer Module, including control break processing and summary and detail printing.
2. If the data-name identifies an `RD` entry, the `GENERATE` statement performs all functions of the Report Writer Module *except detail printing*. In this way, only summary printing is achieved.

TERMINATE Statement

The `TERMINATE` statement completes the processing of a report after all records have been processed. Its format is:

Format

$$\underline{\text{TERMINATE}} \text{ report-name-1} \ldots$$

The `TERMINATE` causes the Report Writer Module to produce all `CONTROL FOOTING` report groups beginning with the minor ones. That is, it forces all control totals to print for the last control group and also prints any final totals. It is usually coded just before the files are closed.

Note that the only report group format in Figure 17.3 that has a name is `DETAIL-LINE`. This is because `DETAIL-LINE` is the only report group accessed in the `PROCEDURE DIVISION`. Unless a `USE BEFORE REPORTING` declarative is coded, which we have not discussed here, only the report group with `TYPE DETAIL` needs to be given a data-name. We `INITIATE` and `TERMINATE` the report-name but `GENERATE` the detail line name (e.g., `DETAIL-LINE`) to achieve detail printing (as well as summary printing if the report contains `CONTROL FOOTINGs`).

Thus, the entire `PROCEDURE DIVISION` for our Report Writer program is:

COBOL 85

```
PROCEDURE DIVISION.
100-MAIN-MODULE.
    OPEN INPUT  FILE-IN
         OUTPUT FILE-OUT
    INITIATE REPORT-LISTING
    PERFORM UNTIL NO-MORE-RECORDS
        READ FILE-IN
            AT END
                MOVE 'NO ' TO ARE-THERE-MORE-RECORDS
            NOT AT END
                PERFORM 200-CALC-RTN
        END-READ
    END-PERFORM
```

COBOL 74 Substitutions

```
READ FILE-IN
    AT END MOVE 'NO ' TO ARE-THERE-MORE-RECORDS.
PERFORM 200-CALC-RTN
    UNTIL NO-MORE-RECORDS.
```

```
                                   TERMINATE REPORT-LISTING
                                   CLOSE FILE-IN
                                            FILE-OUT
                                   STOP RUN.
                           200-CALC-RTN.
                                   GENERATE DETAIL-LINE.
```

COBOL 74 Substitutions

```
READ FILE-IN
    AT END MOVE 'NO ' TO ARE-THERE-MORE-RECORDS.
```
$\longrightarrow$

In summary, we can see that, although the Report Writer Module requires a fairly complex REPORT SECTION of the DATA DIVISION, it results in simplified coding of the PROCEDURE DIVISION.

CHAPTER SUMMARY A. DATA DIVISION Entries

1. Code a REPORT SECTION following the WORKING-STORAGE SECTION.
2. The FD for the output print file references the RD in the REPORT SECTION:

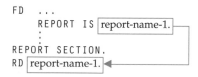

```
FD  ...
        REPORT IS  report-name-1.
         :
REPORT SECTION.
RD  report-name-1.
```

3. RD clauses.
   a. Control fields are listed beginning with major controls as:

   ```
   CONTROLS ARE [FINAL,] major control field ...
                        minor control field.
   ```

   b. The PAGE LIMIT clause describes the number of print lines on each page; it can also include clauses that indicate what line a heading should print on and/or what line a first detail, last detail, and last CONTROL FOOTING should print on.
4. 01 report group description entries can describe REPORT HEADING, PAGE HEADING, CONTROL HEADING, DETAIL, CONTROL FOOTING, PAGE FOOTING, and REPORT FOOTING.
   a. A data-name is required on the 01 level only if the data-name is used in the PROCEDURE DIVISION (e.g., with TYPE DETAIL) or in a USE BEFORE REPORTING declarative, which has not been discussed here.
   b. A LINE NUMBER clause on the 05 level indicates what actual line or relative line the report group should print on.
   c. Specifying individual items within a report group:
      (1) Each entry indicates the columns in which items are to print.
      (2) Each entry can contain a (1) SOURCE—where the sending data is located, (2) VALUE, or (3) SUM if the item is the sum of some other field.
      (3) A data-name is required after the entry's level number only if it is accessed elsewhere (e.g., in a CONTROL FOOTING's SUM clause).
   d. If a REPORT or PAGE HEADING or any detail printing requires more than one line, code each on an 05 level subordinate to the corresponding 01-level item.

B. PROCEDURE DIVISION Statements

1. INITIATE report-name-1 after the files are opened.
2. GENERATE detail-report-group-name for each input record that has been read. The computer will print all headings, detail lines, control lines, and footings as well.
3. Before closing the files, TERMINATE report-name-1.

KEY TERMS

Control break	DETAIL	REPORT FOOTING
CONTROL FOOTING	PAGE FOOTING	REPORT HEADING
CONTROL HEADING	PAGE HEADING	REPORT SECTION

CHAPTER SELF-TEST

1. Page numbers on each page of the report can be automatically generated by the computer if the _____ clause of the _____ SECTION is included in the program.

2. In order to print page numbers, the report group description entries defining the PAGE HEADING should reference a field called _____ .

3. The CONTROL and PAGE-LIMIT clauses are defined in the _____ entry.

4. If a change in DISTRICT requires the printing of TOTAL-SALES, which is accumulated for each DISTRICT, then DISTRICT is called a _____ field.

5. The printing of TOTAL-SALES for each DISTRICT is called _____ printing, whereas the individual printing of each input record is called _____ printing.

6. The report-name referenced in the REPORT clause is defined in a(n) _____ entry of the _____ SECTION.

7. The three verbs required in the PROCEDURE DIVISION for using the Report Writer Module are _____ , _____ , and _____ .

8. The identifier associated with the INITIATE verb is the _____ .

9. The identifier associated with the GENERATE statement is either the _____ for _____ printing or the _____ for _____ printing.

10. The TERMINATE statement has the same format as the _____ and is usually part of the _____ routine.

Solutions

1. PAGE LIMIT; REPORT

2. PAGE-COUNTER

3. RD

4. control

5. summary or group; detail

6. RD; REPORT

7. GENERATE; INITIATE; TERMINATE

8. report name (RD entry)

9. DETAIL report group name; detail; RD name; summary

10. INITIATE; end-of-job

PRACTICE PROGRAM Write a program using the Report Writer Module to generate the report in Figure 17.1 on page 677. The solution is shown in Figure 17.6.

Figure 17.6 Practice Program that uses the Report Writer Module.

COBOL 85

```
IDENTIFICATION DIVISION.
PROGRAM-ID.     REPORT-WRITER2.
AUTHOR.         NANCY STERN.
*********************************************************
*  this is an example of the report writer feature  *
*********************************************************
ENVIRONMENT DIVISION.
INPUT-OUTPUT SECTION.
FILE-CONTROL.
    SELECT FILE-IN ASSIGN TO DATA17.
    SELECT FILE-OUT ASSIGN TO PRINTER.
*
DATA DIVISION.
FILE SECTION.
FD  FILE-IN
    LABEL RECORDS ARE STANDARD.
01  IN-REC.
    05  TERR                          PIC X.
```

Figure 17.6 (continued)

```
                            05   AREA-IN                        PIC X.
                            05   DEPARTMENT                     PIC XX.
                            05   SALESPERSON                    PIC X(20).
                            05   SALES-AMOUNT                   PIC 999V99.
                       FD  FILE-OUT
                           LABEL RECORDS ARE OMITTED
                           REPORT IS REPORT-LISTING.
                       WORKING-STORAGE SECTION.
                       01  ARE-THERE-MORE-RECORDS                  PIC X(3)  VALUE 'YES'.
                            88  NO-MORE-RECORDS                               VALUE 'NO '.
                       REPORT SECTION.
                       RD  REPORT-LISTING
                           CONTROLS ARE FINAL, TERR, AREA-IN, DEPARTMENT
                           PAGE LIMIT IS 60 LINES
                           HEADING 4
                           FIRST DETAIL 10.
                       01   TYPE IS REPORT HEADING.
                            05  LINE NUMBER IS 4.
                                10  COLUMN NUMBER IS 57           PIC X(20)
                                    VALUE 'MONTHLY SALES REPORT'.
                                10  COLUMN NUMBER IS 85           PIC X(4)
                                    VALUE 'PAGE'.
                                10  COLUMN NUMBER IS 92           PIC 99
                                    SOURCE PAGE-COUNTER.
                       01   TYPE IS PAGE HEADING.
                            05  LINE NUMBER IS 8.
                                10  COLUMN NUMBER IS 6            PIC X(9)
                                    VALUE 'TERRITORY'.
                                10  COLUMN NUMBER IS 19           PIC X(4)
                                    VALUE 'AREA'.
                                10  COLUMN NUMBER IS 27           PIC X(10)
                                    VALUE 'DEPARTMENT'.
                                10  COLUMN NUMBER IS 44           PIC X(11)
                                    VALUE 'SALESPERSON'.
                                10  COLUMN NUMBER IS 57           PIC X(15)
                                    VALUE 'AMOUNT OF SALES'.
                       01   DETAIL-LINE TYPE IS DETAIL.
                            05  LINE NUMBER IS PLUS 1.
                                10  COLUMN NUMBER IS 9 GROUP INDICATE  PIC X
                                    SOURCE IS TERR.
                                10  COLUMN NUMBER IS 21           PIC X
                                    SOURCE IS AREA-IN.
                                10  COLUMN NUMBER IS 31           PIC XX
                                    SOURCE IS DEPARTMENT.
                                10  COLUMN NUMBER IS 39           PIC X(18)
                                    SOURCE IS SALESPERSON.
                                10  COLUMN NUMBER IS 60           PIC ZZ9.99
                                    SOURCE IS SALES-AMOUNT.
                       01   TYPE IS CONTROL FOOTING DEPARTMENT.
                            05  LINE NUMBER IS PLUS 3.
                                10  COLUMN NUMBER IS 68           PIC X(16)
                                    VALUE 'TOTAL DEPARTMENT'.
                                10  COLUMN NUMBER IS 85           PIC XX
                                    SOURCE IS DEPARTMENT.
                                10  DEPT-TOT COLUMN NUMBER IS 89  PIC $$$$9.99
                                    SUM SALES-AMOUNT RESET ON DEPARTMENT.
                                10  COLUMN NUMBER IS 98           PIC X
                                    VALUE '*'.
                       01   TYPE IS CONTROL FOOTING AREA-IN.
                            05  LINE NUMBER IS PLUS 2.
                                10  COLUMN NUMBER IS 79           PIC X(10)
                                    VALUE 'TOTAL AREA'.
                                10  COLUMN NUMBER IS 90           PIC X
                                    SOURCE IS AREA-IN.
                                10  AREA-TOT COLUMN NUMBER IS 97  PIC $$$$$.99
                                    SUM DEPT-TOT RESET ON AREA-IN.
```

Figure 17.6   (continued)

```
                                        10   COLUMN NUMBER IS 107              PIC XX
                                             VALUE '**'.
                    01   TYPE IS CONTROL FOOTING TERR NEXT GROUP IS NEXT PAGE.
                        05   LINE NUMBER IS PLUS 2.
                                        10   COLUMN NUMBER IS 81               PIC X(15)
                                             VALUE 'TOTAL TERRITORY'.
                                        10   COLUMN NUMBER IS 97               PIC X
                                             SOURCE IS TERR.
                                        10   TERR-TOT COLUMN NUMBER IS 106     PIC $$$$$9.99
                                             SUM AREA-TOT.
                                        10   COLUMN NUMBER IS 116              PIC XXX
                                             VALUE '***'.
                    01   TYPE IS CONTROL FOOTING FINAL.
                        05   LINE NUMBER IS 60.
                                        10   COLUMN NUMBER IS 16               PIC X(11)
                                             VALUE 'TOTAL SALES'.
                                        10   COLUMN NUMBER IS 36               PIC $$,$$$,$$9.99
                                             SUM TERR-TOT.
                    *
                    PROCEDURE DIVISION.
                    100-MAIN-MODULE.
                        OPEN INPUT FILE-IN
                             OUTPUT FILE-OUT
                        INITIATE REPORT-LISTING
                        PERFORM UNTIL NO-MORE-RECORDS
                            READ FILE-IN
                                AT END
                                    MOVE 'NO ' TO ARE-THERE-MORE-RECORDS
                                NOT AT END
                                    PERFORM 200-CALC-RTN
                            END-READ
                        END-PERFORM
                        TERMINATE REPORT-LISTING
                        CLOSE FILE-IN
                              FILE-OUT
                        STOP RUN.
                    200-CALC-RTN.
                        GENERATE DETAIL-LINE.
```

COBOL 74 Substitutions

```
READ FILE-IN
    AT END MOVE 'NO ' TO
        ARE-THERE-MORE-RECORDS.
PERFORM 200-CALC-RTN
    UNTIL NO-MORE-RECORDS.
```

```
READ FILE-IN
    AT END MOVE 'NO ' TO
        ARE-THERE-MORE-RECORDS.
```

Sample Input Data

```
1 1 01 A NEWMAN           41745
1 1 01 P PETERSON JR       62814
1 1 01 D SILVERS           40455
1 1 02 J ADAMS             37923
1 1 02 B JONES             29816
1 1 03 A BYRNES            55926
1 1 03 F CARLETON          22368
1 2 04 A FRANKLIN          62734
1 2 04 D ROBERTS           57226
1 2 04 S STONE             42632
1 2 05 L DANTON            36522
1 2 05 R JACKSON           42622
```

SALES-AMOUNT
SALESPERSON
DEPARTMENT
AREA-IN
TERR

Figure 17.6 (continued)

Sample Output

```
                                      MONTHLY SALES REPORT   PAGE   01

   TERRITORY   AREA   DEPARTMENT      SALESPERSON   AMOUNT OF SALES

      1          1       01       A NEWMAN            417.45
                 1       01       P PETERSON JR       628.14
                 1       01       D SILVERS           404.55


                                              TOTAL DEPARTMENT 01   $1450.14 *
      1          1       02       J ADAMS             379.23
                 1       02       B JONES             298.16


                                              TOTAL DEPARTMENT 02    $677.39 *
      1          1       03       A BYRNES            559.26
                 1       03       F CARLETON          223.68


                                              TOTAL DEPARTMENT 03    $782.94 *
                                                     TOTAL AREA 1       $2910.47   **
      1          2       04       A FRANKLIN          627.34
                 2       04       D ROBERTS           572.26
                 2       04       S STONE             426.32


                                              TOTAL DEPARTMENT 04   $1625.92 *
      1          2       05       L DANTON            365.22
                 2       05       R JACKSON           426.22


                                              TOTAL DEPARTMENT 05    $791.44 *
                                                     TOTAL AREA 2       $2417.36   **
                                                            TOTAL TERRITORY 1       $5327.83 ***
               TOTAL SALES          $5,327.83
```

REVIEW QUESTIONS

1. What is the Report Writer Module and when is it used?
2. Explain the meaning of the following terms:
   (a) CONTROL HEADING.
   (b) CONTROL FOOTING.
   (c) PAGE HEADING.
   (d) PAGE FOOTING.
3. Explain the differences between detail and group printing.
4. What is a control break and how is it used in group printing?
5. What section of the DATA DIVISION is required for writing reports using the Report Writer Module?

DEBUGGING EXERCISES

Make necessary corrections to the following:

```
01   TYPE REPORT HEADING.
       05   LINE 1.
              10 COLUMN 44      PIC X(19)      VALUE 'COMPENSATION REPORT'.
*
01   TYPE PAGE HEADING.
       05   LINE 3.
              10 COLUMN 11      PIC X(16)      VALUE 'SALESPERSON NAME'.
```

```
                              10 COLUMN 41      PIC X(12)     VALUE 'HOURS WORKED'.
                              10 COLUMN 49      PIC X(11)     VALUE 'TOTAL SALES'.
                              10 COLUMN 62      PIC X(10)     VALUE 'COMMISSION'.
                              10 COLUMN 75      PIC X(05)     VALUE 'BONUS'.
                              10 COLUMN 83      PIC X(10)     VALUE 'AMT. EARNED'.
     *
         01  DETAIL-LINE.
             TYPE DETAIL.
             LINE PLUS 1.
             05 COLUMN 11      PIC X(32)     SOURCE SALESPERSON-NAME-IN.
             05 COLUMN 43      PIC Z9        SOURCE YEARS-EMPLOYED-IN.
             05 COLUMN 49      PIC $ZZZ,ZZ9  SOURCE TOTAL-SALES-IN.
             05 COLUMN 63      PIC $ZZZ,ZZ9  SOURCE SALES-COMMISSION-IN.
             05 COLUMN 74      PIC $ZZ,ZZZ   SOURCE BONUS-IN.
             05 SUM AMT1 COLUMN 85 SOURCE BONUS-IN + SALES-COMMISSION-IN.
     *
         01  TYPE CONTROL FOOTING FINAL
             LINE PLUS 3.
             05 COLUMN 11      PIC X(18)     VALUE 'TOTAL COMPENSATION'.
             05 COLUMN 81 SUM AMT2  PIC $ZZZ,ZZZ,ZZ9.
```

PROGRAMMING ASSIGNMENTS Code the programs at the end of Chapter 10 using the Report Writer Module.

CHAPTER 18

An Introduction to Object-Oriented Programming

THE ADVANTAGES OF OBJECT-ORIENTED PROGRAMMING

We have emphasized throughout this text the importance of writing programs that are easy to read, debug, maintain, and modify. As the need for computer applications increases, the need for well-designed, well-written, and well-documented programs increases as well. Some of the concepts we have focused on that improve the quality of programs include the use of:

1. Structured techniques
2. Top-down design
3. Comments to help document the program
4. Scope terminators with COBOL 85 to delimit instructions
5. Indentation and other COBOL coding techniques for improving readability
6. `COPY` and `CALL` statements to minimize duplication of effort
7. Data validation techniques to minimize input errors

The above techniques are used with most third-generation languages for improving the overall design of programs. But because there is an increasing need for quality programs in a wide variety of application areas, additional concepts are required in the current computer environment to improve programmer productivity.

Many people have become dissatisfied with COBOL as a business language because they believe that the language is cumbersome and that it does not lend itself to improved programmer productivity. Often, companies that are downsizing their operations—moving applications from larger computers to smaller ones—decide to have their existing COBOL programs rewritten in a language considered to be easier to read, debug, maintain, and modify. As a result, there are many pundits who are predicting the demise of the COBOL language. But this prediction may prove to be incorrect, particularly if COBOL becomes more commonly used as an *object-oriented* programming language.

Object-oriented programming is a concept that has the potential for significantly enhancing both the quality and quantity of all programs. This concept is considered by many to be the key to improved productivity in future programs. Several years ago, an Object-Oriented COBOL Task Group approved by the American National Standards Institute (ANSI) was formed to define object-oriented extensions to the COBOL language, with the aim of incorporating these extensions into the COBOL 9x standard. This Task Group has since been renamed ANSI COBOL Technical Committee X3J4. If object-oriented programming realizes its potential and if this COBOL Committee can successfully integrate objects into COBOL programs, then predictions of the demise of COBOL are likely to be greatly exaggerated—indeed, the continued preeminence of COBOL as the major business-oriented language will be assured.

There are several programming languages that already implement the object-oriented approach. Smalltalk is a programming language developed explicitly around the object-oriented concept. C++ is a language that enhances the C programming language with object-oriented extensions. Versions of object-oriented COBOL are currently available as well. When the COBOL 9x standard is approved, COBOL will hopefully become another major language to be standardized around this object-oriented concept.

Keep in mind that the concept of object-oriented programming will be added to the COBOL standard as an *extension*, so that any new compiler incorporating object-oriented techniques will be compatible with previous standards. That is, the new compilers will be able to compile existing programs *in addition to* new object-oriented programs. Moreover, object-oriented COBOL and traditional COBOL will be usable together, making it possible to migrate to object-oriented COBOL in stages.

OVERVIEW OF OBJECT-ORIENTED (OO) PROGRAMMING

Data and procedures are combined and stored in a program as units referred to as objects. An object, then, includes both data and procedures or methods that operate on that data:

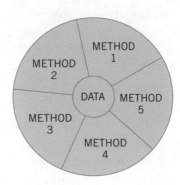

Action occurs when an object receives a message from the user. Services or actions are performed by the program as responses to user messages.

Objects can be written so that they share attributes—data and methods—with other objects; in addition, objects can have any number of other attributes unique to them. Enabling objects to share attributes means that data and procedure components need only be written once and copied to all objects with the same attributes.

A class defines a template for a series of similar objects. The class can be used to define and create objects that are the same except for the value of their data. Every object in a class looks the same when it is first created, but an object can be changed if the need arises. A class, then, is similar to a template or image; each object within a class is created by "filling in the blanks."

By defining classes and objects within classes:

1. Complex applications will be easier to develop. In effect, object-oriented (OO) programming provides the opportunity to build very sophisticated applications based on preexisting modules. Applications that use complex databases, multimedia features, and user-friendly graphical user interfaces are likely to benefit most from object-oriented programming.

2. Programs will become more standardized because they can share components and access collections of objects stored in libraries.

3. Reusable code stored in libraries will reduce duplication of effort, programming and maintenance costs, and errors, as well as improve overall programmer productivity.

4. Once objects are written, debugged, and documented, they can be acted on in any program by responding to the messages provided by the user. The user need not be familiar with the way the objects were developed. Indeed, the objects can be viewed as a "black box" having specified meaning in a program, with data and procedures either unknown by the user or hidden from the user. This means that programmers and users will be able to incorporate fairly complex objects into their programs without needing to understand how they were created or what data and techniques they use. It also means that objects can have a certain amount of security. Users are free to issue messages, but they cannot make changes to the objects themselves.

In summary, data and procedures are combined into a class definition. The class definition is specified in a COBOL program with procedures and global data that look just like standard COBOL code. Multiple instances of a class, each with its own local data, can be created at any point. These instances of a class are the objects that can send and receive messages from other objects. We say that a class defines a template for a series of similar objects.

Object-oriented programming is really more than an added technique to improve productivity; it is a different way of writing programs. With traditional code, actions are accomplished by procedures that act on data. With OO programming, objects that include both data and procedures are prewritten and acted upon in a user program by messages sent to the objects.

We say that objects are **ENCAPSULATED**, meaning that their data and procedures are hidden behind an **INTERFACE**; the user need only be familiar with the interface in order to use the object. These messages can be transmitted to an object by keying commands or by selecting icons using a mouse, or by one object sending a message to another object—it depends on the interface developed.

As an analogy, a driver of a car does not need to know how an engine functions. He or she need only know that using the ignition key will start the engine. The engine is similar to an object in a program, and the ignition key is similar to the interface necessary to invoke the object.

One goal of OO programming, then, is to develop libraries of objects that can be shared and called into user programs as needed. The COBOL COPY and CALL verbs as described in Chapter 16 are existing instructions that can begin to achieve some of the objectives of OO programming. Because COBOL programs have always treated data and procedures as a unit, the language really lends itself to this technique by enabling objects to be developed and called or copied into user programs.

A **CLASS** is a group of objects that share attributes, including data and procedures, which are methods for operating on the data. A **METHOD** is an action achieved by issuing a message to an object. Objects within a class can be acted on by unique methods or by methods shared by all objects in the same class. A method, then, is really an object's way of responding to a message.

Defining classes means placing reusable code in a central location or library, rather than having to redefine it over and over again. The expectation is that organizations will have large numbers of classes stored in their libraries and objects stored in databases so that user programs can retrieve and reuse classes and objects they need when they need them.

To say this in a different way, an object is called an **INSTANCE** of a class. Objects **INHERIT** attributes—data and procedures—from their class. (Remember that objects can also have their own unique attributes as well as inheriting attributes from their class.)

A class, then, can include a group of objects. In addition, an object may be included in another object; we call objects within other objects of a class a **MEMBER** object. Similarly, classes can be defined as part of other classes. A class that is part of another class is called a **DESCENDENT CLASS** or subclass, and the class that includes subclasses is called an **ANCESTOR CLASS**. So we may have ancestor classes that include descendent classes, with each consisting of objects or instances of the class.

Example 1 A bank-account may be defined as a class. It may have checking-account and savings-account as subclasses, each of which shares data attributes (e.g., account number and balance) and procedures (e.g., calculating interest) defined as part of bank-account.

Example 2 Methods that can be applied to a bank-account class include deposit and withdrawal. All objects within bank-account (e.g., checking-account and savings-account) can share deposit and withdrawal services. That means that the mechanisms used for withdrawing or depositing money will be the same for all objects within the class. Each object can have additional methods not inherited from the class but unique to that object. That is, process-check-fee can be a method applied to checking-account but not to savings-account.

Example 3 Data such as account-number can be shared by objects within the class as well. This may be made available to users for processing but may also be protected so that users can enter and retrieve them, but not be able to change them.

Classes and their objects consist of data and procedures. There are two types of data in a class: (1) object data and procedures that are unique for each object in the class, called an **INSTANCE VARIABLE**, and (2) **FACTORY** data and procedures that are data shared by all objects in the class (the word **CLASS** is already a COBOL Reserved Word, so we use **FACTORY** instead). **FACTORY** data such as an interest rate for a bank account class is automatically available to any object in the class. Similarly, procedures or **METHODS** can be (1) object methods unique to each object in the class and (2) **FACTORY** methods shared by all objects in the class. Objects are identified by unique names called **OBJECT HANDLES**.

In COBOL, **FACTORY** data, which is shared by all users, needs to be set to its initial value before processing using the `INITIALIZE` verb or by a `VALUE` clause. That is, before any object is acted upon by a **METHOD**, its **FACTORY** data is initialized.

POLYMORPHISM means that a method can be implemented differently depending on the object. Withdrawal, for example, may be implemented one way for objects like checking-account and savings-account within the bank-account class, and implemented an entirely different way for objects in a credit-card class. The service provided by the method called withdrawal is similar regardless of the class it acts upon but the way that service is provided can differ greatly. The interface that links the **METHOD** to the object may be different but the service provided will be similar. Thus, with **POLY-**

MORPHISM, the same message can result in completely different actions when received by different objects.

Although the term "polymorphism" itself may be new to you, it has relevance to the current COBOL language. The READ statement, for example, is polymorphic in that it results in different actions depending on whether we are reading from a sequential, indexed, or relative file.

The entire set of messages to which an object can respond along with the parameters required by each message is called the object's **INTERFACE.**

The concept of **DATA ABSTRACTION** in OO programming encourages programmers to think of data and methods in abstract terms, as fixed objects; common objects—data and procedures—should be factored out and located in ancestor classes, sometimes referred to as abstract classes.

Consider the following analogies:

Object-Oriented Terms	Traditional Programming Terms
Methods	Procedures, functions, subroutines
Instance variable	Data
Message	Procedure call or function call
Class	Abstract data type
Inheritance	Copy

The use of classes enables data hiding, which means that access privileges for those using data and procedures can be managed and limited. **ENCAPSULATION** is the ability to hide internal details of data and procedures while providing a public interface through a user-defined message. As in a previous analogy, think of program code as a car. It was developed by others, each responsible for different parts. You, as the user of this program, do not need to know how components (e.g., carburetor, transmission, etc.) operate. They can be encapsulated or hidden behind a user interface. Users request services using object handles such as a steering wheel, brake, and so on.

INHERITANCE provides a means of deriving a new class from an existing class called the **BASE CLASS.** The concept of inheritance is extended to permit a **DESCENDENT CLASS** or subclass to modify, replace, or even delete methods in the ancestor class.

Conceptually, we can begin to implement the object-oriented approach with standard COBOL:

The COPY statement enables you to copy class definitions and objects into a program. The CALL enables you to send messages to objects so that results can be obtained. The objects copied or called can have their own COPY so that they inherit properties from classes. The object-oriented extensions to the COBOL standard may use the COPY and CALL, or use a separate verb, such as INVOKE for objects. We may code, for example, INVOKE ASAVINGSACCOUNT 'Withdraw' USING CUSTOMER-ACCT TRANS-AMT RETURNING NEW-BALANCE. ASAVINGSACCOUNT may be an instance of some class object such as ACCOUNT, 'Withdraw' is a method, USING indicates the parameters to pass to the object, and RETURNING indicates the parameters passed back to the user program.

Often you begin by establishing a new instance of an object from a class of objects. MYSAVINGSACCOUNT may be an instance of ASAVINGSACCOUNT. Defining an instance of an object is called **INSTANTIATION.** This may be accomplished by code such as INVOKE ASAVINGSACCOUNT 'New' RETURNING MYSAVINGSACCOUNT. MYSAVINGSACCOUNT will then have all the properties of ASAVINGSACCOUNT, which inherits attributes from a class called ACCOUNT as well as having attributes unique to it.

Another method of achieving inheritance is to have data in each file indexed so that specified fields can be linked to data from other files. Suppose we have a payroll file that includes job classifications and we want to develop a method for producing paychecks. For employees who are salespeople, we can access each salesperson's record to add a commission to their base pay; for employees who are paid on an hourly basis, we can access the employee time-card routine to calculate any overtime hours; for management employees, we can access accounting records to determine bonuses that may be a function of profits. Routines for calculating FICA, federal and state taxes, and so on, are common to all employees.

Similarly, you can, for example, build a BUY method or function that can be applied to buying a house, car, or appliance. Or you can apply an existing BUY method to your file of stock data.

Another important element in object-oriented programs is that there needs to be a mechanism to enable user programs to make changes to **FACTORY** data as well as to objects so that (1) those changes are retained even after the program is terminated, and (2) the program, when executed again, begins just as it ended. This is referred to as **PERSISTENCE**. This is analogous to a "Save on Exit" menu item in some programs.

For objects within a class, we define data and methods shared with other objects in the class as follows:

```
IDENTIFICATION DIVISION.
FACTORY.
ENVIRONMENT DIVISION.
DATA DIVISION.
    <define Factory Data here>
PROCEDURE DIVISION.
    <define Factory Methods here>
END FACTORY.
```

To define methods and data unique to a specific object, we follow the preceding with:

```
IDENTIFICATION DIVISION.
OBJECT.                    <Any number of objects can be defined>
ENVIRONMENT DIVISION.
DATA DIVISION.
   <Object Data>
PROCEDURE DIVISION.
   <Object Methods>
END OBJECT.
```

Example   Consider the following OBJECT data:

```
IDENTIFICATION DIVISION.
CLASS-ID. ACCOUNT.
IDENTIFICATION DIVISION.
OBJECT.
DATA DIVISION.
WORKING-STORAGE SECTION.
01  CUSTOMER.
    05  ACCT-NO          PIC 9(5).
    05  LAST-NAME        PIC X(15).
    05  FIRST-NAME       PIC X(10).
    05  FULL-ADDRESS     PIC X(40).
    05  ACCT-BAL         PIC 9(5)V99.
```

Suppose we want to determine if the customer has a special type of classification such as GOLD-CARD-HOLDER or PLATINUM-CARD-HOLDER. We could code:

```
PROCEDURE DIVISION.
IDENTIFICATION DIVISION.
METHOD-ID. DETERMINE-CLASSIFICATION.
DATA DIVISION.
LINKAGE SECTION.
01  CUSTOMER-IN          USAGE OBJECT CUSTOMER.
01  CLASSIFICATION       PIC X(25).
PROCEDURE DIVISION USING CUSTOMER-IN
        RETURNING CLASSIFICATION.
    :
    :
    EXIT METHOD.
END METHOD DETERMINE-CLASSIFICATION.
```

Summary of Terms

Object—an integrated unit of data and procedures or methods that operate on that data.

Encapsulation—hiding the data and procedures in an object behind a user interface so that the user program need not be concerned about the details and so that security can be maintained.

Class—a set of objects that share attributes (data and procedures).

Inheritance—the ability of objects to share attributes held by other objects in the same class.

Polymorphism—the ability for objects in a class to respond to methods differently from other objects in the class.

Persistence—the ability of a user program to operate on class objects and retain the changes made.

Instantiation—establishing a new instance of an object in a class.

TUTORIAL FOR OBJECT-ORIENTED COBOL

The single most important change in the COBOL 9x standard will be its expected inclusion of an official version of object-oriented COBOL. In anticipation of the release of COBOL 9x, several software developers have already incorporated object-oriented options into their compilers:

Software Developer	Product
Micro Focus	Object COBOL
IBM	Visual Age for COBOL
Computer Associates	Visual Realia COBOL
Netron, Inc.	Netron/Fusion
TechBridge Technology	TechBridge Builder

Micro Focus has been a leader not only in including object COBOL extensions, but also in including graphical user interfaces and client-server features in their products. The following is a brief tutorial, consisting of three lessons, that has been reprinted with permission from Micro Focus's Personal Object COBOL manual.[1] Personal Object COBOL is a version of COBOL available with this text.

LESSON 1: "HELLO WORLD" AND PROCEDURAL COBOL

With Micro Focus's Object COBOL option, you use the key programming tool, the Class Browser, along with some of the fundamental concepts of object-oriented COBOL programming. In going through the tutorial, you'll learn:

- The basic parts of a class.
- The key elements needed to use an object.
- Passing a parameter to an object method.
- Passing a parameter to an object method and getting back a return value.

Along the way, you'll get a feel for Micro Focus's Class Browser and learn how to load, compile, and run code with it. By the time you finish (and it doesn't take long), you should feel familiar with the Browser and its basic controls.

We start with a programming classic: *Hello world*.

---

[1]*Getting Started*, Micro Focus Personal COBOL for Windows 3.1 with Object Orientation, 1995.

Introducing the Class Browser

The Personal COBOL programming environment is the Class Browser, also known as the Browser. The Browser works with a **project file** (a container file that holds one or more program files). By working within a project, a programmer can browse across numerous files down to the code level without ever doing a **File/Open**. The Browser lets you look at source code in special groups. In the case of procedural COBOL, these groups are standard COBOL divisions and sections. In Personal Object COBOL, they are elements within the project's class structure. Instead of scrolling through your code, you click the name of the code group you want to edit. Take a look at the Browser working with the procedural COBOL *Hello world* program:

1. Open the Browser; go to the Program Manager and the Personal Object COBOL program group. Double-click the **Personal COBOL** icon. The Browser asks you what project you want to work on and opens the standard **Open File** dialog.
2. In the dialog box, select **hello0.prj** and press **Enter**. Hello0.prj is a one-file project. It contains the HELLO0.CBL program.
3. Click the Program ID **Hello** in the leftmost **Classes** pane. Its file-name is in the center **Files** pane, and the COBOL division and section names are in the rightmost **Sections/Methods** pane. The text-editing pane shows the contents of the highlighted IDENTIFICATION DIVISION. See Figure 18.1.

The Browser consists of four panes. The three small panes across its top constitute a control panel for selecting text. The selected text appears in the large pane at the bottom, the *text-editing pane*. Typically, you choose the desired class or program name in the leftmost **(Classes)** pane and the item you want to edit in the rightmost **(Sections/Methods)** pane. The center **Files** pane shows the physical file-name of the class or program.

Important: Because this is COBOL, be sure to start in the eighth column. Note that anything typed in columns 1 through 7 (sequence and continuation columns) or in columns 73 through 80 (the identification columns) appears in colored text. Also, the Browser maintains a default warning when you exceed column 72. If you don't want this warning, you can turn it off with **Text/Column Check**. If **Column Check** is checked, the warning is turned on.

Here is the Hello program listing:

```
*************************************************
* HELLO0.CBL                                     *
* A procedural COBOL "hello world" program.      *
* Getting Started hello0.prj                     *
*************************************************
 IDENTIFICATION DIVISION.
 PROGRAM-ID. Hello.
```

Figure 18.1 The Browser.

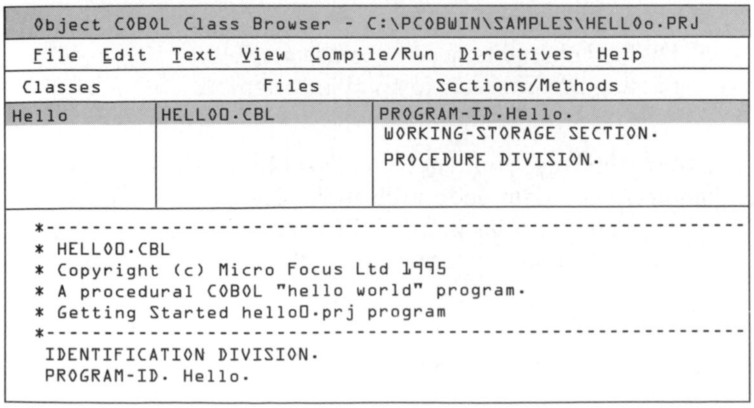

```
Object COBOL Class Browser - C:\PCOBWIN\SAMPLES\HELLO0.PRJ

 File  Edit  Text  View  Compile/Run  Directives  Help

 Classes           Files            Sections/Methods

 Hello      HELLO0.CBL        PROGRAM-ID.Hello.
                              WORKING-STORAGE SECTION.
                              PROCEDURE DIVISION.



 *-------------------------------------------------------
 * HELLO0.CBL
 * Copyright (c) Micro Focus Ltd 1995
 * A procedural COBOL "hello world" program.
 * Getting Started hello0.prj program
 *-------------------------------------------------------
  IDENTIFICATION DIVISION.
  PROGRAM-ID. Hello.
```

```
ENVIRONMENT DIVISION.
DATA DIVISION.
WORKING-STORAGE SECTION.
01  salutation              pic x(20).
PROCEDURE DIVISION.
    move "Hello world" to salutation
    display salutation
    stop run.
```

Even if you've only had one COBOL class, there should be no surprises here. When you loaded the Hello0 project, it showed just one entity in the **Classes** pane. Because this code doesn't include a Class-ID, the Browser shows its Program-ID. Try out the Browser:

1. Click each division name in the **Sections/Methods** pane—displaying the procedural COBOL divisions—to see what the Browser puts in the text-editing pane. Note: You can also choose different data views in the **View** menu. Some views are better for procedural programming and some for object-oriented programming.

2. Make sure that **Hello** (the class name) is selected in the **Classes** pane (meaning that a colored band highlights the word "Hello").

3. Compile and run the program from the **Compile/Run|Compile** option. When the **COBOL Compile** dialog appears, click **OK**.

4. When the compiler has finished its work, go to the **Compile/Run|Run**. The **COBOL Run Time Shell** should appear, displaying the message "Hello world." See Figure 18.2.

5. To retire the display, click **OK**.

A style note: Micro Focus COBOL products let you enter code in uppercase, lowercase, or any mixture of the two. To make divisions and sections more obvious, the programmer put these items in uppercase, and everything else in lowercase or mixed case.

From Procedural COBOL to OO COBOL

The next example is the Hello program written as an object-oriented (OO) program. It has much the same structure as the procedural COBOL program you just compiled and ran. Data declaration, followed by a Procedure Division that, from its Main Section, calls a series of procedures. Object COBOL programming is not that different.

The differences are that the programmer writes and uses classes (source entities that package data and procedures together). Each data item in a class has a particular range of accessibility or *scope*. Typically, you can only change an object's data values by

Figure 18.2 The Run Time Shell Window after running Hello0 in the Browser.

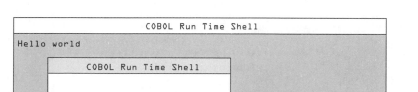

invoking an appropriate object method. Once you see the architecture of a class, you'll see a structure similar to that of procedural COBOL, complete with Data Divisions and Procedure Divisions.

LESSON 2: "HELLO WORLD" AND OO COBOL

How does object-oriented (OO) programming work? Part of what an object programmer must do is a bit like baking cookies. You start with a recipe, which is pretty much like the source code for a class. It describes everything that goes into the cookies. When you mix up the dough, you have something like a *class object*. It's not just words. It's real, but it isn't cookies yet. And it's the thing your cookies/objects will be made of. The object is the final product.

An *object* (defined by its *class*) contains both data (*attributes*) and the procedures (*methods*) to access that data. This packaging of data items with methods is called *encapsulation*. It means that the only way to access a data item is to send a message to the appropriate object method. For example, in the case of a window object, you can summon appropriate methods to set the window's size, position the window on screen, and keep track of user interactions with the window. A class can send a message to another class, as can a *driver* or *trigger* program (any program that activates an object).

Throughout the rest of these lessons, you will find programs presented in pairs. Each pair consists of a driver program and a class program. The driver:

- Registers the class.
- Declares object reference data items.
- Creates an object from the class.
- Sends a message accessing a method within the object.
- Cleans up memory when it's done with the object.

Each pair is packaged in a *project*. A project makes handling multi-file programs easier. The first driver program for the Hello class is HELODRV1.CBL. Take a look at how it works:

1. To change projects, go to the **File|Open/New Project**.
2. From the **Open File** dialog box, choose **hello1.prj** and click **OK**. When the project loads, two items appear in the **Classes** pane: **Hello** and **HeloDrv1**.
3. Click **Hello** and then **HeloDrv1**, and you'll see a different file-name for each. **Hello** is the class name, found in the HELOCLS1.CBL file, and HELODRV1.CBL is the driver file.
4. Make sure **HeloDrv1** is selected (highlighted). The HeloDrv1 listing below shows the whole program. You can look at each individual section by clicking the desired section name in the **Sections/Methods** pane.

```
*****************************************
*  HELODRV1.CBL                         *
*  A driver for the Hello               *
*  class, invoking one method:          *
*      sayHello                         *
*  Getting Started hello.prj, driver    *
*****************************************
 IDENTIFICATION DIVISION.
 PROGRAM-ID. HeloDrv1.
 ENVIRONMENT DIVISION.
 CLASS-CONTROL.
*----Register classes
     Hello is class "helocls1"
     Base is class "base".
 DATA DIVISION.
 WORKING-STORAGE SECTION.
*----Data items of type 'object reference'
 01  helloHandle       usage object reference.
 01  defaultReturn     usage object reference.
```

```
PROCEDURE DIVISION.
*----Create an object instance using Hello class and get handle
     invoke Hello "new" returning helloHandle
*----Invoke a method within the object just created
     invoke helloHandle "sayHello"
*----Clean up; destroy object helloHandle
     invoke helloHandle "finalize" returning defaultReturn
     stop run.
```

You may notice that the driver looks pretty much like a procedural COBOL program with a few new items:

- The Environment Division carries a Class-Control statement that is similar to the familiar File-Control section. In fact, it does much the same thing. Here, the statement equates a logical class name with the class's physical file-name. This also registers the class with the system. Base class is the parent of all classes. Ultimately, unless you want to write a Base class of your own, all classes descend from it. Therefore, the programmer must include it in this statement. You need to put every class directly accessed by your program in this statement. Otherwise, the *Run-Time System (RTS)* won't know where to find them.
- The Data Division's Working-Storage Section declares a new data type: object reference. In the Working-Storage Section, you have two data items declared with the new object reference object-oriented type. When you create an object, you don't deal with the object itself, but with a *handle* to it. (A handle is not the thing itself, but a thing to get hold of, so you can use the thing itself, whether a tea cup, a chain saw, or an object in memory.) Data items of type object reference hold these handles. The example names the handle to the Hello class "helloHandle."
- In the Procedure Division, you'll find a new verb, INVOKE. In the driver, INVOKE causes the Hello class to create an object using the "new" method (inherited from Base class.) Second, it invokes or sends a message to the Hello object's one method, SayHello. This method is the heart of this object. Everything in the example supports this. There's another handle, **defaultReturn**, that is used to destroy (**"finalize"**) an object, when the program is done with it.

Note: Programmers refer to using the INVOKE verb as "sending a message to an object." A *message* has these parts:

- An object reference (the object handle, like helloHandle).
- A method selector (the name of the method the message is invoking, like *SayHello*).
- Optional input and/or output parameters (with the USING and RETURNING clauses).

Four (or Five) Keys to Working with an Object

In the example, the programmer has put these elements into a separate driver program. You can put them into a class that creates objects from other classes and sends messages to them. A driver includes a minimum of four class structural elements. And five isn't a bad idea. As noted earlier, all five are in this driver:

1. The Environment Division's Class-Control statement lists the logical name of each class and the physical name of its disk file. (Personal COBOL permits just one class to a disk file.)

    ```
    ENVIRONMENT DIVISION.
    OBJECT SECTION.
    CLASS-CONTROL.
    *----Register names of classes and their files
         Hello is class "helocls1"
         Base is class "base".
    ```

2. The Data Division's Working-Storage Section declares a data item of type USAGE OBJECT REFERENCE as a handle to the object to be created:

```
DATA DIVISION.
WORKING-STORAGE SECTION.
*----Data items of type 'object reference'
01  helloHandle   usage object reference.
01  defaultReturn usage object reference.
```

3. The Procedure Division creates an object with the formula:

   INVOKE <className> "NEW" RETURNING <handleName>,

   where <handleName> is the same data name as declared in the second key (as USAGE OBJECT REFERENCE).

   ```
   PROCEDURE DIVISION.
   *----Create an object instance using Hello class and get handle
       invoke Hello "new" returning helloHandle
   ```

4. The Procedure Division also sends a message to the created object via <handleName>. This formula includes the optional USING and RETURNING clauses:

   INVOKE <handleName> "<methodName>" USING
   RETURNING <returnValue>

   ```
   *----Invoke a method within the object just created
       invoke helloHandle "sayHello"
   ```

5. Here is some optional good housekeeping within the Procedure Division. When you're finished with the object, destroy it and release the memory to the operating system. The formula is:

   INVOKE <handleName> "FINALIZE" RETURNING DEFAULTRETURN

   ```
   *----Clean up; destroy object helloHandle
       invoke helloHandle "finalize" returning defaultReturn
   ```

   Notice how it follows the formula seen in the previous step.

Believe it or not, you can do most of your object-oriented COBOL programming with these five steps and a few variations on them. Object-oriented COBOL is just that easy.

A Look at a Class

Now, take a look at the Hello class as it was written for the HeloDrv1 driver. Follow these steps:

1. To get at the class description, click **Hello** in the **Classes** pane.
2. To see each item in the class, click the item name in the **Sections/Methods** pane. Here's the listing for the HeloCls1 class:

```
*-----------------------------------------------------------*
* HELOCLS1.CBL
* A "hello world" class with one method:
*     sayHello
* Getting Started hello1.prj, class
*-----------------------------------------------------------*

*---------------- CLASS SHARED DEFINITIONS ----------------*
IDENTIFICATION DIVISION.
CLASS-ID. hello
          data is protected
          inherits from Base
          with data.
ENVIRONMENT DIVISION.
OBJECT SECTION.
CLASS-CONTROL.
*----Register names of classes and their files
      Hello is class "helocls1"
      Base is class "base".
```

```
 DATA DIVISION.
 WORKING-STORAGE SECTION.
*----Scope: class procedure, class object methods, and
*    instance object methods; uninheritable

*---------------- CLASS OBJECT DEFINITION ------------------*
 CLASS-OBJECT.
 OBJECT-STORAGE SECTION.
*----Scope: class object methods; inheritable
 END CLASS-OBJECT.

*--------------- INSTANCE OBJECT DEFINITION ---------------*
 OBJECT.
 OBJECT-STORAGE SECTION.
*----Scope: instance object methods; inheritable
 01  salutation              pic x(20)          value
                                                "Hello world".
*-----------------------------------------------------------
 METHOD-ID. "sayHello".
 DATA DIVISION.
 PROCEDURE DIVISION.
     display salutation
     exit method.
 END METHOD "sayHello".
*-----------------------------------------------------------
 END OBJECT.
 END CLASS hello.
```

Five Key Elements in a Class

The structure of a class includes at least four and preferably five elements:

- A *class header* gives the Class-ID name and describes what classes it inherits from. Personal COBOL offers various clauses for handling data inheritance, but these don't come into play in this example.
- Within the class header, a *Class-Control statement* lists the logical name of each class and the physical name of its disk file. (Personal COBOL permits just one class to a disk file.)
- The *class object definition*—including its data and methods—begins with the CLASS-OBJECT clause and ends with END CLASS-OBJECT. When you register a class, one class object gets created to assist in the creation and maintenance of instance objects.
- The *instance object definition*—complete with its data and methods—is bracketed by the OBJECT and END-OBJECT clauses. (This entity is the central interest of object programming. Whereas you can have only one class object per class, you can have numerous instance objects that belong to the class object.)
- Within the instance object definition, you need at least one miniprogram, a *method*. Look at the listing above and notice the similarity between the instance object descriptions and Hello0, the procedural COBOL program. Each has the salutation data item stored for use by a procedure. Each has a Procedure Division carrying the statement display salutation.

"Real" classes are typically more complex with data positioned at various levels of accessibility. This class declares one item in the instance object definition's Object-Storage Section. Data items in this section are accessible by all object instances belonging to the class and all object instances of subclasses of the current class. This accessibility to data (and methods) by subclasses is called inheritance. A class and its data remain until the application using them ends.

Compiling and Running a Class in the Browser

In the Personal Object COBOL Browser, you must compile one class at a time. You may wonder if the order of compilation makes any difference. It does. Always compile the least dependent programs first. In this case, you compile the class first, because compilation of the driver depends on compiled elements of the class being present. To compile and run the driver and class, follow these steps:

1. In the **Classes** pane, select **Hello** (the class).
2. Choose **Compile/Run|Compile**. When the **COBOL Compile** dialog appears, click **OK**.
3. In the **Classes** pane, select **HeloDrv1** (the driver).
4. Choose **Compile/Run|Compile**. When the **COBOL Compile** dialog appears, click **OK**.
5. To run, make sure HeloDrv1 is selected in the **Classes** pane. If you choose **Hello** and run the program, nothing happens. In this application, the driver makes things happen, not the class. (You don't always need a driver; you can write self-activating classes.)
6. Choose **Compile/Run|Run**. Just as with the procedural version, the COBOL **Run Time Shell** displays the "Hello world" message.
7. Return to the Browser; to retire the display, click **OK**.

LESSON 3: OO PROGRAMMING AND PARAMETER PASSING

The Hello1 project gave you a glimpse of object programming structure, but it made little use of the potential of objects. For example, just as with the procedural COBOL version, a procedure (program) pulled the data from the object's own data storage area and displayed it. Data access was completely internal to the object; no outside program directly accessed the data.

One of the things that happens with real object programming is that any data access always takes place through one of an object's methods. You can't read or write an object's data, unless the object supplies methods for reading and writing. In many cases, you store data in an object (or change the data already there) by passing in new data. Likewise, you can't see data inside an object, unless the object has a method that returns a value. This section shows you how to pass data (*parameters*) to an object method and how to get values returned.

Passing a Parameter to an Object

The single-method class illustrates the basic structure of a class and its relationship to a driver program. But passing a parameter in the message would make things more interesting. It's also very easy, because the conventions are similar to those of a COBOL CALL. To pass a parameter, add the USING clause to the INVOKE verb on the driver side. On the class side, you need a Linkage Section to receive the parameter and the USING clause attached to the method's Procedure Division. Notice the balance; the message sender and the message receiver share a syntax. (As you will see shortly, when requesting a value from a method, both sides must state a RETURNING clause.)

In the Hello2 project, you will meet the following:

- *setValue* is a method that takes two parameters—a greeting and a greetee. It writes these into appropriate data items and then cements them together as a single phrase and stores them in the salutation data item.
- *sayHello* remains as you saw it in the last project. It displays the salutation data item.

Follow these steps to load and examine the new project that demonstrates parameter passing:

1. To change projects, choose **File/Open/New Project**.
2. From the **Open File** dialog box, select **hello2.prj** and click **OK**. When the project loads, two items appear in the **Classes** pane: **Hello** and **HeloDrv2**.
3. Take a look at what the driver is doing. In the **Classes** pane, click **HeloDrv2**.
4. Click your way through the **Sections/Methods** pane. It's slightly more sophisticated than HeloDrv1.

5. For example, click the Working-Storage Section and you'll see new data items (greeting and greetee).

6. Notice too that the Procedure Division has been subdivided into various sections.

7. Click the Greet Section below the Procedure Division and take a look.

```
Greet Section.
*----Invoke methods within the object just created
        invoke helloHandle "setHello" using greeting, greetee
        invoke helloHandle "sayHello"
```

The first message invokes the setHello method, sending it (with USING) two data items as parameters. The second message was carried over from HELODRV1.CBL. This is a simple example of sending data to an object.

Take a look at the two new methods in the class; follow these steps:

1. In the **Classes** pane, select **Hello**.

2. Go to the **Sections/Methods** pane and click **setHello**. The listing for this new method appears below. Notice that Working-Storage Section contains a new data item and that there's a new Data Division section—the Linkage Section.

```
METHOD-ID. "setHello".
DATA DIVISION.
LINKAGE SECTION.
01   greeting                 pic x(10).
01   greetee                  pic x(10).
PROCEDURE DIVISION using greeting, greetee.
    display "Testing raw data: " greeting, greetee
    string greeting delimited by ' '
           ' ' delimited by size
           greetee delimited by ' '
           ' ' delimited by size
           into salutation
    exit method.
END METHOD "setHello".
```

The programmer has put the greeting and the greetee into two data items, each in the Linkage Section. The Linkage Section serves as a transit point for incoming and outgoing data. Here, it contains two incoming items. (You know they're incoming because the Procedure Division defines them as such with the USING clause.) After displaying the two items received (a good check on data flow during development), the programmer concatenates the two items with the COBOL STRING function, storing the result in the Object-Storage Section data item, salutation. With the greeting so stored, the SayHello method only needs to grab it (from salutation) and display it. To see both methods in action, follow these steps:

1. In the **Classes** pane, select **Hello** (the class).

2. Choose **Compile/Run|Compile**. When **COBOL Compile** dialog appears, click **OK**.

3. In the **Classes** pane, select **HeloDrv2** (the driver).

4. Choose **Compile/Run|Compile**. When the **COBOL Compile** dialog appears, click **OK**.

5. Make sure **HeloDrv2** is selected in the **Classes** pane.

6. Choose **Compile/Run|Run**. This time the **COBOL Run Time Shell** displays more than one line of text. (You may need to move the OK message box to see the output.) See Figure 18.3.

7. Return to the Browser. Click the **OK** button to retire the display.

An INVOKE statement can both send data and receive a data item from a method. The next section explores this usage.

Figure 18.3   The Run Time Shell after running the Hello2 project in the Browser.

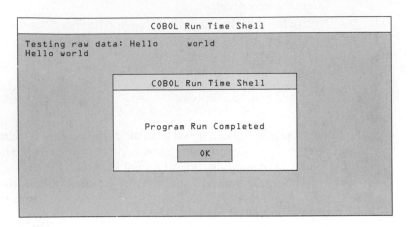

Returning a Value

You may have noticed the RETURNING clause when creating an object and when finalizing one. But those examples are a bit abstract, at least when you're starting out. This section adds a RETURNING clause and an object method to do something with it. Ultimately, what you'll see is that RETURNING is nothing mysterious; it's USING in reverse. In the Hello3 project, you'll see one old friend and make a new one:

- *setValue* is a method that takes two parameters—a greeting and a greetee—the same as in the Hello2 project.
- *getHello* is a method that returns the salutation data item to the driver.

Often, you don't want an object or a *function* to display a value. You want the object to *return* a value. With a Linkage Section in place, returning a value is easy. To load and examine the new class, follow these steps:

1. To change projects, choose **File|Open/New Project**.
2. From the **Open file** dialog box, select **hello3.prj** and click **OK**. When the project loads, two items appear in the **Classes** pane: **Hello** and **HeloDrv3**.
3. In the **Classes** pane, select **Hello**.
4. Go to the **Sections/Methods** pane and click **getHello**. The listing for this third method appears below.

```
METHOD-ID. "getHello".
DATA DIVISION.
LINKAGE SECTION.
01  outBox              pic x(20).
PROCEDURE DIVISION returning outBox.
    move salutation to outBox
    exit method.
END METHOD "getHello".
```

Here, the Linkage Section provides a transit point for returning a value, the data item outBox. The getHello program moves the salutation data item into outBox, and that's it. Here are the statements that invoke and use getHello in the driver:

```
invoke helloHandle "getHello" returning hiho
display "getHello returned: " hiho
```

On the driver side, salutation's data will appear in the hiho data item (newly declared in the driver Data Division). Why does this work? Because both hiho and outBox are linked by the RETURNING clause—one on each end of the transaction. To see it in action, follow these steps:

1. In the **Classes** pane, select **Hello** (the class).

2. Choose **Compile/Run|Compile**. When the **COBOL Compile** dialog appears, click **OK**.

3. In the **Classes** pane, select **HeloDrv3** (the driver).

4. Choose **Compile/Run|Compile**. When the **COBOL Compile** dialog appears, click **OK**.

5. Make sure **HeloDrv3** is selected in the **Classes** pane.

6. To run, in the **Classes** pane, click the driver name, **HeloDrv3**.

7. Choose **Compile/Run|Run**. This time the **COBOL Run Time Shell** displays the setHello output and the new report from getHello. (You may need to move the OK message box to see the output.) See Figure 18.4.

8. Return to the Browser. To retire the display, click **OK**.

Now, you have a statement that sends data to a method with USING and a second statement that receives data returned from method. How about a statement that both sends and receives data?

Passing a Parameter and Returning a Value

There are times when a programmer may want to treat an object method as if it were a function, sending it data and getting back the results of a process. This section shows you how to do this. With a Linkage Section in place, sending parameters and returning a value is easy. Follow these steps to load and examine project 4:

1. To change projects, choose **File|Open/New Project**.

2. From the Open file dialog box, choose **hello4.prj** and click **OK**. When the project loads, two items appear in the **Classes** pane: **Hello** and **HeloDrv4**.

3. In the **Classes** pane, select the class; click **Hello**.

4. Go to the **Sections/Methods** pane and click **getAndPutHello**. The listing for this third method appears below.

```
METHOD-ID. "getAndPutHello".
DATA DIVISION.
LINKAGE SECTION.
01   greeting              pic x(10).
01   greetee               pic x(10).
01   greeted               pic x(20).
PROCEDURE DIVISION using greeting,
                         greetee
                returning greeted.
    invoke self "setHello" using greeting, greetee
    move salutation to greeted
    exit method.
END METHOD "getAndPutHello".
```

Figure 18.4   The Run Time Shell after running the Hello3 project in the Browser.

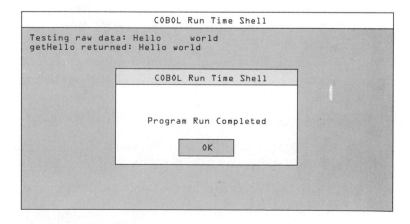

Notice that the Linkage Section contains a third data item, *greeted*, also named in the Procedure Division. How would you (or the compiler) know what to do with this item? By just looking at the three data items, there's no way to tell which one(s) receive data and which one(s) return it. The USING and RETURNING clauses of the Procedure Division sort out usage for the compiler. The greeted item, preceded by the RETURN-ING clause, returns data to the invoking statement. The greeting and greetee data items, on the other hand, are USING received data. In fact, the Procedure Division clauses echo the clauses used with the invoking statement. These clauses make it possible for reciprocal data items to have different data-names, that is, hiho and greeted.

Notice something else interesting. The getAndPutHello method itself includes an INVOKE statement. Here, an object method makes use of a peer method, but instead of stating:

```
invoke helloHandle "setHello" using greeting, greetee
```

it states

```
invoke self "setHello" using greeting, greetee
```

The difference is that instead of using the object handle, helloHandle, this statement substitutes an object COBOL reserved word, *self*. The self data item always holds the object handle data-name for the current object. This use of self shows the pattern for invoking a method *within the same object*. (In the on-line *Beginning Tutorials*, accessed through **Help|Online Tutorials and References**, you'll learn more about self and related words, *super*, and *selfclass*.)

To see the driver, follow these steps:

1. In the **Classes** pane, click **HeloDrv4**.
2. In the **Sections/Methods** pane, click **Greet Section**.

Notice that this time, the programmer doesn't need the setHello method. getAnd-PutHello does all the work with regard to preparing the data:

```
 Greet Section.
*----Invoke methods within the object just created
    invoke helloHandle "getAndPutHello" using greeting,
                                              greetee
                                              returning hiho
     display "getAndPutHello returned the greeting: " hiho
```

To see project 4 in action, follow these steps:

1. In the **Classes** pane, select **Hello** (the class).
2. Choose **Compile/Run|Compile**. When the **COBOL Compile** dialog appears, click **OK**.
3. In the **Classes** pane, select **HeloDrv4** (the driver).
4. Choose **Compile/Run|Compile**. When the **COBOL Compile** dialog appears, click **OK**.
5. Make sure **HeloDrv4** is selected in the **Classes** pane.
6. Choose **Compile/Run|Run**. The **COBOL Run Time Shell** displays the outputs. See Figure 18.5.
7. Return to the Browser. To retire the display, click **OK**.
8. When you're done, exit the Browser; choose **File|Exit**.

PROGRAMMING IN PERSONAL COBOL: A REVIEW

This topic describes how to use the Personal COBOL environment to create a program and its project. Use it as a map to get yourself into the development process.

1. Open the Browser; go to the Program Manager and the **Personal COBOL** pro-

Figure 18.5 The Run Time Shell after running the Hello4 project in the Browser.

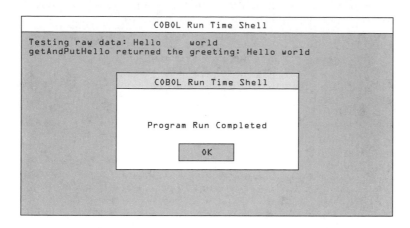

gram group. Double-click the **Personal COBOL** icon. The Browser asks you what project you want to work on and opens the standard **Open File** dialog.

2. In the dialog box, type in the project name, including the .prj extension. For example: **myproj.prj** and press **Enter**.
   Note: To start a new project or open a project from disk once in the Browser, choose **File|Open/New Project**.

3. Now create a source code file. Personal COBOL starts you off with an appropriate template:
   To create a procedural COBOL file, choose **File|New Program**.
   To create an object COBOL class file, choose **File|New Class**.
   In either case, respond to the dialog box with a program name (including the .CBL extension).

4. To edit, click into the text-editing pane, and type (obeying COBOL column rules).

5. To save your efforts, choose **File|Save**.

6. To compile your program, choose **Compile/Run|Compile**.

7. To debug your program, choose **Compile/Run|Animate**.

8. To run your program, choose **Compile/Run|Run**.

9. To quit, choose **File|Exit**.

WHAT YOU'VE LEARNED

You've seen Personal COBOL's basic structures and some amount of interaction between program entities. These are the basic components of all *OO* (object-oriented) programming. Keep in mind that these example projects are sound models. You might consider printing them and seeing if you can follow the flow of data between the two. Keep them handy for reference, too.

What you didn't experience are the concepts of *inheritance* and *polymorphism*. The **Help|Online Tutorials and Reference** *Beginning Tutorials* treats both of these in a series of examples that calculate various aspects of circles and cylinders.

What did you learn? A lot! You learned:

- How to open a project in the Browser and view various program sections.
- How to compile and run a program.
- How important menu items work.
- How to work with a procedural COBOL program in the Browser.
- The object-oriented syntax items in Personal COBOL.
- The basic structure of classes and their objects and how to access them with driver programs.

- Passing a parameter to an object method and returning a value.
- How one object method can access a peer method (with *self*).
- How to print a listing from the Browser.

PRINTING A LISTING

You can print any .CBL file from your favorite text processor or from the Browser. Because the Browser lets you print selections from a source file, keep two things in mind:

- Once you have the code you want to print in the Browser text pane, be sure to execute Edit|Select All or hand select the portion of text you want to print.
- If you want to print the entire source file for the selected file, follow these steps:

1. Make sure your printer is on and ''on line.''
2. Go to the **View** menu, make a mental note of which item is checked in the middle section of the **View** menu, and click **File Only**.
3. Click the file's name in the **Sections/Methods** pane. This causes the listing to appear in the text-editing pane.
4. Choose **Edit|Select All**.

To print the selection, whether it is a portion of the file or the whole thing, follow these steps:

1. Choose **Print|Print Selection**.
2. When you're done, return to the **View** menu and reselect the View you had before printing (possibly, **COBOL Sections**).

Appendixes

APPENDIX A

COBOL Character Set and Reserved Words

See the COBOL Syntax Reference Guide that accompanies this book for full Instruction Formats.

COBOL CHARACTERS

The following lists are in ascending order:

EBCDIC		ASCII	
	space		space
.	period, decimal point	"	quotation mark
<	less than	$	dollar sign
(	left parenthesis	'	single quotation mark
+	plus symbol	(	left parenthesis
$	dollar sign	)	right parenthesis
*	asterisk, multiplication	*	asterisk, multiplication
)	right parenthesis	+	plus symbol
;	semicolon	,	comma
-	hyphen, minus sign	-	hyphen, minus sign
/	slash, division	.	period, decimal point
,	comma	/	slash, division
>	greater than	0–9	digits
'	single quotation mark	;	semicolon
=	equal sign	<	less than
"	quotation mark	=	equal sign
a–z	lowercase letters	>	greater than
A–Z	uppercase letters	A–Z	uppercase letters
0–9	digits	a–z	lowercase letters

COBOL RESERVED WORDS

Each COBOL compiler has a list of reserved words that:

1. Includes all entries in the ANS COBOL standard.
2. Includes additional entries not part of the standard but that are either VAX or IBM compiler extensions. These are called enhancements.

You may find that your computer has additional reserved words. Diagnostic messages will print if you are using a reserved word incorrectly.

New reserved words that are not relevant for COBOL 74, but are relevant only for COBOL 85, are denoted with a single asterisk (*). COBOL 74 reserved words that are *not* reserved in the new standard are denoted with a double asterisk (**). Words marked with a (V) are VAX COBOL 85 extensions. Words marked with an (I) are IBM COBOL 85 extensions.

ACCEPT
ACCESS
ACTUAL (I)
ADD
ADVANCING
AFTER
ALL
ALLOWING (V)
ALPHABET *
ALPHABETIC
ALPHABETIC-LOWER *
ALPHABETIC-UPPER *
ALPHANUMERIC *
ALPHANUMERIC-EDITED *
ALSO
ALTER
ALTERNATE
AND
ANY *
APPLY (V)
ARE
AREA
AREAS
ASCENDING
ASSIGN
AT
AUTHOR
AUTOTERMINATE (V)

BASIS (I)
BATCH (V)
BEFORE
BEGINNING (V)/(I)
BELL (V)
BINARY *
BIT (V)/(I)
BITS (V)/(I)
BLANK
BLINKING (V)
BLOCK
BOLD (V)
BOOLEAN (V)/(I)
BOTTOM
BY

CALL
CANCEL
CBL (I)
CD
CF
CH
CHARACTER
CHARACTERS
CLASS *
CLOCK-UNITS
CLOSE
COBOL
CODE
CODE-SET
COLLATING
COLUMN
COM-REG (I)
COMMA
COMMIT (V)/(I)
COMMON (V)
COMMUNICATION
COMP
COMP-1 (V)/(I)

COMP-2 (V)/(I)
COMP-3 (V)/(I)
COMP-4 (V)/(I)
COMP-5 (V)
COMP-6 (V)
COMPUTATIONAL
COMPUTATIONAL-1 (V)/(I)
COMPUTATIONAL-2 (V)/(I)
COMPUTATIONAL-3 (V)/(I)
COMPUTATIONAL-4 (V)/(I)
COMPUTATIONAL-5 (V)
COMPUTATIONAL-6 (V)
COMPUTE
CONCURRENT (V)
CONFIGURATION
CONNECT (V)/(I)
CONSOLE (I)
CONTAIN (V)
CONTAINS
CONTENT *
CONTINUE *
CONTROL
CONTROLS
CONVERSION (V)
CONVERTING *
COPY
CORE-INDEX (I)
CORR
CORRESPONDING
COUNT
CURRENCY
CURRENT (V)
CURRENT-DATE (I)

DATA
DATE
DATE-COMPILED
DATE-WRITTEN
DAY
DAY-OF-WEEK *
DB (V)
DB-ACCESS-CONTROL-KEY (V)
DB-CONDITION (V)
DB-CURRENT-RECORD-ID (V)
DB-CURRENT-RECORD-NAME (V)
DB-EXCEPTION (V)
DBKEY (V)
DB-KEY (V)
DB-RECORD-NAME (V)
DB-SET-NAME (V)
DB-STATUS (V)
DEBUG-SUB (V)
DB-UWA (V)
DE
DEBUG-CONTENTS
DEBUG-ITEM
DEBUG-LENGTH (V)
DEBUG-LINE
DEBUG-NAME
DEBUG-NUMERIC-CONTENTS (V)
DEBUG-SIZE (V)
DEBUG-START (V)
DEBUG-SUB
DEBUG-SUB-1
DEBUG-SUB-2
DEBUG-SUB-3
DEBUG-SUB-ITEM (V)
DEBUG-SUB-N (V)

DEBUG-SUM-NUM (V)
DEBUGGING
DECIMAL-POINT
DECLARATIVES
DEFAULT
DELETE
DELIMITED
DELIMITER
DEPENDING
DESCENDING
DESCRIPTOR (V)
DESTINATION
DETAIL
DICTIONARY (V)
DISABLE
DISCONNECT
DISP (I)
DISPLAY
DISPLAY-1 (I)
DISPLAY-6 (V)
DISPLAY-7 (V)
DISPLAY-9 (V)
DIVIDE
DIVISION
DOES (V)
DOWN
DUPLICATE
DUPLICATES
DYNAMIC

ECHO (V)
EGCS (I)
EGI
EJECT (I)
ELSE
EMI
EMPTY
ENABLE
END
END-ACCEPT (V)
END-ADD *
END-CALL *
END-COMMIT (V)
END-COMPUTE *
END-CONNECT (V)
END-DELETE *
END-DISCONNECT (V)
END-DIVIDE *
END-ERASE (V)
END-EVALUATE *
END-FETCH (V)
END-FIND (V)
END-FINISH (V)
END-FREE (V)
END-GET (V)
END-IF *
ENDING (V)/(I)
END-KEEP (V)
END-MODIFY (V)
END-MULTIPLY *
END-OF-PAGE
END-PERFORM *
END-READ *
END-READY (V)
END-RECEIVE *
END-RECONNECT (V)
END-RETURN *
END-REWRITE *

END-ROLLBACK (V)
END-SEARCH *
END-START *
END-STORE (V)
END-STRING *
END-SUBTRACT *
END-UNSTRING *
END-WRITE *
ENTER
ENTRY (I)
ENVIRONMENT
EOP
EQUAL
EQUALS
ERASE
ERROR
ESI
EVALUATE *
EVERY **
EXCEEDS (V)
EXCEPTION
EXCLUSIVE (V)
EXIT
EXOR (V)
EXTEND
EXTERNAL *

FAILURE (V)
FALSE *
FD
FETCH (V)
FILE
FILE-CONTROL
FILE-LIMIT (I)
FILE-LIMITS (I)
FILLER
FINAL
FIND (V)
FINISH (V)
FIRST
FOOTING
FOR
FREE (V)
FROM

GENERATE
GET (V)
GIVING
GLOBAL *
GO
GOBACK (I)
GREATER
GROUP

HEADING
HIGH-VALUE
HIGH-VALUES

ID (I)
IDENTIFICATION
IF
IN
INCLUDING (V)
INDEX
INDEXED
INDICATE
INITIAL
INITIALIZE *

INITIATE
INPUT
INPUT-OUTPUT
INSERT (I)
INSPECT
INSTALLATION
INTO
INVALID
I-O
I-O-CONTROL
IS

JUST
JUSTIFIED

KANJI (I)
KEEP (V)
KEY

LABEL
LAST
LD (V)
LEADING
LEAVE (I)
LEFT
LENGTH
LESS
LIMIT
LIMITS
LINAGE
LINAGE-COUNTER
LINE
LINE-COUNTER
LINES
LINKAGE
LOCALLY
LOCK
LOW-VALUE
LOW-VALUES

MATCH (V)
MATCHES (V)
MEMBER (V)
MEMBERSHIP (V)
MEMORY **
MERGE
MESSAGE
MODE
MODIFY
MODULES **
MORE-LABELS (I)
MOVE
MULTIPLE
MULTIPLY

NATIVE
NEGATIVE
NEXT
NO
NOMINAL (I)
NON-NULL (V)
NONE (I)
NOT
NOTE (I)
NULL (V)/(I)
NULLS (I)
NUMBER
NUMERIC

NUMERIC-EDITED

OBJECT-COMPUTER
OCCURS
OF
OFF
OFFSET (V)
OMITTED
ON
ONLY
OPEN
OPTIONAL
OR
ORDER *
ORGANIZATION
OTHER *
OTHERS (V)
OUTPUT
OVERFLOW
OWNER (V)

PACKED-DECIMAL *
PADDING *
PAGE
PAGE-COUNTER
PARAGRAPH (I)
PASSWORD (I)
PERFORM
PF
PH
PIC
PICTURE
PLUS
POINTER
POSITION
POSITIVE
PRESENT (I)
PRINTING
PRIOR
PROCEDURE
PROCEDURES
PROCEED
PROGRAM
PROGRAM-ID
PROTECTED
PURGE *

QUEUE
QUOTE
QUOTES

RANDOM
RD
READ
READERS (V)
READY (V)/(I)
REALM
REALMS (V)
RECEIVE
RECONNECT
RECORD
RECORD-NAME
RECORD-OVERFLOW (I)
RECORDING (I)
RECORDS
REDEFINES
REEL
REFERENCE *

REFERENCE-MODIFIER (V)
REFERENCES
REGARDLESS (V)
RELATIVE
RELEASE
RELOAD (I)
REMAINDER
REMOVAL
RENAMES
REPLACE *
REPLACING
REPORT
REPORTING
REPORTS
REREAD (I)
RERUN
RESERVE
RESET
RETAINING
RETRIEVAL
RETURN
RETURN-CODE (I)
REVERSED
REWIND
REWRITE
RF
RH
RIGHT
RMS-FILENAME (V)
RMS-STS (V)
RMS-STV (V)
ROLLBACK (V)
ROUNDED
RUN

SAME
SCREEN (V)
SD
SEARCH
SECTION
SECURITY
SEGMENT
SEGMENT-LIMIT
SELECT
SEND
SENTENCE
SEPARATE
SEQUENCE
SEQUENCE-NUMBER (V)
SEQUENTIAL
SERVICE (I)
SET
SETS (V)
SHIFT-IN (I)

SHIFT-OUT (I)
SIGN
SIZE
SKIP-1 (I)
SKIP-2 (I)
SKIP-3 (I)
SORT
SORT-CONTROL (I)
SORT-CORE-SIZE (I)
SORT-FILE-SIZE (I)
SORT-MERGE
SORT-MESSAGE (I)
SORT-MODE-SIZE (I)
SORT-RETURN (I)
SOURCE
SOURCE-COMPUTER
SPACE
SPACES
SPECIAL-NAMES
STANDARD
STANDARD-1
STANDARD-2 *
START
STATUS
STOP
STORE
STRING
SUB-QUEUE-1
SUB-QUEUE-2
SUB-QUEUE-3
SUB-SCHEMA
SUBTRACT
SUCCESS (V)
SUM
SUPPRESS
SYMBOLIC
SYNC
SYNCHRONIZED

TABLE
TALLY (I)
TALLYING
TAPE
TENANT
TERMINAL
TERMINATE
TEST
TEXT
THAN
THEN *
THROUGH
THRU
TIME
TIME-OF-DAY (I)

TIMES
TITLE (I)
TO
TOP
TRAILING
TRUE *
TYPE

UNDERLINED (V)
UNEQUAL
UNIT
UNLOCK (V)
UNSTRING
UNTIL
UP
UPDATE
UPDATERS (V)
UPON
USAGE
USAGE-MODE (V)
USE
USING

VALUE
VALUES
VARYING

WAIT
WHEN
WHEN-COMPILED (I)
WHERE (V)
WITH
WITHIN
WORDS **
WORKING-STORAGE
WRITE
WRITE-ONLY (I)
WRITERS (V)

ZERO
ZEROES
ZEROS

+
-
*
/
**
>
<
=
>= *
<= *

FUNCTION NAMES INCLUDED IN THE EXTENSIONS TO COBOL 85

The following is the list of function names included in the extensions to COBOL 85:

ABS
ACOS
ANNUITY
ASIN
ATAN
CHAR
CHAR-NATIONAL

COS
CURRENT-DATE
DATE-OF-INTEGER
DAY-OF-INTEGER
DISPLAY-OF
EXCEPTION-FILE
EXCEPTION-LOCATION

EXCEPTION-STATEMENT
EXCEPTION-STATUS
EXP
FACTORIAL
FRACTION-PART
INTEGER
INTEGER-OF-DATE

INTEGER-OF-DAY	MOD	REVERSE
INTEGER-PART	NATIONAL-OF	SIGN
LENGTH	NUMVAL	SIN
LENGTH-AN	NUMVAL-C	SQRT
LOG	ORD	STANDARD-DEVIATION
LOG10	ORD-MAX	SUM
LOWER-CASE	ORD-MIN	TAN
MAX	PI	UPPER-CASE
MEAN	PRESENT-VALUE	VARIANCE
MEDIAN	RANDOM	WHEN-COMPILED
MIDRANGE	RANGE	
MIN	REM	

NEW COBOL 9X RESERVED WORDS

The following is the list of new COBOL 9x reserved words:

ALIGN	INHERITS	PROPERTY
B-AND	INTERFACE	RAISE
B-NOT	INTERFACE-ID	REPOSITORY
B-OR	INVARIANT	RESERVED
B-XOR	INVOKE	RETURNING
CLASS-ID	METHOD	REUSES
CONFORMING	METHOD-ID	SELF
END-INVOKE	NATIONAL	SUPER
EXCEPTION-OBJECT	NATIONAL-EDITED	SYSTEM-OBJECT
FACTORY	OBJECT	UNIVERSAL
FUNCTION	OVERRIDE	

APPENDIX B

Data Set for Programming Assignment 2 in Each Chapter

The following is a sample data set that can be used with Programming Assignment 2 of each chapter beginning with Chapter 4. Note that your instructor has a data disk for *all* programming assignments in the text.

This data set for Programming Assignment 2 can be used for a number of different applications. For some, columns 1–5 represent a CUST-NO, for others, an EMP-NO, and so on.

```
            1    1    2    2    3    3    4    4    5    5    6    6    7
  ....5....0....5....0....5....0....5....0....5....0....5....0....5....0
00001ADAMSON          01010400000145503242010215000675000400100011593
00002BAKER            01010500000195342500201275508005002500000032094
00003CARTWELL         01011000001278314590502170509752503003204109
00004DORSEY           01010450001128056510201280008005002902702029
00005HAMMOND          01020500000851297500402195009000010004005059
00006NOLTE            01020450001255583250402135009002502200506279
00007REDFORD          01020480001225759830302290758507501801011019
00008JOHNKE           02010550001285320000203220008002501001201159
00009WHITE            02010590000189744370102350006750000500006209
00010MARSHALL         02010530001258021960203270258005000803511299
00011EISEN            02010500001358012770401325009005004504009289
00012SAGER            02020680001955302190201290008002509504007259
00013STERN            02020680000885677240402320759000002001010019
00014SUMMERS          02020675000339955270101375006750002501502019
00015JONES            03010400000113387720903210009957501700905059
00016JOHNSON          03011000001458814770203225258007503201208019
00017NOLAN            03010447500518733230203325008002500200707159
00018CANTWELL         03020682501813795500102255506752508704006289
00019SMITH            03020750000112050300301110008505005203902159
00020HAMMEL           03020591001249867430202280008000000500203209
00021RAMIREZ          03020570430310590900635136290553310400007289
00022WASHINGTON       03020473082100667010314211721017903368400019
00023JAMES            03030457163093240100691078470992184650703219
00024LYONS            04010652029064207550156103510361003986100289
00025GREGORY          04010671905359420320507219131083675210308289
00026LINCOLN          04010432620180735220459163071106950572012289
00027NEWMAN           04020465310429978040245124220560033498211049
00028CARTWELL         04020470823534250770168221890877521043609049
00029DREYFUS          05010831081933063410632132630443940552118179
00030LOPEZ            05020920180374188020314156220932382005712289
00031FRANKLIN         05020445211841103830276034561004850236609209
00032FORTE            05020439723590620890233218310348113219812279
00033BYRON            05020556017210804710121175001069207773407259
00034KEATS            05030438943285144250416203660312960851905209
00035SUMTER           05030716132050821550635214920556354213717019
00036PITERIS          06040450000528795440165478912000124587406029
00037SIMOS            06040689000695525480556888457123110021419039
00038ASHLEY           06040758002357812220256871002145874445508049
00039BUTTERFIELD      06040432000052587770369855821470012457805059
00040CALIOPIS         06030960000239884470900369582147456665416069
00041DESEREY          06020850003695522880803256502584555442513069
00042FIELDSON         07010523001122056990731465589702155446911079
00043GALAGHER         07080890009988025210512258794002548023002159
00044HOUSTONS         07090520000685442130645687111245552020007169
00045JACKSON          07020870000988258770289878232333544801404179
00046KENDERSON        07020360000366651470245781002541479872501189
00047LIPSTERS         07020685000024144470112345556888124770305199
```

```
00048MANATARIS          07040400000699874420302541236987452145218209 5
00049NICHOLSON          08050555000665520310645877123654545781416219 5
00050OBERTON            08060750000114899450645687123002144587508229 3
00051PETERS             08060630000233564780823568711245003254817239 4
00052ROBERTS            08060652004581122000712554542358914725804249 4
00053SERGIS             08090870000458866450700214587012143692511289 3
00054TUCKERSON          08010650000982145660801245870001245558900199 5
00055VRICOLICSON        08020500000652333450912011474453021165815189 5
00056MACALUSO           08020758000639457880900124555241117113319179 5
00057KORNS              08030600005662111400978902235455546958805199 3
00058OKINS              09040756006547888000578978000214501245602129 3
00059FRIEDMAN           09050895009875522010145678780012124654505119 3
00060SANTOS             09050471000369852250178971254565800125504109 3
00061ANDOLINI           09040553000233566640212456547870144411016019 3
00062RUTH               09080500000147888250312354780001425525213029 3
00063APPLESEED          09030908000111245870412350005874144436915039 4
00064RIVERA             09020886230998722330578945123336002525018049 4
00065RIVERSON           09010529000687411470678925142202036985514079 4
```

APPENDIX C

Differences Among the COBOL Standards

The following are some major additions to COBOL 85 that we have discussed in the text. This list does *not* include every change from COBOL 74, just the more significant ones.

1. **Scope Terminators**
   Use the following terminators to produce a more well-designed program:

```
END-ADD              END-MULTIPLY         END-START
END-COMPUTE          END-PERFORM          END-STRING
END-DELETE           END-READ             END-SUBTRACT
END-DIVIDE           END-RETURN           END-UNSTRING
END-EVALUATE         END-REWRITE          END-WRITE
END-IF               END-SEARCH
```

Examples

```
1. IF  AMT1 = AMT2
       READ FILE-1
           AT END MOVE 'NO ' TO ARE-THERE-MORE-RECORDS
       END-READ
   END-IF
2. IF  AMT1 = AMT2
       ADD AMT1 TO TOTAL
           ON SIZE ERROR PERFORM 200-ERR-RTN
       END-ADD
   END-IF
```

2. The reserved word THEN may be used in a conditional, which makes COBOL conform more specifically to an IF-THEN-ELSE structure.

Example

```
IF  AMT1 < 0
THEN
    ADD 1 TO CTR1
ELSE
    ADD 1 TO CTR2
END-IF
```

3. **INITIALIZE Verb**
   A series of elementary items contained within a group item can all be initialized with this verb. Numeric items will be initialized at zero, and nonnumeric items will be initialized with blanks.

```
01  WS-REC-1.
    05                   PIC X(20).
    05   NAME            PIC X(20).
    05                   PIC X(15).
    05   AMT-1           PIC 9(5)V99.
    05                   PIC X(15).
    05   AMT-2           PIC 9(5)V99.
    05                   PIC X(15).
    05   TOTAL           PIC 9(6)V99.
    05                   PIC X(13).
       :
    INITIALIZE WS-REC-1
```

The above will set AMT-1, AMT-2, and TOTAL to zeros and will set all the other fields to spaces.

4. An in-line PERFORM is permitted, making COBOL more like pseudocode.

Example

```
PERFORM
    ADD AMT1 TO TOTAL
    ADD 1 TO CTR1
END-PERFORM
```

5. A TEST AFTER option may be used with the PERFORM ... UNTIL. This means that the test for the condition is made *after* the PERFORM is executed, rather than before, which ensures that the PERFORM is executed at least once.

Example

```
PERFORM 400-READ-RTN WITH TEST AFTER
    UNTIL NO-MORE-RECORDS
```

6. **EVALUATE Verb**

   The EVALUATE verb has been added. A programmer can now test a series of multiple conditions easily when each requires a different set of procedures to be performed. This implements the case structure in COBOL.

Example

```
EVALUATE CODE-IN
    WHEN 0 THRU 30
        PERFORM NO-PROBLEM
    WHEN 31 THRU 40
        PERFORM WARNING
    WHEN 41 THRU 60
        PERFORM ASSIGNED-RISK
    WHEN OTHER
        PERFORM 400-ERR-RTN
END-EVALUATE
```

7. **OCCURS**
   a. Up to seven levels of OCCURS are permitted for COBOL 85; only three levels are permitted for COBOL 74.
   b. An OCCURS item may contain initial contents—for all elements—with one VALUE clause. There is no need to REDEFINE the table or array.

8. **De-Editing: Moving Report Items to Numeric Fields**
   A report item such as one with a PIC $99,999.99 can be moved to a numeric item such as one with a PIC of 9(5)V99. This is called de-editing.

9. **DAY-OF-WEEK**
   DAY-OF-WEEK is a COBOL reserved word with a one-digit value. If the day of the run is Monday, DAY-OF-WEEK will contain a 1; if the day of the run is Tuesday, DAY-OF-WEEK will contain a 2; and so on.

10. **Relative MOVE**
    It is possible to reference a portion of an elementary item. Consider the following:

    ```
    MOVE CODE-IN (4:3) TO CODE-1
    ```

    This moves positions 4–6 of CODE-IN to CODE-1. Suppose CODE-IN is an eight-character field with contents 87325879 and CODE-1 is three positions. The above MOVE will result in 258 being moved to CODE-1.

11. Nonnumeric literals may contain up to 160 characters. With COBOL 74, the upper limit is 120 characters.

12. EXIT need not be the only word in a named paragraph.

13. Procedure names, such as those used in SORT ... INPUT PROCEDURE and SORT ... OUTPUT PROCEDURE can reference paragraph-names as well as section-names, making coding more structured and easier to read.

14. The CONFIGURATION SECTION is optional. In fact, the entire ENVIRONMENT DIVISION is optional, as is the DATA DIVISION.

15. The BLOCK CONTAINS clause may be omitted if the blocking is specified to the operating system some other way (e.g., with an operating system command).

16. The relational operators IS GREATER THAN OR EQUAL TO (>=) and IS LESS THAN OR EQUAL TO (<=) have been added.

17. The word TO in an ADD statement with a GIVING option is now optional. For example, you may code ADD AMT1 TO AMT2 GIVING TOTAL.

18. NOT ON SIZE ERROR, NOT AT END, and NOT INVALID KEY clauses are now permitted.

19. The WITH NO ADVANCING clause has been added to the DISPLAY statement, which means that interaction between the user and the terminal can be made more user-friendly. For example, DISPLAY 'ENTER ACCT NO.' WITH NO ADVANCING means that the prompt for ACCT NO will remain on the same line as the displayed message.

20. Lowercase letters are now included in the character set. They may be used in alphanumeric constants, which will be considered alphabetic and will pass an ALPHABETIC class test. If lowercase letters are used as identifiers, they will be considered equivalent to uppercase letters. The class tests ALPHABETIC-LOWER and ALPHABETIC-UPPER may be used for testing for lowercase or uppercase letters, respectively.

21. The comma, space, or semicolon used as separators are interchangeable.

22. A word following a level number may begin in Area A.

23. The INITIAL clause may be specified in the PROGRAM-ID paragraph to indicate that a program is to be in its initial state on each call to it.

24. The word FILLER is optional.

25. Relative or indexed files can be referenced in the USING and GIVING phrases of the SORT statement.

CHANGES IN THE NEW COBOL STANDARD (199x)

We highlight here some of the changes noted in the text:

1. Although current versions of COBOL require strict adherence to margin rules, COBOL 9x will eliminate these restrictions. Coding rules for Margins A and B will become recommendations, not requirements.

2. The PROGRAM-ID paragraph will be the only one permitted in the IDENTIFICATION DIVISION; all other entries (e.g., AUTHOR through SECURITY) can be specified as a comment.

3. The maximum length of user-defined names will increase from 30 to 60 characters.

4. The LABEL RECORDS clause will be phased out entirely.

5. VALUE clauses will be permitted in the FILE SECTION for defining initial contents of fields.

6. The way nonnumeric literals are continued will change, with the hyphen being eliminated from the continuation column (7). Instead, you will add a hyphen on the line being continued:

```
MOVE 'PART 1 OF LITERAL' -
    'PART 2 OF LITERAL' TO ABC
```

7. Commas and dollar signs will be permissible in numeric literals. Thus, $1,000.00 would be a valid numeric literal.

8. You will be able to code comments on a line with an instruction. *> will be used to add a comment to a line. After *> appears, characters to the end of the line will not be compiled.

9. MOVE CORRESPONDING will be phased out.

10. You will be able to perform arithmetic operations on report items.

11. You will be able to concatenate nonnumeric literals in a MOVE statement. For example:

```
MOVE    '  NAME      TRANSACTION'
    & ' NUMBER    AMOUNT'
       TO COLUMN-HDGS
```

12. If a field contains a VALUE clause, use of the INITIALIZE statement will not change the VALUE.

13. Spaces around arithmetic operators such as *, /, +, −, and ** will no longer be required.

14. The COMPUTE statement will yield the same results regardless of the compiler used by making the precision or number of decimal places in each intermediate calculation fixed.

15. The restrictions on the INSPECT statement limiting the AFTER/BEFORE items to one-character literals or fields in the REPLACING clause will be eliminated.

16. A VALIDATE statement will check the format of data fields and see that the contents of such fields fall within established ranges or have acceptable contents as defined by DATA DIVISION VALUEs.

17. You will be able to assign every occurrence of an element in a table the same initial value using a single VALUE clause.

18. The INDEXED BY and KEY phrases will be permitted in any sequence with an OCCURS. Now, INDEXED BY must precede the KEY clause.

19. You will be able to use the SORT verb to sort table entries as well as files.

20. A DELETE file-name statement will be added, enabling you to delete an entire file with a single instruction.

21. A COBOL screen management section will be added to the standard, making screen handling more consistent among compilers.

APPENDIX D
COBOL for the AS/400

This appendix provides a brief introduction to the COBOL/400 programming language used on the IBM AS/400 system. The COBOL/400 topics selected for this appendix are basic topics that might be helpful to students using this textbook and programming on an AS/400 computer system.

In June of 1988, IBM unveiled the Application System/400 (AS/400) midrange computer as the successor to the System/38 and System/36 models. As a follow-up to these highly successful System/3X lines, the AS/400 provides midrange users with a growth platform for the future. The AS/400 is not just another traditional computer system; it is a generation of computer systems based on advanced technologies and new applications. It is a multiuser system that combines the major strengths of both the System/38 and System/36 into a single product line that has become IBM's new strategic line of midrange computers.

The AS/400 incorporates features that are typically not provided in one computer system by a single vendor. Among these features are its powerful built-in database and support facilities, interactive workstation support, security, development support, and extendable architecture. It also includes a full set of advanced application development tools that has made the AS/400 extremely popular.

COBOL/400 AND THE ANSI COBOL 1985 STANDARD

IBM has implemented two COBOL compilers on the AS/400: RM/COBOL-85 and COBOL/400. Both COBOL compilers for the AS/400 are available from IBM. RM/COBOL-85 is also available from the Liant Corporation. An educational version can be obtained with this textbook.

RM/COBOL-85 is the Ryan McFarland implementation of COBOL that is fully compatible with the ANSI COBOL 85 Standard. In addition, RM/COBOL-85 includes extensions that provide support in writing interactive workstation applications and using externally described files on the AS/400.

With the release of the AS/400, IBM also announced COBOL/400, IBM's own ANSI COBOL 85 compiler. COBOL/400 incorporates many enhancements pertaining to the AS/400 that are not incorporated in the ANSI COBOL 85 Standard. Among them are extensions that aid in writing interactive workstation applications as well as support for AS/400 externally described files.

COBOL/400 RESERVED WORDS

To facilitate the use of COBOL on the AS/400, IBM provides several extensions to the ANSI COBOL 85 Standard. Table D.1 contains a list of the COBOL/400 reserved words that are extensions or enhancements to the 1985 ANSI Standard. Many of these enhancements pertain specifically to COBOL/400 programming in interactive and database environments.

Table D.1	COBOL/400 Reserved Words that Are an *IBM Extension* to the 1985 ANSI Standard			
ACQUIRE	EJECT	INDIC	PROCESS	STARTING
COMMIT	END-ACCEPT	INDICATOR	ROLLBACK	SUBFILE
COMMITMENT	EXTERNALLY-DESCRIBED-KEY	INDICATORS	ROLLING	TITLE
CONTROL-AREA	FORMAT	LIKE	SKIP1	TRANSACTION
DB-FORMAT-NAME	GOBACK	MODIFIED	SKIP2	WHEN-COMPILED
DROP	ID	PRIOR	SKIP3	

For more information about the usage of these reserved words refer to the IBM COBOL/400 User's Guide and Reference Manuals.

In addition to the reserved words unique to COBOL/400, there are many reserved words in the ANSI Standard that are *not* used by the COBOL/400 compiler. If used, a diagnostic message will be generated. These reserved words are listed in Table D.2. The only word in this list discussed in the text is DAY-OF-WEEK (see Chapter 6). Many of the words in Table D.2 are used with the Report Writer feature and since this feature has been rendered obsolete with COBOL 85 it is not supported in COBOL/400.

Table D.2	COBOL Reserved Words from the 1985 ANSI Standard that Are *Not* Used by the COBOL/400 Compiler			
ANY	DETAIL	LENGTH	QUEUE	SEGMENT
CD	DISABLE	LIMIT	RD	SEND
CF	EGI	LIMITS	RECEIVE	SOURCE
CH	EMI	LINE-COUNTER	REFERENCE	SUB-QUEUE-1
CLOCK-UNITS	ENABLE	MESSAGE	REPLACE	SUB-QUEUE-2
COBOL	END-RECEIVE	OTHER	REPORT	SUB-QUEUE-3
CODE	ESI	PADDING	REPORTING	SUM
COMMON	EXTERNAL	PAGE-COUNTER	REPORTS	SYMBOLIC
COMMUNICATION	FALSE	PF	RESET	TABLE
CONTENT	FINAL	PH	RD	TERMINATE
DAY-OF-WEEK	GLOBAL	PLUS	RF	TEXT
DE	GROUP	PURGE	RH	TYPE
DESTINATION	HEADING			

COBOL/400 ENHANCEMENTS

IDENTIFICATION DIVISION

Within the IDENTIFICATION DIVISION, the abbreviation ID may be substituted for IDENTIFICATION. Thus, ID DIVISION may be substituted for the standard division header as shown below:

```
ID DIVISION.
PROGRAM-ID.  EMPMSTLIST.
```

In addition, COBOL/400 uses the first 10 characters of the program-name specified in the PROGRAM-ID paragraph to identify the object program to the system. Thus, EMPMSTLIST could be used as a program-name.

LIKE CLAUSE

The LIKE clause allows the attributes of a data item or identifier to be defined by copying them from a previously defined data item. The characteristics that can be copied include the PICTURE, USAGE, SIGN, and BLANK WHEN ZERO characteristics.

One advantage of this clause is that it allows data items defined in the WORKING-STORAGE SECTION to have the same attributes as data items defined in externally described files and added to a program's DATA DIVISION using the COPY statement. The following two examples illustrate simple usages of the LIKE clause:

Example 1　In this example, a field called WS-NET-PAY specified in the WORKING-STORAGE SECTION is defined to have the same attributes as the field EM-EMPLOYEE-GROSS-PAY defined in a data record using the LIKE clause.

```
        1         2         3         4         5         6
..5..A.0.B..5....0....5....0....5....0....5....0....5....0....5
        05  EM-EMPLOYEE-GROSS-PAY        PIC 9(7)V9(2).
        :
      WORKING-STORAGE SECTION.
      01  WS-NET-PAY  LIKE  EM-EMPLOYEE-GROSS-PAY.
    * PICTURE IS 9(7)V9(2)
```

When the program is compiled, the attributes of the new field, in this example WS-NET-PAY, are listed by the compiler as comments immediately below the field.

Using the LIKE clause, the attributes of one data item can be copied to another data item and changes can be made to the length of the new data item.

Example 2　In this example, an integer (+2) is used to increase the length of the new field WS-YEARLY-SALES. Similarly, an integer can be used to decrease the length of the new field.

```
        1         2         3         4         5         6
..5..A.0.B..5....0....5....0....5....0....5....0....5....0....5
      WORKING-STORAGE SECTION.
      01  WS-MONTHLY-SALES                PIC 9(7)  COMP-3.
      01  WS-YEARLY SALES  LIKE  WS-MONTHLY-SALES (+2).
    * PICTURE IS 9(9)
    * USAGE IS PACKED-DECIMAL
```

In this example, the compiler has added two comment lines following the new field WS-YEARLY-SALES that identify the attributes of the field. Two comment lines have been added by the compiler because the new field WS-YEARLY-SALES acquired two attributes of the original field WS-MONTHLY-SALES: PIC 9(7) and COMP-3.

OVERVIEW OF AS/400 DATABASE CONCEPTS

The database support of the AS/400 system is integrated into both the machine and operating system and provides functions that allow for a high degree of data integrity and programmer productivity.

As noted in the text, a *database* is an organized collection of related files that can be joined to provide information to users. The database model used on the AS/400 is the relational model.

PHYSICAL FILES

A *physical file* is a file that contains data records. All the records have the same format; that is, they are fixed-length records and contain the same fields in the same order. For keyed access, indexes can be built using any field or combination of fields within the physical file.

Physical files are not dynamic. If you change the definition of a field, the change is not dynamically duplicated in all of the programs that refer to the file. Every program affected by the change still needs to be recreated.

EXTERNALLY DESCRIBED FILES

Files defined within a COBOL program are called *program-described files*. This means that both the file and record descriptions for the file are described internally within the DATA DIVISION. COBOL/400, however, enables the programmer to use record descriptions for a file that is defined external to the COBOL/400 program. A file described in this manner is called an *externally described file*. In this way, a file used by many programs within a system is described only once; it need not be described by each program that accesses it.

Using externally described files makes it easier to modify a file; the changes required need to be made only once. Thus, if the format of the file changes, the description of the externally described file is changed and the COBOL/400 code need not be modified at all. The COBOL/400 program would, however, have to be re-compiled to reflect the changes to the externally described file.

File processing within the PROCEDURE DIVISION for an externally described file is the same as for a file that has been described within the program.

USING EXTERNALLY DESCRIBED FILES

The programmer enters the source Data Description Specifications into the system and compiles the DDS to create a file object, usually called a file. After the file is created, data can be entered or modified in the file. The attributes of the file are stored with the DDS, external to any program that might access it. The COBOL/400 program references the externally described file by specifying the Format 2 version of the COPY statement in the FILE SECTION of the DATA DIVISION. When the COBOL/400 program is compiled, the external description of the file is retrieved from the system and included in the compiled COBOL/400 program. Because the fields are defined in the DDS, it is not necessary to define them in the DATA DIVISION.

DATA DESCRIPTION SPECIFICATIONS (DDS)

To define an externally described file, a specification form called Data Description Specifications or DDS is used (see Figure D.1).

Physical files are described to the AS/400 systems with the use of Data Description Specifications (DDS). The DDS defines the characteristics of the physical file. These include data field-names, their length and type, and other attributes such as the actual values (VALUE keyword) that are permissible in that field.

When writing COBOL/400 programs, externally described files are accessed by referencing the DDS entry for the appropriate physical file using the Format 2 version of the COPY statement. When the COBOL/400 program is compiled, the system will copy the pertinent information about the file and fields from the DDS into the program and compile it with the rest of the COBOL/400 program.

ACCESS PATHS

The access path is contained in the Data Description Specifications (DDS) of the externally described file and is the method used by the computer to retrieve input and write output. Records can be retrieved based on (1) an arrival sequence (nonkeyed) access path or (2) a keyed sequence access path.

Arrival Sequence Access Path

When records are added to a physical file they are added to the end of the file, an arrangement known as *arrival sequence*. The arrival sequence access path is based on the

Figure D.1 Data Description Specifications (DDS) form.

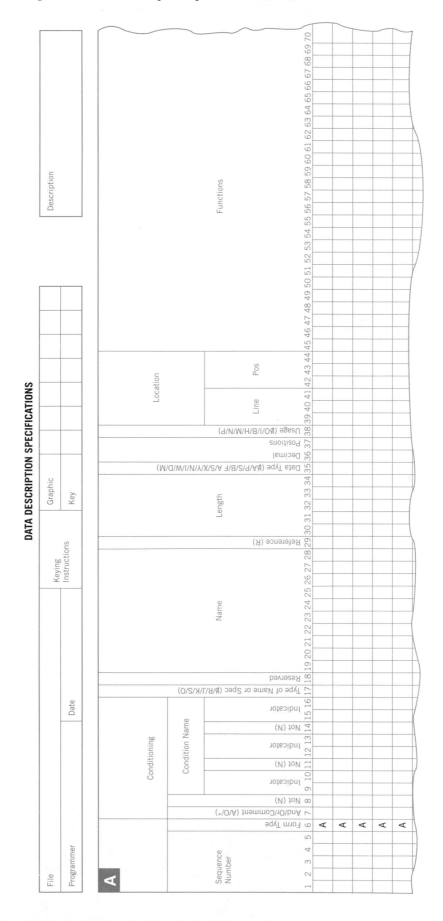

order in which the records are stored in the physical file. Consequently, when retrieving records using an arrival sequence access path, the records are retrieved sequentially from a physical file in the same sequence in which they were added to the file. This is known as the first-in first-out (FIFO) principle.

Keyed Sequence Access Path

A *keyed sequence access path* is based on the content of key fields within a record. When a physical file is created, key fields (indexes) provide the sequence in which records are to be retrieved from the file. When a record is added to a physical file that is indexed, the system automatically adds corresponding index records to all indexes that refer to that file and places those index records in their properly sorted positions in the indexes. For the keyed sequence access path, the sequence in which records are retrieved from the file is based on the contents of the key fields defined in the DDS for the file. This permits random access of records in the file. Thus, while the physical file itself is in arrival sequence, not in order by any set of field values, the indexes effectively provide such orderings.

DESCRIPTION OF THE DDS FOR PHYSICAL FILE (EMPMSTP)

The description of the records in an externally described file is called a record format. Figure D.2 shows the DDS source for the EMPMSTP physical file. A description of each line follows:

All DDS specifications have the letter A in position 6.

Line 100: A comment is indicated by an * in position 7. Comments are used to describe the Data Description Specifications (DDS) source. They do not become part of the object file when the source DDS is compiled.

Line 200: The UNIQUE keyword indicates that the key field, EMPNO, will be unique within the records. That is, an error will occur if a program tries to write a record to the file with a key value equal to an existing record.

Line 300: The record format is identified by a unique name and by the letter R in column 17. The name of the record EMPMSTR is entered in positions 19 through 28. Notice that the record name differs from the file-name. This is to meet a requirement that any names (files or records) must be unique in the program.

TEXT Keyword: A text description (TEXT keyword) is provided to describe the record. It also can be used to describe fields. The TEXT keyword is used for documentation and appears on a COBOL compilation listing that uses the field.

The left side of the form (positions 7 through 44) has specific positions for specific functions. Position 45 to the end of the specification line is the keyword area. The keyword area is more free-form and allows a wide variety of entries. Keywords include TEXT, COLHDG (column heading), and VALUE, which identifies the valid values that are permitted in a field.

Lines 400–500: The EMPNO (EM-EMPLOYEE-NUMBER) field is defined and the 5 in position 34 describes a length of 5 characters. The 0 in position 37 indicates that the field has zero decimal positions. Because there is an entry in the decimal field, the field is defined as *numeric*. The default is that if no decimal positions are defined (position 37 is blank), the field will be defined as a *character* field. The letter S in position 35 indicates that the data type is signed numeric.

COLHDG Keyword: One keyword for the EMPNO field is COLHDG, meaning *column heading*. A column heading is used to help describe the field. If no COLHDG keyword is entered, the column heading assigned is the field-name. Since the data-name EMPNO may not be meaningful to an end user, a column heading can be assigned to this field as well as every field in the physical file. Up to three lines can be used for the column heading.

Figure D.2 Data Description Specifications for the `EMPMSTP` Physical File.

DATA DESCRIPTION SPECIFICATIONS

Sequence Number (1–5)	Form Type (6)	And/Or/Comment (A/O/*) (7)	Not (N) (8)	Indicator (9–10)	Not (N) (11)	Indicator (12–13)	Not (N) (14)	Indicator (15–16)	Type of Name or Spec (ᵬ/R/J/K/S/O) (17)	Reserved (18)	Name (19–28)	Reference (R) (29)	Length (30–34)	Data Type (ᵬA/P/S/B/F A/S/X/Y/N/I/W/D/M) (35)	Decimal Positions (36–37)	Usage (ᵬO/I/B/H/M/N/P) (38)	Location Line (39–41)	Location Pos (42–44)	Functions (45–80)
ØØ1ØØ	A			P	H	YS	I	CA	L		FILE-EMPMS	T	P	E	MP	L	OYE	E M	ASTER FILE
ØØ2ØØ	A																		UNIQUE
ØØ3ØØ	A								R		EMPMSTR								TEXT('EMPLOYEE MASTER')
ØØ4ØØ	A										EMPNO		5	S	Ø				COLHDG('EMPLOYEE NUMBER')
ØØ5ØØ	A																		ALIAS(EM_EMPLOYEE_NUMBER)
ØØ6ØØ	A										ENAME		2Ø	A					COLHDG('EMPLOYEE NAME')
ØØ7ØØ	A																		ALIAS(EM_EMPLOYEE_NAME)
ØØ8ØØ	A										SALARY		7	P	2				COLHDG('EMPLOYEE SALARY')
ØØ9ØØ	A																		ALIAS(EM_EMPLOYEE_SALARY)
Ø1ØØØ	A								K		EMPNO								
	A																		

Line 500: The ALIAS keyword allows a data item to have an alternative name of up to 30 characters. When used, the ALIAS name will be copied to the COBOL/400 program instead of the field-name in positions 19 through 28.

Lines 600–700: The ENAME (EM-EMPLOYEE-NAME) field is described as a 20-byte character field (no decimal positions). A column heading and alias are assigned using the COLHDG and ALIAS keywords.

Lines 800–900: The SALARY (EM-EMPLOYEE-SALARY) field is defined as a five-digit packed-decimal field with no decimals. The letter P in position 35 indicates that the data type is packed-decimal. A column heading and alias are assigned using the COLHDG and ALIAS keywords.

Line 1000: The letter K in position 17 defines the EMPNO (EM-EMPLOYEE-NUMBER) field as the key field for this file.

SAMPLE COBOL/400 PROGRAM THAT ACCESSES AN EXTERNALLY DESCRIBED FILE

In the sample program shown in Figure D.3, there is one input file (EMPMSTP) and one output file (QPRINT). The purpose of this sample program is to print a listing of the Employee Master records read from an externally described file called EMPMSTP (**EMP**loyee **MaST**er **P**hysical file). The output file, a program-described print file, is named QPRINT. No calculations are performed on the data in the input records. Only a detail output listing is to be produced.

The description of the externally described file (EMPMSTP), created by DDS, is stored in the system independently of any program. The DDS that was used to define the EMPMSTP file was shown earlier in Figure D.2.

Figure D.3 Sample COBOL/400 program with compiled DDS included. Coding in color in the first three divisions identifies COBOL/400 code unique to the AS/400.

```
           1         2         3         4         5         6
.......A.0.B..5....0....5....0....5....0....5....0....5....0....5
        ID DIVISION.
        PROGRAM-ID. EMPMSTLIST.
        ************************************************************
        *     this program accesses a keyed employee          *
        *     master file sequentially and prints a report    *
        ************************************************************
        ENVIRONMENT DIVISION.
        CONFIGURATION SECTION.
        SOURCE-COMPUTER. IBM-AS400.
        OBJECT-COMPUTER. IBM-AS400.
        INPUT-OUTPUT SECTION.
        FILE-CONTROL.
            SELECT EMPLOYEE-MASTER-FILE
                ASSIGN TO DATABASE-EMPMSTP
                ORGANIZATION IS INDEXED
                ACCESS IS SEQUENTIAL
                RECORD KEY IS EXTERNALLY-DESCRIBED-KEY.
            SELECT PRINT-FILE ASSIGN TO PRINTER-QPRINT.
        *
        DATA DIVISION.
        FILE SECTION.
        FD  EMPLOYEE-MASTER-FILE
            LABEL RECORDS ARE STANDARD.
        01  EMPLOYEE-MASTER-RECORD.
        COPY DD-EMPMSTR OF EMPLIB-EMPMSTP.
```

The word DATABASE is required for keyed access or when using database features

When EXTERNALLY-DESCRIBED-KEY is used, the key fields are extracted from the DDS

This specification is used for print files

Figure D.3   (continued)

```
+000001*    I-O FORMAT:EMPMSTR    FROM FILE EMPMSTP    OF LIBRARY EMPLIB
+000002*                          EMPLOYEE MASTER RECORD
+000003*THE KEY DEFINITIONS FOR RECORD FORMAT  EMPMSTR
+000004*   NUMBER              NAME              RETRIEVAL    TYPE    ALTSEQ
+000005*   0001   EM-EMPLOYEE-NUMBER             ASCENDING   SIGNED    NO
+000006      05  EM-EMPMSTR.
+000007          06 EM-EMPLOYEE-NUMBER
+000008                                  PIC S9(5).
+000009*                      EMPLOYEE NUMBER
+000010          06 EM-EMPLOYEE-NAME   PIC X(20).
+000011*                      EMPLOYEE NAME
+000012          06 EM-EMPLOYEE-SALARY
+000013                                  PIC S9(5)       COMP-3.
+000014*                      EMPLOYEE SALARY
```

```
     FD  PRINT-FILE
         LABEL RECORDS ARE OMITTED.
     01  PRINT-RECORD               PIC X(132).
     WORKING-STORAGE SECTION.
     01  WORK-AREAS.
         05 ARE-THERE-MORE-RECORDS     PIC X(3)  VALUE 'YES'.
             88 NO-MORE-RECORDS                  VALUE 'NO '.
         05 WS-LINE-COUNTER            PIC 99    VALUE ZEROS.
         05 WS-PAGE-COUNTER  LIKE  WS-LINE-COUNTER VALUE ZEROS.
   * PICTURE IS 9(2)
     01  PRT-HEADING.
         05                            PIC X(55).
         05                            PIC X(43)
                     VALUE 'PAYROLL SUMMARY REPORT'.
         05                            PIC X(4)  VALUE 'PAGE'.
         05 PRT-PAGE-COUNTER           PIC ZZ9.
         05                            PIC X(27) VALUE SPACES.
     01  DETAIL-RECORD.
         05                            PIC X(9)  VALUE SPACES.
         05 PRT-EMPLOYEE-NUMBER        PIC 9(9).
         05                            PIC X(10) VALUE SPACES.
         05 PRT-EMPLOYEE-NAME          PIC X(20).
         05                            PIC X(10) VALUE SPACES.
         05 PRT-EMPLOYEE-SALARY        PIC $ZZ,ZZZ.
         05                            PIC X(62) VALUE SPACES.
   *
     PROCEDURE DIVISION.
     100-MAIN-MODULE.
         OPEN INPUT EMPLOYEE-MASTER-FILE
              OUTPUT PRINT-FILE
         PERFORM 300-HEADING-ROUTINE
         PERFORM UNTIL NO-MORE-RECORDS
             READ EMPLOYEE-MASTER-FILE
                 AT END
                     MOVE 'NO ' TO ARE-THERE-MORE-RECORDS
                 NOT AT END
                     PERFORM 200-DETAIL-PROCESSING
             END-READ
         END-PERFORM
         CLOSE EMPLOYEE-MASTER-FILE
               PRINT-FILE
         STOP RUN.
     200-DETAIL-PROCESSING.
         MOVE EM-EMPLOYEE-NUMBER TO PRT-EMPLOYEE-NUMBER
         MOVE EM-EMPLOYEE-NAME TO PRT-EMPLOYEE-NAME
         MOVE EM-EMPLOYEE-SALARY TO PRT-EMPLOYEE-SALARY
         IF  WS-LINE-COUNTER > 50
             PERFORM 300-HEADING-ROUTINE
         END-IF
```

Figure D.3 (continued)

```
WRITE PRINT-RECORD FROM DETAIL-RECORD
    AFTER ADVANCING 2 LINES
ADD 1 TO WS-LINE-COUNTER.
300-HEADING-ROUTINE.
ADD 1 TO WS-PAGE-COUNTER
MOVE WS-PAGE-COUNTER TO PRT-PAGE-COUNTER
WRITE PRINT-RECORD FROM PRT-HEADING
    AFTER ADVANCING PAGE
MOVE ZEROS TO WS-LINE-COUNTER.
```

With the AS/400, then, externally described files are easily defined and included in COBOL/400 programs. Let us consider two specific entries in this sample program that are unique to COBOL/400.

FORMAT 2 COPY STATEMENT

The Format 2 COPY statement is used to create a record description structure in the FILE SECTION from an externally described file that exists on the AS/400. In our example that follows, the COPY DD-EMPMSTR OF EMPLIB-EMPMSTP statement will import to the COBOL/400 program the record structure, including the field-names and attributes of the AS/400 file, which has already been defined externally to the program in DDS. The Format 2 version of the COPY statement does not copy the description from the source DDS. Instead, it extracts the description from the actual physical file that has been defined by DDS and compiled into a file object on the AS/400.

```
DATA DIVISION.
FILE SECTION.
FD  EMPLOYEE-MASTER-FILE
    LABEL RECORDS ARE STANDARD.
01  EMPLOYEE-MASTER-RECORD.
COPY DD-EMPMSTR OF EMPLIB-EMPMSTP.
```

The purpose of this COPY statement is to retrieve the DDS record description called EMPMSTR defined in the physical file EMPMSTP in library EMPLIB (**EMP**loyee **LIB**rary) and place the record description into the FILE SECTION as shown in Figure D.3.

This version of the COPY statement differs from the ANSI Standard COPY statement. The Format 2 version of the COPY statement is a database enhancement that allows the use of externally described files in a COBOL/400 program. It allows a COBOL/400 program to extract information from a compiled object, a file that was created using DDS and compiled into an object, on the AS/400.

The Format 2 COPY statement has four options: DD, DDR, DDS, or DDSR. Only the DD option will be presented here. The DD option is used to reference ALIAS or alternative names defined with the ALIAS keyword in the DDS. In this way, a data item of up to 30 characters can be included in the COBOL/400 program. All underscores in the ALIAS names are translated into hyphens when they are placed in the COBOL/400 program.

If the DDS option is used, only the field-names specified in positions 19 through 28 of the DDS will be copied into the COBOL/400 program. The DDR and DDSR options do everything the DD and DDS options do. They also replace characters used in the DDS that are not valid COBOL characters with valid COBOL characters when they are copied.

SELECT STATEMENT

The coding below represents the SELECT statement for our sample program:

```
FILE-CONTROL.
    SELECT EMPLOYEE-MASTER-FILE
    ASSIGN TO DATABASE-EMPMSTP
    ORGANIZATION IS INDEXED
    ACCESS IS SEQUENTIAL
    RECORD KEY IS EXTERNALLY-DESCRIBED-KEY.
```

When assigning disk files with the ASSIGN clause, DATABASE is required for keyed access or if special COBOL/400 database features are being used. Using DISK restricts the program to traditional disk processing.

When EXTERNALLY-DESCRIBED-KEY is specified as RECORD KEY in the SELECT statement, the fields that make up the record key are also extracted from DDS. These keys can be noncontiguous. If a file has multiple key fields that are *not* contiguous in each record, the EXTERNALLY-DESCRIBED-KEY must be specified in the RECORD KEY clause.

The SELECT statement for the printer file assigns the printer to QPRINT. The file QPRINT is a standard printer file supplied with the AS/400 operating system.

SAMPLE COBOL/400 INQUIRY PROGRAM

Interactive Processing.   This example illustrates how transactions can be entered interactively from the keyboard into a COBOL/400 program. It performs a basic inquiry into the Employee Master file used in Example 1. To perform this inquiry, Data Description Specifications must be created for the display screens that will be used by the COBOL/400 program. Figure D.4 shows the Data Description Specifications (DDS) for the EMPINQ Display File.

Figure D.4   Data Description Specifications for the EMPINQ Display File.

```
         1         2         3         4         5         6         7         8
6...0....5....0....5....0....5....0....5....0....5....0....5....0....5....0
A*  DISPLAY FILE-EMPINQ        EMPLOYEE MASTER INQUIRY FILE
A*
A                                          CA03(03 'F3=EXIT')
A            R EMPPMT                       TEXT('Employee Prompt')
A                                      1  3'Employee Master Inquiry'
A                                      3  3'Employee Number'
A              SEMPNO         5S 0I    3 20TEXT('Employee Number')
A  81                                      ERRMSG('Employee number not found, +
A                                          press reset, then enter valid numbe+
A                                          r' 81)
A                                      5  3'F3=Exit'
A                                      5 11'ENTER=Continue'
A            R EMPFLDS                      TEXT('Employee Display')
A                                          OVERLAY
A                                      8  3'Name'
A              SNAME         20    O   8  8TEXT('Employee Name')
A                                      9  3'Salary'
A              SSALRY         5    0O   9 12TEXT('Employee Salary')
```

The Data Description Specifications (DDS) for the EMPINQ (**EMP**loyee **INQ**uire) Display file has two record formats: EMPPMT (**EMP**loyee **P**ro**M**p**T**) and EMPFLDS (**EMP**loyee **FieLDS**).

The EMPPMT record format, shown below, allows the user to enter a value for employee number (SEMPNO), which is the key field for the file. The employee number entered by the user is used to randomly retrieve the record from the file:

Display for EMPPMT record format

```
Employee Master Inquiry

Employee Number _____

F3=Exit ENTER=Continue
```

The EMPPMT record format contains the constant 'Employee Master Inquiry', which is used to identify the display. It also contains a prompt, labeled 'Employee Number', and an input field called SEMPNO, where the user will enter the employee number. When the SEMPNO appears on the screen, underscores will also appear where the user is to enter the employee number. These underscores represent the length of the field.

If the employee number requested by the user is not found in the master file, the program will set ON indicator 81 (IN81 = B'0'). When indicator 81 is ON, the error message 'Employee number not found' will be displayed as shown here:

This display appears if the employee number entered by the user on the EMPPMT display was not found in the employee master file EMPMSTP

```
Employee Master Inquiry

Employee Number 12345

F3=Exit ENTER=Continue


Employee number not found, press Reset,
then enter valid number
```

In addition, a function key (F3) is defined that will be used by the user to end the program (EXIT). When the user presses function key F3, indicator 03 is set ON in the COBOL/400 program and the program terminates.

The second record format, EMPFLDS, is used to display two output fields on the screen as shown here:

The EMPFLDS record format appears if a record is found in the EMPMSTP file for the employee number requested by the user on the EMPPMT display

```
Employee Master Inquiry

Employee Number 12345

F3=Exit ENTER=Continue


Name Paul Smith
Salary 42000
```

Along with the fields SNAME (employee name) and SSALRY (employee salary), the record format contains the lengths and number of decimal positions. In addition, there are two constants that are used to identify these fields when they are displayed on the screen.

The record format also defines the line numbers and horizontal positions where the constants and fields will be displayed when the record is written to the screen.

When the EMPFLDS format is displayed on the screen, it will overlay the EMPPMT record as indicated by the OVERLAY keyword. Therefore, when the EMPFLDS record is written to the screen, the information from the EMPPMT record remains on the screen.

DEFINING A TRANSACTION FILE IN THE FILE-CONTROL PARAGRAPH

Interactive Processing.   COBOL/400 allows an input and output file called TRANS-ACTION. The transaction file organization (ORGANIZATION IS TRANSACTION), shown below, allows an interactive program to send or receive records from a workstation:

```
SELECT EMPLOYEE-DISPLAY
    ASSIGN TO WORKSTATION-EMPINQ
    ORGANIZATION IS TRANSACTION.
```

When ORGANIZATION IS TRANSACTION is used in an interactive program, records are read from and written to the display screen using the READ and WRITE statements rather than ACCEPT and DISPLAY.

INDICATORS IN COBOL/400 PROGRAMS

Interactive Processing.   When writing interactive programs, indicators or switches are used to communicate between the COBOL/400 program and the display file. *Indicators* are Boolean data items that can have the values B"0" or B"1". They can be used to (1) condition the attributes of a display file during the processing of an interactive program and (2) reflect function key responses that can control the processing of a program by relating function keys to indicators (switches) within the program.

Our sample program uses indicator 03 to EXIT (end the program) and indicator 81 to represent the 'Employee number not found' error condition. See Figure D.5 for the full sample COBOL/400 inquiry program.

Figure D.5   Sample COBOL/400 inquiry program. Coding in color in the first three divisions identifies COBOL/400 code unique to the AS/400.

```
        1         2         3         4         5         6
......A.O.B..5....0....5....0....5....0....5....0....5....0....5
      ID DIVISION.
      PROGRAM-ID. EMPMSTINQ.
      ***********************************************************
      *     sample inquiry program                        *
      ***********************************************************
      ENVIRONMENT DIVISION.
      CONFIGURATION SECTION.
      SOURCE-COMPUTER. IBM-AS400.
      OBJECT-COMPUTER. IBM-AS400.
      INPUT-OUTPUT SECTION.
      FILE-CONTROL.
          SELECT DISPLAY-FILE
              ASSIGN TO WORKSTATION-EMPINQ          WORKSTATION means that data will be
              ORGANIZATION IS TRANSACTION.          entered at the keyboard and the
          SELECT EMPLOYEE-MASTER-FILE               output will be displayed on a screen
              ASSIGN TO DATABASE-EMPMSTP
              ORGANIZATION IS INDEXED
              ACCESS IS RANDOM
              RECORD KEY IS EXTERNALLY-DESCRIBED-KEY.
      *
      DATA DIVISION.
      FILE SECTION.
      FD  DISPLAY-FILE
          LABEL RECORDS ARE OMITTED.
      01  DISPLAY-RECORD.
      COPY DDS-ALL-FORMATS OF EMPLIB-EMPINQ.
```

Figure D.5 (continued)

```
+000001        05   EMPINQ-RECORD PIC X(25).
+000002*  INPUT FORMAT:EMPPMT    FROM FILE EMPINQ    OF LIBRARY EMPLIB
+000003*                      Employee Prompt
+000004     05   EMPPMT-I      REDEFINES EMPINQ-RECORD.
+000005        06   EMPPMT-I-INDIC.
+000006           07  IN03         PIC 1   INDIC 03.
+000007*                 F3=EXIT
+000008           07  IN81         PIC 1   INDIC 81.
+000009*     Employee number not found, press enter, then valid number
+000010        06   SEMPNO          PIC S9(5).
+000011*                 Employee Number
+000012*  OUTPUT FORMAT:EMPPMT   FROM FILE EMPINQ    OF LIBRARY EMPLIB
+000013*                      Employee Prompt
+000014     05   EMPPMT-O      REDEFINES EMPINQ-RECORD.
+000015        06   EMPPMT-O-INDIC.
+000016           07  IN81         PIC 1   INDIC 81.
+000017*     Employee number not found, press enter, then valid number
+000018*  INPUT FORMAT:EMPFLDS    FROM FILE EMPINQ    OF LIBRARY EMPLIB
+000019*                      Employee Display
+000020     05   EMPFLDS-I     REDEFINES EMPINQ-RECORD.
+000021        06   EMPFLDS-I-INDIC.
+000022           07  IN03         PIC 1   INDIC 03.
+000023*                 F3=EXIT
+000024*  OUTPUT FORMAT:EMPFLDS   FROM FILE EMPINQ    OF LIBRARY EMPLIB
+000025*                      Employee Display
+000026     05   EMPFLDS-O     REDEFINES EMPINQ-RECORD.
+000027        06   SNAME          PIC X(20).
+000028*             Employee Name
+000029        06   SSALRY         PIC S9(5).
+000030*             Employee Salary
```

```
     FD   EMPLOYEE-MASTER-FILE
          LABEL RECORDS ARE STANDARD.
     01   EMPLOYEE-MASTER-RECORD.
          COPY DD-EMPMSTR OF EMPLIB-EMPMSTP.
```

```
+000001*   I-O FORMAT:EMPMSTR   FROM FILE EMPMSTP    OF LIBRARY EMPLIB
+000002*                 EMPLOYEE MASTER RECORD
+000003*THE KEY DEFINITIONS FOR RECORD FORMAT  EMPMSTR
+000004*  NUMBER              NAME              RETRIEVAL     TYPE    ALTSEQ
+000005*  0001   EM-EMPLOYEE-NUMBER            ASCENDING   SIGNED     NO
+000006     05   EM-EMPMSTR.
+000007        06   EM-EMPLOYEE-NUMBER
+000008                          PIC S9(5).
+000009*             EMPLOYEE NUMBER
+000010        06   EM-EMPLOYEE-NAME    PIC X(20).
+000011*             EMPLOYEE NAME
+000012        06   EM-EMPLOYEE-SALARY
+000013                          PIC S9(5)        COMP-3.
+000014*             EMPLOYEE SALARY
```

```
     WORKING-STORAGE SECTION.
     01   ONE                     PIC 1      VALUE B'1'.
     *
     PROCEDURE DIVISION.
     100-MAIN-MODULE.
          OPEN I-O   DISPLAY-FILE
               INPUT  EMPLOYEE-MASTER FILE
          MOVE ZERO TO IN81 OF EMPPMT-O
[1]       WRITE DISPLAY-RECORD FORMAT IS 'EMPPMT'
[2]       READ DISPLAY-FILE RECORD
          PERFORM 200-DETAIL-PROCESSING
               UNTIL IN03 OF EMPPMT-I  IS EQUAL TO ONE
               OR    IN03 OF EMPFLDS-I IS EQUAL TO ONE
          CLOSE DISPLAY-FILE
               EMPLOYEE-MASTER-FILE
          STOP RUN.
```

Figure D.5 (continued)

```
        200-DETAIL-PROCESSING.
            MOVE SEMPNO TO EM-EMPLOYEE-NUMBER
[3]         READ EMPLOYEE-MASTER-FILE RECORD
                INVALID KEY MOVE ONE TO IN81 OF EMPPMT-O
            IF IN81 OF EMPPMT-O IS EQUAL TO ONE
                PERFORM 210-INVALID-EMPLOYEE-NUMBER
            ELSE
                PERFORM 220-WRITE-EMPFLDS-DISPLAY
            END-IF.
        210-INVALID-EMPLOYEE-NUMBER.
            WRITE DISPLAY-RECORD FORMAT IS 'EMPPMT'
            MOVE ZERO TO IN81 OF EMPPMT-O
            READ DISPLAY-FILE RECORD.
        220-WRITE-EMPFLDS-DISPLAY.
            MOVE EM-EMPLOYEE-NAME TO SNAME
            MOVE EM-EMPLOYEE-SALARY TO SSALRY
[4]         WRITE DISPLAY-RECORD FORMAT IS 'EMPFLDS'
            READ DISPLAY-FILE RECORD
            IF IN03 OF EMPFLDS-I IS NOT EQUAL TO ONE
                MOVE ZERO TO IN81 OF EMPPMT-O
                WRITE DISPLAY-RECORD FORMAT IS 'EMPPMT'
                READ DISPLAY-FILE RECORD
            END-IF.
```

The first WRITE operation [1] writes the EMPPMT format to the screen. This display prompts the user to enter an employee number. If the user enters an employee number and presses the Enter key, the next READ operation [2] then reads the record back into the program.

The READ operation [3] for the EMPMSTP file uses the employee number (SEMPNO) field to retrieve the corresponding employee master record (EMPMSTR) from the EMPMSTP file. If no record is found in the EMPMSTP file, indicator 81 is set on. An indicator is used so the program can communicate to the display file that there is an error condition. The message 'Employee number not found' is displayed when the format is written to the screen because it is conditioned by indicator 81 in the DDS for the EMPPMT record format. When the user receives this message, the keyboard locks. The user must press the Reset key in response to this message and unlock the keyboard. Once the keyboard is unlocked, the user can enter another employee number.

If the READ operation is successful in retrieving a record from the EMPMSTP file, the WRITE operation [4] writes the EMPFLDS format to the screen. This format contains the employee name and salary.

Once the user verifies the employee name and salary, he or she can press the Enter key and the program returns to the beginning of the cycle and prompts for a new employee number.

To end the program, the user presses F3, which sets on indicator 03. The ON status of indicator 03 is passed to the program when the record is read from the screen. When indicator 03 is ON, the program closes the two files and processes the STOP RUN statement.

The actual display screens for the sample program are illustrated below:

This display is the initial EMPPMT display written by the WRITE operation [1]

```
Employee Master Inquiry

Employee Number _____

F3=Exit ENTER=Continue
```

This display appears if a record is found in the EMPMSTP file for the employee number requested by the user on the prompt display [4]

```
Employee Master Inquiry

Employee Number 12345

F3=Exit ENTER=Continue


Name Paul Smith
Salary 42000
```

This display appears if the employee number entered by the user on the prompt display was not found in the employee master file EMPMSTP [4]

```
Employee Master Inquiry

Employee Number 12345

F3=Exit ENTER=Continue


Employee number not found, press Reset,
then enter valid number
```

APPENDIX E

Glossary

ACCEPT. A statement used for reading in a low volume of input; unlike a READ, an ACCEPT does not require establishing a file with a SELECT statement, nor does it require an OPEN statement.

ADD. A statement used for performing an addition operation.

AFTER ADVANCING. An option with the WRITE statement that can cause the paper in a printer to space any number of lines *before* an output record is printed.

Alphanumeric field. A field that can contain any character.

Alphanumeric literal. See **nonnumeric literal**.

American National Standards Institute (ANSI). An organization of academic, business, and government users that develops standards in a wide variety of areas, including programming. There are several versions of American National Standard COBOL—1968, 1974, and 1985.

Applications package. A prewritten program or set of programs designed to perform user-specified tasks. Contrast with **customized programs**.

Applications program. A program designed to perform user-specified tasks. It may be part of an applications package or it may be a customized program. Contrast with **operating systems software**.

Applications programmer. The computer professional who writes the set of instructions in an applications program. Same as **software developer**.

Area A. Columns 8–11 of a COBOL coding sheet or program; some COBOL entries must begin in Area A, that is, column 8.

Area B. Columns 12–72 of a COBOL coding sheet or program; most COBOL entries must begin in Area B, that is, anywhere from column 12 on.

Array. A storage area consisting of numerous fields, all with the same format; commonly used for storing totals.

Ascending sequence. The ordering of data so that a key field in the first record is less than the key field in the next, and so on.

ASCII code. A common computer code for representing data; an acronym for *A*merican *Stan*dard *C*ode for *I*nformation *I*nterchange.

AT END. A clause used with a sequential READ statement to indicate the operations to be performed when an end-of-file condition has been reached.

Audit trail. A control listing that specifies changes made to a master file, errors encountered, the number of records processed, and any other data that might be helpful in ensuring the overall validity and integrity of an applications program.

AUTHOR. A paragraph coded in the IDENTIFICATION DIVISION after the PROGRAM-ID. It is typically used for documentation purposes to identify the programmer.

Batch processing. A mode of processing where data is accumulated and processed as a group rather than immediately as the data is generated.

Batch total. A count of records within specific groups (e.g., departments, territories, and so on) used for control purposes to minimize the risk of records being misplaced or incorrectly transmitted.

BEFORE ADVANCING. An option with the WRITE statement that can cause the paper in a printer to space any number of lines *after* an output record is printed.

Binary search. An efficient method of searching a series of entries in a table or array that are in sequence by some key field. Contrast with **serial search**.

BLANK WHEN ZERO. A clause used in the DATA DIVISION to ensure that a field consisting of all zeros will print as blanks.

BLOCK CONTAINS. A clause used in an FD to indicate the blocking factor of disk or tape files.

Blocking. Combining several logical records into one physical record to conserve space on a disk or tape.

Business Information System. An organized set of procedures for accomplishing a set of business operations.

CALL. A COBOL statement for accessing a subprogram.

Called program. A subprogram or program called into a user program as needed.

Calling program. A program that calls a subprogram.

Case structure.   A logical control structure used when there are numerous paths to be followed depending on the contents of a given field. The EVALUATE verb in COBOL 85 is used for implementing the case structure.

Character.   A single letter, digit, or special symbol. Fields such as NAME or SALARY are composed of individual characters.

Check digit.   A computed integer added to a key field and used for minimizing the risk of transposition and transcription errors during the data entry process.

Check protection symbol (∗).   A symbol used to minimize the risk of people tampering with a check amount; e.g., $ 1.25 would print as $∗∗∗∗∗1.25 using the asterisk (∗) as a check protection symbol.

Class.   A set of objects that share attributes (data and procedures).

Class test.   A data validation procedure used to ensure that input is entered in the appropriate data format, that is, numeric, alphabetic, or alphanumeric.

CLOSE.   A statement that deactivates files and devices used in a program.

COBOL character set.   The full set of characters that may be used in a COBOL program. These characters are listed in Appendix A.

Coded field.   A type of field in which a code is used to designate data; for example, 'M' may be a code to designate 'Married' in a Marital Status field; coded fields make records shorter and more manageable.

Coding sheet.   A form that contains the specific columns in which entries are required in a programming language.

Cohesion.   A program exhibits cohesion when it has modules that perform only one self-contained set of operations, leaving unrelated tasks to other modules.

Collating sequence.   The specific order in which characters are represented by a computer; for example, A < B < . . . Z and 0 < 1, . . . < 9. The two common computer codes, ASCII and EBCDIC, have slightly different collating sequences with regard to special characters and lowercase letters.

Compile (Compilation).   The process of translating a symbolic program into machine language so that it can be executed.

Compiler.   A special translator program used to convert source programs into object programs.

Compound conditional.   An IF statement in which there are two or more conditions being tested; each condition is separated by the word OR or AND.

COMPUTE.   A statement used for performing a series of arithmetic operations.

Concatenation.   The process of joining several fields together to form one field; a method of linking records, fields, or characters into one entity.

Conditional statement.   An instruction that uses the word IF to test for the existence of a condition.

Condition-name.   A name assigned to a specific value or a range of values that an identifier can assume; IF (condition-name) is the same as IF (identifier = value), where the value is assigned to the condition-name; used on the 88-level in the DATA DIVISION.

CONFIGURATION SECTION.   A section of the ENVIRONMENT DIVISION that describes the source and object computers and any SPECIAL-NAMES used.

Constant.   A fixed value or literal that is used in a program.

Continuation position.   Column 7 of a COBOL coding form or line can contain a hyphen (-) for continuing a nonnumeric literal from one line to the next.

Continuous form.   A continuous sheet of paper separated only by perforations and typically used by a computer's printer for printed output.

Control break processing.   The use of a control field for causing groups of records to be processed as one unit.

Control field.   A key field used to indicate when totals are to print; used in control break processing.

CONTROL FOOTING.   Produced by the Report Writer Module, a control footing prints at the end of a control group for a given control item.

CONTROL HEADING.   Produced by the Report Writer Module, a control heading prints at the beginning of a control break for each new control group.

Control listing.   A computer-produced report used for control or checking purposes; typically includes (1) identifying information about all input records processed by the computer, (2) any errors encountered, and (3) a total of records processed. See **audit trail.**

COPY.   A statement for copying files, records, routines, and so on from a source statement library.

Counter field.   A field used to sum the number of occurrences of a given condition.

Cursor.   A symbol, such as a blinking square or a question mark, that indicates where on a screen the next character will be entered.

Customized program.   An applications program that is written for a specific user.

Database.   A collection of related files that can be cross-referenced for inquiry and reporting purposes.

DATA DIVISION.   One of the four major divisions of a COBOL program; it defines and describes all data to be used in a program.

Data exception error.   A common logic error that occurs if data is designated in a PIC clause as numeric, but does not actually contain numeric data.

Data-name.   The name assigned to each field, record, and file in a COBOL program. A data-name, unlike an identifier, may *not* be subscripted or qualified.

Data validation.   Techniques used to minimize the risk of errors by checking input, insofar as is possible, before processing it.

DATE.   The COBOL reserved word used for obtaining the date of a program run in yymmdd format.

DATE-COMPILED.   A paragraph in the IDENTIFICATION DIVISION for indicating the date when a program was compiled.

DATE-WRITTEN.   A paragraph in the IDENTIFICATION DIVISION for indicating the date when a program was coded.

Debugging.   The process of testing a program to eliminate errors.

Default.   The computer system's normal options that are implemented unless the programmer specifically requests an alternative.

DELETE.   A statement used to delete records from indexed files.

Descending sequence.   The ordering of data so that a key field in the first record is greater than the key field in the next and so on; that is, the first record has a key field with the greatest value.

Desk checking.   A method of debugging programs by manually checking for typographic, keying, and other errors prior to a compilation; this method of debugging reduces computer time.

DETAIL.   Produced by the Report Writer Module, one or more detail lines are printed for each input record read.

Detail report.   The printing of one or more lines for each input record read. Same as **transaction report**.

Diagnostic message.   An explanation of a syntax error.

Digit extraction.   One of numerous randomizing algorithms for converting a numeric key field to a disk address using the relative method of file organization.

Direct access.   See **random access**.

Direct-referenced table.   A type of table that can be accessed directly by using an input field as a subscript, thereby eliminating the need for a SEARCH.

DISPLAY.   A statement used for printing or displaying a low volume of output; unlike a WRITE, a DISPLAY does not require establishing a file with a SELECT statement, nor does it require the use of an OPEN statement.

DIVIDE.   A statement used for performing a division operation.

Divide exception.   An error that occurs when you attempt to divide a field by zero.

DIVISION.   One of four major parts of a COBOL program.

Division algorithm method.   A hashing technique used to calculate record addresses in a relative file.

Documentation.   The formal set of documents that describes a program or system and how to use it.

EBCDIC code.   A common computer code for representing data on IBM and IBM-compatible mainframes; an acronym for Extended Binary Coded Decimal Interchange Code.

Edit symbol.   A symbol such as $, −, and * used in a report-item to make printed or displayed output more readable.

Editing.   The process of converting data that is typically stored in a concise form into a more readable form; for example, $1,235.46 would be an edited version of 123546.

Elementary item.   A field that contains a PIC clause; a field that is not further subdivided.

Encapsulation.   Hiding the data and procedures in an object behind a user interface so that the user program need not be concerned about the details and so that security can be maintained.

End-of-file.   A condition that indicates when the last data record has been read and processed.

Enhancements. Options that are provided by some COBOL compilers; these options are in addition to the standard requirements of an ANS compiler.

ENVIRONMENT DIVISION. One of four major divisions of a COBOL program, it provides information on the equipment used with the program. This is the only division that may be machine-dependent.

EVALUATE. A COBOL 85 statement used to implement the case structure; it tests for a series of values.

Exception report. The printing of detail records that fall outside established guidelines, that is, records that are "exceptions" to a rule.

Execution error. A major-level syntax error that will prevent program execution. Also called a fatal error.

EXIT. A COBOL reserved word that may be used to terminate a paragraph; for COBOL 74, it is used to indicate that "no operation" is required in the paragraph.

EXIT PROGRAM. The last entry in a called program.

External table. A table stored on disk or other auxiliary storage device that is loaded into the program as needed. Modifying or updating such tables does not require modification of the program using the table. Contrast with **internal table**.

FD. See **file description**.

Field. A group of consecutive characters used to represent a unit of information; for example, a NAME field or an AMOUNT field.

FIFO (first in, first out). The technique of storing records so that the first one entered is the first one available for outputting; analogous to a queue or waiting line where the first entry is the one handled first.

Figurative constant. A COBOL reserved word, such as SPACES or ZEROS, where the word denotes the actual value; for example, MOVE ZEROS TO TOTAL will result in all 0's in the field called TOTAL.

File. A major collection of data consisting of records.

FILE-CONTROL. A paragraph in the INPUT-OUTPUT SECTION of the ENVIRONMENT DIVISION where each file to be used in the program is assigned to a device.

File description (FD). Entries used to describe an input or output file.

FILE SECTION. The section of the DATA DIVISION in which input and output files are defined and described.

FILE STATUS. The FILE STATUS clause can be used with a SELECT statement for determining the result of an input/output operation. If an input or output error has occurred, the FILE STATUS field indicates the specific type of error.

FILLER. A COBOL reserved word used to designate a field that will not be accessed by the program.

Fixed-length records. Records within a file that are all the same length.

Flag. See **switch**.

Floating string. An edit symbol, such as a $, that will appear adjacent to the first significant digit.

Flowchart. A planning tool that provides a pictorial representation of the logic to be used in a program.

Folding. One of numerous randomizing algorithms used to convert a numeric key field to a disk address using the relative method of file organization.

GO TO. A branch instruction that transfers control from one paragraph to another; GO TO statements are to be avoided in structured COBOL programs; that is, PERFORM statements should be used in place of GO TOs.

Group item. A field that is further subdivided into elementary fields with PICTURE clauses.

Group report. The printing of one line of output for groups of input records; usually used to summarize data. Same as **summary report**.

Hashing. A technique for transforming a record's key field into a relative record number.

Header label. The first record recorded on a disk or tape for identification purposes.

Hierarchy chart. A planning tool for specifying the relationships among modules in a program; another term for hierarchy chart is structure chart or visual table of contents (VTOC); a tool used to depict top-down logic.

High-order position. The leftmost, or most significant, character in a field.

HIGH-VALUES. A COBOL reserved word that represents the largest value in the computer's collating sequence; may be used only with fields defined as alphanumeric.

IDENTIFICATION DIVISION. The first division of a COBOL program; used for documentation purposes.

Identifier. The name assigned to fields and records in a COBOL program. An identifier, unlike a data-name, may be subscripted or qualified.

IF-THEN-ELSE. A logical control structure that executes a step or series of steps depending on the existence of a specific condition or conditions. Same as **selection**.

Imperative statement. Begins with a verb and specifies an unconditional action to be taken by the computer; contrast with **conditional statement**.

Implementor-name. A system-dependent term that equates a user-defined entry with a specific device.

Implied decimal point. The place where a decimal point is assumed to be in a field; PIC 99V99, for example, has an implied decimal point between the second and third positions; for example, 1234 in a field with PIC 99V99 is assumed to have a value of 12.34 for arithmetic and comparison purposes.

Index (for an indexed disk file). A reference table that stores the key field and the corresponding disk address for each record that is in an indexed disk file.

Index (INDEXED BY with OCCURS). The indicator used to reference an item defined by an OCCURS clause or subordinate to an item defined by an OCCURS clause. An index functions just like a subscript; unlike a subscript, however, an index is not defined separately in WORKING-STORAGE.

Indexed file. A method of file organization in which each record's key field is assigned a disk address; used when random access of disk records is required.

Infinite loop. An error condition in which a program would continue performing a module indefinitely or until time has run out for the program.

Information system. A set of computerized business procedures in a specific application area.

Inheritance. The ability for objects to share attributes held by other objects in the same class.

INITIALIZE. A COBOL 85 statement that sets numeric fields to zero and nonnumeric fields to spaces.

In-line PERFORM. A PERFORM statement without a paragraph-name, which is followed by all instructions to be executed at that point; it is delimited with an END-PERFORM. Available with COBOL 85.

Input. The data that is entered into a computer system.

INPUT-OUTPUT SECTION. That section of the ENVIRONMENT DIVISION that provides information on the input/output devices used in the program and the names assigned to the devices.

INPUT PROCEDURE. An option used with the SORT statement to process input records prior to sorting them.

INSPECT. A statement for counting the occurrence of specific characters in a field and for replacing one character with another.

INSTALLATION. A paragraph coded in the IDENTIFICATION DIVISION for documentation purposes; used to denote where the program is run.

Instantiation. Establishing a new instance of an object in a class.

Interactive processing. A mode of processing where data is operated on as soon as it is transacted or generated.

Intermediate result field. A field defined in WORKING-STORAGE that is necessary for performing calculations but is not part of either the input or the output areas.

Internal table. A table defined in a program with the use of VALUE clauses. Modifying or updating such tables requires program modification, which always increases the risk of errors. Contrast with **external table**.

Intrinsic function. A built-in function such as SQRT (X), which calculates the square root of X.

INVALID KEY. A clause that can be used with READ, WRITE, and REWRITE statements for indexed files; checks that disk records have valid key fields.

I-O file. An indexed or relative file that is opened as both input and output when the file is to be updated.

Iteration. A logical control structure for indicating the repeated execution of a routine or routines.

Julian date. A date in yyddd format, where yy is a two-digit number that represents the year and ddd is a three-digit number from 001 to 366 that represents the day of the year. For example, the Julian date for January 1, 1998 is 98001.

JUSTIFIED RIGHT. A clause used in the DATA DIVISION with a nonnumeric field to store the data in the rightmost positions rather than the leftmost positions of the field.

Key field. A field that identifies a record; for example, ACCT-NO, EMPLOYEE-NO, or PART-NO could be key fields.

LABEL RECORD(S). A clause in a File Description entry to designate whether header and trailer labels are standard or omitted.

Level number. A number from 01–49 that denotes the hierarchy of data within records.

Library. A file of programs that can be called in by the operating system or program as needed.

Limit test. A data validation procedure used to ensure that a field does not exceed a specified limit.

Line counter. A field used for keeping track of the number of lines printed.

LINKAGE SECTION. A section used when calling subprograms to pass data from a called subprogram back to a calling program.

Logic error. A program error that can be caused by a mistake in the sequencing of instructions or from an improperly coded instruction that does not accomplish what was desired. Contrast with **syntax error**.

Logical control structures. The ways in which instructions in a program may be executed.

Loop. A programming technique for executing a series of steps a fixed number of times or until a specified condition is met.

Low-order position. The rightmost position in a field.

Machine language. The only executable language; the language into which programs must be translated before execution.

Main module. Usually the first module in a top-down program; all other modules are executed from the main module in a top-down program.

Master file. The major collection of data pertaining to a specific application.

Menu. A technique used for interactive processing; the user is offered various options from which to select the procedures or routines required.

MERGE. A statement that combines two or more data files into one main file. The statement has a format similar to the SORT and automatically handles the opening, closing, and input/output operations associated with the files to be merged.

Module. A section, routine, procedure, or paragraph in a structured program.

MOVE. A statement that transmits, or copies, data from a sending field to a receiving field.

MULTIPLY. A statement used for multiplying one field by another.

Murphy's Law. An adage that states that if it is possible for something to go wrong, eventually it will go wrong; should be kept in mind when you prepare test data so that you make sure you test for every conceivable condition.

Negated conditional. An IF statement that tests for the absence of a condition; the word NOT is used in the statement; for example, IF A IS NOT EQUAL TO B ....

Nested conditional. An IF within an IF; an alternative to writing a series of simple conditionals.

Nested PERFORM. A PERFORM within a PERFORM.

Nonnumeric literal. A constant or fixed value that may contain any character in the COBOL character set (except a quote); limited to 120 characters for COBOL 74 and 160 for COBOL 85; such literals are enclosed in quotes.

Numeric literal. A constant that can contain only numbers, a decimal point, and a sign; typically used in arithmetic and comparison operations.

Object. An integrated unit of data and procedures or methods that operate on that data.

OBJECT-COMPUTER. The paragraph of the ENVIRONMENT DIVISION that indicates the computer on which the program is executed or run.

Object-oriented programming. A method of programming that combines data with the procedures and functions that operate on it; such combinations are called objects. This programming method reduces duplication of effort by enabling programmers to reuse code stored in a library.

Object program. The machine-language equivalent of a source program.

OCCURS clause. A clause used for indicating the repeated occurrence of items in the DATA DIVISION, all with the same format.

ON SIZE ERROR. A clause used to indicate what operations are to be performed if a field is not large enough to hold the results of an arithmetic operation.

OPEN. A statement used to designate which files are input and which are output, and to activate the appropriate devices.

OPEN EXTEND.   When a disk or tape file is opened in EXTEND mode, the disk or tape is positioned at the end of the file. This mode is used for adding records to the end of a file.

Operand.   A field or a literal that is specified in an instruction.

Operating systems software.   A set of programs that controls the overall operations of the computer and maximizes the efficient use of computer resources. Contrast with **applications program.**

Output.   The information produced by a computer system.

OUTPUT PROCEDURE.   An option used with the SORT statement to process sorted records before they are produced as output.

Overflow.   See **truncation.**

PAGE.   A reserved word used with the ADVANCING option of a WRITE statement so that the paper advances to a new page.

PAGE FOOTING.   Produced by the Report Writer Module, a page footing prints whenever a page break occurs.

PAGE HEADING.   Produced by the Report Writer Module, a page heading prints at the top of each new page.

Paragraph.   A subdivision of a COBOL program consisting of statements or sentences.

Parallel tables.   Two tables having values that correspond or relate to one another. For example, one table might contain zip codes and a parallel table might contain sales tax rates for each corresponding zip code.

PERFORM.   A logical control statement used for executing a paragraph or series of paragraphs and then returning control to the original module.

PERFORM ... TIMES.   A statement that instructs the computer to iterate, or execute a sequence of steps, a fixed number of times.

PERFORM UNTIL ....   A statement that instructs the computer to iterate, or execute a sequence of steps, until the condition specified is met.

PERFORM ... VARYING.   A statement that instructs the computer to iterate by varying an identifier from an initial value until that identifier contains another value.

Persistence.   The ability of a user program to operate on class objects and retain the changes made.

PICTURE (PIC).   A clause that indicates the size and type of data to be entered in a field.

Polymorphism.   The ability for objects in a class to respond to methods differently from other objects in the class.

Priming READ.   An initial READ used typically in COBOL 74 programs to read the first record.

Printer Spacing Chart.   A tool used to map out the proper spacing of output in a printed report.

PROCEDURE DIVISION.   The division of a COBOL program that contains the instructions to be executed.

Program.   A set of instructions that operates on input data and converts it to output.

PROGRAM-ID.   The only paragraph required in the IDENTIFICATION DIVISION.

Program interrupt.   An abnormal end condition that occurs if there is a major error in a program.

Program sheet.   See **coding sheet.**

Program specifications.   The precise instructions necessary for writing a program; consists of record layout forms for disk or tape input and output, and Printer Spacing Charts for printed output, along with notes specifying the logic required.

Programmer.   The computer professional who writes the set of instructions to convert input to output.

Prompt.   A request by the computer for user input. A prompt can be a blinking cursor, a ?, or a message.

Pseudocode.   A program planning tool that uses English-like expressions rather than diagrams to depict the logic in a structured program.

Random access.   The method of processing data independently of the actual location of that data on disk. This method can be used with disk drives, which are classified as direct-access devices.

Randomizing algorithm.   A method used for randomizing numbers or, with relative files, for determining disk addresses for each record on a random basis.

Range test.   A data validation procedure to determine if a field has a value that falls within preestablished guidelines.

READ.   The statement used to enter a record from an input device.

READ ... INTO.   A statement that reads a record from a file and stores it in a WORKING-STORAGE record area.

Receiving field.   The field that accepts data from a sending field in a MOVE operation; in the statement MOVE AMT-IN TO AMT-OUT, AMT-OUT is the receiving field.

Record.   A set of related fields treated as a unit. A payroll record on magnetic disk, for example, contains fields such as Social Security number, name, and salary.

RECORD CONTAINS.   An optional clause within an FD for indicating the number of characters within a record.

Record description.   Entries used to describe records within a file and within WORKING-STORAGE.

RECORD KEY.   The key field within an indexed record used for establishing an index.

Record layout form.   A form used in a problem definition to describe input and output formats on disk or tape.

REDEFINES.   A clause used to describe a field of data in a different way.

Relative file.   A randomly accessible file in which the key field converts to an actual disk address.

RELATIVE KEY.   The key field in a relative file that is nonblank and uniquely identifies the record.

Relative subscripting.   A subscript with a relative value; (SUB + 12), for example, would be a relative subscript.

RELEASE.   A statement to write sorted records to an output file after they have been processed.

REMAINDER.   A clause that may be used with the DIVIDE instruction for storing the remainder of a division operation.

REPORT FOOTING.   Produced by the Report Writer Module, a report footing prints once, at the end of the report.

REPORT HEADING.   Produced by the Report Writer Module, a report heading prints at the beginning of each report.

Report-item.   A type of field used for storing edit symbols such as $, −, ∗ in addition to numeric data; report-items are typically used when data is to be printed or displayed in a readable form.

REPORT SECTION.   This is a section in the DATA DIVISION that is used by the Report Writer Module for defining print records.

Reserved word.   A word that has special significance to the COBOL compiler, such as ADD, MOVE, DATA.

RETURN.   A statement to read records from a sorted work file after they have been processed.

REWRITE.   A statement for altering existing disk records; used when disk records are to be updated.

ROUNDED.   A clause used for rounding results to the specification of the receiving field.

Routine.   A set of instructions or module used to perform a specific operation.

Run-time error.   An error that occurs if the computer cannot execute an instruction; an example would be an attempt to divide by zero.

Scope terminator.   A word that delimits the end of a logical control construct or the end of a statement with clauses. These include END-IF, END-PERFORM, END-EVALUATE, END-READ, etc., for COBOL 85.

SEARCH.   A statement for looking up an item in a table; used to perform a serial search.

SEARCH ALL.   A statement for looking up an item in a table using a more efficient method of searching that requires table entries to be in sequence; used to perform a binary search.

Search argument.   The incoming field that is used for finding a match with a table entry.

Section.   A series of paragraphs within a COBOL program.

Sector.   A wedge-shaped segment of tracks on a disk.

SECURITY.   A paragraph in the IDENTIFICATION DIVISION used to indicate the security classification for the program.

SELECT.   A statement in the FILE-CONTROL paragraph of the ENVIRONMENT DIVISION that is used to assign an input or output file to a specific device.

Selection.   A logical control structure that performs operations if a given condition is met and can perform other operations if the condition is not met. Same as IF-THEN-ELSE.

Sending field.   The field that is to be transmitted, copied, or sent to another field as a result of a MOVE operation; in the statement MOVE AMT-IN TO AMT-OUT, AMT-IN is the sending field.

Sentence.   A statement or series of statements treated as a unit in a COBOL program and ending with a period.

Sequence.   A logical control structure in which a series of instructions are executed in the order in which they appear.

Sequence checking.   A procedure that ensures that data entered is in the proper sequence, usually by a key field.

Sequential processing.   The method of processing records in the order in which they are located in a file.

Serial search. A table look-up method in which each entry in the table is compared to an item; the entries are consecutively compared, beginning with the first. Contrast with **binary search**.

SET. The statement used to transmit data to an index or to increase or decrease the value of the index.

Sign test. A test performed to determine if a numeric field is positive or negative.

Simple condition. A test for the existence of one condition rather than many conditions. Contrast with **compound conditional**.

Software. A term used to describe all types of programs, including operating system programs and applications programs.

Software developer. See **applications programmer**.

SORT. A statement used to sequence a file so that it is in a specified order.

SOURCE-COMPUTER. The paragraph of the ENVIRONMENT DIVISION that indicates the computer on which the program is compiled or translated.

Source program. A set of instructions that must be compiled or translated into machine language before it can be executed.

Square value truncation. One of numerous randomizing algorithms used to convert a numeric key field to a disk address using the relative method of file organization.

Statement. An instruction.

Stepwise refinement. The process of continually breaking down a procedure into smaller and smaller segments; this is a top-down technique.

STOP RUN. A statement that tells the computer to terminate the program.

STRING. A statement used to join several fields together to form one field.

Structure chart. See **hierarchy chart**.

Structured programming. A technique that makes programs easier to read, debug, and modify; sometimes referred to as GO-TO-less programming; each section of a program is written as an independent module and executed using a PERFORM statement.

Structured walkthrough. See **walkthrough**.

Subprogram. A program or series of modules that can be called into a user program.

Subscript. An identifier used for accessing a specific field in an array or table.

SUBTRACT. A statement that subtracts fields or literals from another field or fields.

Summary report. See **group report**.

Suppression of leading zeros. The process of editing a field so that high-order zeros are replaced with blanks.

Switch. A type of field usually defined in WORKING-STORAGE for indicating the presence of a specific condition; the field is set equal to 1, for example, when a condition is met; at all other times, it remains at zero.

Symbolic programming language. A programming language that is relatively easy for a programmer to learn but that requires a translation process before the program can be run.

Syntax error. An error caused by a violation of a programming rule.

Table. A series of consecutive items, all with the same format, defined in the DATA DIVISION with an OCCURS clause; used for looking up or matching against an item read in or computed by the program.

Table argument. The table entry field that is used to locate the table function.

Table function. The element from the table that is being sought or "looked up."

Table look-up. A procedure where an item is matched against a table entry or argument for purposes of determining the value of some corresponding table entry or function.

Test data. Programmer-supplied data used to test the logic of a program.

Test for reasonableness. A data validation procedure to ensure that data entered as input is not obviously incorrect; for example, a year of transaction designated as 1989 (instead of 1998) would clearly be erroneous.

Top-down programming. A programming technique in which main modules or procedures are coded before minor ones.

Tracks. Concentric circles on a disk that are used to store data.

Trailer label. An end-of-file label placed on disk or tape.

Transaction file. A file that contains changes to be used for updating a master file.

Transaction report. See **detail report**.

Truncation. When a receiving field is not large enough to accept a sending field, one or more significant digits may be truncated or lost.

UNSTRING. A statement used to condense input into a more compact form.

Update procedure. The process of making a master file current.

USAGE clause. A clause that specifies the format in which data is stored.

User. The individual who will actually use the output from a computer run.

User-friendly. A technique for simplifying user interaction with a program.

VALUE clause. A literal or figurative constant to be placed in a WORKING-STORAGE field.

Variable data. Data that changes during each run of a program; contrast with **constant**.

Verification procedure. A procedure used to determine if the data keyed into a computer matches the source document from which it was generated.

Visual Table of Contents (VTOC). See **hierarchy chart**.

Walkthrough. The process of checking a program to see if it will produce the results desired.

WORKING-STORAGE SECTION. A section of the DATA DIVISION that contains data required for processing that is not part of input or output.

WRITE. A statement used to produce output data.

WRITE ... FROM. A statement that moves data to an output area and then produces it as output.

INDEX

COBOL Program Sheet

System		Punching Instructions										Sheet	of
Program		Graphic								Form #		Identification	
Programmer	Date	Key										73] [80	

Sequence		Cont.	A	B	COBOL Statement

(Page)	(Serial)			
1 3	4 6	7	8 12 16 20 24 28 32 36 40 44 48 52 56 60 64 68 72

| 0 1 |
| 0 2 |
| 0 3 |
| 0 4 |
| 0 5 |
| 0 6 |
| 0 7 |
| 0 8 |
| 0 9 |
| 1 0 |
| 1 1 |
| 1 2 |
| 1 3 |
| 1 4 |
| 1 5 |
| 1 6 |
| 1 7 |
| 1 8 |
| 1 9 |
| 2 0 |

COBOL Program Sheet

System		Punching Instructions										Sheet	of
Program		Graphic								Form #		Identification	
Programmer	Date	Key										73] [80	

Sequence		Cont.	A	B	COBOL Statement
(Page)	(Serial)				

| 0 1 |
| 0 2 |
| 0 3 |
| 0 4 |
| 0 5 |
| 0 6 |
| 0 7 |
| 0 8 |
| 0 9 |
| 1 0 |
| 1 1 |
| 1 2 |
| 1 3 |
| 1 4 |
| 1 5 |
| 1 6 |
| 1 7 |
| 1 8 |
| 1 9 |
| 2 0 |

COBOL Program Sheet

System		Punching Instructions		Sheet	of
Program		Graphic		Identification	
Programmer	Date	Key	Form #	73] [80	

Sequence		Cont.	A	B	COBOL Statement
(Page)	(Serial)				
1 3	4 6	7	8	12 16 20 24 28 32 36 40 44 48 52 56 60 64 68 72	
	0 1				
	0 2				
	0 3				
	0 4				
	0 5				
	0 6				
	0 7				
	0 8				
	0 9				
	1 0				
	1 1				
	1 2				
	1 3				
	1 4				
	1 5				
	1 6				
	1 7				
	1 8				
	1 9				
	2 0				